STS. PHILIP & JAMES PRAYER GROUP

Baptized in the Spirit

and

Spiritual Gifts

Steve Clark

Dove Publications
Pecos, New Mexico

Servant Books
Ann Arbor, Michigan

1976

Copyright © Dove Publications 1969, 1970
ISBN 0-89283-033-6
Printed in the United States of America

CONTENTS

Baptized in the Spirit

". . .you will be baptized in the Holy Spirit" (Acts 1:5)

1

Baptized in the Spirit

There is a passage in the third chapter of Paul's letter to the Galatians which is disarming to most Christians. The passage is:

> Are you people in Galatia mad? Has someone put a spell on you, in spite of the plain explanation you have had of the crucifixion of Jesus Christ? Let me ask you one question: was it because you practiced the Law that you received the Spirit, or because you believed what was preached to you? Are you foolish enough to end in outward observances what you began in the Spirit? Have all the favors you received been wasted? And if this were so, they would most certainly have been wasted. Does God give you the Spirit so freely and work miracles among you because you practice the Law, or because you believed what was preached to you? (Gal. 3:1-5)

The main message of the letter is that we come into the right relationship with God (are justified) through faith in Jesus Christ rather than by following the Jewish Law. In the above passage, Paul is making the point that the Galatians are going back on their Christian faith by agreeing to the idea that people need to be circumcised in order to be justified. His main argument is this: isn't it true that you experienced the work of the Spirit among you because you had faith in the Christian message and not because you followed the Law? Therefore you know from experience that you are justified by faith and not by following the Law.

What is so disarming about this passage is the glimpse it offers into the life of early Christian churches. The basis of Paul's argument is the *experience* of the Spirit. In order for his argument to have any force to the Galatians they would have had to have experienced being given the Spirit and experienced miracles being worked among them. If Paul asked a modern parish of Christians, "Does God give you the Spirit so freely and work miracles among you because you practice the Law, or because you believed what was preached to you?" most of them would not be able to make sense of the question. Their instinctive response would be, "What do you mean, 'God gives us the Spirit so freely and work miracles among us'? What are you talking about?"

The challenge of this passage for us comes from the fact that Paul simply takes it for granted that the Christians to whom he is writing have had these experiences. He does not feel that he has to explain what he is referring to or argue that it is possible to experience such things. He just expects that the Christians to whom he is writing know what he is talking about. He expects that they have experienced the giving of the Spirit and the working of miracles, and he expects that these are distinct enough experiences and common enough experiences that he can simply refer to them.

Nowadays in the church it is again possible to refer to our experience of the work of the Spirit and expect people to know what is meant. As the charismatic renewal grows and spreads into all parts of the church, people are beginning to experience the Spirit given freely and miracles being worked through faith. In other words, they are beginning to experience the life of the Spirit.

The Life of the Spirit

For early Christians, the Holy Spirit was an experience before he was a doctrine. When the Lord Jesus was on earth, he promised that he would send the Spirit upon his followers. And he promised them that the Holy Spirit would do things among them that they could experience. He told them that they would be "clothed with the power from on high" (Luke 24:49), that they would "receive power when the Holy Spirit comes on you, and then you will be my witnesses . . . to the ends of the earth" (Acts 1:8). He said that "the Advocate, the Holy Spirit, whom the Father will send in my name, will teach you everything and remind you of all I have said to you" (John 14:26). He said that his followers would know the Holy Spirit: "I shall ask the Father, and he will give you another Advocate to be with you forever, that Spirit of truth whom the world can never receive since it neither sees nor knows him; but you know him, because he is with you, he is in you" (John 14:16-17).

In the life of the early church, the Holy Spirit was someone who was with them and acted among them. When the Christians in Jerusalem prayed for courage to speak the gospel message, "the house where they were assembled rocked; they were all filled with the Holy Spirit and began to proclaim the word of God boldly" (Acts 4:31). Stephen "filled with the Holy Spirit" was able to gaze into heaven and see Jesus (Acts 7:55).

The Holy Spirit guided them. Philip was led by the Spirit when "the Spirit said to Philip, 'Go up and meet that chariot' " (the chariot of the Ethiopian eunuch), and after baptizing the eunuch "Philip was taken away by the Spirit of the Lord" (Acts 8:29, 39). Paul was led by the Spirit in his missionary journeys when "they travelled through Phrygia and the Galatian country, having been told by the Holy Spirit not to preach the word in Asia. When they reached the frontier of Mysia, they thought to cross it into Bithynia, but as the Spirit of Jesus would not allow them, they went through Mysia and came down to Troas" (Acts 16:6-8).

The Holy Spirit spoke to them frequently. When some prophets came from Jerusalem to Antioch, "one of them, Agabus, stood up and foretold by the Spirit that there would be a great famine over all the world, and this took place in the days of Claudius" (Acts 11:28). When some of the leaders of the church at Antioch were praying and fasting, "the Holy

Spirit said, 'I want Barnabas and Saul set apart for the work to which I have called them' " (Acts 13:2). Before Paul was taken prisoner by the Jews and given to the Romans, the Spirit constantly kept warning Paul about what would happen. Paul described this experience to the elders of Ephesus by saying, "I am on my way to Jerusalem, but have no idea what will happen to me there, except that the Holy Spirit, in town after town, has made it clear enough that imprisonment and persecution await me" (Acts 20:22-23).

The Holy Spirit did many other things among the early Christians. Paul lists some of the kinds of things the Spirit does in a Christian community in 1 Corinthians: "To one person is given through the Spirit the utterance of wisdom, and to another the utterance of knowledge according to the same Spirit, to another faith by the same Spirit, to another gifts of healing by the one Spirit, to another the working of miracles, to another prophecy, to another the ability to distinguish between spirits, to another various kinds of tongues, to another the interpretation of tongues. All these are inspired by one and the same Spirit" (1 Cor.12:3-11).

But the most important thing which the

Spirit did for the early Christians was to let them experience God's love for them and his union with them. In the eighth chapter of Romans, Paul says, "The spirit you received is not the spirit of slaves bringing fear into your lives again; it is the spirit of sons, and it makes us cry out, 'Abba, Father!' The Spirit himself and our spirit bear united witness that we are children of God" (Rom.8:15-16).

Paul clearly expects the Christians he is talking to to have had an experience of God's love given through the Spirit. The same thing is true of John, who expects the Christians to be able to use their experience of the Spirit as a test of whether they are living in God or not: "We can know that we are living in him and he is living in us, because he lets us share his Spirit" (1 John 4:13).

The whole New Testament is alive with the fact that the early Christians were able to experience the presence of the Spirit in them and see his work among them. It is this experience which is returning with the charismatic renewal. The very same things are happening now which were happening then. Today people are reporting experiences of being filled with the Spirit, of being led by him, of having him speak to them. They describe experiences of inspired speech, of prophecy, of discernment of spirits, of healing, of miracles. In other words, many Christians are beginning to live the life of the Spirit.

The life of the Spirit is a life in which a Christian can experience the Holy Spirit living in him and working through him. Most Christians today are not living the life of the Spirit. They live their Christian lives on the basis of doctrine. They were taught about Christ and about how to live as Christians. They decided to do it and they have been trying to pattern their lives according to Christ's teaching. They believe that Christ is real and that he hears them and helps them. But they do not feel that they are in much contact with him. They do not experience his presence nor do they see things happen which they can tell are his working.

The life of the Spirit changes that. When a person is living the life of the Spirit, he knows by experience that the Holy Spirit is in him. He does not have to "take it on faith" in the sense of believing it without any experience to indicate it is true. When a person is living the life of the Spirit, he begins to experience the Holy Spirit making it possible for him to praise God and worship God with a new freedom. He experiences the Holy Spirit making the scriptures come to life and giving Christian doctrines new meaning. He experiences a new ability to talk to people about Christ, a deeper peace and joy.

The life of the Spirit also involves an experience of a new kind of community life—a community living "in the Spirit." The life of the Spirit is not meant to be an individual life. The Spirit is given to form us into the body of Christ, and the life of the Spirit is a life lived by communities as well as by individuals. A person who is part of a community that is living the life of the Spirit can experience the community being led in worship by the Spirit, being guided by the Spirit, being taught by the Spirit. The community as a whole experiences the presence of the Spirit.

When I talk about "experiencing" things, I do not necessarily have something emotional in mind. "Experience" to us often means "emotion" or "feeling." We say something is "an experience" if we mean that it is a great event or a striking happening. However, we can have experiences that are not especially emotional. Suppose I meet my friend's cousin. I may have heard of him before, so I knew he existed. Then I met him, and I "experienced" the fact that he existed. The meeting may not have been particularly emotional or striking, but the difference is that before I had just heard of him and now I know him by experience. This is the most important sense in which we experience the Holy Spirit.

Before I first began to hear about the charismatic renewal, I had wanted to experience the life of the Spirit. I had always known that what happened in the New Testament and among the great saints could happen today. I never could see why it should not happen now, among us, if God is the same. And I was always unimpressed by the argument that the workings of the Spirit were only for the beginnings of the church–to get it started. If ever the church needed the work of the Spirit to make it effective and alive in the world, it is today.

I also knew that the presence and working of the Spirit must be something more than just interpreting circumstances or events as the Spirit's working. Many Christians today know that the Holy Spirit should be in their lives, and so they decide to interpret what happens to them as the work of the Spirit. If circumstances turn out a certain way, that is the Spirit leading them. If someone tells them something helpful, that is the Spirit speaking to them. If they get a good idea, that is the Spirit inspiring them. I have never felt very good about that approach. I always know that the experience of the Holy Spirit for the early Christians and for the great saints was more than just interpreting what happened to them as the work of the Spirit. It was a distinct, recognizable experience.

My first exposure to the charismatic renewal came through reading *The Cross and the Switchblade*. In that story, I could see that the leading of the Spirit could be something a person experienced and not just something that he could deduce from circumstances. And I could see that it brought results. I could also see in that story that the Holy Spirit had the power to cure people from drug addiction much more effectively than psychological methods. Shortly after that, I read about the gift of tongues and what that could mean to a person. I discovered at the same time that many people were experiencing the workings of the Spirit that I was reading about.

Soon I began to talk with people who had experiences of being filled with the Spirit. Friends of mine began to tell me about a new ability to pray as the result of the Holy Spirit.

They shared about praying for people for healing, and the results that came from it. They told me about the gift of prophecy, and how it was returning to use. And I soon began to experience all these things myself. I began to see from personal experience that the Lord would do for us today all the things he did for the early Christians.

I also gradually have come to experience a Christian community that lives in the Spirit and grows in the life of the Spirit. I have participated in regular gatherings for worship where there is a free, spontaneous spirit of worship and praise, and where the Spirit of God has brought about a remarkable unity among very different people. I have seen the Spirit give guidance to the community as a whole, with the same message coming through many people, often independently of one another. I have seen a people be knit together and grow in numbers, not so much because of a plan, but because the same Spirit was living in them.

I was convinced at an early stage that we needed these workings of the Spirit if the church was to stay alive and make headway in today's world. I knew from my own experience in trying to bring people to faith in Christ that some kind of power was needed. And as I began to see that these things did not have to happen sporadically, but could happen regularly ("so freely" as Paul said to the Galatians), I began to become convinced that they were normal for Christians. The life in the Spirit—the life in which a person experiences the presence of the Spirit and his working—is the normal Christian life.

When I say "normal" I do not mean "average." I do not mean that most Christians today are experiencing these things. They are not. But I mean that the life in the Spirit is the "norm" for the Christian life. This is the way it was meant to be. This should be the expected standard. There is no good reason why it cannot be.

My experience has been that most Christians would like to live the life of the Spirit, but that they do not know how to begin. Catholics especially have been taught a great deal about the spiritual life. They know a lot about it. Many of them have given up a great deal and entered religious orders so that they can live a deeper spiritual life. But they often do not know how to start. They do not know how to get into that contact with the Spirit that allows them to experience his presence and to let him produce the spiritual life in them. Thus, it is important to understand what it is to be baptized in the Spirit, because the life of the Spirit only becomes possible after having been baptized in the Spirit.

Baptized in the Spirit

We can best understand what it means to be baptized in the Spirit by seeing what happens to people when they are baptized in the Spirit. The New Testament contains a number of passages which describe people receiving the Spirit. From these passages we can discover some interesting things.

In the nineteenth chapter of Acts, Paul comes to Ephesus. When he arrives, he comes across a group of "disciples." He probably noticed something missing right away, because he began by asking a question, "Did you receive the Holy Spirit when you became believers?" Now, think what a strange question this is. What would a group of modern Christians say to this? Probably, "What do you mean, 'receive the Holy Spirit'?" As a matter of fact, that is almost the answer the group of disciples gave Paul. They told him they had not even heard there was such a thing as the Holy Spirit which they could receive. But what is strange about the question is that Paul expected them to know the answer. He expected them to be able to tell whether they had received the Holy Spirit or not.

When Paul heard their answer, he knew that they were not yet fully Christians, and so he told them the good news about Jesus. "When they heard this, they were baptized in the name of the Lord Jesus, and the moment Paul had laid hands on them the Holy Spirit came down on them, and they began to speak with tongues and to prophesy." When Paul was done, these disciples had definitely received the Holy Spirit. They knew it, and so did he. There was a change in them.

The same definite coming of the Holy Spirit characterizes the passages in Acts where there is a description of what happened when Christians received the Holy Spirit. This was certainly true at Pentecost. At Pentecost, the coming of the Spirit was manifested by "what sounded like a powerful wind from heaven" and "something that seemed like tongues of fire." But it also made a distinct change in the apostles, because they began to speak in tongues and even looked like they were drunk.

The same thing was true when the Spirit came upon the group of Samaritans who had believed because of Philip's preaching. Peter and John came and laid hands on them "and they received the Holy Spirit" (Acts 8:17). Acts then goes on to say, "When Simon saw that the Spirit was given through the imposition of hands by the apostles, he offered them some money." In other words, the giving of the Holy Spirit was obvious enough and good enough that Simon could see that something was going on and that it would be worth a small investment to obtain the same power.

Finally, the same thing happened when the Holy Spirit came upon Cornelius and his friends. Peter and some other Christians went to Cornelius' house, because God insisted upon it, and they told them the good news. However, it was clear all along that Peter and the other Jewish Christians were not inclined to feel that these gentiles could become Christians. But "while Peter was still speaking, the Holy Spirit came down on all the listeners. Jewish believers who had accompanied Peter were all astonished that the gift of the Holy Spirit should be poured out on the pagans too, since they could hear them speaking strange tongues and proclaiming the greatness of God. Peter himself then said, 'Could anyone refuse the water of baptism to these people, now they have received the Holy Spirit just as much as we have?' " (Acts 10:44-47). In other words, the coming of the Holy Spirit upon these pagans produced a definite, manifest change. The change had to be obvious for the Jewish Christians to accept it.

From the passages in the New Testment, it is clear that when people are baptized in the Spirit, they know it. They experience the Spirit coming to them in such a way that they can recognize it. They can recognize it not only in themselves but also in others. The result of being baptized in the Spirit is that the Spirit enters their lives and begins to make things happen in a way that they can experience.

Nowadays, people are experiencing the same thing. The Holy Spirit is coming to people in a way that they know it and can recognize it from experience. Increasing numbers of people are being baptized in the Spirit in a way that is similar to what happened in the New Testament.

What happens at the moment when people are baptized in the Spirit varies a great deal. One person I prayed with for the coming of the Spirit said that he felt that an electric current was running through him. Another felt "a strange warmth" fill him. Many simply feel a deep peace, or a joy. Some even laugh. But the most important part of what happens when a person is baptized in the Spirit is not any physical sensation or emotion. It is the change that comes from having the Holy Spirit live in us in a new way. It is a new kind of contact with the Lord. People have described it in the following ways:

> Immediately I was filled with peace. And it wasn't just a feeling. I think it could best be described as if I met Jesus Christ without seeing him. It was just as if Jesus Christ came up to me and said, "Hi." It was just like I knew him all along. That night was the big turning point in my life.

> The next week I was baptized in the Spirit and I spoke in tongues right away. It has made all the change in the world. Now I say I believe in God, but not because of a theory, but because I've met him.

> At one prayer meeting there was silence and I was meditating. It seemed to me that if I had a gift to give in response to Christ's love, it would be myself. And then some-

> thing very curious happened. It was very much like the words came, "do it." So I said, "OK." After the prayer meeting was over, for good measure I went up to the chapel and knelt down and said, "I don't understand, but all right." And I left the chapel and I started to feel a tremendous happiness, more than I've ever felt in my life. It was maybe a week later that I prayed in tongues. There are effects. Basically you are no longer loose and questioning who God is. You know Jesus Christ is risen, loves you, is concerned about you personally.

In other words, the same type of thing is happening now as happened to the early Christians. And from the experiences which people are now having, we can draw the same lessons: that when the Holy Spirit comes to them, they know it; that people can experience the Holy Spirit coming to them in a way that they can recognize; and that the result of being baptized in the Holy Spirit is a change in their lives that involves experiencing the Holy Spirit in their lives in a new way.

What then is it to be baptized in the Holy Spirit? Perhaps the most obvious description of what happens when a person is baptized in the

Holy Spirit is that the Holy Spirit comes to him in a way that he can know it. As a result of this coming of the Holy Spirit, he experiences a new contact with God.

But there is something more to being baptized in the Spirit than that. When a person is baptized in the Spirit, the Holy Spirit not only comes to that person in a new way, but he also makes a change in him. His life is different because his relationship with God has been changed. God is in him in a way in which he was not before. He has made his home in him in a new way.

As a result of the change which the Holy Spirit makes in a person, that person can then begin to experience the presence of God in him. He can know God in a way he never did before—by immediate experience. He can also begin to experience the Holy Spirit working in him in a new way. The Spirit guides him, speaks to him, teaches him, lets him know God and know that God loves him.

Another way of saying what it is to be baptized in the Spirit is that it is an introduction to the life of the Spirit. It is a beginning, the doorway, to the life of the Spirit. What makes the life of the Spirit in a person possible is the presence of the Holy Spirit in him doing all the things which God promised the Holy Spirit would do. Therefore, the only way for a person to experience the life of the Spirit is for the Holy Spirit to be in his life in a new way (to swell in him in a new way). There has to be a change such that the Holy Spirit begins to do all these things. When that change occurs, a person has been baptized in the Spirit.

Being baptized in the Spirit is an introduction to the life of the Spirit, but it is also an introduction to the Christian community. I can remember the first time I went to a "charismatic" prayer meeting. I felt "out of it"—and only partly because some of the things people did were strange to me, such as praying with their hands lifted up. I could pray with my hands lifted up, and did, somewhat self-consciously. But I still could not be fully part of what was happening there, because they had experienced something I had not. The Spirit was moving in them both individually and as a group in a way he was not moving in me. I needed some way of "getting into" what they were "into." Or rather, I should say, I needed to let it into me.

If a community is living in the Spirit, the only way of coming into the life of that community is by being baptized in the Spirit. A person cannot simply join. Even if he "joined" he could not take part in its life. And since we need a community that is living in the Spirit in order to live in the Spirit ourselves, being baptized in the Spirit should not only mean coming into a new life with the Spirit. Normally it should mean coming into a community as well. "In one Spirit we were all baptized into one body" (1 Cor. 12:13).

Being baptized in the Spirit is just a beginning, an introduction. It puts us into the kind of relationship with God that makes it possible for us to live the life of the Spirit. If we do not realize that it is just a beginning but instead start to think of it as a one-time spiritual experience which is an end in itself, we can develop some bad attitudes. For instance, one error is the attitude that once I have had an experience of the Holy Spirit, I have "got it." From now on, all through my life, I am numbered among those who have "got it." From this kind of talk, a person might get the idea that God is mainly concerned about who has once had this experience and who has not. Those who have had it are the sheep, and those who have not are the goats.

Once we are baptized in the Spirit, we have not "got it." But we can have it. The "it" is the Holy Spirit living in us and working through us. Once we have been baptized in the Spirit, we can have the Holy Spirit live in us and work through us. We have experienced the Holy Spirit in a new way and that experience makes it possible for us to live with him in a new way. But that experience is not a guarantee that we always will. People who have been baptized in the Holy Spirit can end up farther away from God and from the life of the Spirit than people who have not. And what God is interested in is not people who once had the experience of being baptized in the Spirit, but he is interested in people who are now living in the Spirit.

Another bad attitude that comes from thinking of being baptized in the Spirit mainly as a single experience is the attitude that once I have been baptized in the Spirit I have all I need to live the Christian life. In a way this is true. The Holy Spirit is all we need to live the Christian life. But in a way it is all wrong. When we are baptized in the Spirit, we are in a new relationship with God, but we have to know how to grow in that relationship. It is like being married. We can be fully and completely married and still not have a good married life. We can be baptized in the Spirit and still not live in the Spirit very well. We have to learn how to live the life of the Spirit.

The key to learning how to live in the Spirit is the experience of living in a community of people who are living the life of the Spirit. Being part of a community that is living in the Spirit is so important that it is almost true to say that when we are baptized in the Spirit, we receive as much of the life of the Spirit as the community we are part of is experiencing. (Fortunately this is not completely true.) If the community we are part of has learned to yield to the gift of tongues, we will speak in tongues much more readily when we are baptized in the Spirit. If the community we are part of is closed to the gift of tongues or has difficulty in yielding to it, we will have a much harder time speaking in tongues when we are baptized in the Spirit. Similarly if the community we are part of experiences the guidance of the Spirit deeply in a regular way, we will experience this ourselves easily and soon. If the community we are part of does not know what the guidance of the Spirit is, we will have a hard time discovering it for ourselves.

The life of the Spirit is something which is shared with us by the community we are a part of. If the community has faith in something (tongues or guidance or whatever it might be), it will be able to impart that faith to us. There are, of course, exceptions. The Holy Spirit often gives an individual more than the community he is part of. But as a general rule, the Lord prefers to work with people as a body and not individually. For instance, he prefers to give the gift of prophecy to a body through an individual, not to an individual for his own use when the body cannot receive it.

In other words, being baptized in the Spirit involves coming into a new relationship, a relationship with God and with a Christian community. It is a beginning. Without it, we cannot live the life of the Spirit. But being baptized in the Spirit is only a beginning. We need to learn how to live the life of the Spirit in a community of Christians who are living the life of the Spirit together.

The Gift of Tongues

The gift of tongues is so important for beginning the life of the Spirit that it is not possible to ignore it when talking about being baptized in the Spirit. Normally when a person is baptized in the Spirit he has a definite experience. Commonly this experience is connected with the gift of tongues. This experience is important for him in being able to live the life of the Spirit.

We saw above that when the Holy Spirit came upon people in the Acts of the Apostles, his coming was something which they could experience. But more than this, their experience was not something hidden inside themselves. It was obvious to others as well. Onlookers could see that they were experiencing the Holy Spirit. It was manifest.

There are three passages which describe how the fact that they were receiving the Spirit was manifest. In Acts 10:45-46 it says:

> Jewish believers who had accompanied Peter were all astonished that the gift of the Holy Spirit should be poured out on the pagans, too, *since* they could hear them speaking strange languages (tongues) and proclaiming the greatness of God. (Emphasis added.)

In Acts 19:6 it says:

> the Holy Spirit came down on them, and they began to speak with tongues and to prophesy.

In Acts 2:4,11 it says:

> And they were all filled with the Holy Spirit and began to speak in other tongues as the Spirit gave them utterance, and the onlookers described what was happening (v.11) by saying, "we hear them telling in our own tongues the mighty works of God."

We can presume that what happened in Acts 8 was the same, even though it is not explicitly stated. Whenever the coming of the Holy Spirit upon people is described in Acts, the gift of tongues is mentioned as one of the results. But the significance of what happened to the early Christians is lost to most Christians today, because they do not understand the gift of tongues.

"Tongues" just means "languages." To "speak in another tongue" means to speak in another language. The same Greek word is sometimes translated "tongue" in English, sometimes "language." Thus, when the Holy Spirit came upon people in the New Testament, they began to speak in a langauge they had not learned (Acts 2:6-11) and did not understand (1 Cor. 14:2, 13-14).

But to realize that they began to speak in another language still does not help very much. Why on earth would they want to speak in a language that neither they nor (usually) anyone else understood? The answer to this can be found in 1 Corinthians 14.

In 1 Corinthians 12-14, Paul is trying to deal with some problems in the Corinthian church. The problems seem to be that some people were speaking in tongues in the church gatherings without having what they said interpreted into a language everyone could understand (14:6-19, 27-28); that a number of people would speak in tongues or prophesy at the same time, producing a kind of babble in the Christian meetings (14:26-33); and that people would prefer to speak in tongues rather than to prophesy (14:1-12). There seems to have been a kind of spiritual rivalry underlying these problems (12:14-26).

Paul wrote 1 Corinthians 12-14 to deal with these problems. Here he presents a framework for understanding how the spiritual gifts should be used in Christian gatherings so that the church would be built up by them. He says that each spiritual gift (tongues included) is a working of the Spirit which is given to build up the church. Therefore, it has to be used in Christian gatherings in a way which does build up the church, a loving way. A person should only speak in tongues in Christian gatherings in a way which builds up the community, i.e., one at a time and with an interpretation.

The explanation Paul gives of the spiritual gifts in 1 Corinthians 12-13 is a good one for providing guidelines for how to use the gift of tongues in public gatherings, but it does not provide a complete explanation for the gift of tongues–as is obvious from 1 Corinthians 14. From what Paul says here, it is clear that people were not praying in tongues only when it was helpful to the community. At times there was a profusion of tongues and such a jumble of sound would not have communicated anything. However, Paul does not imply that when people are speaking in tongues this way, a way that is not helpful to the whole gathering, that they are not speaking in tongues at all. Nor does he say that their speaking in tongues is not an inspiration from God. We might have expected him to say either of these two things if he thought that speaking in tongues was only for building up a community and nothing else. In fact, he even claims to speak in tongues more than everyone else–and he certainly does not do all that speaking in tongues at the community gatherings.

In other words, the inspiration from God to speak in tongues is not always a spiritual gift for the building up of the Christian community. Sometimes it is and sometimes it is not. Part of Paul's advice is: learn when to speak out in tongues to the whole gathering and learn when to keep it to yourself.

What else is the gift of tongues, then? The way Paul talks about it in 1 Corinthians 14 gives us a good understanding of what it is. In 1 Corinthians 14:2-5 he says,

> Anybody with the gift of tongues speaks to God, but not to other people; because nobody understands him when he talks in the spirit about mysterious things. On the other hand, the man who prophesies does talk to other people, to their improvement, their encouragement, and their consolation. The one with the gift of tongues talks for his own benefit, but the man who prophesies does so for the benefit of the community. While I should like you all to have the gift of tongues, I would much rather you could prophesy, since the man who prophesies is of greater importance than the man with the gift of tongues, unless of course the latter offers an interpretation so that the church may get some benefit.

In 1 Corinthians 14:13-19 he says,

That is why anybody who has the gift of tongues must pray for the power of interpreting them. For if I use this gift in my prayers, my spirit may be praying but my mind is left barren. What is the answer to that? Surely, I should pray not only with the spirit but with the mind as well? And sing praises not only with the spirit but with the mind as well? Any uninitiated person will never be able to say Amen to your thanksgiving, if you only bless God with the spirit, for he will have no idea what you are saying. However well you make your thanksgiving, the other gets no benefit from it. I thank God that I have a greater gift of tongues than all of you, but when I am in the presence of the community I would rather say five words that mean something than ten thousand words in a tongue.

In other words, when a person speaks in a tongue, he speaks to God (that is, speaking in tongues is prayer) for his own benefit (it is usually private prayer). When he speaks in tongues his spirit is praying. He is praising God and blessing him (blessing God was the normal form of Jewish and early Christian thanksgiving).

To make the point which I want to make about what happens when a person is baptized in the Spirit, we have to see one other thing: that prophecy is sometimes prayer. Sometimes a prophecy is given that is an inspired prayer to God. A clear example of this occurs in the first chapter of Luke where it says,

> Zechariah was filled with the Holy Spirit and spoke this prophecy:
>
> > Blessed be the Lord, the God of Israel, for he has visited his people, he has come to their rescue. . . .

This is probably the kind of prophecy which happened when the Holy Spirit came down upon the disciples at Ephesus. It would not make sense for the Lord to have inspired a number of them to speak prophetic messages at the same time. Probably he inspired them all to praise God prophetically.

Thus, what could people see when the early Christians were baptized in the Spirit? They could see that as the Holy Spirit came upon these Christians, they began to pray inspired prayers of praise, sometimes in words they did not understand, sometimes in their own language. The first manifestation of the presence of the Spirit in them was an inspired prayer of praise. They were lifted up in the Spirit to praise the Lord because they were having a direct experience of his presence and his glory for the first time.

This is why the gift of tongues is so important. It is a new gift of prayer, a gift of praise (at first, although later it can be other kinds of prayer). It allows us to yield to the Spirit and respond to the presence of the Spirit in a way which we could not before. It is therefore a kind of gateway to the full life of the Spirit.

The scriptures do not say that every Christian must speak in tongues. But the implication of the Acts passages is that the speaking in tongues is very common; perhaps the implication of 1 Corinthians 14:5 is that it is for everyone. My own personal experience is that it can be for everyone. In our community, it is usual for people to pray in tongues when they are prayed with to be baptized in the Spirit (if they have been properly instructed and prepared), and the few exceptions pray in tongues within a matter of days or weeks. The problem with receiving the gift of tongues does not seem to be with God giving it so much as with people being able to yield to it.

Some people, mostly from Pentecostal denominations, hold that tongues is the "initial evidence of receiving the Spirit." They mean by this that until a person has prayed in tongues, he has not been baptized in the Spirit. But a look at Acts has shown us, not that tongues is the initial evidence, but "inspired praise" is the initial evidence. Sometimes this comes in tongues, but it can also come in English.

Do we want to say, then, that only if a person has had this experience of inspired praise has he been baptized in the Spirit? I do not think we can say that from the scripture. From the scripture all we can say is that this experience is the *normal* first sign. This is the way it should happen, not the way it always has to happen.

I know of people who have asked to be baptized in the Spirit and who have not been able to pray in tongues at first. But before the gift of tongues has come, other manifestations of the presence of the Spirit in them have come: they have felt the presence of the Spirit in them, the scriptures have come to life, they feel a new guidance of the Spirit.

It is even true that sometimes people are not aware that something has happened when they are baptized in the Spirit. They have no conscious experience at the time. But they can look back and say that something happened at that point. They know something happened because now they can experience the Holy Spirit in them. I know one girl who told me, when I asked her what happened when she was baptized in the Holy Spirit: "Nothing at all. When they prayed over me, nothing happened at all. Except that since then my whole life has been completely different." And she went on to describe what her life had been like since then, and it was clear to me from the description that she was living the life of the Spirit. Even though the beginning of the life of the Spirit was not a striking experience to her, she was now experiencing the Spirit's presence and action each day.

A person has been baptized in the Spirit when he can experience the Spirit living in him and working through him. If there are no traces at all of the presence of the Spirit in him, he has not been baptized in the Spirit. But even if he did not experience much of anything when he was prayed with for the Spirit, but later notices changes and finds himself living the life of the Spirit as a result of being prayed with, we can tell he was baptized in the Spirit.

Often the reason why some people have difficulty in yielding to this new form of prayer (and to the gift of tongues) even though they have been baptized in the Spirit is a simple one: they have inhibitions which need to be overcome. The Spirit is in them, inspiring them to pray in this way. But they cannot let it come out. Often they have been taught not to be expressive, or are afraid of expression and of their own emotions. Sometimes they are afraid that God will not do it for them, and so they cannot put faith in what the Holy Spirit is trying to do in them. One reason why the gift of tongues is so important for modern Americans is that it is easier for them to yield to the Holy Spirit in tongues than it is in English. They can more easily overcome their inhibitions by by-passing their minds (which is what happens in tongues–1 Corinthians 14:14) than through their minds.

From experience I would say that a person is not fully in the Spirit unless he has yielded to this kind of prayer. It is not until he experiences the presence of the Spirit moving in him, yields to it, and experiences something new that he could not do on his own, that he knows what it is to live the life of the Spirit. He needs a direct experience of what it is to do things "in the Spirit"–to do things with full control and full action and yet to have what we do formed by the Spirit into something more than just our own work.

There is a release and a fullness that comes from praying in tongues. It is in this experience that a person begins to experience the deep joy of the Holy Spirit. Even though a person can be baptized in the Spirit without any experience at the initial moment, I do not think it should happen that way. In the New Testament it was normal for people to receive the Spirit in a way that they and everyone else knew it, and it can still be normal now. Having such an experience is a great help in entering the life of the Spirit.

A couple of weeks ago I happened to be in the hall of one of our parish buildings when the people who had been prayed with to be baptized in the Spirit came out of the prayer room. They were all aglow and joyful. One could hardly speak. They had experienced a fullness of the Spirit and knew it. It was not hard for me to see it either. Once a person sees someone who has been baptized in the Spirit the way the apostles were, it is not hard to see why onlookers might have thought that the apostles were drunk.

What It Is Not

Not conversion: Being baptized in the Spirit is not the same as having a conversion to the Lord or a deeper conversion to the Lord.

Sometimes it is true that people are converted to the Lord at the time of being baptized in the Spirit—or converted to him in a new way. I know of a seminarian who had been getting farther and farther from faith in Christ. He wanted to be a Christian, but he found himself distant from Christ and unable to find a way of having much of a relationship with him. He was tending towards leaving the seminary and maybe the church as well. When he first heard about the charismatic renewal and came to his first prayer meeting, he was curious, but he could not accept what he heard. All he could say was that he would be willing to give it a try and see what would happen. He asked to be prayed with to be baptized in the Spirit. When he was, he experienced God in a way he never had before, and that experience was for him a real conversion. From then he began to live for Christ with full faith.

But being baptized in the Spirit does not always involve having a deeper conversion. When I asked to be prayed with to be baptized in the Spirit, I had been trying to give my whole life to God for a number of years. I had been praying daily for some length of time each day, reading the scriptures and spiritual books regularly, spending most of my time working to bring others to Christ, trying to pattern my life on Christ's teaching, etc. When I was prayed with, something happened. I began to pray in a new way, experience the presence of God in a new way, experience the guidance and working of God in a new way. But I did not become any more dedicated or any more turned toward God. In fact, in a certain sense I became less dedicated, because once I began to experience the Spirit working in me in a new way, I didn't try as hard as I used to. I didn't have to.

Conversion is a turning towards Christ. It is something *we* do. After I was prayed for to be baptized in the Spirit, I was no more converted than I had been before. Baptism in the Spirit, however, is something *Christ* does. He is the baptizer in the Holy Spirit. He gives us something new. The result of it is that God begins to work in us in a new way. More happens in our Christian life because God is doing more.

Our part in being baptized in the Spirit is not conversion. Conversion should come before. Our part is "receiving" or "drinking" or "letting ourselves be baptized." What happens when we are baptized in the Spirit is a gift from the Father. He gives us the Spirit in a new way. Our part is to accept that gift, to receive it, to give the Spirit a welcome into us.

Not a realization: Being baptized in the Spirit is not a new realization of the doctrine of the Holy Spirit in us.

Being baptized in the Holy Spirit is a change in people's relationship with God. The result of it is that the Holy Spirit begins to work in a new way. He begins to speak to them, to guide them, to teach them, to work through them, to make them realize God's presence in them and his love for them.

When people are baptized in the Spirit, they do realize the doctrine of the Holy Spirit in a new way. All of a sudden, whole areas of Christian truth are opened up to them. They read the scriptures, and passages that were flat before become some of the most interesting passages in scripture. They go to mass, and prayers that they had "just said" before become charged with meaning. Every mention of the Holy Spirit produces light and understanding.

Such a new realization of the doctrine of the Holy Spirit is a result of being baptized in the Spirit, but it is not the same thing. What happens when we are baptized in the Holy Spirit is that the Spirit begins to do things in us that he never did before. This is more than a realization. It is a change in what is happening. Something new is happening.

The fact that being baptized in the Holy Spirit is different from having a deeper realization of the doctrine of the Holy Spirit is important when we come to the point of wanting to be baptized in the Holy Spirit. We cannot begin the life in the Spirit solely by realizing more who the Holy Spirit is. Realization on our part cannot by itself produce a change in our relationship with him. It may prepare for it, but it cannot do it.

We are only baptized in the Holy Spirit when the Holy Spirit begins to work in us in a new way. It is something he does in us, not something that we grow into through greater realization. We can only begin the life in the Spirit by receiving the Spirit from the Father.

Not a devotion: Being baptized in the Holy Spirit is not a greater devotion to the Holy Spirit.

What was said above is also true about the difference between being baptized in the Holy Spirit and being devoted to the Holy Spirit. Usually we are given a greater devotion to the Holy Spirit as *a result of* being baptized in the Holy Spirit, but the two are not the same thing. Being baptized in the Spirit comes when the Holy Spirit begins to do new things in us. And it does not come about through trying to be more devoted to the Holy Spirit, but by receiving the Spirit.

Not a sign of spiritual maturity or holiness: Being baptized in the Spirit is not a sign of spiritual maturity or holiness. Rather, it gives a person a relationship with the Holy Spirit which will allow him to grow in holiness more quickly and easily than he could do by himself.

A year after I was prayed with to be baptized in the Spirit, I was reading C. S. Lewis' book *The Four Loves*. It is a book which is filled with spiritual wisdom and it shows that the author was a man of real spiritual maturity. At the end of the book, however, he talks about loving God, and he describes a kind of love of God which he says is the most important kind. But Lewis says that he himself has not experienced this love and does not expect to experience it until he gets to heaven. The kind of love he describes (what he calls an appreciative love of God) is exactly the love people experience when they have been baptized in the Spirit and can praise God in tongues or English. When I got to the end of the book, it was clear to me that C. S. Lewis had not been baptized in the Spirit when he wrote that book.

At the same time, I could see that C. S. Lewis was an excellent Christian. He was a better Christian than many people that I knew who had been baptized in the Spirit. He showed more spiritual wisdom, more faithfulness to God, and more fruit in his service than most who have been baptized in the Spirit.

Shortly after reading *The Four Loves*, I found myself talking to a college student who had had little faith a month previously, and who had not lived a very spiritual life. When she was prayed with to be baptized in the Spirit, she had a deep experience of the Holy Spirit (one which gave her an appreciative love of God right away), and she has gone on from that time to grow in the Christian life. But when she was baptized in the Spirit, she was not even close to the spiritual maturity that

C. S. Lewis had when he wrote *The Four Loves*. She probably isn't close even now.

Spiritual growth takes time. Any process of maturing takes time. Relationships need to grow. Changes in our pattern of living have to develop. If we are going to have a deep relationship with God, and if we are going to be able to live a life that is like the one Christ taught us about, we have to expect it to take time. We need to grow into it.

The work of the Spirit in us, however, is a gift. A gift can be given right away, all at once. And because it is a gift and not something that we have to grow into, it can be given at the beginning of the process of spiritual maturity as well as any place along the way. It happens when a person knows that God is offering the gift to him and seeks it.

The gift of the Spirit is given to us to make spiritual growth much easier, and it does. People who are baptized in the Spirit can grow more quickly than people who are not. I spent a number of years in Christian work before seeing the charismatic renewal and I have spent a number of years since then. Both times I was working with the same kind of people—college students. Since we have been praying with them to be baptized in the Spirit, their spiritual growth has been much more rapid. The Spirit of God is producing a much deeper holiness in them. And it is not that these students are trying so much harder than the others were. Many of the others tried just as hard (and some of them are now experiencing a new rate of growth now that they have been baptized in the Spirit). It is not that they are trying harder, but that they are experiencing more. The Spirit of God is doing more of it in them.

On the other hand, being baptized in the Spirit is not at all the same thing as spiritual perfection. A person who has been baptized in the Spirit still needs to go through a process of spiritual maturing. One of the greatest dangers facing people who have experienced a filling with the Spirit is the misconception that they have arrived at spiritual maturity because of it. Being baptized in the Spirit only introduces a person to a new relationship with the Holy Spirit.

People are sometimes scandalized that a new Christian who has just come to faith in Christ can be baptized in the Spirit while there are many faithful Christians who have dedicated themselves to Christ for years and have not been baptized in the Spirit. Rather than a source of scandal, this should point out to us an important lesson: everything God wants us to have comes in the way he wants us to receive it. Spiritual maturity comes to us through a process of effort and dedication. We cannot have it without putting in time in faithful service of God, no matter how much we pray for it. The gift of the Spirit, on the other hand, comes to us through asking faith. It is a gift. We need to recognize that God is offering it and receive it from him in faith. No amount of dedicated service can earn it. But once we realize he is offering it, we can have it if we ask for it.

That also means that the years we have spent in serving the Lord before we have been baptized in the Spirit are not worthless. If we spent time in growing in our relationship with God before we were baptized in the Spirit, we will be farther along in spiritual maturity after we are baptized in the Spirit than someone who began his Christian life with being baptized in the Spirit.

Not everything we need: Being baptized in the Spirit is only part of what is needed to be fully in Christ.

If a person has been baptized in the Spirit

but is only partly converted to Christ, he will not be much of a Christian. If a person has been baptized in the Spirit but does not understand the basic truths of Christianity or does not love the Lord, he will not be much of a Christian. A person who has a full tank of gas in his car will not get very far if he has four flat tires. Or even with a full tank of gas and four good tires, he will not be able to keep moving if the car has a broken fan belt. In other words, we need everything that is part of being a Christian if we are going to live the Christian life the way it was meant to be lived. We need everything which the Lord has provided for us.

Receiving

When the Jews on the day of Pentecost saw the first Christians who had just been baptized in the Spirit, and when they heard Peter's explanation of what it was that had just happened, they asked, "What must we do?" That is the question. How do we begin the life of the Spirit?

The heart of Peter's talk was the Lord Jesus. He said to the Jews: it is because of Jesus that we can have the Holy Spirit. It is because Jesus is Lord and Christ, because he has died and risen, that we can have the Holy Spirit. Because of what he has done, the Father has given him the Holy Spirit to give to us. Peter said:

> Now raised to the heights by God's right hand, he has received from the Father the Holy Spirit, who was promised, and what you see and hear is the outpouring of that Spirit. (Acts 2:33)

Peter just said the same thing John the Baptist had said when he first pointed Jesus out. Probably the words which Peter heard when he first saw Jesus are:

> Someone is following me, someone who is more powerful than I am, and I am not fit to kneel down and undo the strap of his sandals. I have baptized you with water, but he will baptize you with the Holy Spirit. (Mark 1:7-8)

In other words, Jesus is the baptizer in the Holy Spirit. He is the one we have to come to if we want to be baptized in the Holy Spirit.

Jesus himself said the same thing. He told all the people on the feast of Tabernacles that if they wanted new life, living water, the Holy Spirit, they would have to come to him:

> "If any man is thirsty, let him come to me! Let the man come and drink who believes in me!"
>
> As the scripture says: From his breast shall flow fountains of living water.
>
> He was speaking of the Spirit which those who believed in him were to receive; for the Spirit had not yet been given, because Jesus had not yet been glorified. (John 7:37-39)

Those who want the Holy Spirit and the new life he brings have to come to the Lord Jesus.

Peter went on to assure his listeners on the day of Pentecost that the Holy Spirit was for everyone. The Lord wants everyone to be baptized in the Spirit:

> The promise that was made is for you and your children, and for all those who are far away, for all those whom the Lord our God will call to himself. (Acts 2:39)

The same message came to us in the early days of the charismatic renewal in the Catholic Church when we were wondering if what was happening to us was for everyone. One of the first prophecies we were given contained the words, "My Spirit is for all, for all, for all."

The normal way in which people can make contact with Jesus is through his body, through the community of Christians in whom he lives. Just as people normally first hear about him through Christians and so come to faith, they are normally baptized in the Spirit in a Christian community. And they should be. Since the life of the Spirit is lived in a body–the body of Christ–a person should be baptized in the Spirit in the body of Christ. In being baptized in the Spirit, he should enter into the life of a Christian community.

People can be baptized in the Spirit without the help of any Christians. The Lord himself (the baptizer) and the Holy Spirit are all that is absolutely essential. A number of people in our community have prayed for the Holy Spirit on their own and have been baptized in the Spirit without the help of any other Christian. One girl, in fact, was baptized in the Spirit and given the gift of tongues before she even knew that there was such a thing–simply because the Lord in his mercy knew that she had a special need of it. But it is rarer and more difficult for people to be baptized in the Spirit on their own, because the Lord wants us to be part of a community. Normally, then, what a person who wants to be baptized in the Spirit should do is to go to a community of Christians who have been baptized in the Spirit and ask their help.

In the New Testment (and in the early church) the normal way in which Christians helped someone receive the Spirit was through prayer with the laying on of hands. In the eighth chapter of Acts, it says:

> When the apostles in Jerusalem heard that Samaria had accepted the word of God, they sent Peter and John to them, and they went down there, and prayed for the Samaritans to receive the Holy Spirit, for as yet he had not come down on any of them: they had only been baptized in the name of the Lord Jesus. Then they laid hands on them, and they received the Holy Spirit. When Simon saw that the Spirit was given through the imposition of hands by the apostles . . . (Acts 8:14-18)

The same thing happened in the ninth chapter when Ananias prayed for Paul, and in the nineteenth chapter when Paul prayed for the disciples at Ephesus.

In most communities of people who have been baptized in the Spirit, prayer with the laying on of hands is the normal way of helping someone be baptized in the Spirit. It seems to be a natural way of helping people receive the new life in the Spirit. When people are well prepared and are prayed for with the laying on of hands, it is rare for them not to experience the Holy Spirit coming to them and it is rare for them not to speak in tongues.

But the person who comes to be baptized in the Spirit is not passive. His part is to come to the Lord to be baptized in the Spirit. Prayer with the laying on of hands is not a substitute for coming to the Lord. It is only meant to be a help, and if the person himself does not turn to the Lord and receive the Spirit from him, he will not be baptized in the Spirit.

Therefore, the condition that has to be met before a person can be baptized in the Spirit is simply to turn to Jesus as Lord and Savior and Baptizer. The instructions Peter gave the Jews on the day of Pentecost were,

> You must repent, and every one of you must be baptized in the name of Jesus Christ for the forgiveness of your sins, and you will receive the gift of the Holy Spirit. (Acts 2:38)

The condition, then, is being "in the Lord," being a believer, a person who has turned to Christ. When we are in that condition, he can baptize us in the Holy Spirit. Some people are baptized in the Holy Spirit years after having first accepted Christ as their Lord. Others commit their lives to him only at the time they are baptized in the Holy Spirit. But however it happens, being "in the Lord" is the only condition which qualifies us for being baptized in the Holy Spirit.

Once a person belongs to the Lord, he can pray for the Holy Spirit. All he has to do is ask in faith, simply to ask, knowing that the Lord wants him to be baptized in the Spirit and is offering him the chance. Luke has a passage which I sometimes think was kept in his gospel in its present form because it was used to prepare people to be baptized in the Spirit:

> So I say to you: Ask, and it will be given to you; search and you will find; knock, and the door will be opened to you. For the one who asks always receives; the one who searches always finds; the one who knocks will always have the door opened to him. What father among you would hand his son

> a stone when he asked for bread? Or hand him a snake instead of a fish? Or hand him a scorpion if he asked for an egg? If you then, who are evil, know how to give your children what is good, how much more will the heavenly Father give the Holy Spirit to those who ask him! (Luke 11:9-13)

In other words, what a believer has to do to be baptized in the Holy Spirit is simply to ask. God is anxious for him to have it. In fact, God wants us to have it more than we want it ourselves. He wants us to have it because he loves us and he wants to live in us by his Spirit. We simply need to come to him and receive the gift from him.

There seem to be a variety of obstacles people have that keep them from receiving the fullness of the Spirit. Sometimes people do not want it–or do not want everything God is offering (usually tongues). Because they are asking and yet are telling God they only want certain things, he is not free to give them the full life of the Spirit. Sometimes people do not believe that being baptized in the Spirit is anything all that definite. All they are really asking for is "a blessing," a little bit more devotion to God. And that is usually all they receive–not realizing that God wants to give them much more.

Most often the problem is fear: either fear that it is wrong to ask God for things for ourselves, or fear that what happens will be "just me," that is, psychological and not spiritual at all, or fear that "God won't give it to me." The only answer to such fear is to trust God's love. He loves us and wants us to have the Spirit. It we ask him, he will give it to us.

Often people have difficulties in getting through these obstacles. At root, all these obstacles amount to a lack of faith, and often a person has a difficulty in overcoming his lack of faith by himself. That is perhaps the root reason why the life of the Spirit is lived in a community. A community can impart faith to someone who does not have it–effortlessly and painlessly in fact.

In my experience, if a person comes to a community of Christians who have been baptized in the Spirit, and who have faith in the working of the Spirit and who believe that a full experience of the Spirit is available to everyone, and is well prepared, he can be baptized in the Spirit with no difficulty. Our community seems to be at that point now, and people seem to be entering the life of the Spirit and speaking in tongues with no difficulty at all. It took us a while as a community to grow in faith, and it has taken us a while as a community to learn how to prepare people. (Even now, people are sometimes prayed with before they are ready.) But now there seems to be enough faith and wisdom to help anyone who comes.

The father wants us to experience his love. He wants to give his Spirit to us. He wants his people to be able to lead those who come to them to a full life in the Spirit. He wants to do for us everything he did for the early Christians—and maybe more.

2

Understanding Baptism in the Spirit

In the early church being baptized in the Spirit was easily understood. When a person became a Christian, he asked for the Spirit and received it. He had no previous experience as a Christian before being baptized in the Spirit.

Now it is not so easy. Most people who are baptized in the Spirit in the United States today have been Christians for some length of time before. Many of them have had definite experiences of the presence of the Spirit in them. They usually do not feel that they can say with the simplicity of the early Christians that they just "received the Spirit" when they had the experience which is commonly described as being baptized in the Spirit.

Once we sort out the relationship of the new experience of being baptized in the Spirit to previous spiritual experiences and changes, it becomes clearer that being baptized in the

Spirit means different things for different people. Different people, depending on their situation, can expect different things to happen to them when they are baptized in the Spirit. For this reason, what it means to be baptized in the Spirit deserves some more careful thought.

Talking About It

There are a variety of ways of speaking about the coming of the Holy Spirit into a person's life. The rest of our thinking about what it means to be baptized in the Spirit will be clearer if we first see how some words are used (or could be used).

In the New Testament, there are five descriptions of people entering into a union with the Holy Spirit: the day of Pentecost itself (Acts 2), the "Samaritan Pentecost" (Acts 8:4-25), Paul's conversion (9:10-19), the "Gentile Pentecost" (Acts 10), and the conversion of the disciples at Ephesus (Acts 19:1-12). It seems clear that the same thing happened in all five events. There is another event in which the same thing happened, the Johannine Pentecost (John 20:19-23), but because of the complications in understanding the meaning of this passage, it is better ot omit considering it at this point.

The five events are referred to in the New Testament by the following terms (Other places in the New Testament in which these terms are probably used to describe the same thing are added in parentheses.):

(being sent) what the Father promised	Luke 24:49; Acts 1:4, 2:33
the gift of God	Acts 8:20, 11:17
receiving the gift of the Holy Spirit	Acts 2:38
receiving the Holy Spirit	Acts 8:17,19, 10:47, 19:2 (cf.,John 7:39, 14: 17, 20:22; 1 Cor.2:12; Gal. 3:2; Rom. 8:15)
being filled with the Holy Spirit	Acts 2:4, 9:17 (note: this term is also used for special "fill-ings" subse-

	quent to the initial "filling": Acts 4:8, 4:31, 7:55, 13:9; Eph.5:18; Luke 1:41, 67)
being baptized in the Holy Spirit	Acts 1:5, 11:16 (cf., Mark 1:8; Matt. 3:11; Luke 3:16; John 1:33; 1 Cor. 12:13)
being clothed with power	Luke 24:49 (Acts 1:8–similar)
the Holy Spirit comes on	Acts 19:6 (Luke 2:27)
the Holy Spirit falls upon (comes down on)	Acts 10:44, 11:15
the Holy Spirit is poured out on	Acts 2:33, 10:45

the spirit is given	Acts 8:18 (John 7:39; 1 John 3:24, 4:13; Luke 11:13; 1 Thess. 4:8; 2 Cor. 1:22, 5:5; 2 Tim. 1:6)

What seems to be the same thing is referred to in other places in the New Testament in the following terms: receiving the promise of the Holy Spirit (Gal.3:14); being sealed with the Holy Spirit (Eph.1:13, 4:30); being born of water and the Spirit or being born again from above (John 3:5-8, similar–Gal. 4:29); the Holy Spirit is sent into our hearts (Gal.4:6); the Holy Spirit is supplied (Gal.3:5); and the Holy Spirit descends on and alights or remains –the description of Christ's baptism (Mark 1:10; Luke 3:22; Matt.3:16; John 1:32-33).

The terms which are used in the New Testament to describe the entering into a union with the Holy Spirit are interchangeable. "Being baptized in the Holy Spirit" is used to refer to the same thing as "receiving the Holy Spirit" or "the Holy Spirit falls upon." In other words, "being baptized in the Holy Spirit" does not refer to a special experience of the Holy Spirit that is different from "receiving the Holy Spirit."

The list of terms from the New Testament all suggest that something happens to a person. To be more precise, they suggest that something (the Spirit) comes to him or is given to him and his part is to receive. They are all (except perhaps "being sent what the Father promised") metaphors. The change is described as if water is poured out or on or into a person; as if a gift were being given and received; or as if clothing were being put on a person by someone else. The most commonly used terms are those that say in one form or another: the Holy Spirit is given and received.

An unmetaphorical way of stating what happens is to say that there is a change in our relationship with God. This change is produced by God. Our part is to receive it (let it happen). Because of this change, God (the Holy Spirit) enters our life in a new way, so that we begin to experience him doing in us those things which God promised that the Holy Spirit would do in the life of the believer: he gives us the seven gifts (he teaches us, guides us, deepens our union with God, brings scripture alive, and gives us an apostolic boldness and zeal), the fruits of the Spirit (love, joy, peace, patience, etc.), some of the charismatic gifts (tongues, prophecy, healing, miracles, etc.), and lets us be an active part of the Christian community.

A simple definition of what it is to be baptized in the Spirit is: to be baptized in the Spirit means that we have a change in our relationship with God such that we can begin to experience in our lives all the things which God promised that the Holy Spirit would do for believers.

There is another way we might want to talk about it. Most Christians believe that the Holy Spirit is in them even before they are baptized in the Spirit–through their faith in Christ, through baptism, through confirmation. But they do not experience in their lives all the things which God promised the Holy Spirit would do and which the early Christians experienced. If the Holy Spirit is in us, there must be some barrier or block to our experiencing his presence and working. Therefore, we could describe our being baptized in the Spirit as the release of the Spirit in us or as our being opened in the Spirit.

The most common term for this change in our relationship with God is the term "baptized in the Spirit." For a variety of historical reasons, this was the term which was given to this experience of the Spirit at the beginning of the Pentecostal Movement in 1900. It has been used not only by members of Pentecostal churches, but also by people in the mainline Protestant churches and in the Catholic Church. Probably the best reason for using it is historical: this is the term by which most people talk about it today.

However, there is another reason for using this term. If we were to speak about a person receiving the Spirit or being given the Spirit when they were baptized in the Spirit, many people would assume by that that we were denying that the Spirit had ever been given to the believer before that in any way at all (whether through faith in Christ or through baptism or through confirmation). It is true, in the New Testament, all these terms mean the same thing–they all refer to the same experience. When the New Testament says that the Holy Spirit was given to a believer, it means that he experienced the full working of the Spirit. The giving of the Spirit was experienced. But we can select one of the New Testament terms (being baptized in the Spirit), and use it to refer to the change in a believer's life that comes when he first begins to experience the presence and working of the Spirit. The Spirit may have been given in some way before, but when a person is baptized in the Spirit he begins to experience him in a new way, the same way believers in the New Testament did.

The most common form of this term nowadays is the noun form. People speak about "the baptism of the Spirit" and "receiving the baptism of the Spirit." This is, however, not a scriptural use of the term. In the New Testament what we receive (or have) is the Holy Spirit himself (or the gift of the Holy Spirit). And we are baptized in him.

There is another reason for not using the term "the baptism of the Spirit" any more than necessary. When we start talking about "the baptism of the Spriit," we begin to start thinking of it as a thing. The image that comes to mind is some mark on the soul or some merit badge. People often think of "the baptism of the Spirit" as an assured status. If we have "the baptism of the Spirit," we have made it. All the world is divided into Christians who have "the baptism of the Spirit" and Christians who don't. In other words, to talk about what happens as being baptized in the Spirit helps us to realize that it is only a (past) experience which provided us an introduction to an ongoing life in the Spirit. What is important is not "having the baptism in the Spirit," but actually living the life of the Spirit.

Two Events–or one?

There are some knotty theological problems connected with understanding what it is to be baptized in the Spirit. They are worth considering, however, because once we understand the reason for these problems, we can understand more clearly what happens when a person is baptized in the Spirit.

The most common theological problem connected with being baptized in the Spirit is the question of whether coming to Christ and receiving the Spirit are one event or two. Is a person automatically baptized in the Spirit when he becomes a Christian or is that something that has to happen subsequently? This question is usually raised by conservative evangelical Protestants, but sometimes it is raised by Catholics in a slightly different framework (one that is usually concerned with the sacraments of baptism and confirmation).

First of all, being baptized in the Spirit *can be* different from coming to Christ. This is true in present-day experience; it is true in the scriptures; and it was true in the early church.

Many people today have had two different experiences in their coming into a deeper relationship with Christ, and these experiences have had different effects in their lives. One of the first people I ever knew who could talk about being baptized in the Spirit was a conservative evangelical who had all of his experiences "in proper form." He "received Jesus" at a Billy Graham crusade and then became part of a conservative evangelical church. As a result of his conversion he felt that he "knew the Lord," and he lived a good Christian life because of it, a life that was by no means empty of all Christian experience.

Some years later, he was convinced by some friends of his who had a similar background that there was something more. He could see it in them. So he asked to be baptized in the Spirit and he was, speaking in tongues right away. His prayer life began to be one of praise and worship. The scriptures spoke to him in a new way. The presence of God in him became more experiential and flowing. He could sense the guidance of the Spirit. In other words, he began to live the life of the Spirit. When he was baptized in the Spirit, he had a different experience from when he received Christ.

One of the first Catholics I ever talked to

who had been baptized in the Spirit had a very similar experience. He had come to know Christ in an adult way on a Cursillo. After that he had a personal relationship with him and lived a good Christian life for a number of years. Then he was baptized in the Spirit and received the gift of tongues. As a result of that, he too began to live the life of the Spirit with a new prayer life, a new experience of the presence of God, a new experience of God's working in his life. For both the Protestant and the Catholic, being baptized in the Spirit was different from coming to Christ.

The same thing can be seen in the scriptures. The descriptions of people receiving the Spirit in Acts show that the people involved did not receive the Spirit until after they had turned to Christ, believed in him, and been baptized.

This is especially clear in two accounts. When the disciples at Ephesus received the Spirit, they received him after believing and being baptized when Paul laid hands on them. (I have added emphasis to key words in the following passages.)

> When they heard this they were baptized in the name of the Lord Jesus, and *the*

> *moment Paul laid hands on them*, the Holy Spirit came down on them, and they began to speak in tongues and to prophesy.
>
> (Acts 19:5-7)

Luke seems anxious to emphasize that it was the laying on of hands which was the reason for the coming of the Spirit on them, not baptism.

The same thing is true in the eighth chapter of Acts. The account of how the people in the Samaritan town received the Spirit seems to be designed to emphasize the fact that it was not baptism but the laying on of hands which gave the Holy Spirit:

> When the apostles in Jerusalem heard that Samaria had accepted the word of God, they sent Peter and John to them, and they went down there and prayed for the Samaritans to receive the Holy Spirit, for as yet he had not come down on any of them; they had *only been baptized* in the name of the Lord Jesus. Then they laid hands on them, and they received the Holy Spirit. When Simon saw that the *Spirit was given through* the imposition of hands by the apostles . . .
>
> (Acts 8:14-18)

In other words, in both passages, receiving the Holy Spirit came subsequently to believing and being baptized. The difference between being joined to Christ and receiving the Spirit is confirmed in passages in the New Testament which mention the two in a parallel but separate way. The clearest instance is in Titus 3:5-6:

> It was for no reason except his own compassion that he saved us by means of *the cleansing water of rebirth* and by *renewing us with the Holy Spirit* which he has so generously poured over us through Jesus Christ our savior.

Another instance is in the third chapter of John where Jesus is talking to Nicodemus:

> I tell you most solemnly, unless a man is born through *water* and *the Spirit*, he cannot enter the kingdom of God. (John 3:5)

The early church (in fact the church today) kept an awareness of the difference between being joined to Christ and receiving the Spirit in the two-fold rite of initiation (baptism and "confirmation"). Whenever people were brought into the church, they were both baptized and had hands laid on them for the Holy Spirit (and then were fed with the eucharist).

Many of the writers in the early church spoke about the difference between being joined to Christ and receiving the Spirit. In the earliest "church order," the *Apostolic Tradition* of Hippolytus (c. 217), the prayer for the laying on of hands for the newly baptized is as follows:

> O Lord God, who didst count these thy servants worthy of deserving the forgiveness of sins by the laver of regeneration, make them worthy to be filled with thy Holy Spirit and send upon them thy grace that they may serve thee according to thy will.

Tertullian in *On Baptism* (ch. 6), written about the same time as the *Apostolic Tradition*, shows the same view:

> Not that in the waters we receive the Holy Spirit, but cleansed in water . . . we are prepared for the Holy Spirit.

Augustine in one of his sermons (c. 400) is even emphatic about the point:

> This distinction between the reception of baptism and the reception of the Holy Spirit shows us clearly enough that we should not think that those whom we do not deny to have received baptism forthwith have the Holy Spirit.

The same view can be traced in many other fathers of the church.

But on the other hand, being baptized in the Spirit *should normally not happen at a different time* from coming to Christ. This seems to be true both from the scriptures and from the practice of the early church.

Probably the instance of the reception of the Spirit in Acts which was the most normal was the instance in Acts 19. When Paul brought the group of 12 disciples into the fullness of Christian life, he first baptized them and then laid hands on them for the Holy Spirit. In other words, even though there were two different things which Paul did, they occurred right together. He did not wait for a while between the two. The experience of those disciples of entering the Christian life for all practical purposes was one experience. They entered from Judaism (or semi-Christianity) to the full life of the Spirit.

That this was the most normal way (and the way in which it happened to the Samaritans in Acts 8 was not), is confirmed by the practice of the early church. The normal way in which a person in the early Christian community was led into the full Christian life involved one event in which the new Christian was baptized, anointed, had hands laid on him, and was given communion. All these things were done at the same time. Even though there were a variety of rites in this one event, for all practical purposes there must have been just one experience for those who entered the Christian life. They were baptized and received the Spirit all at once. They went from learning about Christianity to the full life in the Spirit without going through two stages.

If it is true that the normal way in which people came into the Christian life included being introduced to the full life of the Spirit, then when writers in the New Testament wrote about the Christian life, they were addressing communities of Christians who had all been baptized in the Spirit. The only two groups they knew of were non-Christians and Christians baptized in the Spirit. The former were not part of the Christian community. They did not have to deal with Christians who were part of the Christian community but who were not baptized in the Spirit.

The New Testament writings confirm this view. There is never any urging in the letters in the New Testament for some of the Christians to receive the Spirit. New Testament writers never refer to two groups among the Christians–those who have received the Spirit and those who have not yet received the Spirit. In fact, consistently the New Testament writers presuppose that those who are listening to the letters have all been baptized in the Spirit. Even when they are acting in an unspiritual way, the writers do not call into question whether they have received the Spirit. Rather, they say that they are not living up to (or according to) what they have been given. (See 1 Cor.1-6, esp.2:12,16; 3:16; 6:11,17,19; Gal. 3:2; 4:6; 5:25.)

It is for this reason that New Testament writings so easily equate the new life in Christ and the life of the Spirit. In the third chapter of John, when Jesus talks about the new life which is given from above, he is talking about the life of the Spirit. He does not suggest that there are two lives (or two births). There is one: the life from above, the life of the Spirit (rather than of the flesh). When Paul talks in

Romans 8 about what the new life that is given to us through faith in Christ does to us, he sees only two options: living according to the flesh and in sin and living according to the Spirit and in Christ:

> But you are not in the flesh, you are in the Spirit, if the Spirit of God really dwells in you. Any one who does not have the Spirit of Christ does not belong to him. But if Christ is in you, although your bodies are dead because of sin, your spirits are alive because of righteousness. If the Spirit of him who raised Jesus from the dead dwells in you, he who raised Christ Jesus from the dead will give life to your mortal bodies also through his Spirit which dwells in you. . . . For all who are led by the Spirit of God are sons of God.

Even the passage in Titus which indicates a difference between what happens in the baptismal washing and the giving of the Holy Spirit only talks about one result for the two of them:

> It was for no reason except his own compassion that he saved us by means of the

> cleansing water of rebirth and by renewing us with the Holy Spirit which he has so generously poured over us through Jesus Christ our savior. He did this so that we should be justified by his grace, to become heirs looking forward to inheriting eternal life. (Titus 3:5-7)

In other words, the renewal of the Holy Spirit is part of justification by grace, the new birth.

If it is true that there can be a difference between being joined to Christ and receiving the Spirit, then it is permissible to talk about baptism in the Spirit as something different from becoming a Christian, and it is permissible to talk about it as a renewal of confirmation (and not just as a renewal of the whole process of initiation). It is also permissible to appropriate different effects in the believer to the union with Christ and the union with the Holy Spirit.

On the other hand, if being joined to Christ and receiving the Spirit normally come together and are talked about in the New Testament as one event (perhaps a two-fold event, but one event nevertheless), then the two should not normally be separated in thought or action. Normally, therefore, a person should be joined to Christ and baptized in the Spirit at the same time. Normally we should not talk about the difference between the work of Christ and the work of the Spirit in a believer (Christ is at work in us through his Spirit.) And normally coming into the Christian life should be seen as a process including baptism, the laying on of hands, and receiving the eucharist (becoming a full part of the Christian people in their common gathering). Moreover, the purpose of baptism should normally be explained as bringing people into the full life of the Spirit in the Christian community, even though baptism itself (in the sense of the water bath) is only one step in the process.

Evaluating Today's Christianity

We have difficulties in understanding what is going on when people are baptized in the Holy Spirit because we are living in a different situation from the early church. We are confronted with a large number of people who are Christians, but whose experience of the Christian life is not the same as the experience the early Christians had. They are missing something. They are not living the full life of the Spirit. Sometimes, in fact, their relationship with

Christ is perfunctory. When we try to apply New Testament ideas to the modern situation, what can we say about it? Most of the Christians we are dealing with are in the category which probably did not exist in the New Testament: the member of the Christian church who believes in Christ but does not experience the Holy Spirit.

There seem to be two ways of dealing with this situation. The approach which has been taken by many conservative evangelicals is to say that because Christians today do not have the same experience of the Christian life that the early Christians did, they are not Christians at all. (Or they say that becuase they do not have the same experience of the Holy Spirit as the early Christians did, they have not received him at all.)

Conservative evangelical theology grew out of the Evangelical Awakening (mostly begun through the work of Wesley) in the 18th and 19th centuries. The early evangelicals were concerned that Christians of their day seemed to be lukewarm and to lack the kind of experience of Christ that the early Christians had. They also discovered personally that it was possible to have a real experience of Christ. Many of them then made the step of saying that it was this experience which was the experience of salvation and which made people Christians. By "salvation" they meant that which let people go to heaven.

The center of evangelical teaching, then, has been "saving people," that is, bringing them to a salvation experience. This experience comes through turning to the Lord and praying for him to "enter our lives," "be our Lord and savior" or however it is expressed. This experience is described as "being saved," "being born again," or "receiving Jesus." Some evangelicals teach that once a person has had this experience, he will automatically go to heaven, no matter what he does afterwards. Most evangelicals say that it is this experience that makes a person a Christian. All those other people who believe in Christ and are trying to live according to his teachings are simply not Christians at all.

Toward the end of the 19th century, many evangelicals began to feel that they were still not having the same experience as the early Christians had. They began to see that there was more. At the start of the 20th century, some evangelicals (mostly from the Holiness Movement) began to discover that if they prayed in faith to be baptized in the Holy

Spirit, they could experience the same things happening to them that happened to the early Christians. They could experience the full life of the Spirit with all the spiritual gifts. As a result of this discovery, the Pentecostal Movement developed.

The early Pentecostals were mostly evangelicals who took the same approach to the new experience which the evangelicals took to the old. This new experience is the second step. Once you have been "saved" then you get "filled." Moreover, only those who have exactly the same kind of experience that the early Christians had have the Holy Spirit at all. All other Christians, even when they seem to experience something of the Holy Spirit or some of the workings of the Holy Spirit, are simply not "Spirit-filled" at all.

Many evangelicals, however, could not accept the Pentecostal experience. They pointed out (to their own satisfaction) that in the New Testament a person received the Holy Spirit (was baptized in the Holy Spirit) when he was joined to Christ (was saved). The Pentecostals, of course, having experienced something more, were convinced that what the evangelicals were talking about as being baptized in the Spirit was not what the New

Testament was talking about as being baptized in the Spirit. And they could point to New Testament passages where the two experiences were different (Acts 2,8,10,19). Some Pentecostals, in a desire to be accommodating (or "ecumenical") have stressed that they did not mean to imply that when a person was saved he had not received the Holy Spirit at all. They might even try to sort out which New Testament passages referred to the Holy Spirit as he was possessed by those who were "saved" and which passages referred to the Holy Spirit as he was possessed by those who were also "filled." Finally, some Pentecostals have even come up with two different experiences of receiving the Holy Spirit, the first being the one by which a person is "saved," the second the one by which he is "baptized in the Holy Spirit."

A second way of dealing with the present-day situation in which there are many Christians who do not experience the same thing which the early Christians did is found in Catholic teaching. Catholic teaching holds that those who have been properly prayed for to be joined to Christ and to receive the Spirit (baptized and confirmed) are Christians in good standing and have been joined to Christ and received the Spirit even if they do not seem to have any direct experience of Christ or of the Spirit.

Catholic teaching is based on the view that once the church has prayed in faith for someone to be joined to Christ and filled with the Spirit, it has happened. The way Catholics would say this is that these people have been baptized and confirmed and are now part of the church. They may lose their faith (stop believing) and fall into sin (turn away from Christ). In that case they would be no longer "living as Christians/Catholics/in grace" and they are no longer in union with Christ. But as long as they still have faith (believe) and are not living in serious sin (have repented) and have been baptized, they are Christians in good standing.

When a Catholic teacher would take a look at the present situation among Christians and would notice that most of them do not seem to be experiencing what the early Christians experienced (or what the church prayed for in the sacraments of baptism and confirmation), he would not say that therefore they were not Christians or were not joined to Christ at all or had not received the Spirit at all. He would say that they needed to have the sacraments take full effect. They needed some kind of revitalization or growth or release or renewal. But he would never say that they had not received the Spirit at all.

There is strength to both approaches to the present situation. The evangelicals (including the Pentecostals) have discovered that there is no reason not to have the same experience that the early Christians had. They have discovered that those who want to can pray to the Lord in faith and they will have a definite experience which will put them at the same level of experience which the early Christians were at.

The Catholic approach, however, has the advantage of not simply writing off the Christianity of millions of people who believe in Christ and are living good Christian lives, even though they are not experiencing Christ or the Holy Spirit in the same way that the early Christians did. Catholic teaching also has the strength of keeping clear the fact that the most important test for a person's Christian life is the fruits of it. The test is whether he is living the Christian life, not what kind of experience he has had (Matt.7:21-28; 1 Cor.12:1-3; Gal.5; 1 Cor.6:9f; 1 Cor.13; Rev.21:6-8,etc.).

But however the two approaches differ in the way they talk about things and how they make use of the New Testament terms, they agree on two points: 1) what the New Testament describes as the norm of Christian living should be there completely; 2) most Christians today are deficient in their Christian lives. They do not experience what the early Christians experienced or do not have what should be there.

There is, in fact, a problem for all kinds of Christian teachers, whether they are evangelical Pentecostals, Catholic Pentecostals, evangelicals who are not Pentecostals, or Catholics who are not Pentecostals. The problem is how to talk about the person who is in the category which the New Testament writers do not explicitly cover—the Christian who has not experienced being baptized in the Spirit the same way which the early Christains did. Since the passages in the New Testament about life "in Christ" or "in the Spirit" refer to people who have been baptized in the Spirit, they do not simply apply to people who have not been. But since these people are in some way Christians, these passages are not completely inapplicable to them.

We may not be able to work out a way of talking about these things which will satisfy everyone, but we can keep two things clear.

The first thing we need to keep clear is what the early Christians experienced. That way we can know when we are not experiencing what they experienced. That way, too, we will avoid the rationalizations and confusions that come from using New Testament terms to describe situations that are different from those the New Testament writers were talking about. The second thing we need to keep clear is that if we seek in faith, the Lord will work in our lives the same way he worked among the early Christians. We can make the New Testament terms a description of our Christian communities by letting the Lord work among us in full freedom.

The Spiritually Experienced

Before going on to try to say what being baptized in the Spirit means today, we need to consider another category of people–those who have a great deal of spiritual experience, but have not had the same kind of experience which the early Christains had. The people in this category are often monks and nuns and other "religious." They are people who have given their lives completely to seeking a deeply spiritual life, and who have often experienced real workings of the Spirit in their lives. But many of them have not had the same kinds of experiences which the new Christians had in Acts (a definite experience of a filling with the Spirit which involves a gift of inspired praise), and who do not seem to experience the charismatic gifts.

Traditionally, spiritual growth has been described in terms of the purgative way, the illuminative way, and the unitive way. In the purgative way a person is cleansed from sins and imperfections. In the illuminative way, a person comes to know Christ and grow in Christ-like qualities. In the unitive way, he experiences a love of God, and he experiences God doing more in him to give him a deeper relationship with himself. In particular, he begins to experience God giving him a gift of prayer (infused contemplation) so that prayer is no longer something he works at but something God works in him.

It is in the third way, the unitive way, that a person begins to experience the Holy Spirit working in him. In the first two ways, what happens is in large part due to our efforts. In the purgative way, we turn from sin. In the illuminative way, we seek to know Christ and to pattern our lives on the virtues he taught us about. For the unitive way, however, is reserved the direct experience of the Spirit and his working in our lives. As Bouyer puts it in his *Introduction to Spirituality*, "In the unitive way the presence, the activity of the Spirit within us, becomes as it were the object of direct experience." The way in which the activity of the Holy Spirit in us is most commonly experienced is in infused contemplation which is the Spirit inspiring a person to prayer.

A common view of these three "ways" (possibly the most popular view of the three ways, but not the only view) is that they are three stages of the spiritual life, each one of which takes a certain length of time. A person, then, would have to begin with a certain amount of purification before he could begin to be illuminated, and finally after a period of spiritual growth, he could then begin to experience a deep union with God and the work of the Holy Spirit in him. In other words, the Holy Spirit would be given only to people who had received a developed state of spiritual growth.

According to this view, because a person did not experience the presence of the Spirit working in him until he had reached the unitive stage does not mean that the Spirit was not working in him. He could not have grown in the Christian life at all if the Spirit had not been working in him. The whole Christian life is a work of grace. It is the experienced working of the Spirit—what we have described as living the life of the Spirit—that did not come until the unitive stage. In other words, according to the approach summarized in the three ways, a person was not baptized in the Spirit until he had reached a certain degree of spiritual maturity.

The difference between what is happening now in the charismatic renewal and what happened in some traditional forms of spirituality is that people in the charismatic renewal are being baptized in the Spirit at the beginning of their spiritual growth. Before the charismatic renewal, it was not common for people to experience the gift of the Spirit and infused prayer until some years had passed in their spiritual growth. True, traditional spiritual writers have always known that it did not have to take many years. They knew it could happen at any time. But they did not normally expect it to happen until a person had spent many years in spiritual growth. Now we know that the Spirit can be given freely even to beginners in the spiritual life. This is clearly the way it was given in New Testament times.

Many of the people who were baptized in the Spirit in Acts had just heard the gospel for the first time. And the Corinthians and Galatians who were experiencing so many workings of the Spirit had only been converted a few years before. They were "new Christians." Most of the people in the Christian community I am part of began their spiritual growth only after having been baptized in the Spirit.

Probably the main reason for the difference in the two experiences is the difference in expectation. The charismatic renewal is a renewal in what could be called "expectant faith." The basis of it is the discovery that if we expect God to do for us what he did for the early Christians and if we ask for it, we will receive it. Since many spiritual men traditionally did not expect to experience the working of the Spirit until they had gone through a process of purification and illumination, they did not have faith that it would happen sooner, and so they did not see it happen. The Lord seems to give to us according to our faith.

But we should not simply assume that because the experience of the Spirit comes earlier in the charismatic renewal than it comes in most traditional forms of spiritual life, that the people who followed the traditional forms simply have an inferior form of spiritual life. The point of what I have been saying is not necessarily that it is inferior, but that it is different, and we need to understand the difference to see what being baptized in the Spirit can mean to someone brought up in traditional spirituality.

First of all, those who have been growing according to a traditional spirituality often have a great deal of spiritual maturity even if they have not been baptized in the Spirit. They are living at a higher level as Christians than many who have been baptized in the Spirit. They are serving the Lord better, loving God and their neighbor more. They may be deficient in some experience, but they are not therefore worse Christians according to the New Testament standards for judging Christians (doing the will of the Father). In fact, when a person is a new Christian who has just been baptized in the Spirit, he needs to go through much of the same growth process which is sketched out in the treatment of the purgative, illuminative, and unitive ways. He is not a formed Christian when he is baptized in the Spirit.

Secondly, because a person has been formed

in traditional spirituality means that often his experience of the Spirit will be somewhat different from that of those who have been part of the charismatic renewal. Our experiences tend to go according to our expectations, because that is often the only way we will allow them to happen to ourselves. For instance, if a person has a certain view of interpersonal relationships, all his relationships with other people will turn out that way, because that is what he is looking for. As a result, someone in the charismatic renewal will allow the Lord to give him the Holy Spirit quickly in one sudden experience, because that is what he is looking for. At the same time, he will be hesitant about accepting a gradual release of the Spirit as being the real article, because what he has been seeking is the complete experience. On the other hand, someone formed in traditional spirituality will be more inclined to have the Spirit released in him gradually, and he will have trouble yielding to a sudden leap in his spiritual experience.

Third, those who have been brought up in traditional spirituality have been used to a different approach to relating to God than what they find in the charismatic renewal. Almost always, they are not used to making the kind of act of faith in the promises of God which new Christians often find so easy. They are used to waiting patiently with nothing discernible happening. Moreover, sometimes they expect that the Spirit will be given to them because of their submission to God's will (rather than by asking in faith). Sometimes, if their formation has not been healthy, they have even been used to suppressing their own emotions and desires and to having a fear of believing that God wants to give them gifts (rather than wants them to suffer).

Because of the differences between the charismatic renewal and traditional forms of spirituality, people who have been brought up in traditional spirituality often have special difficulties in understanding what it is to be baptized in the Spirit. Sometimes this difficulty comes from their very maturity in the spiritual life. After many years of spiritual growth, they find it difficult to ask for the same thing that some college freshman who has just been converted to Christianity is asking for.

Sometimes this difficulty comes from the fact that they have experienced some of the life of the Spirit. When they hear a description of what happens when a person is baptized in the Spirit, they feel that in some ways they need it and in other ways they do not. So they find that they cannot ask for it unambiguously or in full faith.

Sometimes this difficulty comes from their formation. If they have not been taught to claim the promises of the Lord in the scriptures, but have been given a semi-stoical attitude (wait in patient submission to see if perhaps the Lord might give some favor and have faith in his love even if you do not experience anything) and a fear of their own desires and emotions, they will find it very difficult to open up to the work of the Spirit. They will, as a matter of fact, find it difficult whether the life of the Spirit is described to them in the traditional way or in the way in which it has been lived in the charismatic renewal.

Because of these difficulties, living in a community of people who are living the life of the Spirit is also important for people who have been brought up in traditional spirituality. What the charismatic renewal has to offer them is a new, more effective attitude of faith. This new attitude of faith is not so different from what they have had that they will be able to understand it easily. Nor will it involve a total overthrow of their previous teaching and patterns of life. What they need is a series of adjustments throughout their whole Christian mentality, and usually such adjustments come only through being part of a community that is living in a new way.

Fully in Christ

What then is it to be baptized in the Spirit? In one way it is the same for everyone—a change in their relationship with God such that they experience the full working of the Spirit (everything which the early Christians experienced or which was promised in the New Testament). But, because different people have very different relationships with the Holy Spirit when they are baptized in the Spirit, significantly different things happen to them.

There seem to be three main categories of things that happen to people when they are "baptized in the Spirit." Firstly, it can be a complete coming into the full life of Christ (the full life of the Spirit)—from nothing to everything. It is this for non-Christians (people who did not believe in Christ before they were prayed with to be baptized in the Spirit), for nominal Christians (people who call themselves Christians for one reason or another, but whose "Christian lives" exist without understanding, without conviction, without prayer, without any experience of Christ or any trace that he has affected their lives), and for fallen-away Christians (people who once were Christians but had completely fallen away until they came to be prayed with). For people in this category, when they are baptized in the Spirit, they are joined to Christ and are born anew.

Secondly, being baptized in the Spirit can be a transition from a Christian life lived "according to doctrine" to a Christian life lived "according to the Spirit." It is this for people who believe in Christ and are trying to live the Christian life (with some degree of devotion), but who have no direct experience of the working of the Spirit in them. Their Christianity is a matter of teachings which they believe, practices they do, and a morality they keep. For people in this category, when they are baptized in the Spirit, they are introduced to the work of the Spirit in them in a way which they can experience. They begin the life of the Spirit.

Finally, for some, being baptized in the Spirit can mean something like "a charismatic release." It is this for people who are already "spiritual," who have had some formation in spirituality and have experienced the presence and working of the Spirit in some kind of way. But there are things missing in their life of the Spirit. Usually, they will not have the kind of direct faith that can ask for results and see them happen. Usually they will not be experiencing "inspired praise" (the gift of tongues). Usually they will not be experiencing the other spiritual gifts (prophecy, discernment of spirits, healing, etc.). What being baptized in the Spirit means to people in this category is not a simple reception of the Spirit. Rather it is a freeing of the Spirit in them in such a way that they can experience all the normal workings of the Spirit. It might be even more proper to speak of what happens to them as a freeing of their faith rather than as a filling with the Spirit or as being baptized in the Spirit.

Perhaps we should mention one last group—those who have experienced all the New Testament workings of the Spirit, but have not realized it. There are many people like this, and there have been many through the centuries. Often people have experienced the gift of tongues and not known what has happened to them and did not ever think "that babbling" could be anything as significant as the gift of tongues. Or they have experienced prophetic revelations and promptings, but have not known that such things could be spoken as a message from God. It is only in a climate in which all the workings of the Spirit are accepted and talked about that such gifts can be discovered and grown in.

To recognize that being baptized in the Spirit can mean different things to different people does not mean that being baptized in the Spirit is less important for some than for others. If we are determined to be Christians, we will want to have everything Christ wants us to have. Rather, recognizing the differences points to a need to sometimes help different people in different ways.

Our difficulties in understanding what it is to be baptized in the Spirit illustrates an old truth which is at the basis of all learning: we can understand only what we have experienced. Very learned theologians and exegetes who have never experienced a community in which everyone was baptized in the Spirit and in which the spiritual gifts are a normal part of life often struggle to grasp a passage in the New Testament that is perfectly clear to some new Christian who has just experienced what the passage is referring to. Moreover, people who come from different traditions will often interpret the same truth in different ways, because they are trying to relate it to different experiences.

In order to be able to take the New Testament the way it was written, we have to have communities which are the same as the New Testament communities. For instance, once we have communities in which everyone is baptized in the Spirit, we will be able to read Paul's epistle to the Romans as a clarification of everyone's experience of redemption and not as a great theological mystery that we believe in faith but would never take as an accurate description of what has happened to us.

Our goal is to be fully in Christ. We must want everything which the Lord is offering to us. We should be working to build Christian communities which are experiencing the full life of the Spirit, communities in which every member has been baptized in the Spirit and which are built up by the spiritual gifts. There must be communities which can take those who come seeking Christ and lead them into the full life of the Spirit.

We need, in other words, a restoration of the community life which existed in the early church in the New Testament period and in the first few centuries. And along with this, we need a restoration of the Christian initiation in which new Christians were taught what the

Christian life was, were freed from evil spirits, were baptized in water and in the Spirit and were fed with the body and blood of Christ. Once they are fully in Christ, everything which was said in the New Testament about Christians will apply to them.

Spiritual Gifts

"Now concerning spiritual gifts, brethren,
I do not want you to be uninformed."
(1 Cor. 12:1)

"Now concerning spiritual gifts, brethren, I do not want you to be uninformed." With these words, St. Paul begins Chapter 12 of his first letter to the Corinthians. He wants them to have information about spiritual gifts. He wants the Corinthians to understand what spiritual gifts are and how they should function in the life of the church. He is concerned because he knows that spiritual gifts can be a great source of strength to the church, as well as an occasion of trouble.

It is hard to know what Paul would write to the church today. He did not want to have the Corinthians uninformed, but few Christians today know much about what he wanted the Corinthians to know. Few understand what spiritual gifts are or their place in the life of the church. Now that there is a renewal in the use of the spiritual gifts among us, and many are experiencing prophecy, healing, speaking in tongues, and the rest, it has become even more important to understand the place of these "manifestations of the Spirit" in the life of the church.

Some Christians do not believe that miracles happened after the death of the last apostle. Yet many still expect to have them occur in every century and every land. We have not forgotten that God heals directly, that he speaks through prophecies, that extraordinary events accompany his work.

The great 13th century theologian, Thomas Aquinas, in *Summa Theologiae* (in the section on "Graces Freely Given") taught that Christians need spiritual gifts, because Christian revelation contains truths above the power of man to know. Consequently, a Christian needs special gifts from God to know Christian truth and preach it, and he needs to have his preaching accompanied by signs so that others will believe.

Even in our own time, the Catholic Church at the Vatican Council taught Christians that they should expect spiritual gifts. In the Decree on the Lay Apostolate (sec. 3) the Council fathers say:

> For the exercise of this apostolate (of evangelism) the Holy Spirit who sanctifies the people of God through the ministry and the sacraments, gives to the faithful special gifts as well (cf.,1 Cor.12:7), "alloting to every-

> one according as he will" (1 Cor.12:11). Thus may the individual "according to the gifts that each has received, administer it to one another" and become "good stewards of the manifold grace of God" (1 Pet.4:10) and build up the whole body in charity (cf., Eph.4:16). From the reception of these charisms or gifts, including those which are less dramatic, there arises for each believer the right and duty to use them in the Church and in the world for the good of mankind and for the upbuilding of the Church.

Something similar is stated in the Constitution on the Church (sec. 12). The fact that the Council fathers emphasize what are called the less dramatic gifts indicates that they also expect the more dramatic gifts, the kind Paul talks about in 1 Cor. 12.

We know from the Bible that we should expect spiritual gifts. At the end of the gospel of Mark, the risen Christ says to the apostles:

> Go into all the world and preach the gospel to the whole creation. He who believes and is baptized will be saved; but he who does not believe will be condemned. And these

> signs will accompany those who believe: in my name they will cast out demons; they will speak in new tongues; they will pick up serpents, and if they drink any deadly thing, it will not hurt them; they will lay their hands on the sick, and they will recover.

Or Paul says in 1 Cor. 13:8-10:

> Love never ends; as for prophecies, they will pass away; as for tongues they will cease; as for knowledge it will pass away. For our knowledge is imperfect, and our prophecy is imperfect, but when the perfect comes, the imperfect will pass away.

"The coming of the perfect" must mean the second coming. It is certainly not referring to anything that has happened yet. Who has yet suggested that the perfect has come and we see face to face? Until Christ comes we can expect the spiritual gifts.

We should expect to see spiritual gifts in the life of the church. And it should not surprise us to know that they are becoming as frequent as they were in New Testament times. We know that if the church is to be renewed and if the world can ever be led to Christ, there must be a special work of the Holy Spirit. It was this realization that guided Pope John when he prayed for the Vatican Council, "Renew your wonders this day as by a new Pentecost."

What Are the Spiritual Gifts?

St. Paul wrote about spiritual gifts in his first letter to the Corinthians, chapters 12-14. If we want to understand more fully what spiritual gifts are and how they should be used, we can study these chapters. These chapters are Paul's special instructions about spiritual gifts to the church at Corinth, a church he had founded. He begins the whole section by talking about the spiritual gifts he has in mind: the utterance of wisdom, the utterance of knowledge, faith, healing, miracles, prophecy, the ability to distinguish between spirits, various kinds of tongues, the interpretation of tongues.

At this point we sometimes get confused. We know something about spiritual gifts, but we were taught in the catechism class that there are only seven of them: wisdom, understanding, knowledge, counsel, piety, fortitude, and fear of the Lord. To understand what Paul is talking about, we need to understand that there are different types of spiritual gifts. The seven gifts are gifts that come along with the Spirit for the strengthening of each individual Christian. The nine gifts that St. Paul is talking about are sometimes called charismatic gifts, and are a different type of gift. As we consider what they are, we will see how they differ from the seven gifts.

Paul describes the nine gifts that he is talking about as "manifestations" of the Spirit. In other words, when we see a spiritual gift operating, we realize that the Spirit is at work. A spiritual gift makes us aware of his presence. For instance, when we see someone healed miraculously, or when we hear a prophecy, we know that the Spirit is present and at work. When someone is present at a manifestation of the Spirit, it is hard for him to think that God is dead.

Spiritual gifts also make us aware of God's power. They manifest his ability to change the world. At a recent conference of men in pastoral ministry, several persons were sovereignly healed of physical ailments they had borne for a long time. Many of those in attendance had been very skeptical of healing until they witnessed the gift in operation before their eyes. They returned to their churches with a new faith in the effectiveness of prayer and the action of God. This is the effect authentic spiritual gifts can have in people's lives. If we see a deaf person healed, or if we are given a prophecy and see it fulfilled, we are reassured in an even deeper way that God's power is great enough to do all things. That is why St. Paul speaks of Christians as having "tasted the powers of the age to come" (Heb.6:5).

The spiritual gifts, then, are manifestations of God's presence and power. That is why it would be a mistake to say that the gift of healing is what doctors have, or that the gift of tongues is the ability you acquired in school to speak a foreign language, or that the gift of interpretation is what Berlitz translators have. All these things may in a certain sense be gifts of God, but they are not the kind of spiritual gifts that Paul is talking about. If I were to try to tell a non-Christian doctor that his medical skill was a spiritual gift and a manifestation of the Spirit and that therefore he should become a Christian, he would reply that he could not see that it had anything to do with the Spirit. He learned it in school. Moreover, he could say that if his ability was a manifestation of the Spirit, it was an excellent proof that you could have all the spiritual gifts without any faith in Christ at all. Christian belief, according to this view, would be of no value in obtaining gifts of the Spirit.

For example, it is clear what Paul meant when he talked about gifts of healing. He himself healed people instantaneously, not by using medical techniques, but by a simple command (Acts 14:8). And it was a manifestation for the people that the power of God was present. It is also clear that when he talks about the gift of tongues, he is not speaking about a foreign language that he understands, but he is talking about speaking in a language he does not understand (1 Cor.14:14).

As he begins to talk about the spiritual gifts, St. Paul gives us a list of the kind of gifts that he has in mind. There are other lists of spiritual gifts in the New Testament (Rom.12:4-8 and 1 Pet.4:10-11), and they are not the same as the list in 1 Cor.12:4-11, so it is probable that St. Paul was not trying to give a complete list of all the spiritual gifts. However, he does give us enough examples of spiritual gifts so that we can understand what he is talking about.

Teaching Gifts

The first two gifts which St. Paul mentions are teaching gifts: the *utterance of wisdom,* (sometimes translated as "the word of wisdom") and the *utterance of knowledge* (sometimes translated as "the word of knowledge"). These are special inspirations by which God works through one person to give understanding to another person or to a group of people. A person who is given an utterance of wisdom or an utterance of knowledge can then give a lesson (an instruction or an explanation) in the Christian assembly (1 Cor.14:26) or perhaps a special word of advice or instruction to a particular person. The New Testament in great part, especially the epistles, is made up of utterances of wisdom and knowledge–inspired teaching.

The utterance of wisdom probably refers to something different from the utterance of knowledge. The utterance of wisdom is concerned with the best way to live. It is an expression of God's guidance in how to live as a Christian. When Christ spoke to the rich young man and advised him to sell his possessions and follow him (Mark 10:20), he was giving him a word of wisdom. Or when Peter spoke in the Council of Jerusalem and said that the gentiles should not have to follow the full Mosaic Law, he was given an utterance of wisdom by God. Much of what Paul said in 1

Cor. 12-14 would be examples of the utterance of wisdom–practical spiritual teaching. The utterance of knowledge, on the other hand, is more what we would call doctrinal teaching. It is the Spirit inspiring someone to speak an understanding of a truth of the mystery of Christ. Christ's teaching about the relationship between the Father and the Son in Luke 10:22 would be an example of the utterance of knowledge, as would the first chapter of Ephesians where Paul teaches the Ephesians about God's plan.

When he is speaking about the utterance of knowledge Paul almost certainly does not mean a special knowledge of facts that a person could not have known otherwise. I have been present and seen a person–through the operation of a spiritual gift–tell another person something about his past that he could not have known, or tell us what is happening in a room that he was not present in. Revelation happens often, but it is not what Paul is referring to as "the utterance of knowledge." When such a thing happened in the New Testament, people considered it an indication that a person was a prophet (John 4:16-19; Luke 7:39), but they did not consider it "knowledge," a word which in the New Testament is used to describe knowledge of God and the mysteries of God.

The utterance of wisdom and knowledge are spiritual gifts that work through the understanding. The spirit inspires a person to understand a truth, to understand things the way God understands them, and then to speak about them. There is a difference between natural understanding, acquired by study, and inspired understanding. Inspired understanding feeds the spirit in a way that natural understanding cannot, because it is a manifestation of the presence of the Spirit in a person. It makes a deep change in people, giving them an increase of spiritual life.

I remember being present once when a Christian teacher spoke about the love of God. Even while he spoke, I had a sense of the presence of God and I was praying while I was listening to his words. When he finished, there was a change in the whole room. People had come to life, and there was a new sense of the presence of the Spirit. Even though what he had to say was not naturally very impressive, everyone knew that God had spoken through him.

Another time, I was present while a mature Christian was speaking to a young man who had just been baptized in the Spirit. He was explaining how to live the Christian life, and I could see by the expression on the young man's face that his life was being changed by those words. Moreover, the older man did not know the younger man as well as I did, and I am sure that he could not have known how appropriate what he was saying was for that particular man. The Spirit, however, was working through his mind to instruct a new Christian. When I asked him later how he let these gifts operate, he said that when he felt the presence of the Spirit trying to use him, he yielded his mind to the Spirit and he "saw" what to say and how to say it. He said that very often in such situations, he would learn as much as the person he was speaking to, and that he often found himself knowing things that he had never studied or thought through.

Sign Gifts

The next three gifts which St. Paul mentions could be called sign gifts: *faith, gifts of healing,* and *the working of miracles*. They are gifts which manifest the power of God in the world in a particularly striking way. They call attention to God's reality, and so they bring people to a knowledge of God. The words of Christ at the end of the gospel of Mark tell us that this is God's way of confirming the truth of the message:

> Go into all the world and preach the gospel to the whole creation. He who believes and is baptized will be saved; but he who does not believe will be condemned. And these signs will accompany those who believe: in my name they will cast out demons. They will speak in new tongues; they will pick up serpents; and if they drink any deadly thing, it will not hurt them; they will lay their hands on the sick, and they will recover. . . . And they went forth and preached everywhere, while the Lord worked with them and confirmed the message by the signs that attended it.

I was present at a Kathryn Kuhlman "evangelistic" service in Los Angeles one summer, and there I saw the power of the spiritual gifts to bring men to Christ. The message at the service was simple, without a great deal of power to it. But much of the meeting was devoted to prayer for God to heal people. Early in the service a couple of men spoke who had been healed the time before. One had been healed of crippling arthritis (As he put it, "I couldn't even weed my garden, it was so bad.") Another man had been cured of terminal cancer and had his doctor with X-rays taken a week apart to show the authenticity of the cure. Neither of the men was a Christian when he was cured. In the course of that service, about 35 people came forward and said that they were cured of a variety of things. A young boy had been deaf in one ear and was supposed to be operated on that week to have his eardrum sealed up. Now he could hear. A couple of people were cured of arthritis. A woman whom I had seen before on crutches and in a large brace was able to move around and walk normally for the first time since an automobile accident nine years before. At the end of the service, the woman who was leading it asked how many men wanted to become Christians. About 150 men filled the front of the auditorium to commit their lives to Christ, and there were probably even more women who could not find a place.

Such things have happened for many years. At the shrine at Lourdes in France, many people have turned to Christ because they have seen the power of God operate in extraordinary ways. The lives of the saints like

Anthony, Francis, and Vincent Ferrer contain stories of miracles which converted whole towns. When men see the power of God do something extraordinary, they do wonder, and they do turn to God. When they can see him at work in the world in a way that goes beyond what human beings by themselves can do, they recognize the need to confront him.

The sign gifts, then, are the working of the Spirit in power through certain Christians, so that men might know the truth of the Christian message. The first of these—the gift of faith—is not the same as the faith by which all Christians believe and turn to Christ. That is given to all Christians, not just to "another." That kind of faith is what makes men Christians. This kind of faith is a special spiritual gift.

The charismatic gift of faith seems to be a special gift of prayer. It is a gift of praying with a God-given confidence, and it produces extraordinary results. The person who prays with faith knows through the work of the Spirit in him that what he asks for will be given. It is the kind of faith which Christ was speaking about when he said in the Gospel of Mark (Mark 11:23), "Truly I say to you, whoever says to this mountain, 'Be taken up and cast into the sea,' and does not doubt in his heart, but believes that what he says will come to pass, it will be done for him."

The gift of faith is what the prophet Elijah had when he confronted the prophets of Baal. He challenged them to a contest. Whichever god would send down fire from heaven to consume a burnt offering would be the God of Israel. The prophets of Baal went through every rite they could to get Baal to burn the offering, with no results at all. Elijah, on the other hand, first drenched the offering with water so that there would be no doubt about the power of Yahweh, and then he simply prayed, knowing God would answer. And he did. Such faith is God-given. No matter how a man would try to work himself into such faith, he could not do it on his own.

The gifts of healing are different from the power of prayer for healing which is part of the ordinary life of the Christian community. Christians pray for one another for a variety of things and see results. In our community, we have seen people cured of migraine headaches which they had had for years, of colds and flu, of epileptic seizures. Not every prayer has been answered, but we have seen more than can be explained just by accident. Recently people have been approaching the sacrament of anointing with new faith and seeing results. I know of at least one person who was given up as hopeless, who improved right after receiving the sacrament and is well today. Many priests can tell stories of the differences the sacrament has made. These things are part of the normal life of the Christian community.

There are, however, people who seem to have a special gift of healing. When they pray for healing, results happen, and they happen with greater frequency and with more extraordinary effects than happen with other people. The Spirit works through them to produce "works of power," to produce "things for people to be astonished at," to produce miracles. These people have a special spiritual gift, probably because God wishes to use them to bring others to know Chirst.

Revelational Gifts

The next four gifts are gifts which could be called revelational gifts: *prophecy, the ability to distinguish between spirits* (sometimes called discernment of spirits), *various kinds of tongues*, and *interpretation of tongues*. These are gifts by which God makes known something about the current situation to his people.

Discernment of spirits has been called the protection of the Christian community. This is the gift which allows a man to "distinguish between spirits," to tell whether an evil spirit is at work in a person or a situation, or whether it is the Holy Spirit, or whether it is just a man's own spirit. This is probably the work of the Spirit by which Peter "saw" that Simon was "in the gall of bitterness and the bond of iniquity" when he tried to buy the power to confer the Spirit (Acts 8:23), or by which Paul could "see" that the Holy Spirit had given the cripple the faith to be made well (Acts 14:9).

Discernment of spirits is a kind of vision or a sense. One person described to me how the gift of discernment worked with him by saying that he often could almost see the presence of the Holy Spirit in power like a glow. I asked him what he could discern in some people that he did not know but whom I did know. Like Paul he "peered intently" and then gave me a description of those people that I knew to be accurate and which was beyond the power of even extraordinary psychological sensitivity. Another man once told me how in talking to a girl, he was aware that what was holding her back in turning to Christ was the influence (not possession) of an evil spirit. As he put it, he could just sense that that was what the cause was, without knowing her. His discernment was proven true by the marked change in the girl's attitude toward Christ after he prayed with her for deliverance from the influence of the evil spirit. (She did not realize that he had prayed for her that way, because he prayed in a foreign language.) In other words, discernment is a spiritual revelation about the operation of different types of spirits in a person or situation, a means by which God makes Christians aware of what is happening.

Prophecy is a gift by which God speaks through a person a message to an individual or to the whole Christian community. It is God making use of someone to tell men what he thinks about the current situation or what his intention is for the future, or what he thinks they should know or be mindful of right now. Prophecy is not necessarily for prediction of the future (although this frequently happens). Paul describes some of the uses of prophecy by saying in 1 Cor. 14:3, "he who prophesies, speaks to men for their upbuilding and encouragement and consolation." It is God speaking now, to his people, words which are intended to reveal his current attitude.

Today people use the term prophecy in many different senses. Sometimes it is used to describe any speaking of Christ's message to the world. When the word is used in this sense, teaching is a type of prophecy. When a priest or minister teaches, for instance, he is exercising a prophetic role. Another popular use of the term "prophecy" is to regard it as reading the signs of the times or judging the current situation. There are many today who would consider themselves to be exercising a prophetic role because they condemn many current situations in the name of what Christ has revealed.

However, when Paul is using the term "prophecy," he is probably using it in a way that would not include teaching or judging the current situation. He is referring to the type of speaking that occurred when one of the prophets at Antioch stated that Paul and Barnabas were to be set aside for apostolic work (Acts 13:2), or when Agabus foretold that there would be a great famine (Acts 11:28), or when Agabus predicted how Paul would be taken prisoner (Acts 21:1). These prophecies were given as messages from God. They are given in the words of God (the speaker speaks in the first person). That they are more than just human speech is indicated by the accuracy of the predictions and by the fact that the prophet gives directions from God, something that would be sheer presumption if God himself were not speaking. It is clear that not all prophecies are like this. The book of Acts only reports some of the more extraordinary prophecies, but these are enough to indicate that when the New Testament speaks of prophecy, it uses the word in a special sense to indicate direct messages from God.

Speaking a prophecy is more than a person just saying something that happens to be on his mind as a message from God. The prophet receives a special "anointing," an urging to speak. He realizes that he has a message from God, although often he does not know what it is until he actually yields to God and begins to speak. To the degree he yields to God, to that degree his message will be pure. A prophetic message is different from a teaching. A man gives a teaching with his understanding. He sees the truth of what he is saying. A prophet may not understand what he is saying, and he can never "see" that this is God's message right now. He has received a revelation, a message from God.

Prophecy can be very effective in building

up the Christian community. It is clear from 1 Cor. 14 that prophecy was very common in the early church. The church at Corinth apparently had so many messages that there had to be an order to giving them (1 Cor.14:29-32). When a prophecy is given at a gathering of Christians, it has a powerful effect in drawing them to God and deepening their sense of the presence of God. Prophecies are also an effective way for God to direct his people. Once in our work on campus, God predicted through prophecy that we would have a major change in our situation (leaving one position and moving to another), that he would begin soon to bring many people to the prayer meetings at Ann Arbor and throughout Michigan, that he would give us a period of trials, and that he would end that period of trials and again bring many people and a deeper life in the Spirit. Each time, the prophecies turned out to be literally true, and the guidance given in the prophecies about how to confront these coming situations turned out to be a great help.

Speaking in tongues can be two different things. First of all, it can be a gift of prayer for an individual (1 Cor.14:14). This is the more common gift of tongues, but I will not go into it here. Speaking in tongues can also be a gift for the community when the Spirit urges someone to speak out loud in tongues for the community. In this case, the speaking in tongues should have an interpretation, so that the whole community can understand what is happening. The experience of giving interpretations is similar to the experience of prophecy. The interpreter, like the speaker in tongues, does not understand the tongues (1 Cor.14: 2,14). In other words, the gift of interpretation is not a gift of translation. It is an urging to speak words which are given.

Speaking in tongues simply means speaking in languages. As is clear from Acts and 1 Cor. 12-14, it was common for the Spirit to give Christians other languages to speak which they did not understand. And it is still common today. I was talking to a man about a year and a half ago who told me of an experience that he had had a couple of years back. He went with a choir to a church to give a performance, and many of the choir members had received the baptism of the Spirit. During the concert, at a moment of silence, one of the choir members spoke in tongues and then another one gave the interpretation. The rest of the choir was embarrassed because they that the audience would not under- it turned out that right afterwards, the pastor of the church turned to the choir directoress and asked her if she knew the man who had spoken in tongues and the man who had interpreted the message. When she replied that she did, he asked her if they knew Hebrew. When she replied that they did not, he told her that he knew Hebrew and that the first man had given a message in perfect high Hebrew, and that the second man had given an almost literal translation of the message. It was enough to convince the pastor of the validity of the gift of tongues.

The Purpose of Spiritual Gifts

There are more workings of the Spirit than those Paul enumerates in 1 Cor. 12:4-11. But these are enough to give us an idea of what spiritual gifts can be. In a community in which spiritual gifts operate, Christians are much more vividly aware of the presence and power of God.

Paul says in 1 Cor. 12:7: "To each is given the manifestation of the Spirit for the common good." Another translation might be that to each is given the manifestation of the Spirit for usefulness. Spiritual gifts have a very pragmatic purpose. They are given to build up the community. This is the difference between the seven gifts and the nine charismatic gifts. The seven gifts are given with the Spirit for the building up of the individual, of his relationship with God. The charismatic gifts are given so that the individual can do something for the community.

One term which Paul uses to describe the gifts is "service" (1 Cor.12:5). Looked at from this perspective the gifts are a service for the community. In fact, the term "gift" is somewhat misleading. The gifts are not gifts to the individual Christian. They are gifts *through* the individual Christian to the community. For the individual Christian they are a service, a service he can perform for the community. When he makes himself available to God to be used, he performs a service for the community.

It is no accident that the idea of the "body of Christ" is found in the New Testament at its earliest date in passages that are concerned mainly with charismatic gifts (1 Cor.12 and Rom.12). The idea very likely first came to Paul or some early Christian when he was trying to explain how the spiritual gifts operated in a Christian community, a local church. "All these are inspired by one and the same Spirit, who apportions to each one individually as he wills. For just as the body is one and has many members and all the members of the body, though many, are one body, so it is with Christ" (Rom.12:4). In other words, in the church, different Christians are the channels for different gifts. One prophesies, another heals, another speaks in tongues. And yet all these things are the work of the Spirit, and they all work together for the building up of the community. It is much like the different members of the body. The foot, the hand, the eye, all have different functions, and yet they all make one body and they all work together to build up the one body.

It is clear that in 1 Cor. 12-14, Paul is trying to teach the Corinthians how to use the spiritual gifts with love, in harmony, without envy or jealousy or conflict. No one is to envy the other, or to disdain the other, but they are to be as conscious of their dependence on one another as the different members of one body. But in making this point, Paul brings out in a vivid way the important truth about the charismatic gifts–that they are for the upbuilding of the community. They are not primarily for an individual's benefit, but they are for the benefit of the whole Christian community. They are the way an individual can perform a service to the community—by putting himself at God's disposal to be used in one of his "workings."

The charismatic gifts, then, are intended to equip a Christian for service in the community. They are intended to equip him with the power of God so that he can work in the community with God-given ability to strengthen the community. That is why Paul ends chapter 12 with the paragraph on apostles, prophets, teachers, workers of miracles, healers, helpers, administrators, and speakers in various kinds of tongues. These are the various services Christians can perform in the community. These are stable positions within a community. But in order for a person to truly perform one of these functions in the power of God, he has to have the spiritual gifts which equip him to do what these positions call for. In other words, any Christian community needs a certain number of functions to be performed, and God offers spiritual power—spiritual equipment—through the spiritual gifts for those functions to be performed. Moreover, the whole purpose of the giving of spiritual gifts is so that an individual Christian might be ready to perform a service, to carry out a function within the community.

One way of summarizing the spiritual gifts is to say that the spiritual gifts are like tools or resources. They are the equipment of God for the work he has given Christians to do in the world. Christians need the power of God to do the work of God, because the work of God is something beyond human ability. The spiritual gifts are the empowering of Christians to do God's work–to teach, to speak his message, to perform signs of his presence. They are the Holy Spirit working through men to renew the face of the earth.

The Spiritual Gifts and Holiness

Strange as it may seem, before becoming acquainted with the charismatic renewal, it never occurred to me that 1 Cor. 13 came between 1 Cor. 12 and 1 Cor. 14. It sounds obvious when you say it that way, but I had never thought of it. I was not used to reading chapter 13 in its context in First Corinthians. Like most Christians, I knew chapter 13 as the great hymn to love. But I did not realize that Paul wrote that chapter to explain to the Corinthians how to use the spiritual gifts. I did not realize that the whole point of the chapter was to say that spiritual gifts are to be used in a loving way to build up the community.

First Corinthians 13 contains much wisdom that is important for the proper understanding of spiritual gifts. It is also frequently misunderstood because it is not read in context. Paul begins by saying, "If I speak in the tongues of men and of angels but have not love, I am a noisy gong or a clanging cymbal. And if I have prophetic powers and understand all mysteries and all knowledge, and if I have all faith so as to remove mountains, but have not love, I am nothing. If I give away all that I have, and if I deliver my body to be burned, but have not love, I gain nothing." In this opening section, Paul is not playing down spiritual gifts at all. He is not even saying that spiritual gifts are valueless if I do not have love. (A healing by God's power is, after all, a healing by God's power.) Rather he is saying that *I* am nothing if I do not love. He is making a simple point in a forceful way; namely, that there is a difference between charismatic power and holiness, and that holiness, not charismatic power, is the measure of a person.

Jesus makes the same point in a passage in the seventh chapter of Matthew. He says, "Not every one who says to me, 'Lord, Lord,' shall enter the kingdom of heaven, but he who does the will of my Father who is in heaven. On that day many will say to me, 'Lord, Lord, did we not prophesy in your name, and cast out demons in your name, and do many mighty works (miracles) in your name?' And then will I declare to them, 'I never knew you; depart from me, you evildoers' " (Matt.7:21-23). This is a passage that came home to me with a new force after acquaintance with the new work of the Spirit, because I found that I could take it quite literally. What Christ is saying is sobering. He is not saying that they did not really prophesy or cast out demons or do miracles in his name. Rather, he is saying that that is not what makes a man a genuine disciple of his (someone he "knows"). What makes a man a genuine disciple of his is doing his father's will–living in holiness.

It is not uncommon for someone, when he reads Paul's exhortation in 1 Cor. 12:31 to "earnestly desire the higher gifts," to say that the gift he wants is love. But to say that or to describe love as the "greatest of all" is either to miss the point or to obscure what Paul is saying. In this section, Paul does not consider love one of the spiritual gifts. Rather, he calls it "a way." And in Galatians 5:22 he describes it as a fruit of the Spirit along with "joy, peace, patience, kindness, goodness, faithfulness, gentleness and self-control." In other words, love is not one of the spiritual gifts, one of the tools to build up the life of the Christian community. It is the very life of the Christian community itself. It is the way in which the Christian must walk. It is what he must aim at.

To say that Paul does not describe love as a gift is not to say that there is no sense in which love is a gift. Love is the effect of the Holy Spirit living in us. Paul conveys that idea by using the term "fruit of the Spirit," or something that grows in a person's life from living the life of the Spirit. But love is not a gift in the same sense that prophecy or healing is. A person can prophesy or heal just by allowing the Spirit to work through him. But he loves by growing in holiness, by surrendering his heart and will to God, by growing into maturity of Christian character.

There is a relationship between holiness and the spiritual gifts. The spiritual gifts are not a sign of holiness. They are not merit badges for spiritual achievement. Rather they are equipment for working to build up the Christian community in holiness. They are often given to beginners so that growth is possible for them and also for the community that they are a part of. Perhaps the more extraordinary workings of the Spirit are only entrusted to those who are more mature in Christian character, but the whole of First Corinthians 12-14 is instruction for the use of spiritual gifts for Christians who need much more growth in love.

Seeking Spiritual Gifts

Paul says at the beginning of 1 Cor. 14, "Make love your aim and earnestly desire the spiritual gifts, especially that you may prophesy." This is the second time he urges the Corinthians to "earnestly desire" the spiritual gifts. He has an attitude which is much different from that of many modern Christians who are often reluctant to have spiritual gifts. Paul goes so far as to command the Corinthians to seek spiritual gifts.

Paul's attitude toward seeking spiritual gifts makes a great deal of sense if we understand what the gifts are for. If they really are God's equipment for the building up of the church, they are really valuable to have. In these days, when the church seems to be losing ground in the world and when so much of the life of the church seems to be weakening and losing vitality, God's power is needed desperately. It would not make sense for a carpenter to forego a hammer and try to use his fist, or for a writer to forego a pen or a typewriter. They know they need them for effectiveness in their work. And we need the spiritual gifts, because we need the fullness of God's working among us, the fullness of the power he will put at our disposal.

The scripture does not say a great deal about how a person can obtain spiritual gifts. But the advice to seek the gifts is actually excellent advice on how to obtain them. Perhaps the biggest obstacle to our having the gifts is not being open to them, not wanting them. There are, I think, a couple of reasons why this is so. One of them is fear of God. Many people do not want the spiritual gifts because they bring God too close for comfort. It is one thing to think of God in heaven or as the creator. It is even safe to think of his providence, for that means that everything is God working, and there is no need to confront God directly apart from dealing with things. And it is safe to think of him as speaking in the scriptures, because we can read those when we want to and absorb them as we want to. But when God starts healing my next-door neighbor and speaking to me in prophecy, that is a more frightening thing. That means that I have to confront God more immediately than ever before, and it might become obvious that I have not surrendered fully to him.

Another reason for not wanting spiritual gifts is the desire to do things ourselves. Being used for a spiritual gift involves yielding to God and letting him work through you. There is a certain self-denial involved. There is a surrendering of control and a devaluing of my natural abilities. It seems like a less glorious thing to let God work through me to convert the world than to actually go out and convert the world myself. To be the instrument of a working of God is a humbling thing, and we often have an inner resistance to being humbled.

Another clue which Paul gives to obtaining spiritual gifts is in Gal. 3:5, where Paul asks the Galatians the question, "Does he who supplies the Spirit to you and works miracles among you do so by works of the law, or by hearing with faith?" He apparently is referring to a common experience of the Galatians, because he is using the experience of seeing miracles through faith as a proof that it is not law which justifies a man.

Faith, then, is a means to obtaining the

spiritual gifts, perhaps *the* means. Faith means that we know, first of all, that these things are possible, because we realize that Christ promised them to us. And then it means asking for them with expectancy, being willing to count on them happening. Peter would never have walked on the water if he had not had enough faith to actually step out upon it. And he stopped walking on the water when he started looking at the wind and the waves and started being afraid that it would not happen any longer.

God has a great deal in store for us, a great deal that we really need. But we need to be fully open to him. We need to be ready for everything he is willing to do, in fact earnestly desiring him to do more and more among us, for him to increase and for us to decrease. We need to have faith, faith that his promises are still good. Then we will begin to see the spiritual gifts appearing among us and in our own lives.

Why Now?

Some Christians do not find it difficult to believe that God does give prophecies and miracles, discernment of spirits and healing. But they do not expect to see them around commonly. The shrine at Lourdes and great evangelists like Kathryn Kuhlman maybe, but not my next door neighbor with the raspy voice and the irritating habit of slamming the garage door. A prophet should have a certain prophetic look, and a miracle worker should certainly have some kind of glow.

There is something new about the new movement of the Spirit that is different from what Christians have been accustomed to. It is new not because of the spiritual gifts, but because the spiritual gifts seem to be given much more commonly, and to ordinary people—not only to monks, evangelists, and nuns—but to workers and housewives, lawyers and students. They are being given now. In fact, they are being given in much the same way as they were given to the Christians in New Testament times. Why now?

The fathers of the church noticed in the fourth century that there seemed to be a difference between their church and the church of the Acts of the Apostles in the frequency of spiritual gifts. John Chrysostom in his homilies on First Corinthians put it this way:

> Yes, the church was then a heaven. The Holy Spirit reigned as its master, and in-

spired directly each of its ministers. Today, we have been left with nothing more than the symbols and signs of these gifts. In fact, in our own present day also, we speak in turn, two or three, and when one becomes silent, the other begins. But this is only the vestige and memorial of what used to happen.

The reasons they gave for the departing of the spiritual gifts in their age are also clues to why they are returning in our age.

The first reason for the lack of spiritual gifts is given by St. Cyril of Jerusalem in his work in First Corinthians, Chapter 14:

> When we shall have the proper dispositions of faith, hope, and charity in regard to God and our brethren . . . we shall receive an abundance of the charisms of God.

Cyril is saying that the disappearance of the spiritual gifts is our fault. We lack the right disposition to God which makes them possible. And this is probably one reason why the spiritual gifts are becoming more common. With more and more people being baptized in the Spirit, they are receiving a renewal in the life of the Spirit of the kind that makes it possible for God to work through them in the way he did for the early Christians.

A second reason for an absence of spiritual gifts is offered by St. John Chrysostom in his commentary on the Acts chapter 2. His point was that spiritual gifts are given at God's initiative and he gives them in response to different needs. Throughout the history of the church, the Lord seems to have poured out the spiritual gifts more in some ages than in others. The early church experienced a profusion of gifts, for at that time the Lord was laying a foundation. During periods of renewal and reformation of the church, spiritual gifts operated with greater frequency. The Lord seems to be increasing their occurrence now because our need for them is so great. It is obvious that we are in an age of crisis for the church. Unbelief is increasing in the world. There is a loss of faith within the church. Christians everywhere are becoming uneasy, wondering where God is. The church needs the spiritual gifts now to meet the challenge of our unbelieving, technological society.

The last word has to be: it is a mystery. But like every Christian mystery, man enters in and God enters in. If we wish to see God at work in the way he acted in the early church, we have to go deeper into the life of the Spirit. If we do not, the absence of God's gifts in the world is our fault. But is is also true that God is not tied down by us, and right now, almost despite us, he is renewing his church with spiritual power to meet the challenge of this age.

CONTENTS

THESAURUS STAFF

Editor in Chief

Victoria Neufeldt

Project Editor

Andrew N. Sparks

Editors

Jonathan Goldman
Donald Stewart
Stephen P. Teresi

Production

Fernando de Mello Vianna

Assistants

Laura J. Borovac
Alisa A. Murray
Cynthia M. Sadonick
Betty Dziedzic Thompson

FOREWORD

This new edition of the popular paperback abridgment of Charlton Laird's famous thesaurus is evidence of the continuing relevance of the work of a fine scholar. Professor Laird's original thesaurus, entitled *Laird's Promptory*, published in 1948, was a pioneering work that established the pattern for the now standard "dictionary-style" thesaurus. The present book is a direct descendant of the *Promptory*, adhering to the principles on which that work was based. It is not, however, by any means behind the times, for each succeeding edition of the thesaurus, whether paperback abridgment or hardcover, has built on its predecessors and incorporated the new language of its time.

The present book is somewhat different in style from the first paperback edition. The format of the entries has been changed to a style similar to that of the current large hardcover edition *(Webster's New World Thesaurus*, © 1985), and the typefaces and page layout have been revised to match those of the companion *Webster's New World Dictionary, Warner Books Paperback Edition*, © 1990.

We have kept the introduction to the thesaurus that was written by Professor Laird for the first edition of the paperback abridgment, published in 1974, but with some revision to update it. The reader is urged to read in its entirety this very clear and useful introduction; it will be well worth the effort, not least for the people who believe they know how to use a thesaurus. In addition, there is a short, handy reference on page xv, that consists of six essential points on "How to Use This Book".

Victoria Neufeldt
Editor in Chief

INTRODUCTION

The book in your hands was intended to be a handy word-suggester. It should be easy to use, for the book was planned and designed to make it easy, almost natural, to rely on. Still, some explanation may help, for many people have never learned to use a thesaurus at all.

Mainly, the book is an assortment of synonyms, but we mean something different by the word *synonym* than have some editors, and we have brought terms together differently. Partly we are recognizing that relationships among words are complex and subtle, and this subtlety becomes involved in word choice.

Families of words are like families of people in this, that the family has grown a long time, that each term has gone its own way, and no one of them is exactly like any other. A word may be able to take over the job of a word similar in sound or meaning, but it may not. How is one to know? The knowing is not easy, but good books on words can help, particularly if the user knows what each kind of wordbook can be expected to do.

What a Thesaurus Is Good For

So now we come to what a book like this one can do. It should be able to suggest a word you want but have not been able to think of, or suggest new terms you may want to use. But it cannot tell you very much about such a word. That kind of help should be given, if you need it, by other books, such as dictionaries. Trying to crowd descriptions of words into this book, along with the information that properly belongs here, would be to make the book clumsy and confusing.

Thus, anybody who uses a thesaurus should have at least one other wordbook to tell him more about the words he has found in the thesaurus that are likely candidates. The best single wordbook to fill this need is a good general dictionary.

Seeking Synonyms

A dictionary and a thesaurus can be used well together by a writer or speaker who is looking for synonyms, either to avoid repetition or to express a different shade of meaning or a different level of usage. As an example, let us take the word *explain*. If you look in the present book, you will find the following under the entry **explain:**

> interpret, explicate, account for, elucidate, illustrate, clarify, illuminate, make clear, describe, expound, teach, reveal, point out, demonstrate, tell, read, translate, paraphrase, put in other words, define, justify, untangle, unravel, make plain, come to the point, put across, throw light upon, comment on, remark upon, offer an explana-

tion of, resolve, clear up, get right, set right, put someone on the right track, spell out, go into detail, get to the bottom of, figure out, cast light upon, get across, get through, bring out, work out, solve, put in plain English.

Here you have dozens of possibilities with various shades of meaning and differences in usage.

You may decide at once that some terms like *unravel, untangle,* and *comment on* give you the emphasis upon complexity that you want. You may prefer words like *illustrate* or *demonstrate* to introduce detail. Or you may want to avoid all big or rare words, and welcome phrases made up of common words like *set right* and *get to the bottom of.* If you are not sure about the exact meaning of any of the words or phrases you find in this entry, your dictionary can help you.

Dealing with Words for Things

For rather general words like *explain,* a thesaurus and a dictionary work very well together; the user can go back and forth from one to the other, and sooner or later he can be pretty sure to find what he wants. On the other hand, for concrete and specific words, like *boat, doctor,* and *language,* a dictionary by its nature cannot help much. A good dictionary entry for *boat,* for instance, will tell us what the word *boat* can be used for. But inevitably dictionary definitions do not help us to find many synonyms, except to suggest that *boat* can be a landsman's term for what is more properly called a ship. The fact is, of course, that there are no very good synonyms for *boat,* as *expound* is a good synonym for *explain* in one sense. There is no other common, single word for all small, open watercraft.

A thesaurus, on the other hand, can help by providing words that are not very close synonyms but do provide the writer with a better way of saying what he wants to, especially by using concrete words, names for real things. Consider the entry **boat** in this book; it begins:

> *Types of small boats include the following:* . . . rowboat, shell, scull, kayak, dugout, canoe, scow, raft, launch, motorboat . . . .

The list continues, including *skiff, outrigger,* and even *catamaran.* That is, the book recognizes that often when a writer looks for a better word he may not want a synonym at all. What he is probably seeking is a more concrete, more exact, more picturesque, or more revealing term.

English has many such words for real things, of which the two others mentioned above, *doctor* and *language,* provide examples. The user who looks up **doctor** in this book will find a list of more specific terms for various sorts of doctors—*physician, surgeon, intern, chiropractor, general practitioner,* and the like—along with slang or colloquial terms like *doc* and *sawbones.* Then he will find a highly detailed list of specialists, such as *pediatrician, obstetrician, anesthetist,* and *gynecologist.* The entry **language** gives terms that may be substituted for the word **language,** like *sound* and *utterance*; it provides words useful in the study of language, like *morphology* and *phonetics;* it includes words identifying the types of languages, like *synthetic* and *computer,* and it lists dozens of important languages all over the world. That is, a thesaurus, along with being a reference tool, can within limits become a textbook in composition, suggesting to the user ways in which he can make his writing clearer, sharper, more dramatic, more interesting.

A Thesaurus: A Treasure House

A thesaurus should be made to fit into the way a writer or speaker thinks. A compiler of a thesaurus needs to ask himself: "How would a writer or speaker want to use this book? When would he use it? What would he want to get out of it?" The compiler's job is to try to figure out what the user would want to say, and to suggest it to him. That is the principle behind this volume. It has implications for every part of the book.

Take the entry list, the words printed in boldface at the left of the column, the words the user "looks up." On the whole, these are the words he has thought of, but does not, on this occasion, wish to use. They are likely to include words like *thing, really,* and *order.* They are not likely to include *thermonuclear, Weltschmerz,* and *cotangent,* although those are useful words and may belong among listed synonyms. That is, the entry list of a thesaurus—although not of a dictionary—should be made of the commonest words in the language, those that come most readily to the mind of an average person. A likely word may include even slang and colloquialisms such as *keep the ball rolling* and *get going.* Those are just the sorts of terms a writer may think of, but not want to use on a particular occasion or in a particular context.

Similarly, within the entries, some words and phrases may not be synonyms, or even come very close to being "like-names." For some words there may be nothing even approaching a synonym, but there is always another way to say something. Almost all of the so-called *wh*-words, that is, terms like *who, when, where,* and *what,* have no real synonyms although they are very common words. For example, under **why** the present volume has the following:

> **why** ... for what reason? how so? how? how is it that? on whose account? what is the cause that? to what end? for what purpose? on what foundation? how do you explain that? how come?

These are not all synonyms in the sense that they can be substituted for *why* without change in construction, but they do suggest another way of saying what may be implied in *why.*

The natural way with words is also what determines the order of the words dealt with in this book. Some kind of order we must have; something has to be first and something last. For the entry list, the alphabetical order is the most convenient; the alphabet helps you find a starting place. But within a list of synonyms, the alphabet is not useful. Instead, we have assumed that the user of the book would want to find his preferred synonym as soon as possible, and we have tried to put early those terms we thought he was most likely to want, and to put far on in the list those terms he was less likely to use. In making our judgments we guessed the user was most likely to want another common word: thus the first synonyms for *advertise* in the sense of making known are *publicize, proclaim, herald, announce.* Terms like *propagate* and *promulgate* appear farther down. Or we thought the user might want a relatively exact like-word, even though it is rare, and hence *ascertained* occurs early among the synonyms of *discovered* because it is relatively exact, just what a discriminating writer might be looking for.

This is one of the ways in which we hope the book will be easy and quick to use. You need only look up the word you have thought of. It may well be a main entry, and you are likely to find the synonym you want without working through the whole list. First choose the meaning or use you want, since common words have several or even many uses. For the word *fair,* this book recognizes four, quite different: *just, moderately satisfactory, not stormy or likely to storm,* and *of light complexion.* For the word *get* the editors recognized eleven groups of synonyms and over thirty phrases. Once you have chosen the meaning you have in mind, you are likely to find the synonym you want very quickly just by following the printed order.

Cross-references

The handling of cross-references was determined by the need for convenience and low cost. Cross-references are a nuisance; nobody likes them. They always require looking up at least one more entry. We decided we had to have cross-references, but we would do what we could to keep them from being much bother.

We relied mainly on two devices. One of these is usually identified by the phrase "see also." For example, assume you have intended writing, "We had to consider the language of our proposed bill." For *language,* in this specialized sense, most of the likeliest synonyms appear elsewhere in the book, not under the entry **language,** and consequently after the first use for *language* you will find a cross-reference: "see also DIALECT, JARGON 2, WRITING 1, 2." This means that if you do not find the synonym you want under the entry **language,** try **dialect,** the second meaning of **jargon,** or both the first and second meanings of **writing**. Thus the user of this book will find cross-references at the end of many main entries, which will lead him to different but related lists if he wants them.

Then we included what we thought of as mainly cross-references, although to the casual user of the book they may seem to be small entries. The entry **first-class** will provide an example. This is only one of dozens of terms that mean *good, fine, excellent.* For practical reasons, we had to treat the words *first-class, first-rate,* and dozens more as cross-references to **excellent,** which for a number of reasons we had chosen as a good word to be a main entry.

We guessed that if a user looks up **first-rate** he wants one of a relatively few common but rather exact synonyms. If our guess was correct, we could avoid the nuisance for the reader of his having to look up the main entry. Accordingly, the entry for this word is as follows:

first-rate, *a.* prime, very good, choice; see EXCELLENT.

Here you have, in effect, four synonyms—since the cross-reference will usually supply a synonym in itself, even the most common one—and if we have been moderately shrewd in our guess, in a high percentage of such entries you will have the synonym you want without ever looking up the cross-reference.

A few other matters may warrant attention. First, there are the clusters that are sometimes called verb sets. These are verbs made up of at least two words, which taken together mean something other than the words used separately. Notice the following: *Having inherited money, he* started to live it up, *and got a reputation he could not* live down. That is, *live up* and *live down* do not mean living in two directions. Such verbs have been much neglected in thesauruses; we have tried to be more generous in our inclusion of such phrases than have most wordbooks.

Antonyms and What to Do About Them

Something should be said about antonyms. We considered leaving them out; many words have no antonyms. What is the antonym of *eye* or *who*? Besides, writers do not often need antonyms. To save space we considered doing without them, but occasionally having an antonym is handy. So we compromised; where we found good antonyms we included a few at the end, usually three, but to be sure the user of the book could find as many antonyms as he might need, we usually made one of these antonyms a main entry and printed it in small capitals, like the other cross-references. That is, if you want an antonym for *heavy* in the sense of weighty, you will find that the antonyms provided are *light, buoyant, feather-light.* If you do not want any of these, you have only to look up **light** where you will find dozens more. If, however, you want an antonym for *heavy* in the sense of burdensome, you will find no antonyms at the entry for that term—because we are treating this use mainly as a cross-reference—but you will have references to **difficult 1** and **disturbing.** The entry **difficult,** sense 1 has three antonyms, *easy, wieldy,* and *light,* the first one being a cross-reference that will lead you to more antonyms at **easy.** Thus, in the interest of economy, you may find that antonyms take a little more time than synonyms; you may need to use two cross-references instead of one.

What a Thesaurus Is Not Meant For

Some things this book is not meant for. It will not replace a dictionary. As we noted above, it is intended to suggest terms, not to describe them. It is not a grammar; it does have grammatical categories (abbreviations like *a.* for adjective or adverb appear immediately after the entry), but these are intended as classification, not as grammatical statements. On the whole, if you have a cross-reference from a noun you should look at the noun use of the word provided in the reference. Words are not defined, but we have tried to assort them for convenience into groups. The entry **calm** (adjective) is divided into "*Said especially of persons*" and "*Said often of things*", since this seemed to be the readiest way to distinguish words like *impassive* and *sedate* from words like *windless* and *still.* Incidentally, these groupings of words will often not be the same as the meanings recognized in a dictionary. We have had to devise our own classifications, since a thesaurus is not a special kind of dictionary but a different sort of book, with its own principles.

Other information usual in dictionaries is omitted or treated lightly here. There are no pronunciations or etymologies. We have usually shown only one spelling of a word, although several may be acceptable. We have done little with usage. That is a complex problem, partly because a term that is slang in one context may not be slang in another, and words change their currency and respectability. Some years ago, *teenager* was clearly slang, but now it has become a standard term. We have gone so far as to alert the user of the book to some questionable or local terms by placing an asterisk after them. These asterisks are meant to indicate that the word or phrase may have a slang, informal, dialectal, or archaic flavor in the meaning we have in mind. The reader is cautioned to consider whether that term is appropriate to the context in which he wishes to use it. Here again a dictionary is invaluable to give you the information you need if you are in doubt.

HOW TO USE THIS BOOK

For convenience, here is a summary of things you may want to have in mind while you use the book:

1. Look up any word you have thought of but do not want to use.
2. Unless you have thought of a rare word you should find: (a) a main entry, with many alternate terms, some antonyms, and possibly a "see also" cross-reference, or (b) a brief entry, with three synonyms and one or more cross-references.
3. If you have turned to a main entry, check to see whether more than one meaning is recognized, and if so, pick the one you want. The various meanings will be numbered in boldface figures.
4. Work through the list, looking for a term that will suggest what you need, trying the cross-reference at the end if you need it.
5. If you find a word or phrase you may want, but do not know very well, look it up in at least one dictionary.
6. If you have looked up a brief entry, it is probably for the most part a cross-reference, but it will have a few common synonyms. If you do not want any of them, turn to the main entry or entries provided in the cross-reference. The entry to which you are referred may have more than one grammatical use—*fast* can be an adjective, adverb, noun, or verb. Choose the grammatical category that corresponds to the use of the word from which you got the cross-reference.

Key: *a.* = adjective or adverb (i.e., modifier)
n. = noun
v. = verb
* = slang, colloquial, dialectal, regional, archaic, etc.

A

a *a. & prep.* **1.** [The indefinite article; *before vowels, written "an"*] some, one, any, each, some kind of, some particular, any of, any one of, a certain.—*Ant.* THE, this, that. **2.** [An indication of frequency] per, every, at the rate of; see EACH 2.

abandon *n.* unrestraint, spontaneity, freedom, exuberance, spirit, enthusiasm, vigor.

abandon *v.* **1.** [To give up] leave, quit, withdraw, discontinue, break off, go off from, cast away, cast aside, let go, cease, cast off, discard, vacate, give away, part with, evacuate, surrender, yield, desist, concede, renounce, abdicate, lose hope of, go back on, secede, waive, forgo, back down from, lay aside, dispose of, have done with, throw in the towel*, break the habit. **2.** [To leave someone or something in trouble] desert, forsake, ostracize, back out on, break with, break up with, run away, defect, reject, disown, cast off, maroon, depart from, throw overboard, jettison, leave behind, slip away from, stand up*, leave in the lurch, turn one's back on, run out on*, walk out on*, doublecross*, let down, drop*.

abandoned *a.* deserted, desolate, destitute, desperate, empty, unused, vacated, left, neglected, relinquished, lonely, forsaken, solitary, hopeless, cast off, cast aside, cast away, forgotten, shunned, forlorn, avoided, outcast, rejected, helpless, unfortunate, alone, discarded, scorned, lost, doomed, friendless, wretched, thrown overboard*, out on a limb*, waiting at the church*, left in the lurch, left in the cold, left holding the bag*.—*Ant.* INHABITED, used, in use.

abbreviate *v.* shorten, cut, condense; see DECREASE 2.

abbreviation *n.* contraction, abridgment, sketch, brief, abstract, synopsis, reduction, abstraction, condensation, digest, resumé, outline, summary, short form; see also SUMMARY.

abdicate *v.* relinquish, give up, withdraw; see ABANDON 1.

abdomen *n.* midsection, belly, gut; see STOMACH.

abduct *v.* capture, seize, carry off; see KIDNAP.

abide *v.* **1.** [To lodge] stay, room, reside; see DWELL. **2.** [To submit to] put up with, bear, bear with, withstand; see also ENDURE 2.

abide by *v.* follow, observe, comply with; see FOLLOW 3.

ability *n.* aptitude, intelligence, innate qualities, powers, potency, worth, talent, gift, genius, capability, competence, proficiency, adeptness, qualifications, knowledge, self-sufficiency, tact, finish, technique, craft, skill, artistry, cunning, skillfulness, dexterity, facility, finesse, mastery, cleverness, deftness, experience, ingenuity, strength, understanding, faculty, comprehension, makings, sense, what it takes*, brains, knack, hang, know-how*.—*Ant.* IGNORANCE, incompetence, inexperience.

able *a.* intelligent, ingenious, worthy, talented, gifted, fitted, capable, effective, efficient, qualified, masterful, adequate, competent, expert, experienced, skilled, learned, clever, suitable, smart, crafty, cunning, bright, knowing, dexterous, endowed, deft, apt, agile, adept, alert, adaptable, smooth, ready, versatile, equal to, suited, suited to, well-rounded, mighty, powerful, strong, robust, sturdy, brawny, vigorous, courageous, fit for, sharp*, cut out for*, having an ear for*.—*Ant.* STUPID, bungling, unadaptable.

able-bodied *a.* fit, powerful, sturdy; see STRONG 1.

abnormal *a.* strange, irregular, unnatural; see UNUSUAL 2.

abnormality *n.* peculiarity, singularity, malformation; see IRREGULARITY.

aboard *a.* on board, on ship, shipped, loaded, on board ship, freight on board, being shipped, en route, consigned, in transit, being transported, embarked, afloat, at sea, on deck, traveling.

abolish *v.* suppress, eradicate, terminate, exterminate, obliterate, annul, remove, revoke, end, finish, nullify, set aside, annihilate, repeal, subvert, reverse, rescind, prohibit, extinguish, cancel, erase, root out, pull up, uproot, demolish, invalidate, overturn, overthrow, declare null and void, do away with, stamp out, undo, throw out, put an end to, inhibit, dispense with, cut out, raze, squelch, ravage; see also DESTROY.

A-bomb *n.* nuclear weapon, nuclear device, nuclear warhead; see ATOM BOMB.

abort *v.* miscarry, fall short, miss; see FAIL 1.

about *a. & prep.* **1.** [Approximately] roughly, nearly, in general; see APPROXIMATELY. **2.** [Concerning] regarding, respecting, touching, of, on, in realtion to, relative to, relating to, as regards, in regard to, in which, with respect to, in the matter of, with reference to, referring to, so far as something is concerned, in connection with, concerned with, thereby, wherein, as for, dealing with. **3.** [Around] surrounding, round about, on all sides; see AROUND.

about to* *a. & prep.* on the verge of, at the point of, just about; see ALMOST.

above *a. & prep.* **1.** [High in position] over, high, higher, superior, beyond, raised, above one's head, in a higher place, aloft, overhead, toward the sky; see also HIGHER, OVER 1.—*Ant.* BELOW, low, beneath. **2.** [Referring to something earlier] before, foregoing, earlier; see PRECEDING.

above all *a.* in the first place, chiefly, especially; see PRINCIPALLY.

aboveboard *a.* candidly, honestly, frankly; see OPENLY 1.

abrasive *a.* **1.** grinding, sharpening, cutting; see ROUGH 1. **2.** irritating, annoying, caustic; see DISTURBING.

abreast *a.* in line, equal, side by side; see BESIDE.

abroad *a.* away, at large, adrift, wandering, elsewhere, overseas, traveling, touring, outside, distant, far away, gone, out of the country, removed.

abrupt *a.* **1.** [*Said of things, usually landscape*] uneven, rough, jagged; see STEEP. **2.** [*Said of people or acts of people*] blunt, hasty, gruff; see RUDE.

absence *n.* **1.** [The state of being elsewhere] truancy, nonattendance, nonappearance, loss, vacancy, cut*, hooky. **2.** [The state of lacking something] deficiency, need, inadequacy; see LACK 1.

absent *a.* away, missing, elsewhere, vanished, gone, gone out, not at home, not present, out, wanting, lacking, abroad, lost, astray, nowhere to be found, on vacation, AWOL*, playing hooky.

absent-minded *a.* preoccupied, dreamy, listless, lost, absent, thoughtless, oblivious, inattentive, daydreaming, unconscious, unaware, withdrawn, removed, faraway, distracted, remote, forgetful, in the clouds*.—*Ant.* OBSERVANT, attentive, alert.

absolute *a.* **1.** [Without limitation] total, complete, entire, infinite, unqualified, supreme, full, unrestricted, unlimited, unconditional, unbounded, independent, wholehearted, sheer, pure, unmitigated, utter, unabridged, thorough, clean, outright, downright, ideal, simple, perfect, full, blanket, all-out, out-and-out.—*Ant.* RESTRICTED, limited, qualified. **2.** [Without limit in authority] authoritarian, domineering, supreme, arbitrary, official, autocratic, tyrannical, fascist, haughty, overbearing, czarist, nazi, totalitarian, oppressive, antidemocratic, imperative, dogmatic, commanding, controlling, compelling, despotic, intimidating, fanatic, dictatorial, arrogant, with an iron hand, high and mighty*.—*Ant.* LENIENT, tolerant, temperate. **3.** [Certain] positive, unquestionable, undeniable; see CERTAIN 2.

absolutely *a.* **1.** [Completely] utterly, unconditionally, thoroughly; see COMPLETELY. **2.** [Positively] unquestionably, certainly, definitely; see SURELY.

absolve *v.* pardon, set free, clear; see EXCUSE.

absorb *v.* digest, take in, ingest, use up, assimilate, blot, imbibe, swallow, consume, incorporate, sop up, soak up, sponge up.—*Ant.* EJECT, expel, discharge.

absorbed *a.* assimilated, taken in, swallowed up, consumed, drunk, imbibed, dissolved, fused, united, incorporated, digested.—*Ant.* REMOVED, unassimilated, unconsumed.

absorbent *a.* porous, spongy, permeable, dry, soft, penetrable, receptive, retentive, thirsty.

absorbing *a.* engaging, exciting, enthralling; see INTERESTING.

absorption *n.* assimilation, digestion, osmosis, saturation, penetration, fusion, intake, union, merging, blending, consumption, ingestion, swallowing up, taking in, reception, retention, incorporation, appropriation, drinking in, suction, sopping up, soaking up, sponging up, inhalation.—*Ant.* REMOVAL, ejection, discharge.

abstain *v.* refrain, refrain from, renounce, desist, withhold, avoid, stop, deny oneself, refuse, decline, hold back, shun, evade, cease, dispense with, do without, fast, starve, have nothing to do with, let alone, do nothing, keep from, keep one's hands off, swear off, lay off*, turn over a new leaf, have no hand in, take the pledge.—*Ant.* JOIN, indulge, gorge.

abstinence *n.* abstaining, temperance, denial, self-denial, self-control, self-restraint, continence, fasting, frugality, renunciation, avoidance, sobriety, austerity, refraining, nonindulgence, chastity, moderation, soberness, Puritanism.—*Ant.* INDULGENCE, intemperance, overindulgence.

abstract *a.* general, intellectual, ideal; see OBSCURE 1.

absurd *a.* preposterous, ridiculous, ludicrous; see STUPID.

absurdity *n.* improbability, foolishness, senselessness; see NONSENSE 1, 2.

abundance *n.* bounty, more than enough, profusion; see PLENTY.
abundant *a.* sufficient, ample, copious; see PLENTIFUL 2.
abundantly *a.* plentifully, lavishly, richly, handsomely, in large measure, profusely, amply, sufficiently, generously, affluently, inexhaustibly, many times over*, to one's heart's content, off the fat of the land; see also ADEQUATELY.
abuse *n.* perversion, misuse, debasement, degradation, desecration, injury, damage, harm, hurt, wrong, injustice, insult, mistreatment, violation, malevolence, mishandling, mismanagement, pollution, defilement, prostitution.—*Ant.* CARE, respect, veneration.
abuse *v.* insult, injure, hurt, harm, damage, impair, offend, overwork, ill-treat, misuse, maltreat, mistreat, wrong, persecute, molest, victimize, oppress, ruin, mar, spoil, do wrong to, mishandle, pervert, profane, prostitute, desecrate, pollute, harass, manhandle, do an injustice to, violate, defile, impose upon, deprave, taint, debase, corrupt.—*Ant.* DEFEND, protect, befriend.
abused *a.* wronged, injured, harmed; see HURT.
academic *a.* scholastic, erudite, scholarly; see LEARNED.
academy *n.* preparatory school, boarding school, finishing school, secondary school, prep school; see also SCHOOL 1.
accelerate *v.* quicken, speed up, hurry; see HASTEN 2.
acceleration *n.* speeding up, hastening, increase of speed, quickening, hurrying, stepping up, picking up speed; see also SPEED.
accent *n.* stress, beat, stroke, emphasis, pitch, accentuation, inflection, intonation, rhythm, meter, cadence.
accept *v.* receive, get, admit, be resigned, give into, believe, trust, surrender, suffer, endure, grant, allow, tolerate, take in one's stride, consent, acquiesce; see also AGREE.
acceptable *a.* satisfactory, agreeable, pleasing; see PLEASANT 2.
acceptance *n.* recognition, assent, approval; see AGREEMENT 1.
accepted *a.* taken, received, assumed, approved, adopted, recognized, endorsed, verified, acclaimed, welcomed, engaged, hired, claimed, delivered, used, employed, affirmed, upheld, authorized, preferred, acknowledged, accredited, allowed, settled, established, sanctioned, unopposed, customary, authentic, confirmed, chosen, acceptable, popular, formally admitted, stereotyped, orthodox, standard, conventional, current, taken for granted, credited, OK'd; see also POPULAR 1, 3.—*Ant.* REFUSED, denied, nullified.
access *n.* admittance, entree, introduction; see ENTRANCE 1, 2.
accessible *a.* approachable, obtainable, attainable; see AVAILABLE.
accessories *n.pl.* frills, ornaments, adornments, decorations, additions, attachments, gimmicks*, doodads*.
accessory *n.* **1.** [An accomplice] helper, aid, assistant; see ASSOCIATE. **2.** [Something added] attachment, consequence, attendant, complement, supplement, addition.
accident *n.* luck, fortune, contingency, occurrence, circumstance, event, occasion; see also CHANCE 1.
accidental *a.* adventitious, chance, coincidental; see AIMLESS, UNFORTUNATE.
accidentally *a.* unintentionally, involuntarily, unwittingly, unexpectedly, inadvertently, casually, by chance, haphazardly, incidentally, randomly, not purposely, by a fluke*.—*Ant.* DELIBERATELY, voluntarily, intentionally.
accommodate *v.* **1.** [To render a service] help, aid, comfort, make comfortable, oblige, suit, serve, gratify, please, arrange, settle, provide, benefit, tender, supply, furnish, assist, support, sustain, do a favor, indulge, humor, pamper, accept, put oneself out for, do a service for. **2.** [To suit one thing to another] fit, adapt, correspond; see ADJUST 1. **3.** [To provide lodging] house, rent, give lodging to; see ENTERTAIN 2.
accommodations *n.pl.* quarters, rooms, lodging, housing, apartment, hotel, room and board, roof over one's head; see also HOME 1.
accompanied *a.* attended, escorted, tended, shown around, shown about, chaperoned, not alone.
accompaniment *n.* harmony, instrumental music, musical background; see MUSIC 1.
accompany *v.* escort, attend, tend, be with, follow, keep company with, guard, guide, usher, show in, show around, show the way, conduct, go along, go along with, chaperon, associate with, consort with, look after, go hand in hand with, go side by side with, hang around with*.
accomplice *n.* confederate, helper, aid; see ASSOCIATE.
accomplish *v.* fulfill, perform, finish; see ACHIEVE, SUCCEED 1.
accomplished *a.* **1.** [Done] completed, consummated, concluded; see FINISHED. **2.** [Skilled] proficient, expert, skillful; see ABLE.
accomplishment *n.* execution, fulfillment, attainment; see SUCCESS 2.
accordingly *a.* in consequence, consequently, equally, respectively, duly, subsequently, in respect to, thus, hence, therefore, as a result, as a consequence, as the case may be, on the ground, under the circumstances, as things go, to that end, in that event.

according to *prep.* in accordance with, as, to the degree that, conforming to, just as, in keeping with, in line with, in agreement with, consistent with.

account *n.* bulletin, annual, report; see RECORD 1. **—give a good account of oneself** acquit oneself creditably, do well, do oneself proud*, behave courageously. **—on account** charged, in layaway, on layaway, on call; see also UNPAID 1. **—on account of** because of, by virtue of, since; see BECAUSE. **—on no account** for no reason, no way, under no circumstances; see NEVER. **—on someone's account** because of someone, for someone's sake, in someone's behalf; see BECAUSE. **—take account of** judge, evaluate, investigate; see EXAMINE 1. **—take into account** judge, allow for, weigh; see CONSIDER.

accountant *n.* bookkeeper, auditor, CPA; see CLERK.

account for *v.* clarify, resolve, elucidate; see EXPLAIN.

accumulate *v.* hoard, get together, gather, gather into a mass, collect, heap, store, assemble, concentrate, compile, provide, pile up, accrue, scrape up, stockpile, store up, acquire, gain, load up, rake up, unite, add to, profit, build up, gain control, roll in*, bank*; see also GET 1.

accuracy *n.* efficiency, exactness, precision, correctness, skillfulness, sharpness, incisiveness, mastery, dependability, strictness, certainty, sureness.—*Ant.* ERROR, inaccuracy, mistake.

accurate *a.* **1.** [Free from error] exact, correct, perfect; see RIGHT 1. **2.** [Characterized by precision] deft, reliable, trustworthy, true, correct, exact, specific, dependable, skillful, methodical, systematic, distinct, particular, realistic, authentic, genuine, careful, close, critical, detailed, factual, severe, rigorous, rigid, strict, meticulous, sharp, faithful, punctual, scientific, objective, matter-of-fact, rational, unmistakable, reasonable, right, explicit, definite, defined, on the button*, on the spot*, on the nose*, solid.—*Ant.* INCOMPETENT, faulty, slipshod.

accurately *a.* correctly, precisely, exactly; see CAREFULLY 1.

accusation *n.* indictment, allegation, denunciation, slur, complaint, citation, charge, insinuation, beef*, smear*, frame-up*, rap*.

accuse *v.* denounce, charge, prosecute; see BLAME.

accused *a.* arraigned, indicted, incriminated, charged with, under suspicion, alleged to be guilty, apprehended, held for questioning, liable, involved, under attack, under fire, up for.—*Ant.* DISCHARGED, acquitted, cleared.

accuser *n.* prosecutor, plaintiff, adversary; see OPPONENT 1.

accustomed *a.* usual, customary, habitual; see CONVENTIONAL 1.

accustomed to *a.* in the habit of, used to, inclined to; see ADDICTED (TO).

ace *n.* expert, master, champion; see SPECIALIST.

ace *a.* expert, first-rate, outstanding; see DISTINGUISHED 2, ABLE.

ache *n.* twinge, pang, spasm; see PAIN 2.

ache *v.* pain, throb, be sore; see HURT.

achieve *v.* complete, end, terminate, conclude, finish, finish up, finish off, do, perform, execute, fulfill, carry out, carry through, bring about, settle, effect, bring to a conclusion, close, stop, produce, realize, actualize, discharge, wind up, work out, adjust, resolve, solve, accomplish, make an end of, enact, manage, contrive, negotiate, sign, seal, bring to pass, see it through, get done, close up, put the lid on, carry to completion, follow through, take measures, lose oneself in, deliver, knock off*, fill the bill*, round out*, come through, polish off*, clean up*, mop up*, put across*, pull off*, make short work of, put through, go all the way*, go the limit*, call it a day*, put the finishing touch on*, dispose of.—*Ant.* ABANDON, fail, give up.

achievement *n.* fulfillment, feat, exploit, accomplishment, triumph, hit, success, realization, creation, completion, execution, actualization, masterpiece, performance, deed, act, enactment, victory, conquest, attainment, feather in one's cap.—*Ant.* FAILURE, blunder, collapse.

acid *a.* sharp, tart, biting; see SOUR.

acid *n.* **1.** [A sour substance] strong acid, weak acid, corrosive, Lewis acid. **2.** [A drug] LSD, DMT, mescaline; see DRUG. *Common acids include the following:* vinegar, verjuice, lemon juice; citric, ascorbic, nicotinic, boric, acetic, sulfuric, hydrochloric, formic, stearic, phospheric, carbolic, nitric, benzoic, amino, fatty acid.

acidity *n.* sourness, bitterness, tartness, sharpness, pungency, harshness, causticity.

acknowledge *v.* **1.** [To admit] concede, confess, declare; see ADMIT 2. **2.** [To recognize the authority of] endorse, certify, confirm, uphold, support, recognize, ratify, approve, defend, subscribe to, accede to, attest to, take an oath by, defer to.

acknowledged *a.* admitted, confessed, recognized, unquestioned, accepted, authorized, confirmed, received, sanctioned, accredited, approved, out-and-out.

acknowledgment *n.* greeting, reply, answer, response, nod, confession, statement, apology, guarantee, return, support, signature, receipt, letter, card, contract, applause, vote of thanks, IOU.

acquaintance *n.* **1.** [A person one knows] colleague, associate, neighbor; see FRIEND. **2.** [Acquired knowledge] familiarity, awareness, experience; see AWARENESS, EXPERIENCE.

acquainted (with) *a.* introduced, on speaking terms, having some connections; see FAMILIAR WITH.

acquaint with *v.* introduce, make acquainted, present; see INTRODUCE 3.

acquire *v.* take, earn, procure; see GET 1.

acquired *a.* reached, inherited, given, accrued, derived, granted, endowed, transmitted, handed down, bequeathed, allowed, awarded, passed on, willed to, attained, accomplished, learned, adopted, earned, collected, gathered, harvested, secured, procured, obtained, captured, regained, realized, gotten by the sweat of one's brow*, dug out*, raked in*, cornered*, netted*, salted away*, grabbed; see also WON.

acquisition *n.* inheritance, gift, donation, grant, wealth, riches, fortune, profit, gain, earnings, wages, salary, income, winnings, return, returns, proceeds, benefit, prize, reward, award, accomplishment, achievement, premium, bonus, fee, commission, pension, annuity, allowance, gain, dividend.

acquit *v.* clear, absolve, vindicate; see EXCUSE.

acquittal *n.* absolution, clearance, exoneration, dismissal, deliverance, amnesty, discharge, pardon, reprieve, exemption, liberation, release, freedom.—*Ant.* PUNISHMENT, sentence, imprisonment.

acre *n.* plot, acreage, bit of land, estate; see also PROPERTY 2.

acrobat *n.* tumbler, clown, trampolinist, aerialist, trapeze artist, contortionist, performer, tightrope walker, stunt man, figure skater, vaudeville performer, ballet dancer, gymnast.

across *a. & prep.* crosswise, crossed, to the opposite side of, over, opposite, on the other side, from side to side of, from one side to another, transversely, in front of, opposite to, beyond.

across the board *a.* impartially, fairly, equivalently; see EQUALLY.

act *n.* **1.** [An action] deed, performance, exploit; see ACTION 2. **2.** [An official or legal statement] law, proposal, judgment, commitment, verdict, amendment, order, announcement, edict, ordinance, decree, statute, writ, bull, warrant, summons, subpoena, document, bill, code, clause, law of the land*. **3.** [A division of a play] scene, prologue, epilogue, introduction; first act, second act, third act, etc. **4.** [A pose] falsification, feigning, affectation; see PRETENSE 1.

act *v.* **1.** [To perform an action] do, execute, carry out, carry on, operate, transact, accomplish, achieve, consummate, carry into, effect, perpetrate, persist, labor, work, officiate, function, preside, serve, go ahead, step into, take steps, play a part, begin, move in, enforce, maneuver, operate, create, practice, develop, make progress, interfere, interpose, be active, intrude, commit, fight, combat, respond, keep going, answer, pursue, put forth energy, hustle*, get going*.—*Ant.* WAIT, await, rest. **2.** [To conduct oneself] behave, seem, appear, carry oneself, give the appearance of, represent oneself, take on, play one's part, impress one as, put on airs*; see also BEHAVE. **3.** [To take part in a play] perform, impersonate, represent, act out, simulate, pretend, mimic, burlesque, parody, feign, portray, rehearse, take a part in, dramatize, star, play the part of, debut.

act for *v.* do the work of, replace, fill in; see SUBSTITUTE.

acting *a.* substituting, alternate, assistant; see TEMPORARY.

acting *n.* pretending, feigning, simulating, gesturing, ranting, dramatizing, performing, behaving, playing, showing off, impersonation, depiction, portrayal, pantomime, rendition, dramatics, theatricals, performance, dramatic action, mime.

action *n.* **1.** [Any state opposed to rest and quiet] activity, conflict, business, occupation, work, response, reaction, movement, industry, bustle, turmoil, stir, flurry, animation, vivacity, enterprise, energy, liveliness, alertness, agility, vigor, life, commotion, rush, motion, mobility, haste, speed, go*, life, doings*. **2.** [An individual deed] feat, exploit, performance, performing, execution, blow, stroke, maneuver, step, stunt, achievement, act, deed, thing, stratagem, something done, accomplishment, commission, effort, enterprise, manipulation, move, movement, doing, effect, transaction, exertion, operation, handiwork, dealings, procedure, manufacture. —**bring action** accuse, start a lawsuit, take to court; see SUE. —**see action** do battle, engage in combat, conflict; see FIGHT. —**take action** become active, do, initiate activity; see ACT 1.

actions *n.pl.* deportment, conduct, manners; see BEHAVIOR.

activate *v.* stimulate, initiate, arouse; see BEGIN 1.

active *a.* busy, eventful, lively, dynamic, energetic, alive, mobile, hasty, going, rapid, progressive, speedy, walking, traveling, movable, bustling, humming, efficient, functioning, working, moving, restless, swarming, rustling, flowing, in process, in effect, in force, simmering, overflowing, streaming, stirring, effective, at work, operating, operative, agitated, brisk, industrious, enthusiastic, agile, quick, nimble, rapid, dexterous, spry, fresh, sprightly, frisky, wiry, alert, ready, sharp, keen, wide-awake, animated, enlivened, ardent, purposeful, persevering, resolute, aggressive, forceful, intense, determined, diligent, hard-working, assiduous, enterprising, inventive, vigorous, strenuous, eager, zealous, bold, daring, dashing, high-spirited, hopping*, going full blast, in high gear*, snappy*, on the ball*, peppy*, turned on to*.

activity *n.* motion, movement, liveliness; see ACTION 1.

act one's age *v.* act properly, be good, be orderly; see BEHAVE.

actor *n.* player, performer, character, star, comedian, impersonator, leading man, leading woman, entertainer, artist, television star, villain, motion picture actor, stage player, supporting actor, mimic, mime, clown, ventriloquist, pantomimist, understudy, Thespian, protagonist, headliner, bit player*, ham*, extra, movie idol; see also CAST 2.

actress *n.* comedienne, starlet, leading lady; see ACTOR, CAST 2.

actual *a.* original, real, exact; see GENUINE 1.

actually *a.* truly, in fact, as a matter of fact; see REALLY 1.

act up *v.* goof off*, be naughty, create a disturbance; see MISBEHAVE.

act upon or **on** *v.* **1.** [To act in accordance with] adjust, regulate, behave; see ACT 1, 2. **2.** [To influence] affect, sway, impress; see INFLUENCE.

acute *a.* **1.** [Crucial] decisive, important, vital; see CRITICAL. **2.** [Sharp] severe, keen, cutting; see INTENSE. **3.** [Shrewd] clever, bright, perceptive; see INTELLIGENT.

acutely *a.* keenly, sharply, severely; see VERY.

ad* *n.* announcement, display, notice; see ADVERTISEMENT.

A.D. *abbrev.* of the Christian era, after Christ, post-Christian, year of our Lord.

adage *n.* axiom, saying, maxim; see PROVERB.

adapt *v.* modify, revise, readjust; see ALTER 1.

adaptability *n.* changeability, flexibility, versatility, adjustability, conformability, pliancy, docility, compliancy, pliability, plasticity.

adaptable *a.* adjustable, elastic, pliable; see FLEXIBLE.

add *v.* **1.** [To bring together, usually by mathematics] total, sum up, sum, figure, figure up, count up, compute, calculate, add up, tally, reckon, enumerate, hitch on*.—*Ant.* DECREASE, subtract, take away. **2.** [To make a further remark] append, say further, continue, write further, annex, supplement, affix, add a postscript, reply, tack on.

addict *n.* drug abuser, user, cokehead*, head*, dope fiend*, drug fiend*, mainliner*, junkie*, alcoholic, druggie*, freak*.

addicted (to) *a.* disposed to, inclined, in the habit of, prone, accustomed, attached, abandoned, wedded, devoted, predisposed, used to, imbued with, fanatic about, obsessed with, hooked on*.

addiction *n.* fixation, inclination, bent; see HABIT 2, OBSESSION.

addition *n.* **1.** [That which has been added] interest, raise, additive, gain, profit, dividend, bonus, supplement, reinforcement, appendage, appendix, accessory, attachment, extension, increase, annex.—*Ant.* LOSS, reduction, shrinkage. **2.** [A real estate development] annex, annexation, subdivision, shopping center, development, extension, expansion, branch, construction.

additional *a.* supplementary, new, further; see EXTRA.

address *n.* **1.** [A formal speech] oration, lecture, sermon; see SPEECH 3. **2.** [Place at which one may be reached] residence, legal residence, home, quarters, living quarters, dwelling, headquarters, place of business, box number; see also HOME 1.

address *v.* **1.** [To provide directions for delivery] label, mark, prepare for mailing; see WRITE 2. **2.** [To speak formally to an assemblage] lecture, lecture to, discuss, give a talk, give an address, give a speech, take the floor, harangue, rant, sermonize, spout off*, spiel*.

add to *v.* augment, amplify, expand; see INCREASE.

add up *v.* be plausible, be probable, be reasonable, be logical, stand to reason, hold water; see also MAKE SENSE.

add up to *v.* indicate, signify, imply; see MEAN 1.

adept *a.* skillful, proficient, capable; see ABLE.

adequate *a.* sufficient, equal to the need, satisfactory; see ENOUGH 1.

adequately *a.* sufficiently, appropriately, suitably, fittingly, satisfactorily, abundantly, copiously, acceptably, tolerably, decently, modestly, fairly well, well enough, capably, good enough, to an acceptable degree, competently; see also WELL 2, 3.—*Ant.* INADEQUATELY, badly, insufficiently.

adhere (to) *v.* **1.** [To serve] follow, be devoted to, practice; see OBEY. **2.** [To stick to] attach, cling, hold fast; see STICK 1.

adhesive *a.* gummy, clinging, pasty; see STICKY.

ad infinitum *a.* endlessly, forever, ceaselessly; see REGULARLY.

adjacent *a.* beside, alongside, bordering; see NEAR 1.

adjective *n.* modifier, article, determiner, attribute, attributive, qualifier, descriptive word, limiting word, adjectival construction, identifier, qualifying word, accessory, addition, dependent.

adjourn *v.* leave, postpone, discontinue; see SUSPEND 2.

adjournment *n.* intermission, pause, break; see RECESS 1.

adjust *v.* **1.** [To bring to agreement] settle, arrange, conclude, complete, accord, reconcile, clarify, conform, sort, allocate, grade, tally, regulate, organize, systematize, coordinate, straighten, standardize, clean up. **2.** [To place or regulate parts] fix, connect, square, balance, regulate, tighten, fit, repair, focus, fine-tune, readjust, rectify, correct, set, mend, improve, overhaul, grind, sharpen, renovate, polish, bring into line, align, calibrate, put in working order, temper, service.

adjustable *a.* adaptable, stretchable, tractable; see FLEXIBLE.

adjustment *n.* settlement, arrangement, pay, remuneration, reimbursement, compensation, compromise, reconciliation, agreement, making up, improvement, regulation, fixing, adaptation, correction, mutual understanding.

ad-lib* *v.* improvise, make up, devise; see INVENT 1.

administer *v.* **1.** [To manage] conduct, direct, control; see MANAGE 1. **2.** [To furnish] extend, dispense, give; see OFFER 1.

administration *n.* **1.** [The direction of affairs] government, supervision, command; see MANAGEMENT. **2.** [Those who direct affairs] directors, administrators, officers, supervisors, superintendents, advisers, command, executives, strategists, officials, committee, board, board of directors, executive, executive branch, legislature, president, presidency, chief executive, cabinet, ministry, commander, chairman, general, admiral, commander in chief, central office, headquarters, the management, bureau, consulate, embassy, legation, department, Washington, party in power, brass*, front office*, the powers that be, the man*. **3.** [The period in which a political administration is operative] term of office, regime, reign; see sense 2.

administrative *a.* executive, controlling, ruling; see GOVERNING.

administrator *n.* manager, director, chairman; see EXECUTIVE.

admirable *a.* worthy, attractive, good; see EXCELLENT.

admiration *n.* praise, deference, approval, regard, fondness, esteem, respect, appreciation, favor, adoration, applause, glorification, idolatry, honor, recognition, valuing, liking, love, high regard, high opinion, reverence, veneration, homage.—*Ant.* OBJECTION, disregard, distrust.

admire *v.* esteem, honor, applaud, praise, extol, respect, approve, revere, venerate, laud, boost, glorify, reverence, hold dear, appreciate, credit, commend, value, treasure, prize, look up to, rate highly, pay homage to, idolize, adore, hail, put a high price on, have a high opinion of, think highly of, show deference to, think well of, take great stock in, put great stock in, put on a pedestal.—*Ant.* BLAME, censure, deride.

admirer *n.* supporter, believer, patron; see FOLLOWER.

admissible *a.* proper, suitable, right; see PERMITTED.

admission *n.* **1.** [The act of granting entrance] acceptance, admittance, permission, reception, welcome, recognition, acknowledgment, confirmation, selection, initiation.—*Ant.* REMOVAL, rejection, expulsion. **2.** [The entrance fee] cover charge, fee, price, ticket, charges, toll, tax, minimum, donation, cover*, gate. **3.** [Something acknowledged] statement, disclosure, confession, acknowledgment, affirmation, concession, divulgence, declaration, confirmation, assertion, testimony, allegation, deposition, affidavit.—*Ant.* DENIAL, disallowance, repudiation.

admit *v.* **1.** [To grant entrance] bring in, give access to, allow entrance to; see RECEIVE 4. **2.** [To confess] acknowledge, indicate, disclose, bare, unveil, uncover, expose, proclaim, declare, open up, bring to light, go over, go into details, confide to, tell, relate, narrate, enumerate, divulge, reveal, communicate, make known, tell the whole story, plead guilty, own up to, talk, sing*, cough up*, come clean*, spill the beans*.—*Ant.* HIDE, cover up, obscure.

admonish *v.* reprove, chide, rebuke; see SCOLD.

admonition *n.* advice, notice, exhortation; see WARNING.

adolescence *n.* young adulthood, puberty, teens; see YOUTH 1.

adolescent *a.* pubescent, juvenile, youthful; see YOUNG 1.

adolescent *n.* youngster, minor, teenager; see YOUTH 3.

adopt *v.* **1.** [To take as a son or daughter] pick, choose, select, transfer, father, mother, take in, raise, make one's heir, take as one's own, naturalize, foster. **2.** [To take as one's own] embrace, appropriate, seize, take up, take over, choose, assume, use, utilize, imitate, borrow, mimic.—*Ant.* DENY, repudiate, reject.

adoption *n.* choosing, election, choice; see SELECTION 1.

adorable* *a.* delightful, lovable, cute; see CHARMING.

adoration *n.* devotion, homage, veneration; see WORSHIP 1.

adore *v.* **1.** [To worship] venerate, revere, glorify; see WORSHIP. **2.** [To love] cherish, treasure, prize; see LOVE 1.

adorn *v.* beautify, embellish, ornament; see DECORATE.

adorned *a.* trimmed, decked, garnished; see ORNATE.

adult *a.* of age, grown, developed; see MATURE.

adult *n.* mature person, grown-up, fully developed member of a species; see MAN 2, WOMAN 1.

adulterate *v.* dilute, lessen, taint; see POLLUTE, WEAKEN.

adultery *n.* promiscuity, infidelity, unfaithfulness; see FORNICATION.

advance *n.* **1.** [The act of moving forward] impetus, progression, motion; see PROGRESS 1. **2.** [Promotion] enrichment, betterment, increase; see IMPROVEMENT 1.

advance *v.* **1.** [To move forward physically] progress, proceed, move on, forge ahead, press on, push ahead, go on, go forth, gain ground, make headway, step forward, come to the front, conquer territory, march on, move onward, continue ahead, push on, press on.—*Ant.* STOP, halt, stand still. **2.** [To propose] set forth, introduce, suggest; see PROPOSE 1. **3.** [To promote] further, encourage, urge; see PROMOTE 1. **4.** [To lend] loan, provide with, furnish; see LEND. **5.** [To improve] develop, make progress, get better; see IMPROVE 2.

advanced *a.* **1.** [Superior] precocious, first, exceptional; see EXCELLENT. **2.** [Aged] seasoned, venerable, time-honored; see OLD 1, 3. **3.** [Progressive] radical, unconventional, ahead of the times; see LIBERAL.

advancement *n.* **1.** [Promotion in rank] improvement, elevation, raise; see PROMOTION 1. **2.** [Progress] gain, headway, progression; see PROGRESS 1.

advantage *n.* luck, favor, approval, help, aid, sanction, good, patronage, support, preference, odds, protection, start, leg up*, helping hand, upper hand, leverage, hold, opportunity, dominance, superiority, supremacy, lead, influence, power, mastery, authority, prestige, sway, pull*, edge*, ace in the hole*.—*Ant.* WEAKNESS, handicap, disadvantage. —**have the advantage of** be superior, have the opportunity, be privileged; see SUCCEED 1. —**take advantage of** exploit, profit by, utilize; see USE 1.

adventure *n.* happening, experience, episode; see EVENT.

adventurer *n.* explorer, pirate, soldier of fortune, daredevil, hero, pioneer, mountain climber, wild game hunter, romantic; see also PIONEER 2, TRAVELER.

adventurous *a.* bold, daring, courageous; see BRAVE.

adverse *a.* untimely, improper, unfortunate; see UNFAVORABLE.

adversely *a.* negatively, resentfully, unsympathetically; see UNFAVORABLY.

adversity *n.* misfortune, distress, trouble; see DIFFICULTY 1, 2.

advertise *v.* publicize, proclaim, herald, announce, declare, notify, warn, display, exhibit, show, reveal, expose, disclose, unmask, divulge, uncover, communicate, publish abroad, issue, broadcast, print, circulate, show off, parade, propagate, disseminate, inform, celebrate, spread, call public attention to, promulgate, give out, plug*, play up*; see also DECLARE.

advertised *a.* announced, posted, noted, publicized, billed, printed, published, made public, broadcast, emphasized, pointed out, displayed, exhibited, shown, offered, presented, put on sale, flaunted, plugged*, boosted, built up, pushed*.

advertisement *n.* announcement, notice, publicity, exhibit, exhibition, display, circular, handbill, placard, poster, public notice, broadcast, bill, proclamation, classified advertisement, sample, endorsement, want ad*, buildup*, plug*, ballyhoo, blurb*, spread*, classified*.

advice *n.* guidance, instruction, consultation, suggestion, preaching, information, admonition, forewarning, warning, caution, a word to the wise, injunction, lesson, directions, opinion, counsel, advisement, encouragement, persuasion, prescription, recommendation, proposition, proposal, view, help, aid, judgment.

advise *v.* recommend, prescribe, guide, exhort, direct, admonish, warn, point out, instruct, counsel, advocate, suggest, urge, prompt, show, tell, inform, move, caution, charge, encourage, preach, teach, persuade, offer an opinion to, forewarn, prepare, straighten out.—*Ant.* DECEIVE, misdirect, lead astray.

advisor *n.* counselor, instructor, consultant.—*Ant.* FRIEND, TEACHER.

advisory *a.* consulting, having power to advise, prudential; see HELPING.

advocate *v.* bolster, push, further, advance; see also PROMOTE 1.

aerial *a.* in the air, atmospheric, flying; see HIGH 2.

aesthetic *a.* creative, artistic, inventive; see BEAUTIFUL.

affair *n.* **1.** [Business; *often plural*] concern, responsibility, matter, duty, topic, subject, case, circumstance, thing, question, function, private concern, personal business, calling, employment, occupation, profession, pursuit, avocation, obligation, job, province, realm, interest, mission, assignment, task; see also JOB 1. **2.** [An illicit love affair] liaison, rendezvous, intimacy, romance, relationship.

affect *v.* impress, sway, induce; see INFLUENCE.

affected *a.* **1.** [Being subject to influence] moved, touched, melted, influenced, awakened, sympathetic, stimulated, stirred, grieved, overwhelmed, moved to tears, hurt, injured, excited, struck, impressed, overwrought, devoured by, concerned, reached, compassionate, tender, sorry, troubled, distressed.—*Ant.* INDIFFERENT, unmoved, untouched. **2.** [Insincere or artificial] pretentious, melodramatic, unnatural, stilted, superficial, theatrical, stiff, strained, overdone, ostentatious, hollow, shallow, showy, fake, stuck-up*, put-on*.—*Ant.* SIMPLE, natural, genuine.

affection *n.* love, friendship, liking, attachment, good will, partiality, passion, ardor, zealous attachment, friendliness, concern, regard, desire, closeness, kindness, devotion, tenderness, fondness.—*Ant.* HATRED, dislike, enmity.

affectionate *a.* kind, tender, friendly; see LOVING.

affidavit *n.* testimony, sworn statement, affirmation; see OATH 1.

affinity *n.* **1.** [Attraction based on affection] fondness, liking, closeness; see AFFECTION. **2.** [Similarity] likeness, resemblance, kinship; see SIMILARITY.

affirmative *a.* agreeing, consenting, concurring, approving, assenting, supporting.—*Ant.* NEGATIVE, contradictory, noncommittal. —**in the affirmative** favorably, in assent, in agreement, with an affirmative answer; see also YES.

afflict *v.* injure, torment, trouble; see HURT.

affliction *n.* trouble, hardship, plight; see DIFFICULTY 1, 2.

affluent *a.* wealthy, well-off, well-to-do; see RICH 1.

afford *v.* have enough for, make both ends meet, bear, manage, be able to, have the means for, be financially able, stand, be in the market for.

afire *a.* flaming, on fire, blazing; see BURNING.

afloat *a.* adrift, at sea, sailing; see FLOATING.

afoot *a.* on foot, hiking, marching; see WALKING.

afraid *a.* hesitant, anxious, apprehensive, disturbed, frightened, fearful, nervous, uneasy, fidgety, alarmed, intimidated, discouraged, disheartened, perplexed, worried, perturbed, upset, panic-stricken, cowardly, scared, terrified, terrorized, shocked, frozen, aghast, alarmed, startled, aroused, horrified, petrified, stunned, rattled, struck dumb, trembling, distressed, jittery*, jumpy*, leery*, shaky*.—*Ant.* CONFIDENT, self-assured, poised.

Africa *n. Terms for areas in Africa include the following:* Senegal, Chad, Congo, Zaire, Gabon, Côte d'Ivoire, Rwanda, Togo, Algeria, Libya, Mauritania, Mali, Guinea, Guinea-Bissau, Egypt, Liberia, Nigeria, Niger, Sudan, Ethiopia, Zambia, Mozambique, Kenya, Tanzania, Angola, Uganda, Central African Republic, Cameroon, Ghana, Morocco, Tunisia, Gambia, Somalia, Zimbabwe, South Africa, Sierra Leone, Equatorial Guinea, Malawi, Botswana, Lesotho, Swaziland, Benin, Namibia, Djibouti, Burkina Faso, Burundi.

African *a.* **1.** [Concerning a part of Africa] North African, Moroccan, Egyptian, Libyan, Algerian, Saharan, Sudanese, East African, Kenyan, Tanzanian, Ugandan, Ethiopian, Somalian, West African, Liberian, Ghanaian, Nigerian, Senegalese, Congolese, Angolan, Central African, Zambian, South African. **2.** [Concerning the inhabitants of Africa] Negro, negroid, black, Bantu, Zulu, Swazi, Hottentot, Bushman, Pygmy, Afrikaaner, Boer, Colored, Yoruba, Ibo, Hausa, Masai, Kikuyu, Somali, Ethiopian, Egyptian, Arab, Moorish.

aft *a.* rearward, behind, astern; see BACK.

after *a. & prep.* **1.** [Behind in space] back of, in the rear, behind; see BACK. **2.** [Following] next, later, subsequent; see FOLLOWING.

after all *a.* at last, ultimately, in the end; see FINALLY 2.

afternoon *n.* P.M., siesta time, early afternoon, late afternoon, mid-afternoon.

afterward *a.* later, after, subsequently, in a while, a while later, afterwards, by and by, eventually, soon, on the next day, ultimately, another time, then, at a later time.

again *a.* anew, afresh, newly, once more, once again, repeatedly, over, from the beginning, on and on, another time, over again, a second time, recurrently, ditto.—*Ant.* ONCE, once only, at first. —**as much again** doubled, twice as much, multiplied; see DOUBLE.

again and again *a.* repeatedly, once again, continuously; see AGAIN.

against *a. & prep.* **1.** [Counter to] in the face of, into, toward, opposite to, facing. **2.** [In contact with] on, upon, in collision with, touching; see also NEXT 2. **3.** [Contrary to] in opposition to, opposed to, counter to, adverse to, in violation of, versus, over against. **4.** [Opposite] facing, fronting, corresponding; see OPPOSITE 3.

age *n.* **1.** [The period of one's existence] span, lifetime, duration; see LIFE 4. **2.** [A particular point or time in one's life] infancy, childhood, girlhood, boyhood, adolescence, adulthood, youth, middle age, old age, senility. **3.** [A period of time] epoch, era, period, time, century, decade, generation, interval, term, in the time of something; see also LIFE 4. —**of age** adult, twenty-one, having attained majority; see MATURE.

age *v.* grow feeble, decline, wane, advance in years, wrinkle, waste away, have one foot in the grave*, become long in the tooth.

aged *a.* gray, elderly, worn; see OLD.

agency *n.* **1.** [Place where business is transacted] firm, bureau, company; see OFFICE 3, BUSINESS 4. **2.** [That by which something is done] power, auspices, action; see MEANS 1.

agenda *n.* list, plan, schedule; see PROGRAM 2.

agent *n.* broker, promoter, operator, representative, salesman, assistant, emissary, intermediary, appointee, servant, executor, attorney, lawyer, go-between, surrogate, mediary, deputy, minister, envoy, middleman, commissioner, delegate, proxy, substitute, steward, functionary, ambassador, proctor, negotiator, advocate, coagent, press agent, booking agent, bookie*.

aggravate *v.* exasperate, annoy, provoke; see BOTHER 2.

aggravation *n.* **1.** [A cause of aggravation] worry, affliction, distress; see DIFFICULTY 1, 2, TROUBLE 1. **2.** [Annoyance] irritation, provocation, exasperation; see ANNOYANCE 1.

aggression *n.* offensive, assault, invasion; see ATTACK 1.

aggressive *a.* warlike, attacking, combative, threatening, advancing, offensive, firm, strong, disruptive, disturbing, hostile, intrusive, contentious, destructive, intruding, invading, assailing, barbaric, up in arms, on the warpath.—*Ant.* SERENE, peace-loving, peaceful.

agile *a.* nimble, quick, spry, deft, vigorous, athletic, sure-footed, light-footed, frisky, spirited, lithe, sprightly, supple, dexterous, easy-moving, rapid, active, ready, alive, buoyant, energetic, stirring, brisk, lively, swift, alert, bustling.—*Ant.* AWKWARD, slow, clumsy.

agility *n.* nimbleness, dexterity, spryness, quickness, briskness, swiftness, deftness, adroitness, fleetness, friskiness, liveliness, alertness.

aging *a.* declining, getting on, waning, falling, sinking, crumbling, slumping, mellowing, maturing, stale, developing, fermenting, wasting away, wearing out, growing old, fading.

agitate *v.* stir, move, arouse; see EXCITE.

agitated *a.* disturbed, upset, aroused; see EXCITED.

ago *a.* gone, since, past; see BEFORE.

agony *n.* suffering, torture, anguish; see PAIN 1, 2.

agree *v.* coincide, get along, side with, harmonize with, match up, concur, stand together, parallel, go along with, fit in, suit, say yes to, conform, go hand in hand with, equal, correspond, go together, synchronize, measure up to, square with*, click*, hit it off with, see eye to eye*.—*Ant.* DIFFER, disagree, debate.

agreeable *a.* pleasing, satisfactory, acceptable; see PLEASANT 1, 2.

agreeably *a.* kindly, politely, pleasantly, well, wonderfully, satisfactorily, genially, cheerfully, peacefully; see also FAVORABLY.—*Ant.* OPPOSITE, disagreeably, negatively.

agree about *v.* come to terms, see eye to eye*, settle; see SETTLE 1.

agreement *n.* **1.** [The state of being in accord] conformity, friendship, accordance, accommodation, correspondence, harmony, concord, unison, concert, common view, understanding, brotherhood, affiliation, alliance, fellowship, companionship, goodwill, cooperation, assent, approval, compromise, treaty, pact, contract, bargain, settlement, satisfaction, affinity, closeness, concurrence, reconciliation, uniformity, balance, kinship, peace, love, unity, union, tie.—*Ant.* DISAGREEMENT, enmity, disunity. **2.** [An expression of agreement] approval, treaty, contract; see DEAL 1.

agree on *v.* come to terms, make an arrangement, make a bargain; see SETTLE 1.

agree to *v.* promise, consent, approve; see ACCEPT.

agree with *v.* coincide, accord, harmonize; see AGREE.

agriculture *n.* tillage, cultivation, horticulture; see FARMING.

ahead *a.* before, earlier, in advance, ahead of, advanced, preceding, foremost, leading, in the lead, at the head of, in the foreground, to the fore, in the van, first, in front of, preliminary.—*Ant.* behind, back, toward the end. **—get ahead** advance, prosper, progress; see SUCCEED.

ahead of *a.* in advance of, before, above; see AHEAD. **—get ahead of** outdo, excel, subordinate; see EXCEED.

aid *n.* comfort, benefit, favor; see HELP 1.

ailing *a.* ill, feeble, weak; see SICK.

ailment *n.* sickness, infirmity, disease; see ILLNESS 1, 2.

aim *n.* intention, object, plan; see PURPOSE 1. **—take aim** point, direct, train; see AIM, *v.*

aim *v.* train, steer, level, direct, set up, set the sights, sight, take aim, zero in on, draw a bead on.

aimed *a.* proposed, marked, intended for, directed, designed, calculated, leveled, trained, steered, set, planned, anticipated.

aimless *a.* purposeless, pointless, erratic, thoughtless, careless, heedless, rambling, wandering, blind, random, unsettled, flightly, capricious, wayward, without aim, chance, haphazard, to no purpose, drifting, stray, accidental, undirected, casual, indecisive, irresolute, fitful, fanciful, fickle, eccentric, unplanned, helpless, unpredictable, shiftless.—*Ant.* CAREFUL, purposeful, planned.

air *n.* **1.** [The gaseous envelope of the earth] atmosphere, stratosphere, troposphere, wind, breeze, draft, the open air, sky, oxygen, the open, ventilation, the out-of-doors. **2.** [The apparent quality] look, mien, demeanor; see LOOKS. **—off the air** not being broadcast, closed, signed off; see QUIET. **—on the air** broadcasting, transmitting, reporting; see ON THE AIR. **—up in the**

air undecided, unsettled, unsure; see UNCERTAIN.
air *v.* ventilate, open, freshen, air out, circulate air, air-condition, expose to air, draw in air, fan, refresh, cool, purify.
aired *a.* **1.** [Exposed to the air] ventilated, opened, freshened, purified, hung out, sunned, dried.—*Ant.* CLOSED, stuffy, dark. **2.** [Exposed to public attention] exposed, disclosed, discussed, revealed, told, unveiled; see also EXPOSED.—*Ant.* SECRET, undisclosed, concealed.
air force *n.* aviation service, air power, air cover; see ARMY 1.
airline *n.* air carrier, commercial airline, air freight carrier; see BUSINESS 4.
airman *n.* pilot, copilot, navigator; see PILOT.
airplane *n.* aircraft, aeroplane, airliner; see PLANE 3.
airport *n.* airfield, spaceport, flying field, landing field, airstrip, hangar, heliport, installations.
airs *n.pl.* affectation, pretense, show; see PRETENSE 2.
airtight *a.* impermeable to air, closed, shut tight; see TIGHT 2.
airy *a.* windy, breezy, draughty, exposed, ventilated, open, spacious, lofty, atmospheric, well-ventilated, aerial, out-of-doors, outdoors, in the open.
aisle *n.* passageway, opening, way, walk, path, course, clearing, avenue, corridor, passage, gangway, alley, lane.
alarm *n.* drum, siren, horn, signal, fog horn, fire siren, call, SOS, red light, hoot, blast, shout, warning sound, danger signal, cry, yell, scream, air raid siren.
alarmed *a.* frightened, fearful, aroused; see AFRAID.
alarming *a.* frightening, foreboding, distressing; see DISTURBING.
Alaska *n.* the Klondike, the 49th state, the frozen North, the gold country, land of the sourdough.
album *n.* collection, stamp book, register, index, scrapbook, notebook, photograph album, portfolio, commonplace book.
alcohol *n.* spirits, liquor, intoxicant; see DRINK 2.
alcoholic *a.* spirituous, fermented, distilled; see STRONG 4.
alcoholic *n.* addict, heavy drinker, sot; see DRUNKARD.
alcoholism *n.* intoxication, insobriety, dipsomania; see DRUNKENNESS.
alert *a.* wary, on guard, wide-awake; see OBSERVANT. **—on the alert** watchful, vigilant, on guard; see OBSERVANT.
alert *v.* inform, put on guard, signal; see WARN.
alibi *n.* proof of absence, plea, explanation, declaration, defense, statement, case, allegation, avowal, assurance, profession, excuse, assertion, answer, reply, retort, vindication.
alien *a.* exotic, strange, unknown; see FOREIGN.
alien *n.* foreigner, stranger, refugee, displaced person, outsider, migrant, colonist, immigrant, guest, visitor, newcomer, barbarian, Ishmael, settler, stateless person, intruder, squatter, interloper, invader, noncitizen, man without a country.—*Ant.* INHABITANT, native, citizen.
alienate *v.* estrange, turn away, set against, withdraw the affections of, make unfriendly, come between, disunite, separate, divide, part, turn off*.—*Ant.* UNITE, reconcile, acclimate.
align *v.* arrange, straighten, regulate; see ADJUST 1, 2.
alike *a.* like, same, equal, identical, matching, selfsame, akin, similar, comparable, parallel, resembling, related, approximate, equivalent, allied, of a kind, twin, one, indistinguishable, facsimile, duplicate, matched, mated, one and the same, all one, in the same boat, on all fours with.
alimony *n.* upkeep, maintenance, provision; see PAYMENT 1.
alive *a.* live, animate, living, breathing, existing, existent, vital, not dead, mortal, organic, extant, viable, growing, having life, conscious, alive and kicking*, above ground*, among the living.—*Ant.* DEAD, lifeless, inanimate.
all *a.* **1.** [Completely] totally, wholly, entirely; see COMPLETELY. **2.** [Each] every, any, each and every, any and every, every member of, for everybody, for anybody, for anyone, for anything, for everything, barring no one, bar none, beginning and end, from A to Z.—*Ant.* no, not any, none. **3.** [Exclusively] alone, nothing but, solely; see ONLY 1.
all *n.* everything, everyone, every person, sum, collection, group, ensemble, total, totality, quantity, unit, entity, whole kit and caboodle*; lock, stock and barrel*; the works*.—*Ant.* NONE, nobody, nothing. **—after all** nevertheless, in spite of everything, despite; see ALTHOUGH. **—at all** to the slightest degree, in the least, none; see NEVER, NOT. **—in all** all told, collectively, on the whole; see ALTOGETHER.
allegedly *a.* assertedly, according to the statement, supposedly; see APPARENTLY.
allegiance *n.* fidelity, homage, fealty; see LOYALTY.
allergic to *a.* sensitive to, affected by, subject to, susceptible to, repelled by, oversensitive to.—*Ant.* IMMUNE, unaffected by, hardened to.
allergy *n.* hypersensitive bodily reaction, hypersensitivity, antipathy to certain substances; see ILLNESS 2.

alley *n.* back street, lane, rear way; see ROAD 1. **—up** or **down one's alley*** suited to one's abilities, in keeping with one's tastes, enjoyable, useful, what the doctor ordered*.

alliance *n.* **1.** [The state of being allied] connection, membership, affinity, participation, cooperation, support, union, agreement, common understanding, marriage, kinship, relation, collaboration, federation, friendship, partnership, coalition, association, affiliation, confederation, implication, bond, tie. **2.** [The act of joining] fusion, combination, coupling; see UNION 1. **3.** [A union] league, federation, company; see ORGANIZATION 2.

allied *a.* unified, confederated, associated; see UNITED.

allot *v.* earmark, allocate, dole; see ASSIGN, DISTRIBUTE.

allotment *n.* portion, lot, part; see SHARE.

all-out *a.* total, entire, complete; see ABSOLUTE 1.

allow *v.* permit, let, sanction, grant, consent to, tolerate, favor, yield, bear, approve of, give leave, endorse, certify, have no objection to, release, pass, authorize, license, warrant, put up with, give the green light to*, give the go-ahead to.—*Ant.* DENY, forbid, prohibit.

allowable *a.* permissible, proper, legal; see ADMISSIBLE.

allowance *n.* salary, wage, commission, fee, hire, remittance, stipend, gift, grant, pension, alimony, annuity, settled rate, endowment, scholarship, fellowship, prize, subsidy, pay, bequest, legacy, inheritance, contribution, aid, handout, pocket money. **—make allowances for** weigh, excuse, rationalize; see CONSIDER.

allow for *v.* take into account, take into consideration, provide for; see CONSIDER.

alloy *n.* compound, mixture, combination; see METAL. *Common metal alloys include the following:* ferromanganese, ferrosilicon, pewter, chromesteel, nichrome, tungsten steel, stainless steel, nonmagnetic steel, chromium steel, chrome-nickel steel, high tensile steel, tungsten-chromium-cobalt, cobalt steel, finishing steel, structural steel, carbon steel, brass, bronze, green gold, nickel-silver, zinc-aluminum, aluminum-bronze, boron bronze, copper-aluminum, aluminum-manganese-copper, manganese-copper, tin-manganese, tin-copper, antimony.

all right *a.* **1.** [Adequately] tolerably, acceptably, passably; see ADEQUATELY. **2.** [Yes] agreed, very well, of course; see YES. **3.** [Certainly] without a doubt, definitely, positively; see SURELY. **4.** [Uninjured] safe, well, unhurt; see WHOLE. **5.** [Correct] exact, precise, right; see RIGHT 1.

all-time *a.* unsurpassed, record-breaking, to the greatest extent; see BEST 1.

all told *a.* in all, in toto, on the whole; see ALTOGETHER.

ally *n.* confederate, partner, collaborator; see ASSOCIATE.

almanac *n.* calendar, yearbook, annual, register, world almanac, chronicle, journal, record, register of the year.

almighty *a.* **1.** [Omnipotent] invincible, all-powerful, mighty; see POWERFUL 1. **2.** [Omnipresent] infinite, eternal, godlike, all-knowing, all-seeing, deathless, immortal, celestial, divine, godly, pervading.

almighty *n.* all-ruling, all-powerful, omnipotent; see GOD.

almost *a.* all but, nearly, approximately, roughly, to all intents, as good as, near to, substantially, essentially, in effect, on the verge of, relatively, for all practical purposes, to that effect, not quite, about to, with some exceptions, in the vicinity of, bordering on, within sight of, with little tolerance, close upon, in the neighborhood of, about, just about*, not quite, most*, around*, within a hair of, by a narrow squeak*.

aloft *a.* on high, overhead, up; see ABOVE 1, OVER 1.

alone *a.* lone, lonely, solitary, deserted, abandoned, individual, forsaken, desolate, detached, friendless, unaccompanied, isolated, lonesome, apart, by oneself, single, widowed, unattached, unconnected.—*Ant.* ACCOMPANIED, attended, escorted. **—let alone** **1.** [Besides] not to mention, also, in addition to; see BESIDES. **2.** [Neglect] ignore, isolate, refrain from disturbing; see NEGLECT 2. **—let well enough alone** forget, ignore, let alone; see NEGLECT 2.

along *a.* **1.** [Near] by, at, adjacent; see NEAR 1. **2.** [Ahead] on, onward, forward; see AHEAD. **3.** [Together with] with, accompanying, in addition to, in company with, along with, side by side, coupled with, at the same time, simultaneously. **—all along** all the time, from the beginning, constantly; see REGULARLY. **—get along** **1.** [To succeed] prosper, get by, make ends meet; see SUCCEED 1. **2.** [To advance] progress, move on, push ahead; see ADVANCE 1. **3.** [To agree] accord, stand together, equal; see AGREE.

alongside *a. & prep.* parallel to, close by, close at hand, by the side of, at the side of, along the side, side by side, equal with, on the same plane with, almost touching, neck and neck.—*Ant.* BEYOND, ahead, behind.

aloof *a.* remote, reserved, distant; see INDIFFERENT.

aloud *a.* vociferously, audibly, noisily; see LOUDLY.

alphabet *n.* letters, rune, pictograph, ideograph, characters, symbols, signs, hieroglyphs, cryptograms, phonemes, morphemes, sounds; see also LETTER 1.

alphabetical *a.* systematic, logical, consecutive, progressive, one after another, step by step, graded, planned, ordered, letter by letter, from A to Z, indexed.

alphabetize *v.* arrange alphabetically, index, systematize; see ORDER 3.

alpine *a.* mountainous, high, lofty, snow-capped, rocky, soaring, rangy, snow-clad, elevated, towering; see also HIGH 1, 2.

already *a.* previously, by now, now, even now, by this time, at present, just now, in the past, up to now, by that time, then.

also *a.* too, likewise, besides, as well, in addition, additionally, along with, more than that, over and above, in conjunction with, thereto, together with, ditto, more, moreover, further, furthermore, including, plus, to boot.—*Ant.* WITHOUT, excluding, otherwise.

alter *v.* **1.** [To change for a purpose] vary, turn, diminish, replace, mutate, warp, alternate, remodel, renovate, evolve, translate, disguise, restyle, revolutionize, reduce, substitute, reorganize, increase, intensify, shape, shift, modify, transform, remake, convert, reform, tailor, adjust, adapt, invert, reverse, reconstruct. **2.** [To become different] convert, develop, decay; see CHANGE 2.

alteration *n.* exchange, modification, revision; see CHANGE 1.

altered *a.* modified, qualified, revised; see CHANGED 2.

alternate *a.* alternative, substitute, makeshift; see TEMPORARY.

alternate *n.* replacement, equivalent, double; see SUBSTITUTE.

alternate *v.* **1.** [To take or do by turns] substitute, follow in turn, happen by turns, follow one another, do by turns, do one then the other, relieve, fill in for, exchange. **2.** [To fluctuate] vary, rise and fall, shift; see WAVER.

alternative *n.* option, discretion, opportunity; see CHOICE.

although *conj.* though, even though, despite, still, despite the fact that, in spite of, even if, while, however, for all that.

altitude *n.* elevation, loftiness, eminence; see HEIGHT.

altogether *a.* all told, collectively, on the whole, in the aggregate, in sum total, in a mass, all in all, all things considered, by and large, all, taking all things together, as a whole, for the most part.

always *a.* **1.** [Constantly] periodically, continually, ceaselessly; see REGULARLY. **2.** [Forever] perpetually, eternally, evermore; see FOREVER.

A.M. *abbrev.* after midnight, morning, early hours, before noon, forenoon, dawn, sunup.

amass *v.* gather, hoard, store up; see ACCUMULATE.

amateur *n.* beginner, novice, learner, nonprofessional, dabbler, recruit, dilettante, hopeful, neophyte, initiate, apprentice, freshman, tenderfoot, rookie*, greenhorn, cub.—*Ant.* VETERAN, professional, expert.

amaze *v.* astonish, perplex, astound; see SURPRISE.

amazement *n.* astonishment, awe, bewilderment; see WONDER 1.

amazing *a.* astonishing, astounding, marvelous; see UNUSUAL 1.

ambassador *n.* representative, envoy, minister; see DIPLOMAT.

ambiguity *n.* doubtfulness, incertitude, vagueness; see UNCERTAINTY 2.

ambiguous *a.* equivocal, enigmatic, vague; see OBSCURE 1.

ambition *n.* hope, earnestness, aspiration, yearning, eagerness, longing, craving, passion, lust, itch, hunger, thirst, appetite, energy, ardor, zeal, enthusiasm, spirit, vigor, enterprise, get up and go*, what it takes*.—*Ant.* INDIFFERENCE, apathy, laziness.

ambitious *a.* aspiring, longing, hopeful, zealous, hungry, thirsty, inspired, industrious, goal-oriented, enthusiastic, energetic, avid, sharp, climbing, ardent, designing, earnest, enterprising, aggressive, resourceful, pushy*.

ambush *n.* pitfall, snare, deception; see TRAP 1.

ambush *v.* waylay, ensnare, lay for, set a trap, keep out of sight, decoy, entrap, hook in, lurk, lie in wait for, surround, hem in; see also ATTACK.

amend *v.* correct, mend, revise; see ALTER 1.

amendment *n.* bill, measure, act, clause, motion, revision, supplement, rider.

America *n.* **1.** [One or both of the continents of the Western Hemisphere] North America, Latin America, South America, Central America, the New World, the Western Hemisphere. **2.** [The United States of America] U.S., the fifty states, Land of the Free, Land of Liberty, the U.S. of A.*, Uncle Sam*, the States.

American *a.* **1.** [Related to the Western Hemisphere] continental, North American, Latin American, South American, Central American, Pan-American. *In reference to specific countries of the Western Hemisphere, the following are used:* Canadian, Mexican, Nicaraguan, Costa Rican, Guatemalan, Honduran, San Salvadorian, Panamanian, Cuban, Haitian, Puerto Rican, Colombian, Venezuelan, Guianan, Brazilian, Peruvian, Ecuadorian, Chilean, Argentinian, Uruguayan, Paraguayan, Bolivian, etc. **2.** [Related to the United States of America] republican, constitutional, democratic, patriotic, freedom-loving, all-American.

American *n.* citizen of the United States, United States national, Yankee, Northerner. Southerner, Indian, pioneer.

Americanism *n.* patriotism, nationalism, isolationism, provincialism, flag waving, clean living, fair play, friendly rivalry, free enterprise, America first, the competitive system, spirit of '76*.

amiable *a.* pleasant, genial, charming; see FRIENDLY.

ammunition *n. Types of ammunition include the following:* projectile, charge, grenade, buckshot, gunpowder, cartridge, bullet, bomb, missile, hand grenade, fuse, shrapnel, torpedo, shell, ball, cannonball, shot, ammo*; see also BOMB, BULLET, EXPLOSIVE, GAS 3, SHOT 1.

among *prep.* between, in between, in the midst of, surrounded by, in connection with, amid, amongst, amidst, in the company of.

amount *n.* **1.** [The total of several quantities] sum, product, sum total; see WHOLE. **2.** [Price] expense, output, outlay; see PRICE. **3.** [Quantity] bulk, mass, number; see QUANTITY.

amount to *v.* reach, extend to, come to, effect, be equal to, approximate, check with, total up to, be in all, be in the whole, total, tally with, add up to.

ample *a.* sufficient, plentiful, adequate; see ENOUGH 1.

amplify *v.* expand, augment, elaborate; see INCREASE.

amply *a.* enough, sufficiently, copiously; see ADEQUATELY.

amputate *v.* cut off, sever, cut away; see REMOVE.

amuse *v.* divert, cheer, enliven; see ENTERTAIN 1.

amusement *n.* recreation, pastime, play; see ENTERTAINMENT.

amusing *a.* engaging, diverting, enchanting; see ENTERTAINING.

analysis *n.* study, investigation, search; see EXAMINATION 1.

analyze *v.* dissect, examine, investigate, separate, break down, disintegrate, resolve into elements, determine the essential features of, decentralize.

anarchy *n.* turmoil, chaos, mob rule; see DISORDER.

anatomy *n.* physique, form, figure; see BODY 1.

ancestor *n.* progenitor, forebear, founder of the family; see FOREFATHER.

ancestral *a.* inborn, congenital, inherited; see INHERENT.

ancestry *n.* lineage, heritage, parentage; see FAMILY.

anchor *n.* stay, tie, grapnel, mooring, grappling iron, support, mainstay, ballast, safeguard, security, protection, hold, fastener, grip, defense, protection, foothold.

anchor *v.* make port, tie up, moor, berth, bring a ship in, drop anchor.

ancient *a.* antique, antiquated, aged; see OLD 1, 2, 3.

and *conj.* in addition to, also, including, plus, together with, as well as, furthermore, moreover.

anecdote *n.* tale, incident, episode; see STORY.

anemic *a.* pallid, weak, sickly; see PALE 1.

anesthetic *n.* hypnosis, gas, opiate; see DRUG.

angel *n.* Angel of Death, good angel, dark angel, archangel, guardian angel, spirit, cherub, celestial spirit, winged being, saint.—*Ant.* DEVIL, demon, Satan.

angelic *a.* saintly, good, humble, heavenly, spiritual, kind, radiant, beautiful, divine, holy, pure, lovely, devout, virtuous, above reproach, righteous, cherubic.—*Ant.* WICKED, demonic, evil.

anger *n.* wrath, rage, fury, passion, temper, bad temper, animosity, indignation, hatred, resentment, ire, hot temper, impatience, vexation, annoyance, provocation, violence, turbulence, excitement, frenzy, tantrum, exasperation, huff, irritation, dander*.—*Ant.* PATIENCE, mildness, calm.

anger *v.* infuriate, annoy, irritate; see ENRAGE.

angle *n.* **1.** [Figure or plane formed at an intersection] notch, crotch, elbow, fork, cusp, incline, decline, Y, V, point where two lines meet.—*Ant.* CURVE, arc, oval. **2.** [Point of view] standpoint, outlook, perspective; see VIEWPOINT.

angle for *v.* plot, scheme, maneuver; see PLAN 1.

angler *n.* fisher, fisherwoman, Waltonian; see FISHERMAN.

angrily *a.* heatedly, indignantly, irately, grouchily, crisply, sharply, savagely, hotly, fiercely, tartly, bitterly, furiously, wildly, violently.—*Ant.* CALMLY, softly, quietly.

angry *a.* enraged, fierce, fiery, irate, raging, fuming, infuriated, furious, wrathful, stormy, indignant, cross, vexed, resentful, irritated, bitter, ferocious, offended, sullen, hateful, annoyed, provoked, displeased, riled, affronted, huffy, hostile, rabid, having flown off the handle*, mad, up in the air*, hot under the collar*, boiling, steamed up*, at the boiling point*, with one's back up, all worked up, up in arms.—*Ant.* CALM, quiet, restrained.

anguish *n.* wretchedness, pain, agony; see PAIN 1.

angular *a.* sharp-cornered, intersecting, crossing, oblique, divaricate, with corners, Y-shaped, V-shaped, crotched, forked, bent, crooked, pointed, triangular, rectangular, jagged, staggered, zigzag.—*Ant.* ROUND, parallel, side by side.

animal *a.* bestial, beastly, swinish, brutish, wild, beastlike, untamed, mammalian, bovine, canine, feline, reptilian.

animal *n.* living thing, creature, human being, beast, being, fish, crustacean, amphibian, vertebrate, invertebrate, reptile, insect, bird, wild animal, domestic animal, mammal; see also BIRD, FISH, INSECT, MAN 1.

animate *v.* activate, vitalize, inform, make alive, arouse, give life to, energize, put life into, breathe new life into.

animated *a.* spirited, gay, lively; see HAPPY.

animosity *n.* dislike, enmity, displeasure; see HATRED.

ankle *n.* anklebone, joint, tarsus; see BONE, FOOT 2.

annex *n.* expansion, additional quarters, new wing; see ADDITION 1, 2.

annex *v.* append, attach, affix; see ADD.

annihilate *v.* demolish, exterminate, obliterate; see DESTROY.

anniversary *n.* holiday, saint's day, birth date, birthday, yearly observance of an event, feastday, ceremony, annual meeting, biennial, triennial, quadrennial, quintennial, silver anniversary, golden anniversary, diamond jubilee, jubilee, festival, fiesta, centennial, red-letter day.

announce *v.* proclaim, publish, state; see DECLARE.

announced *a.* reported, given out, told, broadcast, issued, circulated, proclaimed, declared, published, disclosed, divulged, released, made known, disseminated, revealed, publicized, made public.—*Ant.* HIDDEN, unannounced, unrevealed.

announcement *n.* declaration, notification, prediction, proclamation, communication, publication, report, statement, advertisement, decision, news, tidings, returns, brief, bulletin, edict, white paper, message, notice, interim report, survey, advice, item, detail, communiqué, speech, release, handbill, poster, pamphlet, circular, billboard, brochure, form letter, telegram, cablegram, letter, leaflet; see also ADVERTISEMENT.—*Ant.* SECRET, ban, silence.

announcer *n.* program announcer, broadcaster, television announcer, telecaster, commentator, sportscaster, newscaster, radio announcer, disc jockey.

annoy *v.* pester, irritate, trouble; see BOTHER 2.

annoyance *n.* **1.** [A feeling of annoyance] vexation, irritation, pique, uneasiness, disgust, displeasure, provocation, nervousness, exasperation, indignation, touchiness, perturbation, moodiness, mortification, vexation, worry, distress, unhappiness, discontent, heartache, misery, aches and pains, dissatisfaction, impatience, peeve*.—*Ant.* JOY, pleasure, delight. **2.** [A source of annoyance] worry, inconvenience, nuisance; see DIFFICULTY 1, 2, TROUBLE 1.

annoying *a.* irritating, bothersome, vexatious; see DISTURBING.

annual *a.* yearly, each year, every year, once a year, lasting a year, anniversary, seasonal.

annually *a.* each year, once a year, periodically; see YEARLY.

annul *v.* invalidate, render void, repeal, revoke; see also CANCEL.

annulment *n.* invalidation, nullification, dissolution; see CANCELLATION.

anonymous *a.* unsigned, nameless, unknown, unacknowledged, unnamed, unclaimed, unidentified, secret, of unknown authorship, without a name, bearing no name, incognito, pseudo.—*Ant.* NAMED, signed, acknowledged.

another *a.* **1.** [Additional] one more, a further, added; see EXTRA. **2.** [Different] a separate, a distinct, some other; see UNLIKE.

another *n.* someone else, a different person, one more, addition, something else.—*Ant.* ONE, same, each.

answer *n.* **1.** [A reply] response, return, statement, retort, echo, repartee, password, rebuttal, approval, acknowledgment, sign, rejoinder, comeback.—*Ant.* QUESTION, query, request. **2.** [A solution] discovery, find, disclosure, revelation, explanation, interpretation, clue, resolution, key, the why and the wherefore.

answer *v.* **1.** [To reply] reply, respond, rejoin, retort, acknowledge, give answer, say, echo, return, refute, react, rebut, argue, plead, claim, remark, talk back, come back.—*Ant.* QUESTION, inquire, ask. **2.** [To provide a solution] solve, elucidate, clarify; see EXPLAIN.

answerable *a.* responsible, liable, amendable; see RESPONSIBLE 1.

answer for *v.* be responsible for, take the blame for, accept the responsibility for, take upon oneself, sponsor, do at one's own risk, take the rap for*.

answer to *v.* be responsible to, be ruled by, respect the authority of; see RESPECT 2.

antagonism *n.* enmity, hostility, opposition; see HATRED.

antagonistic *a.* opposing, hostile, inimical; see UNFRIENDLY.

antecedent *a.* preliminary, previous, prior; see PRECEDING.

antenna *n.* aerial, TV antenna, receiving wire; see WIRE.

anthem *n.* hymn, divine song, melody; see SONG.

antibiotic *n.* antitoxin, wonder drug, miracle drug; see MEDICINE 2.

antibody *n.* immunizer, neutralizer, immunoglobulin; see PREVENTION.

anticipate *v.* expect, forecast, prophesy, predict, hope for, look forward to, wait for, count on, plan on, have a hunch, bargain for, hold in view, have in prospect, assume, suppose, divine, conjecture, promise oneself, lean upon, entertain the hope, await, reckon on, count on, have a funny feeling*, look into the future, feel it in one's bones.—*Ant.* FEAR, be surprised, be caught unawares.

anticipated *a.* foreseen, predictable, prepared for; see EXPECTED, LIKELY 1.

anticipation *n.* expectancy, outlook, trust, promise, prospect, impatience, preoccupation, hope, prevision, presentiment, intuition, foresight, inkling, premonition, apprehension, foreboding, awareness, forethought, hunch*, a feeling in one's bones.—*Ant.* SURPRISE, shock, wonder.

antidote *n.* antitoxin, counteractant, remedy; see MEDICINE 2.

antique *a.* ancient, archaic, prehistoric; see OLD 3.

antique *n.* relic, artifact, heirloom, survival, rarity, monument, vestige, ruin.

antiseptic *a.* clean, germ-free, sterilized; see PURE 2.

antiseptic *n.* detergent, prophylactic, preservative, preventive, preventative, counterirritant, sterilizer, immunizing agent, germicide, insecticide, disinfectant, deodorant; see also MEDICINE 2.

antitoxin *n.* vaccine, antibody, serum; see MEDICINE 2.

antlers *n.pl.* horns, tusks, prongs; see HORN 2.

anxiety *n.* concern, trouble, misgiving; see FEAR.

anxious *a.* **1.** [Disturbed in mind] apprehensive, concerned, dreading; see TROUBLED. **2.** [Eager] desirous, eager, fervent; see ZEALOUS.

any *a.* either, whatever, any sort, any kind, any one, in general, each, some, several, each and every, all, one and all; see also EACH 1, SOME.—*Ant.* ONE, only, single.

anybody *pron.* anyone, everyone, everybody, all, the whole world, the public, the rabble, the masses, each and every one, any person, any of.—*Ant.* NOBODY, no one, somebody.

anyhow *a.* in any event, at any rate, nevertheless, at all, in spite of, in any case, regardless, anyway, in any way, in whatever way, under any circumstances, in one way or the other, in any respect, in either way, whatever happens, irregardless*, somehow or other.

anyone *pron.* a person, one, anyone at all; see ANYBODY.

anyplace* *a.* everywhere, wherever, in any place; see ANYWHERE.

anything *pron.* everything, all, anything at all, anyone, any one thing, whatever one wants, you name it*, anything around.—*Ant.* NOTHING, something, one thing.

any time *a.* whenever, at your convenience, when you will, no matter when, any time when, at any moment, anytime*.

anyway *a.* in any event, however, in any manner; see ANYHOW.

anywhere *a.* wherever, in any place, all over, everywhere, in whatever place, wherever you go, anyplace*.—*Ant.* NOWHERE, in no place, somewhere. **—get anywhere*** prosper, thrive, advance; see SUCCEED 1.

apart *a.* **1.** [Separated] disconnected, distant, disassociated; see SEPARATED. **2.** [Distinct] separate, special, isolated; see INDIVIDUAL. **3.** [Separately] freely, exclusively, alone; see INDEPENDENTLY. **—take apart** dismember, dissect, reduce; see ANALYZE, DIVIDE. **—tell apart** characterize, discriminate, differentiate; see DISTINGUISH 1.

apartment *n.* rooms, quarters, flat, suite, penthouse, residence, home, duplex, pad*, walk-up.

apartment house *n.* tenement, hotel, apartment building, condominium, high-rise apartments.

apathetic *a.* unemotional, cold, unconcerned; see INDIFFERENT.

apathy *n.* dullness, insensitivity, unconcern; see INDIFFERENCE.

ape *n.* gorilla, orangutan, chimpanzee, baboon, gibbon; see also MONKEY.

ape *v.* copy, mimic, impersonate; see IMITATE 1.

apiece *a.* respectively, separately, individually; see EACH.

apologetic *a.* regretful, self-incriminating, explanatory, atoning, rueful, contrite, remorseful, sorry, penitent, down on one's knees*.—*Ant.* STUBBORN, obstinate, unregenerate.

apologize *v.* beg pardon, excuse oneself, atone, ask forgiveness, make amends, make apology for, purge, give satisfaction, clear oneself, make up with, confess, admit one's guilt, retract, withdraw, eat crow*, eat one's words.—*Ant.* INSULT, offend, hurt.

apology *n.* excuse, plea, justification; see EXPLANATION.

apostle *n.* messenger, witness, companion; see FOLLOWER.

appall *v.* amaze, horrify, dismay; see SHOCK 2.

appalling *a.* horrifying, shocking, dreadful; see FRIGHTFUL.

apparatus *n.* appliances, machinery, outfit; see EQUIPMENT.

apparel *n.* clothes, attire, suit; see DRESS 1.

apparent *a.* **1.** [Open to view] visible, clear, manifest; see OBVIOUS 1. **2.** [Seeming, but not actual] probable, possible, plausible; see LIKELY 1.

apparently *a.* obviously, at first sight, in plain sight, unmistakably, at a glance, indubitably, perceptibly, plainly, patently, evidently, clearly, openly, supposedly, overtly, conspicuously, palpably, tangibly, presumably, possibly, manifestly, most likely, reasonably, seemingly, reputedly, as if, as though, to all appearances, in almost every way, allegedly, as it were, on the face of it, to the eye.—*Ant.* SURELY, certainly, undoubtedly.

appeal *n.* **1.** [A plea] request, bid, claim, suit, petition, question, entreaty, prayer, invocation, supplication, address, demand, call, requisition, application, proposition, proposal.—*Ant.* DENIAL, refusal, renunciation. **2.** [Attractiveness] charm, glamour, interest, seductiveness, sex appeal, class*.

appeal *v.* **1.** [To ask another seriously] urge, request, petition; see BEG. **2.** [To attract] interest, engage, tempt; see FASCINATE.

appear *v.* **1.** [To become visible] emerge, rise, come in view, come forth, come out, come forward, be in sight, become plain, loom, arrive, come to light, enter the picture, recur, materialize, become visible, loom up, break through, show up, crop up, burst forth, turn up, stand out, spring up, bob up, see the light of day*, meet the eye, break cover.—*Ant.* DISAPPEAR, depart, vanish. **2.** [To seem] look, have the appearance, resemble; see SEEM.

appearance *n.* **1.** [Looks] bearing, mien, features; see LOOKS. **2.** [That which only seems to be real] impression, idea, image, reflection, sound, mirage, vision, façade, dream, illusion, semblance, seeming.—*Ant.* FACT, being, substance. **—keep up appearances** be outwardly proper, hide one's faults, keep up with the Joneses*; see DECEIVE. **—make or put in an appearance** appear publicly, be present, come; see ARRIVE.

appease *v.* do, be enough, serve; see SATISFY 1, 3.

appeasement *n.* settlement, amends, reparation, conciliation, compromise; see also SATISFACTION 2.

appendix *n.* supplement, attachment, index; see ADDITION 1.

appetite *n.* hunger, thirst, craving, longing, dryness, need for food, need for liquid, starvation, empty stomach, thirstiness, ravenousness, desire; see also HUNGER, THIRST.—*Ant.* indifference, satiety, surfeit.

appetizing *a.* savory, tasty, delectable; see DELICIOUS.

applaud *v.* cheer, clap, acclaim; see PRAISE 1.

applause *n.* ovation, cheers, hurrahs; see PRAISE 2.

apple of one's eye *n.* pet, idol, ideal; see FAVORITE.

apple polisher* *n.* flatterer, toady, flunky; see FLATTERER.

appliance *n.* instrument, machine, apparatus; see DEVICE 1. *Common household appliances include:* broiler, deep-fryer, electric can opener, electric carving knife, coffee maker, blender, mixer, electric frypan, portable oven, hair dryer, toaster, dishwasher, disposal, clothes dryer, clothes washer, stove, oven, microwave, refrigerator, freezer, water heater, electric toothbrush, waffle iron, iron, sewing machine, vacuum cleaner, air conditioner.

applicable *a.* suitable, appropriate, usable; see FIT.

applicant *n.* petitioner, claimant, appellant; see CANDIDATE.

application *n.* **1.** [Putting to use] employment, appliance, utilization; see USE 1. **2.** [The ability to apply oneself] devotion, zeal, diligence; see ATTENTION. **3.** [A request] petition, entreaty, demand; see APPEAL 1. **4.** [The instrument by which a request is made] petition, form, blank, paper, letter, credentials, certificate, statement, requisition, draft, check, bill.

applied *a.* used, related, enforced, practiced, utilized, brought to bear, adapted, devoted, tested, adjusted, activated.

apply *v.* **1.** [To make a request] petition, demand, appeal; see BEG. **2.** [To make use of] utilize, employ, practice, exploit; see also USE 1. **3.** [To be relevant] be pertinent, pertain, bear on, bear upon, have a bearing on, relate to, allude to, concern, touch on, touch upon, involve, affect, regard, have reference to, connect, refer, suit, be in relationship, hold true, come into play*.

apply oneself *v.* attend to, dedicate oneself, address oneself, be occupied with, keep one's mind on, direct oneself to, concentrate on, persevere, persist in, be industrious, buckle down*.

appoint *v.* select, designate, elect; see DELEGATE 1, 2.

appointed *a.* selected, chosen, delegated; see NAMED 2.

appointment *n.* **1.** [The act of appointing] designation, election, selection, nomination, approval, choice, promotion, assignment, authorization, installation, delegation, certification, empowering. **2.** [An engagement] interview, meeting, rendezvous, assignment, invitation, errand, something to do, date.

appraisal *n.* examination, evaluation, assessment; see ESTIMATE.

appraise *v.* assess, price, assay; see PRICE.

appreciable *a.* considerable, sizable, tangible; see LARGE 1.

appreciate *v.* **1.** [To be grateful] welcome, enjoy, be obliged, be indebted, acknowledge, never forget, give thanks, overflow with gratitude; see also THANK.—*Ant.* COMPLAIN, find fault with, minimize, object. **2.** [To recognize worth] esteem, honor, praise; see ADMIRE.

appreciation *n.* **1.** [Sense of gratitude] thankfulness, recognition, gratefulness; see GRATITUDE. **2.** [Favorable opinion] esteem, enjoyment, love, affection, sensitivity, attraction, commendation, high regard; see also ADMIRATION.

appreciative *a.* grateful, obliged, satisfied; see THANKFUL.

apprehend *v.* **1.** [To understand] perceive, comprehend, grasp; see UNDERSTAND 1. **2.** [To arrest] seize, place under arrest, take into custody; see ARREST.

apprehension *n.* **1.** [Foreboding] trepidation, dread, misgiving; see FEAR. **2.** [Understanding] comprehension, grasp, perspicacity; see JUDGMENT 1. **3.** [Arrest] capture, seizure, detention; see ARREST.

apprehensive *a.* fearful, worried, uncertain; see TROUBLED.

apprentice *n.* beginner, student, learner; see AMATEUR.

approach *n.* **1.** [A way] path, entrance, gate; see WAY 1, 2. **2.** [Plan of action] method, program, procedure; see PLAN 2.

approach *v.* **1.** [To approach personally] appeal to, address, speak to, talk to, propose, request, make advances to, make overtures to, take aside, talk to in private, buttonhole, corner, descend on.—*Ant.* AVOID, shun, turn away. **2.** [To come near in space] drift toward, loom up, creep up, drive up, near, go near, draw near, close in, surround, come near to, come up to, bear down on, edge up to, ease up to, head into*; see also APPEAR 1.—*Ant.* LEAVE, recede, depart. **3.** [To come near in time] be imminent, threaten, near, draw near, impend, stare one in the face*.—*Ant.* INCREASE, extend, stretch out. **4.** [To approximate] come near, take after, come close to; see RESEMBLE.

approaching *a.* nearing, advancing, impending, oncoming, touching, approximating, coming, drawing near, next to come, threatening, rising, moving closer, gaining.

appropriate *a.* proper, suitable, suited, fitting; see also FIT.

appropriate *v.* **1.** [To seize] secure, usurp, take possession of; see GET 1. **2.** [To provide money] set aside, set apart, allocate, assign to a particular use, reserve, apportion, devote, appoint, allow for, budget, allot.

appropriately *a.* fittingly, suitably, justly, aptly, rightly, properly, agreeably, happily, fortunately.—*Ant.* BADLY, inappropriately, improperly.

appropriation *n.* stipend, grant, fund, allotment, allowance, allocation, contribution, cash, budget, gift, remuneration, donation, support, pay.

approval *n.* **1.** [Favorable opinion] regard, esteem, favor; see ADMIRATION. **2.** [Sanction] endorsement, support, consent; see PERMISSION.

approve *v.* ratify, affirm, encourage, support, endorse, seal, confirm, license, favor, consent to, agree to, sanction, empower, charter, validate, legalize, recognize, accredit, recommend, authorize, second, subscribe to, allow, go along with, maintain, vote for, advocate, establish, pass, OK, give the green light to*, hold with.—*Ant.* OPPOSE, reject, veto.

approved *a.* certified, authorized, validated, passed, affirmed, legalized, ratified, sanctioned, permitted, endorsed, vouched for, praised, recognized, recommended, backed, supported, upheld, made official, agreed to, allowed, proven, ordered, established, OK'd.—*Ant.* REFUSED, censured, disapproved.

approximate *a.* rough, inexact, uncertain, guessed, imprecise, imperfect, close, surmised, unscientific, by means of trial and error, almost, more or less, not quite, coming close, fair, nearly correct.

approximately *a.* nearly, closely, roughly, close to, near to, almost, around, about, in general, in round numbers, not quite, not far from, more or less, practically, just about, on the edge of, for all practical purposes, bordering on, generally.

apron *n.* cover, smock, bib; see CLOTHES.

apt *a.* **1.** [Quick to learn] adept, clever, bright; see INTELLIGENT. **2.** [Inclined] prone, tending, liable; see LIKELY 4.

aptitude *n.* capability, competence, capacity; see ABILITY.

Arabia *n.* Arabian Peninsula, Near East, Mesopotamia; see ASIA.

Arabian *a.* Arabic, Semitic, from Arabia, Middle Eastern, Near Eastern, Moorish, Levantine.

arbitrary *a.* willful, tyrannical, unsatisfactory, temporary, unpremeditated, irrational, generalized, deceptive, superficial, unscientific, unreasonable, whimsical, fanciful, determined by no principle, optional, uncertain, inconsistent, discretionary, subject to individual will, halfway.

arbitrate *v.* settle, adjust, reconcile; see NEGOTIATE.

arbitrator *n.* arbiter, referee, mediator; see JUDGE.

arc *n.* bend, curve, segment of a circle; see ARCH.

arch *n.* arc, curve, vault, dome, cupola, bend, arching, archway, curvature, cove.

arch *v.* extend, round, stretch, curve, bend, shape, hunch, cover, hump, hook, arch over.—*Ant.* STRAIGHTEN, unbend, smooth.

archaic *a.* antiquated, old, obsolete; see OLD-FASHIONED.

architect *n.* planner, designer, draftsman, artist, engineer, builder, master builder, designer of buildings.

architecture *n.* construction, planning, designing, building, structure, architectonics, house-building, shipbuilding, bridge-building.

archives *n.pl.* **1.** [Place to store documents] repository, vault, treasury; see MUSEUM. **2.** [Documents] chronicles, annals, public papers; see RECORDS.

arctic *a.* polar, frozen, icy; see COLD 1.

ardent *a.* fervent, impassioned, warm; see ZEALOUS.

arduous *a.* hard, severe, laborious; see DIFFICULT 1.

area *n.* section, lot, neighborhood, plot, zone, sector, patch, square, quarter, block, precinct, ward, field, territory, district, ghetto, township, region, tract, enclosure, parcel, division, city, parish, diocese, principality, dominion, kingdom, empire, state; see also MEASURE 1.

arena *n.* field, pit, ground, park, coliseum, square, stadium, playing field, amphitheater, bowl, stage, platform, course, gymnasium, gym*.

argue *v.* plead, appeal, explain, justify, show, reason with, dispute, contend, wrangle, oppose, battle, demonstrate, establish, have it out, put up an argument, bicker, have a brush with.—*Ant.* NEGLECT, ignore, scorn.

argument *n.* **1.** [An effort to convince] discussion, exchange, contention; see DISCUSSION. **2.** [Verbal disagreement] debate, quarrel, row; see DISPUTE.

argumentative *a.* hostile, contentious, factious; see QUARRELSOME.

arid *a.* parched, barren, dried; see DRY 1.

arise *v.* **1.** [To get up] rise, stand up, turn out, get out of bed, get out of a chair, get to one's feet, jump up, roll out, hit the deck*.—*Ant.* FALL, SIT, LIE. **2.** [To ascend] mount, go up, climb; see RISE 1.

aristocracy *n.* nobility, privileged class, superior group, ruling class, noblemen, the elite, gentry, high society, upper classes, persons of rank, patricians.

aristocrat *n.* nobleman, peer, lord, noble, baron, earl, prince, patrician, ruler, gentleman, thoroughbred, duke, viscount, count, emperor, empress, queen, princess, duchess, countess, baroness, knight, lady, marquis; see also KING 1, LADY 2.

aristocratic *a.* noble, refined, well-bred; see NOBLE 1, 2, 3.

arithmetic *n.* addition, subtraction, calculation; see MATHEMATICS.

arm *n.* **1.** [The upper human limb] member, appendage, forelimb, forearm, fin*, flapper*, soupbone*. **2.** [Anything resembling an arm] bend, crook, projection, cylinder, sofa-end, branch, limb, rod, bough, offshoot, wing, prong, stump, hook, handle, bow. —**at arm's length** at a distance, not friendly, not intimate, aloof. —**with open arms** warmly, affectionately, joyously; see FRIENDLY.

arm *v.* furnish weapons, load, give firearms, issue weapons, equip with arms, outfit, fit out.—*Ant.* DISARM, demilitarize, deactivate.

armchair *n.* easy chair, rocker, recliner; see CHAIR.

armed *a.* equipped, outfitted, in battle formation, loaded, provided with arms, fortified, protected, fitted out, in arms, well-armed, heavily armed.—*Ant.* UNARMED, vulnerable, unprotected.

armistice *n.* treaty of peace, cease-fire, temporary peace; see PEACE.

armor *n.* tanks, tank force, Panzer divisions, armored personnel carriers, armored column, gun carriers, armor divisions.

armory *n.* ordnance headquarters, training center, drilling place, depot, arsenal, gymnasium, drill center, shooting range, National Guard building, reserve corps headquarters.

arms *n.pl.* armament, armor, ammunition, firearms, munitions, guns, small arms, instruments of war, deadly weapons, lethal weapons, pistols, rifles, machine guns, submachine guns, equipment, supplies, ordnance, artillery, material, hardware, ammo*; see also WEAPON. —**bear arms** carry weapons, be armed, be militant; see ARM. —**take up arms** go to war, rebel, do battle; see FIGHT. —**up in arms** hostile, indignant, willing to fight; see ANGRY.

army *n.* **1.** [Military land forces] armed force, standing army, regulars, soldiery, troops, men, cavalry, infantry, artillery, air corps, reserves. **2.** [A unit of an army] division, regiment, armored division, airborne division, infantry division, battalion, company, corps, brigade, flight, wing, amphibious force, task force, detail, detachment, squad, troop, blocking force, patrol, unit, command, formation, point, column, legion, platoon, outfit.

aroma *n.* fragrance, perfume, odor; see SMELL 1, 2.

around *a. & prep.* **1.** [Surrounding] about, in this area, on all sides, on every side, in circumference, neighboring, in the vicinity of, all around, round about, encompassing, nearby, approximately, in a circle, along a circuit, all about, close to, nearly in a circle, on various sides, round and round, right and left.—*Ant.* DISTANT, remote, far-off. **2.** [Approximately] almost, about, close to; see APPROXIMATELY. —**have been around*** worldly, sophisticated, knowledgeable; see EXPERIENCED.

arouse *v.* move, stir up, stimulate; see EXCITE.

arrange *v.* **1.** [To put in order] order, regulate, systematize; see ORDER 3. **2.** [To make arrangements] determine, plan, devise, contrive, prepare for, get ready, make ready, draft, scheme, design, provide, make preparations, set the stage, prepare, put into shape, make plans for, line up, organize, adjust, manage, direct, establish, decide, resolve.—*Ant.* BOTHER, disorganize, disturb.

arrangement *n.* 1. [The result of arranging] method, system, form; see ORDER 3. 2. [An agreement] settlement, adjustment, compromise; see AGREEMENT 1. 3. [A design] pattern, composition, combination; see DESIGN.

arrest *n.* appropriation, imprisonment, apprehension, commitment, confinement, incarceration, capture, captivity, protective custody, taking by force, taking into custody, constraint, duress, seizure, detention, bust*.—*Ant.* FREEDOM, acquittal, release. — **under arrest** arrested, in custody, apprehended; see CAPTURED.

arrest *v.* apprehend, hold, place under arrest, take into custody, capture, imprison, jail, incarcerate, detain, secure, seize, get, catch, take prisoner, nab*, pick up, bust*.—*Ant.* FREE, liberate, parole.

arrival *n.* 1. [The act of arriving] entrance, advent, coming, entry, appearance, landing, homecoming, debarkation, approach, return, meeting.—*Ant.* DEPARTURE, leaving, leave-taking. 2. [That which has arrived] passenger, visitor, tourist, guest, newcomer, delegate, traveler, cargo, freight, mail, shipment, package, parcel.

arrive *v.* enter, land, disembark, alight, dismount, halt, roll up, reach, get in, visit, make shore, drop anchor, reach home, appear, get to, hit*, touch*, blow into*, breeze in*, check in*, pull in, hit town*.—*Ant.* LEAVE, go, depart.

arrogance *n.* insolence, smugness, vanity, audacity, haughtiness; see also PRIDE 2.

arrogant *a.* domineering, autocratic, sneering; see EGOTISTIC.

arrogantly *a.* proudly, haughtily, insolently, loftily, with one's nose in the air*.

arrow *n.* shaft, dart, missile; see WEAPON.

arson *n.* pyromania, firing, deliberate burning of property; see CRIME.

art *n.* representation, illustration, abstraction, imitation, modeling, description, portrayal, design, performance, personification, sketching, molding, shaping, painting, characterization, creating, sculpting, carving; see also ARCHITECTURE, DANCE 1, LITERATURE 1, MUSIC 1, PAINTING, SCULPTURE.

artery *n.* 1. [Main channel of communication or travel] highway, thoroughfare, line, supply route, canal; see also ROAD 1, WAY 2. 2. [Blood vessel] tube, aorta, arterial passageway; see VEIN 3.

artful *a.* clever, adroit, ingenious; see ABLE.

article *n.* 1. [An individual thing] object, substance, commodity; see THING 1. 2. [Nonfiction appearing in a periodical] essay, editorial, commentary; see WRITING 2.

articulate *v.* 1. [To speak clearly] enunciate, pronounce, verbalize; see SPEAK 1. 2. [To join] fit together, combine, connect, link; see also JOIN 1.

artificial *a.* unreal, synthetic, counterfeit; see FALSE 3.

artillery *n.* gunnery, arms, weapons; see ARMS.

artist *n.* master, creator, painter, composer, virtuoso, musician, poet, novelist, dramatist, essayist, actress, actor, playwright, writer, performing artist, cartoonist, opera singer, dancer, ballet performer, ballerina, sculptor, etcher, engraver, designer, architect, photographer.

artistic *a.* inventive, skillful, imaginative, discriminating, creative, graceful, talented, accomplished, well-executed, well-wrought, pleasing, sublime, ideal, cultured, tasteful, exquisite, sensitive, fine, elegant, harmonious, grand, stimulating, elevated, noble, beautiful.

artistry *n.* workmanship, skill, proficiency; see ABILITY.

as *a., conj., & prep.* 1. [While] in the process of, in the act of, on the point of; see WHILE 1. 2. [Because] since, inasmuch as, for the reason that; see BECAUSE. 3. [To a degree] in the same way, in the same manner, equally, comparatively, similarly. 4. [For a given purpose, end, use, etc.] just as, just for, serving as, functioning as, acting as, being, in and of itself, by its nature, essentially.

as a matter of course *a.* ordinarily, commonly, customarily; see REGULARLY.

as a matter of fact *a.* truly, actually, indeed; see REALLY 1.

as a rule *a.* usually, commonly, ordinarily; see REGULARLY.

as a whole *a.* in all, all told, all in all; see ALTOGETHER.

ascend *v.* go upward, sprout, soar; see RISE 1.

ascent *n.* ascendance, climbing, ascension; see RISE 1.

as far as *a.* to the extent that, to the degree that, up to the time that, insofar as.

as good as *a.* the same as, tantamount, practically; see EQUAL.

ashamed *a.* embarrassed, shamed, regretful, meek, repentant, penitent, apologetic, debased, abashed, conscience-stricken, mortified, uncomfortable, hesitant, perplexed, bewildered, shamefaced, bowed down, disconcerted, sputtering, stammering, stuttering, gasping, floundering, rattled, muddled, confused, blushing, flustered, distraught, submissive, feeling like a jackass, off balance, in a hole*, taken down a peg, red in the face*, looking silly, at a loss.

ashes *n.pl.* dust, powder, cinders, slag, embers, charcoal, soot.

Asia *n.* the Orient, the East, the mysterious East. *Terms for parts of Asia include the following—Far East:* China, Taiwan, Japan, North Korea, South Korea, Mongolia, Tibet,

Siberia, Vietnam, Laos, Cambodia, Thailand, Burma or Myanmar, India, Bhutan, Sikkim, Nepal, Pakistan, Bangladesh, Ceylon or Sri Lanka, Malaysia, Indonesia; *Near and Middle East:* Turkey, Syria, Armenia, Kurdistan, United Arab Emirates, Iraq, Iran, Jordan, Israel, Lebanon, Saudi Arabia, Yemen, Oman, Kuwait, Qatar, Afghanistan.

Asian *a.* Oriental, Mongolian, Chinese, Hindu, Japanese, Mongoloid.

aside *a.* to the side, to one side, on one side, at rest, out, by oneself, apart, by the side of, at one side, by itself, alone, alongside, out of the way, aloof, away, in safekeeping, beside, sidewise, sideways, abreast, at a short distance, by.

aside from *prep.* beside, in addition to, excluding; see BESIDES.

as if *a. & conj.* just as if, just as though, as it were, in such a way that, as if it were, supposing, quasi, so to speak, as would be if, as might be, just like.

as is* *a.* as it stands, as usual, just the same, the same way.

as it were *a.* so to speak, figuratively speaking, in a way, as it seems, as it would seem, in some sort, in a manner, so to say, kind of*, in a manner of speaking, sort of*.

ask *v.* request, query, question, interrogate, examine, cross-examine, demand, raise a question, inquire, frame a question, order, command, put questions to, requisition, bid, charge, petition, call upon, invite, urge to, challenge, pry into, scour, investigate, hunt for, quiz, grill, needle*, sound out*, pump*, put through the third degree*.—*Ant.* ANSWER, refute, rejoin.

asleep *a.* sleeping, dreaming, quiet, resting, snoring, in a sound sleep, fast asleep, sound asleep, slumbering, reposing, taking a siesta, hibernating, dozing, wakeless, napping, unconscious, dead to the world*, in the Land of Nod, snoozing*, conked out*, out like a light*.—*Ant.* AWAKE, waking, alert.

as long as *conj.* since, during, whilst; see WHILE 1.

aspect *n.* **1.** [Looks] countenance, face, features; see LOOKS. **2.** [View] perspective, regard, slant; see VIEWPOINT.

aspiration *n.* yearning, eagerness, inclination; see AMBITION.

aspire *v.* strive, struggle, yearn; see TRY 1.

aspiring *a.* ambitious, hopeful, enthusiastic; see ZEALOUS.

as regards *a. & prep.* concerning, regarding, respecting; see ABOUT 2.

ass *n.* **1.** [A stupid person] dolt, dunce, blockhead; see FOOL. **2.** [A donkey] burro, jackass, jennet; see ANIMAL.

assailant *n.* antagonist, foe, enemy; see OPPONENT.

assassin *n.* murderer, slayer, butcher; see KILLER.

assassinate *v.* slay, slaughter, put to death; see KILL 1.

assassination *n.* killing, shooting, slaying; see MURDER.

assault *n.* **1.** [An attack] charge, advance, onslaught; see ATTACK. **2.** [A rape] attack, abduction, violation; see RAPE.

assault *v.* **1.** [To attack] assail, advance, strike; see ATTACK. **2.** [To rape] attack, violate, ravish; see RAPE.

assemble *v.* **1.** [To bring together] rally, call, convoke, muster, round up, group, convene, summon, mobilize, call together, accumulate, amass, invite guests, gather, collect, hold a meeting, unite, pack them in, throw a party*, herd together*, rally round, gather around, gang around*.—*Ant.* SCATTER, break up, send away. **2.** [To put together] piece together, set up, erect, construct, join, unite, solder, mold, weld, glue, model.—*Ant.* BREAK, disassemble, break down.

assembly *n.* **1.** [A gathering of persons] assemblage, meeting, association; see GATHERING. **2.** [The process of bringing parts together] construction, piecing together, fitting in, joining, modeling, assembling, attachment, adjustment, collection, welding, soldering, molding, fixing.—*Ant.* SEPARATION, dismantling, wrecking.

assent *n.* approval, authorization, consent; see PERMISSION.

assert *v.* state, say, affirm; see DECLARE.

assertion *n.* affirmation, statement, report; see DECLARATION.

assess *v.* **1.** [To tax] charge, exact tribute, exact from; see TAX 1. **2.** [To estimate] judge, reckon, guess; see ESTIMATE.

assets *n.pl.* holdings, possessions, capital; see PROPERTY.

assign *v.* commit, commission, authorize, hand over, earmark, allocate, detail, appoint, allot, prescribe, nominate, name, select, hold responsible, empower, entrust, allow, cast, deputize, attach, charge, accredit, hire, elect, ordain, enroll, relegate, draft.—*Ant.* MAINTAIN, reserve, keep back.

assignment *n.* **1.** [An appointment] designation, authorization, nomination; see APPOINTMENT 1. **2.** [Something assigned] job, responsibility, task; see DUTY 2.

assimilate *v.* **1.** [To absorb] take up, digest, osmose; see ABSORB. **2.** [To understand] grasp, learn, sense; see UNDERSTAND 1.

assist *v.* support, aid, serve; see HELP.

assistance *n.* comfort, support, compensation; see HELP 1.

assistant *n.* aid, aide, deputy, henchman, friend, follower, adherent, auxiliary, lieutenant, associate, companion, colleague, partner, helper, apprentice, fellow-worker, secretary, helping hand, patron, backer, bodyguard, aide-de-camp, ally, accessory, clerk, collaborator, confederate, mate, helpmate, accomplice, copartner, co-worker, flunky, man Friday, right arm*, yes man*, right-hand man, friend in need*.—*Ant.* ENEMY, rival, antagonist.

associate *n.* comrade, brother-in-arms, peer, colleague, partner, copartner, friend, ally, buddy*, accomplice, assistant, aid, attendant, henchman, confederate, auxiliary, coworker, helper, collaborator, fellow-worker, helping hand, right-hand man, man Friday, teammate; see also ASSISTANT.—*Ant.* ENEMY, foe, antagonist.

associate *v.* **1.** [To keep company with] work with, join with, get along with, be friendly with; see also GO WITH, JOIN 2. **2.** [To relate] correlate, link, connect, join; see also COMPARE.

association *n.* **1.** [The act of associating] frequenting, fraternization, friendship, acquaintanceship, cooperation, assistance, relationship, affiliation, agreement, participation, companionship, fellowship, familiarity, friendliness, camaraderie, membership, acquaintance, mingling, union, community.—*Ant.* DISAGREEMENT, severance, rupture. **2.** [The process of intellectual comparison] connection, relation, mental connection, train of thought, connection of ideas in thought, recollection, impression, remembrance, suggestibility, combination. **3.** [An organization] union, federation, corporation; see ORGANIZATION 2.

assorted *a.* varied, miscellaneous, mixed; see VARIOUS.

assortment *n.* variety, combination, group; see COLLECTION.

as such *a.* in itself, by itself, alone, per se, intrinsically.

assume *v.* suppose, presume, posit, understand, gather, find, collect, theorize, presuppose, ascertain, draw the inference, judge at random, divine, get the idea, have an idea that, suspect, postulate, regard, consider, infer, hypothesize, guess, conjecture, suppose as fact, deem, imagine, surmise, opine, judge, estimate, speculate, fancy, take the liberty, be of the opinion, dare say, deduce, conclude, put two and two together, be inclined to think, hold the opinion, think, calculate, hope, feel, be afraid, believe, have faith, take it, expect, allow, reckon*.—*Ant.* DOUBT, be surprised, be unaware that.

assumed *a.* presumed, understood, presupposed, counted on, inferred, given, granted, taken as known, conjectured, accepted, supposed, hypothetical, hypothesized.

assumption *n.* **1.** [The act of taking for granted] supposition, presupposition, presumption, conjecture, assuming, accepting, suspicion, surmise, theorization, hypothesization.—*Ant.* PROOF, demonstrating, establishing. **2.** [Something assumed] hypothesis, theory, postulate; see OPINION 1.

assurance *n.* **1.** [A guaranty] insurance, support, pledge; see PROMISE 1. **2.** [Confidence] conviction, trust, certainty; see FAITH 1.

assure *v.* **1.** [To guarantee] vouch for, aver, attest; see GUARANTEE. **2.** [To convince] prove, persuade, induce; see CONVINCE.

assured *a.* **1.** [Certain] sure, undoubted, guaranteed; see CERTAIN. **2.** [Confident] self-possessed, bold, unhesitating; see CONFIDENT.

as though *a. & conj.* just as, just as if, just as though; see AS IF.

astonish *v.* shock, amaze, astound; see SURPRISE.

astonishing *a.* surprising, startling, extraordinary; see UNUSUAL 1.

astonishment *n.* surprise, amazement, bewilderment; see WONDER 1.

astound *v.* amaze, shock, startle; see SURPRISE.

astray *a.* straying, roaming, adrift; see WANDERING 1.

astronaut *n.* space traveler, cosmonaut, spaceman, space pilot, rocket pilot, rocketeer, rocket man, space walker, explorer.

asunder *a.* apart, in two, in half, to shreds, into bits and pieces, dismantled, dissected, in two parts, divided, into separate parts, separated, disjoined, rent, carved, dismembered, torn apart, split; see also BROKEN 1, TORN.—*Ant.* WHOLE, together, sound.

as well as *a.* together with, in addition to, plus; see INCLUDING.

as yet *a.* still, not yet, till now; see YET 2.

at *prep.* **1.** [Position] on, by, near to, about, occupying the precise position of, in the vicinity of, placed at, situated at, found in, in front of, appearing in; see also IN 1, NEAR 1. **2.** [Direction] toward, in the direction of, through; see TO 1.

at all *a.* anyhow, ever, in any way, in any case, in any respect, under any condition, under any circumstances, anywise, in the least, in any manner, to any extent, in the least degree, anyways*.

at all events *a.* anyway, regardless, at least; see ANYHOW.

at a loss *a.* in a quandary, perplexed, puzzled; see DOUBTFUL 1.

at arm's length *a.* distant, afar, off, aloof; see also AWAY.

at ease *a.* relaxed, untroubled, carefree; see COMFORTABLE 1.

at fault *a.* in the wrong, in error, to blame; see GUILTY.

at first *a.* in the beginning, in the first place, first off*; see FIRST.

at hand *a.* **1.** [Near] nearby, accessible, convenient; see AVAILABLE. **2.** [Imminent] approaching, near, impending; see COMING.

atheism *n.* heresy, agnosticism, godlessness, ungodliness, impiety, positivism, denial of God, iconoclasm, disbelief in God, irreverence, rationalism, infidelity, materialism, skepticism, freethinking, disbelief; see also DOUBT.

athlete *n.* acrobat, gymnast, player, contestant, champion, sportsman, amateur, professional, semiprofessional, contender, challenger, letterman, muscle man*, jock*. *Athletes include the following:* baseball player, football player, basketball player, soccer player, boxer, wrestler, swimmer, golfer, tennis player, badminton player, jockey, trackman, javelin thrower, high-jumper, discus thrower, shot putter, skier, ski jumper, slalom racer, runner, relay runner, long jumper, pole vaulter, hurdler, bowler, billiard player, polo player, hockey player, skater, bicyclist, fencer, swordsman, marksman, cricket player, miler.

athletic *a.* muscular, husky, heavy-set, wiry, springy, slim, fast, solid, strapping, hardy, robust, strong, vigorous, powerful, brawny, sinewy, sturdy, well-proportioned, well-built, manly, Herculean, Amazonian, built like an ox*.—*Ant.* SICK, weak, fat.

athletics *n.pl.* gymnastics, acrobatics, games; see SPORT 3.

atlas *n.* book of maps, book of charts, book of tables; see BOOK.

at last *a.* ultimately, in conclusion, at the end; see FINALLY 2.

at length *a.* **1.** [Finally] after a while, at last, in the end; see FINALLY 2. **2.** [Fully] in full, extensively, without omission; see COMPLETELY.

atmosphere *n.* **1.** [The air] layer of air, gaseous envelope, air pressure; see AIR 1. **2.** [A pervading quality] sense, impression, taste; see CHARACTER 1, CHARACTERISTIC.

atmospheric *a.* climatic, meteorological, aerial; see AIRY.

at odds *a.* disagreeing, at variance, discordant; see QUARRELSOME.

atom *n.* grain, mite, speck, particle, molecule, iota; see also BIT 1, ELEMENT. *Parts and forms of atoms include the following:* electron, proton, neutron, positron, neutrino, positive electron, neutral electron, cathode ray, alpha ray, beta ray, gamma ray.

atom bomb *n.* atomic bomb, nuclear weapon, thermonuclear device, hydrogen bomb, A-bomb.

atomic *a.* microscopic, tiny, diminutive; see MINUTE 1.

at once *a.* **1.** [Simultaneously] at the same time, concurrently, contemporaneously; see TOGETHER 2. **2.** [Immediately] directly, without delay, now; see IMMEDIATELY.

atone for *v.* compensate for, do penance, make amends; see PAY FOR.

at one's disposal *a.* ready, on call, accessible; see AVAILABLE.

at rest *a.* relaxed, inactive, undisturbed; see RESTING 1.

atrocity *n.* **1.** [Brutality] inhumanity, wickedness, barbarity; see CRUELTY. **2.** [A cruel deed] offense, outrage, horror; see CRIME.

at stake *a.* in danger, risked, involved, implicated, in jeopardy, in question, hazarded, concerned, endangered.

attach *v.* **1.** [To join] connect, append, add; see JOIN 1. **2.** [To attribute] associate, impute, ascribe; see GIVE 1.

attachment *n.* **1.** [Affection] fondness, liking, devotion; see AFFECTION. **2.** [Something attached] accessory, adjunct, annex; see ADDITION 1.

attack *n.* **1.** [Offensive tactical action] assault, raid, onslaught, advance, charge, thrust, offense, drive, aggression, onset, outbreak, skirmish, encounter, volley, shooting, barrage, siege, firing, trespass, blockade, cross-fire, invasion, offensive, intrusion, intervention, onrush, inroad, encroachment, incursion.—*Ant.* WITHDRAWAL, retreat, retirement. **2.** [Verbal attack] libel, slander, denunciation; see BLAME. **3.** [Illness] seizure, breakdown, relapse; see DISEASE 1. **4.** [Rape] assault, violation, defilement; see RAPE.

attack *v.* **1.** [To fight offensively; *used of an army*] assault, beset, besiege, invade, storm, advance, infiltrate, raid, assail, march against, shell, board, take by surprise, make a push, bombard, bomb, go over the top, lay siege to, open fire, lay into, launch an attack, ambush, strafe, waylay, engage, tilt against, set upon, torpedo, stone, push, combat, attempt violence against, charge, strike the first blow, bayonet, saber, stab, close with, rake, have at.—*Ant.* RETREAT, fall back, recoil. **2.** [To assault; *used of an individual*] molest, beat, overwhelm; see FIGHT, RAPE. **3.** [To assail with words] revile, refute, reprove; see BLAME. **4.** [To proceed vigorously] take up, deal with, start on; see ACT 1.

attacked *a.* assaulted, bombed, bombarded, assailed, stoned, torpedoed, fired upon, stormed, under attack, strafed, invaded, besieged; see also RUINED 1.

attacker *n.* aggressor, fighter, assailant, antagonist, invader, foe, enemy, criminal, plunderer, intruder, trespasser, violator, ravager, spoiler, felon.—*Ant.* VICTIM, prey, martyr.

attain *v.* win, achieve, accomplish; see SUCCEED.

attempt *n.* trial, struggle, endeavor; see EFFORT.

attempt *v.* endeavor, strive, venture; see TRY 1.

attend *v.* be present at, frequent, sit in on, be a guest, revisit, haunt, be a member, be an habitué, make an appearance.—*Ant.* LEAVE, be missing, absent oneself.

attendance *n.* **1.** [The act of attending] presence, participation, appearance, being present, putting in an appearance, being in evidence, turning up, showing up.—*Ant.*

ABSENCE, nonappearance, nonattendance. **2.** [The persons attending] audience, spectators, assembly; see GATHERING.

attendant *n.* aid, orderly, valet, nurse, usher, bellhop, servant, domestic, secretary, understudy, disciple, pupil, auditor, steward, stewardess, maid; see also ASSISTANT.

attend school *v.* undergo schooling, learn, go to school, be educated, receive instruction, matriculate, study, take courses, be a student, enroll; see also REGISTER 4, STUDY.

attention *n.* observation, observance, regard, vigilance, mindfulness, inspection, heed, heedfulness, watching, listening, consideration, intentness, study, alertness, thought, application, diligence, caution, preoccupation, thoroughness, recognition, observance, regard, vigilance, mindfulness, inspection.

attitude *n.* mood, opinion, idea about, belief, air, demeanor, condition of mind, state of feeling, position, reaction, bias, set, leaning, bent, inclination, propensity, cast, emotion, temper, temperament, sensibility, disposition, mental state, notion, philosophy, view, orientation to, nature, make-up, frame of mind, character; see also VIEWPOINT.

attorney *n.* attorney at law, barrister, counsel; see LAWYER.

attract *v.* **1.** [To draw] pull, drag, bring; see DRAW 1. **2.** [To allure] entice, lure, charm; see FASCINATE.

attraction *n.* **1.** [The act of drawing toward] magnetism, drawing power, allurement, fascination, temptation, pull, gravitation, affinity, inclination, tendency, enticement; see also APPEAL 2. **2.** [An event] spectacle, display, demonstration; see EVENT.

attractive *a.* good-looking, winning, engaging; see BEAUTIFUL, HANDSOME.

attribute *n.* peculiarity, quality, trait; see CHARACTERISTIC.

attribute *v.* ascribe, impute, connect with; see GIVE 1.

auction *n.* disposal, bidding, public sale; see SALE.

auction *v.* put on sale, sell at auction, put under the hammer; see SELL.

audible *a.* perceptible, discernible, distinct, actually heard, loud enough to be heard, capable of being heard, within earshot, within hearing distance, hearable, sounding, resounding, loud, deafening, roaring, aloud, clear, plain, emphatic; see also HEARD.

audience *n.* witnesses, spectators, patrons; see GATHERING.

audit *n.* checking, scrutiny, inspection; see EXAMINATION 1.

audit *v.* examine, check, inspect; see EXAMINE 1.

auditorium *n.* hall, lecture room, theater, playhouse, movie house, reception hall, amphitheater, assembly hall, opera house, music hall, concert hall, chapel, assembly room. *Sections of an auditorium include the following:* stage, proscenium, orchestra, parquet, stalls, boxes, pit, orchestra circle, dress circle, balcony, gallery, top gallery, tiers, box office.

auger *n.* bit, twist drill, screw auger; see DRILL 2.

augment *v.* enlarge, expand, magnify; see INCREASE.

aunt *n.* mother's sister, father's sister, uncle's wife, grandaunt, great-aunt, auntie*; see also RELATIVE.

auspices *n.pl.* protection, aegis, support, sponsorship, backing.

austere *a.* harsh, hard, ascetic; see SEVERE 1, 2.

austerity *n.* sternness, severity, strictness, harshness, sharpness, hardness, grimness, stiffness, seriousness, rigidity, gravity, rigor, formality; see also DETERMINATION.

authentic *a.* **1.** [Reliable] trustworthy, authoritative, factual; see RELIABLE. **2.** [Genuine] real, true, actual; see GENUINE 1.

authenticate *v.* verify, confirm, validate; see PROVE.

author *n.* writer, journalist, columnist, dramatist, playwright, poet, novelist, short story writer, essayist, paperback writer, mystery writer, science fiction writer, contributor, script writer, correspondent, reporter, copywriter, ghost writer, encyclopedist, lexicographer, scholar, publicist, critic, annotator, hack writer, freelance, adman; see also EDITOR, WRITER.

authoritative *a.* **1.** [Official] authentic, well-supported, well-documented; see RELIABLE. **2.** [Authorized] lawful, legal, mandatory; see APPROVED, AUTHORIZED. **3.** [Suggestive of authority] dogmatic, autocratic, domineering; see ABSOLUTE 2.

authority *n.* **1.** [Power based on right] right, authorization, jurisdiction; see POWER 2. **2.** [The appearance of having authority] prestige, political influence, esteem; see INFLUENCE. **3.** [One who knows] expert, veteran, professional; see SPECIALIST.

authorization *n.* sanction, signature, support; see PERMISSION.

authorize *v.* **1.** [To allow] permit, tolerate, suffer; see ALLOW. **2.** [To approve] sanction, ratify, endorse; see APPROVE.

authorized *a.* allowed, official, legal, lawful, mandatory, authoritative, decisive, valid, standard, sanctioned, confirmed; see also APPROVED.

auto *n.* car, vehicle, wheels*; see AUTOMOBILE.

autobiography *n.* memoirs, personal history, self-portrayal, confession, life, experiences, diary, adventures, biography, life story, journal, letters, log.

autocratic *a.* dictatorial, domineering, aggressive; see ABSOLUTE 2.

autograph *n.* name, seal, John Hancock*; see SIGNATURE.

automated *a.* mechanical, mechanized, motorized, computerized, automatic, electronic, programmed, cybernetic; see also AUTOMATIC.

automatic *a.* self-starting, motorized, self-regulating, automated, mechanized, under its own power, electric, cybernetic, computerized, self-moving, self-propelling, programmed, electronic, self-activating, push-button, involuntary, unthinking, mechanical, instinctive, spontaneous, reflex, intuitive, unintentional, unforced, unconscious, unwilling.

automobile *n.* motor car, car, vehicle, passenger car, machine, auto, wheels*. *Types of automobiles include the following:* subcompact, squad car, hearse, limousine, sedan, hardtop, compact, sports car, convertible, station wagon, taxicab, hatchback, limo*, van, minivan, conversion van, recreational vehicle, RV, stretch limo*, jeep, crate*, buggy*, clunker*, jalopy*. *Principal parts of an automobile include the following:* wheels, tires, fenders, chassis, motor, radiator, engine, fan, cylinders, carburetor, exhaust, muffler, throttle, gear shift, clutch, steering wheel, transmission, universal joint, generator, distributor, alternator, windshield, windshield wipers, catalytic converter, brakes, starter, speedometer, spark plugs, axles, emergency brake, accelerator, shock absorbers, pistons, intake and exhaust valves, fuel pump, gas tank, control panel, steering column, instrument gauges, water pump, air conditioner, heater, radio, belts, hoses, filters, drive shaft, oil pan, computer module, battery, seats, seat belts, headlights, brake lights, turn signals.

autonomous *a.* self-governing, self-ruling, independent; see FREE 1.

autonomy *n.* liberty, independence, sovereignty; see FREEDOM 1.

autopsy *n.* post-mortem examination, dissection, investigation; see EXAMINATION 1.

autumn *n.* harvest time, Indian summer, fall; see FALL 3.

auxiliary *a.* **1.** [Subsidiary] secondary, accessory, subservient; see SUBORDINATE. **2.** [Supplementary] reserve, supplemental, spare; see EXTRA.

available *a.* accessible, usable, ready, convenient, serviceable, prepared, handy, on call, ready for use, open to, derivable from, obtainable, attainable, practicable, achievable, feasible, possible, procurable, realizable, reachable, within reach, at one's disposal, at one's beck and call, at hand, at one's elbow, on tap*, on deck*.—*Ant.* OCCUPIED, unavailable, unobtainable.

avalanche *n.* **1.** [A mass moving down a slope] mudslide, snowslide, landslide, rockslide, icefall. **2.** [Any overwhelming mass] flood, deluge, torrent; see PLENTY.

avenue *n.* street, boulevard, drive; see ROAD 1.

average *a.* ordinary, medium, mediocre; see COMMON 1.

average *n.* midpoint, standard, center, median, norm, middle, normal individual, standard performance, typical kind, rule, average person.—*Ant.* EXTREME, highest, lowest.

average *v.* **1.** [To compute an average] split the difference, find the mean, find the arithmetic average; see BALANCE 2. **2.** [To do, on an average] complete, make, receive; see DO 1, EARN 2, PERFORM 1. **—average out** stabilize, balance, make even; see EQUALIZE. **—on the average** usually, commonly, ordinarily; see REGULARLY.

avert *v.* turn aside, sidetrack, shove aside, shunt, turn away from, look away, look another way, cast one's eyes down.

aviation *n.* flying, flight, aeronautics, theory of flight, aeronautical engineering, piloting, aerodynamics, airmanship.

aviator *n.* flier, airman, copilot; see PILOT 1.

avid *a.* eager, enthusiastic, desirous; see ZEALOUS.

avoid *v.* keep away from, flee from, abstain from, shrink from, escape from, evade, shun, fall back, elude, dodge, give one the slip, draw back, hold off, turn aside, recoil from, keep at arm's length, withdraw, back out of, shirk, let alone, keep out of the way, keep clear of, keep at a respectful distance, let well enough alone, keep in the background, keep one's distance, keep away from, refrain from, steer clear of, lay off*, pass up*, shake off.—*Ant.* FACE, meet, undertake.

avoidance *n.* evasion, delay, elusion, escape, retreat, restraint, abstention, nonparticipation, evasive action, temperance, flight, recoil, recession, escape mechanism, dodge, duck.—*Ant.* MEETING, encounter, participation.

await *v.* wait for, anticipate, expect; see ANTICIPATE.

awake *a.* alert, vigilant, observant; see CONSCIOUS.

awake *v.* open one's eyes, become aware, gain consciousness, see the light, stir, get up, come out of sleep, rub one's eyes, rise up, stretch one's limbs, show signs of life, arise, wake up, rise and shine*.—*Ant.* SLEEP, doze off, slumber.

awaken *v.* awake, call, play reveille, arouse, rouse, wake up, excite, stir up, stimulate.

awakening *n.* rebirth, arousal, renewal; see REVIVAL 1.

award *n.* citation, honor, scholarship; see PRIZE.

award *v.* grant, confer, bestow; see GIVE 1.
aware *a.* knowledgeable, cognizant, informed; see CONSCIOUS.
awareness *n.* sensibility, mindfulness, discernment, cognizance, consciousness, alertness, keenness, attentiveness, recognition, comprehension, perception, apprehension, appreciation, experience.
away *a.* absent, not present, distant, at a distance, not here, far afield, at arm's length, remote, out of, far off, apart, beyond, off.—*Ant.* HERE, present, at hand. —**do away with** eliminate, get rid of, reject; see ABANDON 1.
awe *n.* fright, wonder, admiration; see REVERENCE.
awesome *a.* striking, moving, impressive; see GRAND.
awful *a.* **1.** [Frightful] horrible, terrible, dreadful; see FRIGHTFUL. **2.** [Shocking] appalling, disgusting, repulsive; see OFFENSIVE 2. **3.** [*Very great] gigantic, colossal, stupendous; see BIG 1.
awfully *a.* **1.** [Badly] poorly, imperfectly, clumsily; see BADLY 1. **2.** [*Very] very much, indeed, truly; see VERY.
awhile *a.* for a moment, briefly, momentarily, for a short time, for some time, not for long, temporarily, for a little while, for a spell*.—*Ant.* FOREVER, permanently, for a long time.
awkward *a.* clumsy, bungling, ungraceful, gawky, floundering, stumbling, ungainly, unwieldy, unable, fumbling, bumbling, lacking dexterity, without skill, unskilled, inept, unfit, inexperienced, shuffling, uncouth, incompetent, rusty, unused to, green, amateurish, butterfingered*, all thumbs, with two left feet*.—*Ant.* ABLE, dexterous, smooth.
awkwardly *a.* clumsily, unskillfully, lumberingly, ineptly, ponderously, uncouthly, gracelessly, inelegantly, incompetently, artlessly, amateurishly, ungracefully, stiffly, woodenly, rigidly, with difficulty, with embarrassment.—*Ant.* GRACEFULLY, skillfully, adroitly.
awkwardness *n.* ineptitude, inability, incompetence, ineptness, artlessness, crudeness, ignorance, heavy-handedness, ungainliness, ungracefulness, oafishness, gracelessness.—*Ant.* ABILITY, grace, competence.
awl *n.* bit, drill, pick; see TOOL 1.
awning *n.* canvas covering, canopy, sunshade; see COVER 1.
ax *n.* hatchet, adz, tomahawk, battle-ax, poleax, pickax, mattock, cleaver, broadax, hand ax. —**get the ax*** be fired, be dismissed, be discharged; see GET IT 2. —**have an ax to grind*** want something, have a purpose, complain about something; see WANT 1.
axis *n.* shaft, pivot, axle, pole, stem, support, dividing line, spindle, arbor, line of symmetry, line of rotation, line of revolution.
axle *n.* shaft, spindle, pin; see AXIS.

B

babble *n.* jabber, chatter, twaddle; see NONSENSE 1.
babble *v.* talk incoherently, talk foolishly, rant, rave, gush, run on, go on*, gossip, murmur, chat, chatter, prattle, tattle, jabber, blurt, run off at the mouth*, talk off the top of one's head*, rattle on, gab*, cackle, blab, sputter, gibber, blabber*, clatter; see also TALK 1.
baby *a.* youthful, babyish, juvenile; see CHILDISH.
baby *n.* suckling, babe, child, toddler, tot, brat, young one, little one, papoose, bambino, chick, kid*, cherub, little shaver*, little newcomer*, bundle of joy*, another mouth to feed*.—*Ant.* MAN, adolescent, grown-up.
baby *v.* pamper, coddle, pet, spoil, fondle, caress, nurse, cherish, foster, cuddle, make much of, humor, indulge; see also PAMPER.
babyhood *n.* infancy, nursery days, diaper days*; see CHILDHOOD.
baby-sit *v.* watch, care for, sit; see GUARD.
bachelor *n.* unmarried man, single man, single, misogynist, woman-hater, lone wolf*.—*Ant.* HUSBAND, married man, benedict.
back *a.* rear, after, backward, hindmost, behind, astern, hind, rearward, aft, to the rear, in the rear, dorsal, caudal, following, posterior, terminal, in the wake, in the background, final.—*Ant.* FRONT, forward, head.
back *n.* **1.** [The rear part or side] hind part, posterior, stern, poop, aft, tailpiece, tail, back end.—*Ant.* FRONT, fore part, fore. **2.** [The rear of the torso] posterior, backside, spinal area; see SPINE. **3.** [One who plays behind the line, especially in football] linebacker, fullback, halfback, quarterback, cornerback, safety, running back, tailback, wingback, slot back, blocking back. —**behind someone's back** in secret, slyly, hidden; see SECRETIVE. —**(flat) on one's back** ill, defeated, helpless; see SICK. —**get off someone's back*** let alone, ignore, stop nagging; see NEGLECT 1. —**get one's back**

up become angry, be stubborn, lose one's temper; see RAGE 1. **—go back on** betray, reject, turn against; see DECEIVE. **—in back of** at the rear, behind, coming after; see FOLLOWING. **—turn one's back on** reject, desert, fail; see ABANDON 1. **—with one's back to the wall** desperate, cornered, stopped; see HOPELESS.

back *v.* **1.** [To push backward] drive back, repel, repulse; see PUSH 2. **2.** [To further] uphold, stand behind, encourage; see SUPPORT 2. **3.** [To equip with a back] stiffen, reinforce, line; see LINE 1, STRENGTHEN.

back and forth *a.* zigzag, in and out, from side to side; see TO AND FRO.

backbone *n.* **1.** [Line of bones in the back supporting the body] spinal column, vertebrae, chine; see SPINE 2. **2.** [Determination] firmness, fortitude, resolution; see DETERMINATION.

back down *v.* withdraw, recoil, back out; see RETREAT.

backed *a.* **1.** [Propelled backward] driven back, shoved, repelled, repulsed, pushed, retracted.—*Ant.* AHEAD, moved forward, impelled. **2.** [Supported] upheld, encouraged, approved, heartened, aided, assisted, advanced, promoted, sustained, fostered, favored, championed, advocated, supplied, maintained, asserted, established, helped, bolstered, propped, furthered, seconded, prompted, served, pushed, boosted, primed.—*Ant.* OPPOSED, discouraged, obstructed. **3.** [Supplied with a back, or backing] stiffened, built up, strengthened; see REINFORCED.

backer *n.* benefactor, supporter, follower; see PATRON.

backfire *v.* **1.** [To explode] burst, erupt, detonate; see EXPLODE. **2.** [To go awry] boomerang, ricochet, have an unwanted result; see FAIL 1.

background *n.* **1.** [Setting] backdrop, framework, environment; see SETTING. **2.** [The total of one's experiences] education, qualifications, preparation, grounding, rearing, credentials, capacities, accomplishments, achievements, attainments, deeds, actions; see also EXPERIENCE, KNOWLEDGE 1.

backhanded *a.* obscure, sarcastic, unfavorable; see INDIRECT.

backhouse *n.* latrine, outdoor toilet, outhouse; see TOILET.

backing *n.* **1.** [Assistance] subsidy, encouragement, aid; see HELP 1. **2.** [Support] reinforcement, buttress, lining; see SUPPORT 2.

backlash *n.* response, repercussion, resentment; see REACTION.

backlog *n.* reserve, supply, stock; see RESERVE 1.

back off *v.* fall back, withdraw, retire; see RETREAT.

back out of *v.* withdraw, shrink from, escape; see RETREAT.

backslide *v.* revert, break faith, fall from grace; see RELAPSE.

backstop *n.* screen, net, barrier; see FENCE.

back up *v.* **1.** [To move backward] fall back, withdraw, reverse; see RETREAT. **2.** [To support] aid, assist, help; see SUPPORT 2.

backward *a.* **1.** [To the rear] rearward, astern, behind, retrograde, regressive.—*Ant.* FORWARD, progressive, onward. **2.** [Reversed] turned around, counterclockwise, inverted; see REVERSED. **3.** [Behind in development] underdeveloped, slow, slow to develop, retarded, delayed, arrested, checked, late, undeveloped, underprivileged; see also DULL 3. **—bend over backward** try hard to please, conciliate, be fair; see TRY 1.

back yard *n.* patio, terrace, enclosure, play area, back lawn, grass, court; see also GARDEN, YARD 1.

bacon *n.* flitch, Canadian bacon, salt pork; see MEAT. **—bring home the bacon*** earn a living, prosper, get paid; see SUCCEED 1.

bacteria *n.pl.* bacilli, microbes, organisms; see GERM.

bad *a.* **1.** [Wicked] evil, sinful, immoral, wrong, corrupt, base, foul, gross, profane, naughty, degenerate, decadent, depraved, heartless, degraded, debauched, indecent, mean, scandalous, nasty, vicious, fiendish, devilish, criminal, murderous, sinister, monstrous, dangerous, vile, rotten*, dirty, crooked.—*Ant.* GOOD, honest, pure. **2.** [Spoiled] rancid, decayed, putrid; see ROTTEN 1, 2. **3.** [Below standard] defective, inferior, imperfect; see POOR 2. **4.** [In poor health] ill, diseased, ailing; see SICK. **5.** [Injurious] hurtful, damaging, detrimental; see HARMFUL. **6.** [*Very good] stylish, nice, pretty; see FASHIONABLE, EXCELLENT. **—not bad*** all right, pretty good, passable; see FAIR 2.

badge *n.* **1.** [Outward evidence] marker, symbol, identification; see EMBLEM. **2.** [A device worn as evidence] pin, emblem, seal, medal, insignia, shield, epaulet, ribbon, medallion, marker, feather, rosette, clasp, button, signet, crest, star, chevron, stripe.

badger *v.* harass, annoy, pester; see BOTHER 2.

badly *a.* **1.** [In an ineffectual or incompetent manner] wrongly, imperfectly, ineffectively, inefficiently, poorly, unsatisfactorily, crudely, boorishly, unskillfully, defectively, weakly, haphazardly, clumsily, carelessly, negligently, incompetently, stupidly, blunderingly, mistakenly, awkwardly, faultily, shiftlessly, abominably, awfully*, terribly*.—*Ant.* CAREFULLY, competently, adequately. **2.** [*To a marked degree] severely, seriously, greatly; see VERY.

baffle *v.* perplex, puzzle, bewilder; see CONFUSE.

bag *n.* purse, sack, pouch, grip, handbag, tote bag, knapsack, backpack, carpetbag, kit, satchel, saddlebag, gunny sack, suitcase, briefcase, attaché case, duffel bag, pack, container, feedbag, quiver, packet, pocketbook, holster, vanity bag, valise, case, wallet, haversack, holdall, carryall. **—in the bag*** absolute, sure, definite; see CERTAIN 2. **—left holding the bag*** deceived, tricked, deserted; see ABANDONED.

bag *v.* trap, seize, get; see CATCH 1.

baggage *n.* luggage, gear, bags, trunks, valises, suitcases, overnight cases, parcels, paraphernalia, effects, equipment, packs, things.

baggy *a.* slack, unshapely, bulging; see LOOSE 1.

bail *n.* bond, surety, recognizance, pledge, warrant, guaranty, collateral.

bail *v.* **1.** [To dip] scoop, spoon out, dredge; see DIP 2. **2.** [To empty] clear, drain, deplete; see EMPTY.

bail out *v.* release, give security for, post bail for, assure, underwrite, guarantee, warrant, insure, deliver, go bail for, spring*.

bait *n.* lure, inducement, bribe; see ATTRACTION.

bait *v.* **1.** [To torment] anger, nag, tease; see BOTHER 2. **2.** [To lure] entice, attract, draw; see FASCINATE.

bake *v.* roast, toast, warm; see COOK.

baked *a.* parched, scorched, dried, toasted, warmed, heated, cooked, grilled, burned, charred, roasted, incinerated.

baker *n.* pastry cook, chef, confectioner; see COOK.

bakery *n.* bake shop, pastry shop, confectionery, bread store, patisserie, cake shop.

balance *n.* **1.** [Whatever remains] excess, surplus, residue; see REMAINDER. **2.** [An equilibrium] poise, counterpoise, symmetry, offset, equivalence, counterbalance, tension, equalization, equality of weight, parity.—*Ant.* INCONSISTENCY, topheaviness, imbalance. **3.** [An excess of credits over debits] surplus, dividend, credit balance; see PROFIT 2. **—in the balance** undetermined, undecided, critical; see UNCERTAIN.

balance *v.* **1.** [To offset] counterbalance, compensate for, allow for; see sense 2. **2.** [To place in balance] place in equilibrium, steady, stabilize, neutralize, set, level, equalize, support, poise, oppose, even, weigh, counteract, make equal, compensate, tie, adjust, square, parallel, coordinate, readjust, pair off, equate, match, level off, attune, harmonize, tune, accord, correspond.—*Ant.* UPSET, turn over, topple. **3.** [To demonstrate that debits and credits are in balance] estimate, compare, audit; see CHECK 2.

balanced *a.* **1.** [Made even] equalized, poised, offset, in equilibrium, evened, counterweighted, equivalent, stabilized, symmetrical, counterpoised, counterbalanced, on an even keel.—*Ant.* UNSTABLE, unbalanced, unequal. **2.** [Audited] validated, confirmed, certified; see APPROVED.

balance of power *n.* equilibrium, distribution, apportionment; see BALANCE 2.

balcony *n.* gallery, mezzanine, terrace; see UPSTAIRS.

bald *a.* hairless, shaven, shaved, bare, featherless, glabrous, shiny, smooth, like a billiard ball*; see also SMOOTH 3.—*Ant.* HAIRY, covered, bearded.

balderdash *n.* senseless talk, gibberish, bombast; see NONSENSE 1.

bale *n.* bundle, bunch, parcel; see PACKAGE.

balk *v.* turn down, demur, desist; see REFUSE.

balky *a.* contrary, obstinate, perverse; see STUBBORN.

ball *n.* **1.** [A spherical body] marble, globe, spheroid, sphere, balloon, rounded object, orb, globule, globular object, pellet, pill, drop, knot. **2.** [A game played with a ball] baseball, football, catch; see SPORT 3. **3.** [A dance] grand ball, promenade, reception; see PARTY 1. **—carry the ball*** assume responsibility, take control, bear the burden; see LEAD 1. **—get the ball rolling*** initiate action, commence, start; see BEGIN 1. **—have something on the ball*** be skilled, have ability, be efficient; see ABLE.

ballad *n.* carol, chant, folk song; see SONG.

ballast *n.* sandbags, counterbalance, counterweight; see WEIGHT 2.

ballet *n.* toe dancing, choreography, tap dancing; see DANCE 1.

ballet dancer *n.* ballerina, danseuse, danseur; see DANCER.

balloon *n.* dirigible, aircraft, airship, weather balloon, hot-air balloon, radiosonde, barrage balloon, lighter-than-air craft, toy balloon, zeppelin, observation balloon, blimp*, gasbag.

ballot *n.* tally, ticket, poll; see VOTE 1.

balm *n.* **1.** [Anything healing and soothing] solace, consolation, comfort, relief, refreshment, remedy, cure. **2.** [An ointment of resin] salve, lotion, dressing; see MEDICINE 2.

bamboozle *v.* swindle, trick, dupe; see DECEIVE.

ban *n.* taboo, prohibition, limitation; see REFUSAL.

ban *v.* outlaw, prevent, declare illegal; see FORBID, PREVENT.

banal *a.* dull, trite, hackneyed; see COMMON 1.

band *n.* **1.** [A beltlike strip] circuit, meridian, latitude, circle, ring, orbit, zodiac, circumference, zone, ribbon, belt, line, strip, stripe, tape, sash, twine, scarf, bandage, girdle, thong, wristband, bond, tie, binding, stay, truss, belt, cord, harness, brace, strap, binding, waistband, collar, hatband, cable, rope, link, chain, line, string, guy wire. **2.** [A company of people] group, collection, association; see GATHERING. **3.** [A group of musicians] orchestra, company, troupe, ensemble, string quartet, group, combo*. *Kinds of bands include the following:* military, brass, marching, concert, parade, jazz, stage, dance, Dixieland, jug, rock, swing.

bandage *n.* compress, cast, gauze; see DRESSING 3.

bandage *v.* tie, fix, bind up; see BIND 1, FASTEN.

bandit *n.* burglar, thief, raider; see ROBBER.

bang *n.* **1.** [A loud report] blast, roar, detonation; see NOISE 1. **2.** [A blow] hit, cuff, whack; see BLOW. **3.** [*A thrill] enjoyment, pleasant feeling, kick*; see EXCITEMENT.

bang *v.* **1.** [To beat] strike, slam, whack; see HIT 1. **2.** [To make a noise] crash, clatter, rattle; see SOUND.

banish *v.* exile, deport, cast out, expel, expatriate, ostracize, sequester, excommunicate, transport, outlaw, extradite, isolate, dismiss.—*Ant.* RECEIVE, welcome, accept.

banishment *n.* expatriation, deportation, expulsion; see EXILE 1.

banister *n.* railing, hand rail, guard rail; see RAIL 1.

bank *n.* **1.** [Ground rising above adjacent water] ledge, embankment, edge; see SHORE. **2.** [A financial establishment] national bank, state bank, commercial bank, savings bank, savings and loan association, thrift, lender, mortgage company, Federal Reserve Bank, private bank, countinghouse, banking house, credit union, trust company, treasury.

bank *v.* **1.** [To deposit money] save, put in the bank, enter in an account; see DEPOSIT 2. **2.** [To tilt on a curve] lean, bend, slope; see LEAN 1.

banker *n.* treasurer, teller, officer of the bank, broker, financier, capitalist, investment banker, moneylender.

banking *n.* investment, funding, moneylending; see BUSINESS 1.

bank on* *v.* depend on, believe in, be sure about; see TRUST 1.

bankrupt *a.* failed, out of business, broke*; see RUINED 3.

bankruptcy *n.* insolvency, destitution, distress; see FAILURE 1.

banner *n.* colors, pennant, flag; see EMBLEM.

banquet *n.* repast, fete, festivity; see DINNER.

baptism *n.* dedication, christening, initiation; see CEREMONY 2.

baptize *v.* immerse, purify, regenerate, sprinkle, dip, christen, name, administer baptism to.

bar *n.* **1.** [A relatively long, narrow object] strip, stake, stick, crossbar, boom, rib, crosspiece, pole, spar, rail, lever, rod, crowbar, shaft, slab. **2.** [A counter serving refreshments, especially drinks] barroom, tavern, cocktail lounge, saloon, public house, counter, hotel, inn, canteen, beer parlor, cabaret, restaurant, cafeteria, roadhouse, brass rail, snack bar, beer garden, watering hole*, dive*, pub (British)*, grill. **3.** [The legal profession] lawyers, counselors, barristers, solicitors, jurists, attorneys, bar association, advocates, judiciary. **4.** [An obstruction] hindrance, obstacle, hurdle; see BARRIER. **5.** [A relatively long, narrow area] strip, stripe, ribbon; see BAND 1.

bar *v.* **1.** [To raise a physical obstruction] barricade, dam, dike, fence, wall, erect a barrier, brick up, blockade, clog, exclude, shut out, lock out, keep out, bolt, cork, plug, seal, stop, impede, roadblock.—*Ant.* OPEN, free, clear. **2.** [To obstruct by refusal] ban, forbid, deny, refuse, prevent, stop, boycott, ostracize, preclude, shut out, keep out, exclude, exile, reject, outlaw, condemn, discourage, interfere with, restrain, frustrate, circumvent, override, segregate, interdict, freeze out*.—*Ant.* ALLOW, admit, welcome. **3.** [To close] shut, lock, seal; see CLOSE 4.

barbarian *n.* savage, brute, cannibal, rascal, ruffian, monster, Yahoo, Philistine, troglodyte, clod; see also BEAST 2.

barbaric *a.* inhuman, brutal, fierce; see CRUEL.

barbarity *n.* savageness, cruelty, brutality; see CRUELTY.

barbecue *n.* **1.** [A grill] roaster, grill, broiler; see APPLIANCE. **2.** [A picnic] cookout, wiener roast, picnic; see MEAL 2.

barbecue *v.* grill, sear, broil; see COOK.

barbed wire *n.* fence wire, fencing, barbwire; see FENCE.

bare *a.* **1.** [Without covering] uncovered, bald, stripped; see NAKED 1, OPEN 4. **2.** [Plain] unadorned, simple, unornamented; see MODEST 2. **3.** [Without content] barren, void, unfurnished; see EMPTY.

barefaced *a.* **1.** [Open] unconcealed, clear, apparent; see OBVIOUS 1, 2. **2.** [Impudent] shameless, audacious, bold; see RUDE 2.

barefoot *a.* shoeless, barefooted, unshod; see NAKED 1.

barely *a.* almost, scarcely, just; see HARDLY.

bargain *n.* **1.** [An agreement] pact, compact, contract; see DEAL 1. **2.** [An advantageous purchase] good value, good deal, discount, reduction, marked-down price, buy*, steal*, giveaway*, deal. —**into the bargain** in addition, too, additionally; see ALSO.

bargain *v.* **1.** [To trade] barter, do business, merchandise; see BUY, SELL. **2.** [To negotiate] make terms, arrange, confer; see NEGOTIATE 1.

bargain for *v.* expect, plan on, foresee; see ANTICIPATE.

bargaining *n.* trade, transaction, haggling; see BUSINESS 1.

bark *n.* **1.** [An outer covering, especially of trees] peel, cork, husk; see COVER 1, SHELL 1. **2.** [A short, explosive sound] yelp, yap, grunt; see NOISE 1.

bark *v.* yelp, yap, bay, howl, cry, growl, snarl, yip, woof, arf.

bark up the wrong tree *v.* miscalculate, misdirect one's effort, make a mistake; see MISJUDGE 2.

barn *n.* outbuilding, shed, outhouse, shelter, lean-to, coop, hutch, sty, pen, kennel, stable.

barnyard *n.* feedyard, pen, corral, stableyard, lot, feedlot, run.

barred *a.* **1.** [Equipped or marked with bars] striped, banded, streaked, pleated, pied, motley, calico, mottled, dappled, veined, ribbed, crosshatched, ridged, marked, piped, lined. **2.** [Prohibited] banned, outlawed, unlawful; see ILLEGAL.

barrel *n.* cask, keg, vat, tub, receptacle, container, vessel.

barren *a.* **1.** [Incapable of producing young] impotent, infertile, childless; see STERILE 1. **2.** [Incapable of producing vegetation] fallow, unproductive, fruitless; see STERILE 2.

barricade *n.* obstacle, bar, obstruction; see BARRIER.

barricade *v.* obstruct, block, fortify; see BAR 1.

barrier *n.* bar, obstruction, difficulty, hindrance, obstacle, hurdle, stumbling block, fence, sound barrier, restriction, restraint, impediment, drawback, check, stop, stay, bulwark, barricade, rampart, wall, earthwork, embankment, blockade, barbed wire, bamboo curtain, iron curtain.—*Ant.* WAY, path, trail.

barroom *n.* tavern, saloon, pub*; see BAR 2.

barter *n.* trade, exchange, traffic; see BUSINESS 1.

barter *v.* trade, bargain, swap*; see BUY, SELL.

base *a.* low, foul, sordid; see VULGAR.

base *n.* **1.** [A point from which the action is initiated] camp, field, landing field, airport, airfield, airstrip, port, headquarters, terminal, base camp, home base, fire base, base of operations, center, depot, supply base, dock, harbor, station. **2.** [The bottom, thought of as a support] root, foot, footing; see FOUNDATION 2. **3.** [Foundation of a belief or statement] principle, authority, evidence; see BASIS. **4.** [A goal, especially in baseball] mark, bound, station, plate, post, goal; first base, second base, third base, home plate. **—off base*** erring, mistaken, incorrect; see WRONG 2.

baseball *n.* ball, little league, the national pastime; see SPORT 3.

baseball player *n.* pitcher, catcher, infielder, batter, shortstop, left fielder, right fielder, center fielder, first baseman, second baseman, third baseman, hitter, slugger*.

based *a.* confirmed, planted, founded; see ESTABLISHED 2.

basement *n.* cellar, excavation, storage room, wine cellar, furnace room, vault, crypt.

base on *v.* institute, found, build; see ESTABLISH.

bashful *a.* retiring, reserved, timid; see HUMBLE 1, MODEST 2.

basic *a.* essential, central, primary; see FUNDAMENTAL, NECESSARY.

basically *a.* fundamentally, primarily, radically; see ESSENTIALLY.

basin *n.* pan, tub, bowl; see CONTAINER.

basis *n.* support, foundation, justification, reason, explanation, background, source, authority, principle, groundwork, assumption, premise, backing, sanction, proof, evidence, nucleus, center.

bask *v.* relax, enjoy, indulge; see WALLOW.

basket *n.* bushel, crate, bin; see CONTAINER.

basketball *n.* court game, cage meet, roundball*; see SPORT 3.

bastard *a.* illegitimate, natural, false, mongrel, baseborn, misbegotten.—*Ant.* TRUE, legitimate, well-born.

bastard *n.* **1.** [An illegitimate child] natural child, whoreson, love child, woods colt*, Sunday's child*. **2.** [*A rascal] scoundrel, cheat, SOB; see RASCAL.

baste *v.* **1.** [To sew temporarily] stitch, catch, tack; see SEW. **2.** [To dress cooking meat with fat or sauce] moisten, grease, season; see COOK.

bat *n.* club, racket, stick; see STICK. **—blind as a bat** sightless, unseeing, blinded; see BLIND 1. **—go to bat for*** intervene for, support, back up; see DEFEND 2. **—have bats in one's belfry*** be mad, be eccentric, be peculiar; see INSANE. **—not bat an eye*** not be surprised, not be shocked, not be amazed, ignore, remain unruffled; see also NEGLECT 1. **—(right) off the bat*** at once, without delay, instantly; see IMMEDIATELY.

bat *v.* strike, whack, sock*; see HIT 1.

batch *n.* stack, group, shipment; see BUNCH.

bath *n.* **1.** [The act of cleansing the body] washing, sponge bath, shower, tub, bath, steam bath, sauna, soak*, dip, soaking*. **2.** [An enclosure prepared for bathing] bathroom, toilet, shower, washroom, powder room, lavatory, steam room, sauna, public baths, shower room.

bathe *v.* soap, scour, scrub; see WASH 1.

bathrobe *n.* robe, dressing gown, kimono; see CLOTHES.

bathroom *n.* shower, toilet, lavatory; see BATH 2, TOILET.

battalion *n.* unit, force, corps; see ARMY 2.

batter *n.* **1.** [One who bats] hitter, pinch-hitter, switch-hitter; see BASEBALL PLAYER. **2.** [Baking mixture] dough, mix, paste, recipe, concoction, mush; see also MIXTURE 1.

battery *n.* 1. [Cells which generate or store electricity] dry cell, storage cells, storage battery, energy unit, flashlight battery, solar battery, atomic battery, electric cell. 2. [The act of beating] assault, attack, thumping, beating, physical violence, mugging.

battle *n.* strife, contention, struggle, combat, bombing, fighting, bloodshed, clash, onslaught, onset, barrage, conflict, warfare, fray, assault, crusade, military campaign, hostilities, havoc, carnage; see also FIGHT. —**give** or **do battle** fight back, struggle, engage in a battle; see ATTACK, FIGHT.

battlefield *n.* field of battle, battleground, front, theater of war, disputed territory, no man's land.

battleship *n.* man of war, floating fortress, battlewagon*; see SHIP.

bawl *v.* weep, shed tears, sob; see CRY 1.

bawl out* *v.* chide, berate, admonish; see SCOLD.

bay *n.* inlet, gulf, bayou, loch, bight, sound, fiord, firth, estuary, strait, narrows, road, arm of the sea, mouth, lagoon, cove, harbor.

bayonet *n.* spike, lance, pike; see KNIFE.

B.C. *abbrev.* before Christ, ante-Christian, pre-Christian; see OLD 3.

be *v.* 1. [To have being] live, stay, be alive, exist, remain, continue, endure, go on, stand, subsist, breathe, last, prevail, abide, survive, move, act, do, hold, have place.—*Ant.* DIE, disappear, stop. 2. [To mean] signify, denote, imply; see MEAN 1.

beach *n.* seaside, sand, the coast; see SHORE.

beached *a.* stranded, marooned, aground; see ABANDONED.

beacon *n.* flare, lantern, guide, signal fire, lighthouse, lamp, beam, radar, sonar, airline beacon, radio beacon, air control beacon.

bead *n.* drop, droplet, pellet, grain, particle, speck, dot, dab, pea, shot, pill, driblet.

beads *n.pl.* necklace, pendant, string of jewels; see NECKLACE.

beak *n.* nose, prow, bill, mandible, projection, proboscis, snout, nozzle.

beam *n.* 1. [A relatively long, stout bar] timber, brace, scantling, rafter, stringer, stud, two-by-four, strut, joist, bolster, axle, girder, sleeper, stay, crosspiece, prop, support, trestle, spar, pole, crossbar, T-beam, I-beam, steel beam, boom, post, column, pillar, sill, jamb, cantilever, shaft, scaffolding; see also BAR 1. 2. [Radio waves intended as a guide] direction finder, unidirectional radio signal, radar; see BEACON. —**off the beam*** faulty, incorrect, inaccurate; see WRONG 2. —**on the beam*** alert, keen, efficient; see ABLE.

beam *v.* 1. [To emit] transmit, broadcast, give out; see SEND 1. 2. [To shine] radiate, glitter, glare; see SHINE 1. 3. [To smile] grin, laugh, smirk; see SMILE.

beaming *a.* 1. [Giving forth beams] radiant, glowing, gleaming; see BRIGHT 1. 2. [In very genial humor] grinning, animated, sunny; see HAPPY.

bean *n.* *Varieties include the following:* kidney, navy, lima, soy, castor, black, pinto, string, black-eyed, black-eye, green, wax; see also VEGETABLE. —**full of beans*** 1. lively, vital, energetic; see ACTIVE. 2. mistaken, erring, incorrect; see WRONG 2. —**spill the beans*** divulge information, tell secrets, talk; see TELL 1.

bear *n.* grizzly, polar bear, brown bear, black bear; see also ANIMAL.

bear *v.* 1. [To suffer] tolerate, support, undergo; see ENDURE 2. 2. [To support weight] sustain, hold up, shoulder; see SUPPORT 1. 3. [To give birth to] be delivered of, bring to birth, bring forth; see PRODUCE 1.

bearable *a.* endurable, tolerable, passable, admissible, supportable, sufferable.

beard *n.* whiskers, brush, Van Dyke, chin whiskers, imperial, muttonchops, goatee, spade beard, forked beard, side whiskers.

bearded *a.* bewhiskered, bushy, unshaven; see HAIRY.

bear down on or **upon** *v.* 1. [To press] squeeze, compress, push; see PRESS 1. 2. [To try] endeavor, strive, attempt; see TRY 1.

bearing *n.* 1. [A point of support] frame, ball bearing, roller bearing; see SUPPORT 2. 2. [Manner of carriage] mien, deportment, manner; see BEHAVIOR, POSTURE 1.

bear out *v.* confirm, substantiate, support; see PROVE.

bear up *v.* persist, persevere, carry on; see ENDURE 2.

bear upon *v.* pertain to, refer to, relate to, regard; see also CONCERN 1.

bear with *v.* tolerate, be patient with, suffer, put up with; see also ENDURE 2.

bear witness *v.* affirm, attest, give evidence; see TESTIFY 2.

beast *n.* 1. [A large animal] brute, creature, lower animal; see ANIMAL. 2. [A person of brutish nature] monster, brute, degenerate, animal, fiend, swine, pervert, lout, savage, barbarian, pig, satyr, goat, hog, monstrosity, glutton, gargoyle, Bluebeard; see also PERVERT.

beastly *a.* brutal, savage, coarse, repulsive, gluttonous, obscene, unclean, piggish, hoggish, irrational, boorish, brutish, depraved, abominable, loathsome, vile, low, degraded, sensual, foul, base, disgusting, inhuman, gross, vulgar.—*Ant.* REFINED, sweet, nice.

beat* *a.* weary, fatigued, worn-out; see TIRED.

beat *n.* 1. [A throb] thump, pound, quake, flutter, pulse, pulsation, cadence, flow, vibration, turn, ripple, pressure, impulse, quiver, shake, surge, swell, palpitation, undulation, rhythm. 2. [A unit of music] accent, vibration, division, stress, measure, rhythm.

beat *v.* **1.** [To thrash] hit, punish, whip, pistol-whip, flog, trounce, spank, scourge, switch, lash, slap, cuff, box, strap, birch, cane, horsewhip, buffet, pommel, tap, rap, strike, bump, pat, knock, pound, club, punch, bat, flail, batter, maul, whack, hammer, clout, smack, bang, swat*, slug*, beat black and blue*, whale*, belt*, whack*, beat the tar out of*, beat the daylights out of*, beat the hell out of*, knock the stuffing out of*, wallop*, lick*, paste*, bash*, work over*, thwack. **2.** [To pulsate] pound, thump, pulse; see THROB. **3.** [To worst] overcome, surpass, conquer; see DEFEAT 2, 3. **4.** [To mix] stir, whip, knead; see MIX 1.

beat around the bush *v.* quibble, avoid the issue, hesitate; see EVADE.

beaten *a.* **1.** [Defeated] worsted, humbled, thwarted, bested, disappointed, frustrated, baffled, conquered, overthrown, subjugated, ruined, mastered, trounced, undone, vanquished, crushed, overwhelmed, overpowered, licked*, done in*, done for*, kayoed*, mugged, skinned*, trimmed*, had it*, washed up*, sunk*.—*Ant.* SUCCESSFUL, victorious, triumphant. **2.** [Made firm and hard] hammered, tramped, stamped, rolled, milled, forged, trod, pounded, tramped down, tamped.—*Ant.* SOFT, spongy, loose. **3.** [Made light by beating] whipped, frothy, foamy, mixed, churned, creamy, bubbly, meringued.

beater *n.* whipper, mixer, egg-beater; see APPLIANCE.

beating *n.* thrashing, whipping, drubbing; see DEFEAT.

beatnik *n.* Bohemian, hippie-type, nonconformist; see RADICAL.

beautiful *a.* lovely, attractive, appealing, comely, pleasing, pretty, fair, fine, nice, dainty, good-looking, delightful, charming, enticing, fascinating, admirable, rich, graceful, ideal, delicate, refined, elegant, symmetrical, well-formed, shapely, well-made, splendid, gorgeous, brilliant, radiant, exquisite, dazzling, resplendent, magnificent, superb, marvelous, wonderful, grand, awe-inspiring, imposing, majestic, excellent, impressive, handsome, divine, blooming, rosy, beauteous, statuesque, well-favored, bewitching, personable, taking, alluring, slender, svelte, lissome, lithe, bright-eyed, classy*, easy on the eyes*, long on looks*, built*.—*Ant.* UGLY, deformed, hideous.

beautifully *a.* gracefully, exquisitely, charmingly, attractively, prettily, delightfully, appealingly, seductively, alluringly, elegantly, gorgeously, splendidly, magnificently, ideally, tastefully, sublimely, handsomely, superbly, divinely.

beauty *n.* **1.** [A pleasing physical quality] grace, comeliness, fairness, pulchritude, charm, delicacy, elegance, attraction, fascination, allurement, shapeliness, majesty, attractiveness, good looks, glamour, loveliness, bloom, class*.—*Ant.* UGLINESS, homeliness, deformity. **2.** [A beautiful woman] goddess, belle, attraction, siren, enchantress, seductress, Venus, *femme fatale* (French), looker*, charmer*.—*Ant.* WITCH, blemish, fright.

because *conj.* on account of, in consequence of, in view of, by reason of, for the reason that, for the sake of, in behalf of, on the grounds that, in the interest of, as a result of, as things go, by virtue of, in that, since, by the agency of, due to*, being as how*, owing to.

be certain *v.* be sure, make certain, have confidence; see KNOW 1.

beckon *v.* signal, motion, sign; see SUMMON.

become *v.* develop into, change into, turn into, grow into, eventually be, emerge as, turn out to be, come to be, shift, assume the form of, be reformed, be converted to, convert, mature, shift toward, incline to, melt into; see also GROW 2.

becoming *a.* attractive, beautiful, neat, agreeable, handsome, seemly, comely, tasteful, well-chosen, fair, trim, graceful, flattering, effective, excellent, acceptable, welcome, nice.

bed *n.* **1.** [A place of rest] mattress, cot, couch, bedstead, berth, bunk, hay*, sack*, rack*, feathers*, roost. *Beds include the following:* single bed, double bed, davenport, cot, four-poster, trundle bed, twin bed, fold-away bed, Murphy bed, hammock, feather bed, double-deck bed, stretcher, folding bed, bunk bed, litter, cradle, crib, bassinet, king-size bed, queen-size bed, water bed, hospital bed, circular bed, day bed. **2.** [A foundation] base, bottom, groundwork; see FOUNDATION 2. **3.** [A seed plot] patch, row, planting; see GARDEN.

bedding *n.* bedclothes, bed linen, thermal blankets, covers, bedcovers, pillows, coverlets, sheets, quilts, spreads, comforters.

bed down *v.* turn in, retire, hit the hay*; see SLEEP.

bedlam *n.* confusion, pandemonium, clamor; see CONFUSION, NOISE 2.

bedridden *a.* incapacitated, confined to bed, laid up; see DISABLED.

bedroom *n.* sleeping room, guest room, master bedroom; see ROOM 2.

bedspread *n.* spread, quilt, comforter; see BEDDING.

bedtime *n.* slumbertime, time to hit the hay*, sack time*; see NIGHT.

beef *n.* **1.** [Bovine flesh used as food] cow's flesh, steer beef, red meat; see MEAT. **2.** [A grown animal of the genus *Bos*] bovine, bull, steer; see COW. **3.** [*A complaint] dispute, protestation, gripe*; see OBJECTION.

beef up* *v.* intensify, augment, increase; see STRENGTHEN.

beer *n.* malt beverage, malt liquor, brew, suds*. *Varieties include the following:* lager, bock beer, ale, stout, porter, pale beer, light beer, dark beer, black beer.

beetle *n.* bug, scarab, crawling thing; see INSECT.

before *a.* previously, earlier, in the past, since, gone by, in old days, heretofore, former, formerly, back, sooner, up to now, ahead, in front, in advance, facing.—*Ant.* AFTERWARD, in the future, to come.

before *prep.* prior to, previous to, in front of, ahead of, under jurisdiction of, antecedent to.—*Ant.* BEHIND, following, at the rear.

beforehand *a.* previously, already, in anticipation; see BEFORE.

befriend *v.* encourage, advise, stand by; see HELP.

beg *v.* entreat, implore, beseech, supplicate, crave, solicit, pray for, urge, plead, sue, importune, petition, apply to, request, press, appeal to, requisition, conjure, adjure, apostrophize, canvass; see also ASK.—*Ant.* ADMIT, concede, accede.

beggar *n.* pauper, poor man, hobo, tramp, indigent, vagrant, poverty-stricken person, destitute person, dependent, ghetto-dweller, bankrupt, panhandler*, moocher*, bum*.

begging *a.* anxious, in need, imploring, supplicating; see also WANTING 1.

begin *v.* **1.** [To initiate] start, cause, inaugurate, make, occasion, impel, produce, effect, set in motion, launch, mount, start in, start on, start up, start off, induce, do, create, bring about, get going, set about, institute, lead up to, undertake, enter upon, open, animate, motivate, go ahead, lead the way, bring on, bring to pass, act on, generate, drive, actualize, introduce, originate, found, establish, set up, trigger, give birth to, take the lead, plunge into, lay the foundation for, break ground.—*Ant.* END, finish, terminate. **2.** [To come into being, or start functioning] commence, get under way, set out, start in, start out, come out, arise, rise, dawn, sprout, originate, crop up, come to birth, come into the world, be born, emanate, come into existence, occur, burst forth, issue forth, come forth, bud, grow, flower, blossom, break out, set to work, kick off, jump off*, go to it*, dig in*, take off*, see the light of day*.—*Ant.* STOP, cease, subside.

beginner *n.* novice, freshman, apprentice; see AMATEUR.

beginning *n.* **1.** [The origin in point of time or place] source, outset, root; see ORIGIN 2. **2.** [The origin, thought of as the cause] germ, heart, antecedent; see ORIGIN 3.

begun *a.* started, initiated, instituted, under way, in motion, in progress, on foot, inaugurated, happening, proceeding, going, active, existing, operative, working, in force.

behalf *n.* interest, benefit, sake; see WELFARE.

behave *v.* act with decorum, observe the golden rule, do unto others as you would have others do unto you, be nice, be good, be civil, mind one's p's and q's, be orderly, play one's part, live up to, observe the law, reform, mind one's manners, comport oneself, deport oneself, behave oneself, be on one's best behavior, act one's age, avoid offense, toe the mark, play fair.

behavior *n.* bearing, deportment, comportment, demeanor, air, presence, carriage, conduct, manners, actions, attitudes, way of life, speech, talk, tone, morals, habits, tact, social graces, correctness, decorum, form, convention, propriety, taste, management, routine, practice, what's done, style, expression, performance, code, role, observance, course, guise, act, deed, ethics, way, front.

behind *a. & prep.* **1.** [To the rear in space] back of, following, after; see BACK. **2.** [Late in time] tardy, dilatory, behind time; see LATE 1, SLOW 2. **3.** [Slow in progress] sluggish, slow-moving, delayed, backward, underdeveloped, retarded, behind schedule, belated; see also SLOW 2.—*Ant.* FAST, rapid, on time.

behind someone's back *a.* deceitfully, foully, faithlessly; see FALSELY.

behind the times *a.* antiquated, out-of-date, obsolete; see OLD-FASHIONED.

being *n.* **1.** [Existence] presence, actuality, animation; see LIFE 1. **2.** [The essential part] nature, core, marrow; see ESSENCE 1. **3.** [A living thing] creature, conscious agent, beast; see ANIMAL. **—for the time being** temporarily, tentatively, for now, for the present; see also BRIEFLY, NOW.

belated *a.* remiss, tardy, overdue; see LATE 1, SLOW 3.

belief *n.* idea, opinion, faith, feeling, hope, intuition, view, expectation, acceptance, trust, notion, persuasion, position, understanding, conviction, confidence, suspicion, knowledge, conclusion, presumption, surmise, hypothesis, thinking, judgment, certainty, impression, assumption, conjecture, fancy, theory, guess, conception, inference.

believable *a.* trustworthy, creditable, acceptable; see CONVINCING.

believe *v.* accept, hold, think, understand, consider, swear by, conceive, affirm, conclude, be of the opinion, have faith, have no doubt, take at one's word, take someone's word for, be convinced, be certain of, give credence to, rest assured.—*Ant.* DENY, doubt, suspect.

believe in *v.* swear by, look to, have faith in; see TRUST 1.

believer *n.* convert, devotee, adherent, apostle, disciple, prophet, confirmed believer; see also FOLLOWER.

believing *a.* maintaining, trusting, presuming, assuming, holding, accepting, under the impression.

belittle *v.* lower, disparage, decry; see ABUSE.
bell *n.* chimes, siren, signal, gong, buzzer; see also ALARM.
belligerent *a.* warlike, pugnacious, hostile; see AGGRESSIVE.
bellow *n.* howl, cry, roar; see CRY 1.
bellow *v.* howl, call, shout; see CRY 2, YELL.
belly *n.* paunch, abdomen, gut; see STOMACH.
bellyache* *v.* whine, grumble, protest; see COMPLAIN.
belong *v.* **1.** [To be properly placed] fit in, have a place, relate; see FIT 1. **2.** [To be acceptable in a group; *said of persons*] fit in, have a place, have its place, be born so, be a member, take one's place with, be one of, be counted among, be included in, owe allegiance to, be a part of, be one of the family.—*Ant.* DIFFER, fight, not fit in.
belongings *n.pl.* possessions, goods, things*; see PROPERTY 1.
belong to *v.* pertain to, relate to, be occupied by, be enjoyed by, be owned by, be in the possession of, be at the disposal of, be the property of, concern, come with, go with, fall under.—*Ant.* ESCAPE, be free, have no owner.
beloved *a.* loved, adored, worshiped, cherished, dear, favorite, idolized, precious, prized, dearest, yearned for, revered, treasured, favored, doted on, nearest to someone's heart, dearly beloved, after someone's own heart, darling, admired, popular, well-liked, cared for, respected, pleasing.—*Ant.* HATED, abhorred, disliked.
beloved *n.* fiancé, sweetheart, object of someone's affection; see LOVER 1.
below *a. & prep.* **1.** [Lower in position] beneath, underneath, down from; see UNDER 1. **2.** [Lower in rank or importance] inferior, subject, under; see SUBORDINATE. **3.** [Farther along in written material] later, on a following page, in a statement to be made, hereafter, subsequently.—*Ant.* ABOVE, earlier, on a former page. **4.** [On earth] existing, in this world, here below, under the sun, on the face of the earth, in this our life, here. **5.** [In hell] in the underworld, damned, condemned; see DAMNED 1.
below par *a.* inferior, below average, second-rate; see POOR 2.
below the belt *a.* unjust, foul, unsporting; see UNFAIR.
belt *n.* girdle, ribbon, string; see BAND 1. —**tighten one's belt** endure hunger, suffer, bear misfortune; see ENDURE 2. —**under one's belt** past, finished, completed; see DONE 1.
bench *n.* **1.** [A long seat] pew, seat, stall; see CHAIR 1. **2.** [A long table] workbench, desk, counter; see TABLE 1.
bend *n.* crook, bow, arch; see CURVE.
bend *v.* twist, contort, deform, round, crimp, flex, spiral, coil, crinkle, detour, curl, buckle, crook, bow, incline, deflect, double, loop, twine, curve, arch, wind, stoop, lean, waver, zigzag, reel, crumple, meander, circle, swerve, diverge, droop.—*Ant.* STRAIGHTEN, extend, stretch.
bending *a.* twisting, veering, curving, buckling, twining, spiraling, looping, doubling, drooping, leaning, inclining, bowing, arching, curling, winding, stooping, crumpling, waving, wavering.
beneath *a. & prep.* **1.** [Under] below, underneath, in a lower place; see UNDER 1. **2.** [Lower in rank or importance] subject to, inferior to, under; see SUBORDINATE.
beneath contempt *a.* offensive, contemptible, despicable; see OFFENSIVE 2.
benefactor *n.* helper, protector, angel*; see PATRON.
beneficiary *n.* recipient, receiver, inheritor; see HEIR.
benefit *n.* gain, profit, good; see ADVANTAGE.
benefit *v.* serve, profit, avail; see HELP.
bent *a.* curved, warped, hooked, beaked, looped, twined, crooked, bowed, contorted, stooped, doubled over, wilted, drooping, humped, slumped, hunched, humpbacked, bowlegged, inclined; see also TWISTED 1.—*Ant.* STRAIGHT, rigid, erect.
bent *n.* leaning, tendency, propensity; see INCLINATION 1.
bequeath *v.* grant, hand down, pass on; see GIVE 1.
berry *n. Common berries include the following:* raspberry, blackberry, blueberry, loganberry, boysenberry, cranberry, huckleberry, gooseberry, currant, strawberry, mulberry.
berth *n.* place, situation, employment; see JOB 1, PROFESSION 1. —**give a wide berth** keep clear of, evade, stay away from; see AVOID.
beside *a. & prep.* at the side of, at the edge of, adjacent to, next to, adjoining, alongside, near, close at hand, by, with, abreast, side by side, bordering on, neighboring, overlooking, next door to, to one side, nearby, connected with.
besides *a.* in addition to, additionally, moreover, over and above, added to, likewise, further, furthermore, beyond, exceeding, secondly, more than, apart from, extra, in excess of, plus, also, in other respects, exclusive of, with the exception of, as well as, not counting, other than, too, to boot, on top of that, aside from, else.
beside the point *a.* extraneous, not pertaining to, not connected with; see IRRELEVANT.
best *a.* **1.** [Generally excellent] first, greatest, finest, highest, transcendent, prime, premium, supreme, incomparable, crowning, paramount, matchless, unrivaled, unparalleled, second to none, unequaled, inimitable, beyond compare, superlative, foremost, peerless, boss*, tough*, cool*,

first-rate; see also EXCELLENT.—*Ant.* WORST, poorest, lowest. **2.** [Applied especially to actions and persons] noblest, sincerest, most praiseworthy; see NOBLE.

best *n.* first, favorite, choice, finest, top, pick, prime, flower, cream, cream of the crop*. —**all for the best** favorable, fortunate, advantageous; see HELPFUL 1, HOPEFUL 2. —**as best one can** skillfully, ably, capably; see ABLE. —**at best** good, highest, most favorable; see BEST. —**at one's best** well, in one's prime, capable; see ABLE, STRONG 1. —**get or have the best of** outdo, surpass, defeat; see EXCEED. —**make the best of** suffer, tolerate, get by; see ENDURE 2. —**with the best** excellently, well, ably; see ABLE.

best *v.* worst, get the better of, overcome; see DEFEAT 3.

bestow *v.* bequeath, present, offer; see GIVE 1.

bet *n.* gamble, wager, venture, pot, hazard, tossup, stake, speculation, betting, raffle, uncertainty, chance, lottery, game of chance, sweepstakes, risk, ante, long shot*, shot in the dark*.

bet *v.* wager, gamble, stake, bet on, bet against, venture, hazard, trust, play against, speculate, play for, put money down, put money on, risk, chance, make a bet, take a chance, lay down*, buy in on*, lay odds, lay even money*. —**you bet** certainly, by all means, yes indeed; see SURELY, YES.

betray *v.* **1.** [To deliver into the hands of an enemy] delude, trick, double-cross; see DECEIVE. **2.** [To reveal] divulge, disclose, make known; see REVEAL.

betrayal *n.* treason, treachery, disloyalty; see DECEPTION, DISHONESTY.

betrayer *n.* renegade, deceiver, conspirator; see TRAITOR.

better *a.* **1.** [Superior] greater, finer, preferred, bigger, stronger, higher; see also BEST. **2.** [Recovering health] convalescent, improved in health, improving, on the road to recovery, on the mend.—*Ant.* SICK, failing, wasting away. —**for the better** favorable, fortunate, helpful; see HOPEFUL 2. —**get or have the better of** outdo, overcome, defeat; see EXCEED.

better *v.* ameliorate, revamp, refine; see IMPROVE 1.

between *prep.* separating, within, bounded by, amidst, amid, among, in, in between, mid, intervening, in the midst of, in the middle, centrally located, surrounded by, midway, halfway, in the thick; see also AMONG.

between you and me *a.* confidentially, privately, personally; see SECRETLY.

beverage *n.* liquor, refreshment, draft; see DRINK 2.

bewilder *v.* confound, disconcert, puzzle; see CONFUSE.

bewildered *a.* confused, amazed, misguided, lost, astonished, thunderstruck, shocked, muddled, upset, dazed, giddy, dizzy, reeling, puzzled, misled, uncertain, surprised, baffled, disconcerted, appalled, aghast, adrift, at sea, off the track, awed, stupefied, astounded, struck speechless, breathless, befuddled, startled, struck dumb, dumbfounded, dazzled, stunned, electrified, confounded, staggered, petrified, awestruck, flabbergasted, flustered, all balled up*, rattled, up in the air*, stumped* goofy*.

beyond *a. & prep.* on the other side, on the far side, over there, in advance of, away, out of range, a long way off, yonder, past, free of, clear of, farther off, ahead, behind, more remote.—*Ant.* HERE, on this side, nearer.

bias *n.* bent, preference, leaning; see INCLINATION 1.

bias *v.* influence, prejudice, sway; see INFLUENCE.

Bible *n.* the Good Book, God's word, the Word, the Scriptures, the Canon, the Testaments, Sacred History, the Writings of the Apostles and Prophets, Holy Writ, the Holy Bible, the Word of God, Testament.

bibliography *n.* catalog, compilation, list of books; see LIST.

bicker *v.* wrangle, squabble, dispute; see QUARREL.

bicycle *n.* cycle, bike*, two-wheeler*; see VEHICLE.

bid *n.* proposal, proposition, declaration; see SUGGESTION 1.

bid *v.* **1.** [To propose a price for purchase] venture, bid for, submit a bid; see OFFER 1. **2.** [To order] tell, charge, direct; see COMMAND 1.

big *a.* **1.** [Of great size] huge, great, swollen, fat, obese, bloated, overgrown, gross, mammoth, wide, grand, vast, immense, considerable, substantial, massive, extensive, spacious, colossal, gigantic, titanic, monstrous, towering, mighty, magnificent, enormous, giant, tremendous, whopping*.—*Ant.* LITTLE, tiny, small. **2.** [Grown, or partially grown] grown-up, full-grown, adult; see MATURE. **3.** [Important] prominent, significant, influential; see IMPORTANT 1, 2. **4.** [Pompous] presumptuous, pretentious, imperious; see EGOTISTIC. **5.** [Generous] magnanimous, liberal, unselfish; see GENEROUS.

bigot *n.* dogmatist, fanatic, opinionated person, partisan, enthusiast, extremist, diehard, crank*, red-neck*; see also RADICAL.

bigoted *a.* biased, dogmatic, opinionated; see PREJUDICED.

bigotry *n.* intolerance, narrowmindedness, injustice; see FANATICISM, PREJUDICE.

big shot* *n.* big wheel*, bigwig*, big man on campus; see EXECUTIVE.

bill *n.* **1.** [A statement of account] itemized account, statement of indebtedness, request for payment; see STATEMENT 2. **2.** [A piece of paper money] Federal Reserve note, bank note, greenback; see MONEY 1. **3.** [A statement prepared for enactment into law] measure, proposal, piece of legislation; see LAW 3. **4.** [A beak] nib, mandible, projection; see BEAK. **—fill the bill** meet requirements, be satisfactory, serve the purpose; see SATISFY 3.

bill *v.* dun, solicit, render account of indebtedness, draw upon.

billboard *n.* bulletin board, display panel, poster board; see ADVERTISEMENT, ANNOUNCEMENT.

billfold *n.* card case, pocketbook, purse; see WALLET.

bin *n.* storeroom, granary, silo; see CONTAINER.

binary *a.* double, twofold, paired; see DOUBLE.

bind* *n.* dilemma, tight situation, quandary; see PREDICAMENT.

bind *v.* **1.** [To constrain with bonds] truss up, tie up, shackle, fetter, cinch, clamp, chain, leash, constrict, manacle, enchain, lace, pin, restrict, hamper, handcuff, muzzle, hitch, secure, yoke, pin down, fix, strap, tether, bind up, lash down, clamp down on*, hogtie*. **2.** [To hold together or in place] secure, attach, adhere; see FASTEN. **3.** [To obligate] oblige, necessitate, compel; see FORCE. **4.** [To dress] treat, dress, bandage; see HEAL. **5.** [To join] unite, put together, connect; see JOIN 1.

binding *a.* obligatory, requisite, required; see NECESSARY.

binding *n.* **1.** [The act of joining] merging, coupling, junction; see UNION 1. **2.** [Anything used to bind] tie, adhesive, binder; see FASTENER. **3.** [A cover] wrapper, jacket, book cover; see COVER 1.

biography *n.* life story, saga, memoir, journal, experiences, autobiography, life, adventures, life history, confessions, personal anecdote, profile, sketch, biographical account; see also RECORD 1, STORY.

biological *a.* organic, life, living, zoological, botanical, concerning life.

biology *n.* science of organisms, ecology, natural science, natural history, nature study, life science; see also SCIENCE 1.

bird *n.* *Common birds include the following:* sparrow, starling, robin, blue jay, hawk, meadow lark, owl, vulture, buzzard, turkey buzzard, woodpecker, cardinal, kingfisher, canary, chickadee, swallow, skylark, nightingale, nuthatch, whippoorwill, thrush, bluebird, cuckoo, bobolink, wren, gull, eagle, osprey, blackbird, dove, duck, goose, pheasant, chicken, parakeet, crane, heron, mockingbird, auk. **—eat like a bird** fast, starve, restrain one's appetite; see DIET. **—for the birds*** ridiculous, absurd, useless; see STUPID, WORTHLESS.

birth *n.* delivery, parturition, nativity, beginning, blessed event*, visit from the stork*.—*Ant.* DEATH, decease, demise. **—give birth to** bring forth, have a child, reproduce; see PRODUCE 1.

birthday *n.* natal day, name day, celebration; see ANNIVERSARY.

biscuit *n.* cracker, wafer, roll; see BREAD.

bishop *n.* father, archbishop, primate; see MINISTER 1, PRIEST.

bit *n.* **1.** [A small quantity] piece, fragment, crumb, dot, particle, jot, trifle, mite, iota, whit, splinter, parcel, portion, droplet, trickle, driblet, morsel, pinch, snip, shred, atom, speck, molecule, shard, chip, fraction, sliver, segment, section, lump, slice, shaving, sample, specimen, scale, flake, excerpt, scrap, part, division, share, trace, item, chunk, paring, taste, mouthful, stub, butt, stump, a drop in the bucket*, peanuts*, chicken feed*, gob*, hunk*. **2.** [A small degree] jot, minimum, inch, hairbreadth, trifle, iota, mite, fraction, tolerance, margin, whisker*, hair*, skin of one's teeth. **—do one's bit** participate, share, do one's share; see JOIN 2. **—every bit** wholly, altogether, entirely; see COMPLETELY.

bite *n.* **1.** [What one takes in the mouth at one time] mouthful, chew, taste, spoonful, forkful, morsel, nibble. **2.** [The result of being bitten] wound, sting, laceration; see INJURY. **3.** [A quick meal] snack, nibble, brunch; see FOOD.

bite *v.* **1.** [To seize or sever with the teeth] snap, gnaw, sink one's teeth in, nip, nibble, chew, mouth, gulp, worry, taste, masticate, clamp, champ, munch, bite into, crunch, mangle, chaw*; see also EAT 1, TASTE 1. **2.** [To be given to biting] snap, be vicious, attack; see HURT. **3.** [To cut or corrode] rot, decay, decompose; see RUST. **—put the bite on*** pressure, ask for a loan, touch*; see BORROW.

biting *a.* **1.** [Acidulous] sharp, keen, tangy; see SOUR. **2.** [Sarcastic] caustic, acrimonious, bitter; see SARCASTIC.

bitten *a.* chewed, torn, lacerated, slashed, gulped, gnawed, nibbled, tasted, devoured, eaten, stung, pierced, mangled, punctured, cut, ripped.

bitter *a.* **1.** [Acrid] astringent, acid, tart; see SOUR. **2.** [Intense] sharp, harsh, severe; see INTENSE. **3.** [Sarcastic] acrimonious, caustic, biting; see SARCASTIC.

bitterness *n.* tartness, piquancy, pungency, acidity, sourness, acridity, brackishness, brininess.

bizarre *a.* odd, fantastic, grotesque; see UNUSUAL 2.

blab *v.* disclose, tell, divulge; see REVEAL.

blabber *v.* chatter, prattle, gabble; see BABBLE.

black *a.* **1.** [Opposite to white] dark, blackish, raven, coal-black, dusky, dingy, murky, inklike, somber, swarthy, swart, jet, inky, ebony, pitch-black, black as coal, sooty, gunmetal, flat black, jet black, black as the ace of spades*, black as night*.—*Ant.* WHITE, colored, colorful. **2.** [Without light] gloomy, shadowy, clouded; see DARK 1. **3.** [Negroid] colored, African, black-skinned; see BLACK *n.* 2.

black *n.* **1.** [A chromatic color least resembling white] carbon, darkest gray, jet, sable, ebony, blackness.—*Ant.* WHITE, blond, brightness. **2.** [A Negro] colored person, negro, African, Afro-American, African-American. —**in the black** successful, lucratively, gainfully; see PROFITABLY.

blacken *v.* darken, deepen, make black; see SHADE 2.

black magic *n.* sorcery, witchcraft, necromancy; see MAGIC 1, 2.

blackmail *n.* hush money, tribute, protection*; see BRIBE.

blackmail *v.* extort, exact, coerce; see BRIBE, FORCE.

blackness *n.* gloom, duskiness, murkiness; see DARKNESS 1.

black out *v.* **1.** [To delete] rub out, eradicate, blot out; see CANCEL, ERASE. **2.** [To faint] pass out, lose consciousness, swoon; see FAINT. **3.** [To darken] put out the lights, make dark, cause a blackout in; see SHADE 2.

blade *n.* **1.** [A cutting instrument] edge, brand, sword; see KNIFE. **2.** [A relatively long leaf] frond, spear, flag; see LEAF.

blame *n.* disapproval, condemnation, denunciation, disparagement, depreciation, opposition, abuse, disfavor, objection, reproach, criticism, repudiation, reprimand, invective, slur, accusation, reproof, attack, chiding, rebuke, impeachment, complaint, diatribe, tirade, charge, indictment, recrimination, arraignment, implication, calumny, frowning upon.—*Ant.* PRAISE, commendation, appreciation. —**be to blame** guilty, at fault, culpable; see WRONG 2.

blame *v.* charge, condemn, criticize, arraign, challenge, involve, attack, brand, implicate, arrest, sue, prosecute, slander, impeach, bring to trial, connect with, indict, impute, put the finger on*, smear*, point the finger at*, bring home to.

blameless *a.* faultless, not guilty, inculpable; see INNOCENT 1.

bland *a.* flat, dull, insipid; see TASTELESS 1.

blank *a.* white, clear, virgin, fresh, plain, empty, untouched, pale, new, spotless, vacant, hollow, meaningless.

blank *n.* **1.** [An empty space] void, hollow, hole, cavity, vacancy, womb, gulf, nothingness, hollowness, abyss, opening, vacuum, gap, interval; see also EMPTINESS. **2.** [A form] questionnaire, data sheet, information blank; see FORM 5. —**draw a blank** be unable to remember, lose one's memory, disremember*; see FORGET.

blanket *n.* quilt, robe, comforter, featherbed, throw, electric blanket, thermal blanket, rug, mat, cloak.

blanket *v.* envelop, conceal, bury; see COVER 1.

blank out *v.* delete, black out, cross out; see CANCEL, ERASE.

blast *n.* **1.** [An explosion] burst, eruption, detonation; see EXPLOSION. **2.** [A loud sound] roar, din, bang; see NOISE 1. **3.** [An explosive charge] gunpowder, TNT, dynamite; see EXPLOSIVE. —**(at) full blast** at full speed, rapidly, quickly; see FAST 1.

blast *v.* blow up, dynamite, detonate; see EXPLODE.

blast off *v.* rocket, climb, soar up; see RISE 1.

blaze *n.* conflagration, combustion, burning; see FIRE.

blaze *v.* flame, flash, flare up; see BURN.

bleach *v.* blanch, wash out, whiten; see FADE.

bleak *a.* dreary, desolate, bare, cheerless, wild, exposed, barren, blank, disheartening, weary, melancholy, lonely, flat, somber, distressing, depressing, comfortless, joyless, uninviting, dull, sad, mournful, monotonous, waste, gloomy, dismal, unsheltered, unpopulated, desert, deserted, scorched, stony, burned over, bulldozed, cleared, frozen.—*Ant.* GREEN, verdant, fruitful.

bleed *v.* lose blood, shed blood, be bleeding, hemorrhage, gush, spurt, be bled, open a vein, draw blood; see also FLOW.

blemish *n.* flaw, defect, stain, spot, smudge, imperfection, disfigurement, defacement, blot, blur, chip, taint, tarnish, smirch, stigma, brand, deformity, dent, discoloration, mole, pock, blister, birthmark, wart, scar, impurity, speckle, bruise, freckle, pimple, patch, lump.—*Ant.* PERFECTION, flawlessness, purity.

blench *v.* flinch, quail, shrink back, wince.

blend *n.* combination, compound, amalgam; see MIXTURE 1.

blend *v.* combine, mingle, compound; see MIX 1.

bless *v.* baptize, canonize, glorify, honor, dedicate, make holy, pronounce holy, exalt, give benediction to, absolve, anoint, ordain, hallow, consecrate, beatify, sanctify, enshrine, offer, render acceptable to, sacrifice, commend.

blessed *a.* **1.** [Marked by God's favor, especially in heaven] saved, redeemed, glorified, translated, exalted, rewarded, resurrected, sanctified, glorious, beatified, holy, spiritual, religious.—*Ant.* DOOMED, lost, accursed. **2.**

[Consecrated] sacred, dedicated, sanctified; see DIVINE.

blessing *n.* **1.** [Benediction] commendation, sanctification, laying on of hands, absolution, baptism, unction, consecration, Eucharist.—*Ant.* CURSE, damnation, anathema. **2.** [Anything that is very welcome] boon, benefit, good, advantage, help, asset, good fortune, stroke of luck, godsend, windfall, miracle, manna from heaven.—*Ant.* NUISANCE, obstacle, disadvantage.

blight *n.* disease, withering, mildew; see DECAY.

blight *v.* decay, spoil, ruin; see SPOIL.

blind *a.* **1.** [Without sight] sightless, unseeing, eyeless, blinded, visionless, in darkness, dim-sighted, groping, deprived of sight, sunblind, undiscerning, stone-blind, moonblind, blind as a bat.—*Ant.* OBSERVANT, perceptive, discerning. **2.** [Without looking] obtuse, unseeing, by guesswork, by calculation, with instruments; see also BLINDLY, UNAWARE. **3.** [Without passage] obstructed, blocked, without egress; see TIGHT 2, 3. **4.** [Random] chance, accidental, unplanned; see AIMLESS.

blind *v.* darken, shadow, dim; see SHADE 2.

blindly *a.* at random, wildly, in all directions, frantically, heedlessly, carelessly, recklessly, passionately, thoughtlessly, impulsively, inconsiderately, willfully, unreasonably, without rhyme or reason, senselessly, instinctively, madly, pell-mell, purposelessly, aimlessly, indiscriminately.—*Ant.* CAREFULLY, directly, considerately.

blindness *n.* sightlessness, stone blindness, purblindness, myopia, astigmatism, night blindness, snow blindness, color blindness.—*Ant.* SIGHT, vision, seeing.

blind spot *n.* oversight, failing, unseen area; see FAULT 1, WEAKNESS 1.

blink *v.* **1.** [To wink rapidly] flicker, bat one's eyes, flutter one's eyelids; see WINK. **2.** [To twinkle] glimmer, flash on and off, shimmer; see SHINE 1.

bliss *n.* joy, rapture, ecstasy; see HAPPINESS.

blister *n.* vesicle, sac, weal, welt, blood blister, water blister, second-degree burn; see also SORE.

blister *v.* scald, irritate, mark; see HURT.

blizzard *n.* snowstorm, tempest, blast; see STORM.

bloc *n.* cabal, group, ring; see FACTION.

block *n.* **1.** [A mass, usually with flat surfaces] slab, chunk, piece, square, cake, cube, slice, segment, loaf, clod, bar, hunk. **2.** [The area between streets] vicinity, square, lots; see NEIGHBORHOOD. **3.** [The distance of the side of a city block] street, city block, intersection; see DISTANCE 3. **4.** [An obstruction] hindrance, bar, obstacle; see BARRIER. **—knock someone's block off*** thrash, hit, beat up*; see BEAT 1.

block *v.* **1.** [To impede] interfere with, prevent, close off; see HINDER. **2.** [In sports, to impede a play] throw a block, tackle, check; see STOP 1.

blockade *n.* barricade, encirclement, bar; see BARRIER.

blockhead *n.* nitwit, fool, imbecile; see FOOL.

block out *v.* **1.** [To obscure] conceal, screen, cover; see HIDE 1. **2.** [To plan] outline, sketch, chart; see PLAN 2.

block up *v.* obstruct, barricade, dam; see BAR 1.

blond *a.* fair, fair-skinned, pale, light, lily-white, white-skinned, creamy, whitish, milky, albino, pearly, platinum, gray-white, towheaded, snowy, light-haired, golden-haired, fair-haired, yellow-haired, sandy-haired, ash-blond, bleached, strawberry-blond, peroxide-blond*.

blood *n.* life's blood, heart's blood, vital fluid, vital juices, gore, sanguine fluid. **—bad blood** malice, rancor, feud; see ANGER, HATRED. **—in cold blood** cruelly, intentionally, indifferently; see DELIBERATELY. **—make someone's blood boil** disturb, infuriate, agitate; see ENRAGE. **—make someone's blood run cold** terrify, horrify, scare; see FRIGHTEN.

bloodless *a.* pallid, wan, anemic; see PALE 1.

bloodshed *n.* slaughter, butchery, gore; see BATTLE, MURDER.

bloodshot *a.* inflamed, streaked, red; see BLOODY 1.

bloody *a.* **1.** [Showing blood] bleeding, bloodstained, blood-spattered, gaping, unstaunched, grisly, crimson, open, wounded, dripping blood, raw, blood-soaked.—*Ant.* WHOLE, unhurt, uninjured. **2.** [Fiercely fought] savage, heavy, murderous; see CRUEL.

bloom *n.* blossom, floweret, efflorescence; see FLOWER.

bloom *v.* flower, burst into bloom, open, bud, prosper, grow, wax, bear fruit, thrive, germinate, flourish, be in health, blossom, come out in flower, be in flower.

blooming *a.* flowering, blossoming, in flower; see BUDDING, GROWING.

blossom *n.* bloom, floweret, bud; see FLOWER.

blossom *v.* flower, blow, burst into blossom; see BLOOM.

blossoming *n.* blooming, flowering, budding; see BUDDING, GROWING.

blot *n.* spot, stain, smudge; see BLEMISH.

blot *v.* smudge, blotch, soil; see DIRTY.

blot out *v.* **1.** [To mark out] deface, cross out, scratch out, delete; see also CANCEL. **2.** [To obscure] darken, blur, shroud; see SHADE 2.

blouse *n.* pullover, overblouse, slipover; see CLOTHES, SHIRT.

blow *n.* hit, strike, swing, bump, wallop, rap, bang, whack, thwack, cuff, box, uppercut, knock, clout, slam, bruise, swipe, kick, stroke, punch, jab, gouge, lunge, thrust, swat, poke, prod, slap, the old one-two*, belt*, lick*, crack*, kayo*, K.O.*.

blow *v.* **1.** [To send forth air rapidly] puff, blast, pant, fan, whiff, whisk, whisper, puff away, exhale, waft, breathe, whistle. **2.** [To carry on the wind] waft, flutter, bear, whisk, drive, fling, whirl, flap, flip, wave, buffet, sweep. **3.** [To play a wind instrument] pipe, toot, mouth; see PLAY 3. **4.** [To sound when blown] trumpet, vibrate, blare; see SOUND. **5.** [To give form by inflation] inflate, swell, puff up, pump up; see also FILL 1. **6.** [*To fail] miss, flounder, miscarry; see FAIL 1. **7.** [*To spend] lay out, pay out, waste, squander; see also SPEND.

blow a fuse* *v.* rant, throw a tantrum, become enraged; see RAGE 1.

blowing *a.* blasting, puffing, fanning, panting, whisking, breathing, gasping, fluttering, flapping, waving, streaming, whipping, drifting, tumbling, gliding, straining; see also FLYING.—*Ant.* FALLING, standing still, hovering.

blown *a.* buffeted, fluttered, fanned; see BLOWING.

blowout *n.* eruption, blast, detonation, tear, break, puncture, rupture, leak, gap, seam, flat tire, flat.

blow out *v.* **1.** [To extinguish] put out, dampen, snuff; see EXTINGUISH. **2.** [To burst] shatter, erupt, rupture; see EXPLODE.

blow up *v.* **1.** [To fill] pump up, puff up, swell, inflate; see also FILL 1. **2.** [To explode] erupt, rupture, go off; see EXPLODE. **3.** [To destroy with explosives] bomb, dynamite, detonate; see ATTACK, DESTROY. **4.** [*To lose one's temper] become enraged, rave, lose self-control; see RAGE 1.

blue *a. & n.* **1.** [One of the primary colors] *Tints and shades of blue include the following:* indigo, sapphire, turquoise, lapis lazuli, aquamarine, blue-black, azure, sky-blue, blue-green; royal, Prussian, navy, powder, baby, cobalt, Chinese, robin's egg, pale, light, dark, deep, livid, electric, etc., blue; see also COLOR. **2.** [Despondent] depressed, moody, melancholy; see SAD 1. **—once in a blue moon** rarely, infrequently, once in a while; see SELDOM. **—out of the blue** without warning, unpredicted, unforeseen; see UNEXPECTED.

blues *n.pl.* **1.** [A state of despondency; *often with "the"*] depressed spirits, melancholy, dejection; see GLOOM. **2.** [Rhythmic lamentation in a minor key] dirge, lament, torch song; see MUSIC 1.

bluff *n.* **1.** [A bank] cliff, precipice, steep; see HILL, MOUNTAIN 1. **2.** [A trick] ruse, deception, delusion; see TRICK 1.

bluff *v.* fool, mislead, trick; see DECEIVE.

blunder *n.* mistake, lapse, oversight; see ERROR.

blunt *a.* **1.** [Dull] unsharpened, unpointed, round; see DULL 1. **2.** [Abrupt] brusque, curt, bluff; see RUDE 2.

blur *v.* obscure, blur, blear; see SHADE 2.

blurt out *v.* speak unthinkingly, jabber, utter; see TALK 1.

blush *v.* change color, flush, redden, turn red, glow, have rosy cheeks.

blushing *a.* coloring, dyeing, staining, reddening, turning red, flushing, glowing, changing color, burning, red as a rose, rosy-red, with burning cheeks*.

bluster *v.* brag, swagger, strut; see BOAST.

board *n.* **1.** [A piece of thin lumber] plank, lath, strip; see LUMBER. **2.** [Meals] food, fare, provisions; see FOOD, MEAL 2. **3.** [A body of persons having specific responsibilities] jury, council, cabinet; see COMMITTEE. **—across the board** general, universal, common; see UNIVERSAL 2. **—go by the board** be lost, go, vanish; see FAIL 1. **—on board** present, in transit, en route; see ABOARD.

board *v.* **1.** [Cover] plank, tile, paper; see COVER 1. **2.** [Go aboard] embark, cast off, go on board ship; see LEAVE 1. **3.** [Take care of] lodge, room, accommodate; see FEED.

boast *n.* brag, vaunt, source of pride, pretension, self-satisfaction, bravado.

boast *v.* gloat, triumph, swagger, bully, exult, show off, vaunt, swell, brag, strut, bluff, flaunt, bluster, flourish, blow*, sound off*, crow, pat oneself on the back*, blow one's own trumpet*, attract attention.—*Ant.* APOLOGIZE, humble oneself, admit defeat.

boastful *a.* bragging, pretentious, bombastic; see EGOTISTIC.

boat *n.* *Types of small boats include the following:* sailboat, rowboat, shell, scull, kayak, dugout, canoe, scow, raft, launch, motorboat, dory, catboat, tartan, hydrofoil, speedboat, yawl, sloop, cutter, ketch, schooner, lifeboat, barge, punt, outrigger, dinghy, racer, hydroplane, catamaran, skiff, gondola, longboat, war canoe, flatboat, riverboat, canal boat. **—in the same boat** in the same situation, in a similar situation, in the same condition, concurrently; see also TOGETHER 2. **—miss the boat*** miss, fall short, neglect; see FAIL 1. **—rock the boat*** upset, disturb, distort; see CONFUSE.

bobsled *n.* sleigh, coaster, toboggan; see SLED.

bodily *a.* carnal, fleshly, gross, somatic, solid, physical, unspiritual, tangible, material, substantial, human, natural, normal, organic; see also BIOLOGICAL, PHYSICAL 1.

body *n.* **1.** [The human organism] frame, physique, form, figure, shape, make, carcass*, build, make-up. **2.** [A corpse] cadaver, *corpus delecti* (Latin), dust, clay, carcass*, dead body, relics, the dead, the deceased, mummy, skeleton, ashes, carrion, bones, remains, cold meat*, stiff*, goner*. **3.** [The central portion of an object] chassis, basis, groundwork, frame, fuselage, assembly, trunk, hull, bed, box, skeleton, scaffold, anatomy, bones*, guts*. **4.** [Individuals having an organization] society, group, party; see ORGANIZATION 2. **5.** [A unified or organized mass] reservoir, supply, variety; see COLLECTION. —**keep body and soul together** stay alive, endure, earn a living; see SURVIVE 1.

boil *v.* steep, seethe, stew, bubble, simmer, steam, parboil, boil over, evaporate; see also COOK.

boil down *v.* condense, summarize, sum up; see DECREASE 2, SUMMARIZE.

boiling *a.* stewing, steeping, percolating, steaming, bubbling, seething, simmering, evaporating, boiling over; see also COOKING.

boisterous *a.* tumultuous, uproarious, noisy; see LOUD 2, RUDE 2.

bold *a.* **1.** [Courageous] intrepid, fearless, daring; see BRAVE. **2.** [Impertinent] brazen, audacious, presumptuous; see RUDE 2. **3.** [Prominent] strong, clear, plain; see DEFINITE 2.

boldly *a.* **1.** [*Said of animate beings*] impetuously, headlong, intrepidly, fearlessly, recklessly, courageously, dauntlessly, daringly, valiantly, stoutly, resolutely, brazenly, firmly.—*Ant.* COWARDLY, fearfully, cravenly. **2.** [*Said of inanimate objects*] prominently, conspicuously, saliently, sharply, clearly, plainly, openly, abruptly, steeply, eminently, vividly, strongly, palpably, commandingly, compellingly, showily.—*Ant.* VAGUELY, inconspicuously, unobtrusively.

boldness *n.* audacity, self-reliance, hardihood; see COURAGE.

bolster *v.* prop, hold up, reinforce, sustain; see also SUPPORT 1, 2.

bolt *n.* staple, brad, nut, skewer, peg, rivet, pin, spike, stud, coupling, key, pin, pipe; see also NAIL, SCREW.

bomb *n.* weapon, high explosive, charge; see EXPLOSIVE. *Types of bombs include the following:* incendiary, multiple warhead, high explosive, demolition glider, time, smoke, delayed action, antipersonnel bomb; atom bomb, atomic bomb, A-bomb, cobalt bomb, hydrogen bomb, H-bomb, torpedo, depth charge, cherry bomb, hand grenade, Molotov cocktail*, stink bomb.

bomb *v.* shell, bombard, torpedo, napalm, blow up, wipe out, blast, attack from the air, zero in on, raid, dive-bomb.

bombing *n.* bombardment, shelling, an attack; see ATTACK.

bond *n.* **1.** [A link] attachment, union, obligation, connection, relation, affinity, affiliation, bond of union, restraint; see also FRIENDSHIP, MARRIAGE, RELATIONSHIP. **2.** [A secured debenture] security, warranty, debenture, certificate, registered bond, government bond, municipal bond, long-term bond, short-term bond. **3.** [Bail] surety, guaranty, warrant; see BAIL.

bondage *n.* servitude, thralldom, subjugation; see SLAVERY 1.

bone *n.* *Bones of the human body include the following:* cranium, skull, frontal bone, temporal bone, parietal bone, occipital bone, cheekbone, mandible, jawbone, spinal column, vertebrae, backbone, rib cage, clavicle, collarbone, shoulder blade, humerus, radius, ulna, carpal, metacarpal, phalanges, pelvis, illium, hipbone, femur, thighbone, patella, kneecap, tibia, shinbone, fibula, tarsal, metatarsal. —**feel in one's bones** be convinced, expect, be sure; see TRUST 1. —**have a bone to pick*** have a complaint, be angry, express an objection; see COMPLAIN. —**make no bones*** confess, reveal, expose; see ADMIT 2.

bonus *n.* gratuity, reward, additional compensation; see GIFT 1, TIP 2.

bony *a.* emaciated, skinny, scrawny; see THIN 2.

book *n.* publication, work, volume, booklet, pamphlet, reprint, preprint, offprint, hardcover, text, edition, brochure, folio, copy, monograph, writing, scroll, periodical, magazine, paperback. *Kinds of books include the following:* manual, handbook, reference book, children's book, atlas, cookbook, guidebook, story book, song book, trade book, textbook, workbook, hymnbook, Bible, treatise, tract. —**by the book** according to the rules, properly, correctly; see WELL 3. —**in one's book** in one's opinion, for oneself, to one's mind; see PERSONALLY 2. —**in the book** practiced, done, established, prevalent; see also KNOWN 2. —**know like a book** understand, comprehend, be aware of; see KNOW 1. —**one for the books*** source of amazement, shock, novelty; see SURPRISE 2. —**on the books** listed, noted, set down; see RECORDED. —**throw the book at*** accuse, charge with every possible offense, be overzealous with; see BLAME.

bookkeeper *n.* controller, comptroller, accountant, auditor; see also CLERK.

boom *n.* **1.** [A loud noise] roar, blast, blare; see NOISE 1. **2.** [Sudden increase, especially sudden prosperity] rush, growth, inflation; see INCREASE.

boom *v.* **1.** [To make a loud sound] roar, reverberate, thunder; see SOUND. **2.** [To increase rapidly] prosper, expand, swell; see GROW 1. —**lower the boom on*** take action against, move against, beat, overcome; see also ATTACK.

boon *n.* benefit, good fortune, help; see BLESSING 2.

boor *n.* peasant, yokel, rustic, lout, clown, bumpkin, churl, oaf, lubber, bear, plowman, lumpkin, gaffer, hick*, rube*, hayseed*, clod, clodhopper.

boorish *a.* awkward, clumsy, churlish; see RUDE 1, 2.

boost *n.* **1.** [Aid] assistance, aid, helping hand; see HELP 1. **2.** [An increase] addition, advance, hike*; see INCREASE.

boost *v.* **1.** [To raise] shove, hoist, advance; see RAISE 1. **2.** [To promote] encourage, support, advertise; see PROMOTE 1, 2. **3.** [To increase] raise, heighten, expand; see INCREASE.

boot *n.* hip-boot, bootie, wader, galosh, laced boot, high shoe, hiking boot, ski boot, cowboy boot, climbing boot, riding boot. **—bet your boots*** be certain, rely on it, trust in it; see DEPEND ON.

booth *n.* stall, counter, nook, corner, pew, berth, compartment, shed, manger, cubbyhole, coop, pen, hut, enclosure, stand, cubicle, box.

bootleg *a.* illegal, unlawful, contraband; see ILLEGAL.

booty *n.* plunder, spoils, winnings, stolen goods, ill-gotten gains, seizure, prize, haul, pickings, loot, take*.

booze* *n.* liquor, alcohol, whiskey; see DRINK 2.

border *n.* **1.** [Edge] hem, end, trim; see DECORATION 2, FRINGE. **2.** [Boundary] frontier, outpost, perimeter; see BOUNDARY, EDGE 1.

border *v.* be adjacent to, adjoin, abut on; see JOIN 3.

bordering *a.* rimming, bounding, neighboring, fringing, edging, lining, verging, connecting, on the edge of; see also NEAR 1.

border on *v.* lie next to, abut, touch; see JOIN 3.

bore *n.* nuisance, pest, tiresome person; see TROUBLE.

bore *v.* **1.** [To pierce by rotary motion] drill, ream, perforate; see PENETRATE. **2.** [To weary] fatigue, tire, put to sleep; see TIRE 2.

bored *a.* wearied, fatigued, jaded, dull, irked, annoyed, bored to death*, in a rut, sick and tired, bored stiff*, bored silly*, fed up*; see also TIRED.—*Ant.* EXCITED, thrilled, exhilarated.

boredom *n.* lack of interest, tiresomeness, apathy, doldrums, listlessness, monotony, tedium, indifference.

boring *a.* tedious, stupid, monotonous; see DULL 3, 4.

born *a.* intrinsic, innate, inherent; see NATURAL 1.

borrow *v.* accept the loan of, obtain the use of, take a loan, go into debt, get temporary use of, use, rent, hire, obtain, give a note for, sponge*, hit up for*, bum*, beg, chisel*, mooch*.—*Ant.* LEND, loan, give back.

borrowed *a.* appropriated, taken, acquired, assumed, adopted, hired, plagiarized, imported, cultivated, imitated.—*Ant.* owned, possessed, titular.

boss *n.* supervisor, manager, administrator; see EXECUTIVE.

botanical *a.* concerning plants, vegetable, floral, arboreal, herbaceous, morphological, cytological, agricultural; see also BIOLOGICAL.

botany *n.* phytology, natural history, study of plant life; see BIOLOGY, SCIENCE.

botch *v.* bungle, spoil, mar, ruin, wreck, mutilate, fumble, distort, blunder, mishandle, do clumsily, muddle, make a mess of, trip, flounder, err, fall down, be mistaken, misjudge, mismanage, miscalculate, misconstrue, misestimate, execute clumsily, do unskillfully, stumble, put one's foot in it*, goof up*, butcher, screw up*, mess up*, put out of whack*; see also FAIL 1.—*Ant.* SUCCEED, fix, do well.

both *a.* the two, both together, the one and the other, the pair, the couple, one as well as the other.

bother *n.* **1.** [Worry] vexation, distress, anxiety; see CARE 2. **2.** [A cause of worry] problem, concern, care; see DIFFICULTY 1, 2, TROUBLE.

bother *v.* **1.** [To take trouble] put oneself out, fret, go out of one's way, make a fuss about, fuss over, take pains, make an effort, exert oneself, concern oneself, be concerned about, worry about. **2.** [To give trouble] plague, vex, annoy, perplex, pester, molest, irritate, irk, provoke, insult, harass, heckle, aggravate, badger, discommode, discompose, mortify, goad, intrude upon, disquiet, pursue, hinder, impede, carp at, scare, exasperate, bore, afflict, taunt, torment, torture, bedevil, browbeat, tease, tantalize, ride, rub the wrong way, pick on, nag, needle*, bug*, get under someone's skin*.—*Ant.* HELP, please, delight.

bothered *a.* annoyed, agitated, disturbed; see TROUBLED.

bothersome *a.* vexatious, vexing, troublesome; see DISTURBING.

bottle *n.* flask, flagon, decanter, cruet, jug, urn, canteen, cruse, jar, gourd, carafe, hip flask, vial, vacuum bottle, glass. **—hit the bottle*** get drunk, imbibe, become an alcoholic; see DRINK 2.

bottom *n.* underside, base, nadir, foot, depths, bed, floor, lowest part, deepest part, sole, ground.—*Ant.* TOP, peak, pinnacle. **—at bottom** fundamentally, basically, actually; see REALLY 1. **—be at the bottom of** originate, be the reason for, activate; see CAUSE. **—bet one's bottom dollar*** bet, risk, wager; see GAMBLE.

bottomless *a.* deep, unfathomable, boundless; see INFINITE.

bottom line* *n.* **1.** [Profits or losses] net income, net loss, net profits; see INCOME, PROFIT 2, LOSS 3. **2.** [Final decision] conclusion, determination, last word; see END 2.

bottoms *n.pl.* low land, marsh, bottomland; see SWAMP.

bough *n.* limb, arm, fork; see BRANCH 2.

bought *a.* purchased, procured, budgeted for, requisitioned, paid for, on order, to be delivered, contracted for, included in the purchase; see also ORDERED 1.—*Ant.* STOLEN, sold, given away.

boulder *n.* stone, slab, crag; see ROCK 2.

boulevard *n.* street, avenue, highway; see ROAD 1.

bounce *v.* ricochet, recoil, glance off, spring back, leap, hop, bolt, vault, skip, bob, buck, jump, bound, jerk up and down, snap back, boomerang, backlash.

bound *a.* **1.** [Literally confined in bonds] fettered, shackled, trussed up, manacled, enchained, handcuffed, hobbled, captive, pinioned, muzzled, in leash, tied up, harnessed, bound hand and foot, lashed fast, pinned down, tethered, picketed, secured, roped, gagged.—*Ant.* FREE, unrestrained, loose. **2.** [Figuratively constrained] impelled, compelled, obliged, obligated, restrained, under compulsion, constrained, forced, coerced, driven, pressed, urged, necessitated, under necessity, made, having no alternative, required.

bound *v.* **1.** [To move in leaps] leap, spring, vault; see JUMP 1. **2.** [To rebound] bounce, ricochet, recoil; see BOUNCE. **3.** [To set limits] restrict, confine, circumscribe; see DEFINE 1. —**out of bounds** off limits, not permitted, restricted; see ILLEGAL.

boundary *n.* outline, border, verge, rim, beginning, end, confine, bounds, radius, terminus, landmark, march, extremity, fence, compass, side, hem, frame, skirt, termination, margin, line, barrier, frontier, outpost, perimeter, parameter, extent, circumference, horizon, periphery, fringe, mark, confines, limit, borderland.

bounded *a.* limited, enclosed, bordered; see SURROUNDED.

boundless *a.* limitless, endless, unlimited; see INFINITE.

bound to *a.* certain to, sure to, destined to; see INEVITABLE.

bounty *n.* prize, premium, bonus; see PAY 1, 2.

bouquet *n.* nosegay, bunch of flowers, garland, vase of flowers, flower arrangement, wreath, spray.

bow *n.* longbow, crossbow, single-piece bow; see WEAPON.

bow *n.* **1.** [Front of a boat] forepart, bowsprit, prow, head, stem, fore; see also FRONT 1. **2.** [A bend from the waist] nod, curtsey, bowing and scraping; see ACKNOWLEDGMENT. —**take a bow** accept praise, be congratulated, feel honored; see BEND.

bow *v.* **1.** [To bend] curtsey, stoop, dip; see BEND. **2.** [To submit] surrender, acquiesce, capitualate; see YIELD 1.

bowels *n.pl.* viscera, entrails, guts; see INSIDES.

bowl *n.* vessel, tureen, pot, saucer, crock, jar, urn, pitcher, basin, casserole, boat; see also CONTAINER, DISH.

bowling *n.* ninepins, tenpins, boccie; see SPORT 3.

bow out *v.* withdraw, resign, quit; see ABANDON 1.

box *n.* receptacle, crate, carton; see CONTAINER.

box *v.* **1.** [To enclose in a box] confine, package, crate; see PACK 2. **2.** [To fight for sport] spar, punch, slug; see FIGHT.

boxer *n.* pugilist, fighter, prizefighter; see FIGHTER 1.

boxing *n.* pugilism, prizefighting, the fights*; see SPORT 3.

boy *n.* lad, youth, stripling, fellow, schoolboy, youngster, whippersnapper, male child, junior, little gentleman; see also CHILD.

boycott *v.* withhold patronage, hold aloof from, ostracize; see AVOID, STRIKE 2.

boyfriend *n.* young man, beau*, companion, steady*, lover, sweetheart, suitor, paramour, main man*, old man*.

boyhood *n.* schoolboy days, formative period, adolescence; see CHILDHOOD, YOUTH 1.

boyish *a.* puerile, boylike, adolescent; see CHILDISH, YOUNG 1.

boy scout *n.* cub scout, explorer scout, troop member; see SCOUT 2.

brace *n.* prop, bolster, stay, support, lever, beam, girder, block, rib, buttress, reinforcement, bearing, upholder, bracket, strengthener, band, bracer, stirrup, arm, splint, boom, bar, staff, rafter, jack, crutch.

brace *v.* prop, bolster, hold up; see SUPPORT 1.

bracelet *n.* arm band, ornament, bangle; see JEWELRY.

brag *v.* swagger, exult, gloat; see BOAST.

braggart *n.* boaster, blowhard*, windbag*, trumpeter, swaggerer, strutter, peacock, blusterer, bragger, know-it-all*.

brain *n.* **1.** [The organ of intelligence] cerebrum, gray matter, brain cells; see HEAD 1. **2.** [The intelligence] intellect, genius, mentality; see MIND 1. **3.** [*A very intelligent person] academician, scholar, egghead*; see INTELLECTUAL. —**have on the brain** be obsessed with, be involved with, fuss over, stew about; see also BOTHER 2.

brainwash* *v.* indoctrinate, instill, catechize; see CONVINCE, INFLUENCE, TEACH.

brake *n.* check, hamper, curb, deterrent, obstacle, damper, hindrance, retarding device, governor.

bramble *n.* brier, thorn, burr, stinging nettle, prickly shrub, goose grass, thistle, shrub, bramble bush, hedge.

branch *n.* **1.** [A part, usually of secondary importance] member, office, bureau; see DIVISION 2. **2.** [A secondary shoot] bough, limb, offshoot, sprig, twig, bud, arm, fork, growth.

branch off *v.* diverge, separate, part; see DIVIDE.

branch out *v.* expand, extend, add to; see GROW 1, INCREASE.

brand *n.* stigma, scar, sear, welt, range brand, earmark, owner's mark.

brand *v.* blaze, stamp, imprint; see MARK 1.

brandish *v.* flourish, gesture, warn; see THREATEN.

brass *n.* **1.** [An alloy of copper and zinc] copper alloy, pinchbeck, brassware, yellow metal. **2.** [*High-ranking officials] officers, front office*, brass hats; see OFFICER 3. **3.** [*Impudence] effrontery, impertinence, audacity; see RUDENESS.

brat *n.* impudent child, unruly child, youngster, kid*; see also CHILD.

brave *a.* fearless, daring, dauntless, valiant, intrepid, undaunted, undismayed, confident, unabashed, chivalrous, valorous, heroic, bold, imprudent, adventurous, reckless, foolhardy, dashing, venturesome, forward, audacious, gallant, resolute, militant, defiant, hardy, unafraid, stout, stout-hearted, lion-hearted, manly, firm, plucky, high-spirited, unshrinking, strong, stalwart, unflinching, game, unyielding, indomitable, unconquerable, spunky*, nervy, gutsy*.—*Ant.* COWARDLY, timid, craven.

bravely *a.* courageously, fearlessly, valiantly, boldly, daringly, dauntlessly, intrepidly, heroically, gallantly, hardily, stoutly, manfully, staunchly, with courage, with fortitude, resolutely, valorously, spiritedly, firmly, audaciously, chivalrously, indomitably, with guts*, like a man*.—*Ant.* COWARDLY, fearfully, timidly.

bravery *n.* valor, intrepidity, fearlessness; see COURAGE, STRENGTH.

brawl *n.* fuss, squabble, riot; see FIGHT 1.

breach *n.* violation, infringement, transgression; see CRIME, VIOLATION.

bread *n.* loaf, baked goods, the staff of life. *Types of bread include the following:* whole wheat, rye, salt-rising, leavened, unleavened, corn, sourdough, raisin, pumpernickel, French, white, black, dark brown, Boston brown, potato, hardtack. *Breadlike foods include the following:* spoon bread, cake, dumpling, turnover, bun, cookie, English muffin, corn bread, scone, shortbread, Indian bread. —**break bread** partake, have a meal, indulge; see EAT 1. —**know which side one's bread is buttered on** be prudent, save, look out for number one*; see UNDERSTAND 1.

breadth *n.* largeness, extent, vastness, compass, magnitude, greatness, extensiveness, scope, broadness, width, comprehensiveness, amplitude; see also SIZE 2.

break *n.* **1.** [The act of breaking] fracture, rift, split, schism, cleavage, breach, rupture, eruption, bursting, failure, division, parting, collapse.—*Ant.* REPAIR, mending, maintenance. **2.** [A pause] intermission, interim, lapse; see PAUSE. **3.** [*Fortunate change or event; *often plural*] good luck, advantage, favorable circumstances; see LUCK 1.

break *v.* **1.** [To start a rupture] burst, split, crack, rend, sunder, sever, fracture, tear, cleave, break into, break through, force open, puncture, split, snap, slash, gash, dissect, slice, disjoin, separate; see also CUT. **2.** [To shatter] smash, shiver, crash, break up, crush, splinter, pull to pieces, burst, break into pieces, break into smithereens*, fall apart, fall to pieces, collapse, break down, come apart, come unglued, go to wrack and ruin, get wrecked, bust*, split up; see also DISINTEGRATE and sense 1. **3.** [To bring to ruin or to an end] demolish, annihilate, eradicate; see DESTROY. **4.** [To happen] come to pass, occur, develop; see HAPPEN 2.

breakable *a.* fragile, delicate, frail; see WEAK 2.

breakage *n.* harm, wreckage, ruined goods; see DAMAGE 2.

breakdown *n.* collapse, stoppage, disruption; see FAILURE 1.

break down *v.* **1.** [To analyze] examine, investigate, dissect; see ANALYZE. **2.** [To malfunction] fail, stop, falter, misfire, give out, go down, crack up*, cease, backfire, conk out*, peter out*, fizzle out*, collapse, go kaput*, come unglued*, run out of gas*.

breakfast *n.* morning meal, first meal of the day, early meal, brunch, breaking the fast; see also MEAL 2.

break in *v.* **1.** [Train] educate, instruct, prepare; see TEACH. **2.** [Intrude] rob, burglarize, trespass; see MEDDLE 2, STEAL.

breaking *a.* bursting, splitting, cracking, rending, sundering, parting, severing, exploding, erupting, shattering, splintering, fracturing, tearing, cleaving, snapping, breaking up, dispersing, separating, smashing, shivering, crashing, splintering, disintegrating, collapsing, caving in, falling, busting*, going to pot*.—*Ant.* STRONG, stable, enduring.

break in on or **upon** *v.* cut in on, intrude, intervene; see INTERRUPT.

break off *v.* end, cease, discontinue; see STOP 2.

break out *v.* **1.** [To start] begin, commence, occur; see BEGIN 2. **2.** [To escape] burst out, flee, depart; see LEAVE 1. **3.** [To erupt] get blemishes, have acne, get a rash, get hives, get pimples.

breakthrough *n.* discovery, finding, invention; see DISCOVERY.

break through *v.* penetrate, force a way, intrude; see PENETRATE.

break up *v.* **1.** [To scatter] disperse, disband, separate; see DISINTEGRATE, DIVIDE. **2.** [To stop] put an end to, halt, terminate; see STOP 2. **3.** [*To distress] hurt, sadden, wound; see HURT. **4.** [*To end relations] discontinue, break off, stop; see END 1.

breakwater *n.* pier, wharf, jetty; see DOCK.

breast *n.* **1.** [The forepart of the body above the abdomen] thorax, heart, bosom; see CHEST 2. **2.** [An enlarged mammary gland or glands] bosom, chest, teat, tit*, nipple, bust, udder, boob*, jug*, knocker*. **—beat one's breast** repent, humble oneself, be sorry; see APOLOGIZE, REGRET 1. **—make a clean breast of** confess, reveal, expose; see ADMIT 2.

breath *n.* inspiration, expiration, inhalation, exhalation, breathing, gasp, sigh, pant, wheeze. **—catch one's breath*** rest, stop, slow down; see PAUSE. **—in the same breath** simultaneously, concurrently, at the same time; see TOGETHER 2. **—out of breath** gasping, choking, out of wind; see BREATHLESS. **—save one's breath*** be quiet, stop talking, never mind; see SHUT UP 1. **—take someone's breath away** thrill, stimulate, invigorate; see EXCITE. **—under one's breath** quietly, in a whisper, murmuring; see WHISPERING.

breathe *v.* respire, use one's lungs, inhale, exhale, draw in, breathe in, breathe out, gasp, pant, wheeze, snort, sigh, take air into one's nostrils, scent, sniff.

breathless *a.* out of breath, winded, spent, exhausted, used up, gasping, choking, windless, wheezing, short-winded, puffing, panting, asthmatic, short of breath, out of wind*.

breed *n.* strain, variety, kind; see RACE 1.

breed *v.* **1.** [To produce] give birth to, deliver, bring forth; see PRODUCE 1. **2.** [To cause] bring about, effect, produce; see BEGIN 1.

breeze *n.* draft, gust, blast; see WIND. **—in a breeze*** effortlessly, readily, simply; see EASILY. **—shoot the breeze*** converse, chat, chatter; see TALK 1.

brew *n.* concoction, preparation, distillation, compound, broth, liquor, blend, beer, ale; see also DRINK 1, 2.

brew *v.* concoct, ferment, mull; see COOK.

bribe *n.* fee, reward, hush money, lure, gift, graft, compensation, remuneration, protection, bait, tip, blackmail, price, present, gratuity.

bribe *v.* corrupt, get to, reward, tip, coax, hire, entice, tempt, pervert, lure, buy, influence, buy off, fix*.

brick *n.* cube, chunk, section, block, slab, cinder block, glass block, adobe brick, building brick, paving stone, floor tile; see also STONE.

bridal *a.* nuptial, marriage, wedding, matrimonial, marital, conjugal, wedded.

bride *n.* spouse, mate, partner; see WIFE.

bridegroom *n.* groom, mate, spouse; see HUSBAND.

bridge *n.* **1.** [An elevated structure] viaduct, platform, catwalk, gangplank, drawbridge, trestle, aqueduct, scaffold. *Types of bridges include the following:* arch, pier, girder, concrete arch, suspension, cantilever, bascule, pontoon, swing, floating, covered, cable-stayed, steel arch, lift, truss. **2.** [A game at cards] contract bridge, auction bridge, duplicate bridge; see GAME 1. **3.** [A link] connection, bond, tie; see JOINT 1, LINK.

bridge *v.* connect, span, link; see JOIN 1.

brief *a.* **1.** [Abrupt] hasty, curt, blunt; see RUDE 2. **2.** [Short in time] short-term, fleeting, concise; see SHORT 2.

briefing *n.* instruction, training session, orientation; see INTRODUCTION 4, PREPARATION 1.

briefly *a.* shortly, curtly, abruptly, quickly, hastily, hurriedly, momentarily, fleetingly, suddenly, temporarily, in passing, casually, lightly, briskly, in brief, in outline, in a few words, in a capsule, in a nutshell.

bright *a.* **1.** [Shining or vivid] gleaming, shiny, glittering, luminous, lustrous, burnished, polished, sparkling, mirrorlike, glowing, flashing, scintillating, shimmering, incandescent, twinkling, illumined, light, golden, silvery, illuminated, shining, irradiated, glistening, radiant, burning, glaring, beaming, glimmering, splendid, resplendent, brilliant, dazzling, alight, aglow, lighted up, full of light, ablaze, flamelike, moonlit, sunlit, on fire, phosphorescent, blazing, glossy, colored, colorful, tinted, intense, deep, sharp, rich, tinged, hued, touched with color, fresh, clear, ruddy, psychedelic.—*Ant.* DULL, clouded, dark. **2.** [Intelligent] clever, quick, alert; see INTELLIGENT. **3.** [Not rainy] clear, sunny, mild; see FAIR 3. **4.** [Cheerful] lively, vivacious, joyful; see HAPPY.

brighten *v.* **1.** [To become brighter] clear up, lighten, grow calm, improve, grow sunny, glow. **2.** [To make brighter] polish, intensify, lighten; see SHINE 3.

brightly *a.* lustrously, radiantly, splendidly, brilliantly, dazzlingly, sparklingly, glowingly, shinily, gaily, freshly, vividly, colorfully, cleverly, sunnily.—*Ant.* dully, dingily, darkly.

brightness *n.* shine, luster, illumination; see LIGHT 1.

brilliant *a.* 1. [Shining] dazzling, gleaming, sparkling; see BRIGHT 1. 2. [Showing remarkable ability] ingenious, profound, smart; see INTELLIGENT.
brilliantly *a.* 1. [Very brightly] shiningly, radiantly, blazingly; see BRIGHTLY. 2. [With superior intelligence] cleverly, shrewdly, knowledgeably; see INTELLIGENTLY.
brim *n.* margin, rim, border; see EDGE 1.
bring *v.* 1. [To transport] convey, take along, bear; see CARRY 1, PICK UP 6. 2. [To be worth in sale] sell for, earn, bring in; see PAY 2. 3. [To cause] produce, effect, make; see BEGIN 1.
bring about *v.* 1. [To achieve] do, accomplish, realize; see ACHIEVE, SUCCEED 1. 2. [To cause] produce, effect, do; see BEGIN 1, MANAGE 1.
bring around *v.* 1. [To convince] persuade, prove, induce; see CONVINCE. 2. [To revive] restore, refresh, resuscitate; see REVIVE 1.
bring forth *v.* deliver, bear, yield; see PRODUCE 1, 2.
bring home the bacon* *v.* provide for, triumph, achieve; see EARN 2, PROVIDE 1, SUCCEED 1, SUPPORT 3.
bring home to *v.* make clear to, convince, impress upon; see EMPHASIZE.
bring in *v.* 1. [To import] ship in, introduce, import; see CARRY. 2. [To produce] bring as a price, sell for, fetch, go for.
bringing *n.* fetching, carrying, transporting, accompanying, introducing, shipping, bearing, hauling, bringing in, getting, providing, procuring.
bring off *v.* accomplish, realize, execute; see ACHIEVE, SUCCEED 1.
bring on *v.* cause, lead to, provoke; see BEGIN 1.
bring out *v.* 1. [To excite] elicit, arouse, evoke; see EXCITE. 2. [To publish] print, issue, put out; see PUBLISH 1. 3. [To produce a play] present, put on the stage, exhibit; see PERFORM 2. 4. [To intensify] heighten, sharpen, magnify; see EMPHASIZE, INCREASE.
bring to bear *v.* exert, apply, concentrate; see EXERCISE 2, INFLUENCE, USE 1.
bring to one's senses *v.* restore, bring to reason, persuade; see CONVINCE.
bring up *v.* 1. [To rear] educate, teach, train; see RAISE 2, SUPPORT 3. 2. [To discuss] tender, submit, advance; see DISCUSS, PROPOSE 1.
brink *n.* limit, brim, rim; see EDGE 1.
brisk *a.* lively, refreshing, invigorating; see STIMULATING.
briskly *a.* energetically, quickly, brusquely, rapidly, impulsively, nimbly, agilely, dexterously, decisively, firmly, actively, promptly, readily, vigorously, in a lively manner; see also EMPHATICALLY.—*Ant.* SLOWLY, listlessly, sluggishly.
bristle *n.* hair, fiber, quill; see POINT 2.
Britain *n.* Great Britain, United Kingdom, England; see ENGLAND.
British *a.* Anglo-Saxon, Celtic, Brit*; see ENGLISH.
brittle *a.* fragile, crisp, inelastic; see WEAK 2.
broad *a.* 1. [Physically wide] extended, large, extensive, ample, spacious, deep, expansive, immense, wide, roomy, outstretched, thick, widespread, full, stocky.—*Ant.* NARROW, thin, slender. 2. [Wide in range] cultivated, experienced, cosmopolitan; see CULTURED. 3. [Tolerant] progressive, open-minded, unbiased; see LIBERAL.
broadcast *n.* radio program, newscast, telecast; see PERFORMANCE.
broadcast *v.* announce, relay, telephone, send out, telegraph, radio, transmit, televise, telecast, air, put on the air, go on the air, be on the air; see also SEND 2.
broadcasting *n.* radio transmission, announcing, television, airing, putting on a radio program, telecasting, newscasting, transmitting, reporting.
broaden *v.* widen, expand, increase; see GROW 1, INCREASE.
broad-minded *a.* tolerant, progressive, unprejudiced; see LIBERAL.
brochure *n.* handout, circular, pamphlet; see ADVERTISEMENT.
broil *v.* sear, bake, roast; see COOK.
broiler *n.* oven, grill, barbecue; see APPLIANCE.
broke* *a.* bankrupt, out of money, indebted; see RUINED 3. **—go for broke*** gamble, wager, risk everything; see RISK. **—go broke*** become bankrupt, lose everything; be reduced to poverty; see FAIL 4, LOSE 2.
broken *a.* 1. [Fractured] shattered, hurt, ruptured, burst, splintered, smashed, in pieces, collapsed, destroyed, pulverized, crumbled, mutilated, bruised, injured, damaged, rent, split, cracked, mangled, dismembered, fragmentary, disintegrated, crippled, shredded, crushed, gashed, defective.—*Ant.* WHOLE, intact, sound. 2. [Not functioning properly] defective, inoperable, in need of repair, in disrepair, out of order, busted*, gone to pot*, screwed up*, shot*, gone haywire*, on the fritz*, on the blink*, gone to pieces, out of whack*, out of commission; see also FAULTY. 3. [Discontinuous] spasmodic, erratic, intermittent; see IRREGULAR 1, 4. 4. [Incoherent; *said of speech*] muttered, unintelligible, mumbled; see INCOHERENT.
broken-down *a.* shattered, dilapidated, battered; see OLD 2.
brokenhearted *a.* despondent, crushed, grieved; see SAD 1.
brood *n.* flock, offspring, young; see FAMILY, HERD.

brood *v.* **1.** [To hatch] set, cover, incubate, warm, sit; see also PRODUCE 1. **2.** [To nurse one's troubles] think, meditate, grieve, fret, sulk, mope, ponder, consider, muse, deliberate, dwell upon, speculate, daydream, reflect, dream, chafe inwardly, give oneself over to reflections, mull over, eat one's heart out; see also WORRY 2.

brook *n.* creek, stream, streamlet; see RIVER.

broom *n.* sweeper, carpet sweeper, whisk broom, mop, feather duster.

broth *n.* brew, concoction, soup, consommé, purée, bouillon, stock, chowder, gumbo, porridge, hodge-podge, potpourri; see also FOOD, SOUP.

brotherhood *n.* fellowship, equality, kinship, intimacy, relationship, affiliation, association, society, fraternity, family, race, comradeship, camaraderie, friendship, amity.

brotherly *a.* kindly, humane, sympathetic; see FRIENDLY, KIND, LOVING.

browbeat *v.* bully, intimidate, frighten; see THREATEN.

brown *n. Shades and tints of brown include the following:* tan, bay, chestnut, nutbrown, copper-colored, mahogany, bronze, russet, chocolate, cinnamon, hazel, reddish-brown, sorrel, sepia, tawny, ochre, rust-colored, rust, brownish, puce, fawn, liver-colored, beige, dust, drab, coffee, khaki, maroon, cocoa, umber, brick, ginger, light brown, dark brown, auburn, buff; see also COLOR.

brown *v.* toast, scorch, sauté; see COOK, FRY.

browse *v.* skim, peruse, scan, glance at, look through, run through, flip through, look over, survey, inspect loosely, examine cursorily, glance over, check over, run over, go through carelessly, dip into, wander here and there*.

bruise *n.* abrasion, wound, swelling; see BLEMISH.

bruise *v.* beat, injure, wound; see DAMAGE, HURT.

brunet *a.* dark, dark-complexioned, tawny, dusky, brown, tanned, swarthy, dark-haired, dark-skinned.—*Ant.* FAIR, light-skinned, light-complexioned.

brush *n.* **1.** [A brushing instrument] *Varieties include the following:* bristle, fiber, nail, clothes, camel's hair, rotary, paint, tooth, scrubbing, floor, hair, wire, scrub. **2.** [A touch] rub, tap, stroke; see TOUCH 2. **3.** [Underbrush] bush, thicket, undergrowth, second growth, chaparral, cover, brushwood, shrubbery, canebrake, hedge, fern, underwood, scrub, brake.

brush *v.* **1.** [To cleanse by brushing] sweep, whisk, wipe; see CLEAN. **2.** [To touch lightly] stroke, smooth, graze; see TOUCH 1.

brush off* *v.* reject, get rid of, send away; see DISMISS.

brush up on *v.* reread, look over again, review; see STUDY.

brutal *a.* pitiless, harsh, unmerciful; see CRUEL.

brutality *n.* savageness, grossness, unfeelingness; see CRUELTY.

brutally *a.* ruthlessly, cruelly, callously, relentlessly, mercilessly, heartlessly, grimly, viciously, meanly, inhumanly, inhumanely, brutishly, savagely, pitilessly, barbarously, remorselessly, unkindly, wildly, fiercely, hardheartedly, murderously, ferociously, animalistically, demoniacally, diabolically, barbarically, in cold blood.—*Ant.* NICELY, kindly, gently.

bubble *n.* sac, air bubble, balloon, foam, froth, spume, effervescence, lather.

bubble *v.* froth, gurgle, gush, well, trickle, effervesce, boil, percolate, simmer, seep, eddy, ferment, erupt, issue, fester.

bucket *n.* pail, canister, can; see CONTAINER, POT 1. —**kick the bucket*** expire, lose one's life, pass away; see DIE 1.

buckle *n.* clasp, harness, fastening; see FASTENER.

buckle down *v.* apply oneself, attend to, keep one's mind on; see CONCENTRATE 2.

buck up* *v.* cheer, comfort, hearten; see ENCOURAGE.

bud *n.* shoot, embryo, germ; see FLOWER. —**nip in the bud** check, halt, stop; see PREVENT.

budding *a.* maturing, developing, opening, blossoming, bursting forth, putting forth shoots, vegetating, flowering, fresh, pubescent, blooming, promising, young, sprouting, germinating, immature, latent, embryonic, in bud; see also GROWING.

buddy* *n.* peer, companion, pal*; see ASSOCIATE, FRIEND.

budge *v.* stir, change position, shift; see MOVE 1.

budget *n.* estimates, estimated expenses, allocations, accounts, financial statement, financial plan, cost of operation, funds; see also ESTIMATE.

budget *v.* allocate expenditures, balance income and expenses, forecast, allow for, figure in, estimate necessary expenditures; see also ESTIMATE.

bug *n.* **1.** [An insect] beetle, pest, gnat; see INSECT. **2.** [*A microbe] bacillus, disease germ, virus; see GERM. **3.** [*A defect] flaw, fault, imperfection; see BLEMISH, DEFECT. **4.** [*An enthusiast] devotee, zealot, fanatic; see FOLLOWER.

bug* *v.* **1.** [To annoy] irritate, plague, pester; see BOTHER 2, DISTURB. **2.** [To install hidden microphones] spy, overhear, listen in on, wiretap, tap; see also EAVESDROP.

build *v.* create, form, erect, frame, raise, make, manufacture, put together, fit together, fabricate, contrive, assemble, put up, model, hammer together, set up, reconstruct, pile stone on stone, sculpture, fashion, compose, evolve, compile, cast, produce, forge, bring about, devise, carve, weave.—*Ant.* DESTROY, demolish, wreck.

building *n.* edifice, erection, construction, fabrication, house, framework, superstructure, frame, structure, apartment house, barn, castle, church, factory, home, hotel, motel, skyscraper, temple, office building, mosque, mall, store, school; see also ARCHITECTURE.

build on *v.* extend, enlarge, develop; see INCREASE.

build up *v.* **1.** [To increase] strengthen, add to, expand; see INCREASE. **2.** [To construct] make, erect, establish; see BUILD.

built *a.* constructed, fabricated, manufactured, made, put together, produced, assembled, contrived, remodeled, completed, joined, perfected, finished, realized, created; see also FORMED.

bulb *n.* globe, globule, ball, knob, corn, tuber, protuberance, head, bunch, swelling, tumor, nodule.

bulge *n.* swelling, bunch, lump, protuberance, hump, bump, bulb, outgrowth, protrusion, nodule, sagging, growth, prominence, excess, bagginess, appendage, projection, tumor, egg, sac, knob, horn, ridge, wart, promontory.

bulge *v.* puff out, distend, protrude; see SWELL.

bulk *n.* greater part, main part, predominant part, better part, most, majority, plurality, biggest share, greater number, nearly all, body, more than half, best, gross, lion's share.—*Ant.* BIT, remnant, fraction.

bulky *a.* massive, big, huge; see HIGH 1, LARGE 1, LONG 1.

bull *n.* **1.** [The male of various cattle] steer, ox, service bull; see COW. **2.** [*Nonsense] balderdash, rubbish, trash; see NONSENSE 1.

bullet *n.* shell, cartridge, ball, projectile, missile, piece of ammunition, slug, ammo*; see also SHOT 1.

bulletin *n.* release, notice, communiqué; see ANNOUNCEMENT.

bully *n.* ruffian, rowdy, tough; see RASCAL.

bully *v.* tease, domineer, harass; see THREATEN.

bum *n.* hobo, tramp, vagrant; see BEGGAR.

bump *n.* **1.** [A jarring collision] knock, bang, bounce, jar, box, smash, pat, crack, jolt, crash, sideswipe, punch, hit, clap, push, shove, thrust, boost, shock, clash, impact, stroke, rap, tap, slap, clout, jab, jerk, crash, prod, jolt, slam, nudge, buffet, swat*, bash*, wallop*, belt*, bat*, swipe*, thump*, whack*, poke*, clump*, clunk*, sock*, whop*, lick*, smack*, cuff, slug*. **2.** [A swelling] projection, protuberance, knob; see BULGE, LUMP.

bump *v.* **1.** [To collide with] collide, run against, strike; see CRASH 4, HIT 1. **2.** [To make a bumping sound] thud, whack, smack; see SOUND.

bumper *n.* cover, guard, protector; see DEFENSE 2, FENDER.

bun *n.* muffin, biscuit, roll; see BREAD, ROLL 4, PASTRY.

bunch *n.* clump, group, batch, spray, sheaf, tuft, shock, stack, thicket, group, gathering, host, galaxy, bundle, knot, accumulation, collection, mess*, slug*, oodles*.

bundle *n.* packet, parcel, pack; see PACKAGE.

bungle *v.* blunder, fumble, mishandle; see BOTCH, FAIL 1.

bungler *n.* fumbler, lout, blunderer, flounderer, muddler, numskull, featherbrain, dolt, scatterbrain, dunce, clod, ignoramus, idiot, duffer, addlebrain, butterfingers, bonehead*, blockhead*, blunderhead*, goof-off*, clumsy oaf, bull in a china shop*, harebrain*, klutz*.

bungling *a.* clumsy, unskillful, inept; see AWKWARD, INCOMPETENT.

bunk *n.* **1.** [A bed] berth, cot, mattress; see BED 1. **2.** [*Anything untrue, silly, or unreliable] rubbish, rot, hogwash; see NONSENSE 1.

buoy *n.* float, drift, floating marker; see FLOAT.

burden *n.* **1.** [Something carried] cargo, freight, pack; see LOAD 1. **2.** [Anything hard to support or endure] encumbrance, punishment, misery; see DIFFICULTY 2, MISFORTUNE.

burden *v.* weigh down, force, hinder, encumber, overwhelm, hamper, strain, load with, saddle with, handicap, obligate, tax, afflict, vex, try, trouble, pile, bog down, crush, depress, impede, overload, oppress, make heavy, press down.—*Ant.* LIGHTEN, relieve, unload.

burdensome *a.* heavy, oppressive, troublesome; see DIFFICULT 1, 2, DISTURBING.

bureau *n.* **1.** [Committee] commission, authority, board; see COMMITTEE. **2.** [Chest of drawers] highboy, dresser, cabinet; see CHEST 1, FURNITURE.

bureaucracy *n.* the Establishment, the authorities, the system; see GOVERNMENT 1, 2.

burglar *n.* thief, housebreaker, robber; see CRIMINAL.

burglary *n.* housebreaking, stealing, robbery; see CRIME, THEFT.

burial *n.* last rites, interment, entombment; see FUNERAL.

burn *n.* scorch, wound, impairment; see BLISTER.

burn *v.* ignite, kindle, incinerate, burn up, burn down, blaze, flame, flare, burst into flame, rage, consume, enkindle, cremate, consume with flames, set a match to, set on fire, set ablaze, set afire, sear, singe, scorch, brand, fire, light, torch, char, roast, toast, heat, bake; see also COOK.—*Ant.* EXTINGUISH, put out, quench.

burned *a.* scorched, charred, seared, burnt, singed, branded, cauterized, marked, blistered, scalded.

burned up* *a.* angered, enraged, infuriated; see ANGRY.

burning *a.* fiery, blazing, glowing, ablaze, afire, on fire, smoking, in flames, aflame, inflamed, kindled, enkindled, ignited, scorching, turning to ashes, searing, in a blaze, blistering, red-hot, white-hot; see also PASSIONATE 2.—*Ant.* COLD, frozen, out.

burnt *a.* scorched, singed, charred; see BURNED.

burst *n.* **1.** [An explosion] blowout, blast, blowup; see EXPLOSION. **2.** [A sudden spurt] rush, outburst, torrent; see FIT 2.

burst *v.* **1.** [To explode] blow up, erupt, rupture; see BREAK 2, DISINTEGRATE, EXPLODE. **2.** [To break] crack, split, fracture; see BREAK 1, DESTROY.

burst into tears *v.* weep, start crying, sob; see CRY 1.

bury *v.* **1.** [To inter] lay in the grave, entomb, enshrine, deposit in the earth, to give burial to, embalm, hold funeral services for, hold last rites for, lay out. **2.** [To cover] conceal, mask, stow away; see HIDE 1. **3.** [To defeat] overcome, win over, conquer; see DEFEAT 2, 3.

bus *n.* autobus, passenger bus, limousine, sightseeing bus, motor coach, common carrier, public conveyance, Greyhound (trademark).

bus *v.* transport, ship, redistrict; see CARRY.

bush *n.* bramble, thicket, hedge, shrubbery, briar bush, rose bush; see also PLANT. —**beat around the bush** speak evasively, avoid the subject, be deceptive; see EVADE.

bushy *a.* fuzzy, disordered, thick, shaggy, rough, full, tufted, fringed, woolly, nappy, fluffy, furry, crinkly, stiff, wiry, rumpled, prickly, feathery, leafy, bristly, heavy.—*Ant.* THIN, sleek, smooth.

busily *a.* diligently, actively, energetically, strenuously, eagerly, earnestly, seriously, intently, rapidly, dexterously, industriously, carefully, intently, studiously, hurriedly, briskly, purposefully, ardently, arduously, fervently, nimbly, zealously, vigorously, restlessly, enthusiatically, speedily, hastily, persistently, like hell*.—*Ant.* SLOWLY, listlessly, idly.

business *n.* **1.** [Industry and trade] commerce, exchange, trade, traffic, barter, commercial enterprise, gainful occupation, buying and selling, negotiation, production and distribution, dealings, affairs, sales, contracts, bargaining, trading, transaction, banking, marketing, undertaking, speculation, market, mercantilism, wholesale and retail, capital and labor, free enterprise, game*, racket*. **2.** [Occupation] trade, profession, vocation; see JOB 1. **3.** [A person's proper concerns] affair, concern, interest; see AFFAIR 1. **4.** [A commercial enterprise] firm, factory, mill, store, company, shop, corporation, concern, combine, conglomerate, cooperative, establishment, enterprise, partnership, institution, house, market, syndicate, cartel, trust, monopoly, holding company. —**do business with** deal with, trade with, patronize; see BUY, SELL, TREAT 1. —**get the business*** be mistreated, be abused, endure; see SUFFER 1. —**give the business*** mistreat, bother, victimize; see ABUSE. —**mean business*** be serious, stress, impress; see EMPHASIZE.

businesslike *a.* purposeful, methodical, systematic; see PRACTICAL.

businessman *n.* industrialist, capitalist, employer, tycoon, broker, retailer, stockbroker, manager, buyer, operator, backer, financier, systems expert, company man, comptroller, accountant, investor, speculator, entrepreneur, purchasing agent, storekeeper, tradesman; see also EXECUTIVE.

busy *a.* **1.** [Engaged] occupied, diligent, employed, working, in conference, in a meeting, in the field, in the laboratory, on an assignment, on duty, on the job, at work, busy with, on the run, on the road, hard-working, busy as a bee*, hustling*, up to one's ears*, hard at it*, having other fish to fry.—*Ant.* IDLE, unemployed, unoccupied. **2.** [In use] employed, occupied, taken; see RENTED.

busybody *n.* meddler, tattletale, troublemaker; see GOSSIP 2.

but *conj. & prep.* **1.** [Indicating contrast] however, on the other hand, in contrast, nevertheless, still, yet, though, on the contrary, but then, but as you see; see also ALTHOUGH. **2.** [Indicating an exception] save, disregarding, without, not including, not taking into account, let alone, aside from, with the exception of, not to mention, passing over, barring, setting aside, forgetting; see also EXCEPT. **3.** [Indicating a limitation] only, merely, simply, barely, solely, purely, just, no more, exactly, no other than, without; see also ONLY 1.

butcher *v.* **1.** [To slaughter for human consumption] stick, pack, dress, clean, cure, smoke, salt, cut, put up. **2.** [To kill inhumanly] slaughter, slay, massacre; see KILL 1. **3.** [To ruin] mess up, spoil, wreck; see BOTCH, DESTROY.

butt *n.* base, tail end, bottom, hilt, extremity, tail, tip, fundament, stump, tub, bottom, seat, posterior; see also BOTTOM.

butt *v.* hit, ram, push headfirst, bump, batter, knock, collide with, run into, smack, strike, gore, buck, toss, crash into.

butter *n. Varieties of butter include the following:* creamery, sweet, dairy, cube, country, tub, vegetable, soy.
button *n.* knob, catch, disk; see FASTENER. —**on the button*** correctly, precisely, accurately; see RIGHT 1.
button *v.* close, clasp, make firm; see FASTEN.
buy* *n.* value, good deal, steal*; see BARGAIN 2.
buy *v.* purchase, get, bargain for, procure, gain, contract for, sign for, get in exchange, go marketing, buy and sell, order, invest in, make an investment, shop for, acquire ownership of, procure title to, pay for, redeem, pay a price for, buy into, score*.
buyer *n.* purchasing agent, purchaser, customer, client, prospect, consumer, representative, patron, user, shopper.—*Ant.* SELLER, vendor, dealer.
buying *n.* purchasing, getting, obtaining, acquiring, paying, investing, exchange, bartering, bargaining, procuring, trafficking.—*Ant.* SELLING, vending, auctioning.
buy off *v.* corrupt, influence, fix*; see BRIBE.
buzz *n.* murmur, buzzing, hum; see NOISE 1.
buzz *v.* drone, hum, whir; see SOUND.
buzzer *n.* siren, signal, bell; see ALARM, WARNING, WHISTLE 1.
by *prep.* **1.** [Near] close to, next to, nigh; see NEAR 1, NEXT 2. **2.** [By stated means] over, with, through, by means of, in the name of, at the hand of, along with, through the medium of, with the assistance of, on, supported by.
bypass *n.* detour, temporary route, side road; see ROAD 1.
bypass *v.* miss, evade, detour around; see AVOID.
bystander *n.* onlooker, watcher, spectator; see OBSERVER.
by the book *a.* strictly, according to rule, rigidly; see LEGALLY, OFFICIALLY 1.
by the same token *a.* similarly, likewise, furthermore; see BESIDES.
by the way *a.* casually, incidentally, offhand; see ACCIDENTALLY.

C

cab *n.* taxi, taxicab, hack*; see AUTOMOBILE, VEHICLE.
cabin *n.* log house, cottage, hut; see HOME 1, SHELTER.
cabinet *n.* council, advisory council, authority, bureaucracy, committee, bureau, governing body, administrators, assembly, assistants, department heads, advisors, United States Cabinet, ministry, backstairs cabinet, brain trust; see also GOVERNMENT 2.
cable *n.* cord, preformed cable, wire twist; see CHAIN, WIRE 1.
cackle *v.* chuckle, snicker, giggle; see LAUGH.
cactus *n. Cactuses include the following:* giant, saguaro, barrel, choya, hedgehog, cochineal, nipple, night-blooming cereus, century plant, prickly pear, mescal; see also PLANT.
cad *n.* rogue, scoundrel, rake; see RASCAL.
cadence *n.* rhythm, meter, flow; see BEAT 2, MEASURE 3.
cafe *n.* cafeteria, lunchroom, coffee shop; see RESTAURANT.
cage *n.* coop, jail, crate; see ENCLOSURE 1, PEN 1.
cake *n.* **1.** [A flattish, compact mass] cube, bar, loaf; see BLOCK 1. **2.** [Sweet baked goods] *Kinds of cake include the following:* wedding, birthday, angel food, devil's-food, corn, sponge, fruit, burnt-sugar, caramel, German chocolate, upside-down, pound, Martha Washington, maple, orange, white lemon, citron, walnut, almond, layer, white mountain, spice, marble, Lady Baltimore, coffeecake, jellyroll, gingerbread, shortbread; see also BREAD, PASTRY. —**take the cake*** excel, outdo, win the prize; see EXCEED.
cake *v.* crust, solidify, pack; see FREEZE 1, HARDEN, THICKEN.
calamity *n.* cataclysm, distress, trial; see CATASTROPHE, DISASTER, MISFORTUNE, TRAGEDY 1.
calculate *v.* count, measure, reckon, enumerate, determine, rate, forecast, weigh, gauge, number, figure, figure up, account, compute, sum up, divide, multiply, subtract, add, work out, cipher, tally, dope out*; see also ESTIMATE.
calculation *n.* **1.** [The act of calculating] adding, totaling, count; see ESTIMATE. **2.** [A forecast] prediction, divination, prognostication; see FORECAST.
calendar *n.* list, program, record, timetable, schedule, annals, journal, diary, daybook, chronology, log, logbook, table, register, almanac, agenda, docket; see also ALMANAC.
calf *n.* young cow, young bull, yearling; see COW.
California *n.* Golden Bear State, Gold Rush State, Golden Poppy State, Bear Flag State, Gold Coast, Sunny California, CA, Cal.
calisthenics *n.* exercises, workout, aerobics; see EXERCISE 1, GYMNASTICS.

call *n.* **1.** [A shout] yell, whoop, hail; see ALARM, CRY 1. **2.** [Characteristic sound] twitter, tweet, shriek; see CRY 2. **3.** [A visit] visiting, a few words, afternoon call; see VISIT. **4.** [Word of command] summons, battle cry, reveille; see ALARM, COMMAND, CRY 1. **5.** [An invitation] bidding, solicitation, proposal; see INVITATION, REQUEST. —**on call** usable, ready, prepared; see AVAILABLE. —**within call** close by, approximate, not far away; see NEAR 1.

call *v.* **1.** [To raise the voice] shout, call out, exclaim; see YELL. **2.** [To bring a body of people together] collect, convene, muster; see ASSEMBLE 2. **3.** [To address] denominate, designate, term; see NAME 1. **4.** [To invite] summon, request, ask; see INVITE.

call a halt to *v.* suspend, check, stop; see HALT.

call attention to *v.* point out, indicate, note; see REMIND, WARN.

call down* *v.* rebuke, chide, admonish; see SCOLD.

called *a.* christened, termed, labeled; see NAMED 1.

call for *v.* **1.** [To ask] ask for, request, make inquiry about; see ASK. **2.** [To need] require, want, lack; see NEED. **3.** [To come to get] come for, collect, fetch; see GET 1, PICK UP 6.

call in *v.* **1.** [To collect] collect, remove, receive; see WITHDRAW. **2.** [To invite] ask for, request, solicit; see BEG, SUMMON.

calling *n.* occupation, vocation, work; see JOB 1, PROFESSION 1, TRADE 2.

call names *v.* defame, slander, attack; see CURSE, INSULT.

call off *v.* cancel, postpone, cease; see HALT, STOP 2.

call on or **upon** *v.* stop in, have an appointment with, go to see; see VISIT.

callous *a.* unfeeling, hardened, insensitive; see INDIFFERENT.

call up *v.* **1.** [To remember] recollect, recall, summon up; see REMEMBER 1, SUMMON. **2.** [To summon] send for, bid, order; see INVITE. **3.** [To telephone] phone, call, ring; see TELEPHONE.

calm *a.* **1.** [*Said especially of persons*] dignified, reserved, cool, composed, collected, unmoved, level-headed, coolheaded, impassive, detached, aloof, unconcerned, disinterested, unhurried, neutral, gentle, sedate, serene, unanxious, unexcited, contented, meek, satisfied, pleased, amiable, temperate, placid, civil, kind, moderate, confident, poised, tranquil, self-possessed, restful, relaxed, dispassionate, mild, still, patient, self-controlled, untroubled, cool as a cucumber, unflappable*; see also RESERVED 3, PATIENT 1.—*Ant.* VIOLENT, excited, furious. **2.** [*Said often of things*] quiet, undisturbed, unruffled, comfortable, moderate, in order, soothing, at peace, placid, smooth, still, restful, harmonious, peaceful, pacific, balmy, waveless, windless, serene, motionless, slow; see also QUIET.—*Ant.* ROUGH, agitated, aroused.

calm *n.* **1.** [Peace] stillness, peacefulness, quiet; see PEACE 2, REST 1, SILENCE 1. **2.** [Composure] serenity, tranquillity, peace of mind; see COMPOSURE, PATIENCE 1, RESTRAINT 1.

calm *v.* tranquilize, soothe, pacify; see QUIET 1.

calm down *v.* compose oneself, control oneself, calm oneself, keep oneself under control, keep cool, take it easy, get organized, rest, get hold of oneself, cool it*, cool off, cool down, simmer down, keep one's shirt on*; see also RELAX.

calmly *a.* quietly, unexcitedly, tranquilly, unconcernedly, serenely, confidently, sedately, collectedly, composedly, placidly, smoothly, restfully, motionlessly, peacefully, naturally, comfortably, unhurried, without anxiety, without fuss, dully; see also EASILY, EVENLY.—*Ant.* EXCITEDLY, agitatedly, disturbedly.

calmness *n.* quietness, tranquillity, calm; see COMPOSURE, PATIENCE 1, PEACE 2.

calumny *n.* slander, defamation, detraction; see LIE.

camera *n. Kinds of cameras include the following:* cinecamera, X-ray machine, microcamera, photomicroscope, photostat, spectrograph, motion-picture, television, TV, video, camcorder, press, movie, film, flash, still, electron-diffraction, box, stereo, zoom-lens, Polaroid (trademark), single-lens reflex, double-lens reflex, spectroscopic, telescopic.

camouflage *n.* dissimulation, masquerade, simulation, cloak, shade, shroud, veil, blackout, masking, paint, netting, deceit; see also DISGUISE, SCREEN 1.

camouflage *v.* cover, conceal, veil; see DECEIVE, DISGUISE, HIDE 1.

camp *n.* **1.** [A temporary living place] camping ground, campground, campsite, encampment, tents, tent city, wigwams, tepees, wickiups. **2.** [Temporary living quarters] tent, lean-to, cottage, tilt, shack, hut, lodge, cabin, chalet, shed, log house, summer home, cottage. —**break camp** dismantle, depart, pack up; see LEAVE 1.

camp *v.* bivouac, stop over, make camp, encamp, dwell, nest, locate, pitch camp, pitch a tent, tent, quarter, lodge, sleep out, station, put up for the night, camp out, rough it, sleep under the stars.

campaign *n.* operations, crusade, warfare; see ATTACK, FIGHT.

campaign *v.* crusade, electioneer, run, agitate, contend for, contest, canvass for, solicit votes, lobby, barnstorm, mend fences, go to the grass roots*, stump, beat the bushes*, whistle-stop; see also COMPETE.

campus *n.* seat of learning, buildings and grounds, physical plant, alma mater, quad; see also COLLEGE, UNIVERSITY.

can *n.* **1.** [A container] tin can, tin (British), canister, receptacle, package, jar, bottle, quart can, bucket, gallon can, vessel; see also CONTAINER. **2.** [*Jail] prison, penitentiary, stir*; see JAIL. **3.** [*A toilet] lavatory, restroom, washroom; see TOILET.

can *v.* **1.** [To preserve] bottle, put up, keep; see PRESERVE 3. **2.** [To be able] could, may, be capable of, be equal to, be up to*, lie in one's power, be within one's control, manage, can do, take care of, make it*, make the grade, make out, cut the mustard*, have it made*.

canal *n.* waterway, trench, ditch; see CHANNEL, WATER 2.

cancel *v.* repudiate, nullify, ignore, invalidate, suppress, countermand, call off, set aside, rule out, refute, rescind, remove, repeal, counteract, recall, retract, abrogate, discharge, void, make void, put an end to, abort, offset, revoke, overthrow, scratch, drop; see also ABOLISH.—*Ant.* SUSTAIN, approve, uphold.

cancellation *n.* cancelling, annulment, nullification, abrogation, dissolution, invalidation, revocation, repudiation, repeal, abolition, retraction, reversal, voiding, recall, overruling, undoing, withdrawing, abandoning; see also REMOVAL.

cancer *n.* growth, tumor, malignancy; see GROWTH 3, ILLNESS 2.

cancerous *a.* carcinogenic, virulent, mortal; see HARMFUL.

candid *a.* straightforward, sincere, open; see FRANK, HONEST 1.

candidate *n.* aspirant, possible choice, nominee, applicant, political contestant, office-seeker, successor, competitor, bidder, solicitor, petitioner; see also CONTESTANT.

candle *n.* taper, rush, torch; see LIGHT 3. —**burn the candle at both ends** dissipate, squander, use up; see WASTE 1, 2. —**not hold a candle to** be unequal to, be subordinate to, be inferior to; see FAIL 1.

candlestick *n.* candelabrum, candelabra, taper holder, flat candlestick, menorah, candleholder.

candy *n.* confection, confectionery, sweetmeat, bonbon. *Varieties of candy include the following:* caramel, taffy, fudge, cream, lemon drop, cotton candy, nougat, peanut brittle, praline, fruit roll, marshmallow, crystallized fruit, coconut bar, Turkish delight, lollipop, halvah, marchpane, gum drop, divinity, toffee, after-dinner mint, Life Saver (trademark), stick, hard, spun-sugar, all-day sucker.

cane *n.* walking stick, staff, pole; see STICK.

canned *a.* bottled, conserved, kept; see PRESERVED 2.

cannon *n. Types of cannon include the following:* self-propelled, muzzle-loading, breech-loading, tank destroyer, turret, mountain, siege, coast defense, field, antiaircraft, railway, antitank gun, knee mortar, recoilless rifle, howitzer.

canoe *n.* kayak, dugout, outrigger; see BOAT.

canon *n.* decree, rule, order; see COMMAND, DECLARATION, LAW 3.

canonize *v.* saint, sanctify, beatify; see BLESS, LOVE 1, WORSHIP.

canopy *n.* awning, sunshade, umbrella; see COVER 1.

canteen *n.* jug, flask, water supply; see BOTTLE, CONTAINER.

canvas *n.* **1.** [A coarse cloth] tenting, awning cloth, sailcloth, duck, coarse cloth; see also CLOTH. **2.** [Anything made of canvas] sail, awning, tarpaulin; see COVER 1, TENT. **3.** [A painting on canvas] portrait, still life, oil; see ART, PAINTING 1.

canyon *n.* gulch, gorge, gully; see RAVINE, VALLEY.

cap *n.* beret, mortarboard, bonnet; see HAT.

capability *n.* capacity, skill, aptitude; see ABILITY, INCLINATION 1.

capable *a.* proficient, competent, fitted; see ABLE, INTELLIGENT.

capacity *n.* contents, limit, space, room, size, volume, holding power, extent, compass, magnitude, spread, expanse, scope, latitude, bulk, dimensions, measure, range, quantity, size, reach, holding ability, sweep, proportions, mass, sufficiency.

cape *n.* **1.** [Land jutting into the water] headland, peninsula, foreland, point, promontory, jetty, head, tongue, neck of land, ness, mole, finger, arm. **2.** [An overgarment] cloak, wrapper, mantilla, mantle, shawl, wrap, overdress, poncho; see also COAT 1.

caper *n.* prank, trick, escapade; see JOKE.

caper *v.* frolic, gambol, cavort; see PLAY 1, 2.

capital *n.* **1.** [A seat of government] metropolis, principal city, capitol; see CENTER 2, CITY. **2.** [Money and property] cash, assets, interests; see ESTATE, PROPERTY 1, WEALTH. **3.** [A letter usually used initially] initial, upper case, majuscule; see LETTER 1.

capitalism *n.* capitalistic system, free enterprise, private ownership; see DEMOCRACY, ECONOMICS, GOVERNMENT 2.

capitalist *n.* entrepreneur, investor, landowner; see BANKER, BUSINESSMAN, FINANCIER.

capitol *n.* statehouse, state capitol, seat of government; see CENTER 2.

capitulate *v.* surrender, submit, give up; see YIELD 1.

capsize *v.* overturn, invert, tip over; see UPSET 1.

caption *n.* inscription, title, subtitle; see HEADING.

captive *a.* restrained, incarcerated, jailed; see BOUND 1, 2, RESTRICTED.

captive *n.* hostage, convict, con*; see PRISONER.

captivity *n.* imprisonment, jail, restraint, slavery, bondage, subjection, servitude, duress, detention, incarceration, enslavement, constraint, the guardhouse, custody; see also CONFINEMENT.—*Ant.* FREEDOM, liberty, independence.

capture *n.* capturing, arrest, recovery, seizing, taking, seizure, acquisition, obtaining, securing, gaining, winning, occupation, appropriation, ensnaring, abduction, laying hold of, grasping, catching, trapping, commandeering, apprehending, confiscation, taking into custody, apprehension, fall.—*Ant.* RESCUE, liberation, setting free.

capture *v.* seize, take, apprehend; see ARREST, SEIZE 2.

captured *a.* taken, seized, arrested, apprehended, detained, grasped, overtaken, grabbed, snatched, kidnapped, abducted, netted, hooked, secured, collared*, nabbed*, bagged; see also UNDER ARREST.—*Ant.* RELEASED, unbound, loosed.

car *n.* auto, motorcar, automotive vehicle; see AUTOMOBILE, VEHICLE. *Types of cars include the following:* passenger car, limousine, sedan, hardtop, compact, subcompact, sports car, convertible, town car, ranch wagon, station wagon, taxicab, squad car, prowl car, staff car, bus, truck, jeep, dune buggy.

carcass *n.* corpse, cadaver, remains; see BODY 2.

card *n.* cardboard, ticket, sheet, square, Bristol board, fiberboard. *Varieties of cards include the following:* poster, window card, show card, ticket, fortunetelling cards, tarot cards, label, badge, tally, check, billet, voucher, pass; calling card, playing card, address card, visiting card, credit card, bank card, greeting card, registration card, filing card, index card, check-cashing card, police card, social security card, identification card, I.D. card; see also PAPER 1. **—in the cards** probable, predicted, possible; see LIKELY 1. **—put one's cards on the table** reveal, tell the truth, expose; see ADMIT 2.

care *n.* **1.** [Careful conduct] heed, concern, caution, consideration, regard, thoughtfulness, forethought, attention, precaution, wariness, vigilance, watchfulness, watching, diligence, nicety, pains, application, conscientiousness, thought, discrimination, exactness, exactitude, watch, concentration; see also ATTENTION, PRUDENCE.—*Ant.* CARELESSNESS, neglect, negligence. **2.** [Worry] concern, anxiety, distress; see WORRY 2. **3.** [Custody] supervision, administration, keeping; see CUSTODY. **4.** [A cause of worry] problem, care, concern; see DISASTER, MISFORTUNE. **—take care** be careful, be cautious, beware, heed; see also MIND 3, WATCH OUT. **—take care of** protect, attend to, be responsible for; see GUARD.

care *v.* **1.** [To be concerned] attend, take pains, regard; see CONSIDER. **2.** [To be careful] look out for, be on guard, watch out; see MIND 3.

care about *v.* cherish, be fond of, hold dear; see LIKE 2, LOVE 1.

career *n.* occupation, vocation, work; see JOB 1, PROFESSION 1.

care for *v.* **1.** [To look after] provide for, attend to, nurse; see RAISE 2, SUPPORT 3. **2.** [To like] be fond of, hold dear, prize; see LIKE 2, LOVE 1.

carefree *a.* lighthearted, cheerful, jovial; see HAPPY, CALM 1.

careful *a.* thorough, concerned, deliberate, conservative, prudent, meticulous, particular, rigorous, fussy, finicky, prim, exacting, wary, sober, vigilant, watchful, suspicious, alert, wide-awake, scrupulous, religious, hard to please, discriminating, sure-footed, precise, painstaking, exact, on one's guard, on the alert, conscientious, attentive, calculating, mindful, cautious, guarded, considerate, shy, circumspect, discreet, noncommittal, self-possessed, cool, calm, self-disciplined, solid, farsighted, frugal, thrifty, stealthy, observant, on guard, apprehensive, leery, choosy, picky*, feeling one's way, seeing how the land lies, going to great lengths.—*Ant.* CARELESS, heedless, haphazard.

carefully *a.* **1.** [Scrupulously] conscientiously, exactly, rigidly, correctly, strictly, precisely, minutely, painstakingly, faithfully, honorably, attentively, rigorously, providently, deliberately, reliable, particularly, solicitously, concernedly, meticulously, laboriously, thoroughly, dependably, in detail.—*Ant.* HAPHAZARDLY, neglectfully, indifferently. **2.** [Cautiously] prudently, discreetly, watchfully; see CAUTIOUSLY.

careless *a.* loose, lax, remiss, unguarded, incautious, forgetful, unthinking, unobservant, reckless, unheeding, indiscreet, inadvertent, unconcerned, wasteful, regardless, imprudent, unconsidered, hasty, inconsiderate, heedless, mindless, untroubled, negligent, neglectful, thoughtless, indifferent, casual, oblivious, absent-minded, listless, abstracted, nonchalant, undiscerning, offhand, slack, blundering; see also RASH.—*Ant.* THOUGHTFUL, attentive, careful.

carelessly *a.* heedlessly, negligently, neglectfully, thoughtlessly, nonchalantly, offhandedly, rashly, unconcernedly, at random, happen what may, incautiously, improvidently, wastefully, without caution, without care, without concern, with no attention, like crazy*.

carelessness *n.* unconcern, nonchalance, heedlessness, rashness, omission, slackness, delinquency, indolence, procrastination, dereliction, neglect, negligence, disregard, imprudence, haphazardness; see also INDIFFERENCE.—*Ant.* CARE, consideration, caution.

caress *n.* embrace, stroke, feel*; see HUG, KISS, TOUCH 2.

caress *v.* embrace, cuddle, pat; see LOVE 2, TOUCH 1.

caretaker *n.* porter, keeper, janitor; see CUSTODIAN, WATCHMAN.

care to *v.* prefer, desire, wish; see LIKE 1, WANT 1.

cargo *n.* shipload, baggage, lading; see FREIGHT, LOAD 1.

carnal *a.* fleshly, bodily, sensuous; see LEWD 2, SENSUAL 2.

carnival *n.* side show, circus, fair; see ENTERTAINMENT, SHOW 1.

carol *n.* hymn, Christmas song, ballad; see SONG.

carpenter *n.* mason, craftsman, builder; see LABORER, WORKMAN.

carpet *n.* wall-to-wall carpet, carpeting, linoleum, floor covering, matting; see also RUG. **—(called) on the carpet** reprimanded, censured, interrogated; see IN TROUBLE.

carriage *n.* **1.** [The manner of carrying the body] walk, pace, step, attitude, aspect, presence, look, cast, gait, bearing, posture, pose, demeanor, poise, air; see also BEHAVIOR. **2.** [A horse-drawn passenger vehicle] buggy, surrey, coach, coach-and-four, buckboard, cart, dogcart, two-wheeler, trap, gig, sulky, hansom, coupe, four-wheeler, stagecoach, chariot, hack, hackney coach; see also WAGON.

carrier *n.* aircraft carrier, escort carrier, flattop*; see SHIP.

carry *v.* **1.** [To transport] convey, move, transplant, transfer, cart, import, transmit, freight, remove, conduct, bear, take, bring, shift, haul, change, convoy, relocate, relay, lug, tote, fetch; see also SEND 1. **2.** [To transmit] pass on, transfer, relay; see SEND 1. **3.** [To support weight] bear, sustain, shoulder; see SUPPORT 1. **4.** [To give support] corroborate, back up, confirm; see APPROVE, SUPPORT 2, STRENGTHEN. **—be** or **get carried away** zealous, aroused, exuberant; see EXCITED.

carry on *v.* **1.** [To continue] keep going, proceed, persist; see ACHIEVE, CONTINUE 1, 2, ENDURE 1. **2.** [To manage] conduct, engage in, administer; see MANAGE 1. **3.** [To behave badly] blunder, be indecorous, raise Cain*; see MISBEHAVE.

carry (oneself) *v.* appear, seem, behave; see ACT 2, WALK 1.

carry out *v.* complete, accomplish, fulfill; see ACHIEVE, COMPLETE, SUCCEED 1.

carry-over *n.* holdover, vestige, remains; see REMAINDER.

carry over *v.* continue, persist, survive; see ENDURE 1.

carry (something) off *v.* do, triumph, accomplish, handle, take care of, make it, make good; see also ACHIEVE, SUCCEED 1.

cart *n.* truck, wheelbarrow, little wagon, tip cart, handcart, gig, dray, two-wheeler, pushcart, gocart, two-wheeled cart; see also CARRIAGE 2, WAGON. **—put the cart before the horse** reverse, be illogical, err; see MISTAKE.

cartoon *n.* caricature, parody, joke; see RIDICULE.

carve *v.* create, form, hew, chisel, engrave, etch, sculpture, incise, mold, fashion, cut, shape, model, tool, block out, scrape, pattern, trim; see also CUT 1, ENGRAVE.

carved *a.* incised, graven, cut, chiseled, chased, furrowed, formed, hewn, hewed, etched, sculptured, scratched, slashed, done in relief, scrolled, grooved, sliced, scissored; see also ENGRAVED.—*Ant.* PLAIN, cast, molded.

case *n.* **1.** [An example] instance, illustration, sample; see EXAMPLE 1. **2.** [Actual conditions] incident, occurrence, fact; see CIRCUMSTANCE 1, EVENT, FACT 2, STATE. **3.** [A legal action] suit, litigation, lawsuit; see TRIAL 2. **4.** [An organized argument] argument, petition, evidence; see CLAIM, PROOF 1. **5.** [A container or its contents] carton, canister, crate, crating, box, baggage, trunk, casing, chest, drawer, holder, tray, receptacle, coffer, crib, chamber, bin, bag, grip, cabinet, sheath, scabbard, wallet, safe, basket, casket; see also CONTAINER. **—in any case** in any event, anyway, however; see ANYHOW. **—in case (of)** in the event that, provided that, supposing; see IF.

cash *n.* money in hand, ready money, liquid assets, currency, legal tender, principal, available means, working assets, funds, payment, capital, finances, stock, resources, wherewithal, investments, savings, riches, reserve, treasure, moneys, security; see also MONEY 1, WEALTH.

cash *v.* cash in, change, draw; see PAY 1.

cashier *n.* purser, treasurer, receiver; see CLERK.

cash in *v.* realize, change, exchange, turn into money, discharge, draw, pay.

cash on delivery *a.* with cash paid when delivered, collect, C.O.D.; see PAID.

cast *n.* **1.** [A plaster reproduction] facsimile, duplicate, replica; see COPY, SCULPTURE. **2.** [Those in a play] persons in the play, list of characters, players, roles, parts, dramatis personae, company, troupe, producers, dramatic artists. **3.** [Aspect] complexion, face, appearance; see LOOKS. **4.** [A surgical dressing] plaster-of-Paris dressing, plaster cast, arm, cast, leg cast, knee cast, body cast, splints; see also DRESSING 3. **5.** [A tinge] hue, shade, tint; see COLOR.

cast *v.* **1.** [To throw] pitch, fling, hurl; see THROW 1. **2.** [To form in a mold] shape, roughcast, wetcast; see FORM 1. **3.** [To select actors for a play] appoint, designate, decide upon, determine, pick, give parts, detail, name; see also ASSIGN, CHOOSE.

cast away *v.* dispose of, reject, throw out; see ABANDON 1.

castle *n.* stronghold, manor, seat, villa, fortress, château, citadel, keep, fort, hold, safehold; see also FORTIFICATION.

cast off *v.* reject, jettison, throw away; see ABANDON 1.

cast out *v.* evict, ostracize, expel; see BANISH, EJECT.

castrate *v.* emasculate, sterilize, asexualize, mutilate, cut, spay, geld, unman, steer, caponize, effeminize, deprive of manhood; see also MAIM.

casual *a.* **1.** [Accidental] chance, unexpected, unplanned; see SPONTANEOUS. **2.** [Nonchalant] blasé, apathetic, unconcerned; see CARELESS, INDIFFERENT.

casually *a.* **1.** [Accidentally] unintentionally, by chance, inadvertently; see ACCIDENTALLY. **2.** [Nonchalantly] indifferently, coolly, unemotionally; see CARELESSLY, EASILY.

casualty *n.* fatalities, losses, death toll; see LOSS 3.

cat *n.* **1.** [A domestic animal] tomcat, kitten, kit, tabby, puss, pussy, mouser, kitty. *House cats include the following:* Maltese, Persian, Siamese, Angora, tortoise shell, alley, tiger, calico; see also ANIMAL. **2.** [A member of the cat family] lion, tiger, leopard, puma, wildcat, cheetah, lynx, bobcat, mountain lion, ocelot, cougar, jaguar; see also ANIMAL. —**let the cat out of the bag** expose, tell a secret, let slip; see REVEAL.

catalog *n.* register, file, directory, schedule, inventory, index, bulletin, syllabus, brief, slate, table, calendar, list, docket, classification, record, draft, roll, timetable, table of contents, prospectus, program, rent roll; see also LIST.

catalog *v.* classify, record, index; see LIST 1.

catastrophe *n.* calamity, mishap, mischance, misadventure, misery, accident, trouble, casualty, infliction, affliction, stroke, havoc, ravage, wreck, fatality, grief, crash, devastation, desolation, hardship, blow, ruin, reverse, emergency, scourge, convulsion, tragedy, adversity, bad luck, upheaval, down; see also DISASTER.

catch* *n.* **1.** [A likely mate] boyfriend, sweetheart, fiancé; see LOVER 1. **2.** [Something stolen] capture, grab, haul*; see BOOTY. **3.** [A trick] puzzle, trick, trap; see JOKE. **4.** [A hook] clasp, clamp, snap; see FASTENER.

catch *v.* **1.** [To seize hold of] snatch, take, take hold of, snag, grab, pick, pounce on, fasten upon, snare, pluck, hook, claw, clench, clasp, grasp, clutch, grip, nab, net, bag*; see also SEIZE. **2.** [To bring into captivity] trap, apprehend, capture; see ARREST, SEIZE 2. **3.** [To come to from behind] overtake, reach, come upon; see PASS 1. **4.** [To contract a disease] get, fall ill with, become infected with, incur, become subject to, be liable to, fall victim to, take, succumb to, break out with, receive, come down with.—*Ant.* ESCAPE, ward off, get over.

catching *a.* contagious, communicable, infectious, epidemic, endemic, pestilential, noxious, dangerous, pandemic; see also CONTAGIOUS.

catch on *v.* **1.** [To understand] grasp, comprehend, perceive; see UNDERSTAND 1. **2.** [To become popular] become fashionable, become prevalent, become common, become widespread, become acceptable, grow in popularity, find favor; see also SUCCEED 1.

catch one's breath *v.* rest, wait, stop; see HESITATE, PAUSE.

catch (on) fire *v.* inflame, ignite, burst into flame; see BURN.

catch the eye *v.* attract notice, engage attention, interest; see FASCINATE.

catch up *v.* catch, join, equal; see REACH 1.

catch up with or **catch up to** *v.* overtake, join, overcome; see REACH 1.

category *n.* level, section, classification; see CLASS 1, DIVISION 2, KIND.

cathedral *n.* temple, house of God, house of prayer, Holy place, basilica; see also CHURCH 1. *Parts of a cathedral include the following:* altar, sanctuary, holy of holies, sacristy, sacrarium, holy table, baptistery, chancel, apse, choir, nave, aisle, transept, crypt, pew, seat, pulpit, confessional. *Famous cathedrals include the following:* St. Peter's, Rome; St. Paul's, London; Notre Dame, Paris; St. John the Divine, New York; St. Patrick's, New York.

cattle *n.* stock, cows, steers, calves, herd, beef cattle, dairy cattle; see also COW.

caught *a.* taken, seized, arrested; see CAPTURED, UNDER ARREST.

cause *n.* **1.** [Purpose] motive, causation, object, purpose, explanation, inducement, incitement, prime mover, motive power, mainspring, ultimate cause, ground, matter, element, stimulation, instigation, foundation, the why and wherefore; see also BASIS, REASON 3.—*Ant.* RESULT, effect, outcome. **2.** [Moving force] agent, case, condition; see CIRCUMSTANCES. **3.** [A belief] principles, conviction, creed; see BELIEF, FAITH 2.

cause *v.* originate, provoke, generate, occasion, let, kindle, give rise to, lie at the root of, be at the bottom of, bring to pass, bring to effect, sow the seeds of; see also BEGIN.

caution *n.* care, heed, discretion; see ATTENTION, PRUDENCE.

caution *v.* forewarn, alert, advise; see WARN.

cautious *a.* circumspect, watchful, wary; see CAREFUL.

cautiously *a.* tentatively, prudently, discreetly, watchfully, wisely, sparingly, thoughtfully, heedfully, delicately, mindfully, anxiously, with care, with caution, gingerly, with forethought, slowly.

cave *n.* rock shelter, cavern, grotto; see HOLE.

cavern *n.* cave, hollow, grotto; see HOLE.

cavity *n.* **1.** [Sunken area] pit, depression, basin; see HOLE. **2.** [Hollow place in a tooth] dental caries, distal pit, gingival pit; see DECAY.

cease *v.* desist, terminate, discontinue; see HALT, STOP 1, 2.

ceaseless *a.* continual, endless, unending; see CONSTANT, ETERNAL.

celebrate *v.* **1.** [To recognize an occasion] keep, observe, consecrate, hallow, dedicate, commemorate, honor, proclaim, ritualize.—*Ant.* FORGET, overlook, neglect. **2.** [To indulge in celebration] feast, give a party, carouse, rejoice, kill the fatted calf, revel, go on a spree, make whoopee*, blow off steam*, let off steam, have a party, have a ball, kick up one's heels*, let loose*, let go, live it up, whoop it up, make merry, kick up a row*, beat the drum*.

celebrated *a.* well-known, renowned, noted; see FAMOUS, IMPORTANT 2.

celebration *n.* commemoration, holiday, anniversary, jubilee, inauguration, installation, coronation, presentation, carnival, revelry, spree, festivity, festival, feast, merrymaking, gaiety, frolic, hilarity, joviality, merriment, remembrance, ceremonial, keeping observance, fete, Mardi Gras, birthday.

celebrity *n.* famous man, famous woman, hero, heroine, leader, notable, magnate, dignitary, worthy, figure, personage, famous person, man of note, someone, somebody, VIP*, luminary, lion, lioness, star, bigwig*, big gun*, big shot*, ace.

cell *n.* **1.** [A unit of living organism] corpuscle, cellule, micro-organism, vacuole, spore, plastid, organism, egg, ectoplasm, embryo, germ, follicle. **2.** [A room] vault, hold, pen, cage, tower, hole, coop, keep, batille, chamber, den, recess, retreat, alcove, manger, crypt, crib, nook, burrow, stall, closet, booth, cloister, compartment, lockup; see also ROOM 2.

cellar *n.* half basement, underground room, basement apartment; see BASEMENT.

cement *n.* glue, putty, tar, gum, mortar, paste, adhesive, rubber cement, epoxy resin, bond.

cement *v.* mortar, plaster, connect; see FASTEN, JOIN 1.

cemetery *n.* burial ground, memorial park, funerary grounds, churchyard, necropolis, potter's field, catacomb, city of the dead, tomb, vault, crypt, charnel house, sepulcher, graveyard, mortuary, last resting place, Golgotha, boneyard*.

censor *n.* inspector, judge, expurgator, guardian of morals; see also EXAMINER.

censor *v.* control, restrict, strike out, forbid, suppress, ban, withhold, enforce censorship, control the flow of news, inspect, oversee, abridge, expurgate, review, criticize, exert pressure, conceal, prevent publication, blacklist, blue pencil, cut, black out; see also RESTRICT.

censorship *n.* licensing, restriction, forbidding, controlling the press, infringing the right of freedom of speech, governmental control, security blackout, news blackout, thought control; see also RESTRAINT.

censure *n.* criticism, reproof, admonition; see BLAME, OBJECTION.

censure *v.* **1.** [To blame] criticize, judge, disapprove; see BLAME. **2.** [To scold] rebuke, reprove, attack; see SCOLD.

census *n.* statistics, enumeration, valuation, account, registration, listing, evaluation, demography, figures, statement, numbering, registering, roll call, tabulation, tally, poll, count, counting, nose count; see also COUNT.

cent *n.* penny, a copper, 100th part of a dollar; see MONEY 1.

center *a.* mid, middle, inmost, inner, midway, medial, deepest, at the inmost, innermost, internal, interior, at the halfway point; see also MIDDLE.—*Ant.* OUTSIDE, outer, exterior.

center *n.* **1.** [A central point] point, middle, focus, nucleus, core, place, heart, hub, navel, point of convergence, point of concentration, focal point, midst, middle point, centrality, marrow, kernel, bull's eye, pivot, axis, pith, dead center; see also MIDDLE. **2.** [A point that attracts people] city, town, metropolis, plaza, capital, shopping center, trading center, station, hub, mart, market, crossroads, mall, social center, meeting place, club, market place. **3.** [Essence] core, gist, kernel; see CHARACTER 1.

center *v.* concentrate, centralize, focus, intensify, unify, unite, combine, converge upon, join, meet, gather, close on, consolidate, bring to a focus, center round, center in, gather together, flock together, collect, draw together, bring together, focus attention, attract; see also MEET 1.—*Ant.* SPREAD, decentralize, branch off.

central *a.* middle, midway, equidistant, medial, focal, nuclear, midmost, mean, inner, median, inmost, middlemost, intermediate, interior, in the center of; see also

MIDDLE.—*Ant.* OUTER, peripheral, verging on.

centrally *a.* in the middle, focal, middlemost, in the center, in the heart of; see also CENTRAL.

century *n.* 100 years, centenary, era; see AGE 3, TIME 1.

ceramics *n.* earthenware, crockery, porcelain; see POTTERY, SCULPTURE.

cereal *n.* corn, breakfast food, seed; see GRAIN 1.

ceremonial *a.* ritual, formal, stately; see CONVENTIONAL 3.

ceremony *n.* **1.** [A public event] function, commemoration, services; see CELEBRATION. **2.** [A rite] observance, ritual, rite, service, solemnity, formality, custom, tradition, liturgy, ordinance, sacrament, liturgical practice, conformity, etiquette, politeness, decorum, propriety, preciseness, strictness, nicety, formalism, conventionality.

certain *a.* **1.** [Confident] calm, assured, sure, positive, satisfied, self-confident, undoubting, believing, secure, untroubled, unconcerned, undisturbed, unperturbed, fully convinced, assertive, cocksure; see also CONFIDENT. **2.** [Beyond doubt] indisputable, unquestionable, assured, positive, real, true, genuine, plain, clear, undoubted, guaranteed, unmistakable, sure, incontrovertible, undeniable, definite, supreme, unqualified, infallible, undisputed, unerring, sound, reliable, trustworthy, evident, conclusive, authoritative, irrefutable, unconditional, incontestable, unquestioned, absolute, unequivocal, inescapable, conclusive, in the bag*, on ice*, done up*, salted away*; see also TRUE 1, 3. **3.** [Fixed] settled, concluded, set; see DEFINITE 1, DETERMINED 1. **4.** [Specific but not named] special, definite, individual, marked, specified, defined, one, some, a few, a couple, several, upwards of, regular, particular, singular, precise, specific, express; see also SOME. —**for certain** without doubt, absolutely, certainly; see SURELY.

certainly *a.* positively, absolutely, unquestionably; see SURELY.

certificate *n.* declaration, warrant, voucher, testimonial, credentials, license, testament, endorsement, affidavit, certification, coupon, document, pass, ticket, warranty, guarantee, testimony, receipt, affirmation, docket, record; see also RECORD 1.

certify *v.* swear, attest, state; see DECLARE, TESTIFY 2.

chain *n.* **1.** [A series of links] series, train, set, string, connection, cable, link, charm bracelet, ring series, shackle, manacle; see also SERIES. **2.** [A sequence] succession, progression, continuity; see SERIES.

chain *v.* connect, attach, secure; see FASTEN, HOLD 1.

chair *n.* **1.** [A single seat] seat, place, room, space, cathedra; see also FURNITURE. *Chairs include the following:* stool, throne, footstool, rocker, wing chair, armchair, easy chair, wheelchair, highchair, occasional chair, dining-room chair, desk chair, kitchen chair, deck chair, lawn chair, swivel chair, folding chair. **2.** [A position of authority] throne, professorship, fellowship; see INFLUENCE.

chairman *n.* chairperson, chairwoman, president, administrator, director, toastmaster, speaker, moderator, monitor, leader, principal, captain, master of ceremonies, MC, emcee; see also LEADER 2.

chalk up *v.* credit, enter, register; see ADD 1, RECORD 1, SCORE 1.

challenge *n.* dare, provocation, threat; see OBJECTION.

challenge *v.* **1.** [To invite to a contest] defy, denounce, invite competition; see DARE 2, THREATEN. **2.** [To question] dispute, inquire, search out; see ASK, DOUBT, QUESTION.

champion *n.* vanquisher, conqueror, victor; see HERO 1, WINNER.

chance *a.* accidental, unplanned, unintentional; see AIMLESS, INCIDENTAL.

chance *n.* **1.** [The powers of uncertainty] fate, fortune, hazard, casualty, lot, accident, luck, good luck, bad luck, destiny, outcome, cast, lottery, gamble, adventure, contingency, happening, future, doom, destination, occurrence, Lady Luck*, turn of the cards, heads or tails*.—*Ant.* PURPOSE, aim, design. **2.** [A possibility] opening, occasion, prospect; see OPPORTUNITY 1, POSSIBILITY 2. **3.** [Probability; *often plural*] likelihood, feasibility, indications; see ODDS. —**by chance** by accident, as it happens, unexpectedly; see ACCIDENTALLY. —**on the off chance** in case, in the event that, supposing; see IF.

chance *v.* venture, stake, hazard, wager, jeopardize, speculate, tempt fate, tempt fortune, play with fire, take a shot, take a leap in the dark, buy a pig in a poke, go out on a limb*, chance it, take a fling at, put all one's eggs in one basket, skate on thin ice, run the risk; see also RISK.

change *n.* **1.** [An alteration] modification, correction, remodeling, switch, reformation, reconstruction, shift, reform, conversion, transformation, revolution, rearrangement, adjustment, readjustment, reorganization, reshaping, renovation, realignment, redirection, reprogramming, variation, addition, refinement, advance, development, diversification, turn, turnover, enlargement, revision, qualification, distortion, compression, contraction, widening, narrowing, lengthening, flattening, shortening, fitting, setting, adjusting, rounding, gone every which way, ups and downs. **2.** [Substitution] switch, replacement, exchange; see SHIFT 1. **3.** [Variety] diversity, novelty, variance; see DIFFERENCE 1, VARIETY 1. **4.** [Small coins] silver, coins, chicken feed*; see MONEY 1.

change *v.* **1.** [To make different] vary, turn, alternate; see ALTER 1. **2.** [To become different] alter, vary, modify, evolve, be converted, turn into, resolve into, grow, ripen, mellow, mature, transform, reform, moderate, adapt, adjust; see also BECOME. **3.** [To put in place of another] displace, supplant, transpose; see EXCHANGE 1, REPLACE 1, SUBSTITUTE. **4.** [To change clothing] undress, disrobe, make one's toilet; see DRESS 1.

changeable *a.* **1.** [*Said of persons*] fickle, flighty, unreliable; see UNSTABLE 2. **2.** [*Said of conditions*] variable, unsteady, unsettled; see UNCERTAIN.

changed *a.* **1.** [Exchanged] substituted, replaced, traded; see RETURNED. **2.** [Altered] qualified, reconditioned, modified, limited, reformed, shifted, moved, mutated, deteriorated, aged, run down, rewritten, conditioned, modernized, remodeled, reprogrammed, rescheduled, redone, done over, brought up to date, edited, moderated, innovated, deviated, diverted, fluctuated, chopped, warped, passed to, recreated, converted, transfigured, metamorphosed, transmuted.—*Ant.* UNCHANGED, PERMANENT, final.

changeless *a.* permanent, unchanging, enduring; see CONSTANT, REGULAR 3.

change one's mind *v.* decide against, alter one's convictions, modify one's ideas; see ALTER 1, CHOOSE.

changing *a.* changeful, changeable, mobile, dynamic, alternative, unstable, inconstant, uncertain, mutable, fluid, mercurial, declining, deteriorating, unsteady, irresolute, degenerating, wavering; see also UNCERTAIN.—*Ant.* FIXED, stable, unchanging.

channel *n.* conduit, tube, canal, duct, course, gutter, furrow, trough, runway, tunnel, strait, sound, race, sewer, main, artery, vein, ditch, aqueduct, canyon; see also WAY 2.

channel *v.* route, send, direct; see SEND 1.

chant *n.* religious song, chorus, incantation; see SONG.

chant *v.* intone, chorus, carol; see SING.

chaos *n.* turmoil, anarchy, discord; see CONFUSION, DISORDER.

chaotic *a.* disorganized, disordered, uncontrolled; see CONFUSED 2.

chapel *n.* place of worship, tabernacle, God's house; see CHURCH 1.

chapter *n.* part, section, book; see DIVISION 2.

character *n.* **1.** [The dominant quality] temper, temperament, attitude, nature, sense, complex, mood, streak, attribute, badge, tone, style, aspect, complexion, spirit, genius, humor, frame, grain, vein; see also CHARACTERISTIC. **2.** [The sum of a person's characteristics] personality, reputation, constitution, repute, individuality, estimation, record, caliber, standing, type, shape, quality, habit, appearance; see also KIND 2. **3.** [A symbol, especially in writing] sign, figure, emblem; see LETTER 1, MARK 1. **4.** [A queer or striking person] personality, figure, personage, original, eccentric, crank*, nut*, oddball*, weirdo*, freak*, psycho*. —**in character** consistent, usual, predictable; see CONVENTIONAL 1. —**out of character** inconsistent, unpredictable, unusual; see UNEXPECTED.

characteristic *a.* innate, fixed, essential, distinctive, distinguishing, marked, discriminative, symbolic, individualizing, representative, specific, personal, original, peculiar, individualistic, individual, idiosyncratic, unique, special, particular, symptomatic, private, exclusive, inherent, inborn, inbred, ingrained, native, indicative, inseparable, in the blood; see also NATURAL 2, TYPICAL.—*Ant.* IRREGULAR, erratic, aberrant.

characteristic *n.* flavor, attribute, quality, faculty, peculiarity, individuality, style, aspect, tone, tinge, feature, distinction, manner, bearing, inclination, nature, personality, temperament, frame, originality, singularity, qualification, virtue, mark, essence, caliber, complexion, particularity, idiosyncrasy, trick, earmark, mannerism, trademark, badge, symptom, disposition, specialty, mood, character, bent, tendency, component, thing, bag*.

characterize *v.* delineate, designate, portray; see DEFINE 2, DESCRIBE.

charge *n.* **1.** [A charged sale] entry, debit, credit; see PRICE. **2.** [An attack] assault, invasion, outbreak; see ATTACK. —**in charge** responsible, controlling, managing; see RESPONSIBLE 1.

charge *v.* **1.** [To ask a price] require, sell for, fix the price at; see PRICE. **2.** [To enter on a charge account] debit, put to account, charge to, run up an account, take on account, put on one's account, incur a debt, put down, credit, encumber, sell on credit, buy on credit, chalk up, put on the books, carry, put on the cuff; see also BUY, SELL. **3.** [To attack] assail, assault, invade; see ATTACK. **4.** [To accuse] indict, censure, impute; see BLAME.

charged *a.* **1.** [Bought but not paid for] debited, placed on the account of, unpaid, on credit, on time, owing, owed, on the cuff*, on the tab*; see also BOUGHT, DUE. **2.** [Accused] taxed, confronted with, arraigned; see ACCUSED.

charitable *a.* open-handed, liberal, philanthropic; see GENEROUS, KIND.

charity *n.* **1.** [Kindness] benevolence, magnanimity, compassion; see KINDNESS 1, TOLERANCE 1. **2.** [An organization to aid the needy] charitable institution, welfare organization, eleemosynary foundation; see FOUNDATION 3.

charm *n.* **1.** [An object thought to possess power] amulet, talisman, fetish, mascot, good-luck piece, lucky piece, rabbit's foot. **2.** [The quality of being charming] grace, attractiveness, attraction; see BEAUTY 1.

charm *v.* enchant, captivate, voodoo, possess, enrapture, enthrall, transport, delight, please, entrance, bewitch, mesmerize; see also FASCINATE.

charmed *a.* enchanted, bewitched, enraptured, entranced, captivated, attracted, lured, tempted, enticed, bedazzled, hypnotized, mesmerized, under a spell, in a trance, spellbound, moonstruck, possessed, obsessed, psyched*, out of it*; see also FASCINATED.

charming *a.* enchanting, bewitching, entrancing, captivating, cute, fascinating, delightful, lovable, sweet, winning, irresistible, attractive, amiable, appealing, alluring, charismatic, pleasing, nice, graceful, winsome, seducing, seductive, desirable, enticing, tempting, inviting, ravishing, enrapturing, glamorous, elegant, infatuating, dainty, delicate, absorbing, tantalizing, engrossing, titillating, engaging, enthralling, rapturous, electrifying, lovely, intriguing, thrilling, fair, exquisite, likable, diverting, fetching, provocative, delectable, sexy*, sharp*, smooth*.—*Ant.* OFFENSIVE, disgusting, unpleasant.

chart *n.* graph, outline, diagram; see MAP, PLAN 1.

chart *v.* map, outline, draft; see PLAN 2.

charter *n.* contract, settlement, pact; see AGREEMENT 2, TREATY.

chase *v.* trail, track, seek; see HUNT 1, PURSUE 1.

chaste *a.* immaculate, unstained, clean, innocent, virginal, unblemished, unsullied, moral, modest, proper, decent, uncontaminated, virgin, celibate, platonic, controlled, unmarried, unwed, spotless, infallible, strong; see also INNOCENT 2.—*Ant.* WEAK, corruptible, frail.

chastise *v.* scold, discipline, spank; see PUNISH.

chastity *n.* innocence, purity, virtue, uprightness, honor, celibacy, integrity, decency, delicacy, cleanness, goodness, bachelorhood, unmarried state, demureness, abstinence, morality, chasteness, modesty, sinlessness, continence, coldness, restraint, virginity, spotlessness.—*Ant.* LEWDNESS, adultery, licentiousness.

chat *v.* converse, prattle, chatter; see TALK 1.

chatter *v.* gossip, chat, prattle; see BABBLE.

cheap *a.* **1.** [Low in relative price] inexpensive, low-priced, moderate, family-size, economy-size, budget, depreciated, slashed, cut-rate, on sale, competitive, lowered, thrifty, bargain, irregular, reduced, cut-priced, low-cost, at a bargain, reasonable, marked down, half-priced, popular-priced, worth the money, dime-a-dozen*, dirt-cheap*, for peanuts*, for a song, second, bargain-basement*; see also ECONOMICAL.—*Ant.* EXPENSIVE, dear, costly. **2.** [Low in quality] inferior, ordinary, shoddy; see COMMON 1, POOR 2. **3.** [Dishonest or base] dirty, tawdry, low; see DISHONEST, MEAN 3, VULGAR.

cheapen *v.* spoil, depreciate, demean; see CORRUPT, DAMAGE.

cheaply *a.* economically, inexpensively, advantageously, at a bargain price, at a good price, on sale, at cost, below cost, discounted, at a discount, reduced, at a reduced price, sacrificed, dirt cheap*, given away*, stolen*.

cheat *n.* rogue, cheater, confidence man, quack, charlatan, conniver, fraud, swindler, chiseler, beguiler, fake, bluff, deceiver, inveigler, hypocrite, trickster, pretender, dodger, humbug, crook, wolf in sheep's clothing, con man*, shark*, fourflusher*, shill*; see also CRIMINAL.

cheat *v.* defraud, swindle, beguile; see DECEIVE.

cheated *a.* defrauded, swindled, deprived of, tricked, imposed upon, victimized, beguiled, trapped, foiled, lured, taken in*, bamboozled, hoodwinked; see also DECEIVED.

cheating *n.* lying, defrauding, deceiving; see DECEPTION, DISHONESTY.

check *n.* **1.** [An order on a bank] money order, letter of credit, traveler's check, bank check, cashier's check, note, remittance; see also MONEY 1. **2.** [A control] poll, roll call, rein; see RESTRAINT 2. **3.** [An examination] investigation, analysis, inquiry; see EXAMINATION 1, 3. **4.** [The symbol √] cross, ex, sign, line, stroke, score, dot; see also MARK 1. **5.** [A pattern in squares] patchwork, checkered design, checkerboard; see DESIGN. —**in check** controlled, under control, checked; see HELD.

check *v.* **1.** [To bring under control] bridle, repress, inhibit, control, checkmate, counteract, discourage, repulse, neutralize, squelch; see also RESTRAIN.—*Ant.* FREE, liberate, loose. **2.** [To determine accuracy] review, monitor, balance accounts, balance the books, keep account of, correct, compare, find out, investigate, vet*, count, tell, call the roll, take account of, take stock, go through, go over with a fine-toothed comb*, keep tabs on*, keep track of; see also EXAMINE. **3.** [To halt] hold, terminate, cut short; see HALT, STOP 1.

check in *v.* appear, sign in, come; see ARRIVE, REGISTER 4.
check off *v.* mark off, notice, correct; see MARK 2.
check out *v.* depart, pay one's bill, settle up; see LEAVE 1, PAY 1.
check up on* *v.* watch, investigate, control; see EXAMINE.
cheek *n.* jowl, gill, chop; see FACE 1.
cheer *n.* **1.** [An agreeable mental state] delight, mirth, glee; see JOY. **2.** [An encouraging shout] roar, applause, hurrah, hurray, college yell, approval; see also YELL.
cheer *v.* **1.** [To hearten] console, inspirit, brighten; see COMFORT 1, ENCOURAGE, HELP. **2.** [To support with cheers] applaud, shout, salute; see SUPPORT 2, YELL.
cheerful *a.* **1.** [*Said especially of persons*] gay, merry, joyful; see HAPPY. **2.** [*Said especially of things*] bright, sunny, sparkling; see COMFORTABLE 2, PLEASANT 2.
cheerfully *a.* cheerily, gladly, willingly, happily, merrily, joyfully, lightheartedly, blithely, brightly, vivaciously, airily, genially, jovially, sportively, elatedly, winsomely, pleasantly, gleefully, gaily, mirthfully, playfully, hopefully, breezily, briskly, with good cheer.—*Ant.* SADLY, unwillingly, reluctantly.
cheers *interj.* here's to you, to your health, *skoal* (Scandinavian); see TOAST 1.
cheer up *v.* enliven, inspirit, exhilarate, inspire, brighten, rally, restore, perk up, boost, buck up*, pat on the back; see also IMPROVE 1.
cheese *n.* *Varieties of cheese include the following:* mild, American, Cheddar, Monterey Jack, Philadelphia cream, creamed cottage, Edam, Roquefort, Brie, mozzarella, provolone, Gorgonzola, Swiss, Camembert, Liederkranz, Neufchâtel, Gruyère, Parmesan, Stilton, Gouda, Limburger, Muenster, Port du Salut, pot, ricotta, feta, Romano; see also FOOD.
chemical *a.* synthetic, artificial, ersatz; see FALSE 3.
chemical *n.* substance, synthetic, compound; see DRUG, MEDICINE 2.
chemistry *n.* *Branches of chemistry include the following:* pure, quantitative, qualitative, organic, inorganic, theoretical, physical, physiological, pathological, metallurgical, mineralogical, geological, applied, agricultural, pharmaceutical, sanitary, industrial, technical, engineering chemistry; biochemistry, electrochemistry, zoochemistry; see also MEDICINE 3, SCIENCE 1.
cherish *v.* treasure, value, adore; see LOVE 1, 2.
cherry *a.* ruddy, reddish, rosy; see RED.
chest *n.* **1.** [A boxlike container] case, box, coffer, cabinet, strongbox, receptacle, crate, locker, bureau, coffin, casket, treasury; see also CONTAINER. **2.** [The ribbed portion of the body] breast, thorax, bosom, rib cage, heart, upper trunk, pulmonary cavity, peritoneum, ribs.
chew *v.* bite, champ, munch, crunch, masticate, nibble, feast upon, gnaw, gulp, grind, rend, scrunch, ruminate; see also EAT 1.
chicken *n.* **1.** [A barnyard fowl] chick, hen, rooster; see FOWL. **2.** [Flesh of the chicken] giblets, dark meat, white meat; see MEAT. **3.** [*A coward] recreant, dastard, craven; see COWARD. **—count one's chickens before they are hatched** rely on, depend on, put trust in; see ANTICIPATE.
chief *a.* leading, first, foremost; see MAIN, PRINCIPAL.
chief *n.* principal, manager, overseer, governor, president, foreman, proprietor, supervisor, director, chairman, ringleader, general, master, dictator, superintendent, head, prince, emperor, duke, majesty, monarch, overlord, lord, potentate, sovereign, chieftain, ruler, captain, commander, bigwig*, prima donna*, boss, it*; see also LEADER.
chiefly *a.* mainly, particularly, in the first place; see PRINCIPALLY.
child *n.* newborn, infant, youth, adolescent, youngster, daughter, son, grandchild, stepchild, offspring, innocent, minor, juvenile, tot, cherub, papoose, moppet*, kid*, kiddie*, whelp*, brat*, imp, small fry; see also BOY, GIRL.—*Ant.* PARENT, forefather, adult. **—with child** carrying a child, going to have a baby, fertile; see PREGNANT.
childbirth *n.* delivery, childbearing, parturition, childbed, labor, nativity, delivering, accouchement, lying in, confinement, procreation, reproduction, propagation, giving birth, blessed event*; see also BIRTH.
childhood *n.* infancy, youth, minority, school days, adolescence, nursery days, babyhood, boyhood, girlhood, teens, puberty, immaturity, tender age.—*Ant.* AGE, maturity, senility.
childish *a.* childlike, foolish, stupid, baby, infantile, juvenile, youthful, babyish, boyish, girlish, adolescent, green, soft, immature; see also NAIVE, SIMPLE 1, YOUNG 2.—*Ant.* MATURE, adult, grown.
chill *n.* crispness, coolness, coldness; see COLD 1.
chill *v.* **1.** [To reduce temperature] frost, refrigerate, make cold; see COOL, FREEZE 1. **2.** [To check] dispirit, dishearten, dampen; see DEPRESS 2, DISCOURAGE.
chilly *a.* brisk, fresh, crisp; see COLD 1, COOL 1.
chime *v.* tinkle, clang, toll; see RING 2, SOUND.
chimney *n.* smokestack, fireplace, furnace, hearth, flue, vent, pipe, funnel, smokeshaft, stack.
chin *n.* mentum, mandible, jawbone; see JAW.

china *n.* earthenware, pottery, crockery; see DISH.

China *n.* an Asiatic country, Chung Kwoh, People's Republic of China, Red China, the Celestial Kingdom, the Middle Kingdom, Chinese Empire, the East, the Orient, the Mysterious East; see also ASIA.

Chinese *a.* Sinaic, Asian, Asiatic; see ORIENTAL.

chip *n.* **1.** [A fragment] fragment, slice, wedge; see BIT 1, FLAKE, PART 1. **2.** [A microcircuit] integrated circuit, semiconductor, microprocessor, computer on a chip. —**having a chip on one's shoulder** ready to fight, disturbed, agitated; see ANGRY. —**when the chips are down** in a crisis, having trouble, in a difficult position; see IN TROUBLE.

chip *v.* slash, hew, hack, crumble, snip, fragment, incise, whittle, crack off, splinter, notch, sliver, cut off, chop, split, slice, chisel, clip, break, crack, flake, cut away, nick, shiver, reduce, shear; see also BREAK.

chip in* *v.* contribute, pay, pitch in*; see SHARE 1.

chirp *v.* twitter, warble, cheep; see SOUND.

chisel *n.* gouge, blade, edge; see KNIFE, TOOL 1.

chisel *v.* **1.** [To work with a chisel] carve, hew, incise; see CUT 1. **2.** [*To get by imposition] impose upon, defraud, gyp*; see DECEIVE, STEAL.

chivalrous *a.* courteous, heroic, valiant; see BRAVE, NOBLE 1, 2, POLITE.

chivalry *n.* valor, gallantry, fairness; see COURTESY 1.

chock-full *a.* packed, crammed, stuffed; see FULL 1.

choice *a.* superior, fine, exceptional; see BEST 1.

choice *n.* selection, preference, alternative, election, substitute, favorite, pick, a good bet; see also JUDGMENT 2.

choke *v.* asphyxiate, strangle, strangulate, stifle, throttle, garrote, drown, noose, smother, grab by the throat, wring the neck of, stop the breath of, gag, gasp, suffocate, choke off, be choked, die out, die by asphyxiation; see also DIE.

choke up* *v.* give way to one's feelings, weep, break down; see CRY 1.

choose *v.* decide, take, pick out, draw lots, cull, prefer, make a choice of, accept, weigh, judge, sort, appoint, embrace, will, call for, fancy, take up, separate, favor, determine, resolve, discriminate, make a decision, adopt, collect, mark out for, cut out, arrange, keep, take up, make one's choice, pick and choose, settle on, use one's discretion, determine upon, fix on, place one's trust in, glean, single out, espouse, exercise one's option, make up one's mind, set aside, set apart, commit oneself, separate the wheat from the chaff, incline toward, opt for, burn one's bridges; see also DECIDE.—*Ant.* DISCARD, reject, refuse.

choosing *n.* selecting, picking, judging; see CHOICE.

chop *v.* fell, cut with an ax, whack; see CUT 1.

chord *n.* harmonizing tones, triad, octave; second, third, fourth, fifth, etc. chord; diminished chord, augmented chord, inverted chord, broken chord; primary, secondary, tertiary chord; tetrachord, perfect fourth, arpeggio, common chord; see also HARMONY 1, MUSIC 1.

chore *n.* task, routine, errand; see JOB 2.

chorus *n.* **1.** [A body of singers] choir, singing group, choristers, voices, glee club, singing society, church singers, male chorus, female chorus, mixed chorus, operatic group; see also MUSIC 1. **2.** [A refrain] melody, strain, tune; see SONG.

chosen *a.* picked, elected, preferred; see NAMED 2.

Christ *n.* the Saviour, Jesus, Jesus of Nazareth, the Redeemer, Messiah, Immanuel, the Word, the Son, the Son of Man, the Son of God, God the Son, the Son of David, the Son of Mary, the Risen, the King of Glory, the Prince of Peace, the Good Shepherd, the King of the Jews, the Lamb of God, the Only Begotten, King of Kings, Lord of Lords, Christ Our Lord, the Way, the Door, the Truth, the Life, the Light of the World, the Incarnate Word, the Word made Flesh, Rose of Sharon; see also GOD 2.

christen *v.* immerse, sprinkle, take into a Christian church; see BAPTIZE, BLESS, NAME 1.

Christian *a.* pious, reverent, devoted; see HUMBLE 1, RELIGIOUS 1, 2.

Christian *n.* Protestant, Catholic, gentile; see CHURCH 3, SAINT.

Christianity *n.* **1.** [A religion based upon the divinity of Christ] teachings of Christ, the Gospel, the Faith; see FAITH 2, RELIGION 2. **2.** [The body of Christian people] Christendom, Christians, followers of Christ; see CHURCH 3. **3.** [An attitude associated with Christianity] Christian spirit, forgiving disposition, loving-kindness; see KINDNESS 1, TOLERANCE 1.

Christmas *n.* Xmas*, Noel, Yule; see HOLIDAY, WINTER.

chronic *a.* inveterate, confirmed, settled, rooted, deep-seated, continuing, persistent, stubborn, incurable, lasting, lingering, deep-rooted, perennial, fixed, continual, incessant, long-standing, recurring, continuous, of long duration, long-lived, protracted, ceaseless, sustained, lifelong, prolonged, recurrent, obstinate, inborn, inbred, ingrained, ever-present; see also CONSTANT, HABITUAL, PERMANENT.—*Ant.* TEMPORARY, acute, casual.

chronicle *n.* narrative, annals, account; see HISTORY, RECORD 1.

chronological *a.* temporal, historical, tabulated, classified, according to chronology, in the order of time, sequential, consecutive, properly dated, measured in time, in sequence, progressive in time, ordered, in order, in due course.

chubby *a.* plump, round, pudgy; see FAT.

chuckle *n.* giggle, smile, grin; see LAUGH.

chuckle *v.* giggle, smile, snigger; see LAUGH.

chummy* *a.* affectionate, intimate, constant; see FRIENDLY.

chunk *n.* piece, mass, lump; see PART 1.

chunky *a.* stocky, thickset, stout; see FAT.

church *n.* **1.** [A building consecrated to worship] cathedral, house of God, Lord's house, temple, synagogue, mosque, house of worship, meeting house, chapel, basilica, tabernacle, abbey, sanctuary, house of prayer, mission, shrine, pagoda. **2.** [A divine service] rite, prayers, prayer meeting, Sunday school, worhsip, Mass, Lord's Supper, sacrament, the holy sacrament, rosary, ritual, religious rite, morning service, evening service, congregational worship, fellowship, devotion, office, revival meeting, chapel service, sermon, communion; see also CEREMONY. **3.** [An organized religious body] congregation, gathering, denomination, sect, chapter, body, order, communion, faith, religion, religious order, affiliation, persuasion, belief, faction, doctrine, creed, cult. *Christian churches include the following:* Methodist, Presbyterian, Unitarian, Episcopalian, Baptist, Christian Science, Mormon, Congregational, Lutheran, Roman Catholic, Eastern Orthodox, Greek, Russian, Pentecostal, Church of England, Church of the Nazarene, Society of Friends.

churn *v.* stir, beat, agitate; see MIX 1.

cigarette *n.* fag*, smoke*, coffin nail*, weed*.

cinema *n.* film, motion pictures, the movies; see MOVIE.

circle *n.* **1.** [A round closed plane figure] ring, loop, wheel, sphere, globe, orb, orbit, zodiac, bowl, vortex, hoop, horizon, perimeter, periphery, circumference, full turn, circuit, disk, meridian, equator, ecliptic, cycle, bracelet, belt, wreath. **2.** [An endless sequence of events] cycle, course, succession; see PROGRESS 1, SERIES, SEQUENCE 1. —**come full circle** go through a cycle, come back, revert; see RETURN 1.

circle *v.* round, encircle, loop, tour, circumnavigate, ring, belt, embrace, encompass, wind about, revolve around, circumscribe, curve around, circuit, enclose, spiral, coil, circulate, detour, wind, roll, wheel, swing past, go round about, evade; see also SURROUND 1.—*Ant.* DIVIDE, bisect, cut across.

circuit *n.* circumference, course, circle; see ORBIT 1, REVOLUTION 1.

circular *a.* spherical, cyclical, globular; see ROUND 1.

circular *n.* handbill, broadside, leaflet; see ADVERTISEMENT, PAMPHLET.

circulate *v.* **1.** [To go about] move around, go about, wander; see TRAVEL, WALK 1. **2.** [To send about] diffuse, report, broadcast; see DISTRIBUTE.

circulation *n.* **1.** [Motion in a circle] rotation, current, flowing; see FLOW, REVOLUTION 1. **2.** [Number of copies distributed] transmission, apportionment, dissemination; see DISTRIBUTION.

circumference *n.* perimeter, periphery, border; see CIRCLE 1.

circumscribe *v.* encircle, encompass, girdle; see SURROUND 1.

circumstance *n.* **1.** [An attendant condition] situation, condition, contingency, phase, factor, detail, item, fact, case, place, time, cause, status, element, feature, point, incident, article, stipulation, concern, matter, event, occurrence, crisis, coincidence, happenstance*. **2.** [An occurrence] episode, happening, incident; see EVENT.

circumstances *n.pl.* **1.** [Condition in life] worldly goods, outlook, prospects, chances, means, assets, prosperity, financial condition, resources, standing, property, net worth, financial standing, credit rating, terms, way of life, rank, class, degree, capital, position, financial responsibility, footing, income, sphere, substance, stock in trade, lot, prestige, what one is worth, place on the ladder; see also STATE 2, WEALTH. **2.** [Attendant conditions] situation, environment, surroundings, facts, particulars, factors, features, motives, controlling factors, governing factors, the times, occasion, basis, grounds, setting, background, needs, requirements, necessities, course of events, legal status, change, life, fluctuation, phase, case, condition, state of affairs, surrounding facts, the score*, the scene*, the story*, where it's at*, how the land lies, the lay of the land, current regime, ups and downs. —**under no circumstances** under no conditions, by no means, absolutely not; see NEVER. —**under the circumstances** conditions being what they are, for this reason, because of; see BECAUSE.

circumstantial *a.* presumptive, inferential, inconclusive; see UNCERTAIN.

circumvent *v.* **1.** [To go around] encircle, encompass, entrap; see SURROUND 1. **2.** [To avoid] dodge, elude, shun; see AVOID, EVADE.

circus *n.* hippodrome, spectacle, fair; see ENTERTAINMENT.

citation *n.* bidding, charge, summons; see COMMAND.

citizen *n.* inhabitant, denizen, national, subject, cosmopolite, commoner, civilian, urbanite, taxpayer, member of the community, householder, native, occupant, settler, voter, dweller, immigrant, naturalized person, townsman, the man on the street, villager, John Q. Public; see also RESIDENT.

city *a.* metropolitan, civil, civic; see MUNICIPAL.

city *n.* town, place, municipality, capital, megalopolis, metropolis, suburb, county seat, trading center, inner city, downtown, shopping center, shopping district, business district, financial district, incorporated town, village, metropolitan area, township; see also CENTER 2.

civic *a.* civil, urban, municipal; see PUBLIC 1, 2.

civil *a.* **1.** [Civic] local, civic, public; see MUNICIPAL. **2.** [Polite] formal, courteous, refined; see POLITE.

civilian *n.* private citizen, noncombatant, person not in the armed forces; see CITIZEN.

civilization *n.* cultivation, polish, enlightenment, refinement, civility, illumination, advancement of knowledge, elevation, edification, culture, advancement, social well-being, degree of cultivation, material well-being, education, breeding; see also CULTURE 1, PROGRESS 1.—*Ant.* barbarism, savagery, degeneration.

civilize *v.* enlighten, cultivate, enrich, reclaim, refine, acculturate, spiritualize, humanize, edify, uplift, tame, foster, instruct, promote, indoctrinate, idealize, elevate, educate, advance, ennoble; see also DEVELOP 1, TEACH.

civilized *a.* enlightened, refined, humanized; see CULTURED, EDUCATED.

civil rights *n.pl.* civil liberties, equality, four freedoms; see CHOICE, FREEDOM 1.

claim *n.* demand, declaration, profession, entreaty, petition, suit, ultimatum, call, request, requirement, application, case, assertion, plea, right, interest, title, part; see also APPEAL 1. **—lay claim to** demand, challenge, stake out a claim to; see OWN 1.

claim *v.* **1.** [To assert a claim to] demand, attach, lay claim to; see OWN 1. **2.** [To assert] insist, pronounce, pretend; see BELIEVE, DECLARE.

clam *n.* bivalve, mollusk, shellfish; see FISH.

clammy *a.* moist, damp, soggy; see COLD 1, WET 1.

clamor *n.* din, outcry, discord; see NOISE 2, UPROAR.

clamp *n.* snap, clasp, catch; see FASTENER, LOCK 1.

clan *n.* group, clique, moiety; see ORGANIZATION 2, RACE 2.

clang *n.* ring, clatter, jangle; see NOISE 1.

clank *n.* chink, bang, clink; see NOISE 1.

clap *v.* **1.** [To applaud] cheer, acclaim, approve; see PRAISE 1. **2.** [To strike] bang, slap, slam; see HIT 1.

clarification *n.* exposition, elucidation, description; see DEFINITION, EXPLANATION, INTERPRETATION.

clarify *v.* interpret, define, elucidate; see EXPLAIN.

clarity *n.* limpidity, clearness, purity, brightness, precision, explicitness, exactness, distinctness, plain speech, openness, directness, evidence, prominence, salience, transparency, conspicuousness, certainty, lucidity.—*Ant.* DARKNESS, haze, obscurity.

clash *n.* **1.** [Collision] crash, encounter, impact; see COLLISION. **2.** [Disagreement] opposition, conflict, argument; see DISAGREEMENT 1, DISPUTE.

clash *v.* be dissimilar, mismatch, not go with; see CONTRAST, DIFFER 1.

clasp *n.* buckle, pin, clamp; see FASTENER.

clasp *v.* clamp, pin, buckle; see FASTEN.

class *n.* **1.** [A classification] degree, order, rank, grade, standing, genus, division, distinction, breed, type, kingdom, subdivision, phylum, subphylum, superorder, family, sect, category, rate, collection, denomination, department, sort, species, variety, branch, group, genre, range, brand, set, kind, section, domain, nature, color, origin, character, frame, temperament, school, designation, sphere, spirit, vein, persuasion, province, make, grain, source, name, mood, habit, form, selection, stamp, status, range, property, aspect, disposition, tone; see also CLASSIFICATION. **2.** [A group organized for study] lecture, seminar, study session; see SCHOOL 1. **3.** [A division of society] set, caste, social level; see FAMILY. **—in a class by itself** unusual, different, one of a kind; see UNIQUE.

class *v.* identify, rank, grade; see CLASSIFY, MARK 2.

classic *n.* opus, masterwork, exemplar; see MASTERPIECE.

classical *a.* **1.** [Of recognized importance] standard, first-rate, established, ideal, flawless, distinguished, paramount, aesthetic, superior, artistic, well-known; see also EXCELLENT.—*Ant.* POPULAR, modern, transitory. **2.** [Concerning ancient Greece or Rome] humanistic, academic, classic; see OLD 3.

classification *n.* arrangement, assortment, grouping, ordering, allotment, organization, gradation, coordination, disposition, categorizing, apportionment, analysis, division, assignment, designation, assorting, distribution, allocation, categorization; see also CLASS 1, ORDER 3.

classified *a.* assorted, grouped, classed, indexed, filed, orderly, recorded, listed, registered, detailed, arranged, regulated, compiled, coordinated, ranked, distributed, cataloged, separated, labeled, numbered, systematized, tabulated, alphabetized, typed, on file, rated.—*Ant.* MIXED, confused, jumbled.

classify *v.* arrange, order, pigeonhole, tabulate, organize, distribute, categorize, systematize, coordinate, correlate, incorporate, label, alphabetize, place in a category, range, form into classes, divide, allocate, number, rate, class, rank, catalog, segregate, distinguish, allot, analyze, regiment, name, group, tag, type, put in order, break down, assort, sort, index, grade, match, size, reduce to order; see also FILE 1, LIST 1.—*Ant.* DISORGANIZE, disorder, disarrange.

clatter *v.* rattle, clash, crash; see SOUND.

clause *n.* **1.** [A provision] condition, codicil, ultimatum; see LIMITATION 2, REQUIREMENT 1. **2.** [A grammatical structure] limiters, sentence modifiers, transformations; see GRAMMAR.

claw *n.* talon, hook, spur, paw, grappling iron, grappling hook, forked end, clutching hand, grapnel, crook, barb, pincers, fingernail.

claw *v.* tear, scratch, rip open; see BREAK 1, HURT, RIP.

clay *n.* loam, earth, till, marl, kaolin, potter's clay, clayware, green pottery, terra cotta, green brick, china clay, porcelain clay, adobe; see also MUD.

clean *a.* **1.** [Not soiled] spotless, washed, stainless, laundered, untarnished, unstained, neat, tidy, clear, blank, white, unblemished, unspotted, snowy, well-kept, dustless, cleansed, immaculate, unsoiled, unpolluted, spic and span*, clean as a whistle*.—*Ant.* DIRTY, soiled, stained. **2.** [Not contaminated] unadulterated, wholesome, sanitary; see PURE 2. **3.** [Having sharp outlines] clear-cut, sharp, distinct; see DEFINITE 2. **4.** [Thorough] complete, entire, total; see ABSOLUTE 1, WHOLE 1. **5.** [Fair] reliable, decent, lawful; see FAIR 1, HONEST 1. —**come clean*** confess, reveal, expose; see ADMIT 2.

clean *v.* cleanse, clean up, clear up, clear out, purify, soak, shake out, wash down, scrub off, disinfect, tidy up, deodorize, swab, polish, sterilize, scrape, sweep out, scour, launder, vacuum, scald, dust, mop, cauterize, rinse, sponge, brush, dress, comb, whisk, scrub, sweep, wipe up, clarify, rake, clean away, make clear, bathe, soap, erase, neaten, shampoo, refine, flush, blot, do up*, spruce up, slick up*; see also WASH 1, 2.—*Ant.* DIRTY, soil, smear.

cleaner *n.* detergent, disinfectant, cleaning agent; see CLEANSER, SOAP.

cleaning *a.* cleansing, purgative, detergent, washing, delousing, dusting, sweeping, scouring, soaking, sterilizing, laundering, vacuuming, scalding, purifying.

cleaning *n.* cleansing, purge, scrubbing, scouring, purification, scrub, sweeping, brush, prophylaxis, sterilizing, washing, brushing, purifying, deodorizing, catharsis.

cleanliness *n.* cleanness, neatness, pureness, tidiness, trimness, spruceness, immaculateness, spotlessness, dapperness, orderliness, whiteness, disinfection, sanitation.—*Ant.* FILTH, dirtiness, griminess.

cleanse *v.* **1.** [To remove dirt from the surface] launder, wash, scrub; see CLEAN. **2.** [To remove impurities from within] refine, disinfect, purge; see CLEAN, PURIFY.

cleanser *n.* cleansing agent, cleaning agent, abrasive, lather, solvent, purgative, deodorant, fumigant, soap flakes, polish, disinfectant, antiseptic, purifier, scouring powder, spray cleaner, cleaner, detergent, soap powder, cleaning fluid, dry cleaner, suds; see also SOAP. *Cleansers include the following:* water, soap and water, soap, washing powder, oven cleaner, naphtha, furniture polish, borax, lye, household ammonia, solvent, bluing, carbon tetrachloride, toilet-bowl cleanser, baking soda, chlorine compound, silver-polish, kerosene, gasoline, vinegar, rug shampoo.

clear *a.* **1.** [Open to the sight or understanding] explicit, plain, manifest; see OBVIOUS 1, 2. **2.** [Offering little impediment to the vision] lucid, pure, transparent, apparent, limpid, translucent, crystal, crystalline, thin, crystal clear.—*Ant.* OPAQUE, dark, muddy. **3.** [Unclouded] sunny, bright, rainless; see FAIR 3. **4.** [Freed from legal charges] free, guiltless, cleared, exonerated, blameless, innocent, sinless, dismissed, discharged, absolved; see also INNOCENT 1.—*Ant.* GUILTY, accused, blamed. **5.** [Audible] loud enough to be heard, distinct, definite; see AUDIBLE. —**in the clear** guiltless, not suspected, cleared; see FREE 2, INNOCENT 1.

clear *v.* **1.** [To free from uncertainty] clear up, relieve, clarify; see EXPLAIN. **2.** [To free from obstacles] disentangle, rid, unloose; see FREE, REMOVE 1. **3.** [To profit] realize, net, make; see RECEIVE 1.

clear-cut *a.* precise, plain, evident; see OBVIOUS 1, 2.

cleared *a.* **1.** [Emptied] cleaned, unloaded, cleared away; see EMPTY. **2.** [Freed of charges] vindicated, absolved, set right; see DISCHARGED, FREE 2.

clearing *n.* **1.** [The act of clearing] clearance, freeing, removing; see REMOVAL. **2.** [A cleared space] open space, opening, clearance; see AREA, COURT, EXPANSE, YARD 1.

clearly *a.* **1.** [Distinctly; *said of sight*] plainly, precisely, lucidly, purely, brightly, perceptibly, unmistakably, in full view, in focus, discernibly, decidedly, incontestably, undoubtedly, noticeably, admittedly, before one's eyes, beyond doubt, prominently, obviously, openly, overtly, observably, certainly, apparently, manifestly, recognizably, conspicuously, in plain sight, definitely, markedly, surely, visibly, positively, seemingly, evidently, at first sight, to all appearances, on the face of.—*Ant.* HAZY, dully, cloudily. **2.** [Distinctly; *said of sounds*] sharply, acutely, ringingly, penetratingly, audibly, bell-like.—*Ant.* indistinct, mutteringly, unclearly.

clearness *n.* brightness, distinctness, lucidity; see CLARITY.

clear out *v.* **1.** [To remove] clean out, dispose of, get rid of; see ELIMINATE, EXCRETE. **2.** [*To leave] depart, go, remove oneself; see LEAVE 1.

clear up *v.* **1.** [To become clear; *said especially of weather*] improve, blow over, stop raining, stop snowing, run its course, die away, pass away, die down, show improvement, pick up, lift, become fair, have fair weather. **2.** [To make clear] explicate, clarify, make plausible, make explicable, make reasonable; see also EXPLAIN.

clench *v.* grip, grasp, double up; see HOLD 1.

clergy *n.* priesthood, prelacy, pastorate; see MINISTRY 2.

clergyman *n.* pastor, rabbi, preacher; see MINISTER 1, PRIEST.

clerical *a.* **1.** [Concerning clerks] stenographic, accounting, bookkeeping, secretarial, typing, written, assistant, subordinate. **2.** [Concerning the clergy] ministerial, priestly, apostolic, monastic, monkish, churchly, cleric, papal, episcopal, canonical, pontifical, ecclesiastic, sacred, holy, ecclesiastical, in God's service, devoted to the Lord, in the Lord's work.

clerk *n.* salesgirl, saleswoman, saleslady, shopgirl, shop assistant, salesclerk, salesman, salesperson, counterman, seller, auditor, bookkeeper, recorder, registrar, stenographer, office girl, office boy, timekeeper, cashier, teller, office worker, notary, controller, copyist, law clerk, switchboard, operator; see also SECRETARY 2.

clever *a.* **1.** [Apt, particularly with one's hands] skillful, expert, adroit; see ABLE. **2.** [Mentally quick] smart, bright, shrewd; see INTELLIGENT, SLY.

cleverly *a.* neatly, skillfully, tactfully, dexterously, ingeniously, resourcefully, deftly, nimbly, agilely, adroitly, proficiently, expertly, smoothly, quickly, speedily, readily; see also EASILY.—*Ant.* AWKWARDLY, clumsily, unskillfully.

cleverness *n.* skill, adroitness, ingenuity; see ABILITY.

cliché *n.* commonplace, platitude, stereotype, proverb, saying, slogan, trite phrase, stereotyped saying, vapid expression, triteness, banality, triviality, staleness, hackneyed phrase, trite idea; see also MOTTO.

click *n.* tick, snap, bang; see NOISE 1.

click *v.* **1.** [To make a clicking sound] tick, snap, bang; see SOUND. **2.** [*To be successful] match, go off well, meet with approval; see SUCCEED 1.

client *n.* customer, patient, patron; see BUYER.

cliff *n.* bluff, crag, steep rock; see HILL, MOUNTAIN 1, WALL 1.

climate *n.* characteristic weather, atmospheric conditions, meteorologic conditions, aridity, humidity, weather conditions; see also COLD 1, HEAT 1, WEATHER.

climax *n.* peak, apex, highest point, culmination, acme, pinnacle, crest, zenith, summit, apogee, extremity, limit, pitch, utmost extent, highest degree, turning point, crowning point; see also MAXIMUM, TOP 1.—*Ant.* DEPRESSION, anticlimax, nadir.

climax *v.* culminate, tower, end, top, conclude, reach a peak, come to a head, reach the zenith, break the record; see also ACHIEVE.

climb *n.* **1.** [The act of climbing] climbing, clamber, mounting; see RISE. **2.** [An ascending place] slope, incline, dune; see GRADE 1, HILL.

climb *v.* scale, work one's way up, ascend gradually, scramble up, clamber up, swarm up, start up, go up, ascend, struggle up, get on, climb on, progress upward, rise, lift, rise hand over hand, come up, creep up, escalate, surmount, shinny up, shoot up.

climb down *v.* step off, come down, dismount; see DESCEND.

cling *v.* adhere, clasp, hold fast; see STICK 1.

clip *v.* snip, crop, clip off; see CUT 1, DECREASE 2.

clippers *n.pl.* shears, cutting instruments, barber's tools; see SCISSORS.

clique *n.* coterie, clan, club; see FACTION, ORGANIZATION 2.

clock *n.* timekeeper, timepiece, time-marker, timer, ticker*. *Kinds of clocks include the following:* alarm, cuckoo, electric, grandfather, pendulum clock; hourglass, stopwatch, sundial, wristwatch; see also WATCH 1. —**around the clock** continuously, continually, twenty-four hours a day; see REGULARLY.

clock *v.* time, measure time, register speed; see MEASURE 1.

clog *v.* stop up, seal, obstruct; see CLOSE 2, HINDER.

close *a.* **1.** [Nearby] neighboring, across the street, around the corner; see NEAR 1. **2.** [Intimate] confidential, intimate, familiar; see PRIVATE. **3.** [Compact] dense, solid, compressed; see THICK 1. **4.** [Stingy] narrow, parsimonious, niggardly; see STINGY. **5.** [Stifling] sticky, stuffy, unventilated, moldy, heavy, motionless, uncomfortable, choky, stale-smelling, musty, stagnant, confined, suffocating, sweltering, tight, stale, oppressive, breathless; see also UNCOMFORTABLE 2.—*Ant.* FRESH, refreshing, brisk. **6.**

[Similar] resembling, having common qualities, much the same; see ALIKE, LIKE.

close *n.* termination, adjournment, ending; see END 2.

close *v.* **1.** [To put a stop to] conclude, finish, terminate; see END 1. **2.** [To put a stopper into] shut, stop down, choke off, stuff, clog, prevent passage, shut off, turn off, lock, block, bar, dam, cork, seal, button; see also CLOSE 2.—*Ant.* OPEN, uncork, unseal. **3.** [To come together] meet, unite, agree; see JOIN 1. **4.** [To shut] slam, close down, shut down, shut up, seal, fasten, bolt, clench, bar, shutter, clap, lock, bring to.

closed *a.* **1.** [Terminated] ended, concluded, final; see FINISHED 1. **2.** [Not in operation] shut down, out of order, out of service, bankrupt, closed up, padlocked, folded up*; see also BROKEN 2. **3.** [Not open] shut, fastened, sealed; see TIGHT 2.

closely *a.* approximately, similarly, exactly, nearly, strictly, firmly, intimately, jointly, in conjunction with; see also ALMOST.—*Ant.* INDIVIDUALLY, separately, one by one.

closet *n.* cabinet, recess, cupboard, buffet, locker, wardrobe, receptacle, safe, bin, drawer, chest of drawers, vault, cold storage, clothes room.

clot *n.* lump, bulk, clotting, curdling, coagulation, mass, clump, coagulum, thickness, coalescence, curd.

clot *v.* coagulate, set, lump; see THICKEN.

cloth *n.* fabric, material, stuff; see GOODS.

clothe *v.* attire, dress up, costume; see DRESS 1.

clothed *a.* clad, invested, costumed, robed, shod, dressed, attired, decked, disguised, covered, draped, veiled.—*Ant.* NAKED, exposed, stripped.

clothes *n.pl.* wearing apparel, raiment, clothing, garments, garb, vesture, vestments, attire, array, casual wear, informal wear, evening clothes, work clothes, suit of clothes, costume, wardrobe, trappings, gear, underclothes, outfit, get-up*, rags, toggery*, togs*, duds*, threads*, things; see also COAT 1, DRESS 1, 2, HAT, PANTS 1, SHIRT. *Men's clothes include the following:* business suit, jacket and slacks, trousers, shorts, breeches, knickers*, tuxedo, tux*, dress suit, dinner jacket, uniform, shirt, body shirt, hiphugger pants, continental suit, socks; long underwear, long johns*. *Women's clothes include the following:* housecoat, negligee, morning dress, evening gown, kimono, shorts, frock, blouse, jumper, slip, shirtwaist, robe, underwear, slacks, panties, brassiere, bra, pantyhose, girdle; nightgown, nightie*, pajamas, pj's*, dress, street dress, suit, cardigan, sweater, pullover, slipover sweater, house dress, dickey, nylon stockings, nylons, miniskirt, shift, muumuu, hiphugger slacks, smock, skirt, coat, petticoat, hat, bonnet. *Clothes worn by both men and women include the following:* blue jeans, levis, turtleneck, sweat shirt, tank top, kimono, raincoat, tights, bell-bottom pants, cutoffs*. *Children's clothes include the following:* rompers, playsuit, coveralls, snowsuit, leggings. *Work clothes include the following:* overalls, windbreaker, blue jeans, coveralls, jumper, cords*.

clothing *n.* attire, raiment, garb; see CLOTHES, DRESS 1.

cloud *n.* haze, mist, fogginess, haziness, film, puff, billow, frost, smoke, veil, cloud cover, overcast. *Types of clouds include the following:* cirrus, cumulus, stratus, nimbus, cirrocumulus, cirro-stratus. **—in the clouds** fanciful, fantastic, romantic; see IMPRACTICAL. **—under a cloud** suspect, dubious, uncertain; see SUSPICIOUS 2.

cloudy *a.* **1.** [Hazy] overcast, foggy, sunless; see DARK 1. **2.** [Not clear] dense, nontransparent, nontranslucent; see OPAQUE.

clown *n.* buffoon, fool, joker, harlequin, punch, funnyman, humorist, jester, comedian, cut-up*; see also ACTOR.

clown (around) *v.* fool around, kid around, cut up*; see JOKE.

club *n.* **1.** [A social organization] association, order, society; see FACTION, ORGANIZATION 2. **2.** [A cudgel] bat, hammer, mallet; see STICK.

club *v.* batter, whack, pound; see BEAT 1, HIT 1.

clue *n.* evidence, trace, mark; see PROOF 1, SIGN 1.

clump *n.* cluster, bundle, knot; see BUNCH.

clumsily *a.* crudely, gawkily, stumblingly: see AWKWARDLY.

clumsiness *n.* crudity, ineptitude, boorishness; see AWKWARDNESS.

clumsy *a.* ungainly, gawky, inexpert; see AWKWARD.

cluster *n.* group, batch, clump; see BUNCH.

clutch *v.* grab, grasp, grip; see HOLD 1, SEIZE 1.

clutches *n.pl.* control, grasp, keeping; see POWER 2.

clutter *n.* disarray, jumble, disorder; see CONFUSION.

coach *n.* **1.** [A carriage] fourwheeler, chaise, victoria; see CARRIAGE 2, VEHICLE. **2.** [An instructor] mentor, drillmaster, physical education instructor; see TEACHER, TRAINER.

coach *v.* train, drill, instruct; see TEACH.

coagulate *v.* curdle, clot, congeal; see THICKEN.

coal *n.* sea coal, stone coal, mineral coal; see FUEL. **—haul or rake or drag over the coals*** reprimand, criticize, castigate; see BLAME.

coalition *n.* compact, conspiracy, association; see FACTION.

coarse *a.* 1. [Not fine] rough, rude, unrefined; see CRUDE. 2. [Vulgar] low, common, base; see RUDE 1, VULGAR.

coast *n.* shoreline, beach, seaboard; see SHORE.

coast *v.* glide, float, ride on the current; see DRIFT, RIDE 1.

coat *n.* 1. [An outer garment] topcoat, overcoat, cloak, suit coat, tuxedo, dinner jacket, sport coat, dress coat, mink coat, fur coat, ski jacket, mackintosh, raincoat, jacket, windbreaker, peacoat, three-quarter length coat, wrap, leather jacket, southwester, slicker; see also CLOTHES. 2. [The covering of an animal] protective covering, husk, shell, crust, scale, fleece, epidermis, rind, ectoderm, pelt, membrane; see also FUR, HIDE, SKIN. 3. [An applied covering] coating, layer, set, wash, primer, finish, glaze, crust, painting, overlay, whitewashing, varnish, lacquer, gloss, tinge, prime coat, plaster; see also FINISH 2.

coat *v.* surface, glaze, enamel; see PAINT 2, VARNISH.

coating *n.* crust, covering, layer; see COAT 3.

coax *v.* persuade, cajole, inveigle; see INFLUENCE, URGE 2.

cocktail *n.* mixed drink, aperitif, highball. *Cocktails include the following:* Manhattan, martini, old-fashioned, champagne, sidecar, Margarita, pink lady, whisky sour, screwdriver, Bloody Mary, black Russian, Daiquiri, Bacardi, Alexander; see also DRINK 2.

code *n.* codex, method, digest; see LAW 2, SYSTEM.

coerce *v.* impel, compel, constrain; see FORCE.

coercion *n.* compulsion, persuasion, constraint; see PRESSURE 2, RESTRAINT 2.

coexist *v.* exist together, synchronize, be contemporary; see ACCOMPANY.

coexistence *n.* order, conformity, accord; see PEACE 1, 2.

coffee *n.* beverage, decoction, java*; see DRINK 2. *Prepared coffee includes the following:* Turkish, Armenian, drip, percolated, vacuum, instant, French roast, coffee with cream, demitasse.

coffin *n.* box, casket, sarcophagus, lead coffin, burial urn, funerary urn, funerary box, mummy case; see also CONTAINER.

cohabit *v.* shack up with*, play house with*, be roommates; see ACCOMPANY.

coherence *n.* stickiness, viscosity, gumminess, cementation, soldering, adhesiveness, sticking together, coagulation, viscidity, adherence, set, fusion, sticking, union, adhesion, cohesiveness, consistency.

coherent *a.* comprehensible, sound, intelligible; see LOGICAL, UNDERSTANDABLE.

coil *n.* curl, turn, ring, wind, convolution, twine, twist, twirl, lap, loop, curlicue, corkscrew, roll, spiral, helix, scroll; see also CIRCLE 1.

coil *v.* scroll, wind, loop, twist, fold, twine, intertwine, entwine, convolute, lap, twirl, spire, wreathe; see also CURL.—*Ant.* UNFOLD, unwind, ravel.

coin *n.* legal tender, silver, copper; see MONEY 1.

coin *v.* 1. [To mint money] mint, strike, stamp; see MANUFACTURE. 2. [To invent a word, etc.] create, originate, make up; see INVENT 1.

coincide *v.* 1. [Correspond] accord, harmonize, match; see AGREE. 2. [Happen] occur, come about, take place; see HAPPEN 2.

coincidence *n.* luck, fortune, circumstance; see ACCIDENT, CHANCE 1.

coincidental *a.* 1. [Occurring simultaneously] concurrent, concomitant, contemporaneous; see SIMULTANEOUS. 2. [Apparently accidental] chance, unpredictable, unplanned; see RANDOM.

cold *a.* 1. [*Said of the weather*] crisp, cool, icy, freezing, frosty, frigid, wintry, bleak, nippy, brisk, keen, penetrating, snowy, frozen, cutting, snappy, piercing, chill, bitter, numbing, severe, stinging, glacial, intense, Siberian, chilly, sharp, raw, nipping, arctic, polar, below zero, biting.—*Ant.* HOT, warm, heated. 2. [*Said of persons, animals, etc.*] cold-blooded, frozen, clammy, stiff, chilled, frostbitten, shivering, blue from cold.—*Ant.* HOT, perspiring, thawed. 3. [*Said of temperament*] unconcerned, apathetic, distant; see INDIFFERENT, RESERVED 3.

cold *n.* 1. [Conditions having a cold temperature] coldness, frozenness, chilliness, frostiness, draft, frostbite, absence of warmth, want of heat, chill, shivers, coolness, shivering, goose flesh, numbness, iciness, frigidity, freeze, glaciation, refrigeration; see also WEATHER.—*Ant.* HEAT, warmth, heat wave. 2. [Head or respiratory congestion] cough, hack, sore throat, sickness, cold in the head, sinus trouble, cold in one's chest, bronchial irritation, common cold, laryngitis, hay fever, whooping cough, influenza, flu, asthma, bronchitis, strep throat*, strep*, sniffles*, frog in one's throat; see also ILLNESS 2. —**catch cold** come down with a cold, become ill, get a cold; see SICKEN 1. —**have** or **get cold feet** go back on one's word, hold back, back down; see FEAR, STOP 2. —**(out) in the cold** forgotten, ignored, rejected; see NEGLECTED. —**throw cold water on** dishearten, squelch, dampen; see DISCOURAGE.

cold-blooded *a.* relentless, callous, unfeeling; see CRUEL.

collaborate *v.* work together, conspire, work with; see COOPERATE.

collapse *n.* breakdown, downfall, destruction; see FAILURE 1, WRECK.

collapse *v.* drop, deflate, give way; see FAIL 1, FALL 1, 2.

collar *n.* neckband, neckpiece, dickey; see CLOTHES.

collateral *n.* security, guarantee, pledge; see INSURANCE, MONEY 1, WEALTH.

colleague *n.* partner, collaborator, teammate; see ASSOCIATE.

collect *v.* **1.** [To bring into one place] amass, consolidate, convoke; see ACCUMULATE, ASSEMBLE 2, CONCENTRATE 1. **2.** [To come together] congregate, assemble, flock; see GATHER. **3.** [To obtain funds] solicit, raise, secure; see GET 1.

collected *a.* **1.** [Composed] self-possessed, poised, cool; see CALM 1. **2.** [Assembled] accumulated, amassed, compiled; see GATHERED.

collection *n.* specimens, samples, examples, extracts, gems, models, assortment, medley, accumulation, pile, stack, group, assemblage, compilation, mass, quantity, selection, treasury, anthology, miscellany, aggregation, combination, number, store, stock, digest, arrangement, concentration, discoveries, finds, batch, mess, lot, heap, bunch.

collector *n.* authority, historian, hobbyist, fancier, serious amateur, gatherer, discoverer, curator, compiler, finder, assembler, hoarder, librarian; see also SCIENTIST, SPECIALIST.

college *n.* institute, institution, community college, liberal arts college, teachers college, junior college, state college, denominational college, nondenominational college, private college, business school, technical school, higher education, graduate school, medical school, law school, seminary; see also UNIVERSITY.

collide *v.* **1.** [To come into violent contact] hit, strike, smash; see CRASH 4. **2.** [To come into conflict] clash, conflict, disagree; see OPPOSE 1.

collision *n.* impact, contact, shock, accident, encounter, crash, colliding, bump, jar, jolt, sideswipe, strike, hit, slam, blow, thud, thump, knock, smash, butt, rap, head-on crash, fender-bender*; see also DISASTER.

colonial *a.* **1.** [Concerning a colony] pioneer, isolated, dependent, settled, provincial, frontier, Pilgrim, emigrant, immigrant, territorial, outland, distant, remote, early American, overseas, protectoral, dominion, established. **2.** [Having qualities suggestive of colonial life] hard, raw, crude, harsh, wild, unsettled, limited, uncultured, new, unsophisticated.

colonization *n.* immigration, settlement, expansion; see FOUNDATION 2.

colonize *v.* found, people, pioneer; see ESTABLISH 2, SETTLE 5.

colony *n.* settlement, dependency, subject state, colonial state, dominion, offshoot, political possession, province, group, new land, protectorate, hive, daughter country, satellite state, community, group migration; see also NATION 1.

color *n.* hue, tone, tint, shade, tinge, dye, taint, dash, touch, complexion, brilliance, undertone, value, iridescence, intensity, coloration, discoloration, pigmentation, coloring, cast, glow, blush, wash, tincture. *Colors include the following—colors in the solar spectrum:* red, orange, yellow, green, blue, violet; *physiological primary colors:* red, green, blue; *psychological primary colors:* red, yellow, green, blue, black, white; *primary colors in painting:* red, blue, yellow; see also BLACK 1, BLUE 1, PURPLE, BROWN, GREEN 1, ORANGE 1, PINK, RED, YELLOW. —**change color** flush, redden, become red in the face; see BLUSH. —**lose color** become pale, blanch, faint; see WHITEN 1.

color *v.* gloss, chalk, daub, gild, enamel, lacquer, suffuse, stipple, pigment, glaze, tinge, tint, stain, tone, shade, dye, wash, crayon, chrome, enliven, embellish, give color to, adorn, imbue, emblazon, illuminate, rouge; see also DECORATE, PAINT 1, 2.

colored *a.* **1.** [Treated with color] hued, tinted, tinged, shaded, flushed, reddened, glowing, stained, dyed, washed, rouged; see also PAINTED 2. **2.** [Belonging to a dark-skinned race] brown, black, red; see NEGRO.

colorful *a.* vivid, glossy, realistic; see BRIGHT 1.

colorless *a.* drab, pale, neutral; see DULL 2, TRANSPARENT 1.

colors *n.pl.* banner, standard, symbol; see EMBLEM.

colossal *a.* huge, enormous, immense; see LARGE 1.

colt *n.* foal, filly, yearling; see HORSE.

column *n.* **1.** [A pillar] support, prop, shaft, monument, totem, pylon, obelisk, tower, minaret, cylinder, mast, monolith, upright, pedestal; see also POST 1. **2.** [Journalistic commentary] comment, article, editorial; see NEWS 1.

columnist *n.* newspaperman, journalist, correspondent; see REPORTER, WRITER.

coma *n.* unconsciousness, trance, stupor; see SLEEP.

comb *n.* pocket comb, pick, currycomb; see BRUSH 1.

comb *v.* untangle, disentangle, cleanse, scrape, arrange, straighten, lay smooth, smooth.

combat *n.* struggle, warfare, conflict; see BATTLE, FIGHT.

combat *v.* battle, oppose, resist; see FIGHT.

combination *n.* **1.** [The act of combining] uniting, joining, unification; see UNION 1. **2.** [An association] union, alliance, federation; see ORGANIZATION 2. **3.** [Something formed by combining] compound, aggregate, blend; see MIXTURE 1.

combine *v.* **1.** [To bring together] connect, couple, link; see JOIN 1. **2.** [To become one] fuse, merge, blend; see MIX 1, UNITE.

combined *a.* linked, mingled, connected; see JOINED.

combustion *n.* flaming, kindling, oxidization; see FIRE 1.

come *v.* **1.** [To move toward] close in, advance, draw near; see APPROACH 2. **2.** [To arrive] appear at, reach, attain; see ARRIVE. **3.** [To be available] appear, be at one's disposal, be ready, be obtainable, be handy, be accessible, be able to be reached, show up, turn up; see also APPEAR 1. **4.** [*To have an orgasm] to reach sexual fulfillment, ejaculate, climax; see ACHIEVE, COPULATE. **—as good as they come** excellent, superior, fine; see BEST. **—how come?*** for what reason?, how so?, what is the cause of that?; see WHY.

come about *v.* occur, take place, result; see HAPPEN 2.

come across *v.* **1.** [To find] uncover, stumble upon, notice; see DISCOVER, FIND. **2.** [*To give] deliver, pay, hand over; see GIVE 1.

come again *v.* **1.** [To return] come back, go again, go back; see RETURN 1. **2.** [*To repeat] reiterate, retell, restate; see REPEAT 3.

come along *v.* **1.** [To accompany] accompany, go with, attend; see ARRIVE, ADVANCE 1. **2.** [To progress] show improvement, do well, prosper; see IMPROVE 2.

come around *v.* **1.** [To recover] improve, recuperate, rally; see RECOVER 3, REVIVE 2. **2.** [*To visit] call on, stop by, drop in on; see VISIT.

comeback* *n.* **1.** [Improvement] revival, progress, betterment; see IMPROVEMENT 1, RECOVERY 1, 2. **2.** [Witty answer] retort, reply, rejoinder; see ANSWER 1.

come back *v.* **1.** [To return] come again, reappear, re-enter; see RETURN 1. **2.** [*To reply] retort, rejoin, respond; see ANSWER 1. **3.** [*To recover] do better, triumph, gain; see IMPROVE 2, WIN 1.

come between *v.* intervene, interfere, interrupt; see HAPPEN 2, MEDDLE 1.

come by *v.* **1.** [To pass] go by, overtake, move past; see PASS 1. **2.** [To acquire] get, win, procure; see GET 1.

come clean* *v.* confess, reveal, acknowledge; see ADMIT 2.

comedian *n.* comic, jester, entertainer; see ACTOR, CLOWN.

comedown *n.* reversal, blow, defeat; see FAILURE 1.

come down *v.* worsen, decline, suffer; see DECREASE 1, FAIL 1.

come down on or **upon** *v.* rebuke, reprimand, criticize; see ATTACK, SCOLD.

comedy *n.* comic drama, tragicomedy, stand-up comedy, situation comedy, sitcom, musical comedy, farce, satire, burlesque, slapstick, light entertainment; see also DRAMA.

come for *v.* call for, come to get, come to collect; see PICK UP 6.

come forward *v.* offer oneself, appear, make a proposal; see VOLUNTEER.

come in *v.* enter, pass in, reenter; see ENTER.

come in for* *v.* get, be eligible for, acquire; see RECEIVE 1.

come in handy* *v.* be useful, have a use, aid; see HELP.

come into *v.* **1.** [To inherit] fall heir to, succeed to, acquire; see INHERIT, RECEIVE 1. **2.** [To join] enter into, associate with, align; see JOIN 2.

come off *v.* **1.** [To become separated] be disconnected, be disengaged, be severed, be parted, be disjoined, be detached, be disunited; see also DIVIDE. **2.** [To happen] occur, turn out, come about; see HAPPEN 2.

come on *v.* encounter, come across, come upon; see MEET 6.

come out *v.* **1.** [To be made public] be published, be made known, be announced, be issued, be brought out, be reported, be revealed, be divulged, be disclosed, be exposed; see also APPEAR 1. **2.** [To result] end, conclude, terminate; see SUCCEED 1.

come out for *v.* announce, state, affirm; see DECLARE, SUPPORT 1.

come out with *v.* report, declare, announce; see ADVERTISE, DECLARE, PUBLISH 1.

come through *v.* **1.** [To be successful] accomplish, score, triumph; see ACHIEVE, SUCCEED 1. **2.** [To survive] live through, persist, withstand; see ENDURE 2. **3.** [To do] accomplish, achieve, carry out; see PERFORM 1.

come to *v.* **1.** [To recover] rally, come around, recuperate; see RECOVER 3, REVIVE 2. **2.** [To result in] end in, terminate by, conclude; see HAPPEN 2, RESULT.

come to life *v.* recover, regain consciousness, live; see REVIVE 2.

come to pass *v.* result, befall, occur; see HAPPEN 2.

come to the point *v.* cut the matter short, make a long story short, get down to brass tacks*; see DEFINE 2.

come up *v.* appear, arise, move to a higher place; see RISE 1.

come upon *v.* locate, identify, recognize; see DISCOVER, FIND.

come up to *v.* **1.** [To equal] match, resemble, rank with; see EQUAL. **2.** [To reach] extend to, get to, near; see APPROACH 1, 2, ARRIVE, REACH 1.

come up with *v.* **1.** [To propose] suggest, recommend, offer; see PROPOSE 1. **2.** [To find] uncover, detect, stumble on; see DISCOVER, FIND.

comfort *n.* rest, quiet, relaxation, repose, relief, poise, well-being, cheer, abundance, sufficiency, gratification, luxury, warmth, plenty, pleasure, happiness, contentment, restfulness, peacefulness, cheerfulness, coziness, exhilaration, complacency, bed of roses*; see also EASE 1, ENJOYMENT, SATISFACTION 2.—*Ant.* WEAKNESS, discomfort, uneasiness.

comfort *v.* **1.** [To console] share with, commiserate, solace, grieve with, cheer, gladden, uphold, hearten, pat on the back, put someone in a good humor, sustain, support, help, aid, confirm, reassure, refresh; see also ENCOURAGE, PITY 1.—*Ant.* DISCOURAGE, be indifferent, depress. **2.** [To make easy physically] alleviate, relieve, make comfortable, assuage, soothe, mitigate, gladden, quiet one's fears, help one in need, lighten one's burden, encourage, calm, revive, sustain, aid, assist, nourish, support, compose, delight, divert, bolster up, invigorate, refresh, put at ease, reassure, warm, lighten, soften, remedy, release, restore, free, make well, revitalize; see also EASE 1, HELP, STRENGTHEN.—*Ant.* WEAKEN, make uneasy, worsen.

comfortable *a.* **1.** [In physical ease] contented, cheerful, easy, at rest, relaxed, at ease, untroubled, healthy, rested, pleased, complacent, soothed, relieved, strengthened, restored, in comfort, at home with, without care, snug as a bug in a rug*; see also HAPPY, SATISFIED.—*Ant.* UNEASY, ill, disturbed. **2.** [Conducive to physical ease] satisfactory, snug, cozy, warm, sheltered, convenient, protected, cared for, appropriate, useful, roomy, spacious, luxurious, rich, satisfying, restful, in comfort, well-off, well-to-do; see also PLEASANT 2.—*Ant.* SHABBY, run-down, uncomfortable.

comfortably *a.* luxuriously, in comfort, restfully, snugly, cozily, pleasantly, warmly, conveniently, adequately, with ease, competently, amply; see also EASILY.—*Ant.* INADEQUATELY, insufficiently, poorly.

comforting *a.* sympathetic, cheering, encouraging, invigorating, health-giving, warming, consoling, sustaining, reassuring, inspiring, refreshing, upholding, relieving, soothing, lightening, mitigating, alleviating, softening, curing, restoring, releasing, freeing, revitalizing, tranquilizing.—*Ant.* DISTURBING, distressing, upsetting.

comic *a.* ridiculous, humorous, ironic; see FUNNY 1.

comical *a.* witty, amusing, humorous; see FUNNY 1.

coming *a.* **1.** [Approaching] advancing, drawing near, progressing, nearing, in the offing, arriving, gaining upon, pursuing, getting near, converging, subsequent, coming in, close at hand, coming on, near at hand, almost upon, immediate, future, in view, preparing, to come, eventual, fated, written, hereafter, at hand, in store, due, about to happen, hoped for, deserving, close, imminent, prospective, anticipated, forthcoming, certain, ordained, impending, to be, expected, near, pending, foreseen, in the cards, in the wind; see also EXPECTED, LIKELY 1.—*Ant.* DISTANT, going, leaving. **2.** [Having a promising future] promising, advancing, probable; see ABLE, AMBITIOUS. **3.** [Future] lying ahead, pending, impending; see EXPECTED, FUTURE.

coming *n.* approach, landing, homecoming; see ARRIVAL 1.

command *n.* order, injunction, direction, dictation, demand, decree, prohibition, interdiction, canon, rule, call, summons, imposition, precept, mandate, charge, behest, edict, proclamation, instruction, proscription, ban, requirement, dictate, subpoena, commandment, dictum, word of command, writ, citation, notification, will, regulation, ordinance, act, fiat, bidding, word, requisition, ultimatum, exaction, enactment, caveat, prescript, warrant; see also LAW 3, POWER 2, REQUEST.

command *v.* **1.** [To issue an order] charge, tell, demand; see ORDER 1. **2.** [To have control] rule, dominate, master; see CONTROL.

commandeer *v.* appropriate, take, confiscate; see SEIZE 2.

commander *n.* commandant, officer, head; see ADMINISTRATION 2, ADMINISTRATOR, CHIEF, LEADER 2.

commanding *n.* **1.** [Ruling] leading, directing, determining, ordering, instructing, dictating, dominating, compelling, managing, checking, curbing, forcing, coercing, requiring, restraining, in command, in authority, in charge, regulating. **2.** [Important] decisive, impressive, significant; see IMPORTANT 1.

commemorate *v.* solemnize, honor, memorialize; see ADMIRE, CELEBRATE 1.

commemoration *n.* recognition, remembrance, observance; see CELEBRATION, CEREMONY, CUSTOM.

commemorative *a.* dedicated to the memory of, in remembrance of, in honor of; see MEMORABLE 1.

commence *v.* start, initiate, set in motion; see BEGIN 2.

commend *v.* laud, support, acclaim; see APPROVE, PRAISE 1.

commendable *a.* praiseworthy, laudable, deserving; see EXCELLENT.

commendation *n.* tribute, approval, approbation; see HONOR, PRAISE 1.

comment *n.* report, commentary, editorial; see DISCUSSION, EXPLANATION, REMARK.

comment *v.* observe, remark, criticize, notice, state, express, pronounce, assert, affirm, mention, interject, say, note, touch upon, disclose, bring out, point out, conclude; see also MENTION, TALK 1.

commentary *n.* criticism, analysis, description; see EXPLANATION, INTERPRETATION.

commerce *n.* buying and selling, trading, marketing; see BUSINESS 1, ECONOMICS.

commercial *a.* trading, business, financial, economic, materialistic, practical, profitable, mercantile, merchandising, bartering, exchange, fiscal, monetary, trade, market, retail, wholesale, marketable, in the market, for sale, profit-making, money-making, across the counter; see also INDUSTRIAL, PROFITABLE.

commercial *n.* message from the sponsor, commercial announcement, plug*; see ADVERTISEMENT.

commercialize *v.* lessen, degrade, cheapen; see ABUSE.

commission *n.* **1.** [An authorization] order, license, command; see PERMISSION. **2.** [A committee] commissioners, representatives, board; see COMMITTEE. **3.** [A payment] royalty, fee, rake-off*; see PAY 2, PAYMENT 1. —**out of commission** damaged, not working, out of order; see BROKEN 2.

commission *v.* send, delegate, appoint, authorize, charge, empower, constitute, ordain, commit, entrust, send out, dispatch, deputize, assign, engage, employ, inaugurate, invest, name, nominate, hire, enable, license, command, elect, select; see also DELEGATE 1.

commissioner *n.* spokesman, magistrate, government official; see EXECUTIVE.

commit *v.* **1.** [To perpetrate] do something wrong, be guilty of, execute; see PERFORM 1. **2.** [To entrust] confide, delegate, relegate to, leave to, give to do, promise, assign, turn over to, put in the hands of, charge, invest, rely upon, depend upon, confer a trust, bind over, make responsible for, put an obligation upon, empower, employ, dispatch, send, vest in, invest with power, authorize, deputize, grant authority to, engage, commission; see also ASSIGN.—*Ant.* DISMISS, relieve of, discharge.

commitment *n.* pledge, responsibility, agreement; see DUTY 1, PROMISE 1.

commit suicide *v.* kill oneself, take an overdose, slash one's wrists, take one's own life, end it all*, commit hara-kiri, poison oneself, jump off a bridge*, blow one's brains out*.

committee *n.* consultants, board, bureau, council, cabinet, investigators, trustees, appointed group, board of inquiry, representatives, investigating committee, executive committee, standing committee, planning board, ad hoc committee, special committee, grand jury, referees, task force, study group, court, subcommittee; see also REPRESENTATIVE 2.

commodity *n.* goods, articles, stocks, merchandise, wares, materials, possessions, property, assets, belongings, things, stock in trade, consumers' goods, line, what one handles, what one is showing.

common *a.* **1.** [Ordinary] universal, familiar, natural, normal, everyday, accepted, commonplace, characteristic, customary, bourgeois, conventional, passable, general, informal, wearisome, unassuming, pedestrian, lower-level, habitual, prevalent, probable, typical, prosaic, simple, current, prevailing, trite, household, second-rate, banal, unvaried, homely, colloquial, trivial, stock, oft repeated, indiscriminate, tedious, worn-out, hackneyed, monotonous, stale, casual, undistinguished, uneducated, artless, workaday, provincial, unsophisticated, unrefined, untutored, plain, uncultured, vulgar, unadorned, ugly, obvious, average, orthodox, mediocre, humdrum, well-known, insipid, stereotyped, patent, moderate, middling, abiding, indifferent, tolerable, temperate, innocuous, undistinguished, run-of-the-mill*, not too bad*, garden variety, fair-to-middling*, so-so, nothing to write home about*; see also CONVENTIONAL 1, DULL 4, POPULAR 1, 3, TRADITIONAL.—*Ant.* UNIQUE, extraordinary, unnatural. **2.** [Of frequent occurrence] customary, constant, usual; see FREQUENT 1, HABITUAL, REGULAR 3. **3.** [Generally known] general, prevalent, well-known; see FAMILIAR, TRADITIONAL. **4.** [Low] cheap, inferior, shoddy; see POOR 2, SUBORDINATE. **5.** [Held or enjoyed in common] shared, joint, mutual; see COOPERATIVE, PUBLIC 2. —**in common** shared, communal, mutually held; see PUBLIC 2.

commonly *a.* usually, ordinarily, generally; see REGULARLY.

commonplace *a.* usual, hackneyed, mundane; see COMMON 1, CONVENTIONAL 1, 3.

common sense *n.* good sense, judgment, horse sense*; see SENSE 2, WISDOM.

commotion *n.* violence, tumult, uproar; see DISTURBANCE 2, FIGHT.

communal *a.* shared, cooperative, mutual; see PUBLIC 2.

commune *n.* community, collective, co-op*; see COOPERATIVE.

communicate *v.* **1.** [To impart information] convey, inform, advise; see TEACH, TELL 1. **2.** [To be in communication] correspond, be in touch, have access to, contact, reach, hear from, be within reach, be in correspondence with, be near, be close to, have the confidence of, associate with, establish contact with, be in agreement with, be in agreement about, confer, talk, converse, chat, speak together, deal with, write to, telephone, wire, cable, fax*, network, reply, answer, have a meeting of minds, find a common denominator; see also AGREE.—*Ant.* AVOID, withdraw, elude.

communication *n.* talk, utterance, announcing, extrasensory perception, telepathy, ESP, publication, writing, drawing, painting, broadcasting, televising, correspondence, disclosure, speaking, disclosing, conference, faxing*, telephoning, wiring, cabling, networking, description, mention, announcement, presentation, interchange, expression, narration, relation, declaration, assertion, elucidation, transmission, reception, reading, translating, interpreting, news, ideas, statement, speech, language, warning, communiqué, briefing, bulletin, summary, information, report, account, publicity, translation, printed work, advice, tidings, conversation. *Means of communication include the following:* book, letter, newspaper, magazine, radio, proclamation, broadcast, dispatch, fax, wire, printout, telecast, telephone call, telegram, cable, broadside, circular, notes, memorandum, post card, poster, billboard; see also MAIL, NEWS 1, 2, RADIO 2, TELEPHONE, TELEVISION.

communications *n.* mail, mass media, telephone; see COMMUNICATION.

communism *n.* state socialism, Marxism, dictatorship of the proletariat, collectivism, state ownership of production; see also GOVERNMENT 2.

communist *n.* Marxist, commie*, red*; see RADICAL.

community *n.* **1.** [A town] village, colony, hamlet; see CITY, TOWN 1. **2.** [Society] the public, the people, the nation; see SOCIETY 2.

commute *v.* **1.** [To exchange for something less severe] reduce, lessen, mitigate; see DECREASE 2. **2.** [Travel] go back and forth, drive, take the train; see TRAVEL.

commuter *n.* suburbanite, city worker, daily traveler; see DRIVER, TRAVELER.

companion *n.* attendant, comrade, escort, chaperon, protector, guide, friend, bodyguard.

companionship *n.* fraternity, rapport, association; see BROTHERHOOD, FELLOWSHIP 1, FRIENDSHIP.

company *n.* **1.** [A group of people] assembly, throng, band; see GATHERING. **2.** [People organized for business] partnership, firm, corporation; see BUSINESS 4. **3.** [A guest or guests] visitors, callers, overnight guests; see GUEST. **—keep (a person) company** stay with, visit, amuse; see ENTERTAIN 1. **—part company** separate, part, stop associating with; see LEAVE 1.

comparable *a.* **1.** [Worthy of comparison] as good as, equivalent, tantamount; see EQUAL. **2.** [Capable of comparison] similar, akin, relative; see ALIKE, LIKE.

comparatively *a.* relatively, similarly, analogously; see APPROXIMATELY.

compare *v.* **1.** [To liken] relate, connect, make like, notice the similarities, associate, link, distinguish between, bring near, put alongside, reduce to a common denominator, declare similar, equate, match, express by metaphor, correlate, parallel, show to be analogous, identify with, bring into meaningful relation with, collate, balance, parallel, bring into comparison, estimate relatively, set over against, compare notes, exchange observations, weigh one thing against another, set side by side, correlate, measure, place in juxtaposition, note the similarities and differences of, juxtapose, draw a parallel between, tie up, come up to, stack up with; see also DISTINGUISH 1. **2.** [To examine on a comparative basis] contrast, set against, weigh; see ANALYZE, EXAMINE. **3.** [To stand in relationship to another] match, vie, rival; see EQUAL, MATCH 3. **—beyond** or **past** or **without compare** incomparable, without equal, distinctive; see UNIQUE.

compare to or **with** *v.* put side by side, relate to, equate; see COMPARE 1.

comparison *n.* likening, metaphor, resemblance, analogy, illustration, correspondence, relation, correlation, parable, allegory, similarity, likening, identification, equation, measurement, example, contrast, association, parallel, connection, paralleling; see also ASSOCIATION 2.

compartment *n.* section, portion, subdivision; see PART 1.

compassion *n.* sympathy, consideration, clemency; see KINDNESS 1, PITY.

compassionate *a.* merciful, humane, sympathetic; see MERCIFUL.

compatible *a.* agreeable, congruous, cooperative; see HARMONIOUS 2.

compel *v.* enforce, constrain, coerce; see FORCE.

compensate *v.* recompense, remunerate, requite; see PAY 1, REPAY 1.

compensation *n.* remuneration, recompense, indemnity, satisfaction, remittal, return for services, commission, gratuity, reimbursement, allowance, deserts, remittance, salary, stipend, wages, hire, earnings, settlement, honorarium, coverage, consideration, damages, repayment, fee, reckoning, bonus, premium, amends, reward, advantage, profit, benefit, gain, kickback*; see also PAY 2, PAYMENT 1.—*Ant.* LOSS, deprivation, confiscation.

compete *v.* enter competition, take part, strive, struggle, vie with, be in the running, become a competitor, enter the lists, run for, participate in, engage in a contest, oppose, wrestle, be rivals, battle, bid, spar, fence, collide, face, clash, encounter, match wits, play, grapple, take on all comers, go in for*, lock horns, go out for; see also FIGHT.

competence *n.* capability, skill, fitness; see ABILITY.

competent *a.* fit, qualified, skilled; see ABLE.

competition *n.* race, match, contest, meet, fight, bout, boxing match, game of skill, trial, sport, athletic event, wrestling; see also GAME 1, SPORT 1, 3.

competitive *a.* competing, antagonistic, opposing; see RIVAL.

competitor *n.* foe, rival, antagonist; see CONTESTANT, OPPONENT 1.

compile *v.* collect, arrange, assemble; see ACCUMULATE, EDIT.

complacent *a.* self-satisfied, contented, self-righteous; see EGOTISTIC, HAPPY, SATISFIED, SMUG.

complain *v.* disapprove, accuse, deplore, criticize, denounce, differ, disagree, dissent, charge, report adversely, reproach, oppose, grumble, whine, whimper, remonstrate, fret, protest, fuss, moan, make a fuss, take exception to, object to, deprecate, enter a demurrer, demur, defy, carp, impute, indict, attack, refute, grouse*, kick*, bitch*, grouch, gripe*, grunt*, beef*, bellyache*, kick up a fuss*.—*Ant.* APPROVE, sanction, countenance.

complaining *a.* objecting, lamenting, murmuring, mourning, regretting, bewailing, deploring, weeping, moaning, protesting, charging, accusing, disapproving, grumbling, fretting, whining, imputing, resenting, dissenting, registering a protest, filing a complaint, making an adverse report, kicking.—*Ant.* enjoying, appreciating, praising.

complaint *n.* 1. [An objection] charge, criticism, reproach; see ACCUSATION, OBJECTION. 2. [An illness] ailment, disease, infirmity; see ILLNESS 1.

complementary *a.* paired, mated, corresponding; see ALIKE, MATCHED.

complete *a.* 1. [Not lacking in any part] total, replete, entire; see FULL 1, WHOLE 1. 2. [Finished] concluded, terminated, ended; see FINISHED 1. 3. [Perfect] flawless, unblemished, impeccable; see PERFECT, WHOLE 2.

complete *v.* execute, consummate, perfect, accomplish, realize, perform, achieve, fill out, fulfill, equip, actualize, furnish, make up, elaborate, make good, make complete, develop, fill in, refine, effect, carry out, crown, get through, round out; see also CREATE.—*Ant.* BEGIN, start, commence.

completed *a.* achieved, ended, concluded; see BUILT, DONE 2, FINISHED 1.

completely *a.* entirely, fully, totally, utterly, wholly, perfectly, exclusively, simply, effectively, competently, solidly, bodily, absolutely, unanimously, thoroughly, en masse, exhaustively, minutely, painstakingly, extensively, conclusively, unconditionally, finally, to the utmost, ultimately, altogether, comprehensively, to the end, from beginning to end, on all counts, in all, in full measure, to the limit, to the full, in full, to completion, to the nth degree, to a frazzle*, downright, through thick and thin, down to the ground, through and through, rain or shine, in one lump, from A to Z, from head to foot; hook, line, and sinker*.—*Ant.* PARTLY, somewhat, partially.

completion *n.* finish, conclusion, fulfillment; see END 2.

complex *a.* 1. [Composed of several parts] composite, heterogeneous, conglomerate, multiple, mosaic, manifold, multiform, compound, complicated, aggregated, involved, combined, compact, compounded, miscellaneous, multiplex, multifarious, variegated; see also MIXED 1. 2. [Difficult to understand] entangled, tangled, circuitous, convoluted, puzzling, mixed, mingled, muddled, jumbled, impenetrable, inscrutable, unfathomable, undecipherable, bewildering, intricate, perplexing, complicated, involved, enigmatic, hidden, knotted, meandering, winding, tortuous, snarled, rambling, twisted, disordered, devious, discursive, cryptic, inextricable, knotty, roundabout; see also CONFUSED 2, DIFFICULT 2.—*Ant.* UNDERSTANDABLE, plain, apparent.

complex *n.* 1. [An obsession] phobia, mania, repressed emotions, repressed desires; see also FEAR, INSANITY. 2. [A composite] conglomerate, syndrome, ecosystem, aggregation, association, totality; see also COLLECTION.

complexion *n.* tone, glow, color, coloration, general coloring, tinge, cast, flush, skin texture, tint, hue, pigmentation; see also SKIN. *Descriptions of complexions include the following:* blond, fair, pale, sallow, sickly, dark, brunet, olive, bronze, sandy, rosy, red, ruddy, brown, yellow, black, peaches-and-cream*.

compliant *a.* obedient, pliant, acquiescent; see DOCILE.

complicate *v.* combine, fold, multiply, twist, snarl up, associate with, involve, obscure, confound, muddle, clog, jumble, interrelate, elaborate, embarrass, implicate, tangle, conceal, mix up, impede, perplex, hinder, hamper, handicap, tie up with, ball up*; see also CONFUSE, ENTANGLE.—*Ant.* SIMPLIFY, clear up, unfold.

complicated *a.* intricate, various, mixed; see COMPLEX 2, CONFUSED 2, DIFFICULT 2.

complication *n.* complexity, dilemma, development; see CONFUSION, DIFFICULTY 1, 2.

compliment *n.* felicitation, tribute, approval, commendation, endorsement, confirmation, sanction, applause, flattery, acclaim, adulation, notice, puff, regards, honor, appreciation, respects, blessing, ovation, veneration, admiration, congratulation, homage, good word, sentiment; see also PRAISE 2.—*Ant.* ABUSE, censure, disapproval.

compliment *v.* wish joy to, remember, commemorate, pay one's respects, honor, cheer, salute, hail, toast, applaud, extol, celebrate, felicitate, pay tribute to, be in favor of, commend, endorse, sanction, confirm, acclaim, please, satisfy, pay a compliment to, sing the praises of, speak highly of, exalt, applaud, worship, eulogize, glorify, magnify, fawn upon, butter up*, puff, hand it to*; see also PRAISE 1.—*Ant.* DENOUNCE, disapprove of, censure.

complimentary *a.* flattering, laudatory, approving, celebrating, honoring, respectful, congratulatory, well-wishing, highly favorable, praising, singing the praises of, with highest recommendations, with high praise; see also POLITE.

compose *v.* **1.** [To be the parts or the ingredients] constitute, comprise*, go into the making of, make up, merge into, be a component, be an element of, belong to, consist of, be made of; see also COMPRISE, INCLUDE 1. **2.** [To create] fabricate, produce, write music, score, orchestrate, forge, discover, design, conceive, imagine, make up, turn out, draw up; see also CREATE, INVENT 1.

composed *a.* **1.** [Made] created, made up, fashioned; see FORMED. **2.** [Calm] poised, confident, cool*; see CALM 1, CONFIDENT 1.

composer *n.* arranger, song-writer, musical author; see AUTHOR, MUSICIAN, POET, WRITER.

composition *n.* creation, making, fashioning, formation, conception, presentation, invention, fiction, novel, tale, essay, play, drama, poem, stanza, symphony, concerto, quartet, song, rhapsody, melody; see also BIOGRAPHY, LITERATURE 2, MUSIC 1, POETRY, WRITING 2.

composure *n.* serenity, peace of mind, calm, calmness, self-possession, nonchalance, cool-headedness, control, self-control, balance, contentment, tranquility, stability, harmony, assurance, self-assurance, poise, composed state of mind, even temper, equanimity, coolness, level-headedness, fortitude, moderation, gravity, sobriety, a cool head, presence of mind, equilibrium, aplomb, self-restraint, ease, evenness, complacence, tolerance, content, quiet, command of one's faculties, forbearance, cool*; see also PATIENCE 1, PEACE.—*Ant.* EXUBERANCE, passion, wildness.

compound *n.* composite, union, aggregate; see MIXTURE 1.

comprehend *v.* grasp, discern, perceive; see KNOW 1, UNDERSTAND 1.

comprehension *n.* understanding, perception, cognizance; see AWARENESS, KNOWLEDGE 1.

comprehensive *a.* extensive, sweeping, complete; see ABSOLUTE 1, GENERAL 1, INFINITE, LARGE 1.

compress *v.* condense, compact, press together, consolidate, squeeze together, tighten, cramp, contract, crowd, constrict, abbreviate, shrivel, make brief, reduce, dehydrate, pack, shorten, shrink, narrow, abridge, bind tightly, wrap closely, wedge, boil down, cram; see also PRESS 1, TIGHTEN 1.—*Ant.* SPREAD, stretch, expand.

comprise *v.* comprehend, contain, embrace, include, involve, enclose, embody, encircle, encompass, sum up, cover, consist of, be composed of, be made up of, constitute, incorporate, span, hold, engross, take into account, be contained in, add up to, amount to, take in; see also COMPOSE 1, INCLUDE 1.—*Ant.* BAR, lack, exclude.

compromise *n.* covenant, bargain, give-and-take; see AGREEMENT.

compromise *v.* agree, conciliate, find a middle ground; see NEGOTIATE 1.

compulsion *n.* **1.** [Force] drive, necessity, need; see REQUIREMENT 2. **2.** [An obsession] preoccupation, obssession, engrossment; see REQUIREMENT 2.

compulsive *a.* driving, impelling, besetting; see PASSIONATE 2.

compulsory *a.* obligatory, required, requisite; see NECESSARY.

compute *v.* count, figure, measure; see CALCULATE.

computer *n.* electronic brain, thinking machine, calculator, data processor, electronic circuit, cybernetic device, analog computer, digital computer, programmer; see also MACHINE.

computer language *n.* macroinstruction system, machine language, programming language, computer-processed instructions. *Some computer languages include the following:* Ada, ALGOL, BASIC, COBOL, FORTRAN, Pascal, PL/I; see also LANGUAGE 1.

comrade *n.* confidant, confidante, intimate; see ASSOCIATE, FRIEND.

con *a.* conversely, opposed to, in opposition; see AGAINST 1.

con* *n.* deception, swindle, fraud; see TRICK 1.

con* *v.* cheat, dupe, mislead; see DECEIVE.

concave *a.* curved, sunken, cupped; see ROUND 2.

conceal *v.* screen, secrete, cover; see HIDE 1.

concealed *a.* covered, obscured, unseen; see HIDDEN.

concealment *n.* hiding, covering, camouflage; see DISGUISE.

concede *v.* yield, grant, acknowledge; see ADMIT 2, ALLOW.

conceit *n.* arrogance, self-admiration, narcissism; see VANITY.

conceited *a.* vain, arrogant, stuck-up*; see EGOTISTIC.

conceivable *a.* understandable, credible, believable; see CONVINCING, IMAGINABLE, LIKELY 1.

conceive *v.* **1.** [To form a concept or image of] consider, formulate, speculate; see IMAGINE, THINK 1. **2.** [To become pregnant] be with child, get pregnant, be impregnated, be in the family way*.

concentrate *v.* **1.** [To bring or come together] amass, mass, assemble, combine, consolidate, compact, condense, reduce, hoard, garner, centralize, store, bring into a small compass, bring toward a central point, embody, localize, strengthen, direct toward one object, constrict, fix, cramp, focus, reduce, intensify, crowd together, flock together, contract, muster, bunch, heap up, swarm, conglomerate, stow away, congest, narrow, compress, converge, center, collect, cluster, congregate, huddle; see also ACCUMULATE, GATHER 2, PACK 2. **2.** [To employ all one's mental powers] think intensely, give attention to, meditate upon, ponder, focus attention on, direct attention to one object, weigh, consider closely, scrutinize, regard carefully, contemplate, study deeply, examine closely, brood over, put one's mind to, be engrossed in, be absorbed in, attend, give exclusive attention to, occupy the thoughts with, fix one's attention, apply the mind, give heed, focus one's thought, give the mind to, direct the mind upon, center, think hard, rack one's brains, be on the beam*, keep one's eye on the ball*, knuckle down, buckle down; see also ANALYZE, EXAMINE, THINK 1.—*Ant.* DRIFT, be inattentive, ignore.

concentrated *a.* **1.** [Undiluted] rich, unmixed, unadulterated, straight; see also STRONG 4, THICK 1. **2.** [Intense] intensive, deep, hard; see INTENSE.

concentration *n.* **1.** [Attention] close attention, concern, application; see THOUGHT 1. **2.** [Density] solidity, consistency, frequency; see CONGESTION, DENSITY.

concept *n.* idea, theory, notion; see THOUGHT 2.

conception *n.* **1.** [The act of conceiving mentally] perception, apprehension, comprehension, imagining, speculating, meditation, dreaming, cogitating, deliberating, concentrating, meditating, realization, consideration, speculation, understanding, cognition, mental grasp, apperception, forming an idea, formulation of a principle; see also THOUGHT 1. **2.** [The act of conceiving physically] inception, impregnation, insemination; see FERTILIZATION 2.

concern *n.* **1.** [Affair] business, matter, interest; see AFFAIR 1. **2.** [Regard] care, interest, solicitude; see ATTENTION.

concern *v.* **1.** [To have reference to] refer to, pertain to, relate to, be related to, have significance for, bear on, regard, be connected with, be about, have to do with, be a matter of concern to, have a bearing on, have connections with, be applicable to, depend upon, be dependent upon, answer to, deal with, belong to, touch upon, figure in; see also INFLUENCE, TREAT 1. **2.** [Concern oneself] be concerned, become involved, take pains; see BOTHER 1, CARE, WORRY 2.

concerning *a.* respecting, touching, regarding; see ABOUT 2.

concert *n.* musical selections, musicale, recital; see PERFORMANCE.

concise *a.* succinct, brief, condensed; see SHORT 1.

conclude *v.* **1.** [To finish] terminate, bring to an end, complete; see ACHIEVE. **2.** [To deduce] presume, reason, gather; see ASSUME.

conclusion *n.* **1.** [An end] finish, termination, completion; see END 2. **2.** [A decision] determination, resolve, resolution; see JUDGMENT 3. —**in conclusion** lastly, in closing, in the end; see FINALLY 1.

conclusive *a.* final, decisive, absolute; see CERTAIN 2.

concord *n.* harmony, consensus, accord; see AGREEMENT, UNITY 1.

concrete *a.* **1.** [Specific] particular, solid, precise; see DEFINITE 1, DETAILED, REAL 2. **2.** [Made of concrete] cement, poured, prefabricated, precast, concrete and steel, compact, unyielding; see also FIRM 2.

concrete *n.* concretion, ferroconcrete, reinforced concrete; see CEMENT, PAVEMENT.

concur *v.* accord with, be consonant with, be in harmony with; see AGREE, APPROVE, EQUAL.

concurrent *a.* synchronal, parallel, coexisting; see SIMULTANEOUS.

concussion *n.* rupture, gash, crack; see FRACTURE, INJURY.

condemn *v.* doom, sentence, damn, pass sentence on, find guilty, seal the doom of, pronounce judgment, prescribe punishment; see also CONVICT, PUNISH.—*Ant.* EXCUSE, acquit, exonerate.

condemnation *n.* denunciation, disapprobation, reproach; see ACCUSATION, BLAME, OBJECTION.

condense *v.* **1.** [To compress] press together, constrict, consolidate; see COMPRESS, CONTRACT 1, DECREASE 1, 2. **2.** [To abridge] abbreviate, summarize, digest; see DECREASE 2.

condensed *a.* **1.** [Shortened] concise, brief, succinct; see SHORT 2. **2.** [Concentrated] undiluted, rich, evaporated; see THICK 3.

condescend *v.* stoop, lower oneself, agree, humble oneself, demean oneself, submit with good grace, assume a patronizing air, lower one's tone, descend, comply, oblige, favor, concede, grant, accord, accommodate to, come down a peg*, come down off one's high horse*; see also PATRONIZE 2.

condescending *a.* patronizing, complaisant, superior; see EGOTISTIC.

condition *n.* **1.** [A state] situation, position, status; see STATE 2. **2.** [A requisite] stipulation, contingency, provision; see REQUIREMENT 1. **3.** [A limitation] restriction, qualification, prohibition; see LIMITATION 2, RESTRAINT 2. **4.** [State of health] fitness, tone, trim, shape*; see also HEALTH. **5.** [*Illness] ailment, infirmity, temper; see ILLNESS 1, 2.

condition *v.* adapt, modify, work out; see PRACTICE 1, TRAIN 1.

conditional *a.* provisional, subject, contingent, limited, restricted, relying on, subject to, restrictive, guarded, not absolute, granted on certain terms; see also DEPENDENT 3.

conditionally *a.* hypothetically, subject to a condition, with reservations, with limitations, tentatively, possible; see also TEMPORARILY.

conditioned *a.* altered, disciplined, modified; see TRAINED.

conditions *n.pl.* environment, surroundings, setting; see CIRCUMSTANCES 2.

condominium *n.* cooperative appartment dwelling, commonly owned apartment house, jointly owned dwelling, condo, coop*; see also APARTMENT, HOME 1.

condone *v.* pardon, excuse, overlook; see APPROVE.

conduct *n.* **1.** [Behavior] deportment, demeanor, manner; see BEHAVIOR. **2.** [Management] supervision, plan, organization; see MANAGEMENT.

conduct *v.* **1.** [To guide] escort, convoy, attend; see ACCOMPANY, LEAD 1. **2.** [To manage] administer, handle, carry on; see MANAGE 1.

conduct oneself *v.* comport oneself, act properly, acquit oneself well; see BEHAVE.

conductor *n.* **1.** [That which conducts] conduit, conveyor, transmitter; see CHANNEL, WIRE 1, WIRING. **2.** [One who conducts] orchestra leader, pilot, head; see ADMINISTRATOR, GUIDE, LEADER 2. **3.** [One in charge of a car or train] trainman, railroad man, ticket taker, brakeman, streetcar conductor, motorman, bus driver; see also DRIVER.

Confederacy *n.* Confederate States of America, rebel states, Confederacy, the South, Dixie; see also SOUTH.

confer *v.* converse, deliberate, parley; see DISCUSS.

conference *n.* conversation, discussion, interchange; see GATHERING.

conferring *a.* discussing, conversing, in conference; see TALKING.

confess *v.* acknowledge, own, concede; see ADMIT 2.

confession *n.* **1.** [The act of confessing] concession, allowance, owning to, owning up, revelation, disclosure, publication, affirmation, assertion, declaration, telling, exposure, narration, exposé, proclamation, making public; see also ACKNOWLEDGMENT.—*Ant.* DENIAL, concealment, disclaimer. **2.** [A sacrament] absolution, contrition, repentance; see SACRAMENT.

confidant *n.* adherent, intimate associate, companion; see FRIEND.

confide *v.* disclose, admit, divulge; see REVEAL, TELL 1.

confidence *n.* self-confidence, self-reliance, morale, fearlessness, boldness, resolution, firmness, sureness, faith in oneself, tenacity, fortitude, certainty, daring, spirit, reliance, grit, cool*, heart, backbone, nerve, spunk*; see also COURAGE, DETERMINATION.

confident *a.* **1.** [Self-assured] self-confident, assured, being certain, fearless, self-reliant, sure of oneself, dauntless, self-sufficient, bold; see also CERTAIN 1. **2.** [Trusting] presumptuous, hopeful, depending on, counting on, relying on, expectant.

confidential *a.* classified, intimate, privy; see PRIVATE, SECRET 1, 3.

confidentially *a.* privately, personally, in confidence; see SECRETLY.

confidently *a.* in an assured way, with conviction, assuredly; see BOLDLY 1, POSITIVELY 1.

confine *v.* **1.** [To restrain] repress, hold back, keep within limits; see HINDER, RESTRAIN. **2.** [To imprison] cage, incarcerate, shut up; see ENSLAVE, IMPRISON.

confined *a.* **1.** [Restricted] limited, hampered, compassed; see BOUND 1, 2, RESTRICTED. **2.** [Bedridden] on one's back, ill, laid up; see SICK. **3.** [In prison] behind bars, locked up, in bonds, in irons, in chains, in jail, imprisoned, jailed, immured, incarcerated, detained, under lock and key.—*Ant.* FREE, released, at liberty.

confinement *n.* restriction, limitation, constraint, repression, control, coercion, keeping, safekeeping, custody, curb, bounds, check, bonds, detention, imprisonment, incarceration; see also JAIL.—*Ant.* FREEDOM, release, independence.

confines *n.pl.* bounds, limits, periphery; see BOUNDARY.

confining *a.* limiting, restricting, bounding, prescribing, restraining, hampering, repressing, checking, enclosing, imprisoning, incarcerating, detaining, keeping locked up, keeping behind bars.

confirm *v.* **1.** [To ratify] sanction, affirm, settle; see APPROVE, ENDORSE 2. **2.** [To prove] verify, authenticate, validate; see EXPLAIN, PROVE.

confirmation *n.* **1.** [The act of confirming] ratification, proving, authentication, corroboration, support, endorsement, sanction, authorization, verification, affirmation, acceptance, passage, validation, approval, attestation, assent, admission, recognition, witness, consent, testimony, agreement, evidence; see also AGREEMENT, PROOF 1.—*Ant.* CANCELLATION, annulment, disapproval. **2.** [A sacrament] rite, consecration, liturgy; see CEREMONY, SACRAMENT.

confirmed *a.* **1.** [Firmly established] proved, valid, accepted; see CERTAIN 2, ESTABLISHED 2, GUARANTEED. **2.** [Inveterate] ingrained, seasoned, regular; see CHRONIC, HABITUAL.

confiscate *v.* appropriate, impound, usurp; see SEIZE 2, STEAL.

conflict *n.* struggle, strife, engagement; see BATTLE, FIGHT.

conflict *v.* clash, contrast, contend; see DIFFER 1, FIGHT, OPPOSE 1, 2.

conform *v.* comply, accord, submit, accommodate, live up to, fit, suit, acclimate, accustom, be regular, harmonize, adapt, be guided by, fit the pattern, be in fashion, reconcile, obey, grow used to, do as others do, get in line, fall in with, go by, adhere to, adjust to, keep to, keep up, get one's bearings, keep up with the Joneses*, chime in with, join the parade, play the game, go according to Hoyle, follow the beaten path, toe the line, follow suit, run with the pack, follow the crowd, when in Rome do as the Romans do; see also AGREE, FOLLOW 2, OBEY.—*Ant.* DIFFER, CONFLICT, disagree.

conforming *a.* agreeing, in line with, in agreement; see HARMONIOUS 2.

conformist *n.* conformer, philistine, advocate; see FOLLOWER.

conformity *n.* **1.** [Similarity] congruity, correspondence, resemblance; see SIMILARITY. **2.** [Obedience] willingness, submission, compliance; see AGREEMENT.

conform to *v.* correspond, parallel, fit; see AGREE, COMPARE 1.

confound *v.* puzzle, perplex, bewilder; see CONFUSE.

confounded *a.* confused, bewildered, disconcerted; see DOUBTFUL.

confront *v.* brave, defy, repel; see DARE 2, FACE 1.

confrontation *n.* meeting, battle, strife; see DISPUTE, FIGHT 1.

confuse *v.* upset, befuddle, mislead, misinform, puzzle, perplex, confound, fluster, bewilder, embarrass, daze, astonish, disarrange, disorder, jumble, blend, mix, mingle, cloud, fog, stir up, disconcert, abash, agitate, amaze, worry, trouble, snarl, unsettle, muddle, clutter, complicate, involve, rattle, derange, baffle, frustrate, perturb, dismay, distract, entangle, encumber, befog, obscure, mystify, make a mess of, throw off the scent, cross up, foul up, mix up, ball up*, lead astray, stump, rattle, make one's head swim; see also DISTURB, TANGLE.—*Ant.* CLEAR UP, clarify, untangle.

confused *a.* **1.** [Puzzled in mind] disconcerted, abashed, perplexed; see DOUBTFUL. **2.** [Not properly distinguished] mistaken, jumbled, snarled, deranged, bewildered, out of order, disarrayed, confounded, mixed, mixed up, chaotic, disordered, muddled, fuddled, befuddled, slovenly, untidy, messy, involved, misunderstood, blurred, obscured, topsy-turvy, balled up*, fouled up*, screwed up*, in a mess, haywire*, snafu*; see also OBSCURE 1, TANGLED.—*Ant.* DISTINGUISHED, discriminated, ordered.

confusing *a.* disconcerting, confounding, baffling, puzzling, disturbing, unsettling, upsetting, embarrassing, obscuring, blurring, befuddling, tangling, snarling, cluttering, muddling, disarranging; see also DIFFICULT 2, OBSCURE 1.—*Ant.* ORDERLY, reassuring, clear.

confusion *n.* complication, intricacy, muss, untidiness, complexity, difficulty, mistake, bewilderment, turmoil, tumult, pandemonium, commotion, stir, ferment, disarray, jumble, convulsion, bustle, trouble, row, riot, uproar, fracas, distraction, agitation, emotional upset, daze, astonishment, surprise, fog, haze, consternation, racket, excitement, chaos, turbulence, dismay, uncertainty, irregularity, maze, interruption, stoppage, clutter, entanglement, backlash, clog, break, breakdown, knot, obstruction, trauma, congestion, interference, nervousness, disorganization, muddle, mass, lump, snarl, to-do*, hubbub, tie-up, botch, rumpus, scramble, shuffle, mess, hodgepodge, stew, going round and round*, jam*, fix*, bull in a china shop; see also DISORDER.—*Ant.* ORDER, quiet, calm.

confute *v.* confound, dismay, invalidate; see DENY, OPPOSE 1.

congenial *a.* kindred, agreeable, genial; see FRIENDLY, HARMONIOUS 2.

congestion *n.* profusion, crowdedness, overpopulation, press, traffic jam, overcrowding, overdevelopment, too many, too much, concentration, surplus; see also EXCESS 1.

congratulate *v.* felicitate, wish joy to, toast; see COMPLIMENT, PRAISE 1.

congratulations *interj.* best wishes, compliments, bless you; see COMPLIMENT.

congregate *v.* convene, meet, converge; see GATHER 1.

congregation *n.* meeting, group, assemblage; see GATHERING.

congress *n.* [*Often capital C*] parliament, assembly, legislative body; see COMMITTEE, GOVERNMENT, LEGISLATURE.

congruent *a.* in agreement, harmonious, corresponding; see HARMONIOUS 2.

congruous *a.* suitable, appropriate, fitting; see HARMONIOUS 2.

conjunction *n.* **1.** [Act of joining together] combination, connection, association; see UNION 1. **2.** [A syntactic connecting word] *Conjunctions include the following:* and, but, if, for, or, nor, so, yet, only, else, than, before, since, then, though, when, where, why, both, either, while, as, neither, although, because, unless, until.

conjure up *v.* call, invoke, materialize; see SUMMON, URGE 2.

connect *v.* **1.** [To join] combine, unite, attach; see JOIN 1. **2.** [To associate] relate, equate, correlate; see COMPARE 1.

connected *a.* **1.** [Joined together] united, combined, coupled; see JOINED. **2.** [Related] associated, applicable, pertinent; see RELATED 2, RELEVANT.

connecting *a.* joining, linking, combining, uniting, associating, relating, tying, cementing, knitting, fusing, hooking, bringing together, clinching, fastening, mixing, mingling, intertwining, welding, pairing, coupling; see also JOINED.

connection *n.* **1.** [Relationship] kinship, association, reciprocity; see ASSOCIATION 2, RELATIONSHIP. **2.** [A junction] combination, juncture, consolidation; see UNION 1. **3.** [A link] attachment, fastening, bond; see LINK. **—in connection with** in conjunction with, associated with, together with; see WITH.

connotation *n.* implication, intention, essence; see MEANING.

conquer *v.* subdue, overcome, crush; see DEFEAT 2.

conqueror *n.* vanquisher, master, champion; see HERO 1, WINNER.

conquest *n.* triumph, success, conquering; see VICTORY.

conscience *n.* moral sense, inner voice, the still small voice; see DUTY 1, MORALS, SHAME 2. **—have on one's conscience** be culpable for, be blamable for, be responsible for; see GUILTY. **—in (all) conscience** rightly, fairly, properly; see JUSTLY 1.

conscience-stricken *a.* remorseful, repentant, chastened; see SORRY 1.

conscientious *a.* fastidious, meticulous, complete; see CAREFUL, RELIABLE.

conscientiousness *n.* exactness, care, honor; see CARE 1, DUTY 1, HONESTY, RESPONSIBILITY 1.

conscious *a.* cognizant, informed, sure, certain, assured, discerning, knowing, sensible, sensitive, acquainted, attentive, watchful, mindful, vigilant, understanding, keen, alert, alert to, alive to, sensitive to, conscious of, mindful of, cognizant of, hip to*, on to*, with it*; see also INTELLIGENT.—*Ant.* UNAWARE, insensitive, inattentive.

consciousness *n.* alertness, cognizance, mindfulness; see AWARENESS, KNOWLEDGE 1.

consecrate *v.* hallow, sanctify, anoint; see BLESS.

consecrated *a.* blessed, sanctified, hallowed; see DIVINE.

consecration *n.* making holy, sanctification, exalting; see CELEBRATION.

consecutive *a.* continuous, chronological, serial, in turn, progressive, connected, in order, in sequence, sequential, going on, continuing, one after another, one after the other, serialized, numerical; see also CONSTANT, REGULAR 3.

consecutively *a.* following, successively, continuously; see GRADUALLY.

consensus *n.* consent, unison, accord; see AGREEMENT.

consent *n.* assent, approval, acquiescence; see PERMISSION.

consent *v.* accede, assent, acquiesce; see AGREE, ALLOW, APPROVE.

consequence *n.* **1.** [Effect] outgrowth, end, outcome; see RESULT. **2.** [Importance] moment, value, weight; see IMPORTANCE. **—take the consequences** accept the results of one's actions, suffer, bear the burden of; see ENDURE 2.

conservation *n.* maintenance, keeping, preservation, preserving, conserving, guarding, storage, protecting, saving, safekeeping, upkeep, economy, keeping in trust; see also PRESERVATION.—*Ant.* WASTE, destruction, misuse.

conservative *a.* conserving, preserving, unchanging, unchangeable, stable, constant, steady, traditional, reactionary, conventional, moderate, unprogressive, firm, obstinate, inflexible, opposed to change, cautious, sober, Tory, taking no chances, timid, fearful, unimaginative, right-wing, in a rut*, in a groove*; see also CAREFUL, MODERATE 3.—*Ant.* RADICAL, risky, changing.

conservative *n.* reactionary, right-winger, die-hard, Tory, Whig, Federalist, champion of the status quo, opponent of change, classicist, traditionalist, unprogressive, conventionalist, John Bircher, mossback*, old fogy, fossil*.—*Ant.* RADICAL, progressive, liberal.

consider *v.* allow for, provide for, grant, take up, concede, acknowledge, recognize, favor, value, take under advisement, deal with, regard, make allowance for, take into consideration, keep in mind, reckon with, play around with*, toss around, see about; see also RECONSIDER, THINK 1.—*Ant.* REFUSE, deny, reject.

considerable *a.* **1.** [Important] noteworthy, significant, essential; see IMPORTANT 1. **2.** [Much] abundant, lavish, bountiful; see MUCH 2, PLENTIFUL 1.

considerate *a.* charitable, kind, solicitous; see POLITE, THOUGHTFUL 2.

consideration *n.* **1.** [The state of being considerate] kindliness, thoughtfulness, attentiveness; see COURTESY 1, KINDNESS 1, TOLERANCE 1. **2.** [Payment] remuneration, salary, wage; see PAYMENT 1. **3.** [Something to be considered] situation, problem, judgment, notion, fancy, puzzle, proposal, difficulty, incident, evidence, new development, occurrence, taste, pass, occasion, emergency, idea, thought, trouble, plan, particulars, items, scope, extent, magnitude; see also IDEA 1, PLAN 2. **—in consideration of** because of, on account of, for; see CONSIDERING. **—take into consideration** take into account, weigh, keep in mind; see CONSIDER. **—under consideration** thought over, discussed, evaluated; see CONSIDERED.

considered *a.* carefully thought about, treated, gone into, contemplated, weighed, meditated, investigated, examined; see also DETERMINED 1.

considering *prep. & conj.* in light of, in view of, in consideration of, pending, taking into account, everything being equal, inasmuch as, insomuch as, with something in view.

consign *v.* convey, dispatch, transfer; see GIVE 1, SEND 1.

consistency *n.* **1.** [Harmony] union, compatibility, accord; see AGREEMENT, SYMMETRY. **2.** [The degree of firmness or thickness] hardness, softness, firmness; see DENSITY, TEXTURE 1.

consistent *a.* compatible, equable, expected; see LOGICAL, RATIONAL 1, REGULAR 3.

consist of *v.* embody, contain, involve; see COMPRISE, INCLUDE 1.

consolation *n.* sympathy, compassion, support; see PITY, RELIEF 1, 4.

console *v.* solace, sympathize with, hearten; see COMFORT 1, ENCOURAGE.

consolidate *v.* connect, mix, unify; see COMPRESS, PACK 2.

consolidation *n.* alliance, association, federation; see UNION 1.

consonant *n. Linguistic terms referring to consonant sounds include the following:* voiceless, voiced; stop, fricative, resonant, sibilant; implosive, plosive, nasal, click, glide, continuant, trill. *In spelling, English consonants are as follows:* b,c,d,f, g,h,j,k,l,m,n,p,q,r,s,t,v,w,x,y,z; see also LETTER, SOUND 2, VOWEL.

conspicuous *a.* outstanding, eminent, distinguished, celebrated, noted, renowned, famed, notorious, important, influential, notable, illustrious, striking, prominent, well-known, arresting, remarkable, noticeable, flagrant, glaring, standing out like a sore thumb*; see also PROMINENT 1.—*Ant.* UNKNOWN, inconspicuous, unsung.

conspiracy *n.* intrigue, collusion, connivance; see TRICK 1.

conspirator *n.* betrayer, schemer, cabalist; see TRAITOR.

conspire *v.* plot, scheme, contrive; see PLAN 1.

constant *a.* steady, uniform, perpetual, unchanging, continual, uninterrupted, unvarying, connected, even, incessant, unbroken, nonstop, monotonous, standardized, regularized; see also REGULAR 3.

constantly *a.* uniformly, steadily, invariably; see REGULARLY.

constituency *n.* the voters, electorate, body politic, electors, voting public, balloters, the people; see also VOTER.

constituent *n.* component, element, ingredient; see PART 1.

constitute *v.* **1.** [To found] establish, develop, create; see ESTABLISH 2. **2.** [To make up] frame, compound, aggregate; see COMPOSE 1.

constitution *n.* **1.** [Health] vitality, physique, build; see HEALTH. **2.** [A basic political document] code, written law, doctrines; see LAW 2.

constitutional *a.* lawful, safeguarding liberty, democratic; see LEGAL, DEMOCRATIC.

constrain *v.* necessitate, compel, stifle; see FORCE, URGE 2.

constraint *n.* **1.** [The use of force] coercion, force, compulsion; see PRESSURE 2. **2.** [Shyness] bashfulness, restraint, humility; see RESERVE 2. **3.** [Confinement] captivity, detention, restriction; see ARREST, CONFINEMENT.

constrict *v.* contract, cramp, choke up; see TIGHTEN 1.

construct *v.* make, erect, fabricate; see BUILD, CREATE.

construction *n.* **1.** [The act of constructing] formation, manufacture, building; see ARCHITECTURE, BUILDING, PRODUCTION 1. **2.** [A method of constructing] structure, arrangement, organization, system, plan, development, steel and concrete, contour, format, mold, cast, outline, type, shape, build, cut, fabric, formation, turn, framework, configuration, brick and mortar, prefab.

constructive *a.* useful, valuable, effective; see HELPFUL 1.

construe *v.* infer, deduce, interpret; see EXPLAIN.

consult *v.* take counsel, deliberate, confer, parley, conspire with, be closeted with, compare notes about, put heads together, commune, treat, negotiate, debate, argue, talk over, call in, ask advice of, turn to, seek advice; see also ASK, DISCUSS.

consultation *n.* interview, conference, deliberation; see DISCUSSION.

consume *v.* **1.** [To use] use, use up, wear out; see SPEND, USE 1. **2.** [To eat or drink] absorb, feed, devour; see EAT 1.

consumer *n.* user, customer, shopper; see BUYER.
consumption *n.* using, spending, expense; see DESTRUCTION 1, USE 1, WASTE 1.
contact *n.* touch, junction, connection; see MEETING 1.
contact *v.* speak to, reach, make contact with; see COMMUNICATE 2, TALK 1.
contagion *n.* poison, virus, illness; see ILLNESS 1.
contagious *a.* communicable, infectious, transmittable, spreading, poisonous, epidemic, deadly, endemic, tending to spread; see also CATCHING.
contain *v.* **1.** [Include] comprehend, embrace, be composed of; see INCLUDE 1. **2.** [Restrict] hold, keep back, stop; see RESTRAIN.
container *n.* receptacle, basket, bin, bowl, dish, tub, holder, cauldron, vessel, capsule, package, packet, chest, purse, pod, pouch, cask, sack, pot, pottery, jug, bucket, canteen, pit, box, carton, canister, crate, pail, kettle; see also BAG, CAN 1, CASE 5, JAR 1, VASE.
contaminate *v.* pollute, infect, defile; see CORRUPT, DIRTY.
contamination *n.* disease, contagion, taint; see POLLUTION.
contemplate *v.* ponder, muse, speculate on; see STUDY, THINK 1.
contemporary *a.* present, fashionable, current; see MODERN 1, 3.
contempt *n.* scorn, derision, slight; see HATRED.
contend *v.* contest, battle, dispute; see FIGHT.
content *a.* appeased, gratified, comfortable; see HAPPY, SATISFIED.
contented *a.* happy, pleased, thankful; see HAPPY, SATISFIED.
contention *n.* **1.** [A quarrel] struggle, belligerency, combat; see COMPETITION, DISPUTE, FIGHT. **2.** [An assertion supported by argument] explanation, stand, charge; see ATTITUDE, DECLARATION.
contentment *n.* peace, pleasure, happiness; see COMFORT, EASE 1, SATISFACTION 2.
contents *n.pl.* gist, essence, meaning, significance, intent, implication, connotation, text, subject matter, sum, substance, sum and substance, details; see also INGREDIENTS, MATTER 1.
contest *n.* trial, match, challenge; see GAME 1, SPORT 1.
contest *v.* oppose, battle, quarrel; see DARE, FIGHT.
contestant *n.* competitor, opponent, participant, rival, challenger, contester, disputant, antagonist, adversary, combatant, player, team member; see also PLAYER 1.
context *n.* connection, text, substance; see MEANING.
continent *n.* mainland, continental land mass, body of land; see AFRICA, AMERICA, ASIA, EUROPE.
continual *a.* uninterrupted, unbroken, connected; see CONSECUTIVE, REGULAR 3.
continually *a.* steadily, continuously, constantly; see FREQUENTLY, REGULARLY.
continuation *n.* succession, line, extension, increase, endurance, sustaining, preservation, perserverance, correction, translation, revision, supplement, complement, new version; see also ADDITION 1, SEQUENCE 1.—*Ant.* END, pause, delay.
continue *interj.* keep on, carry on; keep going, keep talking, keep reading, etc.; keep it up.
continue *v.* **1.** [To persist] persevere, carry forward, maintain, carry on, keep on, go on, run on, live on, never stop, sustain, promote, progress, uphold, forge ahead, remain, press onward, make headway, move ahead, keep the ball rolling, leave no stone unturned*, chip away at*; see also ADVANCE 1, ENDURE 1.—*Ant.* END, cease, give up. **2.** [To resume] begin again, renew, begin over, return to, take up again, begin where one left off, be reestablished, be restored; see also RESUME.—*Ant.* HALT, discontinue, postpone.
continuing *a.* persevering, carrying on, progressing; see CONSTANT, REGULAR 3.
continuity *n.* continuousness, constancy, continuance, flow, succession, unity, sequence, chain, linking, train, progression, dovetailing, extension; see also CONTINUATION.—*Ant.* INTERRUPTION, stop, break.
continuous *a.* unfaltering, repeated, perpetual; see CONSECUTIVE, CONSTANT, REGULAR 3.
contort *v.* deform, misshape, twist; see DISTORT 2.
contortion *n.* deformity, distortion, grimace, twist, ugliness, pout, crookedness.
contour *n.* profile, silhouette, shape; see FORM 1.
contraband *n.* plunder, smuggling, illegal goods; see BOOTY.
contraceptive *n.* prophylactic, birth-control device, preventative. *Contraceptives include the following:* birth-control pill, the Pill*, condom, rubber*, diaphragm, IUD, loop, coil*, foam.
contract *n.* agreement, compact, stipulation, contractual statement, contractual obligation, understanding, promise, pledge, covenant, obligation, guarantee, settlement, gentlemen's agreement, commitment, bargain, pact, arrangement, the papers, deal; see also AGREEMENT, TREATY.
contract *v.* **1.** [To diminish] draw in, draw back, shrivel, weaken, shrink, become smaller, decline, fall away, subside, grow

less, ebb, wane, lessen, lose, dwindle, recede, fall off, wither, waste, condense, constrict, deflate, evaporate; see also DECREASE 1.—*Ant.* STRETCH, expand, strengthen. **2.** [To cause to diminish] abbreviate, narrow, condense; see COMPRESS, DECREASE 2. **3.** [To enter into an agreement by contract] pledge, undertake, come to terms, make terms, adjust, dicker, make a bargain, agree on, limit, bound, establish by agreement, engage, stipulate, consent, enter into a contractual obligation, sign the papers, negotiate a contract, accept an offer, obligate oneself, put something in writing, swear to, sign for, give one's word, shake hands on it, initial, close; see also AGREE. **4.** [To catch; *said of diseases*] get, incur, become infected with; see CATCH 4.

contraction *n.* shrinkage, shrinking, recession, reduction, withdrawal, consumption, condensation, omission, deflation, evaporation, constriction, decrease, shortening, compression, confinement, curtailment, omitting, abridgment, cutting down, consolidating, consolidation, lowering; see also ABBREVIATION, REDUCTION 1, SHRINKAGE.—*Ant.* INCREASE, expansion, extension.

contractor *n.* builder, jobber, constructor; see ARCHITECT.

contradict *v.* differ, call in question, confront; see DARE 2, OPPOSE 1.

contradiction *n.* incongruity, inconsistency, opposition; see DIFFERENCE 1, OPPOSITE.

contrary *a.* **1.** [Opposed] antagonistic to, hostile, counter; see AGAINST 3, OPPOSED. **2.** [Unfavorable] untimely, bad, unpropitious; see UNFAVORABLE. **3.** [Obstinate] willful, contradictory, headstrong; see STUBBORN.

contrast *n.* divergence, incompatibility, variation, variance, dissimilarity, inequality, distinction, oppositeness, contradiction, diversity, disagreement, opposition; see also DIFFERENCE 1.—*Ant.* AGREEMENT, similarity, uniformity.

contrast *v.* contradict, disagree, conflict, set off, be contrary to, diverge from, depart from, deviate from, differ from, vary, show difference, stand out; see also DIFFER 1, OPPOSE 1.—*Ant.* AGREE, concur, be identical.

contribute *v.* add, share, endow, supply, furnish, bestow, present, confer, bequest, commit, dispense, settle upon, grant, afford, donate, dispense, assign, give away, subscribe, devote, will, bequeath, subsidize, hand out, ante up*, chip in*, kick in*, have a hand in, get in the act*, go Dutch*; see also GIVE 1, OFFER 1, PROVIDE 1.—*Ant.* RECEIVE, accept, take.

contributing *a.* aiding, helpful, supporting, secondary, subordinate, valuable, sharing, causative, forming a part of, not to be overlooked, to be considered, coming into the picture*; see also HELPFUL.

contribution *n.* donation, present, bestowal; see GIFT 1, GRANT.

contributor *n.* subscriber, giver, grantor; see DONOR, PATRON.

contrive *v.* make, improvise, devise; see CREATE, INVENT 1.

control *n.* **1.** [The power to direct] dominion, reign, direction; see POWER 2. **2.** [The document executed to bind a contract] deposition, paper, evidence; see PROOF 1, RECORD 1.

control *v.* **1.** [To hold in check] constrain, master, repress; see CHECK 1, RESTRAIN. **2.** [To direct] lead, rule, dominate, direct, determine, master, conquer, conduct, administer, supervise, run, coach, head, dictate, manage, influence, prevail, domineer, constrain, charge, subdue, push, coerce, oblige, train, limit, officiate, drive, move, regulate, take over, rule the roost*, crack the whip*, call the shots*; see also GOVERN.

controlling *a.* ruling, supervising, regulating; see GOVERNING.

controversial *a.* disputable, debatable, suspect; see UNCERTAIN.

controversy *n.* contention, debate, quarrel; see DIFFERENCE 1, DISCUSSION.

convene *v.* unite, congregate, collect; see ASSEMBLE 2, GATHER 1.

convenience *n.* **1.** [The quality of being convenient] fitness, availability, accessibility, suitability, appropriateness, decency, acceptability, receptiveness, openness, accord, consonance, adaptability, usefulness. **2.** [An aid to ease or comfort] ease, comfort, accommodation, help, aid, assistance, means, support, luxury, personal service, relief, cooperation, promotion, advancement, satisfaction, service, benefit, contribution, advantage, utility, labor saver, time saver, lift; see also ADVANTAGE, APPLIANCE. **—at one's convenience** suitable, conveniently, when convenient; see APPROPRIATELY.

convenient *a.* **1.** [Serving one's convenience] ready, favorable, suitable, adapted, available, fitted, suited, adaptable, roomy, well-arranged, appropriate, well-planned, decent, agreeable, acceptable, useful, serviceable, assisting, aiding, beneficial, accommodating, advantageous, conducive, comfortable, opportune, timesaving, laborsaving; see also HELPFUL.—*Ant.* DISTURBING, unserviceable, disadvantageous. **2.** [Near] handy, close by, easy to reach; see NEAR 1.

convention *n.* **1.** [An occasion for which delegates assemble] assembly, convocation, meeting; see GATHERING. **2.** [Custom] practice, habit, fashion; see CUSTOM.

conventional *a.* **1.** [Established by convention] accustomed, prevailing, accepted, customary, regular, standard, orthodox, normal, typical, expected, usual, routine, general, everyday, commonplace, ordinary, plain, current, popular, prevalent, predominant, expected, well-known, stereotyped, in established usage; see also COMMON 1, FAMILIAR, HABITUAL.—*Ant.* UNUSUAL, atypical, unpopular. **2.** [In accordance with convention] established, sanctioned, correct; see POPULAR 3. **3.** [Devoted to or bound by convention] formal, stereotyped, orthodox, narrow, narrow-minded, dogmatic, parochial, strict, rigid, puritanical, inflexible, hidebound, conservative, conforming, believing, not heretical, literal, bigoted, obstinate, straight*, straight-laced; see also PREJUDICED.—*Ant.* LIBERAL, broad-minded, unconventional.

conversation *n.* talk, discussion, communion, consultation, hearing, conference, gossip, chat, rap*, dialogue, discourse, expression of views, mutual exchange, questions and answers, traffic in ideas, getting to know one another, general conversation, question, talking it out, heart-to-heart talk, powwow, bull session*, chitchat, see also COMMUNICATION, SPEECH 3.

converse *n.* inverse, antithesis, reverse; see OPPOSITE.

conversion *n.* turn, spiritual change, regeneration, rebirth, being baptized, seeing the light, new birth.

convert *n.* proselyte, neophyte, disciple; see FOLLOWER.

convert *v.* **1.** [To alter the form or use] turn, transform, alter; see CHANGE 2. **2.** [To alter convictions] regenerate, save, baptize; see REFORM 1.

convertible *n.* open car, sports car, ragtop*; see AUTOMOBILE.

convey *v.* pass on, communicate, conduct; see SEND 1, 2.

convict *n.* captive, malefactor, felon; see CRIMINAL, PRISONER.

convict *v.* find guilty, sentence, pass sentence on, doom, declare guilty of an offense, bring to justice, send up; see also CONDEMN.—*Ant.* FREE, acquit, find not guilty.

conviction *n.* persuasion, confidence, reliance; see BELIEF, FAITH 2.

convince *v.* prove to, persuade, establish, refute, satisfy, assure, demonstrate, argue into, change, effect, overcome, turn, win over, bring around, put across, bring to one's senses, bring to reason, gain the confidence of, cram into one's head, sell a bill of goods; see also PROVE, TEACH.

convinced *a.* converted, indoctrinated, talked into something; see CHANGED 2.

convince oneself *v.* be convinced, be converted, persuade oneself, make up one's mind; see also BELIEVE, PROVE.

convincing *a.* trustworthy, credible, acceptable, reasonable, creditable, plausible, probable, likely, presumable, possible, dependable, hopeful, worthy of confidence, to be depended on; see also RELIABLE.

convulsion *n.* paroxysm, epilepsy, attack; see FIT 1.

cook *n.* short-order cook, chef, head cook; see SERVANT.

cook *v.* prepare, fix, warm up, warm over, stew, simmer, sear, braise, scald, broil, parch, scorch, poach, dry, chafe, fricasee, percolate, steam, bake, griddle, brew, boil down, seethe, barbecue, grill, roast, pan fry, pan broil, deep fry, French fry, brown; see also FRY, HEAT 1.

cooking *a.* simmering, heating, scalding, brewing, stewing, steeping, frying, broiling, griddling, grilling, browning, roasting, baking; see also BOILING.

cooking *n.* cookery, dish, dainty; see FOOD.

cook up* *v.* make up, concoct, falsify; see ARRANGE 2, PLAN 1, 2.

cooky *n.* small cake, sweet wafer, bun; see BREAD, CAKE 2, PASTRY. *Common varieties of cookies include the following:* cream, lemon, icebox, oatmeal, vanilla, chocolate, sugar, ginger, molasses, etc., cooky; gingersnap, fig bar, raisin bar, Scotch shortbread, doughnut, macaroon, tart, fruit bar, brownie, wafer.

cool *a.* **1.** [Having a low temperature] cooling, frigid, frosty, wintry, somewhat cold, chilly, shivery, chill, chilling, refrigerated, air-conditioned, snappy, nippy, biting; see also COLD 1.—*Ant.* WARM, tepid, heated. **2.** [Calm] unruffled, imperturbable, composed; see CALM 1. **3.** [Somewhat angry or disapproving] disapproving, annoyed, offended; see ANGRY, INDIFFERENT. **4.** [*Excellent] neat*, keen*, groovy*; see EXCELLENT. **—play it cool** hold back, underplay, exercise restraint; see RESTRAIN.

cool *v.* lose heat, lessen, freeze, reduce, calm, chill, cool off, become cold, be chilled to the bone, become chilly, moderate, refrigerate, air-cool, air-condition, pre-cool, frost, freeze, quick-freeze; see also FREEZE 1.—*Ant.* BURN, warm, defrost.

cool it* *v.* quiet down, hold back, be sensible; see CALM DOWN.

cooperate *v.* unite, combine, concur, conspire, pool, join forces, act in concert, hold together, stick together, comply with, join in, go along with, make common cause, unite efforts, share in, second, take part, work in unison, participate, work side by side with, side with, take sides with, join hands with, play along with, play fair, throw in with, fall in with, be in cahoots*, chip in*, stand shoulder to shoulder, pull together; see also AGREE.—*Ant.* DIFFER, act independently, diverge.

cooperation *n.* collaboration, participation, combination, concert, union, confederacy, confederation, conspiracy, alliance, society, company, partnership, coalition, federation, clanship, unanimity, concord, harmony; see also AGREEMENT, UNITY 2.—*Ant.* DISAGREEMENT, discord, separation.

cooperative *a.* cooperating, agreeing, joining, combining, collaborating, coactive, uniting, concurring, participating, in joint operation; see also HELPFUL, UNITED.

cooperative *n.* marketing cooperative, consumer's cooperative, communal society, kibbutz, commune, collective, co-op*; see also UNITY 2.

coordinate *v.* harmonize, regulate, organize; see ADJUST 1, AGREE.

coordinator *n.* superintendent, supervisor, organizer; see EXECUTIVE.

cope with *v.* encounter, suffer, confront; see ENDURE 2, FACE 1.

copied *a.* **1.** [Reproduced] dittoed, duplicated, transcribed; see PRINTED, REPRODUCED. **2.** [Imitated] made in facsimile, mimicked, aped; see IMITATED.

copper *n.* biological trace element, major element of the alloys bronze and brass; see ELEMENT 2, METAL.

copulate *v.* sleep with, make love, go to bed, unite, couple, cover, lie with, know, have relations, have sexual relations, have marital relations, have extramarital relations, be carnal, unite sexually, have sexual intercourse, have intercourse, breed, cohabit, fornicate, lay*, fool around*, screw*, do it*, make it*, get it on*, ball*.—*Ant.* ABSTAIN, be continent, be celibate.

copulation *n.* coitus, intercourse, sex, sex act, sexual union, sexual congress, coupling, mating, coition, carnal knowledge, love, screwing*; see also SEX 1, 4.

copy *n.* imitation, facsimile, photostat, likeness, print, similarity, mimeograph sheet, simulation, mirror, impersonation, offprint, xerox, semblance, imitation of an original, forgery, counterfeit, reprint, rubbings, transcript, carbon, replica, typescript, cast, tracing, counterpart, likeness, portrait, model, reflection, representation, study, photograph, carbon copy, certified copy, office copy, typed copy, pencil copy, fair copy, ditto; see also DUPLICATE, REPRODUCTION 2.

copy *v.* **1.** [To imitate] follow, mimic, ape; see IMITATE 1. **2.** [To reproduce] represent, duplicate, counterfeit, forge, cartoon, depict, portray, picture, draw, sketch, paint, sculpture, mold, engrave; see also REPRODUCE 2.

cord *n.* string, cordage, fiber; see ROPE.

cordial *a.* genial, hearty, warm-hearted; see FRIENDLY.

core *n.* **1.** [Essence] gist, kernel, heart; see ESSENCE 1. **2.** [Center] hub, focus, pivot; see CENTER 1.

cork *n.* stopper, tap, spike; see PLUG 1.

corn *n.* oats, millet, maize; see FOOD, GRAIN 1.

corn bread *n.* hoe cakes, corndodgers, corncakes, hot bread, johnnycake, hush puppies, corn pone, spoon bread; see also BREAD, CAKE 2.

corner *n.* **1.** [A projecting edge] ridge, sharp edge, projection; see EDGE 1, RIM. **2.** [A recess] niche, nook, indentation; see HOLE 1. **3.** [A sharp turn] bend, veer, shift; see CURVE, TURN 2. **4.** [The angle made where ways intersect] V, Y, intersection; see ANGLE 1. **5.** [*Difficulty] impediment, distress, knot; see DIFFICULTY 2. **—around the corner** immediate, imminent, next; see NEAR 1, SOON. **—cut corners** cut down, shorten, reduce; see DECREASE 2.

corner *v.* trap, trick, fool; see CATCH 1, DECEIVE.

cornerwise *a.* cornerways, diagonally, cater-corner, obliquely, askew, slanting, aslant, from corner to corner, on the bias, angling, diagonalwise, kitty-cornered, cater-cornered; see also OBLIQUE.

corny* *a.* stale, trite, stereotyped; see DULL 4, STUPID.

corporation *n.* partnership, enterprise, company; see BUSINESS 4.

corps *n.* troops, brigade, regiment; see ARMY 2, ORGANIZATION 2.

corpse *n.* carcass, remains, cadaver; see BODY 2.

correct *a.* **1.** [Accurate] exact, true, right; see ACCURATE 2. **2.** [Proper] suitable, becoming, fitting; see FIT.

correct *v.* better, help, remove the errors of, remove the faults of, remedy, alter, rectify, accommodate for, make right, mend, amend, fix up, do over, reform, remodel, review, reconstruct, reorganize, edit, revise, make corrections, put to rights, put in order, doctor, touch up, polish; see also REPAIR.

corrected *a.* rectified, amended, reformed; see CHANGED 2.

correction *n.* revisal, reexamination, rereading, remodeling, rectification, editing, righting, reparation, mending, fixing, amending, changing; see also REPAIR.

corrective *a.* restorative, curative, healing; see MEDICAL.

correctly *a.* rightly, precisely, perfectly; see RIGHT 1.

correctness *n.* **1.** [Accuracy] precision, exactness, rightness; see ACCURACY, TRUTH. **2.** [Propriety] decency, decorum, fitness; see PROPRIETY.

correlate *v.* connect, equate, associate; see COMPARE 1.

correlation *n.* interdependence, alternation, equivalence; see RELATIONSHIP.

correspond *v.* **1.** [To be alike] compare, match, be identical; see RESEMBLE. **2.** [To communicate with, usually by letter] write to, reply to, drop a line to; see ANSWER 1, COMMUNICATE 2.

correspondence *n.* **1.** [The quality of being like] conformity, equivalence, accord; see AGREEMENT, SIMILARITY. **2.** [Communication, usually by letter] messages, reports, exchange of letters; see COMMUNICATION.
corresponding *a.* identical, similar, coterminous; see LIKE.
correspond to *v.* accord, concur, harmonize; see AGREE.
corrode *v.* rot, degenerate, deteriorate; see RUST.
corrupt *a.* exploiting, underhanded, mercenary, fraudulent, crooked, nefarious, profiteering, unscrupulous, shady*, fixed*, padded*, on the take*; see also DISHONEST.
corrupt *v.* pervert, degrade, demean, lower, pull down, reduce, adulterate, depreciate, deprave, debauch, defile, demoralize, pollute, taint, contaminate, infect, stain, spoil, blight, blemish, undermine, impair, mar, injure, harm, hurt, damage, deface, disfigure, deform, abuse, maltreat, ill-treat, outrage, mistreat, misuse, dishonor, disgrace, violate, waste, ravage, cause to degenerate; see also RAPE, WEAKEN 2.—*Ant.* CLEAN, purify, restore.
corrupted *a.* debased, perverted, depraved; see WICKED.
corruption *n.* **1.** [Vice] baseness, depravity, degradation; see CRIME, EVIL 1. **2.** [Conduct involving graft] extortion, exploitation, fraudulence, misrepresentation, dishonesty, bribery, racket; see also CRIME.
cosmetic *n.* beautifier, beauty preparation, get-up, face*; see also MAKEUP 1. *Cosmetics include the following:* hair, body, sun tan, etc., oil; hair, eye, cold, cleansing, hormone, complexion, skin, hand, etc., cream; aftershave, hand, sun tan, etc., lotion; talcum, face, bath, tooth, etc., powder; eyebrow pencil, mascara, eye shadow, eye liner, lipstick, nail polish, moisturizer, foundation, powder, perfume, toilet water, cologne, hair tonic, hair dye, hair bleach, mouthwash, toothpaste, shampoo, shaving soap, shaving cream, shaving foam, depilatory, deodorant, antiperspirant; see also LOTION, PERFUME, SOAP.
cosmic *a.* vast, empyrean, grandiose; see UNIVERSAL 1.
cosmopolitan *a.* metropolitan, gregarious, catholic; see INTERNATIONAL, PUBLIC 2.
cosmos *n.* solar system, galaxy, star system; see UNIVERSE.
cost *n.* payment, value, charge; see PRICE, VALUE 1.
cost *v.* require, take, be priced at, be marked at, be valued at, be worth, amount to, be for sale at, command a price of, mount up to, bring in, sell for, set one back, go for.
costing *a.* as much as, to the amount of, priced at, no less than, estimated at, selling for, on sale at, reduced to, a bargain at, a steal at.
costly *a.* high-priced, dear, precious; see EXPENSIVE.
costs *n.pl.* price, outgo, living costs; see EXPENSES. **—at all costs** by any means, in spite of difficulties, without fail; see REGARDLESS 2.
costume *n.* attire, apparel, garb; see CLOTHES, DRESS 1.
cottage *n.* cot, cabin, small house; see HOME 1.
cotton *n. Cotton cloth includes the following:* chintz, organdy, dotted swiss, voile, cambric, calico, flannel, denim, ticking, net, muslin, crinoline, flannelette, gingham, jersey, lace, monk's cloth, poplin, velveteen, gabardine, crepe, twill, canvas, percale, terry cloth, sailcloth, cheesecloth, theatrical gauze.
couch *n.* sofa, lounge, davenport; see CHAIR 1, FURNITURE.
cough *n.* hem, hack, frog in one's throat; see COLD 2, ILLNESS 2.
cough *v.* hack, convulse, bark*; see CHOKE.
council *n.* advisory board, cabinet, directorate; see COMMITTEE.
counsel *n.* **1.** [Advice] guidance, instruction, information; see ADVICE, SUGGESTION 1. **2.** [A lawyer] attorney, legal adviser, barrister; see LAWYER. **—keep one's own counsel** be secretive, conceal oneself, keep quiet; see HIDE 1.
counsel *v.* admonish, direct, inform; see ADVISE, TEACH.
counselor *n.* guide, instructor, mentor; see TEACHER.
count *n.* number, enumeration, account, listing, statistics, returns, figures, tabulation, tally, poll, sum, outcome; see also RESULT, WHOLE.
count *v.* compute, reckon, enumerate, number, add up, figure, count off, count up, foot up, count noses; see also ADD, TOTAL.
counter *n.* board, shelf, ledge; see BENCH 2, TABLE 1. **—under the counter** unofficial, black-market, underhanded; see ILLEGAL.
counteract *v.* frustrate, check, invalidate; see HALT, HINDER, PREVENT.
counterfeit *a.* sham, spurious, fictitious; see FALSE 3.
counterfeit *v.* copy money, make counterfeit money, circulate bad money; see FORGE.
countless *a.* innumerable, incalculable, numberless; see INFINITE, MANY.
count off *v.* number, get numbers for, give numbers to; see COUNT, TOTAL.
count on *v.* rely on, depend on, depend upon, lean upon, expect from, take for granted, believe in, swear by; see also TRUST 1.
count out *v.* remove, mark off, get rid of; see ELIMINATE.

country *a.* 1. [*Said of people*] rural, homey, unpolished; see IGNORANT 2, RUDE 1. 2. [*Said of areas*] rustic, agrarian, provincial; see RURAL.

country *n.* 1. [Rural areas] farms, farmland, farming district, rural region, rural area, range, country district, back country, bush, forests, woodlands, backwoods, sparsely settled areas, sticks*, the boondocks*, boonies*; see also FARM, FOREST.—*Ant.* CITY, borough, municipality. 2. [A nation] government, a people, a sovereign state; see NATION 1. 3. [Land and all that is associated with it] homeland, native land, fatherland; see LAND 2.

countryside *n.* rural district, farmland, woods; see COUNTRY 1.

count up *v.* compute, get a total for, bring together; see ADD, TOTAL.

county *n.* province, constituency, shire; see AREA, REGION 1.

couple *n.* 1. [A pair] two, set, brace; see PAIR. 2. [*A few] two, several, a handful; see FEW.

couple *v.* unite, come together, link; see COPULATE, JOIN 1.

coupon *n.* token, box top, order blank, detachable portion, premium certificate, ticket; see also CARD, TICKET 1.

courage *n.* bravery, valor, boldness, fearlessness, spirit, audacity, audaciousness, temerity, manliness, pluck, mettle, enterprise, stoutheartedness, firmness, self-reliance, hardihood, heroism, gallantry, daring, prowess, power, resolution, dash, recklessness, defiance, the courage of one's convictions, spunk*, grit, backbone, guts*, what it takes*, nerve; see also STRENGTH.—*Ant.* FEAR, cowardice, timidity.

courageous *a.* daring, gallant, intrepid; see BRAVE.

course *n.* 1. [A route] passage, path, way; see ROUTE 1. 2. [A prepared way, especially for racing] lap, cinder path, cinder track; see ROAD 1. 3. [A plan of study] subject, studies, curriculum; see EDUCATION 1. 4. [A series of lessons] classes, lectures, seminar; see EDUCATION 1. —**in due course** in due time, properly, conveniently; see APPROPRIATELY. —**in the course of** during, in the process of, when; see WHILE 1. —**of course** certainly, by all means, indeed; see SURELY. —**off course** misdirected, erratic, going the wrong way; see WRONG 2. —**on course** on target, correct, going in the right direction; see ACCURATE 2.

court *n.* 1. [An enclosed, roofless area] square, courtyard, patio; see YARD 1. 2. [An instrument for administering justice] tribunal, bench, magistrate, bar, session. *Types of courts include the following:* the Supreme Court of the United States, appellate court of the United States, Federal court, State supreme court, district court, county court, justice's court, magistrate's court, mayor's court, police court. 3. [A ruler and his surroundings] lords and ladies, attendants, royal household; see GOVERNMENT 2, ROYALTY, RULER 1. 4. [An area for playing certain games] arena, rink, ring; see FIELD 2.

court *v.* attract, allure, solicit, beseech, entice, pursue, accompany, follow, plead, make love, pay court, pay attentions to, pay court to, make overtures, go courting, propose, ask in marriage, set one's cap for*, pop the question*, go steady, go together*, go with*, make a play for*; see also DATE 2.

courteous *a.* courtly, affiable, cultivated; see POLITE.

courteously *a.* civilly, affably, obligingly; see POLITELY.

courtesy *n.* 1. [Courteous conduct] kindness, friendliness, affability, courteousness, gentleness, consideration, thoughtfulness, sympathy, geniality, cordiality, graciousness, tact, good manners, politeness, refinement, chivalry, gallantry, respect, deference, polished manners, good breeding; see also GENEROSITY, KINDNESS 1. 2. [Courteous act] compassion, generosity, charity; see KINDNESS 2.

cousin *n.* kin, an aunt's child, an uncle's child; see RELATIVE.

cove *n.* inlet, sound, lagoon; see BAY.

cover *n.* 1. [A covering object] covering, ceiling, canopy, hood, sheath, sheet, awning, tent, umbrella, dome, stopper, lid, canvas, tarpaulin, book cover, folder, wrapper, wrapping paper, jacket, case, spread, tarp*; see also BLANKET, ENVELOPE, FOLDER, ROOF. 2. [A covering substance] paint, varnish, polish; see COAT 3, SHEET 2. 3. [Shelter] harbor, asylum, refuge; see RETREAT 2, SHELTER. —**take cover** conceal oneself, take shelter, go indoors; see HIDE 1. —**under cover** secretive, hiding, concealed; see HIDDEN.

cover *v.* 1. [To place as a covering] carpet, put on, overlay, surface, board up, superimpose, black in, black out; see also SPREAD 3. 2. [To wrap] envelop, enshroud, encase; see WRAP. 3. [To protect] shield, screen, house; see DEFEND 1, 2, SHELTER. 4. [To hide] screen, camouflage, mask; see DISGUISE, HIDE 1. 5. [To include] embrace, comprise, incorporate; see INCLUDE 1. 6. [To travel] traverse, journey over, cross; see TRAVEL. 7. [To send down in plenty] drench, engulf, overcome; see FLOOD. 8. [To report upon, especially for a newspaper] recount, narrate, relate; see BROADCAST, RECORD 3.

covered *a.* 1. [Provided with cover] topped, lidded, roofed, wrapped, enveloped, bound, painted, varnished, coated, camouflaged, sheltered, shielded, separated, disguised, masked, secreted, protected, concealed; see also HIDDEN.—*Ant.* OBVIOUS, revealed, exposed. **2.** [Plentifully bestrewn] scattered with, sprinkled over, spattered, spangled, dotted, strewn with, starred, starry with, flowered, spotted with, sown, dusted over, powdered, spread with.—*Ant.* EMPTY, bare, unfurnished. **3.** [Attended to] noted, taken note of, reported, recorded, written, included, marked, explored, regarded, scrutinized, examined, surveyed, investigated, observed, looked to, hurdled, cared for; see also DONE 1, RECOGNIZED.—*Ant.* unheeded, unnoticed, passed over.

covering *n.* concealment, top, spread; see COVER 1.

cover up for *v.* lie for, take the rap for*, be the goat*; see DEFEND 1, 2, SHELTER.

covet *v.* desire, envy, wish for; see WANT 1.

cow *n.* heifer, milk cow, dairy cow, critter, bossy; see also CATTLE.

coward *n.* sneak, milksop, shirker, deserter, weakling, alarmist, slacker*, quitter*, chicken*, lily-liver*, scaredy-cat*, chicken-heart*, fraidy-cat*, yellow-belly*.

cowardice *n.* cowardliness, timidity, faint heartedness, fear, weakness, quailing, lack of courage, apprehension, shyness, dread, fearfulness, yellow streak*, cold feet; see also FEAR.—*Ant.* bravery, valor, fearlessness.

cowardly *a.* timid, frightened, afraid, fearful, shy, backward, cowering, apprehensive, nervous, anxious, dismayed, faint-hearted, panicky, scared, scary, jittery*, craven, mean-spirited, weak, soft, chicken-livered*, lily-livered*, yellow*, skulking, sneaking, cringing, trembling, shaken, crouching, running, quaking, shaking like a leaf, shaking in one's boots*; see also AFRAID, WEAK 3.—*Ant.* BRAVE, fearless, open.

cowboy *n.* cowhand, hand, wrangler, rider, herder, cattle-herder, drover, gaucho, cowpuncher*, cowpoke*, buckaroo; see also RANCHER.

cower *v.* cringe, shrink, fear, run, quake, shiver, tremble, shake, snivel, flinch, quail; see also GROVEL.

coy *a.* bashful, shy, demure; see HUMBLE 1.

cozy *a.* secure, sheltered, snug; see COMFORTABLE 2, SAFE 1.

crab *n.* crayfish, crustacean, seafood; see SHELLFISH.

crack* *a.* first-rate, first-class, skilled; see ABLE, EXCELLENT.

crack *n.* **1.** [An incomplete break] chink, split, cut; see HOLE 1. **2.** [A crevice] cleft, fissure, rift; see HOLE 1. **3.** [A blow] hit, thwack, stroke; see BLOW. **4.** [*A witty or brazen comment] return, witticism, jest; see JOKE, REMARK.

crack *v.* **1.** [To become cracked] cleave, burst, split; see BREAK. **2.** [To cause to crack] cleave, split, sever; see BREAK. **3.** [To damage] injure, hurt, impair; see DAMAGE. **4.** [*To become mentally deranged] become insane, go crazy, blow one's mind*; see CRACK UP 2. **5.** [To solve] figure out, answer, decode; see SOLVE. —**get cracking*** get going, go, start; see BEGIN 2, MOVE 1.

crack a book* *v.* study, read, scan; see EXAMINE, STUDY.

crack a joke *v.* quip, jest, jape; see JOKE.

cracked *a.* shattered, split, fractured; see BROKEN 1.

cracker *n.* wafer, cookie, soda cracker, oyster cracker, biscuit, saltine, hardtack, sea biscuit, wheat biscuit; see also BREAD.

crack up *v.* **1.** [*To crash a vehicle] collide, be in an accident, smash up; see CRASH 4. **2.** [*To fail suddenly in health, mind, or strength] go to pieces, fail, deteriorate, sicken, go insane, go crazy, become demented, freak out*, blow one's mind*, go out of one's mind, go off one's rocker*, blow a fuse*, go off the deep end*; see also WEAKEN 1. **3.** [*To laugh] roar, howl, roll in the aisles*; see LAUGH.

cradle *n.* trundle bed, crib, basinet; see BED 1, FURNITURE.

craft *n.* **1.** [Skill] proficiency, competence, aptitude; see ABILITY. **2.** [Trade] occupation, career, work; see JOB 1, PROFESSION 1. **3.** [Ship] vessel, aircraft, spacecraft; see BOAT, SHIP.

craftsman *n.* artisan, skilled worker, journeyman, maker, technician, manufacturer, machinist, handcraftsman, mechanic; see also ARTIST, LABORER, SPECIALIST.

crafty *a.* clever, sharp, shrewd; see INTELLIGENT.

cram *v.* **1.** [To stuff] crush, jam, press; see COMPRESS, PACK. **2.** [To study hurriedly] read, teach, review; see STUDY.

cramp *n.* spasm, crick, pang; see PAIN 2.

cramped *a.* narrow, confined, restraining; see RESTRICTED, UNCOMFORTABLE 1.

cranium *n.* brain, cerebrum, cerebellum, brain encasing, brainpan, skull; see also HEAD 1.

crank *n.* **1.** [A device for revolving a shaft] bracket, turning device, bend; see ARM 2, HANDLE 1. **2.** [A person with an obsession] eccentric, fanatic, monomaniac; see CHARACTER 4. **3.** [*An ill-natured person] eccentric, misanthrope, complainer; see GROUCH.

cranky *a.* disagreeable, cross, perverse; see IRRITABLE.

crash *n.* **1.** [A crashing sound] clatter, clash, din; see NOISE 1, SOUND 2. **2.** [A collision] wreck, accident, shock; see COLLISION.

crash *v.* **1.** [To fall with a crash] overturn, upset, break down, plunge, be hurled, pitch, smash, dive, hurtle, lurch, sprawl, tumble, fall headlong, fall flat, drop, slip, collape; see also FALL 1. **2.** [To break into pieces] shatter, shiver, splinter; see BREAK, SMASH. **3.** [To make a crashing sound] clatter, bang, smash; see SOUND. **4.** [To have a collision] collide, run together, run into, smash into, bang into, meet, jostle, bump, butt, knock, punch, jar, jolt, crack up; see also HIT 1. **5.** [*To collapse] fall asleep, pass out, become unconscious; see FAINT, SLEEP. **6.** [*To go uninvited] disturb, gate-crash, intrude; see INTERRUPT, MEDDLE 1.

crash program *n.* crash project, immediate undertaking, intensive program, around-the-clock endeavor, revised plan, speed-up; see also EMERGENCY.

crass *a.* gross, tasteless, coarse; see IGNORANT 1, 2, VULGAR.

crate *n.* carton, box, cage; see CONTAINER, PACKAGE.

crater *n.* hollow, opening, abyss; see HOLE 1.

craving *n.* need, longing, yearning; see DESIRE 1.

crawl *v.* creep, worm along, wriggle, squirm, slither, move on hands and knees, writhe, go on all fours, worm one's way, go on one's belly; see also GROVEL, SNEAK.

crayon *n.* chalk, pastel, colored wax; see PENCIL.

craze *n.* fad, rage, fashion; see FAD.

crazily *a.* furiously, irrationally, hastily, madly, rashly, insanely, psychotically, maniacally; see also VIOLENTLY, WILDLY.

crazy *a.* crazed, demented, mad; see INSANE 1.

cream *n.* **1.** [The fatty portion of milk] rich milk, creamy milk, crème, coffee cream, whipping cream, ice cream, half-and-half, butterfat; see also MILK. **2.** [A creamy substance] emulsion, salve, jelly; see COSMETIC, LOTION.

creamy *a.* smooth, buttery, creamed; see RICH 2, SOFT 1.

crease *n.* tuck, overlap, pleat; see FOLD, WRINKLE.

crease *v.* double, rumple, plait; see FOLD 1, WRINKLE.

create *v.* make, produce, form, perform, cause to exist, bring into being, bring into existence, build, fashion, constitute, originate, generate, construct, discover, shape, forge, design, plan, fabricate, cause to be, conceive, give birth to; see also COMPOSE 2, INVENT 1, PRODUCE 2.

creation *n.* **1.** [The process of creating] imagination, production, formulation; see CONCEPTION 1, MAKING. **2.** [All that has been created] cosmos, nature, totality; see EARTH 1, UNIVERSE. **3.** [A work of art] labor of love, masterpiece, brainchild*; see PRODUCTION 1.

creative *a.* formative, inventive, productive; see ARTISTIC, ORIGINAL 2.

Creator *n.* First Cause, Deity, Maker; see GOD.

creature *n.* creation, being, beast; see ANIMAL.

credential *n.* declaration, warrant, voucher; see CERTIFICATE, RECORD 1.

credibility *n.* likelihood, probability, chance; see POSSIBILITY 2.

credible *a.* trustworthy, dependable, sincere; see RELIABLE.

credit *n.* **1.** [Belief] credence, reliance, confidence; see FAITH 1. **2.** [Unencumbered funds] assets, stocks, bonds, paper credit, bank account, mortgages, liens, securities, debentures, cash; see also WEALTH. **3.** [Permission to defer payment] extension, respite, continuance, trust; see also LOAN. **—do credit to** bring approval to, please, do honor to; see SATISFY 1. **—give credit to** believe in, rely on, have confidence in; see TRUST 1. **—give one credit for** believe in, rely on, have confidence in; see TRUST 1. **—on credit** on loan, delayed, postponed; see UNPAID 1. **—to one's credit** good, honorable, beneficial; see WORTHWHILE.

credit card *n.* charge card, smart card, plastic*, charge plate.

creditor *n.* realtor, lender, mortgager; see BANKER.

creed *n.* belief, doctrine, dogma; see FAITH 2.

creek *n.* stream, spring, brook; see RIVER. **—up the creek*** in difficulty, desperate, lost; see IN TROUBLE.

creep *v.* slither, writhe, worm along; see CRAWL.

creeping *a.* crawling, worming, squirming, writhing, wriggling, crouching, cowering, slinking, skulking, inching, dragging, lagging, limping, faltering, shuffling, hobbling, sneaking, moving slowly, barely moving, going at a snail's place, worming along.

crevice *n.* chasm, cleft, slit; see GAP 3.

crew *n.* **1.** [Company of seamen] seafarers, sailors, hands, able seamen, ship's company, mariners, sea dogs, gobs*. **2.** [A group of men organized to do a particular job] company, troupe, squad; see ORGANIZATION 2, TEAM 1.

crime *n.* transgression, misdemeanor, vice, outrage, wickedness, immorality, infringement, depravity, evil behavior, wrongdoing, misconduct, corruption, delinquency, wrong, trespass, malefaction, dereliction, lawlessness, atrocity, felony, capital crime, offense, white-collar crime*, scandal, infraction, violation, cold-blooded crime, mortal sin, homicide, voluntary manslaughter, involuntary, manslaughter, simple assault. aggravated assault, battery, larceny, robbery, burglary, holdup, kidnapping, swindling, fraud, defrauding, embezzlement, smuggling, extortion, bribery, mugging, rape, statutory rape, attack, sexual molestation, breach of promise, malicious mischief, breach of the peace, libel, perjury, fornication, sodomy, conspiracy, counterfeiting, inciting to revolt, sedition; see also CORRUP-

TION, EVIL 2, MURDER, RAPE, SIN, THEFT, TREASON.

criminal *a.* unlawful, felonious, illegal; see BAD 1.

criminal *n.* lawbreaker, felon, crook. *Criminals include the following:* murderer, killer, desperado, thug, gangster, gang leader, burglar, safecracker, swindler, clip artist*, confidence man, con man*, thief, bandit, second-story man*, cattle thief, cattle rustler, horse thief, automobile thief, pickpocket, counterfeiter, forger, smuggler, extortionist, kidnapper, gunman, trigger man*, accomplice, informer, stool pigeon*, stoolie*, squealer*, convict, con*, dope peddler, pusher*.

crimson *a.* blood-red, bright red, scarlet; see COLOR *n.*, RED *n.*

cringe *v.* flinch, quail, wince; see COWER, CRAWL.

crinkle *v.* coil, wind, crease; see WRINKLE.

cripple *v.* stifle, mangle, injure; see HURT.

crippled *a.* maimed, mutilated, mangled; see DEFORMED, DISABLED.

crisis *n.* straits, urgency, necessity, dilemma, puzzle, pressure, embarrassment, pinch, juncture, pass, change, contingency, situation, condition, plight, impasse, deadlock, predicament, corner, trauma, quandary, extremity, trial, crux, moment of truth, turning point, critical situation, pickle*, stew*, fix*, mess, big trouble*, hot water*.—*Ant.* STABILITY, normality, regularity.

crisp *a.* **1.** [Fresh and firm] green, plump, firm; see FRESH 1, RIPE 1. **2.** [Brisk] fresh, invigorating, bracing; see STIMULATING.

criterion *n.* basis, foundation, test, standard, rule, proof, scale, prototype, pattern, example, standard of judgment, standard of criticism, archetype, norm, original, precedent, fact, law, principle; see also MEASURE 2, MODEL 2.

critic *n.* **1.** [One who makes adverse comments] faultfinder, censor, quibbler, detractor, slanderer, complainer, doubter, nagger, fretter, scolder, worrier, mud-slinger*.—*Ant.* BELIEVER, praiser, supporter. **2.** [One who endeavors to interpret and judge] commentator, reviewer, analyst, connoisseur, writer of reviews, cartoonist, caricaturist, expert; see also EXAMINER, WRITER.

critical *a.* **1.** [Disapproving] faultfinding, trenchant, derogatory, disapproving, hypercritical, demanding, satirical, cynical, nagging, scolding, condemning, censuring, reproachful, disapproving, disparaging, exacting, sharp, cutting, biting; see also SARCASTIC. **2.** [Capable of observing and judging] penetrating, perceptive, discerning; see DISCREET, OBSERVANT. **3.** [Crucial] decisive, significant, deciding; see IMPORTANT 1.

criticism *n.* **1.** [A serious estimate or interpretation] study, analysis, critique; see JUDGMENT 2, REVIEW 1. **2.** [An adverse comment] caviling, carping, faultfinding; see OBJECTION.

criticize *v.* **1.** [To make a considered criticism] study, probe, scrutinize; see ANALYZE, EXAMINE. **2.** [To make adverse comments] chastise, reprove, reprimand; see BLAME.

crook* *n.* **1.** [Criminal] swindler, thief, rogue; see CRIMINAL. **2.** [A bend] fork, V, notch; see ANGLE 1.

crooked *a.* **1.** [Having a crook] curved, curving, hooked, devious, winding, bowed, spiral, serpentine, not straight, zigzag, twisted, meandering, tortuous, sinuous; see also ANGULAR, BENT, OBLIQUE.—*Ant.* STRAIGHT, unbent, direct. **2.** [Dishonest] iniquitous, corrupt, nefarious; see DISHONEST.

crop *n.* harvest, yield, product, crops, reaping, hay, fodder, grains, vintage, fruits; see also PRODUCE.

cross *a.* jumpy, easily annoyed, pettish; see CRITICAL, IRRITABLE.

cross *n.* **1.** [Religious symbol, especially of Christianity] crucifix, Greek cross, swastika, papal cross, Maltese cross, Latin cross. **2.** [A tribulation] affliction, trial, misfortune; see DIFFICULTY 2. **3.** [A mixed offspring] mongrel, crossbreed, half-breed; see HYBRID, MIXTURE 1.

cross *v.* **1.** [To pass over] traverse, go across, go over, pass, ford, cut across, span. **2.** [To lie across] intersect, lean on, rest across; see DIVIDE. **3.** [To mix breeds] mingle, interbreed, cross-pollinate; see MIX 1.

cross-examine *v.* investigate, check, interrogate; see EXAMINE, QUESTION.

crossing *n.* **1.** [A place to cross] intersection, overpass, crosswalk; see BRIDGE 1. **2.** [A mixing of breeds] hybridization, interbreeding, cross-pollination; see MIXTURE 1.

crossroad *n.* intersecting road, service road, junction; see ROAD 1.

crosswise *a.* across, cross, perpendicular, transversely, vertically, horizontally, at right angles, awry, over, sideways, crisscross, askew, crossways; see also ANGULAR.

crotch *n.* **1.** [Angle] fork, corner, elbow; see ANGLE 1, CURVE. **2.** [Loins] pubic area, groin, pelvic girdle; see BODY 1.

crouch *v.* **1.** [To stoop] dip, duck, bow; see BEND. **2.** [To cower] cringe, flinch, quail; see COWER, CRAWL.

crowd *n.* host, horde, flock, mob, company, swarm, press, crush, surge, legion, rout, group, body, pack, army, drove, party, flood, throng, troupe, deluge, multitude, congregation, cluster, assembly, crew, herd, bunch, gang, batch; see also GATHERING.

crowd *v.* stuff, jam, squeeze; see PACK 2, PUSH 1.

crowded *a.* packed, huddled, crushed; see FULL 1.

crown *n.* diadem, headdress, tiara, coronet, circlet.

crown *v.* commission, authorize, invest, enable, sanction, inaugurate, fix, exalt, raise, heighten, set up, ennoble, establish; see also DELEGATE 1.

crucial *a.* **1.** [Critical] decisive, climactic, deciding; see IMPORTANT 1. **2.** [Severe] trying, taxing, hard; see DIFFICULT 1.

crude *a.* rude, rough, unpolished, in a raw state, homemade, thick, coarse, harsh, rudimentary, homespun, rough-hewn, unfashioned, unformed, undeveloped, in the rough, raw, immature, sketchy; see also UNFINISHED 1.—*Ant.* FINISHED, polished, refined.

crudely *a.* clumsily, coarsely, impudently; see RUDELY.

cruel *a.* malevolent, spiteful, depraved, wicked, vengeful, evil, sinful, degenerate, brutish, demonic, rampant, outrageous, tyrannical, gross, demoralized, evil-minded, vicious, brutal, rough, wild, bestial, ferocious, monstrous, demoniac, debased, destructive, harmful, mischievous, callous, unnatural, merciless, sadistic, unpitying, unmerciful, unyielding, remorseless, pitiless, unfeeling, inflexible, bloodthirsty, unrelenting, relentless, grim, inhuman, atrocious, harsh, heartless, stony, unconcerned, knowing no mercy*, turning a deaf ear*, hard as nails*.—*Ant.* MERCIFUL, kindly, compassionate.

cruelly *a.* savagely, inhumanly, viciously; see BRUTALLY.

cruelty *n.* brutality, barbarity, sadism, inhumanity, barbarism, mercilessness, wickedness, coarseness, ruthlessness, severity, malice, rancor, venom, coldness, unfeelingness, insensibility, indifference, fierceness, bestiality, ferocity, savagery, grimness, monstrousness, inflexibility, fiendishness, hardness of heart, bloodthirstiness, torture, relentlessness, persecution, harshness, heartlessness, atrocity; see also EVIL 1, 2, TYRANNY.—*Ant.* KINDNESS, benevolence, humanity.

cruise *n.* voyage, sail, jaunt; see JOURNEY.

cruise *v.* voyage, navigate, coast; see SAIL 1, TRAVEL.

cruiser *n.* cabin cruiser, boat, privateer; see SHIP.

crumb *n.* particle, scrap, pinch; see BIT 1.

crumble *v.* fall apart, decay, break up; see DISINTEGRATE.

crumbly *a.* breaking up, breaking down, falling to pieces, decayed, degenerated, perishing, deteriorating, soft, corroded, rusted, rotted, worn away, fragile, brittle, frail, rotten, breakable, eroded, disintegrated, tumbling down; see also DECAYING, GRITTY.—*Ant.* FIRM, sound, undecayed.

crumple *v.* rumple, crush, crease; see WRINKLE.

crush *v.* **1.** [To break into small pieces] smash, pulverize, powder; see GRIND. **2.** [To bruise severely] press, mash, bruise; see BEAT 1, BREAK 1. **3.** [To defeat utterly] overwhelm, force down, annihilate; see DEFEAT 2.

crust *n.* **1.** [A crisp covering] hull, rind, pie crust; see SHELL 1. **2.** [The edge] verge, border, band; see EDGE 1.

cry *n.* **1.** [A loud utterance] outcry, exclamation, clamor, shout, call, battle cry, halloo, hurrah, cheer, scream, shriek, yell, whoop, squall, groan, bellow, howl, bawl, holler, uproar, acclamation, roar; see also sense 2 and NOISE 2.—*Ant.* WHISPER, murmur, silence. **2.** [A characteristic call] howl, hoot, wail, bawl, screech, bark, squawk, squeak, yelp, meow, whinny, moo, chatter, bay, cluck, crow, whine, pipe, trill, quack, clack, cackle, caw, bellow, coo, whistle, gobble, hiss, growl; see also YELL. **3.** [A fit of weeping] sobbing, wailing, shedding tears, sorrowing, mourning, whimpering; see also TEARS. —**a far cry (from)** unlike, dissimilar, opposed to; see DIFFERENT.

cry *v.* **1.** [To weep] weep, sob, wail, shed tears, snivel, squall, lament, bewail, bemoan, moan, howl, keen, whimper, whine, weep over, complain, deplore, sorrow, grieve, fret, groan, burst into tears, choke up, cry one's eyes out, break down*, break up*, blubber, bawl.—*Ant.* LAUGH, rejoice, exult. **2.** [To call; *said of other than human creatures*] howl, bark, hoot, scream, screech, squawk, squeak, yelp, grunt, roar, shriek, meow, whinny, moo, bawl, snarl, chatter, bay, cluck, crow, whine, pipe, trill, coo, whistle, caw, bellow, quack, gabble, hiss, growl, croak, cackle, twitter, tweet; see also YELL.

crying *n.* shrieking, sorrow, sobbing; see TEARS. —**for crying out loud*** for God's sake; for heaven's sake; oh, no; see CURSE, NO.

crystallize *v.* become definite, take shape, be outlined; see FORM 4.

cub *n.* young, offspring, whelp; see ANIMAL.

cube *n.* six-sided solid, hexahedron, die; see SOLID.

cuddle *v.* snuggle, huddle, curl up; see NESTLE.

cue *n.* prompt, warning signal, opening bars; see SIGN 1.

cuff *n.* **1.** [Edge of a sleeve or pants leg] French cuff, armband, wristband; see BAND 1. **2.** [A blow] slap, punch, hit; see BLOW. —**off the cuff*** extemporaneous, unofficial, offhand; see INFORMAL. —**on the cuff*** on credit, charged, delayed; see UNPAID 1.

culminate *v.* finish, close, end up*; see END 1.

culprit *n.* offender, felon, fugitive; see CRIMINAL.

cult *n.* clique, clan, band; see FACTION, RELIGION 2.

cultivate *v.* **1.** [Plant] till, garden, seed; see HARVEST, PLANT. **2.** [Educate] nurture, refine, improve; see TEACH.

cultivation *n.* horticulture, agriculture, gardening; see FARMING.

cultural *a.* educational, socializing, refining, refined, constructive, influential, nurturing, disciplining, enlightening, civilizing, instructive, humanizing, beneficial, learned, educative, polishing, enriching, promoting, elevating, uplifting, ennobling, raising, broadening, expanding, widening, developmental.—*Ant.* PRIMITIVE, barbaric, crude.

culture *n.* **1.** [Civilizing tradition] folklore, folkways, instruction, education, study, law, society, family, convention, habit, inheritance, learning, arts, sciences, custom, mores, knowledge, letters, literature, poetry, painting, music, lore, architecture, history, religion, humanism, the arts and sciences; see also CIVILIZATION.—*Ant.* DISORDER, barbarism, chaos. **2.** [Refinement and education] breeding, gentility, enlightenment, learning, capacity, ability, skill, science, lore, education, training, art, perception, discrimination, finish, taste, grace, dignity, politeness, savoir-faire, manners, urbanity, dress, fashion, address, tact, nobility, kindness, polish; see also COURTESY 1, ELEGANCE, EXPERIENCE.—*Ant.* IGNORANCE, crudeness, vulgarity.

cultured *a.* cultivated, educated, informed, advanced, accomplished, enlightened, polished, well-bred, genteel, elegant, courteous, intellectual, sophisticated, sensitive, intelligent, *au courant* (French), able, well-read, up-to-date, well-informed, traveled, experienced, tolerant, understanding, appreciative, civilized, literary, urbane, mannerly, gently bred, chivalrous, erudite, gallant, lettered, high-brow*, high-class*; see also LIBERAL, POLITE, REFINED 2.—*Ant.* PREJUDICED, narrow, backward.

cunning *a.* clever, skillful, ingenious; see INTELLIGENT.

cup *n.* vessel, bowl, goblet, mug, tumbler, beaker, stein, bumper, teacup, coffee cup, measuring cup, chalice; see also CAN 1, CONTAINER.

cupboard *n.* closet, locker, storeroom; see FURNITURE.

curable *a.* improvable, subject to cure, not hopeless, correctable, capable of improvement, healable, restorable, mendable.

curb *n.* **1.** [Restraint] hindrance, chain, check; see BARRIER, RESTRAINT 2. **2.** [Edge] border, ledge, lip; see EDGE 1, RIM.

curb *v.* retard, impede, subdue; see HINDER, RESTRAIN, RESTRICT.

curdle *v.* coagulate, condense, clot; see THICKEN.

cure *n.* restorative, healing agent, antidote; see MEDICINE 2.

cure *v.* make healthy, restore, make whole; see HEAL.

curfew *n.* late hour, time limit, check-in time; see LIMITATION 2.

curiosity *n.* **1.** [Interest] concern, regard, inquiring mind, inquisitiveness, thirst for knowledge, a questing mind, questioning, interest, desire to know, interest in learning, scientific interest, healthy curiosity. **2.** [An unusual object] exoticism, rarity, marvel; see WONDER 2.

curious *a.* **1.** [Strange or odd] rare, queer, unique; see UNUSUAL 2. **2.** [Interested] inquiring, inquisitive, questioning; see INTERESTED 1.

curl *n.* coil, spiral, wave; see HAIR 1.

curl *v.* curve, coil, bend, spiral, crinkle, wind, twine, loop, crimp, scallop, lap, fold, roll, contort, form into a spiral, form into a curved shape, meander, ripple, buckle, zigzag, wrinkle, twirl.—*Ant.* STRAIGHTEN, uncurl, unbend.

curly *a.* curled, kinky, wavy, waving, coiled, crinkly, looped, winding, wound; see also ROLLED 1.

currency *n.* coin, bank notes, cash; see MONEY 1.

current *a.* prevailing, contemporary, in fashion; see FASHIONABLE, MODERN 1.

current *n.* drift, tidal motion, ebb and flow; see FLOW, TIDE.

curse *n.* **1.** [Profanity] oath, blasphemy, obscenity, sacrilege, anathema, ban, cursing, profanity, denunciation, damning, cuss word, cussing, swearword*, four-letter word*. *Common exclamations and curses include the following* (*many of which are old-fashioned*)*:* Lord, oh God, the Devil, bless my soul, bless me, mercy, gracious, goodness, in Heaven's name, gee*, sakes alive*, good night*, darn*, hang it all*, dang*, blast*, damn it*, damn*, by golly*, for crying out loud*, Judas Priest*, Jesus H. Christ*, hell's bells*, geez*. **2.** [*Menstruation] menses, period, red letter days*; see FLOW.

curse *v.* blaspheme, profane, swear, use foul language, be foul-mouthed, be obscene, take the Lord's name in vain, damn, turn the air blue*, abuse, revile, swear at, insult, call down curses on the head of, blast, doom, fulminate, denounce, call names, cuss*, cuss out*.

cursed *a.* blighted, doomed, confounded; see DAMNED 1.

curt *a.* brief, concise, terse; see SHORT 2.

curtain *n.* hanging, screen, shade, drape, drapery, window covering, blind. *Kinds of curtains include the following:* draw curtain, roller shade, shutter, portiere, cafe curtains, vertical blinds, Venetian blinds.

curve *n.* sweep, bow, arch, circuit, curvature, crook. *Types of curves include the following:* bell curve, bell-shaped curve, hairpin curve, S-curve, sine curve, extrapolated curve, hyperbolic curve, parabolic curve, normal curve, logarithmic curve, French curve, circle, ellipse, arc.

curve *v.* bow, crook, twist; see BEND.

curved *a.* bowed, arched, rounded; see BENT.

cushion *n.* mat, seat, rest; see PILLOW.

custodian *n.* superintendent, janitor, porter, cleaner, cleaning man, cleaning woman, attendant, caretaker, building superintendent, keeper, gatekeeper, night watchman; see also WATCHMAN.

custody *n.* care, guardianship, supervision, keeping, safekeeping, watch, superintendence, safeguard; see also MANAGEMENT. —**take into custody** capture, apprehend, seize; see ARREST.

custom *n.* habit, practice, usage, wont, fashion, routine, precedent, use, form, addiction, rule, procedure, observance, characteristic, second nature, matter of course, beaten path*, rut*, manner, way, mode, method, system, style, vogue, convention, habit, rule, practice, formality, form, mold, pattern, design, type, taste, character, ritual, rite, attitude, mores, dictate of society, unwritten law, etiquette, conventionality.—*Ant.* DEPARTURE, deviation, shift.

customarily *a.* usually, commonly, generally; see REGULARLY.

customary *a.* usual, wonted, habitual; see COMMON 1, CONVENTIONAL 1, 2.

customer *n.* clientele, patron, consumer; see BUYER.

cut *a.* **1.** [Formed] shaped, modeled, arranged; see FORMED. **2.** [Reduced] lowered, debased, marked down; see REDUCED 1, 2. **3.** [Severed] split, divided, sliced through; see CARVED.

cut *n.* **1.** [The using of a sharp instrument] slash, thrust, dig, prick, gouge, penetrating, dividing, separation, severance, slitting, hack, slice, carve, chop, stroke, incision, cleavage, penetration, gash, cleft, mark, nick, notch, opening, passage, groove, furrow, slit, wound, fissure; see also HOLE 1, INJURY. **2.** [A reduction] decrease, diminution, lessening; see REDUCTION 1. **3.** [The shape] fashion, figure, construction; see FORM 1. **4.** [A section] segment, slice, portion; see PART 1, PIECE 1. **5.** [A piece of butchered meat] piece, slice, chunk; see MEAT. **6.** [*An insult] indignity, offense, abuse; see INSULT. —**a cut above** superior, higher, more capable or competent or efficient, etc.; see BETTER 1.

cut *v.* **1.** [To sever] separate, slice through, slice, cut into, cleave, mow, prune, reap, shear, dice, chop down, chop, slit, split, cut apart, hew, fell, rip, saw through, chisel, cut away, snip, chip, quarter, clip, behead, scissor, bite, shave, dissect, bisect, amputate, gash, incise, truncate, lacerate, slash, notch, nick, indent, score, mark, scratch, rake, furrow, wound, gouge; see also CARVE. **2.** [To cross] intersect, pass, move across; see CROSS 1. **3.** [To shorten] curtail, delete, lessen; see DECREASE 2. **4.** [To divide] split, break apart, separate; see DIVIDE. **5.** [*To absent oneself] shirk, avoid, stay away; see EVADE. **6.** [To record electronically] make a record, film, tape; see RECORD 3.

cut back *v.* reduce, curtail, shorten; see DECREASE 2.

cute *a.* dainty, attractive, delightful; see CHARMING, PLEASANT 1, 2.

cut off *v.* **1.** [To remove] eliminate, turn off, cut out; see REMOVE 1. **2.** [To interrupt] intrude on, break in on, cut in on; see INTERRUPT.

cut out *v.* pull out, extract, tear out; see REMOVE 1.

cut out for *a.* suitable, adequate, good for; see FIT.

cut short *v.* finish, halt, terminate; see END 1, STOP 1, 2.

cut up *v.* **1.** [To chop] chop up, slice, dice; see CUT 1. **2.** [To cavort] show off, play jokes, fool around*; see JOKE, PLAY 2.

cycle *n.* revolution of time, period, recurrence; see AGE 3, SEQUENCE 1, SERIES.

cylinder *n.* **1.** [An automobile part] compression chamber, combustion chamber, cylinder block; see AUTOMOBILE. **2.** [A geometric form] circular cylinder, right cylinder, barrel; see CIRCLE 1.

cynic *n.* misanthrope, misogynist, mocker, satirist, scoffer, pessimist, sarcastic person, sneerer, unbeliever, egotist, man-hater, skeptic, doubter, questioner, detractor, doubting Thomas; see also CRITIC 1.—*Ant.* BELIEVER, optimist, idealist.

cynical *a.* scornful, disrespectful, sneering; see SARCASTIC.

cynicism *n.* criticism, ridicule, contempt; see SARCASM.

D

dab *n.* small quantity, fragment, lump; see BIT 1.
dab *v.* tap, pat, nudge; see TOUCH 1.
dabble *v.* trifle with, trifle, engage in superficially, amuse oneself with, dally, be an amateur, have sport with, fiddle with, flirt with, toy with, putter, idle away time, work superficially, putter around, fool with*, fool around*, dip into*.—*Ant.* STUDY, work at, become an expert.
dad* *n.* daddy*, male parent, pop*; see FATHER, PARENT.
dagger *n.* stiletto, point, blade; see KNIFE. —**look daggers at** glower, look at with anger, scowl at; see DISLIKE.
daily *a.* diurnal, per diem, every day, occurring every day, issued every day, periodic, cyclic, day after day, once daily, by day, once a day, during the day, day by day, from day to day; see also REGULAR 3.
dainty *a.* delicate, fragile, petite, frail, thin, light, pretty, beautiful, lovely, attractive, trim, graceful, fine, neat, elegant, exquisite, precious, rare, soft, tender, airy, lacy, nice, darling*, cute*, sweet; see also CHARMING, WEAK.—*Ant.* ROUGH, coarse, gross.
dairy *n.* creamery, dairy farm, ice-cream plant, cheese factory, buttery, milk station, pasteurizing plant, cooperative; see also FARM.
dairy products *n.pl.* produce, milk products, farm products; see BUTTER, CHEESE, CREAM 1, MILK, PRODUCE.
dally with *v.* flirt with, trifle with, toy with; see DABBLE.
dam *n.* dike, ditch, wall, bank, embankment, gate, levee, irrigation dam, beaver dam, cofferdam; see also BARRIER.
dam *v.* hold back, check, obstruct, bar, slow, retard, restrict, stop up, close, clog, choke, block up, impede, hold, stop, block, confine; see also HINDER, RESTRAIN.—*Ant.* FREE, release, open up.
damage *n.* **1.** [Injury] harm, hurt, wound, bruise, wrong, casualty, suffering, illness, stroke, affliction, accident, catastrophe, adversity, outrage, hardship, disturbance, mutilation, impairment, mishap, evil, blow, devastation, mischief, reverse; see also DISASTER, INJURY, MISFORTUNE.—*Ant.* BLESSING, benefit, boon. **2.** [Loss occasioned by injury] ruin, breakage, ruined goods, wreckage, deprivation, waste, shrinkage, depreciation, pollution, corruption, blemish, contamination, defacement, degeneration, deterioration, ravage, havoc, erosion, disrepair, debasement, corrosion, wear and tear*, foul play; see also DESTRUCTION 2, LOSS 1.—*Ant.* IMPROVEMENT, betterment, growth.
damage *v.* ruin, wreck, tarnish, burn, scorch, dirty, rot, smash, bleach, drench, batter, discolor, mutilate, scratch, smudge, crack, bang up, abuse, maltreat, mar, deface, disfigure, mangle, contaminate, crumple, dismantle, cheapen, blight, disintegrate, pollute, ravage, sap, stain, tear, undermine, gnaw, corrode, break, split, stab, crack, pierce, lacerate, cripple, rust, warp, maim, mutilate, wound, taint, despoil, incapacitate, pervert, bruise, spoil, wear away, abuse, defile, wrong, corrupt, infect; see also BREAK, DESTROY.
damaged *a.* **1.** [Less valuable than formerly] injured, in need of repair, in poor condition; see BROKEN 1, 2. **2.** [Reduced in value because of damage] secondhand, used, leftover; see CHEAP 1.
damages *n.pl.* reparations, costs, reimbursement; see EXPENSE, EXPENSES.
damn *v.* curse, ban, doom, banish, excommunicate, sentence, convict, excoriate, cast into hell, torment, condemn to hell, condemn to eternal punishment, call down curses on; see also CONDEMN.—*Ant.* FORGIVE, bless, elevate. —**not give a damn*** not care, be indifferent, reject; see NEGLECT 1. —**not worth a damn*** useless, unproductive, valueless; see WORTHLESS.
damnation *n.* damning, condemnation, doom; see BLAME, CURSE.
damned *a.* **1.** [Consigned to hell] cursed, condemned, accursed, lost, infernal, gone to blazes*; see also UNFORTUNATE.—*Ant.* BLESSED, saved, holy. **2.** [*Disapproved of] bad, unwelcome, blankety-blank*, blasted*, bloody*, danged*, darned*, doggone*, lousy*; see also BAD 1, UNDESIRABLE.—*Ant.* WELCOMED, desirable, favorite. —**do (or try) one's damnedest*** endeavor, do one's best, give one's all; see TRY 1.
damp *a.* moist, soaked, soggy; see WET 1.
dampen *v.* sprinkle, water, rinse; see MOISTEN.
dance *n.* **1.** [Rhythmic movement] hop, jig, shuffle, fling, hoedown. *Dances include the following—social:* fox trot, polka, rhumba, tango, cha-cha, disco, mambo, samba, twist, jitterbug, two-step, box-step, Charleston, bunny hop, hokey-pokey; *theatrical:* ballet, modern dance, tap dance, soft-shoe; *traditional:* cotillion, polonaise, waltz, quadrille, pavane, mazurka, bolero, fandango, square dance, minuet, Virginia reel; *folkloristic and primitive:* sun dance, ghost dance, rain

dance, sword dance, snake dance, fertility dance, Highland fling, flamenco, Irish jig, tarantella, hornpipe, clog, hora, hula. **2.** [A dancing party] grand ball, dress ball, reception, ball, sock hop*, hoedown, shindig*, prom; see also PARTY 1.

dance *v.* waltz, shimmy, samba, jitterbug, twist, disco, fox-trot, cha-cha, mambo, tango, polka, hop, skip, jump, leap, bob, scamper, bounce, sway, swirl, sweep, swing, cut a rug*, rock*; see also MOVE 1.

dancer *n.* ballerina, chorus girl, showgirl, stripper*, hoofer*; ballet, tap, toe, hula, belly, go-go, folk, square, modern, flamenco, geisha, break, etc. dancer.

dandy* *n.* very good, fine, first-rate; see EXCELLENT.

danger *n.* uncertainty, risk, peril, jeopardy, threat, hazard, insecurity, instability, exposure, venture, menace, vulnerability; see also CHANCE 1.—*Ant.* SAFETY, security, certainty.

dangerous *a.* perilous, critical, serious, pressing, vital, vulnerable, exposed, full of risk, threatening, alarming, urgent, hazardous, risky, menacing, serious, ugly, nasty, formidable, terrible, deadly, insecure, precarious, ticklish, delicate, unstable, touchy, treacherous, bad, thorny, breakneck, shaky*, on a collision course*, hairy*, under fire*, unhealthy, hot*; see also ENDANGERED, UNCERTAIN, UNSAFE.—*Ant.* CERTAIN, sure, secure.

dangerously *a.* desperately, precariously, severely; see SERIOUSLY 1.

dangle *v.* hover, swing, suspend; see HANG 1, 2.

dare *v.* **1.** [To be courageous] take a chance, venture, adventure, undertake, try, attempt, endeavor, try one's hand, hazard, take the bull by the horns*, go ahead, go for it*; see also CHANCE, RISK, TRY 1.—*Ant.* AVOID, dread, fear. **2.** [To defy] meet, confront, oppose, disregard, brave, scorn, insult, resist, threaten, spurn, denounce, bully, mock, laugh at, challenge, have the nerve, have the courage of one's convictions, face the music*, face up to, call someone's bluff; see also FACE 1.—*Ant.* AVOID, shun, evade.

daredevil *n.* stunt man, madman, gambler; see ADVENTURER.

daring *a.* bold, courageous, fearless; see BRAVE.

dark *a.* **1.** [Lacking illumination] unlighted, unlit, dim, shadowy, somber, cloudy, foggy, sunless, lightless, indistinct, dull, faint, vague, dusky, murky, gloomy, misty, obscure, nebulous, shady, shaded, clouded, darkened, overcast, opaque, without light, inky; see also BLACK 1, HAZY.—*Ant.* BRIGHT, lighted, illuminated. **2.** [Dark in complexion] tan, swarthy, dark-complexioned; see BLACK 1. **3.** [Evil] wicked, immoral, corrupt; see BAD 1.

dark *n.* gloom, evening, dusk; see DARKNESS 1. **—in the dark** uninformed, unaware, naive; see IGNORANT 1.

darken *v.* **1.** [To grow darker] cloud up, cloud over, become dark; see SHADE 3. **2.** [To make darker] cloud, shadow, blacken; see SHADE 2.

darkness *n.* **1.** [Gloom] dark, dusk, murkiness, dimness, shade, blackness, pitch darkness, twilight, eclipse, nightfall, obscurity, cloudiness; see also NIGHT 1. **2.** [Evil] wickedness, sin, corruption; see EVIL 1. **3.** [Secrecy] concealment, isolation, seclusion; see PRIVACY, SECRECY.

darling *n.* lover, sweetheart, dear one, beloved, dear heart, heart's desire, dearest, pet*, angel*, love, sweetie-pie*, sugar*, honey*, precious*, sweetie*, hon*, light of my life*, baby*, one and only*.

darn *v.* mend, knit, embroider; see REPAIR, SEW.

dart *n.* missile, barb, arrow; see WEAPON.

dart *v.* shoot, shoot out, speed, plunge, launch, thrust, hurtle, fling, heave, pitch, dash, spurt, spring, spring up, fly, fire off*, scoot*; see also MOVE 1.—*Ant.* STOP, amble, loiter.

dash *n.* **1.** [A short, swift movement] spurt, charge, rush; see RUN 1. **2.** [Punctuation marking a break in thought] em, em dash, en dash, hyphen; see also MARK 1, PUNCTUATION. **3.** [A little of something] a few drops, hint, sprinkle, scattering, seasoning, touch, grain, trace, suspicion, suggestion, squirt, taste; see also BIT 1, PART 1.—*Ant.* TOO MUCH, quantity, excess.

dash *v.* **1.** [To discourage] dampen, dismay, dispirit; see DISCOURAGE. **2.** [To sprint] race, speed, hurry; see RUN 1.

data *n.* evidence, reports, details, results, notes, documents, abstracts, testimony, facts, raw data, memorandums, statistics, figures, measurements, conclusions, information, circumstances, experiments, info*, dope*; see also DECLARATION, KNOWLEDGE 1, PROOF 1.

date *n.* **1.** [A specified time or period of time] epoch, period, era, generation, day, term, course, spell, duration, span, moment, year, reign, hour, century; see also AGE 3, TIME 2, YEAR. **2.** [An appointment] meeting, rendezvous, engagement, interview, call, visit; see also APPOINTMENT 2. **3.** [Person with whom one has a date] partner, companion, associate; see FRIEND, LOVER 1. **—out of date** obsolete, passé, antiquated; see OLD-FASHIONED. **—to date** until now, as yet, so far; see NOW 1. **—up to date** modern, contemporary, current; see FASHIONABLE.

date *v.* **1.** [To indicate historical time] ascertain the time of, determine, assign a time to, measure, mark with a date, fix the date of, chronicle, isolate, measure, carbon-date; see also DEFINE 1, MEASURE 1, RECORD 1. **2.** [To court or be courted] escort, associate with, take out, keep company with, go out with*, go together*, make a date with*, go steady*; see also ACCOMPANY.

daughter *n.* female child, girl, offspring, descendant, stepdaughter, infant; see also CHILD, GIRL.

dawn *n.* dawning, sunrise, daybreak; see MORNING 1.

day *n.* **1.** [The time of light or work] daylight, daytime, full day, working day, daylight hours, eight-hour day, sizzler*, scorcher*; good, bad, hot, damp, etc. day. **2.** [A special day] feast day, celebration, festival; see HOLIDAY. **3.** [A period of time] era, age, time; see AGE 3. —**call it a day*** finish, quit working, end; see STOP 1. —**from day to day** without thought for the future, sporadically, as well as one can; see IRREGULARLY.

day after day *a.* continually, monotonously, steadily; see REGULARLY.

day by day *a.* gradually, slowly, persistently; see REGULARLY.

daydream *n.* trance, vision, fantasy; see DREAM.

day in and day out *a.* consistently, steadily, every day; see DAILY, REGULARLY.

daylight *n.* daytime, daylight hours, broad daylight; see DAY 1. —**scare** (or **beat** or **knock**) **the daylights out of*** frighten, scare, beat; see THREATEN.

daze *n.* stupor, trance, bewilderment; see CONFUSION.

dazed *a.* confused, bewildered, perplexed; see DOUBTFUL.

dead *a.* **1.** [Without life] not existing, expired, deceased, perished, lifeless, inanimate, late, defunct, breathless, no longer living, devoid of life, departed, brain dead, clinically dead, gone, no more*, done for*, gone the way of all flesh*, gone to one's reward*, gone to meet one's Maker*, at rest with God*, out of one's misery*, snuffed out*, pushing up daisies*, rubbed out*, wasted*, liquidated*, erased*, gone by the board*, resting in peace*.—*Ant.* ALIVE, animate, enduring. **2.** [Without the appearance of life] inert, still, stagnant; see DULL 2. **3.** [Numb] insensible, deadened, anesthetized; see NUMB 1, UNCONSCIOUS. **4.** [*Exhausted] wearied, worn, spent; see TIRED.

deaden *v.* blunt, impair, dull, repress, slow, paralyze, freeze, anesthetize, put to sleep, numb, knock out, incapacitate, depress, stifle, benumb, smother, retard, destroy, KO*; see also HURT, WEAKEN 2.—*Ant.* EXCITE, revitalize, invigorate.

deadlock *n.* standstill, stalemate, cessation; see PAUSE.

deadly *a.* fatal, lethal, murderous, mortal, homicidal, virulent, poisonous, bloody, destructive, venomous, malignant, injurious, carcinogenic, suicidal, bloodthirsty, cannibalistic, harmful, violent; see also DANGEROUS.

deaf *a.* stone-deaf, unable to hear, without hearing, deaf and dumb, deafened, stunned, hard of hearing.

deafening *a.* thunderous, overpowering, shrieking; see LOUD 1, 2.

deal *n.* **1.** [An agreement] pledge, compromise, pact; see AGREEMENT, CONTRACT. **2.** [A secret or dishonest agreement] swindle, robbery, graft; see CRIME, THEFT. **3.** [A lot] much, abundance, superabundance; see PLENTY. —**a good** (or **great**) **deal** a lot, quite a bit, a considerable amount; see MUCH. —**make a big deal out of*** expand, magnify, blow up; see EXAGGERATE.

deal *v.* trade, bargain, barter; see BUY, SELL.

dealer *n.* retailer, trader, vendor; see BUSINESSMAN, MERCHANT.

dealings *n.pl.* business, trade, transactions; see BUSINESS 1, 4.

deal with *v.* handle, manage, have to do with; see TREAT 1.

dear *a.* precious, respected, cherished; see BELOVED.

dear *n.* loved one, sweetheart, love; see DARLING, LOVER 1.

dearly *a.* **1.** [In an affectionate manner] fondly, affectionately, yearningly; see LOVINGLY. **2.** [To a great extent] greatly, extremely, profoundly; see VERY.

death *n.* decease, dying, demise, passing, loss of life, departure, release, parting, end of life, afterlife, other world, grave, tomb, paradise, heaven, hell, extinction, mortality, exit*, end, finish*, the way of all flesh*, the Grim Reaper*, eternal rest, last rest*; see also DESTRUCTION 1.—*Ant.* LIFE, birth, beginning. —**at death's door** failing, wasting away, nearly dead; see DYING 1, 2. —**to death** very much, extremely, to the extreme; see MUCH 1. —**to the death** to the end, constantly, faithfully; see LOYALLY.

debatable *a.* disputable, unsettled, up for discussion; see CONTROVERSIAL, QUESTIONABLE 1.

debate *n.* contest, match, dispute; see DISCUSSION.

debate *v.* refute, oppose, question, contend, contest, reason with, wrangle, answer, ponder, weigh, differ, dispute, quarrel, bandy words with, argue the pros and cons of; see also ARGUE, DISCUSS.—*Ant.* AGREE, concur, concede.

debauched *a.* corrupted, debased, depraved; see WICKED.

debit *n.* deficit, obligation, liability; see DEBT.

debris *n.* rubbish, litter, wreckage; see TRASH 1.

debt *n.* liability, obligation, mortgage, duty, arrears, deficit, note, bill, account payable, indebtedness; see also OBLIGATION.—*Ant.* CASH, asset, capital.

debtor *n.* one that owes, borrower, mortgagor; see BUYER.

debunk *v.* expose, uncover, disclose; see EXPOSE 1.

decadence *n.* deterioration, decline, degeneration; see DECAY, EVIL 1.

decadent *a.* immoral, wicked, degenerate; see BAD 1.

decay *n.* decline, decrease, consumption, decomposition, collapse, downfall, decadence, depreciation, corruption, spoilage, wasting away, degeneration, dry rot, putrefaction, corruption, dissolution, rottenness, spoiling, breakup, breakdown, mold, rust, atrophy, emaciation, blight, mildew, deterioration, ruination, extinction, disintegration, ruin, crumbling, waste, corrosion, wear and tear, crack-up*.

decay *v.* corrode, rot, wither; see SPOIL 1.

decayed *a.* decomposed, putrid, spoiled; see ROTTEN 1.

decaying *a.* rotting, crumbling, spoiling, breaking down, breaking up, wasting away, falling, deteriorating, wearing away, disintegrating, worsening, tumbling down; see also ROTTEN 1.

deceased *a.* late, lifeless, departed; see DEAD 1.

deceit *n.* fraud, trickery, duplicity; see DECEPTION, DISHONESTY.

deceitful *a.* tricky, cunning, insincere; see DISHONEST.

deceive *v.* mislead, swindle, outwit, fool, delude, rob, defraud, not play fair, play a practical joke on, victimize, betray, beguile, take advantage of, entrap, ensnare, hoodwink, dupe, fleece, con*, skin*, sucker*, string along*, screw out of*, do in*, lead astray*, bamboozle*, cross up*, bilk*, gouge*, clip*, fake, gyp*, put on*, burn*, sell out*, chisel*, double-cross*, shake down*, make a sucker out of*, take to the cleaners*, take for a ride*, snow*, put one over on*, take in*, pull the wool over someone's eyes*, flimflam*, give someone the runaround*, do a snow job on*, play upon*, make a monkey of*, stack the cards*; see also TRICK.

deceived *a.* duped, fooled, humbugged, hoaxed, snared, trapped, decoyed, baited, deluded, defrauded, hoodwinked, betrayed, bamboozled*, sucked in*, conned*; see also CHEATED.—*Ant.* TRUSTED, dealt with openly, informed.

deceiver *n.* conniver, swindler, impostor; see CHEAT.

decency *n.* propriety, righteousness, respectability; see HONESTY, VIRTUE 1.

decent *a.* **1.** [In accordance with common standards] accepted, standard, approved; see CONVENTIONAL 3. **2.** [In accordance with the moral code] nice, proper, moral, honest, honorable, chaste, modest, pure, ethical, reserved, spotless, respectable, prudent, mannerly, virtuous, immaculate, delicate, stainless, clean, trustworthy, upright, worthy, untarnished, unblemished, straight; see also GOOD 1.

deception *n.* trickery, double-dealing, untruth, insincerity, craftiness, juggling, treachery, treason, betrayal, mendacity, disinformation, falsehood, trickiness, lying, deceitfulness, deceit, duplicity, cunning, fast one*, snow job*, hokum*; see also DISHONESTY.—*Ant.* HONESTY, frankness, sincerity.

deceptive *a.* misleading, ambiguous, deceitful; see FALSE 2, 3.

decide *v.* settle, determine, judge, conclude, compromise, choose, terminate, vote, poll, make a decision, come to a conclusion, form an opinion, form a judgment, make up one's mind, make a selection, select, pick, make one's choice, commit oneself, come to an agreement, have the final word*; see also AGREE, RESOLVE.—*Ant.* DELAY, hesitate, hedge.

decided *a.* **1.** [Determined] settled, decided upon, arranged for; see DETERMINED 1. **2.** [Certain] emphatic, determined, clear; see DEFINITE 1.

deciding *a.* determining, crucial, conclusive; see IMPORTANT 1, NECESSARY.

decipher *v.* interpret, translate, explain; see SOLVE.

decision *n.* resolution, result, declaration; see JUDGMENT 3, OPINION 1.

decisive *a.* final, definitive, absolute; see DEFINITE 1, DETERMINED 1.

deck *n.* **1.** [The floor of a ship] level, flight, story, layer, tier, topside; see also FLOOR 1, 2. **2.** [Cards sufficient for a game] pack, set, pinochle deck, playing cards, the cards; see also CARD. —**on deck*** prepared, available, on hand; see READY 2.

declaration *n.* statement, assertion, utterance, information, affirmation, profession, manifesto, announcement, document, bulletin, denunciation, proclamation, confirmation, ultimatum, notice, notification, resolution, affidavit, testimony, charge, indictment, allegation, canon, bill of rights, constitution, creed, article of faith, presentation, exposition, communication, disclosure, explanation, revelation, publication, answer, advertisement, saying, report, oath, admission, acknowledgment; see also ACKNOWLEDGMENT, ANNOUNCEMENT.

declare *v.* assert oneself, announce, pronounce, claim, tell, state, point out, affirm, maintain, attest to, testify to, confess, reveal, swear, disclose, impart, represent, indicate, notify, repeat, insist, contend, advance, allege, argue, demonstrate, propound, bring forward, put forward, set forth, stress, cite, advocate, pass, proclaim, acknowledge, profess, give out, certify, swear; see also REPORT 1, SAY.—*Ant.* HIDE, equivocate, withhold.

decline *n.* deterioration, dissolution, lessening; see DECAY.

decline *v.* **1.** [To refuse] desist, beg to be excused, send regrets; see REFUSE. **2.** [To decrease] degenerate, deteriorate, backslide; see DECREASE 1.

decompose *v.* rot, crumble, break up; see DISINTEGRATE.

decomposition *n.* dissolution, breakdown, disintegration; see DECAY.

decontaminate *v.* disinfect, purify, sterilize; see CLEAN.

decor *n.* decoration, ornamentation, adornment; see DECORATION 1.

decorate *v.* adorn, beautify, ornament, deck, paint, color, renovate, enrich, brighten, enhance, festoon, embellish, illuminate, spangle, elaborate, enamel, bead, polish, varnish, grace, garnish, finish, tile, redecorate, add the finishing touches, perfect, dress up, fix up, deck out*, pretty up*.

decorated *a.* adorned, ornamented, embellished; see ORNATE.

decoration *n.* **1.** [The act of decorating] adornment, ornamentation, embellishment; see DESIGN, IMPROVEMENT 1. **2.** [Something used for decorating] tinsel, thread work, lace, ribbon, braid, gilt, color, appliqué, scroll, wreath, glass, flourish, tooling, inlay, figure work, spangle, finery, filigree, design, ornament, extravagance; see also JEWELRY, PAINT 1. **3.** [An insignia of honor] citation, medal, ribbon; see EMBLEM.

decorative *a.* embellishing, beautifying, florid; see ORNATE.

decoy *n.* imitation, bait, fake; see CAMOUFLAGE, TRICK 1.

decrease *n.* shrinkage, lessening, contraction; see DISCOUNT, REDUCTION 1.

decrease *v.* **1.** [To grow less] lessen, diminish, decline, wane, deteriorate, degenerate, dwindle, sink, settle, lighten, slacken, ebb, melt, lower, moderate, subside, shrink, shrivel up, depreciate, soften, quiet, narrow down, waste, fade away, run low, weaken, crumble, let up, dry up, slow down, calm down, burn away, burn down, die away, die down, decay, evaporate, slack off, wear off, wear away, wear out, wear down, slump; see also CONTRACT 1.—*Ant.* GROW, increase, multiply. **2.** [To make less] cut, reduce, check, curb, restrain, quell, tame, compose, hush, still, sober, pacify, blunt, curtail, lessen, lower, subtract, abridge, abbreviate, condense, shorten, minimize, diminish, slash, dilute, shave, pare, prune, modify, digest, limit, level, deflate, compress, strip, thin, make smaller, curtail, clip, lighten, trim, level off, take from, take off, roll back, hold down, step down, scale down, boil down, let up, cut off, cut down, cut short, cut back, chisel*, wind down*, knock off*; see also COMPRESS.—*Ant.* INCREASE, expand, augment.

decree *n.* edict, pronouncement, proclamation; see DECLARATION, JUDGMENT 3.

dedicate *v.* devote, apply, give, appropriate, set aside, surrender, apportion, assign, give over to, donate; see also GIVE 1.

dedication *n.* sanctification, devotion, glorification; see CELEBRATION.

deduct *v.* take away, diminish by, subtract; see DECREASE 2.

deduction *n.* **1.** [The act of deducing] inferring, concluding, reasoning; see THOUGHT 1. **2.** [A conclusion] result, answer, inference; see JUDGMENT 3, OPINION 1. **3.** [A reduction] subtraction, abatement, decrease; see DISCOUNT, REDUCTION 1.

deed *n.* **1.** [An action] act, commission, accomplishment; see ACTION 2. **2.** [Legal title to real property] document, release, agreement, charter, title deed, record, certificate, voucher, indenture, warranty, lease; see also PROOF 1, RECORD 1, SECURITY 2.—**in deed** in fact, actually, really; see SURELY.

deep *a.* **1.** [Situated or extending far down] low, below, beneath, bottomless, submerged, subterranean, submarine, inmost, deep-seated, immersed, dark, dim, impenetrable, buried, inward, underground, down-reaching, of great depth, depthless, immeasurable, yawning; see also UNDER 1.—*Ant.* SHALLOW, near the surface, surface. **2.** [Extending laterally or vertically] extensive, far, wide, yawning, penetrating, distant, thick, fat, spread out, to the bone*, up to the hilt*; see also BROAD, LONG 1.—*Ant.* NARROW, thin, shallow. **3.** [Showing evidence of thought and understanding] penetrating, acute, incisive; see PROFOUND.—**go off the deep end*** **1.** [To act rashly] go to extremes, go too far, rant; see EXAGGERATE, RAGE 1. **2.** [To break down] collapse, lose control of oneself, become insane; see CRACK UP 2.

deepen *v.* intensify, expand, extend; see DEVELOP 1, GROW 1, INCREASE.

deeply *a.* surely, profoundly, genuinely; see SINCERELY, TRULY.

deer *n.* doe, buck, fawn, roe, stag, venison, member of the deer family, cervine animal, cervid animal. *Creatures popularly called deer include the following:* spotted, white-tailed, mule, red, musk; antelope, American elk, wapiti, moose, caribou, reindeer, roebuck.

deface *v.* disfigure, scratch, mutilate; see DESTROY.

default *n.* failure, lack, error, offense, failure to act, wrongdoing, transgression, imperfection, oversight, neglect, shortcoming, inadequacy, insufficiency, failure to appear, failure to pay, lapse, weakness, vice, blunder; see also FAILURE 1. —**in default of** lacking, absent, in the absence of; see WANTING.

defeat *n.* repulse, reverse, rebuff, conquest, rout, overthrow, subjugation, destruction, breakdown, collapse, extermination, annihilation, check, trap, ambush, breakthrough, withdrawal, setback, stalemate, ruin, blow, loss, butchery, massacre, Waterloo, beating, whipping, thrashing, fall, comedown, upset, battering*, pasting*, walloping*, whaling*, slaughter*, massacre*, KO*, the old one-two*; see also LOSS 1.—*Ant.* VICTORY, triumph, conquest.

defeat *v.* **1.** [To get the better of another] master, subjugate, overwhelm; see OVERCOME. **2.** [To worst in war] overcome, vanquish, conquer, rout, entrap, subdue, overrun, best, overthrow, crush, smash, drive off, annihilate, overwhelm, scatter, repulse, halt, reduce, outflank, finish off, encircle, slaughter, butcher, outmaneuver, ambush, demolish, sack, torpedo, sink, swamp, wipe out*, decimate, obliterate, roll back, mop up*, chew up*, mow down*; see also DESTROY, RAVAGE.—*Ant.* YIELD, give up, relinquish. **3.** [To worst in sport or in personal combat] beat, overpower, outplay, trounce, knock out, throw, floor, pommel, pound, flog, outhit, outrun, outjump, thrash, edge*, shade*, lay low*, skin*, lick*, wallop*, clean up on*, beat up*, take*, KO*, put down*, beat the pants off of*, pulverize*, steamroll*, plow under*, smear*, cream*; see also BEAT 1.—*Ant.* FAIL, suffer, be defeated.

defeated *a.* crushed, overcome, conquered; see BEATEN 1.

defect *n.* imperfection, flaw, drawback; see FAULT 1.

defect *v.* fall away from, run away, forsake; see ABANDON 2, DESERT, LEAVE 1.

defective *a.* imperfect, incomplete, inadequate; see FAULTY, POOR 2, UNFINISHED 1.

defend *v.* **1.** [To keep off an enemy; *often used figuratively*] shield, shelter, screen; see PROTECT. **2.** [To support an accused person or thing] plead for, justify, uphold, second, exonerate, back, vindicate, aid, espouse the cause of, befriend, say in defense of, guarantee, endorse, warrant, maintain, recommend, rationalize, plead someone's cause, say a good word for, speak for, stand up for, put in a good word for, apologize for, go to bat for*, cover for*, back up*, stick up for*; see also SUPPORT 2.—*Ant.* CONVICT, accuse, charge.

defendant *n.* the accused, defense, offender; see PRISONER.

defended *a.* protected, guarded, safeguarded; see SAFE 1.

defender *n.* champion, patron, sponsor; see GUARDIAN 1, PROTECTOR.

defense *n.* **1.** [The act of defending] resistance, protection, safeguard, preservation, security, custody, stand, front, backing, guardianship, the defensive, precaution, inoculation, excusing, apologizing, explaining, justifying, exoneration, explanation.—*Ant.* OFFENSE, retaliation, aggression. **2.** [A means or system for defending] trench, bulwark, dike, stockade, machine-gun nest, bastion, fortification, fort, chemical and biological warfare, barricade, garrison, rampart, fence, wall, embankment, citadel, fortress, armor, antiaircraft, camouflage, gas mask, shield, screen, stronghold, parapet, buttress, guard; see also FORTIFICATION, TRENCH.—*Ant.* ATTACK, siege, blitzkrieg. **3.** [In law, the reply of the accused] denial, plea, answer; see DECLARATION, PROOF 1, STATEMENT 1.

defensible *a.* justfiable, proper, permissible; see FIT 1, 2, LOGICAL.

defensive *a.* protecting, guarding, watchful, protective, vigilant; see also CAREFUL.

defensively *a.* protectively, guardedly, suspiciously; see CAREFULLY 1.

defer *v.* **1.** [To postpone] put off, postpone, shelve; see DELAY, SUSPEND 2. **2.** [To yield] submit, accede, concede; see AGREE.

deference *n.* veneration, acclaim, homage; see REVERENCE.

deferred *a.* delayed, prolonged, held up; see POSTPONED.

defiance *n.* insubordination, rebellion, insurgence; see DISOBEDIENCE.

defiant *a.* resistant, obstinate, disobedient; see REBELLIOUS.

deficiency *n.* want, need, absence; see LACK 2.

deficient *a.* insufficient, skimpy, meager; see INADEQUATE.

deficit *n.* shortage, paucity, deficiency; see LACK 2.

defile *v.* ravish, violate, molest; see HURT, RAPE.

define *v.* **1.** [To set limits] bound, confine, limit, outline, fix, settle, circumscribe, mark, set, distinguish, establish, encompass, mark the limits of, determine the boundaries of, fix the limits of, curb, edge, border, enclose, set bounds to, fence in, rim, encircle, hedge in, wall in, envelop, flank, stake out; see also LIMIT.—*Ant.* CONFUSE, distort, mix. **2.** [To provide a name or description] determine, entitle, label, designate, characterize, elucidate, interpret, illustrate, represent, individuate, find out, popularize, spell out, translate, exemplify, specify, prescribe, nickname, dub; see also DESCRIBE, EXPLAIN, NAME 1.—*Ant.* MISUNDERSTAND, misconceive, mistitle.

definite *a.* **1.** [Determined with exactness] fixed, exact, precise, positive, accurate, correct, decisive, absolute, clearly defined, well-defined, limited, strict, explicit, specific, settled, decided, prescribed, restricted, assigned, unequivocal, special, conclusive, categorical, particular, unerring, to the point, beyond doubt; see also CERTAIN 2, DETERMINED.—*Ant.* OBSCURE, indefinite, inexact. **2.** [Clear in detail] sharp, visible, audible, tangible, distinct, vivid, unmistakable in meaning, straightforward, obvious, marked, plain, not vague, well-drawn, clearly defined, well-marked, well-defined, clear-cut, explicit, unmistakable, distinguishable, undistorted, crisp, bold, graphic, downright, undisguised, in plain sight, clear as day, standing out like a sore thumb*.—*Ant.* CONFUSED, vague, hazy. **3.** [Positive] sure, beyond doubt, convinced; see CERTAIN 1.

definitely *a.* clearly, unmistakably, unquestionably; see SURELY.

definition *n.* meaning, terminology, signification, diagnosis, synonym, exposition, interpretation, explication, clue, key, translation, comment, rationale, commentary, explanation, representation, characterization, solution, answer; see also DESCRIPTION, EXPLANATION.

definitive *a.* final, ultimate, conclusive; see ABSOLUTE 1.

deflate *v.* exhaust, flatten, void; see EMPTY 1, 2.

deflect *v.* swerve, diverge, curve; see TURN 3, 6.

deform *v.* disfigure, deface, injure; see DAMAGE.

deformed *a.* damaged, distorted, misshapen, disfigured, crippled, misproportioned, malformed, cramped, badly made, disjointed, unseemly, ill-favored, dwarfed, hunchbacked, warped, mangled, crushed, unshapely, clubfooted, curved, contorted, gnarled, crooked, grotesque, lame, irregular; see also TWISTED 1, UGLY 1.—*Ant.* REGULAR, shapely, well-formed.

deformity *n.* malformation, ugliness, unsightliness; see CONTORTION, DAMAGE 1.

defraud *v.* hoax, dupe, cheat; see DECEIVE.

defy *v.* insult, resist, confront; see DARE 2, OPPOSE 1, 2.

degenerate *a.* depraved, immoral, corrupt; see BAD.

degradation *n.* depravity, corruption, degeneration; see EVIL 1.

degrade *v.* demote, discredit, diminish; see HUMBLE.

degraded *a.* disgraced, debased, depraved; see BAD.

degree *n.* **1.** [One in a series used for measurement] measure, grade, step, mark, interval, space, measurement, gradation, size, dimension, shade, point, line, plane, step in a series, gauge, rung, term, tier, stair, ratio, period, level; see also DIVISION 2. **2.** [An expression of relative excellence, attainment, or the like] extent, station, order, quality, development, height, expanse, length, potency, range, proportion, compass, quantity, standing, strength, reach, intensity, scope, caliber, pitch, stage, sort, status, rate; see also RANK 3. **3.** [Recognition of academic achievement] distinction, testimonial, honor, qualification, dignity, eminence, credit, credentials, baccalaureate, doctorate, sheepskin*; see also DIPLOMA, GRADUATION. —**by degrees** step by step, slowly but surely, inch by inch; see GRADUALLY. —**to a degree** somewhat, partially, to an extent; see PARTLY.

dehydrate *v.* dessicate, parch, drain; see DRY 1.

dejected *a.* depressed, dispirited, cast down; see SAD 1.

delay *n.* deferment, adjournment, putting off, procrastination, suspension, moratorium, reprieve, setback, stay, stop, discontinuation, cooling-off period*, holdup*; see also PAUSE.

delay *v.* postpone, defer, retard, hold up, deter, clog, choke, slacken, keep, hold, keep back, impede, discourage, interfere with, detain, stay, stop, withhold, arrest, check, prevent, repress, curb, obstruct, inhibit, restrict, prolong, encumber, procrastinate, adjourn, block, bar, suspend, table, slow, put aside, hold back, hold off, hold everything, bide one's time, slow up, stall, put off, restrain, put on ice*, shelve*, pigeonhole; see also HINDER, INTERRUPT.—*Ant.* SPEED, accelerate, encourage.

delayed *a.* held up, slowed, put off; see LATE 1, POSTPONED.

delegate *n.* legate, emissary, proxy, deputy, substitute, consul, appointee, minister, alternate, nominee, ambassador, congressman, senator, stand-in*, sub*, pinch hitter*; see also AGENT, REPRESENTATIVE 2.

delegate *v.* **1.** [To give authority to another] authorize, commission, appoint, name, nominate, select, choose, assign, license, empower, deputize, swear in, ordain, invest, elect, give someone the green light*, give someone the go-ahead*; see also APPROVE.—*Ant.* DISMISS, repudiate, reject. **2.** [To give duties to another] entrust, parcel out, hold responsible for; see ASSIGN.

delegation *n.* **1.** [The act of assigning to another] assignment, giving over, nomination, trust, commissioning, ordination, authorization, charge, deputation, referring, transferring; see also APPOINTMENT 1. **2.** [A group with a specific mission] representatives, deputation, commission; see COMMITTEE, GATHERING, ORGANIZATION 2.

deliberate *a.* thought out, predetermined, conscious, advised, prearranged, fixed, with forethought, well-considered, cautious, studied, intentional, planned in advance, done on purpose, willful, considered, thoughtful, purposed, planned, reasoned, calculated, intended, purposeful, premeditated, voluntary, designed, cold-blooded, resolved, cut-and-dried; see also CAREFUL.

deliberately *a.* resolutely, determinedly, emphatically, knowingly, meaningfully, voluntarily, consciously, on purpose, willfully, premeditatedly, in cold blood, with malice aforethought, advisedly, freely, independently, without any qualms, by design, intentionally, purposely, all things considered, pointedly, to that end, with eyes wide open*; see also CAREFULLY 1.

delicacy *n.* **1.** [Fineness of texture] airiness, daintiness, transparency, flimsiness, softness, smoothness, subtlety, tenderness; see also LIGHTNESS 2. **2.** [A rare commodity, especially for the table] tidbit, luxury, gourmet dish, gourmet food, dessert, sweet, delight, party dish, imported food, delicatessen, chef's special*; see also FOOD.

delicate *a.* **1.** [Sickly] susceptible, in delicate health, feeble; see SICK, WEAK 1. **2.** [Dainty] fragile, frail, fine; see DAINTY.

delicately *a.* deftly, skillfully, cautiously; see CAREFULLY 1.

delicatessen *n.* **1.** [Ready-to-serve-foods] *Varieties of delicatessen include the following:* cold meats, luncheon meats, salad, dairy products, salami, pastrami, bologna, wurst, sausage, frankfurters, olives, sauerkraut, pickled peppers, pickled fish, dill pickles, sweet pickles, kosher pickles, gherkins, caviar, anchovies, pâté; see also BREAD, CHEESE, DESSERT, FISH, FRUIT, MEAT, WINE. **2.** [A place that sells delicatessen] food store, butcher store, grocery; see MARKET 1.

delicious *a.* tasty, savory, good, appetizing, choice, well-seasoned, well-done, spicy, sweet, rich, delectable, exquisite, dainty, luscious, tempting, yummy*, fit for a king*; see also EXCELLENT, RICH 4.—*Ant.* ROTTEN, flat, stale.

delight *n.* enjoyment, joy, pleasure; see HAPPINESS.

delight *v.* fascinate, amuse, please; see ENTERTAIN 1.

delighted *a.* **1.** [Greatly pleased] entranced, excited, pleasantly surprised; see HAPPY. **2.** [An expression of acceptance or pleasure] thank you, by all means, to be sure, splendid, excellent, overwhelmed, charmed, so glad.

delightful *a.* charming, amusing, clever; see PLEASANT 1.

delinquent *a.* **1.** [Lax in duty] slack, behindhand, tardy, procrastinating, criminal, neglectful, faulty, blamable, negligent, derelict, remiss; see also CARELESS.—*Ant.* PUNCTUAL, punctilious, scrupulous. **2.** [Not paid on time; *said especially of taxes*] owed, back, overdue; see DUE, UNPAID 1.

delinquent *n.* defaulter, tax evader, offender, dropout, reprobate, loafer, derelict, bad debtor, poor risk, felon, law breaker, wrongdoer, sinner, juvenile offender, juvenile delinquent, JD*, punk*, outlaw, black sheep*; see also CRIMINAL.

delirious *a.* demented, crazy, irrational; see INSANE.

deliver *v.* **1.** [To free] set free, liberate, save; see FREE. **2.** [To transfer] pass, remit, hand over; see GIVE 1. **3.** [To speak formally] present, read, give; see ADDRESS 2. **4.** [To bring to birth] bring forth, be delivered of, provide obstetrical attention; see PRODUCE 2. **5.** [To distribute] allot, dispense, give out; see DISTRIBUTE.

delivered *a.* brought, deposited, transported, checked in, forwarded, expressed, hand-delivered, mailed, dispatched, at the door, sent out by truck, trucked; see also MAILED.

delivery *n.* **1.** [Bringing goods into another's possession] consignment, carting, shipment, transfer, portage, freighting, dispatch, conveyance, mailing, special delivery, parcel post, giving over, handing over, cash on delivery, COD, free on board, FOB; see also TRANSPORTATION. **2.** [Delivery of a child] birth, parturition, confinement, childbirth, labor, bringing forth, midwifery, obstetrics, Caesarean section; see also BIRTH. **3.** [The manner of a speaker] articulation, enunciation, accent, utterance, pronunciation, emphasis, elocution; see also ELOQUENCE.

delusion *n.* **1.** phantasm, hallucination, fancy; see ILLUSION.

deluxe *a.* elegant, luxurious, grand; see LUXURIOUS.

demand *n.* **1.** [A peremptory communication] order, call, charge; see COMMAND. **2.** [Willingness to purchase] trade, request, sale, bid, need, requirement, interest, call, rush, search, inquiry, desire to buy; see also DESIRE 1.—*Ant.* INDIFFERENCE, lack of interest, sales resistance. **—in demand** sought, needed, requested; see WANTED. **—on demand** ready, prepared, usable; see AVAILABLE.

demand *v.* charge, direct, command; see ASK.

demanding *a.* fussy, imperious, exacting; see CRITICAL.

demented *a.* crazy, bemused, unbalanced; see INSANE.

demerit *n.* bad mark, loss of points, poor grade; see FAULT 1, PUNISHMENT.

demobilize *v.* disband, disperse, withdraw; see DISARM.

democracy *n.* justice, the greatest good for the greatest number, equality, popular suffrage, individual enterprise, capitalism, laissez faire, rugged individualism, freedom of religion, freedom of speech, freedom of the press, the right to work, private ownership, emancipation, political equality, democratic spirit, the American Way*; see also EQUALITY, FREEDOM 2.—*Ant.* dictatorship, feudalism, tyranny.

democrat *n.* republican, Social Democrat, state socialist, advocate of democracy, constitutionalist, individualist.—*Ant.* DICTATOR, Nazi, autocrat.

Democrat *n.* Southern Democrat, constitutional Democrat, Jeffersonian Democrat, Dixiecrat*, Fair Dealer*, Great Society Democrat*, New Dealer*; see also REPUBLICAN.—*Ant.* REPUBLICAN, Tory, Socialist.

democratic *a.* popular, constitutional, representative, free, equal, common, bourgeois, individualistic, communal, laissez-faire.

demolish *v.* wreck, devastate, obliterate; see DESTROY.

demolition *n.* extermination, annihilation, wrecking; see DESTRUCTION 1, EXPLOSION.

demon *n.* imp, vampire, incubus; see DEVIL.

demonstrate *v.* **1.** [To prove] show, make evident, confirm; see PROVE. **2.** [To present for effect] exhibit, manifest, parade; see DISPLAY.

demonstration *n.* **1.** [An exhibition] showing, presentation, exhibit; see DISPLAY, SHOW 1. **2.** [A mass rally] picket line, march, sit-in; see PROTEST.

demoralize *v.* weaken, unman, enfeeble; see DISCOURAGE.

demoralized *a.* unnerved, weakened, depressed; see SAD 1.

demote *v.* downgrade, lower, bust*; see DECREASE 2, DISMISS.

den *n.* **1.** [The home of an animal] cavern, lair, cave; see HOLE 1. **2.** [A private or secluded room] study, recreation room, rec room*; see RETREAT 2, ROOM 2.

denial *n.* repudiation, disclaimer, rejection, refutation, rejecting, retraction, dismissal, renunciation, refusal to recognize, the cold shoulder*, the brush-off*; see also OPPOSITION 2.—*Ant.* ACKNOWLEDGMENT, avowal, confession.

denomination *n.* **1.** [A class] category, classification, group; see CLASS 1. **2.** [A religious group] belief, creed, sect; see CHURCH 3.

denounce *v.* condemn, threaten, charge, blame, accuse, indict, arraign, implicate, incriminate, upbraid, impugn, prosecute, revile, stigmatize, ostracize, reproach, castigate, brand, boycott, rebuke, dress down, take to task, damn, impeach, scold, reprimand, reprove, condemn openly, charge with, blacklist, expose, knock*, rip into*, blackball*; see also DENY.—*Ant.* PRAISE, laud, commend.

dense *a.* **1.** [Close together] solid, compact, impenetrable; see THICK 1. **2.** [Slow-witted] stupid, dumb*, imbecilic; see DULL 3, IGNORANT 2.

density *n.* solidity, thickness, impenetrability, consistency, quantity, bulk, heaviness, body, compactness, denseness; see also MASS 1, WEIGHT 1.—*Ant.* LIGHTNESS, rarity, thinness.

dent *n.* indentation, depression, impression, dimple, nick, notch, dip, cavity, cut, incision, sinkhole, pit, trough, furrow, scratch; see also HOLE 1.

dent *v.* hollow, depress, indent, gouge, sink, dig, imprint, mark, dimple, pit, notch, scratch, nick, make a dent in, perforate, ridge, furrow.—*Ant.* STRAIGHTEN, bulge, make protrude.

dentist *n.* DDS, dental practitioner, specialist; see DOCTOR.

deny *v.* contradict, disagree with, disprove, disallow, gainsay, disavow, disclaim, negate, repudiate, controvert, revoke, rebuff, reject, renounce, discard, not admit, take exception to, disbelieve, spurn, doubt, veto, discredit, nullify, say "no" to; see also DENOUNCE, REFUSE.—*Ant.* ADMIT, accept, affirm.

deodorant *n.* disinfectant, deodorizer, fumigator; see CLEANSER, COSMETIC.

depart *v.* go, quit, withdraw; see LEAVE 1.

departed *a.* **1.** [Dead] defunct, expired, deceased; see DEAD 1. **2.** [Gone away] left, disappeared, moved; see GONE 1.

department *n.* **1.** [The field of one's activity] jurisdiction, activity, interest, occupation, province, bureau, business, capacity, dominion, administration, station, function, office, walk of life, vocation, specialty, field, duty, assignment, bailiwick; see also JOB 1. **2.** [An organized subdivision] section, office, bureau, precinct, tract, range, quarter, area, arena, corps, agency, board, administration, circuit, territory, ward, state office, district office, force, staff, beat; see also DIVISION 2.

department store *n.* variety store, supermarket, shopping center, shopper's square, mall, drygoods store, mail-order house, bazaar, fair, bargain store; see also MARKET 1.

departure *n.* going, departing, separation, embarkation, taking leave, sailing, withdrawal, hegira, evacuation, passage, setting out, setting forth, parting, takeoff, taking off, becoming airborne, starting, leaving, flight, exodus, exit, walkout, getaway; see also RETREAT 1.—*Ant.* ARRIVAL, landing, invasion.

dependable *a.* trustworthy, steady, sure; see RELIABLE.

dependence *n.* reliance, servility, inability to act independently, subordination to the direction of another, subjection to control, subservience; see also NECESSITY 3.

dependent *a.* **1.** [Subordinate] inferior, secondary, lesser; see SUBORDINATE. **2.** [Needing outside support] helpless, poor, immature, clinging, not able to sustain itself, on a string*; see also WEAK 5. **3.** [Contingent] liable to, subject to, incidental to, conditioned, sustained by, unable to exist without, subordinate, accessory to, subservient, controlled by, regulated by, determined by; see also CONDITIONAL.

dependent *n.* retired person, old man, old woman, foster child, charge, orphan, minor, delinquent, protegé, hanger-on.

depending (on) *a.* contingent upon, regulated by, controlled by, determined by, in the event of, on the condition that, subject to, providing, provided, secondary to, growing from; see also CONDITIONAL.

depend on *v.* **1.** [To be contingent] be determined by, rest with, rest on, be subordinate to, be dependent on, be based on, be subject to, hinge on, turn on, turn upon, be in the power of, be conditioned by, revolve on, trust to, be at the mercy of. **2.** [To rely on] put faith in, confide in, believe in; see TRUST 1.

depleted *a.* emptied, exhausted, spent; see WASTED.

depletion *n.* exhaustion, consumption, deficiency; see EMPTINESS.

deport *v.* exile, ship out, ship away, expel from a given place; see also BANISH, DISMISS.

deposit *v.* **1.** [To lay down] drop, place, put; see INSTALL. **2.** [To present money for safekeeping] invest, amass, store, keep, stock up, bank, hoard, collect, treasure, lay away, put in the bank, entrust, transfer, put for safekeeping, put aside for a rainy day*, salt away*; see also ACCUMULATE, SAVE 2.—*Ant.* SPEND, withdraw, put out. **—on deposit** hoarded, stored, saved; see KEPT 2.

depot *n.* station, base, lot, freight depot, passenger depot, railway depot, railroad depot, terminal, railway station, railroad yards, stockyards, sidetrack, loading track, ammunition dump, ticket office, waiting room, junction, central station, airport, harbor, station house, stopping-place, destination.

deprave *v.* pervert, debase, degrade; see CORRUPT.

depraved *a.* low, mean, base; see BAD.

depreciate *v.* deteriorate, lessen, worsen; see DECREASE 1.

depreciation *n.* harm, reduction, shrinkage; see LOSS 3.

depress *v.* **1.** [To bring to a lower level] press down, squash, settle; see FLATTEN, PRESS 1. **2.** [To bring to a lower state] reduce, dampen, dishearten, debase, degrade, abase, dismay, sadden, mock, darken, scorn, reduce to tears, deject, weigh down, keep down, cast down, beat down, chill, dull, oppress, lower in spirits, throw cold water on*; see also DISCOURAGE, DISGRACE, HUMBLE, HUMILIATE.—*Ant.* URGE, animate, stimulate.

depressed *a.* discouraged, pessimistic, cast down; see SAD 1.

depressing *a.* discouraging, disheartening, saddening; see DISMAL, SAD 1.

depression *n.* **1.** [Something lower than its surroundings] cavity, dip, sinkhole; see HOLE 1. **2.** [Low spirits] despair, despondency, sorrow, unhappiness, gloom, dejection, melancholy, misery, trouble, worry, discouragement, hopelessness, distress, desperation, desolation, dreariness, dullness, cheerlessness, darkness, bleakness, oppression, gloominess, dumps, blues*, doldrums; see also GRIEF, SADNESS.—*Ant.* JOY, cheer, satisfaction. **3.** [Period of commercial stress] decline, unemployment, slack times, hard times, bad times, inflation, crisis, economic decline, over-production, economic stagnation, recession, panic, crash, slump; see also FAILURE 1.

deprive *v.* strip, despoil, divest; see SEIZE 2.

depth *n.* **1.** [Vertical or lateral distance] lowness, pitch, extent down from a given point, downward measure, perpendicular measurement from the bottom; see also EXPANSE.—*Ant.* HEIGHT, shallowness, flatness. **2.** [Deepness] profundity, intensity, abyss, pit, base, bottom of the sea; see also BOTTOM. **3.** [Intellectual power] profundity, weightiness, acumen; see WISDOM. **—in depth** extensively, broadly, thoroughly, comprehensively.

deputy *n.* lieutenant, appointee, aide; see ASSISTANT, DELEGATE.

derail *v.* run off the rails, be wrecked, fall off; see CRASH 1, WRECK.

derange *v.* madden, craze, unbalance; see CONFUSE, DISTURB.

deranged *a.* demented, crazy, mad; see INSANE.

deride *v.* scorn, jeer, mock; see RIDICULE.

derision *n.* scorn, mockery, disdain; see RIDICULE.

derivation *n.* root, source, beginning; see ORIGIN 3.

derive *v.* draw a conclusion, work out, conclude; see ASSUME.

derogatory *a.* belittling, faultfinding, detracting; see CRITICAL, SARCASTIC.

descend *v.* slide, settle, gravitate, slip, dismount, topple, plunge, sink, dip, pass downward, pitch, light, deplane, tumble, move downward, come down upon, slump, trip, stumble, flutter down, plummet, submerge, step down, climb down, go down, swoop down, get off; see also DIVE, DROP 1, FALL 1.—*Ant.* CLIMB, ascend, mount.

descendants *n.pl.* offspring, kin, children; see FAMILY.

descent *n.* **1.** [A downward incline] declivity, fall, slide; see HILL, INCLINATION 2. **2.** [The act of descending] slump, downfall, drop, lapse, subsiding, falling, coming down, sinking, reduction, landslide, tumble, decline; see also FALL 1.—*Ant.* RISE, mounting, growth. **3.** [Lineal relationship] extraction, origin, lineage; see FAMILY, RELATIONSHIP.

describe *v.* delineate, characterize, portray, depict, picture, illuminate, make clear, make apparent, make vivid, give the details of, specify, give meaning to, elucidate, report, draw, paint, illustrate, detail, make sense of, relate, express, narrate, label, name, call, term, write up, give the dope on*, spell out*; see also DEFINE, EXPLAIN.

description *n.* narration, story, portrayal, word picture, account, report, delineation, sketch, specifications, characterization, declaration, rehearsal, information, definition, record, brief, summary, depiction, explanation, write-up; see also RECORD 1.

descriptive *a.* designating, identifying, definitive, photographic, describing, narrative, expository, interpretive, characterizing, expressive, clear, true to life, illustrative, lifelike, vivid, picturesque, circumstantial, eloquent, detailed, pictorial, indicative, revealing; see also CHARACTERISTIC, EXPLANATORY, GRAPHIC 1, 2.—*Ant.* DULL, analytical, expository.

desert *n.* waste, sand, wastelands, barren plains, arid region, deserted region, sand dunes, lava beds, infertile region, salt flats, abandoned land; see also WILDERNESS.

desert *v.* defect, be absent without leave, abandon one's post, sneak off, run away from duty, violate one's oath, leave unlawfully, go AWOL*, go over the hill*; see also ABANDON 2.—*Ant.* OBEY, stay, do one's duty.

deserted *a.* left, forsaken, relinquished; see ABANDONED, EMPTY.

deserter *n.* runaway, fugitive, refugee, truant, defector, derelict, delinquent, lawbreaker, betrayer, traitor, backslider, slacker; see also CRIMINAL, TRAITOR.

desertion *n.* abandonment, flight, escape, departure, leaving, defection, defecting, renunciation, withdrawal, avoidance, evasion, elusion, truancy, retirement, resignation, divorce, backsliding, running out on*, going back on*; see also ESCAPE.—*Ant.* LOYALTY, cooperation, union.

deserve *v.* merit, be worthy of, earn, be deserving, lay claim to, have the right to, be given one's due, be entitled to, warrant, rate*, have it coming*.—*Ant.* FAIL, be unworthy, usurp.

deserved *a.* merited, earned, justified, appropriate, suitable, equitable, right, rightful, proper, fitting, just, due, well-deserved; see also FIT.

deserving *a.* needy, rightful, fitting; see WORTHY.

design *n.* pattern, layout, conception, diagram, drawing, preliminary sketch, draft, blueprint, picture, tracing, outline, depiction, chart, map, plan, perspective, treatment, idea, study; see also COMPOSITION, FORM 1, PURPOSE 1.—*Ant.* CONFUSION, jumble, mess. —**by design** on purpose, with intent, purposely; see DELIBERATELY.

design *v.* block out, outline, sketch; see PLAN 2.

designate *v.* indicate, point out, name; see CHOOSE.

designation *n.* classification, key word, appellation; see CLASS 1, NAME 1.

designer *n.* planner, draftsman, modeler; see ARCHITECT, ARTIST, SCULPTOR.

desirable *a.* **1.** [Stimulating erotic desires] seductive, fascinating, alluring; see CHARMING. **2.** [Having many good qualities] good, welcome, acceptable; see EXCELLENT.

desire *n.* **1.** [The wish to enjoy] aspiration, wish, motive, will, urge, eagerness, propensity, fancy, frenzy, craze, mania, hunger, thirst, attraction, longing, yearning, fondness, liking, inclination, proclivity, craving, relish, hankering*, itch*, yen*; see also AMBITION, GREED.—*Ant.* INDIFFERENCE, unconcern, apathy. **2.** [Erotic wish to possess] lust, passion, hunger, appetite, fascination, infatuation, fervor, excitement, nymphomania, sexual love, libido, sensual appetite, carnal passion, eroticism, biological urge, rut*, heat*.—*Ant.* ABSTINENCE, coldness, frigidity.

desire *v.* **1.** [To wish for] covet, crave, wish for; see NEED, WANT 1. **2.** [To request] ask for, seek, solicit; see BEG. **3.** [To want sexually] lust after, hunger for, have the hots for*, be turned on by*; see also WANT 1.

desk *n.* **1.** [A piece of furniture] secretary, bureau, box, lectern, frame, case, pulpit; see also FURNITURE, TABLE 1. **2.** [A department of an editorial office] jurisdiction, occupation, bureau; see DEPARTMENT.

desolate *a.* deserted, forsaken, uninhabited; see ABANDONED, ISOLATED.

desolation *n.* bareness, barrenness, devastation, havoc, ruin, dissolution, wreck, demolition, annihilation, extinction; see also DESERT.

despair *n.* hopelessness, depression, discouragement; see DESPERATION, GLOOM.

despair *v.* lose hope, lose faith, lose heart, give up hope, abandon hope, have no hope, have a heavy heart, abandon oneself to fate; see also ABANDON 1.

despairing *a.* hopeless, despondent, miserable; see SAD 1.

desperado *n.* outlaw, bandit, ruffian; see CRIMINAL.

desperate *a.* **1.** [Hopeless] despairing, despondent, downcast; see HOPELESS, SAD 1. **2.** [Reckless] incautious, frenzied, wild; see CARELESS, RASH.

desperately *a.* severely, harmfully, perilously; see CARELESSLY, SERIOUSLY 1.

desperation *n.* despondency, despair, depression, discomfort, dejection, distraction, distress, desolation, anxiety, anguish, agony, melancholy, grief, sorrow, worry, trouble, pain, hopelessness, torture, pang, heartache, concern, misery, unhappiness; see also FEAR, FUTILITY, GLOOM.—*Ant.* HOPE, hopefulness, confidence.

despicable *a.* contemptible, abject, base; see MEAN 3.

despise *v.* scorn, disdain, condemn; see HATE 1.

despite *prep.* in spite of, in defiance of, regardless of, even with.

despondent *a.* dejected, discouraged, depressed; see SAD 1.

dessert *n.* sweet, tart, cobbler, jelly, custard, ice, sundae, compote, fruit salad, pudding, ice cream; see also CAKE 2, CANDY, CHEESE, DELICACY 2, FRUIT, PASTRY, PIE.

destination *n.* objective, goal, aim; see PURPOSE 1.

destined *a.* fated, compulsory, foreordained, menacing, near, forthcoming, threatening, in prospect, predestined, predetermined, compelled, condemned, at hand, impending, inexorable, that is to be, in store, to come, directed, ordained, settled, sealed, closed, predesigned, in the wind, in the cards; see also DOOMED, INEVITABLE.—*Ant.* INVOLUNTARY, at will, by chance.

destiny *n.* fate, future, fortune; see DOOM.

destitute *a.* impoverished, poverty-stricken, penniless; see POOR 1.

destroy *v.* ruin, demolish, exterminate, raze, tear down, plunder, ransack, eradicate, overthrow, root up, root out, devastate, butcher, consume, liquidate, break up, dissolve, blot out, quash, quell, level, abort, stamp out, suppress, squelch, scuttle, undo, annihilate, lay waste, overturn, impair, damage, ravish, deface, shatter, split up, crush, obliterate, knock to pieces, abolish, crash, extinguish, wreck, dismantle, upset, bomb, mutilate, smash, trample, overturn, maim, mar, end, nullify, blast, neutralize, gut, snuff out, erase, sabotage, repeal, pull down, terminate, conclude, finish, bring to ruin, stop, put a stop to, wipe out, do in*, do away with, finish off, make short work of, total*, cream*, destruct, self-destruct, put an end to; see also DEFEAT, RAVAGE, STOP 1.—*Ant.* BUILD, construct, establish.

destroyed *a.* wrecked, annihilated, killed, lost, devastated, wasted, demolished, overturned, overwhelmed, upset, nullified, undone, put to an end, shattered, smashed, scuttled, ravished, engulfed, submerged, overrun, extinguished, eradicated, devoured, consumed, burned up, burned down, gone to pieces, razed, lying in ruins, sacked; see also BROKEN 1, DEAD 1, RUINED 1.—*Ant.* SAVED, protected, restored.

destroyer *n.* **1.** [A destructive agent] assassin, executioner, slayer; see CRIMINAL, KILLER, WEAPON. **2.** [A swift armed surface vessel] warship, battleship, fighting vessel; see SHIP, WARSHIP.

destruction *n.* **1.** [The act of destroying] demolition, annihilation, eradication, slaughter, liquidation, overthrow, extermination, elimination, abolition, murder, assassination, killing, disruption, bombardment, disintegration, extinction, annihilating, wreckage, dissolution, butchery, sabotage, sacking, extinguishing, eliminating, crashing, falling, felling, tearing down; see also DAMAGE 1, DISASTER.—*Ant.* PRODUCTION, formation, erection. **2.** [The condition after destruction] waste, ashes, wreck, annihilation, remnants, devastation, vestiges, desolation, ruins, overthrow, decay, loss, remains, havoc, prostration, injury, downfall, end, starvation, plague, shipwreck, dissolution, disorganization; see also DAMAGE 2, WRECK.

destructive *a.* **1.** [Harmful] hurtful, injurious, troublesome; see HARMFUL. **2.** [Deadly] fatal, ruinous, devastating; see DEADLY, VICIOUS.

detach *v.* separate, withdraw, disengage; see DIVIDE.

detached *a.* **1.** [Cut off or removed] loosened, divided, disjoined; see SEPARATED. **2.** [Indifferent] apathetic, uninvolved, unconcerned; see INDIFFERENT.

detail *n.* item, portion, particular, trait, specialty, feature, aspect, article, peculiarity, fraction, specification, article, technicality; see also CIRCUMSTANCE, PART 1.—*Ant.* WHOLE, entirety, synthesis. —**in detail** item by item, in all details, with particulars, comprehensively, minutely.

detail *v.* itemize, exhibit, show, report, relate, narrate, tell, designate, catalogue, recite, specialize, depict, enumerate, mention, uncover, reveal, recount, recapitulate, analyze, set forth, produce, go into the particulars, get down to cases*; see also DESCRIBE.—*Ant.* DABBLE, summarize, epitomize.

detailed *a.* enumerated, specified, explicit, specific, particularized, individual, individualized, developed, itemized, definite, minute, described, precise, full, narrow, complete, exact, fussy, particular, meticulous, point by point, circumstantial, accurate, unfolded, disclosed, elaborated, complicated, comprehensive, at length, gone into; see also ELABORATE 2.—*Ant.* GENERAL, brief, hazy.

details *n.pl.* analysis, trivia, minutiae, particulars, bill, itemized account, trivialities, fine points, items; see also DETAIL.

detain *v.* hold, keep, inhibit; see DELAY, RESTRAIN.

detect *v.* distinguish, recognize, identify; see DISCOVER.

detection *n.* apprehension, exposure, disclosure; see DISCOVERY, EXPOSURE.

detective *n.* policeman, agent, plainclothesman, private eye*, narcotics agent, police sergeant, police officer, FBI agent, wiretapper, investigator, criminologist, prosecutor, patrolman, sleuth, shadow, eavesdropper, spy, shamus*, flatfoot*, dick*, G-man*, copper*, cop*, fed*, narc*; see also POLICEMAN.

detention *n.* custody, impediment, quarantine; see ARREST, CONFINEMENT, RESTRAINT 2.

deter *v.* caution, stop, dissuade; see PREVENT, WARN.

detergent *n.* cleansing agent, disinfectant, washing substance; see CLEANSER, SOAP.

deteriorate *v.* depreciate, lessen, degenerate; see DECREASE 1.

deterioration *n.* decadence, rotting, degeneration; see DECAY.

determinable *a.* definable, discoverable, capable of being determined; see DEFINITE 2.

determination *n.* resolution, certainty, persistence, stubbornness, obstinacy, resolve, certitude, decision, assurance, conviction, boldness, fixity of purpose, hardihood, tenacity, courage, independence, self-confidence, purposefulness, fortitude, self-assurance, firmness, self-reliance, nerve, heart, bravery, fearlessness, will, energy, vigor, stamina, perseverance, strength of will, a brave front, a bold front, a stout heart, enterprise, guts*, spunk*, a stiff upper lip*; see also CONFIDENCE, FAITH 1, PURPOSE 1.

determine *v.* **1.** [To define] limit, circumscribe, delimit; see DEFINE 1, RESTRICT. **2.** [To find out the facts] ascertain, find out, learn; see DISCOVER. **3.** [To resolve] fix upon, settle, conclude; see DECIDE, RESOLVE.

determined *a.* **1.** [Already fixed or settled] decided, agreed, acted upon, agreed upon, concluded, contracted, set, ended, resolved, closed, terminated, achieved, finished, over, at an end, checked, measured, tested, budgeted, passed, given approval, given the green light*, given the go-ahead, over and done with; see also APPROVED.—*Ant.* UNFINISHED, argued, suspended. **2.** [Having a fixed attitude] resolute, firm, strong-minded; see STUBBORN.

deterrent *n.* hindrance, impediment, obstacle; see RESTRAINT 2.

detest *v.* abhor, loathe, despise; see HATE.

detonate *v.* touch off, discharge, blast; see EXPLODE, SHOOT 1.

detour *n.* temporary route, alternate route, byway, back road, service road, alternate highway, secondary highway, bypass, circuit, roundabout course.

detract *v.* decrease, take away a part, subtract, draw away, diminish, lessen, withdraw, derogate, depreciate, discredit; see also SLANDER.

devalue *v.* revalue, depreciate, mark down; see DECREASE 2.

devastate *v.* ravage, sack, pillage; see DESTROY.

devastation *n.* destruction, defoliation, waste; see DESOLATION.

develop *v.* **1.** [To improve] enlarge, expand, extend, promote, advance, magnify, build up, refine, enrich, cultivate, elaborate, polish, finish, perfect, deepen, lengthen, heighten, widen, intensify, fix up, shape up*; see also GROW 1, IMPROVE 1, 2, STRENGTHEN.—*Ant.* DAMAGE, disfigure, spoil. **2.** [To grow] mature, evolve, advance; see GROW 1. **3.** [To reveal slowly] unfold, disclose, exhibit, unravel, disentangle, uncover, make known, explain, unroll, explicate, produce, detail, tell, state, recount, account for, give an account of; see also REVEAL.—*Ant.* HIDE, conceal, blurt out. **4.** [To work out] enlarge upon, elaborate upon, go into detail; see EXPLAIN, INCREASE.

developed *a.* grown, refined, advanced; see MATURED, PERFECTED.

development *n.* growth, unfolding, elaboration, maturing, progress, ripening, maturation, enlargement, addition, spread, gradual evolution, evolving, advancement, improvement, growing, increasing, spreading, adding to, making progress, advancing; see also IMPROVEMENT 1, INCREASE, PROGRESS 1.—*Ant.* REDUCTION, decrease, lessening.

deviate *v.* deflect, digress, swerve, vary, wander, stray, turn aside, keep aside, stay aside, go out of control, shy away, depart, break the pattern, not conform, go out of the way, veer, go off on a tangent, go haywire*, swim against the stream*; see also DIFFER 1.—*Ant.* CONFORM, keep on, keep in line.

deviation *n.* change, deflection, alteration; see DIFFERENCE 1, VARIATION 2.

device *n.* **1.** [An instrument] invention, contrivance, mechanism, gear, equipment, appliance, contraption, means, agent, material, implement, utensil, construction, apparatus, outfit, article, accessory, gadget, thing, whatnot*, whatsit*, whatchamacallit*; see also MACHINE, TOOL 1. **2.** [A shrewd method] artifice, scheme, design, trap, dodge, trick, pattern, loophole, wile, craft, ruse, expedient, subterfuge, plan, project, plot, racket*, game, finesse, catch*; see also DISCOVERY, METHOD, TRICK 1.

devil *n.* Satan, fiend, adversary, error, sin, imp, mischiefmaker, Beelzebub, fallen angel, hellhound, Mammon, Molloch, Hades, Lucifer, Mephistopheles, diabolical force, the Tempter, Prince of Darkness, Evil One; see also EVIL 1.—*Ant.* GOD, angel, Christ. **—give the devil his due** give one credit, give credit where credit is due, recognize; see ACKNOWLEDGE 2. **—go to the**

devil 1. [To decay] degenerate, fall into bad habits, go to pot*; see FAIL 1. 2. [A curse] go to hell, damn you, be damned; see CURSE. —**raise the devil*** cause trouble, riot, be unruly; see DISTURB, FIGHT.
devious *a.* foxy, insidious, shrewd; see DISHONEST, SLY.
devote *v.* apply, consecrate, give; see BLESS, DEDICATE.
devoted *a.* dutiful, loyal, constant; see FAITHFUL.
devotion *n.* allegiance, service, consecration, devotedness, adoration, piety, zeal, ardor, earnestness, faithfulness, fidelity, deference, sincerity, adherence, observance; see also LOYALTY, WORSHIP 1.—*Ant.* INDIFFERENCE, apathy, carelessness.
devotions *n.pl.* religious worship, church services, prayers; see CHURCH 2, WORSHIP 1.
devour *v.* gulp, swallow, gorge; see EAT 1.
devout *a.* devoted, pious, reverent; see FAITHFUL, HOLY, RELIGIOUS 2.
diagnosis *n.* analysis, determination, investigation; see SUMMARY.
diagonal *a.* slanting, inclining, askew; see OBLIQUE.
diagonally *a.* cornerwise, obliquely, on a slant; see CORNERWISE.
diagram *n.* sketch, layout, picture; see DESCRIPTION, DESIGN, PLAN 1.
dial *n.* face, control, gauge, indicator, meter, register, measuring device, compass; see also INDEX.
dialect *n.* idiom, accent, local speech, regional speech, broken English, pidgin English, brogue, lingo, trade language, lingua franca, usage level, pig Latin, jargon, cant, vernacular, patois; see also LANGUAGE 1.
dialogue *n.* talk, exchange, remarks; see CONVERSATION.
diameter *n.* breadth, measurement across, broadness; see WIDTH.
diametrical *a.* contrary, adverse, facing; see OPPOSITE 3.
diamond *n.* 1. [A crystalline jewel] precious stone, solitaire, engagement ring, brilliant, crystal, ring, stone*, rock*, sparkler*, glass*, ice*; see also JEWEL. 2. [Shape or figure] lozenge, solid, rhombus; see FORM 1. 3. [A baseball playing field, particularly the infield] lot, ball park, sandlot; see FIELD 2, PARK 1.
diary *n.* chronicle, journal, log; see RECORD 1.
dicker *v.* trade, barter, bargain; see ARGUE, BUY, SELL.
dictate *v.* speak, deliver, give forth, interview, compose, formulate, verbalize, record, orate, give an account; see also TALK 1.
dictator *n.* autocrat, despot, tyrant, czar, fascist, absolute ruler, oppressor, terrorist, master, leader, ringleader, magnate, lord, commander, chief, advisor, overlord, taskmaster, disciplinarian, headman, cock of the walk*, man at the wheel*, slave driver*; see also LEADER 2, RULER 1.
dictatorial *a.* despotic, authoritarian, arbitrary; see ABSOLUTE 2.
dictatorship *n.* despotism, unlimited rule, coercion; see GOVERNMENT 2, TYRANNY.
diction *n.* style, enunciation, expression, wording, usage, choice of words, command of language, locution, rhetoric, fluency, oratory, articulation, vocabulary, language, line*, gift of gab*; see also ELOQUENCE, SPEECH 2.
dictionary *n.* word book, word list, lexicon, thesaurus, reference work, glossary, encyclopedia, Webster, dictionary of synonyms.
die *v.* 1. [To cease living] expire, pass away, pass on, depart, perish, succumb, go, commit suicide, suffocate, lose one's life, cease to exist, drown, hang, fall, meet one's death, be no more, drop dead, be done for*, rest in peace*, go to one's final resting place*, pass over to the great beyond*, give up the ghost*, go the way of all flesh*, return to dust*, cash in one's chips*, push up daisies*, buy the farm*, kick the bucket*, bite the dust*, lay down one's life*, breathe one's last*, croak*, check out*, kick off*, go by the board*.—*Ant.* LIVE, thrive, exist. 2. [To cease existing] disappear, vanish, become extinct; see STOP 2. 3. [To decline as though death were inevitable] fade, ebb, wither; see DECAY, WEAKEN 2.
die away *v.* decline, go away, sink; see STOP 2.
die down *v.* decline, disappear, recede; see DIE 2, 3, DECREASE 1.
die-hard *n.* zealot, reactionary, extremist; see CONSERVATIVE.
die off or **out** *v.* go, cease to exist, disappear; see VANISH.
diet *n.* 1. [What one eats] menu, fare, daily bread*; see FOOD. 2. [Restricted intake of food] weight-reduction plan, fast, abstinence from food, starvation diet, bread and water*.
diet *v.* lose weight, go without, starve oneself, slim down, go on a diet, reduce, tighten one's belt*.
differ *v.* 1. [To be unlike] vary, modify, not conform, digress, take exception, turn, reverse, qualify, alter, change, diverge from, contrast with, bear no resemblance, not look like, jar with, clash with, conflict with, be distinguished from, diversify, stand apart, depart from, go off on a tangent*; see also CONTRAST.—*Ant.* RESEMBLE, parallel, take after. 2. [To oppose] disagree, object, fight; see OPPOSE 1.
difference *n.* 1. [The quality of being different] disagreement, divergence, non-conformity, contrariness, deviation, opposition, antithesis, dissimilarity, inequality, diversity, departure, variance, discrepancy, separation, differentiation, distinctness, separateness, asymmetry; see also CON-

TRAST, VARIETY 1.—*Ant.* AGREEMENT, similarity, resemblance. **2.** [That which is unlike in comparable things] deviation, departure, exception; see VARIATION 2. **3.** [Personal dissension] discord, estrangement, dissent; see DISPUTE. —**make a difference** change, have an effect, affect; see MATTER. —**split the difference** compromise, go half way, come to an agreement; see AGREE. —**what's the difference?*** what does it matter?, what difference does it make?, so what?*; see WHY.

different *a.* **1.** [Unlike in nature] distinct, separate, not the same; see UNLIKE. **2.** [Composed of unlike things] diverse, miscellaneous, assorted; see VARIOUS. **3.** [Unusual] unconventional, strange, startling; see UNUSUAL 1, 2.

differentiate *v.* contrast, set apart, separate; see DISTINGUISH 1.

differently *a.* variously, divergently, individually, distinctively, creatively, uniquely, separately, each in his own way, severally, diversely, incongruously, abnormally, not normally, nonconformably, asymmetrically, in a different manner, with a difference, otherwise.—*Ant.* EVENLY, uniformly, invariably.

difficult *a.* **1.** [Hard to achieve] laborious, hard, unyielding, strenuous, exacting, stiff, heavy, arduous, painful, labored, trying, bothersome, troublesome, demanding, burdensome, backbreaking, not easy, wearisome, onerous, rigid, crucial, uphill, challenging, exacting, formidable, ambitious, immense, tough*, heavy*, no picnic*, stiff*; see also SEVERE 1.—*Ant.* EASY, wieldy, light. **2.** [Hard to understand] intricate, involved, perplexing, abstruse, abstract, delicate, hard, knotty, thorny, troublesome, ticklish, obstinate, puzzling, mysterious, mystifying, subtle, confusing, bewildering, confounding, esoteric, unclear, mystical, tangled, hard to explain, hard to solve, profound, rambling, loose, meandering, inexplicable, awkward, complex, complicated, deep, stubborn, hidden, formidable, enigmatic, paradoxical, incomprehensible, unintelligible, inscrutable, inexplicable, unanswerable, not understandable, unsolvable, unfathomable, concealed, unaccountable, ambiguous, equivocal, metaphysical, inconceivable, unknown, deep*, over one's head*, too deep for*, not making sense*, Greek to*; see also OBSCURE 1, 3.—*Ant.* CLEAR, obvious, simple.

difficulty *n.* **1.** [Something in one's way] obstacle, obstruction, stumbling block, impediment, complication, hardship, adversity, misfortune, distress, deadlock, dilemma, hard job, maze, stone wall, barricade, impasse, knot, opposition, quandary, struggle, crisis, trouble, embarrassment, entanglement, thwart, mess, paradox, muddle, emergency, matter, standstill, hindrance, perplexity, bar, trial, check, predicament, hot water*, pickle*, fix*, stew*, scrape*, hard nut to crack*, hitch*, dead end*, snag*, monkey wrench in the works*, pinch, deep water*, jam*, the devil to pay*, hangup*; see also sense 2 and BARRIER.—*Ant.* HELP, aid, assistance. **2.** [Something mentally disturbing] trouble, annoyance, to-do, ado, worry, weight, complication, distress, oppression, depression, aggravation, anxiety, discouragement, touchy situation, embarrassment, burden, grievance, irritation, strife, puzzle, responsibility, frustration, harassment, misery, predicament, setback, pressure, stress, strain, charge, struggle, maze, jam*, hangup*, mess*, pickle*, pinch*, scrape*; see also sense 1 and CRISIS, EMERGENCY.—*Ant.* EASE, comfort, happiness.

dig* *n.* **1.** [Insult] slur, innuendo, cut; see INSULT. **2.** [Excavation] digging, archaeological expedition, exploration; see EXPEDITION.

dig *v.* **1.** [To stir the earth] delve, spade, mine, excavate, channel, deepen, till, drive a shaft, clean, undermine, burrow, dig out, gouge, dredge, scoop out, tunnel out, hollow out, clean out, stope, grub, bulldoze; see also SHOVEL.—*Ant.* BURY, embed, fill. **2.** [To remove by digging] dig up, uncover, turn up; see HARVEST. **3.** [*To like] enjoy, love, appreciate; see LIKE 1, 2. **4.** [*To understand] comprehend, recognize, follow; see UNDERSTAND 1.

digest *n.* epitome, précis, condensation; see SUMMARY.

digest *v.* transform food, consume, absorb; see EAT 1.

digestible *a.* eatable, absorbable, good to eat; see EDIBLE.

dig in *v.* **1.** [To begin] commence, start, get going; see BEGIN 2. **2.** [To entrench] delve, burrow, undermine; see DIG 1.

dig into *v.* investigate, research, probe; see EXAMINE.

digit *n.* symbol, arabic notation, numeral; see NUMBER.

dignified *a.* stately, somber, solemn, courtly, reserved, ornate, elegant, classic, lordly, aristocratic, majestic, formal, noble, regal, superior, magnificent, grand, eminent, sublime, august, grave, distinguished, magisterial, imposing, portly, haughty, honorable, decorous, lofty, proud, classy*, snazzy*, sober as a judge*, high-brow*; see also CULTURED, REFINED 2.—*Ant.* RUDE, undignified, boorish.

dignify *v.* exalt, elevate, prefer; see PRAISE 1.

dignity *n.* nobility, self-respect, lofty bearing, grand air, quality, culture, distinction, stateliness, elevation, worth, character, importance, renown, splendor, majesty, class*; see also HONOR, PRIDE 1.—*Ant.* HUMILITY, lowness, meekness.

dig up *v.* find, uncover, excavate; see DIG 2, DISCOVER.

dilemma *n.* quandary, perplexity, predicament; see DIFFICULTY 1.

diligence *n.* alertness, earnestness, quickness, perseverance, industry, vigor, carefulness, intent, intensity; see also ATTENTION, CARE 1.—*Ant.* CARELESSNESS, sloth, laziness.

dilute *v.* mix, reduce, thin; see WEAKEN 2.

dim *a.* faint, dusky, shadowy; see DARK 1.

dime *n.* ten cents, thin dime, ten-cent piece; see MONEY 1.

dimensions *n.pl.* size, measurements, extent; see HEIGHT, LENGTH 1, 2, WIDTH.

diminish *v.* lessen, depreciate, abbreviate; see DECREASE.

din *n.* clamor, commotion, hubbub; see CONFUSION, NOISE 2.

dine *v.* lunch, feast, sup; see EAT 1.

dingy *a.* grimy, muddy, soiled; see DIRTY 1.

dining room *n. Varieties include the following:* dining hall, breakfast nook, dinette, tea shop, lunch counter, lunch room, cafeteria, café, ice-cream parlor, drug store, grill, coffee shop, fast-food outlet, soda fountain, steak house, sandwich shop, diner, mess hall, galley, automat, greasy spoon*; see also RESTAURANT.

dinner *n.* feast, banquet, main meal, supper, repast; see also MEAL 2.

dip *n.* **1.** [The action of dipping] plunge, immersion, soaking, ducking, drenching, sinking; see also BATH 1. **2.** [Material into which something is dipped] preparation, solution, suspension, dilution, concoction, saturation, mixture; see also LIQUID. **3.** [A low place] depression, slope, inclination; see HOLE 1. **4.** [A swim] plunge, bath, dive; see SWIM.

dip *v.* **1.** [To put into a liquid] plunge, lower, wet, slosh, submerge, irrigate, steep, drench, douse, souse, moisten, splash, slop, water, duck, bathe, rinse, baptize, dunk; see also IMMERSE, SOAK 1, WASH 2. **2.** [To transfer by means of a vessel] scoop, shovel, ladle, bale, spoon, dredge, lift, draw, dish, dip up, dip out, offer; see also SERVE.—*Ant.* EMPTY, pour, let stand. **3.** [To fall] slope, decline, recede, tilt, swoop, slip, spiral, sink, plunge, bend, verge, veer, slant, settle, slump, slide, go down; see also DIVE, DROP 2, FALL 1.

diploma *n.* degree, graduation certificate, credentials, honor, award, recognition, commission, warrant, voucher, confirmation, sheepskin*; see also GRADUATION.

diplomacy *n.* artfulness, skill, discretion; see TACT.

diplomat *n.* ambassador, consul, minister, legate, emissary, envoy, agent; see also REPRESENTATIVE 2, STATESMAN.

diplomatic *a.* tactful, suave, gracious, calculating, shrewd, opportunistic, smooth, capable, conciliatory, conniving, sly, artful, wily, subtle, crafty, sharp, cunning, contriving, scheming, discreet, deft, intriguing, politic, strategic, astute, clever; see also POLITE.

dipped *a.* immersed, plunged, bathed, ducked, doused, drenched, soused, covered, dunked; see also SOAKED, WET 1.

dire *a.* dreadful, terrible, horrible; see FRIGHTFUL 1.

direct *a.* **1.** [Without divergence] in a straight line, straight ahead, undeviating, uninterrupted, unswerving, shortest, nonstop, as the crow flies*, straight as an arrow*, in a beeline*, point-blank; see also STRAIGHT 1.—*Ant.* ZIGZAG, roundabout, crooked. **2.** [Frank] straightforward, outspoken, candid; see FRANK, HONEST. **3.** [Immediate] prompt, succeeding, resultant; see IMMEDIATE.

direct *v.* **1.** [To show the way] conduct, show, guide; see LEAD 1. **2.** [To decide the course of affairs] regulate, govern, influence; see MANAGE 1. **3.** [To aim a weapon] sight, train, level; see AIM. **4.** [To command] command, bid, charge; see ORDER 1.

directed *a.* supervised, controlled, conducted, sponsored, under supervision, assisted, counseled, guided, serviced, managed, organized, orderly, modern, purposeful, functioning; see also AIMED, ORGANIZED.

direction *n.* **1.** [A position] point of the compass, objective, bearing, region, area, place, spot; see also WAY 2. *Points of the compass include the following:* north (N), south (S), east (E), west (W), NE, NW, SE, SW, NNE, NNW, SSE, SSW, ENE, ESE, WNW, WSW. **2.** [Supervision] management, superintendence, control; see ADMINISTRATION 2. **3.** [A tendency] bias, bent, proclivity; see INCLINATION 1.

directions *n.pl.* instructions, advice, notification, specification, indication, orders, assignment, recommendations, summons, directive, regulation, prescription, plans.

directly *a.* instantly, at once, quickly; see IMMEDIATELY.

director *n.* manager, supervisor, executive; see LEADER 2.

directory *n.* list, syllabus, notice, register, record, almanac, roster, dictionary, gazetteer, telephone book, Yellow Pages, city directory, Social Register, Who's Who, blue book; see also CATALOG, INDEX.

dirt *n.* **1.** [Earth] soil, loam, clay; see EARTH 2. **2.** [Filth] rottenness, filthiness, smut; see FILTH.

dirty *a.* **1.** [Containing dirt] soiled, unclean, unsanitary, unhygienic, filthy, polluted, nasty, slovenly, dusty, messy, squalid, sloppy, disheveled, uncombed, unsightly, untidy, straggly, unwashed, stained, tarnished, spotted, smudged, foul, fouled, grimy, greasy, muddy, mucky, sooty, smoked, slimy, rusty, unlaundered, unswept, crummy*, grubby, scuzzy*, scummy.—*Ant.* PURE, unspotted, sanitary. **2.** [Obscene] pornographic, smutty, lewd; see LEWD 1, 2, SENSUAL. **3.** [Nasty] mean, contemptible, disagreeable; see MEAN 3, RUTHLESS.

dirty *v.* soil, sully, defile, pollute, foul, tarnish, spot, smear, blot, blur, smudge, smoke, spoil, sweat up, blotch, spatter, splash, stain, debase, corrupt, taint, contaminate.—*Ant.* CLEAN, cleanse, rinse.

disability *n.* feebleness, inability, incapacity; see INJURY, WEAKNESS 1.

disable *v.* cripple, impair, put out of action; see DAMAGE, WEAKEN 2.

disabled *a.* crippled, helpless, useless, wrecked, stalled, maimed, wounded, mangled, lame, mutilated, run-down, worn-out, weakened, impotent, castrated, paralyzed, handicapped, senile, decrepit, laid up*, done for*, done in*, cracked up*, out of action*; see also HURT, USELESS 1, WEAK 1.—*Ant.* HEALTHY, strong, capable.

disadvantage *n.* **1.** [Loss] damage, harm, deprivation; see LOSS 3. **2.** [A position involving difficulties] bar, obstacle, handicap; see RESTRAINT 2. **3.** [Unfavorable details or prospects; *often plural*] inconvenience, obstacle, drawbacks; see WEAKNESS 1.

disagree *v.* **1.** [To differ] dissent, object, oppose; see DIFFER 1. **2.** [To have uncomfortable effect] nauseate, make ill, be hard on one's stomach*; see BOTHER 2.

disagreeable *a.* **1.** [Having an unpleasant disposition] difficult, obnoxious, offensive; see IRRITABLE, RUDE 2. **2.** [Irritating; *said of things and conditions*] bothersome, unpleasant, upsetting; see DISTURBING, OFFENSIVE 2.

disagreement *n.* **1.** [Discord] contention, strife, conflict, controversy, wrangle, dissension, animosity, ill feeling, ill will, misunderstanding, division, opposition, hostility, breach, discord, feud, clashing, antagonism, bickering, squabble, tension, split, quarreling, falling-out, break, rupture, quarrel, clash, opposition, contest, friction; see also BATTLE, COMPETITION, FIGHT. **2.** [Inconsistency] discrepancy, dissimilarity, disparity; see DIFFERENCE 1. **3.** [A quarrel] fight, argument, feud; see DISPUTE.

disappear *v.* cease, fade, die; see ESCAPE, EVAPORATE, VANISH.

disappearance *n.* vanishing, fading, departure, ebbing away, removal, dissipation, ceasing to exist, ceasing to appear, desertion, flight, retirement, escape, exodus, vanishing point, going, disintegration, exit, withdrawal, decline and fall, eclipse; see also ESCAPE, EVAPORATION.

disappoint *v.* fail, delude, deceive, dissatisfy, disillusion, harass, embitter, chagrin, dumbfound, fall short of, cast down, frustrate, torment, tease, miscarry, abort, thwart, foil, baffle, balk, mislead, bungle, let down, leave in the lurch*, fizzle out*.

disappointed *a.* dissatisified, discouraged, unsatisfied, despondent, depressed, objecting, complaining, distressed, hopeless, balked, disconcerted, aghast, disgruntled, disillusioned; see also SAD.—*Ant.* SATISFIED, pleased, content.

disappointing *a.* unsatisfactory, ineffective, uninteresting, discouraging, unpleasant, inferior, lame, insufficient, failing, at fault, limited, second-rate, mediocre, ordinary, unexpected, unhappy, depressing, disconcerting, disagreeable, irritating, annoying, troublesome, disheartening, unlucky, uncomfortable, bitter, distasteful, disgusting, deplorable, short of expectations; see also INADEQUATE.

disappointment *n.* **1.** [The state of being disappointed] dissatisfaction, frustration, chagrin, lack of success, despondency, displeasure, distress, discouragement, disillusionment, check, disillusion, setback, adversity, hard fortune; see also DEFEAT, FAILURE 1, REGRET 1.—*Ant.* SUCCESS, fulfillment, realization. **2.** [A person or thing that disappoints] miscarriage, misfortune, calamity, blunder, bad luck, setback, downfall, slip, defeat, mishap, error, mistake, discouragement, obstacle, miscalculation, fiasco, no go*, blind alley*, washout*, lemon*, dud*, letdown, bust*, false alarm*; see also sense 1 and FAILURE 2.—*Ant.* ACHIEVEMENT, successful venture, success.

disapproval *n.* criticism, censure, disparagement; see OBJECTION.

disapprove *v.* blame, chastise, reprove; see DENOUNCE.

disapprove of *v.* object to, dislike, deplore; see COMPLAIN, OPPOSE 1.

disarm *v.* demobilize, disable, unarm, weaken, debilitate, incapacitate, muzzle, deprive of weapons, deprive of means of defense, subdue, strip, tie the hands of* clip the wings of*; see also DEFEAT 2, 3.—*Ant.* ARM, outfit, equip.

disarmament *n.* arms reduction, cease-fire, de-escalation; see PEACE 1.

disaster *n.* accident, calamity, mishap, debacle, casualty, emergency, adversity, harm, misadventure, collapse, slip, fall, collision, crash, hazard, setback, defeat, failure, woe, trouble, scourge, grief, undoing, cure, tragedy, blight, cataclysm, downfall, rainy day, bankruptcy, upset, blast, blow, wreck, bad luck, comedown*, crack-up, pileup*, smashup, washout*, flop*, bust*; see also CATASTROPHE, MISFORTUNE.

disastrous *a.* calamitous, ruinous, unfortunate; see HARMFUL, UNFAVORABLE.

disband *v.* scatter, disperse, dismiss; see LEAVE 1.

disbelief *n.* unbelief, skepticism, mistrust; see DOUBT.

disbeliever *n.* doubter, skeptic, agnostic; see CRITIC 1.

disburse *v.* expend, use, contribute; see PAY 1, SPEND.

discard *v.* reject, expel, repudiate, protest, cast aside, cast away, cast out, cast off, throw away, throw aside, throw overboard, throw out, get rid of, give up, renounce, have done with, dump, make away with, dismantle, discharge, write off, banish, eject, divorce, dispossess, dispense with, shake off, pass up, free oneself from, free of, give away, part with, dispose of, do away with, dispense with, shed, relinquish, thrust aside, cast aside, sweep away, cancel, abandon, forsake, desert, cut, have nothing to do with, brush away, scotch*, chuck*, drop, wash one's bands of*, junk*; see also ABANDON 1, DISMISS.—*Ant.* SAVE, retain, preserve.

discarded *a.* rejected, repudiated, cast off, thrown away, dismantled, dismissed, useless, damaged, outworn, worn out, done with, run down, not worth saving, abandoned, obsolete, shelved, neglected, deserted, forsaken, outmoded, out of date, out of style, out of fashion, old-fashioned, old hat*.—*Ant.* KEPT, worthwhile, modern.

discern *v.* find out, determine, discriminate; see DISCOVER.

discerning *a.* discriminating, perceptive, penetrating; see DISCREET.

discharge *v.* **1.** [To unload] unpack, release, remove cargo; see EMPTY, UNLOAD. **2.** [To remove] take off, send, carry away; see REMOVE 1. **3.** [To cause to fire] blast, shoot off, fire; see SHOOT 1. **4.** [To release] emancipate, liberate, let go; see FREE.

discharged *a.* mustered out, sent home, recalled, freed, liberated, released, let go, sent away, emancipated, expelled, ejected, dismissed, fired, ousted, canned*, axed*; see also FREE 2, 3.

disciple *n.* **1.** [A follower] adherent, pupil, believer; see FOLLOWER. **2.** [A follower of Christ] apostle, witness, revealer. *Christ's disciples mentioned in the New Testament include:* Matthew, John, Peter, Bartholomew, James, Philip, Andrew, Thaddaeus, Thomas, James the son of Alphaeus, Judas Iscariot, Simon the Canaanite.

discipline *n.* **1.** [Mental self-training] preparation, development, exercise, drilling, training, regulation, self-disciplining; see also DRILL 3, EDUCATION 1. **2.** [A system of obedience] conduct, regulation, drill, orderliness, restraint, limitation, curb, indoctrination, brainwashing; see also TRAINING.

discipline *v.* chastise, correct, limit; see PUNISH.

disc jockey *n.* radio announcer, commentator, DJ*; see ANNOUNCER, REPORTER.

disclose *v.* make known, confess, publish; see REVEAL.

disclosure *n.* exposé, acknowledgment, confession; see ADMISSION 3, DECLARATION.

discolor *v.* stain, rust, tarnish; see COLOR, DIRTY.

discoloration *n.* blot, blotch, splotch; see BLEMISH, STAIN.

discomfort *n.* trouble, displeasure, uneasiness; see ANNOYANCE, EMBARRASSMENT.

disconnect *v.* separate, detach, disengage; see CUT 1, DIVIDE.

disconnected *a.* broken off, detached, switched off; see SEPARATED.

discontent *n.* envy, uneasiness, depression; see REGRET 1.

discontented *a.* unhappy, disgruntled, malcontented; see SAD 1.

discontinue *v.* finish, close, cease; see END 1, STOP 2.

discontinued *a.* ended, terminated, given up; see ABANDONED.

discord *n.* **1.** [Conflict] strife, contention, dissension; see DISAGREEMENT 1. **2.** [Noise] din, tumult, racket; see NOISE 2.

discount *n.* deduction, allowance, rebate, decrease, markdown, concession, percentage, premium, subtraction, commission, exemption, modification, qualification, drawback, depreciation, cut rate; see also REDUCTION 1.—*Ant.* INCREASE, markup, surcharge. **—at a discount** discounted, cheap, below face value; see REDUCED 2.

discount *v.* reduce, remove, redeem, diminish, depreciate, deduct from, lower, make allowance for, allow, take off, charge off, rebate, mark down, anticipate, discredit, rake off*; see also DECREASE 2.—*Ant.* RAISE, mark up, advance.

discourage *v.* repress, appall, intimidate, break one's heart, deject, unnerve, scare, confuse, dampen, dismay, daunt, bully, demoralize, throw a wet blanket on*, throw cold water on*, dampen the spirits, dash one's hopes; see also DEPRESS 2, FRIGHTEN.—*Ant.* ENCOURAGE, cheer, inspire.

discouraged *a.* downcast, pessimistic, depressed; see SAD 1.

discouragement *n.* **1.** [Dejection] melancholy, despair, the blues*; see DEPRESSION 2, SADNESS. **2.** [A restriction] constraint, hindrance, deterrent; see IMPEDIMENT 1.

discouraging *a.* **1.** [Acting to discourage one] depressing, disheartening, repressing; see DISMAL. **2.** [Suggesting an unwelcome future] inopportune, disadvantageous, dissuading; see UNFAVORABLE.

discourteous *a.* boorish, crude, impolite; see RUDE 2.

discourtesy *n.* impudence, impoliteness, vulgarity; see RUDENESS.

discover *v.* invent, find out, ascertain, detect, discern, recognize, distinguish, determine, observe, explore, hear of, hear about, awake to, bring to light, uncover, ferret out, root out, trace out, unearth, look up, stumble on, stumble upon, come on, come upon, run across, fall upon, strike upon, think of, perceive, glimpse, identify, devise, catch, spot, create, make out, sense, feel, sight, smell, hear, spy, bring out, find a clue, put one's finger on, get wise to*, dig out*, dig up*, turn up*, sniff out, come up with, happen upon, get wind of, hit upon, lay one's hands on; see also FIND, LEARN.—*Ant.* MISS, pass by, omit.

discovered *a.* found, searched out, come on, happened on, happened upon, unearthed, ascertained, detected, revealed, disclosed, unveiled, observed, sighted, shown, exposed, traced out, made out, met with, come across, recognized, identified, laid bare, opened, presented, spotted, perceived, learned; see also REAL 2.—*Ant.* HIDDEN, unfound, lost.

discovery *n.* invention, detection, exploration, identification, discernment, distinction, determination, calculation, experimentation, feeling, hearing, sighting, strike, results, findings, formula, device, find, contrivance, design, machine, invention, process, breakthrough, data, principle, law, theorem, innovation, conclusion, method, way; see also RESULT.

discredit *v.* question, disbelieve, distrust; see DOUBT.

discreet *a.* cautious, prudent, discerning, discriminating, not rash, strategic, noncommittal, heedful, vigilant, civil, sensible, reserved, alert, awake, wary, watchful, wise, circumspect, attentive, considerate, intelligent, guarded, politic, diplomatic, tight-lipped, cagey*; see also CAREFUL, THOUGHTFUL 2.—*Ant.* RASH, indiscreet, imprudent.

discretion *n.* caution, foresight, carefulness, wariness, sound judgment, thoughtfulness, attention, heed, concern, consideration, observation, watchfulness, precaution, good sense, providence, maturity, discernment, forethought, calculation, deliberation, vigilance, discrimination, responsibility, presence of mind; see also CARE 1, PRUDENCE, TACT.—*Ant.* CARELESSNESS, thoughtlessness, rashness. **—at one's discretion** as one wishes, whenever appropriate, discreetly; see APPROPRIATELY.

discriminate *v.* **1.** [To differentiate] specify, separate, tell apart; see DISTINGUISH 1. **2.** [To be (racially) prejudiced] be a bigot, show prejudice, set apart, segregate; see also HATE, SEPARATE 1.

discrimination *n.* **1.** [The power to make distinctions] perception, acuteness, understanding; see INTELLIGENCE 1. **2.** [The act of drawing a distinction] separation, differentiation, difference; see JUDGMENT 2. **3.** [Partiality] unfairness, bias, bigotry; see HATRED, PREJUDICE.

discuss *v.* argue, debate, dispute, talk of, talk about, explain, contest, confer, deal with, reason with, take up, look over, consider, talk over, talk out, take up in conference, engage in conversation, go into, think over, telephone about, have a conference on, discourse about, argue for and against, canvass, consider, handle, present, review, recite, treat of, speak of, converse, discourse, take under advisement, comment upon, have out, speak on, kick around*, toss around*, chew the fat*, jaw*, air out*, knock around*, compare notes*, chew the rag*; see also TALK 1. *Ant.* DELAY, table, postpone.

discussed *a.* talked over, debated, argued; see CONSIDERED.

discussion *n.* conversation, exchange, consultation, interview, deliberation, argumentation, contention, dialogue, talk, conference, argument, debate, panel discussion, summit meeting, dealing with the agenda, controversy, altercation, review, reasons, dispute, symposium, quarrel, powwow*, bull session*; see also CONVERSATION, DISPUTE.—*Ant.* AGREEMENT, decision, conclusion.

disease *n.* **1.** [A bodily infirmity] sickness, malady, ailment; see ILLNESS 1. **2.** [Loosely used term for any ailment] condition, defect, infirmity; see ILLNESS 2.

diseased *a.* unhealthy, unsound, ailing; see SICK.

disengage *v.* loose, undo, disentangle; see FREE.

disengaged *a.* detached, unattached, disjoined; see SEPARATED.

disentangle *v.* disengage, untangle, untwist; see FREE.

disfavor *n.* displeasure, disapproval, disrespect; see DISAPPOINTMENT 1.

disfigure *v.* deface, mar, mutilate; see DAMAGE, HURT.

disgrace *n.* scandal, shame, stain, slur, slight, stigma, brand, spot, slander, dishonor, infamy, reproach, disrepute, humiliation, degradation, taint, tarnish, mark of Cain*, scarlet letter; see also INSULT.—*Ant.* PRIDE, praise, credit.

disgrace *v.* debase, shame, degrade, abase, dishonor, disparage, discredit, deride, disregard, strip of honors, dismiss from favor, disrespect, mock, humble, reduce, put to shame, tarnish, stain, blot, sully, taint, defile, stigmatize, brand, tar and feather, put down*, snub, derogate, belittle, take down a peg*; see also HUMILIATE, RIDICULE, SLANDER.—*Ant.* PRAISE, honor, exalt.

disgraced *a.* discredited, in disgrace, dishonored; see ASHAMED.

disgraceful *a.* dishonorable, disreputable, shocking; see OFFENSIVE, SHAMEFUL 1, 2.

disguise *n.* mask, deceptive covering, make-up, faking, false front, deception, smoke screen, blind, concealment, counterfeit, pseudonym, costume, masquerade, veil, cover, façade, put-on*; see also CAMOUFLAGE.

disguise *v.* mask, conceal, camouflage, pretend, screen, cloak, shroud, cover, veil, alter, obscure, feign, counterfeit, varnish, age, redo, make up, simulate, muffle, dress up, touch up, doctor up; see also CHANGE 2, DECEIVE, HIDE.—*Ant.* REVEAL, open, strip.

disguised *a.* cloaked, masked, camouflaged; see CHANGED 2, COVERED 1, HIDDEN.

disgust *n.* loathing, abhorrence, aversion; see HATRED, OBJECTION.

disgust *v.* repel, revolt, offend, displease, nauseate, sicken, make one sick, fill with loathing, cause aversion, be repulsive, irk, scandalize, shock, upset, turn one's stomach*; see also DISTURB, INSULT.

disgusted *a.* overwrought, offended, sickened, displeased, repelled, unhappy, revolted, appalled, outraged, having had a bellyful*, fed up*, having had it*, having had enough*; see also INSULTED, SHOCKED.

disgusted with *a.* repelled by, sick of*, fed up with*; see INSULTED, SHOCKED.

disgusting *a.* repugnant, revolting, sickening; see OFFENSIVE 2.

dish *n.* **1.** [Plate] vessel, pottery, ceramic; see PLATE 3. *Table dishes include the following:* dinner plate, luncheon plate, salad plate, bread and butter plate, platter, casserole, cake plate, coffee cup, coffee mug, espresso cup, demitasse, teacup, egg cup, saucer, beer mug, cereal bowl, soup bowl, gravy boat, relish tray, cruet, teapot, coffeepot, cream pitcher, water pitcher, lemonade pitcher, sugar bowl, butter dish, salt cellar; see also CONTAINER, CUP, POTTERY. **2.** [Meal] course, serving, helping; see MEAL 2.

dishonest *a.* deceiving, fraudulent, double-dealing, backbiting, treacherous, deceitful, cunning, sneaky, tricky, wily, crooked, deceptive, misleading, elusive, slippery, shady, swindling, cheating, sneaking, traitorous, villainous, sinister, lying, underhanded, two-timing*, two-faced, double-crossing*, unprincipled, shiftless, unscrupulous, undependable, disreputable, questionable, dishonorable, counterfeit, infamous, corrupt, immoral, discredited, unworthy, shabby, mean, low, venial, self-serving, contemptible, rotten*, fishy*, crooked; see also FALSE 1, LYING 1.—*Ant.* HONEST, irreproachable, scrupulous.

dishonesty *n.* infidelity, faithlessness, falsity, falsehood, deceit, trickery, duplicity, insidiousness, cunning, guile, slyness, double-dealing, trickiness, treachery, crookedness, corruption, cheating, stealing, lying, swindle, fraud, fraudulence, forgery, perjury, treason, flim-flam, hocus-pocus*, hanky-panky*; see also DECEPTION, HYPOCRISY, LIE.—*Ant.* HONESTY, virtue, integrity.

dishonor *n.* shame, ignominy, abasement; see DISGRACE.

dish out *v.* hand out, serve, deliver; see DISTRIBUTE, GIVE 1.

dish towel *n.* tea towel, kitchen towel, drying towel; see TOWEL.

disillusion *v.* disenchant, strip of ideals, embitter; see DISAPPOINT.

disinfect *v.* purify, fumigate, use disinfectant upon; see CLEAN.

disinherit *v.* disown, evict, dispossess; see DISMISS, NEGLECT 2.

disintegrate *v.* break down, separate, divide, dismantle, break into pieces, disunite, disperse, crumble, disband, take apart, disorganize, detach, break apart, come apart, fall apart, sever, disconnect, fall to pieces, fade away, reduce to ashes; see also DISSOLVE.—*Ant.* UNITE, put together, combine.

disinterested *a.* impartial, not involved, unconcerned; see INDIFFERENT.

disjoint *v.* dismember, cut up, carve; see CUT 1, DIVIDE, SEPARATE 1.

disjointed *a.* disconnected, divided, unattached; see SEPARATED.

dislike *n.* opposition, offense, distaste; see HATE, HATRED, OBJECTION.

dislike *v.* detest, condemn, deplore, regret, lose interest in, speak down to, have hard feelings toward, not take kindly to, not be able to say much for, not have the stomach for, not speak well of, not have any part of, not care for, bear a grudge, have nothing to do with, keep one's distance from, care nothing for, resent, not appreciate, not endure, be averse to, abhor, hate, abominate, disapprove, loathe, despise, object to, shun, shrink from, mind, shudder at, scorn, avoid, be displeased by, turn up the nose at, look on with aversion, not be able to stomach, regard with displeasure, not like, take a dim view of*, have it in for*, be down on*, look down one's nose at*, have a bone to pick with*; see also HATE.

dislocate *v.* disjoint, disunite, disengage; see BREAK 1, DIVIDE, SEPARATE 1.

dislocation *n.* displacement, discontinuity, luxation; see BREAK 1, DIVISION 1.

dislodge *v.* eject, evict, uproot; see OUST, REMOVE 1.

disloyalty *n.* treason, betrayal, bad faith; see DISHONESTY, TREASON.

dismal *a.* gloomy, monotonous, dim, melancholy, desolate, dreary, sorrowful, morbid, troublesome, horrid, shadowy, overcast, cloudy, unhappy, discouraging, hopeless, black, unfortunate, ghastly, horrible, boring, gruesome, tedious, mournful, dull, disheartening, regrettable, cheerless, dusky, dingy, sepulchral, joyless, funereal, comfortless, murky, wan, bleak, somber, disagreeable, creepy, spooky*, blue; see also DARK 1.—*Ant.* HAPPY, joyful, cheerful.

dismantle *v.* take apart, disassemble, break down, take down, tear down, knock down, undo, demolish, level, ruin, unrig, subvert, raze, take to pieces, fell, take apart; see also DESTROY.

dismay *n.* terror, dread, anxiety; see FEAR.

dismember *v.* dissect, disjoint, amputate; see CUT 1, DIVIDE.

dismiss *v.* discard, reject, decline, repel, let out, repudiate, disband, detach, lay off, pack off, cast off, cast out, relinquish, dispense with, disperse, remove, expel, abolish, relegate, push aside, shed, do without, have done with, dispose of, sweep away, clear, rid, chase, dispossess, boycott, exile, expatriate, banish, outlaw, deport, excommunicate, get rid of, send packing*, drop, brush off*, kick out*, blackball, write off; see also OUST, REFUSE.—*Ant.* MAINTAIN, retain, keep.

dismissal *n.* deposition, displacement, expulsion; see REMOVAL.

dismissed *a.* sent away, ousted, removed; see DISCHARGED, FREE 2, 3.

disobedience *n.* insubordination, defiance, insurgence, disregard, violation, neglect, mutiny, revolt, nonobservance, strike, stubbornness, noncompliance, infraction of the rules, unruliness, sedition, rebellion, sabotage, riot; see also REVOLUTION 2.

disobedient *a.* insubordinate, refractory, defiant; see REBELLIOUS, UNRULY.

disobey *v.* balk, decline, neglect, desert, be remiss, ignore the commands of, refuse submission to, disagree, differ, evade, disregard the authority of, break rules, object, defy, resist, revolt, strike, violate, infringe, transgress, shirk, misbehave, withstand, counteract, take the law into one's own hands, not mind, pay no attention to, go counter to, not listen to; see also DARE 2, OPPOSE 1, REBEL.—*Ant.* OBEY, follow, fulfill.

disorder *n.* tumult, discord, turmoil, complication, chaos, mayhem, terrorism, rioting, mob rule, anarchy, anarchism, lawlessness, entanglement, commotion, agitation, insurrection, revolution, rebellion, strike, disorganization, riot, reign of terror, uproar, dither, static*; see also DISTURBANCE 2, TROUBLE 1.—*Ant.* ORDER, peace, tranquillity.

disorder *v.* disarrange, clutter, scatter; see CONFUSE, DISORGANIZE.

disordered *a.* displaced, misplaced, dislocated, mislaid, out of place, deranged, in disorder, out of kilter, out of hand, in confusion, in a mess, all over the place, in a mess, in a jumble, upset, unsettled, disorganized, disarranged, moved, removed, shifted, tampered with, tumbled, ruffled, rumpled, jumbled, jarred, tossed, stirred up, rolled, jolted, muddled; see also CONFUSED 2, TANGLED.—*Ant.* ORDERED, arranged, settled.

disorderly *a.* **1.** [Lacking orderly arrangement] confused, jumbled, undisciplined, unrestrained, scattered, dislocated, unsystematic, messy, slovenly, untidy, cluttered, unkempt, scrambled, badly managed, in confusion, disorganized, untrained, out of control, topsy-turvy, all over the place*, mixed-up; see also DISORDERED.—*Ant.* REGULAR, neat, trim. **2.** [Creating a disturbance] intemperate, drunk, rowdy; see UNRULY.

disorganization *n.* disunion, dissolution, derangement; see CONFUSION.

disorganize *v.* break up, disperse, destroy, scatter, litter, clutter, break down, put out of order, disarrange, disorder, upset, disrupt, derange, dislocate, disband, jumble, muddle, unsettle, disturb, perturb, shuffle, toss, turn topsy-turvy, complicate, confound, overthrow, overturn, scramble; see also CONFUSE.—*Ant.* SYSTEMATIZE, order, distribute.

disown *v.* repudiate, deny, retract; see DISCARD.

dispatch *v.* **1.** [To send something on its way] transmit, express, forward; see SEND 1. **2.** [To make an end] finish, conclude, perform; see ACHIEVE.

dispel *v.* disperse, deploy, dissipate; see DISTRIBUTE, SCATTER.

dispensable *a.* removable, excessive, unnecessary; see TRIVIAL, USELESS 1.

dispense *v.* apportion, assign, allocate; see DISTRIBUTE, GIVE 1.

dispenser *n.* vendor, tap, vending machine, spray can, spray gun, cigarette machine, Coke machine (trademark), automat, squeeze bottle.

dispense with *v.* ignore, pass over, brush aside; see DISREGARD, NEGLECT 2.

disperse *v.* break up, separate, disband; see SCATTER.

displace *v.* **1.** [To remove] replace, transpose, dislodge; see REMOVE 1. **2.** [To put in the wrong place] mislay, misplace, disarrange; see LOSE 2.

display *n.* exhibition, exhibit, presentation, representation, exposition, arrangement, demonstration, performance, revelation, procession, parade, pageant, example, appearance, waxworks, fireworks, tinsel, carnival, fair, pomp, splendor, unfolding; see also SHOW 1.

display *v.* show, show off, exhibit, uncover, open up, unfold, spread, parade, unmask, present, represent, perform, flaunt, lay out, put out, set out, disclose, unveil, arrange,

make known; see also EXPOSE.—*Ant.* HIDE, conceal, veil.
displayed *a.* presented, visible, on display; see ADVERTISED, SHOWN 1.
displease *v.* vex, provoke, enrage; see ANGER.
displeasure *n.* disapproval, annoyance, resentment; see ANGER.
disposal *n.* action, provision, determination, disposition, distribution, arrangement, conclusion, assortment, settlement, control, winding up; see also RESULT. —**at someone's disposal** ready, prepared, usable; see AVAILABLE.
dispose *v.* settle, adapt, condition; see ADJUST 1, PREPARE 1.
disposed *a.* inclined, prone, apt; see LIKELY 4.
dispose of *v.* relinquish, throw away, part with; see DISCARD, SELL.
disposition *n.* 1. [Arrangement] decision, method, distribution; see ORGANIZATION 1, PLAN 2. 2. [Temperament] character, nature, temper; see MOOD, TEMPERAMENT.
disproportionate *a.* unsymmetrical, incommensurate, excessive; see IRREGULAR 4.
disprove *v.* prove false, throw out, set aside, find fault in, invalidate, weaken, overthrow, tear down, confound, expose, cut the ground from under, poke holes in*; see also DENY.
disputable *a.* debatable, doubtful, dubious; see QUESTIONABLE 1, UNCERTAIN.
dispute *n.* argument, quarrel, debate, misunderstanding, conflict, strife, discussion, polemic, bickering, squabble, disturbance, feud, commotion, tiff, fracas, controversy, altercation, dissension, squall, difference of opinion, rumpus*, row, flare-up, fuss, fireworks*; see also DISAGREEMENT 1.
dispute *v.* debate, contradict, quarrel; see ARGUE, DISCUSS.
disqualify *v.* preclude, disentitle, disbar; see BAR 2.
disquieting *a.* disturbing, troubling, disconcerting; see DISTURBING.
disregard *v.* ignore, pass over, let pass, make light of, have no use for, laugh off, take no account of, brush aside, turn a deaf ear to, be blind to, shut one's eyes to; see also NEGLECT 1.
disrepair *n.* decrepitude, deterioration, dilapidation; see DECAY.
disreputable *a.* low, objectionable, discreditable; see OFFENSIVE 2, SHAMEFUL 1, 2.
disrespect *n.* discourtesy, coarseness, irreverence; see RUDENESS.
disrespectful *a.* ill-bred, discourteous, impolite; see RUDE 2.
disrobe *v.* strip, divest, unclothe; see UNDRESS.
disrupt *v.* fracture, intrude, obstruct; see BREAK 1, INTERRUPT.
disruption *n.* debacle, disturbance, agitation; see CONFUSION.
dissatisfaction *n.* dislike, displeasure, disapproval; see OBJECTION.
dissatisfied *a.* displeased, unsatisfied, fed up*; see DISAPPOINTED.
dissect *v.* dismember, quarter, operate; see CUT 1, DIVIDE.
disseminate *v.* sow, propagate, broadcast; see DISTRIBUTE.
dissension *n.* difference, quarrel, trouble; see DISAGREEMENT 1, DISPUTE.
dissent *n.* nonconformity, difference, heresy; see DISAGREEMENT 1, OBJECTION, PROTEST.
dissent *v.* disagree, refuse, contradict; see DIFFER 1, OPPOSE 1.
dissenter *n.* disputant, dissentient, demonstrator; see NONCONFORMIST, RADICAL, REBEL.
disservice *n.* wrong, injury, outrage; see DAMAGE 1, INJUSTICE, INSULT.
dissipate *v.* 1. [To dispel] spread, diffuse, disseminate; see SCATTER 2. 2. [To squander] use up, consume, misuse; see SPEND, WASTE 2.
dissipated *a.* 1. [Scattered] dispersed, strewn, disseminated; see SCATTERED. 2. [Wasted] squandered, spent, consumed; see EMPTY, WASTED.
dissipation *n.* 1. [Dispersion] scattering, dispersal, spread; see DISTRIBUTION. 2. [Debauchery] indulgence, intemperance, dissolution; see EVIL 1.
dissolve *v.* liquefy, melt, thaw, soften, run, defrost, waste away, cause to become liquid; see also EVAPORATE, MELT 1.—*Ant.* HARDEN, freeze, solidify.
distance *n.* 1. [A degree or quantity of space] reach, span, range; see EXPANSE, EXTENT, LENGTH 1, 2. 2. [A place or places far away] background, horizon, as far as the eye can reach, sky, heavens, outskirts, foreign countries, different worlds, strange places, distant terrain, objective, the country, beyond the horizon.—*Ant.* NEIGHBORHOOD, surroundings, neighbors. 3. [A measure of space] statute mile, rod, yard, foot, kilometer, meter, centimeter, millimeter, league, fathom, span, hand, cubit, furlong, a stone's throw. —**go the distance** finish, bring to an end, see through; see COMPLETE. —**keep at a distance** ignore, reject, shun; see AVOID. —**keep one's distance** be aloof, ignore, shun; see AVOID.
distant *a.* afar, far off, abroad, faraway, yonder, backwoods, removed, abstracted, inaccessible, unapproachable, out-of-the-way, at arm's length, stretching to, out of range, out of reach, out of earshot, out of sight, in the background, in the distance, separate, farther, further, far away, at a distance, abroad, different; see also SEPARATED.—*Ant.* CLOSE, near, next

distaste *n.* aversion, dislike, abhorrence; see HATRED.
distasteful *a.* disagreeable, repugnant, undesirable; see OFFENSIVE 2.
distend *v.* enlarge, widen, inflate; see DISTORT 2, INCREASE, STRETCH 1, 2.
distill *v.* vaporize and condense, steam, precipitate; see CONCENTRATE 1, EVAPORATE.
distinct *a.* **1.** [Having sharp outlines] lucid, plain, obvious; see CLEAR 2, DEFINITE 2. **2.** [Not connected with another] discrete, separate, disunited; see SEPARATED. **3.** [Clearly heard] clear, sharp, enunciated; see AUDIBLE.
distinction *n.* **1.** [The act or quality of noticing differences] separation, difference, refinement; see DEFINITION. **2.** [That which makes a thing distinct] distinctive feature, particular, qualification; see CHARACTERISTIC, DETAIL. **3.** [A mark of personal achievement] repute, renown, prominence; see FAME.
distinctive *a.* peculiar, unique, distinguishing; see CHARACTERISTIC.
distinctly *a.* precisely, sharply, plainly; see CLEARLY 1, 2, SURELY.
distinctness *n.* sharpness, lucidity, explicitness; see CLARITY.
distinguish *v.* **1.** [To make distinctions] discriminate, differentiate, classify, specify, identify, individualize, characterize, separate, divide, collate, sort out, sort into, set apart, mark off, criticize, select, draw the line, tell from, pick and choose, separate the wheat from the chaff, separate the sheep from the goats; see also DEFINE 2. **2.** [To discern] detect, discriminate, notice; see DISCOVER, SEE 1. **3.** [To bestow honor upon] pay tribute to, honor, celebrate; see ACKNOWLEDGE 2, ADMIRE, PRAISE 1.
distinguishable *a.* separable, perceptible, discernible; see AUDIBLE, OBVIOUS, TANGIBLE.
distinguished *a.* **1.** [Made recognizable by markings] characterized, labeled, marked, stamped, signed, signified, identified, made certain, obvious, set apart, branded, earmarked, separate, unique, differentiated, observed, distinct, conspicuous; see also SEPARATED.—*Ant.* TYPICAL, unidentified, indistinct. **2.** [Notable for excellence] eminent, illustrious, venerable, renowned, honored, memorable, celebrated, well-known, noted, noteworthy, highly regarded, well-thought-of, esteemed, prominent, reputable, superior, outstanding, brilliant, glorious, extraordinary, singular, great, special, striking, unforgettable, shining, foremost, dignified, famed, talked of, first-rate, big-name*, headline*; see also FAMOUS.—*Ant.* OBSCURE, insignificant, unimportant.
distinguishing *a.* distinctive, differentiating, different; see CHARACTERISTIC.
distort *v.* **1.** [To alter the meaning] pervert, misinterpret, misconstrue; see DECEIVE. **2.** [To change shape] contort, sag, twist, slump, knot, get out of shape, buckle, writhe, melt, warp, deform, collapse; see also CHANGE 2.
distortion *n.* **1.** [Deformity] twist, malformation, mutilation; see CONTORTION. **2.** [Misrepresentation] perversion, misinterpretation, misuse; see LIE.
distract *v.* detract, occupy, amuse, entertain, draw away, call away, draw one's attention from, lead astray, attract from; see also MISLEAD.
distracted *a.* distraught, panicked, frenzied; see TROUBLED.
distraction *n.* **1.** [Confusion] perplexity, abstraction, complication; see CONFUSION. **2.** [Diversion] amusement, pastime, preoccupation; see ENTERTAINMENT, GAME 1.
distress *n.* worry, anxiety, misery, sorrow, wretchedness, pain, dejection, irritation, suffering, ache, heartache, ordeal, desolation, anguish, affliction, woe, torment, shame, embarrassment, disappointment, tribulation, pang; see also GRIEF, TROUBLE 1.—*Ant.* JOY, happiness, jollity.
distress *v.* irritate, disturb, upset; see BOTHER 1, 2.
distribute *v.* dispense, divide, share, deal, bestow, issue, dispose, disperse, mete out, pass out, parcel out, dole out, hand out, give away, assign, allocate, ration, appropriate, pay dividends, dish out, divvy up*; see also GIVE 1.—*Ant.* HOLD, keep, preserve.
distributed *a.* delivered, scattered, shared, dealt, divided, apportioned, assigned, awarded, peddled from door to door, sowed, dispensed, dispersed, appropriated, budgeted, made individually available, equally divided, spread evenly, returned, rationed, given away, handed out, parceled out, spread.
distribution *n.* dispersal, allotment, partitioning, partition, dividing up, deal, circulation, disposal, apportioning, prorating, arrangement, scattering, dissemination, sorting, spreading, parceling out, handing out, peddling, assorting, frequency, occurrence, ordering, pattern, combination, relationship, appearance, configuration, scarcity, number, plenty, saturation, population, spread, concentration; see also DIVISION 1, 2, ORDER 3.—*Ant.* COLLECTION, retention, storage.
distributor *n.* wholesaler, jobber, merchant; see BUSINESSMAN.
district *a.* community, provincial, territorial; see LOCAL 1.
district *n.* neighborhood, community, vicinity; see AREA.
distrust *v.* mistrust, suspect, disbelieve; see DOUBT.
distrustful *a.* distrusting, doubting, fearful; see SUSPICIOUS 1.

disturb *v.* trouble, worry, agitate, perplex, rattle, startle, shake, amaze, astound, alarm, excite, arouse, badger, plague, fuss, perturb, vex, upset, outrage, molest, grieve, depress, distress, irk, ail, tire, provoke, afflict, irritate, pain, make uneasy, harass, exasperate, pique, gall, displease, complicate, involve, astonish, fluster, ruffle, burn up*; see also BOTHER 2, CONFUSE.—*Ant.* QUIET, calm, soothe.

disturbance *n.* **1.** [Interpersonal disruption] quarrel, brawl, fisticuffs; see FIGHT 1. **2.** [Physical disruption] turmoil, rampage, tumult, clamor, violence, restlessness, uproar, riot, disruption, agitation, turbulence, change, bother, stir, racket, ferment, spasm, convulsion, tremor, shock, explosion, eruption, earthquake, flood, shock wave, storm, whirl; see also TROUBLE. **3.** [A political or social uprising] revolt, insurrection, riot; see REVOLUTION 2.

disturbed *a.* **1.** [Disturbed physically] upset, disorganized, confused; see DISORDERED. **2.** [Disturbed mentally] agitated, disquieted, upset; see TROUBLED.

disturbing *a.* disquieting, upsetting, tiresome, perturbing, bothersome, unpleasant, provoking, annoying, alarming, painful, discomforting, inauspicious, foreboding, aggravating, disagreeable, troublesome, worrisome, burdensome, trying, frightening, startling, perplexing, threatening, distressing, galling, difficult, severe, hard, inconvenient, discouraging, pessimistic, gloomy, depressing, irritating, harassing, unpropitious, unlikely, embarrassing, ruffling, agitating; see also OMINOUS.

disunite *v.* dissociate, disjoin, separate; see DIVIDE.

ditch *n.* canal, moat, furrow; see CHANNEL, TRENCH.

ditch* *v.* desert, forsake, leave; see ABANDON 2, DISCARD.

ditto *n.* ditto mark ("), the very same, as is; see ALIKE.

dive *n.* **1.** [A sudden motion downward] plunge, leap, spring, nosedive, headlong leap, pitch, ducking, swim, swoop, dip; see also FALL 1, JUMP 1. **2.** [*An establishment offering accommodation] saloon, tavern, cafe; see BAR 2, RESTAURANT.

dive *v.* plunge, spring, jump, vault, leap, go headfirst, plummet, sink, dip, duck, submerge, nose-dive; see also FALL 1, JUMP 1.

diver *n.* high diver, fancy diver, submarine diver, deep-sea diver, aquanaut, pearl diver, skin diver, scuba diver, swimmer, athlete, frogman; see also ATHLETE.

diverge *v.* radiate, veer, swerve; see DEVIATE.

diverse *a.* different, assorted, distinct; see VARIOUS.

diversify *v.* vary, expand, alter; see CHANGE 2, INCREASE.

diversion *n.* **1.** [The act of changing a course] detour, alteration, deviation; see CHANGE 1. **2.** [Entertainment] amusement, recreation, play; see ENTERTAINMENT, SPORT 1.

divert *v.* **1.** [To deflect] turn aside, redirect, avert; see TURN 3. **2.** [To distract] attract the attention of, lead away from, disturb; see DISTRACT.

diverted *a.* deflected, turned aside, redirected, perverted, averted, turned into other channels, rechanneled, taken, adopted, used, made use of, taken over; see also CHANGED 2.—*Ant.* UNTOUCHED, undiverted, left.

divide *v.* part, cut up, fence off, detach, disengage, dissolve, sever, rupture, dismember, sunder, split, unravel, carve, cleave, intersect, cross, bisect, rend, tear, segment, halve, quarter, third, break down, divorce, dissociate, isolate, count off, pull away, chop, slash, gash, carve, splinter, pull to pieces, tear apart, break apart, segregate, fork, branch, tear limb from limb*, split off, split up; see also BREAK 1, CUT 1, SEPARATE 1.—*Ant.* UNITE, combine, connect.

dividend *n.* pay, check, coupon, proceeds, returns, quarterly dividend, annual dividend, share, allotment, appropriation, remittance, allowance, cut*, rakeoff*; see also PROFIT 2.

divine *a.* sacred, hallowed, spiritual, sacramental, ceremonial, ritualistic, consecrated, dedicated, devoted, venerable, pious, religious, anointed, sanctified, ordained, sanctioned, set apart, sacrosanct, scriptural, blessed, worshiped, revered, venerated, mystical, adored, solemn, faithful; see also HOLY.

divine *v.* predict, prophesy, prognosticate; see FORETELL.

divinity *n.* deity, godhead, higher power; see GOD.

divisible *a.* separable, distinguishable, distinct, divided, fractional, fragmentary, detachable; see also SEPARATED.—*Ant.* INSEPARABLE, indivisible, fast.

division *n.* **1.** [The act or result of dividing] separation, detachment, apportionment, partition, parting, distribution, severance, cutting, subdivision, dismemberment, distinction, distinguishing, selection, analysis, diagnosis, reduction, splitting, breakdown, fracture, disjuncture.—*Ant.* UNION, joining, glueing. **2.** [A part produced by dividing] section, kind, sort, portion, compartment, share, split, member, subdivision, parcel, segment, fragment, department, category, branch, fraction, dividend, degree, piece, slice, lump, wedge, cut, book, chapter, verse, class, race, clan, tribe, caste; see also PART 1. **3.** [Discord or disunion] trouble, words, difficulty; see DISAGREEMENT 1, DIS-

PUTE. **4.** [A military unit] armored division, airborne division, infantry division; see ARMY 2. **5.** [An organized area] state, government, range; see NATION.

divorce *n.* separation, partition, divorcement, bill of divorcement, annulment, separate maintenance, parting of the ways, dissolution, split-up*.—*Ant.* MARRIAGE, betrothal, wedding.

divorce *v.* separate, annul, nullify, put away, split up*; see also CANCEL.

divorced *a.* dissolved, parted, disunited, divided, split*, washed up*; see also SEPARATED.—*Ant.* MARRIED, joined, mated.

divulge *v.* disclose, impart, confess; see ADMIT 2, EXPOSE 1.

dizzy *a.* confused, lightheaded, giddy, bemused, staggering, upset, dazzled, dazed, dumb, faint, with spots before one's eyes, out of control, weak-kneed, wobbly; see also UNSTABLE 1.

DNA *n.* genetic alphabet, double helix, hereditary information, dexoyribonucleic acid, genetic code.

do *v.* **1.** [To discharge one's responsibilities] effect, execute, achieve, act, perform, finish, complete, work, labor, produce, create, effect, accomplish; see also ACHIEVE, PERFORM 1, SUCCEED 1. **2.** [To execute commands or instructions] carry out, complete, fulfill; see OBEY. **3.** [To suffice] serve, be sufficient, give satisfaction; see SATISFY 3. **4.** [To solve] figure out, work out, decipher, decode; see also SOLVE. **5.** [To present a play, etc.] give, put on, produce; see PERFORM 2. **6.** [To act] perform, portray, render the role of; see ACT 3. **7.** [To conduct oneself] behave oneself, comport oneself, acquit oneself, seem, appear; see also BEHAVE. **—have to do with** be related to, be connected with, bear on; see CONCERN 1. **—make do** get by, get along, manage, survive; see also ENDURE 2.

do about *v.* make better, take care of, correct; see HELP, IMPROVE 1, REPAIR.

do away with *v.* **1.** [To eliminate] get rid of, cancel, take away; see ELIMINATE, REMOVE 1. **2.** [To kill] slay, execute, put to death; see KILL 1.

do by *v.* handle, act toward, deal with; see TREAT 1.

docile *a.* meek, mild, tractable, pliant, submissive, accommodating, adaptable, resigned, agreeable, willing, obliging, well-behaved, manageable, tame, yielding, teachable, easily influenced, easygoing, usable, soft, childlike; see also GENTLE 3, HUMBLE 1, OBEDIENT 1.

docility *n.* obedience, gentleness, adaptability; see HUMILITY, SHYNESS.

dock *n.* landing pier, wharf, lock, boat landing, marina, dry dock, embarcadero, waterfront.

dock *v.* lessen, withhold, deduct; see DECREASE 2.

doctor *n.* Doctor of Medicine (M.D.), physician, general practitioner (G.P.), surgeon, medical attendant, consultant, specialist, intern, house physician, resident, veterinarian, chiropractor, homeopath, osteopath, acupuncturist, faith healer, witch doctor, shaman, medicine man, quack, doc*, sawbones*. *Types of doctors include the following:* heart specialist; eye, ear, nose, and throat specialist; inhalation therapist, anesthetist, dentist, pediatrician, gynecologist, oculist, obstetrician, psychiatrist, psychoanalyst, orthopedist, neurologist, cardiologist, pathologist, dermatologist, endocrinologist, ophthalmologist, urologist, hematologist; see also MEDICINE 3.

doctor* *v.* tamper with, change, alter; see ALTER 1.

doctrine *n.* principle, proposition, precept, article, concept, conviction, opinion, convention, attitude, tradition, unwritten law, natural law, common law, teachings, accepted belief, article of faith, canon, regulation, rule, pronouncement, declaration; see also LAW 2, 4.

document *n.* paper, diary, report; see RECORD 1.

dodge *n.* trick, strategy, scheme; see METHOD, PLAN 1.

dodge *v.* duck, elude, evade; see AVOID.

do dirt to* *v.* hurt, mistreat, injure; see ABUSE, SLANDER.

doer *n.* actor, performer, instrument; see MEANS 1.

do for *v.* care for, assist, look after; see HELP, SUPPORT 3.

dog *n.* hound, bitch, puppy, pup, mongrel, stray, canine, cur, pooch*, mutt*. *Types and breeds of dogs include the following:* hunting dog, field dog, racing dog, boxer, shepherd dog, bloodhound, wolfhound, greyhound, whippet, St. Bernard, Great Dane, German shepard, Doberman pinscher, Afghan hound, Irish wolfhound, Labrador retriever, Chesapeake Bay retriever, malamute, husky, collie, Old English sheep dog, Irish setter, pointer, spaniel, cocker spaniel, basset, beagle, dachshund, Dalmatian, poodle, French poodle, Pekingese, Chihuahua, Airedale, schnauzer, fox terrier, wirehaired terrier, Scottie, bull terrier, Boston terrier. **—a dog's life*** wretched existence, bad luck, trouble; see POVERTY 1. **—go to the dogs*** deteriorate, degenerate, weaken; see WEAKEN 1, 2. **—let sleeping dogs lie*** ignore, leave well enough alone, pass over; see NEGLECT 1. **—put on the dog*** show off, entertain lavishly, exhibit; see DISPLAY. **—teach an old dog new tricks*** influence, convince, change; see PERSUADE.

dog-eat-dog *a.* vicious, ferocious, brutal; see CRUEL, RUTHLESS.
dogged *a.* stubborn, tenacious, firm; see STUBBORN.
dogmatic *a.* **1.** [Based on an assumption of absolute truth] authoritarian, on faith, by nature; see ABSOLUTE 1. **2.** [Acting as though possessed of absolute truth] dictatorial, stubborn, egotistical, bigoted, fanatical, intolerant, opinionated, overbearing, magisterial, arrogant, domineering, tyrannical, obstinate, confident, downright, arbitrary, unequivocal, definite, formal, stubborn, determined, emphatic, narrow-minded, one-sided, hidebound, high and mighty*, pig-headed, bullheaded, stubborn as a mule*; see also ABSOLUTE 2.—*Ant.* LIBERAL, tolerant, dubious.
do in* *v.* eliminate, slay, murder; see DESTROY, KILL 1.
doing *n.* performing, accomplishing, achieving; see PERFORMANCE.
doings *n.pl.* activities, conduct, dealings; see ACTION 1.
do justice to *v.* esteem, pay tribute, honor; see ADMIRE, CONSIDER, RESPECT 2.
dole out *v.* share, assign, parcel out; see DISTRIBUTE.
doll *n.* baby, figurine, manikin, model, dolly, doll baby*; see also TOY 1.
dollar *n.* coin, legal tender, dollar bill, silver dollar, currency, bank note, greenback, folding money*, buck*; see also MONEY 1.
dollop *n.* bit, touch, dash; see DASH 3, BIT 1.
doll up *v.* fix up, put on one's best clothes, primp; see DRESS 1.
dolt *n.* simpleton, nitwit, blockhead; see FOOL.
domain *n.* dominion, field, specialty; see AREA.
dome *n.* ceiling, top, vault; see ROOF.
domestic *a.* **1.** [Home-loving] houseloving, domesticated, stay-at-home, household, family, quiet, sedentary, indoor, tame, settled; see also CALM 1, 2, TRANQUIL.—*Ant.* UNRULY, roving, restless. **2.** [Home-grown] indigenous, handcrafted, native; see HOME-MADE.
domesticate *v.* tame, breed, housebreak; see TEACH, TRAIN 2.
domesticated *a.* tamed, trained, house-broken; see TAME 1.
dominant *a.* commanding, authoritative, assertive; see AGGRESSIVE, POWERFUL 1.
dominate *v.* rule, manage, control, dictate to, subject, subjugate, tyrannize, have one's own way, have influence over, domineer, lead by the nose, boss*, keep under one's thumb; see also GOVERN.
domination *n.* rule, control, mastery; see COMMAND, POWER 2.
domineering *a.* despotic, imperious, oppressive; see EGOTISTIC.
dominion *n.* region, district, state; see AREA, NATION 1.
donate *v.* grant, bestow, bequeath; see DISTRIBUTE, GIVE 1, PROVIDE 1.
donation *n.* contribution, offering, present; see GIFT 1.
done *a.* **1.** [Accomplished] over, through, completed, realized, effected, executed, performed, fulfilled, brought to pass, brought about, perfected; see also FINISHED 1.—*Ant.* UNFINISHED, unrealized, failed. **2.** [Cooked] brewed, stewed, broiled, boiled, crisped, crusted, fried, browned, done to a turn; see also BAKED.—*Ant.* RAW, burned, uncooked.
done for* *a.* defeated, conquered, vanquished; see BEATEN 1.
done in* *a.* exhausted, worn out, weary; see TIRED.
done out of* *a.* defrauded, bilked, taken*; see CHEATED, DECEIVED.
done up *a.* prepared, packaged, finished; see WRAPPED.
done with* *a.* finished with, dispatched, no longer in need of; see FINISHED 1.
Don Juan *n.* Lothario, pursuer, Romeo, libertine, philanderer, rake, seducer, lecher, wolf*.
donkey *n.* burrow, ass, jackass; see HORSE.
donor *n.* benefactor, contributor, patron, philanthropist, giver, subscriber, altruist, Good Samaritan, fairy godmother*; see also PATRON.
doom *n.* fate, lot, destination, predestination, future, fortune, ruin, goal.
doomed *a.* ruined, cursed, sentenced, lost, condemned, unfortunate, ill-fated, foreordained, predestined, threatened, menaced, suppressed, wrecked; see also DESTROYED, FATED.
door *n.* entry, portal, hatchway, doorway, gateway, opening; see also ENTRANCE 2, GATE. **—out of doors** outside, in the air, out; see OUTDOORS. **—show someone the door** show out, ask to leave, eject; see OUST.
do out of* *v.* cheat, trick, beat out of*; see DECEIVE, STEAL.
do over *v.* redo, do again, rework; see REPEAT 1.
dope *n.* **1.** [*A drug] narcotic, stimulant, opiate; see DRUG. **2.** [*Pertinent information] details, account, developments; see INFORMATION 1, KNOWLEDGE 1, NEWS 1. **3.** [*A dull-witted person] dunce, dolt, simpleton; see FOOL.
dope *v.* anesthetize, drug, put to sleep; see DEADEN.
dormitory *n.* barracks, residence hall, dorm*; see HOTEL.
dos and don'ts* *n.pl.* rules, regulations, instructions; see ADVICE, COMMAND, DIRECTIONS.

dose *n.* prescription, dosage, treatment, spoonful, portion, doctor's orders*; see also QUANTITY, SHARE.

dot *n.* point, spot, speck; see MARK 1. **—on the dot*** precisely, accurately, punctually; see PUNCTUAL.

dote *v.* adore, pet, admire; see LOVE 1.

do time* *v.* serve a sentence, be in jail, pay one's debt to society; see SERVE TIME.

double *a.* twofold, two times, paired, coupled, binary, doubled, redoubled, duplex, renewed, dual, both one and the other, repeated, second, increased, as much again, duplicated; see also TWICE, TWIN.—*Ant.* ALONE, single, apart. **—on the double*** hastily, rapidly, hurriedly; see QUICKLY.

double *v.* **1.** [To make or become double] make twice as much, duplicate, multiply; see GROW 1, INCREASE. **2.** [To replace] substitute, stand in, fill in; see SUBSTITUTE.

double back *v.* backtrack, reverse, circle; see RETURN 1, TURN 2, 6.

double-cross *v.* cheat, defraud, trick; see DECEIVE.

double-dealing *n.* deceit, cheating, trickery; see DISHONESTY, HYPOCRISY.

double meaning *n.* play on words, innuendo, pun; see JOKE.

double up *v.* combine, join, share; see JOIN 1, 2, UNITE.

doubly *a.* twofold, redoubled, increased; see AGAIN, DOUBLE, TWICE.

doubt *n.* distrust, mistrust, disbelief, suspicion, misgiving, skepticism, apprehension, agnosticism, incredulity, lack of faith, lack of confidence, jealousy, rejection, scruple, misgiving, indecision, lack of conviction, ambiguity, dilemma, reluctance, quandary, feeling of inferiority; see also UNCERTAINTY 1, 2.—*Ant.* BELIEF, conviction, certainty. **—beyond (or without) doubt** doubtless, certainly, without doubt; see SURELY. **—no doubt** doubtless, in all likelihood, certainly; see PROBABLY, SURELY.

doubt *v.* wonder, question, query, ponder, dispute, be dubious, be uncertain, be doubtful, refuse to believe, demur, have doubts about, have one's doubts, stop to consider, have qualms, call in question, give no credit to, throw doubt upon, have no conception, not know which way to turn, not know what to make of, close one's mind, not admit, not believe, refuse to believe, not buy*; see also ASK, DENY, QUESTION 1.—*Ant.* TRUST, believe, confide.

doubter *n.* questioner, unbeliever, agnostic; see CYNIC.

doubtful *a.* **1.** [Uncertain in mind] dubious, doubting, questioning, undecided, unsure, wavering, hesitating, undetermined, uncertain, unsettled, confused, disturbed, lost, puzzled, perplexed, flustered, baffled, distracted, unresolved, in a quandary, of two minds, unable to make up one's mind, troubled with doubt, having little faith, of little faith, in question, not knowing what's what, not following, up a tree*, not able to make head or tail of, going around in circles*, out of focus, up in the air, wishy-washy*, iffy; see also SUSPICIOUS 1. **2.** [Improbable] probably wrong, questionable, unconvincing; see OBSCURE 1, UNCERTAIN.

doubting *a.* questioning, dubious, skeptical; see DOUBTFUL 1, SUSPICIOUS 1.

doubtless *a.* positively, certainly, unquestionably; see SURELY.

dough *n.* **1.** [A soft mixture] paste (especially of flour), pulp, mash; see BATTER 2, MIXTURE 1. **2.** [*Money] dollars, change, silver; see MONEY 1, WEALTH.

doughnut *n.* friedcake, cruller, sinker*; see CAKE 2, PASTRY.

douse *v.* submerge, splash, drench; see IMMERSE, SOAK 1.

dove *n.* peacemaker, activist, pacifier; see PACIFIST.

dowdy *a.* untidy, slovenly, plain; see SHABBY.

do well by *v.* aid, favor, treat well; see HELP.

do without *v.* dispense with, get along without, forego; see ENDURE 1, 2, NEED.

down *a. & prep.* forward, headlong, bottomward, downhill, on a downward course, from higher to lower, to the bottom, to a lower position, declining, falling, descending, gravitating, slipping, sliding, sagging, slumping, dropping, sinking, earthward, groundward, downward; see also BACKWARD 1.—*Ant.* UP, upward, rising.

down *n.* feathers, fluff, fur; see HAIR 1.

down *v.* put down, throw down, knock down, throw, fell, subdue, tackle, trip, overthrow, overpower, upset, overturn; see also DEFEAT 3, HIT 1.—*Ant.* RAISE, lift, elevate.

down and out *a.* ruined, defeated, finished; see BEATEN.

downcast *a.* discouraged, dejected, unhappy; see SAD 1.

downfall *n.* drop, comedown, ruin; see DESTRUCTION 2.

downgrade *v.* minimize, deprecate, lower; see DECREASE 2.

downhearted *a.* dejected, despondent, downcast; see SAD 1.

down on* *a.* against, disillusioned about, furious with; see OPPOSED.

downpour *n.* rain, deluge, flood, monsoon; see also STORM.

downright *a.* total, complete, utter; see ABSOLUTE 1, WHOLE 1.

downstairs *a.* underneath, below decks, on the floor below; see BELOW 4, UNDER 1.

downstairs *n.* first floor, ground floor, cellar; see BASEMENT.

down-to-earth *a.* sensible, mundane, practicable; see COMMON 1, PRACTICAL, RATIONAL 1.

downtown *a.* city, central, inner-city, main, midtown, in the business district, on the main street, metropolitan, business, shopping; see also URBAN.—*Ant.* RURAL, suburban, residential.

downtown *n.* hub, crossroads, inner city; see CENTER 2, CITY.

downtrodden *a.* tyrannized, subjugated, overcome; see OPPRESSED.

downward *a.* earthward, descending, downwards; see DOWN.

downy *a.* woolly, fuzzy, fluffy; see LIGHT 5, SOFT 2.

doze *v.* nap, drowse, slumber; see SLEEP.

dozen *a.* twelve, baker's dozen, long dozen, handful, pocketful.

drab *a.* **1.** [Dismal] dingy, colorless, dreary; see DULL 2, 4. **2.** [Dun-colored] yellowish-brown, dull brown, dull gray; see BROWN, GRAY.

draft *n.* **1.** [A preliminary sketch] plans, blueprint, sketch; see DESIGN. **2.** [A breeze] current of air, gust, puff; see WIND. **3.** [An order for payment] cashier's check, bank draft, money order; see CHECK 1. **4.** [The selection of troops] conscription, induction, recruiting; see SELECTION 1.

draft *v.* **1.** [Make a rough plan] outline, delineate, sketch; see PLAN 1, 2. **2.** [Select for military service] select, conscript, choose; see RECRUIT 1.

draftsman *n.* sketcher, designer, drawer; see ARCHITECT, ARTIST.

drag *n.* **1.** [A restraint] hindrance, burden, impediment; see BARRIER. **2.** [*An annoying person, thing, or situation] bother, annoyance, hang-up*; see NUISANCE 3.

drag *v.* **1.** [To go slowly; *said of animate beings*] lag, straggle, dawdle; see LOITER, PAUSE. **2.** [To go slowly; *said of an activity*] slow down, be delayed, fail to show progress, crawl*; see also DELAY.—*Ant.* IMPROVE, progress, pick up. **3.** [To pull an object] haul, move, transport; see DRAW 1.

dragon *n.* mythical beast, serpent, hydra; see MONSTER 1, SNAKE.

drag on *v.* go on slowly, keep going, persist; see CONTINUE 1, ENDURE 1.

drag one's feet* *v.* lag behind, obstruct, hold back; see HESITATE, HINDER, PAUSE, RESIST.

drain *n.* duct, channel, sewer; see CHANNEL, PIPE 1. —**down the drain*** wasted, ruined, gone; see LOST 1.

drain *v.* **1.** [To withdraw fluid] tap, draw off, remove; see EMPTY 2. **2.** [To withdraw strength] exhaust, weary, tire out; see SPEND, WEAKEN 2. **3.** [To seep away] run off, run out, flow away, seep out, exude, trickle out, filter off, ooze, find an opening, decline, diminish, leave dry; see also FLOW.

drama *n.* play, theatrical piece, theatrical production, dramatization, stage show, theatre. *Types of drama include the following:* melodrama, tragicomedy, comedy of manners, burlesque, pantomime, mime, grand opera, operetta, light opera, musical comedy, musical, mystery, murder mystery, farce, classical drama, historical drama, theatre of the absurd, epic, pageant, miracle play, revival; see also ACTING, COMEDY, PERFORMANCE.

dramatic *a.* tense, climactic, moving; see EXCITING.

dramatist *n.* playwright, script writer, scenario writer, scripter*; see also AUTHOR, WRITER. *Major dramatists include the following—Great Britain:* Christopher Marlowe, Ben Jonson, William Shakespeare, Oscar Wilde, George Bernard Shaw, Sean O'Casey, Harold Pinter; United States: Thornton Wilder, Eugene O'Neill, William Inge, Tennessee Williams, Arthur Miller, Edward Albee; Greece: Aeschylus, Sophocles, Euripides; France: Moliere, Pierre Corneille, Jean Racine, Jean Anouilh, Eugene Ionesco, Jean Genet, Jean Cocteau; Germany: Wolfgang von Goethe, Friedrich Schiller, Bertolt Brecht; other: Maxim Gorky, Anton Chekov, Henrik Ibsen, August Strindberg, Samuel Beckett, Karel Capek.

dramatize *v.* enact, produce, execute; see PERFORM 2.

drape *v.* clothe, wrap, model; see DRESS.

drapes *n.pl.* window covering, drapery, hanging; see CURTAIN.

drastic *a.* extravagant, exorbitant, radical; see EXTREME.

draw *v.* **1.** [To move an object] pull, drag, attract, move, bring, tug, lug, tow, carry, jerk, wrench, yank, haul, extract.—*Ant.* REPEL, repulse, reject. **2.** [To make a likeness by drawing] sketch, describe, etch, pencil, outline, tract, make a picture of, depict, model, portray, engrave, chart, map; see also PAINT 1. —**beat to the draw*** be quicker than another, forestall, stop; see ANTICIPATE, PREVENT.

draw away *v.* pull away from, gain on, increase a lead; see ADVANCE 1, DEFEAT 1, LEAVE 1.

drawback *n.* detriment, hindrance, check; see LACK 1.

draw back *v.* withdraw, recede, draw in; see RETREAT.

drawing *n.* sketching, designing, illustrating, tracing, etching, design, illustration, commercial designing; see also PICTURE 3, REPRESENTATION.

draw on *v.* take from, extract from, employ; see USE 1.

draw out *v.* **1.** [To induce to talk] make talk, lead on, interrogate; see INTERVIEW. **2.** [To pull] drag, tug, attract; see DRAW 1.

draw up *v.* draft, execute, prepare; see WRITE 1.

draw upon *v.* rely upon, employ, make use of; see USE 1.

dread *n.* awe, horror, terror; see FEAR.

dreadful *a.* hideous, fearful, shameful; see FRIGHTFUL 1.

dream *n.* nightmare, apparition, hallucination, image, trance, idea, impression, emotion, reverie, daydream, castle in the air, castle in Spain, chimera; see also FANTASY, ILLUSION, THOUGHT 2, VISION 3, 4.—*Ant.* REALITY, verity, truth.

dream *v.* **1.** [To have visions, usually during sleep or fever] hallucinate, fancy, visualize; see IMAGINE. **2.** [To entertain or delude oneself with imagined things] fancy, imagine, conceive, have notions, conjure up, create, picture, idealize, daydream, fantasize, be in the clouds, pipedream*; see also INVENT 1.

dreamer *n.* visionary, utopist, theorizer; see RADICAL.

dreaming *a.* thinking, daydreaming, in a reverie; see THOUGHTFUL 1.

dream up* *v.* devise, contrive, concoct; see IMAGINE.

dreamy *a.* whimsical, fanciful, daydreaming, visionary, given to reverie, illusory, introspective, otherworldly, idealistic, mythical, utopian, romantic; see also IMAGINARY, IMPRACTICAL.—*Ant.* PRACTICAL, ACTIVE, REAL.

dreary *a.* damp, raw, windy; see COLD 1, DISMAL.

dregs *n.pl.* scum, grounds, remains; see RESIDUE.

drench *v.* wet, saturate, flood; see IMMERSE, SOAK 1.

dress *n.* **1.** [Clothing] ensemble, attire, garments, outfit, garb, apparel, array, costume, wardrobe, uniform, habit, livery, formal dress, evening clothes, trappings, things, get-up*, threads*, rags*, duds*; see also CLOTHES, COAT 1, PANTS 1, SHIRT, SUIT 3, UNDERWEAR. **2.** [A woman's outer garment] frock, gown, wedding dress, evening gown, formal, cocktail dress, suit, skirt, robe, shift, sundress, wraparound, housedress, smock; see also CLOTHES.

dress *v.* **1.** [To put on clothes] don, wear, garb, clothe, robe, attire, drape, array, cover, spruce up, dress up, bundle up, get into*, doll up*, put on the dog*, dress to the nines*; see also WEAR 1. **2.** [To provide with clothes] costume, outfit, clothe; see SUPPORT 3. **3.** [To give medical treatment] treat, bandage, give first aid; see HEAL.

dressed up *a.* dressed formally, in full dress, dolled up*; see FANCY, FASHIONABLE, ORNATE.

dresser *n.* dressing table, chest of drawers, bureau; see FURNITURE, TABLE 1.

dressing *n.* **1.** [A food mixture] stuffing, filling, forcemeat. *Dressings include the following:* bread, giblet, oyster, chestnut, potato, prune, plum, apple, duck, turkey, chicken, fish, clam, wild rice. **2.** [A flavoring sauce] *Salad dressings include the following:* ranch, French, Russian, Thousand Island, blue cheese, Roquefort, Italian, Caesar, oil and vinegar; see also SAUCE. **3.** [An external medical application] bandage, plaster cast, adhesive tape, Band-Aid (trademark), compress, gauze, tourniquet, pack; see also CAST 4.

dressmaker *n.* seamstress, designer, dress fitter; see TAILOR.

dress up *v.* primp, deck out, put on the dog*; see DRESS 1.

dressy *a.* dressed up, elegant, elaborate; see FANCY, FASHIONABLE, ORNATE.

dribble *v.* trickle, spout, squirt; see DROP 1.

dried *a.* drained, dehydrated, desiccated; see DRY 1, PRESERVED 2.

drift *n.* **1.** [The tendency in movement] bent, trend, tendency, end, inclination, impulse, propulsion, aim, scope, goal, push, bias, set, leaning, progress, disposition, bearing, line, set; see also DIRECTION 1, WAY 2.—*Ant.* INDIFFERENCE, aimlessness, inertia. **2.** [The measure or character of movement] current, diversion, sweep; see FLOW.

drift *v.* float, ride, sail, wander, sweep, move with the current, gravitate, tend, be carried along by the current, move toward, go with the tide, be caught in the current, move without effort, move slowly; see also FLOW, MOVE 1.—*Ant.* LEAD, steer, pull.

drill *n.* **1.** [Practice] preparation, repetition, learning by doing; see PRACTICE 3. **2.** [A tool for boring holes] borer, wood bit, steel drill, steam drill, diamond drill, compressed-air drill, boring tool, tap-borer, auger, corkscrew, awl, riveter, jackhammer; see also TOOL 1. **3.** [Exercise, especially in military formation] training, maneuvers, marching, close-order drill, open-order drill, conditioning, survival training, guerrilla training; see also PARADE 1. **4.** [Device for planting seed in holes] planter, seeder, implement; see TOOL 1.

drill *v.* **1.** [To bore] pierce, sink in, puncture; see DIG 1, PENETRATE. **2.** [To train] practice, rehearse, discipline; see TEACH.

drink *n.* **1.** [A draft] gulp, sip, potion, drop, bottle, glass, refreshment, tall drink, shot*, stiff one*, slug*, belt*, nip*, swig*, spot*, short one*, nightcap*, hair of the dog*, one for the road*. **2.** [Something drunk] rye, bourbon, Scotch, Irish whiskey, ale, stout, rum, liqueur, tequila, vodka, distilled water, mineral water, carbonated water, mixer, tonic, seltzer, cocoa, hot chocolate, chocolate milk, milkshake, frappé, lemonade, punch, soft drink, soda water, ginger ale, ice-cream soda; orange juice, tomato juice, grapefruit juice, etc.; pop, soda, soda pop;

see also BEER, COFFEE, MILK, WATER 1, WHISKEY, WINE.

drink *v.* **1.** [To swallow liquid] gulp down, take in, sip, suck in, guzzle, imbibe, wash down, gargle; see also SWALLOW. **2.** [To consume alcoholic liquor] tipple, swill, swig, guzzle, belt*, take a drop*, take a nip, wet one's whistle*, down*, booze*, hit the bottle*, go on a binge*.

drinker *n.* tippler, alcoholic, lush*; see DRUNKARD.

drip *v.* dribble, trickle, plop; see DROP 1.

drive *n.* **1.** [A ride in a vehicle] ride, trip, outing, airing, tour, excursion, jaunt, spin, Sunday drive*; see also JOURNEY. **2.** [A road] approach, avenue, boulevard, entrance, street, roadway, parkway, lane, track, path, pavement; see also ROAD 1. **3.** [Impelling force] energy, effort, impulse; see FORCE 2.

drive *v.* **1.** [To urge on] impel, propel, instigate, incite, animate, hasten, egg on, urge on, compel, coerce, induce, force, press, stimulate, hurry, provoke, arouse, make, put up to, inspire, prompt, rouse, work on, act upon; see also sense 2 and ENCOURAGE, PUSH 2.—*Ant.* STOP, hinder, drag. **2.** [To manage a propelled vehicle] direct, manage, handle, run, wheel, bicycle, bike*, cycle, transport, float, drift, dash, put in motion, start, set going, speed, roll, coast, get under way, keep going, back up, burn up the road*, go like hell*, step on it*, floor it*, gun it*, burn rubber*, give it the gas*; see also RIDE 1.—*Ant.* WALK, crawl, stay.

drive a bargain *v.* deal, close a deal, bargain; see BUY, SELL.

drive at *v.* allude to, indicate, signify; see MEAN 1.

drive away *v.* drive off, disperse, banish; see SCATTER 2.

drive crazy or **mad** *v.* anger, perplex, infuriate; see BOTHER 2.

driven *a.* blown, drifted, herded, pushed, pounded, washed, guided, steered, directed, urged on, forced, shoved, sent, hard pressed, impelled, unable to help oneself, with one's back to the wall.

driver *n.* chauffeur, motorist, licensed operator, bus driver, truck driver, cab driver, person in the driver's seat, cabbie*, hack*.

driveway *n.* drive, entrance, approach; see DRIVE 2, ROAD 1.

drizzle *v.* spray, shower, sprinkle; see DROP 1, RAIN.

drone *n.* **1.** [A continuous sound] hum, buzz, vibration; see NOISE 1. **2.** [An idle person] idler, loafer, parasite; see LOAFER.

drone *v.* hum, buzz, vibrate; see SOUND.

drool *v.* drivel, drip, salivate, spit, dribble, trickle, ooze, run; see also DROP 1.

droop *v.* settle, sink, hang down; see LEAN 1.

drop *n.* **1.** [Enough fluid to fall] drip, trickle, droplet, bead, teardrop, dewdrop, raindrop; see also TEAR. **2.** [A lowering or falling] fall, tumble, reduction, decrease, slide, descent, slump, lapse, slip, decline, downfall, upset; see also FALL 1. **3.** [A small quantity] speck, dash, dab; see BIT 1. **—at the drop of a hat*** without warning, at the slightest provocation, quickly; see IMMEDIATELY.

drop *v.* **1.** [To fall in drops] drip, fall, dribble, trickle, descend, leak, ooze, seep, drain, filter, sink, bleed, bead, splash, hail; see also RAIN.—*Ant.* RISE, spurt, squirt. **2.** [To cause or to permit to fall] let go, give up, release, shed, relinquish, abandon, loosen, lower, floor, ground, shoot, knock down, fell, topple; see also DUMP.—*Ant.* RAISE, elevate, send up. **3.** [To discontinue] give up, quit, leave; see STOP 2. **4.** [To break off an acquaintance] break with, part from, cast off; see ABANDON 1.

drop a hint *v.* suggest, intimate, imply; see HINT, PROPOSE 1.

drop a line *v.* write to, post, communicate with; see COMMUNICATE, WRITE 1.

drop back *v.* lag, fall back, retire; see RECEDE 2, RETREAT.

drop behind *v.* slow down, worsen, decline; see FAIL 1, LOSE 3.

drop dead* *v.* expire, collapse, succumb; see DIE.

drop in *v.* call, stop, look in on; see VISIT.

drop off *v.* **1.** [*To sleep] fall asleep, doze, drowse; see SLEEP. **2.** [*To deliver] leave, hand over, present; see GIVE 1.

dropout *n.* failing student, truant, quitter; see FAILURE 1.

drop out *v.* withdraw, cease, quit; see ABANDON 1, RETREAT.

dropped *a.* discontinued, released, expelled; see ABANDONED.

drought *n.* dry season, dehydration, dry spell; see WEATHER.

drove *n.* flock, pack, rout; see CROWD, HERD.

drown *v.* **1.** [To cover with liquid] swamp, inundate, overflow; see FLOOD. **2.** [To lower into a liquid] dip, plunge, submerge; see IMMERSE, SINK 2. **3.** [To kill or die by drowning] go down three times, suffocate, asphyxiate; see DIE, KILL 1.

drowned *a.* suffocated, sunk, foundered; see DEAD 1, GONE 2.

drown out *v.* silence, hush, muffle; see QUIET 2.

drowsy *a.* sleepy, languid, indolent; see LAZY 1.

drudge *n.* slave, menial, hard worker; see LABORER, WORKMAN.

drug *n.* sedative, potion, essence, smelling salts, powder, tonic, opiate, pills, uppers*, downers*. *Kinds of drugs include the following—general:* caffeine, alcohol, adrenalin, amphetamine, nicotine, dope*; *hallucinogens:* marijuana, pot*, grass*, weed*; peyote, mescaline, psilocybin; *D*-lysergic acid diethylamide, LSD, acid*; *stimulants:* cocaine, coke*, snow*, crack*; benzedrine, bennies*, pep pills*; dexedrine, dexies*; methedrine, meth*, speed*; amyl nitrate, poppers*; *narcotics:* opium; morphine; heroin, H*, horse*, junk*, smack*; codeine; see also MEDICINE 2.

drug *v.* anesthetize, desensitize, dope*; see DEADEN.

drugged *a.* comatose, doped, stupefied; see UNCONSCIOUS.

druggist *n.* apothecary, chemist, registered pharmacist, licensed pharmacist, manufacturing pharmacist, proprietor, drugstore owner, merchant; see also DOCTOR.

drum *n.* snare drum, skins*, traps; see MUSICAL INSTRUMENT.

drum up *v.* attract, provide, succeed in finding; see DISCOVER, FIND.

drunk *a.* intoxicated, inebriated, befuddled, tipsy, overcome, sottish, drunken, stoned*, feeling no pain*, out of it*, seeing double*, smashed*, blotto*, gassed*, plowed*, under the table*, tanked*, wiped out*, soused*, high*, pickled*, stewed*, boozed up*, tight*, higher than a kite*; see also DIZZY.—*Ant.* SOBER, steady, temperate.

drunkard *n.* sot, inebriate, heavy drinker, tippler, alcoholic, drunken sot, drunk*, sponge*, boozer*, barfly*, pub-crawler*, wino*, lush*, alky*; see also ADDICT.

drunkenness *n.* inebriety, intoxication, intemperance, insobriety, alcoholism, jag*.—*Ant.* ABSTINENCE, sobriety, temperance.

dry *a.* **1.** [Having little or no moisture] arid, parched, waterless, hard, dried up, evaporated, desiccated, barren, dehydrated, drained, rainless, not irrigated, bare, thirsty, waterproof, rainproof, baked, shriveled, desert, dusty, depleted, dry as a bone*; see also STERILE 2.—*Ant.* WET, moist, damp. **2.** [Thirsty] parched, dehydrated, athirst; see THIRSTY. **3.** [Lacking in interest] boring, uninteresting, tedious; see DULL 4. **4.** [Possessed of intellectual humor] sarcastic, cynical, biting; see FUNNY 1.

dry *v.* **1.** [To become dry] dry up, shrivel, wilt; see EVAPORATE, WITHER. **2.** [To cause to become dry] air-dry, condense, concentrate, dehydrate, freeze-dry, blot, sponge, parch, scorch, dry up, exhaust; see also DRAIN 1, EMPTY 2.

dry goods *n.pl.* cloth, yard goods, yardage; see COTTON, LINEN, WOOL.

dryness *n.* aridity, lack of moisture, drought; see THIRST.

dry out or **up** *v.* drain, dehydrate, undergo evaporation; see DRY 1, 2.

dual *a.* binary, twofold, coupled; see DOUBLE, TWIN.

dubious *a.* **1.** [Doubtful] indecisive, perplexed, hesitant; see DOUBTFUL, UNCERTAIN. **2.** [Vague] ambiguous, indefinite, unclear; see OBSCURE 1.

dubiously *a.* doubtfully, doubtingly, indecisively; see SUSPICIOUSLY.

duck *n.* teal, mallard, fresh water duck, sea duck; see also BIRD. —**like water off a duck's back*** ineffective, ineffectual, weak; see USELESS 1.

duck *v.* **1.** [To immerse quickly] plunge, submerge, drop; see DIP 1, IMMERSE. **2.** [*To avoid] dodge, escape, elude; see AVOID, EVADE.

duct *n.* tube, canal, channel; see PIPE 1.

dud* *n.* failure, flop, debacle; see FAILURE 1.

duds* *n.pl.* garb, garments, gear; see CLOTHES.

due *a.* payable, owed, owing, overdue, collectible, unsatisfied, unsettled, not met, receivable, to be paid, chargeable, outstanding, in arrears; see also UNPAID 1, 2. —**become** (or **fall**) **due** be owed, payable, remain unsatisfied, mature.

duel *n.* combat, engagement, contest; see FIGHT 1.

dues *n.pl.* contribution, obligation, toll, duty, levy, collection, fee, annual assessment, tax, rates; see also PAY 1, TAX 1.

due to *a. & conj.* because of, resulting from, accordingly; see BECAUSE.

dull *a.* **1.** [Without point or edge] blunt, blunted, unsharpened, pointless, unpointed, round, square, flat, nicked, broken, toothless.—*Ant.* SHARP, sharpened, keen. **2.** [Lacking brightness or color] gloomy, sober, somber, drab, dismal, dark, dingy, dim, dusky, colorless, plain, obscure, tarnished, opaque, leaden, grave, grimy, pitchy, sooty, inky, dead, black, coal-black, unlighted, sordid, dirty, muddy, gray, lifeless, rusty, flat.—*Ant.* BRIGHT, colorful, gleaming. **3.** [Lacking intelligence; *said usually of living beings*] slow, retarded, witless; see STUPID. **4.** [Lacking interest; *said usually of writing, speaking, or inanimate things*] heavy, prosaic, trite, hackneyed, monotonous, humdrum, tedious, dreary, dismal, dry, arid, colorless, insipid, boring, vapid, flat, senseless, long-winded, stupid, commonplace, ordinary, common, usual, old, ancient, stale, moth-eaten, out-of-date, archaic, worn-out, tiring, banal, tired, uninteresting, driveling, pointless, uninspiring, piddling, senile, proverbial, tame, routine, familiar, known, well-known, conventional, depressing, sluggish, repetitious, repetitive, soporific, tiresome, lifeless, wearying, unexciting, flat, stereotyped, stock, the usual thing, the same old thing, the same thing day after day, slow, dry as a bone*, cut and dried, dead as a doornail*.—*Ant.* EXCITING, fascinating, exhilarating. **5.** [Not loud or distinct] low, soft, softened; see FAINT 3. **6.** [Showing little activity] still, routine, regular; see SLOW

1. 7. [Gloomy] cloudy, dim, unlit; see DARK 1.

dullness *n.* 1. [Quality of being boring] flatness, sameness, routine, evenness, aridity, depression, dimness, commonplaceness, mediocrity, tedium, tameness, familiarity; see also BOREDOM, MONOTONY.—*Ant.* ACTION, liveliness, interest. 2. [Stupidity] stupidness, insensibility, slow-wittedness; see STUPIDITY 1.

duly *a.* rightfully, properly, decorously; see JUSTLY 1.

dumb *a.* 1. [Unable to speak] silent, inarticulate, deaf and dumb, voiceless, speechless, having a speech impediment; see also MUTE 1, QUIET. 2. [Slow of wit] simpleminded, feebleminded, moronic; see DULL 3, STUPID.

dumbbell* *n.* blockhead, fool, dunce; see FOOL.

dummy *n.* 1. [*Fool] dolt, blockhead, oaf; see FOOL. 2. [Imitation] sham, counterfeit, duplicate; see COPY, IMITATION 2.

dump *n.* refuse heap, junk pile, garbage dump, city dump, dumping ground, swamp, garbage lot.

dump *v.* empty, unload, deposit, unpack, discharge, evacuate, drain, eject, exude, expel, throw out, throw over, throw overboard; see also DISCARD.—*Ant.* LOAD, fill, pack.

dumps *n.* despondency, dejection, despair; see DESPERATION, GLOOM.

dunce *n.* dolt, lout, moron; see FOOL.

dune *n.* rise, knoll, ridge; see HILL.

dung *n.* offal, defecation, compost, manure, guano, fertilizer, excreta; horse dung, cow dung, etc.; chips, pellets, leavings, muck, feces, filth, garbage, sludge, slop, sewage; see also EXCREMENT, FERTILIZER.

duo *n.* couple, two, twosome; see PAIR.

duplicate *n.* double, second, mate, facsimile, replica, carbon copy, likeness, counterpart, analogue, parallel, correlate, repetition, duplication, recurrence, match, twin, Xerox (trademark), chip off the old block; see also COPY, IMITATION. —**in duplicate** duplicated, doubled, copied; see REPRODUCED.

duplicate *v.* 1. [To copy] reproduce, counterfeit, make a replica of; see COPY. 2. [To double] make twofold, multiply, make twice as much; see INCREASE. 3. [To repeat] redo, remake, rework; see REPEAT 1.

durability *n.* durableness, stamina, persistence; see ENDURANCE.

durable *a.* strong, firm, enduring; see PERMANENT.

duration *n.* span, continuation, continuance; see TERM 2.

duress *n.* compulsion, discipline, control; see PRESSURE 2, RESTRAINT 2.

during *a. & prep.* as, at the time, at the same time as, the whole time, the time between, in the course of, in the middle of, when, all along, pending, throughout, in the meanwhile, in the interim, all the while, for the time being; see also MEANWHILE, WHILE 1.

dusk *n.* gloom, twilight, dawn; see NIGHT 1.

dust *n.* dirt, lint, soil, sand, flakes, ashes, cinders, grime, soot, grit, filings, sawdust; see also EARTH 2, FILTH. —**bite the dust*** be killed, fall in battle, succumb; see DIE. —**make the dust fly** move swiftly, work hard, be active; see ACT 1, MOVE 1.

dust *v.* sprinkle, sift, powder; see SCATTER 2.

dusty *a.* undusted, unused, untouched; see DIRTY 1.

dutiful *a.* devoted, respectful, conscientious; see FAITHFUL, OBEDIENT 1.

duty *n.* 1. [A personal sense of what one should do] moral obligation, conscience, liability, charge, accountability, faithfulness, pledge, burden, good faith, honesty, integrity, sense of duty, call of duty; see also RESPONSIBILITY 1, 2.—*Ant.* DISHONESTY, irresponsibility, disloyalty. 2. [Whatever one has to do] work, task, occupation, function, business, province, part, calling, charge, office, service, mission, obligation, contract, station, trust, burden, undertaking, commission, engagement, assignment, routine, chore, pains, responsibility; see also JOB 2.—*Ant.* ENTERTAINMENT, amusement, sport. 3. [A levy, especially on goods] charge, revenue, custom; see TAX 1. —**off duty** not engaged, free, inactive; see UNEMPLOYED. —**on duty** employed, engaged, at work; see BUSY 1.

dwarf *a.* dwarfed, low, diminutive; see LITTLE 1.

dwarf *v.* minimize, overshadow, dominate, predominate over, tower over, detract from, belittle, rise over, rise above, look down upon.—*Ant.* INCREASE, magnify, enhance.

dwell *v.* live, inhabit, stay, lodge, stop, settle, remain, live in, live at, continue, go on living, rent, tenant, have a lease on, make one's home at, have one's address at, keep house, be at home, room, bunk*; see also OCCUPY 2.

dweller *n.* tenant, inhabitant, occupant; see RESIDENT.

dwelling *n.* house, establishment, lodging; see HOME 1.

dwell on *v.* involve oneself in, think about, be engrossed in; see CONSIDER, EMPHASIZE.

dye *n.* tinge, stain, tint; see COLOR.

dye *v.* tint, stain, impregnate with color; see COLOR.

dying *a.* 1. [Losing life] sinking, passing away, fated, going, perishing, failing, expiring, moribund, withering away, at death's door*, done for*, cashing in one's chips*, with one foot in the grave; see also WEAK 2. 2. [Becoming worse or less] declining, going down, receding, retarding, decreasing, disappearing, dissolving, disintegrating, vanishing, failing, fading, ebbing, decaying, overripe, decadent, passé, doomed, neglected; see also SICK, WEAK 2.

dynamic *a.* energetic, potent, compelling, forceful, changing, progressive, productive, vigorous, magnetic, electric, effective, influential, charismatic, high-powered, peppy*, hopped up*; see also ACTIVE, POWERFUL 1.

dynamite *n.* trinitrotoluene, TNT, detonator; see EXPLOSIVE.

dynasty *n.* sovereignty, empire, absolutism; see NATION 1.

E

each *a.* **1.** [Every] all, any, one by one, separate, particular, specific, private, several, respective, various, piece by piece, individual, personal, without exception. **2.** [For each time, person, or the like] individually, proportionately, respectively, for one, per unit, singly, per capita, apiece, separately, every, without exception, by the, per, a whack*, a throw*, a shot*.

each *pron.* each one, one, each for himself, each in his own way, every last one, one another, each other.

eager *a.* anxious, keen, fervent; see ZEALOUS.

eagerly *a.* zealously, intently, anxiously, sincerely, vigorously, readily, earnestly, willingly, heartily, strenuously, fiercely, rapidly, hungrily, thirstily, fervently, actively, with enthusiasm, gladly, lovingly, with zeal, with open arms, with all the heart, from the bottom of one's heart, with delight.—*Ant.* SLOWLY, unwillingly, grudgingly.

eagerness *n.* zest, anticipation, excitement; see ZEAL.

eagle *n.* hawk, falcon, bird of prey; see BIRD.

eagle-eyed *a.* discerning, keen-sighted, clear-sighted; see OBSERVANT.

ear *n.* outer ear, middle ear, inner ear, eardrum, labyrinth, acoustic organ, auditory apparatus. **—all ears** attentive, hearing, paying attention; see LISTENING. **—bend someone's ear*** jabber, chatter, gossip; see TALK 1. **—fall on deaf ears** be ignored, fail to attract notice, be received with indifference; see FAIL 1, WAIT 1. **—have** (or **keep**) **an ear to the ground*** be aware of, observe, keep one's eyes open; see LISTEN, MIND 3. **—in one ear and out the other** ignored, forgotten, received with indifference; see NEGLECTED. **—play it by ear*** improvise, concoct, go along; see INVENT 1. **—set on its ear*** stir up, agitate, arouse; see EXCITE. **—turn a deaf ear (to)** disregard, ignore, shun; see NEGLECT 1.

earlier *a.* former, previous, prior; see PRECEDING.

early *a.* **1.** [Near the beginning] recent, primitive, prime, new, brand-new, fresh, budding.—*Ant.* LATE, old, superannuated. **2.** [Sooner than might have been expected] quick, premature, in advance, far ahead, in the bud, preceding, advanced, immediate, unexpected, speedy, ahead of time, direct, prompt, punctual, briefly, shortly, presently, beforehand, on short notice, on the dot*, with time to spare.—*Ant.* SLOW, late, tardy.

earmark *n.* characteristic, attribute, quality; see CHARACTERISTIC.

earmark *v.* reserve, set aside, keep back; see MAINTAIN 3.

earn *v.* **1.** [To deserve as reward] win, merit, gain; see DESERVE. **2.** [To receive in payment] obtain, attain, get, procure, realize, obtain a return, make money by, acquire, profit, net, clear, score, draw, gather, secure, derive, make money, bring home, bring in, collect, pick up, scrape together*.—*Ant.* SPEND, consume, exhaust.

earnest *a.* ardent, zealous, warm; see ENTHUSIASTIC.

earnestly *a.* solemnly, soberly, thoughtfully; see SERIOUSLY 2.

earnings *n.pl.* net proceeds, balance, receipts; see PAY 2.

earring *n.* pendant, ornament, jewel; see JEWELRY.

earth *n.* **1.** [The world] globe, sphere, planet, *terra*, mundane world, creation, terrestrial sphere, orb, cosmos, universe, star. **2.** [The earthly crust] dirt, clean dirt, loam, humus, clay, gravel, sand, land, dry land, terrain, mud, muck, soil, ground, fill, compost, topsoil, alluvium, terrane, surface, shore, coast, deposit. **—come back** (or **down**) **to earth** be practical, be sensible, return to one's senses, quit dreaming; see also CALM DOWN, WORK 1. **—down to earth** earthly, realistic, mundane; see PRACTICAL. **—on earth** of all things, of everything, what; see WHATEVER.

earthen *a.* clay, stone, mud, dirt, rock, fictile, made of earth, made of baked clay.

earthenware *n.* crockery, ceramics, china; see POTTERY.

earthly *a.* human, mortal, global, mundane, worldly, under the sun, in all creation.—*Ant.* UNNATURAL, unearthly, superhuman.

earthquake *n.* tremor, temblor, trembler, earthquake shock, shock, quake, fault, slip, movement of the earth's crust, earth tremor, earth shock, volcanic quake.

earthy *a.* **1.** [Characteristic of earth] dusty, made of earth, muddy; see EARTHEN. **2.** [Unrefined] coarse, dull, unrefined; see CRUDE.

ease *n.* **1.** [Freedom from pain] comfort, rest, quietness, peace, prosperity, leisure, repose, satisfaction, calm, calmness, restfulness, tranquility, solace, consolation.—*Ant.* PAIN, discomfort, unrest. **2.** [Freedom from difficulty] expertness, facility, efficiency, knack, readiness, quickness, skillfulness, dexterity, cleverness, smoothness; child's play, clear sailing*, snap*, breeze*, cinch*, pushover*.—*Ant.* DIFFICULTY, trouble, clumsiness. —**at ease** relaxed, collected, resting; see CALM 1.

ease *v.* **1.** [To relieve of pain] alleviate, allay, drug, keep under sedation, tranquilize, sedate, anesthetize, give relief, comfort, relieve pressure, cure, attend to, doctor, nurse, relieve, soothe, set at ease, cheer.—*Ant.* HURT, injure, pain. **2.** [To lessen pressure or tension] prop up, lift, bear, hold up, make comfortable, raise, unburden, release, soften, relieve one's mind, lighten, let up on, give rest to, relax, quiet, calm, pacify. **3.** [To move carefully] induce, remove, extricate, set right, right, insert, join, slide, maneuver, handle.—*Ant.* HURRY, rush, blunder.

easily *a.* readily, with ease, in an easy manner, effortlessly, simply, with no effort, without trouble, evenly, regularly, steadily, efficiently, smoothly, plainly, comfortably, calmly, coolly, surely, just like that*, with one hand tied behind one's back*.

easiness *n.* carelessness, nonchalance, facility; see ABILITY.

east *a.* **1.** [Situated to the east] eastward, in the east, on the east side of, toward the sunrise, east side, eastern, easterly, easternmost. **2.** [Going toward the east] eastbound, eastward, to the east, headed east, in an easterly direction. **3.** [Coming from the east] westbound, headed west, out of the east, westward, westerly, tending to the west.

East *n.* **1.** [The eastern part of the United States] the eastern states, the Atlantic seaboard, the Eastern seaboard, land east of the Alleghenies, east of the Appalachians, land east of the Mississippi. *Areas in the East include the following:* East Coast, Atlantic Coast, Appalachia, Middle Atlantic States, New England, down East, the Thirteen Colonies; see also AMERICA 2, UNITED STATES. **2.** [The eastern part of Eurasia] Asia, Asia Minor, Near East, Far East, Middle East, Siberia, Mongolia, southeast Asia, Arabia, Orient, Levant; see also ASIA for countries in the East.

eastern *a.* **1.** [Concerning the direction to the east] easterly, eastward, on the east side of; see EAST 1. **2.** [Concerning the eastern part of the United States] East, Atlantic, Atlantic Seaboard, east of the Appalachian Mountains, Allegheny, Appalachian, New England, Middle Atlantic, South Atlantic. **3.** [Concerning the Near East or Middle East] Southwest Asian, Egyptian, of the Holy Land, Arab, Arabic, Israeli, Hellenic, Hebraic, in Asia Minor. **4.** [Concerning the Orient] Far Eastern, East Asian, Asian; see ORIENTAL.

easy *a.* **1.** [Free from constraint] secure, at ease, prosperous, leisurely, unembarrassed, spontaneous, calm, peaceful, tranquil, careless, contented, carefree, untroubled, moderate, hospitable, soft*.—*Ant.* DIFFICULT, impoverished, hard. **2.** [Providing no difficulty] simple, facile, obvious, apparent, yielding, easily done, smooth, manageable, accessible, wieldy, slight, little, paltry, inconsiderable, nothing to it*, simple as ABC*, pushover*, easy as pie*, like taking candy from a baby*.—*Ant.* HARD, difficult, complicated. **3.** [Lax] lenient, indulgent, easygoing; see KIND. —**take it easy** relax, rest, slow down; see CALM DOWN.

easygoing *a.* tranquil, carefree, patient; see CALM 1.

eat *v.* **1.** [To take as food] consume, bite, chew, devour, swallow, feast on, dine out, get away with, peck at, gorge, gobble up, eat up, digest, masticate, feed on, breakfast, dine, eat out, sup, lunch, feed, feast, banquet, fall to, live on, feed on, take in, enjoy a meal, have a bite*, put away*, make a pig of oneself*, eat out of house and home*.—*Ant.* FAST, starve, vomit. **2.** [To reduce gradually] eat up, eat away, liquefy, melt, disappear, vanish, waste, rust away, spill, dissipate, squander, drain, spill, fool away, run through.—*Ant.* INCREASE, swell, build. **3.** [To bother] worry, vex, disturb; see BOTHER 2.

eatable *a.* digestible, nutritious, delicious; see EDIBLE.

eating *n.* consuming, consumption, devouring, feasting on, gorging on, feeding on, biting, chewing, dining, breakfasting, lunching, eating out, dining out, eating up, having a coffee break, having a lunch break, having a bite, having a snack, breaking bread, making a pig of oneself, bolting, swallowing, gulping down, gobbling up, gobbling down, putting on the feed bag*, eating out of house and home*.

eat one's heart out *v.* fret, pine, grieve; see WORRY 2.

eat one's words *v.* retract a statement, take back, rescind; see ABANDON 1.

eat out* *v.* rebuke, reprove, admonish.

eat out of house and home *v.* devour, be ravenous, have a huge appetite; see EAT 1.

eat out of one's hand *v.* be tame, submit, acquiesce; see YIELD 1.
eats* *n.pl.* food, victuals, meal; see FOOD.
eavesdrop *v.* overhear, wiretap, listen, listen in on, try to overhear, bend an ear*, bug*, tap.
ebb *n.* recession, decline, outward flow, outward sweep, shrinkage, wane, waste, depreciation, reduction, lessening, ebb tide, regression, withdrawal, decrease, depreciation.—*Ant.* INCREASE, flow, rise.
ebb *v.* recede, subside, retire, flow back, sink, decline, decrease, drop off, melt, fall away, peter out, wane, fall off, decay.—*Ant.* INCREASE, flow, rise.
eccentric *a.* odd, queer, strange; see UNUSUAL 2.
eccentricity *n.* peculiarity, abnormality, idiosyncrasy; see CHARACTERISTIC.
echo *n.* repetition, imitation, reply; see ANSWER 1.
echo *v.* repeat, mimic, impersonate; see IMITATE 1.
eclipse *n.* solar eclipse, lunar eclipse, total eclipse; see DARKNESS 1.
ecologist *n.* environmentalist, conservationist, naturalist, ecological engineer, oceanographer, biologist, botanist; see also SCIENTIST.
ecology *n.* ecological engineering, human environment, anti-pollution projects, pollution control, survival studies, study of ecosystems, conservation of natural resources; see also SCIENCE 1, ZOOLOGY.
economic *a.* industrial, business, financial; see COMMERCIAL.
economical *a.* **1.** [Careful of expenditures] saving, sparing, careful, economizing, thrifty, prudent, frugal, miserly, stingy, mean, close, watchful, tight*, closefisted, penny-pinching*; see also STINGY.—*Ant.* GENEROUS, liberal, wasteful. **2.** [Advantageously priced] cheap, sound, low, reasonable, fair, moderate, inexpensive, marked down, on sale. **3.** [Making good use of materials] practical, efficient, methodical; see EFFICIENT 1.
economics *n.* commerce, finance, public economy, political economy, science of wealth, economic theory, commerical theory, theory of business, theory of finance, principles of business, principles of finance, study of industry, study of production and distribution, theory of trade, economic principles; see also LAW 4, SCIENCE 1.
economist *n.* statistician, business analyst, efficiency expert; see SCIENTIST.
economize *v.* husband, manage, stint, conserve, scrimp, skimp, be frugal, be prudent, pinch, cut costs, cut corners, meet expenses, keep within one's means, cut down, meet a budget, make both ends meet, tighten one's belt*, save for a rainy day*, pinch pennies; see also ACCUMULATE, MAINTAIN 3, SAVE 3.—*Ant.* SPEND, waste, splurge.
economy *n.* curtailment, cutback, business recession, retrenchment, rollback, reduction, layoff, wage decrease, cut in wages.—*Ant.* INCREASE, outlay, raise.
ecstasy *n.* joy, rapture, delight; see HAPPINESS.
edge *n.* **1.** [The outer portion] border, frontier, extremity, threshold, brink, boundary, end, limit, brim, rim, margin, ring, frame, side, corner, point, bend, peak, turn, crust, verge, bound, ledge, skirt, outskirt, lip, limb, hem, seam, fringe, frill, mouth, shore, strand, bank, beach, curb, periphery, circumference.—*Ant.* CENTER, surface, interior. **2.** [Anything linear and sharp] blade, cutting edge, razor edge; see KNIFE. **3.** [*Advantage] upper hand, handicap, head start; see ADVANTAGE. —**on edge** nervous, tense, uptight*; see IRRITABLE. —**set one's teeth on edge** irritate, annoy, provoke; see BOTHER 2. —**take the edge off** weaken, subdue, dull; see SOFTEN.
edge *v.* **1.** [To trim] border, fringe, bind; see TRIM 2, DECORATE. **2.** [*To defeat narrowly] nose out, slip past, squeeze by; see DEFEAT 3.
edgy *a.* irritable, touchy, excitable; see NERVOUS.
edible *a.* palatable, good, delicious, satisfying, fit to eat, savory, tasty, culinary, yummy*, nutritious, digestible; see also DELICIOUS.
edifice *n.* structure, architectural monument, pile; see BUILDING.
edit *n.* revise, alter, rewrite, arrange materials for publication, prepare for the press, compose, compile, select, arrange, set up, censor, polish, finish, analyze, revise and correct, delete, condense, discard, strike out, write, proofread, cut, trim, blue-pencil, doctor up*.
edition *n.* printing, reprint, revision; see BOOK.
editor *n.* reviser, copyreader, supervisor, director, manager, editor-in-chief, proofreader, reader, editorial writer, desk man, newspaperman; see also AUTHOR, WRITER.
editorial *n.* essay, article, column; see COMPOSITION.
educate *v.* tutor, instruct, train; see TEACH.
educated *a.* trained, accomplished, skilled, well-taught, scientific, scholarly, intelligent, learned, well-informed, well-read, well-versed, well-grounded, disciplined, prepared, instructed, developed, civilized, fitted, versed in, informed in, acquainted with, professional, expert, polished, cultured, finished, initiated, enlightened, literate, lettered, tutored, schooled.—*Ant.* IGNORANT, illiterate, unlettered.
education *n.* **1.** [The process of directing learning] schooling, study, training, direc-

tion, instruction, guidance, apprenticeship, teaching, tutelage, learning, reading, discipline, preparation, adult education, book learning, information, indoctrination, brainwashing, cultivation, background, rearing. **2.** [Knowledge acquired through education] learning, wisdom, scholarship; see KNOWLEDGE 1. **3.** [The teaching profession] teaching, tutoring, pedagogy, instruction, training, the field of education, the educational profession, progressive education, lecturing.

educational *a.* enlightening, instructive, enriching; see CULTURAL.

educator *n.* pedagogue, instructor, tutor; see TEACHER.

eerie *a.* strange, ghostly, weird; see FRIGHTFUL 1.

effect *n.* conclusion, consequence, outcome; see RESULT. **—in effect** as a result, in fact, actually; see REALLY 1. **—take effect** work, produce results, become operative; see ACT 1. **—to the effect (that)** as a result, so that, therefore; see FOR.

effect *v.* produce, cause, make; see BEGIN 1, CAUSE.

effective *a.* efficient, serviceable, useful, operative, effectual, sufficient, adequate, productive, capable, competent, yielding, practical, valid, resultant.—*Ant.* USELESS, inoperative, inefficient.

effectively *a.* efficiently, completely, finally, expertly, conclusively, definitely, persuasively, adequately, capably, productively; see also WELL 2, 3.

effects *n.pl.* personal property, baggage, possessions; see PROPERTY 1.

effectual *a.* adequate, efficient, qualified; see EFFECTIVE.

efficiency *n.* productivity, capability, capableness; see ABILITY.

efficient *a.* **1.** [*Said of persons*] competent, businesslike, good at, apt, adequate, fitted, able, capable, qualified, skillful, clever, talented, energetic, skilled, adapted, familiar with, deft, adept, expert, experienced, equal to, practiced, practical, proficient, accomplished, active, productive, dynamic, decisive, tough, shrewd.—*Ant.* INCOMPETENT, inefficient, incapable. **2.** [*Said of things*] economical, fitting, suitable, suited, effectual, effective, adequate, serviceable, useful, saving, profitable, valuable, expedient, handy, conducive, well-designed, streamlined, good for.—*Ant.* INADEQUATE, unsuitable, ineffectual.

effluent *a.* emanating, issuing forth, seeping; see FLOWING.

effort *n.* attempt, enterprise, undertaking, struggle, battle, try, trial, work, venture, aim, aspiration, purpose, intention, resolution, exercise, discipline, drill training, crack*, go*, whirl*; see also ACTION 1, 2.

effortless *a.* simple, offhand, smooth; see EASY 2.

egg *n.* ovum, seed, germ, spawn, bud, embryo, nucleus, cell. *Prepared eggs include the following:* fried, scrambled, poached, deviled, hard boiled, soft boiled, soufflé, raw, buttered, on toast, egg salad, ham or bacon and eggs, over easy, sunnyside up. **—lay an egg*** be unsuccessful, err, make a mistake; see FAIL 1. **—put** (or **have**) **all one's eggs in one basket** chance, gamble, bet; see RISK.

egg on *v.* encourage, goad, incite; see DRIVE 1, 2, URGE 2, 3.

egg-shaped *a.* rounded, oval, pear-shaped; see ROUND 1.

ego *n.* personality, individuality, self; see CHARACTER 1, 2.

egotism *n.* egoism, conceit, vanity, pride, assurance, self-love, self-confidence, self-glorification, self-worship, arrogance, insolence, overconfidence, haughtiness.—*Ant.* MODESTY, humility, meekness.

egotist *n.* conceited person, boaster, egoist; see BRAGGART.

egotistic *a.* conceited, vain, boastful, inflated, pompous, arrogant, insolent, puffed up, affected, self-centered, self-glorifying, presumptuous, blustering, showy, boisterous, haughty, snobbish, contemptuous, proud, bullying, sneering, aloof, pretentious, assuming, cocky*, brazen, impertinent, selfish, bragging, insulting, theatrical, garish, gaudy, spectacular, reckless, impudent, inflated, stiff, overbearing, domineering, bold, rash, overconfident, self-satisfied, stuck up*, looking down one's nose*, snooty*, uppity, wrapped up in oneself*, on one's high horse*, high and mighty*, too big for one's breeches*, big as you please*.—*Ant.* HUMBLE, meek, modest.

egotistically *a.* vainly, boastfully, arrogantly, haughtily, pretentiously, loftily.

either *a. & conj.* on the one hand, whether or not, unless, it could be that, it might be that.

either *pron.* one, one or the other, this one, either/or, each of two, as soon one as the other, one of two.

eject *v.* dislodge, discard, reject, run out, kick out, throw out, put out, force out, spit out, turn out, squeeze out, oust, do away with, evict, banish, throw off, vomit, excrete, dump, get rid of, send packing, give the boot*, ditch*, bounce*.

ejection *n.* eviction, expulsion, dismissal; see REMOVAL.

elaborate *a.* **1.** [Ornamented] gaudy, decorated, garnished, showy, fussy, dressy, refined, flowery, flashy; see also ORNATE.—*Ant.* COMMON, ordinary, unpolished. **2.** [Detailed] complicated, extensive, laborious, minute, intricate, involved, many-faceted, complex, a great many, painstaking, studied.—*Ant.* GENERAL, usual, unified.

elaborate *v.* embellish, bedeck, deck; see DECORATE.

elaborate upon *v.* expand, discuss, comment upon; see EXPLAIN.

elapse *v.* transpire, pass away, slip by; see PASS 2.

elastic *a.* plastic, tempered, pliant; see FLEXIBLE.

elasticity *n.* resiliency, buoyancy, pliability; see FLEXIBILITY.

elbow *n.* joint, angle, funny bone; see BONE. —**rub elbows with** mingle with, associate with, be friends with; see JOIN 2. —**up to the elbows (in)** engaged, employed, working at; see BUSY 1.

elbowroom *n.* sweep, range, margin; see SPACE 2.

elder *n.* veteran, old lady, old man, old woman, superior, old timer, senior, one of the old folks, one of the older generation, patriarch, chief, tribal head, dignitary, counselor, father, uncle, grandfather, ancestor.

elderly *a.* declining, retired, venerable; see OLD 1.

elect *v.* choose, name, select; see CHOOSE.

elected *a.* chosen, duly elected, picked; see NAMED 2.

election *n.* poll, polls, ballot, balloting, ticket, bote, voting, vote-casting, primaries, suffrage, referendum, franchise, constitutional right.

elective *a.* voluntary, selective, not compulsory; see OPTIONAL.

electric *a.* electrical, magnetic, galvanic, electronic, power driven, telegraphic, electrified, pulsing, vibrating, dynamic, energetic.—*Ant.* OLD-FASHIONED, manual, steam.

electricity *n.* power, current, service, heat, light, ignition, spark, utilities, alternating current (AC), direct current (DC), voltage, 110 volts, 220 volts, high voltage, high tension, kilowatts, kilowatt hours, kilocycles, megacycles.

electrify *v.* wire, charge, power, heat, light, equip, lay cables, provide service, magnetize, galvanize, energize, subject to electricity, pass an electric current through, give an electric shock to, charge with electricity.

electrocute *v.* execute, put to death, kill by electric shock, put in the electric chair, send to the hot seat*, fry*, burn*.

electron *n.* negative particle, negatron, electrically charged element; see ATOM.

electronic *a.* photoelectric, cathodic, anodic, voltaic, photoelectronic, autoelectronic, computerized, automatic, automated; see also ELECTRIC.

electronics *n.* radionics, electron physics, radar, physics, photoelectronics, automatics, cybernetics, computer electronics; see also SCIENCE 1.

elegance *n.* culture, tastefulness, taste, cultivation, politeness, polish, grace, delicacy, splendor, beauty, balance, purity, grace, gracefulness, delicacy, magnificence, courtliness, nobility, charm, sophistication, propriety, style.

elegant *a.* ornate, polished, perfected, elaborate, finished, ornamented, adorned, embellished, embroidered, flowing, artistic, fancy, rich, pure, fluent, neat.—*Ant.* DULL, ill-chosen, inarticulate.

element *n.* **1.** [A constitution] portion, particle, detail, component, constituent, ingredient, factor; see also PART 1. **2.** [A form of matter] *The older sciences determined the following elements:* earth, air, fire, water; *modern chemistry and physics identify the following elements:* actinium (Ac), aluminum (Al), americium (Am), antimony (Sb), argon (A), arsenic (As), astatine (At), barium (Ba), berkelium (Bk), beryllium (Be), bismuth (Bi), boron (B), bromine (Br), cadmium (Cd), calcium (Ca), californium (Cf) carbon (C), cerium (Ce), cesium (Cs), chlorine (Cl), chromium (Cr), cobalt (Co), copper (Cu), curium (Cm), dysprosium (Dy), einsteinium (E), erbium (Er), europium (Eu), fermium (Fm), fluorine (F), francium (Fr), gadolinium (Gd), gallium (Ga), germanium (Ge), gold (Au), hafnium (Hf), hahnium (Ha), helium (He), holmium (Ho), hydrogen (H), indium (In), iodine (I), iridium (Ir), iron (Fe), krypton (Kr), lanthanum (La), lawrencium (Lr), lead (Pb), lithium (Li), lutetium (Lu), magnesium (Mg), manganese (Mn), mendelevium (Mv), mercury (Hg), molybdenum (Mo), neodymium (Nd), neon (Ne), neptunium (Np), nickel (Ni), niobium *or* columbium (Nb), nitrogen (N), nobelium (No), osmium (Os), oxygen (O), palladium (Pd), phosphorus (P), platinum (Pt), plutonium (Pu), polonium (Po), potassium (K), praseodymium (Pr), promethium (Pm), protactinium (Pa), radium (Ra), radon (Rn), rhenium (Re), rhodium (Rh), rubidium (Rb), ruthenium (Ru), rutherfordium (Rf), samarium (Sm), scandium (Sc), selenium (Se), silicon (Si), silver (Ag), sodium (Na), strontium (Sr), sulfur (S), tantalum (Ta), technetium (Tc), tellurium (Te), terbium (Tb), thallium (Ti), thorium (Th), thulium (Tm), tin (Sn), titanium (Ti), tungsten (W), uranium (U), vanadium (V), xenon (Xe), ytterbium (Yb), yttrium (Y), zinc (Zn), zirconium (Zr).

elementary *a.* **1.** [Suited to beginners] primary, introductory, rudimentary; see EASY 2. **2.** [Fundamental] foundational, essential, basic; see FUNDAMENTAL.

elements *n.pl.* basic material, fundamentals, grammar, ABC's, initial stage, basis, beginning, first step, principles, rudiments, groundwork.

elevate *v.* **1.** [To lift bodily] hoist, heave, tilt; see RAISE 1. **2.** [To promote] advance, appoint, further; see PROMOTE 1.

elevated *a.* aerial, towering, tall; see HIGH 2, RAISED 1.

elevation *n.* top, roof, platform; see HEIGHT.

elevator *n.* **1.** [Machine for lifting] lift, escalator, conveyor, elevator shaft, chair lift, passenger elevator, freight elevator, automatic elevator, hoist, chute. **2.** [A building handling grain] bin, storage plant, silo; see BARN.

elf *n.* brownie, sprite, leprechaun; see FAIRY.

eligibility *n.* fitness, acceptability, capability; see ABILITY.

eligible *a.* qualified, fit, suitable, suited, equal to, worthy of being chosen, capable of, fitted for, satisfactory, trained, employable, usable, becoming, likely, in the running, in line for, up to*.—*Ant.* UNFIT, ineligible, disqualified.

eliminate *v.* take out, wipe out, clean out, throw out, stamp out, blot out, cut out, phase out, drive out, dispose of, get rid of, do away with, put aside, set aside, exclude, eject, cast off, disqualify, oust, depose, evict, cancel, eradicate, erase, expel, discharge, dislodge, reduce, invalidate, abolish, repeal, exterminate, annihilate, kill, murder, throw overboard, be done with, discard, dismiss, obliterate, discount, exile, banish, deport, expatriate, maroon, blackball, ostracize, fire, dump*, can*, ditch*, scrap, bounce*, sack*, drop.—*Ant.* INCLUDE, accept, welcome.

elimination *n.* **1.** [The act of removing] dismissal, expulsion, exclusion; see REMOVAL. **2.** [The act of declining to consider] rejection, repudiation, denial, disqualification, avoidance.

elite *n.* society, nobility, celebrities; see ARISTOCRACY.

ellipse *n.* oval, conic section, curve; see CIRCLE 1.

elongate *v.* prolong, lengthen, extend; see STRETCH.

eloquence *n.* fluency, wit, wittiness, expression, expressiveness, appeal, ability, diction, articulation, delivery, power, force, vigor, facility, style, poise, expressiveness, flow, command of language, gift of gab*.

eloquent *a.* vocal, articulate, outspoken; see FLUENT.

elsewhere *a.* gone, somewhere else, not here, in another place, in some other place, to some other place, away, absent, abroad, hence, removed, remote, outside, formerly, subsequently.—*Ant.* HERE, at this point, in this spot.

elude *v.* dodge, shun, escape; see AVOID.

elusive *a.* slippery, fleeting, fugitive; see TEMPORARY.

emaciated *a.* gaunt, famished, wasted; see THIN 2.

emanate *v.* exude, radiate, exhale; see EMIT.

emancipate *v.* release, liberate, deliver; see FREE.

emancipation *n.* liberty, release, liberation; see FREEDOM.

emasculate *v.* geld, unman, mutilate; see CASTRATE.

embalm *v.* preserve, process, freeze, anoint, wrap, mummify, prepare for burial, lay out.

embankment *n.* dike, breakwater, pier; see DAM.

embargo *n.* restriction, prohibition, impediment; see RESTRAINT 2.

embark *v.* set out, leave port, set sail; see LEAVE 1.

embarrass *v.* perplex, annoy, puzzle, vex, distress, disconcert, agitate, bewilder, confuse, chagrin, confound, upset, bother, plague, tease, worry, trouble, distract, discomfort, disturb, let down, perturb, fluster, irk, shame, stun, rattle, put on the spot*, make a monkey out of*.—*Ant.* ENCOURAGE, cheer, please.

embarrassed *a.* abashed, perplexed, disconcerted; see ASHAMED.

embarrassing *a.* difficult, disturbing, confusing, distracting, bewildering, puzzling, rattling, perplexing, delicate, unbearable, distressing, disconcerting, upsetting, discomforting, ticklish, flustering, troublesome, worrisome, uncomfortable, awkward, disagreeable, helpless, unseemly, impossible, uneasy, mortifying, shameful, annoying, irksome, exasperating, inconvenient, unmanageable, sticky*.—*Ant.* COMFORTABLE, easy, agreeable.

embarrassment *n.* confusion, chagrin, mortification, discomfiture, shame, humiliation, shyness, timidity, inhibition, dilemma, puzzle, perplexity, tangle, strait, pinch, quandary, mistake, blunder, clumsiness, indebtedness, uncertainty, hindrance, poverty, destitution, distress, difficulties, involvement, obligation, indiscretion, awkward situation, predicament, plight, pinch*, fix*, snag*, hitch*, hot seat*, hot water*, pickle*, stew.

embassy *n.* commission, mission, delegation; see COMMITTEE, DIPLOMAT.

embed *v.* plant, implant, secure; see FASTEN.

embezzle *v.* thieve, forge, pilfer; see STEAL.

embezzlement *n.* fraud, misappropriation, stealing; see THEFT.

embezzler *n.* thief, robber, defaulter; see CRIMINAL.

embitter *v.* irritate, aggravate, annoy; see BOTHER 2.

emblem *n.* symbol, figure, image, design, token, sign, insignia, banner, seal, colors, crest, coat of arms, representation, effigy, reminder, mark, badge, souvenir, keepsake, medal, character, motto, hallmark, flag, pennant, banner, standard.

embodiment *n.* incarnation, matter, structure; see CHARACTERISTIC, ESSENCE 1, IMAGE 2.
emboss *v.* raise, design, enchase; see DECORATE.
embrace *v.* enfold, squeeze, grip; see HUG.
embroider *v.* stitch, knit, quilt; see SEW.
embryo *n.* fetus, incipient organism, nucleus; see EGG.
embryonic *a.* incipient, immature, undeveloped; see EARLY 1.
emerald *n.* green beryl, valuable gem, precious stone; see JEWEL.
emerge *v.* rise, arrive, come out; see APPEAR 1.
emergence *n.* rise, evolution, visibility; see VIEW.
emergency *n.* accident, unforeseen occurrence, misadventure, strait, urgency, necessity, pressure, tension, distress, turn of events, obligation, pass, crisis, predicament, turning point, impasse, dilemma, quandary, pinch, fix*, hole*; see also DIFFICULTY 1, 2.
emigrant *n.* exile, expatriate, colonist, migrant, displaced person, D.P., traveler, foreigner, pilgrim, refugee, fugitive, wayfarer, wanderer, immigrant, alien, outcast, man without a country.
emigrate *v.* migrate, immigrate, quit; see LEAVE 1.
emigration *n.* reestablishing, departure, removal, leaving, expatriation, displacement, moving away, crossing, migrating, exodus, exile, trek, journey, movement, trend, march, travel, voyage, wayfaring, wandering, migration, shift, settling, homesteading.—*Ant.* immigration, arriving, remaining.
émigré *n.* exile, emigrant, refugee; see REFUGEE.
eminence *n.* standing, prominence, distinction; see FAME.
eminent *a.* renowned, celebrated, prominent; see DIGNIFIED, DISTINGUISHED 2.
emissary *n.* intermediary, ambassador, consul; see AGENT.
emission *n.* ejection, effusion, eruption; see RADIATION 1.
emit *v.* give off, let off, give out, let out, send forth, send out, throw up, throw out, spill out, pour out, give forth, eject, blow, hurl, gush, secrete, spurt, shoot, erupt, squirt, shed, expel, expend, vomit, belch, excrete, issue, perspire, spew, spit, ooze, exhale, emanate; see also EMPTY 2.
emotion *n.* agitation, tremor, commotion, excitement, disturbance, sentiment, feeling, tumult, turmoil, sensation. *Emotions include the following:* love, passion, ecstasy, warmth, glow, fervor, ardor, zeal, thrill, elation, joy, satisfaction, happiness, sympathy, tenderness, concern, grief, remorse, sorrow, sadness, melancholy, despondency, despair, depression, worry, disquiet, uneasiness, dread, fear, apprehension, hate, resentment, conflict, jealousy, greed, anger, rage, ire, shame, pride, sensuality, lust, desire.
emotional *a.* hysterical, demonstrative, fiery, warm, zealous, sensuous, fervent, ardent, enthusiastic, passionate, excitable, impulsive, spontaneous, ecstatic, impetuous, nervous, wrought-up, overwrought, temperamental, irrational, sensitive, oversensitive, hypersensitive, sentimental, maudlin, overflowing, affectionate, loving, neurotic, fickle, wearing one's heart on one's sleeve, high-strung, mushy*.—*Ant.* COLD, rational, hard.
emotionalism *n.* hysteria, sentimentality, excitement; see EMOTION.
empathy *n.* vicarious emotion, insight, understanding; see PITY.
emperor *n.* monarch, sovereign, dictator; see RULER 1.
emphasis *n.* stress, accent, weight; see IMPORTANCE.
emphasize *v.* make clear, make emphatic, underline, underscore, highlight, dramatize, pronounce, enunciate, articulate, accentuate, accent, stress, point up, point out, strike, call to the attention of, reiterate, repeat, insist, maintain, impress, affirm, indicate, rub in*, pound into one's head*, drum into one's head*, labor the point, make a fuss about.
emphatic *a.* assured, strong, determined, forceful, forcible, earnest, positive, energetic, potent, powerful, dynamic, stressed, pointed, flat, definitive, categorical, dogmatic, explicit.
emphatically *a.* definitely, certainly, of course, undoubtedly, decidely, decisively, absolutely, entirely, flatly, distinctly.—*Ant.* SLOWLY, hesitantly, indistinctly.
empire *n.* union, people, federation; see NATION 1.
employ *v.* **1.** [To make use of] operate, manipulate, apply; see USE 1. **2.** [To obtain services for pay] engage, contract, procure; see HIRE.
employed *a.* working, occupied, busy, laboring, gainfully employed, not out of work, in one's employ, on the job, hired, operating, active, engaged, on duty, on the payroll.—*Ant.* UNEMPLOYED, out of work, jobless.
employee *n.* worker, laborer, servant, domestic, agent, representative, hired hand, salesman, salesperson, assistant, associate, attendant, apprentice, operator, workman, laboring man, workingman, breadwinner, craftsman, wage earner, hireling, lackey, underling, flunky.
employer *n.* owner, manager, proprietor, management, head, director, executive, superintendent, supervisor, president, chief, businessman, manufacturer, corporation, company, boss, front office, big shot*.

employment *n.* job, profession, vocation; see BUSINESS 1, TRADE 2, WORK 2.

emptiness *n.* void, vacuum, vacancy, gap, chasm, blankness, blank, exhaustion, hollowness.

empty *a.* hollow, bare, clear, blank, unfilled, unfurnished, unoccupied, vacated, vacant, void, vacuous, void of, devoid, lacking, wanting, barren, emptied, abandoned, exhausted, depleted, deserted, stark, deprived of, dry, destitute, negative, deflated, evacuated.—*Ant.* FULL, filled, occupied.

empty *v.* **1.** [To become empty] discharge, leave, pour, flow out, ebb, run out, open into, be discharged, void, release, exhaust, leak, drain off, drain, rush out, escape.—*Ant.* ABSORB, flow in, enter. **2.** [To cause to become empty] dump, dip, ladle, tap, void, pour, spill out, let out, deplete, exhaust, deflate, drain, bail out, clean out, clear out, evacuate, eject, expel, draw off, draw out, disgorge, suck dry, drink.—*Ant.* FILL, pack, stuff.

emulate *v.* challenge, contend, imitate; see COMPETE, FOLLOW 2.

enable *v.* make possible, sanction, give power to, give authority to, invest, endow, authorize, allow, let, permit, license; see also APPROVE.

enact *v.* decree, sanction, ordain, order, dictate, make into law, legislate, pass, establish, ratify, vote in, proclaim, vote favorably, determine, authorize, appoint, institute, railroad through*, get the floor, put in force, make laws, put through, constitute, fix, set, formulate.

enactment *n.* edict, decree, statute; see LAW 3.

enamel *n.* lacquer, coating, finish, polish, gloss, top coat, varnish, glaze, veneer.

enamel *v.* lacquer, glaze, gloss, paint, veneer, coat, varnish, finish, paint.

encampment *n.* village, campsite, bivouac; see CAMP 1.

enchant *v.* entrance, entice, allure; see FASCINATE.

enchanted *a.* enraptured, entranced, captivated; see FASCINATED.

encircle *v.* encompass, circle, throw a cordon about; see SURROUND 1.

enclose *v.* insert, jail, corral, impound, confine, blockade, imprison, block off, fence off, set apart, lock up, lock in, keep in, box in, close in, shut in, wall in, box off, box up.—*Ant.* FREE, liberate, open.

enclosed *a.* locked in, penned in, jailed, packed up, wrapped up, shut up, buried, encased, imprisoned.

enclosure *n.* **1.** [A space enclosed] pen, sty, yard, jail, garden, corral, cage, asylum, pound, park, zone, precinct, plot, court, patch, coop, den, cell, dungeon, vault, paddock, stockade, concentration camp, prison; see also BUILDING, PLACE 2, ROOM 2. **2.** [Something inserted] information, check, money, circular, copy, questionnaire, forms, documents, printed matter.

encompass *v.* encircle, compass, gird; see SURROUND 1.

encounter *n.* **1.** [A coming together] interview, rendezvous, appointment; see MEETING 1. **2.** [Physical violence] conflict, clash, collision; see FIGHT 1.

encounter *v.* **1.** [To meet unexpectedly] meet, confront, come across; see FIND. **2.** [To meet in conflict] battle, attack, struggle; see FIGHT.

encourage *v.* cheer, refresh, enliven, exhilarate, inspire, cheer up, praise, restore, revitalize, gladden, fortify, console, ease, relieve, help, aid, comfort, approve, reassure, assist, befriend, uphold, reinforce, back, bolster, brace, further, favor, strengthen, side with, cheer on, back up, egg on, root for*, pat on the back.—*Ant.* RESTRAIN, discourage, caution.

encouraged *a.* inspired, enlivened, renewed, aided, supported, hopeful, confident, enthusiastic, roused, cheered; see also HELPED.—*Ant.* SAD, discouraged, disheartened.

encouragement *n.* aid, faith, help, assistance, support, cheer, confidence, trust, advance, promotion, reward, reassurance, incentive, backing, optimism, comfort, consolation, hope, relief, pat on the back, lift, shot in the arm.

encouraging *a.* bright, good, promising; see HOPEFUL 1, 2.

encyclopedia *n.* book of facts, book of knowledge, compilation, general reference work, encyclopedic reference work, cyclopedia.

encyclopedic *a.* exhaustive, broad, all-encompassing; see COMPREHENSIVE, GENERAL 1, WIDESPREAD.

end *n.* **1.** [Purpose] aim, object, intention; see PURPOSE 1. **2.** [The close of an action] expiration, completion, target date, termination, adjournment, final event, ending, close, finish, conclusion, finis, finale, retirement, accomplishment, attainment, determination, achievement, fulfillment, pay-off, realization, period, consummation, culmination, execution, performance, last line, curtain, terminus, last word*, wrap-up*, windup, cutoff, end of the line*.—*Ant.* ORIGIN, beginning, opening. **3.** [A result] conclusion, effect, outcome; see RESULT. **4.** [The extremity] terminal, termination, terminus, boundary, limit, borderline, point, stub, stump, tail end, edge, tip, top, head, butt end.—*Ant.* CENTER, middle, hub. **5.** [The close of life] demise, passing, doom; see DEATH.

end *v.* **1.** [To bring to a halt] stop, finish, quit, close, halt, shut down, settle, bring to an end, make an end of, break off, break up, put an end to, discontinue, postpone, delay, conclude, interrupt, dispose of, drop, call it a day*, cut short, wind up, get done, call off, give up, wrap up*.—*Ant.* BEGIN, initiate, start. **2.** [To bring to a conclusion] settle, conclude, terminate; see ACHIEVE. **3.** [To come to an end] desist, cease, die; see STOP 2. **4.** [To die] expire, depart, pass away; see DIE. —**keep one's end up*** do one's share, join, participate; see SHARE 1. —**make ends meet** manage, get by, survive; see ENDURE 2. —**no end*** very much, extremely, greatly; see MUCH, VERY. —**on end 1.** [Endless] ceaseless, without interruption, constant; see ENDLESS. **2.** [Upright] erect, vertical, standing up; see STRAIGHT 1. —**put an end to** stop, finish, cease; see END 1.

endanger *v.* imperil, jeopardize, expose to danger, expose to hazard, expose to peril, be careless with, lay open, put on the spot*, leave in the middle.—*Ant.* SAVE, protect, preserve.

endangered *a.* exposed, imperiled, in a dilemma, in a predicament, jeopardized, in danger, in jeopardy, in a bad way*, on thin ice*, hanging by a thread*.

endeavor *n.* effort, try, attempt; see EFFORT.

endeavor *v.* attempt, aim, essay; see TRY 1.

ended *a.* done, completed, concluded; see FINISHED 1.

ending *n.* finish, closing, terminus; see END 2.

endless *a.* infinite, interminable, untold, without end, unbounded, unlimited, immeasurable, limitless, boundless, incalculable, unfathomable.

endorse *v.* **1.** [To inscribe one's name] sign, put one's signature to, put one's signature on, countersign, underwrite, sign one's name on, subscribe, notarize, add one's name to, put one's John Hancock on*, sign on the dotted line*. **2.** [To indicate one's active support of] approve, confirm, sanction, ratify, guarantee, underwrite, support, stand up for, stand behind, be behind, vouch for, uphold, recommend, praise, give one's word for, OK, back up, go to bat for*.—*Ant.* BLAME, censure, condemn.

endorsed *a.* signed, notarized, legalized, ratified, sealed, settled, approved, upheld, supported, recommended, sanctioned, advocated, backed*, OK'd.

endorsement *n.* support, sanction, permission; see SIGNATURE.

endow *v.* enrich, provide, supply; see GIVE 1.

endowment *n.* benefit, provision, bequest, gratuity, grant, pension, stipend, legacy, inheritance, subsidy, revenue, trust, nest egg.

end up *v.* finish, cease, come to a close; see END 1, STOP 2.

endurable *a.* sustainable, tolerable, supportable; see BEARABLE.

endurance *n.* sufferance, fortitude, capacity to endure, long-suffering, resignation, patience, tolerance, courage, perseverance, stamina, restraint, resistance, will, backbone, guts*, spunk*.—*Ant.* WEAKNESS, feebleness, infirmity.

endure *v.* **1.** [To continue] persist, remain, last, continue, exist, be, stay, prevail, wear, sustain, survive, outlast, carry on, live on, go on, hold on, hang on, keep on, linger, outlive, hold out, never say die*, stick to*, ride out.—*Ant.* DIE, cease, end. **2.** [To sustain adversity] suffer, tolerate, bear with, bear up, allow, permit, support, undergo, sit through, take, withstand, bear up under, stand, accustom oneself to, submit to, sustain, go through, get through, encounter, be patient with, keep up, resign oneself, weather, brave, face, put up with, live through, stand for*, swallow, stomach, never say die*, grin and bear it, take it*, brace oneself, like it or lump it*, hang on, keep one's chin up.—*Ant.* AVOID, resist, refuse.

enduring *a.* lasting, abiding, surviving; see PERMANENT.

enemy *n.* foe, rival, assailant, competitor, attacker, antagonist, opponent, adversary, public enemy, criminal, opposition, guerrillas, guerrilla force, fifth column, saboteur, spy, foreign agent, assassin, murderer, betrayer, traitor, terrorist, revolutionary, rebel, invader.—*Ant.* FRIEND, ally, supporter.

energetic *a.* industrious, vigorous, forcible; see ACTIVE.

energy *n.* **1.** [One's internal powers] force, power, virtility; see STRENGTH. **2.** [Power developed or released by a device] horsepower, power, pressure, potential energy, kinetic energy, atomic energy, solar energy, high pressure, foot-pounds, magnetism, friction, voltage, kilowatt-hours, current, electricity, gravity, heat, suction, radioactivity, potential, fuel consumption.

enfold *v.* envelope, encase, enclose; see SURROUND 1, WRAP.

enforce *v.* urge, compel, incite, exert, drive, demand, carry out vigorously, put in force, dictate, exact, require, execute, coerce, oblige, insist upon, emphasize, necessitate, press, impel, make, sanction, force upon, goad, stress, spur, hound, crack down.—*Ant.* ABANDON, neglect, evade.

enforced *a.* compelled, established, exacted, required, executed, pressed, sanctioned, forced upon, kept, dictated, admonished, advocated, charged, meted out, cracked down.

enforcement *n.* requirement, enforcing, prescription, compulsion, constraint, coercion, pressure, duress, obligation, necessity, insistence, carrying out, fulfilling.

engage *v.* **1.** [To hire] employ, contract, retain; see HIRE. **2.** [To engross] absorb, captivate, bewitch; see FASCINATE. **3.** [To enmesh, especially gears] interlock, mesh, interlace; see FASTEN.

engaged *a.* **1.** [Promised in marriage] bound, pledged, betrothed, matched, hooked*.—*Ant.* FREE, unpledged, unbetrothed. **2.** [Not at liberty] working, occupied, employed; see BUSY 1. **3.** [In a profession, business, or the like] employed, practicing, performing, dealing in, doing, interested, absorbed in, pursuing, at work, involved with, engaged with, involved in, engaged in, working at, connected with; see also EMPLOYED.—*Ant.* UNEMPLOYED, out of a job, without connection.

engage in *v.* take part in, attack, undertake; see PERFORM 1.

engagement *n.* **1.** [A predetermined action] meeting, rendezvous, errand; see APPOINTMENT 2. **2.** [The state of being betrothed] contract, promise, match, betrothal, espousal, betrothing.

engine *n.* motor, power plant, dynamo, generator, turbine, diesel engine, traction engine, source of power, diesel.

engineer *n.* **1.** [A professional engineer] surveyor, designer, planner, builder. *Types of engineers include the following:* mining, civil, metallurgical, geological, electrical, architectural, chemical, construction, military, naval, flight, industrial. **2.** [The operator of a locomotive] motorman, brakeman, stoker; see DRIVER.

engineering *n.* design, planning, blueprinting, structure, structures, surveying, metallurgy, architecture, shipbuilding, installations, stresses, communications.

England *n.* Britain, Great Britain, British Isles, United Kingdom, Britannia, member of the British Commonwealth of Nations, Albion, the mother country, John Bull*.

English *a.* British, Britannic, Anglian, Anglican, Anglo-, England's, His Majesty's, Her Majesty's, Commonwealth, anglicized, English-speaking, Norman.

engrave *v.* etch, bite, stipple, lithograph, cut, burn, incise, grave, chisel, crosshatch.

engraved *a.* carved, decorated, etched, scratched, bitten into, embossed, furrowed, incised, deepened, marked deeply, lithographed.

engraving *n.* print, wood engraving, etching, aquatint, graphotype, rotogravure, lithograph, cut, woodcut, illustration, impression, copy, proof.

engross *v.* absorb, busy, fill; see OCCUPY 3.

engulf *v.* swallow up, submerge, inundate; see SINK 2.

enhance *v.* heighten, magnify, amplify; see INCREASE.

enigma *n.* problem, riddle, parable; see PUZZLE 3.

enjoy *v.* **1.** [To get pleasure from] relish, luxuriate in, delight in; see LIKE 1. **2.** [To have the use or benefit of] experience, partake of, share, undergo, make use of, use.

enjoyable *a.* agreeable, welcome, genial; see PLEASANT 1, 2.

enjoyment *n.* satisfaction, gratification, triumph, loving, enjoying, rejoicing, having, using, occupation, use, diversion, entertainment, luxury, sensuality, indulgence, self-indulgence, hedonism.—*Ant.* ABUSE, dislike, displeasure.

enjoy oneself *v.* take pleasure, celebrate, have a good time, revel in, delight in, luxuriate in, be pleased with; see also PLAY 1.

enlarge *v.* **1.** [To increase] expand, spread, swell; see GROW 1. **2.** [To cause to increase] extend, augment, expand; see INCREASE.

enlarged *a.* increased, augmented, expanded, developed, exaggerated, extended, amplified, spread, added to, lengthened, broadened, widened, thickened, magnified, filled-out, inflated, stretched, heightened, intensified, blown up*.

enlargement *n.* **1.** [Growth or extension] augmentation, amplification, expansion; see INCREASE. **2.** [An enlarged photograph] view, enlarged print, blowup; see PHOTOGRAPH, PICTURE 2.

enlighten *v.* inform, divulge, acquaint; see TEACH, TELL 1.

enlightened *a.* instructed, learned, informed; see EDUCATED.

enlightenment *n.* wisdom, culture, education; see KNOWLEDGE 1.

enlist *v.* **1.** [To enroll others] sign up, press into service, hire, retain, call up, recruit, mobilize, induct, register, list, initiate, employ, place, admit, draft, conscribe, muster, call to arms.—*Ant.* REFUSE, neglect, turn away. **2.** [To enroll oneself] enter, sign up, serve; see JOIN 2, REGISTER 4.

enlisted *a.* recruited, commissioned, registered; see ENROLLED.

enlistment *n.* conscription, levy, recruitment; see ENROLLMENT 1, INDUCTION 3.

en masse *a.* bodily, ensemble, together; see TOGETHER 2, UNIFIED.

enmity *n.* animosity, malice, rancor; see HATRED.

enormous *a.* monstrous, immense, huge; see LARGE 1.

enough *a.* **1.** [Sufficient] plenty, abundant, adequate, acceptable, ample, satisfactory, complete, copious, plentiful, satisfying, unlimited, suitable.—*Ant.* INADEQUATE, deficient, insufficient. **2.** [Sufficiently] satisfactorily, amply, abundantly; see ADEQUATELY. **3.** [Fully] quite, rather, just; see VERY. **4.** [Just adequately] tolerably, fairly, barely; see ADEQUATELY.

enough *n.* abundance, sufficiency, adequacy; see PLENTY.
enrage *v.* anger, incite, provoke, irk, bother, annoy, tease, pester, agitate, arouse, stir, goad, bait, inflame, incense, infuriate, madden; see also INCITE.
enrich *v.* adorn, better, decorate; see IMPROVE 1.
enriched *a.* improved, bettered, embellished; see IMPROVED.
enrichment *n.* advancement, promotion, endowment; see IMPROVEMENT 1.
enroll *v.* **1.** [To obtain for service] recruit, obtain, employ; see HIRE. **2.** [To register oneself] enter, sign up, enlist; see JOIN 2, REGISTER 4.
enrolled *a.* joined, inducted, registered, installed, settled, pledged, enlisted, commissioned, employed, recruited, signed up.—*Ant.* SEPARATED, mustered out, discharged.
enrollment *n.* **1.** [The act of enrolling] registering, listing, inducting, recording, enlistment, matriculation, induction, entry, enlisting, selecting, registration. **2.** [The persons enrolled] group, students, student body, conscript, volunteers, number enrolled, response, registration, entrance, subscription.
en route *a.* on the way, in transit, flying, driving, traveling, midway, in passage, on the road, making headway toward, bound, heading toward.—*Ant.* MOTIONLESS, delayed, stalled.
enslave *v.* bind, imprison, incarcerate, shut in, enclose, confine, hold under, hold, subjugate, restrain, oppress, restrict, fetter, coerce, check, subdue, capture, suppress, make a slave of, hold in bondage, compel, chain, jail, deprive, tie, shackle.
enslavement *n.* oppression, subjection, servitude; see SLAVERY 1.
ensnare *v.* entrap, trap, snare; see CATCH 1.
ensure *v.* secure, assure, warrant; see GUARANTEE.
entail *v.* require, necessitate, evoke; see NEED.
entangle *v.* ensnare, entrap, trap, implicate, complicate, involve, snarl, corner, catch, embroil, tangle, ravel, unsettle, foul up*, mess up*, goof up*.—*Ant.* FREE, liberate, disentangle.
entanglement *n.* complexity, intricacy, complication; see DIFFICULTY 1, 2.
enter *v.* invade, set foot in, pass into, come in, drive in, burst in, rush in, go in, break into, get in, barge in, penetrate, intrude, reenter, slip, sneak, infiltrate, insert, move in, fall into*, crowd in, worm oneself into.—*Ant.* LEAVE, depart, exit.
entered *a.* filed, listed, posted; see RECORDED.
enter into *v.* engage in, take part in, become part of; see JOIN 2.
enter on or **upon** *v.* start, take up, make a beginning; see BEGIN 2.
enterprise *n.* undertaking, endeavor, affair; see BUSINESS.
entertain *v.* **1.** [To keep others amused] amuse, cheer, please, interest, enliven, delight, divert, beguile, charm, captivate, inspire, stimulate, satisfy, humor, enthrall, elate, tickle, distract, indulge, flatter, relax, make merry, comfort.—*Ant.* TIRE, bore, weary. **2.** [To act as host or hostess] receive, host, invite, treat, charm, feed, dine, wine, give a party, do the honors, welcome, give a warm reception to, receive with open arms.—*Ant.* NEGLECT, ignore, bore.
entertained *a.* amused, diverted, pleased, occupied, charmed, cheered, interested, relaxed, delighted, engrossed, enjoying oneself, happy, in good humor, in good company.—*Ant.* BORED, depressed, irritated.
entertainer *n.* performer, player, artist; see ACTOR.
entertaining *a.* diverting, amusing, engaging, enchanting, sprightly, lively, witty, clever, interesting, gay, charming, enjoyable, delightful, funny, pleasing, edifying, engrossing, compelling, rousing, cheerful, relaxing, moving, inspiring, captivating, thrilling, entrancing, stirring, poignant, impressive, soul-stirring, stimulating, absorbing, exciting, provocative, fascinating, ravishing, satisfying, seductive; see also FUNNY 1.—*Ant.* BORING, irritating, dull.
entertainment *n.* amusement, enjoyment, merriment, fun, pleasure, sport, recreation, pastime, diversion, relaxation, distraction, play, feast, banquet, picnic, show, television, the movies, treat, game, party, reception, spree.
enthused* *a.* excited, approving, eager; see ENTHUSIASTIC.
enthusiasm *n.* fervor, ardor, eagerness; see ZEAL.
enthusiast *n.* **1.** [A zealous person] zealot, fanatic, partisan; see BELIEVER. **2.** [One who has strong interest in something] hobbyist, supporter, participant; see FOLLOWER.
enthusiastic *a.* interested, fascinated, willing, thrilled, feverish, concerned, passionate, raging, pleased, excited, attracted, exhilarated, anxious, eager, yearning, dying to*, inflamed, absorbed, devoted, diligent, ardent, fiery, longing, desiring, spirited, zestful, fervent, ecstatic, impatient, delighted, enraptured, avid, wild about*, crazy about*, mad about*, hot for*, gung-ho, aching to*.—*Ant.* OPPOSED, reluctant, apathetic.
entice *v.* lure, allure, attract; see FASCINATE.
enticement *n.* lure, bait, promise; see ATTRACTION.
entire *a.* complete, untouched, undamaged; see WHOLE 1, 2.

entirely *a.* **1.** [Completely] totally, fully, wholly; see COMPLETELY. **2.** [Exclusively] uniquely, solely, undividedly; see ONLY 1.
entirety *n.* total, aggregate, sum; see WHOLE.
entitle *v.* authorize, empower, qualify; see ALLOW.
entity *n.* item, article, something; see THING 1.
entourage *n.* retinue, associates, followers; see FOLLOWING.
entrails *n.pl.* viscera, guts, insides; see INTESTINES.
entrance *n.* **1.** [The act of coming in] arrival, entry, passage, approach, induction, initiation, admission, admittance, appearance, introduction, penetration, trespass, debut, enrollment, baptism, invasion, immigration.—*Ant.* ESCAPE, exit, issue. **2.** [The opening that permits entry] gate, door, doorway, vestibule, entry, gateway, portal, port, inlet, opening, passage, staircase, porch, hall, hallway, path, way, entrance, passageway, threshold, lobby, corridor, approach.
entrance *v.* charm, captivate, hypnotize; see FASCINATE.
entrap *v.* catch, ensnare, decoy; see CATCH 1.
entrapment *n.* snare, ambush, ruse; see TRAP 1.
entree *n.* main course, main dish, meat dish; see MEAL.
entrepreneur *n.* capitalist, employer, owner; see BUSINESSMAN.
entrust *v.* deposit with, trust to, leave with; see TRUST 4.
entry *n.* approach, hall, lobby, foyer, door, gate; see also ENTRANCE 2.
enumerate *v.* list, mention, identify; see RECORD 1.
enumeration *n.* inventory, catalog, register; see RECORD 1.
envelop *v.* encompass, contain, hide; see SURROUND 1, WRAP.
envelope *n.* receptacle, pouch, pocket, bag, container, box, covering, case, wrapper, enclosure, cover, sheath, casing.
enviable *a.* welcome, good, superior; see EXCELLENT.
envious *a.* covetous, desirous, resentful, desiring, wishful, longing for, aspiring, greedy, grasping, craving, begrudging, green-eyed, hankering, green with envy; see also JEALOUS.—*Ant.* GENEROUS, trustful, charitable.
environment *n.* conditions, living conditions, circumstances, surroundings, scene, external conditons, background, milieu, setting, habitat, situation.
envoy *n.* emissary, ambassador, intermediary; see AGENT.
envy *n.* jealousy, ill-will, spite, rivalry, opposition, grudge, malice, prejudice, malevolence, covetousness, enviousness, backbiting, maliciousness, the green-eyed monster*.
envy *v.* begrudge, covet, lust after, crave, be envious of, feel ill toward, have hard feelings toward, feel resentful toward, have a grudge against, object to.
eon *n.* eternity, cycle, time; see AGE 3.
epic *a.* heroic, classic, grand; see IMPORTANT 1.
epic *n.* narrative poem, saga, legend; see POEM, STORY.
epidemic *n.* plague, scourge, pestilence; see ILLNESS 1.
epidermis *n.* cuticle, dermis, hide; see SKIN.
episode *n.* happening, occurrence, incident; see EVENT.
epoch *n.* era, period, time; see AGE 3.
equal *a.* even, regular, like, same, identical, similar, uniform, invariable, fair, unvarying, commensurate, just, impartial, unbiased, to the same degree, on a footing with, without distinction, equitable, one and the same, level, parallel, corresponding, equivalent, proportionate, comparable, tantamount.—*Ant.* IRREGULAR, unequal, uneven.
equal *n.* parallel, match, counterpart, complement, peer, fellow, twin, double, likeness, companion, copy, duplicate, rival, competitor, opposite number.
equal *v.* match, equalize, rank with, be the same, rival, equate, approach, live up to, come up to, amount to, consist of, comprise, be composed of, be made of, measure up to, even off, break even, come to, compare, square with, tally with, agree, correspond, be tantamount to, be identical, keep pace with, be commensurate, meet, rise to.
equality *n.* balance, parity, uniformity, sameness, likeness, identity, evenness, equalization, equilibrium, impartiality, fairness, civil rights, equivalence, tolerance, all for one and one for all*, six of one and half a dozen of the other*, even-steven*, fair shake.—*Ant.* INJUSTICE, inequality, unfairness.
equalize *v.* make even, make equal, balance, equate, match, level, adjust, establish equilibrium, even up.
equally *a.* evenly, symmetrically, proportionately, coordinately, equivalently, on a level, both, either ... or, impartially, justly, fairly, across the board, on even terms, as well as, the same for one as for another.
equal to *a.* adequate, capable, qualified; see ABLE.
equate *v.* **1.** [To equalize] make equal, average, balance; see EQUALIZE. **2.** [To compare] match, link, relate; see COMPARE 1.
equation *n.* mathematical statement, formal statement of equivalence, chemical statement. *Kinds of equations include the following:* linear, quadratic, conic, cubic, balanced, unbalanced.
equator *n.* middle, circumference of the earth, tropics; see JUNGLE.

equatorial *a.* tropical, mediterranean, central; see HOT 1.
equilibrium *n.* stability, center of gravity, steadiness; see BALANCE 2.
equip *v.* furnish, outfit, supply; see PROVIDE 1.
equipment *n.* material, materiel, tools, facilities, implements, utensils, apparatus, furnishings, appliances, paraphernalia, belongings, devices, outfit, accessories, attachments, extras, conveniences, articles, tackle, rig, machinery, fittings, trappings, fixtures, contraptions, supplies, accompaniments, gear, fixings, stuff, gadgets, things; see also MACHINE, PART 3.
equipped *a.* outfitted, furnished, supplied, rigged up, fitted out, arrayed, dressed, accoutered, assembled, readied, provided, implemented, decked, bedecked, appareled, completed, supplemented, set up.
equitable *a.* impartial, just, moral; see FAIR 1.
equity *n.* investment, money, capital; see PROPERTY 1.
equivalent *a.* commensurate, comparable, similar; see EQUAL.
era *n.* epoch, period, date; see AGE 3, TIME 2.
eradicate *v.* eliminate, exterminate, annihilate; see DESTROY.
eradication *n.* extermination, annihilation, elimination; see DESTRUCTION 1.
erase *v.* delete, expunge, omit, obliterate, cut, clean, nullify, eradicate; see also CANCEL.
erect *a.* upright, vertical, perpendicular; see STRAIGHT 1.
erect *v.* construct, raise, fabricate; see BUILD.
erected *a.* constructed, completed, raised; see BUILT.
erection *n.* building, erecting, constructing; see CONSTRUCTION 2.
erode *v.* decay, corrode, consume; see DISINTEGRATE.
erosion *n.* wearing away, decrease, carrying away; see DESTRUCTION 1, 2.
erotic *a.* amorous, stimulating, carnal; see SENSUAL 1, 2.
err *v.* misjudge, blunder, be mistaken; see FAIL 1.
errand *n.* mission, task, commission; see DUTY 2.
erratic *a.* **1.** [Wandering] nomadic, rambling, roving; see WANDERING 1. **2.** [Strange] eccentric, queer, irregular; see UNUSUAL 2. **3.** [Variable] inconsistent, unpredictable, variable; see IRREGULAR 1.
erring *a.* mistaken, faulty, blundering; see WRONG 1.
erroneous *a.* untrue, inaccurate, incorrect; see FALSE 2.
error *n.* blunder, mistake, fault, oversight, inaccuracy, omission, deviation, misdoing, faux pas, fall, slip, wrong, lapse, miss, failure, slight, misunderstanding, flaw, boner*, bad job, blooper*, muff, boo-boo*, botch.
ersatz *a.* artificial, synthetic, imitation; see FALSE 3.
erupt *v.* go off, eject, emit; see EXPLODE.
eruption *n.* burst, outburst, flow; see EXPLOSION.
escalate *v.* heighten, intensify, make worse; see INCREASE.
escalation *n.* intensification, growth, acceleration; see INCREASE, RISE 2.
escapade *n.* caper, adventure, prank; see JOKE.
escape *n.* flight, retreat, disappearance, evasion, avoidance, leave, departure, withdrawal, liberation, deliverance, desertion, abdication, break, rescue, freedom, release.—*Ant.* IMPRISONMENT, retention, bondage.
escape *v.* flee, fly, leave, depart, elude, avoid, evade, shun, run off, run away, make off, disappear, vanish, steal off, steal away, flow out, get away, break out, wriggle out, break away, desert, slip away, elope, run out*, go scot-free, take flight, duck out*, get clear of, break loose, cut and run, worm out of, clear out*, bail out*, crawl out of, save one's neck, scram*, make a break*.—*Ant.* RETURN, come back, remain.
escaped *a.* out, at liberty, liberated; see FREE 2.
escort *n.* guide, attend, guard; see COMPANION.
escort *v.* go with, attend, take out*; see ACCOMPANY, DATE 2.
esophagus *n.* gullet, food tube, neck; see THROAT.
especially *a.* **1.** [To an unusual degree] particularly, unusually, abnormally, extraordinarily, uncommonly, peculiarly, unexpectedly, pre-eminently, eminently, supremely, remarkably, strangely, curiously, notably, uniquely, singularly, to a marked degree, above all. **2.** [For one more than for others] chiefly, mainly, primarily; see PRINCIPALLY.
espionage *n.* undercover work, reconnaissance, spying; see INFORMATION 1.
espouse *v.* advocate, adopt, uphold; see SUPPORT 2.
essay *n.* dissertation, treatise, article; see WRITING 2.
essence *n.* **1.** [Basic material] pith, core, kernel, spirit, gist, root, nature, basis, being, essential quality, reality, constitution, substance, nucleus, vital part, base, quintessence, primary element, germ, heart, marrow, backbone, soul, bottom, life, grain, structure, principle, character, fundamentals. **2.** [Distinctive quality] principle, nature, essential quality; see CHARACTERISTIC.
essential *a.* **1.** [Necessary] imperative, required, indispensable; see NECESSARY. **2.**

[Rooted in the basis or essence] basic, primary, quintessential; see FUNDAMENTAL.

essentially *a.* basically, fundamentally, radically, at bottom, at heart, centrally, originally, intimately, chiefly, naturally, inherently, permanently, necessarily, primarily, significantly, importantly, at the heart of, in effect, in essence, materially, in the main, at first, characteristically, intrinsically, substantially, typically, approximately, precisely, exactly, actually, truly, really; see also PRINCIPALLY.

establish *v.* **1.** [To set up in a formal manner] institute, found, authorize; see ORGANIZE 2. **2.** [To work or settle in a permanent place] build up, set up, install, build, erect, plant, root, place, settle, practice, live, stay, start.—*Ant.* LEAVE, break up, depart. **3.** [To prove] verify, authenticate, confirm; see PROVE. **4.** [To make secure] fix, secure, stabilize; see FASTEN.

established *a.* **1.** [Set up to endure] endowed, founded, organized, instituted, set up, originated, chartered, incorporated, settled, begun, initiated, realized, codified, produced, completed, finished; see also FINISHED 1, CERTAIN.—*Ant.* TEMPORARY, unsound, insolvent. **2.** [Conclusively proved] approved, verified, guaranteed, endorsed, demonstrated, determined, confirmed, substantiated, assured, concluded, authenticated, ascertained, achieved, upheld, certain, validated, identified, proved, undeniable.—*Ant.* FALSE, invalidated, untrue.

establishing *n.* verifying, demonstrating, confirming; see PROOF 1.

establishment *n.* **1.** [A business, organization, or the like] company, corporation, enterprise; see BUSINESS 4. **2.** [The act of proving] verification, substantiation, demonstration; see PROOF 1.

estate *n.* property, bequest, inheritance, fortune, endowment, wealth, legacy, heritage, belongings, effects, earthly possessions, personal property, private property.

esteem *n.* regard, respect, appreciation; see ADMIRATION.

esteem *v.* prize, respect, appreciate; see ADMIRE.

esthetic *a.* creative, appreciative, sensitive; see ARTISTIC, BEAUTIFUL.

estimate *n.* evaluation, assessment, valuation, guess, appraisal, estimation, calculation, gauging, rating, survey, measure, reckoning; see also JUDGMENT 2.

estimate *v.* rate, value, measure, calculate, appraise, assess, account, compute, evaluate, count, number, reckon, guess, expect, judge, figure, plan, outline, run over, rank, furnish an estimate, set a value on, set a figure, appraise, assay, consider, predict, suppose, suspect, reason, think through, surmise, determine, decide, budget.

estimated *a.* supposed, approximated, guessed at; see LIKELY 1.

estimation *n.* opinion, appraisal, valuation; see JUDGMENT 2.

et cetera (etc.) *a.* and so forth, and so on, and others; see AND.

etching *n.* print, cut, work of art; see ENGRAVING.

eternal *a.* endless, interminable, continual, unbroken, continuous, continued, unceasing, ceaseless, constant, unending, incessant, relentless, undying, enduring, persistent, always, uninterrupted, everlasting, perpetual, indestructible, unconquerable, never-ending, indefinite, permanent, ageless, boundless, timeless, immortal, forever, indeterminable, immeasurable, having no limit, imperishable, to one's dying day, for ever and ever*.—*Ant.* TEMPORARY, finite, ending.

eternally *a.* endlessly, continually, perpetually; see REGULARLY.

eternity *n.* endlessness, forever, infinite, duration, timelessness, world without end, the future, infinity, all eternity, other world, after life, life after death, for ever and ever*.—*Ant.* INSTANT, moment, second.

ethical *a.* humane, moral, respectable; see DECENT 2, HONEST, NOBLE 1, 2.

ethics *n.* conduct, morality, mores, decency, integrity, moral conduct, social values, moral code, principles, right and wrong, natural law, honesty, goodness, honor, social laws, human nature, the Golden Rule.

etiquette *n.* conduct, manners, social graces; see BEHAVIOR.

Eucharist *n.* sacrament, host, communion; see SACRAMENT.

eulogize *v.* laud, extol, applaud; see PRAISE 1.

eulogy *n.* tribute, glorification, commendation; see PRAISE 2.

euphoria *n.* joy, delight, glee; see HAPPINESS.

Europe *n.* the Continent, continental Europe, Old World, Motherland. *Terms associated with countries, areas, and political divisions in Europe include the following:* western, northern, southern, central, eastern, etc. Europe; the Mediterranean world, the Low Countries, Balkan states, Adriatic states, Baltic states, Slavic countries, Scandinavian peninsula, Holy Roman Empire, Hellenic peninsula, Albania, Austria, Belgium, Andorra, Bulgaria, Crete, Czechoslovakia, Denmark, Norway, Sweden, Iceland, Finland, Lapland, France, Provence, Normandy, Brittany, Gascony, Germany, West Germany, East Germany, Prussia, Bavaria, Greece, Hungary, Republic of Ireland, Eire, Ulster, Italy, San Marino, Sardinia, Corsica, Sicily, Liechtenstein, Luxembourg, Malta, Monaco, the Netherlands, Holland, Poland, Portugal, Romania, Spain, Gibraltar, Switzerland, Turkey, Union of Soviet Socialist

Republics, USSR, Russia, the Ukraine, Crimea, Armenia, Moldavia, Byelorussia, Lithuania, Latvia, Estonia, Georgia, United Kingdom of Great Britain and Northern Ireland, England, Britain, Scotland, Wales, the British Isles, the Vatican, Vatican City, Yugoslavia, Serbia, Croatia, Montenegro; see also ENGLAND, FRANCE, GERMANY, ITALY.

European *a.* Continental, Old Country, Old World, Eurasian, Indo-European, West European, East European. *Terms associated with particular areas include the following:* Anglo-Saxon, British, English, Irish, Scottish, Scots, Welsh, Cornish, French, Norman, Gallic, German, Germanic, Dutch, Belgian, Flemish, Low German, Saxon, Bavarian, Prussian, Gothic, Teutonic, Nordic, Scandinavian, Danish, Swedish, Norwegian, Icelandic, Swiss, Greek, Hellenic, Athenian, Corinthian, Spartan, Peloponnesian, Mycenean, Cretan, Thracian, Ionian, Slovak, Romanian, Bulgarian, Slavic, Slav, Aegean, Balkan, Adriatic, Yugoslavian, Serbian, Croatian, Austrian, Hungarian, Czechoslovakian, Czech, Bohemian, Turk, Turkish, Russian, Polish, Baltic, Latvian, Lithuanian, Ukranian, Finnish, Lap, Italian, Latin, Corsican, Roman, Venetian, Florentine, Neapolitan, Sicilian, Maltese, Sardinian, Tyrolese, Apennine, Spanish, Hispanic, Iberian, Portuguese, Catalan, Basque, Majorcan, Castilian, Andalusian, Jewish, Yiddish; see also ENGLISH, GERMAN, GREEK, ITALIAN, ROMAN, SPANISH.

European *n. Terms associated with Europeans from particular areas include the following:* Englishman, Briton, Scotsman, Scot, Highlander, Welshman, Irishman, Celt, Anglo-Saxon, Frenchman, Norman, Basque, German, Teuton, Prussian, Bavarian, Saxon, Swiss, Dutchman, Hollander, Belgian, Scandinavian, Dane, Norwegian, Swede, Norseman, Icelander, Finn, Lapp, Italian, Roman, Sicilian, Venetian, Florentine, Spaniard, Castilian, Andalusian, Portuguese, Austrian, Hungarian, Czechoslovakian, Czech, Bohemian, Slovak, Slav, Russian, Pole, Lithuanian, Latvian, Estonian, Ukrainian, White Russian, Yugoslavian, Bulgarian, Romanian, Balkan, Greek, Turk, Jew, Gypsy; see also EUROPEAN, *a.*, FRENCH, GERMAN, GREEK.

evacuate *v.* **1.** [To empty] void, exhaust, deplete; see REMOVE 1. **2.** [To abandon] vacate, desert, leave; see ABANDON 1.

evacuation *n.* **1.** [Removal] draining, depletion, exhaustion; see REMOVAL. **2.** [Withdrawal] abandonment, removal, retreat; see DEPARTURE.

evade *v.* lie, prevaricate, dodge, shun, put off, avoid, elude, trick, baffle, quibble, shift, mystify, cloak, cover, conceal, deceive, screen, veil, hide, drop the subject, pretend, confuse, dodge the issue, beat around the bush, give someone the run-around*, throw off the scent*, lead on a merry chase, pass up, put off, get around, lie out of; see also AVOID.—*Ant.* EXPLAIN, make clear, elucidate.

evaluate *v.* appraise, judge, assess; see DECIDE, ESTIMATE.

evangelical *a.* pious, fervent, spiritual; see RELIGIOUS 2.

evangelist *n.* preacher, missionary, revivalist; see MINISTER 1.

evangelize *v.* proselytize, instruct, convert; see PREACH.

evaporate *v.* diffuse, vanish, fade, dissolve, dissipate, steam, steam away, boil away, fume, distill, turn to steam, rise in a mist.

evaporation *n.* drying, dehydration, vanishing, steaming away, boiling away, vaporization, distillation, dissipation, disappearance, vanishing into thin air.

evasion *n.* quibble, subterfuge, equivocation; see LIE, TRICK 1.

evasive *a.* elusory, fugitive, shifty; see SLY.

eve *n.* evening before, night preceding, evening; see NIGHT 1.

even *a.* **1.** [Lying in a smooth plane] smooth, level, surfaced; see FLAT 1. **2.** [Similar] uniform, unbroken, homogeneous; see ALIKE, REGULAR 3. **3.** [Equal] commensurate, coterminous, equivalent; see EQUAL. **4.** [In addition] also, too, as well; see AND. —**break even** make nothing, tie, neither win nor lose; see BALANCE 2.

evening *n.* twilight, dusk, late afternoon; see NIGHT 1.

evenly *a.* **1.** [On an even plane] smoothly, regularly, without bumps, without lumps, uniformly, placidly, unvaryingly, steadily, constantly, fluently, on an even keel, without variation, neither up nor down. **2.** [Equally proportioned or distributed] exactly, justly, fairly, precisely, equally, impartially, identically, equitably, symmetrically, proportionately, synonymously, analogously, correspondingly, tied, alike, fifty-fifty*, squarely*.—*Ant.* WRONGLY, unfairly.

evenness *n.* smoothness, similarity, likeness; see REGULARITY.

event *n.* occurrence, happening, episode, incident, circumstance, affair, phenomenon, development, function, transaction, experience, appearance, turn, tide, shift, phase, accident, chance, pass, situation, story, case, matter, occasion, catastrophe, mishap, mistake, experience, parade, triumph, coincidence, miracle, adventure, holiday, wonder, marvel, celebration, crisis, predicament, misfortune, situation, calamity, emergency, something to write home about*; see also DISASTER, HOLIDAY, WONDER 2. —**in any event** anyway, no matter what happens, however; see ANYHOW. —**in the event of** (or **that**) in case of, if it should happen that, if there should happen to be; see IF.

eventful *a.* momentous, memorable, signal; see IMPORTANT 1.

eventual *a.* inevitable, ultimate, consequent; see LAST 1.

eventually *a.* in the end, at last, ultimately; see FINALLY 2.

ever *a.* eternally, always, at all times; see REGULARLY. —**for ever and a day*** always, for ever and ever, perpetually; see FOREVER.

evergreen *n.* coniferous tree, ornamental shrub, fir; see PINE, TREE.

everlasting *a.* permanent, unending, perpetual; see ETERNAL.

every *a.* each one, all, without exception; see EACH 1.

everybody *n.* each one, every one, all, the public, old and young; men, women, and children; the people, the populace, the voters; the buying public, the voting public; generality, anybody, all sorts, the masses, the man in the street*, you and I; see also MAN 1.—*Ant.* NOBODY, no one, not a one.

everyday *a.* commonplace, normal, plain; see COMMON 1.

every day *a.* always, all the time, frequently; see REGULARLY.

every now and then or **every so often*** *a.* sometimes, occasionally, once in a while; see FREQUENTLY.

everyone *pron.* all, each person, whoever; see EVERYBODY.

everything *pron.* all, all things, the universe, the whole complex, the whole, many things, all that, every little thing, the whole kit and kaboodle*; lock, stock, and barrel; the works, the lot.

everywhere *a.* everyplace, here and there, at all points, wherever one turns, at each point, without exception, universally, at all times and places; here, there and everywhere; in every direction, on all hands, all over the place, throughout, to the four winds*, in all creation*, to hell and back*, inside and out*, from beginning to end*, high and low, all around, the world over.

evict *v.* remove, expel, oust; see DISMISS.

eviction *n.* ouster, ejection, dispossession; see REMOVAL.

evidence *n.* testimony, data, confirmation; see PROOF 1. —**in evidence** evident, visible, manifest; see OBVIOUS 1, 2.

evident *a.* apparent, visible, manifest; see OBVIOUS 1.

evidently *a.* seemingly, obviously, so far as one can see; see APPARENTLY.

evil *a.* immoral, sinful, corrupt; see BAD.

evil *n.* 1. [The quality of being evil] sin, wickedness, depravity, crime, sinfulness, corruption, vice, immorality, iniquity, perversity, badness, vileness, baseness, meanness, malevolence, indecency, hatred, viciousness, wrong, debauchery, lewdness, wantonness, grossness, foulness, degradation, obscenity.—*Ant.* VIRTUE, good, goodness. **2.** [A harmful or malicious action] ill, harm, mischief, misfortune, scandal, calamity, pollution, contamination, catastrophe, blow, disaster, plague, outrage, foul play, ill wind*, crying shame*, double cross*, raw deal*.

evildoer *n.* malefactor, sinner, wrongdoer; see CRIMINAL.

evoke *v.* summon forth, call out, invoke; see SUMMON.

evolution *n.* growth, unfolding, natural process; see DEVELOPMENT.

evolve *v.* result, unfold, emerge; see DEVELOP 3, GROW 2.

exact *a.* **1.** [Accurate] precise, correct, perfect; see ACCURATE 2, DEFINITE 1. **2.** [Clear] sharp, distinct, clear-cut; see DEFINITE 2.

exacting *a.* precise, careful, critical; see DIFFICULT 1, 2.

exactly *a.* precisely, specifically, correctly; see DETAILED.

exactness *n.* precision, nicety, scrupulousness; see ACCURACY.

exaggerate *v.* overestimate, overstate, misrepresent, falsify, magnify, expand, amplify, pile up, heighten, intensify, distort, enlarge on, stretch, overdo, misquote, go to extremes, give color to, misjudge, elaborate, romance, embroider, color, make too much of, lie, fabricate, corrupt, paint in glowing colors*, carry too far*, lay it on thick*, make a mountain out of a molehill, cook up*, build up, make much of, make the most of.—*Ant.* UNDERESTIMATE, tell the truth, minimize.

exaggerated *a.* colored, magnified, overwrought, extravagant, preposterous, impossible, fabulous, sensational, spectacular, melodramatic, out of proportion, fantastic, high-flown, farfetched, false, distorted, fabricated, strained, artificial, glaring, pronounced, unrealistic, whopping*, too much.—*Ant.* ACCURATE, exact, precise.

exaggeration *n.* overestimation, misrepresentation, extravagance, elaboration, coloring, flight of fancy, fantasy, fancy, stretch of the imagination, figure of speech, yarn, making a mountain out of a molehill, tall story*, whopper*.—*Ant.* TRUTH, accuracy, understatement.

exalt *v.* commend, glorify, laud; see PRAISE 1.

exaltation *n.* rapture, elation, rhapsody; see HAPPINESS.

examination *n.* **1.** [The act of seeking evidence] search, research, survey, scrutiny, investigation, inquiry into, inspection, observation, checking, exploration, analysis, audit, study, questioning, testing program, inquest, test, trial, cross-examination, third degree*. **2.** [A formal test] experiment, review, questionnaire, battery, quiz, exam, make-up*, midterm*, final, blue book, orals, writtens*; see also TEST. **3.** [A medical checkup] checkup, physical examination, physical; see TEST.

examine *v.* 1. [To inspect with care] inspect, analyze, criticize, scrutinize, investigate, go into, inquire into, scan, probe, sift, explore, reconnoiter, audit, take stock of, take note of, make an inventory of, consider, canvass, find out, search out, review, assay, check, check out, check up on, re-examine, go back over, concentrate on, give one's attention to, look at, look into, look over, conduct research on, run checks on, put to the test, sound out, feel out, subject to scrutiny, peer into, look into, pry into, hold up to the light, finger, pick over, sample, experiment with, give the once-over*, size up*, smell around, see about, see into, poke into, nose around, look up and down, go over with a fine-toothed comb*, dig into*. 2. [To test] question, interrogate, cross-examine; see TEST.

examined *a.* checked, tested, inspected; see INVESTIGATED.

examiner *n.* tester, questioner, observer; see INSPECTOR.

example *n.* 1. [A representative] illustration, representation, warning, sample, citation, case in point, concrete example, case, prototype, archetype, stereotype, original, copy, instance, quotation. 2. [Something to be imitated] standard, pattern, sample; see MODEL 2. **—set an example** instruct, behave as a model, set a pattern; see TEACH.

excavate *v.* shovel, empty, hollow out; see DIG 1.

excavation *n.* cavity, hollow, pit; see HOLE 1, TUNNEL.

exceed *v.* excel, outdo, overdo, outdistance, pass, outrun, beat, get the better of, go beyond, surpass, transcend, eclipse, rise above, pass over, run circles around*, get the edge on*, excel in, have it all over someone*, get the drop on*, beat to the draw*, break the record*, have the best of, have the jump on*, be ahead of the game, have the advantage, gain the upper hand.

exceedingly *a.* greatly, remarkably, in a marked degree; see VERY.

excel *v.* surpass, transcend, improve upon; see EXCEED.

excellence *n.* superiority, worth, distinction; see PERFECTION.

excellent *a.* first-class, premium, choice, first, choicest, prime, high, picked, the best obtainable, select, exquisite, high-grade, very fine, finest, good, desirable, admirable, distinctive, attractive, great, highest, superior, exceptional, superb, striking, supreme, unique, custom-made, incomparable, surprising, transcendent, priceless, rare, invaluable, highest priced, magnificent, wonderful, skillfull, above par, superlative, worthy, refined, well-done, cultivated, to be desired, competent, skilled, notable, first-rate, terrific*, sensational*, sharp*, groovy*, all right, A-1*, grade A*, classy*, top-notch*, cream*, tops*.—*Ant.* POOR, inferior, imperfect.

excellently *a.* perfectly, exquisitely, splendidly; see WELL 2.

except *prep.* excepting, excluding, rejecting, omitting, barring, save, but, with the exception of, other than, if not, not for, without, outside of, aside from, leaving out, exempting, minus.

except *v.* exclude, reject, leave out; see BAR 1.

exception *n.* exclusion, omission, making an exception of, rejection, barring, reservation, leaving out, segregation, limitation, exemption, elimination, expulsion, excusing. **—take exception (to)** 1. [To differ] object, disagree, demur; see DIFFER 1. 2. [To dislike] resent, be offended, take offense; see DISLIKE.

exceptional *a.* uncommon, extraordinary, rare; see UNUSUAL 1, 2.

exceptionally *a.* unusually, particularly, abnormally; see ESPECIALLY 1.

excerpt *n.* selection, extract, citation; see QUOTATION.

excess *n.* 1. [More than is needed] profusion, abundance, surplus, remainder, too much, too many, exorbitance, waste, wastefulness, luxuriance, lavishness, over-supply, plenty, bellyful*, too much of a good thing*.—*Ant.* LACK, dearth, deficiency. 2. [Conduct that is not temperate] prodigality, dissipation, intemperance; see GREED, WASTE 1. **—in excess of** additional, surplus, more than; see EXTRA. **—to excess** too much, excessively, extravagantly; see EXTREME.

excessive *a.* immoderate, extravagant, exorbitant; see EXTREME.

excessively *a.* extravagantly, extremely, unreasonably; see VERY.

exchange *n.* 1. [The act of replacing one thing with another] transfer, substitute, replacement, change, rearrangement, shift, revision, sleight-of-hand, reciprocity, barter, correspondence, interdependence, buying and selling, negotiation, transaction, commerce, trade, give and take. 2. [A substitution] change, shift, swap*, trade, interchange, replacing, shuffle, reciprocation, replacement, switch.

exchange *v.* 1. [To replace one thing with another] substitute, transfer, replace, go over to, give in exchange, remove, pass to, reverse, provide a replacement, shuffle, shift, revise, rearrange, change, interchange, transact, reset, change hands, borrow from Peter to pay Paul, swap*. 2. [To give and receive reciprocally] reciprocate, barter, trade with, buy and sell, deal with, do business with, correspond, swap*.

exchanged *a.* restored, traded, brought back; see RETURNED.

excitable *a.* sensitive, high-strung, impatient; see NERVOUS.

excite *v.* stimulate, inflame, arouse, anger, delight, move, tease, worry, infuriate, madden, stir up, fire up, work up, goad, taunt, mock, provoke, incite, astound, amaze, annoy, jolt, fan the flames, carry away, warm, irritate, offend, bother.

excited *a.* aroused, stimulated, inflamed, agitated, hot, annoyed, seething, wrought up, frantic, flushed, overwrought, restless, feverish, apprehensive, roused, disturbed, perturbed, flustered, upset, angry, tense, discomposed, embarrassed, hurt, angered, distracted, distraught, edgy, furious, beside oneself, delighted, eager, enthusiastic, frenzied, troubled, ruffled, moved, avid, hysterical, passionate, provoked, quickened, inspired, wild, nervous, animated, ill at ease, jumpy, jittery*, turned on*, hyped up*, hopped up*, worked up*, in a tizzy*, up tight*, all nerves*, blue in the face*, on fire*.—*Ant.* CALM, reserved, self-confident.

excitedly *a.* tensely, apprehensively, hysterically; see EXCITED.

excitement *n.* confusion, disturbance, tumult, enthusiasm, rage, turmoil, stir, excitation, agitation, movement, feeling, exhilaration, emotion, stimulation, drama, melodrama, activity, commotion, fuss*, hullabaloo, bother, dither, hubbub, bustle, to-do*.—*Ant.* PEACE, calm, quiet.

exciting *a.* stimulating, moving, animating, provocative, arousing, arresting, stirring, thrilling, dangerous, breathtaking, overwhelming, interesting, new, mysterious, overpowering, inspiring, impressive, soul-stirring, sensational, astonishing, bracing, appealing, bloodcurdling, racy, hair-raising*, mindblowing*.—*Ant.* DULL, pacifying, tranquilizing.

exclaim *v.* cry out, call out, burst out, assert, shout, call aloud, say loudly; see also YELL.

exclamation *n.* yell, clamor, vociferation; see CRY 1.

exclude *v.* shut out, reject, ban; see BAR 1, 2.

exclusion *n.* keeping out, rejection, elimination, prohibition, nonadmission, omission, segregation, isolation, blockade, repudiation, separation, eviction, dismissal, suspension, refusal, expulsion, barring.—*Ant.* WELCOME, invitation, inclusion.

exclusive *a.* restricted, restrictive, fashionable, aristocratic, preferential, privileged, particular, licensed, select, private, segregated, prohibitive, clannish, independent, swank*.—*Ant.* FREE, inclusive, unrestricted.

exclusively *a.* particularly, solely, completely; see ONLY 1.

excommunicate *v.* expel, curse, oust; see DISMISS.

excommunication *n.* expulsion, dismissal, suspension; see REMOVAL.

excrement *n.* excretion, stool, fecal matter, offal, droppings, discharge, dung, manure, urine, effluvium, feces, sweat, perspiration, excreta, poop*.

excrete *v.* remove, eliminate, eject, defecate, urinate, discharge, secrete, go to the bathroom, go to the toilet, answer a call of nature, pass, expel, exude, perspire, sweat, squeeze out, give off, dump*, poop*.

excretion *n.* eliminating, elimination, urinating, discharging, secreting, secretion, defecation, ejecting, ejection, passing off.

excruciating *a.* torturing, intense, agonizing; see PAINFUL 1.

excursion *n.* jaunt, ramble, tour; see JOURNEY.

excusable *a.* pardonable, forgivable, understandable, justifiable, reasonable, defensible, permissible, trivial, passable, slight, plausible, allowable, explainable, not excessive, not fatal, not too bad, not inexcusable, not injurious, moderate, temperate, all right, fair, within limits, OK.

excuse *n.* apology, reason, defense; see EXPLANATION. **—a poor excuse for** inferior, poor, unsatisfactory; see INADEQUATE. **—make one's excuses** regret, apologize, offer an explanation; see APOLOGIZE, EXPLAIN.

excuse *v.* pardon, forgive, justify, discharge, vindicate, apologize for, release from, dispense with, free, set free, overlook, purge, exempt from, rationalize, acquit, condone, appease, reprieve, absolve, exonerate, clear of, give absolution to, pass over, give as an excuse, make excuses for, make allowances for, make apologies for, grant amnesty to, provide with an alibi for, plead ignorance of, whitewash, let off easy, let go scot-free, wink at*, wipe the slate clean, shrug off, take the rap for*.

excused *a.* forgiven, freed, permitted; see PARDONED.

excuse me *interj.* pardon me, forgive me, begging your pardon, I'm sorry.

execute *v.* **1.** [To carry out instructions] act, do, effect; see PERFORM 1. **2.** [To put to death] electrocute, hang, behead; see KILL 1.

executed *a.* **1.** [Performed] completed, done, carried out; see FINISHED 1. **2.** [Formally put to death] killed, hanged, electrocuted, gassed, shot at sunrise, sent before a firing squad, beheaded, guillotined, crucified, sent to the chair*, fried*, cooked*.

execution *n.* punishment, capital punishment, killing, electrocution, hanging, gassing, beheading, decapitation, guillotining, crucifixion, martyrdom.

executive *a.* administrative, governing, ruling; see MANAGING.

executive *n.* businessman, president, vice-president, secretary, treasurer, supervisor, chairman, dean, head, chief, superintendent, bureaucrat, leader, governor, controller, organizer, commander, director, boss, big shot, official, manager; see also BUSINESSMAN, LEADER 2.

exemplify *v.* illustrate, give an example, represent; see EXPLAIN.

exempt *a.* freed, cleared, liberated, privileged, excused, absolved, not subject to, released from, not responsible to, not responsible for, set apart, excluded, released, not liable, unrestrained, unbound, uncontrolled, unrestricted, freed from, not restricted by, not restricted to, outside.—*Ant.* RESPONSIBLE, liable, subject.

exempt *v.* free, liberate, pass by; see EXCUSE.

exemption *n.* exception, immunity, privilege; see FREEDOM.

exercise *n.* **1.** [Action undertaken for training] practice, exertion, drill, drilling, gymnastics, sports, calisthenics, workout. **2.** [The means by which training is promoted] performance, action, activity; see ACTION. **3.** [Use] application, employment, operation; see USE 1.

exercise *v.* **1.** [To move the body] stretch, bend, pull, tug, hike, work, promote muscle tone, labor, strain, loosen up, discipline, drill, execute, perform exercises, practice, take a walk, work out, limber up, warm up; see also TRAIN 1. **2.** [To use] employ, practice, exert, apply, operate, execute, sharpen, handle, utilize, devote, put in practice; see also USE 1. **3.** [To train] drill, discipline, give training to; see TEACH, TRAIN 1.

exert *v.* put forth, bring to bear, exercise; see USE 1.

exertion *n.* struggle, attempt, endeavor; see EFFORT.

exert oneself *v.* strive, attempt, endeavor; see TRY 1.

exhalation *n.* emanation, vapor, air; see BREATH.

exhaust *v.* **1.** [To consume strength] debilitate, tire, wear out, wear down; see also WEAKEN 1, 2, WEARY 1, 2. **2.** [To use entirely] use up, take the last of, deplete; see WEAR 3.

exhausted *a.* **1.** [Without further physical resources] debilitated, wearied, worn; see TIRED, WEAK 1. **2.** [Having nothing remaining] all gone, consumed, used; see EMPTY.

exhaustion *n.* weariness, fatigue, depletion; see FATIGUE.

exhibit *n.* show, performance, presentation; see DISPLAY.

exhibit *v.* show, present, manifest; see DISPLAY.

exhibited *a.* shown, presented, advertised; see SHOWN 1.

exhibition *n.* exposition, fair, carnival; see SHOW 1.

exile *n.* **1.** [Banishment] expulsion, deportation, expatriation, ostracism, displacement, separation. **2.** [An outcast] fugitive, outlaw, man without a country; see REFUGEE.

exile *v.* ostracize, outlaw, cast out; see BANISH.

exist *v.* **1.** [To have being] breathe, live, survive; see BE 1. **2.** [To carry on life] be alive, endure, go on; see SURVIVE 1.

existence *n.* **1.** [The carrying on of life] being, actuality, reality; see LIFE 1. **2.** [The state of being] presence, actuality, permanence; see REALITY.

existing *a.* for the time being, temporary, just now; see PRESENT 1.

exit *n.* **1.** [A means of egress] way out, outlet, opening; see DOOR. **2.** [The act of leaving] going, farewell, exodus; see DEPARTURE.

exorbitant *a.* excessive, extravagant, too much; see WASTEFUL.

exotic *a.* **1.** [Foreign] imported, not native, extrinsic; see FOREIGN. **2.** [Peculiar] strange, fascinating, different; see FOREIGN, UNUSUAL 2.

expand *v.* extend, augment, dilate; see GROW 1.

expanse *n.* breadth, width, length, extent, reach, stretch, distance, area, belt, space, field, territory, span, spread, room, scope, range, compass, sphere, margin, sweep, radius, wilderness, region, immensity.

expansion *n.* enlargement, augmentation, extension; see INCREASE.

expatriate *n.* exile, emigrant, outcast; see REFUGEE.

expatriate *v.* exile, ostracize, deport; see BANISH.

expect *v.* **1.** [To anticipate] await, look for, look forward to, count on, plan on, assume, suppose, lean on, feel it in one's bones*, wait for, hope for; see also ANTICIPATE. **2.** [To require] demand, insist upon, exact; see REQUIRE 2. **3.** [To assume] presume, suppose, suspect; see ASSUME.

expectancy *n.* hope, prospect, likelihood; see ANTICIPATION.

expectant *a.* **1.** [Characterized by anticipation] expecting, hoping, hopeful, waiting, awaiting, in anticipation, watchful, vigilant, eager, ready, prepared, in suspense, gaping, wide-eyed, on edge, itching.—*Ant.* INDIFFERENT, UNPREPARED, nonchalant. **2.** [Anticipating birth] pregnant, parturient, expecting; see PREGNANT.

expectation *n.* hope, belief, prospect; see ANTICIPATION.

expected *a.* looked for, counted upon, contemplated, looked forward to, hoped for, relied upon, forseen, predictable, predetermined, foretold, prophesied, planned for, prepared for, budgeted, within normal expectations, in the works, in the cards, coming up, in the bag*; see also LIKELY.

expecting *a.* expectant, due, about to become a mother; see PREGNANT.

expediency *n.* advantageousness, efficiency, profitableness; see USEFULNESS.

expedient *a.* profitable, useful, convenient; see PRACTICAL.

expedition *n.* **1.** [Travel undertaken] excursion, voyage, campaign; see JOURNEY. **2.** [That which undertakes travel] party, hunters, explorers, pioneers, traders, soldiers, scouts, archaeologist, tourists, sightseers, caravan, posse; see also CROWD.

expel *v.* **1.** [To eject] get rid of, cast out, dislodge; see EJECT. **2.** [To dismiss] suspend, discharge, oust; see DISMISS.

expend *v.* pay out, write checks for, lay out; see SPEND.

expenditure *n.* outgo, investment, payment; see EXPENSE.

expense *n.* expenditure, responsibility, obligation, loan, mortgage, lien, debt, liability, investment, insurance, upkeep, alimony, debit, account, cost, price, outlay, charge, payment, outgo, value, worth, sum, amount, risk, capital, rate, tax, carrying charges, budgeted items, cost of materials, overhead, time, payroll, investment.—*Ant.* PROFIT, income, receipts. **—at the expense of** paid by, at the cost of, charged to; see OWED.

expenses *n.pl.* expenses, living expenses, costs, lodging, room and board, incidentals, carrying charge.

expensive *a.* dear, precious, valuable, invaluable, rare, high-priced, costly, prized, choice, rich, priceless, high, too high, unreasonable, exorbitant, extravagant, at a premium, out of sight*, at great cost, sky-high, steep*, stiff*.—*Ant.* CHEAP, inexpensive, low.

experience *n.* background, skill, knowledge, wisdom, practice, maturity, judgment, practical knowledge, sense, patience, caution, know-how*; see also BACKGROUND 2.

experience *v.* undergo, feel, live through; see ENDURE 2, FEEL 2.

experienced *a.* skilled, practiced, instructed, accomplished, versed, qualified, able, skillful, knowing, trained, wise, expert, veteran, mature, with a good background, rounded, knowing the score*, knowing the ropes*, having all the answers, having been around*, having been through the mill*, broken in*.—*Ant.* NEW, apprentice, beginning.

experiment *n.* analysis, essay, examination, trial, inspection, search, organized observation, research, scrutiny, speculation, check, proof, operation, test, exercise, quiz, investigation.

experiment *v.* analyze, investigate, probe, search, venture, explore, test, rehearse, try out, sample, subject to discipline, prove, conduct an experiment, research, study, examine, scrutinize, weigh, play around with, fool with*.

experimental *a.* tentative, trial, temporary, test, provisional, preliminary, preparatory, under probation, on approval, on trial, pending verification, momentary, primary, beginning, laboratory, in its first stage.—*Ant.* PERMANENT, tried, tested.

expert *a.* skillful, practiced, proficient; see ABLE.

expert *n.* graduate, master, trained personnel; see SPECIALIST.

expiration *n.* close, closing, finish; see END 2.

expire *v.* stop, finish, quit; see END 1.

explain *v.* interpret, explicate, account for, elucidate, illustrate, clarify, illuminate, make clear, describe, expound, teach, reveal, point out, demonstrate, tell, read, translate, paraphrase, put in other words, define, justify, untangle, unravel, make plain, come to the point, put across, throw light upon, comment on, remark upon, remark on, offer an explanation of, resolve, clear up, get right, set right, put someone on the right track, spell out, go into detail, get to the bottom of, figure out, cast light upon, get across, get through, bring out, work out, solve, put in plain English*.—*Ant.* CONFUSE, puzzle, confound.

explainable *a.* explicable, accountable, intelligible; see UNDERSTANDABLE.

explained *a.* made clear, interpreted, elucidated; see KNOWN 2, OBVIOUS 2.

explanation *n.* information, answer, account, reason, illustration, description, comment, justification, narrative, story, tale, footnote, anecdote, example, analysis, criticism, exegesis, key, commentary, note, summary, report, brief, the details, budget, breakdown; see also PROOF 1.

explanatory *a.* expository, illustrative, informative, allegorical, interpretative, instructive, guiding, descriptive, analytical, graphic, critical.

explicit *a.* express, sure, plain; see DEFINITE 1, UNDERSTANDABLE.

explode *v.* blow up, blow out, blow a fuse, break out, erupt, go off, detonate, discharge, backfire, shatter, fracture, split, collapse, blow off, blast, blow to smithereens*.

exploit *n.* deed, venture, escapade; see ACHIEVEMENT.

exploit *v.* utilize, take advantage of, employ; see USE 1.

exploited *a.* taken advantage of, utilized, worked; see USED.

exploration *n.* investigation, research, search; see EXAMINATION 1.

explore *v.* search, investigate, seek; see EXAMINE.

explorer *n.* adventurer, traveler, pioneer, wayfarer, pilgrim, voyager, space traveler, astronaut, cosmonaut, deep-sea diver, seafarer, mountaineer, mountain climber, scientist, navigator, colonist.

explosion *n.* detonation, blast, burst, discharge, blowout, blowup, eruption, combustion, outburst, firing, ignition, backfire.

explosive *a.* stormy, fiery, forceful, raging, wild, violent, uncontrollable, vehement, sharp, hysterical, frenzied, savage.—*Ant.* MILD, gentle, uneventful.

explosive *n.* mine, gunpowder, ammunition, TNT, plastic, dynamite, nitroglycerine, bomb, missile, grenade, charge, shell, Molotov cocktail; see also AMMUNITION, WEAPON.

export *n.* shipping, trading, overseas shipment, commodity, international trade, foreign trade.

export *v.* send out, sell abroad, trade abroad, ship, transport, consign, dump*.

expose *v.* **1.** [To uncover] disclose, smoke out, show up, present, prove, reveal, air, exhibit, unmask, lay open, lay bare, bring to light, open, dig up, give away, bring into view, unfold, let the cat out of the bag, drag through the mud, put the finger on*. **2.** [To endeavor to attract attention] show, show off, bare; see DISPLAY. **3.** [To open to danger] lay open to, subject to, imperil; see ENDANGER.

exposed *a.* disclosed, defined, revealed, divulged, made public, laid bare, dug up, brought to light, solved, resolved, discovered, found out, see through.—*Ant.* HIDDEN, concealed, disguised.

exposition *n.* **1.** [The process of making clear] elucidation, delineation, explication; see EXPLANATION. **2.** [A popular exhibition] exhibit, showing, performance; see DISPLAY.

ex post facto *a.* subsequently, retroactively, retrospectively; see FINALLY 2.

exposure *n.* disclosure, betrayal, display, exhibition, publication, showing, revelation, confession, unveiling, acknowledgment, exposé, giveaway*, bombshell, stink*.—*Ant.* SECRECY, protection, concealment.

express *a.* **1.** [Explicit] definite, specific, exact; see DEFINITE 1. **2.** [Nonstop] fast, direct, high-speed; see FAST 1.

express *v.* declare, tell, signify; see UTTER.

expression *n.* **1.** [Significant appearance] look, cast, character; see LOOKS. **2.** [Putting into understandable form] representation, art product, utterance, narration, interpretation, invention, creation, declaration, commentary, diagnosis, definition, explanation, illustration; see also COMPOSITION, WRITING 1. **3.** [A traditional form of speech] locution, idiom, speech pattern; see PHRASE, WORD 1. **4.** [Facial cast] grimace, smile, smirk, mug, sneer, pout, grin; see also SMILE.

expressionless *a.* wooden, dull, vacuous; see BLANK.

expressive *a.* eloquent, demonstrative, revealing, indicative, representative, dramatic, stirring, sympathetic, articulate, touching, significant, meaningful, pathetic, spirited, emphatic, strong, forcible, energetic, lively, tender, passionate, warm, colorful, vivid, picturesque, brilliant, stimulating.—*Ant.* INDIFFERENT, impassive, dead.

express oneself *v.* communicate, declare, enunciate; see UTTER.

expulsion *n.* ejection, suspension, purge; see REMOVAL.

exquisite *a.* fine, scrupulous, precise; see DAINTY.

extemporaneous *a.* spontaneous, impromptu, unprepared; see AUTOMATIC, IMMEDIATE, IMMEDIATELY.

extend *v.* **1.** [To make larger] lengthen, enlarge, prolong; see INCREASE. **2.** [To occupy space to a given point] continue, go as far as, spread; see REACH 1.

extended *a.* **1.** [Outspread] spread, widespread, expansive; see WIDESPREAD. **2.** [Very long] elongated, drawn-out, lengthened; see LONG 1.

extending *a.* reaching, continuing, continual, perpetual, ranging, stretching, spreading, spanning, going on, running to, drawn out to, lengthening; see also ENDLESS.

extension *n.* section, branch, additional telephone; see ADDITION 2.

extensive *a.* wide, broad, long; see LARGE 1.

extensively *a.* widely, broadly, greatly; see WIDELY.

extent *n.* degree, limit, span, space, area, measure, size, bulk, length, compass, scope, reach, weep, wideness, width, range, amount, expanse, magnitude, intensity; see also EXPANSE.

exterior *a.* outer, outlying, outermost; see OUTSIDE.

exterior *n.* surface, covering, visible portion; see OUTSIDE 1.

exterminate *v.* annihilate, eradicate, abolish; see DESTROY.

external *a.* surface, visible, open to the air; see OBVIOUS 1.

extinct *a.* dead, ended, terminated, exterminated, deceased, lost, unknown, no longer known.

extinction *n.* abolition, extermination, extirpation; see DESTRUCTION 1, MURDER.

extinguish *v.* smother, choke, quench, douse, put out, snuff out, drown out, blow out, stifle, suffocate.

extort *v.* extract, wrench, force; see STEAL.

extortion *n.* fraud, stealing, blackmail; see THEFT.

extortionist *n.* thief, blackmailer, oppressor; see CRIMINAL.

extra *a.* additional, in addition, other, one more, spare, reserve, supplemental, increased, another, new, auxiliary, added, adjunct, besides, also, further, more, beyond, over and above, plus, supplementary, accessory, unused.—*Ant.* LESS, short, subtracted.

extract *n.* distillation, infusion, concentration; see ESSENCE 1.

extract *v.* evoke, derive, secure; see OBTAIN 1.

extradite *v.* obtain, apprehend, bring to justice; see ARREST.

extraordinarily *a.* remarkably, notably, peculiarly; see VERY.

extraordinary *a.* remarkable, curious, amazing; see UNUSUAL 1.

extravagance *n.* lavishness, expenditures, improvidence; see WASTE 1.

extravagant *a.* lavish, prodigal, immoderate; see WASTEFUL.

extravagantly *a.* expensively, beyond one's means, without restraint; see RASHLY, WASTEFULLY.

extreme *a.* radical, intemperate, immoderate, imprudent, excessive, inordinate, extravagant, flagrant, outrageous, unreasonable, irrational, improper, preposterous, thorough, far, fanatical, desperate, severe, intense, drastic, sheer, total, advanced, violent, sharp, acute, unseemly, beyond control, fantastic, to the extreme, absurd, foolish, monstrous, exaggerated.—*Ant.* RESTRAINED, cautious, moderate.

extreme *n.* height, apogee, apex; see END 4, LIMIT 2. —**go to extremes** be excessive, overreact, act rashly; see EXCEED. —**in the extreme** extremely, to the highest degree, inordinately; see MUCH.

extremely *a.* greatly, remarkably, notably; see MUCH.

extremist *n.* zealot, fanatic, die-hard; see RADICAL.

exuberance *n.* fervor, eagerness, exhilaration; see ZEAL.

exuberant *a.* ardent, vivacious, passionate; see ZEALOUS.

eye *n.* **1.** [The organ of sight] instrument of vision, compound eye, simple eye, naked eye, optic, orb, peeper*, lamp*. *Parts of the eye include the following:* eyeball, pupil, retina, iris, cornea, eye muscles, optic nerve, white, lens. **2.** [Appreciation] perception, taste, discrimination; see TASTE 1, 3. **3.** [A center] focus, core, heart; see CENTER 1. —**private eye*** detective, investigator, gumshoe*; see POLICEMAN. —**all eyes*** attentive, aware, perceptive; see OBSERVANT. —**an eye for an eye** punishment, retaliation, vengeance; see REVENGE 1. —**catch one's eye** attract one's attention, cause notice, stand out; see FASCINATE. —**easy on the eyes*** attractive, appealing, pleasant to look at; see BEAUTIFUL. —**give a person the eye*** attract, charm, invite; see SEDUCE. —**have an eye for** appreciate, be interested in, desire; see WANT 1. —**have an eye to** watch out for, be mindful of, attend to; see WATCH OUT. —**have eyes for*** appreciate, be interested in, desire; see WANT 1. —**in a pig's eye*** under no circumstances, impossible, no way; see NEVER. —**in the public eye** well-known, renowned, celebrated; see FAMOUS. —**keep an eye on** look after, watch over, protect; see GUARD. —**keep an eye out for** watch for, be mindful of, attend to; see WATCH OUT. —**keep one's eyes open** (or **peeled**) be aware, be watchful, look out; see WATCH. —**lay eyes on** look at, stare, survey; see SEE 1. —**make eyes at** attract, charm, invite; see SEDUCE. —**open one's eyes** make aware, inform, apprise; see TELL 1. —**shut one's eyes to** refuse, reject, ignore; see REFUSE. —**with an eye to** considering, mindful of, aware of; see OBSERVANT.

eyesight *n.* vision, sense of seeing, visual perception; see SIGHT 1.

eyesore *n.* ugly thing, distortion, deformity; see UGLINESS.

eyewitness *n.* onlooker, passerby, observer; see WITNESS.

F

fable *n.* allegory, tale, parable; see STORY.

fabled *a.* mythical, legendary, unreal; see LEGENDARY.

fabric *n.* textile, stuff, material; see GOODS.

fabricate *v.* **1.** [To construct] erect, make, form; see BUILD, MANUFACTURE. **2.** [To misrepresent] make up, contrive, prevaricate; see LIE 1.

fabulous *a.* remarkable, amazing, immense; see UNUSUAL 1.

façade *n.* face, appearance, look; see FRONT 3.

face *n.* **1.** [The front of the head] visage, countenance, appearance, features, silhouette, profile, front, mug*. **2.** [A plane surface] front, surface, finish; see PLANE 1. **3.** [Prestige] status, standing, social position; see REPUTATION 2. **—make a face** distort one's face, grimace, scowl; see FROWN. **—on the face of it** to all appearances, seemingly, according to the evidence; see APPARENTLY. **—pull (or wear) a long face*** look sad, scowl, pout; see FROWN. **—show one's face** be seen, show up, come; see APPEAR 1. **—to one's face** candidly, openly, frankly; see BOLDLY 1.

face *v.* **1.** [To confront conflict or trouble] confront, oppose, defy, meet, dare, brave, challenge, withstand, encounter, risk, tolerate, endure, sustain, suffer, bear, tell to one's face, make a stand, meet face to face, cope with, allow, stand, submit, abide, go up against, swallow, stomach, take, take it.—*Ant.* EVADE, elude, shun. **2.** [To put a face on a building] refinish, front, redecorate; see COVER 1, PAINT 2. **3.** [To look out on] front, border, be turned toward; see LIE 2.

facet *n.* aspect, face, side; see PLANE 1.

facetious *a.* humorous, whimsical, ridiculous; see FUNNY 1.

face to face *a.* eye to eye, cheek by jowl, facing; see OPPOSITE 3.

facile *a.* simple, obvious, apparent; see EASY 2.

facilitate *v.* promote, aid, make easy; see HELP.

facility *n.* **1.** [Material means; *usually plural*] tools, plant, buildings; see EQUIPMENT. **2.** [Administrative agency] department, bureau, company; see OFFICE 3.

facsimile *n.* duplicate, reproduction, mirror; see COPY.

fact *n.* **1.** [A reliable generality] certainty, truth, appearance, experience, matter, the very thing, not an illusion, what has really happened, something concrete, what is the case, matter of fact, hard evidence, actuality, naked truth, gospel, reality, law, basis, state of being, hard facts*.—*Ant.* FANCY, fiction, imagination. **2.** [An individual reality] circumstance, detail, factor, case, evidence, event, action, deed, happening, occurrence, creation, conception, manifestation, being, entity, experience, affair, episode, performance, proceeding, phenomenon, incident, thing done, act, plain fact, accomplishment, accomplished fact, *fait accompli* (French).—*Ant.* error, illusion, untruth. **—as a matter of fact** in reality, in fact, actually; see REALLY 1.

faction *n.* cabal, combine, party, conspiracy, plot, gang, crew, wing, block, junta, clique, splinter group, set, clan, club, lobby, camp, inner circle, sect, coterie, partnership, cell, unit, mob, side, machine, band, team, knot, circle, concern, guild, schism, outfit, crowd*, bunch*.

factor *n.* portion, constituent, determinant; see PART 1, 3.

factory *n.* manufactory, plant, shop, industry, workshop, machine shop, mill, laboratory, assembly plant, foundry, forge, loom, mint, carpenter shop, brewery, sawmill, supply house, warehouse, processing plant, works, workroom, firm, packing plant.

facts *n.pl.* reality, certainty, information; see FACT 1.

factual *a.* exact, specific, descriptive; see ACCURATE 1.

faculty *n.* **1.** [A peculiar aptitude] peculiarity, strength, forte; see ABILITY. **2.** [A group of specialists, usually engaged in instruction or research] staff, teachers, research workers, personnel, instructors, university, college, institute, teaching staff, research staff, teaching assistants, professorate, society, body, organization, mentors, professors, assistant professors, associate professors, docents, tutors, foundation, department, pedagogues, lecturers, advisors, masters, scholars, fellows, profs*.

fad *n.* fancy, style, craze, fashion, humor, fit, prank, quirk, kink, eccentricity, popular innovation, vogue, fantasy, whimsy, passing fancy, latest word, all the rage, the latest thing, the last word*; see also FASHION 2.—*Ant.* CUSTOM, convention, practice.

fade *v.* **1.** [To lose color or light] bleach, tone down, wash out, blanch, tarnish, dim, discolor, pale, grow dim, neutralize, become dull, lose brightness, lose luster, lose color.—*Ant.* COLOR, brighten, glow. **2.** [To diminish in sound] hush, quiet, sink; see DECREASE 1.

faded *a.* used, bleached, shopworn; see DULL 2.

fail *v.* 1. [To be unsuccessful] fall short, miss, back out, abandon, desert, neglect, slip, lose ground, come to naught, come to nothing, falter, flounder, blunder, break down, get into trouble, abort, fault, come down, fall flat, go amiss, go astray, fall down, get left, be found lacking, go down, go under, not hold a candle to, fold up, go on the rocks, not have it in one, miss the boat*, not measure up, lose out, give out, fall short of, not make the grade*, miss the mark, lose control, fall down on the job, go wrong, be out of it, blow it*, fizzle out*, hit rock bottom, go up in smoke, bomb*, not get to first base*, get hung up*, get bogged down*, flunk out*, flop*, conk out*, peter out*.—*Ant.* WIN, succeed, triumph. 2. [To prove unsatisfactory] lose out, come short of, displease; see DISAPPOINT. 3. [To grow less] lessen, worsen, sink; see DECREASE 1. 4. [To become insolvent] go bankrupt, go out of business, go broke*; see sense 1. —**without fail** constantly, dependably, reliably; see REGULARLY.

failing *a.* declining, feeble, faint; see WEAK 1.

failure *n.* 1. [An unsuccessful attempt] fiasco, misadventure, abortion, bankruptcy, miscarriage, frustration, misstep, faux pas, breakdown, checkmate, stoppage, collapse, defeat, overthrow, downfall, total loss, stalemate, flop*, bust*, dud*, washout*, sinking ship*, mess.—*Ant.* SUCCESS, accomplishment, triumph. 2. [An unsuccessful person] incompetent, underachiever, bankrupt, derelict, dropout, loser*, lemon*, bum*, dud*.—*Ant.* SUCCESS, winner, star.

faint *a.* 1. [Having little physical strength] shaky, faltering, dizzy; see WEAK 1. 2. [Having little light or color] vague, thin, hazy; see DULL 2. 3. [Having little volume of sound] whispered, breathless, murmuring, inaudible, indistinct, low, stifled, dull, hoarse, soft, heard in the distance, quiet, low-pitched, muffled, hushed, distant, subdued, gentle, softened, from afar, deep, rumbling, far-off, out of earshot.—*Ant.* LOUD, audible, raucous.

faint *v.* lose consciousness, become unconscious, fall, go into a coma, drop, collapse, succumb, pass out, go out like a light*, keel over*, black out.—*Ant.* RECOVER, awaken, come to.

fainthearted *a.* irresolute, halfhearted, weak; see WEAK 3, COWARDLY.

fair *a.* 1. [Just] forthright, impartial, plain, scrupulous, upright, candid, generous, frank, open, sincere, straightforward, honest, lawful, clean, legitimate, decent, honorable, virtuous, righteous, temperate, unbiased, reasonable, civil, courteous, blameless, uncorrupted, square, equitable, fair-minded, dispassionate, uncolored, objective, unprejudiced, evenhanded, good, principled, moderate, praiseworthy, aboveboard, trustworthy, due, fit, appropriate, on the level*, on the up-and-up*, fair and square*, straight*.—*Ant.* UNFAIR, unjust, biased. 2. [Moderately satisfactory] average, pretty good, not bad, up to standard, ordinary, mediocre, usual, common, all right, commonplace, fair to middling*, so-so, OK; see also COMMON 1.—*Ant.* POOR, bad, unsatisfactory. 3. [Not stormy or likely to storm] clear, pleasant, sunny, bright, calm, placid, tranquil, favorable, balmy, mild.—*Ant.* STORMY, threatening, overcast. 4. [Of light complexion] blond, light-colored, light-complexioned, pale, white, bleached, white-skinned, flaxen, fair-haired, snow-white, snowy, whitish, light, lily-white, faded, neutral, platinum blond, peroxide blond, bleached blond*, pale-faced, white as a sheet, white as a ghost.—*Ant.* DARK, brunet, black.

fair *n.* exposition, county fair, state fair, world's fair, carnival, bazaar, exhibition, display, festival, market, exchange, centennial, observance, celebration.

fairground *n.* enclosure, coliseum, race track, racecourse, exhibition place, fairway, concourse, rink, midway, exposition.

fairly *a.* 1. [In a just manner] honestly, reasonably, honorably; see JUSTLY 1. 2. [A qualifying word] somewhat, moderately, reasonably; see ADEQUATELY.

fairness *n.* decency, honesty, uprightness, truth, integrity, charity, impartiality, justice, tolerance, honor, moderation, consideration, good faith, decorum, propriety, courtesy, reasonableness, rationality, humanity, equity, justness, goodness, measure for measure, give-and-take, fair-mindedness, open-mindedness, just dealing, good sense, fair treatment, even-handed justice, due, accuracy, scrupulousness, correctness, virtue, duty, dutifulness, legality, rightfulness, lawfulness, square deal*, fair play, fair shake*.—*Ant.* INJUSTICE, unfairness, partiality.

fairy *n.* spirit, sprite, good fairy, elf, goblin, hobgoblin, nymph, pixy, mermaid, siren, bogie, genie, imp, enchantress, witch, warlock, banshee, werewolf, ogre, demon, succubus, devil, ghoul, harpy, poltergeist, troll, gnome, leprechaun, satyr, fiend, Fate, Weird Sister.

fairy tale *n.* folk tale, children's story, romance; see STORY.

faith *n.* 1. [Complete trust] confidence, trust, credence, credit, assurance, acceptance, troth, dependence, conviction, sureness, fidelity, loyalty, certainty, allegiance, reliance.—*Ant.* DOUBT, suspicion, distrust. 2. [A formal system of beliefs] creed, doctrine, dogma, tenet, revelation, credo, gospel, profession, conviction, canon, principle, church, worship, teaching, theology, denomination, cult, sect. —**bad faith** insincerity, duplicity, infidelity; see DISHONESTY. —**break faith** be disloyal, abandon, fail; see DECEIVE. —**good faith** sincerity, honor, trustworthiness; see HONESTY. —**in faith** indeed, in fact, in reality; see REALLY 1. —**keep faith** be loyal, adhere, follow; see SUPPORT 2.

faithful *a.* reliable, genuine, dependable, incorruptible, straight, honest, upright, honorable, scrupulous, firm, sure, unswerving, conscientious, enduring, unchanging, steady, staunch, attached, obedient, steadfast, sincere, resolute, on the level*, devoted, true, dutiful; see also LOYAL.—*Ant.* FALSE, fickle, faithless.

faithfully *a.* trustingly, conscientiously, truly; see LOYALLY.

faithfulness *n.* trustworthiness, care, duty; see DEVOTION.

fake *a.* pretended, fraudulent, bogus; see FALSE 3.

fake *n.* deception, counterfeit, sham, copy, cheat, imitation, charlatan, fraud, make-believe, pretense, fabrication, forgery, cheat, humbug, trick, swindle, phony*, gyp*, put-on*, flimflam.—*Ant.* FACT, original, reality.

fake *v.* feign, simulate, disguise; see PRETEND 1.

fall *n.* **1.** [The act of falling] drop, decline, lapse, collapse, breakdown, tumble, spill, downfall, overthrow, defeat, degradation, humiliation, descent, plunge, slump, recession, ebb.—*Ant.* RISE, elevation, ascent. **2.** [That which falls] rainfall, snowfall, precipitation; see RAIN 1, SNOW. **3.** [The season after summer] autumn, the fall of the year, harvest, September, October, November, harvest time. —**ride for a fall** endanger oneself, take chances, act indiscreetly; see RISK.

fall *v.* **1.** [To pass quickly downward] sink, topple, drop, settle, droop, stumble, trip, plunge, tumble, descend, totter, break down, cave in, make a forced landing, decline, subside, collapse, drop down, pitch, be precipitated, fall down, fall flat, fall in, fold up, keel over, tip over, slip, recede, ebb, diminish, flop.—*Ant.* RISE, ascend, climb. **2.** [To be overthrown] submit, yield, surrender, succumb, be destroyed, be taken, bend, defer to, obey, resign, capitulate, back down, fall to pieces, break up.—*Ant.* ENDURE, prevail, resist. —**fall in love (with)** lose one's heart, take a fancy to, take a liking to, become attached to, become fond of; see also FALL IN LOVE.

fallacy *n.* inconsistency, quibbling, evasion, fallacious reasoning, illogical reasoning, mistake, deceit, deception, subterfuge, inexactness, perversion, bias, prejudice, preconception, ambiguity, paradox, miscalculation, quirk, flaw, irrelevancy, erratum, heresy; see also ERROR.—*Ant.* LAW, theory, reason.

fall asleep *v.* go to sleep, doze, drop off*; see SLEEP.

fallen *a.* sinful, shamed, shameless; see CORRUPT.

fall for* *v.* become infatuated with, desire, flip over*; see FALL IN LOVE.

fallibility *n.* imperfection, misjudgment, frailty; see UNCERTAINTY 2.

fallible *a.* deceptive, frail, imperfect, ignorant, uncertain, erring, unpredictable, unreliable, in question, prone to error, untrustworthy, questionable; see also WRONG 2.

fall in *v.* get into line, form ranks, take a place; see LINE UP.

falling *a.* dropping, sinking, descending, plunging, slipping, sliding, declining, settling, toppling, tumbling, tottering, diminishing, weakening, decreasing, ebbing, subsiding, collapsing, crumbling, dying.—*Ant.* INCREASING, improving, mounting.

fall in love *v.* become enamoured, lose one's heart, take a fancy to, have eyes for, take a liking to, become attached to, become fond of, fancy.

fall off *v.* decline, lessen, wane; see DECREASE 1.

fall out *v.* argue, disagree, fight; see QUARREL.

fallow *a.* unplowed, unplanted, unproductive; see VACANT 2.

fall short *v.* fail, be deficient, be lacking; see NEED.

false *a.* **1.** [*Said of persons*] faithless, treacherous, unfaithful, disloyal, dishonest, lying, foul, hypocritical, double-dealing, malevolent, mean, malicious, deceitful, underhanded, corrupt, wicked, unscrupulous, untrustworthy, dishonorable, two-faced.—*Ant.* FAITHFUL, true, honorable. **2.** [*Said of statements or supposed facts*] untrue, spurious, fanciful, lying, untruthful, fictitious, deceptive, fallacious, incorrect, misleading, delusive, imaginary, illusive, erroneous, invalid, inaccurate, deceiving, misrepresentative, fraudulent, trumped up.—*Ant.* ACCURATE, correct, established. **3.** [*Said of things*] sham, counterfeit, fabricated, manufactured, synthetic, bogus, spurious, make-believe, assumed, unreal, copied, forged, pretended, faked, made-up, simulated, pseudo, hollow, mock, feigned, bastard, alloyed, artificial, contrived, colored, disguised, deceptive, adulterated, so-called, fake, phony*, shoddy, not what it's cracked up to be*.—*Ant.* REAL, genuine, authentic.

falsehood *n.* deception, prevarication, story; see LIE.

falsely *a.* traitorously, treacherously, deceitfully, foully, faithlessly, behind one's back, disloyally, underhandedly, maliciously, malevolently, unfaithfully, dishonestly, unscrupulously, dishonorably.—*Ant.* TRULY, justly, honorably.

falsify *v.* adulterate, counterfeit, misrepresent; see DECEIVE.

falter *v.* waver, fluctuate, be undecided; see HESITATE.

fame *n.* renown, glory, distinction, eminence, honor, celebrity, esteem, name, estimation, public esteem, credit, note, greatness, dignity, rank, splendor, position, standing, preeminence, superiority, regard, character, station, place, degree, popularity.

familiar *a.* everyday, well-known, customary, frequent, homely, humble, usual, intimate, habitual, accustomed, common, ordinary, informal, unceremonious, plain, simple, matter-of-fact, workaday, prosaic, commonplace, homespun, natural, native, unsophisticated, old hat*, garden-variety.—*Ant.* UNUSUAL, exotic, strange.

familiarity *n.* **1.** [Acquaintance with people] friendliness, acquaintanceship, fellowship; see FRIENDSHIP. **2.** [Acquaintance with things] the feel of, being at home with, comprehension; see AWARENESS, EXPERIENCE.

familiarize (oneself with) *v.* acquaint, accustom, habituate, make the acquaintance of, get acquainted with, gain the friendship of, make friends with, awaken to, come to know, become aware of.

familiar with *a.* well-acquainted with, acquainted with, aware of, informed of, on speaking terms with, having some connections with, cognizant of, attuned to.—*Ant.* UNAWARE, UNKNOWN, unacquainted.

family *n.* kin, folk, clan, relationship, relations, tribe, dynasty, breed, house, kith and kin, blood, blood tie, progeny, offspring, descendants, forebears, heirs, race, ancestry, pedigree, genealogy, descent, parentage, extraction, paternity, inheritance, kinship, lineage, line, one's own flesh and blood, strain, siblings, in-laws, people.

famine *n.* starvation, want, misery; see HUNGER.

famished *a.* starving, hungering, starved; see HUNGRY.

famous *a.* eminent, foremost, famed, preeminent, acclaimed, illustrious, celebrated, noted, conspicuous, far-famed, prominent, honored, reputable, renowned, recognized, notable, important, well-known, of note, notorious, exalted, remarkable, extraordinary, great, powerful, noble, grand, mighty, imposing, towering, influential, leading, noteworthy, talked of, outstanding, distinguished, excellent, memorable, elevated, in the spotlight, in the limelight.—*Ant.* UNKNOWN, obscure, humble.

fan *n.* **1.** [An instrument for creating currents of air] ventilator, agitator, blower, forced draft, vane, air conditioner, propeller, electric fan, Japanese fan, windmill. **2.** [*Supporter] follower, enthusiast, devotee; see FOLLOWER.

fanatic *n.* devotee, bigot, enthusiast; see ZEALOT.

fanatical *a.* obsessed, passionate, devoted; see ZEALOUS.

fanaticism *n.* bigotry, intolerance, obsession, prejudice, hatred, superstition, narrow-mindedness, injustice, obstinacy, stubbornness, bias, unfairness, partiality, devotion, violence, immoderation, zeal, willfulness, single-mindedness, infatuation, dogma, arbitrariness, unruliness, enthusiasm, frenzy, passion, rage.—*Ant.* INDIFFERENCE, tolerance, moderation.

fanciful *a.* unreal, incredible, whimsical; see FANTASTIC.

fancy *a.* elegant, embellished, rich, adorned, ostentatious, gaudy, showy, intricate, baroque, lavish; see also ELABORATE, ORNATE.

fancy *n.* **1.** [The mind at play] whimsy, frolic, caprice, banter, sport, diversion, whim, notion, quip, prank, wit, buffoonery, fooling, facetiousness, merriment, levity, humor. **2.** [The product of a playful mind] whim, notion, impulse; see IDEA. **3.** [Inclination] wishes, will, preference; see DESIRE 1.

fang *n.* tusk, prong, venom, duct; see also TOOTH.

fantastic *a.* whimsical, capricious, extravagant, freakish, strange, odd, queer, quaint, peculiar, outlandish, farfetched, wonderful, comical, humorous, foreign, exotic, extreme, ludicrous, ridiculous, preposterous, grotesque, frenzied, absurd, vague, hallucinatory, high-flown, affected, artificial, out of sight*.—*Ant.* COMMON, conventional, routine.

fantasy *n.* vision, appearance, illusion, flight, figment, fiction, romance, mirage, nightmare, fairyland.

far *a.* **1.** [Distant from the speaker] removed, faraway, remote; see DISTANT. **2.** [To a considerable degree] extremely, incomparably, notably; see VERY. **—by far** very much, considerably, to a great degree; see MUCH 1, VERY. **—few and far between** scarce, sparse, in short supply; see RARE 2. **—(in) so far as** to the extent that, in spite of, within limits; see CONSIDERING. **—so far** thus far, until now, up to this point; see NOW 1. **—so far, so good** all right, favorable, going well; see SUCCESSFUL.

farce *n.* travesty, burlesque, horseplay; see FUN.

fare *n.* **1.** [A fee paid, usually for transportation] ticket, charge, passage, passage money, toll, tariff, expenses, transportation, check, token. 2. [Served food] menu, rations, meals; see FOOD.

fare *v.* prosper, prove, turn out; see HAPPEN 2.

farewell *n.* goodbye, valediction, parting; see DEPARTURE.

farfetched *a.* forced, strained, unbelievable; see FANTASTIC.

farm *n.* plantation, ranch, homestead, claim, holding, field, kibbutz, pasture, meadow, grassland, truck farm, estate, land, acres, freehold, cropland, soil, acreage, garden, patch, vegetable garden, orchard, nursery, vineyard.

farm *v.* cultivate land, produce crops, cultivate, till, garden, work, run, ranch, crop, graze, homestead, produce, pasture, till the soil.

farmer *n.* planter, grower, livestock breeder, stockman, feeder, agriculturist, rancher, dirt farmer, lessee, homesteader, producer, tiller of the soil, peasant, peon, herdsman, plowman, sharecropper, hired man, cropper, grazer, cattleman, sheepman, harvester, truck gardener, gardener, nurseryman, horticulturist, settler, sodbuster*, farm hand, hired hand, help.

farming *n.* agriculture, tillage, cultivation, husbandry, farm management, soil culture, ranching, sharecropping, homesteading, plantation, horticulture, agronomy, grazing, livestock raising, taking up a claim, hydroponics, growing, crop-raising.

farm out *v.* lease, rent, allot; see DISTRIBUTE, RENT 1.

farmyard *n.* barnyard, yard, farmstead; see FARM.

far-off *a.* far, remote, strange; see DISTANT.

farsighted *a.* aware, perceptive, sagacious; see INTELLIGENT.

farther *a.* at a greater distance, more distant, beyond, further, more remote, remoter, longer.

farthest *a.* remotest, ultimate, last; see FURTHEST.

fascinate *v.* charm, entrance, captivate, enchant, bewitch, ravish, enrapture, delight, overpower, please, attract, compel, lure, seduce, entice, tempt, draw, engage, excite, stimulate, overwhelm, provoke, arouse, intoxicate, thrill, stir, kindle, absorb, tantalize, win, interest, enthrall, influence, capture, coax, tease, lead on, knock dead*, cast a spell over*, catch one's eye, carry away, invite attention.—*Ant.* DISGUST, repel, horrify.

fascinated *a.* enchanted, bewitched, dazzled, captivated, attracted, seduced, enraptured, charmed, hypnotized, delighted, infatuated, thrilled, spellbound; see also CHARMED.—*Ant.* DISGUSTED, repelled, disenchanted.

fascinating *a.* engaging, attractive, delightful; see CHARMING.

fascination *n.* charm, power, enchantment; see ATTRACTION.

fascism *n.* dictatorship, totalitarianism, Nazism; see GOVERNMENT 2.—*Ant.* DEMOCRACY, self-government, socialism.

fascist *n.* reactionary, Nazi, rightist; see RADICAL.

fashion *n.* 1. [The manner of behavior] way, custom, convention, style, vogue, mode, tendency, trend, formality, formula, procedure, practice, device, usage, observance, new look. 2. [Whatever is temporarily in vogue] craze, sport, caprice, whim, hobby, innovation, custom, amusement, eccentricity, rage, cry. **—after** (or **in**) **a fashion** somewhat, to some extent, in a way; see MODERATELY.

fashion *v.* model, shape, form; see CREATE.

fashionable *a.* in fashion, in style, in vogue, being done, well-liked, favored, smart, stylish, chic, hot*, in*, trendy*, up to the minute.

fashioned *a.* molded, shaped, intended; see FORMED.

fast *a.* 1. [Rapid] swift, fleet, quick, speedy, brisk, accelerated, hasty, nimble, active, electric, agile, ready, quick as lightning, like a flash, racing, like a bat out of hell*, like a house afire*.—*Ant.* SLOW, sluggish, tardy. 2. [Firmly fixed] adherent, attached, immovable; see FIRM 1.

fast *n.* abstinence, day of fasting, Lent; see ABSTINENCE.

fast *v.* not eat, go hungry, observe a fast; see ABSTAIN.

fasten *v.* lock, fix, tie, lace, close, bind, tighten, make firm, attach, secure, anchor, grip, zip up, hold, screw up, screw down, clasp, clamp, pin, nail, tack, bolt, rivet, set, weld, cement, glue, hold fast, make secure, make fast, cinch, catch, buckle, bolt, bar, seal up.—*Ant.* RELEASE, loosen, unfasten.

fastened *a.* locked, fixed, tied; see TIGHT 2.

fastener *n.* buckle, hook, hasp, lock, clamp, tie, stud, vise, grip, grappling iron, clasp, snap, bolt, bar, lace, cinch, grip, pin, safety pin, nail, rivet, tack, thumbtack, screw, dowel, hook, brake, binder, binding, button, padlock, catch, bond, band, mooring, rope, cable, anchor, chain, harness, strap, thong, girdle, latch, staple, zipper.

fastening *n.* catch, clasp, hook; see FASTENER.

fat *a.* portly, stout, obese, corpulent, fleshy, potbellied, beefy, brawny, solid, plumpish, plump, burly, bulky, unwieldy, heavy, husky, puffy, on the heavy side, in need of reducing, swollen, inflated, ponderous, lumpish, fat as a pig, tubby*.—*Ant.* THIN, lean, skinny. **—chew the fat*** chat, gossip, confer; see TALK 1.

fat *n.* blubber, lard, oil; see GREASE.

fatal *a.* inevitable, mortal, lethal; see DEADLY.
fatality *n.* casualty, dying, accident; see DEATH.
fate *n.* fortune, destination, luck; see DOOM.
fated *a.* lost, destined, elected; see DOOMED.
fateful *a.* **1.** [Momentous] portentous, critical, decisive; see CRUCIAL 1. **2.** [Fatal] destructive, ruinous, lethal; see DEADLY.
father *n.* **1.** [A male parent] sire, progenitor, procreator, forebear, ancestor, head of the household, papa, dad*, daddy*, pa*, the old man*, pappy*, pop*. **2.** [An originator] founder, inventor, promoter; see AUTHOR. **3.** [A priest, especially a Catholic priest] pastor, ecclesiastic, parson; see PRIEST.
Father *n.* Supreme Being, Creator, Author; see GOD 1.
father-in-law *n.* spouse's father, parent, in-law*; see RELATIVE.
fatherland *n.* mother country, homeland, native land; see NATION 1.
fatherly *a.* paternal, patriarchal, benevolent; see KIND.
fatigue *n.* weariness, lassitude, exhaustion, weakness, feebleness, faintness, battle fatigue, nervous exhaustion, dullness, heaviness, listlessness, tiredness.
fatness *n.* plumpness, obesity, weight, flesh, heaviness, grossness, corpulence, bulkiness, girth, breadth, largeness, protuberance, inflation, fleshiness, stoutness, heftiness*.
fatten *v.* feed, stuff, prepare for market, plump, cram, fill, round out.—*Ant.* STARVE, reduce, constrict.
fatty *a.* greasy, blubbery, containing fat; see OILY 1.
faucet *n.* tap, fixture, petcock, drain, spigot, plumbing, hot-water faucet, cold-water faucet.
fault *n.* **1.** [A moral delinquency] misdemeanor, weakness, offense, wrongdoing, transgression, crime, sin, impropriety, juvenile delinquency, misconduct, malpractice, failing; see also MISTAKE. **2.** [An error] blunder, mistake, misdeed; see ERROR. **3.** [Responsibility] liability, accountability, blame; see RESPONSIBILITY 2. —**at fault** culpable, blamable, in the wrong; see GUILTY. —**find fault (with)** complain about, carp at, criticize; see BLAME.
faulty *a.* imperfect, flawed, blemished, deficient, distorted, weak, tainted, leaky, defective, damaged, unsound, spotted, cracked, warped, injured, broken, wounded, hurt, impaired, worn, battered, frail, crude, botched, insufficient, inadequate, incomplete, out of order, below par, incorrect, unfit; see also UNSATISFACTORY.—*Ant.* WHOLE, perfect, complete.
favor *n.* **1.** [Preference] help, support, encouragement; see ENCOURAGEMENT. **2.** [Kindness] service, courtesy, boon; see KINDNESS 2. —**find favor** please, suit, become welcome; see SATISFY 1. —**in favor** liked, esteemed, wanted; see FAVORITE. —**in favor of** approving, endorsing, condoning; see FOR. —**in one's favor** to one's advantage, on one's side, creditable; see FAVORABLE 3.
favor *v.* prefer, like, approve, sanction, praise, regard favorably, be in favor of, pick, choose, lean toward, incline toward, value, prize, esteem, think well of, set great store by, look up to, think the world of*, be partial to, grant favors to, promote, play favorites, show consideration for, spare, make an exception for, pull strings for; see also PROMOTE 1.—*Ant.* HATE, dislike, disesteem.
favorable *a.* **1.** [Friendly] well-disposed, kind, well-intentioned; see FRIENDLY. **2.** [Displaying suitable or promising qualities] propitious, convenient, beneficial; see HOPEFUL 2. **3.** [Commendatory] approving, commending, assenting, complimentary, well-disposed toward, in favor of, agreeable, in one's favor.
favorably *a.* approvingly, agreeably, kindly, helpfully, fairly, willingly, heartily, cordially, genially, graciously, courteously, receptively, in an approving manner, positively, without prejudice.—*Ant.* UNFAVORABLY, adversely, discouragingly.
favorite *a.* liked, beloved, personal, favored, intimate, to one's taste, to one's liking, choice, pet, desired, wished-for, preferred, adored.—*Ant.* UNPOPULAR, unwanted, unwelcome.
favorite *n.* darling, pet, idol, ideal, favored one, mistress, love, favorite son, favorite child, fair-haired boy*, teacher's pet, odds-on favorite, apple of one's eye.
favoritism *n.* bias, partiality, inequity; see INCLINATION 1.
fawn *n.* baby deer, baby doe, baby buck; see DEER.
faze *v.* bother, intimidate, worry; see DISTURB.
fear *n.* fright, terror, horror, panic, dread, dismay, awe, scare, revulsion, aversion, tremor, mortal terror, cowardice, dread, timidity, misgiving, trembling, anxiety, phobia, foreboding, despair, agitation, hesitation, worry, concern, suspicion, doubt, qualm, funk*, cold feet*, cold sweat.—*Ant.* COURAGE, intrepidity, dash. —**for fear of** avoiding, lest, in order to prevent, out of apprehension concerning.
fear *v.* be afraid, shun, avoid, falter, lose courage, be alarmed, be frightened, be scared, live in terror, dare not, have qualms about, cower, flinch, shrink, quail, cringe, turn pale, tremble, break out in a sweat*.—*Ant.* DARE, outface, withstand.
fearful *a.* timid, shy, apprehensive; see COWARDLY.
fearfully *a.* apprehensively, shyly, with fear and trembling, for fear of, in fear.

fearless *a.* bold, daring, courageous; see BRAVE.

feasible *a.* **1.** [Suitable] fit, expedient, worthwhile; see CONVENIENT 1. **2.** [Likely] probable, practicable, attainable; see LIKELY 1.

feast *n.* banquet, entertainment, festival, treat, merrymaking, fiesta, barbecue, picnic; see also DINNER.

feat *n.* act, effort, deed; see ACHIEVEMENT.

feather *n.* quill, plume, plumage, down, wing, tuft, crest, fringe. —**in fine** or **high** or **good feather** well, in good humor, in good health; see HAPPY.

feature *n.* **1.** [Anything calculated to attract interest] innovation, highlight, prominent part, drawing card, main bout, specialty, special attraction, featured attraction. **2.** [Matter other than news published in a newspaper] article, editorial, feature story; see STORY. **3.** [A salient quality] point, peculiarity, notability; see CHARACTERISTIC.

features *n.pl.* lineaments, looks, appearance; see FACE 1.

featuring *a.* presenting, showing, recommending, calling attention to, giving prominence to, emphasizing, making much of, pointing up, drawing attention to, turning the spotlight on, centering attention on, starring.

February *n.* winter month, second month of the year, shortest month of the year; see MONTH, WINTER.

feces *n.* excretion, waste, dung; see EXCREMENT.

federal *a.* general, central, governmental; see NATIONAL 1.

federation *n.* confederacy, alliance, combination; see ORGANIZATION 2.

fee *n.* remuneration, salary, charge; see PAY 2.

feeble *a.* fragile, puny, strengthless; see WEAK 1, 2.

feebleminded *a.* foolish, retarded, senile; see DULL 3.

feed *n.* provisions, supplies, fodder, food for animals, pasture, forage, roughage. *Common feeds include the following:* grain, small grain, corn, oats, barley, rye, wheat, peanuts, hay, clover, sweet clover, alfalfa, sorghum, kale, soybeans, beets, straw.

feed *v.* feast, give food to, satisfy the hunger of, nourish, supply, support, satisfy, fill, stuff, cram, gorge, banquet, dine, nurse, maintain, fatten, provide food for, cater to, stock, furnish, nurture, sustain, encourage, serve.—*Ant.* STARVE, deprive, quench.

feel *n.* touch, quality, air; see FEELING 2.

feel *v.* **1.** [To examine by touch] finger, explore, stroke, palm, caress, handle, manipulate, press, squeeze, fondle, tickle, paw, feel for, fumble, grope, grasp, grapple, grip, clutch, clasp, run the fingers over, pinch, poke, contact. **2.** [To experience] sense, perceive, receive, be aware of, observe, be moved by, respond, know, acknowledge, appreciate, accept, be affected, be impressed, be excited by, have the experience of, take to heart.—*Ant.* IGNORE, be insensitive to, be unaware of. **3.** [To believe] consider, hold, know; see THINK 1. **4.** [To give an impression through touch] appear, exhibit, suggest; see SEEM.

feeler *n.* hint, tentative proposal, trial balloon; see TEST.

feeling *n.* **1.** [The sense of touch] tactile sensation, tactility, power of perceiving by touch, tangibility. **2.** [State of the body, or of a part of it] sense, sensation, sensibility, feel, sensitiveness, sensory response, perception, perceptivity, susceptibility, activity, consciousness, receptivity, responsiveness, excitability, excitement, awareness, enjoyment, sensuality, pain, pleasure, reaction, motor response, reflex, excitation.—*Ant.* INDIFFERENCE, apathy, numbness. **3.** [A personal reaction] opinion, thought, outlook; see ATTITUDE. **4.** [Sensitivity] taste, emotion, passion, tenderness, discrimination, delicacy, discernment, sentiment, sentimentality, refinement, culture, cultivation, capacity, faculty, judgment, affection, sympathy, imagination, intelligence, intuition, spirit, soul, appreciation, response.—*Ant.* RUDENESS, crudeness, coldness.

feign *v.* simulate, imagine, fabricate; see PRETEND 1.

feigned *a.* imagined, fictitious, simulated; see IMAGINARY.

fell *v.* pull down, knock down, cause to fall; see CUT 1.

fellow *n.* **1.** [A young man] youth, lad, boy, person, teenager, stripling, novice, cadet, apprentice, adolescent, juvenile, youngster, guy*, kid*, squirt*. **2.** [An associate] peer, associate, colleague; see FRIEND.

fellowship *n.* **1.** [Congenial social feeling] comradeship, conviviality, sociality, sociability, intimacy, acquaintance, friendliness, familiarity, good-fellowship, amity, affability, camaraderie, togetherness.—*Ant.* RUDENESS, unsociability, surliness. **2.** [Subsistence payment to encourage study] stipend, scholarship, honorarium, subsidy, teaching fellowship, assistantship.

felon *n.* outlaw, delinquent, convict; see CRIMINAL.

felony *n.* misconduct, offense, transgression; see CRIME.

female *a.* reproductive, fertile, childbearing, of the female gender.—*Ant.* MALE, masculine, virile.

feminine *a.* soft, womanly, delicate, gentle, ladylike, female, matronly, maidenly, tender, womanish, fair; see also WOMANLY.—*Ant.* MALE, masculine, virile.

fence *n.* 1. [That which surrounds an enclosure] picket fence, wire fence, board fence, barbed-wire fence, rail fence, chain fence, iron fence, hedge, backstop, rail, railing, barricade, net, barrier, wall, dike. 2. [A receiver of stolen goods] accomplice, front*, uncle*; see CRIMINAL. —**mend one's fences** renew contacts, look after one's political interests, solicit votes; see CAMPAIGN. —**on the fence** undecided, uncommitted, indifferent; see UNCERTAIN.

fender *n.* guard, mudguard, shield, apron, buffer, mask, cover, frame, cushion, protector, bumper.

fend for oneself *v.* take care of oneself, stay alive, eke out an existence; see SURVIVE 1.

fend off *v.* keep off, ward off, repel; see DEFEND 1.

ferment *v.* effervesce, sour, foam, froth, bubble, seethe, fizz, sparkle, boil, work, ripen, dissolve, evaporate, rise.

fermentation *n.* souring, foaming, seething; see DECAY.

fern *n.* greenery, bracken, lacy plant; see PLANT.

ferocious *a.* fierce, savage, wild; see FIERCE.—*Ant.* GENTLE, meek, mild.

ferocity *n.* fierceness, brutality, barbarity; see CRUELTY.

ferry *n.* passage boat, barge, packet; see BOAT.

fertile *a.* fruitful, rich, productive, fat, teeming, yielding, arable, flowering.—*Ant.* STERILE, barren, desert.

fertility *n.* fecundity, richness, fruitfulness, potency, virility, pregnancy, productiveness, productivity, generative capacity.

fertilization *n.* 1. [The enrichment of land] manuring, dressing, mulching; see PREPARATION 1. 2. [Impregnation of the ovum] insemination, impregnation, pollination, implantation, breeding, propagation, generation, procreation.

fertilize *v.* 1. [To enrich land] manure, dress, lime, mulch, cover, treat. 2. [To impregnate] breed, make pregnant, generate, germinate, pollinate, inseminate, propagate, procreate, get with child, beget, knock up*.

fertilizer *n.* manure, chemical fertilizer, plant food, compost, humus, mulch. *Common fertilizers include the following:* barnyard manure, guano, sphagnum, peat moss, phosphate, dung, litter, crushed limestone, bone dust, kelp, bone meal, nitrogen, ammonium sulphate, potash.

fervent *a.* zealous, eager, ardent; see ENTHUSIASTIC.

fervor *n.* fervency, ardor, enthusiasm; see ZEAL.

fester *v.* rankle, putrefy, rot; see SPOIL.

festival *n.* festivity, feast, competition; see CELEBRATION.

festive *a.* merry, gay, joyful; see HAPPY.

festivity *n.* revelry, pleasure, amusement; see ENTERTAINMENT.

fetch *v.* bring, get, retrieve; see CARRY 1.

fete *n.* festival, entertainment, ball; see CELEBRATION, PARTY 1.

fetish *n.* fixation, craze, mania; see OBSESSION.

fetus *n.* organism, embryo, the young of an animal in the womb; see CHILD.

feud *n.* quarrel, strife, bickering; see FIGHT.

fever *n.* abnormal temperature and pulse, febrile disease, high body temperature; see ILLNESS 1.

feverish *a.* burning, above normal, running a temperature; see HOT 1.

few *a.* not many, scarcely any, less, sparse, scanty, thin, widely spaced, inconsiderable, negligible, infrequent, not too many, some, any, scarce, rare, seldom, few and far between.—*Ant.* MANY, numerous, innumerable.

few *pron.* not many, a small number, a handful, scarcely any, not too many, several, a scattering, three or four, a sprinkling.—*Ant.* MANY, a multitude, a great many. —**quite a few** several, some, a large number; see MANY.

fiancé *n.* intended, betrothed, person engaged to be married; see LOVER.

fib *n.* prevarication, fabrication, misrepresentation; see LIE.

fiber *n.* thread, cord, string, strand, tissue, filament, vein, hair, strip, shred. *Some common fibers include the following:* vegetable fiber, animal fiber, synthetic fiber, silk, linen, hemp, cotton, wool, jute, rayon, nylon, orlon, polyester, acetate.

fibrous *a.* veined, hairy, coarse; see STRINGY.

fickle *a.* capricious, whimsical, mercurial; see CHANGING.

fiction *n.* novel, tale, romance; see STORY.

fictitious *a.* made-up, untrue, counterfeit; see FALSE 1, 2.

fiddle* *n.* violin, stringed instrument, cornstalk fiddle; see MUSICAL INSTRUMENT. —**fit as a fiddle** healthy, strong, sound; see WELL 1.

fidelity *n.* fealty, loyalty, devotion; see LOYALTY.

fidget *v.* stir, twitch, worry; see WIGGLE.

fidgety *a.* nervous, uneasy, apprehensive; see RESTLESS.

field *n.* 1. [Open land] grainfield, hayfield, meadow, pasture, range, acreage, plot, patch, garden, cultivated ground, grassland, green, ranchland, arable land, plowed land, cleared land, cropland, tract, vineyard. 2. [An area devoted to sport] diamond, gridiron, track, rink, court, course, racecourse, golf course, racetrack, arena, stadium, theater, amphitheater, playground, park, turf, green, fairground. 3. [An area devoted to a specialized activity] airfield, airport, flying field, terminal, battlefield, battleground, sector, field of fire, terrain, no man's land, theater of war, field of battle, field of honor, parade ground, range, parking lot. —**play the field** experiment, explore, look elsewhere; see DISCOVER, EXAMINE, TRY 1.

fielder *n.* infielder, outfielder, gardener*; see BASEBALL PLAYER.

fiend *n.* **1.** [A wicked or cruel person] monster, barbarian, brute; see BEAST. **2.** [*An addict] fan, aficionado, monomaniac; see ADDICT.

fiendish *a.* diabolical, demoniac, infernal; see BAD.

fierce *a.* ferocious, wild, furious, enraged, raging, impetuous, untamed, angry, passionate, savage, primitive, brutish, animal, raving, outrageous, terrible, vehement, frightening, awful, horrible, venomous, bold, malevolent, malign, brutal, monstrous, severe, rough, rude, vicious, dangerous, frenzied, mad, insane, desperate, ravening, frantic, wrathful, irate, fanatical, bestial, boisterous, violent, threatening, stormy, thunderous, howling, tumultuous, turbulent, uncontrolled, raging, storming, blustering, cyclonic, torrential, frightful, fearful, devastating, hellish, rip-roaring*.—*Ant.* MILD, moderate, calm.

fiercely *a.* ferociously, violently, wildly, terribly, vehemently, angrily, threateningly, frighteningly, awfully, horribly, mightily, passionately, impetuously, boldly, irresistibly, furiously, riotously, brutally, monstrously, forcibly, forcefully, convulsively, hysterically, severely, roughly, rudely, viciously, dangerously, madly, insanely, desperately, outrageously, savagely, frantically, wrathfully, irately, virulently, relentlessly, turbulently, overpoweringly, strongly, deliriously, fanatically, with rage, in a frenzy, tooth and nail.—*Ant.* PEACEFULLY, mildly, reasonably.

fiesta *n.* festival, holiday, feast; see CELEBRATION.

fifty *a.* half a hundred, half a century, two score and ten, many, five times ten, a considerable number.

fight *n.* **1.** [A violent physical struggle] strife, contention, feud, quarrel, contest, encounter, row, dispute, disagreement, battle, confrontation, controversy, brawl, bout, match, fisticuffs, round, fracas, difficulty, altercation, bickering, wrangling, riot, argument, debate, competition, rivalry, conflict, skirmish, clash, scuffle, collision, brush, action, engagement, combat, blow, exchange of blows, wrestling match, squabble, game, discord, estrangement, fuss, tussle, scrap*, free-for-all, ruckus*, run-in*, tiff, flare-up, go*, row, set-to*, difference of opinion. **2.** [Willingness or eagerness to fight] mettle, hardihood, boldness; see COURAGE.

fight *v.* strive, war, struggle, resist, assert oneself, challenge, meet, contend, attack, carry on war, withstand, give blow for blow, do battle, war against, persevere, force, go to war, exchange blows, encounter, oppose, tussle, grapple, flare up, engage with, combat, wrestle, box, spar, skirmish, quarrel, bicker, dispute, have it out, squabble, come to grips with, row, light into*, tear into*, mix it up with*.—*Ant.* RETREAT, submit, yield.

fight back *v.* defend oneself, resist, retaliate; see OPPOSE 2.

fighter *n.* **1.** [One who fights] contestant, disputant, contender, party to a quarrel, warrior, soldier, combatant, belligerent, assailant, aggressor, antagonist, rival, opponent, champion, bully, competitor, controversialist, scrapper*. **2.** [A professional pugilist] boxer, prize fighter, pug*, bruiser*.

fighting *a.* combative, battling, brawling, unbeatable, resolute, argumentative, angry, ferocious, quarrelsome, ready to fight, belligerent, boxing, wrestling, warlike, contending, up in arms.

fighting *n.* combat, struggle, strife; see FIGHT.

fight off *v.* defend from, hold back, resist; see DEFEND 1.

figurative *a.* not literal, metaphorical, allegorical; see ILLUSTRATIVE.

figure *n.* **1.** [A form] shape, mass, structure; see FORM 1. **2.** [The human torso] body, frame, torso, shape, form, development, configuration, build, appearance, outline, posture, attitude, pose, carriage. **3.** [A representation of quantity] sum, total, symbol; see NUMBER. **4.** [Price] value, worth, terms; see PRICE.

figure *v.* **1.** [To compute] reckon, number, count; see CALCULATE. **2.** [To estimate] set a figure, guess, fix a price; see ESTIMATE. **3.** [*To come to a conclusion] suppose, think, opine; see DECIDE. **4.** [To figure out] comprehend, master, reason; see DISCOVER.

figure of speech *n. Varieties include the following:* image, comparison, metaphor, simile, metonymy, synecdoche, trope, personification, hyperbole, litotes, allegory, parable, allusion, euphemism, analogue, parallel, irony, satire, understatement, paradox.

file *n.* **1.** [An orderly collection of papers] card index, card file, portfolio, record, classified index, list, register, dossier, notebook. **2.** [Steel abrasive] rasp, steel, sharpener. *Types of files include the following:* flat, rattail, ignition, triangular, fingernail, wood. **3.** [A line] rank, row, column; see LINE 1. —**on file** filed, cataloged, registered; see RECORDED.

file *v.* 1. [To arrange in order] classify, index, deposit, categorize, catalog, record, register, list, arrange. 2. [To use an abrasive] abrade, rasp, scrape, smooth, rub down, level off, finish, sharpen.

fill *n.* enough, capacity, satiety; see PLENTY.

fill *v.* 1. [To pour to the capacity of the container] pack, stuff, replenish, furnish, supply, satisfy, blow up, fill up, pump up, fill to capacity, fill to overflowing, brim over, swell, charge, inflate.—*Ant.* EMPTY, exhaust, drain. 2. [To occupy available space] take up, pervade, overflow, stretch, bulge out, distend, brim over, stretch, swell, blow up, run over at the top, permeate, take over.

filled *a.* finished, completed, done; see FULL 1.

fill in *v.* 1. [To insert] write in, answer, sign; see ANSWER. 2. [To substitute] replace, act for, represent; see SUBSTITUTE.

filling *n.* stuffing, dressing, contents, mixture, center, layer, filler, fill, sauce, insides, lining, wadding, padding, cement, innards*, guts*.

fill out *v.* 1. [To enlarge] swell out, expand, overgrow; see GROW 1. 2. [To insert] fill in, sign, apply; see ANSWER.

fill up *v.* saturate, pack, stuff; see FILL 1.

film *n.* 1. [Thin, membranous matter] gauze, tissue, fabric, sheet, membrane, layer, transparency, foil, fold, skin, coat, coating, scum, veil, cobweb, web, mist, cloud. 2. [A preparation containing a light-sensitive emulsion] negative, positive, microfilm, color film. 3. [A moving picture film] motion picture, cinema, photoplay; see MOVIE.

film *v.* record, take, shoot; see PHOTOGRAPH.

filter *v.* 1. [To soak slowly] seep, penetrate, percolate; see SOAK 1. 2. [To clean by filtering] strain, purify, sift, sieve, refine, clarify, clean, separate.

filth *n.* dirt, dung, feces, contamination, corruption, pollution, foul matter, sewage, muck, manure, slop, squalor, trash, grime, mud, smudge, silt, garbage, carrion, slush, slime, sludge, foulness, filthiness, excrement, dregs, lees, sediment, rottenness, impurity.—*Ant.* CLEANLINESS, purity, spotlessness.

filthy *a.* foul, squalid, nasty; see DIRTY 1.

fin *n.* membrane, paddle, propeller, balance, guide, blade, ridge, organ, spine, pectoral fin, ventral fin, dorsal fin, caudal fin, flipper, fishtail.

final *a.* terminal, concluding, ultimate; see LAST 1.

finalized *a.* concluded, decided, completed; see FINISHED 1.

finally *a.* 1. [As though a matter were settled] with finality, with conviction, settled, in a final manner, certainly, officially, irrevocably, decisively, definitely, beyond recall, permanently, for all time, conclusively, assuredly, done with, once and for all, for good, beyond the shadow of a doubt.—*Ant.* TEMPORARILY, momentarily, for the time being. 2. [After a long period] at length, at last, in the end, subsequently, in conclusion, lastly, after all, after a while, eventually, ultimately, at long last, at the final point, at the last moment, at the end, tardily, belatedly, when all is said and done, in spite of all.

finance *n.* business, commerce, financial affairs; see ECONOMICS.

finance *v.* fund, pay for, provide funds for; see PAY FOR.

finances *n.* revenue, capital, funds; see WEALTH.

financial *a.* economic, business, monetary; see COMMERCIAL.

financier *n.* capitalist, banker, merchant; see EXECUTIVE.

find *n.* fortunate discovery, findings, acquisition; see DISCOVERY.

find *v.* discover, detect, notice, observe, perceive, arrive at, discern, hit upon, encounter, uncover, recover, expose, stumble on, happen upon, come across, track down, dig up, turn up, scare up*, run across, run into, lay one's hands on, bring to light, spot; see also SEE 1.—*Ant.* LOSE, mislay, miss.

finder *n.* acquirer, discoverer, search party; see OWNER.—*Ant.* LOSER, seeker, failure.

find fault *v.* blame, criticize, condemn; see BLAME.

finding *n.* verdict, decision, sentence; see JUDGMENT 3.

findings *n.pl.* data, discoveries, conclusions; see SUMMARY.

find out *v.* recognize, learn, identify; see DISCOVER.

fine *a.* 1. [Not coarse] light, powdery, granular; see LITTLE 1. 2. [Of superior quality] well-made, supreme, fashionable; see EXCELLENT. 3. [Exact] precise, distinct, strict; see ACCURATE 2, DEFINITE 2.

fine *n.* penalty, damage, forfeit; see PUNISHMENT.

fine *v.* penalize, exact, tax, confiscate, levy, seize, extort, alienate, make pay; see also PUNISH.

finger *n.* digit, organ of touch, tactile member, forefinger, thumb, index finger, extremity, pointer, feeler, tentacle, pinky*. —**have (or keep) one's fingers crossed*** wish, aspire to, pray for; see HOPE. —**lift a finger** make an effort, attempt, endeavor; see TRY 1. —**put one's finger on** indicate, ascertain, detect; see DISCOVER. —**put the finger on*** inform on, turn in, fink on*; see TELL 1.

finger *v.* 1. [To feel] handle, touch, manipulate; see FEEL 1. 2. [*To choose or specify] appoint, point out, name; see CHOOSE.

fingernail *n.* nail, talon, matrix; see CLAW.

finish *n.* **1.** [The end] close, termination, ending; see END 2. **2.** [An applied surface] shine, polish, glaze, surface. *Finishes include the following:* shellac, oil, plastic, turpentine, lacquer, stain, varnish, polish, wallpaper, wash, whitewash, paint, casein paint, enamel, gold leaf, wax, veneer, cement, stucco, luster.

finish *v.* **1.** [To bring to an end] complete, end, perfect; see ACHIEVE. **2.** [To develop a surface] polish, wax, stain; see COVER 1, PAINT 2. **3.** [To come to an end] cease, close, end; see STOP.

finished *a.* **1.** [Completed] done, accomplished, perfected, achieved, ended, performed, executed, dispatched, concluded, complete, through, fulfilled, closed, over, decided, brought about, ceased, stopped, resolved, settled, made, worked out, rounded out, discharged, satisfied, disposed of, realized, finalized, effected, put into effect, all over with, attained, done with, made an end of, brought to a close, said and done, sewed up*, wound up.—*Ant.* UNFINISHED, imperfect, incomplete. **2.** [Given a finish] polished, coated, varnished; see PAINTED 2.

fire *n.* **1.** [Burning] flame, conflagration, blaze, campfire, coals, flame and smoke, blazing fire, hearth, burning coals, tinder, bonfire, bed of coals, embers, source of heat, sparks, heat, glow, warmth, luminosity, combustion. **2.** [The discharge of ordinance] artillery attack, bombardment, rounds, barrage, explosions, bombings, curtain of fire, volley, sniping, mortar attack, salvos, shells, pattern of fire, fire superiority, cross-fire, machine-gun fire, rifle fire, small-arms fire, antiaircraft fire; see also ATTACK. **—catch (on) fire** begin burning, ignite, flare up; see BURN. **—on fire 1.** [Burning] flaming, fiery, hot; see BURNING. **2.** [Excited] full of ardor, enthusiastic, zealous; see EXCITED. **—open fire** start shooting, shoot, attack; see SHOOT 1. **—play with fire** gamble, endanger one's interests, do something dangerous; see RISK. **—set fire to** ignite, oxidize, make burn; see BURN. **—set the world on fire** achieve, become famous, excel; see SUCCEED 1. **—under fire** criticized, censured, under attack; see QUESTIONABLE 1, 2.

fire *v.* **1.** [To set on fire] kindle, enkindle, ignite, inflame, light, burn, set fire to, put a match to, start a fire, set burning, touch off, rekindle, relight.—*Ant.* EXTINGUISH, smother, quench. **2.** [To shoot] discharge, shoot off, hurl; see SHOOT 1. **3.** [To dismiss] discharge, let go, eject; see DISMISS.

fired *a.* **1.** [Subjected to fire] set on fire, burned, baked, ablaze, afire, on fire, aflame, burning, incandescent, scorched, glowing, kindled, enkindled, smoking, smoldering, heated. **2.** [Discharged] dropped, let go, given one's walking papers*; see DISCHARGED.

fireman *n.* **1.** [One who extinguishes fires] firefighter, engineman, ladderman, fire chief. **2.** [One who fuels engines or furnaces] stoker, engineer's helper, railroad man, trainman, attendant, oil feeder, cinder monkey*, hellholer*.

fireplace *n.* hearth, chimney, hearthside, stove, furnace, blaze, bed of coals, grate.

fireproof *a.* noninflammable, noncombustible, nonflammable, fire-resistant, incombustible, concrete and steel, asbestos.

fireworks *n.pl.* rockets, Roman candles, sparklers; see EXPLOSIVE.

firm *a.* **1.** [Stable] fixed, solid, rooted, immovable, fastened, motionless, secured, steady, substantial, durable, rigid, bolted, welded, riveted, soldered, imbedded, nailed, tightened, fast, secure, sound, immobile, unmovable, mounted, stationary, set, settled.—*Ant.* LOOSE, movable, mobile. **2.** [Firm in texture] solid, dense, compact, hard, stiff, impenetrable, impervious, rigid, hardened, inflexible, unyielding, thick, compressed, substantial, heavy, close, condensed, impermeable.—*Ant.* SOFT, porous, flabby. **3.** [Settled in purpose] determined, steadfast, resolute; see CONSTANT. **—stand** or **hold firm** be steadfast, endure, maintain one's resolution; see FIGHT, RESOLVE.

firmly *a.* **1.** [Not easily moved] immovably, solidly, rigidly, stably, durably, enduringly, substantially, securely, heavily, stiffly, inflexibly, soundly, strongly, thoroughly.—*Ant.* LIGHTLY, tenuously, insecurely. **2.** [Showing determination] resolutely, steadfastly, doggedly, stolidly, tenaciously, determinedly, staunchly, constantly, intently, purposefully, persistently, obstinately, stubbornly, unwaveringly, unchangeably, through thick and thin.

firmness *n.* stiffness, hardness, toughness, solidity, impenetrability, durability, imperviousness, temper, impermeability, inflexibility.

first *a.* beginning, original, primary, prime, primal, antecedent, initial, virgin, earliest, opening, introductory, primeval, leading, in the beginning, front, head, rudimentary.—*Ant.* LAST, ultimate, final. **—in the first place** firstly, initially, to begin with; see FIRST.

first aid *n.* emergency medical aid, emergency relief, field dressing; see MEDICINE 2, TREATMENT 2.

first-class *a.* superior, supreme, choice; see EXCELLENT.

first-rate *a.* prime, very good, choice; see EXCELLENT.

fiscal *a.* monetary, economic, financial; see COMMERCIAL.

fish *n.* seafood, panfish, denizen of the deep. *Types of fish include the following:* catfish, pickerel, pike, perch, trout, flounder, sucker, sunfish, bass, crappy, mackerel, cod, salmon, carp, minnow, eel, bullhead, herring, shad, barracuda, swordfish, goldfish, gar, octopus, dogfish, flying fish, whitefish, tuna, pompano, haddock, hake, halibut, mullet, loach, muskellunge, sardine, smelt; see also SHELLFISH. **—drink like a fish** drink heavily, get drunk, become inebriated; see DRINK 2. **—like a fish out of water** out of place, alien, displaced; see UNFAMILIAR 1.
fish *v.* go fishing, troll for, net, bob, shrimp, bait the hook, trawl, angle, cast one's net.
fisherman *n.* angler, fisher, harpooner, sailor, seaman, whaler, fish catcher.
fish for *v.* hint at, elicit, try to evoke; see HINT.
fishing *n.* angling, casting, trawling; see SPORT 1.
fishy* *a.* improbable, dubious, implausible; see UNLIKELY.
fist *n.* clenched hand, clenched fist, hand, clutch, clasp, grasp, grip, hold.
fit *a.* **1.** [Appropriate by nature] suitable, proper, fitting, fit, likely, expedient, appropriate, convenient, timely, opportune, feasible, practicable, wise, advantageous, favorable, preferable, beneficial, desirable, adequate, tasteful, becoming, agreeable, seasonable, due, rightful, equitable, legitimate, decent, harmonious, pertinent, according, relevant, in keeping, consistent, applicable, compatible, admissible, concurrent, to the point, adapted to, fitted, suited, calculated, prepared, qualified, competent, matched, ready-made, accommodated, right, happy, lucky, cut out for*.—*Ant.* unfit, unseemly, inappropriate. **2.** [In good physical condition] trim, competent, robust; see HEALTHY.
fit *n.* **1.** [Sudden attack of disease] muscular convulsion, rage, spasm, seizure, stroke, epileptic attack, paroxysm, spell*; see also ILLNESS 1. **2.** [Transitory spell of action or feeling] impulsive action, burst, rush, outbreak, torrent, tantrum, mood, outburst, whimsy, huff, rage, spell. **—have** (or **throw**) **a fit*** become angry, lose one's temper, give vent to emotion; see RAGE 1.
fit *v.* **1.** [To be suitable in character] agree, suit, accord, harmonize, apply, belong, conform, consist, fit right in, be in keeping, parallel, relate, concur, match, correspond, be comfortable, respond, have its place, answer the purpose, meet, click*.—*Ant.* OPPOSE, disagree, clash. **2.** [To make suitable] arrange, alter, adapt; see ADJUST 1.
fitness *n.* appropriateness, suitability, propriety, expediency, convenience, adequacy, correspondence, decency, decorum, harmony, keeping, consistency, applicability, compatibility, rightness, timeliness, adaptation, qualification, accommodation, competence.
fit out *v.* supply, equip, outfit; see PROVIDE 1.
fitted *a.* suited, proper, adapted; see FIT 1.
fix *v.* **1.** [To make firm] plant, implant, secure; see FASTEN. **2.** [To prepare a meal] prepare, heat, get ready; see COOK. **3.** [To put in order] correct, improve, settle, put into shape, reform, patch, rejuvenate, touch up, revive, refresh, renew, renovate, rebuild, make compatible, clean, align, adapt, mend, adjust.
fixed *a.* **1.** [Firm] solid, rigid, immovable; see FIRM 1. **2.** [Repaired] rebuilt, in order, timed, synchronized, adjusted, settled, mended, rearranged, adapted, corrected, restored, renewed, improved, patched up, put together, in working order. **3.** [*Prearranged] predesigned, put-up*, set-up*; see PLANNED.
fixings *n.pl.* parts, components, constituents; see INGREDIENTS.
fixture *n.* convenience, gas appliance, electric appliance; see APPLIANCE.
fix up* *v.* fix, mend, rehabilitate; see REPAIR.
fizz *n.* hissing, sputtering, bubbling; see NOISE 1.
fizzle* *n.* disappointment, fiasco, defeat; see FAILURE 1.
flabby *a.* limp, tender, soft; see FAT.
flag *n.* banner, standard, colors; see EMBLEM.
flag *v.* signal, wave, give a sign to; see SIGNAL.
flagrant *a.* notorious, disgraceful, infamous; see OUTRAGEOUS.
flair *n.* talent, aptitude, gift; see ABILITY.
flake *n.* scale, cell, sheet, wafer, peel, skin, slice, sliver, layer, leaf, shaving, plate, section, scab.
flake *v.* scale, peel, sliver, shed, drop, chip, scab, slice, pare, trim, wear away.
flamboyant *a.* baroque, bombastic, ostentatious; see ORNATE.
flame *n.* blaze, flare, flash; see FIRE 1.
flame *v.* blaze, oxidize, flare up; see BURN.
flaming *a.* blazing, ablaze, fiery; see BURNING.
flannel *n.* woolen, cotton flannel, flannelette; see WOOL.
flap *n.* fold, tab, lapel, fly, cover, pendant, drop, tail, appendage, tag, accessory, apron, skirt, strip, wing.
flap *v.* flutter, flash, swing; see WAVE 1.
flare *n.* glare, brief blaze, spark; see FLASH.
flare *v.* blaze, glow, burn; see FLASH.
flare out *v.* widen out, spread out, splay; see GROW 1.
flare up *v.* **1.** [*Said of persons*] lose one's temper, rant, seethe; see RAGE 1. **2.** [*Said of fire*] glow, burst into flame, blaze; see BURN.
flash *n.* glimmer, sparkle, glitter, glisten, gleam, beam, blaze, flicker, flame, glare, burst, impulse, vision, dazzle, shimmer, shine, glow, twinkle, twinkling, phosphores-

cence, reflection, radiation, ray, luster, spark, streak, stream, illumination, incandescence.

flash *v.* glimmer, sparkle, glitter, glisten, gleam, beam, blaze, flame, glare, dazzle, shimmer, shine, glow, twinkle, reflect, radiate, shoot out beams, flicker; see also SHINE 1, 2.

flashlight *n.* flash lamp, spotlight, torch; see LIGHT 1.

flashy *a.* gaudy, showy, ostentatious; see ORNATE.

flask *n.* decanter, jug, canteen; see BOTTLE.

flat *a.* **1.** [Lying in a smooth plane] level, even, smooth, spread out, extended, prostrate, horizontal, low, on a level, fallen, level with the ground, prone.—*Ant.* ROUGH, raised, uneven. **2.** [Lacking savor] unseasoned, insipid, flavorless; see TASTELESS 1.

flatten *v.* level off, even out, smooth, spread out, depress, squash, smash, level, even, knock down, wear down, beat down, fell, floor, ground, smooth, roll out, straighten, deflate.—*Ant.* RAISE, elevate, inflate.

flattened *a.* leveled, depressed, smoothed; see FLAT 1.

flatter *v.* overpraise, adulate, glorify; see PRAISE 1.

flattered *a.* praised, lauded, exalted; see PRAISED.

flatterer *n.* parasite, toady, sycophant, flunky, slave, puppet, groveler, sniveler, yes man*, bootlicker*, apple polisher*, doormat*.

flattering *a.* pleasing, favorable, unduly favorable; see COMPLIMENTARY.

flattery *n.* adulation, compliments, blandishment, sycophancy, applause, false praise, commendation, tribute, gratification, pretty speeches, soft words, fawning, blarney, soft soap*, hokum*, mush*.—*Ant.* HATRED, criticism, censure.

flaunt *v.* vaunt, display, brandish; see BOAST.

flaunting *a.* gaudy, ostentatious, pretentious; see ORNATE.

flavor *n.* taste, savor, tang, relish, smack, twang, gusto. *Individual flavors include the following:* tartness, sweetness, acidity, saltiness, spiciness, pungency, piquancy, astringency, bitterness, sourness, pepperiness, hotness, gaminess, greasiness, fishy taste.

flavor *v.* season, salt, pepper, spice, give a tang to, make tasty, bring out a flavor in, put in flavoring.

flavoring *n.* essence, extract, seasoning, spice, additive, condiment, sauce, relish; see also HERB, SPICE.

flavorless *a.* insipid, vapid, mawkish; see TASTELESS 1.

flaw *n.* defect, imperfection, stain; see BLEMISH.

flawless *a.* faultless, sound, impeccable; see PERFECT.

flea *n.* dog flea, sand flea, flea louse; see INSECT.

fleck *n.* mite, speck, dot; see BIT 1.

flee *v.* desert, escape, run; see RETREAT.

fleet *n.* armada, naval force, task force; see NAVY.

flesh *n.* meat, fat, muscle, brawn, tissue, cells, flesh and blood, protoplasm, plasm, plasma, body parts, heart, insides*. **—one's (own) flesh and blood** family, kindred, kin; see RELATIVE.

fleshy *a.* obese, plump, corpulent; see FAT.

flexibility *n.* pliancy, plasticity, flexibleness, pliableness, suppleness, elasticity, extensibility, limberness, litheness.

flexible *a.* limber, lithe, supple, plastic, elastic, bending, malleable, pliable, soft, extensile, spongy, tractable, moldable, yielding, formable, bendable, formative, impressionable, like putty, like wax, adjustable, stretchable.—*Ant.* STIFF, hard, rigid.

flicker *v.* sparkle, twinkle, glitter; see FLASH, SHINE 1.

flight *n.* **1.** [Act of remaining aloft] soaring, winging, flying, journey by air, avigation. **2.** [Travel by air] aerial navigation, aeronautics, flying, gliding, space flight, air transport, aviation. **3.** [Act of fleeing] fleeing, running away, retreating; see RETREAT 1. **4.** [Stairs] steps, staircase, stairway; see STAIRS.

flighty *a.* capricious, fickle, whimsical; see CHANGING.

flimsy *a.* slight, infirm, frail, weak, unsubstantial, inadequate, defective, wobbly, fragile, makeshift, decrepit; see also POOR 2.

flinch *v.* start, shrink back, blench; see COWER.

fling *n.* indulgence, party, good time; see CELEBRATION.

fling *v.* toss, sling, dump; see THROW 1.

flippancy *n.* impertinence, impudence, sauciness; see RUDENESS.

flippant *a.* impudent, saucy, smart; see RUDE 2.

flirt *n.* coquette, tease, siren; see LOVER.

flirt *v.* coquet, make advances, make eyes at; see SEDUCE.

float *n.* buoy, air cell, air cushion, lifesaver, bobber, cork, raft, diving platform, life preserver.

float *v.* waft, stay afloat, swim; see DRIFT.

floating *a.* buoyant, hollow, unsinkable, lighter-than-water, light, swimming, inflated, sailing, soaring, volatile, loose, free.—*Ant.* HEAVY, submerged, sunk.

flock *n.* group, pack, litter; see HERD.

flock *v.* throng, congregate, crowd; see GATHER 1.

flood *n.* deluge, surge, tide, high tide, overflow, torrent, wave, flood tide, tidal flood, tidal flow, inundation.

flood *v.* inundate, swamp, overflow, deluge, submerge, immerse, brim over.

floor *n.* 1. [The lower limit of a room] floorboards, deck, flagstones, tiles, planking, ground, carpet, rug, linoleum. 2. [The space in a building between two floors] story, stage, landing, level, flat, basement, cellar, ground floor, ground story, lower story, first floor, mezzanine, upper story, downstairs, upstairs, loft, attic, garret, penthouse.

flooring *n.* floors, woodwork, oak flooring, hardwood flooring, tile, flagstones, boards, cement, floor covering, linoleum.

flop *v.* 1. [To move with little control] wobble, teeter, stagger, flounder, wriggle, squirm, stumble, tumble, totter, flounce, quiver, flap, wiggle, spin, jerk. 2. [To fall without restraint] tumble, slump, drop; see FALL 1. 3. [*To be a complete failure] founder, fall short, bomb*; see FAIL 1.

flounder *v.* struggle, wallow, blunder; see FLOP 1, TOSS 2.

flour *n.* meal, pulp, powder, grit, bran, starch, wheat germ, white flour, wheat flour, rye flour, potato flour, barley meal, corn meal, oatmeal, rolled oats, cake flour, pancake flour, soybean flour, soyabean flour, soyflour.

flourish *v.* thrive, increase, wax; see SUCCEED 1.

flourishing *a.* thriving, doing well, growing; see RICH 1, SUCCESSFUL.

flow *n.* current, movement, progress, stream, tide, run, river, flood, ebb, gush, spurt, spout, leakage, dribble, oozing, flux, overflow, issue, discharge, drift, course, draft, downdraft, up-current, wind, breeze.

flow *v.* stream, course, slide, slip, glide, move, progress, run, pass, float, sweep, rush, whirl, surge, roll, swell, ebb, pour out, spurt, squirt, flood, jet, spout, rush, gush, well up, drop, drip, seep, trickle, overflow, spill, run, spew, stream, brim, surge, leak, run out, ooze, splash, pour forth, bubble.

flower *n.* blossom, bud, spray, cluster, shoot, posy, herb, vine, annual, perennial, flowering shrub, potted plant; see also FRUIT. *Common flowers include the following:* daisy, violet, cowslip, jack-in-the-pulpit, goldenrod, orchid, primrose, bluebell, salvia, geranium, begonia, pansy, calendula, forsythia, daffodil, jonquil, crocus, dahlia, zinnia, tulip, iris, lily, petunia, gladiolus, aster, rose, peony, nasturtium, chrysanthemum, poppy, morning-glory, lily of the valley, clematis, buttercup, bougainvillea, dandelion, fuchsia, bridal wreath, lilac, stock, sweet william, bachelor's button, tuberose, bleeding heart, phlox.

flower *v.* open, blossom, bud; see BLOOM.

flowery *a.* elaborate, ornamented, rococo; see ORNATE.

flowing *a.* sweeping, sinuous, spouting, running, gushing, pouring out, rippling, issuing, fluid, tidal, liquid.

fluctuate *v.* vacillate, waver, falter; see HESITATE.

fluctuation *n.* vacillation, variation, inconstancy; see CHANGE 1.

fluency *n.* facility of speech, volubility, command of language; see ELOQUENCE.

fluent *a.* eloquent, voluble, glib, wordy, smooth, talkative, smooth-spoken, garrulous, verbose, chatty, argumentative, articulate, vocal, cogent, persuasive, silver-tongued*, having the gift of gab*.—*Ant.* DUMB, tongue-tied, stammering.

fluffy *a.* fleecy, fuzzy, lacy; see SOFT 1.

fluid *a.* liquid, fluent, flowing, running, watery, molten, liquefied, juicy.—*Ant.* STIFF, solid, frozen.

fluid *n.* liquor, vapor, solution; see LIQUID.

flunk* *v.* miss, drop, have to repeat; see FAIL 1.

flute *n.* pipe, piccolo, wind instrument, fife, panpipe, recorder; see also MUSICAL INSTRUMENT.

flutter *v.* flap, ripple, wiggle; see WAVE 1, 3.

fly *n.* 1. [An insect] housefly, bluebottle, bug, winged insect, gnat, horsefly, fruit fly, tsetse fly. 2. [A ball batted into the air] infield fly, high fly, fly ball, fungo, pop fly*. 3. [A hook baited artificially] lure, fish lure, dry fly, wet fly, spinner, trout fly, bass fly, minnow.

fly *v.* 1. [To pass through the air] wing, soar, float, glide, remain aloft, take flight, take wing, hover, sail, swoop, dart, drift, flutter, circle. 2. [To move swiftly] rush, dart, flee; see SPEED. 3. [To flee from danger] retreat, hide, withdraw; see ESCAPE. 4. [To manage a plane in the air] pilot, navigate, control, jet, take off, operate, glide, climb, dive, manipulate, maneuver.

flyer *n.* aviator, navigator, airman; see PILOT 1.

flying *a.* floating, making flight, passing through the air, on the wing, soaring, gliding, winging, swooping, darting, plummeting, drifting, rising, airborne, in midair.

foam *n.* fluff, bubbles, lather; see FROTH.

focus *n.* focal point, locus, point of convergence; see CENTER 1. —**in focus** distinct, obvious, sharply defined; see CLEAR 2. —**out of focus** indistinct, unclear, blurred; see OBSCURE 1.

focus *v.* 1. [To draw toward a center] attract, converge, convene; see CENTER. 2. [To make an image clear] adjust, bring out, get detail; see SHARPEN 2.

foe *n.* opponent, antagonist, adversary; see ENEMY.

fog *n.* mist, haze, cloud, film, steam, wisp, smoke, smog, soup*, pea soup*.

foggy *a.* dull, misty, gray; see HAZY.

fold *n.* lap, pleat, lapel, tuck, folded portion, part turned over, part turned back, doubled material, crease, turn, folded edge, crimp, wrinkle.

fold *v.* **1.** [To place together, or lay in folds] double, crease, curl, crimp, wrinkle, ruffle, pucker, gather, double over, lap, overlap, overlay.—*Ant.* UNFOLD, straighten, expand. **2.** [*To fail] become insolvent, declare oneself bankrupt, close; see FAIL 4.

folder *n.* **1.** [A folded sheet of printed matter] circular, pamphlet, paper, bulletin, advertisement, enclosure, brochure, throwaway, insert. **2.** [A light, flexible case] envelope, binder, portfolio, Manila folder.

folk *n.* race, nation, community, tribe, society, nationality, population, state, settlement, culture, ethnic group, clan, confederation.

folklore *n.* traditions, folk tales, oral tradition, folk wisdom, oral literature, ballad lore, customs, superstitions, legends, folkways, folk wisdom, traditional lore; see also MYTH.

folks *n.pl.* relatives, relations, kin; see FAMILY.

follow *v.* **1.** [To be later in time] come next, ensue, postdate; see SUCCEED 2. **2.** [To regulate one's action] conform, observe, imitate, copy, take after, match, mirror, reflect, follow the example of, do as, mimic, follow suit, do like, tag along, obey, abide by, adhere to, comply, be in keeping, be consistent with.—*Ant.* NEGLECT, disregard, depart from. **3.** [To observe] heed, regard, keep an eye on; see WATCH. **4.** [To understand] comprehend, catch, realize; see UNDERSTAND 1. **5.** [To result] proceed from, happen, ensue; see BEGIN 2. **—as follows** the following, next, succeeding; see FOLLOWING.

follower *n.* henchman, attendant, hanger-on, companion, lackey, helper, partisan, recruit, disciple, pupil, protegé, imitator, apostle, adherent, supporter, zealot, backer, participant, sponsor, witness, devotee, believer, advocate, member, admirer, patron, promoter, upholder, copycat*, yes man*.—*Ant.* OPPONENT, deserter, heretic.

following *a.* succeeding, next, ensuing, subsequent, later, after a while, by and by, when, later on, a while later, then, henceforth, afterwards, presently, afterward, coming after, directly after, in the wake of, pursuing, in pursuit of, in search of, resulting, latter, rear, back.—*Ant.* PRECEDING, former, earlier.

following *n.* group, clientele, public, audience, train, adherents, supporters, hangers-on, patrons.

fond *a.* enamored, attached, affectionate; see LOVING.

fondness *n.* partiality, attachment, kindness; see AFFECTION.

food *n.* victuals, foodstuffs, meat and drink, meat, nutriment, refreshment, edibles, table, comestibles, provisions, stores, sustenance, subsistence, rations, board, cooking, cookery, cuisine, nourishment, fare, grub*, vittles*, eats*, chow*; see also MEAL 2. For food in the menu, see also BREAD, BUTTER, CAKE 2, CANDY, CHEESE, DELICATESSEN 1, DESSERT, DRINK 2, EGG, FISH, FLAVORING, FOWL, FRUIT, JAM 1, JELLY, MEAT, MILK, NUT 1, PASTRY, SALAD, SOUP, SPICE, STEW, VEGETABLE.

fool *n.* nitwit, simpleton, dunce, oaf, ninny, cretin, nincompoop, dolt, idiot, jackass, ass, buffoon, blockhead, numskull, boob*, goose, ignoramus, imbecile, moron, clown, loon, dullard, fathead*, half-wit, bonehead*, dope*, sap*, birdbrain*, jerk*, dum-dum*.—*Ant.* PHILOSOPHER, sage, scholar. **—no** (or **nobody's**) **fool** shrewd, calculating, capable; see ABLE, INTELLIGENT. **—play the fool** be silly, show off, clown; see JOKE.

fool *v.* trick, dupe, mislead; see DECEIVE.

fool around *v.* waste time, idle, dawdle; see PLAY 1, 2, WASTE 1, 2.

fooled *a.* tricked, duped, deluded; see DECEIVED.

fooling *a.* joking, jesting, humorous, deceitful, gay, witty, smart, frivolous, flippant, laughable, insincere, misleading, absurd, clever, playful, merry, kidding*, spoofing*.—*Ant.* SERIOUS, grave, earnest.

foolish *a.* silly, simple, half-witted; see STUPID.

foolishly *a.* stupidly, irrationally, idiotically, insanely, imprudently, ineptly, mistakenly, illogically, unwisely, ill-advisedly, crazily, thoughtlessly, carelessly, senselessly, irresponsibly, absurdly, preposterously, ridiculously, with bad judgment, without good sense.

foolishness *n.* folly, weakness, silliness; see STUPIDITY 1.

foot *n.* **1.** [A unit of measurement] twelve inches, running foot, front foot, board foot, square foot, cubic foot. **2.** [End of the leg] pedal extremity, hoof, paw, pad, dog*, tootsy*. **3.** [A foundation] footing, base, pier; see FOUNDATION 2. **4.** [A metrical unit in verse] measure, accent, interval, meter, duple meter, triple meter. *Metrical feet include the following:* iamb, dactyl, spondee, trochee, anapest. **—on foot** running, hiking, moving; see WALKING. **—on one's feet 1.** [Upright] standing, erect, vertical; see STRAIGHT. **2.** [Established] sound, settled, secure; see ESTABLISHED 1. **—on the wrong foot** unfavorably, ineptly, incapably; see WRONGLY. **—put one's best foot forward*** do one's best, appear at one's best, try hard; see DISPLAY. **—put one's foot down*** be firm, act decisively, determine; see RESOLVE. **—under foot** on the ground, at one's feet, in the way; see UNDER 1.

football *n.* **1.** [A sport] American football, Canadian football, association football, soccer, gridiron pastime*, the pigskin sport*. **2.** [The ball used in football] leather oval, pigskin*, sphere; see BALL 1.
football player *n. In the United States, football players include the following:* right end, left end, right tackle, left tackle, right guard, left guard, center, quarterback, left halfback, right halfback, fullback; safety, linebacker, tight end, wide end, cornerback, flanker, nose guard.
foothold *n.* ledge, footing, niche; see STEP 2.
footing *n.* basis, resting place, foot; see STEP 2.
footprint *n.* trace, trail, footstep; see TRACK 2.
footstep *n.* trace, trail, evidence; see TRACK 2. **—follow in someone's footsteps** emulate, succeed, resemble a predecessor; see IMITATE 1.
for *conj.* as, since, in consequence of the fact that; see BECAUSE.
for *prep.* toward, to, in favor of, intended to be given to, in order to get, under the authority of, in the interest of, during, in order to, in the direction of, to go to, to the amount of, in place of, in exchange for, as, in spite of, supposing, concerning, with respect to, with regard to, notwithstanding, with a view to, for the sake of, in consideration of, in the name of, on the part of.
forasmuch (as) *conj.* since, inasmuch as, whereas; see BECAUSE.
for a while *a.* for a short time, for a few minutes, briefly; see AWHILE.
forbid *v.* prohibit, debar, embargo, restrain, inhibit, preclude, oppose, cancel, hinder, obstruct, bar, prevent, censor, outlaw, declare illegal, withhold, restrict, deny, block, check, disallow, deprive, exclude, ban, taboo, say no to, put under an injunction.—*Ant.* APPROVE, recommend, authorize.
forbidden *a.* denied, taboo, kept back; see REFUSED.
forbidding *a.* unpleasant, offensive, repulsive; see GRIM 1.
force *n.* **1.** [Force conceived as a physical property] power, might, energy; see STRENGTH. **2.** [Force conceived as part of one's personality] forcefulness, dominance, competence, energy, persistence, willpower, drive, determination, effectiveness, efficiency, authority, impressiveness, ability, capability, potency, sapience, guts*.—*Ant.* INDIFFERENCE, impotence, incompetence. **3.** [An organization] group, band, unit; see ORGANIZATION 2, POLICE. **—in force 1.** [Powerfully] in full strength, totally, all together; see ALL 2. **2.** [In operation] operative, valid, in effect; see WORKING.
force *v.* compel, coerce, press, drive, make, impel, constrain, oblige, obligate, necessitate, require, enforce, demand, order, command, inflict, burden, impose, insist, exact, put under obligation, contract, charge, restrict, limit, pin down, bring pressure to bear upon, bear down, ram down someone's throat*, high-pressure*, strong-arm*, put the squeeze on*.
forced *a.* compelled, coerced, constrained; see BOUND 2.
forceful *a.* commanding, dominant, electric; see POWERFUL 1.
forcefully *a.* forcibly, stubbornly, willfully; see VIGOROUSLY.
foreboding *n.* premonition, dread, presentiment; see ANTICIPATION.
forecast *n.* prediction, guess, estimate, prognosis, divination, forethought, foresight, prescience, foreknowledge, conjecture, prophecy, calculation, foreseeing.
forecast *v.* predetermine, predict, guess; see FORETELL.
forefather *n.* ancestor, progenitor, forebear, father, parent, sire, forerunner, author, predecessor, originator, precursor, grandfather, procreator, patriarch, relative, begetter, founder, kinsman.
for effect *a.* artificially, hypocritically, ostentatiously; see DELIBERATELY.
forego *v.* quit, relinquish, waive; see ABANDON 1.
foregoing *a.* prior, former, previous; see PRECEDING.
foreground *n.* face, forefront, frontage, façade, neighborhood, proximity, nearness, adjacency, range, reach, view.—*Ant.* BACKGROUND, shadow, perspective.
forehead *n.* brow, countenance, temples; see FACE 1.
foreign *a.* remote, exotic, strange, far, distant, inaccessible, unaccustomed, different, unknown, alien, imported, borrowed, immigrant, outside, expatriate, exiled, from abroad, coming from another land, not native, not domestic, nonresident, alienated, faraway, far-off, outlandish.—*Ant.* LOCAL, national, indigenous.
foreigner *n.* stranger, immigrant, newcomer; see ALIEN.
foreknowledge *n.* foresight, prescience, premonition; see FEELING 4, FORECAST.
foreman *n.* overseer, manager, supervisor, superintendent, head, head man, shop foreman, boss, slave driver.
foremost *a.* fore, original, primary; see FIRST.
forerunner *n.* herald, harbinger, precursor; see FOREFATHER, MESSENGER.
foresee *v.* prophesy, understand, predict; see FORETELL.
foreseen *a.* anticipated, predictable, prepared for; see EXPECTED, LIKELY 1.
foreshadow *v.* imply, presage, suggest; see FORETELL.

foresight *n.* economy, carefulness, husbandry; see PRUDENCE.

forest *n.* wood, jungle, timber, growth, stand of trees, grove, woodland, park, greenwood, cover, clump, forested area, shelter, brake, backwoods, tall timber; see also TREE.

forestall *v.* thwart, prevent, preclude; see HINDER.

forestry *n.* forest management, horticulture, dendrology, woodcraft, forestation, reclamation, woodmanship; see also CONSERVATION.

foretell *v.* predict, prophesy, divine, foresee, announce in advance, prognosticate, augur, portend, foreshadow.—*Ant.* RECORD, confirm, recount.

forethought *n.* judgment, planning, foresight; see PRUDENCE.

forever *a.* everlastingly, permanently, immortally, on and on, ever, perpetually, always, in perpetuity, world without end, eternally, interminably, infinitely, enduringly, unchangingly, durably, ever and again, indestructibly, endlessly, forevermore, for good, till hell freezes over*, for keeps*, for always, now and forever, for life, till death do us part.—*Ant.* TEMPORARILY, for a time, at present.

forewarn *v.* alert, advise, caution; see WARN.

for example *a.* for instance, as a model, as an example, to illustrate, to cite an instance, to give an illustration, a case in point, like.

forfeit *v.* sacrifice, give up, relinquish; see ABANDON 1.

for fun *a.* for no reason, for the fun of it, in fun; see HAPPILY.

forge *v.* falsify, counterfeit, fabricate, trump up, invent, feign, make, fashion, design, imitate, copy, duplicate, reproduce, trace.

forger *n.* falsifier, counterfeiter, con man*; see CRIMINAL.

forgery *n.* imitation, copy, counterfeit, fake, fabrication, sham, phony*.—*Ant.* ORIGINAL, real thing, real article.

forget *v.* lose consciousness of, put out of one's head, fail to remember, be forgetful, have a short memory, overlook, ignore, omit, neglect, slight, disregard, lose sight of, pass over, skip, think no more of, close one's eyes to, not give another thought, draw a blank*, dismiss from the mind, kiss off*, laugh off*.—*Ant.* REMEMBER, recall, recollect.

forget about *v.* omit, let slip one's memory, miss; see FORGET, NEGLECT 2.

forgetful *a.* inattentive, neglectful, heedless; see CARELESS.

forgetfulness *n.* negligence, neglect, inattention; see CARELESSNESS.

forget oneself *v.* offend, go astray, lose control; see MISBEHAVE.

forgivable *a.* venial, trivial, pardonable; see EXCUSABLE.

forgive *v.* pardon, forgive and forget, let pass, excuse, condone, remit, forget, relent, bear no malice, exonerate, exculpate, let bygones be bygones, laugh it off, let up on, let it go, kiss and make up, bury the hatchet, turn the other cheek, make allowance, write off.—*Ant.* HATE, resent, retaliate.

forgiven *a.* reinstated, taken back, welcomed home; see PARDONED.

forgiveness *n.* absolution, pardon, acquittal, exoneration, remission, dispensation, reprieve, justification, amnesty, respite.

forgiving *a.* charitable, open-hearted, generous; see KIND.

for good *a.* permanently, for all time, henceforth; see FOREVER.

forgotten *a.* not remembered, not recalled, not recollected, lost, out of one's mind, erased from one's consciousness, beyond recollection, past recall, not recoverable, blanked out, lapsed; see also ABANDONED.

fork *n.* **1.** [A forked implement] table fork, hay fork, pitchfork, salad fork, cooking fork, trident, prong. **2.** [A branch of a road or river] bend, turn, crossroad, tributary, byway, junction, branch, stream, creek, confluence.

form *n.* **1.** [Shape] figure, appearance, plan, arrangement, design, outline, configuration, formation, structure, style, construction, fashion, mode, scheme, framework, contour, stance, profile, silhouette, skeleton, anatomy. **2.** [The human form] body, frame, torso; see FIGURE 2. **3.** [The approved procedure] manner, mode, custom; see METHOD. **4.** [Anything intended to give form] pattern, model, die; see MOLD 1. **5.** [A standard letter or blank] mimeographed letter, duplicate, form letter, data sheet, information blank, chart, card, reference form, order form, questionnaire, application; see also COPY.

form *v.* **1.** [To give shape to a thing] mold, pattern, model, arrange, make, block out, fashion, construct, devise, plan, design, contrive, produce, invent, frame, scheme, plot, compose, erect, build, cast, cut, carve, chisel, hammer out, put together, whittle, assemble, conceive, create, outline, trace, develop, cultivate, work, complete, finish, perfect, fix, regulate, establish, sculpture, bend, twist, knead, set, determine, arrive at, reach.—*Ant.* DESTROY, demolish, shatter. **2.** [To give character to a person] instruct, rear, breed; see TEACH. **3.** [To comprise] constitute, figure in, act as; see COMPOSE 1. **4.** [To take form] accumulate, condense, harden, set, settle, rise, appear, take shape, grow, develop, unfold, mature, materialize, become a reality, take on character, become visible, shape up*, fall into place*, get into shape*.—*Ant.* DISAPPEAR, dissolve, waste away.

formal *a.* 1. [Notable for arrangement] orderly, precise, set; see REGULAR 3. 2. [Concerned with etiquette and behavior] reserved, distant, stiff; see CONVENTIONAL 3, POLITE. 3. [Official] confirmed, directed, lawful; see APPROVED, LEGAL. 4. [In evening clothes] full dress, black-tie, dressed up; see SOCIAL.

formality *n.* decorum, etiquette, correctness; see BEHAVIOR.

format *n.* make-up, arrangement, construction; see FORM 1.

formation *n.* arrangement, crystallization, accumulation, production, composition, development, fabrication, deposit, generation, creation, genesis, constitution.—*Ant.* DESTRUCTION, dissolution, annihilation.

formed *a.* shaped, molded, patterned, modeled, carved, outlined, developed, cultivated, completed, finished, built, forged, created, invented, concocted, designed, accomplished, manufactured, produced, born, perfected, fixed, established, arrived at, solidified, hardened, set, determined.—*Ant.* SHAPELESS, formless, nebulous.

former *a.* earlier, previous, past; see PRECEDING.

formerly *a.* before now, some time ago, once, once upon a time, already, in former times, previously, earlier, in the early days, eons ago, centuries ago, in the past, in the olden days, used to be, long ago, before this, in time past, heretofore, a while back*.—*Ant.* RECENTLY, subsequently, immediately.

formula *n.* specifications, description, recipe; see METHOD.

formulate *v.* express, give form to, set down; see FORM 1.

fornication *n.* adultery, incontinence, carnality, lechery, illicit intercourse, lewdness, licentiousness, unfaithfulness, fooling around*, promiscuousness, coitus, debauchery, libertinism, copulation, sex, prostitution.

for rent *a.* on the market, renting, selling, for hire, available, offered, advertised, to let, salable.

forsake *v.* desert, leave, quit; see ABANDON 2.

forsaken *a.* destitute, deserted, rejected; see ABANDONED.

for sale *a.* selling, salable, on the block, on the market, on auction, advertised, listed, up for sale, to be cleared out*, for clearance.

fort *n.* fortress, citadel, stockade; see FORTIFICATION.

forth *a.* first, out, into; see AHEAD. —**and so forth** and so on, similarly, and the like; see OTHER.

forthcoming *a.* expected, inevitable, anticipated, future, impending, pending, resulting, awaited, destined, fated, predestined, approaching, in store, at hand, inescapable, imminent, in prospect, prospective, in the wind, in preparation, in the cards.

for the time being *a.* at the moment, for now, for the present; see TEMPORARILY.

forthright *a.* at once, straight away, directly; see IMMEDIATELY.

fortification *n.* fort, fortress, defense, dugout, trench, entrenchment, gun emplacement, barricade, battlement, stockade, outpost, citadel, support, wall, barrier, earthwork, castle, pillbox, bastion, bulwark, breastwork, blockhouse.

fortified *a.* defended, guarded, safeguarded, protected, manned, garrisoned, barricaded, armed, barbed, secured, entrenched, strong, covered, strengthened, supported, surrounded, fortressed, walled, enclosed, stockaded, armored, dug in, hidden, camouflaged.—*Ant.* OPEN, unprotected, unguarded.

fortify *v.* 1. [To strengthen against attack] barricade, entrench, buttress; see DEFEND 1. 2. [To strengthen physically or emotionally] sustain, invigorate, toughen; see STRENGTHEN.

fortitude *n.* firmness, resolution, persistence; see DETERMINATION.

fortunate *a.* lucky, blessed, prosperous, successful, having a charmed life, in luck, favored, well-to-do, happy, triumphant, victorious, overcoming, affluent, thriving, flourishing, healthy, wealthy, well-fixed*, well-heeled*, born with a silver spoon in one's mouth*.—*Ant.* UNFORTUNATE, unlucky, cursed.

fortunately *a.* luckily, happily, in good time, auspiciously, favorably, prosperously, in the nick of time.—*Ant.* UNFORTUNATELY, unluckily, unhappily.

fortune *n.* 1. [Chance] luck, fate, uncertainty; see CHANCE 1. 2. [Great riches] possessions, inheritance, estate; see WEALTH. —**a small fortune** a high price, a great expense, a large amount of money; see PRICE.

forward *a.* 1. [Going forward] advancing, progressing, ahead, leading, progressive, onward, propulsive, in advance.—*Ant.* BACKWARD, retreating, regressive. 2. [Bold] presumptuous, impertinent, fresh; see RUDE 2.

forwarded *a.* shipped, expressed, dispatched; see DELIVERED.

fossil *n.* remains, reconstruction, specimen, skeleton, relic, find, impression, trace, petrified deposit; see also RELIC.

foster *v.* cherish, nurse, nourish; see RAISE 2.

foul *a.* 1. [Disgusting] nasty, vulgar, coarse; see OFFENSIVE 2. 2. [Unfair] vicious, inequitable, unjust; see DISHONEST.

foul *v.* 1. [To make dirty] defile, pollute, sully; see DIRTY. 2. [To become dirty] soil, spot, stain; see DIRTY.

found *a.* unearthed, revealed, detected; see DISCOVERED.

found *v.* establish, endow, set up; see ESTABLISH 2.

foundation *n.* **1.** [An intellectual basis] reason, justification, authority; see BASIS. **2.** [A physical basis] footing, base, foot, basement, pier, groundwork, bed, ground, bottom, substructure, wall, underpinning, solid rock, infrastructure, pile, roadbed, support, prop, stand, shore, post, pillar, skeleton, column, shaft, pedestal, buttress, framework, scaffold, beam. **3.** [That which has been founded] institution, organization, endowment, institute, society, establishment, company, guild, corporation, association, charity, scholarship fund, trust.

founded *a.* organized, endowed, set up; see ESTABLISHED 1.

founder *n.* originator, sponsor, prime mover; see AUTHOR, FOREFATHER.

fountain *n.* **1.** [A jet of water] jet, stream, gush, spout, geyser, spurt, spring, pond, basin, pool; see also WATER 1, 2. **2.** [A soda-water dispensary] soda fountain, ice-cream parlor, drugstore fountain; see BAR 2.

fowl *n.* barnyard fowl, wild fowl, poultry, chicken, duck, goose, turkey, cock, hen, Cornish hen, pheasant, partridge, prairie chicken, grouse, capon, ptarmigan, swan; see also BIRD.

fox *n.* **1.** [A clever person] cheat, trickster, con man*; see RASCAL. **2.** [An animal] red fox, gray fox, silver fox; see DOG.

fraction *n.* section, portion, part; see DIVISION 2.

fractional *a.* partial, sectional, fragmentary; see UNFINISHED 1.

fracture *n.* rupture, wound, crack, cleaving, shattering, breach, fragmentation, displacement, dislocation, broken bone, shearing, severing, separating, dismembering.

fragile *a.* brittle, frail, delicate; see DAINTY, WEAK 1, 2.

fragment *n.* piece, scrap, remnant; see BIT 1.

fragrance *n.* perfume, aroma, odor; see SMELL 1.

fragrant *a.* aromatic, sweet, perfumed; see SWEET 3.

frail *a.* feeble, breakable, tender; see DAINTY.

frailty *n.* brittleness, delicacy, feebleness; see WEAKNESS 1.

frame *n.* **1.** [The structural portion] skeleton, scaffold, framework, scaffolding, casing, framing, support, substructure, infrastructure, stage, groundwork, organization, anatomy, fabric, architecture, enclosure, span, block, window frame, doorjamb. **2.** [A border intended as an ornament] margin, fringe, hem, flounce, trim, trimming, outline, mounting, molding.

frame *v.* **1.** [To make] construct, erect, raise; see BUILD. **2.** [To enclose in a frame] mount, border, enclose; see SUPPORT 1. **3.** [To act as a frame] encircle, confine, enclose; see SURROUND 1. **4.** [*To cause a miscarriage of justice] conspire against, double-cross, fix; see DECEIVE.

framed *a.* **1.** [Surrounded by a frame] mounted, enclosed, bordered, encircled, fringed, enveloped, outlined, confined, enclosed, wrapped, clasped. **2.** [*Arranged beforehand] faked, fixed*, planted*; see FALSE 3.

frame-up* *n.* deception, fraud, conspiracy; see TRICK 1.

framework *n.* skeleton, structure, core; see FRAME.

France *n.* French nation, French people, the French, French Republic, Fifth Republic, French empire, Franks, Gaul; see also EUROPE.

frank *a.* candid, sincere, free, easy, familiar, open, direct, unreserved, uninhibited, downright, ingenuous, unsophisticated, unaffected, plain, aboveboard, forthright, outspoken, tactless, guileless, straightforward, plain-spoken, natural, blunt, matter-of-fact.—*Ant.* DISHONEST, insincere, secretive.

frankfurter *n.* wiener, wiener sausage, weenie*, hot dog*, frank*, dog*, link.

frankly *a.* freely, honestly, candidly; see OPENLY 1.

frankness *n.* openness, sincerity, candidness; see HONESTY.

frantic *a.* distracted, mad, wild, frenetic, furious, raging, raving, frenzied, violent, agitated, deranged, crazy, delirious, insane, angry; see also EXCITED.—*Ant.* CALM, composed, subdued.

fraternity *n.* brotherhood, club, fellowship; see ORGANIZATION 2.

fraud *n.* **1.** [Deceit] trickery, duplicity, guile; see DECEPTION. **2.** [An imposter] pretender, charlatan, fake; see CHEAT.

fraudulent *a.* deceitful, tricky, swindling; see DISHONEST.

freak *n.* monstrosity, monster, rarity, malformation, freak of nature, oddity, aberration, curiosity, hybrid, anomaly, mutation; see also MONSTER.

freckle *n.* mole, patch, blotch; see BLEMISH.

free *a.* **1.** [Not restricted politically] sovereign, independent, released, autonomous, self-ruling, freed, liberated, self-governing, democratic, at liberty, unconstrained.—*Ant.* RESTRICTED, enslaved, subject. **2.** [Not restricted in space; *said of persons*] unconfined, at large, cast loose, escaped, let out, scot-free, free as air, free to come and go, unfettered, foot-loose and fancy-free, free-wheeling*, on the loose*.—*Ant.* CONFINED, imprisoned, restrained. **3.** [Not restricted in space; *said of things*] unimpeded, unobstructed, unhampered, unattached, loose, not attached, clear from, unentangled, unengaged, disengaged, unfastened.—*Ant.* FIXED, fastened, rooted. **4.** [Given without charge] gratuitous, gratis, for nothing, without charge, free of cost, complimentary, for free*, on the house.—*Ant.* PAID, charged, costly. —**for free*** without cost, gratis, for nothing; see FREE 4. —**set free** release, liberate, emancipate; see FREE.

free *v.* release, discharge, deliver, save, emancipate, rescue, extricate, loosen, unbind, disengage, undo, set free, let out, let loose, bail out, cut loose, relieve, absolve, acquit, dismiss, pardon, clear, ransom, redeem, unbind, unchain, disentangle, untie, let go, unlock, unhand, let out of prison, open the cage, turn loose, unfetter, unshackle.—*Ant.* SEIZE, capture, incarcerate.

freedom *n.* **1.** [Political liberty] independence, sovereignty, autonomy, democracy, self-government, citizenship, representative government, self-determination; see also LIBERTY 4.—*Ant.* SLAVERY, bondage, regimentation. **2.** [Exemption from necessity] privilege, immunity, license, indulgence, facility, range, latitude, scope, play, own accord, free rein, leeway, plenty of rope*.—*Ant.* RESTRAINT, constraint, hindrance. **3.** [Natural ease and facility] readiness, forthrightness, spontaneity; see EASE 2.

freeing *n.* emancipation, releasing, salvation; see RESCUE.

freely *a.* **1.** [Without physical restriction] loosely, without encumbrance, unhindered, without restraint, as one pleases, easily, smoothly.—*Ant.* with difficulty, uneasily, stressfully. **2.** [Without mental restriction] voluntarily, willingly, fancy-free, of one's own accord, at will, at pleasure, of one's own free will, purposely, deliberately, intentionally, advisedly, spontaneously, frankly, openly.—*Ant.* UNWILLINGLY, under compulsion, hesitantly.

freeway *n.* turnpike, superhighway, toll road; see HIGHWAY, ROAD 1.

free will *n.* willingness, volition, intention, purpose, choice, free choice, power of choice, freedom, pleasure, discretion, inclination, desire, wish, intent, option, determination, mind, consent, assent.—*Ant.* RESTRAINT, predestination, unwillingness.

freeze *v.* **1.** [To change to a solid state] congeal, harden, solidify, ice, quick-freeze, glaciate, chill, benumb, cool, ice up*.—*Ant.* MELT, thaw, liquefy. **2.** [To control] seal, terminate, immobilize; see CONTROL.

freezing *a.* frosty, wintry, frigid; see COLD 1.

freight *n.* burden, load, contents, weight, bulk, encumbrance, bales, shipment, cargo, shipping, consignment, goods, tonnage, packages, ware.

freighter *n.* tanker, transport, cargo ship; see SHIP.

French *a.* **1.** [Referring to the French culture or people] Gallic, Latin, Frenchified, Parisian. **2.** [Referring to the French language] Romance, Romantic, Parisian, Gallic.

French *n.* **1.** [The French people] Gallic nation, Parisians, Frenchmen, Latins, Basques, Gauls, Normans, Provençals, French provincials. **2.** [The French tongue] Romance language, modern French, Middle French, Old French, Norman, Parisian French, Anglo-Norman.

frenzy *n.* rage, craze, furor; see EXCITEMENT, INSANITY.

frequency *n.* recurrence, number, reiteration; see REGULARITY.

frequent *a.* **1.** [Happening often] many, repeated, numerous, common, habitual, monotonous, profuse, incessant, continual, customary, intermittent, familiar, commonplace, expected, various, a good many.—*Ant.* RARE, infrequent, occasional. **2.** [Happening regularly] recurrent, usual, periodic; see REGULAR 3.

frequent *v.* visit often, go to, be seen at daily, attend regularly, be at home in, be often in, be accustomed to, hang around*, hang out*; see also VISIT.

frequently *a.* often, regularly, usually, commonly, successively, many times, in many instances, all the time, notably, repeatedly, intermittently, generally, every now and then, at times, not infrequently, often enough, not seldom, periodically, at regular intervals; see also REGULARLY.—*Ant.* SELDOM, infrequently, rarely.

fresh *a.* **1.** [Newly produced] new, green, crisp, raw, recent, current, late, this season's, factory-fresh, garden-fresh, farm-fresh, brand-new, newborn, immature, young, beginning, hot off the press*, just out, newfangled.—*Ant.* OLD, stale, musty. **2.** [Not preserved] unsalted, uncured, unsmoked; see sense 1. **3.** [Unspoiled] uncontaminated, green, not stale, good, undecayed, well-preserved, odor-free, in good condition, unblemished, unspotted, preserved, new, virgin, unimpaired.—*Ant.* DECAYED, spoiled, contaminated. **4.** [Not faded] colorful, vivid, sharp; see BRIGHT 1, DEFINITE 2. **5.** [Not salt; *said of water*] potable, drinkable, cool, clear, pure, clean, sweet, fit to drink, safe.—*Ant.* DIRTY, brackish, briny. **6.** [Refreshed] rested, restored, rehabilitated, like new, unused, new, relaxed, stimulated, relieved, freshened, revived.—*Ant.* TIRED, exhausted, worn-out. **7.** [Inexperienced] untrained, untried, unskilled; see INEXPERIENCED.

freshman *n.* beginner, novice, frosh*; see AMATEUR.

fret *v.* disturb, agitate, vex; see BOTHER 2.

friar *n.* brother, padre, father; see MONK.

friction *n.* **1.** [The rubbing of two bodies] attrition, abrasion, erosion; see GRINDING.

2. [Trouble between individuals or groups] animosity, quarrel, discontent; see HATRED.

fried *a.* grilled, cooked, browned; see DONE 2.

friend *n.* familiar, schoolmate, playmate, best friend, roommate, companion, intimate, confidant, comrade, mate, amigo, fellow, pal*, chum*, crony*, buddy*, sidekick*.—*Ant.* ENEMY, foe, stranger. —**make** or **be friends with** befriend, stand by, become familiar with; see ASSOCIATE 1.

friendless *a.* deserted, alone, forlorn; see ABANDONED.

friendliness *n.* kindness, amiability, geniality; see FRIENDSHIP.

friendly *a.* kind, kindly, helpful, sympathetic, amiable, well-disposed, neighborly, well-intentioned, sociable, civil, peaceful, loving, affectionate, fond, warm-hearted, attentive, brotherly, agreeable, genial, affable, benevolent, accommodating, unoffensive, pleasant, tender, companionable, with open arms, cordial, familiar, intimate, close, devoted, dear, attached, loyal, faithful, steadfast, true, responsive, understanding, congenial, approachable, cheerful, convivial, good-humored, good-natured, generous, gracious, cooperative, whole-hearted, big-hearted*, chummy*, folksy*, thick*, arm in arm.—*Ant.* UNFRIENDLY, antagonistic, spiteful.

friendship *n.* harmony, friendliness, brotherly love; see FELLOWSHIP 1.

fright *n.* panic, dread, horror; see FEAR.

frighten *v.* scare, scare away, scare off, dismay, terrify, cow, shock, intimidate, threaten, badger, petrify, panic, demoralize, disrupt, give cause for alarm, terrorize, horrify, astound, awe, perturb, disturb, startle, frighten out of one's wits, take someone's breath away, chill to the bone, make someone's hair stand on end, make someone's blood run cold, make someone's flesh creep*, scare one stiff*, curdle the blood.

frightened *a.* terrorized, scared, startled; see AFRAID.

frightful *a.* 1. [Causing fright] fearful, awful, dreadful; see TERRIBLE 1, 2. 2. [Very unpleasant] calamitous, shocking, terrible; see OFFENSIVE 2.

frigid *a.* 1. [Thermally cold] freezing, frosty, refrigerated; see COLD 1. 2. [Unresponsive] unloving, distant, chilly; see COLD 2, INDIFFERENT.

fringe *n.* hem, trimming, border; see EDGE 1.

frisky *a.* spirited, dashing, playful; see ACTIVE.

frivolity *n.* silliness, levity, folly; see FUN.

frivolous *a.* superficial, petty, trifling; see TRIVIAL.

frog *n.* amphibian, tree frog, toad, bullfrog, horned frog, horned toad, polliwog.

from *prep.* in distinction to, out of possession of, outside of; see OF.

from side to side *a.* back and forth, wobbly, unstable; see IRREGULAR 1.

front *a.* fore, forward, frontal, foremost, head, headmost, leading, in the foreground.—*Ant.* BACK, rear, hindmost.

front *n.* 1. [The forward part or surface] exterior, forepart, anterior, bow, foreground, face, head, breast, frontal area.—*Ant.* REAR, posterior, back. 2. [The fighting line] front line, no man's land, advance position, line of battle, vanguard, outpost, field of fire, advance guard. 3. [The appearance one presents before others] mien, demeanor, aspect, countenance, face, presence, expression, figure, exterior. —**in front of** before, preceding, leading; see AHEAD.

frontier *n.* hinterland, remote districts, outskirts; see COUNTRY 1.

frost *n.* frozen dew, permafrost, rime; see ICE.

frosting *n.* icing, topping, finish, covering, coating.

frosty *a.* frigid, freezing, chilly; see COLD 1.

froth *n.* bubbles, scum, fizz, effervescence, foam, ferment, head, lather, suds, spray.

frothy *a.* fizzing, bubbling, foaming, soapy, sudsy, bubbly, fizzy, foamy, with a head on.

frown *n.* scowl, grimace, wry face, gloomy countenance, forbidding aspect, dirty look.

frown *v.* scowl, grimace, pout, glare, sulk, glower, gloom, look stern.—*Ant.* SMILE, laugh, grin.

frozen *a.* chilled, frosted, iced; see COLD 1, 2.

frugal *a.* thrifty, prudent, parsimonious; see CAREFUL.

frugality *n.* carefulness, conservation, management; see ECONOMY.

fruit *n.* berry, grain, nut, root; see also VEGETABLE. *Common fruits include the following:* apple, pear, peach, plum, nectarine, orange, grapefruit, banana, pineapple, watermelon, cantaloupe, honeydew melon, papaya, mango, guava, grape, lime, lemon, persimmon, pomegranate, raspberry, blackberry, blueberry, huckleberry, date, fig, apricot, cherry, raisin, avocado, gooseberry, strawberry.

fruitful *a.* prolific, productive, fecund; see FERTILE.

fruitless *a.* vain, unprofitable, empty; see FUTILE.

frustrate *v.* defeat, foil, balk; see PREVENT.

frustration *n.* disappointment, impediment, failure; see DEFEAT.

fry *v.* sauté, sear, singe, brown, grill, pan-fry, deep-fry, French fry, sizzle; see also COOK. —**small fry** children, infants, toddlers; see BABY, CHILD.

fudge *n.* penuche, chocolate fudge, divinity fudge; see CANDY.

fuel *n.* propellant, combustibles, firing material. *Fuels include the following:* coal, gas, oil, coke, charcoal, anthracite, propane, bituminous coal, peat, slack, stoker coal, lignite, carbon, turf, cordwood, firewood, log, kindling, timber, diesel oil, crude oil, fuel oil, natural gas, gasoline, kerosene, wax.

fuel *v.* fill up, tank up*, gas up*; see FILL 1.

fugitive *n.* outlaw, refugee, truant, runaway, exile, vagabond, waif, stray, derelict, outcast, recluse, hermit.

fulfill *v.* accomplish, effect, complete; see ACHIEVE.

fulfilled *a.* accomplished, completed, achieved, realized, effected, finished, obtained, perfected, attained, reached, actualized, executed, concluded, brought about, performed, carried out, put into effect, made good, brought to a close.—*Ant.* DISAPPOINTED, unfulfilled, unrealized.

fulfillment *n.* attainment, accomplishment, realization; see ACHIEVEMENT.

full *a.* **1.** [Filled] running over, abundant, weighted, satisfied, saturated, crammed, packed, stuffed, jammed, glutted, gorged, loaded, chock-full, stocked, satiated, crowded, stuffed to the gills*, jam-packed, crawling with*, up to the brim, packed like sardines*.—*Ant.* EMPTY, exhausted, void. **2.** [Well supplied] abundant, complete, copious, ample, plentiful, sufficient, adequate, competent, lavish, extravagant, profuse.—*Ant.* INADEQUATE, scanty, insufficient. **3.** [Not limited] broad, unlimited, extensive; see ABSOLUTE 1, 2. —**in full** for the entire amount, fully, thoroughly; see COMPLETELY.

full blast *a.* at full capacity, full throttle, to the utmost; see FAST 1.

full-grown *a.* adult, prime, grown-up; see MATURE.

fully *a.* entirely, thoroughly, wholly; see COMPLETELY.

fumble *n.* mistake, blunder, dropped ball; see ERROR.

fumble *v.* mishandle, bungle, mismanage; see BOTCH.

fun *n.* play, game, sport, jest, amusement, relaxation, pastime, diversion, frolic, mirth, entertainment, solace, merriment, pleasure, caper, foolery, romping, joke, absurdity, playfulness, laughter, festivity, carnival, tomfoolery, ball*, escapade, antic, romp, prank, comedy, teasing, celebration, holiday, rejoicing, good humor, joking, enjoyment, gladness, good cheer, delight, glee, treat, lark, recreation, joy, time of one's life, blast*, big time*, picnic*, riot*.—*Ant.* UNHAPPINESS, tedium, sorrow. —**for** or **in fun** for amusement, not seriously, playfully; see HAPPILY. —**make fun of** mock, satirize, poke fun at; see RIDICULE.

function *n.* employment, capacity, faculty; see USE 1.

function *v.* perform, run, work; see OPERATE 2.

functional *a.* occupational, utilitarian, anatomic; see PRACTICAL.

fund *n.* endowment, trust fund, capital; see GIFT 1.

fundamental *a.* basic, underlying, primary, first, rudimentary, elemental, supporting, elementary, cardinal, organic, theoretical, structural, sustaining, central, original.—*Ant.* SUPERFICIAL, incidental, consequent.

fundamentally *a.* basically, radically, centrally; see ESSENTIALLY.

fundamentals *n.pl.* essentials, basics, foundation; see BASIS.

funds *n.pl.* capital, wealth, cash, collateral, money, assets, currency, savings, revenue, wherewithal, proceeds, hard cash, stocks and bonds, money on hand, money in the bank, accounts receivable, property, means, affluence, belongings, resources, securities, stakes, earnings, winnings, possessions, profits, stocks, nest egg; see also MONEY.

funeral *n.* interment, last rites, burial, burial ceremony, entombment, requiem, cremation.

fungus *n.* mushroom, mold, rust; see DECAY, PARASITE 1.

funnel *n.* duct, shaft, conduit; see PIPE 1.

funny *a.* **1.** [Stirring to laughter] laughable, comic, comical, whimsical, amusing, entertaining, diverting, humorous, witty, jesting, jocular, waggish, droll, facetious, clever, mirthful, ludicrous, jolly, absurd, ridiculous, sly, sportive, playful, merry, joyful, joyous, good-humored, glad, gleeful, hilarious, jovial, farcical, joking, side-splitting.—*Ant.* SAD, serious, melancholy. **2.** [*Likely to arouse suspicion] curious, unusual, odd; see SUSPICIOUS 2.

fur *n.* pelt, hide, hair, coat, brush. *Types of fur include the following:* sable, mink, chinchilla, karakul, seal, muskrat, ermine, monkey, beaver, skunk, otter, marten, stone marten, weasel, squirrel, leopard, raccoon, wolverine; white fox, blue fox, red fox, etc.; sheepskin, bearskin, calfskin, rabbit, coney. —**make the fur fly*** fight, bicker, stir up trouble; see EXCITE.

furious *a.* enraged, raging, fierce; see ANGRY.

furnace *n.* heater, heating system, boiler, hot-air furnace, steam furnace, hot-water furnace, oil burner, gas furnace, electric furnace, kiln, blast furnace, open-hearth furnace, stove, forge.

furnish *v.* fit out, equip, stock; see PROVIDE 1.

furnished *a.* supplied, provided, fitted out; see EQUIPPED.

furniture *n.* movables, household goods, home furnishings. *Furniture includes the following—home:* table, chair, rug, carpeting, drapes, sofa, davenport, couch, cabinet, picture, chest, bureau, buffet, cupboard, stove, washing machine, washer, clothes dryer, dishwasher, refrigerator, bed, dresser, mirror, commode, chiffonier, tapestry, footstool, secretary, sideboard, clock, bookcase; *office:* desk, filing cabinet, stool, chair, table, counter, typewriter table.

furor *n.* tumult, excitement, stir; see DISTURBANCE 2.

further *a.* more, at a greater distance, in addition; see DISTANT.

furthermore *a.* moreover, too, in addition; see BESIDES.

furthest *a.* most remote, most distant, remotest, farthest, uttermost, outermost, ultimate, extreme, outmost.

fury *n.* wrath, fire, rage; see ANGER.

fuse *n.* wick, tinder, kindling; see FUEL. —**blow a fuse*** become angry, lose one's temper, rant; see RAGE 1.

fuss *n.* trouble, complaint, bother; see DISTURBANCE 2.

fuss *v.* whine, whimper, object; see COMPLAIN.

fussy *a.* fastidious, particular, meticulous; see CAREFUL.

futile *a.* vain, useless, in vain, fruitless, hopeless, impractical, worthless, unprofitable, to no effect, not successful, to no purpose, unneeded, unsatisfactory, unsatisfying, ineffective, ineffectual, unproductive, idle, empty, hollow, unreal.—*Ant.* HOPEFUL, practical, effective.

futility *n.* uselessness, falseness, hollowness, frivolity, idleness, emptiness, fruitlessness, hopelessness, worthlessness, illusion, folly, unimportance, carrying water in a sieve*, wild-goose chase*, running around in circles*, carrying coals to Newcastle*.—*Ant.* IMPORTANCE, fruitfulness, significance.

future *a.* coming, impending, imminent, destined, fated, prospective, to come, in the course of time, expected, inevitable, approaching, eventual, ultimate, planned, scheduled, budgeted, booked, looked toward, likely, coming up, in the cards.—*Ant.* PAST, completed, recorded.

future *n.* infinity, eternity, world to come, subsequent time, coming time, events to come, prospect, tomorrow, the hereafter, by and by.—*Ant.* PAST, historic ages, recorded time.

fuzz *n.* nap, fluff, fur; see HAIR 1.

fuzzy *a.* **1.** [Like or covered with fuzz] hairy, woolly, furry; see HAIRY. **2.** [Not clear] blurred, indistinct, out of focus, hazy, foggy; see also OBSCURE 1, HAZY.

G

gab* *n.* gossip, idle talk, prattle; see NONSENSE 1. —**gift of (the) gab*** loquacity, volubility, verbal ability; see ELOQUENCE.

gab* *v.* gossip, jabber, chatter; see BABBLE.

gadget *n.* mechanical contrivance, object, contraption; see DEVICE 1.

gag *v.* **1.** [To stop the mouth] choke, muzzle, muffle, obstruct, stifle, throttle, tape up, deaden. **2.** [To retch] be nauseated, sicken, choke; see VOMIT.

gaiety *n.* jollity, mirth, exhilaration; see HAPPINESS.

gaily *a.* showily, brightly, vivaciously, spiritedly, brilliantly, splendidly, gaudily, expensively, colorfully, extravagantly, in a sprightly manner.—*Ant.* PEACEFULLY, quietly, modestly.

gain *n.* increase, accrual, accumulation; see ADDITION 1.

gain *v.* **1.** [To increase] augment, expand, enlarge; see GROW 1, INCREASE. **2.** [To advance] progress, overtake, move forward; see ADVANCE 1. **3.** [To achieve] attain, realize, reach; see SUCCEED 1.

gainful *a.* lucrative, productive, useful; see PROFITABLE.

gainfully *a.* productively, profitably, usefully; see PROFITABLY.

gait *n.* walk, run, motion, step, tread, stride, pace, tramp, march, carriage, movements.

galaxy *n.* cosmic system, star cluster, nebula; see STAR.

gale *n.* hurricane, blow, typhoon; see STORM, WIND.

gall *n.* effrontery, insolence, impertinence; see RUDENESS.

gall *v.* annoy, irk, irritate; see BOTHER 2.

gallant *a.* bold, courageous, intrepid; see BRAVE.

gallantry *n.* heroism, valor, bravery; see COURAGE.

gallery *n.* **1.** [An elevated section of seats] arcade, upstairs, balcony; see UPSTAIRS. **2.** [Onlookers, especially from the gallery] spectators, audience, public; see LISTENER. **3.** [A room for showing works of art] salon, museum, exhibition room, studio, hall, exhibit, showroom.

gallon *n.* 231 cubic inches, 3.7853 liters, liquid measure, four quarts, eight pints.

gallop *v.* run, spring, leap, jump, go at a gallop, bound, hurdle, swing, stride, lope, amble, trot.

galoshes *n.pl.* overshoes, rubbers, boots; see SHOE.
gamble *n.* chance, lot, hazard; see CHANCE 1.
gamble *v.* game, wager, bet, play, plunge, play at dice, cut the cards, bet against, speculate, back, lay money on, lay odds on, try one's luck, go for broke*, shoot craps; see also RISK.
gambler *n.* backer, sharper, card-sharp, speculator, confidence man, bettor, bookmaker, croupier, banker, player, sport*, highroller*, shark*, shill*, bookie*, con man*.
gambling *n.* betting, staking, venturing, gaming, laying money on, speculating.
game *a.* spirited, hardy, resolute; see BRAVE.
game *n.* **1.** [Entertainment] *Card games include the following:* poker, bridge, contract bridge, duplicate bridge, five hundred, casino, war, seven-up, cribbage, solitaire, hearts, twenty-one, blackjack, baccarat. *Children's games include:* hide-and-go-seek, tag, hopscotch, jacks, ball, fox and geese, marbles, crack the whip, statues, London Bridge, ring around the roses, drop the handkerchief, blindman's buff, follow the leader, Simon says, catch, post office, favors, musical chairs, streets and alleys, cops and robbers, soldier, cowboys and Indians, mother-may-I. *Board games include:* chess, checkers, Chinese checkers, backgammon, go, Monopoly, Sorry, Clue, Parcheesie, mahjongg. **2.** [Sport] play, recreation, merrymaking; see SPORT 1. **3.** [Wild meat, fish, or fowl] quarry, prey, wildlife; see FISH, FOWL, MEAT. —**ahead of the game*** winning, doing well, thriving; see SUCCESSFUL. —**play the game*** behave properly, act according to custom, do what is expected; see BEHAVE.
gang *n.* horde, band, troop; see ORGANIZATION 2.
gangster *n.* gunman, underworld leader, racketeer; see CRIMINAL.
gang up on or **against*** *v.* combat, overwhelm, fight with; see ATTACK.
gap *n.* **1.** [A breach] cleft, break, rift; see HOLE 1. **2.** [A break in continuity] hiatus, recess, lull; see PAUSE. **3.** [A mountain pass] way, chasm, hollow, cleft, ravine, gorge, arroyo, canyon, passageway, notch, gully, gulch.
garage *n.* car stall, parking space, parking garage, parking, parking lot, carport.
garbage *n.* refuse, waste, table scrapings; see TRASH 1.
garden *n.* vegetable patch, melon patch, cultivated area, truck garden, enclosure, field, plot, bed, herb garden, rock garden, rose garden, formal garden, kitchen garden, hotbed, greenhouse, patio, terrace, back yard, nursery, flower garden, garden spot, oasis.
gardener *n.* vegetable grower, caretaker, landscaper; see FARMER.
gardening *n.* truck farming, vegetable raising, tillage; see FARMING.
gargantuan *a.* enormous, huge, immense; see LARGE 1.
gargle *v.* swash, rinse the mouth, use a mouthwash; see CLEAN.
garish *a.* showy, gaudy, ostentatious; see ORNATE.
garment *n.* dress, attire, apparel; see CLOTHES.
garnish *v.* embellish, beautify, deck; see DECORATE.
gas *n.* **1.** [A state of matter] vapor, volatile substance, fumes, aeriform fluid, gaseous mixture. **2.** [Gasoline] propellant, petrol, motor fuel; see GASOLINE. **3.** [Poisonous gas] systemic poison, mustard gas, tear gas; see POISON. **4.** [An anesthetic] ether, general anesthetic, chloroform, nitrous oxide, laughing gas. **5.** [A fuel] natural gas, propane, bottled gas, acetylene, coal gas; see also FUEL. —**step on the gas*** rush, hasten, move fast; see HURRY 1.
gaseous *a.* vaporous, effervescent, in the form of gas; see LIGHT 5.
gash *n.* slash, slice, wound; see CUT.
gasoline *n.* petrol, motor fuel, propellant, gas, juice, low octane gasoline, high octane gasoline, ethyl gasoline, gasohol.
gasp *v.* labor for breath, gulp, have difficulty in breathing, pant, puff, wheeze, blow, snort.
gate *n.* entrance, ingress, passage, way, bar, turnstile, revolving door, barrier; see also DOOR.
gather *v.* **1.** [To come together] assemble, meet, gather around, congregate, flock in, pour in, rally, crowd, throng, come together, convene, collect, unite, reunite, associate, hold a meeting, hold a reunion, swarm, huddle, draw in, group, converge, concentrate.—*Ant.* SCATTER, disperse, part. **2.** [To bring together] collect, aggregate, amass; see ACCUMULATE, ASSEMBLE 2. **3.** [To conclude] infer, deduce, find; see ASSUME.
gathered *a.* assembled, met, congregated, joined, rallied, crowded together, thronged, collected, united, associated, swarmed, huddled, grouped, massed, amassed, accumulated, picked, garnered, harvested, stored, combined, brought together, convened, convoked, summoned, compiled, mobilized, lumped together, raked up, concentrated, heaped, stacked, piled, stowed away.—*Ant.* SCATTERED, dispersed, separated.
gathering *n.* assembly, meeeting, conclave, caucus, parley, council, conference, band, congregation, company, rally, crowd, throng, bunch, collection, union, association, society, committee, legislature, house, senate, parliament, swarm, huddle, group, body, mass, herd, turnout, flock, combination, convention, discussion, panel, reunion,

meet, congress, attendance, multitude, audience, horde, mob, crush, party, social gathering, crew, gang, school, bevy, troop, drove, concentration, convocation, get-together, bull session*.

gaudy *a.* showy, flashy, tawdry; see ORNATE.

gauge *n.* scale, criterion, standard; see MEASURE 2.

gauge *v.* check, weigh, calibrate, calculate; see also MEASURE 1.

gaunt *a.* emaciated, scraggy, skinny; see THIN 2.

gauze *n.* veil, bandage, dressings; see DRESSING 3.

gawk *v.* stare, ogle, gaze; see LOOK 2.

gay *a.* **1.** [Happy] cheerful, merry, vivacious; see HAPPY. **2.** [Homosexual] homophile, homoerotic, lesbian; see HOMOSEXUAL.

gaze *v.* stare, watch, gape; see LOOK 2.

gear *n.* **1.** [Equipment] material, tackle, things; see EQUIPMENT. **2.** [A geared wheel] cog, cogwheel, pinion, toothed wheel, sprocket. *Driving gears include:* first, low, second, intermediate, third, high, fourth, reverse, overdrive. **—in gear** usable, efficient, productive; see WORKING 1. **—out of gear** inefficient, not working, broken; see USELESS 1.

gem *n.* **1.** [A jewel] precious stone, bauble, ornament; see JEWEL. *Types of gems include the following:* diamond, emerald, ruby, pearl, brilliant, aquamarine, amethyst, topaz, turquoise, jade, opal, sapphire, garnet, carnelian, jacinth, beryl, cat's eye, chrysoprase, chalcedony, agate, bloodstone, moonstone, onyx, sard, lapis lazuli, chrysolite, carbuncle, coral. **2.** [Anything excellent, especially if small and beautiful] jewel, pearl of great price, paragon, ace, nonpareil, perfection, ideal.

gender *n.* sexuality, sort, variety; see KIND 2, SEX 3.

genealogy *n.* derivation, lineage, extraction; see FAMILY.

general *a.* **1.** [Having wide application] comprehensive, comprehending, widespread, universal, limitless, unlimited, extensive, ecumenical, all-embracing, ubiquitous, unconfined, broad, taken as a whole, not particular, not specific, blanket, inclusive, wide, infinite, worldwide, endless.—*Ant.* SPECIAL, particular, limited. **2.** [Of common occurrence] usual, customary, prevailing; see COMMON 1. **3.** [Not specific] indefinite, uncertain, imprecise; see VAGUE 2. **—in general** generally, usually, ordinarily; see REGULARLY.

generality *n.* abstraction, universality, principle; see LAW 4.

generalize *v.* theorize, speculate, postulate; see UNDERSTAND.

generally *a.* usually, commonly, ordinarily; see REGULARLY.

generate *v.* form, make, beget, create; see also PRODUCE 1.

generation *n.* **1.** [The act of producing offspring] procreation, reproduction, breeding; see BIRTH. **2.** [One cycle in the succession of parents and children] age, stage, crop, rank, age group. **3.** [The time required for a generation] span, 20 to 30 years, period; see AGE 3.

generic *a.* universal, general, nonexclusive; see UNIVERSAL 3, GENERAL 1.

generosity *n.* hospitality, benevolence, charity, liberality, philanthropy, altruism, unselfishness; see also KINDNESS 2.—*Ant.* GREED, miserliness, stinginess.

generous *a.* **1.** [Open-handed] bountiful, liberal, charitable, altruistic, free-handed, beneficient, lavish, profuse, unselfish, hospitable, philanthropic, prodigal, unsparing, unstinting.—*Ant.* STINGY, close, tight-fisted. **2.** [Considerate] kindly, magnanimous, reasonable; see KIND.

generously *a.* **1.** [With a free hand] bountifully, liberally, lavishly, unsparingly, unstintingly, in full measure, handsomely, freely, profusely, with open hands, abundantly, munificently, charitably, copiously.—*Ant.* SELFISHLY, grudgingly, sparingly. **2.** [With an open heart] charitably, liberally, magnanimously, wholeheartedly, unreservedly, nobly, majestically, royally, genially, honestly, candidly, enthusiastically, unselfishly, disinterestedly, chivalrously, benevolently, warmly.—*Ant.* SELFISHLY, coldly, heartlessly.

genetic *a.* sporogenous, hereditary, genic, patrimonial; see also HISTORICAL.

genetics *n.* heredity, inheritance, eugenics; see HEREDITY.

genial *a.* cordial, kind, warmhearted; see FRIENDLY.

genitals *n.pl.* organs, sexual organs, genitalia, private parts, reproductory organs, pudenda, gonads, testicles, testes, privates.

genius *n.* **1.** [The highest degree of intellectual capacity] ability, talent, intellect, brains, intelligence, inspiration, imagination, gift, aptitude, wisdom, astuteness, penetration, grasp, discernment, acumen, acuteness, power, capability, accomplishment, sagacity, understanding, reach, enthusiasm, creative gift, knack, bent, turn. **2.** [One having genius] gifted person, prodigy, adept; see ARTIST, AUTHOR, DOCTOR, PHILOSOPHER, POET, WRITER.

gentility *n.* decorum, propriety, refinement; see BEHAVIOR.

gentle *a.* **1.** [Soft] tender, smooth, sensitive; see FAINT 3, SOFT 2, 3. **2.** [Kind] tender, considerate, benign; see KIND. **3.** [Tamed] domesticated, housebroken, disciplined, educated, trained, civilized, tractable, pliable, taught, cultivated, tame.—*Ant.* WILD, savage, untamed.

gentleman *n.* man of honor, man of his word, sir, gentleman and a scholar.

gentlemanly *a.* polite, polished, gallant; see REFINED 2.

gentleness *n.* tenderness, softness, delicacy, smoothness, fragility, sweetness.—*Ant.* ROUGHNESS, hardness, imperviousness.

gently *a.* considerately, tenderly, benevolently; see GENEROUSLY 2.

genuine *a.* **1.** [Authentic; *said of things*] real, true, actual, original, veritable, unadulterated, official, whole, accurate, proved, tested, good, natural, unimpeachable, pure, unquestionable, authenticated, existent, essential, substantial, factual, palpable, exact, precise, positive, valid, literal, sound, plain, certain, legitimate, legit*, for real*, honest-to-goodness*, in the flesh*.—*Ant.* VULGAR, spurious, sham. **2.** [Sincere] real, actual, unaffected, unquestionable, certain, absolute, unimpeachable, definite, incontrovertible, well-established, known, reliable, bona fide, staunch, trustworthy, certain, valid, positive, frank.

geographical *a.* terrestrial, geographic, earthly; see PHYSICAL 1, WORLDLY.

geography *n.* earth science, geology, topography, economic geography, political geography, geopolitics, geopolitical study, physiography, cartography; see also SCIENCE 1.

geology *n.* applied geology, mining geology, paleontology; see GEOGRAPHY, SCIENCE 1.

geometrical *a.* square, many-sided, multilateral, bilateral, triangular, trilateral, quadrilateral.

germ *n.* microbe, antibody, bacteria, disease germ, microorganism, virus, parasite, bug*.

German *a.* Germanic, Teutonic, Prussian, Saxon, Bavarian.

German *n.* **1.** [The German Language] Teutonic language, Proto-Germanic, High German, Low German, Old High German, Middle High German, Modern German, New High German; see also LANGUAGE. **2.** [A German person] East German, West German, Teuton, Berliner, East Berliner, West Berliner, Bavarian, Hanoverian, Prussian, Franconian, Rhinelander, Saxon, Swabian, Hitlerite, Nazi, Aryan.

Germany *n.* German nation, German Reich, German people, West Germany, East Germany, Axis power, Third Reich, German Empire, Nazi state, Weimar Republic; see also EUROPE.

germinate *v.* generate, live, develop; see GROW 1.

gestation *n.* reproduction, gravidity, fecundation; see PREGNANCY.

gesture *n.* gesticulation, indication, intimation; see SIGN 1.

gesture *v.* make a sign, motion, signal, pantomime, act out, use sign language, use one's hands, indicate, signalize, point, nod; see also MOVE 1.

get *v.* **1.** [To obtain] gain, procure, occupy, reach, capture, recover, take, grab, accomplish, attain, gain, win, secure, achieve, collect, purchase, earn, receive, realize, possess, get possession of, take title to, acquire. **2.** [To become] grow, develop into, go; see BECOME. **3.** [To receive] be given, take, accept; see RECEIVE 1. **4.** [To induce] persuade, talk into, compel; see URGE 2. **5.** [*To overcome] beat, vanquish, overpower; see DEFEAT 2, 3. **6.** [To prepare] make, arrange, dress; see PREPARE 1. **7.** [To contract; *said of bodily disorders*] fall victim to, succumb to, get sick; see CATCH 4. **8.** [To learn] acquire, gain, receive; see LEARN. **9.** [*To understand] comprehend, perceive, know; see UNDERSTAND 1. **10.** [*To irritate] annoy, provoke, vex; see BOTHER 2. **11.** [To arrive] come to, reach, land; see ARRIVE.

get across* *v.* impart, convey, pass on; see COMMUNICATE 1.

get ahead *v.* climb, prosper, thrive; see SUCCEED 1.

get along *v.* **1.** [To be successful] thrive, prosper, flourish; see SUCCEED 1. **2.** [To proceed] progress, move on, push ahead; see ADVANCE 1.

get angry *v.* become enraged, become furious, lose one's temper, get mad, blow up*, blow one's cool*, lose one's cool*, get hot under the collar*, get steamed up*, fly off the handle*, blow a fuse*.

get at *v.* **1.** [To arrive at] achieve, reach, ascertain; see ARRIVE. **2.** [To intend] mean, aim, purpose; see INTEND 1.

get away (from) *v.* flee, run away, elude; see ESCAPE.

get away with* *v.* escape notice, manage, succeed in; see ACHIEVE, SATISFY 3.

get back *v.* retrieve, reclaim, salvage; see RECOVER 1.

get back at* *v.* get even with, pay back, retaliate; see REVENGE.

get behind *v.* loiter, fall behind, hesitate; see LAG.

get by* *v.* manage, get along, do well enough; see SURVIVE 1.

get down *v.* dismount, come down, alight; see DESCEND.

get even with *v.* settle a score, avenge, pay back; see REVENGE.

get going* *v.* start, progress, move; see BEGIN 1, 2.

get in *v.* **1.** [To arrive] come, land; reach the airport, hotel, etc.; see ARRIVE. **2.** [To enter] get inside, find a way in, gain ingress; see ENTER.

get in touch (with) *v.* call, telephone, write to, contact, wire, telegraph, correspond with, communicate with, reach, keep in contact with, make overtures.

get it* *v.* **1.** [To understand] comprehend, perceive, know; see UNDERSTAND 1. **2.** [To be punished] suffer, get what is coming to one, be reprimanded, suffer for, catch it*, get in trouble.

get mad *v.* lose one's temper, become angry, rant and rave; see GET ANGRY.

get off *v.* **1.** [To go away] depart, escape, go; see LEAVE 1. **2.** [To dismount] alight, light, disembark; see DESCEND.

get on *v.* **1.** [To mount] go up, mount, scale; see CLIMB. **2.** [To succeed] manage, do well enough, get along; see SUCCEED 1. **3.** [To age] grow older, advance in years, approach retirement; see AGE.

get out *interj.* leave, begone, be off, go away, get away*, scram*, clear out*, split*, beat it*, get the hell out*.

get out *v.* **1.** [To leave] go, depart, take one's departure; see LEAVE 1. **2.** [To escape] break out, run away, flee; see ESCAPE.

get out of *v.* **1.** [To obtain] get from, secure, gain; see GET 1. **2.** [To escape from] flee from, fly from, run away from; see ESCAPE. **3.** [To leave] depart from, go away from, withdraw from; see LEAVE 1.

get over *v.* overcome, recuperate, survive; see RECOVER 3.

get ready *v.* make preparations, arrange, plan; see PREPARE 1.

get rid of *v.* eject, expel, remove; see ELIMINATE.

get set *v.* be on the alert, be ready, consolidate one's position; see PREPARE 1.

get sick *v.* become sick or ill, contract a disease, take sick; see SICKEN 1.

get the hang of* *v.* comprehend, become acquainted with, grasp; see UNDERSTAND 1.

get through *v.* **1.** [To complete] discharge, enact, finish; see ACHIEVE. **2.** [To endure] live through, survive, subsist; see ENDURE 1, 2.

get through to *v.* make understand, reach, come to an agreement with; see INFLUENCE.

getting *n.* taking, obtaining, gaining, catching, earning, winning, seizing, securing, capturing, mastering, confiscating, appropriating.

get to *v.* **1.** [To arrive] reach, approach, land at; see ARRIVE. **2.** [To make listen or understand] reach, talk to, approach; see INFLUENCE.

get together *v.* **1.** [To gather] collect, accumulate, congregate; see ASSEMBLE 2. **2.** [To reach an agreement] come to terms, settle, make a bargain; see AGREE.

get up *v.* **1.** [To climb] ascend, mount, go up; see CLIMB. **2.** [To arise] get out of bed, rise, turn out; see ARISE 1.

ghastly *a.* **1.** [Terrifying] hideous, horrible, frightening; see FRIGHTFUL. **2.** [*Unpleasant] repulsive, disgusting, abhorrent; see OFFENSIVE 2.

ghost *n.* vision, specter, apparition, spirit, demon, shade, phantom, appearance, spook; see also DEVIL.

giant *a.* monstrous, colossal, enormous; see LARGE 1.

giant *n.* ogre, Cyclops, Titan, colossus, Goliath, Hercules, Atlas, mammoth, behemoth, monster, whale, elephant, leviathan, mountain, hulk, lump, bulk; see also MONSTER 1.

gibberish *n.* jargon, chatter, claptrap; see NONSENSE 1.

giddy *a.* high, towering, lofty; see STEEP.

gift *n.* **1.** [A present] presentation, donation, grant, gratuity, alms, endowment, bequest, bounty, charity, favor, legacy, award, reward, offering, souvenir, token, remembrance, courtesy, bonus, subsidy, tribute, subvention, contribution, subscription, relief, ration, benefit, tip, allowance, handout, hand-me-down. **2.** [An aptitude] faculty, capacity, capability; see ABILITY. — **look a gift horse in the mouth** carp, criticize, be ungrateful; see JUDGE.

gifted *a.* smart, skilled, talented; see ABLE.

gigantic *a.* massive, huge, immense; see LARGE 1.

giggle *n.* titter, chuckle, snicker; see LAUGH.

gild *v.* varnish, whitewash, paint in rosy colors; see PAINT 2.

gimmick* *n.* catch, secret device, method; see TRICK.

girder *n.* truss, rafter, mainstay; see BEAM 1.

girdle *n.* belt, cincher, sash; see UNDERWEAR.

girdle *v.* encircle, enclose, clasp; see SURROUND 1.

girl *n.* schoolgirl, miss, lass, young woman, coed, lassie, damsel, maid, maiden, tomboy, chick*, skirt*, dame*, babe*.

girlish *a.* juvenile, naive, unsophisticated fresh, unaffected; see also YOUNG 1.—*Ant.* MATURE, matronly, sophisticated.

girth *n.* circumference, distance around, bigness; see SIZE 2.

gist *n.* substance, essence, significance; see BASIS, SUMMARY.

give *v.* **1.** [To transfer] grant, bestow, confer, impart, present, endow, bequeath, award, dispense, subsidize, contribute, hand out, dole out, hand in, hand over, deliver, let have, tip, pass down, convey, deed, sell, will, make over to, put into the hands of, contribute to, consign, relinquish, cede, lease, invest, dispose of, part with, lay upon, turn over, come through with*, come across with*, shell out*, fork over*, kick in*, palm off*.—*Ant.* MAINTAIN, withhold, take. **2.** [To yield under pressure] give way, retreat, collapse, fall, contract, shrink, recede, open, relax, sag, bend, flex, crumble, yield.—*Ant.* RESIST, remain rigid, stand firm. **3.** [To allot] assign, dispense, deal; see DISTRIBUTE. **4.** [To pass on] communicate, transmit, transfer; see SEND 1. 5. [To administer] minister, provide with, dispense; see PROVIDE 1.

give away *v.* 1. [*To reveal] betray, divulge, disclose; see REVEAL. 2. [To give] bestow, award, present; see GIVE 1.

give back *v.* return, refund, reimburse; see REPAY 1.

give in *v.* capitulate, submit, surrender; see ADMIT 2, YIELD 1.

given *a.* granted, supplied, donated, bestowed, presented, awarded, bequeathed, dispensed, handed out, contributed, offered.—*Ant.* KEPT, taken, withheld.

give out *v.* 1. [To emit] emanate, expend, exude; see EMIT, SMELL 1. 2. [To deliver] dole out, hand out, pass out; see DISTRIBUTE. 3. [To publish] proclaim, make known, announce; see ADVERTISE, DECLARE. 4. [To weaken] faint, fail, break down; see TIRE 1, WEAKEN 1.

give over *v.* give up, deliver, relinquish; see GIVE 1.

giver *n.* provider, supplier, donator; see DONOR.

give up *v.* 1. [To surrender] stop fighting, cede, hand over; see YIELD 1. 2. [To stop] quit, halt, cease; see END 1.

give way *v.* 1. [To collapse] sag, fall, crumble; see GIVE 2. 2. [To concede] yield, accede, grant; see ADMIT 2.

giving *n.* donating, granting, supplying, awarding, presenting, dispensing, passing out, handing out, contributing, conferring, distributing, remitting, transferring, consigning, yielding, giving up, furnishing, allowing, expending, offering, tipping, parting with, pouring forth, discharging, emitting.—*Ant.* GETTING, taking, appropriating.

giving up *n.* quitting, losing, giving in; see END 2.

glacial *a.* icy, frozen, polar; see COLD 1.

glacier *n.* ice floe, floe, iceberg, berg, glacial mass, snow slide, icecap, ice field, ice stream, glacial table.

glad *a.* exhilarated, animated, jovial; see HAPPY.

gladly *a.* joyously, happily, gaily, blithely, cheerfully, ecstatically, blissfully, contendedly, readily, gratefully, enthusiastically, merrily, heartily, willingly, zealously, pleasantly, pleasurably, zestfully, complacently, delightfully, gleefully, cheerily, warmly, passionately, ardently, lovingly, cordially, genially, sweetly, joyfully, with relish, with satisfaction, with full agreement, with full approval, with delight.—*Ant.* SADLY, unwillingly, gloomily.

gladness *n.* cheer, mirth, delight; see HAPPINESS.

glamorous *a.* fascinating, alluring, captivating, bewitching, dazzling; see also CHARMING.

glamour *n.* allurement, charm, attraction; see BEAUTY 1.

glance *n.* glimpse, sight, fleeting impression; see LOOK 3.

glance *v.* 1. [To look] see, peep, glimpse; see LOOK 2. 2. [To ricochet] skip, slide, rebound; see BOUNCE.

gland *n.* endocrine organ, pancreas, kidney, liver, testicle, spleen, epithelial cell. *Kinds of glands include the following:* simple, compound, tubular, sacular, ductless, adrenal, carotid, endocrine, lymphatic, parathyroid, parotid, pineal, pituitary, thyroid, thymus, sweat, lacrimal, salivary, mammary, seminal, prostrate, urethral, vaginal.

glare *v.* 1. [To shine fiercely] beam, glow, radiate; see SHINE 1, 2. 2. [To stare fiercely] pierce, glower, scowl; see FROWN, LOOK 2.

glaring *a.* 1. [Shining] blinding, dazzling, blazing; see BRIGHT 1. 2. [Obvious] evident, conspicuous, obtrusive; see OBVIOUS 2.

glass *n.* *Objects referred to as* glass *include the following:* tumbler, goblet, beaker, chalice, cup, looking glass, mirror, barometer, thermometer, hourglass, windowpane, watch crystal, monocle, telescope, microscope, spyglass, burning glass, eyeglass, lens, optical glass.

glasses *n.pl.* spectacles, eyeglasses, bifocals, trifocals, goggles, field glasses, opera glasses, contact lenses, specs*.

glassware *n.* crystal, glasswork, glass; see GLASS. *Types of common glassware include the following:* tumbler, jug, decanter, bottle, fruit jar, tableware, glass ovenware, vase, flower bowl, goblet, sherbet glass, wine glass, liqueur glass, champagne glass, cocktail glass, highball glass, old-fashioned glass, brandy snifter, shot glass, cake tray, parfait glass, beer mug.

glassy *a.* vitreous, lustrous, polished; see SMOOTH 1.

glaze *n.* enamel, polish, varnish; see FINISH 2.

glaze *v.* coat, enamel, gloss over; see SHINE 3.

glazed *a.* glassy, translucent, transparent, enameled, varnished, filmed over, shiny, encrusted, burnished, lustrous, smooth.—*Ant.* ROUGH, fresh, unglazed.

glee *n.* joviality, merriment, mirth; see HAPPINESS.

gleeful *a.* joyous, jolly, merry; see HAPPY.

glide *n.* floating, continuous motion, smooth movement, flowing, slide, drift, swoop, skimming, flight, soaring, slither.

glide *v.* float, slide, drift, waft, skim, skip, trip, fly, coast, flit, wing, soar, coast along, slide along, skim along.—*Ant.* HIT, rattle, lurch.

glimmer *n.* gleam, flash, flicker; see LIGHT 1.

glimpse *n.* flash, impression, sight; see LOOK 3.

glisten *v.* sparkle, shimmer, flicker; see SHINE 1.

glitter *n.* sparkle, shimmer, gleam; see LIGHT 1.

glitter *v.* glare, shimmer, sparkle; see SHINE 1.

globe *n.* balloon, orb, spheroid; see BALL 1.

gloom *n.* woe, sadness, depression, dejection, melancholy, melancholia, dullness, despondency, misery, sorrow, morbidity, pessimism, foreboding, low spirits, cheerlessness, heaviness of mind, weariness, apprehension, misgiving, distress, affliction, despair, anguish, grief, horror, mourning, bitterness, chagrin, discouragement, the blues, the dumps.—*Ant.* HAPPINESS, optimism, gaiety.

gloomy *a.* dreary, depressing, discouraging; see DISMAL.

glorify *v.* laud, commend, acclaim; see PRAISE 1.

glorious *a.* famous, renowned, famed, well-known, distinguished, splendid, excellent, noble, exalted, grand, illustrious, notable, celebrated, esteemed, honored, eminent, remarkable, brilliant, great, heroic, memorable, immortal, time-honored, admirable, praiseworthy, remarkable; see also FAMOUS.—*Ant.* UNIMPORTANT, inglorious, ignominious.

glory *n.* **1.** [Renown] honor, distinction, reputation; see FAME. **2.** [Splendor] grandeur, radiance, majesty, brilliance, richness, beauty, fineness.—*Ant.* tawdriness, meanness, baseness.

glossy *a.* shining, reflecting, lustrous; see BRIGHT 1.

glove *n.* mitten, mitt, finger mitten; see CLOTHES.

glow *n.* warmth, shine, ray; see HEAT 1, LIGHT 1.

glow *v.* gleam, redden, radiate; see BURN, SHINE 1.

glowing *a.* gleaming, lustrous, phosphorescent; see BRIGHT 1.

glue *n.* paste, mucilage, cement; see ADHESIVE.

glue *v.* paste, gum, cement; see REPAIR.

glum *a.* moody, morose, sullen; see SAD 1.

glut *n.* oversupply, overabundance, excess; see EXCESS 1.

glut *v.* **1.** [To oversupply] overwhelm, overstock, fill; see FLOOD. **2.** [To overeat] stuff, cram, gorge, eat one's fill, gobble up, eat out of house and home, fill, feast, wolf, bolt, devour, eat like a horse*.—*Ant.* DIET, starve, fast.

glutton *n.* greedy person, hog, pig; see BEAST 2.

gluttony *n.* voracity, piggishness, intemperance; see GREED.

gnarled *a.* knotted, twisted, contorted; see BENT.

gnaw *v.* crunch, chomp, masticate; see BITE, CHEW.

go *v.* **1.** [To leave] quit, withdraw, take leave, depart, move, set out, go away, take off, start, leave, vanish, retire, vacate, flee, get out, fly, run along, say goodby, escape, run away, clear out*, pull out, push off*, scram*, split*, blow*, beat it*, take a powder*, get along*, fade away; see also LEAVE 1. **2.** [To proceed] travel, progress, proceed; see ADVANCE 1, MOVE 1. **3.** [To function] work, run, perform; see OPERATE 2. **4.** [To fit or suit] conform, accord, harmonize; see AGREE, FIT 1. **5.** [To extend] stretch, cover, spread; see REACH 1. **6.** [To elapse] be spent, waste away, transpire; see PASS 2. **7.** [To fail] miss, flunk, fall short; see FAIL 1. **8.** [To continue] maintain, carry on, persist; see CONTINUE 1. **9.** [To die] pass on, depart, succumb; see DIE. **10.** [To end] terminate, finish, conclude; see STOP 2. **11.** [To endure] persevere, go on, persist; see ENDURE 1. **—as people (or things) go** in comparison with others, by all standards, according to certain criteria; see ACCORDING TO. **—from the word "go"** from the outset, at the start, beginning with; see FIRST. **—have a go at*** attempt, endeavor, try one's hand at; see TRY 1. **—let go** let free, give up, release; see ABANDON 1. **—let oneself go** be unrestrained, free oneself, have fun; see RELAX. **—no go*** impossible, worthless, without value; see USELESS 1. **—on the go*** in constant motion, moving, busy; see ACTIVE.

go about *v.* engage in, busy oneself with, be employed at; see WORK 1, 2.

goad *v.* prod, urge, prick, prompt, spur, drive, whip, press, push, impel, force, stimulate, provoke, tease, excite, needle*, instigate, arouse, animate, encourage, bully, coerce; see also URGE 2.—*Ant.* RESTRAIN, curb, rein in.

go after *v.* **1.** [To chase] seek, try to catch, hunt; see PURSUE 1. **2.** [To follow in time] come after, supersede, supplant; see SUCCEED 2.

go against *v.* be opposed to, contradict, counteract; see OPPOSE 1, 2.

go ahead *v.* move on, proceed, progress; see ADVANCE 1.

goal *n.* object, aim, intent; see END 2, PURPOSE 1.

go all out *v.* attempt, make a great effort, strive; see TRY 1.

go along *v.* carry on, keep up, go; see CONTINUE 1.

go along with *v.* **1.** [To agree with] concur, conspire, collaborate; see AGREE. **2.** [To cooperate] work together, act jointly, share in; see COOPERATE. **3.** [To accompany] escort, squire, go with; see ACCOMPANY.

goat *n.* nanny goat, buck, kid; see ANIMAL. **—get one's goat*** annoy, irritate, anger; see BOTHER 2.

go back on *v.* desert, be unfaithful, forsake; see ABANDON 2.

go bad *v.* degenerate, deteriorate, rot; see SPOIL.

go badly *v.* miscarry, fall short, dissatisfy; see DISAPPOINT, FAIL 1.

gobble *v.* bolt, cram, stuff; see EAT 1.

go-between *n.* middleman, referee, mediator; see AGENT, MESSENGER.

go beyond *v.* overdo, distance, surpass; see EXCEED.

go by *v.* move onward, make one's way, proceed; see PASS 1.

go crazy *v.* become insane, lose one's wits, get angry; see RAGE 1.

god *n.* deity, divinity, divine being, spirit, numen, power, demigod, oversoul, prime mover, godhead, omnipotence, world soul, universal life force, infinite spirit. *Greek gods and their Roman counterparts include:* Zeus or Jupiter or Jove, Phoebus or Apollo, Ares or Mars, Hermes or Mercury, Poseidon or Neptune, Hephaestus or Vulcan, Dionysius or Bacchus, Hades or Pluto, Kronos or Saturn, Eros or Cupid. *Norse gods include:* Balder, Frey, Loki, Odin or Woden or Wotan, Thor. For specific female deities see also GODDESS.

God *n.* **1.** [The Judeo-Christian deity] Lord, Jehovah, Yahweh, the Almighty, the King of Kings, the Godhead, the Creator, the Maker, the Supreme Being, the Ruler of Heaven, Our Father in Heaven, Almighty God, God Almighty, the Deity, the Divinity, Providence, the All-knowing, the Infinite Spirit, the First Cause, the Lord of Lords, the Supreme Soul, the All-wise, the All-merciful, the All-powerful; the Trinity, the Holy Trinity, Threefold Unity; Father, Son, and the Holy Ghost; God the Son, Jesus Christ, Christ, Jesus, Jesus of Nazareth, the Nazarene, the Messiah, the Savior, the Redeemer, the Son of God, the Son of Man, the Son of Mary, the Lamb of God, Immanuel, Emmanuel, the King of the Jews, the Prince of Peace, the Good Shepherd, the Way, the Door, the Truth, the Life, the Light, the Christ Child, the Holy Spirit, the Spirit of God. **2.** [The supreme deity of other religions] Allah (Islam); Brahma (Hinduism); Buddha (Buddhism); Mazda or Ormazd (Zoroastrianism).

goddess *n.* female deity, she-god, beauty; see GOD. *Greek goddesses and their Roman counterparts include the following:* Hera or Juno, Ceres or Demeter, Proserpina or Persephone, Artemis or Diana, Minerva or Athena, Aphrodite or Venus. *Hindu and Brahmanic goddesses include:* Devi, Kali, Parvati, Sarasvati.

godly *a.* righteous, devout, pious; see HOLY 1.

go down *v.* **1.** [To sink] descend, decline, submerge; see SINK 1. **2.** [To lose] be defeated, submit, succumb; see FAIL 1, LOSE 3. **3.** [To decrease] fall, decline, lessen; see DECREASE 1.

go easy *v.* skimp, be sparing, be careful; see PITY 2, SAVE 2.

go far *v.* **1.** [To extend] reach, buy, reinforce; see INCREASE. **2.** [To succeed] rise, achieve, rise in the world; see SUCCEED 1.

go for *v.* **1.** [To reach for] try to get, aim at, clutch at; see REACH 2. **2.** [*To attack] rush upon, run at, spring at; see ATTACK. **3.** [*To like] be fond of, fancy, care for; see LIKE 2.

go in for* *v.* **1.** [To advocate] endorse, favor, back; see PROMOTE 1. **2.** [To like] care for, be fond of, fancy; see LIKE 1.

going *a.* flourishing, thriving, profitable; see SUCCESSFUL. **—be going to** shall, be intending to, be prepared to; see WILL 3. **—get one going*** annoy, excite, enrage; see BOTHER 2. **—have (something) going for one*** have an advantage, be talented, have opportunity; see SUCCEED 1. **—going strong*** flourishing, surviving, thriving; see SUCCESSFUL.

go into *v.* **1.** [To investigate] analyze, probe, look into; see EXAMINE. **2.** [To take up an occupation, hobby, etc.] develop, undertake, enter into, participate in, take upon oneself, engage in, take up, take on, get involved with, be absorbed in.

go in with *v.* form a partnership with, join, merge with; see UNITE.

gold *a.* yellow, gold-colored, red-gold, greenish gold, flaxen, wheat-colored, deep tan, tawny.

gold *n.* **1.** [A color] dark yellow, bright yellow, tawny; see COLOR, GOLD *a.* **2.** [A precious metal] green gold, white gold, red gold, gold foil, gold leaf, gold plate, filled gold, commercial gold, gold alloy, cloth of gold, gold thread, gold wire; see also METAL. **—as good as gold*** very good, well-behaved, obedient; see EXCELLENT.

golf *n.* match play, medal play, nine holes, eighteen holes, front nine, back nine, game; see also SPORT 1.

gone *a.* **1.** [Having left] gone out, gone away, moved, removed, traveling, transferred, displaced, shifted, withdrawn, retired, left, taken leave, departed, deserted, abandoned, quit, disappeared, not here, no more, flown, run off, decamped.—*Ant.* HERE, returned, remained. **2.** [Being no longer in existence] dead, vanished, dissipated, disappeared, dissolved, burned up, disintegrated, decayed, rooted away, extinct. **—far gone** **1.** advanced, deeply involved, absorbed; see INTERESTED 2. **2.** crazy, mad, eccentric; see INSANE.

good *a.* **1.** [Moral] upright, just, honest, worthy, respectable, noble, ethical, fair, guiltless, blameless, pure, truthful, decent, kind, conscientious, honorable, charitable. **2.** [Kind] considerate, tolerant, generous; see KIND. **3.** [Proper] suitable, becoming, desirable; see FIT 1. **4.** [Reliable] trustworthy, dependable, loyal; see RELIABLE. **5.** [Sound] safe, solid, stable; see RELIABLE. **6.** [Pleasant] agreeable, satisfying, enjoyable; see PLEASANT 1, 2. **7.** [Qualified] suited, competent, suitable; see ABLE. **8.** [Of approved quality] choice, select, high-grade; see EXCELLENT. **9.** [Healthy] sound, normal, vigorous; see HEALTHY. **10.** [Obedient] dutiful, tractable, well-behaved; see OBEDIENT 1. **11.** [Genuine] valid, real, sound; see GENUINE 1. **12.** [Delicious] tasty, flavorful, tasteful; see DELICIOUS. **13.** [Considerable] great, big, immeasurable; see LARGE 1, MUCH. **14.** [Favorable] approving, commendatory, commending; see FAVORABLE 3. —**as good as** in effect, virtually, nearly; see ALMOST. —**come to no good** come to a bad end, get into trouble, have difficulty; see FAIL 1. —**make good** fulfill, satisfy the requirements, accomplish; see SATISFY 3. —**no good** useless, valueless, unserviceable; see WORTHLESS. —**to the good** favorable, advantageous, beneficial; see PROFITABLE.

good *n.* **1.** [A benefit] welfare, gain, asset; see ADVANTAGE. **2.** [That which is morally approved] ethic, merit, ideal; see VIRTUE 1.

goodbye *interj.* farewell, fare you well, God bless you and keep you, God be with you, adieu, adios, so long, bye, bye-bye, see you later, take it easy, have a nice day.

good for *a.* **1.** [Helpful] useful, beneficial, salubrious; see HELPFUL 1. **2.** [Financially sound] safe, competent, worth it; see VALID 2.

good-for-nothing *n.* loafer, vagabond, bum; see VAGRANT.

good humor *n.* cordiality, levity, geniality; see HAPPINESS.

good-looking *a.* clean-cut, attractive, impressive; see BEAUTIFUL, HANDSOME.

good luck *interj.* cheers, best wishes, God bless you, peace be with you.

good luck *n.* prosperity, fortune, affluence; see SUCCESS 2.

good morning *interj.* good day, good morrow*, greetings; see HELLO.

good-natured *a.* cordial, kindly, amiable; see FRIENDLY.

goodness *n.* decency, morality, honesty; see VIRTUE 1, 2.

good night *interj.* sleep well, have a good evening, nighty-night; see GOODBYE.

goods *n.pl.* **1.** [Effects] equipment, personal property, possessions; see PROPERTY 1. **2.** [Commodities] merchandise, materials, wares; see COMMODITY.

goodwill *n.* benevolence, charity, kindness, cordiality, sympathy, tolerance, helpfulness, altruism.—*Ant.* HATRED, malevolence, animosity.

goof* *v.* err, make a mistake, flub; see FAIL 1.

go off *v.* **1.** [To leave] quit, depart, part; see LEAVE 1. **2.** [To explode] blow up, detonate, discharge; see EXPLODE.

go on *v.* **1.** [To act] execute, behave, conduct; see ACT 1, 2. **2.** [To happen] occur, come about, take place; see HAPPEN 2. **3.** [To persevere] persist, continue, bear; see ENDURE 1. **4.** [*To talk] chatter, converse, speak; see TALK 1.

goose *n.* gray goose, snow goose, Canada goose; see BIRD.

go out *v.* cease, die, darken, flicker out, flash out, become dark, become black, burn out, stop shining.

go over *v.* **1.** [To rehearse] repeat, say something repeatedly, practice; see REHEARSE 3. **2.** [To examine] look at, investigate, analyze; see EXAMINE, STUDY.

gorge *n.* chasm, abyss, crevasse; see RAVINE.

gorge *v.* glut, devour, stuff oneself; see EAT 1, FILL 1.

gorgeous *a.* superb, sumptuous, impressive; see BEAUTIFUL, GRAND.

gory *a.* blood-soaked, bloodstained, bloody; see OFFENSIVE 2.

gospel *n.* **1.** [A record of Christ] New Testament, Christian Scripture, Evangelist; see BIBLE. **2.** [Belief or statement supposedly infallible] creed, certainty, dogma; see DOCTRINE, FAITH 2, TRUTH.

gossip *n.* **1.** [Local, petty talk] babble, chatter, meddling, small talk, malicious talk, hearsay, rumor, scandal, news, slander, defamation, injury, blackening, skinny*, the grapevine*. **2.** [One who indulges in gossip] snoop, busybody, meddler, tattler, newsmonger, scandalmonger, muckraker, backbiter, chatterbox, talkative person, babbler.

gossip *v.* tattle, prattle, tell tales, talk idly, chat, chatter, rumor, report, tell secrets, blab, babble, repeat.

go through *v.* **1.** [To inspect] search, audit, investigate; see EXAMINE. **2.** [To undergo] withstand, survive, suffer; see ENDURE 2. **3.** [To spend] consume, deplete, expend; see SPEND.

go through with *v.* fulfill, finish, follow through with; see ACHIEVE, COMPLETE.

go together *v.* **1.** [To harmonize] be suitable, match, fit; see AGREE. **2.** [To keep company] go steady*, escort, go with; see DATE 2, KEEP COMPANY (WITH).

go to the dogs* *v.* deteriorate, backslide, decline; see SPOIL.

gouge *v.* scoop, chisel, channel; see DIG 1.

go under *v.* **1.** [Drown] sink, drown, suffocate; see DIE. **2.** [To become bankrupt] default, go broke, go bankrupt; see LOSE 2.

go up *v.* increase, rise, double; see GROW 1.

govern *v.* command, administer, reign, rule, legislate, oversee, assume command, hold office, administer the laws, exercise authority, be in power, supervise, direct, dictate, tyrannize.

governed *a.* commanded, administered, under authority, supervised, directed, dictated to, conducted, guided, piloted, mastered, led, driven, subjugated, subordinate, determined, guided, influenced, swayed, inclined, regulated, directed, ordered, dependent, obedient, under one's jurisdiction.—*Ant.* UNRULY, self-determined, capricious.

governing *a.* commanding, administrative, executive, authoritative, supervisory, regulatory, controlling, directing, overseeing, dictatorial, conducting, guiding, mastering, dominating, dominant, determining, supreme, influential, presidential, absolute, ruling, checking, curbing, inhibiting, limiting.—*Ant.* SUBORDINATE, powerless, tributary.

government *n.* **1.** [The process of governing] rule, control, command, regulation, bureaucracy, direction, dominion, sway, authority, jurisdiction, sovereignty, direction, power, management, authorization, mastery, supervision, superintendence, supremacy, domination, influence, politics, state, political practice; see also ADMINISTRATION 2. **2.** [The instrument of governing] administration, assembly, legislature, congress, cabinet, excutive power, authority, party, council, parliament, senate, department of justice, soviet, synod, convocation, convention, court, house. *Types of government include the following:* absolute monarchy, dictatorship, empire, tyranny, fascism, imperialism, colonialism, despotism, limited monarchy, constitutional monarchy, oligarchy, aristocracy, democracy, popular government, representative government, democratic socialism, communism, socialism, party government. *Divisions of government include:* state, province, kingdom, territory, colony, dominion, commonwealth, soviet, republic, shire, city, county, town, village, township, municipality, borough, commune, ward, district, department, parish.

governmental *a.* political, administrative, executive, regulatory, bureaucratic, legal, supervisory, sovereign, presidential, official, gubernatorial, national.

governor *n.* director, leader, head, presiding officer, ruler; see also LEADER 2.

go with *v.* **1.** [*To keep company with] escort, attend, be with; see ACCOMPANY, DATE 2, KEEP COMPANY (WITH). **2.** [To be appropriate to] match, correspond, not clash, go well with, harmonize, complement, fit; see also AGREE.

go without *v.* lack, fall short, want; see NEED.

gown *n.* garb, garment, clothes; see DRESS 2.

go wrong *v.* slip, break down, go amiss; see FAIL 1.

grab *v.* clutch, grasp, take; see SEIZE 1, 2.

grace *n.* **1.** [The quality of being graceful] suppleness, ease of movement, nimbleness, agility, pliancy, smoothness, form, poise, dexterity, symmetry, balance, style, harmony.—*Ant.* AWKWARDNESS, stiffness, maladroitness. **2.** [Mercy] forgiveness, love, charity; see MERCY. **—in the bad graces of** in disfavor, rejected, disapproved; see HATED. **—in the good graces of** favored, accepted, admired; see APPROVED.

graceful *a.* **1.** [*Said of movement*] supple, agile, lithe, pliant, nimble, elastic, springy, easy, dexterous, adroit, smooth, controlled, light-footed, willowy, poised, practiced, skilled, rhythmic, sprightly, elegant.—*Ant.* AWKWARD, fumbling, stiff. **2.** [*Said of objects*] elegant, neat, well-proportioned, trim, balanced, symmetrical, dainty, pretty, harmonious, beautiful, comely, seemly, handsome, fair, delicate, tasteful, slender, decorative, artistic, exquisite, statuesque.—*Ant.* UGLY, shapeless, cumbersome. **3.** [*Said of conduct*] cultured, seemly, becoming; see POLITE.

gracefully *a.* lithely, agilely, harmoniously, daintily, nimbly, elegantly, trimly, symmetrically, beautifully, delicately, tastefully, artistically, easily, dexterously, smoothly, skillfully, fairly, adroitly, handsomely, rhythmically, exquisitely, neatly, delightfully, charmingly, imaginatively, becomingly, suitably, pleasingly, appropriately, happily, decoratively, prettily.—*Ant.* AWKWARDLY, insipidly, grotesquely.

gracious *a.* **1.** [Genial] amiable, courteous, condescending; see POLITE. **2.** [Merciful] tender, loving, charitable; see KIND.

grade *n.* **1.** [An incline] slope, inclined plane, gradient, slant, inclination, pitch, ascent, descent, ramp, upgrade, downgrade, climb, elevation, height; see also HILL. **2.** [An embankment] fill, causeway, dike; see DAM. **3.** [Rank or degree] class, category, classification; see DEGREE 2. **4.** [A division of a school] standard, form, rank; see GATHERING. **—make the grade** win, prosper, achieve; see SUCCEED 1.

grade *v.* rate, give a grade to, assort; see RANK 2.

gradual *a.* creeping, regular, continuous; see REGULATED.

gradually *a.* step by step, by degrees, steadily, increasingly, slowly, regularly, a little at a time, little by little, bit by bit, inch by inch, by installments, in small doses, continuously, progressively, successively, sequentially, constantly, unceasingly, imperceptibly, deliberately.—*Ant.* QUICKLY, haphazardly, by leaps and bounds.

graduate *n.* recipient of a degree, recipient of a certificate, recipient of a diploma, alumnus, alumna, former student, holder of a degree, bearer of a degree, holder of a certificate, bearer of a certificate, baccalaureate, grad*, alum*.

graduate *v.* receive a degree, receive a certificate, receive a diploma, be awarded a degree, be awarded a certificate, be awarded a diploma, earn a degree, earn a certificate, earn a diploma, become an alumna, become an alumnus, get out, finish up; get a B.A., M.A., Ph.D., M.D., etc.; get a sheepskin*.

graduated *a.* **1.** [Granted a degree] certified, ordained, passed; see OFFICIAL 1. **2.** [Arranged or marked according to a scale] graded, sequential, progressive; see ORGANIZED.

graduation *n.* commencement, convocation, granting of diplomas, promotion, bestowal of honors, commissioning.

grain *n.* **1.** [Seeds of domesticated grasses] cereals, corn, small grain, seed. *Varieties of grain include the following:* rice, wheat, oats, barley, maize, corn, rye, millet, Indian corn, hybrid corn, popcorn. **2.** [Character imparted by fiber] texture, warp and woof, warp and weft, tendency, fabric, tissue, current, direction, tooth, nap. **—against the grain** disturbing, irritating, bothersome; see OFFENSIVE 2.

grammar *n.* syntax, morphology, structure, syntactic structure, sentence structure, language pattern, sentence pattern, linguistic science, generative grammar, stratificational grammar, transformational grammar, universal grammar, tagmemics, synthetic grammar, inflectional grammar, analytic grammar, distributive grammar, traditional grammar, the new grammar; see also LANGUAGE. *Terms in grammar include the following:* tense, mood, aspect, case, modification, incorporation, inflection, concord, agreement, sentence, nexus, coordination, subordination, structure, phrase structure, structural linguistics, phoneme, phonemics, string, head word, morpheme, transform.

grammatical *a.* **1.** [Having to do with grammar] linguistic, syntactic, morphological, logical, philological, analytic, analytical. **2.** [Conforming to rules of grammar] grammatically correct, conventional, accepted; see CONVENTIONAL 1.

grand *a.* lofty, stately, dignified, elevated, high, regal, noble, illustrious, sublime, great, ambitious, august, majestic, solemn, grave, preeminent, extraordinary, monumental, stupendous, huge, chief, commanding, towering, overwhelming, impressive, imposing, awe-inspiring, mighty, terrific*.—*Ant.* POOR, low, mediocre.

grandeur *n.* splendor, magnificence, pomp, circumstance, impressiveness, eminence, distinction, fame, glory, brilliancy, richness, luxury, stateliness, beauty, ceremony, importance, celebrity, solemnity, fineness, majesty, sublimity, nobility, scope, dignity, elevation, preeminence, height, greatness, might, breadth, immensity, amplitude, vastness.

grandfather *n.* elder, forefather, ancestor, patriarch, grandpa*, granddaddy*, grandpappy*.

grandmother *n.* matriarch, dowager, ancestor, grandma*, gram*, granny*.

grant *n.* gift, boon, reward, present, allowance, stipend, donation, matching grant, benefaction, gratuity, endowment, concession, bequest, privilege, federal grant.—*Ant.* DISCOUNT, deprivation, deduction.

grant *v.* **1.** [To permit] yield, cede, impart; see ALLOW. **2.** [To accept as true] concede, accede, acquiesce; see ACKNOWLEDGE 2.

granted *a.* **1.** [Awarded] conferred, bestowed, awarded; see GIVEN. **2.** [Allowed] accepted, admitted, acknowledged; see ASSUMED. **—take for granted** accept, presume, consider settled; see ASSUME.

grape *n.* wine grapes, raisin grapes, Concord grapes; see FRUIT.

graph *n.* diagram, chart, linear representation; see DESIGN, PLAN 1.

graphic *a.* **1.** [Pictorial] visible, illustrated, descriptive, photographic, visual, depicted, seen, drawn, portrayed, traced, sketched, outlined, pictured, painted, engraved, etched, chiseled, penciled, printed.—*Ant.* UNREAL, imagined, chimerical. **2.** [Vivid] forcible, telling, picturesque, intelligible, comprehensible, clear, explicit, striking, definite, distinct, precise, expressive, eloquent, moving, stirring, concrete, energetic, colorful, strong, figurative, poetic.—*Ant.* OBSCURE, ambiguous, abstract.

grasp *v.* **1.** [To clutch] grip, enclose, clasp; see SEIZE 1, 2. **2.** [To comprehend] perceive, apprehend, follow; see UNDERSTAND 1.

grasp *n.* hold, clutch, cinch; see GRIP 2.

grass *n.* **1.** [Plant for food, grazing, etc.] *Wild grasses include the following:* Johnson grass, salt grass, bluegrass, foxtail, buffalo grass, sandbur, crab grass, deer grass, bunch grass, meadow grass, fescue, orchard grass, pampas grass, June grass, redtop, river grass, ribbon grass, sweet grass, cattail, wild rice. **2.** [Grassed area] grassland, meadow, lawn, turf, pasture, prairie, hayfield; see also FIELD 1, YARD 1. **3.** [*A drug] marijuana, cannabis, pot*; see DRUG.

grassland *n.* plains, meadow, prairie; see FIELD 1.

grassy *a.* grass-grown, verdant, green, reedy, lush, matted, tangled, carpeted, sowed, luxurious, deep.

grate *v.* rasp, grind, abrade; see RUB 1.

grateful *a.* appreciative, pleased, obliged; see THANKFUL.

gratefully *a.* appreciatively, thankfully, with a sense of obligation, delightedly, responsively, admiringly.—*Ant.* RUDELY, ungratefully, thanklessly.

gratitude *n.* thankfulness, appreciation, acknowledgment, response, sense of indebtedness, feeling of obligation, responsiveness, thanks, praise, recognition, honor, thanksgiving, grace.—*Ant.* INDIFFERENCE, ingratitude, thanklessness.

grave *a.* **1.** [Important] momentous, weighty, consequential; see IMPORTANT 1. **2.** [Dangerous] critical, serious, ominous; see DANGEROUS. **3.** [Solemn] serious, sober, earnest; see SOLEMN.

grave *n.* vault, sepulcher, tomb, pit, crypt, mausoleum, catacomb, long home, six feet of earth, final resting place, place of interment, mound, burial place, charnel house, last home*. **—make one turn (over) in one's grave** do something shocking, sin, err; see MISBEHAVE. **—one foot in the grave** old, infirm, near death; see DYING 2.

gravel *n.* sand, pebbles, shale, macadam, screenings, crushed rock, washings, alluvium, tailings.

graveyard *n.* burial ground, necropolis, God's acre; see CEMETERY.

gravity *n.* **1.** [Weight] heaviness, pressure, force; see PRESSURE 1. **2.** [Importance] seriousness, concern, significance; see IMPORTANCE.

gravy *n.* sauce, dressing, brown gravy, white gravy, milk gravy, pan gravy, chicken gravy, meat gravy.

gray *a.* neutral, dusky, silvery, dingy, somber, shaded, drab, leaden, grayish, ashen, grizzled. *Shades of gray include the following:* blue-gray, silver-gray, smoke-gray, slate, bat, mouse-colored, iron-gray, lead, ash-gray, pepper-and-salt, dusty, smoky.

gray *n.* shade, drabness, dusk; see COLOR.

graze *v.* **1.** [To touch or score lightly] brush, scrape, rub; see TOUCH 1. **2.** [To pasture] browse, feed, crop, gnaw, nibble, bite, uproot, pull grass, forage, eat, munch, ruminate.

grazing *a.* cropping, feeding, gnawing, nibbling, biting, uprooting, pasturing, pulling grass, foraging, eating, munching, ruminating.

grease *n.* oil, wax, fat, lubricant, salve, petrolatum, petroleum jelly, vaseline, olive oil, cottonseed oil, peanut oil, axle grease; see also OIL 1.

grease *v.* oil, lubricate, smear, salve, coat with oil, cream, pomade, grease the wheels, anoint, swab, give a grease job*.

greasy *a.* creamy, oleaginous, fatty; see OILY 1.

great *a.* **1.** [Eminent] noble, grand, majestic, dignified, exalted, commanding, famous, renowned, widely acclaimed, famed, celebrated, distinguished, noted, conspicuous, elevated, prominent, high, stately, honorable, magnificent, glorious, regal, royal, kingly, imposing, preeminent, unrivaled, fabulous, fabled, storied.—*Ant.* OBSCURE, retired, anonymous. **2.** [Large] numerous, big, vast; see LARGE 1. **3.** [*Excellent] exceptional, surpassing, transcendent; see EXCELLENT.

greatly *a.* exceedingly, considerably, hugely; see VERY.

greatness *n.* **1.** [Eminence] prominence, renown, importance; see FAME. **2.** [Size] bulk, extent, largeness; see SIZE 2.

Greece *n.* Hellas, Greek peninsula, Hellenic peoples; see EUROPE.

greed *n.* greediness, selfishness, eagerness, voracity, excess, gluttony, piggishness, indulgence, hoggishness, niggardliness, acquisitiveness, intemperance, covetousness, desire, grabbiness, an itching palm*.—*Ant.* GENEROSITY, liberality, kindness.

greedy *a.* avid, grasping, rapacious, selfish, miserly, parsimonious, close, closefisted, tight, tight-fisted, niggardly, exploitative, grudging, devouring, ravenous, omnivorous, carnivorous, intemperate, gobbling, indulging one's appetites, mercenary, stingy, covetous, pennypinching.—*Ant.* GENEROUS, munificent, bountiful.

Greek *a.* Grecian, Hellenic, Hellenistic, Minoan, Dorian, Attic, Athenian, Spartan, Peloponnesian, Ionian, Corinthian, Thessalian, ancient, classic; see also CLASSICAL 2.

Greek *n.* **1.** [A citizen of Greece] Hellene, Athenian, Spartan; see EUROPEAN. **2.** [The Greek language] Hellenic, Ionic, New Ionic; see LANGUAGE 1.

Greeks *n.pl.* Greek culture, Hellenes, the Ancients, Hellenism, classical times, Athens, the glory that was Greece, the Golden Age.

green *a.* **1.** [Of the color green] *Tints and shades of green include the following:* emerald, blue-green, sage, aquamarine, chartreuse, lime, kelly, bronze-green, yellow-green, bottle-green, pea-green, sea-green, apple-green, grass-green, forest-green, moss-green, spinach-green, pine-green, olive-green, jade. **2.** [Verdant] growing, leafy, sprounting, grassy, grass-grown, flourishing, lush. **3.** [Immature] young, growing, unripe, maturing, developing, half-formed, fresh.—*Ant.* MATURE, ripe, gone to seed. **4.** [Inexperienced] youthful, callow, raw; see INEXPERIENCED.

green *n.* greenness, verdure, virescence; see COLOR.

greet *v.* welcome, speak to, salute, address, hail, recognize, embrace, shake hands, nod, receive, call to, stop, acknowledge, bow to, approach, give one's love, hold out one's hand, herald, bid good day, bid hello, bid welcome, exchange greetings, usher in, attend, pay one's respects.—*Ant.* IGNORE, snub, slight.

greeting *n.* welcome, address, notice, speaking to, ushering in, acknowledgment, one's compliments, regards. *Common greetings include the following:* hello, how do you do, how are you, good morning, good day, good afternoon, good evening, hi*, hey*, yo*.

grey *a.* dun, drab, grayish; see GRAY.

grief *n.* sorrow, sadness, regret, melancholy, mourning, misery, trouble, anguish, despondency, pain, worry, harassment, anxiety, woe, heartache, malaise, disquiet, discomfort, affliction, gloom, unhappiness, desolation, despair, agony, torture, purgatory.—*Ant.* HAPPINESS, exhilaration, pleasure.

grievance *n.* complaint, injury, case; see OBJECTION.

grieve *v.* lament, bewail, sorrow for; see MOURN.

grill *v.* roast, sauté, barbecue; see COOK.

grim *a.* **1.** [Sullen] sour, crusty, gloomy, sulky, morose, churlish, forbidding, glum, grumpy, scowling, grouchy, crabby, glowering, stubborn, cantankerous.—*Ant.* HAPPY, cheerful, gay. **2.** [Stern] austere, strict, harsh; see SEVERE 1. **3.** [Relentless] unrelenting, implacable, inexorable; see SEVERE 2.

grimace *n.* smirk, smile, sneer; see EXPRESSION 4.

grime *n.* soil, smudge, dirt; see FILTH.

grimy *a.* begrimed, dingy, soiled; see DIRTY 1.

grin *n.* smirk, simper, delighted look; see SMILE.

grin *v.* smirk, simper, beam; see SMILE.

grind *v.* crush, powder, mill, grate, granulate, disintegrate, rasp, scrape, file, abrade, pound, reduce to fine particles, crunch, roll out, pound out, chop up, crumble.—*Ant.* ORGANIZE, mold, solidify.

grinding *a.* abrasive, crushing, pulverizing, grating, rasping, rubbing, milling, powdering, cracking, bone-crushing, crunching, splintering, shivering, smashing, crumbling, scraping, chopping, wearing away, eroding.

grip *n.* **1.** [The power and the application of the power to grip] grasp, hold, manual strength, clutch, clasp, catch, cinch, vise, clench, clinch, embrace, handhold, fist, handshake, anchor, squeeze, wrench, grab, enclosure, fixing, fastening, crushing, clamp, hoops of steel, vicelike grip, jaws. **2.** [Something suited to grasping] knocker, knob, ear; see HANDLE 1. **3.** [A traveling bag] valise, suitcase, satchel; see BAG.

grip *v.* clutch, grasp, clasp; see SEIZE 1. —**come to grips** engage, encounter, cope with; see FIGHT, TRY 1.

gripe* *n.* complaint, grievance, beef*; see OBJECTION.

gripe* *v.* grumble, mutter, fuss; see COMPLAIN.

gristle *n.* ossein, cartilage, bony matter; see BONE.

grit *n.* sand, dust, crushed rock; see GRAVEL.

gritty *a.* rough, abrasive, sandy, rasping, lumpy, gravelly, muddy, dusty, powdery, granular, crumbly, loose, scratchy.

groan *n.* moan, sob, grunt; see CRY 1.

groan *v.* moan, murmur, keen; see CRY 1.

groceries *n.pl.* food, edibles, produce, comestibles, foodstuffs, perishables, vegetables, staples, green groceries, fruits, dairy products, processed foods, frozen foods, freeze-dried foods, dried foods, packaged foods, canned foods.

grocery *n.* food store, vegetable market, corner store; see MARKET 1.

groggy *a.* sleepy, dizzy, reeling; see TIRED.

groom *n.* bridegroom, married man, successful suitor; see HUSBAND.

groom *v.* rub down, comb, brush; see PREPARE 1.

groove *n.* channel, trench, gouge, depression, scratch, canal, valley, notch, furrow, rut, incision, slit, gutter, ditch, crease. —**in the groove*** efficient, skillful, operative; see WORKING 1.

grope *v.* fumble, touch, feel blindly; see FEEL 1.

gross *a.* **1.** [Fat] corpulent, obese, huge; see FAT. **2.** [Obscene] foul, swinish, indecent; see LEWD 1, 2. **3.** [Without deduction] in sum, total, entire; see WHOLE 1.

gross *n.* total, aggregate, total amount; see WHOLE.

gross *v.* earn, bring in, take in; see EARN 2.

grotesque *a.* malformed, ugly, distorted; see DEFORMED.

grouch *n.* complainer, grumbler, growler, bear*, sourpuss*, sorehead*, crab*, crank*, bellyacher*.

grouch *v.* mutter, grumble, gripe*; see COMPLAIN.

grouchy *a.* surly, ill-tempered, crusty; see IRRITABLE.

ground *n.* **1.** [Soil] sand, dirt, clay; see EARTH 2. **2.** [An area] spot, terrain, territory; see AREA. —**break ground** start, initiate, commence; see BEGIN 1. —**cover ground** move, go on, progress; see ADVANCE 1. —**from the ground up** thoroughly, wholly, entirely; see COMPLETELY. —**gain ground** move, go on, progress; see ADVANCE 1. —**get off the ground** start, commence, come into being; see BEGIN 2. —**hold (or stand) one's ground** maintain one's position, defend, sustain; see ENDURE 2. —**lose ground** withdraw, fall behind, drop back; see LAG. —**run into the ground*** exaggerate, do too much, press; see OVERDO 1.

ground *v.* 1. [To bring to the ground] floor, bring down, prostrate; see TRIP 2. 2. [To restrict] cause to remain on the ground, confine, prevent from driving; see RESTRICT. 3. [To instruct in essentials] train, indoctrinate, educate; see TEACH.

grounds *n.pl.* 1. [Real estate] lot, environs, territory; see PROPERTY 2. 2. [Basis] reasons, arguments, proof; see BASIS. 3. [Sediment] dregs, lees, leavings; see RESIDUE.

groundwork *n.* background, base, origin; see BASIS, FOUNDATION 2.

group *n.* 1. [A gathering of persons] assembly, assemblage, crowd; see GATHERING. 2. [Collected things] accumulation, assortment, combination; see COLLECTION. 3. [An organized body of people] association, club, society; see ORGANIZATION 2.

group *v.* file, assort, arrange; see CLASSIFY.

grovel *v.* crawl, beg, sneak, stoop, kneel, crouch before, kowtow to, sponge, cower, snivel, beseech, wheedle, flatter, cater to, humor, pamper, curry favor with, court, act up to, play up to, beg for mercy, prostrate oneself, soft-soap, butter up*, make up to, kiss one's feet*, lick another's boots*, knuckle under, polish the apple*, eat dirt*, brown-nose*.—*Ant.* HATE, spurn, scorn.

grow *v.* 1. [To become larger] increase, expand in size, swell, wax, thrive, gain, enlarge, advance, dilate, stretch, mount, build, burst forth, spread, multiply, develop, mature, flourish, grow up, rise, sprout, shoot up, jump up, start up, spring up, spread like wildfire.—*Ant.* WITHER, lessen, shrink. 2. [To change slowly] become, develop, alter, tend, pass, evolve, flower, shift, flow, progress, advance; get bigger, larger, etc.; wax, turn into, improve, mellow, age, better, ripen into, blossom, open out, resolve itself into, mature. 3. [To cultivate] raise, nurture, tend, nurse, foster, produce, plant, breed.—*Ant.* HARM, impede, neglect.

growing *a.* increasing, ever-widening, expanding, budding, germinating, maturing, waxing, enlarging, amplifying, swelling, developing, mushrooming, spreading, thriving, flourishing, stretching, living, sprouting, viable, organic, animate, spreading like wildfire.—*Ant.* CONTRACTION, withering, shrinking.

growl *n.* snarl, gnarl, moan, bark, bellow, rumble, roar, howl, grumble, grunt.

growl *v.* snarl, bark, gnarl; see CRY 2.

grown *a.* of age, adult, grown up; see MATURE.

grown-up *n.* adult, grown person, big person, grown man, grown woman.

growth *n.* 1. [The process of growing] extension, organic development, germination; see INCREASE. 2. [The result of growing] completion, adulthood, fullness; see MAJORITY 2. 3. [A swelling] tumor, cancer, mole, fungus, parasite, outgrowth, thickening.

grubby *a.* dirty, sloppy, grimy; see DIRTY 1.

grudge *n.* spite, rancor, animosity; see HATRED.

grudge *v.* begrudge, covet, be reluctant; see ENVY.

grueling *a.* exhausting, tiring, fatiguing; see DIFFICULT 1, 2.

gruesome *a.* grim, grisly, fearful; see FRIGHTFUL, OFFENSIVE 2.

gruff *a.* harsh, grating, rough; see HOARSE.

grumble *v.* whine, protest, fuss; see COMPLAIN.

grumpy *a.* sullen, grouchy, cantankerous; see IRRITABLE.

grunt *v.* snort, squawk, squeak; see CRY 2.

guarantee *v.* attest, testify, vouch for, declare, assure, answer for, be responsible for, pledge, give bond, go bail, wager, stake, give a guarantee, stand good for, back, sign for, become surety for, endorse, secure, make certain, warrant, insure, witness, prove, reassure, support, affirm, confirm, cross one's heart.

guaranteed *a.* warranted, certified, bonded, secured, endorsed, insured, pledged, confirmed, assured, approved, attested, sealed, certificated, protected, affirmed, sure-fire*.—*Ant.* ANONYMOUS, unsupported, unendorsed.

guaranty *n.* warrant, warranty, bond, contract, certificate, charter, testament, security.

guard *n.* sentry, sentinel, protector; see WATCHMAN. —**off one's guard** unaware, unprotected, defenseless; see UNPREPARED. —**on one's guard** alert, mindful, vigilant; see READY 2.

guard *v.* watch, observe, superintend, patrol, picket, police, look out, look after, see after, supervise, tend, keep in view, keep an eye on, attend, overlook, hold in custody, stand over, babysit, care for, see to, chaperone, oversee, ride herd on*, keep tabs on*.—*Ant.* NEGLECT, disregard, forsake.

guarded *a.* 1. [Protected] safeguarded, secured, defended; see SAFE 1. 2. [Cautious] circumspect, attentive, overcautious; see CAREFUL.

guardian *n.* 1. [One who regulates or protects] overseer, safeguard, curator, guard, protector, preserver, trustee, custodian, keeper, patrol, warden, defender, supervisor, babysitter, sponsor, superintendent, sentinel. 2. [A foster parent] adoptive parent, foster mother, foster father; see FATHER 1, MOTHER 1.

guerrilla *a.* auxiliary, independent, predatory; see FIGHTING.
guerrilla *n.* irregular soldier, saboteur, independent; see SOLDIER.
guess *n.* conjecture, surmise, supposition, theory, hypothesis, presumption, opinion, postulate, estimate, suspicion, guesswork, view, belief, assumption, speculation, fancy, inference, conclusion, deduction, induction, shot in the dark.
guess *v.* conjecture, presume, infer, suspect, speculate, imagine, surmise, theorize, hazard a guess, suggest, figure, venture, suppose, presume, imagine, think likely, reckon, calculate.
guess at *v.* reckon, calculate, survey; see ESTIMATE.
guessing *n.* guesswork, supposition, imagination, fancy, inference, deduction, presupposition, reckoning, surmise, theorizing, taking for granted, postulating, assuming, presuming, jumping to conclusions.
guest *n.* visitor, caller, house guest, dinner guest, luncheon guest, visitant, confidant, confidante, friend.
guidance *n.* direction, leadership, supervision; see ADMINISTRATION 2.
guide *n.* pilot, captain, pathfinder, scout, escort, courier, director, explorer, lead, guru, conductor, pioneer, leader, superintendent.
guide *v.* conduct, escort, show the way; see LEAD 1.
guilt *n.* culpability, blame, error, fault, crime, sin, offense, liability, criminality, sinfulness, misconduct, misbehavior, malpractice, delinquency, transgression, indiscretion, weakness, failing, felonious conduct.—*Ant.* INNOCENCE, blamelessness, honor.
guilty *a.* found guilty, guilty as charged, condemned, sentenced, criminal, censured, impeached, incriminated, indicted, liable, condemned, convictable, judged, damned, doomed, at fault, sinful, to blame, in the wrong, in error, wrong, blameable, reproachable, chargeable.—*Ant.* INNOCENT, blameless, right.
gulch *n.* gully, ditch, gorge; see RAVINE.
gulf *n.* **1.** [Chasm] abyss, gap, depth; see RAVINE. **2.** [An arm of the sea] inlet, sound, cove; see BAY.
gullible *a.* innocent, trustful, simple; see NAIVE.
gully *n.* ditch, chasm, crevasse; see RAVINE.
gulp *v.* swig, choke down, toss off; see SWALLOW.
gum *n.* resin, glue, pitch, tar, pine tar, amber, wax. *Commercial gums include the following:* chewing gum, sealing wax, rosin, mucilage, chicle, latex, gum arabic.
gummy *a.* sticky, cohesive, viscid; see STICKY.
gun *n.* *Types include the following:* rifle, automatic rifle, repeating rifle, repeater, recoilless rifle, air rifle, shotgun, sawed-off shotgun, musket, hand gun, automatic, semiautomatic pistol, squirrel gun, carbine, long rifle, laser gun, revolver, pistol, rod*; see also MACHINE GUN. —**jump the gun*** start too soon, act inappropriately, give oneself away; see BEGIN 1, HURRY 1.
gunfire *n.* bombardment, fire to pin down someone, artillery support, air support, air strike, mortar fire, heavy arms attack, explosion, shooting, shot, report, artillery, volley, discharge, detonation, blast, firing, burst, barrage, cannonade, fire superiority, salvo, fire power.
gunman *n.* killer, thug, gangster; see CRIMINAL.
gunner *n.* machine gunner, rocketeer, missile launcher, bazooka launcher, sniper, sharpshooter, aerial gunner, artilleryman, cannoneer.
gurgle *v.* ripple, murmur, pour; see FLOW.
gush *v.* pour, well, spew; see FLOW.
gust *n.* blast, blow, breeze; see WIND.
gusto *n.* zeal, fervor, ardor; see ZEAL.
gut *n.* small intestine, large intestine, duodenum; see INTESTINES.
guts *n.pl.* **1.** [Bowels] viscera, insides, belly; see INTESTINES. **2.** [*Fortitude] pluck, hardihood, effrontery; see COURAGE. —**hate someone's guts*** detest, dislike, despise; see HATE.
gutter *n.* canal, gully, sewer, watercourse, channel, dike, drain, moat, trough; see also TRENCH.
guttural *a.* throaty, gruff, deep; see HOARSE.
guy *n.* chap, lad, person; see FELLOW 1.
guzzle *v.* swill, quaff, swig; see DRINK 1.
gymnasium *n.* health center, recreation center, playing floor, exercise room, sports center, field house, court, athletic club, arena, coliseum, theater, circus, stadium, ring, rink, pit, gym*.
gymnast *n.* acrobat, tumbler, jumper; see ATHLETE.
gymnastics *n.* trapeze performance, health exercises, acrobatics, aerobatics, therapeutics, body-building exercises, tumbling, vaulting, work on the rings, bars, balance beam, horizontal bars, horse.
gyp* *n.* cheat, fraud, trick; see FAKE, TRICK 1.
gyp* *v.* cheat, defraud, swindle; see DECEIVE.
gypsy *n.* tramp, Bohemian, vagrant; see TRAVELER.

H

habit *n.* **1.** [A customary action] mode, wont, routine, rule, characteristic, practice, disposition, way, fashion, manner, propensity, bent, turn, proclivity, addiction, predisposition, susceptibility, weakness, bias, persuasion, second nature; see also CUSTOM. **2.** [An obsession] addiction, fixation, hang-up; see OBSESSION.

habitat *n.* locality, territory, natural surroundings; see ENVIRONMENT, HOME 1, POSITION 1.

habitual *a.* ingrained, confirmed, frequent, periodic, continual, routine, mechanical, automatic, seasoned, permanent, perpetual, fixed, rooted, systematic, recurrent, periodical, methodical, repeated, disciplined, practiced, accustomed, established, set, repetitious, cyclic, reiterated, settled, trite, stereotyped, in a groove, in a rut.—*Ant.* DIFFERENT, exceptional, departing.

hack *n.* **1.** [A literary drudge] pulp-story writer, ghost writer, propagandist, commercial writer, popular novelist; see also WRITER. **2.** [A cut] notch, nick, cleavage; see CUT 1. **3.** [*Commercial driver, especially of a taxicab] cab driver, chauffeur, cabbie*; see DRIVER.

hack *v.* chop, whack, mangle; see CUT 1.

hag *n.* crone, virago, withered old woman, shrew, ogress, hellcat, fishwife, harridan, old witch, battle-ax*; see also WITCH.

haggle *v.* deal, wrangle, argue; see BUY, SELL.

hail *n.* hailstorm, sleet, icy particles, ice; see also RAIN 1.

hail *v.* cheer, welcome, honor; see GREET.

hail from *v.* come from, be born in, be a native of; see BEGIN 2.

hair *n.* **1.** [Threadlike growth] locks, wig, moustache, whiskers, eyebrow, eyelash, sideburn, mane, fluff; see also BEARD, FUR. **2.** [Anything suggesting the thickness of a hair] a hairbreadth, a narrow margin, hair trigger, hairspring, splinter, shaving, sliver; see also BIT 1. **—get in one's hair*** irritate, annoy, disturb; see BOTHER 2. **—let one's hair down*** be informal, have fun, let oneself go; see RELAX. **—make one's hair stand on end** terrify, scare, horrify; see FRIGHTEN.

haircut *n.* trim, trimming, bob, crew cut, flattop*, Beatle, page boy, pigtails, French roll, bun, ponytail, braid, feathercut, bangs, butch*, DA*, ducktail*.

hairdo *n.* coiffure, hairdressing, hair style; see HAIRCUT.

hairless *n.* clean-shaven, beardless, smooth-faced; see BALD, SMOOTH 3.

hairpin *n.* bobby pin, hair clip, barrette; see FASTENER.

hairsplitting *a.* unimportant, minute, subtle; see TRIVIAL, IRRELEVANT, UNIMPORTANT.

hair style *n.* hairdo, coiffure, haircut; see HAIRCUT.

hairy *a.* bristly, shaggy, woolly, unshorn, downy, fleecy, whiskered, tufted, unshaven, bearded, bewhiskered, furry, fuzzy, hirsute, fluffy.—*Ant.* BALD, hairless, smooth.

half *a.* partial, divided by two, equally distributed in halves, mixed, divided, halved, bisected; see also HALFWAY.—*Ant.* FULL, all, whole. **—by half** considerably, many, very much; see MUCH. **—in half** into halves, split, divided; see HALF. **—not the half of it** not all of it, partial, incomplete; see UNFINISHED.

halfback *n.* right halfback, left halfback, back; see FOOTBALL PLAYER.

half-baked *a.* senseless, brainless, indiscreet; see STUPID.

half-breed *a.* half-caste, crossbreed, half-blood; see HYBRID.

half dollar *n.* fifty cents, fifty-cent piece, four bits*; see MONEY 1.

halfhearted *a.* lukewarm, indecisive, irresolute; see INDIFFERENT.

halfway *a.* midway, half the distance, in the middle, incomplete, unsatisfactory, partially, fairly, imperfectly, in part, partly, nearly, insufficiently, to a degree, to some extent, comparatively, moderately, at half the distance, in some measure, middling*; see also HALF.—*Ant.* COMPLETELY, wholly, entirely.

halfway house *n.* addiction facility, referral center, rest home; see HOSPITAL.

hall *n.* **1.** [A large public or semi-public building or room] legislative chamber, assembly room, meeting place, banquet hall, town hall, concert hall, dance hall, music hall, arena, ballroom, clubroom, church, salon, lounge, chamber, stateroom, gymnasium, dining hall, armory, amphitheater, council chamber, reception room, waiting room, lecture room, gallery, gym*, mess hall. **2.** [An entrance way] foyer, corridor, hallway; see ENTRANCE 2, ROOM 2.

hallelujah *interj.* praise God, praise the Lord, glory be; see YELL.

hallmark *n.* endorsement, seal, mark of acceptance; see EMBLEM.

hallowed *a.* sacred, sacrosanct, consecrated; see DIVINE.

hallway *n.* foyer, entrance way, corridor; see ENTRANCE 2.

halt *v.* pull up, check, terminate, suspend, put an end to, interrupt, break into, block, cut short, adjourn, hold off, cause to halt, stem, deter, bring to a standstill, stall, bring to an end, curb, stop, restrict, arrest, hold in check, defeat, thwart, hamper, frustrate, suppress, clog, intercept, extinguish, blockade, obstruct, repress, inhibit, hinder, barricade, impede, overthrow, vanquish, override, dam, upset, stand in the way of, baffle, contravene, overturn, reduce, counteract, quell, prohibit, outdo, put down, finish, forbid, oppose, crush, nip in the bud*, break it up, put on the brakes*, hold on*, throw a wet blanket on*, throw a monkey wrench in the works*, clip one's wings*, tie one's hands*, take the wind out of one's sails, squelch*.—*Ant.* BEGIN, start, instigate.

halter *n.* leash, bridle, rein; see ROPE.

halve *v.* split, bisect, cut in two; see DIVIDE.

ham *n.* **1.** [Smoked pork thigh] sugar-cured ham, Virginia ham, picnic ham; see MEAT. **2.** [An incompetent actor] inferior player, nonprofessional, ham actor*; see AMATEUR.

hamburger *n.* ground round, ground beef, burger; see MEAT.

hammer *n.* maul, mallet, mace, club, gavel, steam hammer, triphammer, jackhammer, sledge; see also STICK, TOOL 1.

hammer *v.* strike, bang, pound away at; see BEAT 1, HIT.

hammer out *v.* work out, fight through, get settled; see DECIDE.

hammock *n.* porch swing, hanging bed, bunk; see BED 1.

hamper *v.* impede, thwart, embarrass; see HINDER.

hand *n.* **1.** [The termination of the arm] fingers, palm, grip, grasp, hold, knuckles; see also FIST. **2.** [A workman] helper, worker, hired hand; see LABORER. **3.** [Handwriting] chirography, script, penmanship; see HANDWRITING. **4.** [Aid] help, guidance, instruction; see HELP 1. **5.** [Applause] standing ovation, thunderous reception, handclapping; see PRAISE 2. **6.** [Round of cards] single hand, deal, round; see GAME 1. —**at hand** immediate, approximate, close by; see NEAR 1. —**by hand** handcrafted, handmade, manual; see HOMEMADE. —**change hands** transfer, pass on, shift; see GIVE 1. —**from hand to hand** shifted, given over, changed; see TRANSFERRED. —**from hand to mouth** from day to day, by necessity, in poverty; see POOR 1. —**hold hands** touch, press, squeeze; see HOLD 1. —**in hand** under control, in order, all right; see MANAGED 2. —**join hands** unite, associate, agree; see JOIN 1. —**keep one's hand in** carry on, continue, make a practice of; see PRACTICE 1. —**not lift a hand** do nothing, be lazy, not try; see NEGLECT 1, 2. —**off one's hands** out of one's responsibility, no longer one's concern, not accountable for; see IRRESPONSIBLE. —**on hand** ready, close by, usable; see AVAILABLE. —**on one's hands** in one's care or responsibility, chargeable to one, accountable to; see RESPONSIBLE 1. —**on the other hand** otherwise, conversely, from the opposite position; see OTHERWISE 1, 2. —**out of hand** out of control, wild, unmanageable; see UNRULY. —**take in hand** take responsibility for, take over, handle; see TRY 1. —**throw up one's hands** give up, resign, quit; see YIELD 1. —**wash one's hands of** deny, reject, refuse; see DENOUNCE.

hand *v.* deliver, give to, return; see GIVE 1.

hand around *v.* hand out, pass around, allot; see DISTRIBUTE, GIVE 1.

handbag *n.* lady's pocketbook, bag, clutch purse; see PURSE.

handbook *n.* textbook, directory, guidebook; see BOOK.

hand down *v.* pass on, bequeath, grant; see GIVE 1.

handed *a.* given to, conveyed, bestowed; see GIVEN.

handful *n.* a small quantity, some, a sprinkling; see FEW.

handicap *n.* **1.** [A disadvantage] hindrance, obstacle, block; see BARRIER. **2.** [A physical injury] impairment, affliction, chronic disorder; see IMPEDIMENT 2, INJURY.

handicapped *a.* thwarted, crippled, impeded, burdened, hampered, obstructed, encumbered, put at a disadvantage, checked, blocked, limited, restrained, wounded, curbed, put behind; see also DISABLED, RESTRICTED.—*Ant.* HELPED, aided, supported.

handily *a.* skillfully, intelligently, smoothly; see CLEVERLY, EASILY.

hand in *v.* deliver, submit, return; see GIVE 1, OFFER 1.

hand in hand *a.* closely associated, working together, related; see TOGETHER 2, UNITED.

handiwork *n.* handicraft, creation, handwork; see WORKMANSHIP.

handkerchief *n.* kerchief, rag*, hanky*; see TOWEL.

handle *n.* **1.** [A holder] handhold, hilt, grasp, crank, knob, stem, grip, arm; see also HOLDER. **2.** [*A title] nickname, designation, moniker*; see NAME 1, TITLE 3. —**fly off the handle** become angry, lose one's temper, blow off steam*; see RAGE 1.

handle *v.* **1.** [To deal in] retail, market, offer for sale; see SELL. **2.** [To touch] finger, check, examine; see FEEL 1, TOUCH 1. **3.** [To do whatever is necessary] manipulate, operate, work; see MANAGE 1.

handling *n.* treatment, approach, styling; see MANAGEMENT.

handmade *a.* made by hand, handicraft, handcrafted; see HOMEMADE.

hand-me-down *n.* secondhand article, discard; old clothes, etc.; see SECONDHAND.
handout *n.* contribution, donation, free meal; see GIFT 1, GRANT.
hand out *v.* give to, deliver, distribute; see GIVE 1, PROVIDE 1.
hand over *v.* deliver, surrender, give up; see GIVE 1, YIELD 1.
hands off *interj.* keep away, don't touch, stay back; see AVOID.
handsome *a.* smart, impressive, stately, good-looking, attractive, athletic, personable, strong, muscular, robust, well-dressed, slick*; see also BEAUTIFUL.—*Ant.* UGLY, homely, unsightly.
hand-to-hand *a.* face-to-face, facing, close; see NEAR 1.
handwriting *n.* penmanship, hand, writing, cursive, script, longhand, scrawl, scribble, manuscript, a style of writing, calligraphy, scratching*, chicken scratch*.
handwritten *a.* in writing, in long hand, not typed; see REPRODUCED, WRITTEN 2.
handy *a.* **1.** [Near] nearby, at hand, close by; see NEAR 1. **2.** [Useful] beneficial, advantageous, gainful; see HELPFUL 1, PROFITABLE, USABLE.
hang *v.* **1.** [To suspend] dangle, attach, drape, hook up, hang up, nail on the wall, put on a clothesline, fix, pin up, tack up, drape on the wall, fasten up; see also FASTEN.—*Ant.* DROP, throw down, let fall. **2.** [To be suspended] overhang, wave, flap, be loose, droop, flop, be in midair, swing, dangle, be fastened, hover, stay up.—*Ant.* FALL, come down, drop. **3.** [To kill by hanging] execute, lynch, hand by the neck until dead; see KILL 1. —**get** (or **have**) **the hang of** have the knack of, comprehend, learn; see UNDERSTAND 1. —**not care** (or **give**) **a hang about** be indifferent toward, not care about, ignore; see NEGLECT 2.
hang around *v.* associate with, get along with, have relations with; see KEEP COMPANY (WITH).
hanged *a.* lynched, strung up, brought to the gallows; see EXECUTED 2.
hanger *n.* coat hook, nail, peg, coat hanger, clothes hanger, holder, clothes rod, wire hanger, collapsible hanger; see also HOLDER.
hanger-on *n.* leech, nuisance, parasite; see DEPENDENT.
hanging *a.* dangling, swaying, swinging, overhanging, projecting, suspended, fastened to, pendulous, drooping.
hang on *v.* persist, remain, continue; see ENDURE 1, 2.
hangout* *n.* bar, joint*, hole*; see BAR 2, HEADQUARTERS, ROOM 2.
hang out *v.* loiter, spend time, haunt; see VISIT.
hangover *n.* nausea, sickness, headache; see DRUNKENNESS, ILLNESS 1.
hang up *v.* finish a telephone call, ring off, hang up the phone; see END 1.
hang-up* *n.* problem, predicament, disturbance; see DIFFICULTY 1, 2.
haphazard *a.* offhand, casual, random, careless, slipshod, incidental, unthinking, unconscious, uncoordinated, reckless, unconcerned, unpremeditated, loose, indiscriminate, unrestricted, irregular, blind, purposeless, unplanned, hit-or-miss, willy-nilly; see also AIMLESS.—*Ant.* CAREFUL, studied, planned.
haphazardly *a.* unexpectedly, casually, every now and then; see ACCIDENTALLY, CARELESSLY.
happen *v.* **1.** [To be by chance] come up, come about, turn up, crop up, chance, occur unexpectedly, come face to face with, befall, hit one like a ton of bricks*, be just one's luck. **2.** [To occur] take place, come to pass, arrive, ensue, befall, come after, arise, take effect, come into existence, recur, come into being, spring, proceed, follow, come about, fall, repeat, appear, go on, become a fact, turn out, become known, be found, come to mind, transpire, come off; see also RESULT.
happening *n.* incident, affair, accident; see EVENT.
happily *a.* joyously, gladly, joyfully, cheerily, gaily, laughingly, smilingly, jovially, merrily, brightly, vivaciously, hilariously, with pleasure, peacefully, blissfully, cheerfully, gleefully, playfully, heartily, lightheartedly, lightly, to one's delight, optimistically, with all one's heart, with relish, with good will, in a happy manner, with zeal, with good grace, zestfully, with open arms, sincerely, willingly, freely, graciously, tactfully, lovingly, agreeably.—*Ant.* SADLY, morosely, dejectedly.
happiness *n.* mirth, merrymaking, cheer, merriment, joyousness, vivacity, laughter, delight, gladness, good spirits, hilarity, playfulness, exuberance, gaiety, cheefulness, good will, rejoicing, exhilaration, glee, geniality, good cheer, lightheartedness, joy; see also JOY.
happy *a.* joyous, joyful, merry, mirthful, glad, gleeful, delighted, cheerful, gay, laughing, contented, genial, satisfied, enraptured, congenial, cherry, jolly, hilarious, sparkling, enchanted, transported, rejoicing, blissful, jovial, delightful, delirious, exhilarated, pleased, gratified, peaceful, comfortable, intoxicated, debonair, light, bright, ecstatic, charmed, pleasant, hearty, overjoyed, lighthearted, radiant, vivacious, sunny, smiling, content, animated, lively, spirited, exuberant, good-humored, elated, jubilant, rollicking, playful, thrilled, fun-loving, carefree, at peace, in good spirits, in high spirits, happy as a lark, in ecstasy, beside oneself, bubbling over, tickled pink, tickled to death, tickled

silly, happy-go-lucky, in seventh heaven*.—*Ant.* SAD, sorrowful, melancholy.

happy-go-lucky *a.* cheerful, easygoing, unconcerned; see IRRESPONSIBLE.

harass *v.* tease, vex, irritate; see BOTHER 2.

harbinger *n.* indication, sign, signal; see MESSENGER, SIGNAL.

harbor *n.* port, pier, inlet; see DOCK.

harbor *v.* **1.** [To protect] shelter, provide refuge, secure; see DEFEND 2. **2.** [To consider] entertain, cherish, regard; see CONSIDER.

hard *a.* **1.** [Compact] unyielding, thick, solid, heavy, strong, impermeable, tough, tempered, hardened, dense; see also FIRM 2. **2.** [Difficult] arduous, tricky, impossible, trying, tedious, complex, abstract, puzzling, troublesome, laborious; see also DIFFICULT 1, 2. **3.** [Cruel] perverse, unrelenting, vengeful; see CRUEL. **4.** [Severe] harsh, exacting, grim; see SEVERE 1, 2. **5.** [Alcoholic] intoxicating, inebriating, stimulating; see STRONG 4. **6.** [With difficulty] strenuously, laboriously, with great effort; see CAREFULLY 1, VIGOROUSLY. —**be hard on** treat severely, be harsh toward, be painful to; see ABUSE.

hard-core *a.* dedicated, steadfast, unwavering; see FAITHFUL.

harden *v.* steel, temper, solidify, precipitate, crystallize, freeze, coegulate, clot, granulate, make firm, make compact, make tight, make hard, petrify, starch, cure, bake, dry, flatten, cement, compact, concentrate, sun, fire, fossilize, vulcanize, toughen, concrete, encrust; see also STIFFEN.—*Ant.* SOFTEN, unloose, melt.

hardened *a.* **1.** [Made hard] compacted, stiffened, stiff; see FIRM 2. **2.** [Inured to labor or hardship] accustomed, conditioned, tough; see HABITUAL.

hardening *n.* thickening, crystallization, setting; see SOLIDIFICATION.

hard going *n.* trouble, emergency, competition; see DIFFICULTY.

hardheaded *a.* willful, stubborn, headstrong; see STUBBORN.

hardhearted *a.* cold, unfeeling, heartless; see CRUEL.

hardly *a.* scarcely, barely, just, merely, imperceptibly, not noticably, gradually, not markedly, no more than, not likely, not a bit, almost not, only just, with difficulty, with trouble, by a narrow margin, not by a great deal, seldom, almost not at all, but just, in no manner, by no means, little, infrequently, somewhat, not quite, here and there, simply, not much, rarely, slightly, sparsely, not often, once in a blue moon*, by the skin of one's teeth*; see also ONLY.—*Ant.* EASILY, without difficulty, readily.

hard-nosed *a.* stubborn, unyielding, hardheaded; see OBSTINATE, RESOLUTE.

hard of hearing *a.* almost deaf, having a hearing problem, in need of a hearing aid; see DEAF.

hard on *a.* unjust to, brutal, inclined to blame; see CRUEL, HARMFUL.

hardship *n.* trial, sorrow, worry; see DIFFICULTY 2, GRIEF.

hard up *a.* in trouble, poverty-stricken, in the lower income brackets; see POOR 1.

hardware *n.* domestic appliances, fixtures, metal manufactures, casting, plumbing, metalware, implements, tools, housewares, fittings, aluminum ware, cutlery, house furnishings, kitchenware, household utensils, equipment.

hardy *a.* tough, toughened, in good shape, in good condition, hardened, resistant, solid, staunch, seasoned, capable of endurance, able-bodied, physically fit, well-equipped, acclimatized, rugged, mighty, well, fit, robust, hearty, sound, fresh, hale, brawny, able, vigorous, powerful, firm, sturdy, solid, substantial; see also STRONG.—*Ant.* WEAK, unaccustomed, unhabituated.

harm *n.* **1.** [Injury] hurt, infliction, impairment; see INJURY. **2.** [Evil] wickedness, outrage, foul play; see ABUSE, EVIL 1, WRONG.

harm *v.* injure, wreck, cripple; see HURT.

harmed *a.* damaged, injured, wounded; see HURT.

harmful *a.* injurious, detrimental, hurtful, noxious, evil, mischievous, ruinous, adverse, sinister, subversive, incendiary, virulent, cataclysmic, corroding, toxic, baleful, painful, wounding, crippling, bad, malicious, malignant, sinful, pernicious, unwholesome, corrupting, menacing, dire, prejudicial, damaging, corrupt, vicious, insidious, treacherous, catastrophic, disastrous, wild, murderous, destructive, unhealthy, killing, fatal, mortal, serious, dangerous, fraught with evil, doing harm, doing evil, painful, sore, distressing, diabolic, brutal, unhealthful, satanic, grievous, lethal, venomous, cruel, unfortunate, disadvantageous, felonious, objectionable, fiendish, unlucky, malign, devilish, corrosive.

harmless *a.* pure, innocent, painless, powerless, controllable, manageable, safe, sure, reliable, trustworthy, sanitary, germproof, sound, sterile, disarmed.—*Ant.* HARMFUL, injurious, poisonous.

harmonica *n.* mouth organ, harmonicon, mouth harp; see MUSICAL INSTRUMENT.

harmonious *a.* **1.** [Harmonic] melodious, tuneful, musical, rhythmical, melodic, symphonic, in tune, in unison. **2.** [Congruous] agreeable to, corresponding, suitable, adapted, similar, like, peaceful, cooperative, in step, in accordance with, in concord with, in favor with, in harmony with, on a footing with, friendly, conforming, well-matched, evenly blalanced, symmetrical, congruent; see also FIT.—*Ant.* OPPOSED, incongruous, incompatible.

harmonize *v.* blend, arrange, put to harmony, adapt, set, orchestrate, tune, sing a duet, sing in harmony.

harmony *n.* **1.** [Musical concord] chord, consonance, accord, symphony, harmonics, counterpoint, concert, music, chorus, blending, unity, accordance, chime, unison, overtone, musical pattern, musical blend. **2.** [Social concord] compatibility, equanimity, unanimity; see AGREEMENT 1, PEACE 2. **3.** [Musical composition] melody, piece, arrangement; see COMPOSITION, MUSIC 1.

harness *n.* tackle, gear, yoke, apparatus, bridle, rigging, fittings; see also EQUIPMENT.

harness *v.* fetter, saddle, yoke, outfit, bridle, hold in leash, hitch up, control, limit, cinch, strap, collar, put in harness, rig up, rig out, tie, secure, rein in, curb, check, constrain.

harp *n.* lyre, multi-stringed instrument, claviharp; see MUSICAL INSTRUMENT.

harp on *v.* repeat, pester, nag; see COMPLAIN, TALK 1.

harsh *a.* discordant, jangling, cacophonous, grating, rusty, dissonant, assonant, strident, creaking, clashing, sharp, jarring, jangled, clamorous, cracked, hoarse, out of tune, unmelodious, rasping, screeching, earsplitting, disturbing, noisy, flat, sour, out of key, tuneless, unmusical, off-key; see also SHRILL.

harshly *a.* sternly, powerfully, grimly; see BRUTALLY, FIRMLY 2, LOUDLY, SERIOUSLY 1, 2.

harshness *n.* crudity, brutality, roughness; see ANGER, CRUELTY, TYRANNY.

harvest *n.* reaping, yield, crop; see CROP, FRUIT, GRAIN 1, PRODUCE, VEGETABLE.

harvest *v.* gather, accumulate, pile up, collect, garner, crop, cut, pluck, pick, cull, take in, draw in, glean, gather in the harvest, hoard, mow.—*Ant.* sow, plant, seed.

hash *n.* ground meat and vegetables, leftovers, casserole; see MEAT, STEW.

hash over* *v.* debate, argue about, review; see DISCUSS.

hassle* *n.* quarrel, squabble, row; see DISPUTE.

hassle* *v.* bother, annoy, harass; see BOTHER 2.

haste *n.* hurry, scramble, bustle, scurry, precipitation, flurry, hurly-burly, impetuosity, rashness, dispatch, impetuousness, foolhardiness, want of caution, hustling, press, recklessness, rush, hastiness, carelessness, irrationality, rashness, giddiness, impatience, heedlessness, plunge, testiness, excitation, outburst, abruptness, anticipation.—*Ant.* PRUDENCE, caution, attention. **—in haste** hastening, in a hurry, moving fast; see FAST. **—make haste** hurry, act quickly, speed up; see HURRY 1.

hasten *v.* **1.** [To make haste] rush, fly, sprint; see HURRY 1. **2.** [To expedite] accelerate, speed up, advance, move up, quicken, stimulate, hurry up, push, make short work of, urge, goad, press, agitate, push ahead, put into action, get started, give a start, drive on, set in motion, take in hand, blast off, gear up; see also SPEED.—*Ant.* DELAY, defer, put off.

hastily *a.* **1.** [Rapidly] hurriedly, speedily, nimbly; see QUICKLY. **2.** [Carelessly] thoughtlessly, recklessly, rashly; see CARELESSLY.

hasty *a.* **1.** [Hurried] quick, speedy, swift; see FAST 1. **2.** [Careless] ill-advised, precipitate, foolhardy; see CARELESS, RASH.

hat *n.* headgear, millinery, headpiece, helmet, chapeau, bonnet. *Hatlike coverings include the following—for men:* cap, yarmulke, derby, straw hat, felt hat, sombrero, cowboy hat, top hat, bowler, panama, fedora, beret, turban; *for women:* hood, snood, cowl, kerchief, beret, bandanna, cloche, boater, bonnet, turban, pillbox, scarf, babushka. **—take one's hat off to** salute, cheer, congratulate; see PRAISE 1. **—talk through one's hat*** chatter, talk nonsense, make foolish statements; see BABBLE. **—throw one's hat into the ring** enter a contest, run for office, enter politics; see CAMPAIGN. **—under one's hat*** confidential, private, hidden; see SECRET 1.

hatch *v.* bear, lay eggs, give birth; see PRODUCE 1.

hate *n.* ill will, animosity, enmity; see HATRED.

hate *v.* **1.** [To detest] abhor, abominate, loathe, scorn, despise, have an aversion toward, look at with loathing, spit upon, curse, dislike intensely, shudder at, not care for, have enough of, be repelled by, feel repulsion for, have no use for, object to, bear a grudge against, shun, denounce, resent, curse, be sick of, be tired of, reject, revolt against, deride, have no stomach for, disfavor, look down upon, hold in contempt, be disgusted with, view with horror, be down on*, have it in for*.—*Ant.* LOVE, adore, worship. **2.** [To dislike; *often used with infinitive or participle*] object to, shudder at, not like; see DISLIKE.

hated *a.* despised, loathed, abhorred, detested, disliked, cursed, unpopular, avoided, shunned, out of favor, condemned; see also UNDESIRABLE.

hateful *a.* odious, detestable, repugnant; see OFFENSIVE 2, UNDESIRABLE.

hater *n.* enemy of, racist, antagonist; see BIGOT, ENEMY.

hatred *n.* abhorrence, loathing, rancor, detestation, antipathy, repugnance, repulsion, disgust, contempt, intense dislike, scorn, abomination, distaste, disapproval, horror, hard feelings, displeasure, ill will, bitterness, antagonism, animosity, pique, grudge, malice, malevolence, revulsion, prejudice, spite, revenge, hate, venom, envy, spleen, coldness, distaste, contempt, hostility, alienation, bad blood, chip on one's shoulder*, grudge; see also ANGER.—*Ant.* DEVOTION, friendship, affection.

haughty *a.* arrogant, disdainful, proud; see EGOTISTIC.

haul *n.* **1.** [A pull] tug, lift, wrench; see PULL 1. **2.** [The distance something is hauled] trip, voyage, yards; see DISTANCE 3. **3.** [*Something obtained, especially loot] find, spoils, take; see BOOTY. —**in** (or **over**) **the long haul** over a long period of time, for a long time, in the end; see FINALLY 2.

haul *v.* pull, drag, bring; see DRAW 1.

haunt *v.* **1.** [To frequent persistently] habituate, visit often, hang around; see LOITER. **2.** [To prey upon] recur in one's mind, obsess, torment, beset, possess, trouble, weigh on one's mind, craze, madden, hound, terrify, plague, vex, harass, prey on, pester, worry, tease, terrorize, frighten, annoy, cause regret, cause sorrow, molest, appall, agitate, drive one nuts*; see also BOTHER 2, DISTURB.

haunted *a.* frequented, visited by, preyed upon; see TROUBLED.

haunting *a.* eerie, unforgettable, seductive; see FRIGHTFUL, REMEMBERED.

have *v.* **1.** [To be in possession of] own, possess, keep, retain, guard, use, maintain, control, treasure, keep title to, hold; see also OWN 1. **2.** [To be obliged; *used with infinitive*] be compelled to, be forced to, should, ought, be one's duty to, fall on, be up to, have got to; see also MUST. **3.** [To bear] beget, give birth to, bring forth; see PRODUCE 1. **4.** [To have sexual intercourse with] seduce, sleep with, deflower; see COPULATE.

have a ball* *v.* revel, have fun, celebrate; see PLAY 1.

have a heart* *v.* take pity on, be merciful to, be considerate of; see PITY 1, 2.

have had it* *v.* be out, be defeated, come to the end of everything; see LOSE 3, SUFFER 1.

have in mind *v.* expect, foresee, hope; see ANTICIPATE, THINK 1.

have it good* *v.* do well, thrive, have it easy; see SUCCEED 1.

haven *n.* port, harbor, roadstead; see REFUGE 1, SHELTER.

have on *v.* be clothed in, be wearing, try on; see WEAR 1.

have something on one *v.* be able to expose, have special knowledge of, be able to control; see CONVICT, KNOW 1.

have something on the ball* *v.* be alert, be quick, be in tune, have a keen mind, be industrious, be with it*; see also SUCCEED 1.

having *a.* owning, possessing, enjoying, commanding, holding, controlling; see also COMMANDING.

havoc *n.* devastation, plunder, ruin; see DESTRUCTION 2.

hawk *n.* **1.** [A member of the Accipitridae] bird of prey, osprey, falcon; see BIRD. **2.** [A warlike person] militarist, chauvinist, warmonger; see CONSERVATIVE, RADICAL.

hay *n.* fodder, roughage, forage, feed; see also GRASS 1. *Hay includes the following:* red clover, wild hay, timothy, alsike, sweet clover, soybeans, swamp hay, alfalfa, oat hay, millet. —**hit the hay*** go to bed, rest, recline; see SLEEP.

hazard *n.* risk, peril, jeopardy; see DANGER.

hazard *v.* stake, try, guess; see CHANCE, GAMBLE, RISK.

hazardous *a.* perilous, uncertain, precarious; see DANGEROUS.

haze *n.* mist, smog, cloudiness, see FOG.

hazy *a.* cloudy, foggy, murky, misty, unclear, overcast, steaming, screened, filmy, gauzy, vaporous, smoky, dim, dull, indistinct, nebulous, shadowy, dusky, obscure, thick, opaque, frosty, veiled, blurred, semitransparent, blurry, faint; see also DARK 1.—*Ant.* CLEAR, bright, cloudless.

he *pron.* this one, the male, the above-named, the man, the boy, third person, masculine singular.

head *n.* **1.** [The skull] brainpan, scalp, crown, headpiece, bean*, noggin*, noodle*. **2.** [A leader or supervisor] commander, commanding officer, ruler; see LEADER 2. **3.** [The top] summit, peak, crest; see TOP 1. **4.** [The beginning] front, start, source; see ORIGIN 2. **5.** [An attachment] cap, bottle top, cork; see COVER 1. **6.** [*Intelligence] brains, foresight, ingenuity; see JUDGMENT 1. **7.** [Drug addict] habitual user of drugs, acidhead*, pothead*; see ADDICT. —**come to a head** culminate, reach a crisis, come to a climax; see CLIMAX. —**get it through one's head** learn, comprehend, see; see UNDERSTAND 1. —**go to one's head** stir mentally, stimulate, intoxicate; see EXCITE. —**hang** (or **hide**) **one's head** repent, be sorry, grieve; see REGRET 1. —**keep one's head** remain calm, keep one's self-control, hold one's emotions in check; see RESTRAIN. —**lose one's head** become excited, become angry, rave; see RAGE 1. —**make head or tail of** comprehend, apprehend, see; see UNDERSTAND 1. —**one's head off** greatly, extremely, considerably; see MUCH. —**on** (or **upon**) **one's head** burdensome, taxing, strenuous; see DIFFICULT 1. —**out of** (or **off**) **one's head** crazy, delirious, raving; see INSANE. —**over one's head** incomprehensible, not understandable, hard; see DIFFICULT 2.

head *v.* direct, oversee, supervise; see COMMAND 2, MANAGE 1.

headache *n.* 1. [A pain in the head] migraine, sick headache, neuralgia; see PAIN 2. 2. [*A source of vexation and difficulty] problem, jumble, mess; see DIFFICULTY 1, 2, TROUBLE 1.

headed *a.* in transit, in motion, en route, going, directed, started, aimed, slated for, on the way to, pointed toward, consigned to, on the road to.

heading *n.* headline, subtitle, address, caption, legend, head, banner head, subject, capital, superscription, ticket, headnote, display line, preface, prologue, streamer, preamble, topic, designation, specification.

headless *a.* 1. [Unthinking] witless, fatuous, brainless; see DULL 3, STUPID. 2. [Without a head] decapitated, lifeless, truncated; see DEAD 1.

headlight *n.* searchlight, beacon, spotlight; see LIGHT 3.

headline *n.* heading, caption, title; see HEADING.

head off *v.* block off, interfere with, intervene; see STOP 1.

head over heels *a.* entirely, precipitately, unreservedly; see COMPLETELY.

headquarters *n.* main office, home office, chief office, central station, central place, distributing center, police station, meeting place, meeting house, manager's office, quarters, base, military station, military town, post, center of operations, base of operations, HQ.

headstone *n.* gravestone, marker, stone; see GRAVE.

headstrong *a.* determined, strong-minded, stubborn; see STUBBORN.

headway *n.* advance, increase, promotion; see PROGRESS 1.

heal *v.* restore, renew, treat, attend, make healthy, return to health, fix, repair, regenerate, bring around, remedy, purify, rejuvenate, medicate, make clean, dress a wound, rebuild, revive, rehabilitate, work a cure, cause to heal, resuscitate, salve, help to get well, ameliorate, doctor*, put one on his feet again, breathe new life into*.—*Ant.* EXPOSE, make ill, infect.

healing *a.* restorative, invigorating, medicinal; see HEALTHFUL.

health *n.* vigor, wholeness, good condition, healthfulness, good health, fitness, bloom, soundness of body, physical fitness, tone, hardiness, well-being, stamina, energy, full bloom, rosy cheeks*, good shape*, clean bill of health*; see also STRENGTH.

healthful *a.* nutritious, restorative, bodybuilding, sanitary, hygienic, salutary, invigorating, tonic, stimulating, bracing, salubrious, wholesome, beneficial, health-giving, nutritive, nourishing, energy-giving, fresh, pure, clean, corrective, cathartic, sedative, regenerative, substantial, sustaining, benign, good for one, desirable, harmless, innocuous, healing, preventive, disease-free, unpolluted, unadulterated, favorable.—*Ant.* UNHEALTHY, sickly, unwholesome.

healthy *a.* sound, trim, all right, normal, robust, hale, vigorous, well, hearty, athletic, rosy-cheeked, hardy, able-bodied, virile, muscular, blooming, sturdy, safe and sound, in good condition, in full possession of one's faculties, in good health, full of pep*, never feeling better, fresh, whole, firm, lively, undecayed, flourishing, good, physically fit, clear-eyed, in fine fettle, youthful, free from disease, fine, fine and dandy*, hunky-dory*, in the pink of condition*, rugged, fit as a fiddle, feeling one's oats*; see also SANE 1, STRONG 1.—*Ant.* UNHEALTHY, ill, diseased.

heap *n.* pile, mass, stack; see QUANTITY.

heap *v.* pile, add, lump; see LOAD 1, PACK 2.

hear *v.* 1. [To perceive by ear] listen to, give attention, attend to, make out, become aware of, catch, apprehend, take in, eavesdrop, detect, perceive by the ear, overhear, take cognizance of, keep one's ears open, have the sense of hearing, read loud and clear, strain one's ears, listen in, get an earful*. 2. [To receive information aurally] overhear, eavesdrop, find out; see LISTEN. 3. [To hold a hearing] preside over, put on trial, summon to court; see JUDGE. —**not hear of** not allow, refuse to consider, reject; see FORBID.

heard *a.* perceived, listened, witnessed, caught, made out, understood, heeded, noted, made clear.

hearer *n.* listener, witness, bystander; see LISTENER.

hear from *v.* get word from, be informed, learn through; see RECEIVE 1.

hearing *n.* 1. [An opportunity to be heard] audition, interview, test, fair hearing, tryout, attendance, conference, audit, notice, performance, consultation, council, reception, presentation, audience, attention; see also TRIAL 2. 2. [The act of hearing] detecting, recording, distinguishing; see LISTENING. 3. [The faculty for hearing] ear, auditory faculty, perception, listening ear, sense of hearing, audition, act of perceiving sound, acoustic sensation. 4. [Range of hearing] earshot, hearing distance, reach, sound, carrying distance, range, auditory range; see also EXTENT.

hear of *v.* know about, be aware of, discover; see KNOW 1, 3.

hear out *v.* listen to, yield the floor to, remain silent; see LISTEN.

hearsay *n.* noise, scandal, report; see GOSSIP 1, RUMOR.

heart *n.* 1. [The pump in the circulatory system] vital organ, vascular organ, blood pump, cardiac organ, ventricle, ticker*, clock*; see also ORGAN 2. **2.** [Feeling] response, sympathy, sensitivity; see EMOTION, FEELING 4, PITY. **3.** [The center] core, middle, pith; see CENTER 1. **4.** [The most important portion] gist, essence, root; see SOUL 1. **5.** [Courage] fortitude, gallantry, spirit; see COURAGE, MIND 1, SOUL 2. —**after one's own heart** suitable, pleasing, lovable; see PLEASANT 2. —**break one's heart** grieve, disappoint, pain; see HURT. —**by heart** from memory, memorized, learned; see REMEMBERED. —**change of heart** change of mind, reversal, alteration; see CHANGE 1. —**do one's heart good** please, make content, delight; see SATISFY 1. —**eat one's heart out** worry, regret, nurse one's troubles; see BROOD 2. —**from the bottom of one's heart** deeply, honestly, frankly; see SINCERELY. —**have a heart** be kind, empathize, take pity; see SYMPATHIZE. —**lose one's heart to** love, cherish, adore; see FALL IN LOVE. —**set one's heart at rest** calm, placate, soothe; see COMFORT 1. —**set one's heart on** long for, need, desire; see WANT 1. —**take to heart** think about, take into account, believe; see CONSIDER. —**wear one's heart on one's sleeve** disclose, divulge, confess; see REVEAL. —**with all one's heart** honestly, deeply, frankly; see SINCERELY.

heartache *n.* sorrow, despair, anguish; see GRIEF, REGRET.

heartbeat *n.* pulsation, throb of the heart, cardiovascular activity; see BEAT 1.

heartbreaking *a.* cheerless, deplorable, joyless; see PITIFUL, TRAGIC.

heartbroken *a.* melancholy, sorrowful, doleful; see SAD 1.

heartburn *n.* indigestion, nervous stomach, stomach upset; see ILLNESS 2.

heart disease *n.* heart failure, coronary illness, thrombosis; see ILLNESS 2.

hearth *n.* **1.** [A fireplace] grate, fireside, hearthstone; see FIREPLACE. **2.** [Home] dwelling, abode, residence; see HOME 1.

heartily *a.* enthusiastically, earnestly, cordially; see SERIOUSLY 2, SINCERELY.

heartless *a.* unkind, unthinking, insensitive; see CRUEL, RUTHLESS.

hearty *a.* warm, zealous, sincere, cheery, cheerful, jovial, wholehearted, neighborly, well-meant, animated, jolly, ardent, genial, glowing, enthusiastic, genuine, avid, deepest, passionate, deep, intense, exuberant, profuse, eager, devout, deep-felt, unfeigned, fervent, warm-hearted, authentic, impassioned, heartfelt, responsive; see also FRIENDLY.—*Ant.* FALSE, mock, sham.

heat *n.* **1.** [Warmth] torridity, high temperature, hot wind, heat wave, fever, hot weather, temperature, hotness, warmness, sultriness, white heat, torridness, tropical heat, dog days; see also WARMTH.—*Ant.* COLD, frost, frigidity. **2.** [Fervor] ardor, passion, excitement; see DESIRE 2. **3.** [Sources of heat] flame, radiation, solar energy; see ENERGY 2, FIRE 1, 2.

heat *v.* **1.** [To make hot] warm, fire, heat up, inflame, kindle, enkindle, subject to heat, put on the fire, make hot, make warm, scald, thaw, boil, char, roast, chafe, seethe, toast, oxidize, set fire to, melt, cauterize, reheat, steam, incinerate, sear, singe, scorch, fry, turn on the heat; see also BURN, COOK, IGNITE.—*Ant.* COOL, freeze. **2.** [To become hot] glow, warm up, rise in temperature, grow hot, blaze, flame, seethe, burst into flame, kindle, ignite, thaw, swelter, perspire.

heated *a.* **1.** [Warmed] cooked, fried, burnt; see BAKED, BURNED. **2.** [Fervent] fiery, ardent, avid; see EXCITED, PASSIONATE 2.

heater *n.* radiator, car heater, electric heater; see FURNACE.

heathen *n.* infidel, non-Christian, atheist; see BARBARIAN.

heating *n.* boiling, warming, cooking; see HEAT.

heave *n.* throw, hurl, fling, cast, wing, toss; see also PITCH 2.

heave *v.* rock, bob, pitch, go up and down, lurch, roll, reel, sway, swell, dilate, expand, be raised, swirl, throb, waft, ebb and flow, wax and wane, puff, slosh, wash; see also WAVE 3.—*Ant.* REST, lie still, quiet.

heaven *n.* **1.** [The sky; *often plural*] firmament, stratosphere, heights, atmosphere, azure, beyond, heavenly spheres, upstairs. **2.** [The abode of the blessed] Paradise, Great Beyond, Abode of the Dead, Home of the Gods, Heavenly Home, God's Kingdom, Valhalla, Holy City, Nirvana, throne of God, the New Jerusalem, afterworld, heavenly city, the city of God, our eternal home, Kingdom of Heaven, next world, world to come, our Father's house, world beyond the grave, happy hunting grounds*, the eternal rest*, Kingdom Come, the hereafter.—*Ant.* HELL, underworld, inferno. **3.** [A state of great comfort] bliss, felicity, harmony; see HAPPINESS.

heavenly *a.* **1.** [Concerning heaven] divine, celestial, supernal; see ANGELIC, DIVINE, HOLY 1. **2.** [*Much approved of or liked] blissful, sweet, enjoyable; see EXCELLENT, PLEASANT 1, 2.

heavily *a.* laboriously, tediously, weightily, massively, ponderously, gloomily, with difficulty, wearily, profoundly, densely; see also GRADUALLY.—*Ant.* LIGHTLY, gently, easily.

heaviness *n.* burden, denseness, ballast; see DENSITY, MASS 1, WEIGHT 1.

heavy *a.* **1.** [Weighty] bulky, massive, unwieldy, ponderous, huge, overweight, top-heavy, of great weight, burdensome, weighty, stout, big, hard to carry, dense, fat, substantial, ample, hefty*, chunky*; see also LARGE 1.—*Ant.* LIGHT, buoyant, feather-light. **2.** [Burdensome] troublesome, oppressive, vexatious; see DIFFICULT 1, DISTURBING. **3.** [Dull] listless, slow, apathetic; see DULL 4, INDIFFERENT. **4.** [Gloomy] dejected, cloudy, overcast; see DARK 1, DISMAL, SAD 1.

heavy-handed *a.* oppressive, harsh, coercive; see CRUEL, SEVERE 2.

heckle *v.* torment, disturb, pester; see BOTHER 2, RIDICULE.

hectic *a.* unsettled, boisterous, restless; see CONFUSED 2, DISORDERED.

hedge *n.* shrubbery, bushes, thicket; see PLANT.

heed *v.* pay attention to, notice, be aware; see LOOK OUT.

heel *n.* **1.** [Hind part of the foot] hock, hind toe, Achilles' tendon; see FOOT 2. **2.** [The portion of the shoe under the heel] low, spring, wedge sole; see BOTTOM, FOUNDATION 2, SHOE. **3.** [*A worthless individual] scamp, skunk, trickster; see RASCAL. —**down at the heel(s)** shabby, seedy, rundown; see WORN 2. —**kick up one's heels** be lively, have fun, enjoy oneself; see PLAY 1, 2. —**on** (or **upon**) **the heels of** close behind, in back of, behind; see FOLLOWING. —**take to one's heels** run away, flee, take flight; see ESCAPE.

heel *v.* follow, stay by one's heel, attend; see OBEY.

hefty* *a.* sturdy, husky, stout, beefy, strapping, substantial, massive; see also STRONG 1.

heifer *n.* yearling, baby cow, calf; see ANIMAL, COW.

height *n.* elevation, extent upward, prominence, loftiness, highness, perpendicular distance, upright distance, tallness, stature; see also EXPANSE, EXTENT, LENGTH 1.—*Ant.* DEPTH, breadth, width.

heighten *v.* **1.** [Increase] sharpen, redouble, emphasize; see INCREASE, STRENGTHEN. **2.** [Raise] uplift, elevate, lift; see RAISE 1.

heir *n.* future possessor, legal heir, heir apparent, successor, descendent, one who inherits, heiress, beneficiary, inheritor, crown prince.

heiress *n.* female inheritor, crown princess, inheritress; see HEIR.

heirloom *n.* inheritance, legacy, bequest; see GIFT 1.

held *a.* grasped, controlled, occupied, guarded, taken, gripped, clutched, defended, stuck, detained, sustained, believed.—*Ant.* LOST, released, freed.

held over *a.* returned, presented again, retold; see REPEATED 1.

held up *a.* **1.** [Robbed] assaulted, shot at, beaten; see ATTACKED. **2.** [Postponed] withheld, put off, delayed; see POSTPONED.

hell *n.* **1.** [Place of the dead, especially of the wicked dead; *often capitalized*] underworld, inferno, place of departed spirits, the lower world, the grave, infernal regions, abyss, Satan's Kingdom, purgatory, nether world, hell-fire, Hades, bottomless pit, perdition, place of the lost, place of torment, limbo, the hereafter.—*Ant.* HEAVEN, earth, paradise. **2.** [A condition of torment] trial, agony, ordeal; see CRISIS, DIFFICULTY 1, 2, EMERGENCY. —**catch** (or **get**) **hell*** get into trouble, be scolded, receive punishment; see GET IT 2. —**for the hell of it*** for no reason, for the fun of it, playfully; see LIGHTLY.

hellish *a.* diabolical, fiendish, destructive; see BAD 1.

hello *interj.* how do you do, greetings, welcome, how are you, good morning, good day, hi*, hey*, howdy*, lo*, hyah*, how goes it.—*Ant.* GOODBYE, farewell, so long.

hell of a* *a.* helluva*, extremely, very bad or good; see POOR 2, EXCELLENT.

hell on* *a.* hard on, prejudiced against, strict with; see CRUEL, HARMFUL.

helmet *n.* football helmet, diver's helmet, hard hat; see HAT.

help *n.* **1.** [Assistance] advice, comfort, aid, favor, support, gift, reward, charity, encouragement, advancement, advice, subsidy, service, relief, care, endowment, cooperation, guidance. **2.** [Employees] aides, representatives, hired help; see ASSISTANT, FACULTY 2, STAFF 2. **3.** [Physical relief] maintenance, sustenance, nourishment; see RELIEF 4, REMEDY. —**cannot help but** be obliged to, cannot fail to, have to; see MUST. —**cannot help oneself** be compelled to, have a need to, be the victim of habit; see MUST. —**so help me (God)** as God is my witness, by God, I swear; see OATH 1.

help *v.* assist, uphold, advise, encourage, stand by, cooperate, intercede for, befriend, accommodate, work for, back up, maintain, sustain, benefit, bolster, lend a hand, do a service, see through, do one's part, give a hand, be of use, come to the aid of, be of some help, help along, do a favor, promote, back, advocate, abet, stimulate, uphold, further, work for, stick up for*, take under one's wing, go to bat for*, side with, give a lift, boost, pitch in*; see also SUPPORT 2.—*Ant.* OPPOSE, rival, combat.

helped *a.* aided, maintained, supported, advised, befriended, relieved, sustained, nursed, encouraged, assisted, accompanied, taken care of, subsidized, upheld.—*Ant.* HURT, impeded, harmed.

helper *n.* apprentice, aide, secretary; see ASSISTANT.

helpful *a.* **1.** [Useful] valuable, important, significant, crucial, essential, cooperative, symbiotic, serviceable, profitable, advantageous, favorable, convenient, suitable, practical, operative, usable, applicable, conducive, improving, bettering, of service, all-purpose, desirable, instrumental, contributive, good for, to one's advantage, at one's command; see also CONVENIENT 1.—*Ant.* USELESS, ineffective, impractical. **2.** [Curative] healthy, salutary, restorative; see HEALTHFUL. **3.** [Obliging] accommodating, considerate, neighborly; see KIND.

helpfully *a.* usefully, constructively, advantageously; see EFFECTIVELY.

helpfulness *n.* assistance, convenience, help; see USE 2, USEFULNESS.

helping *a.* aiding, assisting, cooperating, collaborating, synergistic, working, cooperating, collaborating, being assistant to, being consultant to, in cooperation with, in combination with, contributing to, accessory to, going along with, in cahoots with*, thick as thieves*, in the same boat with; see also HELPFUL 1.

helping *n.* serving, plateful, portion; see FOOD, MEAL 2, SHARE.

helpless *a.* **1.** [Dependent] feeble, unable, invalid; see DEPENDENT 2, DISABLED, WEAK 1, 5. **2.** [Incompetent] incapable, unfit, inexpert; see INCOMPETENT.

helplessness *n.* **1.** [Disability] poor health, disorder, convalescence; see ILLNESS 1, WEAKNESS 1. **2.** [Incompetence] incapacity, weakness, failure; see WEAKNESS 1.

help oneself *v.* aid oneself, promote oneself, further oneself, live by one's own efforts, get on, get along; see also HELP.

help oneself to *v.* take, grab, pick up; see SEIZE 1, 2, STEAL.

hem *n.* border, skirting, edging; see EDGE 1, FRINGE, RIM.

hemisphere *n.* half of the globe, Western Hemisphere, Eastern Hemisphere, Northern Hemisphere, Southern Hemisphere, territory; see also EARTH 1.

hemorrhage *n.* discharge, bleeding, bloody flux; see ILLNESS 1, INJURY.

hen *n.* female chicken, pullet, egger*; see BIRD, FOWL.

hence *a.* **1.** [Therefore] consequently, for that reason, on that account; see SO 2, THEREFORE. **2.** [From now] henceforth, henceforward, from here; see HEREAFTER.

henpeck *v.* bully, suppress, intimidate; see BOTHER 2, THREATEN.

henpecked *a.* dominated by a wife, subjected to nagging, browbeaten, intimidated, passive, constrained, compliant, in bondage, yielding, without freedom or independence, acquiescent, in subjection, subject, obedient, resigned, submissive, docile, meek, cringing, unresisting, unassertive, led by the nose, under one's thumb, at one's beck and call, tied to one's apron strings, nagged, in harness; see also OBEDIENT 1.

herb *n.* seasoning, flavoring, spice, medicine. *Herbs include the following:* ginger, peppermint, thyme, savory, mustard, chicory, chives, cardamom, coriander, sweet basil, parsley, anise, cumin, fennel, caraway, rosemary, tarragon, oregano, wintergreen; see also SPICE.

herd *n.* flock, drove, pack, brood, swarm, lot, bevy, covey, gaggle, nest, brood, flight, school, clan; see also GATHERING.

herdsman *n.* shepherd, herder, sheepherder; see COWBOY, RANCHER.

here *a.* in this place, hereabout, in this direction, on this spot, over here, up here, down here, right here, on hand, on board, on deck*, in the face of, within reach.

hereafter *a.* hence, henceforth, from now on, after this, in the future, hereupon, in the course of time.

hereafter *n.* underworld, abode of the dead, the great beyond; see HEAVEN 2, HELL 1.

here and there *a.* often, patchily, sometimes; see EVERYWHERE, SCATTERED.

hereby *a.* at this moment, with these means, with this, thus, herewith.

hereditary *a.* inherited, genetic, paternal; see GENETIC.

heredity *n.* inheritance, ancestry, hereditary transmission, genetics, eugenics.

heresy *n.* nonconformity, dissidence, protestantism, dissent, heterodoxy, sectarianism, agnosticism, schism, unorthodoxy, secularism.

heretic *n.* schismatic, apostate, sectarian; see CYNIC.

heritage *n.* **1.** [Inheritance] legacy, birthright, heirship, ancestry, right, dowry; see also DIVISION 2, HEREDITY, SHARE. **2.** [Tradition] convention, endowment, cultural inheritance; see CULTURE 1, CUSTOM, FASHION 2, METHOD, SYSTEM.

hermit *n.* holy man, ascetic, anchorite, solitary, recluse, solitarian, anchoress, pillar saint.

hero *n.* **1.** [One distinguished for action] brave man, model, conqueror, victorious general, god, martyr, champion, prize athlete, master, brave, warrior, saint, man of courage, star, popular figure, great man, knight-errant, a man among men, man of the hour; see also HEROINE 1. **2.** [Principal male character in a literary composition] protagonist, male lead, leading man; see ACTOR.

heroic *a.* valiant, valorous, fearless; see BRAVE, NOBLE 1, 2.

heroine *n.* **1.** [A female hero] courageous woman, champion, goddess, ideal, intrepid woman, resourceful woman, supremely courageous woman, woman of heroic character, woman of the hour; see also HERO 1. **2.** [Leading female character in a literary composition] protagonist, leading lady, prima donna; see ACTOR.

heroism *n.* rare fortitude, valor, bravery; see COURAGE, STRENGTH.

hesitancy *n.* wavering, delaying, procrastination; see DELAY, PAUSE.

hesitant *a.* **1.** [Doubtful] skeptical, unpredictable, irresolute; see DOUBTFUL, UNCERTAIN. **2.** [Slow] delaying, wavering, dawdling; see LAZY 1, SLOW 2.

hesitantly *a.* dubiously, falteringly, shyly; see CAUTIOUSLY.

hesitate *v.* falter, fluctuate, vacillate, pause, stop, hold off, hold back, be dubious, be uncertain, flounder, alternate, ponder, think about, defer, delay, think it over, change one's mind, recoil, not know what to do, pull back, catch one's breath, weigh, consider, hang back, swerve, debate, shift, wait, deliberate, linger, balance, think twice, drag one's feet, hem and haw, blow hot and cold, dillydally, straddle the fence, leave up in the air.—*Ant.* RESOLVE, decide, conclude.

hesitation *n.* **1.** [Doubt] equivocation, skepticism, irresolution; see DOUBT, UNCERTAINTY 2. **2.** [Delay] wavering, delaying, dawdling; see DELAY, PAUSE.

hey *interj.* you there, say, hey there; see HALT, HELLO.

heyday *n.* adolescence, bloom, prime of life; see YOUTH 1.

hibernate *v.* sleep through the winter, lie dormant, hole up*; see SLEEP.

hidden *a.* secluded, out of sight, private, covert, concealed, undercover, occult, in the dark, in a haze, in a fog, in darkness, masked, screened, veiled, cloaked, obscured, disguised, invisible, clouded, sealed, unobserved, blotted, impenetrable, unseen, eclipsed, camouflaged, shrouded, shadowy, unknown, buried, undetected, deep, unsuspected, inscrutable, illegible, puzzling, unobserved, out of view, dim, clandestine, subterranean, cloistered, suppressed, dark, inward, underground, unrevealed, withheld, surreptitious, underhand, kept in the dark, under wraps; see also PRIVATE.—*Ant.* OBVIOUS, open, apparent.

hide *n.* pelt, rawhide, pigskin, chamois, bearskin, goatskin, jacket, sheepskin, sealskin, snakeskin, alligator skin, calfskin; see also FUR, LEATHER, SKIN. —**neither hide nor hair** nothing whatsoever, no indication, not at all; see NOTHING.

hide *v.* **1.** [To conceal] shroud, curtain, veil, camouflage, cover, mask, cloak, not give away, screen, blot out, bury, suppress, withhold, keep underground, stifle, keep secret, hush up, shield, eclipse, not tell, lock up, confuse, put out of sight, put out of the way, hold back, keep from, secrete, smuggle, shadow, conceal from sight, keep out of sight, stow away, protect, hoard, store, seclude, closet, conceal, hush, obscure, wrap, shelter, throw a veil over, keep in the dark, keep under one's hat*, seal one's lips*, put the lid on*, salt away*; see also DISGUISE.—*Ant.* EXPOSE, lay bare, uncover. **2.** [To keep oneself concealed] disguise oneself, change one's identity, cover one's traces, keep out of sight, go underground, lie in ambush, sneak, prowl, burrow, skulk, avoid notice, lie in wait, hibernate, lie concealed, lie low, conceal oneself, lurk, shut oneself up, seclude oneself, lie hidden, keep out of the way, stay in hiding, hide out, cover up, duck*, keep in the background; see also DECEIVE.

hide-and-seek *n.* evasion, mystification, elusiveness; see GAME.

hideous *a.* ghastly, grisly, frightful; see UGLY 1.

hideout *n.* lair, den, hermitage; see REFUGE 1, RETREAT 2, SHELTER.

hiding *a.* concealing, in concealment, out of sight; see HIDDEN.

hierarchy *n.* ministry, regime, theocracy; see GOVERNMENT 1, 2.

high *a.* **1.** [Tall] towering, gigantic, big, colossal, tremendous, great, giant, huge, formidable, immense, long, sky-scraping, steep, sky-high; see also LARGE 1.—*Ant.* SHORT, diminutive, undersized. **2.** [Elevated] lofty, uplifted, soaring, aerial, high-reaching, flying, hovering, overtopping, jutting; see also RAISED 1.—*Ant.* LOW, depressed, underground. **3.** [Exalted] eminent, leading, powerful; see DISTINGUISHED 2, NOBLE 1, 2. **4.** [Expensive] high-priced, costly, precious; see EXPENSIVE. **5.** [To an unusual degree] great, extraordinary, special; see UNUSUAL 1, 2. **6.** [Shrill] piercing, sharp, penetrating; see LOUD 1, SHRILL. **7.** [*Drunk] intoxicated, tipsy, inebriated; see DRUNK. **8.** [*Under the influence of drugs] stoned*, freaked-out*, wasted*, turned-on*, on a trip*, tripping*, hyped-up*, spaced-out*, zonked out*.

high and low *a.* in every nook and corner, in all possible places, exhaustively; see COMPLETELY, EVERYWHERE.

high and mighty *a.* pompous, vain, conceited; see EGOTISTIC.

higher *a.* taller, more advanced, superior to, over, larger than, ahead, surpassing, bigger, greater; see also ABOVE 1, BEYOND.—*Ant.* SHORTER, smaller, inferior.

highest *a.* topmost, superlative, supreme, maximal, most, top, maximum, head, preeminent, capital, chief, paramount, tiptop, crown.

highly *a.* extremely, profoundly, deeply; see VERY.

highness *n.* **1.** [Quality of being high] length, tallness, loftiness; see HEIGHT. **2.** [Term of respect, usually to royalty; *often capitalized*] majesty, lordship, ladyship; see ROYALTY.

high-pressure *a.* forceful, potent, compelling; see POWERFUL 1.

high-priced *a.* costly, precious, extravagant; see EXPENSIVE.

high school *n.* public school, secondary school, preparatory school, private academy, military school, upper grades, trade school, seminary, junior high school, vocational school; see also SCHOOL 1.

high-speed *a.* swift, rapid, quick; see FAST 1.

high-spirited *a.* daring, dauntless, reckless; see BRAVE.

high-strung *a.* nervous, tense, impatient; see RESTLESS.

highway *n.* roadway, parkway, superhighway, freeway, turnpike, toll road, state highway, national highway; see also ROAD 1.

hijack* *v.* highjack, privateer, capture; see SEIZE 2.

hike *n.* trip, backpack, tour; see JOURNEY, WALK 3.

hike *v.* **1.** [To tramp] take a hike, tour, explore; see TRAVEL, WALK 1. **2.** [*To raise] lift, advance, pull up; see INCREASE.

hiking *a.* hitchhiking, backpacking, exploring; see WALKING.

hilarious *a.* amusing, lively, witty; see ENTERTAINING, FUNNY 1.

hill *n.* mound, knoll, butte, bluff, promontory, precipice, cliff, range, rising ground, headland, upland, downgrade, inclination, descent, slope, ascent, slant, grade, incline, height, highland, rise, foothill, dune, climb, elevation, ridge, heap, hillside, upgrade, hilltop, vantage point, gradient, summit; see also MOUNTAIN 1.

hillside *n.* grade, gradient, acclivity; see HILL.

hilltop *n.* peak, height, elevation; see HILL, TOP 1.

hilly *a.* steep, sloping, rugged; see MOUNTAINOUS, ROUGH 1, STEEP.—*Ant.* LEVEL, even, regular.

hinder *v.* impede, obstruct, interfere with, check, retard, fetter, block, thwart, bar, clog, encumber, burden, cripple, handicap, cramp, preclude, inhibit, shackle, interrupt, arrest, curb, resist, oppose, baffle, deter, hamper, frustrate, outwit, stop, counteract, offset, neutralize, tie up, hold up, embarrass, delay, postpone, keep back, set back, dam, close, box in, end, terminate, shut out, choke, intercept, bottleneck, defeat, trap, control, conflict with, deadlock, hold back, clash with, be an obstacle to, cross, exclude, limit, shorten, go against, prohibit, withhold, slow down, stall, bring to a standstill, smother, disappoint, spoil, gag, annul, silence, invalidate, detain, stalemate, taboo, suspend, set against, clip one's wings*, tie one's hands, get in the way of, hold up, throw a monkey wrench into the works*, knock the props from under*.—*Ant.* HELP, assist, aid.

hindrance *n.* obstacle, intervention, trammel; see BARRIER, INTERFERENCE 1.

hinge *n.* hook, pivot, juncture, articulation, link, elbow, ball-and-socket joint, knee, butt, strap, articulated joint, flap; see also JOINT 1.

hinge *v.* connect, add, couple; see JOIN 1.

hint *n.* allusion, inkling, insinuation, implication, reference, advice, observation, reminder, communication, notice, information, announcement, inside information, tip, clue, token, idea, omen, scent, cue, trace, notion, whisper, taste, suspicion, evidence, reminder, innuendo, symptom, sign, bare suggestion, impression, supposition, inference, premonition, broad hint, gentle hint, word to the wise, indication, tip-off, pointer*; see also SUGGESTION 1.

hint *v.* touch on, allude to, intimate, inform, hint at, imply, acquaint, remind, impart, bring up, recall, cue, prompt, insinuate, indicate, wink, advise, cause to remember, make an allusion to, jog the memory, give a hint of, suggest, make mention of, remark in passing, drop a hint, whisper, give an inkling of, tip off*.—*Ant.* HIDE, conceal, cover.

hinted at *a.* signified, intimated, referred to; see IMPLIED, SUGGESTED.

hip* *a.* aware, informed, enlightened; see MODERN 1, OBSERVANT.

hip *n.* side, hipbone, pelvis; see BONE.

hippie *n.* dissenter, bohemian, nonconformist; see RADICAL.

hire *v.* engage, sign up, draft, obtain, secure, enlist, give a job to, take on, put to work, bring in, occupy, use, fill a position, appoint, delegate, authorize, retain, commission, empower, book, utilize, select, pick, contract, procure, fill an opening, find help, find a place for, exploit, make use of, use another's services, add to the payroll.—*Ant.* DISMISS, discharge, fire.

hired *a.* contracted, signed up, given work; see BUSY, EMPLOYED, ENGAGED 3.

hiring *n.* engaging, contracting, employing; see EMPLOYER.

hiss *n.* buzz, sibilance, escape of air; see NOISE 1.

hiss *v.* sibilate, fizz, seethe; see SOUND.

historical *a.* factual, traditional, chronicled; see OLD 3, PAST 1.

history *n.* annals, records, archives, recorded history, chronicle, historical knowledge, historical writings, historical evidence, historical development; see also RECORD 1, SOCIAL SCIENCE. **—make history** accomplish, do something important, achieve; see SUCCEED 1.

hit *a.* shot, struck, slugged, cuffed, slapped, smacked, clouted, punched, boxed, slammed, knocked, beaten, pounded, thrashed, spanked, banged, smashed, tapped, rapped, whacked, thwacked, thumped, kicked, swatted, mugged, pasted*, knocked out; see also HURT.—*Ant.* UNTOUCHED, unhurt, unscathed.

hit *n.* **1.** [A blow] slap, rap, punch; see BLOW. **2.** [A popular success] favorite, sellout*, smash; see SUCCESS 2. **3.** [In baseball, a batted ball that cannot be fielded] base hit or single, two-base hit or double, three base-hit or triple, home run, Texas leaguer, two-bagger*, three-bagger*, homer*.

hit *v.* **1.** [To strike] knock, beat, sock*, slap, jostle, butt, knock against, scrape, bump, run against, thump, collide with, bump into, punch, punish, hammer, strike down, bang, whack, thwack, jab, tap, smack, kick at, pelt, flail, thrash, cuff, kick, rap, clout*, club, bat around, lash out at, hit at, hit out at, let have it, crack, pop*, bash*; see also BEAT 1. **2.** [To fire in time; *said of an internal combustion motor*] catch, go, run; see OPERATE 2. **3.** [In baseball, to hit safely] make a hit, get on, get on base.

hit-and-run *a.* leaving without offering assistance, fugitive, illegally departed; see ILLEGAL.

hitch *n.* **1.** [A knot] loop, noose, yoke; see KNOT 1, TIE 1. **2.** [A difficulty] block, obstacle, tangle; see DIFFICULTY.

hitch *v.* tie up, strap, hook; see FASTEN, JOIN 1.

hitchhike *v.* take a lift, hitch a ride, thumb a ride; see RIDE 1, TRAVEL.

hit it off *v.* get along well, become friends, become friendly; see AGREE, LIKE 1, 2.

hit on or **upon** *v.* realize, come upon, stumble on; see DISCOVER, FIND, RECOGNIZE 1.

hit or miss *a.* at random, uncertainly, sometimes; see SCATTERED.

hit the jackpot* *v.* be lucky, be well paid, strike it rich; see WIN 1.

hive *n.* apiary, swarm, colony; see COLONY.

hoard *v.* store up, acquire, keep; see ACCUMULATE, SAVE 3.

hoarse *a.* grating, rough, uneven, harsh, raucous, discordant, gruff, husky, thick, growling, croaking, cracked, guttural, dry, piercing, scratching, indistinct, squawking, jarring, rasping.—*Ant.* PURE, sweet, mellifluous.

hoax *n.* falsification, fabrication, deceit; see DECEPTION, LIE.

hobby *n.* avocation, pastime, diversion, side interest, leisure-time activity, specialty, whim, fancy, whimsy, labor of love, play, craze, sport, amusement, craft, fun, art, game, sideline; see also ENTERTAINMENT.

hobo *n.* vagrant, vagabond, wanderer; see BEGGAR.

hock* *v.* sell temporarily, pledge, deposit; see PAWN, SELL.

hockey *n.* ice hockey, field hockey, hockey game; see GAME 1, SPORT 3.

hodgepodge *n.* jumble, combination, mess; see MIXTURE 1.

hoe *n.* digger, scraper, garden hoe; see TOOL 1.

hog *n.* **1.** [A pig] swine, sow, boar, shoat, razorback, wild boar, wart hog, peccary, porker, piggy, pork; see also ANIMAL. **2.** [A person whose habits resemble a pig's] pig, glutton, filthy person; see SLOB. —**high on** (or **off**) **the hog*** luxuriously, extravagantly, richly; see EXPENSIVE.

hogtie *v.* fetter, shackle, tie up; see BIND.

hogwash *n.* foolishness, absurdity, ridiculousness; see NONSENSE 1.

hoist *n.* crane, lift, derrick; see ELEVATOR 1.

hold *v.* **1.** [To have in one's grasp] grasp, grip, clutch, carry, embrace, cling to, detain, enclose, restrain, confine, check, take hold of, contain, hold down, hold onto, not let go, hang on, squeeze, press, hug, handle, fondle, have in hand, keep in hand, get a grip on, retain, keep, clasp, hold fast, hold tight, keep a firm hold on, tie, take, catch; see also SEIZE 1.—*Ant.* DROP, let fall, release. **2.** [To have in one's possession] keep, retain, possess; see HAVE 1. **3.** [To remain firm] resist, persevere, keep staunch; see CONTINUE 1, ENDURE 2. **4.** [To adhere] attach, cling, take hold; see FASTEN, STICK 1. **5.** [To be valid] exist, continue, operate; see BE 1.—*Ant.* STOP, expire, be out of date. **6.** [To contain] have capacity for, carry, be equipped for; see INCLUDE 1. **7.** [To support; *often used with "up"*] sustain, brace, buttress, prop, lock, stay, shoulder, uphold, bear up; see also SUPPORT 1.

hold back *v.* **1.** [To restrain] inhibit, control, curb; see CHECK 1, PREVENT, RESTRAIN. **2.** [To refrain] desist, hesitate, forbear; see ABSTAIN, AVOID.

holder *n.* **1.** [An instrument used in holding] sheath, container, holster, bag, sack, fastener, clip, handle, rack, knob, stem; see also CONTAINER, FASTENER. **2.** [An owner or occupant] leaseholder, renter, dweller; see OWNER, RESIDENT, TENANT.

hold fast *v.* clasp, lock, clamp; see FASTEN, STICK 1.

holdings *n.pl.* lands, possessions, security; see ESTATE, PROPERTY 1.

hold off *v.* be above, keep aloof, stave off; see AVOID, PREVENT.

hold office *v.* be in office, direct, rule; see GOVERN, MANAGE 1.

hold on *v.* hang on, attach oneself to, cling; see SEIZE 1.

hold one's own *v.* keep one's advantage, stand one's ground, do well, keep up; see also SUCCEED 1.

hold one's tongue or **one's peace** *v.* be silent, conceal, keep secret, not say a word; see also HIDE 1.

holdout *n.* die-hard, objector, resister; see RESISTANCE 4.

hold out *v.* **1.** [To offer] proffer, tempt with, grant; see GIVE 1, OFFER 1. **2.** [To endure] suffer, hold on, withstand; see CONTINUE 1, ENDURE 2.

hold out for *v.* persist, go on supporting, stand firmly for; see CONTINUE 1.

holdover *n.* remnant, relic, surplus; see REMAINDER.

hold over *v.* do again, show again, play over; see REPEAT 1.

holdup *n.* robbery, burglary, stickup*; see CRIME, THEFT.

hold up *v.* **1.** [To show] exhibit, raise high, elevate; see DISPLAY. **2.** [To delay] stop, pause, interfere with; see DELAY, HINDER, INTERRUPT. **3.** [To rob at gunpoint] waylay, burglarize, steal from; see ROB. **4.** [To support] brace, prop, shoulder; see HOLD 7, SUPPORT 1.

hole *n.* **1.** [A perforation or cavity] notch, puncture, slot, eyelet, keyhole, porthole, buttonhole, peephole, loophole, air hole, window, crack, rent, split, tear, cleft, opening, fissure, gap, gash, rift, rupture, fracture, break, leak, aperture, space, chasm, breach, slit, nick, cut, chink, incision, orifice, eye, acupuncture, crater, mouth, gorge, throat, gullet, cranny, dent, opening, depression, indentation, impression, corner, pockmark, pocket, dimple, dip, drop, gulf, depth, pit, abyss, hollow, chasm, crevasse, mine, shaft, chamber, valley, ravine, burrow, rift, cell, niche. **2.** [A cave] burrow, den, lair; see sense 1. **3.** [*Serious difficulty] impasse, tangle, mess; see CRISIS, DIFFICULTY 1, EMERGENCY. **—in a hole*** in trouble, suffering, caught; see ABANDONED. **—in the hole*** broke, without money, in debt; see POOR 1.

holiday *n.* feast day, fiesta, legal holiday, holy day, festival, centennial, carnival, jubilee, red-letter day; see also ANNIVERSARY, CELEBRATION. *Common holidays include the following:* Sunday, Independence Day, Veterans Day, Memorial Day, Mardi Gras, New Year's Day, Saint Valentine's Day, Christmas, Easter Sunday, Lincoln's Birthday, Thanksgiving Day, Washington's Birthday, Presidents' Day, Columbus Day, Labor Day, Halloween, Election Day, Good Friday.

holiness *n.* devoutness, humility, saintliness; see DEVOTION, WORSHIP 1.

hollow *a.* **1.** [Concave] curving inward, bell-shaped, curved, carved out, sunken, depressed, arched, vaulted, cup-shaped, excavated, hollowed-out, indented, cupped; see also BENT, ROUND 2.—*Ant.* RAISED, convex, elevated. **2.** [Sounding as though from a cave] cavernous, echoing deep, resonant, booming, roaring, rumbling, reverberating, muffled, dull, resounding, sepulchral, vibrating, low, ringing, deep-toned, thunderous; see also LOUD 1.—*Ant.* DEAD, mute, silent.

hollow *n.* dale, bowl, basin; see VALLEY.

hollow (out) *v.* excavate, indent, remove earth; see DIG 1, SHOVEL.

holy *a.* **1.** [Sinless] devout, pious, blessed, righteous, moral, just, good, angelic, godly, reverent, venerable, immaculate, pure, spotless, clean, humble, saintly, innocent, godlike, saintlike, perfect, faultless, undefiled, untainted, chaste, upright, virtuous, revered, sainted, heavensent, pious, believing, profoundly good, sanctified, devotional, reverent, spiritual, unstained, pure in heart, dedicated, unspotted; see also FAITHFUL, RELIGIOUS 2.—*Ant.* BAD, wicked, sinful. **2.** [Concerned with worship] devotional, religious, ceremonial; see DIVINE.

Holy Ghost *n.* Holy Spirit, the Dove, third person of the Holy Trinity; see GOD.

homage *n.* respect, adoration, deference; see DEVOTION, REVERENCE, WORSHIP 1.

home *a.* in one's home, at ease, at rest, homely, domestic, familiar, being oneself, homey, in the bosom of one's family, down home, in one's element; see also COMFORTABLE 1.

home *n.* **1.** [A dwelling place] house, dwelling, residence, habitation, tenement, abode, lodging, quarters, homestead, domicile, dormitory, apartment house, flat, living quarters, chalet, shelter, asylum, hut, cabin, cottage, mansion, castle, summer home, rooming house, place, address, hovel, lodge, hotel, inn, farmhouse, tent, pad*, hang-out*, digs*, nest; see also APARTMENT. **2.** [An asylum] orphanage, sanatorium, mental hospital; see HOSPITAL. **—at home** relaxed, at ease, familiar; see COMFORTABLE 1, HOME. **—come home** come back, return home, regress; see RETURN 1.

homecoming *n.* homecoming celebration, entry, revisitation; see ARRIVAL 1.

homeless *a.* desolate, outcast, destitute, vagrant, wandering, itinerant, friendless, banished, derelict, without a country, exiled, having no home, vagabond, forsaken, friendless, unsettled, unwelcome, dispossessed, disinherited, left to shift for oneself, without a roof over one's head; see also ABANDONED, POOR 1.—*Ant.* ESTABLISHED, at home, settled.

homely *a.* **1.** [Unpretentious] snug, simple, cozy; see MODEST 2. **2.** [Ill-favored] plain, unattractive, uncomely; see UGLY 1.

homemade *a.* homespun, domestic, do-it-yourself, self-made, made at home, home, not foreign.

home run *n.* inside-the-park home run, round-tripper*, homer*; see SCORE 1.

homesick *a.* nostalgic, pining, yearning for home, ill with longing, unhappy, alienated, rootless; see also LONELY.

homesickness *n.* nostalgia, isolation, unhappiness; see LONELINESS.

homespun *a.* handicrafted, domestic, handspun; see HOMEMADE.

homestead *n.* house, ranch, estate; see HOME 1, PROPERTY 2.

homeward *a.* toward home, back home, on the way home, homewards, home, homeward bound, to one's family, to one's native land.

homework *n.* outside assignment, library assignment, preparation; see EDUCATION 1.
homey *a.* enjoyable, livable, familiar; see COMFORTABLE 2, PLEASANT 2.
homosexual *a.* monoclinius, gynandrous, hermaphroditic, lesbian, Sapphic, androgynous, homoerotic, epicene, gay.
homosexual *n.* lesbian, gay, gynandroid, androgyne, hermaphrodite, transvestite.
honest *a.* **1.** [Truthful] true, trustworthy, correct, exact, verifiable, undisguised, candid, straightforward, aboveboard, just, frank, impartial, respectful, factual, sound, unimpeachable, legitimate, unquestionable, realistic, true-to-life, reasonable, naked, plain, square, honest as the day is long, on the level*, kosher*, fair and square*, straight.—*Ant.* deceptive, false, misleading. **2.** [Frank] candid, straightforward, aboveboard; see sense 1 and FRANK. **3.** [Fair] just, equitable, impartial; see FAIR 1.
honestly *a.* **1.** [In an honest manner] uprightly, fairly, genuinely; see JUSTLY 1, SINCERELY. **2.** [Really] indeed, truly, naturally; see REALLY 1.
honesty *n.* honor, fidelity, scrupulousness, self-respect, straightforwardness, trustworthiness, confidence, soundness, right, principle, truthfulness, candor, frankness, openness, morality, goodness, responsibility, loyalty, faithfulness, good faith, probity, courage, moral strength, virtue, reliability, character, conscience, worth, conscientiousness, trustiness, faith, justice, respectability.—*Ant.* DISHONESTY, deception, deceit.
honey *n.* comb honey, extracted honey, wild honey; see FOOD.
honk *n.* croak, quack, blare; see NOISE 1.
honk *v.* blare, trumpet, bellow; see SOUND.
honor *n.* **1.** [Respect] reverence, esteem, worship, adoration, veneration, high regard, trust, faith, confidence, righteousness, recognition, praise, attention, deference, notice, consideration, renown, reputation, elevation, credit, tribute, popularity; see also ADMIRATION.—*Ant.* DISGRACE, opprobrium, disrepute. **2.** [Integrity] courage, character, truthfulness; see HONESTY. **—do the honors** act as host or hostess, present, host; see SERVE. **—on (or upon) one's honor** by one's faith, on one's word, staking one's good name; see SINCERELY.
honor *v.* **1.** [To treat with respect] worship, sanctify, venerate; see PRAISE 1. **2.** [To recognize worth] esteem, value, look up to; see ADMIRE. **3.** [To recognize as valid] clear, pass, accept; see ACKNOWLEDGE 2.
honorable *a.* proud, reputable, creditable; see DISTINGUISHED 2, FAMOUS, NOBLE 2, 3.
honorably *a.* nobly, fairly, virtuously; see JUSTLY 1.
honorary *a.* titular, nominal, privileged; see COMPLIMENTARY.
honored *a.* respected, revered, decorated, privileged, celebrated, reputable, well-known, esteemed, eminent, distinguished, dignified, noble, recognized, highly regarded, venerated; see also FAMOUS.—*Ant.* CORRUPT, disgraced, shamed.
honors *n.pl.* **1.** [Courtesies] ceremony, privilege, duties; see DUTY 2. **2.** [Distinction] high honors, award, prize; see FAME.
hood *n.* **1.** [Covering worn over the head] cowl, shawl, bonnet, protector, veil, capuchin, kerchief, mantle; see also HAT. **2.** [A covering for vehicles and the like] canopy, awning, auto top; see COVER 1. **3.** [*A criminal] gangster, hoodlum, crook*; see CRIMINAL.
hoodlum *n.* outlaw, gangster, crook*; see CRIMINAL.
hoof *n.* ungula, animal foot, paw; see FOOT 2.
hook *n.* lock, catch, clasp; see FASTENER.
hook *v.* **1.** [To curve in the shape of a hook] angle, crook, curve; see ARCH. **2.** [To catch on a hook] pin, catch, secure; see FASTEN.
hooked up *a.* connected, linked together, attached; see JOINED.
hookup *n.* attachment, connection, consolidation; see LINK, UNION 1.
hook up *v.* combine, connect, attach; see JOIN 1, UNITE.
hoop *n.* wooden wheel, band, circlet; see CIRCLE 1.
hoot *n.* howl, whoo, boo; see CRY 2.
hop *n.* spring, bounce, leap; see JUMP 1.
hop *v.* leap, skip, jump on one leg; see BOUNCE, JUMP 1.
hope *n.* **1.** [Reliance upon the future] faith, expectation, confidence; see ANTICIPATION, OPTIMISM 2. **2.** [The object of hope] wish, goal, dream; see DESIRE 1, END 2, PURPOSE 1.
hope *v.* be hopeful, lean on, wish, desire, live in hope, rely, depend, count on, aspire to, doubt not, keep one's fingers crossed, hope for the best, be of good cheeer, pray, cherish the hope, look forward to, await, dream, presume, watch for, bank on, foresee, think to, promise oneself, suppose, deem likely, believe, suspect, surmise, hold, be assured, feel confident, anticipate, be prepared for, make plans for, have faith, rest assured, be sure of, be reassured, take heart, hope to hell*, knock on wood*; see also EXPECT 1, TRUST 1.
hopeful *a.* **1.** [Optimistic] expectant, assured, sanguine, buoyant, enthusiastic, trustful, reassured, emboldened, full of hope, cheerful, anticipating, trusting, expecting, in hopes of, forward-looking, lighthearted, serene, calm, poised, comfortable, eager, elated, looking through rose-colored glasses; see also CONFIDENT, TRUSTING. **2.** [Encouraging] promising, reassuring, favorable, bright, cheering, flattering, gracious, opportune, timely, fortunate, pro-

pitious, auspicious, well-timed, fit, suitable, convenient, beneficial, fair, uplifting, heartening, inspiring, exciting, pleasing, fine, lucky, stirring, making glad, helpful, rosecolored, rosy, animating, attractive, satisfactory, refreshing, probable, good, conducive, advantageous, pleasant, of promise, happy, cheerful.—*Ant.* UNFORTUNATE, discouraging, unfavorable.

hopefully *a.* **1.** [Optimistically] confidently, expectantly, with confidence, with hope, trustingly, naively, with some reassurance, trustfully; see also BOLDLY 1, POSITIVELY 1, SURELY.—*Ant.* HOPELESSLY, doubtfully, gloomily. **2.** [Probably] expectedly, conceivably, feasibly; see PROBABLY.

hopeless *a.* unfortunate, threatening, bad, sinister, unyielding, incurable, past hope, past cure, vain, irreversible, irreparable, without hope, with no hope, impracticable, ill-fated, disastrous, menacing, foreboding, unfavorable, dying, worsening, past saving, tragic, fatal, desperate, helpless, lost, to no avail, gone, empty, idle, useless, pointless, worthless; see also ABANDONED, IMPOSSIBLE.—*Ant.* FAVORABLE, heartening, cheering.

hopelessly *a.* cynically, pessimistically, despondently, dejectedly, desperately, mechanically, automatically, emptily, darkly, gloomily, dismally, desolately, down in the mouth*; see also SADLY.—*Ant.* HOPEFULLY, confidently, expectantly.

hoping *a.* believing, expecting, wishing; see TRUSTING.

horde *n.* pack, throng, swarm; see CROWD, GATHERING.

horizon *n.* range, border, limit; see BOUNDARY, EXTENT.

horizontal *a.* **1.** [Level] plane, aligned, parallel; see FLAT 1, LEVEL 3, STRAIGHT 1. **2.** [Even] flush, uniform, regular; see FLAT 1, SMOOTH 1.

horn *n.* **1.** [A hornlike sounding instrument] *Horns include the following:* bugle, trombone, saxophone, cornet, clarinet, bassoon, pipe, fife, flute, picolo, oboe, English horn, French horn, tuba; see also MUSICAL INSTRUMENT. **2.** [Hard process protruding from the head of certain animals] tusk, antler, outgrowth, pronghorn, frontal bone, spine, spike, point; see also BONE, TOOTH. **—lock horns** disagree, conflict, defy; see OPPOSE 1.

horn in (on)* *v.* intrude, impose upon, get in on; see ENTER, MEDDLE 1.

horny *a.* **1.** [Callous] hard, firm, bony; see TOUGH 2. **2.** [*Sexually excited] sensual, aroused, lecherous; see EXCITED, LEWD 2.

horrendous *a.* horrible, frightful, terrible; see POOR 2, FAULTY.

horrible *a.* **1.** [Offensive] repulsive, dreadful, disgusting; see OFFENSIVE 2. **2.** [Frightful] shameful, shocking, awful; see FRIGHTFUL, TERRIBLE 1.

horrid *a.* hideous, disturbing, shameful; see OFFENSIVE 2, PITIFUL.

horror *n.* awe, terror, fright; see FEAR.

horse *n.* nag, draft animal, plow horse, racer, saddlehorse, steed, mount, charger, hunter, cutting horse, stallion, gelding, hack, mare, thoroughbred, pacer, trotter, courser; see also ANIMAL. **—from the horse's mouth*** originally, from an authority, according to the original source of the information; see OFFICIALLY 1. **—hold one's horses*** curb one's impatience, slow down, relax; see RESTRAIN. **—on one's high horse*** arrogant, haughty, disdainful; see EGOTISTIC.

horse around* *v.* fool around, cavort, cause trouble; see MISBEHAVE, PLAY 2.

horseman *n.* equestrian, rider, jockey; see COWBOY, RIDER 1.

horseplay *n.* clowning, play, fooling around; see FUN, JOKE.

horsepower *n.* strength, pull, power; see ENERGY 2.

hose *n.* **1.** [Stocking] men's or women's hose, tights, panty hose; see HOSIERY. **2.** [A flexible conduit] garden hose, fire hose, line, tubing; see also PIPE 1, TUBE 1.

hosiery *n.* silk stockings, rayon stockings, nylon stockings, woolen stockings, seamless hose, full-fashioned hose, socks, anklets, tights, panty hose, leotards, knee socks, body stocking.

hospitable *a.* cordial, courteous, open; see FRIENDLY.

hospital *n.* clinic, infirmary, sanatorium, sanitarium, dispensary, mental hospital, army hospital, city hospital, public hospital, veteran's hospital, medical center, lying-in hospital, health service, outpatient ward, sick bay, rest home.

hospitality *n.* good cheer, companionship, good fellowship; see ENTERTAINMENT, WELCOME.

host *n.* **1.** [A person who entertains] man of the house, woman of the house, entertainer, toastmaster, master of ceremonies. **2.** [A large group] throng, multitude, army; see CROWD, GATHERING. **3.** [Organism on which a parasite subsists] host mother, host body, animal; see PARASITE 1.

host *v.* receive, treat, wine and dine; see ENTERTAIN 2.

hostage *n.* security, captive, victim of a kidnapping; see PRISONER.

hostess *n.* society lady, socialite, clubwoman, social leader, social climber, entertainer, lady of the house, mistress of the household, toastmistress, mistress of ceremonies.

hostile *a.* antagonistic, hateful, opposed; see UNFRIENDLY.

hostility *n.* abhorrence, aversion, bitterness; see HATRED.

hot *a.* 1. [Having a high temperature] torrid, burning, fiery, flaming, blazing, very warm, baking, roasting, smoking, scorching, blistering, searing, sizzling, tropical, warm, broiling, red-hot, grilling, piping hot, white-hot, scalding, parching, sultry, on fire, at high temperature, incandescent, smoldering, thermal, toasting, simmering, blazing hot*, boiling hot*, like an oven*, hotter than blazes*; see also BOILING, COOKING, MOLTEN.—*Ant.* COLD, frigid, chilly. 2. [Aroused] furious, ill-tempered, indignant; see ANGRY. 3. [*Erotic] spicy, salacious, carnal; see SENSUAL 2. —**get hot*** become excited, become enthusiastic, burn with fervor, get angry, rave; see also RAGE 1. —**make it hot for*** create discomfort for, cause trouble for, vex; see DISTURB.

hotel *n.* stopping place, inn, lodging house, halfway house, boarding house, hostel, motel, motor hotel, resort, tavern, spa, rooming house, flop-house*.

hotheaded *a.* unmanageable, wild, reckless; see RASH, UNRULY.

hot under the collar* *a.* furious, mad, resentful; see ANGRY.

hound *n.* greyhound, bloodhound, beagle; see ANIMAL, DOG.

hound *v.* badger, provoke, annoy; see BOTHER 2.

hour *n.* time unit, sixty minutes, man-hour, planetary hour, horsepower hour, class hour, supper hour, study hour, rush hour; see also TIME 1.

hour after hour *a.* continually, steadily, on and on; see REGULARLY.

hourly *a.* each hour, every hour, every sixty minutes; see FREQUENTLY, REGULARLY.

house *n.* 1. [A habitation] dwelling, apartment house, residence; see APARTMENT, HOME 1. 2. [A family] line, family tradition, ancestry; see FAMILY. 3. [A legislative body] congress, council, parliament; see LEGISLATURE. —**bring down the house*** receive applause, create enthusiasm, please; see EXCITE. —**clean house** arrange, put in order, tidy up; see CLEAN. —**keep house** manage a home, run a house, be a housekeeper; see MANAGE 1. —**like a house on fire** actively, vigorously, energetically; see QUICKLY. —**on the house*** without expense, gratis, complimentary; see FREE 4.

household *n.* family unit, house, domestic establishment; see FAMILY, HOME 1.

housekeeper *n.* wife and mother, caretaker, serving woman; see SERVANT.

housekeeping *n.* household management, domestic science, home economy; see HOUSEWORK.

housewife *n.* mistress, lady of the house, housekeeper, home economist, homemaker, family manager, wife and mother, stay-at-home*; see also WIFE.

housework *n.* house cleaning, spring cleaning, window-washing, sweeping, cooking, baking, dusting, mopping, washing, laundering, bed-making, sewing, ironing, mending; see also JOB 2.

housing *n.* habitation, home construction, housing development, low-cost housing, house-building program, sheltering, installation, abode, domicile, house, accommodations, quarters, roof, dwelling, lodging, pad*, residence, headquarters; see also HOME 1, SHELTER.

hover *v.* float, flutter, be in midair; see FLY 1, HANG 2.

how *a. & conj.* in what way, to what degree, by what method, in what manner, according to what specifications, from what source, by whose help, whence, wherewith, by virtue of what, whereby, through what agency, by what means.

however *a. & conj.* 1. [But] still, though, nevertheless; see BUT 1, YET 1. 2. [In spite of] despite, without regard to, nonetheless; see NOTWITHSTANDING.

howl *n.* wail, lament, shriek; see CRY 1, YELL.

howl *v.* bawl, wail, lament; see CRY 1, YELL.

hub *n.* core, heart, middle; see CENTER 1.

hubbub *n.* turmoil, fuss, disorder; see CONFUSION, NOISE 2, UPROAR.

huddle *v.* crouch, press close, crowd, bunch, draw, together, mass, cluster, throng, nestle, cuddle, hug, curl up, snuggle.

hue *n.* hue, shade, dye; see TINT.

huff *n.* annoyance, offense, perturbation; see ANGER, RAGE 1.

huffy *a.* offended, piqued, huffish; see ANGRY, INSULTED, IRRITABLE.

hug *n.* embrace, squeeze, tight grip, caress, clinch, bearhug; see also TOUCH 2.

hug *v.* embrace, squeeze, clasp, press, love, hold, be near to, cling, fold in the arms, clutch, seize, envelop, enfold, nestle, welcome, cuddle, lock, press to the bosom, snuggle.

huge *a.* tremendous, enormous, immense; see LARGE 1.

hulk *n.* bulk, hunk, lump; see MASS 1, PART 1.

hull *n.* 1. [The body of a vessel] framework, skeleton, main structure; see FRAME 1. 2. [A shell] peeling, husk, shuck; see SHELL 1.

hullabaloo *n.* tumult, chaos, clamor; see CONFUSION, NOISE 2, UPROAR.

hum *v.* buzz, drone, murmur, sing low, hum a tune, croon, whisper, moan, make a buzzing sound, whir, vibrate, purr.

human *a.* anthropoid, animal, biped, civilized, man-made, anthropomorphic, manlike, of man, belonging to man, humanistic, individual, man's, personal, humane; see also ANIMAL.—*Ant.* DIVINE, bestial, nonhuman.

human being *n.* being, mortal, individual; see MAN 1, PERSON 1, WOMAN 1.

humane *a.* benevolent, sympathetic, understanding, pitying, compassionate, kindhearted, human, tenderhearted, forgiving, gracious, charitable, gentle, tender, friendly, generous, lenient, tolerant, democratic, good-natured, liberal, open-minded, broadminded, altruistic, philanthropic, helpful, magnanimous, amiable, genial, cordial, unselfish, warmhearted, bighearted, softhearted, good, soft, easy; see also KIND.—*Ant.* CRUEL, barbaric, inhuman.

humanitarian *n.* altruist, philanthropist, benefactor; see PATRON.

humanity *n.* **1.** [The human race] man, mankind, men; see MAN 1. **2.** [An ideal of human behavior] tolerance, sympathy, understanding; see KINDNESS 1, VIRTUE 1, 2.

humble *a.* **1.** [Meek] lowly, submissive, gentle, quiet, unassuming, diffident, simple, retiring, bashful, shy, timid, reserved, deferential, self-conscious, soft-spoken, sheepish, mild, withdrawn, unpretentious, hesitant, fearful, tentative, poor in spirit, sedate, unpresuming, manageable, ordinary, unambitious, commonplace, free from pride, without arrogance, peaceable, obedient, passive, tame, restrained, unostentatious, unimportant, gentle as a lamb, resigned, subdued, tolerant, content, eating humble pie; see also MODEST 2.—*Ant.* PROUD, haughty, conceited. **2.** [Lowly] unpretentious, unassuming, modest, seemly, becoming, homespun, natural, low, proletarian, servile, undistinguished, pitiful, sordid, shabby, underprivileged, meager, beggarly, commonplace, unimportant, insignificant, small, poor, rough, hard, base, meek, little, of low birth, obscure, inferior, plain, common, homely, simple, uncouth, miserable, scrubby, ordinary, humdrum, trival, vulgar.—*Ant.* NOBLE, upper-class, privileged.

humble *v.* shame, mortify, chasten, demean, demote, lower, crush, bring low, put to shame, silence, reduce, humiliate, degrade, overcome, strike dumb, put down, pull down, bring down, snub, discredit, deflate, upset, make ashamed, take down a peg, pull rank on*, squelch*, squash*.—*Ant.* PRAISE, exalt, glorify.

humbly *a.* meekly, submissively, simply, obscurely, apologetically.

humbug *n.* lie, fraud, faker; see DECEPTION, NONSENSE 1.

humdrum *a.* monotonous, common, uninteresting; see DULL 4.

humid *a.* stuffy, sticky, muggy; see CLOSE 5, WET 1.

humidity *n.* moisture, wetness, dampness, mugginess, dankness, heaviness, sogginess, thickness, fogginess, wet, sultriness, steaminess, steam, evaporation, dewiness, stickiness, moistness; see also RAIN 1.

humiliate *v.* debase, chasten, mortify, make a fool of, put to shame, humble, degrade, crush, shame, confuse, snub, confound, lower, dishonor, depress, fill with shame, break, demean, bring low, conquer, make ashamed, vanquish, take down a peg; see also DISGRACE, EMBARRASS.

humiliation *n.* chagrin, mortification, degradation; see DISGRACE, EMBARRASSMENT, SHAME 2.

humility *n.* meekness, timidity, submissiveness, servility, reserve, subservience, subjection, humbleness, submission, obedience, passiveness, nonresistance, resignation, bashfulness, shyness, inferiority complex.—*Ant.* PRIDE, vainglory, conceit.

humor *n.* **1.** [Comedy] amusement, jesting, raillery, joking, merriment, clowning, farce, facetiousness, whimsy, black humor; see also ENTERTAINMENT, FUN. **2.** [An example of humor] witticism, pleasantry, banter; see JOKE. **3.** [The ability to appreciate comedy] good humor, sense of humor, wittiness, high spirits, jolliness, gaiety, joyfulness, playfulness, happy frame of mind.

humor *v.* indulge, pamper, baby, play up to, gratify, please, pet, coddle, spoil, comply with, appease, placate, soften, be playful with; see also COMFORT 1.—*Ant.* ANGER, provoke, enrage.

humorous *a.* comical, comic, entertaining; see FUNNY 1.

humorously *a.* comically, ridiculously, playfully, absurdly, ludicrously, amusingly, jokingly, ironically, satirically, facetiously, merrily, genially, jovially, in a comical manner, in an amusing manner, just for fun.

hump *n.* protuberance, mound, bump, swelling, camel hump, humpback, hunchback, hummock, protrusion, knob, prominence, eminence, projection, swell, hunch, lump, dune.

hunch *n.* idea, notion, feeling, premonition, forecast, presentiment, instinct, expectation, anticipation, precognition, prescience, forewarning, clue, foreboding, hint, portent, apprehension, misgiving, qualm, suspicion, inkling, glimmer; see also THOUGHT 2.

hundred *n.* ten tens, five score, century; see NUMBER.

hung *a.* suspended, swaying, dangling; see HANGING.

hunger *n.* craving, longing, yearning, mania, lust, desire for food, famine, gluttony, hungriness, panting, drought, want, vacancy, void, greed, sweet tooth*.—*Ant.* SATISFACTION, satiety, glut.

hungry *a.* starved, famished, ravenous, desirous, hankering, unsatisfied, unfilled, starving, insatiate, voracious, half-starved, omnivorous, piggish, hoggish, on an empty stomach*, hungry as a wolf*, empty*.—*Ant.* FULL, satisfied, fed.

hung up* *a.* 1. [Troubled] disturbed, psychotic, psychopathic; see TROUBLED. 2. [Intent] absorbed, engrossed, preoccupied; see THOUGHTFUL 1.

hunk *n.* lump, large piece, good-sized bit, portion, a fair quantity, a good bit, chunk, bunch, mass, clod, a pile, thick slice, morsel, a lot, slice, gob, loaf, wad; see also PIECE 1.

hunt *n.* chase, shooting, field sport; see HUNTING, SPORT 3.

hunt *v.* 1. [To pursue with intent to kill] follow, give chase, stalk, hound, trail, dog, seek, capture, kill, shoot, track, heel, shadow, chase, hunt out, snare, look for, fish, fish for, poach, gun for*, go gunning for*; see also TRACK 1. 2. [To try to find] investigate, probe, look for; see SEEK.

hunted *a.* pursued, followed, tracked, sought, trailed, chased, stalked, hounded, tailed, wanted, driven out, searched for.

hunter *n.* huntsman, stalker, chaser, sportsman, pursuer, big-game hunter, gunner, poacher, horsewoman, huntress, horseman, archer, deerstalker, angler, fisherman, bowman, shooter.

hunting *a.* looking for, looking around, seeking, in search of; see also SEARCHING.

hunting *n.* the chase, the hunt, sporting, shooting, stalking, preying, trapping, big-game hunting, deer hunting, fox hunting, pheasant shooting, angling, fishing, steeplechase, riding to hounds, gunning; see also SPORT 3.

hurdle *n.* barricade, obstacle, blockade; see BARRIER.

hurdle *v.* jump over, scale, leap over; see JUMP 1.

hurl *v.* cast, fling, heave; see THROW 1.

hurrah *interj.* three cheers, hurray, yippee; see CHEER 2, CRY 1, ENCOURAGEMENT, YELL 1.

hurricane *n.* typhoon, tempest, monsoon; see STORM.

hurry *interj.* run, hasten, move, hustle, gain time, get a move on*, on the double*.

hurry *n.* dispatch, haste, rush; see SPEED.

hurry *v.* 1. [To act hastily] hasten, be quick, make haste, scurry, scuttle, fly, tear, dash, sprint, be in a hurry, lose no time, move quickly, move rapidly, bolt, bustle, rush, make short work of, scoot*, work at high speed, dash on, hurry about, hurry off, hurry up, run off, waste no time, plunge, skip, gallop, zoom, dart, spring, make haste, make good time, whip, go by forced marches, speed, work under pressure, run like mad*, go at full tilt, make strides, act on a moment's notice, turn on the steam*, floor it*, get cracking*, step on it*, shake a leg*.—*Ant.* DELAY, lose time, procrastinate. 2. [To move rapidly] fly, bustle, dash off; see RACE 1, RUN 1. 3. [To urge others] push, spur, goad on; see DRIVE 1, URGE 2.

hurrying *a.* speeding, in a hurry, running; see FAST.

hurt *a.* injured, damaged, harmed, marred, wounded, in critical condition, impaired, shot, struck, bruised, stricken, battered, mauled, hit, stabbed, mutilated, disfigured, in pain, suffering, distressed, tortured, unhappy, grazed, scratched, nicked, winged*; see also WOUNDED.

hurt *n.* 1. [A wound] blow, gash, ache; see INJURY, PAIN 1. 2. [Damage] ill-treatment, harm, persecution; see DAMAGE 1, DISASTER, MISFORTUNE.

hurt *v.* 1. [To cause pain] cramp, squeeze, cut, bruise, tear, torment, afflict, kick, puncture, do violence to, slap, abuse, flog, whip, torture, gnaw, stab, pierce, maul, cut up, harm, injure, wound, lacerate, sting, bite, inflict pain, burn, crucify, tweak, thrash, punch, pinch, spank, punish, trounce, scourge, lash, cane, switch, work over*, wallop*, slug*.—*Ant.* EASE, comfort, soothe. 2. [To harm] maltreat, injure, spoil; see DAMAGE, DESTROY. 3. [To give a feeling of pain] ache, throb, sting; see sense 1.

hurtful *a.* aching, injurious, bad; see DANGEROUS, DEADLY, HARMFUL.

husband *n.* spouse, married man, mate, bedmate, helpmate, consort, bridegroom, breadwinner, provider, man, common-law husband, hubby*, lord and master*, the man of the house*, old man*; see also MAN 2.

hush *interj.* quiet, be quiet, pipe down*; see SHUT UP 1.

hush *n.* peace, stillness, quiet; see SILENCE 1.

hush *v.* silence, gag, stifle; see QUIET 2.

hush (up) *v.* cover, conceal, suppress; see HIDE 1.

husk *n.* shuck, covering, outside; see COVER 1, SHELL 1.

husky *a.* 1. [Hoarse] throaty, growling, gruff; see HOARSE. 2. [Strong] muscular, sinewy, strapping; see STRONG 1.

hustle* *v.* act quickly, rush, push; see HURRY 1, RACE 1, RUN 1, SPEED.

hustler* *n.* 1. [A professional gambler] gamester, bookmaker, plunger*; see GAMBLER. 2. [A prostitute] whore, harlot, call girl; see PROSTITUTE. 3. [An energetic worker] dynamo, go-getter, workaholic; see EXECUTIVE, ZEALOT.

hut *n.* shanty, lean-to, shack, bungalow, bunkhouse, refuge, lodge, dugout, hovel, cottage, cabin, hogan, tepee, log cabin, wigwam, dump*; see also HOME 1, SHELTER.

hybrid *a.* crossed, alloyed, crossbred, cross, half-blooded, half-breed*, half-caste*, heterogeneous, intermingled, half-and-half.

hybrid *n.* crossbreed, cross, mixture, composite, half-breed, half-blood, half-caste, combination, mestizo, mulatto, outcross; see also MIXTURE 1.

hydraulics *n.* science of liquids in motion, hydrodynamics, hydrology; see SCIENCE 1.
hygiene *n.* cleanliness, hygienics, preventive medicine, public health, sanitary measures; see also HEALTH.
hygienic *a.* healthful, sanitary, clean; see PURE 2, STERILE 3.
hymn *n.* chant, psalm, spiritual; see SONG.
hypnosis *n.* trance, anesthesia, lethargy; see SLEEP.
hypnotic *a.* sleep-inducing, opiate, narcotic, anesthetic, soporific, sleep-producing, soothing, calmative, trance-inducing.
hypnotism *n.* bewitchment, suggestion, hypnotherapy, deep sleep, self-hypnosis, autohypnosis, hypnotic, suggestion, charm, fascination.
hypnotize *v.* mesmerize, lull to sleep, dull the will, hold under a spell, bring under one's control, stupefy, drug, soothe, fascinate, anesthetize, subject to suggestion, make drowsy.
hypnotized *a.* entranced, mesmerized, enchanted; see CHARMED.
hypochondria *n.* depression, imagined ill-health, hypochondriasis; see PRETENSE 1.
hypochondriac *n.* malingerer, melancholic, self-tormentor; see FAKE.
hypocrisy *n.* affectation, deception, bad faith, hollowness, display, lip service, bigotry, sham, fraud, pretense of virtue, quackery, empty ceremony, sanctimony, cant; see also DISHONESTY, LIE.—*Ant.* VIRTUE, devotion, piety.
hypocrite *n.* pretender, fraud, faker, fake, deceiver, charlatan, bigot, quack, pharisee, sham, actor, cheat, informer, trickster, confidence man, malingerer, humbug, imposter, swindler, informer, rascal, traitor, wolf in sheep's clothing, masquerader, four-flusher*, two-timer*, two-face*; see also FAKE.
hypocritical *a.* deceptive, double-dealing, insincere; see DISHONEST.
hypothesis *n.* supposition, theory, assumption; see GUESS, OPINION 1.
hypothetical *a.* **1.** [Supposed] imagined, uncertain, vague; see ASSUMED, LIKELY 1. **2.** [Characterized by hypothesis] postulated, academic, philosophical; see LOGICAL.
hysteria *n.* delirium, agitation, feverishness; see CONFUSION, EXCITEMENT, NERVOUSNESS.
hysterical *a.* convulsed, uncontrolled, raving, delirious, wildly emotional, unnerved, neurotic, spasmodic, emotional, rabid, emotionally disordered, distracted, fuming, distraught, unrestrained, possessed, fanatical, irrepressible, convulsive, carried away, seething, beside oneself, rampant, out of one's wits, mad, uncontrollable, agitated, raging, frenzied, confused, tempestuous, maddened, crazy, impetuous, crazed, furious, violent, impassioned, panic-stricken, nervous, vehement, overwrought, fiery, passionate, jittery*, wild-eyed, on a crying jag*; see also ANGRY, EXCITED, TROUBLED.

I

I *pron.* myself, *ego* (Latin), self; see CHARACTER 2.
ICBM *n.* Intercontinental Ballistic Missile, guided missile, strategic deterrent; see ROCKET, WEAPON.
ice *n.* crystal, hail, floe, glacier, icicle, ice cube, cube ice, dry ice, black ice, white ice, chunk ice, iceberg, permafrost; see also FROST. **—break the ice** make a start, initiate, commence; see BEGIN 1. **—on ice*** in reserve, held, in abeyance; see SAVED 2. **—on thin ice*** in a dangerous situation, imperiled, insecure; see ENDANGERED.
ice *v.* frost, coat, mist; see FREEZE 1.
iceberg *n.* ice field, berg, icecap; see ICE.
icebox *n.* cooler, freezer, fridge*; see REFRIGERATOR.
ice cream *n.* mousse, spumoni, *glacé* (French), sherbet, ice, ice milk, soft serve, frozen custard, parfait, frozen dessert; see also DESSERT.
icy *a.* frozen over, iced, freezing, glacial, frostbound, frosted, frosty, smooth as glass; see also SLIPPERY.
idea *n.* **1.** [A concept] conception, plans, view, fancy, impression, image, understanding, conception, observation, belief, feeling, opinion, guess, inference, theory, hypothesis, supposition, assumption, intuition, conjecture, design, approach, mental impression, notion. **2.** [Fancy] whimsy, whim, fantasy; see FANCY 1, IMAGINATION. **3.** [Meaning] sense, import, purport; see MEANING.
ideal *a.* **1.** [Typical] prototypical, model, archetypical; see TYPICAL. **2.** [Perfect] supreme, fitting, exemplary; see EXCELLENT, PERFECT.
ideal *n.* paragon, goal, prototype; see MODEL 1.
idealism *n.* principle, conscience, philosophy; see ETHICS.

idealistic *a.* lofty, noble, exalted; see IMPRACTICAL, NOBLE 1.

idealize *v.* romanticize, glorify, build castles in the air; see DREAM 2, INVENT 1.

ideals *n.pl.* standards, principles, goals; see ETHICS, MORALS.

identical *a.* like, twin, indistinguishable; see ALIKE.

identification *n.* **1.** [The act of identifying] classifying, naming, cataloging; see CLASSIFICATION, DESCRIPTION. **2.** [Means of identifying] credentials, letter of introduction, testimony, letter of credit, badge, papers, ID; see also PASSPORT.

identify *v.* classify, catalog, analyze; see DESCRIBE, NAME 1, 2.

identity *n.* identification, character, individuality, uniqueness, antecedents, true circumstances, parentage, status, citizenship, nationality, connections; see also NAME 1.

ideology *n.* beliefs, ideas, philosophy; see CULTURE 2, ETHICS.

idiot *n.* simpleton, nincompoop, booby; see FOOL.

idiotic *a.* thickwitted, dull, moronic; see STUPID.

idle *a.* unoccupied, fallow, vacant, deserted, not in use, barren, void, empty, abandoned, still, quiet, motionless, inert, dead, rusty, dusty, out of action, out of a job, out of work, resting; see also UNEMPLOYED.—*Ant.* ACTIVE, busy, engaged.

idle *v.* slack, shirk, slow down; see LOAF.

idleness *n.* loitering, time-killing, dawdling, inertia, inactivity, indolence, sluggishness, unemployment, dormancy, lethargy, stupor, loafing.—*Ant.* ACTION, industry, occupation.

idol *n.* icon, graven image, god, Buddha, false god, figurine, fetish, totem, golden calf, pagan deity.

idolatry *n.* infatuation, fervor, transport; see ZEAL.

idolize *v.* glorify, adore, canonize; see WORSHIP.

I don't know *interj.* Beats me!*, Who knows?, How should I know?, You've got me!*, Ask me another!.

if *conj.* provided that, with the condition that, supposing that, conceding that, on the assumption that, granted that, assuming that, whenever, wherever. **—as if** as though, assuming that, in a way; see AS IF.

iffy *a.* unsettled, doubtful, uncertain; see UNCERTAIN.

ignite *v.* enkindle, light, strike a light, start up, burst into flames, touch off, touch a match to, set off; see also BURN.

ignition *n.* **1.** [Igniting] combustion, bursting into flame, kindling; see FIRE 1. **2.** [A system for igniting] distributor, firing system, wiring system; see ENGINE, MACHINE, MOTOR.

ignorance *n.* unconsciousness, incomprehension, bewilderment, incapacity, inexperience, disregard, illiteracy, denseness, stupidity, dumbness, empty-headedness, unintelligence, rawness, blindness, simplicity, lack of education, insensitivity, shallowness, fog, vagueness, half-knowledge, a little learning.—*Ant.* ABILITY, learning, erudition.

ignorant *a.* **1.** [Unaware] unconscious of, uninformed about, unknowing, uninitiated, inexperienced, unwitting, unmindful, disregardful, misinformed, unsuspecting, unaware of, unmindful of, unconscious of, mindless, witless, not conversant with, unintelligent, obtuse, thick, dense, unscientific, birdbrained*, lowbrow*, sappy*, green; see also sense 2 and DULL 3, SHALLOW 2, STUPID.—*Ant.* INTELLIGENT, alert, aware. **2.** [Untrained] illiterate, uneducated, unlettered, untaught, uninstructed, uncultivated, unenlightened, untutored, unschooled, unread, benighted, shallow, superficial, gross, coarse, vulgar, crude, green, knowing nothing, misinformed, misguided, just beginning, apprenticed, unbriefed; see also INEXPERIENCED, NAIVE, UNAWARE.—*Ant.* LEARNED, cognizant, tutored.

ignore *v.* disregard, overlook, pass over; see DISCARD, NEGLECT 2.

ill *a.* **1.** [Bad] harmful, evil, noxious; see BAD 1. **2.** [Sick] unwell, unhealthy, ailing; see SICK.

ill *n.* depravity, misfortune, mischief; see EVIL 2, INSULT, WRONG.

ill at ease *a.* anxious, uneasy, uncomfortable; see DOUBTFUL, RESTLESS, SUSPICIOUS 1, 2.

illegal *a.* illicit, unlawful, contraband, unwarranted, banned, unconstitutional, outside the law, extralegal, outlawed, not legal, unauthorized, unlicensed, lawless, actionable, illegitimate, prohibited, forbidden, criminal, against the law, not approved, uncertified, unlicensed, smuggled, bootlegged, hot*.—*Ant.* LEGAL, lawful, authorized.

illegible *a.* faint, unintelligible, difficult to read; see CONFUSED 2, OBSCURE 1.

illegibly *a.* faintly, unintelligibly, indistinctly; see CONFUSED 2.

illegitimate *a.* **1.** [Unlawful] contraband, wrong, illicit; see BAD 1, ILLEGAL. **2.** [Misbegotten] born out of wedlock, unlawfully begotten, unfathered; see BASTARD.

illicit *a.* unlawful, prohibited, unauthorized; see BAD 1, ILLEGAL, WRONG 1.

illiteracy *n.* lack of education, stupidity, idiocy; see IGNORANCE.

illiterate *a.* uneducated, unenlightened, dumb*; see IGNORANT 2.

ill-mannered *a.* impolite, uncouth, rough; see RUDE 2.

illness *n.* **1.** [Poor health] sickness, failing health, seizure, ailing, infirmity, disorder, relapse, attack, fit, convalescence, complaint, delicate health, collapse, breakdown, confinement, disturbance, ill health; see also WEAKNESS 1. **2.** [A particular disease] sickness, ailment, malady, ache, infection, stroke, allergy; see also COLD 2, IMPEDIMENT 2, INSANITY, PAIN 2.

illogical *a.* irrational, unreasonable, absurd, fallacious, unsubstantial, incorrect, inconsistent, false, unscientific, contradictory, untenable, unsound, preposterous, invalid, self-contradictory, unproved, groundless, implausible, hollow, irrelevant, inconclusive, prejudiced, biased, unconnected, without foundation, not following, without rhyme or reason; see also WRONG 2.—*Ant.* LOGICAL, sound, reasonable.

ill-suited *a.* inappropriate, unsuitable, mismatched; see UNSUITABLE.

ill-tempered *a.* cross, touchy, querulous; see IRRITABLE, SULLEN.

illuminate *v.* **1.** [To make light(er)] lighten, irradiate, illume; see BRIGHTEN 1, LIGHT 1. **2.** [To explain] interpret, elucidate, clarify; see EXPLAIN.

illumination *n.* **1.** [A light] gleam, flame, brilliance, lighting; see also FLASH, LIGHT 1, 3. **2.** [Instruction] teaching, education, information; see KNOWLEDGE 1.

illusion *n.* fancy, hallucination, mirage, apparition, ghost, delusion, figment of the imagination, image, trick of vision, myth, make-believe; see also DREAM.

illustrate *v.* picture, represent, portray, depict, imitate; see also DRAW 2, PAINT 1.

illustrated *a.* engraved, decorated, portrayed; see DESCRIPTIVE.

illustration *n.* engraving, tailpiece, frontispiece, cartoon, vignette, etching, inset picture, newsphoto; see also PICTURE 3.

illustrative *a.* symbolic, representative, pictorial; see DESCRIPTIVE, EXPLANATORY, GRAPHIC 1, 2.

ill will *n.* malevolence, dislike, hostility; see BLAME, HATRED, OBJECTION.

image *n.* 1. [Mental impression] concept, conception, perception; see IDEA 1, THOUGHT 2. **2.** [Representation] idol, carved figure, effigy, form, drawing, model, illustration, portrait, photograph, reproduction, copy, likeness, facsimile, counterpart, replica; see also PICTURE 2.

imagery *n.* illustration, metaphor, representation; see COMPARISON.

imaginable *a.* conceivable, comprehensible, credible, thinkable, sensible, possible, plausible, believable, reasonable; see also LIKELY 1.—*Ant.* UNBELIEVABLE, unimaginable, inconceivable.

imaginary *a.* fancied, illusory, visionary, shadowy, dreamy, dreamlike, hypothetical, theoretical, deceptive, imagined, hallucinatory, ideal, whimsical, fabulous, nonexistent, apocryphal, fantastic, mythological, legendary, fictitious, imaginative; see also UNREAL.—*Ant.* REAL, factual, existing.

imagination *n.* intelligence, thoughtfulness, inventiveness, conception, mental agility, wit, sensitivity, fancy, visualization, realization, cognition, awareness, dramatization, pictorialization, insight; see also MIND 1.

imaginative *a.* creative, inventive, originative; see ARTISTIC, ORIGINAL 2.

imagine *v.* conceive, picture, conjure up, envisage, envision, see in one's mind, invent, fabricate, formulate, devise, think of, make up, conceptualize, dream, dream up*, perceive, dramatize, create.

imagined *a.* not real, insubstantial, thought-up; see FALSE 1, 2, 3, IMAGINARY.

imbalance *n.* lack of balance, unevenness, inequality; see IRREGULARITY.

imbibe *v.* ingest, gorge, guzzle; see DRINK 1, SWALLOW.

imitate *v.* **1.** [To mimic] impersonate, mirror, copy, mime, ape, simulate, duplicate, act, repeat, echo, parody, emulate, do like, reflect, pretend, play a part, take off*. **2.** [To copy] duplicate, counterfeit, falsify; see COPY, REPRODUCE 2. **3.** [To resemble] be like, simulate, parallel; see RESEMBLE.

imitated *a.* copied, duplicated, mimicked, mocked, aped, counterfeited, caricatured, parodied.

imitation *a.* copied, feigned, bogus; see FALSE 3.

imitation *n.* **1.** [The act of imitating] simulation, counterfeiting, copying, duplication, patterning after, picturing, representing, mimicry, aping, impersonation, echoing, matching, mirroring, paralleling; see also COPY. **2.** [An object made by imitating] counterfeit, mime, sham, fake, picture, replica, echo, reflection, match, parallel, resemblance, transcription, image, mockery, takeoff*, caricature, parody, satire, substitution, forgery; see also COPY.—*Ant.* ORIGINAL, novelty, pattern.

imitative *a.* forged, sham, deceptive; see FALSE 2, 3.

imitator *n.* follower, copier, impersonator, mime, mimic, pretender, counterfeiter, forger, copycat.

immaculate *a.* unsullied, spotless, stainless; see BRIGHT 1, CLEAN 1.

immature *a.* youthful, sophomoric, half-grown; see NAIVE.

immaturity *n.* imperfection, incompleteness, childlike behavior; see INSTABILITY.

immediate *a.* at once, instant, now, on the moment, at this moment, at the present time, next, prompt; see also FOLLOWING.—*Ant.* SOMEDAY, later, any time.

immediately *a.* at once, without delay, instantly, directly, right away, at the first opportunity, at short notice, now, this instant, speedily, quickly, promptly, on the spot, on the dot, rapidly, instantaneously, shortly, on the double*, in a jiffy*; see also URGENTLY.—*Ant.* LATER, in the future, in a while.

immense *a.* gigantic, tremendous, enormous; see LARGE 1.

immensity *n.* infinity, vastness, greatness; see EXTENT.

immerse *v.* submerge, dip, douse, plunge, duck, cover with water, drown, bathe, steep, soak, drench, dunk, souse; see also SOAK 1.

immersed *a.* drowned, plunged, bathed; see DIPPED, SOAKED, WET 1.

immigrant *n.* newcomer, naturalized citizen, adoptive citizen; see ALIEN, EMIGRANT.

immigrate *v.* migrate, colonize, seek political asylum; see ENTER.

immigration *n.* colonization, settlement, migration; see ENTRANCE 1.

imminent *a.* approaching, in store, about to happen; see COMING 1, DESTINED.

immodest *a.* brazen, shameless, bold; see EGOTISTIC, RUDE 2.

immoral *a.* sinful, corrupt, shameless; see BAD 1.

immorality *n.* vice, depravity, dissoluteness; see EVIL 1.

immorally *a.* sinfully, wickedly, unrighteously; see WRONGLY.

immortal *a.* **1.** [Deathless] undying, permanent, imperishable, endless, timeless, everlasting, death-defying, unfading, neverending, perennial, constant, ceaseless, indestructible, enduring; see also ETERNAL.—*Ant.* MORTAL, perishable, corrupt. **2.** [Illustrious] celebrated, eminent, glorious; see FAMOUS.

immortality *n.* deathlessness, everlasting life, permanence, endlessness, timelessness, divinity, indestructibility, continuity, perpetuation, endless life, unlimited existence, perpetuity; see also ETERNITY.—*Ant.* DEATH, mortality, decease.

immovable *a.* solid, stable, fixed; see FIRM 1.

immune *a.* free, unaffected by, hardened to, unsusceptible, privileged, not liable, excused; see also SAFE 1.

immunity *n.* **1.** [Exemption] favor, privilege, license; see FREEDOM 2. **2.** [Freedom from disease] resistance, immunization, protection, active immunity, passive immunity; see also SAFETY 1.

impact *n.* shock, impression, contact; see COLLISION.

impair *v.* spoil, injure, hurt; see BREAK 2, DAMAGE, DESTROY.

impart *v.* **1.** [To give] bestow, grant, present; see ALLOW, GIVE 1. **2.** [To inform] tell, announce, divulge; see ADMIT 2, REVEAL.

impartial *a.* unbiased, unprejudiced, disinterested; see EQUAL, FAIR 1.

impartiality *n.* objectivity, candor, justice; see EQUALITY, FAIRNESS.

impasse *n.* deadlock, standstill, cessation; see PAUSE.

impatience *n.* agitation, restlessness, anxiety; see EXCITEMENT, NERVOUSNESS.

impatient *a.* anxious, eager, feverish; see RESTLESS.

impeach *v.* criticize, charge, arraign, denounce, indict, discredit, reprimand, blame, incriminate, try, bring charges against, question; see also BLAME.—*Ant.* FREE, acquit, absolve.

impediment *n.* **1.** [An obstruction] hindrance, obstacle, difficulty; see BARRIER. **2.** [An obstruction in speech] speech impediment, speech difficulty, stutter, stammer, lisp, halting, harelip, cleft palate.

impending *a.* in the offing, threatening, menacing; see OMINOUS.

impenetrable *a.* **1.** [Dense] impervious, hard, compact; see FIRM 2, THICK 3. **2.** [Incomprehensible] unintelligible, inscrutable, unfathomable; see OBSCURE 1.

imperative *a.* **1.** [Necessary] inescapable, immediate, crucial; see IMPORTANT 1, NECESSARY, URGENT 1. **2.** [Authoritative] masterful, commanding, dominant; see AGGRESSIVE, POWERFUL 1.

imperfect *a.* flawed, incomplete, deficient; see FAULTY.

imperfection *n.* fault, flaw, stain; see BLEMISH.

imperialism *n.* empire, international domination, power politics; see POWER 2.

impersonal *a.* detached, disinterested, cold; see INDIFFERENT.

impersonate *v.* mimic, portray, act out, pose as, pass for, double for, put on an act, pretend to be, act the part of, take the part of, act a part, dress as, represent; see also IMITATE 1.

impersonation *n.* imitation, role, enactment; see PERFORMANCE.

impertinence *n.* impudence, insolence, disrespectfulness; see RUDENESS.

impertinent *a.* saucy, insolent, impudent; see RUDE 2.

impervious *a.* impenetrable, watertight, hermetic; see TIGHT 2.

impetus *n.* force, cause, stimulus; see INCENTIVE, PURPOSE 1, REASON 3.

impious *a.* sinful, profane, blasphemous; see BAD 1.

implant *v.* stick in, insert, root; see PLANT.

implement *n.* utensil, device, instrument; see EQUIPMENT, MACHINE, TOOL 1.

implicate *v.* connect, cite, associate, tie up with, charge, link, catch up in, relate, compromise; see also BLAME.

implicated *a.* under suspicion, suspected, known to have been associated with; see GUILTY, INVOLVED, SUSPICIOUS 1, 2.

implication *n.* **1.** [Assumption] reference, indication, inference; see ASSUMPTION 1, GUESS. **2.** [A link] connection, involvement, entanglement; see JOINT 1, LINK, UNION 1.

implicit *a.* unquestionable, certain, absolute; see ACCURATE 2, DEFINITE 1, INEVITABLE.

implied *a.* implicit, indicated, foreshadowed, involved, tacit, signified, figured, intended, meant, alluded to, latent, hidden, insinuated, hinted at, understood, symbolized, indicative, potential, indirectly meant, inferred, inferential, undeclared; see also SUGGESTED.

imply *v.* **1.** [To indicate] intimate, hint at, suggest; see HINT, MENTION, REFER 2. **2.** [To mean] import, indicate, signify; see INTEND 2, MEAN 1.

impolite *a.* discourteous, moody, churlish; see IRRITABLE, RUDE 2, SULLEN.

import *v.* introduce, bring in, buy abroad; see CARRY 1, SEND 1.

importance *n.* import, force, sense, consequence, bearing, denotation, gist, effect, distinction, influence, usefulness, moment, weightiness, momentousness, emphasis, standing, stress, accent, weight, concern, attention, interest, seriousness, point, substance, relevance, sum and substance; see also MEANING.—*Ant.* INSIGNIFICANCE, triviality, emptiness.

important *a.* **1.** [Weighty; *said usually of things*] significant, considerable, momentous, essential, great, decisive, critical, determining, chief, paramount, primary, foremost, principal, influential, marked, of great consequence, ponderous, of importance, never to be overlooked, of note, valuable, crucial, substantial, vital, serious, grave, relevant, pressing, far-reaching, extensive, conspicuous, heavy, big-league*, big*; see also NECESSARY.—*Ant.* TRIVIAL, inconsequential, unimportant. **2.** [Eminent; *said usually of persons*] illustrious, well-known, influential; see FAMOUS. **3.** [Relevant] material, influential, significant; see FIT 1, RELATED 2, RELEVANT.

imported *a.* shipped in, produced abroad, exotic, alien; see also FOREIGN.—*Ant.* NATIVE, domestic, made in America.

impose *v.* force upon, compel, fix; see FORCE.

impose on or **upon** *v.* intrude, interrupt, presume; see BOTHER 2, DISTURB.

imposing *a.* stirring, exciting, overwhelming; see IMPRESSIVE.

imposition *n.* demand, restraint, encumbrance; see COMMAND, PRESSURE 2.

impossibility *n.* hopelessness, impracticality, impractibility, difficulty, unlikelihood, failure, unworkability; see also FUTILITY.

impossible *a.* inconceivable, vain, unachievable, unattainable, out of the question, too much, insurmountable, useless, inaccessible, unworkable, preposterous, unimaginable, unobtainable, not to be thought of, hardly possible, like finding a needle in a haystack*, a hundred to one*, out of the question; see also FUTILE, HOPELESS.—*Ant.* REASONABLE, possible, likely.

impostor *n.* pretender, charlatan, quack; see CHEAT.

impotence *n.* **1.** [Sterility] unproductiveness, frigidity, infecundity; see EMPTINESS. **2.** [Weakness] inability, feebleness, infirmity; see WEAKNESS 1.

impotent *a.* **1.** [Weak] powerless, inept, infirm; see UNABLE, WEAK 1. **2.** [Sterile] barren, frigid, unproductive; see STERILE 1.

impound *v.* appropriate, take, usurp; see SEIZE 2.

impounded *a.* kept, seized, confiscated; see HELD, RETAINED 1.

impoverish *v.* make poor, bankrupt, exhaust; see DESTROY.

impoverished *a.* poverty-stricken, bankrupt, broke*; see POOR 1, RUINED 3.

impractical *a.* unreal, unrealistic, unworkable, improbable, illogical, unreasonable, absurd, wild, abstract, impossible, idealistic, unfeasible, out of the question.—*Ant.* PRACTICAL, logical, reasonable.

impregnate *v.* **1.** [To permeate] fill up, pervade, overflow; see FILL 2, SOAK 1. **2.** [To beget] procreate, conceive, reproduce; see FERTILIZE 2.

impregnated *a.* **1.** [Full] saturated, shot through and through, full of; see FULL 1. **2.** [Pregnant] bred, in a family way*, with child; see PREGNANT.

impress *v.* **1.** [To make an impression] indent, emboss, imprint; see DENT, MARK 1, PRINT 2. **2.** [To attract attention] stand out, be conspicuous, cause a stir, create an impression, make an impression on, direct attention to, make an impact upon, engage the thoughts of, engage the attention of, be listened to, find favor with, make a hit*, make a dent in; see also FASCINATE.

impressed *a.* aroused, awakened, awed; see AFFECTED 1, EXCITED.

impression *n.* **1.** [An imprint] print, footprint, fingerprint, dent, mold, indentation, depression, cast, form, track, pattern; see also MARK 1. **2.** [An effect] response, consequence, reaction; see RESULT. **3.** [A notion based on scanty evidence] theory, conjecture, supposition; see GUESS, OPINION 1.

impressionable *a.* perceptive, impressible, receptive; see AFFECTED 1.

impressive *a.* stirring, moving, inspiring, effective, affecting, eloquent, impassioned, thrilling, excited, intense, well-done, dramatic, absorbing, deep, profound, penetrating, remarkable, extraordinary, notable, important, momentous, vital; see also PROFOUND.—*Ant.* DULL, uninteresting, common.

imprint *n.* 1. [A printed identification] firm name, banner, trademark, direction, heading; see also EMBLEM, SIGNATURE. 2. [An impression] dent, indentation, print; see MARK 1.

imprint *v.* print, stamp, designate; see MARK 1, 2.

imprison *v.* jail, lock up, confine, incarcerate, immure, impound, detain, keep in, hold, intern, shut in, lock in, box in, fence in, cage, send to prison, keep as captive, hold captive, hold as hostage, enclose, keep in custody, put behind bars, put away*, send up*.—*Ant.* FREE, liberate, release.

imprisoned *a.* arrested, jailed, incarcerated; see CONFINED 3.

imprisonment *n.* captivity, isolation, incarceration, duress, durance, bondage; see also CONFINEMENT.—*Ant.* FREEDOM, liberty, emancipation.

improbable *a.* not likely, doubtful, not to be expected; see UNLIKELY.

improper *a.* at odds, ill-advised, unsuited, incongruous, out of place, ludicrous, incorrect, preposterous, unwarranted, undue, imprudent, abnormal, irregular, inexpedient, unseasonable, inadvisable, untimely, inopportune, unfit, malapropos, unfitting, inappropriate, unbefitting, ill-timed, awkward, inharmonious, inapplicable, odd; see also UNSUITABLE.

improperly *a.* poorly, inappropriately, clumsily; see AWKWARDLY, BADLY 1, INADEQUATELY.

improve *v.* 1. [To make better] mend, update, refine; see CHANGE 1, REPAIR. 2. [To become better] regenerate, advance, progress, renew, enrich, enhance, augment, gain strength, develop, get better, grow better, grow, make progress, widen, increase, mellow, mature, come along, get on, look up, shape up*, pick up, perk up, come around, make headway, snap out of*; see also CHANGE 2, RECOVER 3.—*Ant.* WEAKEN, worsen, grow worse.

improved *a.* corrected, bettered, amended, mended, reformed, elaborated, refined, modernized, brought up-to-date, enhanced, repaired, bolstered up, rectified, remodeled, reorganized, made-over, better for, doctored up*, polished up*; see also CHANGED 2.

improvement *n.* 1. [The process of becoming better] amelioration, betterment, rectification, change, alteration, reformation, progression, advance, advancement, development, growth, rise, civilization, gain, cultivation, increase, enrichment, promotion, elevation, recovery, regeneration, renovation, reorganization, amendment, reform, revision, elaboration, refinement, modernization, enhancement, remodeling.—*Ant.* DECAY, deterioration, retrogression. 2. [That which has been improved] addition, supplement, repair, extra, attachment, correction, reform, remodeling, repairing, refinement, luxury, advance, latest thing, last word; see also CHANGE 1.

improve on or **upon** *v.* make better, develop, refine; see CORRECT, REPAIR.

improving *a.* reconstructing, repairing, elaborating, bettering, correcting, developing, fixing, remodeling, on the mend.

impudence *n.* insolence, impertinence, effrontery; see RUDENESS.

impudent *a.* forward, insolent, shameless; see RUDE 2.

impugn *v.* question, attack, challenge, call into question, contradict, assail, knock*; see also DOUBT.

impulse *n.* 1. [A throb] surge, pulse, pulsation; see BEAT 1. 2. [A sudden urge] fancy, whim, caprice, motive, motivation, spontaneity, drive, appeal, notion, inclination, disposition, wish, whimsy, inspiration, hunch, flash, thought.

impulsive *a.* offhand, unpremeditated, extemporaneous; see AUTOMATIC, SPONTANEOUS.

impulsively *a.* imprudently, hastily, abruptly; see CARELESSLY, RASHLY.

impure *a.* 1. [Adulterated] not pure, loaded, weighted, salted, diluted, debased, contaminated, mixed, watered down, polluted, corrupted, raw, tainted, cut, adulterated, doctored*, tampered with; see also UNCLEAN. 2. [Not chaste] unclean, unchaste, corrupt; see BAD 1, LEWD 2.

impurity *n.* 1. [Lewdness] indecency, profligacy, pornography; see LEWDNESS. 2. [Filth] dirt, defilement, excrement; see FILTH, POLLUTION.

in *prep.* 1. [Within] surrounded by, in the midst of, within the boundaries of, in the area of, within the time of, concerning the subject of, as a part of, inside of, enclosed in, not out of; see also WITHIN. 2. [Into] to the center of, to the midst of, in the direction of, within the extent of, under, near, against; see also INTO, TOWARD. 3. [While engaged in] in the act of, during the process of, while occupied with; see DURING, MEANWHILE, WHILE 1. —**have it in for*** wish to harm, be out to destroy, detest; see HATE 1.

inability *n.* 1. [Lack of competence] incapacity, incompetence, shortcoming; see FAILURE 1, WEAKNESS 1. 2. [A temporary lack] disability, failure, frailty; see LACK 2, NECESSITY 2.

inaccessible *a.* unobtainable, unworkable, out of reach; see AWAY, BEYOND, DIFFICULT 2, DISTANT, RARE 2, REMOTE 1, SEPARATED.

inaccuracy *n.* exaggeration, mistake, deception; see ERROR.

inaccurate *a.* fallacious, in error, incorrect; see MISTAKEN 1, WRONG 2.

inactive *a.* dormant, stable, still; see IDLE, MOTIONLESS 1.

inadequacy *n.* **1.** [Inferiority] ineptitude, incompetence, insufficiency; see WEAKNESS 1. **2.** [A defect] flaw, drawback, shortcoming; see BLEMISH, DEFECT, LACK 2.

inadequate *a.* lacking, scanty, short, meager, failing, unequal, not enough, sparing, stinted, stunted, feeble, sparse, too little, small, thin, deficient, incomplete, inconsiderable, spare, bare, niggardly, miserly, scarce, barren, depleted, low, weak, impotent, unproductive, dry, sterile, imperfect, defective, lame, skimpy*; see also UNSATISFACTORY.—*Ant.* ENOUGH, adequate, sufficient.

inadequately *a.* insufficiently, not enough, partly, partially, incompletely, scantily, deficiently, perfunctorily, ineffectively, inefficiently, ineptly, not up to standards, not up to specifications, not up to requirements, meagerly, not in sufficient quantity, not in sufficient quality, to a limited degree, below par, not up to snuff*; see also BADLY 1.

in advance *a.* ahead of, earlier, in time; see BEFORE.

inadvisable *a.* unsuitable, inappropriate, inconvenient; see IMPROPER, WRONG 2.

inadvisedly *a.* impulsively, regrettably, unwisely; see FOOLISHLY, RASHLY.

in all respects *a.* entirely, altogether, totally; see COMPLETELY.

in a minute *a.* before long, shortly, presently; see SOON.

in and about or **around** *a.* close to, there, approximately; see ABOUT 2, NEAR 1.

inane *a.* pointless, foolish, ridiculous; see ILLOGICAL, SILLY, STUPID.

inanimate *a.* dull, inert, inoperative; see IDLE, MOTIONLESS 1.

in any case *a.* regardless, nonetheless, no matter what; see ANYHOW.

in a pinch *a.* in an emergency, if necessary, under pressure; see IN TROUBLE.

inappropriate *a.* improper, irrelevant, inapplicable; see UNSUITABLE.

inarticulate *a.* **1.** [Mute] reticent, wordless, mute; see DUMB 1. **2.** [Indistinct] unintelligible, inaudible, vague; see OBSCURE 1.

inasmuch as *conj.* in view of, making allowance for, while; see BECAUSE, SINCE 1.

inattentive *a.* preoccupied, indifferent, negligent; see CARELESS, DIVERTED.

inaudible *a.* low, indistinct, silent; see OBSCURE 1, VAGUE.

inaugurate *v.* introduce, initiate, originate; see BEGIN 1.

inauguration *n.* initiation, commencement, installment; see INSTALLATION 1.

inborn *a.* essential, intrinsic, inbred; see NATIVE 1.

inbred *a.* innate, inborn, ingrained; see NATIVE 1.

in brief *a.* concisely, to the point, cut short, abbreviated; see also BRIEFLY.

incalculable *a.* unpredictable, unforeseen, unfixed; see UNCERTAIN.

incandescent *a.* radiant, glowing, brilliant; see BRIGHT 1.

incapable *a.* unsuited, poor, inadequate; see INCOMPETENT, INEXPERIENCED, NAIVE.

incapable of *a.* ineffective, inadequate, unsuited; see INCOMPETENT.

incapacity *n.* inadequacy, insufficiency, uselessness; see WEAKNESS 1.

in case *a.* in the event that, provided, if it should happen that; see IF.

in case of *a.* in the event of, in order to be prepared for, as a provision against; see IF.

incense *n.* scent, fragrance, essence; see PERFUME.

incentive *n.* spur, inducement, motive, stimulus, stimulation, impetus, provocation, enticement, temptation, bait, consideration, excuse, rationale, urge, influence, lure, persuasion, inspiration, encouragement, insistence, instigation, incitement, reason why; see also PURPOSE 1.

incessant *a.* ceaseless, continuous, monotonous; see CONSTANT.

incessantly *a.* steadily, monotonously, perpetually; see REGULARLY.

inch *n.* **1.** [Twelfth of a foot] finger-breadth, measurement, 1/36 yard; see MEASURE 1. **2.** [Small degree] jot, little bit, iota; see BIT 2. —**by inches** slowly, by degrees, step by step; see GRADUALLY. —**every inch** in all respects, thoroughly, entirely; see COMPLETELY.

inch *v.* creep, barely move, make some progress; see CRAWL.

inchoate *a.* incipient, rudimentary, preliminary, beginning; see also UNFINISHED 1.

incident *n.* episode, happening, occurrence; see EVENT.

incidental *a.* subsidiary, relative to, contributing to; see RELATED 2, SUBORDINATE.

incidentally *a.* subordinately, by chance, by the way, as a side effect, as a by-product, unexpectedly, not by design, remotely; see also ACCIDENTALLY.

incidentals *n.pl.* minor needs, incidental expenses, per diem; see EXPENSES, NECESSITY 2.

incinerate *v.* cremate, parch, burn up; see BURN.

incise *v.* dissect, chop, split; see CUT 1, DIVIDE.

incision *n.* gash, slash, surgery; see CUT 1, HOLE 1.

incite *v.* arouse, rouse, impel, stimulate, instigate, provoke, excite, spur, goad, persuade, influence, induce, taunt, activate, animate, inspirit, coax, stir up, motivate, prompt, urge on, inspire, force, work up*, talk into*, egg on, fan the flame*; see also URGE 2.—*Ant.* DISCOURAGE, dissuade, check.

incited *a.* driven, pushed, motivated; see URGED 2.

inclination *n.* **1.** [A tendency] bias, bent, propensity, predilection, penchant, attachment, capability, capacity, aptness, leaning, fondness, disposition, liking, preference, movement, susceptibility, weakness, drift, trend, turn, slant, impulse, attraction, affection, desire, temperament, whim, idiosyncrasy, urge, persuasion. **2.** [A slant] pitch, slope, incline, angle, ramp, bank, lean, list; see also GRADE 1.

incline *n.* slope, inclined plane, approach; see GRADE 1, INCLINATION 2.

incline *v.* **1.** [To lean] bow, nod, cock; see LEAN 1. **2.** [To tend toward] prefer, be disposed, be predisposed; see FAVOR.

inclined *a.* prone, slanted, willing; see LIKELY 4.

include *v.* **1.** [To contain] hold, admit, cover, embrace, involve, consist of, take in, entail, incorporate, constitute, accommodate, be comprised of, be composed of, embody, be made up of, number among, carry, bear; see also COMPOSE 1.—*Ant.* BAR, omit, stand outside of. **2.** [To place into or among] enter, introduce, take in, incorporate, make room for, build, work in, inject, interject, add on, insert, combine, make a part of, make allowance for, give consideration to, count in.—*Ant.* DISCARD, exclude, reject.

included *a.* counted, numbered, admitted, covered, involved, constituted, embodied, inserted, entered, incorporated, combined, placed, fused, merged; see also WITHIN.—*Ant.* REFUSED, excluded, left out.

including *a.* together with, along with, as well as, in conjunction with, not to mention, to say nothing of, among other things, with the addition of, in addition to, counting, made up of; see also PLUS.—*Ant.* BESIDES, not counting, aside from.

incoherence *n.* disagreement, dissimilarity, incongruity; see INCONSISTENCY.

incoherent *a.* mumbling, stammering, confused, speechless, puzzling, indistinct, faltering, stuttering, unintelligible, muttered, mumbled, jumbled, gasping, breathless, disconnected, tongue-tied, muffled, indistinguishable, incomprehensible, muddled.—*Ant.* CLEAR, eloquent, distinct.

incoherently *a.* frantically, drunkenly, confusedly, spasmodically, chaotically, randomly, ineptly, unsystematically, aimlessly, casually, sloppily, ambiguously, equivocally, illegibly, incomprehensibly, unrecognizably, uncertainly, inaudibly; see also WILDLY.

in cold blood *a.* heartlessly, ruthlessly, unmercifully; see BRUTALLY.

income *n.* earnings, salary, wages, returns, profit, dividends, assets, proceeds, benefits, receipts, gains, commission, drawings, rent, royalty, honorarium, net income, gross income, taxable income, cash, take; see also PAY 2.—*Ant.* EXPENSE, expenditures, outgo.

incomparable *a.* unequaled, exceptional, superior; see EXCELLENT, PERFECT.

incompatibility *n.* variance, conflict, animosity; see DISAGREEMENT 1.

incompatible *a.* inconsistent, contrary, clashing, inappropriate, contradictory, disagreeing, inconstant, unadapted, opposite, jarring, discordant, incoherent, inadmissible; see also OPPOSED, UNSUITABLE.

incompetence *n.* inadequacy, inexperience, worthlessness; see WEAKNESS 1.

incompetent *a.* incapable, inefficient, unskillful, not qualified, inadequate, unfit, unskilled, bungling, inexpert, ineffectual, unsuitable, untrained, clumsy, awkward, uninitiated, raw, inexperienced, unadapted, not equal to, amateurish; see also UNABLE.—*Ant.* ABLE, fit, qualified.

in competition with *prep.* opposed to, competing against, over; see AGAINST 3.

incomplete *a.* rough, half-done, under construction; see UNFINISHED 1.

inconceivable *a.* fantastic, unimaginable, incredible; see IMPOSSIBLE.

inconclusive *a.* indecisive, deficient, lacking; see FAULTY, INADEQUATE, UNSATISFACTORY.

in condition *a.* physically fit, conditioned, in the pink*; see HEALTHY, STRONG 1.

incongruous *a.* uncoordinated, unconnected, contradictory; see ILLOGICAL, UNSUITABLE.

in consequence of *a.* because of, owing to, consequently; see BECAUSE.

inconsequential *a.* unimportant, immaterial, insignificant; see IRRELEVANT, TRIVIAL, UNNECESSARY.

inconsiderate *a.* boorish, impolite, discourteous; see RUDE 2, THOUGHTLESS 2.

inconsistency *n.* discrepancy, disagreement, dissimilarity, disparity, variance, incongruity, inequality, divergence, deviation, disproportion, paradox; see also DIFFERENCE 1.—*Ant.* SIMILARITY, consistency, congruity.

inconsistent *a.* contradictory, illogical, incoherent; see ILLOGICAL.

inconspicuous *a.* concealed, indistinct, retiring; see HIDDEN, OBSCURE 1, 3, SECRETIVE.

inconspicuously *a.* slyly, surreptitiously, not openly; see SLYLY.

in contact with *a.* **1.** [Contiguous] meeting, joining, connecting, bordering, adjacent, close; see also NEAR 1.—*Ant.* DISTANT, out of contact, far. **2.** [Communicating with] in touch with, writing to, corresponding with, in communication.

in contrast to or **with** *a.* as against, opposed to, contrasting; see AGAINST 1, OPPOSED.

inconvenience *n.* bother, trouble, awkward detail; see DIFFICULTY 1.
inconvenient *a.* bothersome, awkward, badly arranged; see DISTURBING.
in cooperation (with) *a.* cooperating, collaborating, assisting; see HELPING.
incorporate *v.* add to, combine, fuse; see INCLUDE 2, JOIN 1.
incorporated *a.* entered, placed, fused; see INCLUDED, JOINED.
incorporation *n.* embodiment, adding, fusion; see ADDITION 1.
incorrect *a.* inaccurate, not trustworthy, false; see MISTAKEN 1, UNRELIABLE, WRONG 2.
incorrectly *a.* mistakenly, inaccurately, clumsily; see BADLY 1, WRONGLY.
increase *n.* development, spread, enlargement, expansion, escalation, elaboration, swelling, addition, incorporation, merger, inflation, heightening, extension, dilation, multiplication, rise, broadening, advance, intensification, deepening, swell, amplification, progression, improvement, boost, hike*, jump, boom; see also PROGRESS 1.—*Ant.* REDUCTION, decline, decrease. **—on the increase** growing, developing, spreading; see INCREASING.
increase *v.* extend, enlarge, expand, dilate, broaden, widen, thicken, deepen, heighten, build, lengthen, magnify, add on, augment, escalate, let out, branch out, further, mark up, sharpen, build up, raise, enhance, amplify, reinforce, supplement, annex, double, triple, stretch, multiply, intensify, exaggerate, prolong, redouble, boost, step up, rev up*.—*Ant.* DECREASE, reduce, abridge.
increased *a.* marked up, raised, heightened, elevated, added on, doubled.
increasing *a.* developing, maturing, multiplying, broadening, widening, intensifying, heightening, growing, dominant, advancing, growing louder, sharpening, accentuating, aggravating, emphasizing, accelerating, deepening, flourishing, rising, expanding, enlarging, accumulating, piling up, shooting up, getting big, swelling, on the rise, on the increase, booming; see also GROWING.
increasingly *a.* with continual acceleration, more and more, with steady increase; see MORE 1, 2.
incredible *a.* unbelievable, improbable, ridiculous; see IMPOSSIBLE.
incriminate *v.* implicate, blame, charge; see IMPLICATE.
incriminating *a.* damning, damaging, accusatory; see SUSPICIOUS 2.
inculcate *v.* instill, implant, impress; see INSTILL, TEACH.
incurable *a.* fatal, serious, hopeless; see DEADLY.
in danger *a.* imperiled, threatened, in jeopardy; see ENDANGERED.
indebted *a.* obligated, grateful, appreciative; see RESPONSIBLE 1, THANKFUL.
indebtedness *n.* deficit, responsibility, obligation; see DEBT.
indecency *n.* impurity, immodesty, vulgarity, impropriety, obscenity, raciness, four-letter word, lewdness, foulness; see also EVIL 1.—*Ant.* CHASTITY, purity, delicacy.
indecent *a.* immoral, shocking, shameless; see BAD 1, LEWD 2, SHAMEFUL 1, 2.
indecision *n.* hesitation, question, irresolution; see DOUBT, UNCERTAINTY 2.
indecisive *a.* irresolute, unstable, wishy-washy*; see DOUBTFUL.
indeed *a.* **1.** [Surely] naturally, of course, certainly; see REALLY 1, SURELY. **2.** [Really] For sure?, Honestly?, So?; see OH.
indefensible *a.* bad, unforgivable, unpardonable; see WRONG 1.
indefinite *a.* unsure, unsettled, loose; see UNCERTAIN, VAGUE 2.
indefinitely *a.* **1.** [Vaguely] loosely, unclearly, ambiguously, indistinctly, incoherently, obscurely, indecisively, incompletely, lightly, briefly, momentarily, generally; see also VAGUELY.—*Ant.* POSITIVELY, clearly, exactly. **2.** [Without stated limit] endlessly, continually, considerably; see FREQUENTLY, REGULARLY.
indelible *a.* ingrained, enduring, strong; see PERMANENT.
in demand *a.* desired, requisite, on the market; see WANTED.
indent *v.* make a margin, range, space inward; see ORDER 3.
indentation *n.* imprint, recession, depression; see DENT.
independence *n.* sovereignty, autonomy, license; see FREEDOM 1, 2.
independent *a.* self-ruling, autonomous, unregimented; see FREE 1.
independently *a.* alone, autonomously, unilaterally, without support, separately, exclusively, regardlessly, by oneself, on one's own*; see also FREELY 2.
indestructible *a.* durable, unchangeable, immortal; see PERMANENT.
in detail *a.* minutely, item by item, part by part, step by step, inch by inch, systematically, intimately.—*Ant.* VAGUELY, generally, indefinitely.
index *n.* **1.** [An indicator] formula, rule, average; see MODEL 2. **2.** [An alphabetic arrangement] tabular matter, book index, guide to publications, bibliography, bibliographical work, card file, book list, appendix, end list, directory, dictionary; see also FILE 1, LIST, RECORD 1.
index *v.* alphabetize, arrange, tabulate; see FILE 1, LIST 1, RECORD 1.
India *n.* The Indian Empire, The East, The Fabulous East, British India, Crown Jewel, Mother India, Hindustan; see also ASIA.

Indian *a.* native-American, pre-Columbian, Amerindian; see INDIAN, *n.* 1.

Indian *n.* **1.** [American native] American aborigine, American Indian, Amerindian, red man. *Terms for Indian groups having had historical or social importance include the following—United States and Canada: Arctic Indians:* Eskimo, Aleut; *eastern or Woods Indians*; Iroquois *or* Six Nations, Mohawk, Oneida, Seneca, Cayuga, Huron, Algonquin, Mohican, Delaware, Ojibway *or* Chippewa, Sauk, Fox, Pottawattamic, Seminole, Cherokee, Choctaw, Chicasaw, Creek, Natchez, Winnebago; *Plains Indians:* Sioux, Oglala, Mandan, Iowa, Omaha, Comanche, Dakota, Crow, Osage, Apache, Kiowa, Arapahoe, Cheyenne, Pawnee; *Great Basin Indians:* Blackfoot, Ute, Paiute, Shoshone, Bannock, Modoc, Digger, Pueblo, Hopi, Navaho, Zuni; *west coast Indians;* Athabascan, Costanoa, Chinook, Nez Perce, Tlingit, Flathead, Kwakiutl, Bella Coola, Klamath, Luiseno, Pomo; *Mexico and Central America:* Maya, Aztec, Toltec, Nahuatl, Zacateca, Quiche; *South America:* Inca, Quechua, Carib, Tupi, Arawak. **2.** [A native of India] Hindu, Muslim, Brahmin; see ORIENTAL.

indicate *v.* **1.** [To signify] symbolize, betoken, intimate; see MEAN 1. **2.** [To designate] show, point to, register; see NAME 2.

indication *n.* evidence, sign, implication; see HINT, SUGGESTION 1.

indicator *n.* notice, pointer, symbol; see SIGN 1.

indict *v.* charge, face with charges, arraign; see BLAME.

indictment *n.* detention, censure, incrimination; see BLAME.

indifference *n.* unconcern, nonchalance, aloofness, coldness, insensitivity, callousness, alienation, disregard, neutrality, isolationism, heedlessness, detachment, dullness, sluggishness, stupor, coldbloodedness, disdain, cool*.

indifferent *a.* listless, cold, cool, unemotional, unsympathetic, heartless, unresponsive, unfeeling, uncommunicative, nonchalant, impassive, detached, callous, uninterested, stony, reticent, remote, reserved, distant, unsocial, scornful, apathetic, heedless, unmoved, not inclined toward, neutral, uncaring, aloof, silent, disdainful, haughty, superior, condescending, snobbish, arrogant, not caring about; see also UNMOVED 2.—*Ant.* EXCITED, aroused, warm.

indifferently *a.* **1.** [Rather badly] poorly, not very well done, in a mediocre manner; see BADLY 1, INADEQUATELY. **2.** [In an indifferent manner] nonchalantly, coolly, detached; see CALMLY.

indigestible *a.* inedible, rough, hard, unripe, green, tasteless, unhealthy, undercooked, raw, poisonous, toxic, moldy, bad-smelling, rotten, uneatable, icky*.—*Ant.* DELICIOUS, appetizing, tasty.

indigestion *n.* heartburn, nausea, acid indigestion; see ILLNESS 1, PAIN 2.

indignant *a.* upset, displeased, piqued; see ANGRY.

indirect *a.* roundabout, out-of-the-way, tortuous, twisting, long, complicated, devious, erratic, sidelong, zigzag, crooked, backhanded, obscure, sinister, rambling, long-winded, secondary, implied, oblique.—*Ant.* DIRECT, straight, immediate.

indirectly *a.* by implication, by indirection, in a roundabout way, from a secondary source, secondhand, not immediately, discursively, obliquely.—*Ant.* IMMEDIATELY, directly, primarily.

indiscreet *a.* naive, inopportune, misguided; see RASH, TACTLESS.

indiscretion *n.* recklessness, tactlessness, rashness; see CARELESSNESS.

indiscriminate *a.* random, confused, chaotic; see AIMLESS.

indispensable *a.* required, needed, essential; see NECESSARY.

indisputable *a.* undeniable, undoubted, unquestionable; see CERTAIN 2.

indistinct *a.* vague, confused, indefinite; see OBSCURE 1.

indistinguishable *a.* **1.** [Identical] like, same, equivalent; see ALIKE, EQUAL. **2.** [Indistinct] vague, invisible, dull; see OBSCURE 1, UNCERTAIN.

individual *a.* specific, personal, special, proper, own, particular, definite, lone, alone, solitary, secluded, original, distinct, distinctive, personalized, individualized, exclusive, select, single, only, reserved, separate, sole; see also PRIVATE, SPECIAL.—*Ant.* PUBLIC, collective, social.

individual *n.* human being, self, somebody; see CHILD, MAN 2, PERSON 1, WOMAN 1.

individuality *n.* personality, distinctiveness, particularity, separateness, dissimilarity, singularity, idiosyncrasy, air, manner, habit, eccentricity, oddity, rarity, way of doing things; see also ORIGINALITY.

individually *a.* separately, severally, one by one, one at a time, personally, exclusively, singly, by oneself, alone, independently, without help, distinctively, apart; see also ONLY 1.—*Ant.* TOGETHER, collectively, cooperatively.

indoctrinate *v.* inculcate, imbue, implant; see CONVINCE, INFLUENCE, TEACH.

indoctrination *n.* propagandism, instruction, brainwashing; see EDUCATION 1, TRAINING.

indoors *a.* in the house, at home, under a roof; see INSIDE 2, WITHIN.

in doubt *a.* unsure, dubious, perplexed; see DOUBTFUL, QUESTIONABLE 1, UNCERTAIN.

induce *v.* produce, effect, make; see BEGIN 1.
induced *a.* **1.** [Brought about] effected, achieved, caused; see FINISHED 1. **2.** [Inferred] thought, concluded, reasoned; see ASSUMED, CONSIDERED, DETERMINED 1.
induct *v.* conscript, initiate, draft; see ENLIST 1, RECRUIT 1.
inducted *a.* conscripted, called up, drafted; see INITIATED 2.
induction *n.* **1.** [Logical reasoning] inference, rationalization, generalization, conclusion, judgment, conjecture; see also REASON 2. **2.** [The process of electrical attraction] electric induction, magnetic induction, electromagnetic action; see ELECTRICITY. **3.** [The process of being initiated] initiation, introduction, ordination, consecration, entrance into service.
in due time *a.* eventually, at an appropriate time, in the natural course of events; see FINALLY 2, ULTIMATELY.
indulge *v.* **1.** [To humor] tickle, nourish, coddle; see ENTERTAIN 1, HUMOR. **2.** [To take part in] go in for, revel, give way to; see JOIN 2.
indulgence *n.* **1.** [Humoring] coddling, pampering, petting, fondling, babying, spoiling, placating, pleasing, toadying, favoring, kowtowing, gratifying. **2.** [Revelry] intemperance, overindulgence, self-indulgence; see GREED, WASTE 1.
indulgent *a.* fond, considerate, tolerant; see KIND.
industrial *a.* manufacturing, manufactured, mechanized, automated, industrialized, in industry, factory-made, machine-made, modern, streamlined, technical; see also MECHANICAL 1.—*Ant.* HOMEMADE, handmade, domestic.
industrious *a.* intent, involved, diligent; see ACTIVE, BUSY 1.
industriously *a.* diligently, energetically, busily; see CAREFULLY 1, VIGOROUSLY.
industry *n.* **1.** [Attention to work] activity, persistence, application, patience, intentness, perseverance, enterprise, hard work, zeal, energy, dynamism, pains, inventiveness; see also ATTENTION.—*Ant.* LAZINESS, lethargy, idleness. **2.** [Business as a division of society] big business, management, corporation officers, shareholders, high finance, entrepreneurs, capital, private enterprise, monied interests, stockholders.
inebriated *a.* intoxicated, tipsy, plastered*; see DRUNK.
in effect *a.* in reality, in fact, absolutely; see REALLY 1.
ineffective *a.* not effective, worthless, neutralized; see INCOMPETENT, WEAK 1, 2.
inefficiency *n.* incompetence, incapability, incapacity; see FAILURE 1, WEAKNESS 1.
inefficient *a.* extravagant, prodigal, improvident; see WASTEFUL.
ineligible *a.* inappropriate, unavailable, unsuitable; see INCOMPETENT, UNFIT.
ineluctable *a.* certain, inevitable, unavoidable; see INEVITABLE.
inept *a.* clumsy, gauche, ungraceful; see AWKWARD.
inequality *n.* disparity, dissimilarity, irregularity; see CONTRAST, DIFFERENCE 1, VARIATION 2.
in error *a.* mistakenly, inaccurately, by mistake; see BADLY 1, WRONG 2, WRONGLY.
inert *a.* still, dormant, inactive; see IDLE.
inertia *n.* passivity, indolence, inactivity; see LAZINESS.
in essence *a.* ultimately, fundamentally, basically; see ESSENTIALLY.
inevitable *a.* faded, sure, unavoidable, impending, inescapable, necessary, unpreventable, irresistible, destined, assured, unalterable, compulsory, obligatory, binding, irrevocable, inexorable, without fail, undeniable, fateful, doomed, determined, decreed, fixed, ordained, foreordained, decided, sure as shooting*, in the cards, come rain or shine*.—*Ant.* DOUBTFUL, contingent, indeterminate.
inevitably *a.* unavoidably, inescapably, surely; see NECESSARILY.
inexcusable *a.* unpardonable, reprehensible, indefensible; see WRONG 1.
inexpensive *a.* thrifty, low-priced, modest; see CHEAP 1, ECONOMICAL 2.
inexperience *n.* naiveté, inability, incompetence; see IGNORANCE.
inexperienced *a.* unused, unaccustomed, unadapted, unskilled, common, ordinary, unlicensed, untried, youthful, undeveloped, naive, amateur, untrained, untutored, inefficient, fresh, ignorant, innocent, uninformed, unacquainted, undisciplined, new, immature, tender, not dry behind the ears, soft, raw, green.—*Ant.* EXPERIENCED, seasoned, hardened.
inexplicable *a.* unexplainable, incomprehensible, puzzling; see OBSCURE 1.
in fact *a.* certainly, in truth, truly; see REALLY 1.
infallibility *n.* supremacy, impeccability, consummation; see PERFECTION.
infallible *a.* perfect, reliable, unquestionable; see ACCURATE 1, 2, CERTAIN 2.
infamous *a.* shocking, disgraceful, heinous; see OFFENSIVE 2, SHAMEFUL 2.
infancy *n.* cradle, babyhood, early childhood; see CHILDHOOD.
infant *n.* small child, tot, little one; see BABY, CHILD.
infantile *a.* babyish, childlike, juvenile; see CHILDISH, NAIVE.
infantry *n.* foot soldiers, infantrymen, combat troops; see ARMY 1, 2.
in fashion *a.* stylish, modish, à la mode; see FASHIONABLE, POPULAR 1.

in favor *a.* favored, feted, honored; see APPROVED, POPULAR 1.

in favor of *a.* approving, supporting, encouraging; see ENTHUSIASTIC.

infect *v.* defile, taint, spoil; see POISON.

infection *n.* **1.** [The spread of disease] contagion, communicability, epidemic, taint, corruption; see also POLLUTION. **2.** [Disease] virus, impurity, germs; see GERM.

infectious *a.* transferable, diseased, communicable; see CATCHING, CONTAGIOUS, DANGEROUS.

infer *v.* deduce, gather, reach the conclusion that; see ASSUME, UNDERSTAND 1.

inference *n.* deduction, conclusion, answer; see JUDGMENT 3, RESULT.

inferior *a.* mediocre, common, second-rate; see POOR 2.

inferiority *n.* deficiency, mediocrity, inadequacy; see FAILURE 1, WEAKNESS 1.

infest *v.* **1.** [To contaminate] pollute, infect, defile; see CORRUPT, DIRTY. **2.** [To swarm] overrun, swarm about, crowd, press, harass, jam, pack, teem, fill, flood, throng, flock, be thick as flies*; see also SWARM.

infested *a.* **1.** [Overrun] swarming with, full of, overwhelmed; see FULL 1. **2.** [Diseased] wormy, lousy, grubby; see SICK.

infielder *n.* first baseman, second baseman, third baseman; see BASEBALL PLAYER.

infiltrate *v.* permeate, pervade, penetrate; see JOIN 2.

infinite *a.* unlimited, incalculable, unbounded, boundless, unconfined, countless, interminable, measureless, inexhaustible, bottomless, without end, limitless, tremendous, immense, having no limit, never-ending, immeasurable; see also ENDLESS, UNLIMITED.—*Ant.* RESTRICTED, limited, bounded.

infinite *n.* boundlessness, infinity, the unknown; see ETERNITY, SPACE 1.

infinitely *a.* extremely, very much, unbelievably; see VERY.

infinity *n.* boundlessness, endlessness, the beyond, limitlessness, expanse, extent, continuum, continuity, eternity, infinite space; see also SPACE 1.

infirmary *n.* clinic, sickroom, sick bay; see HOSPITAL.

infirmity *n.* frailty, deficiency, debility; see WEAKNESS 1.

inflame *v.* **1.** [To arouse emotions] incense, aggravate, disturb; see EXCITE. **2.** [To cause physical soreness] redden, break into a rash, swell; see HURT 1. **3.** [To burn] kindle, set on fire, scorch; see BURN, IGNITE.

inflamed *a.* **1.** [Stirred to anger] aroused, incited, angered; see ANGRY. **2.** [Congested] raw, blistered, swollen; see HURT, PAINFUL 1, SORE 1.

inflammable *a.* combustible, burnable, liable to burn, risky, hazardous, dangerous, unsafe, flammable.—*Ant.* SAFE, fireproof, nonflammable.

inflammation *n.* congestion, soreness, infection; see PAIN 2, SORE.

inflate *v.* **1.** [To fill with air or gas] pump up, expand, swell; see FILL 1. **2.** [To swell] exaggerate, bloat, cram, expand, balloon, distend, swell up, widen, augment, spread out, enlarge, magnify, exalt, build up, raise, maximize, overestimate; see also STRETCH 1, SWELL.

inflated *a.* distended, swollen, extended, dilated, puffed, filled, grown, stretched, spread, enlarged, amplified, augmented, pumped up, exaggerated, bloated, crammed, magnified, overestimated, pompous, verbose.—*Ant.* REDUCED, deflated, minimized.

inflation *n.* **1.** [Increase] expansion, extension, buildup; see INCREASE. **2.** [General rise in price levels] financial crisis, boom, move toward higher price levels; see RISE 3.

inflection *n.* pronunciation, enunciation, intonation; see ACCENT, SOUND 2.

inflexibility *n.* stability, toughness, rigidity, stiffness, ossification, fossilization, solidity, crystallization; see also FIRMNESS.

inflexible *a.* rigid, hardened, taut; see FIRM 2, STIFF 1.

inflict *v.* deliver, strike, dispense; see CAUSE.

influence *n.* control, weight, authority, supremacy, command, domination, esteem, political influence, monopoly, rule, fame, prominence, prestige, character, reputation, force, importance, money, power behind the throne*, pull*, clout*; see also LEADERSHIP, POWER 2.

influence *v.* sway, affect, impress, carry weight, be influential, determine, make oneself felt, have influence over, lead to believe, bring pressure to bear, bribe, seduce, talk one into, alter, change, act upon, act on, lead, brainwash, direct, modify, regulate, rule, compel, urge, incite, bias, prejudice, train, channel, mold, form, shape, carry weight, exert influence, get at, be recognized, induce, convince, cajole, persuade, motivate, have an in*, pull strings, have a finger in the pie*, lead by the nose, fix*.

influenced *a.* changed, swayed, persuaded; see AFFECTED 1.

influential *a.* prominent, substantial, powerful; see FAMOUS.

influx *n.* introduction, penetration, coming in; see ENTRANCE 1.

inform *v.* instruct, relate, teach; see TELL 1.

informal *a.* intimate, relaxed, frank, open, straightforward, ordinary, everyday, inconspicuous, habitual, free, extemporaneous, spontaneous, congenial, easygoing, unrestrained, unconventional, without ceremony; see also FRIENDLY.—*Ant.* RESTRAINED, ceremonial, ritualistic.

informality *n.* casualness, familiarity, ease; see COMFORT.

information *n.* 1. [Derived knowledge] acquired facts, evidence, knowledge, reports, details, results, notes, documents, testimony, facts, figures, statistics, measurements, conclusions, deductions, plans, field notes, lab notes, learning, erudition; see also KNOWLEDGE 1. 2. [News] report, notice, message; see NEWS 1, 2.

informative *a.* instructive, informing, accurate; see DETAILED.

informed *a.* versed, knowledgeable, well-read; see EDUCATED, LEARNED 1.

infraction *n.* violation, infringement, breach; see VIOLATION.

infrastructure *n.* foundation, basic structure, base; see FOUNDATION 2.

infrequent *a.* sparse, occasional, scarce; see RARE 2.

infrequently *a.* occasionally, rarely, hardly ever; see SELDOM.

infringe *v.* transgress, violate, trespass; see MEDDLE 1.

in full *a.* complete, entire, inclusive; see WHOLE 1.

in full measure *a.* completely, sufficiently, amply; see ADEQUATELY.

infuriate *v.* aggravate, enrage, provoke; see ANGER.

infuriated *a.* furious, enraged, incensed; see ANGRY.

in general *a.* on the whole, usually, generally; see REGULARLY.

ingenious *a.* original, skillful, gifted; see ABLE, INTELLIGENT.

ingenuity *n.* inventiveness, imagination, productiveness; see ORIGINALITY.

ingrain *v.* imbue, fix, instill; see TEACH.

ingrained *a.* congenital, inborn, indelible; see NATIVE 1.

ingratitude *n.* thanklessness, disloyalty, ungratefulness, callousness, boorishness, lack of appreciation, inconsiderateness, thoughtlessness; see also RUDENESS.—*Ant.* GRATITUDE, appreciation, consideration.

ingredient *n.* constituent, component, element; see FUNDAMENTAL.

ingredients *n.pl.* parts, elements, additives, constituents, pieces, components, makings, fixings*.

inhabit *v.* occupy, stay, live in; see DWELL.

inhabitant *n.* occupant, dweller, settler, denizen, lodger, permanent resident, roomer, boarder, occupier, householder, addressee, inmate, tenant, settler, colonist, squatter, native; see also CITIZEN, RESIDENT.—*Ant.* ALIEN, transient, nonresident.

inhabited *a.* settled, owned, lived in, dwelt in, sustaining human life, peopled, occupied, colonized, developed, pioneered.

inhale *v.* gasp, smell, sniff; see BREATHE.

inherent *a.* innate, inborn, inbred; see NATURAL 1, NATIVE 1.—*Ant.* SUPERFICIAL, incidental, extrinsic.

inherently *a.* naturally, intrinsically, by birth; see ESSENTIALLY.

inherit *v.* succeed to, acquire, receive, obtain, get one's inheritance, fall heir to, come into, come in for*, take over, receive an endowment; see also GET 1.—*Ant.* LOSE, be disowned, miss.

inheritance *n.* bequest, legacy, heritage; see GIFT 1.

inhibit *v.* repress, frustrate, hold back; see HINDER, RESTRAIN.

inhibition *n.* prevention, restraint, hindrance; see BARRIER, INTERFERENCE 1.

inhuman *a.* mean, heartless, coldblooded; see CRUEL, FIERCE, RUTHLESS.

inhumanity *n.* savagery, barbarity, brutality; see CRUELTY, EVIL 1, TYRANNY.

initial *a.* basic, primary, elementary; see FIRST, FUNDAMENTAL.

initially *a.* at first, in the beginning, originally; see FIRST.

initiate *v.* open, start, inaugurate; see BEGIN 1.

initiated *a.* 1. [Introduced into] proposed, sponsored, originated, entered, brought into, admitted, inserted, put into, instituted; see also PROPOSED. 2. [Having undergone initiation] installed, inducted, instructed, grounded, passed, admitted, approved, made part of, made a member of, received, acknowledged, accepted, introduced, drafted, called up, levied, confirmed.

initiation *n.* baptism, induction, indoctrination; see INTRODUCTION 3.

initiative *n.* action, enterprise, first step; see RESPONSIBILITY 1.

inject *v.* inoculate, shoot, mainline*; see VACCINATE.

injection *n.* dose, vaccination, inoculation; see TREATMENT 2.

injure *v.* harm, damage, wound; see HURT 1.

injured *a.* spoiled, damaged, harmed; see HURT, WOUNDED.

injurious *a.* detrimental, damaging, bad; see DANGEROUS, DEADLY, HARMFUL, POISONOUS.

injury *n.* harm, sprain, damage, mutilation, blemish, cut, gash, scratch, stab, impairment, bite, fracture, hemorrhage, sting, bruise, sore, cramp, trauma, abrasion, burn, lesion, swelling, wound, scar, laceration, affliction, deformation; see also PAIN 1.

injustice *n.* wrongdoing, malpractice, offense, crime, villainy, injury, unfairness, miscarriage, infringement, violation, abuse, criminal negligence, transgression, grievance, breach, damage, infraction, a crying shame*; see also EVIL 1, WRONG.—*Ant.* RIGHT, just decision, honest verdict.

ink *n.* dye, paint, watercolor; see COLOR.

inkling *n.* indication, clue, suspicion; see HINT, SUGGESTION 1.

inland *a.* toward the interior, backcountry, backland, hinterland, interior, midland, provincial, domestic, inward; see also CENTRAL.—*Ant.* FOREIGN, international, outlying.

in light of *a.* in view of, since, taking into account; see CONSIDERING.

in line *a.* even, regular, balanced; see FLAT 1.

in line with *a.* similar to, in accord with, consonant; see HARMONIOUS 2, FIT 1.

inmate *n.* patient, convict, captive; see PATIENT, PRISONER.

in memory *a.* for, in honor of, in memoriam; see REMEMBERED.

in motion *a.* traveling, going, under way; see MOVING 1.

inn *n.* tavern, hostel, saloon; see BAR 2, HOTEL, MOTEL, RESORT 2.

inner *a.* innate, inherent, essential, inward, internal, interior, inside, nuclear, central, spiritual, private, subconscious, intrinsic, deep-seated, deep-rooted, intuitive.—*Ant.* OUTER, surface, external.

innocence *n.* 1. [Freedom from guilt] guiltlessness, blamelessness, integrity, clear conscience, faultlessness, clean hands; see also HONESTY.—*Ant.* GUILT, culpability, dishonesty. 2. [Freedom from guile] frankness, candidness, sincerity, simple-mindedness, plainness, forthrightness, inoffensiveness; see also SIMPLICITY 1. 3. [Lack of experience] purity, virginity, naiveté; see CHASTITY, IGNORANCE, VIRTUE 1.

innocent *a.* 1. [Guiltless] not guilty, blameless, impeccable, faultless, safe, upright, free of, uninvolved, above suspicion, clean*; see also HONEST 1.—*Ant.* GUILTY, culpable, blameworthy. 2. [Without guile] open, fresh, guileless; see FRANK, CHILDISH, NAIVE, NATURAL 3, SIMPLE 1. 3. [Morally pure] sinless, unblemished, pure, unsullied, undefiled, spotless, unspotted, wholesome, upright, unimpeachable, clean, virtuous, virginal, immaculate, impeccable, righteous, uncorrupted, irreproachable, unstained, stainless, moral, angelic.—*Ant.* DISHONEST, sinful, corrupt. 4. [Harmless] innocuous, powerless, inoffensive; see HARMLESS, SAFE 1.

innocently *a.* without guilt, with good intentions, ignorantly, with the best of intentions; see also NICELY 1, POLITELY.

innovation *n.* change, alteration, addition; see CHANGE 1.

innuendo *n.* aside, intimation, insinuation; see HINT, SUGGESTION 1.

inoculate *v.* immunize, inject, vaccinate; see TREAT 3.

inoculation *n.* vaccination, injection, shot; see TREATMENT 2.

inoffensive *a.* innocuous, pleasant, peaceable; see CALM 1, FRIENDLY.

in (or **over**) **the long haul** over a long period of time, for a long time, in the end; see FINALLY 2.

in part *a.* partially, somewhat, to some extent; see PARTLY, UNFINISHED 1.

in particular *a.* especially, particularly, mainly; see PRINCIPALLY.

in pieces *a.* shattered, damaged, busted*; see BROKEN 1, DESTROYED, RUINED 1, 2.

input *n.* information, knowledge, facts; see DATA.

in question *a.* open for discussion, in debate, at issue; see CONTROVERSIAL, QUESTIONABLE 1, UNCERTAIN.

inquire *v.* make an inquiry, probe, interrogate; see ASK, QUESTION.

inquiry *n.* probe, analysis, hearing; see EXAMINATION.

inquisitive *a.* curious, inquiring, speculative, questioning, meddling, searching, intrusive, challenging, analytical, scrutinizing, prying, forward, presumptuous, impertinent, snoopy*, nosy*; see also INTERESTED 1.—*Ant.* INDIFFERENT, unconcerned, aloof.

in reality *a.* in truth, truly, honestly; see REALLY 1.

in regard or **respect to** *a.* as to, concerning, with regard to; see ABOUT 2, REGARDING.

in reserve *a.* withheld, out of circulation, stored away; see KEPT 2, RETAINED 1, SAVED 2.

insane *a.* 1. [Deranged] crazy, crazed, wild, raging, frenzied, lunatic, balmy, schizophrenic, psychotic, psychopathic, paranoid, maniacal, raving, demented, rabid, unhinged, mentally unsound, mentally ill, suffering from hallucinations, deluded, daft, possessed, stark mad, out of one's mind, obsessed, touched, cracked*, screwy*, nutty*, nuts*, schizo*, loco*, wacko*, wacky*, haywire*, batty*, unglued*, off one's rocker*, not all there*; see also SICK.—*Ant.* SANE, rational, sensible. 2. [Utterly foolish] madcap, daft, idiotic; see STUPID.

insanely *a.* furiously, psychopathically, fiercely; see CRAZILY, VIOLENTLY, WILDLY.

insanity *n.* mental derangement, delusions, hysteria, anxiety, obsession, compulsion, madness, dementia, lunacy, psychosis, alienation, neurosis, phobia, mania.—*Ant.* SANITY, reason, normality.

inscription *n.* engraving, saying, legend; see WRITING 2.

in season *a.* legal to hunt, ready to pick, mature; see LEGAL, READY 2, RIPE 1, 3.

insect *n.* bug, beetle, mite, vermin, arthropod, cootie*; see also PEST 1. *Creatures commonly called insects include the following:* spider, ant, bee, flea, fly, mosquito, gnat, silverfish, hornet, leafhopper, squash bug, earwig, mayfly, walking stick, dragonfly, termite, cicada, aphid, aphis, mantis, beetle, butterfly, moth, wasp, locust, bedbug, caterpillar, grasshopper, cricket, bumblebee, honeybee, cockroach, potato bug, corn borer, boll weevil, stinkbug, firefly, Japanese beetle, yellow jacket; see also FLY 1, SPIDER.

insecticide *n.* DDT, insect poison, pesticide; see POISON.

insecure *a.* anxious, vague, uncertain; see TROUBLED.

insecurity *n.* **1.** [Anxiety] vacillation, indecision, instability; see DOUBT, UNCERTAINTY 2. **2.** [Danger] risk, hazard, vulnerability; see CHANCE 1, DANGER.

inseparable *a.* indivisible, as one, tied up, intertwined, integrated, integral, interwoven, entwined, whole, connected, attached, conjoined, united; see also JOINED, UNIFIED.—*Ant.* DIVISIBLE, separable, apart.

insert *n.* inclusion, insertion, new material; see ADDITION 1.

insert *v.* enter, introduce, inject; see INCLUDE 2.

inserted *a.* introduced, added, stuck in; see INCLUDED.

insertion *n.* insert, injection, inclusion; see ADDITION 1.

in short *a.* in summary, to put it briefly, and so; see BRIEFLY.

inside *a.* **1.** [Within] inner, in, within the boundaries of, bounded, surrounded by; see also INNER, UNDER.—*Ant.* BEYOND, after, outside. **2.** [Within doors] indoors, under a roof, in a house, out of the open, behind closed doors, under a shelter, in the interior; see also WITHIN.—*Ant.* OUTSIDE, out-of-doors, in the open.

inside *n.* inner wall, sheathing, plaster, facing, wadding; see also LINING.

insides *n.pl.* interior, inner portion, bowels, recesses, inland, middle, belly, womb, heart, soul, breast; see also CENTER 1, STOMACH.

insight *n.* intuition, acuteness, shrewdness; see JUDGMENT 1.

insignia *n.* ensign, coat of arms, symbol; see EMBLEM.

insignificance *n.* unimportance, worthlessness, indifference, triviality, nothingness, smallness, pettiness, matter of no consequence, nothing to speak of, nothing particular, trifling matter, drop in the bucket*, molehill*.

insignificant *a.* irrelevant, petty, trifling; see TRIVIAL, UNIMPORTANT.

insincere *a.* deceitful, pretentious, shifty; see DISHONEST, FALSE 1, HYPOCRITICAL, SLY.

insincerity *n.* deceit, treachery, lies; see DECEPTION, DISHONESTY, HYPOCRISY.

insinuate *v.* imply, suggest, purport; see HINT, MENTION, PROPOSE 1, REFER 2.

insinuation *n.* implication, veiled remark, innuendo; see HINT, SUGGESTION 1.

insistence *n.* persistence, perseverance, obstinacy; see DETERMINATION.

insistent *a.* persistent, obstinate, continuous; see STUBBORN.

insist upon *v.* expect, request, order; see ASK.

insolvent *a.* bankrupt, failed, broke*; see RUINED 3.—*Ant.* RUNNING, solvent, in good condition.

inspect *v.* scrutinize, probe, investigate; see EXAMINE.

inspected *a.* tested, checked, authorized; see APPROVED, INVESTIGATED.

inspection *n.* inventory, investigation, inquiry; see EXAMINATION 1.

inspector *n.* police inspector, chief detective, investigating officer, customs officer, immigration inspector, government inspector, checker, FBI agent, narc*, postal inspector; see also POLICEMAN.

inspiration *n.* **1.** [An idea] notion, hunch, whim; see FANCY 1, IMPULSE 2, THOUGHT 2. **2.** [A stimulant to creative activity] stimulus, motivation, influence; see INCENTIVE.

inspire *v.* fire, be the cause of, start off, urge, stimulate, cause, put one in the mood, give one the idea for, motivate, give an impetus.

inspired *a.* roused, animated, motivated, stimulated, energized, stirred, excited, exhilarated, influenced, set going, started, activated, moved; see also ENCOURAGED.

inspiring *a.* illuminating, encouraging, revealing; see EXCITING, STIMULATING.

in spite of *a.* nevertheless, in defiance of, despite; see REGARDLESS 2.

instability *n.* inconstancy, changeability, immaturity, variability, inconsistency, irregularity, imbalance, unsteadiness, restlessness, anxiety, fluctuation, alternation, disquiet, fitfulness, impermanence, transience, vacillation, hesitation, oscillation, flightiness, capriciousness, wavering, fickleness; see also CHANGE 1, UNCERTAINTY 2.

install *v.* set up, establish, build in, put in, place, invest, introduce, inaugurate, furnish with, fix up.

installation *n.* **1.** [The act of installing] placing, induction, ordination, inauguration, launching, coronation, establishment. **2.** [That which has been installed] machinery, wiring, lighting, insulation, power, power plant, heating system, furnishings, foundation, base.

installed *a.* set up, started, put in; see ESTABLISHED 1, FINISHED 1.

installment *n.* partial payment, periodic payment, down payment; see PART 1, PAYMENT 1.

instance *n.* case, situation, occurrence; see EXAMPLE. —**for instance** as an example, by way of illustration, in this fashion; see FOR EXAMPLE.

instant *n.* short while, second, flash, split second, wink of the eye, jiffy*; see also MOMENT 1. —**on the instant** instantly, without delay, simultaneously; see IMMEDIATELY.

instantly *a.* directly, at once, without delay; see IMMEDIATELY.
instead *a.* in place of, as a substitute, alternative, on second thought, in lieu of, on behalf of, alternatively; see also RATHER 2.
instead of *prep.* rather than, in place of, as a substitute for, in lieu of, as an alternative for.
instill *v.* inject, infiltrate, inoculate, impregnate, inseminate, implant, inspire, impress, brainwash, introduce, inculcate, indoctrinate, impart, insert, force in, imbue, put into someone's head*; see also TEACH.—*Ant.* REMOVE, draw out, extract.
instinct *n.* drive, sense, intuition; see FEELING 4.
instinctive *a.* spontaneous, accustomed, normal; see NATURAL 2.
instinctively *a.* inherently, intuitively, by instinct; see NATURALLY 2.
institute *v.* found, organize, launch; see ESTABLISH 2.
institution *n.* system, company, association; see BUSINESS 4, OFFICE 3, UNIVERSITY.
institutionalize *v.* standardize, incorporate into a system, make official; see ORDER 3, REGULATE 2, SYSTEMATIZE.
instruct *v.* educate, give lessons, guide; see TEACH.
instructed *a.* told, advised, informed; see EDUCATED, LEARNED 1.
instruction *n.* guidance, preparation, direction; see EDUCATION 1.
instructions *n.pl.* orders, plans, directive; see ADVICE, DIRECTIONS.
instructor *n.* professor, tutor, lecturer; see TEACHER.
instrument *n.* means, apparatus, implement; see DEVICE 1, MACHINE, TOOL 1.
instrumental *a.* partly responsible for, contributory, conducive; see EFFECTIVE, HELPFUL 1, NECESSARY.
in style *a.* current, chic, stylish; see FASHIONABLE, POPULAR 1.
insubordinate *a.* disobedient, dissident, defiant; see REBELLIOUS.
insubordination *n.* disobedience, defiance, disregard; see DISOBEDIENCE.
insubstantial *a.* petty, slight, inadequate; see FLIMSY, POOR 2.
insufficient *a.* skimpy, meager, thin; see INADEQUATE, UNSATISFACTORY.
insufficiently *a.* barely, incompletely, partly; see BADLY 1, INADEQUATELY.
insulate *v.* protect, coat, treat, apply insulation, tape up, glass in, pad, caulk, weatherstrip, paint.
insulation *n.* nonconductor, protector, covering, packing, lining, resistant material, caulking, weatherstripping, padding.
insult *n.* indignity, offense, affront, abuse, outrage, impudence, insolence, blasphemy, mockery, derision, impertinence, discourtesy, invective, disrespect, slight, slander, libel, slap in the face, black eye*; see also RUDENESS.—*Ant.* PRAISE, tribute, homage.
insult *v.* revile, libel, offend, outrage, vilify, humiliate, mock, vex, tease, irritate, annoy, aggravate, provoke, taunt, ridicule, abuse, deride, jeer, step on one's toes; see also CURSE, SLANDER.
insulted *a.* slandered, libeled, reviled, disgraced, defamed, vilified, cursed, dishonored, mocked, ridiculed, jeered at, humiliated, mistreated, offended, hurt, outraged, affronted, slighted, shamed; see also HURT.—*Ant.* PRAISED, admired, extolled.
insulting *a.* outrageous, offensive, degrading, humiliating, debasing, embarrassing, humbling, deriding, contemptuous.—*Ant.* RESPECTFUL, complimentary, honoring.
in support of *a.* for, condoning, approving; see FOR.
insurance *n.* indemnity, assurance, warrant, backing, allowance, safeguard, protection, coverage, support, something to fall back on*; see also SECURITY 2.
insure *v.* warrant, protect, cover; see GUARANTEE.
insured *a.* safeguarded, defended, warranteed; see GUARANTEED, PROTECTED.
insurmountable *a.* unconquerable, unbeatable, hopeless; see IMPOSSIBLE.
insurrection *n.* riot, revolt, rebellion; see DISORDER, REVOLUTION 2.
intact *a.* together, entire, uninjured; see WHOLE 2.
intake *n.* **1.** [Contraction] alteration, shortening, constriction; see ABBREVIATION, REDUCTION 1. **2.** [Profit] harvest, gain, accumulation; see PROFIT 2.
intangible *a.* indefinite, unsure, hypothetical; see UNCERTAIN, VAGUE 2.
integrate *v.* unify, combine, desegregate; see MIX 1, UNITE.
integrated *a.* nonsegregated, not segregated, for both black and white, interracial, nonracial, for all races, nonsectarian, without restriction as to race, creed or color, combined; see also FREE 1, 2, OPEN 3.
integration *n.* unification, combination, cooperation; see ALLIANCE 1, MIXTURE 1, UNION 1.
integrity *n.* uprightness, honor, probity; see HONESTY.
intellect *n.* intelligence, brain, mentality; see MIND 1.
intellectual *a.* mental, inventive, creative; see INTELLIGENT, LEARNED 1.
intellectual *n.* genius, philosopher, academician, highbrow, member of the intelligentsia, egghead*, brain*, Einstein*; see also ARTIST, PHILOSOPHER, SCIENTIST, WRITER.
intelligence *n.* **1.** [Understanding] perspicacity, discernment, comprehension; see JUDGMENT 1. **2.** [Secret information] report, statistics, facts, inside information,

account, info*, the dope*; see also KNOWLEDGE 1, NEWS 1, SECRET. **3.** [The mind] intellect, brain, mentality; see MIND 1.

intelligent *a.* clever, bright, exceptional, astute, smart, brilliant, perceptive, well-informed, resourceful, profound, penetrating, original, keen, imaginative, inventive, reasonable, capable, able, ingenious, knowledgeable, creative, responsible, understanding, alert, quick-witted, clear-headed, quick, sharp, witty, ready, calculating, comprehending, discerning, discriminating, knowing, intellectual, studious, contemplative, having a head on one's shoulders, talented, apt, wise, shrewd, smart as a whip*, on the ball*, on the beam*, not born yesterday*.—*Ant.* DULL, slow-minded, shallow.

intelligently *a.* skillfully, admirably, reasonably, logically, judiciously, capably, diligently, sharply, astutely, discerningly, knowingly, knowledgeably, farsightedly, sensibly, prudently, alertly, keenly, resourcefully, aptly, discriminatingly; see also EFFECTIVELY.—*Ant.* BADLY, foolishly, stupidly.

intelligible *a.* plain, clear, obvious; see UNDERSTANDABLE.

intend *v.* **1.** [To propose] plan, purpose, aim, expect, be resolved, be determined to, aspire to, have in mind, hope to, contemplate, think, aim at, take into one's head. **2.** [To destine for] design, mean, devote to, reserve, appoint, set apart, aim at, aim for; see also ASSIGN, DEDICATE. **3.** [To mean] indicate, signify, denote; see MEAN 1.

intended *a.* designed, advised, expected, predetermined, calculated, prearranged, predestined, meant; see also PLANNED, PROPOSED.

intense *a.* intensified, deep, profound, extraordinary, exceptional, heightened, marked, vivid, ardent, powerful, passionate, impassioned, diligent, hard, full, great, exaggerated, violent, excessive, acute, keen, piercing, cutting, bitter, severe, concentrated, intensive, forceful, sharp, biting, stinging, shrill, high-pitched, strenuous, fervent, earnest, zealous, vehement, harsh, strong, brilliant.

intensely *a.* deeply, profoundly, strongly; see VERY.

intensify *v.* heighten, sharpen, emphasize; see INCREASE, STRENGTHEN.

intensity *n.* strain, force, concentration, power, vehemence, passion, fervor, ardor, severity, acuteness, depth, deepness, forcefulness, high pitch, sharpness, emphasis, magnitude.

intensive *a.* accelerated, speeded up, hard; see FAST 1, SEVERE 1, 2.

intention *n.* aim, end, plan; see PURPOSE 1.

intentional *a.* intended, meditated, prearranged; see DELIBERATE.

intentionally *a.* specifically, with malice aforethought, in cold blood; see DELIBERATELY.

intently *a.* hard, with concentration, keenly; see CLOSELY.

intercept *v.* cut off, stop, ambush, block, catch, take away, appropriate, hijack*, head off; see also PREVENT.

interception *n.* blocking, interfering with, interposing; see INTERFERENCE 1.

interchange *n.* **1.** [The act of giving and receiving reciprocally] barter, trade, reciprocation; see EXCHANGE 1. **2.** [A highway intersection] cloverleaf, intersection, off-ramp; see HIGHWAY, ROAD 1.

intercourse *n.* **1.** [Communication] association, dealings, interchange; see COMMUNICATION. **2.** [Sex act] coitus, coition, sexual relations; see COPULATION, SEX 4.

interest *n.* **1.** [Concern] attention, curiosity, excitement; see ATTENTION. **2.** [Advantage] profit, benefit, gain; see ADVANTAGE. **3.** [Premium] credit, gain, earnings; see ADDITION 1, PROFIT 2. —**in the interest(s) of** for the sake of, on behalf of, in order to promote; see FOR.

interest *v.* intrigue, amuse, please; see ENTERTAIN 1, FASCINATE.

interested *a.* **1.** [Having one's interest aroused] stimulated, attentive, curious, drawn, touched, moved, affected, inspired, sympathetic to, responsive, struck, impressed, roused, awakened, stirred, open to suggestion, all for, all wrapped up in.—*Ant.* BORED, tired, annoyed. **2.** [Concerned with or engaged in] occupied, engrossed, partial, prejudiced, biased, taken, obsessed with, absorbed in; see also INVOLVED.—*Ant.* INDIFFERENT, impartial, disinterested.

interesting *a.* pleasing, pleasurable, fine, satisfying, fascinating, arresting, engaging, readable, absorbing, stirring, affecting, exotic, unusual, lovely, gracious, impressive, attractive, captivating, enchanting, beautiful, inviting, winning, magnetic, delightful, amusing, genial, refreshing; see also EXCITING.—*Ant.* DULL, shallow, boring.

interfere *v.* intervene, interpose, interlope; see MEDDLE 1.

interference *n.* **1.** [Taking forcible part in the affairs of others] meddling, interruption, prying, trespassing, tampering, barging in, back-seat driving; see also INTERRUPTION. **2.** [That which obstructs] obstruction, check, obstacle; see BARRIER, RESTRAINT 2.

interior *a.* inner, internal, inward; see CENTRAL, INSIDE 2.

interior *n.* **1.** [Inside] inner part, lining, heart; see CENTER 1, INSIDE. **2.** [The inside of a building] rooms, halls, stairway, vestibule, lobby, chapel, choir, gallery, basement.

interjection *n.* **1.** [Insertion] interpolation, insinuation, inclusion; see ADDITION 1. **2.** [Exclamation] utterance, ejaculation, exclamation; see CRY 1.

intermediate *a.* mean, between, medium, half-way, compromising, intermediary, neutral, standard, median, moderate, average; see also CENTRAL, COMMON 1, MIDDLE.

intermission *n.* interim, wait, respite; see PAUSE, RECESS 1.

intermittent *a.* periodic, coming and going, recurrent; see CHANGING, IRREGULAR 1.

internal *a.* **1.** [Within] inside, inward, interior, private, intrinsic, innate, inherent, under the surface, intimate, subjective, enclosed, circumscribed; see also INNER.—*Ant.* OUTER, external, outward. **2.** [Within the body] intestinal, physiological, physical, neurological, abdominal, visceral.—*Ant.* FOREIGN, alien, external.

internally *a.* within the body, beneath the surface, inwardly, deep down, spiritually, mentally, invisibly, by injection, out of sight; see also INSIDE 1, WITHIN.

international *a.* world-wide, worldly, world, intercontinental, between nations, all over the world, universal, all-embracing, foreign, cosmopolitan; see also UNIVERSAL 3.—*Ant.* DOMESTIC, national, internal.

internationally *a.* interculturally, interracially, cooperatively, globally, universally, concerning the intercourse of nations, not provincial; see also ABROAD, EVERYWHERE.

interpret *v.* give one's impression of, render, play, perform, depict, delineate, enact, portray, make sense of, read into, improvise on, re-enact, mimic, gather from, view as, give one an idea about, make something of*; see also DEFINE, DESCRIBE.

interpretation *n.* account, rendition, exposition, statement, diagnosis, description, representation, definition, presentation, argument, answer, solution; see also EXPLANATION.

interpreter *n.* commentator, writer, artist, editor, reviewer, biographer, analyst, scholar, spokesman, delegate, speaker, exponent, demonstrator, philosopher, professor, translator, linguist, language expert.

interrogate *v.* cross-examine, ask, give the third degree; see EXAMINE, QUESTION.

interrogation *n.* inquiry, query, investigation; see EXAMINATION 1.

interrupt *v.* intrude, intervene, cut in on, break into, interfere, infringe, cut off, break someone's train of thought, come between, butt in*, burst in, crash*.

interrupted *a.* stopped, checked, held up, obstructed, delayed, interfered with, disordered, hindered, suspended, cut short.

interruption *n.* check, break, suspension, intrusion, obstruction, holding over; see also DELAY, INTERFERENCE 1.

intersect *v.* cut across, break in two, intercross; see DIVIDE.

interstate *a.* internal, interior, domestic; see LOCAL 1.

interval *n.* period, interlude, interim; see PAUSE.

intervene *v.* step in, intercede, mediate; see NEGOTIATE 1, RECONCILE 2.

intervention *n.* **1.** [The act of intervening] intercession, interruption, breaking in; see INTERFERENCE 1, INTRUSION. **2.** [Armed interference] invasion, military occupation, armed aggression; see ATTACK.

interview *n.* meeting, audience, conference; see COMMUNICATION, CONVERSATION.

interview *v.* converse with, get someone's opinion, consult with, interrogate, hold an inquiry, give an oral examination to, get something for the record.

intestines *n.pl.* entrails, bowels, viscera, vitals, digestive organs, guts*; see also INSIDES.

in the air *a.* prevalent, abroad, current; see FASHIONABLE, POPULAR 1.

in the background *a.* retiring, unseen, out of sight; see OBSCURE 3, UNNOTICED, WITHDRAWN.

in the bag* *a.* assured, definite, clinched; see DEFINITE 1.

in the dark *a.* uninformed, uninstructed, confused; see DECEIVED, IGNORANT 1.

in the end *a.* at length, in conclusion, as a result; see FINALLY 2.

in the future *a.* eventually, sometime, in due time; see FINALLY 2, SOMEDAY.

in the lead *a.* ahead, winning, leading; see TRIUMPHANT.

in the market *a.* negotiating, purchasing, prepared to buy; see BUYING *n.*

in the meantime *a.* in anticipation, at the same time, meanwhile; see DURING, WHILE 1.

in the way *a.* bothersome, nagging, obstructing; see DISTURBING.

intimacy *n.* closeness, familiarity, confidence; see AFFECTION, FRIENDSHIP.

intimate *a.* close, near, trusted; see PRIVATE, SECRET 1, SPECIAL.

intimate *n.* associate, constant companion, close friend; see FRIEND, LOVER 1.

intimate *v.* suggest, imply, hint; see HINT.

intimately *a.* closely, personally, informally, familiarly, confidentially, without reserve, privately; see also LOVINGLY, SECRETLY.—*Ant.* OPENLY, reservedly, publicly.

in time *a.* eventually, in the end, at the last; see FINALLY 2, ULTIMATELY.

into *prep.* inside, in the direction of, through, to, to the middle of; see also IN 1, 2, TOWARD, WITHIN.

intolerable *a.* insufferable, unendurable, unbearable; see IMPOSSIBLE, OFFENSIVE 2, PAINFUL 1, UNDESIRABLE.

intolerance *n.* racism, chauvinism, nationalism; see FANATICISM, PREJUDICE.

intolerant *a.* dogmatic, narrow, bigoted; see PREJUDICED, STUPID.

in touch *a.* knowing, acquainted with, in communication; see FAMILIAR WITH.

intoxicant *n.* **1.** [Alcohol] alcoholic drink, liquor, booze*; see DRINK 2. **2.** [Drug] narcotic, hallucinogen, dope*; see DRUG.

intoxicate *v.* befuddle, inebriate, muddle; see CONFUSE.

intoxicated *a.* inebriated, high*, stoned*; see DIZZY, DRUNK.

intoxication *n.* infatuation, inebriation, intemperance; see DRUNKENNESS.

intricacy *n.* complication, elaborateness, complexity; see CONFUSION, DIFFICULTY 1, 2.

intricate *a.* involved, tricky, abstruse; see COMPLEX 2, DIFFICULT 1, 2, OBSCURE 1.

intrigue *n.* scheme, conspiracy, ruse; see TRICK 1.

intrigue *v.* delight, please, attract; see CHARM, ENTERTAIN 1, FASCINATE.

intrigued *a.* attracted, delighted, pleased; see CHARMED, ENTERTAINED, FASCINATED.

intriguing *a.* engaging, attractive, delightful; see BEAUTIFUL, CHARMING, HANDSOME, PLEASANT 1.

introduce *v.* **1.** [To bring in] freight, carry in, transport; see CARRY, SEND 1. **2.** [To present] set forth, submit, advance; see OFFER 1, PROPOSE 1. **3.** [To make strangers acquainted] present, give an introduction, make known, put on speaking terms with, do the honors, break the ice. **4.** [To insert] put in, add, enter; see INCLUDE 2.

introduced *a.* **1.** [Brought in] made known, put on the market, advanced, proposed, offered, imported, popularized; see also RECEIVED. **2.** [Made acquainted] acquainted with, befriended, acknowledged, recognized, on speaking terms, not unknown to one another; see also FAMILIAR WITH.

introduction *n.* **1.** [The act of bringing in] admittance, initiation, installation; see ENTRANCE 1. **2.** [The act of making strangers acquainted] presentation, debut, meeting, formal acquaintance, preliminary encounter. **3.** [Introductory knowledge] first acquaintance, elementary statement, first contact, start, awakening, first taste, baptism, preliminary training, basic principles; see also KNOWLEDGE 1. **4.** [An introductory explanation] preface, preamble, foreword, prologue, prelude, overture; see also EXPLANATION. **5.** [A work supplying introductory knowledge] primer, manual, handbook; see BOOK.

introductory *a.* initial, opening, early, prior, starting, beginning, preparatory, primary, original, provisional.—*Ant.* PRINCIPAL, substantial, secondary.

in trouble *a.* in a quandary, never free from, in bad*, in hot water*, in for it*, in the doghouse*, in a jam*, out on a limb*; see also TROUBLED.

intrude *v.* interfere, interrupt, interpose; see MEDDLE 1.

intruder *n.* prowler, thief, unwelcome guest, meddler, invader, snooper, unwanted person, interferer, interrupter, trespasser; see also ROBBER, TROUBLE 1.

intrusion *n.* interruption, forced entrance, trespass, intervention, meddling, encroachment, invasion, infraction, overstepping, transgression, nose-in*, horn-in*, muscle-in*; see also INTERFERENCE 1.

in trust *a.* in escrow, on deposit, held; see RETAINED 1.

intuition *n.* presentiment, foreknowledge, inspiration; see FEELING 4.

intuitive *a.* instantaneously apprehended, emotional, instinctive; see AUTOMATIC, NATURAL 1, SPONTANEOUS.

invade *v.* **1.** [To enter with armed force] force a landing, penetrate, fall on; see ATTACK. **2.** [To encroach upon] infringe on, trespass, interfere with; see MEDDLE 1.

invader *n.* trespasser, alien, attacking force; see ATTACKER, ENEMY.

in vain *a.* futilely, purposelessly, unprofitably; see USELESS.

invalid *a.* irrational, unreasonable, fallacious; see ILLOGICAL, WRONG 2.

invalid *n.* disabled person, incurable, paralytic, cripple, tubercular, leper, inmate; see also PATIENT.

invalidate *v.* annul, refute, nullify; see CANCEL.

invaluable *a.* priceless, expensive, dear; see VALUABLE.

invariable *a.* unchanging, uniform, static; see CONSTANT, REGULAR 3.

invariably *a.* perpetually, constantly, habitually; see CUSTOMARILY, REGULARLY.

invasion *n.* forced entrance, intrusion, aggression; see ATTACK.

invent *v.* **1.** [To create or discover] originate, devise, fashion, form, project, design, find, improvise, contrive, execute, come upon, conceive, author, plan, think up, make up, bear, turn out, forge, make, hatch, dream up*, cook up*. **2.** [To fabricate] misrepresent, fake, make believe; see LIE 1.

invention *n.* contrivance, contraption, design; see DISCOVERY.

inventive *a.* productive, imaginative, fertile; see ARTISTIC, ORIGINAL 2.

inventor *n.* author, originator, creator; see ARCHITECT, ARTIST.

inventory *n.* **1.** [A list] stock book, itemization, register; see INDEX 2, LIST, RECORD 1. **2.** [The act of taking stock] inspection, examination, investigation; see SUMMARY.

inventory *v.* take stock of, count, audit; see FILE 1, LIST 1, RECORD 1.

invert *v.* **1.** [To upset] overturn, turn upside-down, tip; see UPSET 1. **2.** [To reverse] change, rearrange, transpose; see EXCHANGE.

invest *v.* lay out, spend, put one's money into, advance, give money over, buy stocks, make an investment, loan, buy into, sink money in*, put up the dough*; see also BUY.
investigate *v.* look into, interrogate, review; see EXAMINE, STUDY.
investigated *a.* examined, tried, tested, inspected, searched, questioned, probed, considered, measured, checked, studied, researched, made the subject of an investigation, worked on, thought out, thought through, scrutinized, put to the test, gone over, gone into, cross-examined.
investigation *n.* inquiry, search, research; see EXAMINATION 1.
investigator *n.* reviewer, spy, auditor; see DETECTIVE, INSPECTOR.
investment *n.* grant, loan, expenditure, expense, backing, speculation, financing, finance, purchase, advance, bail, interest. *Types of investment include the following:* stocks, bonds, shares, securities, property, real estate, mortgage, capital, goods, insurance liens, debentures, futures, gold, grain.
in view of *a.* in consideration of, because, taking into consideration; see CONSIDERING.
invigorate *v.* stimulate, freshen, exhilarate; see ANIMATE, EXCITE.
invigorating *a.* refreshing, exhilarating, bracing; see STIMULATING.
invincible *a.* unconquerable, insuperable, impregnable; see POWERFUL 1, STRONG 1, 2.
invisibility *n.* obscurity, concealment, camouflage, indefiniteness, seclusion, cloudiness, haziness, fogginess, mistiness, duskiness, darkness, gloom, intangibility, disappearance, vagueness, indefiniteness.
invisible *a.* intangible, out of sight, microscopic, beyond the visual range, unseen, undisclosed, vaporous, gaseous.—*Ant.* REAL, substantial, material.
invisibly *a.* imperceptibly, undetectibly, out of sight; see VAGUELY.
invitation *n.* note, card, message, encouragement, proposition, proposal, call, petition, overture, offer, temptation, attraction, lure, prompting, urge, pressure, reason, motive, ground.
invite *v.* bid, request, beg, suggest, encourage, entice, solicit, pray, petition, persuade, insist, press, ply, propose, appeal to, implore, call upon, ask, have over, have in, formally invite, send an invitation to; see also ASK.
invited *a.* asked, requested, solicited, persuaded, bade, summoned; see also WELCOME.
inviting *a.* appealing, alluring, tempting, attractive, captivating, agreeable, open, encouraging, delightful, pleasing, persuasive, magnetic, fascinating, provocative, bewitching.—*Ant.* PAINFUL, unbearable, insufferable.
invoice *n.* bill of lading, receipt, bill of shipment; see STATEMENT 2.
involuntary *a.* unintentional, uncontrolled, instinctive; see AUTOMATIC, HABITUAL.
involve *v.* draw into, compromise, implicate, entangle, link, connect, incriminate, associate, relate, suggest, prove, comprise, point to, commit, bring up.
involved *a.* brought into difficulties, entangled in a crime, incriminated, embarrassed, embroiled, caught up in; see also INCLUDED.
involvement *n.* **1.** [Difficulty] quandary, crisis, embarrassment; see DIFFICULTY 1, 2. **2.** [Engrossment] intentness, study, preoccupation; see REFLECTION 1.
invulnerable *a.* strong, invincible, secure; see SAFE 1.
inward *a.* **1.** [Moving into] penetrating, ingoing, through, incoming, entering, inbound, infiltrating, inflowing. **2.** [Placed within] inside, internal, interior; see IN 1, WITHIN. **3.** [Private] spiritual, intellectual, intimate; see PRIVATE, RELIGIOUS 2.
inwardly *a.* from within, fundamentally, basically; see NATURALLY, WITHIN.
iota *n.* grain, particle, speck; see BIT 1.
irate *a.* enraged, furious, incensed; see ANGRY.
Irish *a.* Celtic, Gaelic, from the old sod*; see EUROPEAN.
irk *v.* annoy, harass, disturb; see BOTHER 1, 2.
iron *a.* ferrous, ironclad, hard, robust, strong, unyielding, dense, inflexible, heavy; see also FIRM 2, THICK 3.
iron *n.* **1.** [A metallic element] pig iron, cast iron, wrought iron, sheet iron, coke; see also METAL. **2.** [An appliance] pressing device, presser, steam iron; see APPLIANCE.
iron *v.* use a steam iron on, press, mangle, roll, finish, smooth out; see also SMOOTH.
ironical *a.* contradictory, twisted, ridiculous, mocking, satiric, paradoxical, critical, derisive, exaggerated, caustic, biting, incisive, scathing, satirical, bitter; see also SARCASTIC.
iron out *v.* compromise, settle differences, reach an agreement about; see AGREE, NEGOTIATE 1.
irony *n.* satire, wit, ridicule, mockery, quip, banter, derision, criticism, paradox, twist, humor, reproach, repartee, back-handed compliment; see also SARCASM.
irrational *a.* **1.** [Illogical] unreasonable, specious, fallacious; see ILLOGICAL, WRONG 2. **2.** [Stupid] senseless, silly, ridiculous; see STUPID.
irrationally *a.* illogically, unreasonably, stupidly; see FOOLISHLY.
irregular *a.* **1.** [Not even] uneven, spasmodic, fitful, uncertain, random, unsettled, inconstant, unsteady, fragmentary, unsystematic, occasional, infrequent, fluctuating, wavering, intermittent, sporadic, changeable, capricious, variable, shifting, unme-

thodical, jerky, up and down.—*Ant.* REGULAR, even, punctual. **2.** [Not customary] unique, extraordinary, abnormal; see UNUSUAL 2. **3.** [Questionable] strange, overt, debatable; see QUESTIONABLE 2, SUSPICIOUS 2. **4.** [Not regular in form or in outline] not uniform, unsymmetrical, uneven, unequal, craggy, hilly, broken, jagged, notched, eccentric, bumpy, meandering, variable, wobbly, lumpy, off balance, off center, lopsided, pock-marked, scarred, bumpy, sprawling, out of proportion; see also BENT.

irregularity *n.* peculiarity, singularity, abnormality, strangeness, uniqueness, exception, excess, malformation, deviation, allowance, exemption, privilege, noncomformity, innovation, oddity, eccentricity, rarity; see also CHARACTERISTIC.—*Ant.* CUSTOM, regularity, rule.

irregularly *a.* periodically, at irregular intervals, intermittently, fitfully, off and on; see also UNEXPECTEDLY.

irrelevant *a.* inapplicable, impertinent, off the topic, inappropriate, unrelated, extraneous, unconnected, off the point, foreign, beside the question, out of order, out of place, pointless, beside the point, not pertaining to, without reference to, out of the way, remote, neither here nor there; see also TRIVIAL, UNNECESSARY.

irreparable *a.* incurable, hopeless, irreversible; see BROKEN 1, DESTROYED, RUINED 1.

irresistible *a.* compelling, overpowering, invincible; see OVERWHELMING, POWERFUL 1.

irresponsible *a.* untrustworthy, capricious, flighty, fickle, thoughtless, rash, undependable, unstable, loose, lax, immoral, shiftless, unpredictable, wild, devil-may-care; see also UNRELIABLE.—*Ant.* RESPONSIBLE, trustworthy, dependable.

irrevocable *a.* permanent, indelible, lost; see CERTAIN 2, INEVITABLE.

irrigate *v.* water, pass water through, inundate; see FLOOD.

irrigation *n.* watering, flooding, inundation; see FLOOD.

irritability *n.* anger, peevishness, impatience; see ANGER, ANNOYANCE.

irritable *a.* sensitive, touchy, testy, peevish, ill-tempered, huffy, petulant, tense, resentful, fretting, carping, crabbed, hypercritical, quick-tempered, easily offended, glum, complaining, brooding, dissatisfied, snarling, grumbling, surly, gloomy, ill-natured, morose, moody, snappish, waspish, in bad humor, cantankerous, fretful, hypersensitive, annoyed, cross, churlish, grouchy, sulky, sullen, high-strung, thin-skinned, grumpy; see also ANGRY.—*Ant.* PLEASANT, agreeable, good-natured.

irritant *n.* bother, burden, nuisance; see ANNOYANCE.

irritate *v.* **1.** [To bother] provoke, exasperate, pester; see BOTHER 1, CONFUSE, DISTURB. **2.** [To inflame] redden, chafe, swell, erupt, pain, sting; see also BURN, HURT 1, ITCH.

irritated *a.* disturbed, upset, bothered; see TROUBLED.

irritating *a.* annoying, bothersome, trying; see DISTURBING.

irritation *n.* **1.** [The result of irritating] soreness, tenderness, rawness; see FEELING 4. **2.** [A disturbed mental state] excitement, upset, provocation; see ANGER, ANNOYANCE.

is *v.* lives, breathes, transpires, happens, amounts to, equals, comprises, signifies, means.

island *n.* **1.** [Land surrounded by water] isle, sandbar, archipelago; see LAND 1. **2.** [An isolated spot] haven, retreat, sanctuary; see REFUGE 1, SHELTER.

isolate *v.* confine, detach, seclude; see DIVIDE.

isolated *a.* secluded, apart, backwoods, insular, segregated, confined, withdrawn, rustic, separate, lonely, forsaken, hidden, remote, out-of-the-way, lonesome, God-forsaken; see also ALONE, PRIVATE, SOLITARY.

isolation *n.* detachment, solitude, loneliness, seclusion, segregation, confinement, separation, self-sufficiency, obscurity, retreat, privacy; see also WITHDRAWAL.

Israel *n.* Palestine, Judea, Canaan, the State of Israel, the Promised Land; see also ASIA.

issue *n.* **1.** [Question] point, matter, problem, concern, point in question, argument; see also MATTER. **2.** [Result] upshot, culmination, effect; see RESULT. **3.** [Edition] number, copy, impression; see COPY. —**at issue** in dispute, unsettled, controversial; see CONTROVERSIAL. —**take issue** differ, disagree, take a stand against; see OPPOSE 1.

issue *v.* **1.** [To emerge] flow out, proceed, come forth; see APPEAR 1. **2.** [To be a result of] rise from, spring, originate; see BEGIN 2, RESULT. **3.** [To release] circulate, send out, announce; see ADVERTISE, DECLARE, PUBLISH 1.

issued *a.* circulated, broadcast, televised, made public, announced, published, sent out, spread; see also DISTRIBUTED.

it *pron.* such a thing, that which, that object, this thing, the subject; see also THAT, THIS. —**with it*** alert, aware, up-to-date; see READY 2.

Italian *a.* Latin, Etruscan, Roman, Florentine, Milanese, Venetian, Neapolitan, Sicilian.

italicize *v.* stress, underline, print in italic type, draw attention to; see also DISTINGUISH 1, EMPHASIZE.

Italy *n.* Italia, Italian peninsula, Italian people, Italian Republic, Rome.

itch *n.* tingling, prickling, crawling, creeping sensation, rawness, psoriasis, scabbiness.
itch *v.* creep, prickle, be irritated, crawl, tickle; see also TINGLE.
item *n.* piece, article, matter; see DETAIL, PART 1.
itemize *v.* inventory, enumerate, number; see DETAIL, LIST 1.
itemized *a.* counted, particularized, enumerated; see DETAILED.
itinerant *a.* roving, nomadic, peripatetic; see VAGRANT, WANDERING 1.
itinerant *n.* nomad, wanderer, vagrant; see TRAMP 1.
itinerary *n.* course, travel plans, route; see PATH, PLAN 2, PROGRAM 2, WAY 2.
ivory *a.* creamy, cream-colored, off-white; see WHITE 1.
ivy *n.* climber, creeper, plant; see VINE.

J

jab *n.* poke, punch, hit; see BLOW.
jabber *v.* gibber, babble, mutter; see MURMUR 1, SOUND.
jack *n.* automobile jack, pneumatic jack, hydraulic jack; see DEVICE 1, TOOL 1.
jacket *n.* tunic, jerkin, parka; see CAPE 2, CLOTHES, COAT 1.
jackknife *n.* clasp knife, case knife, Barlow knife; see KNIFE.
jack-of-all-trades *n.* handyman, factotum, versatile person; see LABORER, WORKMAN.
jackpot *n.* bonanza, find, winnings; see LUCK 1, PROFIT 2, SUCCESS 2.
jack up* *v.* lift, add to, accelerate; see INCREASE, RAISE 1.
jaded *a.* cold, nonchalant, impassive; see INDIFFERENT.
jagged *a.* serrated, ragged, rugged; see IRREGULAR 4, ROUGH 1.
jail *n.* penitentiary, cage, cell, dungeon, bastille, pound, reformatory, stockade, detention camp, gaol, concentration camp, penal institution, house of detention, prison, lockup, death house, pen*, stir*, clink*, jug*, can*; see also PRISON.
jail *v.* confine, lock up, incarcerate, sentence, impound, detain, put behind bars, put in the clink*, throw away the keys*; see also IMPRISON.—*Ant.* FREE, liberate, discharge.
jailed *a.* arrested, incarcerated, in jail; see CONFINED 3, HELD, UNDER ARREST.
jam *n.* **1.** [Preserves] conserve, fruit butter, spread, marmalade, candied fruit; blackberry jam, plum jam, strawberry jam, etc.; see also JELLY. **2.** [*A troublesome situation] dilemma, problem, trouble; see DIFFICULTY 1.
jam *v.* **1.** [To force one's way] jostle, squeeze, crowd, throng, press, thrust, pack; see also PUSH 1. **2.** [To compress] bind, squeeze, push; see COMPRESS, PACK 2, PRESS 1.
jammed *a.* **1.** [Stuck fast] wedged, caught, frozen; see TIGHT 2. **2.** [Thronged] crowded, busy, congested; see FULL 1.
janitor *n.* building custodian, watchman, doorman; see ATTENDANT, CUSTODIAN.
January *n.* New Year, the new year, first month of the year; see MONTH, WINTER.
Japan *n.* the Japanese Empire, Nippon, the Land of the Rising Sun; see ASIA.
Japanese *a.* Ainu, Nipponese, East Asiatic; see ORIENTAL.
jar *n.* **1.** [A glass or earthen container] crock, pot, fruit jar, can, vessel, basin, beaker, jug, cruet, vat, decanter, pitcher, bottle, flagon, flask, phial, vase, chalice, urn; see also CONTAINER. **2.** [A jolt] jounce, thud, thump; see BUMP 1.
jar *v.* jolt, bounce, bump; see CRASH 4, HIT 1.
jargon *n.* **1.** [Trite speech] banality, patter, hackneyed terms, overused words, commonplace phrases, shopworn language, trite vocabulary, hocus-pocus; see also LANGUAGE 1. **2.** [Specialized vocabulary or pronunciation, etc.] argot, patois, lingo, broken English, idiom, pidgin English, vernacular, colloquialism, coined words, pig Latin, localism, rhyming slang, doubletalk, officialese, newspeak, journalese; see also DIALECT, SLANG.
jarring *a.* **1.** [Discordant] unharmonious, grating, rasping; see HARSH, LOUD 1, 2, SHRILL. **2.** [Jolting] bumpy, rough, uneven; see UNSTABLE 1.
jaunt *n.* excursion, trip, tour; see JOURNEY, WALK 3.
jaw *n.* jawbone, muzzle, jowl, mandible, maxilla, chops; see also BONE.
jaywalk *v.* cross a street obliquely, walk in a forbidden traffic zone, cross against a light, cut across, cross illegally.
jazz *n.* Dixieland, ragtime, modern jazz, traditional jazz, improvisation, hot music, bop, hard bop, mainstream, fusion, free jazz, swing, boogie-woogie; see also MUSIC 1.
jealous *a.* possessive, demanding, monopolizing, envious, watchful, resentful, mistrustful, doubting, apprehensive; see also SUSPICIOUS 1.—*Ant.* TRUSTING, confiding, believing.
jealousy *n.* resentment, possessiveness, suspicion; see DOUBT, ENVY.

jeep *n.* four-wheel-drive vehicle, army car, general-purpose vehicle; see AUTOMOBILE, VEHICLE.

jell *v.* set, crystallize, condense; see FREEZE 1, HARDEN, STIFFEN, THICKEN.

jelly *n.* jell, extract, preserve, gelatin; apple jelly, currant jelly, raspberry jelly, etc.; see also JAM 1.

jellyfish *n.* medusa, coelenterate, hydrozoan; see FISH.

jeopardize *v.* imperil, expose, venture; see ENDANGER, RISK.

jeopardy *n.* risk, peril, exposure; see CHANCE 1, DANGER.

jerk *n.* **1.** [A twitch] tic, shrug, wiggle, shake, quiver, flick, jiggle; see also BUMP 1. **2.** [*A contemptible person] scoundrel, rat*, twerp*; see FOOL, RASCAL.

jerk *v.* **1.** [To undergo a spasm] have a convulsion, quiver, shiver; see SHAKE 1, TWITCH 2. **2.** [To move an object with a quick tug] snatch, grab, flick; see SEIZE 1, 2.

jester *n.* comedian, buffoon, joker; see ACTOR, CLOWN, FOOL.

Jesus *n.* Saviour, Redeemer, the Son of God; see CHRIST, GOD 1.

jet *n.* **1.** [A stream of liquid or gas] spray, stream, spurt; see FOUNTAIN 1. **2.** [A jet-propelled airplane] jet plane, twin jet, supersonic transport; see PLANE 3.

jet *v.* **1.** [To gush out in a stream] spout, squirt, spurt; see FLOW. **2.** [To travel by jet airplane] take a jet, go by jet, fly; see TRAVEL.

Jew *n.* Hebrew, Israelite, Semite.

jewel *n.* bauble, gem, trinket; see DIAMOND. *Jewels include the following:* emerald, amethyst, sapphire, opal, pearl, jade, aquamarine, moonstone, agate, ruby, turquoise, topaz, garnet, jasper, coral, peridot, lapis lazuli, bloodstone, onyx, zircon.

jeweler *n.* goldsmith, diamond setter, lapidary; see ARTIST, CRAFTSMAN, SPECIALIST.

jewelry *n.* gems, jewels, baubles, trinkets, adornments, frippery, ornaments, costume jewelry, bangles; see also JEWEL.

Jewish *a.* Hebrew, Semitic, Yiddish.

jibe* *v.* agree, match, correspond; see RESEMBLE, AGREE.

jiggle *v.* shake, twitch, wiggle; see JERK 2.

jingle *n.* tinkle, jangle, clank; see NOISE 1.

jingle *v.* tinkle, clink, rattle; see SOUND.

jinx *n.* evil eye, hex, spell; see CHANCE 1.

job *n.* **1.** [Gainful employment] situation, place, position, appointment, operation, task, line, calling, vocation, handicraft, career, craft, pursuit, office, function, means of livelihood; see also BUSINESS 1, PROFESSION 1, TRADE 2, WORK 2. **2.** [Something to be done] task, business, action, act, mission, assignment, affair, concern, obligation, enterprise, undertaking, project, chore, errand, care, matter in hand, commission, function, responsibility, office, tour of duty, operation; see also DUTY 1. **3.** [The amount of work done] assignment, day's work, output; see DUTY 1. **—odd jobs** miscellaneous duties, chores, occasional labor; see WORK 2. **—on the job** busy, engaged, occupied; see BUSY 1.

jog *n.* **1.** [A slow run] trot, amble, pace; see RUN 1. **2.** [A bump] nudge, poke, shake; see BLOW, BUMP 1.

jog *v.* jog along, take one's exercise, trot; see RUN 1.

jog someone's memory *v.* bring up, recall, suggest; see REMIND.

John Doe *n.* the average citizen, John Q. Public, anyone; see MISTER.

join *v.* **1.** [To unite] put together, blend, combine, bring in contact with, touch, connect, couple, mix, assemble, bind together, fasten, attach, annex, pair with, link, yoke, marry, wed, copulate, cement, weld, clasp, fuse, lock, grapple, clamp, entwine; see also UNITE.—*Ant.* SEPARATE, sunder, sever. **2.** [To enter the company of] go to, seek, associate with, join forces, go to the aid of, place by the side of, follow, register, team up with, take up with, be in, sign on, sign up, go in with, fall in with, consort, enlist, fraternize, throw in with*, pair with, affiliate, side with, make one of, take part in, seek a place among, advance toward, seek reception, go to meet.—*Ant.* DESERT, leave, abandon. **3.** [*To adjoin] lie next to, neighbor, border, fringe, verge upon, be adjacent to, open into, be close to, bound, lie beside, be at hand, touch, skirt, parallel, rim, hem.

joined *a.* linked, yoked, coupled, allied, akin, intertwined, blended, connected, united, federated, banded, wedded, married, mixed, tied together, combined, touching, cemented, welded, fused, locked, grappled, clipped together, accompanying, associated, confederated, mingled, spliced, affixed, attached, joint, incorporated, involved, inseparable, affiliated, related, pieced together, coupled with, bound up with; see also UNIFIED.—*Ant.* SEPARATED, disparate, apart.

joint *n.* **1.** [A juncture] union, coupling, hinge, tie, swivel, link, connection, point of union, bond, splice, bend, hyphen, junction, bridge; see also BOND 1. **2.** [A section] piece, unit, portion; see LINK, PART 3. **3.** [*An establishment, particularly one providing entertainment] hangout*, dive*, hole in the wall*; see BAR 2, RESTAURANT. **4.** [*A marijuana cigarette] roach*, doobie*, reefer*, stick*; see also DRUG. **—out of joint** dislocated, disjointed, wrong; see DISORDERED.

jointly *a.* conjointly, mutually, combined; see TOGETHER.

joke *n.* prank, put-on*, game, sport, frolic, practical joke, jest, pun, witticism, play on words, quip, pleasantry, banter, drollery, retort, repartee, crack*, wisecrack*, clowning, caper, mischief, escapade, tomfoolery, play, antic, spree, farce, monkeyshine*, shenanigan*, horseplay, stunt, gag*; see also TRICK 1.

joke *v.* jest, quip, banter, laugh, raise laughter, poke fun, play, frolic, play tricks, pun, twit, trick, fool, make merry, play the fool, wisecrack*, pull someone's leg*.

joking *a.* humorous, facetious, not serious; see FUNNY 1.

jokingly *a.* facetiously, amusingly, not seriously; see HUMOROUSLY.

jolly *a.* gay, merry, joyful; see HAPPY.

jolt *n.* **1.** [A bump] jar, punch, bounce; see BLOW, BUMP 1. **2.** [A surprise] jar, start, shock; see SURPRISE 2, WONDER 1.

jostle *v.* nudge, elbow, shoulder; see PRESS 1, PUSH 1.

jot *v.* scribble, indicate, list; see RECORD 1, WRITE 1.

journal *n.* **1.** [A daily record] diary, almanac, chronicle; see RECORD 1. **2.** [A periodical] publication, annual, daily; see MAGAZINE, NEWSPAPER.

journalism *n.* reportage, news coverage, the fourth estate; see WRITING 3.

journalist *n.* commentator, publicist, member of the fourth estate; see ANNOUNCER, REPORTER, WRITER.

journey *n.* trip, visit, run, passage, tour, excursion, jaunt, pilgrimage, voyage, crossing, expedition, patrol, beat, venture, adventure, drive, flight, cruise, course, route, sojourn, traveling, travels, trek, migration, caravan, roaming, quest, safari, exploration, hike, airing, outing, march, picnic, survey, mission, ride.

journey *v.* tour, jaunt, take a trip; see TRAVEL.

jovial *a.* affable, amiable, merry; see HAPPY.

jowl *n.* mandible, chin, cheek; see JAW.

joy *n.* mirth, cheerfulness, delight, pleasure, gratification, treat, diversion, sport, refreshment, revelry, frolic, playfulness, gaiety, geniality, good humor, merriment, merrymaking, levity, rejoicing, liveliness, high spirits, good spirits, jubilation, celebration; see also LAUGHTER.—*Ant.* COMPLAINING, weeping, wailing.

joyful *a.* joyous, cheery, glad; see HAPPY.

joyous *a.* blithe, glad, gay; see HAPPY.

joy ride* *n.* reckless trip, car theft, pleasure trip; see DRIVE 1, RACE 3.

Judaism *n.* Jewish religion, Hebraism, Zionism; see RELIGION 2.

Judas *n.* betrayer, fraud, informer; see HYPOCRITE, TRAITOR.

judge *n.* **1.** [A legal official] justice, executive judge, magistrate, justice of the peace, chief justice, associate justice, judiciary, circuit judge, county judge, judge of the district court, appellate judge. **2.** [A connoisseur] expert, man of taste, professional; see CRITIC 2, SPECIALIST.

judge *v.* adjudge, adjudicate, rule on, pass on, sit in judgment, sentence, give a hearing to, hold the scales; see also CONDEMN, CONVICT.

judged *a.* found guilty or innocent, convicted, settled; see DETERMINED 1, GUILTY.

judgment *n.* **1.** [Discernment] discrimination, taste, shrewdness, sapience, understanding, knowledge, wit, keenness, sharpness, critical faculty, rational faculty, reason, rationality, intuition, mentality, acuteness, intelligence, awareness, experience, profundity, depth, brilliance, mentality, sanity, intellectual power, capacity, comprehension, mother wit, quickness, readiness, grasp, apprehension, perspicacity, soundness, genius, good sense, common sense, astuteness, prudence, wisdom, gray matter*, brains, savvy*, horse sense*.—*Ant.* STUPIDITY, simplicity, naiveté. **2.** [The act of judging] decision, consideration, appraisal, examination, weighing, sifting the evidence, determination, inspection, assessment, estimate, estimation, probing, appreciation, evaluation, review, contemplation, analysis, inquiry, inquisition, inquest, search, quest, pursuit, scrutiny, exploration, close study, observation, exhaustive inquiry; see also EXAMINATION 1. **3.** [A pronouncement] conclusion, appraisal, estimate, opinion, report, view, summary, belief, idea, conviction, inference, resolution, deduction, induction, determination, decree, opinion, supposition, commentary, finding, recommendation; see also VERDICT.

Judgment Day *n.* doomsday, Day of Judgment, retribution, visitation, chastisement, correction, castigation, mortification, end of the world, last day, particular judgment; see also JUDGMENT 1, 2.

judicial *a.* legalistic, authoritative, administrative; see LAWFUL.

judiciary *n.* justices, bench, bar; see COURT 2.

judicious *a.* well-advised, prudent, sensible; see DISCREET, RATIONAL 1.—*Ant.* RASH, ill-advised, hasty.

jug *n.* crock, flask, pitcher; see CONTAINER.

juggle *v.* **1.** [To keep in the air by tossing] toss, keep in motion, perform sleight of hand; see BALANCE 2. **2.** [To alter, usually so as to deceive] shuffle, trick, delude; see DECEIVE.

juice *n.* sap, extract, fluid; see LIQUID.

juicy *a.* **1.** [Succulent] moist, wet, watery, humid, dewy, sappy, dank, dripping, sodden, soaked, liquid, oily, sirupy; see also WET.—*Ant.* DRY, dehydrated, bone-dry. **2.** [*Full of interest] spicy, piquant, intriguing, racy, risqué, fascinating, colorful. **3.** [*Profitable] lucrative, remunerative, fruitful; see PROFITABLE.

July *n.* summer month, midsummer, baseball season; see MONTH, SUMMER.

jumble *n.* clutter, mess, hodgepodge; see CONFUSION, MIXTURE 1.

jumbo *a.* immense, mammoth, gigantic; see LARGE 1.

jump *n.* **1.** [A leap up or across] skip, hop, rise, pounce, lunge, jumping, broad jump, high jump, vault, bounce, hurdle, spring, bound, caper. **2.** [A leap down] plunge, plummet, fall; see DIVE, DROP 2. **3.** [Distance jumped] leap, stretch, vault; see HEIGHT, LENGTH 1. **4.** [*An advantage] upper hand, handicap, head start; see ADVANTAGE. **5.** [A sudden rise] ascent, spurt, inflation; see INCREASE, RISE 3.

jump *v.* **1.** [To leap across or up] vault, leap over, spring, lurch, lunge, pop up, bound, hop, skip, high-jump, broad-jump, hurdle, top. **2.** [To leap down] drop, plummet, plunge; see DIVE, FALL 1. **3.** [To pass over] cover, take, skip, traverse, remove, nullify; see also CANCEL, CROSS 1. **4.** [To vibrate] jiggle, wobble, rattle; see BOUNCE. **5.** [*To accost belligerently] attack suddenly, assault, mug*; see ATTACK.

jumping *a.* vaulting, hopping, skipping; see ACTIVE.

jumpy *a.* sensitive, restless, nervous; see EXCITED.

junction *n.* **1.** [A meeting] joining, coupling, reunion; see JOINT 1, UNION 1. **2.** [A place of meeting, especially of roads] crossroads, crossing, intersection; see ROAD 1.

June *n.* spring or summer month, month of brides, month of roses, beginning of summer; see also MONTH, SUMMER.

jungle *n.* wilderness, undergrowth, wood; see FOREST.

junior *a.* subordinate, lesser, lower; see SUBORDINATE.

junk *n.* waste, garbage, filth; see TRASH 1.

junk* *v.* dump, scrap, wreck; see DISCARD.

junkie* *n.* dope addict, doper*, head*; see ADDICT.

jurisdiction *n.* authority, range, supervision, control, discretion, province, commission, inquisition, scope, arbitration, reign, domain, extent, empire, sovereignty.

jurist *n.* attorney, judge, legal advisor; see LAWYER.

jury *n.* tribunal, panel, board; see COURT 2.

just *a.* **1.** [Precisely] exactly, correctly, perfectly; see ACCURATE. **2.** [Hardly] barely, scarcely, by very little; see HARDLY. **3.** [Only] merely, simply, no more than; see ONLY 2. **4.** [Recently] just a while ago, lately, a moment ago; see RECENTLY. **5.** [Fair] impartial, equal, righteous; see FAIR 1.

justice *n.* **1.** [Fairness] right, truth, equity; see FAIRNESS. **2.** [Lawfulness] legality, equity, prescriptive right, statutory right, established right, legitimacy, sanction, legalization, constitutionality, authority, code, charter, decree, rule, legal process, authorization; see also CUSTOM, LAW 1, POWER 2.—*Ant.* WRONG, illegality, illegitimacy. **3.** [The administration of law] adjudication, settlement, arbitration, hearing, legal process, due process, judicial procedure, jury trial, trial by jury, regulation, decision, pronouncement, review, appeal, sentence, consideration, taking evidence, litigation, prosecution; see also JUDGMENT 2, LAW 1, TRIAL 2.—*Ant.* DISORDER, lawlessness, despotism. **4.** [A judge] magistrate, umpire, chancellor; see JUDGE 1. **—do justice to** treat fairly, do right by, help; see TREAT 1. **—do oneself justice** be fair to oneself, give oneself credit, behave in a worthy way; see APPROVE.

justifiable *a.* proper, suitable, probable; see FIT 1, LOGICAL.

justification *n.* excuse, defense, reason; see APPEAL 1, EXPLANATION.

justify *v.* **1.** [To vindicate] absolve, acquit, clear; see EXCUSE. **2.** [To give reasons for] support, apologize for, excuse; see DEFEND, EXPLAIN.

justly *a.* **1.** [Honorably] impartially, honestly, frankly, candidly, straightforwardly, reasonably, fairly, moderately, temperately, even-handedly, rightly, equitably, equably, tolerantly, charitably, respectably, lawfully, legally, legitimately, rightfully, properly, duly, in justice, as it ought to be. **2.** [Exactly] properly, precisely, rationally; see ACCURATELY.

just the same *a.* nevertheless, however, in spite of that; see BUT 1.

jut *v.* extend, bulge, stick out; see PROJECT 1.

juvenile *a.* youthful, adolescent, teenage; see YOUNG 1.

K

keen *a.* **1.** [Sharp] pointed, edged, acute; see SHARP 1. **2.** [Astute] bright, clever, shrewd; see INTELLIGENT. **3.** [Eager] ardent, interested, intent; see ZEALOUS.

keenly *a.* acutely, sharply, penetratingly; see CLEARLY 1, 2, VERY, VIGOROUSLY.

keep *v.* **1.** [To hold] retain, grip, own, possess, have, take, seize, save, grasp; see also HOLD 1. **2.** [To maintain] preserve, conserve, care for; see MAINTAIN 3. **3.** [To continue] keep going, carry on, sustain; see CONTINUE 1, ENDURE 1. **4.** [To operate] administer, run, direct; see MANAGE 1. **5.** [To tend] care for, minister to, attend; see TEND 1. **6.** [To remain] stay, continue, abide; see SETTLE 5, 6. **7.** [To store] deposit, hoard, retain, store, preserve, reserve, put away, conserve, warehouse, stash away*, put away, cache; see also SAVE 3, STORE. **8.** [To prevent; *used with "from"*] stop, block, avert; see HINDER, PREVENT. **9.** [To retain] not spoil, season, put up; see PRESERVE 3. —**for keeps*** permanently, changelessly, perpetually; see FOREVER.

keep after *v.* **1.** [To pursue] track, trail, follow; see PURSUE 1. **2.** [To nag] push, remind, pester; see BOTHER 2, DISTURB.

keep an appointment *v.* show up, be on time, be there; see ARRIVE.

keep an eye on *v.* observe, investigate, look after; see GUARD, WATCH.

keep at *v.* persist, persevere, endure; see CONTINUE 1.

keep away *v.* **1.** [To remain] stay away, hold back, not come; see WAIT 1. **2.** [To restrain] keep off, hold back, defend oneself from; see HINDER, PREVENT, RESTRICT.

keep back *v.* **1.** [To delay] check, hold, postpone; see DELAY, HINDER, SUSPEND. **2.** [To restrict] enclose, inhibit, oppose; see FORBID, RESTRICT.

keep calm *v.* take one's time, keep cool, be patient; see CALM DOWN, RELAX.

keep company (with) *v.* fraternize, accompany, associate, go together, date, go with*, take up with*, hang around with*, pal around with*.

keep down *v.* reduce, deaden, muffle; see DECREASE 2, SOFTEN.

keeper *n.* guard, official, attendant; see WARDEN, WATCHMAN.

keep from *v.* **1.** [To abstain] desist, refrain, avoid; see ABSTAIN. **2.** [To prevent] prohibit, forestall, impede; see HINDER, PREVENT.

keep going *v.* progress, promote, proceed; see ADVANCE 1, IMPROVE 2.

keeping *n.* care, custody, guard; see PROTECTION 2. —**in keeping with** similar to, much the same as, in conformity with; see ALIKE.

keep in line *v.* **1.** [To behave] obey, be good, restrain oneself; see BEHAVE. **2.** [To manage] check, watch over, be responsible for; see RESTRAIN.

keep off or **out** *interj.* hands off, stay away, stop, keep off the grass, no trespassing, no hunting or fishing, private property.

keep on *v.* finish, repeat, pursue; see CONTINUE 1, ENDURE 1.

keep safe *v.* care for, chaperone, protect; see GUARD, WATCH.

keepsake *n.* memento, token, remembrance; see REMINDER.

keep to oneself *v.* be a recluse, be a hermit, cultivate solitude, avoid human companionship, stay away, keep one's own counsel; see also HIDE.

keep up *v.* support, care for, safeguard; see SUSTAIN 2.

keep up with *v.* keep step with, keep pace with, run with; see COMPETE.

keg *n.* cask, drum, vat; see BARREL, CONTAINER.

kennel *n.* doghouse, den, pound; see ENCLOSURE 1, PEN 1.

kept *a.* **1.** [Preserved] put up, pickled, stored; see PRESERVED 2. **2.** [Retained] maintained, withheld, held, guarded, watched over, reserved, on file, at hand; see also SAVED 2. **3.** [Observed] obeyed, honored, continued, discharged, maintained, carried on; see also FULFILLED.—*Ant.* ABANDONED, dishonored, forgotten.

kernel *n.* nut, core, germ; see GRAIN 1, SEED.

ketchup *n.* tomato sauce, mushroom sauce, condiment; see RELISH.

kettle *n.* cauldron, saucepan, stewpot; see POT 1.

key *n.* **1.** [Instrument to open a lock] latchkey, opener, master key, passkey, skeleton key. **2.** [A means of solution] clue, code, indicator; see ANSWER 2.

keyed up* *a.* stimulated, spurred on, nervous; see EXCITED.

keynote *a.* main, leading, official; see IMPORTANT 1, PRINCIPAL.

kick *n.* **1.** [*A blow with the foot] boot, swift kick, jolt, jar, hit; see also BLOW. **2.** [In sports, a kicked ball] punt, drop kick, place kick; see sense 1. **3.** [*Pleasant reaction] joy, pleasant sensation, refreshment; see ENJOYMENT.

kick *v.* **1.** [To give a blow with the foot] boot, jolt, punt, drop-kick, place-kick, kick off; see also BEAT 1, HIT 1. **2.** [*To object] make a complaint, criticize, carp; see COMPLAIN, OPPOSE 1.
kick about or **around** *v.* mistreat, treat badly, misuse; see ABUSE.
kickoff *n.* opening, beginning, launching; see ORIGIN 2.
kick off *v.* start, open, get under way; see BEGIN 1.
kick out* *v.* reject, throw out, eject; see DISMISS, REMOVE 1.
kid *n.* **1.** [The young of certain animals] lamb, lambkin, fawn, calf, yearling; see also ANIMAL. **2.** [*A child] son, daughter, tot; see BOY, CHILD, GIRL.
kid* *v.* tease, pretend, fool; see BOTHER 2, JOKE.
kidnap *v.* abduct, ravish, capture, steal, rape, carry away, hold for ransom, shanghai, carry off, make off with, make away with, grab, spirit away, pirate, snatch*, bundle off.—*Ant.* RESCUE, ransom, release.
kidnapped *a.* made off with, abducted, ravished, stolen, carried away, held for ransom, shanghaied, waylaid, manhandled, seized, held under illegal restraint; see also CAPTURED.—*Ant.* FREE, rescued, freed.
kidney *n.* excretory organ, urinary organ, abdominal gland; see ORGAN 2.
kill *v.* **1.** [To deprive of life] slay, slaughter, murder, assassinate, massacre, butcher, hang, lynch, electrocute, dispatch, execute, knife, sacrifice, shoot, strangle, poison, choke, smother, suffocate, asphyxiate, drown, behead, guillotine, crucify, dismember, decapitate, disembowel, quarter, tear limb from limb, destroy, give the death blow, give the *coup de grâce*, put to death, deprive of life, put an end to, exterminate, stab, cut the throat, shoot down, mangle, cut down, bring down, mow down, machine-gun, pick off, liquidate, put someone out of his misery, starve, do away with, commit murder, bump off*, rub out*, wipe out*, do in*, knock off*, finish off*, blow someone's brains out*, put to sleep*, brain*, zap*.—*Ant.* RESCUE, resuscitate, animate. **2.** [To cancel] annul, nullify, counteract; see CANCEL. **3.** [To turn off] turn out, shut off, stop; see HALT, TURN OFF. **4.** [To veto] cancel, prohibit, refuse; see FORBID.
killer *n.* murderer, manslayer, gunman, gangster, shooter, butcher, hangman, assassin, slayer, sniper, cutthroat, thug, Cain; see also CRIMINAL.
killing *a.* mortal, lethal, fatal; see DEADLY.
killing *n.* slaying, assassination, slaughter; see CRIME.
kin *n.* blood relation, member of the family, sibling; see FAMILY, RELATIVE.
kind *a.* tender, well-meaning, considerate, charitable, loving, pleasant, amiable, soft, softhearted, compassionate, sympathetic, understanding, solicitous, sweet, generous, helpful, obliging, neighborly, accommodating, indulgent, delicate, tactful, gentle, tenderhearted, kindhearted, good-natured, inoffensive, benevolent, altruistic, other-directed, lenient, easy-going, patient, tolerant, mellow, genial, sensitive, courteous, agreeable, thoughtful, well-disposed.—*Ant.* ROUGH, brutal, harsh.
kind *n.* **1.** [Class] classification, species, genus; see CLASS 1. **2.** [Type] sort, variety, description, stamp, character, tendency, gender, habit, breed, set, tribe, denomination, persuasion, manner, connection, designation.
kindergarten *n.* class for small children, pre-elementary grade, preschool training; see SCHOOL 1.
kindhearted *a.* amiable, generous, good; see HUMANE, KIND.
kindle *v.* light, catch fire, set fire; see BURN, IGNITE.
kindling *n.* firewood, tinder, coals; see FUEL, WOOD 2.
kindly *a.* generous, helpful, good; see HUMANE, KIND.
kindness *n.* **1.** [The quality of being kind] tenderness, good intention, consideration, sympathy, sweetness, helpfulness, tact, benignity, mildness, courtesy, thoughtfulness, humanity, courteousness, understanding, compassion, unselfishness, altruism, warmheartedness, softheartedness, politeness, kindliness, clemency, benevolence, goodness, philanthropy, charity, friendliness, affection, loving kindness, cordiality, mercy, amiability, forbearance, graciousness, kindheartedness, virtue.—*Ant.* CRUELTY, brutality, selfishness. **2.** [A kindly act] good service, relief, charity, benevolence, philanthropy, favor, good deed, good turn, self-sacrifice, mercy, lift, boost; see also HELP 1.—*Ant.* INJURY, transgression, wrong.
kind of* *a.* somewhat, having the nature of, sort of*; see MODERATELY.
kindred *n.* kin, relations, relatives; see FAMILY, RELATIVE.
king *n.* **1.** [A male sovereign] monarch, tyrant, prince, autocrat, czar, caesar, lord, emperor, overlord, crowned head, imperator, majesty, regal personage, sultan, caliph, shah, rajah, maharajah; see also RULER 1.—*Ant.* SERVANT, slave, subordinate. **2.** [A very superior being] lord, chief, head; see LEADER 2.
kingdom *n.* realm, domain, country, empire, lands, possessions, principality, state, dominions, sway, rule, crown, throne, subject territory.
kingship *n.* supremacy, divinity, majesty; see POWER 2, ROYALTY.

king-size *a.* big, large-size, giant; see BROAD 1, LARGE 1.

kink *n.* 1. [A twist] tangle, crimp, crinkle; see CURL, CURVE. 2. [A difficulty] hitch, defect, complication; see DIFFICULTY 1.

kinky *a.* 1. [Full of kinks] fuzzy, curled, crimped; see CURLY. 2. [*Bizarre] weird, odd, sick*; see UNUSUAL 2.

kinship *n.* affiliation, kindred, relationship, affinity, cohesion, unity, familiarity, intimacy, connection, alliance; see also FAMILY, RELATIONSHIP.

kiss *n.* embrace, endearment, touch of the lips, butterfly kiss, caress, smack*, peck*; see also TOUCH 2.

kiss *v.* salute, osculate, make love, play post office*, smack*, smooch*, pet*, neck*, make out*, blow a kiss*; see also LOVE 2.

kit *n.* 1. [Equipment] material, tools, outfit; see EQUIPMENT. 2. [A pack] poke*, knapsack, satchel; see BAG, CONTAINER.

kitchen *n.* scullery, galley, canteen, cook's room, kitchenette, mess.

kite *n.* box kite, Chinese kite, tailless kite; see TOY 1.

kitten *n.* pussy, kitty, baby cat; see ANIMAL, CAT.

knack *n.* trick, skill, faculty; see ABILITY.

knapsack *n.* backpack, kit, rucksack; see BAG, CONTAINER.

knead *v.* work, shape, twist; see PRESS 1.

knee *n.* knee joint, crook, bend, hinge, kneecap, articulation of the femur and the tibia; see also BONE.

kneel *v.* bend the knee, rest on the knees, genuflect, bend, stoop, bow down, curtsey.

knickknack *n.* gadget, bric-a-brac, curio, ornament, trifle, bauble, trinket, toy, plaything, showpiece, gewgaw*; see also TOY 1.

knife *n.* blade, cutter, sword, bayonet, cutting edge, dagger, stiletto, lance, machete, poniard, scalpel, edge, dirk, sickle, scythe, sabre, scimitar, broadsword, point, pigsticker*, toad-stabber*, shiv*; see also RAZOR. *Knives include the following:* carving, chopping, table, dinner, breakfast, dessert, grapefruit, fish, pocket, hunting, Bowie, cane, butcher, skinning, surgical, paper, pruning, oyster, putty, palette, bread, cake, serving, Boy Scout, Swiss Army.

knife *v.* 1. [To stab] spit, lance, thrust through; see HURT 1, KILL 1, STAB. 2. [*To injure in an underhanded way] trick, give a coward's blow, strike below the belt; see DECEIVE.

knight *n.* cavalier, champion, knight-errant; see ARISTOCRAT.

knit *v.* 1. [To form by knitting] spin, crochet, web, cable, net; see also SEW, WEAVE 1. 2. [To combine or join closely] intermingle, connect, affiliate; see JOIN 1.

knitted *a.* knit, crocheted, stitched; see WOVEN.

knob *n.* 1. [A projection] hump, bulge, knot, node, bend, bump, protuberance; see also LUMP. 2. [A door handle] doorknob, latch, door latch; see HANDLE 1.

knobby *a.* knobbed, lumpy, bumpy; see BENT, CROOKED 1.

knock *n.* rap, thump, whack; see BEAT 1, BLOW, INJURY.

knock *v.* tap, rap, thump; see BEAT 2, HIT 1, HURT 1.

knock down *v.* thrash, drub, kayo*; see BEAT 1, HIT 1, KNOCK OUT 2.

knock off* *v.* 1. [To kill] murder, stab, shoot; see KILL 1. 2. [To accomplish] complete, finish, eliminate; see ACHIEVE, SUCCEED 1. 3. [To stop] quit, leave, halt; see STOP 2.

knock oneself out* *v.* slave, labor, do one's utmost; see WORK 1.

knockout *n.* 1. [A blow that knocks unconscious] knockout blow, final blow, kayo*; see BLOW. 2. [*A success] excellent thing, sensation, perfection; see SUCCESS 1.

knock out *v.* 1. [To anesthetize] etherize, put to sleep, stupefy; see DEADEN. 2. [To strike down] strike senseless, render unconscious, knock a person out of his senses, knock cold*, kayo*, knock for a loop*, put out like a light*.

knock up* *v.* impregnate, make pregnant, inseminate; see FERTILIZE 2.

knot *n.* 1. [An arrangement of strands] tie, clinch, hitch, splice, ligature, bond. 2. [A hard or twisted portion] snarl, gnarl, snag, bunch, coil, entanglement, tangle, twist, twirl, whirl.

knot *v.* bind, tie, cord; see FASTEN.

knotted *a.* tied, twisted, tangled, snarled, entangled, bunched, clustered, whirled, looped, hitched, spiced, fastened, bent, warped, clinched, banded, lassoed, braided, linked, involved.—*Ant.* FREE, loose, separate.

know *v.* 1. [To possess information] be cognizant, be acquainted, be informed, be in possession of the facts, have knowledge of, be schooled in, be versed in, be conversant with, recognize, know full well, have at one's fingertips, be master of, know by heart, know inside and out, be instructed, awaken to, keep up on, have information about, know what's what*, know all the answers, have someone's number*, have the jump on*, have down cold*, know one's stuff*, know the score*, know the ropes*.—*Ant.* NEGLECT, be oblivious of, overlook. 2. [To understand] comprehend, apprehend, see into; see UNDERSTAND 1. 3. [To recognize] perceive, discern, be familiar with, have the friendship of, acknowledge, be accustomed to, associate with, get acquainted.

know how *v.* be able, have the necessary background, be trained for; see UNDERSTAND 1.

know-how* *n.* skill, background, wisdom; see ABILITY, EXPERIENCE, KNOWLEDGE 1.

knowing *a.* sharp, clever, acute; see INTELLIGENT, REASONABLE 1.

knowingly *a.* intentionally, purposely, consciously; see DELIBERATELY.

knowledge *n.* **1.** [Information] learning, lore, scholarship, facts, wisdom, instruction, book learning, enlightenment, expertise, intelligence, light, theory, science, principles, philosophy, awareness, insight, education, substance, store of learning, know-how*; see also INFORMATION 1.—*Ant.* IGNORANCE, emptiness, pretension. **2.** [Culture] dexterity, cultivation, learning; see EXPERIENCE, REFINEMENT 2.

known *a.* **1.** [Open] discovered, disclosed, revealed; see OBVIOUS 1, PUBLIC 1. **2.** [Established] well-known, published, recognized, notorious, received, accepted, noted, proverbial, certified, down pat*; see also FAMILIAR.

know-nothing *n.* imbecile, clod, illiterate; see FOOL.

knuckle under *v.* give in, give up, acquiesce; see YIELD 1.

kook* *n.* eccentric, crackpot*, loony*, cuckoo*, ding-a-ling*, nut*, screwball*, crazy*, weirdo*, wacko*, flake*, dingbat*.

kudos *n.* praise, credit, glory, fame, honor; see also PRAISE 2, HONOR 1.

L

label *n.* tag, marker, mark, stamp, hallmark, insignia, design, number, identification, description, classification; see also NAME 1.

label *v.* specify, mark, identify; see NAME 1, 2.

labeled *a.* identified, provided with identification, stamped; see MARKED 1, 2.

labor *n.* **1.** [The act of doing work] activity, toil, operation; see WORK 2. **2.** [Work to be done] task, employment, undertaking; see JOB 2. **3.** [Exertion required in work] exertion, energy, industry, diligence, strain, stress, drudgery; see also EFFORT, EXERCISE 1. **4.** [The body of workers] laborers, workers, workingmen, proletariat, work force, labor force, working people, employees.—*Ant.* EMPLOYER, capitalist, businessman. **5.** [Childbirth] parturition, giving birth, labor pains; see BIRTH.

labor *v.* toil, strive, get cracking*; see WORK 1.

laboratory *n.* workroom, lab*, research room, testing room; see also OFFICE 3.

laborer *n.* day laborer, unskilled worker, hand, manual laborer, ranch hand, farm hand, apprentice, hired man, transient worker, toiler, seasonal laborer, ditchdigger, pick and shovel man, roustabout, stevedore, miner, street cleaner, instrument, peon, flunky, lackey, hireling, hack, beast of burden*, doormat*.

labor union *n.* organized labor, American Federation of Labor and Congress of Industrial Organizations (AFL-CIO), independent union, local, labor party; see also ORGANIZATION 2.

lace *n.* **1.** [Ornamental threadwork] border, tissue, net; see DECORATION 2. **2.** [Material for binding through openings] thong, cord, band; see ROPE.

lace *v.* strap, bind, close; see FASTEN, TIE 2.

lacing *n.* bond, hitch, tie; see FASTENER, KNOT 1.

lack *n.* **1.** [The state of being lacking] destitution, absence, need, shortage, paucity, deprivation, deficiency, scarcity, insufficiency, inadequacy, privation, poverty, distress, scantiness.—*Ant.* PLENTY, sufficiency, abundance. **2.** [That which is lacking] need, decrease, want, loss, depletion, shrinkage, shortage, defect, inferiority, paucity, stint, curtailment, reduction; see also NECESSITY 2.—*Ant.* WEALTH, overflow, satisfaction.

lack *v.* want, require, have need of; see NEED.

lacking *a.* needed, deprived of, missing; see WANTING.

lacy *a.* sheer, thin, gauzy; see TRANSPARENT 1.

lad *n.* fellow, youth, stripling; see BOY, CHILD.

ladder *n. Ladders include the following:* stepladder, rope ladder, ship's ladder,aerial ladder, extension ladder, step-stool, gangway, fire escape; see also STAIRS.

ladle *n.* skimmer, scoop, vessel; see SILVERWARE.

lady *n.* **1.** [A woman] female, adult, matron; see WOMAN 1. **2.** [A woman of gentle breeding] gentlewoman, well-bred woman, woman of quality, cultured woman, highborn lady, mistress of an estate, noblewoman, titled lady; see also WOMAN 1.

ladylike *a.* womanly, cultured, well-bred; see POLITE, REFINED 2.

lag *n.* slack, slowness, tardiness, falling behind, sluggishness, backwardness.—*Ant.* PROGRESS, progression, advance.

lag *v.* dawdle, linger, fall back, loiter, tarry, straggle, get behind, slacken, slow up, fall behind, procrastinate, plod, trudge, lounge, shuffle, falter, stagger, limp, get no place fast*; see also DELAY.—*Ant.* HURRY, hasten, keep pace with.

lagoon *n.* inlet, sound, pool; see BAY, LAKE.

lair *n.* cave, home, den; see PEN 1.

lake *n.* pond, creek, loch, pool, inland sea; see also SEA. *Famous lakes include the following:* Yellowstone, Geneva, Lucerne, Arrowhead, Great Salt, Superior, Huron, Michigan, Erie, Ontario, Champlain, Tahoe, Tanganyika, Nyasa, Como, Loch Lomond.

lamb *n.* young sheep, young one, yeanling; see ANIMAL.

lame *a.* **1.** [Forced to limp] crippled, unable to walk, halt, weak, paralyzed, impaired, handicapped, defective, limping; see also DEFORMED, DISABLED. **2.** [Weak; *usually used figuratively*] inefficient, ineffective, faltering; see UNSATISFACTORY, WANTING.

lamp *n.* light, light bulb, lighting device; see LIGHT 3. *Types and forms of lamps include the following:* wick, oil, gas, electric, sun, hanging, bracket, portable, table, standing, floor, miner's, street, arc, incandescent, gasoline, night, chandelier, lantern, torch.

lampoon *n.* satire, pasquinade, travesty, parody, burlesque.

lance *n.* lancet, foil, point; see SPEAR, WEAPON.

land *n.* **1.** [The solid surface of the earth] ground, soil, dirt, clay, loam, gravel, subsoil, clod, sand, rock, mineral, metal, pebble, stone, dry land, valley, desert, hill, bank, seaside, shore, beach, crag, cliff, boulder, ledge, peninsula, delta, promontory; see also EARTH 2, MOUNTAIN 1, PLAIN.—*Ant.* SEA, stream, ocean. **2.** [Land as property] estate, tract, ranch, farm, home, lot, real estate; see also AREA, PROPERTY 2. **3.** [A country] continent, province, region; see NATION 1.

land *v.* **1.** [To come into port; *said of a ship*] dock, berth, make port, tie up, come to land, drop anchor, put in; see also ARRIVE.—*Ant.* LEAVE, weigh anchor, cast off. **2.** [To go ashore] disembark, come ashore, arrive, alight, leave the boat or ship, go down the gangplank, hit the beach*. **3.** [To bring an airplane to earth] touch down, ground, take down, alight, come in, settle, level off, come down, descend upon, make a forced landing, crash-land, nose over, overshoot, splash down, check in, undershoot, pancake, settle her down hot*, fishtail down; see also ARRIVE.

landing *n.* **1.** [The act of reaching shore] arriving, docking, making port, anchoring, dropping anchor; see also ARRIVAL 1. **2.** [The place where landing on the shore is possible] marina, pier, wharf; see DOCK. **3.** [The act of reaching the earth] setting down, grounding, getting in, arriving, deplaning, reaching an airport, splashing down, completing a mission, settling, splashdown.

landlady *n.* homeowner, apartment manager, innkeeper; see OWNER.

landlord *n.* homeowner, apartment manager, realtor, landowner, lessor, property owner, innkeeper; see also OWNER.

landmark *n.* **1.** [A notable relic] remnant, vestige, souvenir; see MONUMENT 1, RELIC. **2.** [A point from which a course may be taken] vantage point, mark, blaze, guide, marker, stone, tree, hill, mountain, bend, promontory, duck on a rock*.

landscape *n.* scene, scenery, panorama; see VIEW.

landscape *v.* do the landscaping, finish up, put in the lawn and shrubbery; see DECORATE.

landscaping *n.* lawn, shrubbery, garden; see DECORATION 2.

landslide *n.* slide, avalanche, rock slide; see DESCENT 2.

lane *n.* way, alley, passage; see PATH, ROAD 1.

language *n.* **1.** [A means of communication] voice, utterance, expression, vocalization, sound, phonation, tongue, mother tongue, articulation, metalanguage, physical language; language of diplomacy, language of chemistry, language of flowers, etc.; accent, word, sign, signal, pantomime, gesture, vocabulary, diction, dialect, idiom, local speech, broken English, pidgin English, polyglot, patois, vernacular, lingua franca, gibberish, pig Latin, debased speech; see also DIALECT, JARGON 2, WRITING 1. 2. **2.** [The study of language] morphology, phonology, phonemics, morphemics, morphophonemics, phonics, phonetics, criticism, letters, linguistic studies, history of language, etymology, dialectology, linguistic geography; see also GRAMMAR, LINGUISTICS, LITERATURE 1. *Types of languages include the following:* synthetic, inflectional, analytic, distributive, incorporating, agglutinative, computer, artificial, polysynthetic. *Indo-European languages include the following—Germanic:* Gothic, Old Saxon, Old English or Anglo-Saxon, English, Frisian, Old High German, German, Yiddish, Dutch, Afrikaans, Flemish, Old Norse, Danish, Swedish, Norwegian, Icelandic; *Celtic:* Breton, Welsh or Cymric, Cornish, Irish or Erse, Scots Gaelic, Manx; *Italic:* Oscan, Umbrian, Venetic, Latin; *Romance:* Portuguese, Galician, Spanish, Catalan, Provençal, French, Haitian Creole, Walloon, Italian, Sardinian, Romanian, Rhaeto-Romantic or Romansh or Ladin; *Greek:* Attic, Ionic, Doric, Koine; *Slavic:* Old Church Slavonic, Russian, Byelorussian, Ukrainian, Polish, Czech, Slovak, Slovene, Serbo-Croatian, Bulgarian; *Baltic:* Old Prussian, Lithuanian, Latvian or Lettish; Albanian; Armenian; *Iranian:* Old Persian, Avestan, Pahlavi, Kurdish, Persian, Pushtu or Afghan; *Indic:* Sanskrit, Pali, Prakrit, Hindi, Urdu; Tocharian; Hittite. *Other Eurasian languages include the following—Uralic:* Finnish, Estonian, Hungarian, Samoyed; *Altaic:* Turkish, Mongolian; Georgian; Abkhasian, Kabardian, Chechen; Basque; Etruscan. *For terms applying to African, Asian, and Oceanic languages see* AFRICA, ASIA, OCEANIA. *North American languages include the following—Algonquian:* Massachusetts, Delaware, Mohegan, Pasamaquoddy, Fox-Sauk-Kickapoo, Cree, Penobscot, Menomini, Shawnee, Blackfoot, Arapaho, Cheyenne; Wiyot, Yorok; Kutenai; *Salishan:* Tillamook, Lillooet; *Wakashan:* Nootka, Kwakiutl; *Muskogean;* Creek, Chocktaw-Chickasaw, Seminole; Natchez, Chitimacha; *Iroquoian:* Cherokee, Huron or Wayondot, Erie, Oneida, Mohawk, Seneca, Cayuga, Susquehanna or Conestoga; *Siouan:* Biloxi, Dakota, Mandan, Winnebago, Hidatsa, Crow; *Caddoan:* Caddo, Wichita, Pawnee; Yuchi; Aleut, Eskimo; *Penutian:* Tsimshian, Maidu, Miwok, Klamath-Modoc; Zuni; *Hokan:* Karok, Shasta, Washo, Pomo; *Mayan:* Kekchi, Quiche, Yucatec; Totonac; Mixe, Zoque, Vera Cruz; Huave; Zapotec, Chatino; Mixtec; Pueblo or Popoluca; Otomi, Pame; Tarascan; *Uto-Aztecan:* Tubatulabal, Luiseño, Tepehuan, Pima-Papago, Hopi, Huichol, Nahuatl or Aztec, Northern Paiute or Paviotso, Southern Päiute-Ute, Mono, Shoshoni-Comanche, Chemehuevi; Kiowa-Tanoan; Keresan; *Na-Dene:* Haida, Tlingit, Athabaskan; Chippewayan, Apachean, Navaho, Hupa. —**speak the same language** understand one another, communicate, get along; see AGREE.

languor *n.* lethargy, listlessness, lassitude; see INDIFFERENCE, LAZINESS.

lanky *a.* lean, bony, rangy; see THIN 2.

lantern *n.* torch, lamp, lighting device; see LIGHT 3.

lap *n.* **1.** [That portion of the body that is formed when one sits down] knees, legs, thighs, front. **2.** [The portion that overlaps] extension, projection, fold; see FLAP. **3.** [Part of a race] circuit, round, course; see DISTANCE 3, RACE 3. —**drop into someone's lap** transfer responsibility, shift blame, pass the buck*; see GIVE 1. —**in the lap of luxury** surrounded by luxury, living elegantly, prospering; see RICH 1.

lapse *n.* slip, mistake, failure; see ERROR.

lapse *v.* slip, deteriorate, decline; see WEAKEN 1.

larceny *n.* burglary, thievery, robbery; see CRIME, THEFT.

large *a.* **1.** [Of great size] huge, big, wide, grand, great, considerable, substantial, vast, massive, immense, spacious, bulky, colossal, gigantic, mountainous, immeasurable, extensive, plentiful, copious, populous, ample, abundant, liberal, comprehensive, lavish, swollen, bloated, puffy, obese, monstrous, towering, mighty, magnificent, enormous, giant, tremendous, monumental, stupendous, voluminous, cumbersome, ponderous, gross, immoderate, extravagant, super*, booming, bumper, whopping*; see also BIG 1, BROAD 1, DEEP 2, EXTENSIVE, HIGH 1.—*Ant.* LITTLE, small, tiny. **2.** [Involving great plans] extensive, extended, considerable; see GENERAL 1.

largely *a.* **1.** [In large measure] mostly, mainly, chiefly; see PRINCIPALLY. **2.** [In a large way] extensively, abundantly, comprehensively; see WIDELY.

largeness *n.* magnitude, proportion, breadth; see MEASURE 1, MEASUREMENT 2, QUANTITY, SIZE.

lariat *n.* lasso, tether, line; see ROPE.

lark *n.* songbird, warbler, philomel; see BIRD.

larva *n.* maggot, grub, caterpillar; see WORM.

lash *v.* cane, scourge, strap; see BEAT 1, HIT 1.

lass *n.* young woman, damsel, maiden; see GIRL, WOMAN.

lasso *n.* tether, lariat, noose; see ROPE.

last *a.* **1.** [Final] untimate, utmost, lowest, meanest, least, end, extreme, remotest, furthest, outermost, farthest, uttermost, concluding, hindmost, far, far-off, ulterior, once and for all, definitive, after all others, ending, at the end, terminal, eventual, settling, resolving, decisive, crowning, climactic, closing, ending, finishing, irrefutable.—*Ant.* FIRST, foremost, beginning. **2.** [Most recent] latest, newest, current, freshest, immediate, in the fashion, modish, the last word*, trendy*; see also FASHIONABLE, MODERN 1.—*Ant.* OLD, stale, outmoded.

last *n.* tail end, last one, ending; see END 4. —**at (long) last** after a long time, in the end, ultimately; see FINALLY 2. —**see the last of** see for the last time, dispose of, get rid of; see END 1.

last *v.* **1.** [To endure] remain, carry on, survive, hold out, suffer, stay, overcome, persist, sustain, maintain, stick it out*, stick with it*, go on; see also CONTINUE 1, ENDURE 1, 2. **2.** [To be sufficient] hold out, be adequate, be enough, serve, do, accomplish the purpose, answer; see also SATISFY 3.

lasting *a.* enduring, abiding, constant; see PERMANENT.

latch *n.* catch, hook, bar; see FASTENER, LOCK 1.

latch *v.* lock, cinch, close up; see CLOSE 4, FASTEN.

late *a.* **1.** [Tardy] too late, held up, overdue, stayed, postponed, put off, not on time, belated, behind time, lagging, delayed, backward, not in time; see also SLOW 2, 3.—*Ant.*

EARLY, punctual, on time. **2.** [Recently dead] defunct, deceased, departed; see DEAD 1. **3.** [Recent] new, just out, recently published; see FRESH 1. **4.** [Far into the night] nocturnal, night-loving, advanced, tardy, toward morning, after midnight. **—of late** lately, in recent times, a short time ago; see RECENTLY.

lately *a.* a short time ago, in recent times, of late; see RECENTLY.

lateness *n.* belatedness, procrastination, hesitation, tardiness, retardation, protraction, prolongation, slowness, backwardness, advanced hour, late date.—*Ant.* ANTICIPATION, earliness, promptness.

latent *a.* underdeveloped, potential, dormant, inactive.

later *a.* succeeding, next, more recent; see FOLLOWING.

lateral *a.* oblique, sidelong, side by side; see SIDE.

latest *a.* most recent, immediately prior, just finished; see LAST 1, 2.

lather *n.* suds, foam, bubbles; see FROTH.

Latin *a.* **1.** [Pertaining to ancient Rome or to its language] Roman, Romanic, Latinic. **2.** [Pertaining to southwestern Europe] Roman, Mediterranean, Italian; see EUROPEAN.

Latin *n.* Romance language, Classical Latin, Late Latin; see LANGUAGE 2.

latitude *n.* meridional distance, degree, measure, degrees of latitude; see also MEASURE 1.

latter *a.* late, last, recent; see FOLLOWING, LAST 1.

latter *n.* the most recent person referred to, the subsequent person referred to, the last named; see END 4.

laugh *n.* mirth, merriment, amusement, rejoicing, gesture, crow, shout, chuckle, chortle, cackle, peal of laughter, horselaugh, guffaw, titter, snicker, giggle, roar, snort; see also LAUGHTER.—*Ant.* CRY, sob, whimper. **—have the last laugh** defeat finally, beat in the end, overcome all obstacles; see WIN 1. **—no laughing matter** serious, grave, significant; see IMPORTANT 1.

laugh *v.* chuckle, chortle, guffaw, laugh off, snicker, titter, giggle, burst out laughing, shriek, roar, beam, grin, smile, smirk, shout, die laughing*, break up*, crack up*, howl, roll in the aisles*, be in stitches; see also SMILE.—*Ant.* CRY, sob, weep.

laughable *a.* ludicrous, comic, comical; see FUNNY 1.

laugh at *v.* deride, taunt, make fun of; see RIDICULE.

laughing *a.* chortling, giggling, chuckling; see HAPPY.

laughter *n.* chortling, chuckling, guffawing, tittering, giggling, shouting, roaring, howling, snorting; see also LAUGH.—*Ant.* CRY, weeping, wailing.

launch *v.* **1.** [To initiate] originate, start, set going; see BEGIN 1. **2.** [To send off] set in motion, propel, drive, thrust, fire off, send forth, eject; see also DRIVE 1, 2, PROPEL.

launched *a.* started, sent, set in motion; see BEGIN, DRIVEN, SENT.

launder *v.* cleanse, do the wash, wash and iron; see CLEAN, WASH 2.

laundry *n.* ironing, washing, clothes; see WASH 1.

lavatory *n.* privy, bathroom, washroom; see BATH 2, TOILET.

lavender *a. & n.* lilac, lilac-purple, bluish-red; see COLOR, PURPLE.

lavish *a.* generous, unstinted, unsparing; see PLENTIFUL 1, 2.

lavish *v.* scatter freely, give generously, squander; see SPEND, WASTE 2.

lavishly *a.* profusely, richly, expensively; see CARELESSLY, FOOLISHLY, WASTEFULLY.

law *n.* **1.** [The judicial system] judicial procedure, legal process, the legal authorities, the police, due process, precept, summons, notice, warrant, search warrant, warrant of arrest, subpoena. **2.** [Bodies of law] code, constitution, criminal law, statute law, civil law, martial law, military law, private law, public law, commercial law, probate law, statutory law, statutes, civil code, ordinances, equity, cases, common law, canon law, decisions, unwritten law, natural law. **3.** [An enactment] statute, edict, decree, order, ordinance, judicial decision, ruling, injunction, summons, act, enactment, requirement, demand, canon, regulation, commandment, mandate, dictate, instruction, legislation; see also COMMAND, ORDER 1. **4.** [A principle] foundation, fundamental, origin, source, ultimate cause, truth, axiom, maxim, ground, base, reason, rule, theorem, guide, precept, usage, postulate, proposition, generalization, assumption, hard and fast rule; see also REASON 3. **5.** [Officers appointed to enforce the law] sheriff, state police, city police; see JUDGE 1, LAWYER, POLICE. **—lay down the law** establish rules, order, prohibit; see ORDER 1.

lawbreaker *n.* felon, offender, violator; see CRIMINAL.

lawful *a.* legalized, legitimate, statutory, passed, decreed, judged, judicial, juridical, commanded, ruled, ordered, constitutional, legislated, enacted, official, enforced, protected, vested, within the law, legitimatized, established; see also LEGAL, PERMITTED.—*Ant.* ILLEGAL, unlawful, illegitimate.

lawfully *a.* licitly, in accordance with the law, by law; see LEGALLY.

lawless *a.* **1.** [Without law] wild, untamed, uncivilized, savage, native, uncultivated, barbarous, fierce, violent, barbarous, fierce, violent, tempestuous, disordered, agitated, disturbed, warlike; see also UNCON-

TROLLED.—*Ant.* CULTURED, cultivated, controlled. **2.** [Not restrained by law] riotous, insubordinate, disobedient; see UNRULY.

lawlessness *n.* irresponsibility, terrorism, chaos; see DISORDER, DISTURBANCE 2.

lawmaker *n.* lawgiver, congressman, councilman; see GOVERNOR.

lawn *n.* green, grassplot, grassland; see GRASS 2, YARD 1.

lawsuit *n.* action, prosecution, suit; see CLAIM, TRIAL 2.

lawyer *n.* professional man, legal adviser, jurist, defender, prosecuting attorney, prosecutor, attorney, solicitor, counsel, counselor, counselor-at-law, barrister, advocate, professor of law, attorney at law, public attorney, private attorney, attorney general, district attorney, Philadelphia lawyer*, legal eagle*, shyster*, mouthpiece*.

lax *a.* slack, remiss, soft; see CARELESS, INDIFFERENT.

laxative *n.* physic, purgative, diuretic, cathartic, purge, remedy, cure, dose; see also MEDICINE 2. *Common laxatives include the following;* castor oil, mineral oil, agar-agar, cascara sagrada, flaxseed, milk of magnesia, croton oil, epsom salts, cascarin compound.

lay *v.* **1.** [To knock down] trounce, defeat, club; see BEAT 1, HIT 1. **2.** [To place] put, locate, settle, deposit, plant, lodge, store, stow, situate, deposit, set; see also SET 1. **3.** [To put in order] arrange, organize, systematize; see ORDER 3.

lay aside *v.* **1.** [To place] deposit, put, set; see SET 1. **2.** [To save] lay away, collect, keep; see SAVE 3, STORE.

lay away *v.* lay aside, keep, collect; see STORE.

lay claim to *v.* appropriate, demand, take; see SEIZE 2.

lay down *v.* **1.** [To declare] assert, state, affirm; see DECLARE, REPORT 1, SAY. **2.** [To bet] game, put up, wager; see BET, GAMBLE.

lay down the law *v.* demand, stress, emphasize; see ORDER 1.

layer *n.* thickness, fold, band, overlay, lap, overlap, seam, floor, story, tier, zone, stripe, coating, flap, panel.

lay eyes on *v.* stare at, view, notice; see SEE 1.

lay hands on *v.* get, acquire, grasp; see SEIZE 1, 2.

lay into* *v.* battle, invade, fire at; see ATTACK, FIGHT.

layman *n.* nonprofessional, novice, dilettante; see AMATEUR, RECRUIT.

laymen *n.* laity, converts, congregation, neophytes, parish, parishioners, the faithful, communicants, members, believers; see also FOLLOWING.

lay off *v.* **1.** [To discharge employees, usually temporarily] fire, discharge, let go; see DISMISS, OUST. **2.** [*To stop] cease, halt, desist; see END 1, STOP 2.

layout *n.* arrangement, design, draft; see ORGANIZATION 2, PLAN 1, PURPOSE 1.

lay out *v.* lend, put out at interest, put up; see INVEST, SPEND.

layover *n.* break, stop, rest; see DELAY, PAUSE.

lay over *v.* delay, stay over, break a journey; see STOP 1.

lay plans (for) *v.* draft, design, think out; see FORM 1, INTEND 1, PLAN 2.

lay to rest *v.* inter, give burial to, take to a last resting place; see BURY 1.

lay up *v.* **1.** [To save] conserve, preserve, hoard; see SAVE 3, STORE. **2.** [To disable] injure, harm, beat up*; see HURT.

lazily *a.* indolently, nonchalantly, slackly; see GRADUALLY, SLOWLY.

laziness *n.* indolence, sloth, lethargy, inactivity, slackness, sluggishness, dullness, heaviness, inertia, drowsiness, passivity, listlessness, laxness, negligence, sleepiness, dullness, stupidity, dreaminess, weariness, apathy, indifference, tardiness, shiftlessness, procrastination; see also IDLENESS.—*Ant.* ACTION, promptitude, agility.

lazy *a.* **1.** [Indolent] indolent, idle, remiss, sluggish, lagging, apathetic, loafing, dallying, passive, asleep on the job, procrastinating, neglectful, indifferent, dilatory, tardy, slack, inattentive, careless, flagging, weary, tired.—*Ant.* ACTIVE, businesslike, indefatigable. **2.** [Slow] slothful, inactive, lethargic; see SLOW 1, 2.

lead *a.* leading, head, foremost; see BEST, FIRST, PRINCIPAL.

lead *n.* **1.** [The position at the front] head, advance, first place, point, edge, front rank, first line, scout, outpost, scouting party, patrol, advance position, forerunner; see also FRONT.—*Ant.* END, rear, last place. **2.** [Leadership] direction, guidance, headship; see LEADERSHIP. **3.** [A clue] evidence, trace, hint; see PROOF 1, SIGN 1. **4.** [A leading role] principal part, important role, chief character; see ROLE.

lead *n.* metallic lead, galena, blue lead; see ELEMENT 2, METAL.

lead *v.* **1.** [To conduct] guide, steer, pilot, show the way, point the way, show in, point out, escort, accompany, protect, guard, safeguard, watch over, drive, discover the way, find a way through, be responsible for.—*Ant.* FOLLOW, be conveyed, be piloted. **2.** [To exercise leadership] direct, manage, supervise; see MANAGE 1. **3.** [To extend] traverse, pass along, span; see REACH 1.

leaden *a.* **1.** [Made of lead] metal, pewter, galena; see METALLIC 1. **2.** [Heavy] burdensome, oppressive, weighty; see HEAVY 1. **3.** [Lead-colored] dull, pewter, blue-gray; see GRAY.

leader *n.* **1.** [A guide] conductor, lead, pilot; see GUIDE. **2.** [One who provides leadership] general, commander, director, manager, head, officer, captain, master, chieftain, governor, ruler, executor, boss, brains*; see also EXECUTIVE.

leadership *n.* authority, control, administration, effectiveness, superiority, supremacy, skill, initiative, foresight, energy, capacity; see also INFLUENCE, POWER 2.

leading *a.* foremost, chief, dominating; see BEST, PRINCIPAL.

lead on *v.* lure, entice, intrigue; see DECEIVE.

lead up to *v.* prepare for, introduce, make preparations for; see BEGIN 2, PROPOSE 1.

leaf *n.* leaflet, needle, blade, stalk, scale, floral leaf, seed leaf, sepal, petal. **—turn over a new leaf** make a new start, redo, begin again; see CHANGE 2.

leaflet *n.* handbill, circular, broadside; see PAMPHLET.

leafy *a.* leafed out, in leaf, shaded; see SHADY.

league *n.* band, group, unit; see ORGANIZATION 2.

leak *n.* **1.** [Loss through leakage] leakage, loss, flow, seepage, escape, falling off, expenditure, decrease; see also WASTE 1. **2.** [An aperture through which a leak may take place] puncture, chink, crevice; see HOLE 1. **3.** [Surreptitious news] news leak, exposé, slip; see NEWS 1, 2.

leak *v.* **1.** [To escape by leaking] drip, ooze, drool; see FLOW. **2.** [To permit leakage] be cracked, be split, have a fissure, be out of order, have a slow leak.

leakproof *a.* watertight, impervious, waterproof; see TIGHT 2.

leaky *a.* punctured, cracked, split; see BROKEN 1, OPEN 4.

lean *a.* **1.** [Thin] lank, meager, slim; see THIN 2. **2.** [Containing little fat] fibrous, muscular, sinewy, meaty, free from fat, all-meat, protein-rich.

lean *v.* **1.** [To incline] slope, slant, sag, sink, decline, list, tip, bow, roll, veer, droop, drift, pitch, bend, be slanted, be off; see also BEND, TILT. **2.** [To tend] favor, be disposed, incline; see TEND 2.

leaning *a.* inclining, tilting, out of perpendicular; see OBLIQUE.

lean on *v.* **1.** [To be supported by] rest on, be upheld by, bear on, put one's weight on, hang on, fasten on; see also LEAN 1. **2.** [To rely upon] believe in, count on, put faith in; see TRUST 1.

lean-to *n.* shelter, shanty, cabin; see HUT.

leap *v.* spring, vault, bound; see BOUNCE, JUMP 1.

learn *v.* acquire, receive, get, take in, drink in, pick up, read, master, ground oneself in, pore over, gain information, ascertain, determine, unearth, hear, find out, learn by heart, memorize, be taught a lesson, improve one's mind, build one's background, get up on*, get the signal*; see also STUDY.

learned *a.* **1.** [Having great learning; *said of people*] scholarly, erudite, academic, accomplished, conversant with, lettered, instructed, collegiate, well-informed, bookish, pedantic, professorial; see also CULTURED, EDUCATED.—*Ant.* IGNORANT, incapable, illiterate. **2.** [Showing evidence of learning; *said of productions*] deep, sound, solemn; see PROFOUND.

learned *a.* memorized, word for word, by heart; see KNOWN 2.

learning *n.* lore, scholarship, training; see EDUCATION 1, KNOWLEDGE 1.

lease *n.* document of use, permission to rent, charter; see CONTRACT, RECORD 1.

lease *v.* let, charter, rent out; see RENT 1.

leash *n.* cord, chain, strap; see ROPE.

least *a.* **1.** [Smallest] tiniest, infinitesimal, microscopic; see MINUTE 1. **2.** [Least important] slightest, piddling, next to nothing; see TRIVIAL, UNIMPORTANT. **3.** [In the lowest degree] minimal, most inferior, bottom; see LOWEST, MINIMUM. **—at (the) least** in any event, with no less than, at any rate; see ANYHOW. **—not in the least** not at all, in no way, not in the slightest degree; see NEVER.

leather *n.* tanned hide, parchment, calfskin, horsehide, buckskin, deerskin, elk hide, goatskin, sheepskin, rawhide, cowhide, snakeskin, sharkskin, lizard, shoe leather, glove leather, chamois skin, alligator hide; see also HIDE, SKIN.

leave *n.* **1.** [Permission] consent, dispensation, allowance; see PERMISSION. **2.** [Authorized absence] leave of absence, holiday, furlough; see VACATION. **—on leave** away, gone, on a vacation; see ABSENT. **—take one's leave** go away, depart, remove oneself; see LEAVE 1.

leave *v.* **1.** [To go away] go, depart, take leave, withdraw, move, set out, come away, go forth, take off, start, step down, quit a place, part company, defect, vanish, walk out, walk away, get-out, get away, slip out, slip away, break away, break out, ride off, ride away, go off, go out, go away, move out, move away, vacate, abscond, flee, flit, migrate, fly, run along, embark, say goodbye, emigrate, clear out*, cut out, pull out, push off*, cast off, scram*, split*, sign out, check out, beat it*, take a powder*, pull up stakes*.—*Ant.* ARRIVE, get to, reach. **2.** [To abandon] back out, forsake, desert; see ABANDON 2. **3.** [To allow to remain] let stay, leave behind, let continue, let go, drop, lay down, omit, forget; see also NEGLECT 1, 2.—*Ant.* SEIZE, take away, keep. **4.** [To allow to fall to another] bequeath, hand down, transmit; see GIVE 1.

leave home *v.* run off, play truant, depart; see LEAVE 1.

leave out *v.* cast aside, reject, dispose of; see DISCARD, ELIMINATE.

leave out in the cold *v.* ignore, slight, neglect; see ABANDON 2.

leave to *v.* bequeath, hand down, pass on; see GIVE 1.

leave word *v.* inform, let know, report; see TELL 1.

leavings *n.pl.* remains, residue, garbage; see TRASH 1.

lecture *n.* **1.** [A speech] discourse, instruction, lesson; see EDUCATION 1, SPEECH 3. **2.** [A reprimand] rebuke, talking to, dressing down.

lecture *v.* **1.** [To give a speech] talk, instruct, teach; see ADDRESS 2, TEACH. **2.** [To rebuke] scold, reprimand, admonish, give a going-over*, give a piece of one's mind*; see also SCOLD.

led *a.* taken, escorted, guided; see ACCOMPANIED.

ledge *n.* shelf, mantle, strip, bar, step, ridge, reef, rim, bench, edge, path, route, way, walk, track, trail.

leech *n.* **1.** [A parasite] tapeworm, hookworm, bloodsucker; see PARASITE 1. **2.** [Dependent] parasite, hanger-on, sponger*; see WEAKLING.

leeward *a.* protected, screened, safe; see CALM 2.

leeway *n.* space, margin, latitude; see EXTENT.

left *a.* **1.** [Opposite to right] leftward, left-hand, near, sinister, larboard, port, port-side.—*Ant.* RIGHT, right-hand, starboard. **2.** [Remaining] staying, continuing, over; see EXTRA. **3.** [Radical] left-wing, liberal, progressive; see RADICAL 2, REVOLUTIONARY 1. **4.** [Departed] gone out, absent, lacking; see GONE 1.

left *n.* left hand, left side, left part, port, not the right, not the center; see also POSITION 1.

leftist *n.* socialist, anarchist, communist; see LIBERAL, RADICAL.

left out *a.* lost, neglected, removed; see LOST 1.

leftover *a.* remaining, unwanted, unused, residual, uneaten, unconsumed, untouched, perfectly good; see also EXTRA.

leftovers *n.pl.* leavings, scraps, debris; see FOOD, TRASH 1.

left-wing *a.* leftist, not conservative, reform; see LIBERAL, RADICAL 2.

leg *n.* part, member, lower appendage, hind leg, foreleg, back leg, front leg, left leg, right leg, shank; see also LIMB 2. **—not have a leg to stand on*** be unreasonable, make rash statements, have no defense; see MISTAKE. **—on one's (or its) last legs*** decaying, not far from breakdown, old; see DYING 2, WORN 2. **—pull someone's leg*** make fun of, fool, play a trick on; see DECEIVE.

legal *a.* lawful, constitutional, permissible, allowable, allowed, proper, legalized, sanctioned, legitimate, right, just, justifiable, justified, fair, authorized, accustomed, due, rightful, warranted, admitted, sound, granted, acknowledged, equitable, within the law, protected, enforced, judged, decreed, statutory, contractual, customary, chartered, clean*, legit*, straight*, on the up and up*; see also LAWFUL, PERMITTED.—*Ant.* ILLEGAL, unlawful, prohibited.

legality *n.* legitimacy, lawfulness, authority; see LAW 1.

legalize *v.* authorize, formulate, sanction; see APPROVE.

legally *a.* lawfully, legitimately, permissibly, licitly, enforcibly, allowably, admittedly, juridically, constitutionally, with due process of law, by statute, by law, in the eyes of the law, in accordance with law, in accordance with the constitution; see also RIGHTFULLY.—*Ant.* illegally, unconstitutionally, illicitly.

legend *n.* folk tale, saga, fable; see MYTH, STORY.

legendary *a.* fabulous, mythical, mythological, fanciful, imaginative, created, invented, allegorical, apocryphal, improbable, imaginary, dubious, not historical, doubtful, romantic, storied, unverifiable; see also IMAGINARY.

legerdemain *n.* deceit, trickery, deception; see DECEPTION, TRICK 1.

legible *a.* distinct, plain, sharp; see CLEAR 2.

legion *n.* multitude, body, group; see CROWD, GATHERING.

legislate *v.* make laws, pass, constitute; see ENACT.

legislation *n.* bill, enactment, act; see LAW 3.

legislative *a.* lawmaking, enacting, decreeing, ordaining, lawgiving, congressional, parliamentarian, senatorial, parliamentary, by the legislature.

legislator *n.* lawmaker, lawgiver, assemblyman, representative, congressman, congresswoman, senator, member of parliament, floor leader, councilman, councilwoman, alderman; see also EXECUTIVE.

legislature *n.* lawmakers, congress, parliament, chamber, assembly, senate, house, congress, elected representatives, soviet, plenum, law-making body, voice of the people.

legitimate *a.* **1.** [In accordance with legal provisions] licit, statutory, authorized; see LAWFUL, LEGAL. **2.** [Logical] reasonable, probable, consistent; see LOGICAL, UNDERSTANDABLE. **3.** [Authentic] verifiable, valid, reliable; see GENUINE 1, 2.

leisure *n.* freedom, free time, spare time, spare moments, relaxation, recreation, ease, recess, holiday, leave of absence, convenience, idle hours, opportunity; see also REST 1, VACATION.—*Ant.* WORK, toil, travail. —**at leisure** idle, resting, not busy; see RESTING 1. —**at one's leisure** when one has time, at one's convenience, at an early opportunity; see WHENEVER.

leisurely *a.* slowly, unhurriedly, lazily, deliberately, calmly, inactively, taking one's time, gradually, sluggishly, lethargically, indolently, listlessly.—*Ant.* QUICKLY, rapidly, hastily.

lemon *n.* citrus fruit, citron, food; see FRUIT.

lend *v.* advance, provide with, let out, furnish, permit to borrow, allow, trust with, lend on security, extend credit, entrust, accommodate.—*Ant.* BORROW, repay, pay back.

lend a hand *v.* assist, aid, succor; see HELP.

lender *n.* moneylender, bank, loan company; see BANKER, DONOR.

length *n.* **1.** [Linear distance] space, measure, span, reach, range, longitude, remoteness, magnitude, compass, portion, dimension, unit, radius, diameter, longness, mileage, stretch, extensiveness, spaciousness, tallness, height, expansion; see also EXPANSE, EXTENT.—*Ant.* NEARNESS, shortness, closeness. **2.** [Duration] period, interval, season, year, month, week, day, minute, limit; see also TIME 1.

lengthen *v.* **1.** [To make longer] extend, stretch, protract; see INCREASE. **2.** [To grow longer] produce, increase, expand; see GROW 1.

lengthwise *a.* longitudinally, the long way, along, endlong, from end to end, from stem to stern, overall, from head to foot, from top to bottom; see also ALONGSIDE.

lengthy *a.* tedious, not brief, long; see DULL 4.

lenient *a.* soft, mild, tolerant; see KIND.

lens *n.* microscope, camera, spectacles; see GLASS.

leopard *n.* panther, hunting leopard, jaguar; see ANIMAL, CAT 2.

lesbian *n.* gay, Sapphist, homosexual; see HOMOSEXUAL.

less *a.* smaller, lower, not so much as, not as much, lesser, minor, fewer, reduced, declined, in decline, depressed, inferior, secondary, subordinate, beneath, minus, deficient, diminished, shortened, limited; see also SHORTER.—*Ant.* MORE, more than, longer.

lessen *v.* **1.** [To grow less] diminish, dwindle, decline; see DECREASE 1. **2.** [To make less] reduce, diminish, slack up; see DECREASE 2.

lessening *a.* decreasing, declining, waning, dropping, diminishing, abating, slowing down, dwindling, sinking, sagging, subsiding, moderating, slackening, ebbing, lowering, shrinking, drying up, shriveling up, softening, weakening, decaying, narrowing down, drooping, wasting, running low, running down, dying away, dying down, wearing off, wearing out, wearing away, wearing down, falling off, slacking off, growing less and less, losing momentum, slumping, plunging, plummeting, going down, in reverse, getting worse, getting slower.

lesser *a.* inferior, minor, secondary; see SUBORDINATE.

lesson *n.* drill, assignment, reading; see JOB 2.

let *v.* **1.** [To permit] suffer, give permission, allow, condone, approve, authorize, consent, permit, tolerate; see also ALLOW. **2.** [To rent] lease, hire, sublet; see RENT 1.

let alone *v.* ignore, forsake, abandon; see LEAVE 3, NEGLECT 2.

letdown *n.* frustration, setback, disillusionment; see DISAPPOINTMENT 1.

let down *v.* disappoint, disillusion, not support; see ABANDON 2, FAIL 1.

let go *v.* dismiss, release, part with; see ABANDON 1.

lethal *a.* fatal, mortal, malignant; see DEADLY, HARMFUL, POISONOUS.

let in *v.* admit, allow to enter, give admission to; see RECEIVE 4.

let off *v.* leave, excuse, let go, remove; see also ABANDON 1.

let on* *v.* imply, indicate, suggest; see HINT.

let out *v.* liberate, let go, eject; see FREE.

letter *n.* **1.** [A unit of the alphabet] capital, upper case, lower case, small letter, vowel, consonant, digraph, rune, stop, plosive, fricative, diphthong, nasal, dental, glottal, gutteral; see also CONSONANT, VOWEL. **2.** [A written communication] note, epistle, missive, message, memorandum, report, line. *Types of letters include the following:* business, form, circular, drop, open, personal; billet-doux, postcard, postal, direct mail advertising, junk mail*. —**to the letter** just as directed, perfectly, precisely; see PERFECTLY.

let the cat out of the bag *v.* divulge, disclose, let out; see REVEAL, TELL 1.

letup *n.* interval, recess, respite; see PAUSE.

let up *v.* cease, release, slow down; see SLOW 1, STOP 2.

level *a.* **1.** [Smooth] polished, rolled, planed; see FLAT 1, SMOOTH 1. **2.** [Of an even height] regular, equal, uniform, flush, of the same height, same, constant, straight, balanced, steady, stable, trim, precise, exact, matched, unbroken, on a line, lined up, aligned, uninterrupted, continuous; see also SMOOTH 1.—*Ant.* IRREGULAR, uneven, crooked. **3.** [Horizontal] plane, leveled, lying prone, in the same plane, on one plane; see also FLAT 1. —**one's level best*** one's best, the best one can do, all one's effort; see BEST. —**on the level*** fair, sincere, truthful; see HONEST 1.

level *v.* **1.** [To straighten] surface, bulldoze, equalize; see SMOOTH, STRAIGHTEN. **2.** [To demolish] ruin, waste, wreck; see DESTROY. **3.** [*To be honest with] be frank with, come to terms, be open and aboveboard; see DECLARE.

level-headed *a.* wise, practical, prudent; see RATIONAL 1, REASONABLE 1.

level off *v.* level out, find a level, reach an equilibrium; see DECREASE 1, STRAIGHTEN.

lever *n.* lifter, pry, leverage, pry bar, pinch bar, crowbar, handspike, arm, advantage; see also TOOL 1.

leverage *n.* purchase, lift, hold; see SUPPORT 2.

levied *a.* exacted, taken, collected; see TAXED 1.

levy *n.* toll, duty, custom; see TAX 1.

lewd *a.* **1.** [Suggestive of lewdness] ribald, smutty, indecent; see sense 2 and SENSUAL 2. **2.** [Inclined to lewdness] lustful, wanton, lascivious, libidinous, licentious, lecherous, profligate, dissolute, carnal, sensual, debauched, corrupt, unchaste, depraved, unbridled, ruttish, nymphomaniacal, prurient, concupiscent, incontinent, incestuous, goatish, horny*, in heat*; see also VULGAR.—*Ant.* PURE, chaste, modest.

lewdly *a.* wantonly, shockingly, indecently, lasciviously, lecherously, libidinously, unchastely, carnally, dissolutely, immodestly, voluptuously, sensually, incontinently, indelicately, in a lewd manner, with lewd gestures, in a suggestive manner.

lewdness *n.* indecency, unchastity, incontinence, vulgarity, lechery, wantonness, lasciviousness, sensuality, licentiousness, voluptuousness, lecherousness, profligacy, dissoluteness, obscenity, scurrility, coarseness, carnal passion, grossness, sensuous desire, salaciousness, pornography, lust, depravity, carnality, nymphomania, corruption, raunchiness*, dirtiness, incest, indelicacy, eroticism, erotism, smut, impurity, debauchery.—*Ant.* MODESTY, decency, continency.

liability *n.* obligation, indebtedness, answerability; see RESPONSIBILITY 2.

liable *a.* **1.** [Responsible] answerable, subject, accountable; see RESPONSIBLE 1. **2.** [Likely] tending, apt, inclined; see LIKELY 4.

liar *n.* prevaricator, false witness, deceiver, perjurer, trickster, cheat, misleader, falsifier, storyteller*, equivocator, fibber, fabricator; see also CHEAT.

libel *n.* calumny, slander, lying; see LIE.

liberal *a.* tolerant, receptive, nonconformist, progressive, advanced, left, radical, interested, wide-awake, broad-minded, understanding, permissive, indulgent, impartial, unprejudiced, reasonable, rational, unbiased, detached, dispassionate, unconventional, avant-garde, left-wing, objective, magnanimous; see also FAIR 1.—*Ant.* PREJUDICED, intolerant, biased.

liberal *n.* individualist, insurgent, rebel, revolutionary, nonconformist, nonpartisan, independent; believer in civil rights, welfare, reform, etc.; socialist, eccentric, freethinker, left-winger; see also RADICAL.

liberate *v.* set free, loose, release; see FREE.

liberation *n.* rescue, freedom, deliverance; see RESCUE 1.

liberty *n.* **1.** [Freedom from bondage] deliverance, emancipation, enfranchisement; see RESCUE 1. **2.** [Freedom from occupation] rest, leave, relaxation; see FREEDOM 2, LEISURE, RECREATION. **3.** [Freedom to choose] permission, alternative, decision; see CHOICE, SELECTION 1. **4.** [The rights supposedly natural to man] freedom, independence, power of choice; see DEMOCRACY. —**at liberty** unrestricted, unlimited, not confined; see FREE 1, 2. —**take liberties** be too impertinent, act too freely, use carelessly; see ABUSE.

librarian *n.* keeper, caretaker, curator; see EXECUTIVE.

library *n.* books, book collection, manuscripts, manuscript collection, institution, public library, private library, book room, lending library, reference collection, archives, museum, treasury, memorabilia, rare books, reading room.

license *n.* **1.** [Unbridled use of freedom] looseness, excess, immoderation; see FREEDOM 2. **2.** [A formal permission] permit, form, identification, tag, card, consent, grant; see also PERMISSION.

license *v.* permit, authorize, privilege; see ALLOW.

lick *v.* **1.** [To pass the tongue over] stroke, rub, touch, pass over, pass across, caress, wash, graze, brush, glance, tongue, fondle, soothe, tranquilize, calm, quiet. **2.** [To play over; *said of flames*] rise and fall, fluctuate, leap; see BURN, DART, WAVE 3. **3.** [*To beat] whip, trim*, thrash; see BEAT 1. **4.** [*To defeat] overcome, vanquish, frustrate; see DEFEAT 3.

lid *n.* cap, top, roof; see COVER 1, HOOD 1.

lie *n.* falsehood, untruth, fiction, inaccuracy, misstatement, myth, fable, deceptiveness, misrepresentation, lying, prevarication, falsification, falseness, defamation, tall story*, fabrication, deception, slander, aspersion, tale, perjury, libel, forgery, distortion, fib, white lie, fish story*, whopper*.—*Ant.* TRUTH, veracity, truthfulness.

lie *v.* **1.** [To utter an untruth] falsify, prevaricate, tell a lie, lie out of, deceive, mislead, misinform, exaggerate, distort, concoct, equivocate, be untruthful, be a liar, break one's word, bear false witness, go back on, say one thing and mean another, misrepresent, dissemble, perjure oneself, delude, invent.—*Ant.* DECLARE, tell the truth, be honest. **2.** [To be situated] extend, be on, be beside, be located, be fixed, be established, be placed, be seated, be set, be level, be smooth, be even, exist in space, stretch along, reach along, spread along. **3.** [To be prostrate] be flat, be prone, sprawl, loll, be stretched out; see also REST 1.—*Ant.* STAND, be upright, sit. **4.** [To assume a prostrate position] lie down, recline, stretch out, go to bed, turn in, retire, take a nap, take a siesta, hit the sack*, hit the hay*; see also REST 1, SLEEP.—*Ant.* RISE, get up, arise. **—take lying down** submit, surrender, be passive; see YIELD 1.

lie down on the job* *v.* dawdle, slack off, fool around*; see LOITER.

lie low *v.* keep out of sight, conceal oneself, go underground; see HIDE 2, SNEAK.

life *n.* **1.** [The fact or act of living] being, entity, growth, animation, endurance, survival, presence, living, consciousness, breath, continuance, flesh and blood, viability, metabolism, vitality, vital spark; see also EXPERIENCE.—*Ant.* DEATH, discontinuance, nonexistence. **2.** [The sum of one's experiences] life experience, conduct, behavior, way of life, reaction, response, participation, enjoyment, joy, suffering, happiness, tide of events, circumstances, realization, knowledge, enlightenment, attainment, development, growth, personality. **3.** [A biography] life story, memoir, memorial; see BIOGRAPHY, STORY. **4.** [Duration] lifetime, one's natural life, period of existence, duration of life, endurance, continuance, span, history, career, course, era, epoch, century, decade, days, generation, time, period, life span, season, cycle, record; see also TIME 1. **5.** [One who promotes gaiety] animator, entertainer, life of the party*; see HOST 1, HOSTESS. **6.** [Vital spirit] vital force, vital principle, *élan vital* (French); see EXCITEMENT, ZEAL. **—as large** (or **big**) **as life** actually, truly, in actual fact; see TRULY. **—for dear life** intensely, desperately, for all one is worth; see STRONGLY. **—for life** for the duration of one's life, for a long time, as long as one lives; see FOREVER. **—for the life of me*** by any means, as if one's life were at stake, whatever happens; see ANYHOW. **—matter of life and death** crisis, grave concern, something vitally important; see IMPORTANCE. **—not on your life*** by no means, certainly not, never; see NO. **—take one's own life** kill oneself, die by one's own hand, murder; see COMMIT SUICIDE. **—true to life** true to reality, realistic, representational; see GENUINE 1.

life-giving *a.* invigorating, animating, productive; see STIMULATING.

lifeless *a.* **1.** [Without life] inert, inanimate, departed; see DEAD 1. **2** [Lacking spirit] lackluster, listless, heavy; see DULL 3, 4, SLOW 2.

lifelike *a.* simulated, exact, imitative; see GRAPHIC 1, 2.

life or death *a.* decisive, necessary, critical; see IMPORTANT 1.

lifetime *a.* lifelong, continuing, enduring; see PERMANENT.

lifetime *n.* existence, endurance, continuance; see LIFE 4, RECORD 2.

lift *n.* **1.** [The work of lifting] pull, lifting, ascension, raising, weight, foot pounds, elevation, escalation, ascent, mounting. **2.** [A ride] transportation, drive, passage; see JOURNEY. **3.** [Aid] help, assistance, support; see HELP 1.

lift *v.* hoist, elevate, upheave; see RAISE 1.

light *a.* **1.** [Having illumination] illuminated, radiant, luminous; see BRIGHT 1. **2.** [Having color] vivid, rich, clear; see CLEAR 2. **3.** [Having little content] superficial, slight, frivolous; see TRIVIAL, UNIMPORTANT. **4.** [Having gaiety and spirit] lively, merry, animated; see ACTIVE. **5.** [Having little weight] airy, fluffy, feathery, slender, downy, floating, lighter than air, light as air, floatable, light as a feather, frothy, buoyant, dainty, thin, sheer, insubstantial, ethereal, graceful, weightless, atmospheric.—*Ant.* HEAVY, ponderous, weighty. **6.** [Digestible] slight, edible, moderate; see EATABLE. **7.** [Small in quantity or number] wee, small, tiny, minute, thin, inadequate, insufficient, hardly enough, not much, hardly any, not many, slender, scanty, slight, sparse, fragmentary, fractional; see also FEW.—*Ant.* LARGE, great, immense.

light *n.* **1.** [The condition opposed to darkness] radiance, brilliance, splendor, glare, brightness, clearness, lightness, incandescence, shine, luster, sheen, sparkle, glitter, glimmer, flood of light, blare, radiation, gleam.—*Ant.* DARKNESS, blackness, blankness. **2.** [Emanations from a source of light] radiation, stream, blaze; see FLASH, RAY. **3.** [A source of light] match, wick, sun, planet, star, moon, lightning, torch, flashlight, chandelier, spotlight, halo, corona. **4.** [Day] daylight, sun, sunrise; see DAY 1. **5.** [Aspect] point of view, condition, standing; see CIRCUMSTANCES 2. **—in (the) light of** with knowledge of, because of, in view of; see CONSIDERING. **—see the light (of day)** **1.** come into being, exist, begin; see BE. **2.** comprehend, realize, be aware; see UNDERSTAND 1.

light *v.* **1.** [To provide light] illuminate, illumine, lighten, give light to, shine upon, furnish with light, light up, turn on the electricity, make a light, make visible, provide adequate illumination, switch on a light, floodlight, make bright, flood with light, fill with light; see also BRIGHTEN 1.—*Ant.* SHADE, put out, darken. **2.** [To cause to ignite] inflame, spark, kindle; see BURN,

IGNITE. 3. [To become ignited] take fire, become inflamed, flame; see BURN, IGNITE. 4. [To come to rest from flight or travel] rest, come down, stop; see ARRIVE. —**make light of** make fun of, mock, belittle; see NEGLECT 1, RIDICULE.

lighted *a.* 1. [Illuminated] brilliant, alight, glowing; see BRIGHT 1. 2. [Burning] blazing, flaming, aflame; see BURNING.

lighten *v.* unburden, make lighter, reduce the load of, lessen the weight of, uplift, buoy up, alleviate, take off a load, remove, take from, pour out, throw overboard, reduce, cut down, put off, make buoyant, take off weight, eradicate, shift, change; see also UNLOAD.—*Ant.* LOAD, burden, overload.

lighter *a.* smaller, thinner, more buoyant; see LESS.

lighter *n.* cigarette lighter, igniter, flame; see LIGHT 3, MATCH 1.

lightheaded *a.* 1. [Giddy] inane, fickle, frivolous; see SILLY. 2. [Faint] tired, delirious, dizzy; see WEAK 1.

lighthearted *a.* gay, joyous, cheerful; see HAPPY.

lighting *n.* brilliance, flame, brightness; see FLASH, LIGHT 1, 3.

light into* *v.* rebuke, blame, assault; see SCOLD.

lightly *a.* delicately, airily, buoyantly, daintily, readily, gently, subtly, mildly, softly, tenderly, carefully, leniently, effortlessly, smoothly, blandly, sweetly, comfortably, restfully, peacefully, quietly; see also EASILY.—*Ant.* HEAVILY, ponderously, roughly.

lightness *n.* 1. [Illumination] sparkle, blaze, shine; see FLASH, LIGHT 1, 3. 2. [The state of being light] airiness, etherealness, downiness, thinness, sheerness, fluffiness. 3. [Agility] balance, deftness, nimbleness; see AGILITY, GRACE 1.

lightning *n.* electrical discharge, bolt, streak of lightning, thunderstroke, firebolt, fireball, thunderbolt; see also ELECTRICITY.

likable *a.* agreeable, amiable, attractive; see FRIENDLY.

like *a.* similar, same, alike, near, resembling, close, not far from, according to, conforming with, matching, equaling, not unlike, akin, related, analogous, twin, corresponding, allied to, much the same, the same form, comparable, identical, in the manner of, parallel, homologous, to the effect that, consistent, approximating.—*Ant.* UNLIKE, different, unrelated.

like *prep.* similar to, same, near to; see ALIKE, LIKE.

like *n.* counterpart, resemblance, parallelism; see SIMILARITY. —**and the like** and so forth, and so on, similar kinds; see OTHERS. —**more like it*** acceptable, good, improved; see BETTER 1. —**nothing like** dissimilar, contrasting, opposed; see UNLIKE. —**something like** similar, resembling, akin; see LIKE *a.*

like *v.* 1. [To enjoy] take delight in, relish, derive pleasure from, be keen on, be pleased by, revel in, indulge in, rejoice in, find agreeable, find appealing, be gratified by, take satisfaction in, savor, fancy, dote on, take an interest in, develop interest for, delight in, regard with favor, have a liking for, love. have a taste for, care to, get a kick out of*, be tickled by, eat up*, go in for.—*Ant.* ENDURE, detest, dislike. 2. [To be fond of] have a fondness for, admire, take a fancy to feel affectionately toward, prize, esteem, hold dear, care about, care for, approve, b pleased with, take to, have a soft spot in one's heart for, hanker for, dote on, have yen for*, become attached to, be sweet on* have eyes for*; see also LOVE 1.—*Ant.* HATE, disapprove, dislike. 3. [To be inclined] choose, feel disposed, wish, desire, have a preference for, prefer, fancy, feel like, incline toward, want.

liked *a.* popular, loved, admired; see BELOVED, HONORED.

likely *a.* 1. [Probable] apparent, probable, seeming, credible, possible, feasible, presumable, conceivable, reasonable, workable, attainable, achievable, believable, rational, thinkable, imaginable, ostensible, plausible, anticipated, expected, imminent.—*Ant.* IMPOSSIBLE, doubtful, questionable. 2. [Promising] suitable, apt, assuring; see FIT 1, HOPEFUL 2. 3. [Believable] plausible, true, acceptable; see CONVINCING. 4. [Apt] inclined, tending, disposed, predisposed, prone, liable, subject to, on the verge of, in the habit of, given to, in favor of, having a weakness for.

likeness *n.* 1. [Similarity] resemblance, correspondence, affinity; see SIMILARITY. 2. [A representation] image, effigy, portrait; see COPY, PICTURE 3.

likewise *a.* in like manner, furthermore, moreover; see BESIDES.

liking *n.* desire, fondness, devotion; see AFFECTION, LOVE 1.

limb *n.* 1. [A tree branch] arm, bough, offshoot; see BRANCH 2. 2. [A bodily appendage] arm, leg, part, wing, fin, flipper, member; see also ARM 1, LEG.

limber *a.* nimble, spry, deft; see AGILE, GRACEFUL 1.

limit *n.* 1. [The boundary] end, frontier, border; see BOUNDARY. 2. [The ultimate] utmost, farthest point, farthest reach, destination, goal, conclusion, extremity, eventuality, termination, absolute, the bitter end, deadline, cut-off point; see also END 4.—*Ant.* ORIGIN, start.

limit *v.* bound, confine, curb; see DEFINE 1 RESTRICT.

limitation *n.* **1.** [The act of limiting] restriction, restraint, control; see ARREST, INTERFERENCE 1, INTERRUPTION, PREVENTION. **2.** [That which limits] condition, definition, qualification, reservation, control, curb, check, injunction, bar, obstruction, stricture, taboo, inhibition, modification; see also ARREST, BARRIER, BOUNDARY, REFUSAL, RESTRAINT 2.—*Ant.* FREEDOM, latitude, liberty. **3.** [A shortcoming] inadequacy, insufficiency, definciency, shortcoming, weakness, want, blemish, defect, lack, imperfection, failing, fault, frailty, flaw; see also FAULT 1.—*Ant.* STRENGTH, perfection, ability.

limited *a.* **1.** [Restricted] confined, checked, curbed; see BOUND 1, 2, RESTRICTED. **2.** [Having only moderate capacity] cramped, insufficient, short; see FAULTY, INADEQUATE, POOR 2, UNSATISFACTORY.

limitless *a.* unending, boundless, immeasurable; see ENDLESS, INFINITE, UNLIMITED.

limp *a.* pliant, soft, flaccid, flabby, supple, pliable, limber, relaxed, flexible, droopy, unsubstantial, bending readily, plastic, yielding, lax, slack, loose, flimsy.—*Ant.* STIFF, rigid, wooden.

limp *v.* walk lamely, proceed slowly, shuffle, lag, stagger, totter, dodder, hobble, falter.

line *n.* **1.** [A row] array, list, rank, file, catalogue, order, group, arrangement, ridge, range, seam, series, sequence, succession, procession, chain, train, string, column, formation, division, queue, channel, furrow, scar, trench, groove, mark, thread, fissure, crack, straight line. **2.** [A mark] outline, tracing, stroke; see MARK 1. **3.** [A rope] string, cable, towline; see ROPE, WIRE 1. **4.** [Lineal descent] ancestry, pedigree, lineage; see FAMILY, HEREDITY. **5.** [A border line] border, mark, limit; see BOUNDARY, EDGE 1. **6.** [Matter printed in a row of type] row, words, letters; see COPY. **7.** [A military front] disposition, formation, position; see FRONT 2. **8.** [A transportation system] trunk line, bus line, steamship line, railroad line, airline. **9.** [Goods handled by a given company] wares, merchandise, produce; see MATERIAL 2. **10.** [*Talk intended to influence another] sermon, rhetoric, lecture, propaganda, advertising; see also CONVERSATION, SPEECH 3. **—all along the line** at every turn, completely, constantly; see EVERYWHERE. **—bring** (or **come** or **get**) **into line** align, make uniform, regulate; see ORDER 3. **—draw the** (or a) **line** set a limit, prohibit, restrain; see RESTRICT. **—get a line on*** find out about, investigate, expose; see DISCOVER. **—in line** agreeing, conforming, uniform; see REGULAR 3. **—in line for** being considered for, ready, thought about; see CONSIDERED. **—lay** (or **put**) **it on the line** elucidate, define, clarify; see EXPLAIN. **—on a line** straight, even, level; see DIRECT 1, STRAIGHT 1. **—out of line** misdirected, not uniform, not even; see IRREGULAR 1, 4. **—read between the lines** read meaning into, discover a hidden meaning, expose; see UNDERSTAND 1.

line *v.* **1.** [To provide a lining] interline, stuff, wad, panel, pad, quilt, fill. **2.** [To provide lines] trace, delineate, outline; see DRAW 2, MARK 1. **3.** [To be in a line] border, edge, outline, rim, bound, fall in, fall into line, fringe, follow. **4.** [To arrange in a line] align, queue, marshal, arrange, range, array, group, set out, bring into a line with others, fix, place, draw up; see also LINE UP.—*Ant.* SCATTER, disarrange, disperse.

linear *a.* long, elongated, successive; see DIRECT 1, STRAIGHT 1.

lined *a.* interlined, stuffed, coated; see FULL 1.

linen *n.* material, sheeting, linen cloth; see GOODS. *Articles called linens include the following:* handkerchiefs, towels, bedding, sheets, pillowcases, underwear, shirts, dishtowels, tablecloths, napkins, doilies.

lineup *n.* starters, entrants, first string; see LIST.

line up *v.* fall in, form in line, take one's proper place in line, queue up, form ranks, get in line, get set, get into formation.

linger *v.* tarry, saunter, lag, hesitate, trail, vacillate, delay, plod, trudge, falter, dawdle, procrastinate, slouch, shuffle, crawl, loll, take one's time, wait, putter, be tardy, be long, sit around, hang around*; see also LOITER.—*Ant.* HURRY, hasten, speed.

lingerie *n.* women's underwear, undergarmets, unmentionables*; see CLOTHES, UNDERWEAR.

linguist *n.* student of language, language expert, philologist, lexicographer, polyglot, translator, grammarian, etymologist; see also SCIENTIST.

linguistics *n.pl.* grammar, semantics, phonology, etymology, prosody, morphology, syntax, philology; see also GRAMMAR, LANGUAGE 2.

liniment *n.* ointment, cream, lotion; see MEDICINE 2, SALVE.

lining *a.* edging, outlining, rimming; see BORDERING.

lining *n.* interlining, inner coating, inner surface, filling, quilting, stuffing, wadding, padding, sheathing, covering, wall, reinforcement, partition, paneling.

link *n.* ring, loop, coupling, coupler, section, seam, weld, hitch, intersection, copula, connective, connection, fastening, splice, interconnection, junction, joining, ligature, articulation; see also JOINT 1.

link *v.* connect, associate, combine; see JOIN 1.

linked *a.* connected, combined, associated; see JOINED.

linking *a.* combining, joining, associating; see CONNECTING.
lint *n.* thread, fluff, fiber; see DUST.
lion *n.* king of beasts, king of the jungle, lioness; see ANIMAL, CAT 2.
lip *n.* edge of the mouth, liplike part, labium; see MOUTH 1. —**keep a stiff upper lip*** take heart, be encouraged, remain strong; see ENDURE 2.
liquid *a.* **1.** [In a state neither solid nor gaseous] watery, molten, damp, moist, aqueous, liquefied, dissolved, melted, thawed; see also FLUID, WET 1. **2.** [Having qualities suggestive of fluids] flowing, running, splashing, thin, moving, viscous, diluting; see also FLUID, JUICY.
liquid *n.* liquor, fluid, juice, sap, extract, secretion, flow; see also WATER 1.
liquidate *v.* **1.** [To change into money] sell, convert, change; see EXCHANGE. **2.** [To abolish] annul, cancel, destroy; see ABOLISH, ELIMINATE.
liquor *n.* whiskey, booze*, alcohol; see COCKTAIL, DRINK 2.
lisp *v.* mispronounce, sputter, stutter; see UTTER.
lissome *a.* lithe, supple, flexible; see AGILE, FLEXIBLE.
list *n.* roll, record, schedule, agenda, arrangement, enrollment, slate, draft, panel, brief, invoice, register, memorandum, inventory, account, outline, tally, bulletin, directory, roster, subscribers, subscription list, muster, poll, ballot, table of contents, menu, dictionary, thesaurus, glossary, lexicon, vocabulary, docket.
list *v.* **1.** [To enter in a list] set down, arrange, bill, catalogue, schedule, enter, note, add, place, file, record, insert, enroll, register, tally, inventory, index, draft, enumerate, tabulate, book, take a census, poll, slate, keep count of, run down, call the roll.—*Ant.* REMOVE, wipe out, obliterate. **2.** [To lean] pitch, slant, incline; see LEAN 1.
listed *a.* filed, cataloged, indexed; see RECORDED.
listen *v.* attend, keep one's ears open, be attentive, listen in, pick up, overhear, monitor, tap, give attention to, give ear, listen to, pay attention, hear, tune in*, lend an ear*, strain one's ears*.—*Ant.* IGNORE, be deaf to, turn a deaf ear to.
listener *n.* spy, student, monitor, spectator, audience, eavesdropper, witness.
listening *a.* hearing, paying attention, interested, involved, attentive, heeding, overhearing, straining to hear, receiving, lending an ear*.—*Ant.* INDIFFERENT, giving no attention, inattentive.
listless *a.* passive, sluggish, lifeless; see INDIFFERENT, SLOW 2.
lit *a.* illuminated, lighted, resplendent; see BRIGHT 1, BURNING.
literacy *n.* scholarship, ability to read and write, verbal competence; see EDUCATION 1, KNOWLEDGE 1.
literal *a.* true, verbatim, methodical; see ACCURATE 2.
literally *a.* really, actually, precisely, exactly, completely, indisputably, correctly, strictly, to the letter, faithfully, rigorously, straight, unmistakably, truly, not metaphorically, not figuratively, word for word, verbatim, letter by letter.—*Ant.* FREELY, figuratively, fancifully.
literary *a.* scholarly, bookish, literate; see LEARNED 1.
literate *a.* informed, scholarly, able to read and write; see EDUCATED, INTELLIGENT, LEARNED 1.
literature *n.* **1.** [Artistic production in language] letters, lore, belles lettres, literary works, literary productions, the humanities, classics, books, writings. **2.** [Written matter treating a given subject] discourse, composition, treatise, dissertation, thesis, paper, treatment, essay, discussion, research, observation, comment, critique, findings, abstract, report, summary.
litter *n.* **1.** [Trash] rubbish, debris, waste; see TRASH 1. **2.** [The young of certain animals] piglets, puppies, kittens; see OFFSPRING.
litter *v.* scatter, discard, spread; see DIRTY.
litterbug *n.* slob*, pig, polluter; see SLOB.
little *a.* **1.** [Small in size] diminutive, small tiny, wee, undersized, stubby, truncated, stunted, limited, cramped, imperceptible. light, slight, microscopic, short, runty, shriveled, toy, miniature, puny, pygmy, dwarfed, bantam, half-pint*, pocket-sized*, pint-sized*.—*Ant.* LARGE, big, huge. **2.** [Inadequate] a lack of, deficient, insufficient; see INADEQUATE. **3.** [Few in number] scarce, not many, hardly any; see FEW. **4.** [Brief] concise, succinct, abrupt; see SHORT 2. **5.** [Small in importance] trifling, shallow, petty, superficial, frivolous, irrelevant, meaningless, slight, paltry, insignificant, inconsiderable; see also TRIVIAL, UNIMPORTANT. **6.** [Small in character] base, weak, shallow, small-minded, prejudiced, bigoted, low, sneaky, mean, petty; see also VULGAR. **7.** [Weak] stunted, runty, undersized; see WEAK 1. —**make little of** make fun of, mock, abuse; see RIDICULE.
little *n.* some, a few, trifle; see BIT 1.
livable *a.* habitable, endurable, inhabitable; see BEARABLE, COMFORTABLE 2.
live *a.* **1.** [Active] energetic, lively, dynamic; see ACTIVE. **2.** [Not dead] aware, conscious, existing; see ALIVE. **3.** [Not taped or filmed] broadcast direct, unrehearsed, on stage; see REAL 2.

live *v.* **1.** [To have life] exist, continue, subsist, prevail, survive, breathe, be alive; see also BE 1. **2.** [To enjoy life] relish, savor, experience, love, delight in, make every moment count, experience life to the full, live it up*, make the most of life, take pleasure in, get a great deal from life.—*Ant.* SUFFER, endure pain, be discouraged. **3.** [To dwell] live in, inhabit, settle; see DWELL. **4.** [To gain subsistence] earn a living, support oneself, earn money, get ahead, provide for one's needs, make ends meet, subsist, maintain oneself; see also SURVIVE 1. **5.** [To persist in human memory] remain, last, be remembered; see ENDURE 1. —**where one lives*** personally, in a vulnerable area, at one's heart; see PERSONALLY 2.

live and let live *v.* be tolerant, accept, ignore; see ALLOW.

live at *v.* inhabit, reside, occupy; see DWELL.

live down *v.* overcome, survive, outgrow; see ENDURE 2.

live it up* *v.* have fun, enjoy, paint the town*; see CELEBRATE 2.

livelihood *n.* career, occupation, job; see PROFESSION 1.

lively *a.* vigorous, brisk, industrious; see ACTIVE.

live on *v.* be supported, earn, subsist on; see LIVE 4.

livestock *n.* cows, sheep, domestic animals; see CATTLE, HERD.

live up to *v.* meet expectations, do well, give satisfaction; see SATISFY 3.

living *a.* **1.** [Alive] existing, breathing, having being; see ALIVE. **2.** [Vigorous] awake, brisk, alert; see ACTIVE.

living *n.* **1.** [A means of survival] existence, sustenance, maintenance; see SUBSISTENCE 2. **2.** [Those not dead; *usually used with "the"*] the world, everyone, people; see ANIMAL, PERSON, PLANT.

living room *n.* lounge, front room, den; see ROOM 2.

load *n.* **1.** [A physical burden] weight, encumbrance, truckload, carload, wagonload, shipload, cargo, haul, charge, pack, mass, payload, shipment, contents, capacity, bundle.—*Ant.* LIGHTNESS, buoyancy, weightlessness. **2.** [Responsibility] charge, obligation, trust; see DUTY 1. **3.** [A charge; *said especially of firearms*] shot, clip, round; see AMMUNITION. **4.** [A measure] quantity, portion, amount; see MEASUREMENT 2, QUANTITY.

load *v.* **1.** [To place a load] arrange, stow away, store, burden, stuff, put goods in, put goods on, freight, weight, pile, heap, fill, cram, put aboard, stack, pour in, take on cargo; see also PACK 1.—*Ant.* UNLOAD, unpack, take off cargo. **2.** [To overload] encumber, saddle, weigh down; see BURDEN. **3.** [To charge; *said especially of firearms*] prime, ready, make ready to fire; see SHOOT 1.

loaded *a.* **1.** [Supplied with a load] laden, burdened, weighted; see FULL 1. **2.** [Ready to discharge; *said of firearms*] charged, primed, ready to shoot. **3.** [*Intoxicated] inebriated, drunken, smashed*; see DRUNK.

loaf *n.* roll, bun, pastry; see BREAD, CAKE 2.

loaf *v.* idle, trifle, lounge, kill time, be inactive, be slothful, be lazy, take it easy, not lift a finger, putter, rest, dally, let down, slack off, vegetate, loll, malinger, drift, relax, slack, shirk, waste time, slow down, evade, dilly-dally, stand around, dream, goof off*, bum*, stall, piddle.

loafer *n.* idler, lounger, lazy person, ne'er-do-well, good-for-nothing, lazybones, malingerer, waster, slacker, shirker, wanderer, bum*, goldbrick*.

loafing *a.* careless, apathetic, shirking; see LAZY 1.

loan *n.* lending, trust, advance, giving credit, mortgage, time payment, installment loan, student loan, car loan, home equity loan, personal loan.

loan *v.* provide with, share, furnish; see LEND.

loaned *a.* lent, advanced, invested, granted, furnished, put out at interest, let, risked, leased; see also GIVEN.—*Ant.* BORROWED, pledged, pawned.

lobby *n.* vestibule, entryway, foyer; see HALL 1, ROOM 2.

lobby *v.* induce, put pressure on, promote; see INFLUENCE.

local *a.* **1.** [Associated with a locality] sectional, divisional, territorial, district, provincial, neighborhood, town, civic, small-town, grass-roots, geographical, parochial; see also REGIONAL, TRADITIONAL. **2.** [Restricted to a locality] limited, confined, bounded; see RESTRICTED.

locale *n.* vicinity, territory, district; see AREA, REGION 1.

locality *n.* **1.** [Area] district, section, sector; see AREA, REGION 1. **2.** [Position] spot, location, site; see POSITION 1. **3.** [Neighborhood] block, vicinity, district; see NEIGHBORHOOD.

locally *a.* regionally, sectionally, provincially, in the neighborhood, in the town, close by, nearby.

locate *v.* **1.** [To determine a location] discover, search out, find, come across, position, ferret out, stumble on, discover the location of, get at, hit upon, come upon, lay one's hands on, track down, unearth, establish, determine, station, place; see also FIND. **2.** [To take up residence] settle down, establish oneself, inhabit; see DWELL, SETTLE 5.

located *a.* **1.** [Discovered] traced, found, happened on; see DISCOVERED. **2.** [Situated] positioned, seated, fixed; see PLACED.

location *n.* **1.** [A position] place, spot, section; see POSITION 1. **2.** [A site] situation, place, scene; see AREA, NEIGHBORHOOD.

lock *n.* **1.** [A device for locking] hook, catch, latch, bolt, bar, hasp, bond, fastening, padlock, safety catch, clamp, clasp, tumblers, barrier, device, fixture, grip; see also FASTENER. **2.** [A tuft of hair] tress, ringlet, curl; see HAIR 1. **—under lock and key** locked up, imprisoned, in jail; see CONFINED 3.

lock *v.* bolt, bar, turn the key; see FASTEN.

locked *a.* secured, padlocked, closed; see TIGHT 2.

locker *n.* cabinet, footlocker, cupboard; see CLOSET, FURNITURE.

locket *n.* memento case, pendant, keepsake; see JEWELRY, NECKLACE.

lockup *n.* prison, jail, penitentiary; see JAIL.

lock up *v.* confine, put behind bars, shut up; see IMPRISON.

lodge *n.* inn, hostel, ski lodge; see HOTEL, MOTEL, RESORT 2.

lodge *v.* **1.** [To become fixed] catch, stay, abide; see STICK 1. **2.** [To take (temporary) residence] room, stay over, board; see DWELL.

lodger *n.* guest, roomer, resident; see TENANT.

lodging *n.* **1.** [Place of protection] sanctuary, retreat, asylum; see REFUGE 1, SHELTER. **2.** [A (temporary) living place; *usually plural*] room, apartment, suite; see HOTEL, MOTEL, RESORT 2.

lofty *a.* tall, elevated, towering; see HIGH 2, RAISED 1.

log *n.* **1.** [The main stem of a fallen or cut tree] timber, trunk, lumber; see WOOD 2. **2.** [The record of a voyage] journal, account, diary; see RECORD 1.

logic *n.* reasoning, deduction, induction; see PHILOSOPHY 1, THOUGHT 1.

logical *a.* coherent, consistent, probable, sound, pertinent, germane, legitimate, cogent, relevant, congruent with, as it ought to be; see also REASONABLE 1.

logically *a.* rationally, by reason, inevitably; see REASONABLY 1, 2.

logy* *a.* dull, sluggish, drowsy; see LAZY 1.

loiter *v.* saunter, stroll, dawdle, delay, lag, shuffle, waste time, procrastinate, tarry, fritter away time, loll, loaf, dabble, wait, pause, dillydally, hang back, trail, drag, ramble, idle; see also LINGER.—*Ant.* HURRY, hasten, stride along.

lone *a.* solitary, lonesome, deserted; see ALONE.

loneliness *n.* detachment, separation, solitude, desolation, isolation, aloneness, lonesomeness, forlornness.

lonely *a.* abandoned, homesick, forlorn, forsaken, friendless, deserted, desolate, homeless, left, lone, lonesome, solitary, empty, companionless, renounced, withdrawn, secluded, unattended, by oneself, apart, reclusive, single, rejected, unaccompanied; see also ALONE.—*Ant.* ACCOMPANIED, joined, associated.

lonesome *a.* solitary, forlorn, alone; see HOMESICK, LONELY.

long *a.* **1.** [Extended in space] lengthy, extended, outstretched, elongated, interminable, boundless, endless, unending, limitless, stretching, great, high, deep, drawn out, enlarged, expanded, spread, tall, lofty, towering, lengthened, stringy, rangy, lanky, gangling, far-reaching, distant, running, faraway, far-off, remote; see also LARGE 1.—*Ant.* SHORT, small, stubby. **2.** [Extended in time] protracted, prolonged, enduring, unending, meandering, long-winded, spun out, lengthy, for ages, without end, perpetual, forever and a day, lasting, continued, long-lived, sustained, lingering; day after day, hour after hour, etc.—*Ant.* SHORT, brief, uncontinued. **3.** [Tedious] hard, boring, long-drawn; see DULL 4. **4.** [Having (a certain commodity) in excess] rich, profuse, abundant; see PLENTIFUL 1. **—as (or so) long as** seeing that, provided, since; see BECAUSE. **—before long** in the near future, immediately, shortly; see SOON.

long *v.* desire, yearn for, wish; see WANT 1.

long and short of it *n.* gist, totality, outcome; see RESULT, WHOLE.

longing *n.* yearning, pining, hunger; see DESIRE 1, WISH.

long-lived *a.* long-lasting, perpetual, enduring; see PERMANENT.

look *n.* **1.** [Appearance] features, demeanor, shape; see EXPRESSION 4, LOOKS. **2.** [An effort to see] gaze, stare, scrutiny, inspection, examination, contemplation, speculation, attending, noticing, regarding, marking, observation, reconnaissance, keeping watch, once-over*; see also ATTENTION. **3.** [A quick use of the eyes] glance, survey, squint, glimpse, peek, peep, leer, flash.

look *v.* **1.** [To appear] seem to be, look like, resemble; see SEEM. **2.** [To endeavor to see] view, gaze, glance at, scan, stare, behold, contemplate, watch, survey, scrutinize, regard, inspect, discern, spy, observe, attend, examine, mark, gape, give attention, peer, ogle, have an eye on, study, peep, look at, take a gander at*, get a load of*; see also SEE 1. **—it looks like** probably, it seems that there will be, it seems as if; see SEEM.

look after *v.* look out for, support, watch; see GUARD.

look for *v.* research, pry, hunt; see SEARCH, SEEK.

look into *v.* investigate, study, probe; see EXAMINE.

lookout *n.* **1.** [A place of vantage] wa[illegible] tower, observatory, patrol station, [illegible] crow's nest, observation tower. **2.** [C[illegible] tioned at a lookout] observer, sentinel, scout; see WATCHMAN.

look out *interj.* be careful, pay attention, listen, notice, heads up*, hey*; see also WATCH OUT.

looks *n.pl.* appearance, countenance, aspect, manner, demeanor, face, expression, features, form, shape, posture, bearing, presence.

look up *v.* **1.** [*To improve] get better, advance, progress; see IMPROVE 2. **2.** [To find by search] come upon, research, find; see DISCOVER, SEARCH, SEEK.

look up to *v.* respect, idolize, honor; see ADMIRE.

loom *v.* **1.** [To appear] come into view, come on the scene, rise; see APPEAR 1. **2.** [To appear large or imposing] menace, overshadow, hulk, emerge, shadow, top, tower, impress, hang over, rise gradually, seem huge, be near, hover, approach, come forth; see also THREATEN.

loop *n.* ring, eye, circuit; see CIRCLE 1. —**knock** (or **throw**) **for a loop*** confuse, disturb, startle; see SHOCK 2.

loop *v.* curve, connect, tie together; see BEND.

loophole *n.* avoidance, means of escape, deception; see LIE, TRICK 1.

loose *a.* **1.** [Unbound] unfastened, undone, untied, insecure, relaxed, unattached, unconnected, disconnected, untethered, unbuttoned, unclasped, unhooked, unsewed, unstuck, slack, loosened, baggy, unconfined, unlatched, unlocked, unbolted, unscrewed, unhinged, worked free; see also FREE 3.—*Ant.* TIGHT, confined, bound. **2.** [Movable] unattached, free, wobbly; see MOVABLE. **3.** [Vague] disconnected, random, detached; see OBSCURE 1, VAGUE 2. **4.** [Wanton] dissolute, licentious, disreputable; see LEWD 2. —**on the loose*** unconfined, unrestrained, wild; see FREE. —**set** (or **turn**) **loose** set free, release, untie; see FREE.

loosen *v.* **1.** [To make loose] extricate, untie, unbind, undo, disentangle, let go, unlock, release, unfix; see also FREE. **2.** [To become loose] relax, slacken, work free, break up, let go, become unstuck.—*Ant.* TIGHTEN, tighten up, become rigid.

loot *n.* spoils, plunder, take*; see BOOTY.

loot *v.* plunder, thieve, rifle; see ROB, STEAL.

lop *v.* trim, prune, chop; see CUT 1.

lopsided *a.* uneven, unbalanced, crooked; see IRREGULAR 4.

lord *n.* **1.** [A master] ruler, governor, prince; see LEADER 2. **2.** [A member of the nobility] nobleman, count, titled person; see ARISTOCRAT, ROYALTY.

Lord *n.* Divinity, the Supreme Being, Jehovah; see GOD 1.

lordly *a.* grand, dignified, honorable; see NOBLE 1, 2, 3.

lore *n.* enlightenment, wisdom, learning; see KNOWLEDGE 1.

lose *v.* **1.** [To bring about a loss] mislay, misfile, disturb, disorder, confuse, mix, scatter, mess, muss, disorganize, forget, be careless with. **2.** [To incur loss] suffer, miss, be deprived of, fail to keep, suffer loss, be impoverished from, become poorer by, let slip through the fingers*; see also WASTE 1.—*Ant.* PROFIT, gain, improve. **3.** [To fail to win] be defeated, suffer defeat, go down in defeat, succumb, fall, be the loser, miss, have the worst of it, be humbled, take defeat at the hands of, go down for the count*, be sunk*; see also FAIL 1.—*Ant.* WIN, triumph, be victorious. **4.** [To suffer financially] squander, expend, dissipate; see SPEND, WASTE 2.

loser *n.* sufferer, victim, prey, failure, defeated, forfeiter, dispossessed, underdog, disadvantaged, underprivileged, fallen.—*Ant.* WINNER, gainer, conqueror.

losing *a.* **1.** [*Said of one who loses*] failing, having the worst of it, on the way out; see RUINED 1. **2.** [*Said of an activity in which one must lose*] futile, desperate, lost; see HOPELESS.

loss *n.* **1.** [The act or fact of losing] ruin, destruction, mishap, misfortune, giving up, ill fortune, accident, calamity, trouble, disaster, sacrifice, catastrophe, trial, failure. **2.** [Damage caused by losing something] hurt, injury, wound; see DAMAGE 1, 2. **3.** [The result of unprofitable activity] privation, want, bereavement, deprivation, need, destitution, being without, lack, waste, deterioration, impairment, degeneration, decline, disadvantage, wreck, wreckage, undoing, annihilation, bane, end, undoing, disorganization, breaking up, suppression, relapse.—*Ant.* ADVANTAGE, advancement, supply. —**at a loss** confused, puzzled, unsure; see UNCERTAIN.

losses *n.pl.* casualties, damage, deaths; see DESTRUCTION 2.

lost *a.* **1.** [Not to be found] misplaced, mislaid, missing, hidden, obscured, gone astray, nowhere to be found, strayed, lacking, wandered off, absent, forfeited, vanished, wandering, without, gone out of one's possession.—*Ant.* FOUND, come back, returned. **2.** [Ignorant of the way] perplexed, bewildered, ignorant; see DOUBTFUL 1. **3.** [Destroyed] demolished, devastated, wasted; see DESTROYED, RUINED 1. **4.** [No longer to be gained] gone, passed, costly; see UNPROFITABLE. **5.** [Helpless] feeble, sickly, disabled; see WEAK 1, 3. —**get lost*** go away!, leave!, begone!; see GET OUT.

lot *n.* **1.** [A small parcel of land] parcel, part, division, patch, clearing, piece of ground, plat, plot, field, tract, block, portion, parking lot, piece, property, acreage. **2.** [A number of individual items, usually alike] batch, consignment, requisition; see LOAD 1. **3.** [Destiny] doom, portion, fate; see CHANCE 1. **4.** [*A great quantity] large amount, abundance, plenty, considerable amount, great numbers, bundle, bunch, cluster, group, pack, large numbers, very much, very many, quite a lot, quite a bit, a good deal, a whole bunch*, loads*, oodles*; see also PLENTY.

lotion *n.* liniment, hand lotion, cream, wash, unguent; see also COSMETIC, MEDICINE 2, SALVE.

loud *a.* **1.** [Having volume of sound] deafening, ringing, ear-piercing, earsplitting, booming, intense, resounding, piercing, blaring, sonorous, resonant, crashing, deep, full, powerful, emphatic, thundering, heavy, big, deep-toned, full-tongued, roaring, enough to wake the dead; see also SHRILL.—*Ant.* SOFT, faint, feeble. **2.** [Producing loud sounds] clamorous, noisy, uproarious, blatant, vociferous, turbulent, tumultuous, blustering, lusty, loud-voiced, boisterous, cacophonous, raucous; see also HARSH.—*Ant.* QUIET, soft-voiced, calm. **3.** [*Lacking manners and refinement] loud mouthed, brash, offensive; see RUDE 2, VULGAR. **4.** [*Lacking good taste, especially in colors] garish, flashy, tawdry; see ORNATE.

loudly *a.* audibly, fully, powerfully, crashingly, shrilly, deafeningly, piercingly, resonantly, emphatically, vehemently, thunderingly, in full cry, clamorously, noisily, uproariously, blatantly, at the top of one's lungs.

loud-speaker *n.* speaker, amplifier, public address system, PA, high-fidelity speaker, high-frequency speaker, low-frequency speaker, tweeter, woofer, bullhorn.

lounge *v.* idle, repose, kill time; see LOAF, REST 1.

lousy *a.* **1.** [Having lice] infested with lice, crawling with lice, pediculous, pedicular; see also CREEPING. **2.** [*Bad] horrible, disliked, unwelcome; see OFFENSIVE 2.

lovable *a.* winning, winsome, lovely; see FRIENDLY.

love *n.* **1.** [Passionate and tender devotion] attachment, devotedness, passion, infatuation, yearning, flame, rapture, enchantment, ardor, emotion, sentiment, fondness, tenderness, adoration, crush*; see also AFFECTION.—*Ant.* HATE, aversion, antipathy. **2.** [Affection based on esteem] respect, regard, appreciation; see ADMIRATION. **3.** [A lively and enduring interest] involvement, concern, enjoyment; see DEVOTION. **4.** [A beloved] dear one, loved one, cherished one; see LOVER 1. —**for the love of** for the sake of, with fond concern for, because of; see FOR. —**in love** enamored, infatuated, charmed; see LOVING. —**make love** fondle, embrace, sleep with; see COPULATE, LOVE 2. —**not for love or money** under no conditions, by no means, no; see NEVER.

love *v.* **1.** [To be passionately devoted] adore, be in love with, care for, hold dear, choose, fancy, be enchanted by, be passionately attached to, have affection for, dote on, glorify, idolize, prize, be fascinated by, hold high, think the world of, treasure, prefer, yearn for, be fond of, admire, long for, flip over*, fall for*, be nuts about*, be crazy about*, go for*.—*Ant.* HATE, detest, loathe. **2.** [To express love by caresses] cherish, fondle, kiss, make love to, embrace, cling to, clasp, hug, take into one's arms, hold, pet, stroke, draw close, bring to one's side; see also KISS.—*Ant.* REFUSE, exclude, spurn. **3.** [To possess a deep and abiding interest] enjoy, delight in, relish; see ADMIRE, LIKE 1.

loved *a.* desired, cherished, well beloved; see BELOVED.

loveliness *n.* appeal, charm, fairness; see BEAUTY 1.

lovely *a.* **1.** [Beautiful] attractive, comely, fair; see sense 2 and BEAUTIFUL, HANDSOME. **2.** [Charming] engaging, enchanting, captivating; see CHARMING. **3.** [*Very pleasing] nice, splendid, delightful; see PLEASANT 1, 2.

lover *n.* **1.** [A suitor] sweetheart, admirer, escort, paramour, fiancé, fiancée, gentleman friend, boyfriend*, girlfriend*, steady*. **2.** [A willing student or practitioner] practitioner, fan, hobbyist; see ZEALOT. **3.** [An epithet for a beloved] beloved, sweetheart, dear; see DARLING.

loving *a.* admiring, respecting, valuing, liking, fond, tender, kind, enamored, attached, devoted, appreciative, attentive, thoughtful, passionate, ardent, amiable, warm, amorous, affectionate, anxious, concerned, sentimental, earnest, benevolent, cordial, caring, considerate, loyal, generous.

lovingly *a.* tenderly, devotedly, adoringly, warmly, ardently, fervently, zealously, earnestly, loyally, generously, kindly, thoughtfully, dotingly, fondly, affectionately, passionately, longingly, rapturously, admiringly, respectfully, reverently, with love, attentively.

low *a.* **1.** [Close to the earth] squat, flat, level, low-lying, prostrate, crouched, below, not far above the horizon, low-hanging, knee-high, beneath, under, depressed, sunken, nether, inferior, lying under.—*Ant.* HIGH, lofty, elevated. **2.** [Far down on a scale] muffled, hushed, quiet; see FAINT 3. **3.** [Low in spirits] dejected, moody, blue; see SAD 1. **4.** [Vulgar] base, mean, coarse; see VULGAR. **5.** [Faint] ill, dizzy, feeble; see SICK, WEAK 1. **6.** [Simple] economical, moderate, inexpensive; see CHEAP 1. —**lay low** bring to ruin, overcome, kill; see DESTROY. —**lie low** wait, conceal oneself, take cover; see HIDE 2.

lower *a.* beneath, inferior, under; see LOW 1.

lower *v.* bring low, cast down, depress; [illegible] DECREASE 1, 2, DROP 2.

lowest *a.* shortest, littlest, smallest, slightest, least, rock-bottom, ground, base; see also MINIMUM.

low-key *a.* subdued, relaxed, laid-back*; see CALM.

lowly *a.* unpretentious, cast down, meek; see HUMBLE 2.

loyal *a.* true, dependable, firm; see FAITHFUL.

loyally *a.* faithfully, conscientiously, truly, devotedly, constantly, sincerely, obediently, resolutely, earnestly, steadfastly, in good faith.

loyalty *n.* allegiance, faithfulness, fidelity, trustworthiness, constancy, integrity, attachment, sincerity, adherence, bond, tie, honor, reliability, good faith, conscientiousness, dependability, devotedness, support, zeal, ardor, earnestness, resolution, obedience, duty, honesty, truthfulness; see also DEVOTION.—*Ant.* DISHONESTY, disloyalty, faithlessness.

lubricant *n.* cream, ointment, oil; see GREASE.

lubricate *v.* oil, daub, put grease on or in; see GREASE.

luck *n.* **1.** [Good fortune] good luck, prosperity, wealth, streak of luck, windfall, advantage, profit, triumph, victory, win, happiness, blessings, opportunity, lucky break, break*, the breaks*.—*Ant.* FAILURE, ill-fortune, bad luck. **2.** [Chance] unforeseen occurrence, happenstance*, fate; see ACCIDENT, CHANCE 1. **—crowd (or push) one's luck*** gamble, take risks, chance; see RISK. **—in luck** lucky, successful, prosperous; see FORTUNATE. **—out of luck** unlucky, in misfortune, in trouble; see UNFORTUNATE. **—try one's luck** attempt, risk, endeavor; see TRY 1.

luckily *a.* opportunely, happily, favorably; see FORTUNATELY.

lucky *a.* **1.** [Enjoying good luck] blessed, wealthy, victorious, happy, favored, winning, in luck, successful, prosperous; see also FORTUNATE. **2.** [Supposed to bring good luck] providential, propitious, auspicious; see MAGIC.

lucrative *a.* fruitful, productive, gainful; see PROFITABLE.

ludicrous *a.* comical, odd, farcical; see FUNNY 1.

lug *v.* carry, tug, lift; see DRAW 1.

luggage *n.* trunks, bags, valises; see BAGGAGE.

lukewarm *a.* cool, tepid, room-temperature; see WARM 1.

lull *n.* quiet, stillness, calm; see SILENCE 1, PAUSE.

lull *v.* calm, quiet down, bring repose; see QUIET 1, 2.

lullaby *n.* good-night song, bedtime song, cradlesong; see SONG.

lumber *n.* cut timber, logs, sawed timber, forest products, boards, hardwood, softwood, lumbering products; see also WOOD 2.

luminescence *n.* fluorescence, incandescence, radiance; see LIGHT 1.

luminous *a.* lighted, glowing, radiant; see BRIGHT 1.

lump *n.* handful, protuberance, bunch, bump, hump, block, bulk, chunk, piece, portion, section; see also HUNK.

lumpy *a.* knotty, clotty, uneven; see IRREGULAR 4, THICK 1, 3.

lunacy *n.* madness, dementia, mania; see INSANITY.

lunatic *a.* **1.** [Insane] demented, deranged, psychotic; see INSANE. **2.** [Foolish] irrational, idiotic, daft; see STUPID.

lunatic *n.* crazy person, psychotic, insane person; see MADMAN.

lunch *n.* meal, luncheon, brunch, refreshment, sandwich, snack, high tea.

lunch *v.* dine, have lunch, take a lunch break; see EAT 1.

lunge *v.* surge, lurch, bound; see JUMP 1.

lurch *v.* stagger, weave, lunge; see TOTTER.

lure *n.* bait, decoy, fake; see CAMOUFLAGE, TRICK 1.

lure *v.* enchant, bewitch, allure; see CHARM, FASCINATE.

lurk *v.* wait, crouch, conceal oneself; see HIDE 2.

lurking *a.* hiding out, sneaking, hidden; see HIDDEN.

luscious *a.* sweet, toothsome, palatable; see DELICIOUS.

lush *a.* **1.** [Green] verdant, dense, grassy; see GREEN 2. **2.** [Delicious] rich, juicy, succulent; see DELICIOUS. **3.** [Elaborate] extensive, luxurious, ornamental; see ELABORATE 1, ORNATE.

lust *n.* appetite, passion, sensuality; see DESIRE 2.

lust (after) *v.* long for, desire, hunger for; see WANT 1.

luster *n.* glow, brilliance, radiance; see LIGHT 1.

lusty *a.* hearty, robust, vigorous; see HEALTHY.

luxurious *a.* comfortable, easy, affluent; see EXPENSIVE, RICH 2.

luxury *n.* **1.** [Indulgence of the senses, regardless of the cost] gratification, costliness, expensiveness, richness, idleness, leisure, high-living, lavishness; see also INDULGENCE 1.—*Ant.* POVERTY, poorness, lack. **2.** [An indulgence beyond one's means] extravagance, exorbitance, wastefulness; see EXCESS 1, WASTE 1.

lying *a.* **1.** [In the act of lying] falsifying, prevaricating, swearing falsely, committing perjury, fibbing, misrepresenting, inventing.—*Ant.* FRANK, truthful, veracious. **2.** [Given to lying] deceitful, unreliable, double-dealing; see DISHONEST. **3.** [Not reliable] unsound, tricky, treacherous; see FALSE

2. 4. [Prostrate] supine, reclining, resting, horizontal, reposing, recumbent, flat, fallen, prone, powerless.

lying down *a.* reclining, reposing, sleeping; see ASLEEP, RESTING 1.

lynch *v.* hang, string up*, murder; see KILL 1.

lyric *n.* **1.** [Verses set to music] the words, the lyrics, the verse; see POEM. **2.** [A short, songlike poem] lyrical poem, ode, sonnet, hymn, roundel; see also POETRY, SONG, VERSE 1.

lyrical *a.* melodious, sweet, rhythmical; see MUSICAL 1, POETIC.

M

ma* *n.* mama*, mommy*, mom*; see MOTHER 1.

machine *n.* instrument, appliance, vehicle, implement, gadget; see also DEVICE 1, ENGINE, MOTOR, TOOL 1.

machine gun *n.* automatic rifle, semiautomatic rifle, automatic arms, light ordnance, Tommy gun*, burp gun*, Gatling gun; see also GUN, WEAPON.

machinery *n.* appliances, implements, tools; see APPLIANCE, DEVICE 1, ENGINE, MACHINE, MOTOR.

mad *a.* **1.** [Insane] demented, deranged, psychotic; see INSANE. **2.** [Angry] provoked, enraged, exasperated; see ANGRY. **3.** [Afflicted with rabies] frenzied, raging, foaming at the mouth; see SICK.

madden *v.* craze, infuriate, enrage; see ANGER.

maddening *a.* annoying, infuriating, offensive; see DISTURBING.

made *a.* fashioned, shaped, finished; see BUILT, FORMED, MANUFACTURED. **—have** (or **have got**) **it made*** succeed, be assured, be prosperous; see SUCCEED 1.

made easy *a.* reduced, made plain, uncomplicated; see EASY 2, SIMPLIFIED.

made-up *a.* **1.** [False] invented, concocted, devised, fabricated, exaggerated, prepared, fictitious; see also FALSE 2, 3, UNREAL. **2.** [Marked by the use of make-up] rouged, powdered, painted, colored, freshened, reddened, cosmeticized.

madhouse *n.* mental hospital, asylum, bedlam; see HOSPITAL.

madly *a.* rashly, crazily, hastily; see VIOLENTLY, WILDLY.

madman *n.* lunatic, psychopath, maniac, raver, insane person, deranged person, psychiatric patient, nut*, screwball*, oddball*, psycho*, wacko*, schizo*, cuckoo*.

madness *n.* derangement, aberration, delusion; see INSANITY.

magazine *n.* publication, broadside, pamphlet, booklet, manual, circular, journal, periodical, weekly, monthly, quarterly, annual, bulletin, transactions, review, supplement, gazette, report, brochure, pulp, glossy*, slick*.

maggot *n.* grub, slug, larva; see PARASITE 1, WORM 1.

magic *a.* magical, mystic, diabolic, Satanic, necromantic, fiendish, demoniac, malevolent, shamanist, voodooistic, conjuring, spellbinding, enchanting, fascinating, cryptic, transcendental, supernatural, alchemistic, spooky, ghostly, haunted, weird, uncanny, eerie, disembodied, immaterial, astral, spiritualistic, psychic, supersensory, otherworldly, fairylike, mythical, mythic, charmed, enchanted, bewitched, entranced, spellbound, under a spell, cursed, prophetic, telepathic, clairvoyant, telekinetic, parapsychological; see also MYSTERIOUS 2.

magic *n.* **1.** [The controlling of supernatural powers] occultism, legerdemain, necromancy, incantation, spell, wizardry, alchemy, superstition, enchantment, sorcery, prophecy, divination, astrology, taboo, witchcraft, black magic, voodooism, fire worship; see also WITCHCRAFT. **2.** [An example of magic] incantation, prediction, soothsaying, fortunetelling, foreboding, exorcism, ghost dance.

magical *a.* occult, enchanting, mystic; see MAGIC, MYSTERIOUS 2.

magician *n.* enchanter, necromancer, conjurer, seer, soothsayer, diviner, sorcerer, wizard, warlock, medicine man, shaman, exorcist; see also PROPHET, WITCH.

magnet *n.* lodestone, magnetite, magnetic iron ore, natural magnet, artificial magnet, bar magnet, electromagnet, horseshoe magnet.

magnetic *a.* irresistible, captivating, fascinating; see CHARMING.

magnetism *n.* lure, influence, charm; see ATTRACTION.

magnificence *n.* grandeur, majesty, stateliness, nobleness, glory, radiance, grace, beauty, style, flourish, luxuriousness, glitter, nobility, greatness, lavishness, brilliance, splendor, richness, pomp, swank*; see also GRANDEUR.—*Ant.* DULLNESS, simplicity, unostentatiousness.

magnificent *a.* exalted, great, majestic; see GRAND.

magnify *v.* amplify, blow up, expand; see INCREASE.

magnitude *n.* **1.** [Size] extent, breadth, dimension; see MEASURE 1, MEASUREMENT 2, QUANTITY, SIZE. **2.** [Importance] greatness, consequence, significance; see DEGREE 2, IMPORTANCE.

maid *n.* **1.** [A female servant] maidservant, nursemaid, housemaid, chambermaid, barmaid; see also SERVANT. **2.** [A girl] child, maiden, kid*; see GIRL, WOMAN 1.

maiden *a.* earliest, beginning, virgin; see FIRST.

maiden name *n.* family name, inherited name, surname; see NAME 1.

mail *n.* letter, post, communication, correspondence, airmail letters, postal*, junk mail, postcard, printed matter; see also LETTER 2.

mail *v.* post, send by mail, drop into a mailbox; see SEND 1.

mailed *a.* posted, sent by post, transmitted by post, in the mail, shipped, consigned, dispatched, sent by mail, dropped in a mailbox; see also SENT.

maim *v.* mutilate, disable, disfigure; see DAMAGE, HURT.

main *a.* **1.** [Principal] chief, dominant, first, authoritative, significant, most important, superior, foremost, leading; see also MAJOR 1. **2.** [Only] utter, pure, simple; see ABSOLUTE.

mainland *n.* shore, beach, dry land; see LAND 1, REGION 1.

mainly *a.* chiefly, largely, essentially; see PRINCIPALLY.

maintain *v.* **1.** [To uphold] hold up, advance, keep; see SUPPORT 2, SUSTAIN 1. **2.** [To assert] state, affirm, attest; see DECLARE, REPORT 1, SAY. **3.** [To keep ready for use] preserve, keep, conserve, repair, withhold, renew, reserve, defer, hold back, have in store, care for, save, put away, set aside, store up, keep for, lay aside, lay away, set by, keep on hand, keep in reserve, set apart, keep up, keep aside, control, hold over, manage, direct, have, own, sustain, secure, stick to, stand by; see also KEEP 1.—*Ant.* WASTE, neglect, consume. **4.** [To continue] carry on, persevere, keep on; see CONTINUE 1. **5.** [To support] provide for, take care of, keep; see SUPPORT 3, SUSTAIN 2.

maintenance *n.* sustenance, livelihood, resources; see PAY 1, 2, SUBSISTENCE 2.

majestic *a.* dignified, sumptuous, exalted; see GRAND, NOBLE 1, 3.

majesty *n.* **1.** [Grandeur] nobility, illustriousness, greatness; see GRANDEUR. **2.** [A form of address; *usually capital*] Lord, King, Emperor, Prince, Royal Highness, Highness, Sire, Eminence, Queen.

major *a.* **1.** [Greater] higher, larger, dominant, primary, upper, exceeding, extreme, ultra, over, above; see also SUPERIOR. **2.** [Important] significant, main, influential; see IMPORTANT 1, PRINCIPAL.

majority *n.* **1.** [The larger part] more than half, preponderance, most, best, gross, lion's share*, greater number. **2.** [Legal maturity] legal age, adulthood, voting age; see MANHOOD 1.

make *v.* **1.** [To manufacture] construct, fabricate, assemble, fashion, compose, compile, create, effect, produce; see also BUILD, MANUFACTURE. **2.** [To total] add up to, come to, equal; see AMOUNT TO. **3.** [To create] originate, actualize, effect, generate, compose, plan, devise, construct, cause, conceive; see also COMPOSE 2, CREATE , INVENT 1, PRODUCE 2. **4.** [To acquire] gain, get, secure; see GET 1. **5.** [To force] constrain, compel, coerce; see FORCE. **6.** [To cause] start, effect, initiate; see BEGIN 1, CAUSE. **7.** [To wage] carry on, conduct, engage in; see ACT 2. **8.** [To prepare] get ready, arrange, adjust; see COOK, PREPARE 1.

make amends *v.* atone, make up for, compensate; see RECONCILE 2, REPAY 1, SETTLE 7.

make as if or **as though** *v.* make believe, simulate, affect; see PRETEND 1, 2.

make believe *v.* feign, simulate, counterfeit; see DREAM 2, PRETEND 1, 2.

make-believe *a.* pretended, fraudulent, acted; see FALSE 3, FANTASTIC, UNREAL.

make-believe *n.* sham, unreality, fairy tale; see FANTASY, PRETENSE 2.

make certain (of) *v.* make sure of, check into, find out, investigate; see also EXAMINE, GUARANTEE.

make do *v.* employ, suffice, accept; see ENDURE 2, SURVIVE 1, USE 1.

make ends meet *v.* survive, subsist, get along; see BUDGET, ESTIMATE, MANAGE 3.

make fun of *v.* tease, embarrass, mimic; see BOTHER 2, IMITATE 1.

make good *v.* **1.** [To repay] compensate, adjust, reimburse; see PAY 1, REPAY 1. **2.** [To justify] maintain, support, uphold; see SUPPORT 2. **3.** [To succeed] arrive, pay off, prove oneself; see PAY 2, SUCCEED 1.

make headway *v.* progress, achieve, become better; see ADVANCE 1, IMPROVE 2.

make it* *v.* achieve, triumph, accomplish; see SUCCEED 1.

make known *v.* tell, advise, announce; see ADVERTISE, DECLARE.

make love *v.* sleep with, have intercourse, have sex; see COPULATE, JOIN 1, LOVE 2.

make merry *v.* frolic, revel, enjoy; see PLAY 1.

make of *v.* interpret, translate, understand; see THINK 1.

make off with *v.* abduct, rob, kidnap; see STEAL.

make out *v.* **1.** [To understand] perceive, recognize, see; see UNDERSTAND 1. **2.** [To succeed] accomplish, achieve, prosper; see SUCCEED 1. **3.** [To see] discern, perceive, detect; see DISCOVER, SEE 1.

make over *v.* **1.** [To improve] amend, correct, restore; see IMPROVE 1, REDECORATE, REMODEL. **2.** [To rebuild] renovate, refashion, refurbish; see REPAIR, RESTORE 3.

make peace *v.* propitiate, negotiate, make up; see RECONCILE 2.

make progress *v.* go forward, progress, proceed; see ADVANCE 1, IMPROVE 2.

make ready *v.* arrange, get ready, prearrange; see COOK, PREPARE 1.

make sense *v.* be reasonable, be intelligible, be clear, be understandable, be logical, be coherent, articulate, add up, follow, infer, deduce, hang together*, hold water*, put two and two together, straighten out, stand to reason.

makeshift *a.* substitute, alternative, stopgap; see TEMPORARY.

make sure of *v.* ensure, determine, review; see CHECK 2, DISCOVER.

make the most of *v.* take advantage of, employ, promote; see USE 1.

make the rounds *v.* inspect, scrutinize, check up on; see EXAMINE 1.

make time *v.* gain, speed up, make good time; see SPEED, TRAVEL.

makeup *n.* **1.** [Cosmetics] greasepaint, mascara, eyeliner, powder, foundation, eye shadow, lipstick, war paint*; see also COSMETIC. **2.** [*Anything offered to make good a shortage] atonement, compensation, conciliation; see PAYMENT. **3.** [Composition] scheme, structure, arrangement; see COMPOSITION, DESIGN, FORMATION.

make up *v.* **1.** [To compose] compound, combine, mingle; see JOIN 1, MIX 1. **2.** [To constitute] comprise, belong to, go into the making of, be contained in, be an element of, be a portion of, include, consist of; see also COMPOSE 1. **3.** [To invent] fabricate, devise, fashion; see COMPOSE 2, CREATE, INVENT 1. **4.** [To reconcile] conciliate, pacify, accommodate; see RECONCILE 2. **5.** [To apply cosmetics] powder; apply face powder, apply lipstick, apply eye shadow, etc.; beautify, do up*, put one's face on.

make up for *v.* compensate, balance, counterbalance; see BALANCE 2.

make up one's mind *v.* choose, pick, elect; see DECIDE, RESOLVE.

make use of *v.* need, employ, utilize; see USE 1.

make war *v.* battle, combat, encounter; see FIGHT.

make way *v.* progress, proceed, break ground; see ADVANCE 1.

making *n.* imagination, conception, formulation, devising, producing, constituting, causation, fashioning, building, origination, shaping, forging, designing, planning, fabrication, composition; see also PRODUCTION 1.

male *a.* manlike, virile, powerful; see MASCULINE.

male *n.* male sex, man, he; see BOY, FATHER 1.

malformed *a.* distorted, grotesque, abnormal; see DEFORMED, TWISTED 1.

malfunction *n.* slip, bad performance, failure to function; see FAILURE 1.

malice *n.* spite, animosity, resentment; see EVIL 1, HATRED.

malicious *a.* ill-disposed, spiteful, hateful; see BAD 1.

malignant *a.* **1.** [Diseased] cancerous, lethal, poisonous; see DEADLY. **2.** [Harmful] deleterious, corrupt, sapping; see DANGEROUS, HARMFUL.

malpractice *n.* negligence, misbehavior, neglect; see CARELESSNESS, VIOLATION.

mama* *n.* female progenitor, mamma*, parent; see MOTHER 1.

mammal *n.* vertebrate, creature, beast; see ANIMAL.

man *n.* **1.** [The human race] mankind, human beings, race, humanity, human species, human nature, persons, mortals, individuals, earthlings, civilized society, creatures, fellow creatures, people, folk, society, *Homo sapiens* (Latin). **2.** [An adult male] he, gentleman, Sir, Mr., fellow, mister, master, chap*, guy*; see also BOY. **3.** [Anyone] human being, an individual, fellow creature; see PERSON 1. **4.** [An employee] hand, worker, representative; see EMPLOYEE. **5.** [*Husband] married man, spouse, partner; see HUSBAND. **—as a man** in unison, united, all together; see UNANIMOUSLY. **—be one's own man** be independent, stand alone, be free; see ENDURE 1. **—to a man** all, everyone, with no exception; see EVERYBODY.

man *v.* garrison, protect, fortify; see DEFEND 1, GUARD.

manage *v.* **1.** [To direct] lead, oversee, indicate, designate, instruct, mastermind, engineer, show, disburse, distribute, execute, handle, watch, guide, supervise, conduct, engage in, officiate, pilot, steer, run, minister, regulate, administer, manipulate, officiate, superintend, preside, suggest, advocate, counsel, request, call upon, maintain, care for, take over, take care of, carry on, watch over, have in one's charge, look after, see to, run the show*, call the shots*, run a tight ship*.—*Ant.* OBEY, follow, take orders. **2.** [To contrive] accomplish, bring about, effect; see ACHIEVE, SUCCEED 1. **3.** [To get along] bear up, survive, get by; see ENDURE 2.

manageable *a.* controllable, docile, compliant, governable, teachable, tractable, willing, obedient, submissive, yielding, adaptable, flexible, dutiful, humble, meek, easy; see also GENTLE 3, OBEDIENT 1, WILLING.—*Ant.* REBELLIOUS, ungovernable, unruly.

managed *a.* **1.** [Trained] handled, guided, persuaded, influenced, driven, counselled, urged, taught, instructed, coached, groomed, primed, given a workout; see also EDUCATED, TRAINED.—*Ant.* WILD, undisciplined, uneducated. **2.** [Governed] ruled, controlled, dominated, commanded, directed, swayed, mastered, run, regulated, ordered, compelled, supervised, piloted, cared for, taken care of; see also GOVERNED.—*Ant.* FREE, ungoverned, unsupervised.

management *n.* **1.** [Direction] supervision, superintendence, government, command, guidance, conduct, organization, handling, policy, order, power, control; see also COMMAND. **2.** [Those who undertake management; *usually preceded by "the"*] directors, administrators, executives; see ADMINISTRATION 2.

manager *n.* director, handler, superintendent, supervisor; see also EXECUTIVE.

managing *n.* directing, supervising, superintending, advising, overseeing, controlling, taking charge of, caring for, administering, executing, organizing, regulating, leading, piloting, steering, handling, charging, manipulating; see also OPERATING.

mandate *n.* command, decree, order; see COMMAND.

mandatory *a.* compulsory, forced, obligatory; see NECESSARY.

man-eating *a.* cannibal, carnivorous, omnivorous; see DANGEROUS, DEADLY.

maneuver *n.* **1.** [A movement, usually military] stratagem, movement, procedure; see PLAN 2, TACTICS. **2.** [A trick] subterfuge, finesse, ruse; see TRICK 1. **3.** [Extensive practice in arms; *plural*] imitation war, exercise, war games; see DRILL 3, EXERCISE 1, PARADE 1.

maneuver *v.* plot, scheme, move, manage, contrive, design, devise, trick, cheat, conspire, sham, angle for*; see also PLAN 1.

mangle *v.* **1.** [To mutilate] tear, lacerate, wound, injure, cripple, maim, rend, disfigure, cut, slit, butcher, slash, slice, carve, bruise, mutilate; see also HURT 1. **2.** [To iron with a power roller] steam press, smooth, iron; see IRON.

manhandle *v.* damage, maul, mistreat; see ABUSE, BEAT 1.

manhood *n.* **1.** [Male maturity] legal age, post-pubescence, coming of age, prime of life, middle age, voting age, adulthood. **2.** [Manly qualities] virility, resoluteness, honor, gallantry, nobility, forcefulness, daring, boldness, tenacity, self-reliance, potency.

mania *n.* craze, lunacy, madness; see DESIRE 1, INSANITY, OBSESSION.

maniac *n.* lunatic, insane person, crazy person; see MADMAN.

manipulate *v.* handle, shape, mold; see FORM 1, MANAGE 1, PLAN 1.

manipulation *n.* guidance, use, direction; see MANAGEMENT 1.

mankind *n.* humanity, human race, society; see MAN 1.

manlike *a.* anthropoid, simian, anthropomorphic; see HUMAN.

manly *a.* masculine, courageous, fearless, firm, noble, valiant, high-spirited, intrepid, gallant, resolute, bold, confident, dauntless, self-reliant; see also MASCULINE.—*Ant.* COWARDLY, timid, effeminate.

man-made *a.* manufactured, artificial, synthetic, unnatural, counterfeit, not organic, ersatz, false, faux, not genuine.

manner *n.* **1.** [Personal conduct] mien, deportment, demeanor; see BEHAVIOR. **2.** [Customary action] use, way, practice; see CUSTOM, HABIT 1. **3.** [Method] mode, fashion, style; see METHOD. —**in a manner of speaking** in a way, so to speak, so to say; see RATHER.

mannerism *n.* idiosyncrasy, pretension, peculiarity; see CHARACTERISTIC, QUIRK.

mannerly *a.* polished, considerate, charming; see POLITE.

manners *n.pl.* **1.** [Personal behavior] conduct, deportment, bearing; see BEHAVIOR. **2.** [Culture] urbanity, taste, refinement; see COURTESY 1, CULTURE 2, ELEGANCE.

manpower *n.* youth, men of military age, males; see LABOR 4.

mansion *n.* villa, house, hall; see ESTATE, HOME 1.

manslaughter *n.* killing, homicide, assassination; see CRIME, MURDER.

mantle *n.* fireplace, mantlepiece, chimney piece; see SHELF 2.

manual *a.* hand-operated, not automatic, standard; see OLD-FASHIONED.

manual *n.* guidebook, reference book, textbook; see BOOK.

manufacture *n.* fashioning, forming, assembling; see PRODUCTION 1.

manufacture *v.* make, construct, fabricate, produce, form, fashion, carve, mold, cast, frame, put together, turn out, stamp out, print out, cut out, have in production, have on the assembly line, print, shape, execute, accomplish, complete, tool, machine, mill, make up; see also BUILD.—*Ant.* DESTROY, demolish, tear down.

manufactured *a.* made, produced, constructed, fabricated, erected, fashioned, shaped, forged, turned out, tooled, executed, done, assembled, ready for the market, in shape, complete, completed; see also BUILT, FORMED.

manufacturer *n.* maker, producer, fabricator, constructor, builder, operator, craftsman, corporation, entrepreneur, company.

manufacturing *a.* producing, industrial, fabricative; see MAKING.

manufacturing *n.* fabrication, building, construction, assembling, preparing for market, putting in production, continuing production, keeping in production, forging, formation, erection, composition, accomplishment, completion, finishing, doing, turning out; see also PRODUCTION 1.—*Ant.* DESTRUCTION, wreck, demolition.

manure *n.* guano, plant-food, compost; see DUNG, FERTILIZER.

manuscript *n.* composition, parchment, tablet, paper, document, original, copy, letterpress, autograph, translation, facsimile, book, script; see also WRITING 2.

many *a.* numerous, multiplied, manifold, multitudinous, multifarious, diverse, sundry, profuse, innumerable, not a few, numberless, a world of, countless, uncounted, alive with, teeming, in heaps, several, of every description, prevalent, no end of, no end to, everywhere, crowded, common, usual, plentiful, abundant, galore; see also VARIOUS.—*Ant.* FEW, meager, scanty.

many *n.* a great number, abundance, thousands*; see PLENTY. —**a good** or **(great) many** a great number, abundance, thousands*; see PLENTY. —**as many (as)** as much as, an equal number, a similar amount; see SAME.

many-sided *a.* **1.** [Multilateral] polyhedral, geometric, bilateral, dihedral, trilateral, quadrilateral, tetrahedral; see also GEOMETRICAL. **2.** [Gifted] endowed, talented, adaptable; see ABLE, VERSATILE.

map *n.* chart, graph, plat, sketch, delineation, drawing, picture, portrayal, draft, tracing, outline, ground plan. —**put on the map** make famous, bring fame to, glorify; see ESTABLISH 2. —**wipe off the map** eliminate, put out of existence, ruin; see DESTROY.

map *v.* outline, draft, chart; see PLAN 2.

mar *v.* **1.** [To damage slightly] harm, bruise, scratch; see BREAK 2, DAMAGE. **2.** [To impair] deform, deface, warp; see DESTROY.

marble *a.* petrified, granitelike, unyielding; see ROCK *n.* 1, STONE.

marble *n.* **1.** [Metamorphic limestone] *Marbles include the following:* Parian, Pentelic, Carrian, Serpentine, Algerian, Tecali (onyx marbles), Tuscan, Gibraltar, Vermont, Georgia, fire, black, ophicalcite; see also STONE. **2.** [A piece of carved marble] carving, figurine, figure; see ART, SCULPTURE, STATUE. **3.** [A ball used in marbles] nib*, shooter*, aggie; see TOY 1.

march *n.* **1.** [The act of marching] progression, movement, advancing, advancement, countermarch, goose step, military parade; see also STEP 1, WALK 3. **2.** [The distance or route marched] walk, trek, hike; see JOURNEY. **3.** [Music for marching] martial music, wedding march, processional; see MUSIC.

march *v.* move, advance, step out, go on, proceed, step, tread, tramp, patrol, prowl, parade, goose step, file, range, strut, proceed, progress, go ahead, forge ahead.—*Ant.* PAUSE, halt, retreat. —**on the march** proceeding, advancing, tramping; see MOVING 1.

March *n.* spring month, beginning of spring, month that comes in like a lion and goes out like a lamb; see MONTH, SPRING 2.

marching *a.* advancing, parading, pacing; see MOVING 1, TRAVELING, WALKING.

mare *n.* female horse, brood mare, breeding stock; see ANIMAL, HORSE.

margin *n.* border, lip, shore; see BOUNDARY, EDGE 1.

marginal *a.* rimming, edging, verging; see BORDERING.

marijuana *n. cannabis sativa*, grass*, pot*; see DRUG.

marine *a.* maritime, of the sea, oceanic; see MARITIME, NAUTICAL.

marital *a.* conjugal, connubial, nuptial; see MARRIED.

maritime *a.* naval, marine, oceanic, seagoing, hydrographic, seafaring, aquatic, natatorial, Neptunian; see also NAUTICAL.

mark *n.* **1.** [The physical result of marking] brand, stamp, blaze, imprint, impression, line, trace, check, stroke, streak, dot, point, nick. **2.** [A target] butt, prey, bull's-eye. **3.** [Effect] manifestation, consequence, value; see RESULT. —**hit the mark** achieve, accomplish, do well; see SUCCEED 1. —**make one's mark** accomplish, prosper, become famous; see SUCCEED 1. —**miss the mark** be unsuccessful, err, mistake; see FAIL 1.

mark *v.* **1.** [To make a mark] brand, stamp, imprint, blaze, print, check, chalk, label, sign, identify, check off, trace, stroke, streak, dot, point, nick, x, underline. **2.** [To designate] earmark, point out, stake out, indicate, check off, mark off, signify, denote; see also MEAN 1. **3.** [To distinguish] characterize, signalize, qualify; see DISTINGUISH 1. **4.** [To put prices upon] ticket, label, tag; see PRICE.

mark down *v.* reduce, put on sale, cut the price of; see PRICE.

marked *a.* **1.** [Carrying a mark] branded, signed, sealed, stamped, imprinted, inscribed, characterized by, distinguished by, recognized by, identified by. **2.** [Priced] labeled, trade-marked, price-marked, marked down, marked up, ticketed, priced, tagged; see also COSTING.

marked down *a.* lowered, priced lower, discounted; see REDUCED 2.

marked up *a.* added on, more expensive, raised; see RAISED 1.

marker *n.* ticket, price mark, trademark, seal, brand, stamp, boundary mark, inscription, pencil, pen; see also LABEL.

market *n.* **1.** [A place devoted to sale] trading post, mart, shopping mall, shopper's square, emporium, exchange, city market, public market, supermarket, meat market, fish market, stock market, stock exchange, fair, dime store, drug store, discount store, department store, variety store, bazaar, warehouse, business, delicatessen; see also SHOP, STORE. **2.** [The state of trade] supply and demand, sale, run; see BUSINESS 1, 4, DEMAND 2. **—be in the market (for)** want to buy, be willing to purchase, need; see WANT 1. **—on the market** salable, ready for purchase, available; see FOR SALE.

market *v.* vend, exchange, barter; see SELL.

mark off *v.* segregate, separate, indicate; see MARK 2.

mark out *v.* delete, omit, erase; see ELIMINATE.

mark time *v.* put off, postpone, kill time; see DELAY, WAIT 1.

markup *n.* raise, margin, gross profit; see INCREASE, PROFIT 2.

mark up *v.* raise the price, adjust, add to; see INCREASE.

marriage *n.* wedding, espousal, spousal, nuptials, pledging, mating, matrimony, conjugality, union, match, wedlock, wedded state, wedded bliss, holy matrimony.

married *a.* wedded, mated, espoused, united, given in marriage, pledged in marriage, living in the married state, in the state of matrimony, hitched*.—*Ant.* SINGLE, unwedded, unmarried.

marry *v.* **1.** [To take a spouse] wed, espouse, enter the matrimonial state, take wedding vows, pledge in marriage, mate, lead to the altar, tie the knot*, get hitched*, get hooked*.—*Ant.* DIVORCE, separate, reject. **2.** [To join in wedlock] unite, give, join in matrimony, pronounce man and wife; see also JOIN 1.—*Ant.* DIVORCE, annul, separate.

marsh *n.* morass, bog, quagmire; see SWAMP.

marshy *a.* swampy, wet, sloppy; see MUDDY 1, 2.

martial *a.* warlike, soldierly, combative; see AGGRESSIVE.

martyr *n.* sufferer, offering, scapegoat; see SAINT, VICTIM.

martyrdom *n.* agony, suffering, devotion; see TORTURE.

marvel *n.* miracle, phenomenon, curiosity; see WONDER 2.

marvel *v.* stare, stand in awe, stare with open mouth; see WONDER 1.

marvelous *a.* fabulous, astonishing, spectacular; see UNUSUAL 1.

masculine *a.* courageous, male, virile, potent, vigorous, forceful, aggressive, adult, honorable; see also MANLY.

masculinity *n.* virility, power, manliness; see MANHOOD 2, STRENGTH.

mash *n.* mix, pulp, paste; see FEED, MIXTURE 1.

mash *v.* crush, bruise, squash, chew, masticate, smash, pound, reduce, squeeze, brew, pulverize; see also GRIND, PRESS 1.

mashed *a.* crushed, pressed, mixed, pulpy, battered, pounded, smashed, squashed, softened, reduced, spongy, pasty, pulverized, masticated, chewed, bruised; made into a powder, made into a paste, etc.—*Ant.* WHOLE, hard, uncrushed.

mask *n.* **1.** [A disguise] cover, false face, veil, hood, costume, theater device; see also CAMOUFLAGE, DISGUISE. **2.** [A protection] gas mask, catcher's mask, fencing mask, fireman's mask, respirator; see also PROTECTION 2. **3.** [A masquerade] revel, party, carnival; see PARTY 1.

mask *v.* cloak, conceal, veil; see DISGUISE, HIDE 1.

masquerade *n.* Mardi Gras, masked ball, pretense; see DANCE 1, ENTERTAINMENT, PARTY 1.

mass *n.* **1.** [A body of matter] lump, bulk, piece, portion, section, batch, block, body, core, clot, coagulation, wad*, gob*; see also HUNK. **2.** [A considerable quantity] heap, volume, crowd; see QUANTITY, SIZE 2. **3.** [Size] magnitude, volume, span; see EXTENT, SIZE 2.

mass *n.* eucharistic rite, Catholic service, Eucharist, Lord's Supper, Holy Communion, ceremony, observance; see also CELEBRATION, WORSHIP 1. *Masses include the following:* High Mass, Low Mass, Solemn High Mass, Requiem Mass, Votive Mass.

massacre *n.* butchering, killing, slaughter; see MURDER.

massacre *v.* exterminate, mass murder, annihilate; see KILL 1.

massage *v.* stimulate, caress, press; see RUB 1.

masses *n.pl.* proletariat, the rank and file, multitude; see PEOPLE 3.

massive *a.* huge, heavy, cumbersome; see LARGE 1.

mass production *n.* mass producing, assembly-line methods, automation; see MANUFACTURING, PRODUCTION 1.

mast *n.* spar, pole, post, timber, trunk; see also POST 1.

master *a.* leading, supreme, main; see EXCELLENT, MAJOR 1, PRINCIPAL.

master *n.* **1.** [One who directs others] chief, director, boss; see EXECUTIVE, LEADER 2. **2.** [A teacher] instructor, preceptor, mentor; see TEACHER. **3.** [One who possesses great skill] genius, maestro, sage, scientist, past master, champion, prima donna, connoisseur, fellow, doctor; see also ARTIST.—*Ant.* DISCIPLE, beginner, undergraduate.

master *v.* **1.** [To conquer] subdue, rule, humble; see SUCCEED 1. **2.** [To become proficient in] gain mastery in, understand, comprehend; see LEARN, STUDY.

masterful *a.* commanding, expert, skillful; see EXCELLENT.

masterpiece *n.* perfection, model, standard, cream of the crop, masterwork, *magnum opus* (Latin).

mastery *n.* **1.** [Control] dominance, sovereignty, government; see COMMAND, POWER 2. **2.** [Ability to use to the full] skill, capacity, proficiency; see ABILITY, EDUCATION 1.

masturbation *n.* sexual self-gratification, onanism, self-love, self-abuse*.

mat *n.* covering, floor covering, doormat, place mat, network, table mat, place setting, web, mesh, cloth, straw mat; see also COVER 1, RUG.

mat *v.* braid, tangle, snarl; see TWIST, WEAVE 1.

match *n.* **1.** [An instrument to produce fire] safety match, sulphur match, matchstick, fuse; see also LIGHT 3. **2.** [An article that is like another] peer, equivalent, mate, analogue, counterpart, approximation; see also EQUAL. **3.** [A formal contest] race, event, rivalry; see COMPETITION, SPORT 3.

match *v.* **1.** [To find or make equals] equalize, liken, equate, make equal, pair, coordinate, level, even, match up, balance, mate, marry, unite; see also EQUAL. **2.** [To be alike] harmonize, suit, be twins, be counterparts, be doubles, check with, go together, go with, rhyme with, take after; see also AGREE, RESEMBLE.—*Ant.* DIFFER, be unlike, bear no resemblance. **3.** [To meet in contest] equal, meet, compete with; see COMPETE.

matched *a.* doubled, similar, equated, evened, coordinated, harmonized, paired, mated; see also ALIKE, BALANCED 1.—*Ant.* UNLIKE, unequal, different.

matching *a.* comparable, analogous, parallel; see EQUAL.

mate *n.* **1.** [One of a pair] complement, analogue, counterpart; see MATCH 2. **2.** [A companion] playmate, classmate, buddy; see FRIEND. **3.** [A marriage partner] spouse, bride, groom, bedmate, the old man*, the old lady*; see also HUSBAND, WIFE.

material *a.* palpable, sensible, corporeal; see PHYSICAL 1, REAL 2, TANGIBLE.

material *n.* **1.** [Matter] body, corporeality, substance; see ELEMENT 2, MATTER 1. **2.** [Unfinished matter; *often plural*] raw material, stuff, stock, staple, ore, stockpile, crop, supply, accumulation; see also ALLOY, ELEMENT 2, GOODS, METAL, MINERAL, PLASTIC, ROCK 1, WOOL.

materialistic *a.* possessive, acquisitive, opportunistic; see GREEDY, WORLDLY.

materialize *v.* be realized, take on form, become real, actualize, become concrete, metamorphose, reintegrate; see also BECOME.—*Ant.* DISSOLVE, disintegrate, disperse.

maternal *a.* parental, sympathetic, protective; see MOTHERLY.

maternity *n.* parenthood, motherhood, motherliness; see PARENT.

mathematical *a.* arithmetical, numerical, computable; see NUMERICAL.

mathematics *n.* science of real numbers, science of numbers, language of numbers, computation, reckoning, calculation, new math, math. *Types of mathematics include the following:* arithmetic, algebra, plane geometry, spherical geometry, trigonometry, trig*, analytical geometry, differential calculus, integral calculus, programming, applied mathematics, probability, statistics, topology, transforms, logarithms.

matriarch *n.* female ruler, dowager, matron; see QUEEN.

matrimony *n.* conjugality, wedlock, union; see MARRIAGE.

matron *n.* lady, wife, mother; see WOMAN 1.

matronly *a.* middle-aged, grave, sedate; see MATURE, MOTHERLY.

matted *a.* snarled, rumpled, disordered; see TANGLED, TWISTED 1.

matter *n.* **1.** [Substance] body, material, substantiality, corporeality, constituents, stuff, object, thing, physical world; see also ELEMENT 2.—*Ant.* NOTHING, nothingness, immateriality. **2.** [Subject] interest, focus, resolution; see SUBJECT, THEME 1. **3.** [An affair] undertaking, circumstance, concern; see AFFAIR 1. **—as a matter of fact** in fact, in actuality, truly; see REALLY 1. **—for that matter** in regard to that, as far as that is concerned, concerning that; see AND. **—no matter** it doesn't matter, it is of no concern, regardless of; see REGARDLESS 2.

matter *v.* signify, be substantive, be important, have influence, imply, express, be of consequence, involve, be worthy of notice, cut ice*; see also MEAN 1.

matter of course *n.* expected result, routine event, the usual thing; see EVENT, RESULT.

matter-of-fact *a.* objective, prosaic, feasible; see PRACTICAL.

matter of life or death *n.* significance, seriousness, concern; see IMPORTANCE.

mattress *n.* innerspring, springs, box spring, bedding, cushion, crib mattress; see also BED.

mature *a.* full-grown, middle-aged, grown, grown-up, of age, in full bloom, womanly, manly, matronly, developed, prepared, settled, cultivated, cultured, sophisticated; see also EXPERIENCED.—*Ant.* YOUNG, adolescent, immature.

mature *v.* grow up, become a man, become a woman, come of age, become experienced, settle down, ripen, reach perfection, attain majority, culminate, become wise, become perfected, grow skilled, fill out; see also AGE, DEVELOP 1.

matured *a.* grown, full-grown, aged; see FINISHED.

maturity *n.* **1.** [Mental competence] development, sophistication, cultivation, culture, civilization, advancement, mental power, capability. **2.** [Physical development] prime of life, post-pubescence, adulthood; see MAJORITY 2. **3.** [Ripeness] readiness, mellowness, sweetness; see DEVELOPMENT.

maul *v.* pound, whip, trample; see BEAT 1, HIT 1.

maxim *n.* aphorism, adage, epithet; see PROVERB, SAYING.

maximum *a.* supreme, highest, greatest; see BEST.

maximum *n.* supremacy, height, pinnacle, pre-eminence, culmination, matchlessness, preponderance, apex, peak, greatest number, highest degree, summit; see also CLIMAX.—*Ant.* MINIMUM, foot, bottom.

may *v.* **1.** [Grant permission] be permitted, be allowed, can, be privileged to, be authorized, be at liberty to. **2.** [Concede possibility] will, shall, be going to, should, be conceivable, be possible, be practicable, be within reach, be obtainable; see also WILL 3.

May *n.* spring month, baseball season, fifth month; see MONTH, SPRING 2.

maybe *a.* perhaps, possibly, it might be, it could be, maybe so, as it may be, conceivably, God willing.—*Ant.* HARDLY, scarcely, probably not.

mayor *n.* magistrate, Lord Mayor, burgomaster, president of a city council, civil administrator, civil judge, city father; see also EXECUTIVE.

maze *n.* tangle, entanglement, twist, winding, convolution, intricacy, confusion, meandering, puzzle.—*Ant.* ORDER, disentanglement, simplicity.

meadow *n.* grass, pasture, mountain meadow, upland pasture, meadow land, bottom land, bottoms, pasturage; hay meadow, clover meadow, bluegrass meadow, etc.; salt marsh, steppe, heath, pampa, savanna; see also FIELD 1.

meager *a.* lank, lanky, gaunt, starved, emaciated, lean, bony, slender, slim, spare, little, bare, scant, stinted, lacking, wanting, scrawny, withered, lithe, narrow, tenuous, slightly-made, skinny; see also THIN 2.—*Ant.* FAT, plump, stout.

meal *n.* **1.** [Ground feed] bran, farina, grits, fodder, provender, forage; see also FEED, FLOUR, GRAIN 1. *Types of meal include the following:* corn meal, corn grits, hominy, corn starch, barley meal, oatmeal, soybean meal, soybean flour. **2.** [The quantity of food taken at one time] repast, feast, refreshment, mess, feed bag*, eats*, grub*, chow*, spread*, square meal*, snack. *Meals include the following:* breakfast, dinner, lunch, banquet, brunch, snack, tea, picnic, luncheon, dessert, midnight supper; see also BREAKFAST, DINNER, LUNCH.

mean *a.* **1.** [Small-minded] base, low, debased; see VULGAR. **2.** [Of low estate] servile, pitiful, shabby; see HUMBLE 2. **3.** [Vicious] shameless, dishonorable, degraded, contemptible, evil, infamous, treacherous, crooked, fraudulent, faithless, unfaithful, ill-tempered, dangerous, despicable, degenerate, knavish, unscrupulous, hard as nails. **4.** [Average] mediocre, middling, halfway; see COMMON 1.

mean *n.* middle, median, midpoint; see AVERAGE, CENTER 1.

mean *v.* **1.** [To have as meaning] indicate, spell, denote, signify, add up, determine, symbolize, imply, involve, speak of, touch on, stand for, drive at, point to, connote, suggest, express, designate, intimate, tell the meaning of, purport. **2.** [To have in mind] anticipate, propose, expect; see INTEND 1. **3.** [To design for] destine for, aim at, set apart; see INTEND 2.

meander *v.* twist and turn, roam, flow; see RAMBLE 2, RUN 1, WALK 1.

meaning *n.* sense, import, purport, purpose, definition, object, implication, application, intent, suggestion, connotation, aim, drift, context, significance, essence, worth, intrinsic value, interest.—*Ant.* NONSENSE, aimlessness, absurdity.

meaningful *a.* significant, exact, essential; see IMPORTANT 1.

meaningless *a.* vague, absurd, insignificant; see TRIVIAL, UNIMPORTANT.

meanness *n.* **1.** [The quality of being mean] small-mindedness, debasement, degradation, degeneracy, unscrupulousness, stinginess, disrepute, malice, unworthiness, ill-temper, unkindness, covetousness, avarice, miserliness; see also GREED.—*Ant.* GENEROSITY, nobility, worthiness. **2.** [A mean action] belittling, defaming, groveling, cheating, sneaking, quarreling, scolding, taking advantage of, deceiving, coveting, grudging, dishonoring, defrauding, shaming, degrading, stealing.

means *n.pl.* **1.** [An instrumentality or instrumentalities] machinery, mechanism, agency, organ, channel, medium, factor, agent, power, organization; see also METHOD, SYSTEM. **2.** [Wealth] resources, substance, property; see WEALTH. **—by all means** of course, certainly, yes indeed; see SURELY, YES. **—by any means** in any way, at all, somehow; see ANYHOW. **—by means of** with the aid of, somehow, through; see BY 2. **—by no (manner of) means** in no way, not possible, definitely not; see NEVER, NO.

meanwhile *a.* meantime, during the interval, in the interim, ad interim, for the time being, until, till, up to, in the meantime, when; see also DURING.

measurable *a.* weighable, definite, limited, determinable, knowable, recognizable, detectable, calculable, real, present, fathomable, assessible.

measure *n.* **1.** [A unit of measurement] dimension, capacity, weight, volume, distance, degree, quantity, area, mass, frequency, density, intensity, rapidity, speed, caliber, bulk, sum, duration, magnitude, amplitude, size, pitch, ratio, depth, scope, height, strength, breadth, amplification. *Common units of measure include the following—linear:* inch, foot, yard, rod, mile, millimeter, centimeter, decimeter, meter, kilometer; *surface:* square inch, square foot, square yard, acre, square rod, square mile; *volume:* dram, pint, quart, gallon, centiliter, liter; *weight:* gram, ounce, pound; milligram, gram, kilogram; *relationship:* revolutions per minute (r.p.m.), miles per hour (m.p.h.), feet per second (f.p.s.), per second per second, erg, foot-pound, kilowatt-hour, acre-foot, decibel, man-hour, ohm, watt, volt, octane number. **2.** [Anything used as a standard] rule, test, trial, example, standard, yardstick, norm, pattern, type, model; see also CRITERION. **3.** [A beat] rhythm, tempo, time, step, throb, stroke, accent, meter, cadence, tune, melody, stress, vibration, division; see also BEAT 2. —**for good measure** added, as a bonus, additionally; see EXTRA. —**take measures** take action, do things to accomplish a purpose, employ; see ACT 1.

measure *v.* **1.** [To apply a standard of measurement] rule, weigh, mark, lay out, grade, graduate, gauge, sound, pitch, beat, stroke, time, mark off, scale, rank, even, level, gradate, line, align, line out, regulate, portion, set a standard, average, equate, square, calibrate, block in, survey, map. **2.** [To contain by measurement] hold, cover, contain; see INCLUDE 1.

measured *a.* **1.** [Steady] orderly, systematic, deliberate; see REGULAR 3. **2.** [Determined] checked, evaluated, calculated; see DETERMINED 1.

measurement *n.* **1.** [The act of measuring] estimation, analysis, computation; see JUDGMENT 2. **2.** [The result of measuring] distance, dimension, weight, degree, pitch, time, height, depth, density, volume, area, length, measure, thickness, quantity, magnitude, extent, range, scope, reach, amount, capacity, frequency, intensity, pressure, speed, caliber, grade, span, step, strength, mass. **3.** [A set of measures] inch, foot, yard; see MEASURE 1.

measuring *n.* weighing, grading, gauging; see JUDGMENT 1.

meat *n.* veal, mutton, lamb, chicken, turkey, goose, duck, rabbit, venison, horsemeat; see also FOOD. *Cuts and forms of meat include the following:* roast, cutlet, steak, filet, leg, shoulder, loin, tenderloin, rib, round, rump, flank, chop, liver, brains, kidneys, heart, bacon, tripe, shank, sausage, frankfurter, ground meat, chipped meat, dried meat, salted meat, pickled meat.

mechanic *n.* machinist, repair man, skilled workman; see WORKMAN.

mechanical *a.* **1.** [Concerning machinery] engineering, production, manufacturing, tooling, tuning, implementing, fabricating, forging, machining, building, construction, constructing. **2.** [Like a machine] made to a pattern, machinelike, stereotyped, standardized, without variation, unchanging, monotonous.—*Ant.* ORIGINAL, varied, changing. **3.** [Operated by the use of machinery] power-driven, involuntary, programmed; see AUTOMATED, AUTOMATIC.

mechanically *a.* automatically, unreasoningly, unchangeably; see REGULARLY.

mechanism *n.* working parts, mechanical action, system of parts; see DEVICE 1, TOOL 1.

mechanize *v.* equip, computerize, industrialize, motorize, automate, put on the assembly line, make mechanical, introduce machinery into.

medal *n.* reward, commemoration, badge; see DECORATION 3.

medallion *n.* ornament, emblem, necklace; see JEWELRY.

meddle *v.* **1.** [To interfere in others' affairs] interfere, obtrude, interlope, intervene, pry, snoop, impose oneself, infringe, break in upon, make it one's business, abuse one's rights, push in, chime in, force an entrance, encroach, intrude, be officious, obstruct, impede, hinder, encumber, busy oneself with, come uninvited, tamper with, inquire, be curious, stick one's nose in*, monkey with*, bust in*, muscle in*, barge in, have a finger on*, butt in*, horn in*; see also INTERRUPT.—*Ant.* NEGLECT, ignore, let along. **2.** [To handle others' things] tamper, molest, pry, fool with, trespass, snoop, nose, use improperly.

meddlesome *a.* obtrusive, interfering, officious, meddling, intrusive, impertinent, interposing, interrupting, obstructive, impeding, hindering, encumbering, curious, tampering, prying, snooping, troublesome, snoopy*, nosy*, kibitzing*, chiseling*.

meddling *n.* interfering, interrupting, snooping; see INTERFERENCE 1, RUDENESS.

media *n.pl.* radio, television, newspaper, journalism, news, reporters, reportage, programming, audiovisual devices.

medic* *n.* physician, practitioner, surgeon; see DOCTOR.

medical *a.* healing, medicinal, curative, therapeutic, restorative, prophylactic, preventive, alleviating, medicating, pharmaceutical, sedative, narcotic, tonic, disinfectant, corrective, pathological, cathartic, health-bringing, demulcent, balsamic, emollient.—*Ant.* HARMFUL, destructive, disease-giving.

medication *n.* remedy, pill, vaccination; see MEDICINE 2.

medicinal *a.* curative, healing, therapeutic; see HEALTHFUL.

medicine *n.* **1.** [The healing profession] medical men, healers, practitioners, doctors, physicians, surgeons, osteopaths, chiropractors. **2.** [A medical preparation] drug, dose, potion, prescription, pills, tablet, capsule, draft, patent medicine, remedy, cure, antipoison, antibiotic, medication, vaccination, inoculation, injection, draught, herb, specific, nostrum, elixir, tonic, balm, salve, lotion, ointment, emetic, shot. **3.** [The study and practice of medicine] medical science, physic, healing art, medical profession. *Branches of medicine include the following:* surgery, therapy, therapeutics, anesthesiology, internal medicine, general practice, psychiatry, psychotherapy, psychoanalysis, ophthalmology, obstetrics, gynecology, pediatrics, orthopedics, neurology, cardiology, dermatology, pathology, endocrinology, immunology, urology, hematology, inhalation therapy, diagnostics, radiotherapy, geriatrics, veterinary medicine.

medieval *a.* pertaining to the Middle Ages, feudal, antiquated; see OLD 3.

mediocre *a.* average, ordinary, standard; see COMMON 1, DULL 4.

mediocrity *n.* commonplaceness, commonness, normality; see REGULARITY.

meditate *v.* **1.** [To muse] ponder, study, contemplate, muse over, revolve, say to oneself, reflect, view, brood over, dream; see also THINK 1. **2.** [To think over] weigh, consider, speculate; see THINK 1.

meditation *n.* examination, contemplation, speculation; see REFLECTION 1, THOUGHT 1.

medium *a.* commonplace, mediocre, ordinary; see COMMON 1.

medium *n.* **1.** [A means] mechanism, tool, factor; see MEANS 1, PART 3. **2.** [A means of expression] symbol, sign, token, interpretation, manifestation, revelation, evidence, mark, statement; see also COMMUNICATION, SPEECH 2. **3.** [A supposed channel of supernatural knowledge] oracle, seer, spiritualist; see PROPHET.

medley *n.* mingling, melee, conglomeration; see MIXTURE 1, VARIETY 1.

meek *a.* **1.** [Humble] unassuming, plain, mild; see HUMBLE 1, MODEST 2. **2.** [Long-suffering] passive, resigned, serene; see PATIENT 1. **3.** [Lacking spirit] submissive, compliant, subdued; see DOCILE, RESIGNED.

meekness *n.* submission, mildness, timidity; see HUMILITY.

meet *n.* match, athletic event, tournament; see COMPETITION, EVENT.

meet *v.* **1.** [To come together] converge, assemble, crowd, rally, convene, collect, associate, unite, swarm, get together, enter in; see also GATHER 1. **2.** [To go to a place of meeting] resort, be present at, gather together, convene, congregate, muster, appear, go to the meeting; see also ASSEMBLE 1, ATTEND.—*Ant.* LEAVE, disperse, scatter. **3.** [To touch] reach, coincide, adhere; see JOIN 1. **4.** [To become acquainted] make the acquaintance of, be presented to, be introduced, present oneself, make oneself known, get next to*, get to know; see also FAMILIARIZE (ONESELF WITH). **5.** [To fulfill] answer, fit, suffice; see SATISFY 3. **6.** [To encounter] fall in with, come upon, meet by accident, come across, meet face to face, face up to, bump into, touch shoulders with, meet at every turn, engage, join issue with, battle, match, push, brush against, shove; see also FACE 1, FIGHT.—*Ant.* ABANDON, turn one's back on, leave.

meeting *n.* **1.** [The act of coming together] encounter, juxtaposition, joining, juncture, unifying, unification, adherence, convergence, confrontation, contacting, connection, conflict, contention, accord, agreement, compromising.—*Ant.* SEPARATION, departure, dispersal. **2.** [A gathering, usually of people] conference, assemblage, rally; see GATHERING.

meet (up) with *v.* encounter, become acquainted with, be introduced; see MEET 4.

meet with *v.* observe, experience, suffer; see FIND.

melancholy *a.* depressed, unhappy, dispirited; see SAD 1.

melancholy *n.* wistfulness, despair, unhappiness; see DEPRESSION 2, GRIEF, SADNESS.

meld *v.* blend, merge, unite; see MIX 1, UNITE.

mellow *a.* **1.** [Ripe] sweet, soft, perfected; see RIPE 1. **2.** [Culturally mature] cultured, fully developed, broad-minded; see MATURE.

mellowed *a.* mature, ripened, softened; see RIPE 1, SOFT 3.

melodious *a.* agreeable, pleasing, resonant; see HARMONIOUS 1, MUSICAL 1.

melodrama *n.* play, opera, theater; see DRAMA.

melodramatic *a.* artificial, spectacular, sensational; see EXAGGERATED.

melody *n.* **1.** [The quality of being melodious] concord, unison, chime; see HARMONY

1. 2. [A melodious arrangement] air, lyric, strain; see SONG.
melon *n.* watermelon, cantaloupe, muskmelon; see FOOD, FRUIT.
melt *v.* 1. [To liquefy] thaw, fuse, blend, merge, soften, flow, run, disintegrate, waste away; see also DISSOLVE.—*Ant.* FREEZE, harden, coagulate. 2. [To relent] forgive, show mercy, become lenient; see YIELD 1. 3. [To decrease] vanish, pass away, go; see DECREASE 1.
melted *a.* softened, thawed, liquefied, dwindled, blended, merged, wasted away, disintegrated, vanished, decreased, diminished, tempered, relaxed.
melting *a.* softening, liquefying, reducing; see SOFT 2.
member *n.* 1. [A person or group] constituent, charter member, active member, member in good standing, honorary member, affiliate, brother, sister, comrade, chapter, post, branch, lodge, district, county, town, township, state, country, countries, company, battalion, regiment, division. 2. [A part] portion, segment, fragment; see DIVISION 1, PART 1. 3. [A part of the body] organ, arm, leg; see LIMB 2.
membership *n.* club, society, association; see MEMBER 1.
memorable *a.* 1. [Historic] momentous, critical, unforgettable, crucial, famous, illustrious, distinguished, great, notable, significant, decisive, enduring, lasting, monumental, eventful, interesting; see also FAMOUS. 2. [Unusual] remarkable, exceptional, singular; see sense 1 and UNUSUAL 1.
memorandum *n.* notice, record, jotting; see NOTE 2, REMINDER.
memorial *a.* dedicatory, commemorative, remembering; see REMEMBERED.
memorial *n.* remembrance, testimonial, tablet, slab, pillar, tombstone, headstone, column, monolith, mausoleum, record, inscription, memento, statue; see also CELEBRATION, CEREMONY 2, MONUMENT.
memorize *v.* fix in the memory, make memorable, record, commemorate, memorialize, retain, commit to memory, imprint in one's mind, bear in mind, give word for word, get down pat*, have in one's head*, have at one's fingertips*, learn by heart; see also LEARN, REMEMBER 2.—*Ant.* NEGLECT, forget, fail to remember.
memory *n.* 1. [The power to call up the past] recollection, retrospection, reminiscence, thought, consciousness, subconsciousness, unconscious memory, retentive memory, photographic memory, visual memory, auditory memory; see also MIND 1. 2. [That which can be recalled] mental image, picture, vision; see THOUGHT 2.
menace *n.* 1. [A threat] caution, intimidation, foretelling; see WARNING. 2. [An imminent danger] hazard, peril, threat; see DANGER.
menace *v.* intimidate, portend, loom; see THREATEN.
menacing *a.* imminent, impending, threatening; see DANGEROUS, OMINOUS.
mend *v.* 1. [To repair] heal, patch, fix; see REPAIR. 2. [To improve] aid, remedy, cure; see CORRECT.
mended *a.* restored, put in shape, patched up, renovated, refreshed, renewed, corrected, helped, bettered, lessened, remedied, cured, relieved, rectified, rejuvenated, remodeled, altered, changed, fixed, regulated, rebuilt, regenerated, reorganized, revived, touched up, doctored*; see also REPAIRED.
menial *a.* common, servile, abject; see HUMBLE 1, 2.
menstruation *n.* menses, lady's time, time of the month, monthlies*, the curse*; see also FLOW.
mental *a.* 1. [Concerning the mind] reasoning, cerebral, thinking; see RATIONAL 1, THOUGHTFUL 1. 2. [Existing only in the mind] subjective, subliminal, subconscious, telepathic, psychic, clairvoyant, imaginative; see also IMAGINARY.—*Ant.* OBJECTIVE, BODILY, SENSUAL.
mentality *n.* intellect, comprehension, reasoning; see MIND 1.
mentally *a.* rationally, psychically, intellectually; see REASONABLY 1.
mention *n.* notice, naming, specifying; see REMARK. **—not to mention** in addition, too, without even mentioning; see ALSO.
mention *v.* notice, specify, cite, introduce, state, declare, quote, refer to, discuss, touch on, instance, intimate, notify, communicate, suggest, make known, point out, speak of, throw out, toss off; see also TELL 1.—*Ant.* OVERLOOK, take no notice of, disregard.
mentioned *a.* noticed, cited, specified, named, quoted, introduced, referred to, discussed, declared, revealed, brought up, considered, communicated, made known, spoken of; see also TOLD.
menu *n.* bill of fare, cuisine, food; see LIST.
merchandise *n.* wares, commodities, stock; see COMMODITY.
merchandise *v.* market, distribute, promote; see SELL.
merchant *n.* trader, storekeeper, retailer, shopkeeper, wholesaler, exporter, shipper, dealer, jobber, tradesman; see also BUSINESSMAN.
merciful *a.* lenient, feeling, compassionate, softhearted, mild, tolerant, kindly, indulgent; see also KIND.—*Ant.* CRUEL, pitiless, unsparing.
merciless *a.* pitiless, unsparing, relentless; see CRUEL, FIERCE, RUTHLESS.
mercy *n.* leniency, soft-heartedness, mildness, clemency, tenderness, gentleness,

compassion; see also GENEROSITY, TOLERANCE 1.—*Ant.* INDIFFERENCE, intolerance, selfishness. —**at the mercy of** in the power of, vulnerable to, controlled by; see SUBJECT.
mere *a.* small, minor, insignificant; see LITTLE 1, POOR 2.
merely *a.* slightly, solely, simply; see HARDLY, ONLY 3.
merge *v.* fuse, join, blend; see MIX 1, UNITE.
merger *n.* pool, consolidation, alliance; see ORGANIZATION 2.
merit *n.* **1.** [Worth] credit, benefit, advantage; see QUALITY 3, VALUE 3. **2.** [A creditable quality] worthiness, excellence, honor; see CHARACTER 2, VIRTUE 1.
merit *v.* be worth, warrant, justify; see DESERVE.
merited *a.* earned, proper, fitting; see DESERVED, FIT 1.
merrily *a.* joyfully, gleefully, genially; see CHEERFULLY, HAPPILY.
merriment *n.* joy, cheerfulness, gaiety; see HAPPINESS, HUMOR 3.
merry *a.* gay, joyous, mirthful; see HAPPY.
mesa *n.* plateau, table, tableland, butte, table mountain; see also HILL, MOUNTAIN 1.
mesh *v.* coincide, suit, be in gear; see AGREE, FIT 1.
mess *n.* **1.** [A mixture] combination, compound, blend; see MIXTURE 1. **2.** [A confusion] jumble, muss, chaos, clutter, clog, congestion, snag, scramble, complexity, mayhem, hodgepodge; see also CONFUSION, DISORDER.
message *n.* tidings, information, intelligence; see ADVICE, BROADCAST, COMMUNICATION, DIRECTIONS. —**get the message*** get the hint, comprehend, perceive; see UNDERSTAND 1.
mess around (with) *v.* dawdle, fool around, play the fool; see LOITER, PLAY 1, 2.
messenger *n.* bearer, minister, herald, carrier, courier, runner, crier, errand boy, intermediary, envoy, emissary, angel, prophet, go-between; see also AGENT.
Messiah *n.* Saviour, Redeemer, Jesus Christ; see CHRIST, GOD 1.
mess up *v.* spoil, ruin, foul up*, damage; see also BOTCH, DESTROY.
messy *a.* rumpled, untidy, slovenly; see DIRTY, DISORDERED.
metal *n.* element, native rock, ore deposit, free metal, refined ore, smelted ore. *Types of metal include the following:* gold, silver, copper, iron, steel, aluminum, manganese, nickel, lead, cobalt, platinum, zinc, tin, barium, cadmium, chromium, tungsten, mercury, molybdenum, sodium, potassium, radium, magnesium, calcium, titanium, arsenic, uranium.
metallic *a.* **1.** [Made of metal] hard, rock-like, iron, leaden, silvery, golden, metallurgic, mineral, geologic. **2.** [Suggestive of metal; *said especially of sound*] ringing, resounding, resonant, bell-like, clanging.
metaphor *n.* trope, simile, implied comparison; see COMPARISON. —**mix metaphors** be inconsistent, garble, talk illogically; see CONFUSE.
metaphorical *a.* symbolical, allegorical, figurative; see DESCRIPTIVE, GRAPHIC 1, 2.
metaphysical *a.* mystical, abstract, spiritual; see DIFFICULT 2.
meteor *n.* falling star, shooting star, meteorite, fireball, meteroid.
meteorology *n.* climate science, climatology, aerology; see SCIENCE 1, WEATHER.
meter *n.* measure, rhythm, metrical feet, common meter, long meter, ballad meter, tetrameter, pentameter, sprung rhythm, dipodic rhythm.
method *n.* mode, style, standard procedure, fashion, way, means, process, proceeding, adjustment, disposition, practice, routine, technique, attack, mode of operation, manner of working, ways and means, habit, custom, manner, formula, process, course, rule; see also SYSTEM.
methodical *a.* well-regulated, systematic, exact; see ORDERLY 2, REGULAR 3.
métier *n.* trade, profession, occupation; see JOB 1, PROFESSION 1.
metropolis *n.* capital, megalopolis, municipality; see CENTER 2, CITY.
metropolitan *a.* city, municipal, cosmopolitan; see MODERN 2, URBAN.
Mexican *a.* Latin American, south of the border, Hispanic; see AMERICAN 1.
Mexico *n.* the other side of the Rio Grande, land south of the border, the republic to the south; see AMERICA 1.
mickey mouse* *a.* trite, platitudinous, simplistic; see DULL 4, EASY 2, NAIVE.
microbe *n.* microorganism, bacterium, bacillus; see GERM.
microphone *n.* sound transmitter, receiver, pickup instrument, mike*, bug*, walkie-talkie.
microscope *n.* lens, magnifying glass, optical instrument, scope. *Microscopes include the following:* high-powered, compound, photographic, electron, electronic.
microscopic *a.* diminutive, tiny, infinitesimal; see LITTLE 1, MINUTE 1.
middle *a.* mean, midway, medial, average, equidistant; see also CENTRAL, HALFWAY, INTERMEDIATE.
middle *n.* mean, focus, core, nucleus, heart, navel, midst, marrow, pivot, axis, medium, midpoint; see also CENTER 1.
middle age *n.* adulthood, prime, maturity; see MAJORITY 2.
middle-aged *a.* adult, in one's prime, matronly; see MATURE.
middle-class *a.* white-collar, bourgeois, substantial; see COMMON 1, POPULAR 3, 4.

midget *n.* pygmy, dwarf, manikin; see PERSON.

midnight *n.* dead of night, stroke of midnight, twelve midnight, noon of night, witching hour; see also NIGHT 1. —**burn the midnight oil** stay up late, work late, keep late hours; see STUDY, WORK 1.

midst *n.* midpoint, nucleus, middle; see CENTER 1. —**in our** (or **your** or **their**) **midst** between us, with, accompanying; see AMONG. —**in the midst of** in the course of, engaged in, in the middle of; see CENTRAL.

midway *a.* in the thick of, between, in the middle of the way; see CENTRAL, HALFWAY, INTERMEDIATE, MIDDLE.

might *n.* strength, force, sway; see STRENGTH.

mightily *a.* energetically, strongly, forcibly; see POWERFULLY, VIGOROUSLY.

mighty *a.* **1.** [Strong] powerful, stalwart, muscular; see STRONG 1. **2.** [Powerful through influence] great, all-powerful, omnipotent; see POWERFUL 1. **3.** [Imposing] great, extensive, impressive, gigantic, magnificent, towering, dynamic, notable, extraordinary, grand, considerable, monumental, tremendous; see also LARGE 1.—*Ant.* PLAIN, unimpressive, ordinary. **4.** [*To a high degree] exceedingly, greatly, extremely; see VERY.

migrate *v.* move, emigrate, immigrate; see LEAVE 1.

migration *n.* emigration, immigration, voyage; see DEPARTURE, JOURNEY, MOVEMENT 2.

migratory *a.* wandering, migrant, vagrant; see TEMPORARY.

mild *a.* **1.** [Gentle; *said especially of persons*] meek, easygoing, patient; see KIND. **2.** [Temperate; *said especially of weather*] bland, untroubled, tropical, peaceful, summery, tepid, cool, balmy, breezy, gentle, soft, lukewarm, clear, moderate, mellow, fine, uncloudy, sunny, warm.—*Ant.* ROUGH, COLD, STORMY. **3.** [Easy; *said especially of burdens or punishment*] soft, light, tempered; see MODERATE 4. **4.** [Not irritating] bland, soothing, soft, smooth, gentle, moderate, easy, mellow, delicate, temperate.

mildly *a.* gently, meekly, calmly, genially, tranquilly, softly, lightly, moderately, tenderly, compassionately, tolerantly, patiently, temperately, indifferently, quietly.—*Ant.* VIOLENTLY, harshly, roughly.

mildness *n.* tolerance, tenderness, gentleness; see KINDNESS 1.

mile *n.* 5,280 feet, statute mile, geographical mile, nautical mile, Admiralty mile; see also DISTANCE 3, MEASURE 1.

mileage *n.* rate, space, measure; see DISTANCE 3, LENGTH 1.

militant *a.* combative, belligerent, offensive; see AGGRESSIVE.

militant *n.* rioter, violent objector, demonstrator; see RADICAL.

military *a.* armed, militant, combative; see AGGRESSIVE.

militia *n.* military force, civilian army. National Guard; see ARMY 1.

milk *n.* fluid, juice, sap; see LIQUID. *Types of milk include the following:* whole, skim, raw, pasteurized, homogenized, certified; grade-A, grade-B, etc.; loose, condensed, dried, evaporated, powdered; two-percent, four-percent, etc.; goat's, mare's, mother's; cream, half-and-half, buttermilk, kefir. —**cry over spilt milk** mourn, lament, sulk; see REGRET.

milky *a.* opaque, pearly, cloudy; see WHITE 1.

mill *n.* **1.** [A factory] manufactory, plant, millhouse; see FACTORY. **2.** [A machine for grinding, crushing, pressing, etc.] *Types of mills include the following:* flour, coffee, cotton, weaving, spinning, powder, rolling, cider, cane, lapidary, sawmill, coin press.

millionaire *n.* man of means, capitalist, tycoon, rich man, plutocrat, Croesus, nabob, Midas, big-money man*, robber baron, fat cat*.—*Ant.* BEGGAR, poor man, pauper.

mimic *n.* mime, impersonator, comedian; see ACTOR, IMITATOR.

mimic *v.* **1.** [To imitate] copy, simulate, impersonate; see IMITATE. **2.** [To mock] make fun of, burlesque, caricature; see RIDICULE.

mimicry *n.* mime, pretense, mockery; see IMITATION 2.

mind *n.* **1.** [Intellectual potentiality] soul, spirit, intellect, brain, consciousness, thought, mentality, intuition, perception, conception, intelligence, intellectuality, capacity, judgment, understanding, wisdom, genius, talent, reasoning, instinct, wit, mental faculties, intellectual faculties, creativity, ingenuity, intellectual powers, gray matter*, brainpower. **2.** [Purpose] intention, inclination, determination; see PURPOSE 1. —**bear** (or **keep**) **in mind** heed, recollect, recall; see REMEMBER 1. —**be in one's right mind** be mentally well, be rational, be sane; see SANE. —**be of one mind** have the same opinion, concur, be in accord; see AGREE. —**call to mind** recall, recollect, bring to mind; see REMEMBER 1. —**change one's mind** alter one's opinion, change one's views, decide against, modify one's ideas. —**give someone a piece of one's mind** rebuke, confute, criticize; see SCOLD. —**have a good mind to** be inclined to, propose, tend to; see INTEND 1. —**have half a mind to** be inclined to, propose, tend to; see INTEND 1. —**have in mind** **1.** recall, recollect, think of; see REMEMBER 1. **2.** purpose, propose, be inclined to; see INTEND 1. —**know one's own mind** know oneself, be deliberate, have a plan; see KNOW 1. —**make up one's**

mind form a definite opinion, choose, finalize; see DECIDE. **—meeting of the minds** concurrence, unity, harmony; see AGREEMENT 1. **—on one's mind** occupying one's thoughts, causing concern, worrying one; see IMPORTANT 1. **—out of one's mind** mentally ill, raving, mad; see INSANE. **—take one's mind off** turn one's attention from, divert, change; see DISTRACT.

mind *v.* **1.** [To obey] be under the authority of, heed, do as told; see BEHAVE, OBEY. **2.** [To give one's attention] heed, regard, be attentive to; see ATTEND. **3.** [To be careful] tend, watch out for, take care, be wary, be concerned for, mind one's *p's* and *q's**; see also CONSIDER.—*Ant.* NEGLECT, ignore, be careless. **4.** [*To remember] recollect, recall, bring to mind; see REMEMBER 1. **5.** [To object to] complain, deplore, be opposed to; see DISLIKE.

minded *a.* disposed, inclined, leaning toward; see WILLING.

mindful *a.* attentive, heedful, watchful; see CAREFUL.

mindless *a.* **1.** [Careless] inattentive, oblivious, neglectful; see CARELESS, INDIFFERENT, RASH. **2.** [Stupid] foolish, senseless, unintelligent; see STUPID.

mine *a.* my own, belonging to me, possessed by me, mine by right, owned by me, left to me, from me, by me; see also OUR.

mine *n.* **1.** [A source of natural wealth] pit, well, shaft, diggings, excavation, workings, quarry, deposit, vein, lode, ore bed, placer, pay dirt, bonanza, strip mine, open-pit mine, surface mine, hard-rock mine. **2.** [An explosive charge] landmine, ambush, trap; see BOMB, EXPLOSIVE, WEAPON.

mine *v.* **1.** [To dig for minerals] excavate, work, quarry; see DIG 1. **2.** [To lay mines] sow with mines, prepare mine fields, set booby traps; see DEFEND 1.

miner *n.* excavator, digger, driller, dredger, mine worker, prospector, mucker, driller, placer miner, hard-rock miner, mine superintendent, mining engineer, desert rat*, sourdough*, forty-niner*; see also LABORER, WORKMAN.

mineral *a.* geologic, rock, metallurgic; see METALLIC 1.

mineral *n.* earth's crust, geologic formation, geologic rock, rock deposit, ore deposit, igneous rock, metamorphic rock, magma, petroleum, crystal; see also METAL.

mingle *v.* combine, blend, merge; see MIX 1.

miniature *a.* diminutive, small, tiny; see LITTLE 1, MINUTE 1.

minimize *v.* lessen, depreciate, reduce; see DECREASE 2.

minimum *a.* smallest, tiniest, merest, lowest.

minimum *n.* smallest, least, lowest, narrowest, atom, molecule, particle, dot, jot, iota, spark, shadow, gleam, grain, scruple.

mining *n.* excavating, hollowing, opening, digging, boring, drilling, delving, burrowing, tunneling, honeycombing, placer mining, hard-rock mining, prospecting.

minister *n.* **1.** [One authorized to conduct Christian worship] pastor, parson, preacher, clergyman, rector, monk, abbot, prelate, canon, curate, vicar, deacon, chaplain, servant of God, shepherd, churchman, cleric, padre, ecclesiastic, bishop, archbishop, confessor, reverend, diocesan, divine, missionary; see also PRIEST.—*Ant.* LAYMAN, church member, parishioner. **2.** [A high servant of the state] ambassador, consul, liaison officer; see DIPLOMAT, REPRESENTATIVE 2, STATESMAN.

minister *v.* administer to, tend, wait on; see HELP.

ministry *n.* **1.** [The functions of the clergy] preaching, prayer, spiritual leadership; see RELIGION 2. **2.** [The clergy] the cloth, clergymen, ecclesiastics, clerics, the clerical order, priesthood, clericals, prelacy, vicarage, clergy. **3.** [A department of state] bureau, administrative agency, executive branch; see DEPARTMENT.

minor *a.* secondary, lesser, insignificant; see TRIVIAL, UNIMPORTANT.

minor *n.* person under eighteen or twenty-one, underage person, boy, girl, child, infant, little one, lad, schoolboy, schoolgirl; see also YOUTH 3.

minority *n.* **1.** [An outnumbered group] opposition, less than half, the outvoted, the few, the outnumbered, the losing side, splinter group. **2.** [The time before one is of legal age] childhood, immaturity, adolescence; see YOUTH 1.

minor-league *a.* second-rate, minor, small-time; see UNIMPORTANT, TRIVIAL.

mint *v.* strike, coin, issue; see PRINT 2.

minus *a.* diminished, negative, deficient; see LESS.

minute *a.* **1.** [Extremely small] microscopic, diminutive, wee, tiny, atomic, miniature, puny, microbic, molecular, exact, precise, fine, inconsiderable, teeny*, weeny*, teeny-weeny*, teensy*, itty-bitty*, invisible; see also LITTLE 1.—*Ant.* LARGE, huge, immense. **2.** [Trivial] immaterial, nonessential, paltry; see TRIVIAL, UNIMPORTANT. **3.** [Exact] particular, circumstantial, specialized; see DETAILED, ELABORATE 2.

minute *n.* **1.** [The sixtieth part of an hour] sixty seconds, unit of time, space of time; see TIME 1. **2.** [A brief time] short time, second, flash, twinkling, breath, jiffy*, bat of an eye*.—*Ant.* FOREVER, eternity, long time. **—the minute that** as soon as, the second that, at the time that; see WHEN 2. **—up to the minute** modern, contemporary, in the latest style; see FASHIONABLE.

miracle *n.* marvel, revelation, supernatural occurrence; see WONDER 2.

miraculous *a.* **1.** [Caused by divine intervention] supernatural, marvelous, superhuman, beyond understanding, phenomenal, unimaginable, stupendous, awesome, monstrous; see also MYSTERIOUS 2.—*Ant.* NATURAL, familiar, imaginable. **2.** [So unusual as to suggest a miracle] extraordinary, freakish, wondrous; see UNUSUAL 1, 2.

mirage *n.* phantasm, delusion, hallucination; see FANTASY, ILLUSION.

mirror *n.* looking glass, speculum, reflector, polished metal, hand glass, pier glass, mirroring surface, camera finder, hand mirror, full-length mirror; see also GLASS.

mirth *n.* frolic, jollity, entertainment; see FUN.

misbehave *v.* do wrong, sin, fail, trip, blunder, offend, trespass, behave badly, misdo, err, lapse, be delinquent, be at fault, be culpable, be guilty, be bad, forget oneself, be dissolute, be indecorous, carry on*, be naughty, go astray, sow one's wild oats*, cut up*.—*Ant.* BEHAVE, be good, do well.

miscalculate *v.* blunder, miscount, err; see MISTAKE.

miscarriage *n.* **1.** [Failure] malfunction, defeat, mistake; see FAILURE 1. **2.** [A too premature delivery] unnatural birth, untimely delivery, birth interruption, premature delivery.

miscellaneous *a.* **1.** [Lacking unity] diverse, disparate, unmatched; see UNLIKE. **2.** [Lacking order] mixed, muddled, scattered; see CONFUSED 2, DISORDERED.

mischief *n.* troublesomeness, harmfulness, prankishness, playfulness, acting like a brat, impishness, misbehavior, misconduct, fault, transgression, wrongdoing, misdoing, naughtiness, mischiefmaking, friskiness.—*Ant.* DIGNITY, demureness, sedateness.

mischievous *a.* playful, roguish, prankish; see NAUGHTY, RUDE 2.

misconception *n.* delusion, blunder, fault; see ERROR, MISTAKE 2, MISUNDERSTANDING 1.

misconduct *n.* misbehavior, offense, wrongdoing; see EVIL 2, MISCHIEF.

misdemeanor *n.* misconduct, misbehavior, misdeed; see CRIME.

miser *n.* extortioner, usurer, misanthropist, stingy person, skinflint, Scrooge, moneygrubber.—*Ant.* BEGGAR, spendthrift, waster.

miserable *a.* distressed, afflicted, sickly, ill, wretched, sick, ailing, unfortunate, uncomfortable, suffering, hurt, wounded, tormented, tortured, in pain, strained, injured, convulsed; see also TROUBLED.—*Ant.* HELPED, aided, comfortable.

miserably *a.* poorly, unsatisfactorily, imperfectly; see BADLY 1, INADEQUATELY.

miserly *a.* covetous, parsimonious, closefisted; see STINGY.

misery *n.* **1.** [Pain] distress, suffering, agony; see PAIN 2. **2.** [Dejection] worry, despair, desolation; see DEPRESSION 2, GRIEF, SADNESS. **3.** [Trouble] grief, anxiety, problem; see DIFFICULTY 2.

misfit *n.* paranoid, psychotic, maladjusted person; see PERVERT.

misfortune *n.* misadventure, ill luck, ill fortune, disadvantage, mischance, disappointment, adversity, discomfort, burden, annoyance, nuisance, unpleasantness, inconvenience, worry, anxiety; see also DIFFICULTY 1.—*Ant.* ADVANTAGE, good fortune, stroke of fortune.

misgiving *n.* distrust, mistrust, unbelief; see DOUBT, UNCERTAINTY 2.

misguided *a.* misled, deceived, confused; see MISTAKEN 1.

mishap *n.* accident, mischance, misadventure; see CATASTROPHE, DISASTER, MISFORTUNE.

misinform *v.* mislead, report inaccurately to, misstate; see DECEIVE, LIE.

misinterpret *v.* falsify, distort, miscalculate; see MISTAKE, MISUNDERSTAND.

misinterpretation *n.* distortion, misreckoning, delusion; see MISTAKE 2, MISUNDERSTANDING 1.

misjudge *v.* **1.** [To make a wrong judgment, usually of a person] be overcritical, be unfair, come to a hasty conclusion; see MISUNDERSTAND. **2.** [To make an inaccurate estimate] miss, miscalculate, misconceive, misthink, misconstrue, overestimate, underestimate, bark up the wrong tree*; see also MISTAKE.—*Ant.* UNDERSTAND, estimate, calculate.

misjudgment *n.* distortion, misinterpretation, misconception; see MISTAKE 2.

mislead *v.* delude, cheat, defraud, bilk, take in, outwit, trick, entangle, advice badly, victimize, lure, beguile, hoax, dupe, bait, misrepresent, bluff, give a bum steer*, throw off the scent*, bamboozle, hoodwink, put on*; see also DECEIVE.

misled *a.* misguided, deluded, wronged; see DECEIVED, MISTAKEN 1.

mismanage *v.* bungle, blunder, mess up, foul up*; see also FAIL 1.

mismatched *a.* incompatible, discordant, inconsistent; see UNFIT.

misplace *v.* mislay, displace, shuffle, disarrange, remove, disturb, take out of its place, disorder, tumble, confuse, mix, scatter, unsettle, muss, disorganize; see also LOSE 2.—*Ant.* FIND, LOCATE, place.

misplaced *a.* displaced, mislaid, out of place; see LOST 1.

mispronounce *v.* falter, misspeak, mouth; see HESITATE, STAMMER.

misrepresent *v.* distort, falsify, understate; see DECEIVE, LIE 1, MISLEAD.

misrepresentation *n.* untruth, deceit, disguise; see DECEPTION, LIE.

miss *n.* **1.** [A failure] slip, blunder, mishap; see MISTAKE 2. **2.** [A young woman] lass, maid, female; see GIRL.

miss *v.* **1.** [To feel a want] desire, crave, yearn; see NEED, WANT 1. **2.** [To fail to catch] snatch at, drop, fumble, have butterfingers*, muff*, boot*.—*Ant.* CATCH, grab, hold. **3.** [To fail to hit] miss one's aim, miss the mark, be wide of the mark, overshoot, undershoot, fan the air*.—*Ant.* HIT, shoot, get.

missed *a.* **1.** [Not found or noticed] gone, misplaced, mislaid, forgotten, unrecalled, unnoticed, not in sight, put away, in hiding, hidden, strayed, moved, removed, unseen; see also LOST 1.—*Ant.* REMEMBERED, found, located. **2.** [Longed for] needed, desired, wished for, pined for, wanted, yearned for, clung to, craved for, hungered for.—*Ant.* HATED, disliked, unwanted.

missile *n.* cartridge, projectile, ammunition; see BULLET, SHOT 1, WEAPON. *Terms for types of missiles include the following:* Polaris, Poseidon, RPV or remotely piloted vehicle, Minuteman, guided missile, cruise missile, ICBM or intercontinental ballistic missile, ABM or antiballistic missile, ASW or anti-submarine warfare, MIRV or multiple independently targetable reentry vehicle.

missing *a.* disappeared, lacking, removed; see ABSENT, LOST 1.

mission *n.* charge, sortie, commission; see PURPOSE 1.

missionary *n.* apostle, evangelist, preacher; see MESSENGER, MINISTER 1.

misspent *a.* wasted, squandered, thrown away; see WASTED.

mist *n.* cloud, rain, haze; see FOG.

mistake *n.* **1.** [A blunder] false step, blunder, slip, error, omission, failure, confusion, wrongdoing, sin, crime, goof*; see also ERROR. **2.** [A misunderstanding] misapprehension, confusion, muddle, misconception, delusion, illusion, overestimation, underestimation, impression, confounding, misinterpretation, perversion, perplexity, bewilderment, misjudgment; see also EXAGGERATION, MISUNDERSTANDING 1.—*Ant.* KNOWLEDGE, certainty, interpretation.

mistake *v.* err, blunder, slip, lapse, miss, overlook, omit, underestimate, overestimate, substitute, misjudge, misapprehend, misconceive, misunderstand, confound, misinterpret, confuse, botch, bungle, have the wrong impression, tangle, snarl, slip up, make a mess of*, miss the boat*, open one's mouth and put one's foot in it*.—*Ant.* SUCCEED, be accurate, explain.

mistaken *a.* **1.** [In error] misinformed, deceived, confounded, confused, having the wrong impression, deluded, misinformed, misguided, at fault, off the track; see also WRONG 2. **2.** [Ill-advised] unadvised, duped, fooled, misled, tricked, unwarranted; see also DECEIVED. **3.** [Taken for another] wrongly identified, unrecognized, confused with, taken for, in a case of mistaken identity, misnamed, misconstrued.

mistakenly *a.* badly, falsely, inadvisedly; see WRONGLY.

mister *n.* Mr., man, sir, *monsieur* (French), *Herr* (German), *signor* (Italian), *señor* (Spanish).

mistreat *v.* harm, injure, wrong; see ABUSE.

mistress *n.* **1.** [A woman in authority] housekeeper, chaperone, housemother; see LADY 2. **2.** [An illegitimate consort] courtesan, paramour, kept woman; see PROSTITUTE.

mistrust *v.* suspect, distrust, scruple; see DOUBT.

misty *a.* dim, foggy, hazy, murky, shrouded, obscure; see also DARK 1.

misunderstand *v.* err, misconceive, misinterpret, miscomprehend, misjudge, miscalculate, misconstrue, be perplexed, be bewildered, confuse, confound, have the wrong impression, fail to understand, misapprehend, overestimate, underestimate, be misled, be unfamiliar with, have the wrong slant on*, not register; see also MISTAKE.—*Ant.* UNDERSTAND, grasp, apprehend.

misunderstanding *n.* **1.** [Misapprehension] delusion, miscalculation, confusion, misinterpretation, confounding; see also MISTAKE 2.—*Ant.* UNDERSTANDING, conception, apprehension. **2.** [Mutual difficulty] debate, dissension, quarrel; see DISAGREEMENT 1, DISPUTE.

misunderstood *a.* misinterpreted, badly interpreted, misconceived; see MISTAKEN 1, WRONG 2.

mitt *n.* baseball glove, catcher's mitt, first baseman's mitt; see EQUIPMENT.

mitten *n.* mitt, gauntlet, glove; see CLOTHES.

mix *v.* **1.** [To blend] fuse, merge, coalesce, brew, unite, combine, cross, interbreed, amalgamate, incorporate, alloy, mingle, compound, intermingle, weave, interweave, throw together, adulterate, infiltrate, twine, knead, stir, suffuse, instill, transfuse, synthesize, stir around, infuse, saturate, dye, season. **2.** [To confuse] mix up, jumble, tangle; see CONFUSE. **3.** [To associate] fraternize, get along, consort with; see JOIN 2.

mixed *a.* **1.** [Commingled] blended, fused, mingled, compounded, combined, amalgamated, united, brewed, merged, transfused, crossed, assimilated, married, woven, kneaded, incorporated.—*Ant.* SEPARATED, severed, raveled. **2.** [Various] miscellaneous, unselected, diverse; see VARIOUS. **3.** [Confused] mixed up, jumbled, disordered; see CONFUSED 2.

mixer *n.* **1.** [An instrument used to mix materials] blender, food processor, juicer, egg beater, cake mixer, food mixer, cocktail shaker, converter, carburetor, cement mixer, paint mixer; see also MACHINE. **2.** [A substance used in a mixture] ingredient, component, combining element; see PART 1.

mixture *n.* **1.** [A combination] blend, compound, composite, amalgam, miscellany, mishmash, mingling, medley, mix, potpourri, alloy, fusion, jumble, brew, merger, hybrid, crossing, infiltration, transfusion, infusion, mélange, saturation, assimilation, incorporation, hodgepodge. **2.** [A mess] mix-up, muddle, disorder; see CONFUSION.

mix-up *n.* turmoil, chaos, commotion; see CONFUSION, DISORDER.

moan *n.* plaint, groan, wail; see CRY 1.

moan *v.* groan, wail, whine; see CRY 1.

mob *n.* **1.** [A disorderly crowd of people] swarm, rabble, throng, press, multitude, populace, horde, riot, host, lawless element; see also CROWD, GATHERING. **2.** [The lower classes] bourgeoisie, plebeians, proletariat; see PEOPLE 3.

mob *v.* hustle, crowd, swarm; see ATTACK, REBEL.

mobile *a.* unstationary, loose, free; see MOVABLE.

mobility *n.* changeability, versatility, flow; see MOVEMENT 1.

mobilize *v.* assemble, prepare, gather; see ENLIST 1.

moccasin *n.* heelless shoe, slipper, sandal; see SHOE.

mock *a.* counterfeit, sham, pretended; see FALSE 3, UNREAL.

mock *v.* **1.** [To ridicule] deride, scorn, taunt; see RIDICULE. **2.** [To mimic] mime, burlesque, caricature; see IMITATE.

mockery *n.* disparagement, imitation, sham; see RIDICULE.

model *n.* **1.** [A person worthy of imitation] archetype, prototype, exemplar, paradigm, ideal, good man, good woman, good example, hero, demigod, saint. **2.** [Anything that serves as a copy] original, text, guide, copy, tracing, facsimile, duplicate, pattern, design, gauge, ideal, shape, form, specimen, mold, principle, basis, standard, sketch, painting, precedent, archetype, prototype; see also CRITERION. **3.** [A duplicate on a small scale] miniature, image, illustration, representation, reduction, statue, figure, figurine, effigy, mock-up, skeleton, portrait, photograph, relief, print, engraving; see also COPY, DUPLICATE. **4.** [One who poses professionally] poser, sitter, mannequin; see NUDE.

model *v.* **1.** [To form] shape, mold, fashion; see CREATE, FORM 1. **2.** [To imitate a model] trace, duplicate, sketch, reduce, represent, print, counterfeit, caricature, parody; see also ILLUSTRATE, PAINT 1. **3.** [To serve as a model] sit, act as model, set an example; see POSE 2. **4.** [To demonstrate] show off, wear, parade in; see DISPLAY.

moderate *a.* **1.** [Not expensive] inexpensive, low-priced, reasonable; see CHEAP 1, ECONOMICAL 2. **2.** [Not violent] modest, cool, tranquil; see CALM 1, RESERVED 3. **3.** [Not radical] tolerant, judicious, nonpartisan, liberal, middle-of-the-road, unopinionated, not given to extremes, measured, low-key, evenly balanced, neutral, impartial, straight, midway, in the mean, average, restrained, sound, cautious, considered, considerate, respectable, middle-class, compromising; see also CONSERVATIVE.—*Ant.* RADICAL, unbalanced, partial. **4.** [Not intemperate] pleasant, gentle, soft, balmly, inexcessive, tepid, easy, not rigorous, not severe, temperate, favorable, tolerable, bearable, tame, untroubled, unruffled, monotonous, even; see also FAIR 3, MILD 2.—*Ant.* SEVERE, rigorous, bitter. **5.** [Not indulgent] sparing, frugal, regulated, self-denying, abstinent, non-indulgent, self-controlled, disciplined, careful, on the wagon*, sworn off*, teetotalling; see also SOBER.—*Ant.* WASTEFUL, excessive, self-indulgent.

moderate *v.* abate, modify, decline; see DECREASE 1.

moderately *a.* tolerantly, tolerably, temperately, somewhat, to a degree, enough, to some extent, to a certain extent, a little, to some degree, fairly, not exactly, in moderation, within reason, within bounds, within reasonable limits, as far as could be expected, within the bounds of reason, in reason; see also REASONABLY 2, SLIGHTLY.—*Ant.* MUCH, extremely, remarkably.

moderation *n.* **1.** [Restraint] toleration, steadiness, sobriety, coolness, the golden mean, quiet, temperance, patience, fairness, justice, constraint, forbearance, poise, balance; see also RESTRAINT 1. **2.** [The act of moderating] settlement, regulation, limitation; see RESTRAINT 2.

modern *a.* **1.** [Up-to-date] stylish, modish, chic, smart, up-to-the-minute, late, current, recent, of the present, prevailing, prevalent, avant-garde, present-day, latest, most recent, advanced, streamlined, breaking with tradition, new, newest, untraditional, contemporary, in vogue, in use, common, newfangled, cool*, sharp*, smooth*, just out, mod*, jet-age; see also FASHIONABLE.—*Ant.* OLD-FASHIONED, out-of-date, out-of-style. **2.** [Having the comforts of modern life] modernistic, modernized, renovated, functional, with modern conveniences, done over, having modern improvements; see also CONVENIENT 1, IMPROVED. **3.** [Concerning recent times] contemporary, contemporaneous, recent, concurrent, present-day, coincident, twentieth-century, latter-day, mechanical, of the Machine Age, automated, of modern times, modernist; see also NEW 1, 2, NOW 1.—*Ant.* OLD, medieval, primordial.

modest *a.* **1.** [Humble] unassuming, meek, diffident; see HUMBLE 1, RESIGNED. **2.** [Not showy] unpretentious, plain, unostentatious, unobtrusive, demure, quiet, seemly, proper, decorous, simple, natural, unassuming, humble, tasteful, unadorned, unaffected, homely. **3.** [Moderate] reasonable, inexpensive, average; see CHEAP 1, ECONOMICAL 2. **4.** [Proper] pure, chaste, seemly; see DECENT 2, HONEST 1. **5.** [Lowly] plain, simple, unaffected; see HUMBLE 2.

modestly *a.* unobtrusively, retiringly, quietly, unpretentiously, diffidently, bashfully, unassumingly, chastely, virtuously, purely, shyly, demurely.—*Ant.* BOLDLY, boastfully, pretentiously.

modesty *n.* **1.** [The attitude that leads one to make a modest self-estimate] humility, delicacy, reticence, constraint, unobtrusiveness, meekness; see also COURTESY 1, DIGNITY, RESTRAINT 1.—*Ant.* VANITY, conceit, egotism. **2.** [Shyness] inhibition, timidity, diffidence; see SHYNESS. **3.** [Chastity] decency, innocence, celibacy; see CHASTITY, VIRTUE 1.

modification *n.* qualification, alteration, correction; see ADJUSTMENT, CHANGE 2.

modified *a.* varied, mutated, adjusted; see CHANGED 2.

modify *v.* **1.** [To change] alter, modify, vary; see BECOME, CHANGE 2. **2.** [To moderate] mitigate, restrain, curb; see DECREASE 2, RESTRICT.

moist *a.* humid, dank, moistened; see WET 1.

moisten *v.* sprinkle, dampen, saturate, drench, waterlog, steep, sog, sop, dip, rinse, wash over, wet down, water down, squirt, shower, rain on, splash, splatter, bathe, steam, spray, sponge.

moisture *n.* precipitation, mist, drizzle; see FOG, WATER 1.

mold *n.* **1.** [A form] matrix, womb, cavity, shape, frame, pattern, design, die, cast, cup, image, kind, molding, casting, reproduction, form, pottery, shell, core. **2.** [A parasitic growth] rust, parasite, fungus, lichen; see also DECAY.

mold *v.* **1.** [To give physical shape to] make, round into, fashion; see FORM 1. **2.** [To decay through the action of mold] rot, mildew, rust; see SPOIL.

moldy *a.* musty, mildewed, dank; see ROTTEN 1.

mole *n.* flaw, birthmark, blotch; see BLEMISH.

molecular *a.* miniature, microscopic, atomic; see LITTLE 1, MINUTE 1.

molecule *n.* **1.** [Unit] particle, fragment, unit; see BIT 1. **2.** [Atom] electron, ion, particle; see ATOM.

molest *v.* **1.** [To disturb objects] displace, meddle, disorganize; see DISTURB. **2.** [To disturb people] bother, interrupt, break in upon, intrude, encroach upon, annoy, worry, irritate, plague, badger, bait, pester, hinder, tease, irk, vex, trouble, confuse, perturb, frighten, terrify, scare; see also BOTHER 2.

molten *a.* heated, melted, fused, liquefied, running, fluid, seething; see also HOT 1.—*Ant.* COLD, cool, solid.

moment *n.* **1.** [A brief time] minute, instant, millisecond, trice, second, bit, while, flash, jiffy*; see also MINUTE 2. **2.** [Importance] significance, note, consequence; see IMPORTANCE.

momentarily *a.* immediately, right now, instantly; see NOW 1.

momentary *a.* fleeting, quick, passing, flitting, flashing, transient, impermanent, shifting, ephemeral, vanishing, cursory, temporary, dreamlike, in the wink of an eye*.—*Ant.* ETERNAL, continual, ceaseless.

momentum *n.* impulse, force, drive; see ENERGY 2.

mommy* *n.* mom*, female parent, mama*; see MOTHER 1, PARENT.

monarch *n.* despot, sovereign, autocrat; see KING 1.

monarchy *n.* kingship, sovereignty, command; see POWER 2.

monastery *n.* abbey, priory, religious community; see CHURCH 1.

monetary *a.* pecuniary, financial, fiscal; see COMMERCIAL.

money *n.* **1.** [A medium of exchange] gold, silver, cash, currency, check, bills, notes, specie, legal tender, Almighty Dollar*, gravy*, wampum*, shekels*, dough*, long green*, coins*, lucre, folding money*, wad*, bucks*, hard cash*, bread*. *Money includes the following:* cent, dollar, penny, pound, *centime, franc, centesimo, lira, centavo, peso, kopek, ruble, ore, krone, yuan, sen, yen, Pfennig, Mark.* **2.** [Wealth] funds, capital, property; see WEALTH. **3.** [Merged interest] financiers, corporate interests, capitalists; see BUSINESS 4. **4.** [Pay] payment, salary, wages; see PAY 2. **—for one's money*** for one's choice, in one's opinion, to one's mind; see PERSONALLY 2. **—in the money*** wealthy, flush*, loaded*; see RICH 1. **—make money** gain profits, become wealthy, earn; see PROFIT 2. **—one's money's worth** full value, gain, benefit; see VALUE 1, 3. **—put money into** invest in, support, underwrite; see INVEST.

monk *n.* hermit, religious, ascetic, solitary, recluse, abbot, prior; see also PRIEST.

monkey *n.* primate, lemur, anthropoid ape; see ANIMAL. *Monkeys include the following:* chimpanzee, orangutan, baboon, marmoset, gibbon, gorilla, mandrill; spider, squirrel, capuchin.

monkey* *v.* pry, fool around, tamper with; see MEDDLE 2.

monkey business* *n.* deceit, conniving, misconduct; see DECEPTION, LIE.

monologue *n.* talk, speech, discourse; see ADDRESS 1.

monopolize *v.* engross, acquire, exclude, own exclusively, absorb, consume, manage, have, hold, corner, restrain, patent, copyright, corner the market*.—*Ant.* INCLUDE, give, invite.

monopoly *n.* trust, syndicate, cartel; see BUSINESS 1.

monotonous *a.* **1.** [Tiresome] tedious, wearisome, wearying; see DULL 4. **2.** [Having but one tone] monotonic, unvarying, lacking, variety, in one key, unchanged, reiterated, recurrent, single, uniform.—*Ant.* VARIOUS, varying, multiple.

monotony *n.* invariability, likeness, tediousness, similarity, continuity, continuance, oneness, evenness, levelness, flatness, the same old thing; see also BOREDOM.—*Ant.* VARIETY, difference, variability.

monster *n.* **1.** [A great beast] beastlike creature, centaur, monstrosity, sphinx, chimera, unicorn, dragon, griffin, cyclops, phoenix, mermaid, sea serpent, rhinoceros, elephant, werewolf. **2.** [An unnatural creation] abnormality, monstrosity, malformation; see FREAK. **3.** [An inhuman person] brute, beast, cruel person; see CRIMINAL, RASCAL.

monstrous *a.* **1.** [Huge] stupendous, prodigious, enormous; see LARGE 1. **2.** [Unnatural] abnormal, preposterous, uncanny; see UNNATURAL 1, UNUSUAL 2.

month *n.* measure of time, thirty days, one-twelfth of a year, four weeks. *Months of the year are the following:* January, February, March, April, May, June, July, August, September, October, November, December.

monthly *a.* once a month, every month, menstrual, punctually, steadily, recurrent, cyclic, cyclical, repeated, rhythmic, methodically, periodically, from month to month; see also REGULARLY.

monument *n.* **1.** [Anything erected to preserve a memory] tomb, shaft, column, pillar, headstone, tombstone, gravestone, mausoleum, obelisk, shrine, statue, building, tower, monolith, tablet, slab, stone; see also MEMORIAL. **2.** [A landmark in the history of creative work] work of art, magnum opus, permanent contribution; see ACHIEVEMENT, MASTERPIECE.

monumental *a.* lofty, impressive, majestic; see GRAND, GREAT 1.

mood *n.* **1.** [A state of mind] state, condition, frame of mind, temper, humor, disposition, inclination, caprice, whim, fancy, pleasure, freak, wish, desire. **2.** [A quality of mind] bent, propensity, tendency; see ATTITUDE. **3.** [Grammatical mode] aspect, inflection, mode. *Moods in English grammar include the following:* indicative, subjunctive, imperative, interrogative, conditional, potential.

moody *a.* pensive, unhappy, low-spirited; see SAD 1.

moon *n.* celestial body, heavenly body, planet, planetoid, crescent, new moon, half-moon, full moon, old moon, Luna, moon goddess, dry moon, wet moon.

moonlight *n.* effulgence, radiance, luminescence; see LIGHT 3.

moonshine *n.* **1.** [Moonlight] effulgence, radiance, luminosity; see LIGHT 3. **2.** [Whiskey distilled illicitly] mountain dew*, hooch*, white lightning*; see WHISKEY.

mop *n.* swab, duster, sweeper; see BROOM.

mop *v.* swab, wipe, rub, dab, pat, polish, wash, dust, wipe up; see also CLEAN.

mope *v.* fret, pine away, grieve, sorrow, sink, lose heart, brood, pine, yearn, despair, grumble, chafe, lament, regret, look glum, sulk, pull a long face*.—*Ant.* CELEBRATE, revive, cheer up.

mopped *a.* swabbed, washed, polished; see CLEAN.

mop up *v.* finish off, dispatch, clean up; see DEFEAT 2, ELIMINATE.

moral *a.* **1.** [Characterized by conventional virtues] trustworthy, kindly, courteous, respectable, proper, scrupulous, conscientious, good, truthful, decent, just, honorable, honest, high-minded, saintly, pure, worthy, correct, seemly, aboveboard, dutiful, principled, conscientious, chaste, ethical; see also NOBLE 1, 2, RELIABLE.—*Ant.* LYING, DISHONEST, unscrupulous. **2.** [Having to do with approved relationships between the sexes] virtuous, immaculate, decent; see CHASTE, INNOCENT 2.

morale *n.* assurance, resolve, spirit; see CONFIDENCE.

morality *n.* righteousness, uprightness, honesty; see VIRTUE 1.

morally *a.* **1.** [In accordance with accepted standards of conduct] conscientiously, truthfully, honestly, honorably, appropriately, respectably, courteously, scrupulously, uprightly, righteously, trustworthily, decently, properly, in a manner approved by society; see also JUSTLY 1, SINCERELY.—*Ant.* WRONGLY, worthlessly, dishonorably. **2.** [In a chaste manner] chastely, virtuously, purely; see MODESTLY.

morals *n.pl.* ideals, customs, standards, mores, policies, beliefs, dogmas, social standards, principles; see also ETHICS.

morbid *a.* **1.** [Diseased] sickly, unhealthy, ailing; see SICK. **2.** [Pathological] gloomy, melancholic, depressed; see INSANE, SAD 1.

more *a.* **1.** [Additional] also, likewise, and, over and above, more than that, in addition, further, besides, added; see also EXTRA.—*Ant.* LESS, less than, subtracted from. **2.**

[Greater in quantity, amount, degree, or quality] numerous, many, exceeding, extra, expanded, increased, major, augmented, extended, enhanced, added to, larger, higher, wider, deeper, heavier, solider, stronger, above the mark.—*Ant.* weaker, lessened, decreased.

more and more *a.* increasingly, more frequently, increasing in number; see FREQUENTLY, INCREASING.

more or less *a.* about, somewhat, in general; see APPROXIMATE, APPROXIMATELY.

moreover *a.* further, by the same token, furthermore; see BESIDES.

morning *n.* **1.** [Dawn] the East, morn, daybreak, break of day, first blush of morning, daylight, cockcrow, sun-up, the wee small hours*, crack of dawn*. **2.** [The time before noon] forenoon, morningtide, after midnight, before noon, breakfast time, before lunch.

mornings *a.* in the morning, every morning, before noon; see DAILY, REGULARLY.

moron *n.* feeble-minded person, imbecile, idiot, simpleton, goose, dullard, dunce, blockhead, cretin, dunce, dunderhead*, numskull, loony*, dummy*; see also FOOL.—*Ant.* PHILOSOPHER, sage, scientist.

moronic *a.* foolish, mentally retarded, dumb*; see STUPID.

morsel *n.* bite, chunk, piece; see BIT 1, PART 1.

mortal *a.* **1.** [Causing death] malignant, fatal, lethal; see DEADLY, POISONOUS. **2.** [Subject to death] human, transient, temporal, passing, frail, impermanent, perishable, fading, passing away, momentary; see also TEMPORARY.—*Ant.* ETERNAL, perpetual, everlasting.

mortal *n.* creature, being, human; see ANIMAL, MAN 1.

mortality *n.* dying, extinction, fatality; see DEATH, DESTRUCTION 1.

mortgage *n.* lease, title, debt; see CONTRACT.

mortuary *n.* charnel house, funeral parlor, funeral home; see FUNERAL.

mosaic *a.* diapered, varied, inlaid; see ORNATE.

moss *n.* lichen, Iceland moss, peat moss; see PLANT.

mossy *a.* tufted, velvety, plushy, downy, smooth, fresh, damp, moist, resilient, soft, covered, overgrown.—*Ant.* DRY, bare, prickly.

most *a.* nearly all, all but, not quite all, close upon all, in the majority. **—at the most** in toto, not more than, at the outside; see MOST. **—make the most of** exploit, utilize, take advantage of; see USE 1.

mostly *a.* **1.** [Frequently] often, many times, in many instances; see FREQUENTLY, REGULARLY. **2.** [Largely] chiefly, essentially, for the most part; see PRINCIPALLY.

motel *n.* motor inn, inn, cabins, stopping place, road house, court, motor court; see also HOTEL, RESORT 2.

moth *n.* silkworm moth, gypsy moth, clothes moth; see INSECT.

mother *n.* **1.** [A female parent] parent, matriarch, dam, mama, mammy*, mum*, ma*, mom*, mommy*, maw*, mater; see also PARENT, RELATIVE. **2.** [A matron] superintendent, mother superior, housemother; see EXECUTIVE. **3.** [The source] fountainhead, source, beginning; see ORIGIN 2.

mother-in-law *n.* husband's mother, wife's mother, mother by marriage; see RELATIVE.

motherly *a.* maternal, devoted, careful, watchful, kind, warm, gentle, tender, sympathetic, supporting, protective; see also LOVING.

motion *n.* **1.** [A movement] change, act, action; see MOVEMENT 2. **2.** [The state of moving] passage, translating, changing; see MOVEMENT 1. **3.** [An act formally proposed] suggestion, consideration, proposition; see PLAN 2.

motionless *a.* **1.** [Not moving] still, unmoving, dead, deathly still, inert, stock-still, stagnant, quiet.—*Ant.* MOVING, CHANGING, shifting. **2.** [Firm] unmovable, fixed, stationary; see FIRM 1.

motion picture *n.* moving picture, cinema, the silver screen; see MOVIE.

motivate *v.* impel, inspire hope, stimulate, incite, propel, spur, goad, move, induce, prompt, arouse, whet, instigate, fire, provoke, cause, touch off*, egg on*, trigger*; see also DRIVE 1, EXCITE, URGE 2.

motive *n.* cause, purpose, idea; see REASON 3.

motor *n.* machine, device, instrument; see ENGINE. *Types of motors include the following:* internal combustion, diesel, spark diesel, compound, steam, external combustion, Wankel, piston, turbine, gas turbine, jet, rotary, radial, airplane, automobile, truck, AC electric, DC electric, high compression, low compression.

motorboat *n.* speedboat, putt-putt*, hop-up, skip-jack; see also BOAT. *Types of motorboats include the following:* open, outboard, electric-powered, gasoline-powered; cruiser, runabout.

motorcycle *n.* motorized two-wheeled vehicle, cycle, hog*, bike*, chopper*; see also VEHICLE.

motorist *n.* automobile operator, autoist*, gear grinder*; see DRIVER.

motorized *a.* motor-driven, motor-powered, electric-driven, gasoline-driven, oil-driven, motor-equipped, motor-operated.

motto *n.* maxim, adage, saw, epigram, aphorism, sentiment, slogan, catchword, axiom; see also PROVERB, SAYING. *Familiar mottoes* *include the following:* in God we trust, *e pluribus unum* (Latin), time flies, rest in peace, peace be with you, one for all and all for one, home sweet home, God bless our home, don't tread on me, give me liberty or give me death, all or nothing, you can't take it with you, all men are created free and equal; liberty, equality, fraternity; for God and country, what's worth doing is worth doing well, don't give up the ship, don't fire until you see the whites of their eyes; remember the Alamo, remember the Maine, remember Pearl Harbor, etc.; our Country, right or wrong; hew to the line and let the chips fall where they may, praise the Lord and pass the ammunition, put your trust in God and keep your powder dry; abandon hope, all ye who enter here; to err is human, to forgive, divine; make hay while the sun shines, Pike's Peak or bust*.

mound *n.* pile, heap, knoll; see HILL.

mount *v.* **1.** [To rise] ascend, arise, uprise; see RISE 1. **2.** [To climb] ascend, scale, clamber; see CLIMB.

mountain *n.* **1.** [A lofty land mass] mount, elevation, peak, sierra, butte, hill, alp, range, ridge, pike, bluff, headland, volcano, crater, tableland, mesa, plateau, height, crag, precipice, cliff, earth mass.—*Ant.* VALLEY, ravine, flatland. *Famous chains of mountains include the following:* Alps, Himalayas, Caucasus, Urals, Pyrenees, Andes, Rockies, Canadian Rockies, Appalachians, Cascades, Adirondacks, White Mountains, Sierra Nevada, Sierra Madre, Cordillera, Apennine chain. *Famous peaks include the following:* Mont Blanc, Mt. Aetna, Vesuvius, the Matterhorn, Pike's Peak, Mt. Whitney, Mt. Shasta, Mt. Washington, the Jungfrau, the Grand Teton, Mt. McKinley, Krakatoa, Pelee, Popocatepetl, Mt. Cook, Mt. Everest, Annapurna, Mount of Olives, Mt. Sinai, Fujiyama, Mt. Kenya, Mt. Kilimanjaro. **2.** [A pile] mass, mound, glob; see HEAP.

mountaineer *n.* mountain man, mountain dweller, hillman, highlander, uplander, native of mountains, mountain climber, rock climber, mountain guide, mountain scaler, hillbilly*.

mountainous *a.* mountainlike, with mountains, difficult, barbarous, wild, untamed, strange, remote, uncivilized, rude, unpopulated, solitary, unfamiliar, isolated, steep, lofty, hilly, alpine, upland, elevated, volcanic, towering, craggy, cliffy, rugged.—*Ant.* LOW, small, flat.

mounted *a.* **1.** [On horseback] seated, riding, in the saddle, cavalry, horsed*, up.—*Ant.* AFOOT, unhorsed, dismounted. **2.** [Firmly fixed] supported, set, attached; see FIRM 1. **3.** [Backed] pasted on, set off, strengthened; see REINFORCED.

mourn *v.* deplore, grieve, fret, sorrow, rue, regret, bemoan, sigh, long for, miss, droop, languish, yearn, pine, anguish, complain, agonize, weep, suffer, wring one's hands, be brokenhearted, be in distress, be sad.—*Ant.* CELEBRATE, rejoice, be happy.

mourner *n.* lamenter, griever, keener, weeper, wailer, sorrower, pallbearer, friend of the deceased, member of the family.

mournful *a.* sorrowful, mourning, unhappy; see SAD 1.

mourning *n.* **1.** [The act of expressing grief] sorrowing, grieving, yearning, sorrow, lamentation, pining, sighing, regretting, deploring, weeping over, wailing, crying, moaning, murmuring, complaining, sobbing; see also DEPRESSION 2, GRIEF, SADNESS.—*Ant.* CELEBRATION, rejoicing, being glad. **2.** [Symbols of mourning] black, mourning coach, arm band, mourning veil, widow's weeds, black suit, black tie.

mouse *n.* rodent, vermin, rat; see ANIMAL.

mouth *n.* **1.** [The principal facial opening] *Parts of the mouth include the following:* lips, roof, floor, tongue, jaws, gums, teeth, soft palate, alveolar ridge, hard palate, uvula. **2.** [Any opening resembling a mouth] orifice, entrance, aperture; see ENTRANCE 2. **3.** [The end of a river] estuary, firth, delta, portal, harbor, roads, sound, tidewater. —**down in** (or **at**) **the mouth*** depressed, discouraged, unhappy; see SAD 1. —**have a big mouth*** talk loudly, exaggerate, brag; see TALK 1.

mouthful *n.* portion, piece, morsel; see BITE 1.

movable *a.* not fastened, portable, adjustable, adaptable, not fixed, mobile, detachable, turnable, removable, separable, transferable, loose, unfastened, free, unattached, in parts, in sections, knocked down, on wheels.—*Ant.* FIXED, fastened, stationary.

move *n.* motility, transit, progress; see MOVEMENT 1, 2. —**get a move on*** go faster, start moving, get cracking*; see HURRY 1. —**on the move*** moving, busy, acting; see ACTIVE.

move *v.* **1.** [To be in motion] go, walk, run, glide, travel, drift, budge, stir, shift, pass, cross, roll, flow, march, travel, progress, proceed, traverse, drive, ride, fly, hurry, head for, bustle, climb, crawl, leap, hop to it*, get a move on*, get going, get cracking*; see also ADVANCE 1.—*Ant.* STOP, remain stationary, stay quiet. **2.** [To set in motion] impel, actuate, propel; see PUSH 2. **3.** [To arouse the emotions of] influence, stir, instigate, stimulate, touch, play on, sway, induce, rouse, prevail upon, work upon, strike a sympathetic chord; see also DRIVE 1, ENCOURAGE, EXCITE.—*Ant.* QUIET, lull, pacify. **4.** [To take up another residence] pack up, move out, move in; see LEAVE 1.

5. [To propose an action formally] suggest, introduce, submit; see PROPOSE 1.

moved *a.* 1. [Transported] conveyed, carried, sent, taken, shifted, transferred, reassigned, changed, flown, driven, drawn, pushed, lifted, elevated, lowered, let down, displaced, withdrawn, replaced, sent abroad, trucked, hauled, dragged; see also SENT. 2. [Gone to a different residence] emigrated, migrated, vacated, removed, departed, gone away, changed residences, left, gone for good; see also GONE 1.—*Ant.* RESIDENT, remaining, still here. 3. [Proposed] recommended, submitted, introduced; see PROPOSED. 4. [Excited] disturbed, stimulated, upset; see EXCITED.

move in *v.* take up residence, take occupancy, get a home; see ARRIVE, ESTABLISH 2.

movement *n.* 1. [The act of moving] move, transit, passage, progress, journey, advance, mobility, change, shift, alteration, ascension, descension, propulsion, flow, flux, action, flight, wandering, journeying, voyaging, migration, emigration, transplanting, evolving, shifting, changing, locomotion, drive, evolution, undertaking, regression.—*Ant.* QUIET, rest, fixity. 2. [An example of movement] journey, trip, immigration, migration, march, crusade, patrol, sweep, emigration, evolution, unrest, transition, change, transfer, displacement, withdrawal, ascension, descension, progression, regression, transportation, removal, departure, shift, flight, slip, slide, step, footfall, stride, gesture, act, action, pilgrimage, expedition, locomotion. 3. [A trend] drift, tendency, bent; see INCLINATION 1.

move off *v.* depart, be in motion, go; see LEAVE 1.

move on *v.* keep moving, continue, go; see TRAVEL, WALK 1.

move up *v.* go forward, do well, get ahead; see ADVANCE 1, RISE 1.

movie *n.* moving picture, motion picture, photoplay, cinema, film, show, screenplay, cartoon, animated cartoon, serial, comedy, foreign film, travelogue, short, documentary, videotape, flick*; see also DRAMA.

movies *n.pl.* 1. [A showing of a moving picture] motion picture, film, photoplay; see MOVIE. 2. [The motion picture industry] moving pictures, the cinematic industry, Hollywood, the screen world, the silver screen*, the industry*, pictures*, the flicks*, celluloids*.

moving *a.* 1. [In motion] going, changing, progressing, advancing, shifting, evolving, withdrawing, rising, going down, descending, ascending, getting up, traveling, journeying, on the march, moving up, starting, proceeding, flying, climbing, up-tempo, on the jump*, going great guns*. 2. [Going to another residence] migrating, emigrating, vacating, removing, departing, leaving, going away, changing residences. 3. [Exciting] affecting, emotional, touching; see EXCITING.

mow *v.* scythe, reap, lay in swaths; see HARVEST.

much *a.* 1. [To a great degree or extent] important, weighty, notable, considerable, prominent, memorable, momentous, stirring, eventful, serious, urgent, pressing, critical, paramount, principal, leading, significant, telling, first-rate, in the front rank.—*Ant.* LITTLE, inconsiderable, trivial. 2. [In great quantity] full, many, very many, abundant, satisfying, enough, sufficient, adequate, considerable, substantial, ample, everywhere, copious, voluminous, plentiful, profuse, complete, lavish, generous, immeasurable, endless, countless, extravagant, hell of a lot*, all over the place*, no end*.—*Ant.* INADEQUATE, insufficient, limited. 3. [Very] greatly, enormously, extremely; see VERY.

much *n.* a great quantity, abundance, quantities, a great deal, riches, wealth, volume, very much, breadth, plentifulness, fullness, completeness, lavishness, lot*, lots*, quite a bit*, gobs*, thousands*, tons*, oodles*; see also PLENTY.—*Ant.* LITTLE, penury, scarcity. —**as much as** practically, virtually, in effect; see ALMOST, EQUAL. —**make much of** treat with importance, expand, exaggerate; see OVERDO 1. —**not much of a** inferior, mediocre, unsatisfactory; see POOR 2.

muck *n.* refuse, dung, waste; see TRASH 1.

mud *n.* dirt, muck, clay, mire, slush, silt, muddiness, stickiness, ooze, bog, marsh, swamp.

muddle *n.* trouble, disarrangement, disarray; see CONFUSION, DISORDER.

muddle *v.* stir up, disarrange, entangle, foul, mix, jumble, derange, shake up, mess, botch, clutter, snarl, complicate, disorder; see also CONFUSE.

muddled *a.* uncertain, addled, stupid; see CONFUSED 2.

muddy *a.* 1. [Containing sediment] stirred, dull, dark, cloudy, murky, indistinct, roiled, roily, confused, obscure, opaque; see also DIRTY 1.—*Ant.* CLEAR, translucent, pellucid. 2. [Deep with mud] sloppy, swampy, soggy, sodden, slushy, watery, boggy, soaked.—*Ant.* DRY, barren, parched.

muffle *v.* deaden, mute, stifle; see DECREASE 2, SOFTEN.

muffled *a.* suppressed, stifled, indistinct; see OBSCURE 1.

muffler *n.* chest protector, scarf, neckpiece, babushka, neckerchief, kerchief, neckband, neck cloth, Ascot, choker, mantle, stole; see also CLOTHES.

mug *n.* vessel, stein, flagon; see CUP.

muggy *a.* damp, humid, moist; see WET 1.

mule *n.* hinney, army mule, Missouri mule; see ANIMAL.
mull *v.* reflect, meditate, ponder; see THINK 1.
multicolored *a.* dappled, motley, spotted; see COLORED 1.
multiple *a.* **1.** [Various] complicated, more than one, many, manifold, compound, having many uses, multifold, multitudinous, aggregated, many-sided, versatile, increased, varied, compound, added; see also VARIOUS.—*Ant.* SIMPLE, UNITED, centralized. **2.** [Repeated] reoccurring, repetitious, duplicated; see MULTIPLIED.
multiplication *n.* duplication, reproduction, addition, increase, repetition, compounding, recurrence, amplification, making more, reproducing, repeating, augmenting; see also MATHEMATICS.—*Ant.* REDUCTION, subtraction, decrease.
multiplied *a.* compounded, added, reproduced, amplified, repeated, augmented, duplicated, reduplicated, made many.—*Ant.* REDUCED, divided, decreased.
multiply *v.* **1.** [To increase] add, augment, double; see INCREASE. **2.** [To bring forth young] generate, produce, populate; see REPRODUCE 3. **3.** [To employ multiplication as an arithmetical process] square, cube, raise to a higher power; see INCREASE.
multitude *n.* throng, drove, mob; see CROWD, GATHERING, PEOPLE 3.
mumble *v.* mutter, utter, whine, whimper, grumble, murmur, maunder, ramble on, whisper, speak indistinctly, say to oneself; see also HESITATE, STAMMER.—*Ant.* SAY, articulate, enunciate.
mumbo jumbo *n.* gibberish, double talk, drivel; see NONSENSE 1.
munch *v.* crunch, bite, crush; see CHEW, EAT.
mundane *a.* normal, ordinary, everyday; see WORLDLY.
municipal *a.* self-governing, metropolitan, city, town, community, local, civil, incorporated, corporate; see also PUBLIC.—*Ant.* PRIVATE, national, state.
municipality *n.* district, village, borough; see CITY, TOWN 1.
munitions *n.pl.* materiel, weapons, ordnance; see AMMUNITION, BOMB, BULLET, CANNON, EXPLOSIVE, GUN, MACHINE GUN, ROCKET, SHOT 1.
murder *n.* killing, homicide, death, destruction, annihilation, carnage, putting an end to, slaying, shooting, knifing, assassination, lynching, crime, felony, killing with malice aforethought, murder in the first degree, first-degree murder, contract killing, murder in the second degree, murder in the third degree, massacre, genocide, butchery, patricide, matricide, infanticide, fratricide, genocide, suicide, foul play. **—get away with murder*** escape punishment, take flight, avoid punishment; see EVADE.
murder *v.* **1.** [To kill unlawfully] slay, assassinate, butcher; see KILL 1. **2.** [*To ruin, especially by incompetence] spoil, mar, misuse; see BOTCH, DESTROY, FAIL 1.
murdered *a.* killed, assassinated, massacred; see DEAD 1.
murderer *n.* slayer, assassin, butcher; see CRIMINAL, KILLER.
murderous *a.* killing, cruel, criminal; see DEADLY.
murky *a.* dim, dusky, dingy; see DARK 1, DIRTY 1.
murmur *v.* **1.** [To make a low, continuous sound] ripple, moan, trickle, burble, babble, tinkle, gurgle, meander, flow gently; see also HUM, WHISPER.—*Ant.* SOUND, peal, clang. **2.** [To mutter] mumble, rumble, growl; see MUTTER 2.
muscle *n.* fiber, flesh, protoplasm, brawn, beef*.
muscular *a.* brawny, powerful, husky; see STRONG 1.
museum *n.* institution, building, hall, place of exhibition, foundation, art gallery, library, picture gallery, archives, treasury, storehouse, depository, vault, aquarium, menagerie, zoological garden, zoo, botanical garden, herbarium, arboretum.
mush *n.* **1.** [Boiled meal] Indian meal, hasty pudding, hominy, cereal, grain; see also FOOD. **2.** [*Sentimentality] sentimentalism, excessive sentiment, mawkishness, affectation, superficiality, romanticism, puppy love, heart and flowers*, sob story*.
mushroom *n.* toadstool, fungus, *champignon* (French); see FOOD, PLANT.
mushroom *v.* augment, spread, sprout; see GROW 1, INCREASE.
mushy *a.* **1.** [Soft] pulpy, mashy, muddy; see SOFT 2. **2.** [*Sentimental] romantic, maudlin, effusive; see EMOTIONAL, SENTIMENTAL.
music *n.* **1.** [A combination of tone and rhythm] harmony, melody, tune, air, strain, harmonics, song, measure, refrain, phrasing; see also BEAT 2, HARMONY 1. *Terms used in music include the following:* scale, clef, note, tone, pitch, sharp, flat, major, minor, key, mode, bridge, theme, movement, orchestration, instrumentation, variation, improvisation, rhythm, accent, beat, down-beat, upbeat, off-beat, chord, counterpoint, timbre, volume, resonance; see also SONG. *Musical forms for instruments include the following:* symphony (the conventional four movements of a symphony are sonata, andante, scherzo, finale), concerto, suite; trio, quartet, quintet, etc.; overture, prelude, sonata, mass, scherzo, nocturne, fugue, étude, tone poem, variations, rhapsody, serenade, ballade, march, rhythm and blues, dance; see also OVERTURE 2. *Musical dance forms*

include the following: waltz, tango, foxtrot, rhumba, polka; see also DANCE 1. *General styles of music include the following:* classical, long-hair*, serious, medieval, modern, folk, primitive, popular, national, sacred, baroque, modernistic, formal, romantic, jazz, blues, rhythm-and-blues, boogie-woogie, folk-rock, heavy metal, acid rock, rock-and-roll, pop, bebop, bop, soul, ragtime, swing; see also JAZZ. **2.** [Responsiveness to music] musical appreciation, sensitivity, aesthetic sense; see APPRECIATION 2, FEELING 4. **—face the music*** accept the consequences of one's actions, suffer, undergo; see ENDURE 2.

musical *a.* **1.** [Having the qualities of music] tuneful, sweet, pleasing, agreeable, symphonic, lyric, mellow, vocal, choral, consonant, rhythmical; see also HARMONIOUS 1.—*Ant.* HARSH, tuneless, discordant. **2.** [Having aptitude for music] gifted, talented, musically inclined; see ARTISTIC.

musical *n.* musicale, musical comedy, burlesque; see PERFORMANCE, SHOW 1.

musical instrument *n. Types of musical instruments include the following:* recorder, grand piano, concert piano, lyre, bell, flute, piccolo, violin, fiddle*, oboe, clarinet, bassoon, fife, bagpipe, trombone, French horn, tuba, cornet, trumpet, saxophone, dulcimer, harpsichord, harmonica, organ, harp, tambourine, ukelele, guitar, electric guitar, banjo, mandolin, lute, viola, cello, double bass, xylophone, marimba, cymbal, drum, accordion, concertina, tom-tom, sitar, calliope.

musician *n.* player, performer, composer; see ARTIST. *Musicians include the following:* singer, instrumentalist, soloist, soprano, alto, contralto, tenor, baritone, bass, conductor, director, leader, basso profundo, folk singer, drummer, pianist, violinist, cellist; performer on a woodwind instrument, performer on a brass instrument, percussion performer, etc.; jazzman.

muss* *n.* chaos, disarrangement, turmoil; see CONFUSION, DISORDER.

muss *v.* rumble, tousle, dishevel, ruffle, crumple, jumble, disarrange, disturb, mess up; see also TANGLE.

mussy* *a.* messy, chaotic, rumpled; see TANGLED.

must* *n.* requirement, need, obligation; see NECESSITY 2.

must *v.* ought, should, have to, have got to, be compelled, be obliged, be required, be doomed, be destined, be ordered, be made, have no choice, be one's fate; see also NEED.

mustache *n.* moustachio, handlebar*, soup-strainer*; see BEARD, WHISKERS.

musty *a.* moldy, fusty, rank; see ROTTEN 1.

mutation *n.* modification, deviation, variation; see CHANGE 1, VARIETY 1, 2.

mute *a.* **1.** [Without power of speech] tongueless, deaf-mute, deaf-and-dumb*, inarticulate, voiceless, tongue-tied; see also DUMB 1, QUIET.—*Ant.* VOCAL, noisy, unimpaired. **2.** [Suddenly deprived of speech] speechless, wordless, silent; see BEWILDERED, SURPRISED.

mutilate *v.* **1.** [To maim] cut, batter, scratch; see WEAKEN 2. **2.** [To damage] injure, deface, ravage; see DAMAGE, HURT 1.

mutilated *a.* disfigured, distorted, maimed; see DEFORMED.

mutiny *n.* insurrection, revolt, resistance; see REVOLUTION 2.

mutter *v.* **1.** [To make a low, mumbling sound] rumble, growl, snarl; see SOUND. **2.** [To speak as if to oneself] murmur, grunt, grumble, sputter, whisper, speak inarticulately, speak indistinctly, speak in an undertone, swallow one's words*; see also MUMBLE, MURMUR 1. **3.** [To complain] grumble, moan, groan; see COMPLAIN.

mutual *a.* **1.** [Reciprocal] interchangeable, two-sided, given and taken; see COMPLEMENTARY. **2.** [Common] joint, shared, belonging equally to each; see COMMON 5.

mutually *a.* commonly, cooperatively, jointly, reciprocally, in combination, by common consent, in conjunction; see also TOGETHER 2.

muzzle *v.* **1.** [To fasten a muzzle upon] wrap, muffle, deaden; see BIND 1, GAG 1. **2.** [To silence] gag, restrain, restrict, repress, suppress, check, stop, stop someone's mouth, hush, still, shush*; see also QUIET 2.

myriad *a.* variable, infinite, innumerable; see ENDLESS, MULTIPLE 1.

myself *pron.* me, me personally; the speaker, the writer, etc.; on my own authority, on my own responsibility, yours truly*, your humble servant, me myself.

mysterious *a.* **1.** [Puzzling] enigmatic, enigmatical, strange; see DIFFICULT 2, UNNATURAL 1. **2.** [Concerning powers beyond those supposedly natural] mystic, occult, dark, mystifying, transcendental, spiritual, symbolic, subjective, mystical, magical, dark, veiled, strange, astrological, unknowable, unfathomable, esoteric, cryptic, oracular, unrevealed, incredible; see also MAGIC. **3.** [Not generally known] obscure, hidden, ambiguous; see SECRET 1.

mystery *n.* **1.** [The quality of being mysterious] inscrutability, occultism, cabalism; see MAGIC 1, 2, STRANGENESS. **2.** [Something difficult to know] riddle, conundrum, enigma; see DIFFICULTY 2, PUZZLE 2. **3.** [A trick] sleight-of-hand, trick of magic, juggle; see TRICK 1. **4.** [A mystery story] detective story, mystery play, mystery movie; see STORY.

mystic *a.* occult, transcendental, spiritual; see MYSTERIOUS 2, SECRET 1.

mysticism *n.* occultism, cabala, quietism, orphism.
mystify *v.* perplex, trick, hoodwink; see DECEIVE, LIE 1.
mystique *n.* attitude, complex, nature; see CHARACTER 1, TEMPERAMENT.
myth *n.* fable, folk tale, legend, lore, saga, folk ballad, allegory, parable, tale; see also STORY.
mythical *a.* mythological, fabricated, fictitious; see FALSE 3, UNREAL.
mythological *a.* whimsical, fictitious, chimerical; see FANTASTIC, IMAGINARY.
mythology *n.* belief, conviction, mythicism; see FAITH 2, RELIGION 1.

N

nab *v.* grab, take, snatch; see SEIZE 2.
nag *v.* vex, annoy, pester; see BOTHER 2.
nail *n.* brad, pin, peg, stud, spike; see also TACK 1.
nail *v.* **1.** [To hammer] drive, pound, spike; see HIT 1. **2.** [To fasten with nails] secure, hold, bind; see FASTEN. **3.** [*To arrest] capture, detain, apprehend; see ARREST, SEIZE 2. **—hard as nails** callous, unfeeling, remorseless; see CRUEL. **—hit the nail on the head*** do what is exactly right, be accurate, come to the point; see DEFINE 2.
naive *a.* unaffected, childish, plain, artless, innocent, untrained, countrified, callow, natural, unschooled, ignorant, untaught, provincial, unsophisticated, unworldly, guileless, spontaneous, instinctive, impulsive, simple-minded, innocuous, unsuspecting, unsuspicious, harmless, gullible, credulous, trusting, original, fresh, unpolished, rude, primitive, ingenuous, sincere, open, candid, forthright, aboveboard, romantic, fanciful, unpretentious, transparent, straightforward, uncomplicated, easily imposed upon; see also INEXPERIENCED.—*Ant.* EXPERIENCED, sophisticated, complicated.
naively *a.* childishly, innocently, stupidly; see FOOLISHLY, OPENLY 1.
naiveté *n.* simplicity, childishness, inexperience; see INNOCENCE 2.
naked *a.* **1.** [Nude] unclothed, undressed, stripped, unclad, unrobed, disrobed, leafless, hairless, bare, undraped, exposed, having nothing on, unappareled, denuded, unveiled, uncovered, uncloaked, stark naked, topless, bald, in one's birthday suit*, in the buff, peeled*, without a stitch, in the raw. **2.** [Unadorned] plain, simple, artless; see MODEST 2, NATURAL 3.
nakedness *n.* nudity, bareness, undress, exposure, the raw, nudism.
name *n.* **1.** [A title] proper name, Christian name, given name, cognomen, appellation, designation, first name, family name, title, denomination, surname, sign, handle*. **2.** [Reputation] renown, honor, repute; see FAME. **3.** [An epithet] nickname, pen name, pseudonym, sobriquet, stage name, *nom de plume* (French), *nom de guerre* (French), pet name, fictitious name, alias. *Insulting names include the following:* devil, imbecile, idiot, rat*, skunk*, dog*, pig*, fool, moron, brute, bum, boob*, oaf, goon, sourpuss*, dummy*, jerk*, swine, bigmouth*, schmuck*, weasel, beanpole*, bitch*, bastard*, four-eyes*, skinny, fatty*, windbag*. **4.** [A famous person] star, hero, a person of renown; see CELEBRITY. **—call names** swear at, insult, slander; see SCOLD. **—in the name of** by authority of, in reference to, as representative of; see FOR. **—know only by name** be familiar with, not know personally, have heard of; see KNOW 3. **—to one's name** belonging to one, in one's possession, possessed by; see OWNED.
name *v.* **1.** [To give a name] call, christen, baptize, style, term, label, identify, designate, classify, denominate, title, entitle, nickname, characterize, label, ticket, dub*; see also DESCRIBE, DEFINE. **2.** [To indicate by name] refer to, specify, signify, denote, single out, mark, suggest, connote, point to, note, remark, index, list, cite; see also MENTION. **3.** [To appoint] elect, nominate, select; see DELEGATE 1.
name calling *n.* disrespect, insolence, abuse; see INSULT.
named *a.* **1.** [Having as a name] called, designated, entitled, titled, termed, specified, styled, denominated, christened, baptized, nicknamed, labeled, tagged*, dubbed*. **2.** [Chosen] appointed, commissioned, delegated, authorized, nominated, elected, invested, vested, assigned, ordained, entrusted, picked, selected, decided upon, settled on, picked out, preferred, favored, supported, approved, certified, called, anointed, consecrated, sanctioned, drafted, opted, declared, announced, singled out.
nameless *a.* inconspicuous, undistinguished, obscure; see UNKNOWN 2.

namely *a.* specifically, to wit, that is to say, particularly, by way of explanation, strictly speaking, in other words, in plain English.

naming *n.* identifying, giving a name to, finding a name for; see CLASSIFICATION, DESCRIPTION.

nap *n.* **1.** [A short sleep] siesta, cat nap, doze; see SLEEP. **2.** [The finish of certain goods, especially fabric] pile, shag, surface; see GRAIN 2, OUTSIDE 1, TEXTURE 1.

napkin *n.* paper napkin, paper towel, table linen; see TOWEL.

narcotic *n.* depressant, sedative, opiate; see DRUG.

narrate *v.* detail, describe, depict; see REPORT 1, TELL 1.

narrative *a.* storylike, historical, sequential; see CHRONOLOGICAL.

narrow *a.* **1.** [Lacking breadth] close, cramped, tight, confined, shrunken, compressed, slender, thin, fine, linear, threadlike, tapering, tapered, slim, scant, scanty, lanky, small, meager; see also THIN 1.—*Ant.* BROAD, wide, extensive. **2.** [Lacking tolerance] dogmatic, narrow-minded, parochial; see CONSERVATIVE, CONVENTIONAL 3, PREJUDICED. **3.** [Lacking a comfortable margin] close, near, precarious; see DANGEROUS, ENDANGERED, UNSAFE.

narrowly *a.* nearly, closely, by a narrow margin; see ALMOST.

narrow-minded *a.* bigoted, biased, provincial; see CONSERVATIVE, CONVENTIONAL 3, PREJUDICED.

narrowness *n.* **1.** [A physical restriction] confinement, slimness, restriction; see BARRIER, INTERFERENCE 1. **2.** [A mental restriction] intolerance, bigotry, bias; see PREJUDICE, STUBBORNNESS.

nasty *a.* **1.** [Offensive to the senses] foul, gross, revolting; see OFFENSIVE 2, VULGAR. **2.** [Indecent] immoral, immodest, smutty; see LEWD 1, SHAMEFUL 1. **3.** [Unkind] sarcastic, critical, mean; see CRUEL, FIERCE, RUTHLESS.

nation *n.* **1.** [An organized state] realm, country, commonwealth, republic, democracy, state, monarchy, dominion, body politic, land, domain, empire, kingdom, principality, sovereignty, colony; see also GOVERNMENT 1. **2.** [A people having some unity] populace, community, public; see POPULATION, RACE 2, SOCIETY 2.

national *a.* **1.** [Concerning a nation] racial, ethnic, political, sovereign, state, social, civic, civil, societal, communal, royal, imperial, federal; see also GOVERNMENTAL, PUBLIC 2. **2.** [Operative throughout a nation] nationwide, country-wide, interstate, internal, social, widespread, sweeping; see also GENERAL 1.

nationalism *n.* provincialism, chauvinism, allegiance; see LOYALTY, PATRIOTISM.

nationality *n.* native land, country, citizenship; see ORIGIN 2.

nationally *a.* politically, governmentally, as a state, as a country, publicly, of the people, throughout the country, transcending state boundaries, for the general welfare.

native *a.* **1.** [Natural] innate, inherent, inborn, implanted, inbred, ingrained, congenital, fundamental, hereditary, inherited, essential, constitutional; see also NATURAL 1.—*Ant.* UNNATURAL, foreign, alien. **2.** [Characteristic of a region] aboriginal, indigenous, original, primitive, primary, primeval, vernacular, domestic, local, found locally; see also REGIONAL.—*Ant.* IMPORTED, brought in, transplanted.

native *n.* **1.** [Aborigine] primitive, tribesman, hunter-gatherer; see MAN 1. **2.** [Citizen] national, inhabitant, occupant; see CITIZEN, RESIDENT.

natural *a.* **1.** [Rooted in nature] intrinsic, original, essential, true, fundamental, inborn, ingrained, inherent, instinctive, implanted, innate, inbred, incarnate, subjective, inherited, congenital, genetic; see also NATIVE 1.—*Ant.* FOREIGN, alien, acquired. **2.** [To be expected] normal, typical, characteristic, usual, customary, habitual, accustomed, involuntary, spontaneous, uncontrolled, uncontrollable, familiar, common, universal, prevailing, prevalent, general, probable, uniform, constant, consistent, ordinary, logical, reasonable, anticipated, looked for, hoped for, counted on, relied on; see also REGULAR 3.—*Ant.* UNKNOWN, unexpected, unheard of. **3.** [Not affected] ingenuous, simple, artless, innocent, unstudied, spontaneous, impulsive, childlike, unfeigned, open, frank, candid, unsophisticated, unpolished, homey, unpretentious, forthright, sincere, straightforward, being oneself, unsuspecting, credulous, trusting, plain, direct, rustic; see also NAIVE.—*Ant.* ORNATE, pretentious, sophisticated. **4.** [Concerning the physical universe] actual, tangible, according to nature; see PHYSICAL 1, REAL.

naturalist *n.* botanist, zoologist, biologist; see SCIENTIST.

naturally *interj.* certainly, absolutely, of course; see SURELY, YES.

naturally *a.* **1.** [In an unaffected manner] artlessly, spontaneously, innocently, candidly, openly, impulsively, freely, readily, easily, without restraint, directly; see also SIMPLY, SINCERELY.—*Ant.* AWKWARDLY, restrainedly, clumsily. **2.** [As a matter of course] casually, according to expectation, as anticipated, characteristically, typically, normally, commonly, usually, ordinarily, habitually, by nature, instinctively, intuitively, by birth, uniformly, generally, consistently; see also REGULARLY.—*Ant.* STRANGELY, astonishingly, amazingly.

nature *n.* **1.** [The external universe] cosmos, creation, macrocosm; see UNIVERSE. **2.** [The complex of essential qualities] characteristics, quality, constitution; see CHARACTER 1, ESSENCE 1. **3.** [Natural surroundings] outside world, out-of-doors, scenery, natural setting, view, seascape, landscape, the outdoors, natural scenery, recreational facilities, the great outdoors; see also ENVIRONMENT, REALITY. **4.** [Natural forces] natural law, natural order, underlying cause, cosmic process, physical energy, kinetic energy, potential energy, water power, fission, fusion, atomic power, the sun, radiation, rays; see also ENERGY 2. **5.** [Vital forces in an organism] creation, generation, regeneration; see LIFE 1, 2, STRENGTH. **6.** [Kind] species, sort, type; see KIND 2, VARIETY 1, 2. —**by nature** inherently, by birth, as a matter of course; see NATURALLY 2. —**of** (or **in**) **the nature of** similar to, having the essential character of, as compared to; see LIKE.

naughty *a.* wayward, disobedient, mischievous, impish, fiendish, badly behaved, roguish, bad, unmanageable, ungovernable, insubordinate, wanton, recalcitrant; see also RUDE 2, UNRULY.

nausea *n.* motion sickness, queasiness, vomiting; see ILLNESS 2.

nauseate *v.* sicken, offend, repulse; see BOTHER 2, DISGUST, DISTURB.

nauseous *a.* queasy, ill, squeamish; see SICK.

nautical *a.* ocean-going, marine, naval, oceanic, deep-sea, aquatic, sailing, seafaring, seaworthy, sea-going, boating, yachting, cruising, whaling, oceanographic, rowing, navigating; see also MARITIME.

naval *a.* seagoing, marine, aquatic; see MARITIME, NAUTICAL.

navel *n.* abdomen, depression, umbilicus; see CENTER 1.

navigable *a.* passable, deep enough, open; see SAFE 1.

navigate *v.* pilot, steer, lie to, head out for, ride out, lay a course, operate; see also DRIVE 2.

navigation *n.* navigating, seamanship, yachting, piloting, aeronautics, flying, sailing, seafaring, ocean travel, exploration, voyaging, shipping, cruising, plotting a course, boating, pilotage, dead reckoning.

navigator *n.* seaman, explorer, mariner; see PILOT 1, SAILOR.

navy *n.* fleet, carrier group, squadron, flotilla, armada, task force, submarine force, ships, amphibious force, coast guard.

near *a.* **1.** [Not distant in space] proximate, adjacent, adjoining, neighboring, not remote, close at hand, contiguous, handy, near by, next door to, at close quarters, beside, side by side, in close proximity; see also BORDERING.—*Ant.* DISTANT, removed, far off. **2.** [Not distant in relationship] touching, close, akin; see FRIENDLY, RELATED 3. **3.** [Not distant in time] at hand, approaching, next; see COMING 1, EXPECTED.

nearly *a.* within a little, all but, approximately; see ALMOST.

nearness *n.* **1.** [Nearness in time or space] closeness, proximity, vicinity, approximation, approach, intimacy, resemblance, likeness, handiness, close quarters, imminence, immediacy, loom, threat, menace, prospectiveness.—*Ant.* DISTANCE, remoteness, difference. **2.** [Nearness in feeling] familiarity, affection, intimacy; see ADMIRATION, FRIENDSHIP.

neat *a.* **1.** [Clean and orderly] tidy, trim, prim, spruce, dapper, smart, correct, shipshape, methodical, regular, orderly, systematic, spotless, nice, meticulous, elegant, spick-and-span, immaculate, chic, well-groomed, exact, precise, proper, neat as a pin, in good order, spruced up; see also CLEAN 1.—*Ant.* DISORDERED, messy, slovenly. **2.** [Clever; *said of something done*] dexterous, deft, skillful, expert, proficient, handy, apt, ready, artful, nimble, quick, agile, adept, speedy, finished, practiced, easy, effortless; see also ABLE.—*Ant.* AWKWARD, clumsy, fumbling.

neatly *a.* **1.** [Arranged so as to present a neat appearance] tidily, orderly, systematically, methodically, correctly, exactly, uniformly, levelly, flatly, smoothly, regularly, precisely, immaculately; see also EVENLY 1, ORGANIZED. **2.** [In an adroit manner] skillfully, deftly, agilely; see CLEVERLY, EASILY.

neatness *n.* cleanness, tidiness, orderliness; see CLEANLINESS.

necessarily *a.* vitally, fundamentally, importantly, indispensably, unavoidably, undeniably, certainly, as a matter of course, inescapably, irresistibly, inevitably, assuredly, significantly, undoubtedly, indubitably, positively, unquestionably, no doubt, without fail, of necessity, of course, by force, come what may, without recourse, beyond one's control, by its own nature, from within, by definition; see also SURELY.

necessary *a.* important, needed, requisite, expedient, needful, indispensable, required, urgent, wanted, imperative, prerequisite, pressing, vital, fundamental, quintessential, cardinal, significant, momentous, compulsory, mandatory, basic, paramount, obligatory, essential, compelling, incumbent upon, all-important, binding, specified, unavoidable, decisive, crucial, elementary, chief, principal, prime, intrinsic, fixed, constant, permanent, inherent, ingrained, innate, without choice.

necessitate *v.* compel, constrain, oblige; see FORCE.

necessity *n.* **1.** [The state of being required] need, essentiality, indispensability; see REQUIREMENT 2. **2.** [That which is needed] need, want, requisite, vital part, essential, demand, imperative, fundamental, claim; see also LACK 2. **3.** [The state of being forced by circumstances] exigency, pinch, stress, urgency, destitution, extremity, privation, obligation, case of life or death; see also EMERGENCY, POVERTY 1. **—of necessity** inevitably, importantly, surely; see NECESSARILY.

neck *n.* **1.** [The juncture of the head and the trunk] cervical vertebrae, nape, scruff; see THROAT. **2.** [The part of a dress at the neck] neckband, neckline, collar line; see DRESS 1, 2. **—risk one's neck** endanger oneself, gamble, take a chance; see RISK. **—stick one's neck out** endanger oneself, take a chance, gamble; see RISK.

necklace *n.* ornament, accessory, string of beads, jewels, chain, neckband, pearls, diamonds, choker; see also JEWELRY.

necktie *n.* neckwear, knot, ascot; see TIE 2.

need *n.* **1.** [Poverty] want, destitution, pennilessness; see POVERTY 1. **2.** [Lack] insufficiency, shortage, inadequacy; see LACK 1, 2. **3.** [A requirement] obligation, necessity, urgency; see REQUIREMENT 2. **—if need be** if it is required, if the occasion demands, if necessary; see IF.

need *v.* lack, require, feel the necessity for, be in need of, suffer privation, be in want, be destitute, be short, be inadequate, have occasion for, have use for, miss, be without, do without, be needy, be poor, be deficient, go hungry, live from hand to mouth, feel the pinch*, be down and out*, be hard up*, be up against it*; see also WANT 2.—*Ant.* OWN, have, hold.

needed *a.* wanted, required, desired; see NECESSARY.

needle *n.* awl, spike, hypodermic needle, syringe, phonograph needle, stylus, electric needle, probe, skewer, pin, darning needle, sewing needle, knitting needle.

needle* *v.* provoke, goad, tease; see BOTHER 2, EXAMINE.

needless *a.* unwanted, excessive, groundless; see UNNECESSARY, USELESS 1.

need to *v.* have to, be obligated to, have reason to; see MUST.

needy *a.* destitute, indigent, penniless; see POOR 1.

negate *v.* repeal, retract, nullify; see CANCEL.

negation *n.* opposition, contradiction, repudiation; see DENIAL, REFUSAL.

negative *a.* **1.** [Involving a refusal] denying, contradictory, contrary, disavowing, repugnant, contravening, rejecting, disallowing.—*Ant.* FAVORABLE, encouraging, accepting. **2.** [Lacking positive qualities] absent, removed, neutralizing, counteractive, annulling, invalidating.—*Ant.* EMPHATIC, validating, affirmative.

negative *n.* **1.** [A refusal] contradiction, disavowal, refutation; see DENIAL, REFUSAL. **2.** [A negative image] film, plate, developed film; see IMAGE 2, PICTURE 2.

neglect *n.* **1.** [The act of showing indifference to a person] slight, disregard, thoughtlessness, disrespect, carelessness, scorn, oversight, heedlessness, inattention, unconcern, inconsideration, disdain, coolness; see also INDIFFERENCE. **2.** [The act of neglecting duties or charges] negligence, slovenliness, neglectfulness; see CARELESSNESS.

neglect *v.* **1.** [To treat with indifference] slight, scorn, overlook, disregard, disdain, detest, rebuff, affront, despise, ignore, depreciate, spurn, underestimate, undervalue, shake off, make light of, laugh off, keep one's distance, pass over, pass up, have nothing to do with, let alone, let go, not care for, pay no attention to, pay no heed, leave alone, not give a darn*, let the grass grow under one's feet, leave well enough alone, let it ride, play possum*, keep at arm's length.—*Ant.* CONSIDER, appreciate, value. **2.** [To fail to attend to responsibilities] pass over, defer, procrastinate, suspend, dismiss, discard, let slip, miss, skip, omit, skimp, gloss over, be remiss, be derelict, let go, ignore, trifle, postpone, lose sight of, look the other way, let it go, not trouble oneself with, evade, be careless, be irresponsible.—*Ant.* WATCH, care for, attend.

neglected *a.* slighted, disregarded, scorned, disdained, despised, affronted, overlooked, ignored, spurned, omitted, undervalued, deferred, dismissed, passed over, postponed, evaded, deteriorated, underestimated, declined, lapsed, uncared for, unwatched, unheeded, depreciated, unconsidered, shaken off, unused, unwanted, tossed aside, abandoned, forgotten, out in the cold, dropped, put on the shelf.—*Ant.* CONSIDERED, cared for, heeded.

negligence *n.* disregard, inconsideration, disrespect; see CARELESSNESS, INDIFFERENCE NEGLECT 1.

negligent *a.* indifferent, inattentive, neglectful; see CARELESS.

negotiate *v.* **1.** [To make arrangements for] arrange, bargain, confer, consult, parley, transact, mediate, make peace, contract, settle, adjust, conciliate, accomodate, arbitrate, referee, umpire, compromise, bring to terms, make terms, make the best of, treat with, moderate, work out, dicker*, haggle, bury the hatchet. **2.** [To transfer] barter, allocate, transmit; see ASSIGN, SELL.

negotiation *n.* compromise, intervention, mediation; see AGREEMENT.

negro *a.* black, negroid, African, black-skinned, dark-skinned, Afro-American, Afro-Asian, Ethiopian, brown; see also BLACK 2.

Negro *n.* black, Ethiopian, African, Afro-American, Afro-Asian, colored person, Negroid person, black person, person of color.

neighbor *n.* acquaintance, companion, associate, next-door-neighbor, nearby resident; see also FRIEND.

neighborhood *n.* environs, block, vicinity, locality, proximity, district, area, parish, ward, precinct, community, region, zone, section, suburb, tract. **—in the neighborhood of*** about, approximately, close to; see NEAR 1.

neighboring *a.* adjacent, adjoining, contiguous; see BORDERING, NEAR 1.

neighborly *a.* sociable, hospitable, helpful; see FRIENDLY.

neither *a. & conj.* nor yet, also not, not either, not, not at all.

neither *pron.* no one, nobody, neither one, not this one, nor this nor that, no one of two, not the one, not any one; see also NONE 1, NOTHING.

nephew *n.* brother's son, sister's son, grandnephew, son of a brother-in-law, son of a sister-in law, nephew by marriage; see also NIECE, RELATIVE.

nerve *n.* **1.** [The structure that carries nervous impulses] nerve fiber, nerve tissue, nerve filament, nerve cord, nerve ending. *Types of nerves include the following:* motor, sensory, efferent, afferent, effector, receptors. **2.** [Courage] resolution, spirit, mettle; see COURAGE. **3.** [Impudence] temerity, audacity, effrontery; see RUDENESS.

nerve-racking *a.* exhausting, horrible, wearisome; see DIFFICULT 1, PAINFUL 1.

nerves *n.pl.* strain, tension, hysteria, emotional stress, sleeplessness; see also NERVOUSNESS. **—get on one's nerves*** exasperate, irritate, annoy; see BOTHER 2.

nervous *a.* **1.** [Excitable] sensitive, irritable, impatient, moody, peevish, restless, uneasy, impulsive, rash, hasty, reckless, touchy, readily upset, high-strung, neurotic; see also UNSTABLE 2. **2.** [Excited] agitated, bothered, annoyed; see EXCITED.

nervousness *n.* stimulation, agitation, animation, intoxication, sensitivity, delirium, excitability, irascibility, impulsiveness, impetuosity, moodiness, anger, elation, discomfiture, hastiness, vehemence, impatience, feverishness, stage fright, butterflies in the stomach*, the jitters*, the shakes; see also EMBARRASSMENT, EXCITEMENT.—*Ant.* REST, calm, relaxation.

nest *n.* den, cradle, incubator; see RETREAT 2.

nest egg* *n.* personal savings, personal property, real property, something for a rainy day*; see also MONEY 1, SAVINGS.

nestle *v.* cuddle, snuggle, settle down, take shelter, lie close, make oneself snug, huddle, move close to, lie against, curl up to.

net *a.* clear, pure, remaining, exclusive, excluding, irreducible, undeductible.

net *n.* screen, mesh, fabric; see WEB. *Varieties of nets include the following:* hair, mosquito, tennis, ping-pong, volleyball, goal, casting, bird, butterfly, fish, draw, drag, drop, hand, scoop.

net *v.* make, clear, gain above expenses; see PROFIT 2.

network *n.* **1.** [System of channels] tracks, circuitry, channels, system, labyrinth, artery, arrangement; see also CHAIN, WIRING. **2.** [Netting] fiber, weave, mesh; see GOODS, WEB.

neurosis *n.* compulsion, instability, mental disorder; see INSANITY, NERVOUSNESS, OBSESSION.

neurotic *a.* disturbed, unstable, sick; see INSANE, TROUBLED.

neurotic *n.* paranoid, sick person, psychotic; see MADMAN.

neutral *a.* **1.** [Not fighting] noncombatant, nonpartisan, on the side lines, nonparticipating, inactive, disengaged, uninvolved, bystanding, standing by, inert, on the fence.—*Ant.* ENGAGED, involved, active. **2.** [Without opinion] nonchalant, disinterested, impartial; see INDIFFERENT. **3.** [Without distinctive color] drab, indeterminate, vague; see DULL 2.

never *a.* not ever, at no time, not at any time, not in the least, not in any way, in no way, not at all, not under any condition, nevermore, never again, no ways.

never-ending *a.* timeless, endless, persistent; see CONSTANT, ETERNAL.

never mind *interj.* forget it, it doesn't matter, ignore it, don't bother, let it go, drop it*; see also STOP.

nevertheless *a.* not the less, nonetheless, notwithstanding; see ALTHOUGH, BUT 1.

new *a.* **1.** [Recent] current, brand-new, newborn, young, new-fangled, latest, just out; see also FRESH 1. **2.** [Modern] modish, popular, faddish, up to the minute, contemporary, latest; see also FASHIONABLE, MODERN 1. **3.** [Novel] unique, original, bizarre; see UNUSUAL 1, 2. **4.** [Different] unlike, dissimilar, distinct; see UNLIKE. **5.** [Additional] further, increased, supplementary; see EXTRA. **6.** [Inexperienced] unseasoned, unskilled, untrained; see INCOMPETENT, INEXPERIENCED. **7.** [Recently] newly, freshly, lately; see RECENTLY.

newcomer *n.* immigrant, outsider, foreigner, tenderfoot, maverick*, Johnny-come-lately*; see also ALIEN, STRANGER.

newfangled *a.* novel, unique, new; see FASHIONABLE, MODERN 1.

newly *a.* lately, anew, afresh; see RECENTLY.

newlywed *n.* bride, bridegroom, honeymooner; see HUSBAND, WIFE.

newness *n.* uniqueness, modernity, recentness; see ORIGINALITY.

news *n.* 1. [Information] intelligence, tidings, advice, discovery, recognition, the scoop*, the goods*, headlines, front-page news; see also DATA, KNOWLEDGE 1. 2. [A specific report] telling, narration, recital, account, description, message, copy, communication, release, communiqué, telegram, cable, radiogram, broadcast, telecast, bulletin, dispatch, news story, scoop*, big news, eye opener*; see also ANNOUNCEMENT. —**make news** become famous, accomplish, create events; see EXPOSE, REVEAL.

newscast *n.* news broadcasting, telecast, newscasting; see ANNOUNCEMENT, NEWS 2.

newscaster *n.* news analyst, commentator, broadcaster; see REPORTER, WRITER.

newspaper *n.* publication, daily paper, journal, press, fourth estate, public press, sheet, tabloid, gazette; see also RECORD 1. *Varieties of newspapers include the following:* daily, weekly, biweekly, metropolitan, rural, county, country, trade, provincial, community. *Parts of newspapers include the following:* front page section, news section, foreign news section, editorial page, state news section, city news section, local news section, domestic news section, magazine, business section, society section, family section, living section, women's section, sports section, entertainment section, amusement section, comics page, advertising section, syndicated section, boiler plate*.

newspaperman *n.* newsperson, journalist, member of the editorial department; see AUTHOR, EDITOR, REPORTER, WRITER.

New York *n.* Manhattan, Greater New York, Metropolitan New York, Gotham, the Big Apple, Brooklyn, the Bronx, the Town, the Garment Capital, Wall Street, Financial Capital; see also CITY.

next *a.* 1. [Following in order] succeeding, later, afterwards, presently, resulting, subsequent, ensuing; see also FOLLOWING. 2. [Adjacent] beside, close, alongside, on one side, on the side, adjoining, neighboring, meeting, touching, bordering on, cheek by jowl, side by side, attached, abutting, back to back, to the left, to the right; see also NEAR 1.

nibble *n.* morsel, peck, cautious bite; see BIT 1, BITE 1.

nibble *v.* nip, gnaw, snack; see BITE 1, EAT 1.

nice *a.* 1. [Approved] likable, superior, admirable; see EXCELLENT. 2. [Behaving in a becoming manner] pleasing, agreeable, winning, refined, cultured, amiable, delightful, charming, inviting, pleasant, cordial, courteous, considerate, kind, kindly, helpful, gracious, obliging, genial, gentle, becoming, unassuming, modest, demure; see also FRIENDLY.—*Ant.* RUDE, indecorous, crude.

nicely *a.* 1. [In a welcome manner] pleasantly, perfectly, pleasingly, amiably, winningly, creditably, acceptably, excellently, distinctively, happily, triumphantly, admirably, desirably, pleasurably, attractively, likably, enjoyably, beautifully, graciously, finely; see also AGREEABLY.—*Ant.* BADLY, unfortunately, unsuccessfully. 2. [In a becoming manner] winsomely, invitingly, charmingly; see MODESTLY, POLITELY.

niceness *n.* discernment, taste, refinement; see CARE 1, DISCRETION, KINDNESS 1.

niche *n.* cranny, corner, cubbyhole; see HOLE 1.

nick *n.* indentation, notch, slit; see CUT 1, DENT.

nick *v.* indent, notch, slit; see CUT 1, DENT.

nickel *n.* 1. *Ni*, chemical element, plating material; see ELEMENT 2, METAL, MINERAL. 2. [A coin made of nickel] five-cent piece, coin, five cents; see MONEY 1.

niece *n.* sister's daughter, brother's daughter, niece by marriage, grandniece, daughter of a brother-in-law, daughter of a sister-in law; see also NEPHEW, RELATIVE.

niggling *a.* trifling, petty, piddling; see TRIVIAL, UNIMPORTANT.

night *n.* 1. [The diurnal dark period] after dark, evening, from dusk to dawn, nightfall, after nightfall, twilight, nighttime, bedtime, midnight, before dawn, the dark hours, dead of night. 2. [The dark] blackness, duskiness, gloom; see DARKNESS 1.

night club *n.* casino, discotheque, cabaret; see BAR 2, RESTAURANT.

nightly *a.* nocturnal, in the hours of night, every twenty-four hours, during the hours of darkness, at night, each night, every night, by night; see also REGULARLY.—*Ant.* DAILY, by day, diurnal.

nightmare *n.* bad dream, horror, incubus; see DREAM.

nighttime *n.* darkness, bedtime, dark of night; see NIGHT 1.

nimble *a.* 1. [Agile] quick, spry, active; see AGILE, GRACEFUL 1. 2. [Alert] quick-witted, bright, clever; see INTELLIGENT.

nip *v.* nibble, snap, munch; see BITE 1, PINCH.

nipple *n.* mamilla, mammary gland, teat; see BREAST 2.

nitwit *n.* blockhead, dummy*, dimwit*; see FOOL.

no *a. & interj.* absolutely not, not at all, by no means, the answer is in the negative, not by any means, none, *nyet* (Russian), nix*; see also NEGATIVE 2, NEITHER, NEVER.

nobility *n.* [*Usually used with "the"*] ruling class, gentry, peerage; see ARISTOCRACY, ROYALTY.

noble *a.* 1. [Possessing an exalted mind and character] generous, princely, magnanimous, magnificent, courtly, lofty, elevated, splendid, excellent, supreme, eminent, lordly, dignified, great, good, superior, greathearted, high-minded, honorable, distinguished, liberal, tolerant, gracious, humane, benevolent, charitable, sympathetic, bounteous, brilliant, extraordinary, remarkable, devoted, heroic, resolute, valorous; see also WORTHY.—*Ant.* CORRUPT, low, ignoble. **2.** [Possessing excellent qualities or properties] meritorious, virtuous, worthy, valuable, useful, first-rate, refined, cultivated, chivalrous, trustworthy, candid, liberal, gracious, princely, magnanimous, generous, sincere, truthful, constant, faithful, upright, honest, warmhearted, true, incorruptible, distinctive, reputable, respectable, admirable, good, aboveboard, fair, just, estimable; see also EXCELLENT, PERFECT 2.—*Ant.* POOR, inferior, second-rate. **3.** [Belonging to the nobility] titled, aristocratic, patrician, highborn, wellborn, blue-blooded, of gentle birth, imperial, lordly, highbred, princely, of good breed, kingly; see also ROYAL.—*Ant.* COMMON, plebeian, lowborn. **4.** [Grand] stately, impressive, imposing; see GRAND.

nobly *a.* **1.** [Majestically] aristocratically, illustriously, royally; see GENEROUSLY 2, POLITELY. **2.** [Honorably] fairly, respectably, honestly; see JUSTLY 1.

nobody *a.* **1.** [No one at all] no person, no one, not anybody; see NONE 1. **2.** [A person of little importance] upstart, cipher, nonentity, whippersnapper, no great shakes*, nix*, zero.

nocturnal *a.* at night, night-loving, nighttime; see LATE 4, NIGHTLY.

nod *n.* dip, inclination, greeting; see GREETING.

nod *v.* **1.** [To make a nodding movement] assent, sign, signal, greet, bend, curtsy, incline the head, bow, nod yes, acquiesce, consent, respond, fall in with, concur, acknowledge, recognize; see also AGREE, APPROVE.—*Ant.* DENY, dissent, disagree. **2.** [To become sleepy or inattentive] drowse, nap, drift off; see SLEEP.

noise *n.* **1.** [A sound] sound, something heard, impact of sound waves. *Kinds of noises include the following—brief, loud noises:* bang, boom, crash, thud, blast, blast off, roar, bellow, blat, shout, peal, cry, yelp, squawk, blare, clang, ring, shot, sonic boom, jangle, eruption, explosion, detonation; *brief, faint noises:* peep, squeak, squawk, cackle, cluck, tweet, clink, tinkle, pop, whisper, stage whisper, sigh, splash, swish, sob, whine, whimper, plunk, plop, pat, ping, rustle, murmur, beat, stir, purr, still small voice; *continuing noises:* reverberation, ringing, tone, tune, clanging, tinkling, resonance, cacophony, rattle, whir, whistle, dissonance, discord, shouting, roaring, bellowing, rumble, rumbling, grunting, murmuring, drone, droning, thundering, whine, screeching, screaming, banging, clanging, hum, humming, laughing, chuckle, swishing, rustling, ripple, strumming, beating, pattering, clattering, trilling, whinneying, neighing, cawing, cackling. **2.** [Clamor] racket, fracas, din; see UPROAR.

noiseless *a.* **1.** [Containing no noise] silent, still, soundless; see QUIET. **2.** [Making no noise] voiceless, speechless, wordless; see DUMB 1, MUTE 1.

noiselessly *a.* inaudibly, quietly, without a sound; see SILENTLY.

noisy *a.* clamorous, vociferous, boisterous; see LOUD 1, 2.

nomad *n.* wanderer, migrant, vagabond; see TRAVELER.

nominal *a.* professed, pretended, in effect only; see GIVEN, NAMED 1.

nominate *v.* propose as a candidate, designate for election, put up; see CHOOSE, DECIDE.

nominated *a.* designated, called, suggested; see APPROVED, NAMED 2.

nomination *n.* naming, designation, proposal; see APPOINTMENT 1.

nonchalance *n.* apathy, disregard, insouciance; see INDIFFERENCE.

nonchalant *a.* **1.** [Cool and casual] uncaring, unconcerned, untroubled, apathetic, cold, frigid, unfeeling, impassive, imperturbable, easygoing, listless, lackadaisical, unruffled, lukewarm, composed, collected, aloof, detached, calm, serene, placid, disinterested, easy, effortless, light, smooth, neutral; see also DIFFERENT.—*Ant.* WARM, ardent, enthusiastic. **2.** [Careless] negligent, neglectful, trifling; see CARELESS.

nonchalantly *a.* coolly, indifferently, casually; see CALMLY.

nonconformist *n.* rebel, eccentric, maverick, malcontent, dissenter, demonstrator, hippie, protester, dissident, a different breed of cat; see also RADICAL.

nonconformity *n.* dissent, opposition, difference; see INDIVIDUALITY.

none *pron.* **1.** [No person] no one, not one, not anyone, no one at all, not a person, not a soul, neither one nor the other; see also NEITHER.—*Ant.* MANY, some, a few. **2.** [No thing] not a thing, not anything, not any; see NOTHING.

nonetheless *a.* nevertheless, in spite of that, anyway; see ALTHOUGH, BUT 1.

nonexistent *a.* missing, unsubstantial, fictitious; see IMAGINARY, UNREAL.

nonhero *n.* antihero, protagonist, nontraditional hero.

no-nonsense *a.* matter-of-fact, serious, purposeful, dedicated, resolute; see also PRACTICAL.

nonpartisan *a.* unprejudiced, unbiased, independent; see NEUTRAL 1.

nonpayment *n.* failure, delinquency, bankruptcy; see DEFAULT.

nonproductive *a.* unproductive, waste, not producing; see IDLE, USELESS 1.

nonprofit *a.* charitable, altruistic, humane; see GENEROUS.

nonresident *a.* absentee, out-of-state, living abroad; see FOREIGN.

nonsense *n.* **1.** [Matter that has no meaning] balderdash, rubbish, trash, scrawl, inanity, senselessness, buncombe, idle chatter, prattle, rant, bombast, claptrap, bull*, baloney*, hooey*, bunk*, poppycock*, guff*, hot air*. **2.** [Frivolous behavior] unsteadiness, flightiness, stupidity, thoughtlessness, fickleness, foolishness, giddiness, rashness, infatuation, extravagance, imprudence, madness, irrationality, senselessness, inconsistency, shallowness.—*Ant.* CONSIDERATION, steadiness, thoughtfulness. **3.** [Pure fun] absurdity, jest, joke; see FUN.

nonstop *a.* uninterrupted, unbroken, continuous; see CONSTANT.

nonviolent *a.* passive, resistant, without violence; see CALM 1, QUIET.

nook *n.* niche, cubbyhole, cranny; see HOLE 1.

noon *n.* noontime, noontide, noonday, midday, twelve noon, meridian, noon hour; see also TIME 1, 2.

no one *pron.* no man, not one, nobody; see NEITHER, NONE 1.

noose *n.* hitch, running knot, lasso; see KNOT 1, ROPE.

nor *conj.* and not, not any, not either, not one, nor yet; see also NEITHER.

normal *a.* **1.** [Usual] ordinary, run-of-the-mill, typical; see COMMON 1, CONVENTIONAL 1, 3. **2.** [Regular] routine, orderly, methodical; see REGULAR 3. **3.** [Sane] lucid, wholesome, right-minded; see RATIONAL, REASONABLE, SANE 1. **4.** [Showing no abnormal bodily condition] in good health, whole, sound; see HEALTHY.

normality *n.* **1.** [Mediocrity] ordinariness, uniformity, commonness; see REGULARITY. **2.** [Sanity] normalcy, mental balance, reason; see SANITY.

normally *a.* usually, commonly, in accordance with the norm; see FREQUENTLY, REGULARLY.

north *a.* **1.** [Situated to the north] northward, northern, in the north, on the north side of, northerly, northmost, northernmost, toward the North Pole. **2.** [Moving toward the north] northerly, northbound, northward, to the north, headed north, in a northerly direction; see also SOUTH 2. **3.** [Coming from the north] northerly, southbound, headed south, out of the north, moving toward the equator, moving toward the South Pole; see also SOUTH 3. **4.** [Associated with the north] polar, frozen, boreal; see COLD 1.

north *n.* the Barrens, tundra, northern section, northland, Northern Hemisphere, the north country, the north woods, Arctic regions, polar regions, the frozen north, land of ice and snow; see also DIRECTION 1.

northeast *a.* NE, northeastern, northeasterly, northeastward, north-northeast, northeast by east, northeast by north; see also DIRECTION 1.

northerly *a.* boreal, northern, polar; see NORTH 2.

northern *a.* northerly, arctic, polar; see NORTH 1.

northwest *a.* NW, nor'west, northwestern, northwesterly, northwestward, northwest by west, north-north-west, northwest by north; see also DIRECTION 1.

nose *n.* **1.** [The organ of smell] nasal organ, nasal cavity, nares, nasal passages, nostrils, olfactory nerves, snoot*, beak, bill; see also ORGAN 2. **2.** [A projection] snout, nozzle, muzzle; see BEAK. **—by a nose** by a very small margin, too close for comfort, barely; see ALMOST. **—look down one's nose at*** disdain, snub, be disgusted by; see ABUSE. **—on the nose*** precisely, to the point, correctly; see ACCURATE. **—turn up one's nose at** sneer at, refuse, scorn; see ABUSE. **—under one's very nose** in plain sight, visible, at one's fingertips; see OBVIOUS 1.

nostalgia *n.* remorse, wistfulness, sentimentality; see LONELINESS.

nostalgic *a.* lonesome, regretful, sentimental; see HOMESICK, LONELY.

nosy *a.* snoopy*, snooping*, unduly curious; see INQUISITIVE, INTERESTED 2.

not *a.* no, non-, un-, in-; see also NEGATIVE 2.

notable *a.* distinguished, important, striking; see FAMOUS, UNUSUAL 1.

not a little *a.* great, large, copious; see MANY, MUCH 1, 2.

not always *a.* not usually, sometimes, occasionally; see SELDOM.

not at all *a.* by no means, definitely not, in no way; see NEGATIVE 2, NO.

notch *n.* nock, nick, indent; see CUT 1, DENT, GROOVE.

notch *v.* indent, nick, chisel; see CUT 1, DENT.

notched *a.* nicked, jagged, saw-toothed; see IRREGULAR 4, ROUGH 1.

note *n.* **1.** [A representation] sign, figure, mark; see REPRESENTATION. **2.** [A brief record] notation, jotting, scribble, reminder, scrawl, annotation, agenda, entry, memorandum, journal, inscription, calendar, diary; see also NOTES, SUMMARY. **3.** [A brief communication] dispatch, epistle, announcement; see LETTER 2. **4.** [A musical tone, or its symbol] tone, key, scale, shape note, interval, degree, step, sharp, flat, natural; see also MUSIC 1.

note *v.* **1.** [To notice] remark, heed, perceive; see REGARD 1, SEE 1. **2.** [To record] write down, enter, transcribe; see RECORD 1, WRITE.

notebook *n.* memorandum book, record book, diary; see JOURNAL 1, RECORD 1.
noted *a.* well-known, celebrated, notorious; see FAMOUS.
notes *n.pl.* commentary, interpretation, explanation, findings, recordings, field notes, observations; see also DATA, RECORDS. **—compare notes** exchange views, confer, go over; see DISCUSS. **—take notes** write down, keep a record, enter; see RECORD 1.
nothing *n.* not anything, no thing, trifle, blank, emptiness, nothingness, nonexistence, inexistence, nonbeing, nullity, zero, extinction, oblivion, obliteration, annihilation, nonentity, neither hide nor hair. **—for nothing 1.** gratis, without cost, unencumbered; see FREE 4. **2.** in vain, for naught, emptily; see UNNECESSARY. **—have nothing on** have no evidence, be without proof, be only guessing; see GUESS. **—in nothing flat** in almost no time at all, speedily, rapidly; see QUICKLY. **—think nothing of** minimize, underplay, disregard; see NEGLECT 1.
nothing but *a. & prep.* only that, nothing else, without exception; see ONLY 1, 3.
nothing doing* *interj.* certainly not, by no means, the reply is in the negative; see NO.
nothingness *n.* **1.** [Void] vacuum, blank, hollowness; see EMPTINESS, NOTHING. **2.** [Worthlessness] pettiness, unimportance, smallness; see INSIGNIFICANCE.
nothing to it* *a.* facile, slight, like taking candy from a baby; see EASY 2.
notice *n.* **1.** [A warning] note, notification, intimation; see SIGN 1, WARNING. **2.** [An announcement] comments, remark, enlightenment; see ANNOUNCEMENT, DECLARATION, REPORT 1. **—serve notice** give warning, notify, announce; see DECLARE. **—take notice** become aware, pay attention, observe; see SEE 1.
notice *v.* mark, remark, look at; see SEE 1.
noticeable *a.* observable, appreciable, conspicuous; see OBVIOUS 1.
noticed *a.* seen, remarked, observed; see RECORDED.
notify *v.* declare, announce, inform; see ADVERTISE, COMMUNICATE, TELL 1.
notion *n.* **1.** [Opinion] idea, assumption, sentiment; see OPINION 1, THOUGHT 2. **2.** [Conception] whim, fancy, imagination; see AWARENESS, KNOWLEDGE 1.
not now *a.* sometime, later, at another time; see SOMEDAY.
notoriety *n.* repute, renown, name; see FAME.
notorious *a.* ill-famed, infamous, disreputable; see BAD 1.
not really *a.* not entirely, doubtful, uncertain; see QUESTIONABLE 1.
notwithstanding *a. & prep.* despite, in spite of, in any case; see ALTHOUGH, BUT 1.
not worth it *a.* not good enough, too poor, inadequate; see POOR 2, WORTHLESS.
noun *n.* substantive, common noun, proper noun; see LABEL, NAME 1.
nourish *v.* feed, supply, sustain; see PROVIDE 1, SUPPORT 3.
nourishing *a.* healthy, nutritious, full of vitamins; see HEALTHFUL.
nourishment *n.* nurture, nutriment, provender; see FOOD.
novel *a.* new, odd, strange; see UNIQUE, UNUSUAL 1, 2.
novel *n.* paperback, best-seller, fiction; see BOOK, STORY. *Types of novels include the following:* romance, detective story, love story, novella, adventure story, ghost story, mystery, western, science fiction, fantasy; historical, regional, naturalistic, Gothic, biographical, psychological, pornographic, satirical, adventure, etc., novel; thriller, porn*.
novelist *n.* fiction writer, fictionist, storyteller, narrative writer, writer of novels, writer of prose fiction, hack; see also AUTHOR, WRITER.
novelty *n.* **1.** [The quality of being novel] recentness, modernity, freshness; see ORIGINALITY. **2.** [Something popular because it is new] innovation, origination, creation; see FAD.
November *n.* autumn month, Thanksgiving season, hunting season; see MONTH.
novice *n.* beginner, learner, neophyte; see AMATEUR.
now *a.* **1.** [At the present] at this time, right now, at the moment, just now, momentarily, this day, these days, here and now. **2.** [In the immediate future] promptly, in a moment, in a minute; see SOON. **3.** [Immediately] at once, forthwith, instantly; see IMMEDIATELY.
nowadays *a.* in these days, in this age, in the present age; see NOW 1.
now and then *a.* sometimes, infrequently, occasionally; see SELDOM.
noway *a.* not at all, on no account, by no means, not a bit of it, nowhere near, in no respect.
nowhere *a.* not anywhere, not in any place, not at any place, nowhere at all, in no place, to no place.
nozzle *n.* spout, outlet, vent; see END 4.
nuance *n.* subtlety, refinement, distinction; see DIFFERENCE 1.
nub* *n.* essence, crux, core, nitty-gritty*; see also ESSENCE 1.
nuclear bomb *n.* nuclear warhead, hydrogen bomb, H-bomb, atomic bomb, A-bomb, cobalt bomb, atomic weapon, nuclear weapon; see also ARMS.
nucleus *n.* **1.** [Essence] core, gist, kernel; see ESSENCE 1, MATTER 1. **2.** [Center] hub, focus, pivot; see CENTER 1.

nude *a.* stripped, unclothed, bare; see NAKED 1.

nude *n.* naked body, naked man, naked woman, nudist, pinup, model, stripper*, peeler*.

nudge *n.* tap, poke, shove; see BUMP 1, PUSH, TOUCH 2.

nudge *v.* poke, bump, tap; see PUSH 1, TOUCH 1.

nudity *n.* bareness, nudeness, undress; see NAKEDNESS.

nugget *n.* ingot, bullion, chunk; see GOLD, ROCK 1.

nuisance *n.* **1.** [A bother] annoyance, vexation, bore; see TROUBLE 2. **2.** [An offense against the public] breach, infraction, affront; see CRIME. **3.** [An unpleasant or unwelcome person] problem child, frump, bother, holy terror*, bad egg*, insect*, louse*, pain in the neck*, poor excuse*, bum*; see also TROUBLE 1.

null *a.* invalid, vain, unsanctioned; see VOID.

numb *a.* **1.** [Insensible] deadened, dead, unfeeling, numbed, asleep, senseless, anesthetized, comatose; see also PARALYZED. **2.** [Insensitive] apathetic, lethargic, phlegmatic; see INDIFFERENT.

numb *v.* paralyze, stun, dull; see DEADEN.

number *n.* amount, sum total, totality, aggregate, whole, whole number, product, measurable quantity, estimate, the lot, plenty, abundance; see also QUANTITY. **—get** (or **have**) **one's number*** discover one's true character, find out about, know; see UNDERSTAND 1. **—one's number is up*** one's time to die has arrived, one's time has come, one's destiny is fulfilled; see DOOMED. **—without number** too numerous to be counted, innumerable, countless; see MANY.

number *v.* count, calculate, enumerate; see ADD 1, TOTAL.

numbered *a.* designated, told, enumerated, checked, specified, indicated; see also MARKED 1.

numbness *n.* deadness, anesthesia, dullness, insensitivity, insensibility, paralysis, loss of sensation.

numeral *n.* character, cipher, digit; see NUMBER.

numerical *a.* arithmetical, statistical, fractional, exponential, logarithmic, differential, integral, digital, mathematical, binary.

numerous *a.* copious, various, diverse; see INFINITE, MANY.

nun *n.* sister, religious woman, one who has taken vows, anchorite, prioress, mother superior, ecclesiastic; see also MINISTRY.

nuptials *n.pl.* wedding, matrimony, marriage ceremony; see MARRIAGE.

nurse *n.* **1.** [One who cares for the sick] attendant, male nurse, practical nurse, private nurse, registered nurse, RN, floor nurse, night nurse, day nurse, doctor's assistant, student nurse, nurse's aide, therapist, Red Cross nurse, Florence Nightingale*. **2.** [One who cares for the young] nursemaid, babysitter, tutor; see ATTENDANT.

nurse *v.* attend to, aid, medicate; see HEAL, SUSTAIN 2, TEND 1, TREAT 2.

nursery *n.* **1.** [A place for children] child's room, playroom, nursery school; see SCHOOL 1. **2.** [A place for plants] hothouse, hotbed, greenhouse; see BUILDING.

nurture *v.* nourish, care for, provide for; see FEED, SUSTAIN 2.

nut *n.* **1.** [The dry fruit] seed, kernel, stone; see FRUIT. *Common nuts include the following:* acorn, beechnut, peanut, hazelnut, black walnut, English walnut, almond, nutmeg, pecan, filbert, coconut, pistachio, cashew, pignut, chestnut, butternut, hickory, kola nut, Brazil nut, betel nut. **2.** [A threaded metal block] bur, lock nut, cap, ratchet nut; see also BOLT. **3.** [*An eccentric or insane person] eccentric, fanatic, maniac; see ZEALOT.

nutriment *n.* nourishment, provisions, sustenance; see FOOD.

nutrition *n.* diet, nourishment, victuals; see FOOD, SUBSISTENCE 1.

nutritive *a.* edible, wholesome, nutritious; see HEALTHFUL.

nuts* *a.* crazy, deranged, ridiculous; see INSANE, UNUSUAL 2.

nuzzle *v.* caress, cuddle, snuggle; see NESTLE.

nylon *n.* synthetic, polyamide product; synthetic fiber; see PLASTIC.

nymph *n.* nature goddess, sprite, mermaid; see FAIRY.

O

oak *n.* **1.** [An oak tree] willow, laurel, casuarina; see TREE. **2.** [Oak woods] hardwood, oaken wood, oak paneling; see WOOD 2.
oar *n.* pole, sweep, scull; see TOOL 1.
oasis *n.* green area, fertile area, irrigated land, watered tract, garden spot, desert garden, water hole, watering place, desert resting place; see also REFUGE 1, RETREAT 2.
oath *n.* **1.** [An attestation of the truth] affirmation, declaration, affidavit, vow, sworn statement, testimony, word, contract, pledge; see also PROMISE 1.—*Ant.* DENIAL, disavowal, lie. **2.** [The name of the Lord taken in vain] malediction, swearword, blasphemy; see CURSE 1.
obedience *n.* docility, submission, compliance; see WILLINGNESS.
obedient *a.* **1.** [Dutiful] loyal, law-abiding, governable, resigned, devoted, respectful, controllable, attentive, obliging, willing, tractable, deferential, under the control of, at one's command, at one's beck and call, on a string*, wrapped around one's little finger*; see also FAITHFUL.—*Ant.* UNRULY, disobedient, undutiful. **2.** [Docile] pliant, acquiescent, compliant; see DOCILE.
obediently *a.* dutifully, submissively, loyally; see WILLINGLY.
obese *a.* corpulent, plump, stout; see FAT.
obey *v.* submit, answer to, respond, act upon, act on, bow to, surrender, yield, perform, do, carry out, attend to orders, do what one is told, accept, consent, do what is expected of one, do one's duty, do as one says, serve, concur, assent, conform, acquiesce, mind, take orders, do one's bidding, comply, fulfill; see also AGREE.—*Ant.* REBEL, disobey, mutiny.
obfuscate *v.* obscure, muddle, confuse; see MUDDLE, CONFUSE.
object *n.* **1.** [A corporeal body] article, something, gadget; see THING 1. **2.** [A purpose] objective, aim, wish; see PURPOSE 1. **3.** [One who receives] recipient, target, victim; see RECEIVER.
object *v.* protest, take exception to, dispute; see COMPLAIN.
objection *n.* disapproval, scruple, hesitation, question, criticism, complaint, charge, accusation, reprimand, exception, admonition, reproach, dispute, opposition, adverse comment, rejection, ban, countercharge, grievance, contradiction, censure, abuse, scolding, denunciation, lecture, disagreement, difference, disdain, insistence, condemnation, grumbling, faultfinding, reproof, dissent, insinuation, complaining, frown, blame, sarcasm, wail, groan, murmur, lament, regret, aspersion, beef*, gripe*, demurring, reluctance, unwillingness, rejection, dislike, dissatisfaction, discontent, displeasure, low opinion, abhorrence, dubiousness; see also DOUBT.—*Ant.* PERMISSION, acceptance, desire.
objectionable *a.* **1.** [Revolting] gross, repugnant, abhorrent; see OFFENSIVE 2. **2.** [Undesirable] unacceptable, unsatisfactory, inexpedient; see UNDESIRABLE.
objective *a.* **1.** [Existing independently of the mind] actual, external, material, scientific, sure, extrinsic, measurable, extraneous, reified, tactile, corporeal, bodily, palpable, physical, sensible, outward, outside, determinable, unchangeable, invariable; see also REAL 2.—*Ant.* MENTAL, subjective, introspective. **2.** [Free from personal bias] detached, impersonal, unbiased; see ACCURATE 2, FAIR 1.
objective *n.* goal, aim, aspiration; see PURPOSE 1.
objectively *a.* impartially, indifferently, neutrally, open-mindedly, dispassionately, justly, equitably, detachedly, soberly, accurately, candidly, considerately, not subjectively, with objectivity, with impartiality, with consideration, with good judgment, without prejudice, without bias, without partiality, without passion.
object to *v.* disapprove, doubt, question; see OPPOSE 1.
obligate *v.* bind, restrict, constrain; see FORCE.
obligation *n.* responsibility, burden, debt; see DUTY 1.
obligatory *a.* required, essential, binding; see NECESSARY.
oblige *v.* **1.** [To accommodate] assist, aid, contribute; see ACCOMMODATE 1, HELP. **2.** [To require] compel, coerce, bind; see FORCE, REQUIRE 2.
obliged *a.* compelled, obligated, required; see BOUND 2.
obliging *a.* amiable, accommodating, helpful; see KIND.
obligingly *a.* helpfully, thoughtfully, graciously; see AGREEABLY.
oblique *a.* inclined, inclining, diverging, leaning, sloping, angled, askew, asymmetrical, turned, twisted, awry, strained, askance, distorted, off level, sideways, slanted, tipping, tipped, at an angle, on the bias; see also BENT, CROOKED 1.—*Ant.* STRAIGHT, vertical, perpendicular.

oblivion *n.* nonexistence, obscurity, void; see EMPTINESS, NOTHING.

oblivious *a.* abstracted, preoccupied, absorbed; see ABSENT-MINDED, DREAMY.

oblong *a.* elongated, rectangular, oval, elliptical, egg-shaped.—*Ant.* SQUARE, circle, circular.

obnoxious *a.* annoying, disagreeable, displeasing; see OFFENSIVE 2.

obscene *a.* wanton, lustful, lascivious; see LEWD 2.

obscenity *n.* vulgarity, impropriety, smut; see INDECENCY, LEWDNESS.

obscure *a.* **1.** [Vague] indistinct, ambiguous, indefinite, indecisive, unintelligible, impenetrable, inscrutable, unfathomable, unclear, vague, involved, undefined, intricate, illegible, incomprehensible, hazy, dark, dim, inexplicable, inconceivable, unbelievable, incredible, complicated, illogical, unreasoned, mixed up, doubtful, questionable, dubious, inexact, unreasoned, loose, ill-defined, unidentified, invisible, undisclosed, perplexing, cryptic, escaping notice, mystical, secret, enigmatic, concealed, mysterious, esoteric, puzzling, lacking clarity, unreadable, contradictory, out of focus, unrelated, clear as mud*, over one's head, deep, far out*; see also COMPLEX 2, CONFUSED 2, CONFUSING, DIFFICULT 2.—*Ant.* CLEAR, definite, distinct. **2.** [Dark] cloudy, dense, hazy; see DARK 1. **3.** [Little known] unknown, rare, hidden, covered, remote, reticent, secretive, seldom seen, unseen, inconspicuous, humble, invisible, mysterious, deep, cryptic, enigmatic, esoteric, arcane, undisclosed, dark; see also DISTANT, IRRELEVANT, PROFOUND.

obscure *v.* **1.** [To dim] shadow, cloud, screen; see SHADE 2. **2.** [To conceal] cover, veil, wrap up; see DISGUISE, HIDE 1.

obscurely *a.* dimly, darkly, thickly; see VAGUELY.

obscurity *n.* vagueness, dimness, fuzziness; see UNCERTAINTY 1, 2.

observable *a.* perceptible, noticeable, discernible; see OBVIOUS 1.

observance *n.* **1.** [A custom] ritual, practice, rite; see CUSTOM. **2.** [Attention] awareness, observation, notice; see ATTENTION.

observant *a.* keen, alert, penetrating, wide-awake, discerning, perceptive, sharp, eager, interested, discovering, detecting, discriminating, judicious, searching, understanding, questioning, deducing, surveying, considering, sensitive, clear-sighted, comprehending, bright, intelligent, on the ball*, one one's toes*; see also INTELLIGENT.—*Ant.* THOUGHTLESS, unobservant, insensitive.

observation *n.* **1.** [The power of observing] seeing, recognizing, perception; see SIGHT 1. **2.** [A remark] comment, note, commentary; see REMARK, SPEECH 3.

observe *v.* **1.** [To watch] scrutinize, inspect, examine; see SEE, WATCH. **2.** [To comment] note, remark, mention; see COMMENT. **3.** [To commemorate] dedicate, solemnize, keep; see CELEBRATE 1. **4.** [To abide by] conform to, comply, adopt; see FOLLOW 2, OBEY.

observed *a.* **1.** [Noticed] seen, noted, marked; see RECOGNIZED. **2.** [Commemorated] kept, celebrated, recalled; see REMEMBERED.

observer *n.* watcher, watchman, sentinel, lookout, sentry, guard, detective, policeman, spy, spectator, eyewitness, beholder, onlooker, bystander, passerby, meddler, peeper, voyeur, prying person, peeping Tom*; see also WITNESS.

obsess *v.* dominate, possess, hound; see HAUNT 2.

obsessed *a.* haunted, beset, controlled; see TROUBLED.

obsession *n.* fixation, fascination, passion, fancy, phantom, craze, delusion, mania, infatuation, fixed idea, compulsion, bee in one's bonnet*, hang-up*; see also FANTASY.

obsolete *a.* antiquated, archaic, out-of-date; see OLD 1, 2, OLD-FASHIONED.

obstacle *n.* restriction, obstruction, hindrance; see BARRIER.

obstinate *a.* firm, headstrong, opinionated; see STUBBORN.

obstinately *a.* doggedly, bullheadedly, persistently; see STUBBORNLY.

obstruct *v.* stop, interfere, bar; see HINDER, PREVENT.

obstruction *n.* difficulty, trouble, roadblock; see BARRIER, IMPEDIMENT 1.

obtain *v.* **1.** [To gain possession] take, acquire, seize; see GET 1. **2.** [Pertain] be pertinent to, appertain to, bear upon; see CONCERN 1.

obtainable *a.* ready, attainable, achievable; see AVAILABLE.

obvious *a.* **1.** [Clearly apparent to the eye] clear, visible, apparent, public, transparent, observable, perceptible, exposed, noticeable, plain, conspicuous, overt, glaring, prominent, standing out, light, bright, open, unmistakable, evident, recognizable, discernible, in evidence, in view, in sight, perceivable, discoverable, distinguishable, palpable, distinct, clear as a bell*, clear as day*, hitting one in the face*; see also DEFINITE 2.—*Ant.* OBSCURE, hidden, indistinct. **2.** [Clearly apparent to the mind] lucid, apparent, conclusive, explicit, understood, intelligible, comprehensible, self-evident, indisputable, unquestionable, undeniable, proverbial, aphoristic, reasonable, broad, unambiguous, on the surface, as plain as the nose on one's face*, going without saying*, staring one in the face*, open-and-shut*; see also UNDERSTANDABLE.—*Ant.* PROFOUND, ambiguous, equivocal.

obviously *interj.* of course, yes, evidently; see SURELY.

obviously *a.* without doubt, unmistakably, certainly; see CLEARLY 1, 2.

occasion *n.* **1.** [An event] occurrence, incident, happening; see EVENT. **2.** [An opportunity] chance, excuse, opening; see OPPORTUNITY 1, POSSIBILITY 2. —**on occasion** once in a while, sometimes, occasionally; see HARDLY, SELDOM.

occasional *a.* **1.** [Occurring at odd times] sporadic, random, infrequent; see IRREGULAR 1. **2.** [Intended for special use] especial, particular, specific; see EXCLUSIVE, SPECIAL.

occasionally *a.* infrequently, at random, irregularly; see HARDLY, SELDOM.

occult *a.* secret, magical, supernatural; see MYSTERIOUS 2.

occupancy *n.* possession, occupation, inhabitance; see DEED 2, OWNERSHIP.

occupant *n.* lessee, inhabitant, renter; see RESIDENT, TENANT.

occupation *n.* **1.** [The act of occupying] seizure, entering, invasion; see ATTACK, CAPTURE. **2.** [A vocation] calling, affair, chosen work; see JOB 1, PROFESSION 1, TRADE 2.

occupational *a.* professional, career, vocational, technical, workaday, official, industrial.

occupied *a.* **1.** [Busy] engaged, working, engrossed; see BUSY 1. **2.** [Full] in use, leased, taken; see RENTED.

occupy *v.* **1.** [To take possession] conquer, take over, invade; see GET 1, SEIZE 2. **2.** [To fill space] remain, tenant, reside, live in, hold, take up, pervade, keep, own, command, be in command, extend, control, maintain, involve, permeate; see also FILL 2.—*Ant.* EMPTY, remove, move. **3.** [To absorb attention] engage, engross, attend, monopolize, interest, immerse, arrest, absorb, take up, utilize, involve, keep busy, busy, be active with, be concerned with; see also FASCINATE.

occupying *a.* **1.** [Filling a place] holding, remaining, situated, posted, assigned to, tenanting, residing, living in, taking up, possessing, pervading, covering, settled on, controlling, maintaining, commanding, sitting, staying, established in, established at, owning, set up*, running*; see also PLACED.—*Ant.* GONE, leaving, removing. **2.** [Engaging attention] absorbing, engrossing, concerned with, monopolizing, engaging, arresting, working at, attracting, focusing, drawing, exacting, requiring; see also EXCITING, INTERESTING.

occur *v.* take place, transpire, befall; see HAPPEN 1, 2.

occurrence *n.* happening, incident, episode; see EVENT.

occur to *v.* come to mind, present itself, offer itself, suggest itself, spring, issue, rise, appear, catch one's attention, strike one, pass through one's mind, impress one, enter one's mind, cross one's mind, crop up.

ocean *n.* great sea, high seas, salt water, seashore, seaside, shores, the mighty deep, the main, the great waters, the Seven Seas; see also SEA.—*Ant.* EARTH, lake, river. *Oceans include the following:* Atlantic, Pacific, Arctic, Antarctic, Indian, North Atlantic, South Atlantic, North Pacific, South Pacific.

ocean floor *n.* sea bed, bottom of the sea, offshore lands; see SEA BOTTOM.

Oceania *n.* islands, South Sea Islands, Pacific Islands, Hawaii, Polynesia, Samoa, desert islands, tropics.

oceanic *a.* marine, aquatic, pelagic; see MARITIME, NAUTICAL.

October *n.* fall month, autumn month, harvest month, Indian summer, hunting season; see also AUTUMN, MONTH.

odd *a.* **1.** [Unusual] queer, unique, strange; see UNUSUAL 2. **2.** [Miscellaneous] fragmentary, odd-lot, varied; see VARIOUS. **3.** [Single] sole, unpaired, unmatched; see ALONE. **4.** [Not even] remaining, over and above, leftover; see IRREGULAR 1, 4.

oddly *a.* curiously, ridiculously, inexplicably; see FOOLISHLY, STRANGELY.

odds *n.pl.* **1.** [An advantage] allowance, edge, benefit, difference, superiority, place money*, show money*; see also ADVANTAGE. **2.** [A probability] favor, superiority, chances; see CHANCE 1.

odds and ends *n.pl.* miscellany, scraps, particles; see REMNANTS.

odor *n.* perfume, fragrance, bouquet; see SMELL 1, 2.

odorless *a.* flat, scentless, unaromatic, unperfumed, unsmelling, unscented, without odor, odor-free, unfragrant, lacking fragrance.

odorous *a.* **1.** [Having an offensive odor] smelly, stinking, putrid; see OFFENSIVE 2, ROTTEN 1. **2.** [Having a pleasant odor] spicy, sweet-smelling, fragrant; see SWEET 3.

of *prep.* from, out of, out from, away from, proceeding from, coming from, going from, about, concerning, as concerns, appropriate to, pertaining to, peculiar to, attributed to, characterized by, regarding, as regards, in regard to, referring to, in reference to, like, belonging to, related to, having relation to, native to, consequent to, based on, akin to, connected with; see also ABOUT 2.

off *a. & prep.* **1.** [Situated at a distance] ahead, behind, up front, to one side, divergent, beside, aside, below, beneath, above, far, absent, not here, removed, apart, in the distance, at a distance, gone, away; see also DISTANT.—*Ant.* HERE, at hand, present. **2.** [Moving away] into the distance, away from, farther away, disappearing, vanishing, removing, turning aside; see also AWAY.—*Ant.* APPROACHING, returning, coming. **3.** [Started] initiated, commenced, originated; see BEGUN. **4.** [Mistaken] erring, in error, confused; see MISTAKEN 1, WRONG 2. **5.** [*Crazy] odd, peculiar, queer; see INSANE. **6.** [*Not employed] not on duty, on vacation, gone; see UNEMPLOYED.

off and on *a.* now and then, sometimes, occasionally; see SELDOM.

off balance *a.* unbalanced, tipsy, eccentric; see IRREGULAR 1, UNSTEADY.

off base* *a.* incorrect, faulty, erroneous; see MISTAKEN 1, WRONG 2.

off center *a.* off-centered, not centered, eccentric; see IRREGULAR 1, UNSTABLE.

off-color *a.* racy, spicy, indelicate; see RISQUÉ.

off course *a.* strayed, drifting, misguided; see LOST 1.

offend *v.* annoy, affront, outrage; see BOTHER 2.

offended *a.* vexed, provoked, exasperated; see ANGRY, INSULTED.

offense *n.* **1.** [A misdeed] misdemeanor, malfeasance, transgression; see CRIME, SIN. **2.** [An attack] assault, aggression, battery; see ATTACK. *Styles of offense in football include the following:* running attack, ground attack, passing attack, aerial attack, shotgun offense, T-formation, wishbone, power plays, flying wedge, razzle-dazzle. **3.** [Resentment] umbrage, pique, indignation; see ANGER.

offensive *a.* **1.** [Concerned with an attack] assaulting, attacking, invading; see AGGRESSIVE. **2.** [Revolting] disgusting, horrid, repulsive, shocking, gross, dreadful, detestable, repugnant, obnoxious, hideous, horrible, displeasing, disagreeable, repellent, nauseating, invidious, nauseous, revolting, distasteful, unspeakable, accursed, unutterable, terrible, grisly, ghastly, bloody, gory, hateful, low, foul, corrupt, bad, indecent, nasty, dirty, unclean, filthy, sickening, malignant, rancid, putrid, vile, impure, beastly, monstrous, coarse, loathsome, abominable, stinking, reeking, obscene, smutty, damnable, distressing, irritating, unpleasant, contaminated, frightful, unattractive, forbidding, repelling, incompatible, unsavory, intolerable, unpalatable, disatisfactory, unpleasing, unsuited, objectionable, to one's disgust, beneath contempt, icky*, lousy*; see also REVOLTING.—*Ant.* PLEASANT, agreeable, likable. **3.** [Insolent] impertinent, impudent, insulting; see RUDE 2.

offensive *n.* position of attack, invasion, assault; see ATTACK.

offer *n.* proposal, presentation, proposition; see SUGGESTION 1.

offer *v.* **1.** [To present] proffer, tender, administer, donate, put forth, advance, extend, submit, hold out, grant, allow, award, volunteer, accord, place at one's disposal, lay at one's feet, put up; see also CONTRIBUTE, GIVE 1.—*Ant.* REFUSE, withhold, keep. **2.** [To propose] suggest, submit, advise; see PROPOSE 1.

offering *n.* contribution, donation, present; see GIFT 1.

offhand *a.* at the moment, unprepared, impromptu, informal, extemporaneous, extemporary, unpremeditated, spontaneous, unstudied, unrehearsed, improvised, by ear.

office *n.* **1.** [A position involving responsibility] employment, business, occupation; see JOB 1, PROFESSION 1, TRADE 2. **2.** [A function] performance, province, service; see DUTY 1. **3.** [A place in which office work is done] room, office building, factory, bureau, agency, warehouse, facility, school building; see also BUILDING, DEPARTMENT. *Types of offices include the following:* governmental, school principal's, counseling, secretarial, insurance, data processing, real estate, brokerage, law, bank, foreign, consular, doctor's, dentist's, advertising agency, booking office, box office.

officer *n.* **1.** [An executive] manager, director, president; see EXECUTIVE, LEADER 2. **2.** [One who enforces civil law] magistrate, military police, deputy; see POLICEMAN. **3.** [One holding a responsible post in the armed forces] *American officers include the following — Army commissioned and special officers:* Commander in Chief, Five-star General, Four-star General, Three-star General, Two-star General, General of the Army, Lieutenant General, Major General, Brigadier General, Colonel, Lieutenant Colonel, Major, Captain, First Lieutenant, Second Lieutenant, Chief of Staff; *Navy commissioned officers:* Admiral of the Fleet, Fleet Admiral, Admiral, Rear Admiral, Vice Admiral, Captain, Commander, Lieutenant Commander, Lieutenant; Lieutenant, junior grade; Ensign; *Army noncommissioned officers:* Chief Warrant Officer, Warrant Officer, junior grade; Master Sergeant, First Sergeant, Technical Sergeant, Staff Sergeant, Sergeant, Corporal.

official *a.* **1.** [Having to do with one's office] formal, fitting, suitable, precise, established, according to precedent, according to protocol, proper, correct, accepted, recognized, customary; see also CONVENTIONAL 1, 3, FIT 1.—*Ant.* INFORMAL, ill-fitting, unceremonious. **2.** [Authorized] ordered, endorsed, sanctioned; see APPROVED. **3.** [Reliable] authoritative, authentic, trustworthy; see CERTAIN 3, GENUINE 1, RELIABLE.

official *n.* **1.** [Administrator] comptroller, director, executive; see EXECUTIVE, LEADER 2. **2.** [A sports official] referree, umpire, linesman; see UMPIRE.

officially *a.* **1.** [In an official manner] regularly, formally, orderly, suitably, according to form, ceremoniously, in set form, precisely, according to precedent, conventionally, in an established manner, as prescribed, according to protocol, all in order, correctly, properly, customarily. **2.** [With official approval] authoritatively, authorized, sanctioned; see APPROVED.

offset *v.* counterbalance, compensate, allow for; see BALANCE 2.

offspring *n.* progeny, issue, descendants, children, kids, siblings, lineage, generation, brood, seed, family, heirs, offshoots, heredity, succession, successors, next generation; see also BABY, CHILD.

off the record *a.* not for publication, restricted, confidential; see SECRET 1, 3.

off work *a.* not working, gone home, not employed; see UNEMPLOYED.

often *a.* usually, many times, oftentimes; see FREQUENTLY.

oh *interj.* indeed!, oh-oh!, oh, no!, oh, yes!, oops; see also NO, YES.

oil *n.* **1.** [Liquid, greasy substance] melted fat, unction, lubricant; see GREASE. *Common oils include the following:* vegetable, animal, mineral, saturated, polyunsaturated, fatty, volatile, essential, machine, crude, lubricating, cottonseed, olive, castor, palm, corn, safflower, coconut, whale, cocoa, linseed, drying, nondrying, soybean, sesame, cod-liver, fish; lard, tallow, oleo, Vaseline (trademark), turpentine. **2.** [Liquid substance used for power or illumination] petroleum, kerosene, coal oil, crude oil, liquid coal, fossil oil; see also FUEL.

oil *v.* lubricate, smear, coat with oil; see GREASE.

oily *a.* **1.** [Rich with oil] fatty, greasy, buttery, oil-soaked, rich, lardy, bland, oleaginous, soapy, soothing, creamy, oil-bearing.—*Ant.* DRY, dried, gritty. **2.** [Having a surface suggestive of oil] oiled, waxy, sleek, slippery, smooth, polished, lustrous, bright, brilliant, gleaming, glistening, shining; see also SMOOTH 1, 2.—*Ant.* ROUGH, dull, unpolished. **3.** [Unctuous] fulsome, suave, flattering; see AFFECTED 2, TREACHEROUS.

ointment *n.* unguent, lotion, cream; see MEDICINE 2.

OK *interj.* all right, correct, surely; see YES.

OK *n.* approval, endorsement, affirmation; see PERMISSION.

OK *v.* confirm, condone, notarize; see APPROVE, ENDORSE 2.

old *a.* **1.** [No longer vigorous] aged, elderly, patriarchal, gray, venerable, not young, of long life, past one's prime, far advanced in years, matured, having lived long, full of years, seasoned, infirm, inactive, enfeebled, decrepit, superannuated, exhausted, tired, impaired, broken down, wasted, doddering, senile, ancient, having one foot in the grave, gone to seed.—*Ant.* YOUNG, fresh, youthful. **2.** [Worn] time-worn, worn-out, thin, patched, ragged, faded, used, in holes, rubbed off, mended, broken-down, fallen to pieces, fallen in, given way, out of use, rusted, crumbled, dilapidated, battered, shattered, shabby, castoff, decayed, decaying, stale, useless, tattered, in rages, torn, moth-eaten.—*Ant.* FRESH, new, unused. **3.** [Ancient] archaic, time-honored, prehistoric, bygone, early, antique, forgotten, immemorial, antediluvian, olden, remote, past, distant, former, of old, gone by, classic, medieval, in the Middle Ages, out of the dim past, primordial, primeval, before history, dateless, unrecorded, handed down, of earliest time, of the old order, ancestral, traditional, time out of mind, in the dawn of history, old as the hills; see also senses 1, 2.—*Ant.* MODERN, recent, late.

old age *n.* seniority, dotage, infirmity; see AGE 2.

older *a.* elder, senior, sooner, former, preceding, prior, more aged, less young, not so new, earlier, first, first-born, having come before, more ancient, lower, of an earlier time, of an earlier vintage, of a former period; see also OLD 3.—*Ant.* YOUNG, newer, of a later vintage.

oldest *a.* most aged, initial, primeval; see FIRST, ORIGINAL 1.

old-fashioned *a.* antiquated, out-of-date, obsolete, obsolescent, outmoded, *démodé* (French), unfashionable, traditional, unstylish, passé, before the War, Victorian, not modern, old-time, time-honored, not current, antique, ancient, no longer prevailing, bygone, archaic, grown old, primitive, quaint, amusing, odd, neglected, outworn, of long standing, unused, past, behind the times, gone by, of the old school, extinct, out, gone out, out of it*; see also OLD 3.—*Ant.* MODERN, fashionable, stylish.

old lady* *n.* female spouse, woman, female member of the family; see MOTHER 1, PARENT, WIFE.

old man* *n.* head of the house, male spouse, man; see FATHER 1, HUSBAND, PARENT.

Old Testament *n.* the Covenant, Hebrew Scripture, Jewish Law; see BIBLE.

old-time *a.* outmoded, ancient, obsolete; see OLD-FASHIONED.

Old World *n.* Europe, Asia, mother country; see EAST 2, EUROPE.

Olympics *n.* Olympic Games, world championships, international amateur athletic competion; see COMPETITION, SPORT 3.

omen *n.* portent, augury, indication; see SIGN 1.

ominous *a.* threatening, forbidding, foreboding, menacing, dark, suggestive, fateful, premonitory, dire, grim, gloomy, haunting, perilous, ill-starred, ill-fated, impending, fearful, prophetic; see also DANGEROUS, DISMAL, DOOMED.—*Ant.* FAVORABLE, encouraging, auspicious.

omission *n.* **1.** [The act of omitting] overlooking, missing, leaving out; see CARELESSNESS, EXCLUSION, NEGLECT 1.—*Ant.* ADDITION, mention, insertion. **2.** [Something omitted] need, want, imperfection; see LACK 2.

omit *v.* **1.** [To fail to include] leave out, reject, exclude; see BAR 2, DISMISS, ELIMINATE. **2.** [To neglect] ignore, slight, overlook; see DISREGARD, NEGLECT 2.

omitted *a.* left out, overlooked, unmentioned; see MISSED 1, NEGLECTED.

on *a. & prep.* **1.** [Upon] above, in contact with, touching, supported by, situated upon, resting upon, on top of, about, held by, moving across, moving over, covering; see also UPON 1.—*Ant.* UNDER, underneath, below. **2.** [Against] in contact with, close to, leaning on; see NEXT 2. **3.** [Toward] proceeding, at, moving; see APPROACHING, TOWARD. **4.** [Forward] onward, ahead, advancing; see FORWARD 1. **5.** [Near] beside, close to, adjacent to; see BORDERING, NEAR 1. **—and so on** and so forth, also, in addition; see AND.

on account *a.* on credit, payable, credited; see BOUGHT, CHARGED 1, DUE.

on account of *a.* since, for the sake of, for the reason that; see BECAUSE.

on and off *a.* now and then, sometimes, infrequently; see SELDOM.

on board *a.* loaded, shipped, in transit; see ABOARD.

on call *a.* alerted, ready, handy; see AVAILABLE.

once *a.* **1.** [One time] this time, but once, once only, before, one time before, already, one, just this once, not more than once, never again, a single time, one time previously, on one occasion, only one time.—*Ant.* FREQUENTLY, twice, many times. **2.** [Formerly] long ago, previously, earlier; see FORMERLY. **—all at once** simultaneously, all at the same time, unanimously; see TOGETHER 2. **—at once** now, quickly, this moment; see IMMEDIATELY. **—for once** for at least one time, once only, uniquely; see ONCE 1.

once and for all* *a.* with finality, permanently, unalterably; see FINALLY 1.

once in a while *a.* sometimes, occasionally, on occasion; see SELDOM.

once or twice *a.* a few times, infrequently, not much; see SELDOM.

once-over* *n.* look, inspection, checkup; see EXAMINATION 1.

oncoming *a.* impending, expected, imminent; see APPROACHING.

one *a.* individual, peculiar, special, specific, separate, single, singular, odd, one and only, precise, definite, sole, uncommon; see also SPECIAL, UNIQUE, UNUSUAL 2.—*Ant.* COMMON, several, imprecise.

one *n.* unit, 1, whole, person, thing, identity, ace, integer, item, example, digit, singleness, individual, individuality, individuation.—*Ant.* MANY, plural, several. **—all one** making no difference, insignificant, of no importance; see UNIMPORTANT. **—at one** in accord, agreeing, of the same opinion; see UNITED. **—tie one on*** go on a drinking spree, get drunk, imbibe; see DRINK 2.

one another *pron.* each other, reciprocally, each to the other; see EACH.

oneness *n.* integrity, harmony, indivisibility; see UNITY 1.

one-sided *a.* **1.** [Unilateral] single, uneven, partial; see IRREGULAR 4. **2.** [Prejudiced] biased, partial, narrow-minded; see PREJUDICED, UNFAIR.

one-time *a.* prior, former, previous; see PAST 1.

one-way *a.* directional, with no return, restricted; see NARROW 1.

on file *a.* preserved, at hand, filed; see RECORDED.

on fire *a.* aflame, blazing, afire; see BURNING.

ongoing *a.* open-ended, continuous, in process; see REGULAR 3.

on hand *a.* in stock, stocked, present; see AVAILABLE.

only *a.* **1.** [Solely] exclusively, uniquely, wholly, entirely, particularly, and no other, and no more, and nothing else, nothing but, totally, utterly, first and last, one and only; see also SINGLY. **2.** [Merely] just, simply, plainly, barely, solely; see also HARDLY. **3.** [Sole] single, companionless, without another, by oneself, isolated, apart, unaccompained, exclusive, unique; see also ALONE.

on occasion *a.* occasionally, at certain times, sometimes; see SELDOM.

on one hand *a.* on one side of the question, from one viewpoint, from one direction.

on one's hands *a.* in one's care, charged with, responsible for; see RESPONSIBLE 1.

on or about *prep.* at about, approximately, in the vicinity of; see AT.

on or before *prep.* at about the time of, prior to, in anticipation of; see BEFORE.

on purpose *a.* knowingly, meaningfully, consciously; see DELIBERATELY.

on sale *a.* marked down, reduced, cut, at a bargain, at a cut rate, in the bargain basement, among the remnants; see also REDUCED 2.

on second thought *a.* on mature consideration, as afterthought, in reality; see INCIDENTALLY.

onset *n.* incipience, opening, start; see ORIGIN 2.

on the air *a.* broadcasting, going on, televising, in progress, speaking, performing, telecasting, being telecast, live.
on the ball* *a.* competent, qualified, alert; see ABLE.
on the contrary *a.* conversely, antithetically, inversely, contrasting, on the other hand, at the opposite pole, on the other side; see also NOT.
on time *a.* prompt, on schedule, dependable; see PUNCTUAL.
onto *a. & prep.* **1.** [To] toward, in contact with, adjacent; see AGAINST 1. **2.** [Upon] over, out upon, above; see UPON 1.
on trial *a.* **1.** [In court] in litigation, up for investigation, at the bar, before the bar, before a judge, before a jury, being tried, contested, appealed, indicted; see also ACCUSED. **2.** [Experimental] on a trial basis, for a trial period, on approval; see UNCERTAIN.
onward *a.* on ahead, beyond, in front of; see FORWARD 1, MOVING 1.
ooze *n.* slime, fluid, mire; see MUD.
ooze *v.* seep, exude, leak; see FLOW.
opaque *a.* not transparent, dim, dusky, darkened, murky, gloomy, smoky, thick, misty, cloudy, clouded, shady, muddy, dull, blurred, frosty, filmy, foggy, sooty, dirty, dusty, coated over, covered.—*Ant.* CLEAR, transparent, translucent.
open *a.* **1.** [Not closed] unclosed, accessible, clear, open to view, uncovered, disclosed, divulged, introduced, initiated, begun, full-blown, unfurled, susceptible, ajar, gaping, wide, rent, torn, spacious, unshut, expansive, extensive, spread out, revealed; see also senses 2, 4.—*Ant.* CLOSED, tight, shut. **2.** [Not obstructed] unlocked, unbarred, unbolted, unblocked, unfastened, cleared away, removed, made passable, unsealed, unobstructed, unoccupied, vacated, unburdened, emptied; see also sense 1.—*Ant.* TAKEN, barred, blocked. **3.** [Not forbidden] free of entrance, unrestricted, permitted, allowable, free of access, public, welcoming, not posted; see also PERMITTED.—*Ant.* REFUSED, restricted, forbidden. **4.** [Not protected] unguarded, unsecluded, liable, exposed, uncovered, apart, unshut, unroofed, insecure, unsafe, conspicuous, unhidden, unconcealed, subject, sensitive; see also sense 1 and UNSAFE.—*Ant.* SAFE, secluded, secure. **5.** [Not decided] in question, up for discussion, debatable; see QUESTIONABLE 1, UNCERTAIN. **6.** [Frank] plain, candid, straightforward; see FRANK.
open *v.* **1.** [To begin] start, inaugurate, initiate; see BEGIN 1, 2. **2.** [To move aside a prepared obstruction] unbar, unlock, unclose, clear, admit, reopen, open the lock, lift the latch, free, loosen, disengage, unfasten, undo, unbolt, turn the key, turn the knob.—*Ant.* CLOSE, shut, lock. **3.** [To make an opening] force an entrance, breach, cut in, tear down, push in, shatter, destroy, burst in, break open, cave in, burst out from, penetrate, pierce, force one's way into, smash, punch a hole into, slit, puncture, crack, muscle in*, jimmy*; see also FORCE, REMOVE 1.—*Ant.* REPAIR, seal, mend. **4.** [To make available] make accessible, put on sale, put on view, open to the public, make public, put forward, free, make usable, prepare, present, make ready.—*Ant.* REMOVE, put away, lock up. **5.** [To expose to fuller view] unroll, unfold, uncover; see EXPOSE 1, REVEAL.
open-door *a.* unrestricted, unlimited, hospitable; see FREE 1, 2, 3.
opened *a.* unlocked, made open, not closed; see FREE 3, OPEN 2.
open-ended *a.* going on, without specified limits, optional; see CONSTANT, UNCERTAIN.
opening *a.* initial, beginning, primary; see FIRST.
opening *n.* **1.** [A hole] break, crack, tear; see HOLE 1. **2.** [An opportunity] chance, availability, occasion; see OPPORTUNITY 1, POSSIBILITY 2.
openly *a.* **1.** [Frankly] naturally, simply, artlessly, naively, unsophisticatedly, out in the open, candidly, aboveboard, straightforwardly, honestly, unreservedly, fully, readily, willingly, without restraint, plainly, without reserve, to one's face, in public, face to face; see also SINCERELY.—*Ant.* SECRETLY, furtively, surreptitiously. **2.** [Shamelessly] immodestly, brazenly, not caring, regardlessly, insensibly, unconcernedly, crassly, insolently, flagrantly, wantonly, unblushingly, notoriously, without pretense, in defiance of the law; see also CARELESSLY, LEWDLY.—*Ant.* CAREFULLY, prudently, discreetly.
open-minded *a.* tolerant, fair-minded, just; see FAIR 1, LIBERAL.
open-mouthed *a.* astonished, amazed, aghast; see SURPRISED.
open out *v.* fan out, diverge, enlarge; see GROW 1, SPREAD 2.
open up *v.* enlarge, grow, start; see BEGIN 1, 2, SPREAD 2.
opera *n.* musical drama, libretto, score, operetta, grand opera, light opera, comic opera, rock opera, opera performance; see also PERFORMANCE.
operate *v.* **1.** [To keep in operation] manipulate, conduct, administer; see MANAGE 1. **2.** [To be in operation] function, work, serve, carry on, run, revolve, act, behave, fulfill, turn, roll, spin, pump, lift, spark, burn, move, progress, advance, proceed, go, contact, hit, engage, transport, convey, contain, click*, tick*.—*Ant.* STOP, stall, break down. **3.** [To produce an effect] react, act on, influence, bring about, deter-

[illegible]urn, bend, contrive, work, accom[illegible], fulfill, finish, complete, benefit, [illegible]pel, promote, concern, enforce, take effect, have effect, work on, succeed, get results, get across; see also ACHIEVE, PRODUCE 1. **4.** [To perform a surgical operation] remove diseased tissue, amputate, transplant; see TREAT 2.

operated *a.* conducted, handled, run, carried on, regulated, ordered, maintained, supervised, superintended, governed, administered, transacted, performed, conveyed, transported, moved, determined, achieved, contrived, accomplished, fulfilled, promoted, enforced, worked, served, guided, executed, sustained, used, practiced, put into effect, finished, driven, brought about, bent, manipulated, negotiated; see also DIRECTED, MANAGED 2.

operating *a.* managing, conducting, directing, executing, manipulating, administering, ordering, regulating, supervising, running, wielding, transacting, guiding, putting into effect, sustaining, maintaining, performing, practicing, revolving, promoting, determining, moving, turning, spinning, driving, contriving, fulfilling, accomplishing, finishing, effecting, bringing about, serving, enforcing, in operation, at work; see also USING.

operation *n.* **1.** [The act of causing to function] execution, guidance, superintendence, carrying out, ordering, order, maintenance, handling, manipulating, manipulation, supervision, control, conduct, agency, enforcement, advancement, regulating, running, supervising, directing, transacting, conducting; see also MANAGEMENT 1, REGULATION 1. **2.** [An action] performance, act, employment, labor, service, carrying on, transaction, deed, doing, proceeding, handiwork, workmanship, enterprise, movement, progress, development, engagement, undertaking; see also ACTION 1, WORK 2. **3.** [A method] process, formula, procedure; see METHOD, PLAN 2. **4.** [Surgical treatment] surgery, transplant, amputation, dismemberment, vivisection, dissection, biopsy, emergency operation, acupuncture, exploratory operation, section, excision, removal, tonsillectomy, appendectomy, open-heart surgery, abortion, autopsy, the knife*; see also MEDICINE 3.

operator *n.* **1.** [One who operates a machine] engineer, operative, skilled employee; see LABORER, WORKMAN. *Kinds of operators include the following:* telephone, computer, switchboard, PBX, long-distance, information, emergency. **2.** [One who operates workable property] executive, supervisor, director; see EXECUTIVE. **3.** [*Manipulator] speculator, scoundrel, fraud; see RASCAL.

opinion *n.* **1.** [A belief] notion, view, sentiment, conception, idea, surmise, impression, inference, conjecture, inclination, fancy, imagining, supposition, suspicion, notion, assumption, guess, theory, thesis, theorem, postulate, hypothesis, point of view, presumption, presupposition, persuasion, mind; see also BELIEF. **2.** [A considered judgment] estimation, estimate, view, summary, belief, idea, resolution, determination, recommendation, finding, conviction, conclusion; see also JUDGMENT 3, VERDICT.

opinionated *a.* bigoted, stubborn, unyielding; see OBSTINATE, PREJUDICED.

opium *n.* opiate, soporific, dope*; see DRUG.

opponent *n.* **1.** [A rival] competitor, contender, challenger, candidate, equal, entrant, the opposition, aspirant, bidder.—*Ant.* SUPPORTER, defender, abettor. **2.** [An opposing contestant] antagonist, contestant, litigant; see PLAYER 1. **3.** [An enemy] foe, adversary, assailant; see ENEMY.

opportunity *n.* **1.** [Favorable circumstances] chance, occasion, suitable circumstance, excuse, happening, event, probability, good fortune, luck, break; see also POSSIBILITY 2. **2.** [A suitable time] occasion, moment, time and tide; see TIME 2.

oppose *v.* **1.** [To hold a contrary opinion] object, disapprove, debate, dispute, disagree, contradict, argue, deny, run counter to, protest, defy, cross, speak against, confront, thwart, neutralize, reverse, turn the tables, be opposed to, oppose change, not have any part of, face down, interfere with, disapprove of, cry out against, disagree with, not conform, run against, run counter to, come in conflict with, go contrary to, frown at, not be good for, not accept, call into question, conflict with, grapple with, doubt, be against, be unwilling, reject, dislike, take exception, repudiate, question, probe, resist, confound, confute, refute, buck*, turn thumbs down*; see also sense 2 and DARE 2, FACE 1.—*Ant.* AGREE, approve, accept. **2.** [To fight] resist, battle, encounter, assault, attack, assail, storm, protest, clash, meet, skirmish, engage, contest, face, restrain, go against, turn against, uphold, defend, rebel, revolt, mutiny, strike back, combat, run counter to, defy, snub, grapple with, fight off, withstand, repel, guard, counterattack, struggle, outflank, antagonize, retaliate, impede, overpower, take on all comers*, lock horns with; see also FIGHT.

opposed *a.* antagonistic to, averse, adverse, opposite, contrary, hostile to, at odds, disputed, counter to, at cross purposes, up against, against the grain; see also OPPOSITE 2.

opposing *a.* **1.** [In the act of opposition] conflicting, clashing, unfriendly; see OPPOSED. **2.** [Situated opposite] contrary, facing, fronting; see OPPOSITE 3.

opposite *a.* **1.** [Contrary] antithetical, diametric, reversed; see UNLIKE. **2.** [In conflict] adverse, inimical, antagonistic, rival, unfavorable, averse, argumentative, contradictory, hostile; see also AGAINST 1. **3.** [So situated as to seem to oppose] facing, fronting, in front of, on different sides of, on opposite sides, in opposition to, contrasting, on the other side of, contrary, over against, front to front, back to back, nose to nose, on the farther side, opposing, diametrical, eyeball to eyeball*.—*Ant.* MATCHED, on the same side, side by side.

opposite *n.* contradiction, contrary, converse, direct opposite, opposition, vice versa, antithesis, antonym, counter term, counterpart, inverse, reverse, adverse, the opposite pole, the other extreme, the other side, the opposite idea.—*Ant.* EQUAL, like, similar thing.

opposition *n.* **1.** [The act of opposing] hostilities, conflict, combat; see BATTLE, FIGHT 1. **2.** [The attitude suggestive of opposition] dislike, disagreement, hostility, antagonism, defiance, antipathy, abhorrence, aversion, constraint, restriction, restraint, hindrance, discord, distaste, disfavor, dissatisfaction, discontent, displeasure, irritation, offense, chagrin, humiliation, anger, loathing, disapproval, complaint, repugnance; see also HATRED, RESENTMENT.—*Ant.* SUPPORT, enthusiasm, accord. **3.** [The individual or group that opposes] antagonist, disputant, adversary; see ENEMY, OPPONENT 1.

oppress *v.* suppress, harass, maltreat; see ABUSE, BOTHER 2.

oppressed *a.* misused, downtrodden, enslaved; see HURT.

oppression *n.* tyranny, hardness, domination, coercion, dictatorship, fascism, persecution, severity, harshness, abuse, conquering, overthrowing, compulsion, force, torment, martial law; see also CRUELTY.—*Ant.* FREEDOM, liberalism, voluntary control.

opt (for) *v.* choose, decide, pick; see CHOOSE, DECIDE.

optical *a.* ocular, seeing, visible; see VISUAL.

optimism *n.* **1.** [Belief in the essential goodness of the universe] mysticism, philosophy of goodness, belief in progress; see FAITH 1. **2.** [An inclination to expect or to hope for the best] cheerfulness, hopefulness, confidence, assurance, encouragement, happiness, brightness, enthusiasm, good cheer, trust, calmness, elation, expectancy, expectation, anticipation, certainty.—*Ant.* GLOOM, despair, melancholy.

optimist *n.* Pollyanna, dreamer, positivist.

optimistic *a.* cheerful, sanguine, assured; see CONFIDENT, HOPEFUL 1, TRUSTING.

option *n.* **1.** [A choice] selection, alternative, dilemma; see CHOICE. **2.** [A privilege to purchase] right, prerogative, grant, claim, license, lease, franchise, advantage, security, immunity, benefit, title, prior claim, dibs*.

optional *a.* discretionary, elective, noncompulsory, free, unrestricted, arbitrary, not required, with no strings attached*, take it or leave it*; see also VOLUNTARY.—*Ant.* NECESSARY, compulsory, enforced.

or *conj.* **1.** [A suggestion of choice] or only, or but, as an alternative, on the other hand, in turn, conversely, in other words, or else, in preference to; see also EITHER.—*Ant.* NOR, neither, without choice. **2.** [A suggestion of correction] or not, or not exactly, in reverse, reversing it, on the contrary, contrary to, oppositely, or rather, instead of, correctly speaking; see also INSTEAD. **3.** [A suggestion of approximation] roughly, about, practically; see APPROXIMATELY.

oral *a.* vocal, verbal, uttered, voiced, unwritten, phonetic, sounded, not written, by word of mouth; see also SPOKEN.—*Ant.* WRITTEN, PRINTED, unspoken.

orange *a.* reddish, ocherous, glowing; see ORANGE, *n.* 2.

orange *n.* **1.** [Color] red-yellow, apricot, tangerine, burnt orange, peach, coral, salmon; see also COLOR. **2.** [Fruit] citrus fruit, tropical fruit, sour orange; see FOOD, FRUIT.

orbit *n.* **1.** [Path described by one body revolving around another] ellipse, circle, ring, circuit, apogee, course, perigee, lap, round, cycle, curve, flight path; see also REVOLUTION 1. **2.** [Range of activity or influence] range, field, boundary; see AREA.

orbit *v.* **1.** [To revolve around another body] encircle, encompass, ring, move in a circuit, go around, revolve; see also CIRCLE. **2.** [To put into orbit] fire, lift off, project; see LAUNCH 2.

orbited *a.* sent into orbit, put up, rocketed; see DRIVEN, SENT.

orchard *n.* fruit trees, fruit farm, apple orchard; see FARM.

orchestra *n.* musical ensemble, symphony, trio, quartet, quintet; see also BAND.

ordain *v.* **1.** [To establish] install, institute, appoint; see ENACT. **2.** [To destine] determine, foreordain, intend; see INTEND 2. **3.** [To invest with priestly functions] install, confer holy orders upon, consecrate, frock, delegate, invest; see also BLESS.

ordained *a.* **1.** [Ordered] commanded, determined, established by law; see ESTABLISHED 2, ORDERED 2. **2.** [Invested into the ministry] consecrated, anointed, received into the ministry; see NAMED 2.

ordeal *n.* tribulation, distress, calamity; see DIFFICULTY 1, 2.

[illegible] [illegible]ommand] direction, [illegible]le, edict, charge, require- [illegible]e, act, warrant, mandate, [illegible]e also COMMAND, LAW 3. **2.** [illegible] progression, succession, procession; [illegible] LINE 1, SEQUENCE 1, SERIES. **3.** [[illegible]y arrangement] regulation, plan, disposition, management, establishment, method, distribution, placement, scale, rule, computation, adjustment, adaptation, ordering, ranging, standardizing, lining up, trimming, grouping, composition, cast, assortment, disposal, scheme, form, routine, array, procedure, method, index, regularity, uniformity, symmetry, harmony, placement, layout, lineup, setup; see also CLASSIFICATION, SYSTEM.—*Ant.* CONFUSION, disarray, displacement. **4.** [Organization] society, sect, company; see ORGANIZATION 2. **5.** [A formal agreement to purchase] engagement, reserve, application, requisition, request, stipulation, booking, arrangement; see also BUYING, RESERVATION 1. **6.** [Kind] hierarchy, rank, degree; see CLASS 1, CLASSIFICATION. **7.** [Customary method] ritual, rite, plan; see CUSTOM. **—in order** working, efficient, operative; see EFFECTIVE. **—in order to** for the purpose of, as a means to, so that; see FOR. **—in short order** rapidly, without delay, soon; see QUICKLY. **—on order** requested, on the way, sent for; see ORDERED 1.

order *v.* **1.** [To give a command] direct, command, instruct, bid, tell, demand, impose, give directions, dictate, decree; see also REQUIRE 2. **2.** [To authorize a purchase] secure, reserve, request; see BUY, OBTAIN 1. **3.** [To put in order] arrange, plan, furnish, regulate, establish, manage, systematize, space, file, put away, classify, distribute, alphabetize, regularize, pattern, formalize, settle, fix, locate, dress up, sort out, index, put to rights, set guidelines for, adjust, adapt, set in order, assign, place, align, standardize, plan, group; see also ORGANIZE 1.—*Ant.* CONFUSE, disarrange, disarray.

ordered *a.* **1.** [On order] requested, requisitioned, sent for, spoken for, engaged, booked, arranged for, retained, written for, telephoned for; see also RESERVED 1. **2.** [Commanded] directed, ordained, commanded, charged, dictated, regulated, decreed, ruled, enjoined, stipulated, bidden, imposed, authorized, exacted, forbidden, required, announced, by order, as ordered, under one's jurisdiction; see also APPROVED, REQUESTED.—*Ant.* NEGLECTED, omitted, revoked. **3.** [Put in order] arranged, regulated, placed; see CLASSIFIED, ORGANIZED.

orderly *a.* **1.** [Ordered; *said of objects and places*] neat, tidy, arranged; see CLEAN 1, NEAT 1. **2.** [Methodical; *said of persons*] systematic, correct, formal, businesslike, systematical, exact, tidy, neat, thorough, precise; see also CAREFUL.—*Ant.* IRREGULAR, inaccurate, unmethodical.

ordinance *n.* direction, mandate, authorization; see LAW 3.

ordinarily *a.* usually, generally, habitually; see FREQUENTLY, REGULARLY.

ordinary *a.* **1.** [In accordance with a regular order or sequence] customary, normal, regular, constant, usual, habitual, routine, mundane, everyday; see also COMMON 1, POPULAR 1, 3, TRADITIONAL. **2.** [Lacking distinction] average, mediocre, familiar, natural, everyday, accepted, typical, commonplace, characteristic, prosaic, simple, banal, bland, trite, monotonous, stale, tedious, plain, normal; see also COMMON 1, CONVENTIONAL 3, DULL 4. **—out of the ordinary** extraordinary, uncommon, special; see UNUSUAL 2.

ore *n.* unrefined, rock, ore bed, native mineral; see also MINERAL.

organ *n.* **1.** [An instrument] medium, means, way; see TOOL 1. **2.** [A part of an organism having a specialized use] vital part, functional division, process; see GLAND. *Human organs include the following:* brain, heart, eye, ear, nose, tongue, lung, kidney, stomach, intestine, pancreas, gall bladder, liver, penis, womb. **3.** [A musical instrument] wind instrument, keyboard instrument, calliope, hurdy-gurdy, accordion; see also MUSICAL INSTRUMENT. *Types of organs include the following:* choir, orchestral, solo, pipe, echo, pedal, reed, electric, hand.

organic *a.* basic, vital, essential; see FUNDAMENTAL, NATURAL 1.

organically *a.* by nature, inevitably, wholly; see ESSENTIALLY, NATURALLY 2.

organism *n.* person, organic structure, physiological individual; see ANIMAL, BODY 1, PLANT.

organization *n.* **1.** [The process or manner of organizing] establishment, plan, planning, ordering, creation, grouping, design, provision, working out, assembling, construction, regulation, systematization, system, method, coordination, adjustment, harmony, unity, correlation, standard, standardization, settlement, arrangement, disposition, classification, alignment, institution, foundation, preparation, rehearsal, direction, structure, situation, formation, association, uniformity; see also CLASSIFICATION, ORDER 3.—*Ant.* CONFUSION, bedlam, chance. **2.** [An organized body] aggregation, association, federation, combine, corporation, union, institute, trust, cartel, confederation, monopoly, combination, machine, business, industry, company, society, league, club, fraternity, house, order, alliance, party, cooperative, guild, profession, trade, coalition, syndicate, fellowship, lodge, brotherhood, confederacy, affiliation, body, band, team, squad, crew, clique, circle, set, troupe, group; see also SYSTEM.

organize *v.* **1.** [To put in order] arrange, fix, straighten, standardize, compose, combine, systematize, methodize, coordinate, adjust, put in order, line up, regulate; see also CLASSIFY, ORDER 3. **2.** [To form an organization] establish, build, found; see PLAN 2.

organized *a.* established, methodized, coordinated, systematized, systematic, constituted, directed, adjusted, assigned, distributed, grouped, fixed up, standardized, in order, in succession, in good form, placed, put away, orderly, in sequence, arranged, prepared, made ready, constructed, settled, composed, framed, planned, ranked, put in order, ordered, regulated, ranged, disposed, formulated, formed, fashioned, shaped, made, projected, designed, harmonized, related, correlated, founded, associated; see also CLASSIFIED.

Orient *n.* **1.** [Eastern Asia] Far East, Asia, China, India, Japan, Vietnam, Thailand, Laos, Indo-China, Cambodia, Korea, Myanmar, the mysterious East, land of the rising sun; see also ASIA, EAST 2.—*Ant.* EUROPE, Occident, Western World. **2.** [Southwestern Asia] Near East, Middle East, Levant, Egypt, Mohammedan world, Turkey, Syria, Lebanon, Israel, Jordan, Iraq, Iran, Persia, Muslim world, Arabia, the Golden Crescent, the cradle of mankind; see also EAST 2.

Oriental *a.* Far Eastern, Near Eastern, Asian, Chinese, Indian, Japanese, Vietnamese, Cambodian, Laotian, Thai, Korean, Siberian, Arabic, Jewish, Iraqi, Iranian, Malaysian, Hindustani, Ceylonese.

orientation *n.* familiarization, bearings, introduction; see ADJUSTMENT, INTRODUCTION 3, 4.

origin *n.* **1.** [The act of beginning] rise, start, foundation; see BIRTH. **2.** [The place or time of beginning] source, spring, issue, fountain, inlet, derivation, root, stem, shoot, twig, sapling, portal, door, gate, gateway, fountainhead, wellspring, font, fount, birthplace, cradle, nest, womb, reservoir, infancy, babyhood, childhood, youth.—*Ant.* RESULT, outcome, issue. **3.** [Cause] seed, germ, stock, parentage, ancestry, parent, ancestor, egg, sperm, embryo, principle, element, nucleus, first cause, author, creator, prime mover, producer, causation, source, influence, generator, occasion, root, spring, antecedent, motive, inspiration; see also CAUSE.—*Ant.* RESULT, consequence, conclusion.

original *a.* **1.** [Pertaining to the source] primary, primeval, primordial, rudimentary, elementary, inceptive, in embryo, fundamental, primitive, initial, beginning, commencing, starting, opening, dawning, incipient; see also FIRST.—*Ant.* LATE, recent, developed. **2.** [Creative] originative, productive, causal, causative, generative, imaginative, inventive, formative, resourceful, ready, quick, seminal, envisioning, sensitive, archetypal, inspiring, devising, conceiving, fertile, fashioning, molding.—*Ant.* STUPID, imitative, unproductive. **3.** [Not copied] primary, principal, first, genuine, new, firsthand, uncopied, fresh, novel, independent, one, sole, lone, single, solitary, authentic, unique, pure, rare, unusual, not translated, not copied, not imitated, real, absolute, sheer.—*Ant.* IMITATED, copied, repeated.

originality *n.* creativeness, inventiveness, invention, ingenuity, conception, authenticity, novelty, freshness, newness, individuality, brilliance; see also IMAGINATION.

originally *a.* **1.** [In an original manner] imaginatively, creatively, ingeniously, inventively, freshly, startlingly, in a new fashion, independently, artistically. **2.** [In the beginning] first, incipiently, basically; see FORMERLY.

originate *v.* start, introduce, found; see BEGIN 1.

originated *a.* introduced, started, commenced; see BEGUN.

ornament *n.* embellishment, adornment, beautification; see DECORATION 2.

ornamental *a.* **1.** [Intended for ornament] fancy, luxurious, showy; see ELABORATE 1, ORNATE. **2.** [Beautiful] delicate, exquisite, spiritual; see BEAUTIFUL.

ornate *a.* showy, gaudy, sumptuous, lavish, bright, colored, tinseled, jeweled, embroidered, glossy, burnished, polished, gorgeous, pompous, stylish, magnificent, adorned, trimmed, gilded, embellished, inlaid, garnished, flowered, glowing, vivid, radiant, fine, alluring, dazzling, sparkling, shining, flashing, glistening, glamorous, artificial, pretentious, baroque, rococo, tawdry, flashy; see also ELABORATE 1.

orphan *n.* foundling, ragamuffin, parentless child, orphaned child, waif, stray; see also CHILD.

orphanage *n.* orphans' home, institution, foundling home; see SCHOOL 1.

other *a.* one of two, the remaining one, another, one beside, some beside, additional, different, separate, distinct, opposite, across from, lately, recently, not long ago, other than; see also EXTRA.

other *pron.* the one remaining, the part remaining, the alternate, the alternative; see also ANOTHER.—*Ant.* THIS, that, the first choice.

others *n.pl.* unnamed persons, the remainder, some, a few, any others, a number, a handful, a small number, not many, hardly any, two or three, more than one, many, a great number, a great many, they, folks, the rest; see also EVERYBODY.—*Ant.* NONE, no one, not any.

otherwise *a.* **1.** [In another way] in a different way, contrarily, in an opposed way, under other conditions, in different circumstances, on the other hand, in other respects, in other ways.—*Ant.* LIKE, so, in like manner. **2.** [Introducing an alternative threat] unless you do, with this exception, except on these conditions, barring this, in any other circumstances, except that, without this, unless...then, other than; see also UNLESS.—*Ant.* THEREFORE, hence, as a result.

ought (to) *v.* should, have to, is necessary, is fitting, is becoming, is expedient, behooves, is reasonable, is logical, is natural, requires, is in need of, is responsible for; see also MUST.

ounce *n.* measure, troy ounce, avoirdupois ounce, fluid ounce, one sixteenth of a pound (avoirdupois), one sixteenth of a pint, one twelfth of a pound (troy); see also MEASURE 1.

our *a.* ours, our own, belonging to us, owned by us, used by us, due to us, a part of us, of interest to us, done by us, accomplished by us, in our employ, with us, near us, of us.

ourselves *pron.* us, the speakers, individually, personally, privately, without help, our own selves*; see also WE.

oust *v.* eject, discharge, dispossess, evict, dislodge, remove, deprive, expel, drive out, force out, show the door, chase out, cast out, depose, dethrone, disinherit, banish, boot out*, bundle off*, send packing*, give the gate*, pack off*.

out *a. & prep.* **1.** [In motion from within] out of, away from, from, from within, out from, out toward, outward, on the way.—*Ant.* IN, in from, into. **2.** [Not situated within] on the outer side, on the surface, external, extrinsic, outer, outdoors, out-of-doors, unconcealed, open, exposed, in the open; see also OUTSIDE, WITHOUT.—*Ant.* WITHIN, inside, on the inner side. **3.** [Beyond] distant, removed, removed from; see AWAY, BEYOND. **4.** [Continued to the limit or near it] ended, accomplished, fulfilled; see DONE 1, FINISHED 1. **5.** [Not at home or at one's office] not in, away, busy, on vacation, at lunch, gone, left; see also ABSENT.—*Ant.* IN, receiving, not busy. **6.** [*Unconscious] insensible, out cold, blotto*; see UNCONSCIOUS. **7.** [Wanting] lacking, missing, without; see WANTING 1. —**all out*** wholeheartedly, with great effort, entirely; see COMPLETELY.

out* *n.* means of escape, way out, excuse; see ESCAPE, EXPLANATION.

outage *n.* interruption of service, blackout, dimout, brownout, failure of electrical service; see also INTERRUPTION.

out-and-out *a.* complete, entire, total; see COMPLETELY.

outbid *v.* offer higher than, raise the price, bid something up; see PAY 1.

outbreak *n.* **1.** [A sudden violent appearance] eruption, explosion, outburst, disruption, burst, bursting forth, detonation, thunder, commotion, rending, break, breaking out, breaking forth, gush, gushing forth, outpouring, pouring forth, tumult, discharge, blast, blowup, crash, roar, earthquake, squall, paroxysm, spasm, convulsion, fit, effervescence, boiling, flash, flare, crack.—*Ant.* PEACE, tranquillity, quiet. **2.** [Sudden violence] fury, mutiny, brawl; see DISORDER, REVOLUTION 2.

outburst *n.* discharge, upheaval, eruption; see DISTURBANCE 2, OUTBREAK 1.

outcast *a.* vagabond, driven out, hounded, untouchable, rejected, thrown aside, pushed out, disgraced, hunted, not accepted by society, cast out, degraded, expelled, outlawed, cast away, exiled, expatriated, serving a life sentence, having a price on one's head.

outcast *n.* fugitive, pariah, untouchable; see REFUGEE.

outcome *n.* issue, upshot, consequence; see END 2, RESULT.

outcrop *n.* bared soil, exposed surface, projecting land mass; see EARTH 2, LAND 1.

outcry *n.* complaint, clamor, scream; see OBJECTION.

outdated *a.* outmoded, out of fashion, antiquated; see OLD 3.

outdo *v.* surpass, best, beat; see EXCEED.

outdone *a.* defeated, bettered, improved upon; see BEATEN 1.

outdoor *a.* outside, airy, out-of-doors, open-air, out of the house, out in the open, free, unrestricted, rustic, free and easy, healthful; see also OUTDOORS.—*Ant.* interior, indoor, in the house.

outdoors *a.* out-of-doors, outdoor, without, out of the house, outside, on the outside, in the yard, in the open, in the garden, into the street.

outdoors *n.* the out-of-doors, natural scenery, fresh air, garden, patio, woods, hills, mountains, stream, Mother Nature, the great outdoors, countryside, the country.—*Ant.* INSIDE, domestic matters, household concerns.

outer *a.* outward, without, external, exterior, foreign, alien to, beyond, exposed; see also OUTSIDE.—*Ant.* INNER, inward, inside.

outer space *n.* infinity, the heavens, the universe; see SPACE 1.

outfield *n.* left field, deep left, center field, deep center, right field, deep right; see also BASEBALL, FIELD 2.

outfielder *n.* right fielder, center fielder, left fielder; see BASEBALL PLAYER.

outfit *n.* trappings, outlay, gear; see EQUIPMENT.
outfit *v.* equip, fit out, supply; see PROVIDE 1.
outflank *v.* bypass, surround, outmaneuver; see DEFEAT 2, PASS 1.
outgo *n.* costs, losses, outflow; see EXPENSES.
outgoing *a.* sociable, civil, kind; see FRIENDLY.
outgrowth *n.* end result, outcome, effect; see END 2, RESULT.
outing *n.* excursion, airing, drive; see VACATION.
outlast *v.* outlive, outwear, remain; see ENDURE 1, SURVIVE 1.
outlaw *n.* fugitive, bandit, badman; see CRIMINAL.
outlaw *v.* make illegal, stop, ban; see BANISH, CONDEMN.
outlawed *a.* stopped, banned, made illegal; see ILLEGAL.
outlet *n.* **1.** [An opening] break, crack, tear; see HOLE 1. **2.** [An electric terminal] plug-in, socket, double socket, triple socket, wall plug, floor plug, electric service connection.
outline *n.* **1.** [A skeletonized plan] frame, skeleton, framework; see PLAN 1. **2.** [The line surrounding an object; *often plural*] contour, side, boundary; see EDGE 1, FRAME 2. **3.** [A shape seen in outline] silhouette, profile, configuration, shape, figure, formation, aspect, appearance; see also FORM 1.
outline *v.* **1.** [To draw] sketch, paint, describe; see DRAW 2. **2.** [To plan] block out, draft, sketch; see PLAN 2.
outlined *a.* **1.** [Marked in outline] bounded, edged, bordered, circumscribed, marked, zoned, girdled, banded, configurated. **2.** [Given in summary] charted, summarized, surveyed; see PLANNED.
outlive *v.* live longer than, outlast, last; see ENDURE 1.
outlook *n.* **1.** [Point of view] scope, vision, standpoint; see VIEWPOINT. **2.** [Apparent future] probability, prospects, likelihood, possibility, chances, opportunity, appearances, probable future, openings, normal course of events, probabilities, risk, law of averages.
out loud *a.* aloud, above a whisper, audibly; see HEARD, LOUD 1, LOUDLY.
outlying *a.* afar, far-off, external; see DISTANT.
outnumbered *a.* exceeded, bested, overcome; see BEATEN 1.
out of *a.* **1.** [Having none in stock] all out of stock, not in stock, gone; see SOLD OUT. **2.** [From] out from, away from, from within; see FROM. **3.** [Beyond] outside of, on the border of, in the outskirts; see BEYOND.
out of bounds *a.* outlawed, forbidden, controlled; see ILLEGAL.
out of breath *a.* exhausted, gasping, winded; see BREATHLESS.
out of control *a.* gone, doomed, uncontrolled; see LOST 1, UNRULY.
out-of-date *a.* obsolete, passé, antiquated; see OLD-FASHIONED.
out of hand *a.* beyond control, out of control, unchecked; see UNCONTROLLED, UNRULY.
out of it* *a.* uninformed, behind the times, square*; see IGNORANT 1, OLD-FASHIONED.
out of line *a.* **1.** [Crooked] not lined up, uneven, devious; see CROOKED, IRREGULAR 4. **2.** [Disrespectful] outspoken, dissident, insolent; see RADICAL 2, REBELLIOUS, UNRULY.
out of one's mind or **head** *a.* crazy, deranged, irresponsible; see INSANE.
out of order *a.* broken down, defective, faulty; see BROKEN 2.
out of place *a.* mislaid, displaced, gone; see LOST 1.
out of print *a.* sold out, not available, all gone; see SOLD.
out-of-the-way *a.* far-off, secluded, isolated; see DISTANT.
out of work *a.* out of a job, dismissed, without work; see UNEMPLOYED.
outplay *v.* overcome, surpass, beat; see DEFEAT 3.
outpost *n.* forward position, listening post, point of attack; see BOUNDARY, POSITION 1.
output *n.* yield, amount, crop; see PRODUCE.
outrage *n.* indignity, abuse, affront; see INSULT.
outrage *v.* offend, wrong, affront; see ABUSE, INSULT.
outrageous *a.* wanton, notorious, shameless, disgraceful, brazen, barefaced, gross, scandalous, disorderly, insulting, affronting, abusive, oppressive, dishonorable, injurious, glaring, immoderate, extreme, flagrant, contemptible, ignoble, malevolent, odious, monstrous, atrocious, nefarious, vicious, iniquitous, wicked, shocking, violent, unbearable, villainous, infamous, corrupt, degenerate, criminal, sinful, abandoned, vile, abominable.—*Ant.* EXCELLENT, laudable, honorable.
outright *a.* out-and-out, unmitigated, unconditional; see COMPLETELY, OBVIOUS 1.
outset *n.* start, beginning, source; see ORIGIN 2.
outside *a.* extreme, outermost, farthest, apart from, external, away from, farther; see also OUTER.—*Ant.* INNER, inside, interior.
outside *n.* **1.** [An outer surface] exterior, outer side, surface, skin, cover, covering, topside, upper side, front side, face, appearance, outer aspect, seeming.—*Ant.* INSIDE, interior, inner side. **2.** [The limit] outline, border, bounds; see BOUNDARY, EDGE 1, END 4. **—at the outside** at the most, at the absolute limit, not more than; see MOST.
outsider *n.* foreigner, stranger, refugee; see ALIEN.

outskirts *n.pl.* border, suburbs, limits; see BOUNDARY, EDGE 1.
outspoken *a.* blunt, candid, artless; see FRANK.
outspread *a.* spread out, expanded, extended; see WIDESPREAD.
outstanding *a.* conspicuous, leading, notable; see DISTINGUISHED 2.
outward *a.* **1.** [In an outward direction] out, toward the edge, from within; see OUTER, OUTSIDE. **2.** [To outward appearance] on the surface, visible, to the eye; see OBVIOUS 1, OPEN 1.
outwear *v.* sustain, last longer than, outlast; see CONTINUE 1, ENDURE 1, SURVIVE 1.
outweigh *v.* **1.** [To exceed in weight] overbalance, overweigh, weigh more than, go beyond; see also BURDEN. **2.** [To exceed in importance] excel, surpass, outrun; see EXCEED.
outwit *v.* baffle, trick, bewilder; see CONFUSE, DECEIVE.
outwitted *a.* tricked, outsmarted, taken*; see DECEIVED.
oval *a.* egg-shaped, elliptical, ellipsoid; see OBLONG.
oven *n.* hot-air chamber, oil burner, broiler; see FURNACE, STOVE.
over *a. & prep.* **1.** [Situated above] aloft, overhead, up beyond, covering, roofing, protecting, upper, higher than, farther up, upstairs, in the sky, straight up, high up, up there, in the clouds, among the stars, in heaven, just over, up from, outer, on top of; see also ABOVE.—*Ant.* under, below, beneath. **2.** [Passing above] overhead, aloft, up high; see ACROSS. **3.** [Again] once more, afresh, another time; see AGAIN. **4.** [Beyond] past, farther on, out of sight; see BEYOND. **5.** [Done] accomplished, ended, completed; see DONE 1, FINISHED 1. **6.** [*In addition] over and above, extra, additionally; see BESIDES. **7.** [Having authority] superior to, in authority, above; see HIGHER, SUPERIOR.
overall *a.* complete, thorough, comprehensive; see GENERAL 1.
overalls *n.pl.* an overall garment, jump suit, coveralls; see CLOTHES, PANTS 1.
overbearing *a.* despotic, tyrannical, dictatorial; see ABSOLUTE 3.
overboard *a.* over the side, out of the boat, into the water; see WET 1.
overcast *a.* cloudy, gloomy, not clear or fair; see DARK 1.
overcoat *n.* greatcoat, topcoat, raincoat; see CLOTHES, COAT 1.
overcome *a.* conquered, overwhelmed, overthrown; see BEATEN 1.
overcome *v.* overwhelm, best, vanquish, conquer, outdo, surpass, overpower, overwhelm, beat, trounce, subdue, master; see also DEFEAT 2, 3, WIN 1.
overconfident *a.* reckless, imprudent, heedless; see CARELESS, RASH.
overcritical *a.* domineering, harsh, hypercritical; see SEVERE 1, 2.
overcrowd *v.* crowd, stuff, fill; see PACK 2, PRESS 1.
overcrowded *a.* congested, overbuilt, overpopulated; see FULL 1.
overdo *v.* **1.** [To do too much] magnify, amplify, overestimate, overreach, stretch, go too far, overrate, exaggerate, go to extremes, overstate, enlarge, enhance, exalt, bite off more than one can chew*, run into the ground*, do to death, go overboard*, burn the candle at both ends, lay it on*, have too many irons in the fire, have one's cake and eat it too*; see also EXCEED.—*Ant.* NEGLECT, underdo, slack. **2.** [To overtax oneself physically] tire, fatigue, exhaust; see WEARY 2.
overdone *a.* excessive, too much, pushed too far; see EXAGGERATED.
overdose *n.* excessive dose, too much, overtreatment; see EXCESS 1.
overdrawn *a.* exhausted, depleted, all paid out; see GONE 2.
overdue *a.* delayed, belated, tardy; see LATE 1.
overeat *v.* overindulge, stuff, gorge; see EAT 1.
overemphasize *v.* stress, make a big thing of*, make something out of*; see EMPHASIZE, EXCEED.
overestimate *v.* overvalue, overprice, overrate; see EXAGGERATE, EXCEED.
overflow *n.* **1.** [The act of overflowing] redundancy, inundation, overproduction; see FLOOD. **2.** [That which overflows] superfluity, surplus, surplusage; see EXCESS 1.
overflow *v.* **1.** [To flow over the top, or out at a vent] spill over, run over, pour out, waste, shed, cascade, spout forth, jet, spurt, drain, leak, squirt, spray, shower, gush, shoot, issue, rush, wave, surge, overtop, brim over, bubble over; see also LEAK 1. **2.** [To flow out upon] inundate, water, wet; see FLOOD.
overflowing *a.* abundant, in plenty, bountiful; see PLENTIFUL 2.
overfly *v.* survey, fly across, fly over; see FLY 1, 4.
overgrown *a.* disproportionate, excessive, huge; see LARGE 1.
overgrowth *n.* growth, abundance, luxuriance; see EXCESS 1.
overhang *v.* jut, be suspended, dangle over; see PROJECT 1.
overhaul *v.* modernize, fix, renew; see REPAIR.
overhead *a.* above, aloft, hanging; see OVER 1.

overhear *v.* hear intentionally, listen in on, catch; see EAVESDROP, HEAR 1.
overheard *a.* listened to, recorded, bugged*; see HEARD.
overheat *v.* heat too much, bake, blister; see HEAT 2.
overindulgence *n.* overeating, overdrinking, eating or drinking too much; see DRUNKENNESS, EATING, GREED.
overlap *n.* extension, overlay, addition; see FLAP.
overlap *v.* overlie, overhang, lap over, fold over, extend alongside, flap, project upon, overlay; see also PROJECT 1.
overload *v.* oppress, weigh down, encumber; see BURDEN, LOAD 1.
overlook *v.* **1.** [To occupy a commanding height] look over, top, survey, inspect, watch over, look out, view, give upon, give on, front on, have a prospect of. **2.** [To ignore deliberately] slight, make light of, disdain; see NEGLECT 1. **3.** [To fail to see] miss, leave out, neglect; see NEGLECT 2.
overlooked *a.* missed, left out, forgotten; see NEGLECTED.
overlooking *a.* **1.** [Providing a view] looking over, looking out on, commanding; see SEEING. **2.** [Disregarding] missing, neglecting, forgetting.
overnight *a.* one night, lasting one night, during the night; see LATE 4.
over one's dead body* *a.* not if one can help it, only with great difficulty, by no means; see NEVER.
overpass *n.* span, footbridge, walkway; see BRIDGE 1.
overpower *v.* overwhelm, master, subjugate; see DEFEAT 2, 3.
overpowering *a.* irresistible, uncontrollable, overwhelming; see INTENSE.
overproduction *n.* excess, excessive production, overstock; see PRODUCTION 1.
overrate *v.* build up, magnify, overestimate; see EXAGGERATE, EXCEED.
overrated *a.* not very good, overblown, not satisfactory; see POOR 2, UNSATISFACTORY.
override *v.* **1.** [To dismiss] pass over, not heed, take no account of; see DISREGARD, NEGLECT 1. **2.** [To thwart] make void, reverse, annul; see CANCEL, REVOKE.
overrule *v.* **1.** [To nullify] invalidate, rule against, override; see CANCEL, REVOKE. **2.** [To rule] direct, control, manage; see GOVERN.
overrun *v.* **1.** [To defeat] overwhelm, invade, occupy; see DEFEAT 2. **2.** [To infest] ravage, invade, overwhelm; see INFEST 2.
overseas *a.* away, across, in foreign countries; see ABROAD.
oversee *v.* superintend, supervise, look after; see MANAGE 1.
overseer *n.* supervisor, manager, superintendent; see FOREMAN.
overshoes *n.pl.* rubber shoes, galoshes, rubbers; see SHOE.
overshoot *v.* overreach, overdo, overact; see EXCEED.
oversight *n.* failure, overlooking, mistake; see ERROR.
oversleep *v.* sleep late, miss the alarm, stay in bed; see SLEEP.
overspecialize *v.* limit oneself, specialize too much, be a specialist; see RESTRAIN, RESTRICT.
overstay *v.* stay too long, stop, outstay one's welcome; see REMAIN 1.
overstep *v.* violate, encroach, trespass; see EXCEED, MEDDLE 1.
overtake *v.* overhaul, catch up with, get to; see REACH 1.
overtaken *a.* caught up with, reached, apprehended; see BEATEN 1, CAPTURED.
overthrow *v.* overcome, overrun, overpower; see DEFEAT 2.
overthrown *a.* overcome, overwhelmed, vanquished; see BEATEN 1.
overtime *n.* extra pay, additional wages, late hours; see PAY 2.
overtone *n.* tone, implication, hint; see MEANING, SUGGESTION 1.
overture *n.* **1.** [Preliminary negotiations; *sometimes plural*] approach, advance, tender; see SUGGESTION 1. **2.** [A musical introduction] prelude, prologue, *Vorspiel* (German), voluntary, proem, preface; see also INTRODUCTION 3.
overturn *v.* reverse, upturn, overthrow; see UPSET 1.
overwhelm *v.* **1.** [To defeat] overcome, overthrow, conquer; see DEFEAT 2, 3, WIN 1. **2.** [To astonish] puzzle, bewilder, confound; see CONFUSE, SURPRISE.
overwhelmed *a.* beaten, worsted, submerged; see BEATEN 2.
overwhelming *a.* overpowering, ruinous, overthrowing, crushing, smashing, extinguishing, invading, ravaging, overriding, upsetting, inundating, drowning, deluging, surging, obliterating, dissolving, blotting out, wrecking, erasing, effacing, expunging, burying, immersing, engulfing, engrossing, covering; see also HARMFUL, TRIUMPHANT.
overwork *n.* extra work, overtime, exhaustion; see ABUSE.
overwork *v.* overdo, exhaust, wear out; see BURDEN, WEARY 1.
overworked *a.* too busy, overburdened, worked too hard; see TIRED.
owe *v.* be under obligation, be indebted to, be obligated to, have an obligation, ought to, be bound, get on credit, feel bound, be bound to pay, be contracted to, be in debt for, have signed a note for, have borrowed, have lost.
owed *a.* owing, becoming due, indebted; see DUE, UNPAID 1.

owl *n.* bird of prey, night bird, nocturnal bird; see BIRD.

own *a.* personal, individual, owned, very own*; see also PRIVATE.

own *v.* **1.** [To possess] hold, have, enjoy, fall heir to, have title to, have rights to, be master of, occupy, control, dominate, have claim upon, reserve, retain, keep, have in hand, have a deed for.—*Ant.* LACK, want, need. **2.** [To acknowledge] assent to, grant, recognize; see ADMIT 2, DECLARE. **—come into one's own** receive what one deserves, gain proper recognition, thrive; see PROFIT 2. **—of one's own** personal, private, belonging to one; see OWNED. **—on one's own** by oneself, acting independently, singly; see INDEPENDENTLY.

owned *a.* possessed, had, bought, purchased, kept, inherited, enjoyed, in hand, bound over, in the possession of, among the possessions of.

owner *n.* one who has, keeper, buyer, purchaser, heir, heiress, proprietor, landlord, landlady, sharer, partner, title holder, master, heir-apparent.

ownership *n.* possession, having, holding, claim, deed, title, control, buying, purchasing, heirship, proprietorship, occupancy, use, residence, tenancy, dominion.

own up *v.* be honest, admit error, confess; see ADMIT 2.

oyster *n.* bivalve, mollusk, seafood; see FISH, SHELLFISH.

P

pa* *n.* sire, paterfamilias, dad*; see FATHER 1, PARENT.

pace *n.* step, velocity, movement; see SPEED. **—change of pace** variation, alteration, diversity; see CHANGE 1. **—keep pace (with)** go at the same speed, maintain the same rate of progress, keep up with; see EQUAL. **—set the pace** begin, initiate, establish criteria; see LEAD 1.

pace *v.* determine, pace off, step off; see MEASURE 1.

Pacific *n.* North Pacific, South Pacific, South Seas; see OCEAN.

pacifist *n.* man of peace, peace-lover, conscientious objector; see RADICAL, RESISTER.

pacify *v.* conciliate, appease, placate; see QUIET 1.

pack *n.* **1.** [A package] bundle, parcel, load; see PACKAGE. **2.** [Kit] outfit, baggage, luggage; see EQUIPMENT. **3.** [A group] number, gang, mob; see CROWD. **4.** [A medical dressing] application, hot pack, ice pack; see DRESSING 3. **5.** [A set of cards] bridge deck, pinochle deck, set; see DECK 2.

pack *v.* **1.** [To prepare for transportation] prepare, gather, collect, ready, get ready, put in order, stow away, dispose, tie, bind, brace, fasten.—*Ant.* UNDO, untie, take out. **2.** [To stow compactly] stuff, squeeze, bind, compress, condense, arrange, ram, cram, jam, insert, press, contract, put away.—*Ant.* SCATTER, loosen, fluff up.

package *n.* parcel, packet, burden, load, kit, bunch, sheaf, pack, batch, baggage, luggage, grip, suitcase, bag, handbag, valise, trunk, box, carton, crate, bundle, bale, can, tin, sack, bottle; see also CONTAINER.

packed *a.* **1.** [Ready for storage or shipment] prepared, bundled, wrapped; see READY 2. **2.** [Pressed together] compact, compressed, pressed down; see FULL 1.

packet *n.* pack, receptacle, parcel; see CONTAINER, PACKAGE.

packing *n.* preparation, arrangement, compression, consignment, disposal, disposition, sorting, grading, laying away.

pact *n.* settlement, compact, bargain; see TREATY.

pad *n.* **1.** [Material for writing] note pad, stationery, notebook, parchment; see also PAPER 4, TABLET 2. **2.** [An article that cushions] mat, cushion, support; see PILLOW, MAT. **3.** [*A residence] room, apartment, living quarters; see HOME.

pad *v.* **1.** [To stuff] pack, fill out, pad out; see FILL 1. **2.** [To increase] inflate, build up, falsify; see DECEIVE, INCREASE.

padded *a.* stuffed, filled, quilted; see FULL 1.

padding *n.* stuffing, wadding, waste; see FILLING.

paddle *n.* oar, pole, paddle wheel; see TOOL 1.

paddle *v.* **1.** [To propel by paddling] scull, boat, cruise, drift, navigate, cut water, shoot rapids, run rapids; see also DRIVE 2. **2.** [To beat, usually rather lightly] spank, thrash, rap; see BEAT 1, PUNISH.

padlock *n.* latch, fastener, catch; see LOCK 1.

pagan *a.* unchristian, idolatrous, heathenish.

pagan *n.* pantheist, heathen, doubter, scoffer, unbeliever, atheist, infidel.

paganism *n.* heathenism, agnosticism, idolatry; see ATHEISM.

page *n.* leaf, sheet, folio, side, surface, recto, verso.

page *v.* **1.** [To call] hunt for, seek for, call the name of; see SUMMON. **2.** [To mark the pages] number, check, paginate; see CHECK 2.

pageant *n.* exhibition, celebration, pomp; see PARADE 1.

paid *a.* rewarded, paid off, reimbursed, indemnified, remunerated, solvent, unindebted, unowed, recompensed, salaried, hired, out of debt, refunded; see also REPAID.

paid for *a.* purchased, bought and paid for, owned; see BOUGHT.

paid off *a.* leaving nothing still owed, completely paid, unowed; see PAID.

pail *n.* pot, receptacle, jug; see CONTAINER.

pain *n.* **1.** [Suffering, physical or mental] hurt, anguish, distress, discomfort, disorder, agony, misery, martyrdom, wretchedness, shock, torture, torment, passion; see also INJURY.—*Ant.* HEALTH, well-being, ease. **2.** [Suffering, usually physical] ache, twinge, catch, throe, spasm, cramp, torture, malady, sickness, laceration, soreness, fever, burning, torment, distress, agony, affliction, discomfort, hurt, wound, strain, sting, burn, crick; see also ILLNESS 1, INJURY. **3.** [Suffering, usually mental] despondency, worry, anxiety; see DEPRESSION 2, GRIEF, SADNESS. **—feeling no pain*** intoxicated, inebriated, stoned*; see DRUNK.

pain *v.* distress, grieve, trouble; see HURT 1.

painful *a.* **1.** [Referring to physical anguish] raw, aching, throbbing, burning, torturing, hurtful, biting, piercing, sharp, severe, caustic, tormenting, smarting, extreme, grievous, stinging, bruised, sensitive, tender, irritated, distressing, inflamed, burned, unpleasant, ulcerated, abcessed, uncomfortable; see also SORE 1.—*Ant.* HEALTHY, comfortable, well. **2.** [Referring to mental anguish] worrying, depressing, saddening; see DISTURBING.

paint *n.* **1.** [Pigment] coloring material, chroma, chlorophyll; see COLOR. *Paints and colorings include the following—artist's materials:* oil, acrylic, pastel, crayon, charcoal, watercolor, tempera; *architectural finishes:* house paint, enamel, varnish, redwood stain, oil, wax, whitewash, tempera, fresco, luminous paint, plastic paint, cold-water paint, flat paint, high-gloss paint, metallic paint, barn paint, inside paint, outside paint, white lead. **2.** [Covering] overlay, varnish, veneer; see FINISH 2.

paint *v.* **1.** [To represent by painting] portray, paint in oils, sketch, outline, picture, depict, catch a likeness, design, shade, tint, fresco, wash; see also DRAW 2. **2.** [To protect or decorate by painting] coat, decorate, apply, brush, tint, touch up, ornament, gloss over, swab, daub, slap on; see also COVER 1, SPREAD 3.

painted *a.* **1.** [Portrayed] outlined, pictured, drawn, sketched, designed, depicted, washed on; see also COLORED 1. **2.** [Finished] coated, covered, enameled, decorated, ornamented, brushed over, tinted, washed, daubed, touched up, smeared; see also FINISHED 1.

painter *n.* **1.** [House painter] interior decorator, dauber, paint-slinger*; see WORKMAN. **2.** [An artist] craftsman, artisan, illustrator, draftsman, etcher, sketcher, cartoonist, animator; see also ARTIST. *Major painters include the following:* Giotto, Sandro Botticelli, Jan van Eyck, Albrecht Dürer, Hieronymus Bosch, Pieter Brueghel (the elder), Leonardo da Vinci, Raphael, Michelangelo, Titian, Tintoretto, El Greco, Peter Paul Rubens, Anthony Van Dyck, Rembrandt van Rijn, Jan Vermeer, Sir Joshua Reynolds, Thomas Gainsborough, Diego Velázquez, Francisco Goya, Eugène Delacroix, Auguste Renoir, Edgar Degas, James Whistler, Winslow Homer, Edouard Manet, Claude Monet, Paul Cézanne, Vincent van Gogh, Paul Gauguin, Henri de Toulouse-Lautrec, Pablo Picasso, Henri Matisse, Paul Klee, Salvador Dali, Jackson Pollock.

painting *n.* **1.** [A work of art] oil painting, watercolor, abstract design, landscape, sketch, picture, likeness, artwork, canvas, mural, fresco, depiction, delineation; see also ART. **2.** [The act of applying paint] enameling, covering, coating; see ART.

pair *n.* couple, mates, two, two of a kind, twosome, twins, fellows, duality, brace.

pair *v.* combine, match, balance; see JOIN 1, 2.

pajamas *n.pl.* nightwear, lounging pajamas, lounging robe, PJ's*, jamas*, nightie*; see also CLOTHES.

pal* *n.* companion, bosom friend, buddy*; see FRIEND.

palace *n.* royal residence, manor, mansion; see CASTLE.

pale *a.* **1.** [Wan] pallid, sickly, anemic, bloodless, ghastly, cadaverous, haggard, deathlike, ghostly; see also DULL 2. **2.** [Lacking color] white, colorless, bleached; see DULL 2.

pale *v.* grow pale, lose color, blanch; see WHITEN 1.

paleness *n.* whiteness, anemia, colorlessness; see ILLNESS 1.

palmy *a.* prosperous, glorious, delightful; see HAPPY, PLEASANT 2.

paltry *a.* small, insignificant, trifling; see UNIMPORTANT.

pamper *v.* spoil, indulge, pet, cater to, humor, gratify, yield to, coddle, overindulge, please, spare the rod and spoil the child*.

pamphlet *n.* booklet, brochure, pocketbook, chapbook, leaflet, bulletin, circular, broadside, handbill; see also ANNOUNCEMENT.

pan *n.* vessel, kettle, container, pail, bucket, baking pan, gold pan; see also CONTAINER. *Kitchen pans include the following:* kettle, stew pan, saucepan, double boiler, roaster, casserole, cake pan, bread pan, pie pan, cookie sheet, frying pan or skillet, dishpan.

pan* *v.* criticize, review unfavorably, jeer at; see BLAME.

pancake *n.* flapjack, hot cake, griddlecake; see FOOD.

pandemonium *n.* uproar, anarchy, riot; see CONFUSION.

pane *n.* window glass, stained glass, mirror; see GLASS.

panel *n.* ornament, tablet, inset; see DECORATION 2.

pang *n.* throb, sting, bite; see PAIN 2.

panhandle* *v.* solicit, ask alms, bum*; see BEG.

panhandler* *n.* vagrant, bum*, mendicant; see BEGGAR.

panic *n.* dread, alarm, fright; see FEAR.

panic-stricken *a.* terrified, hysterical, fearful; see AFRAID.

panorama *n.* spectacle, scenery, prospect; see VIEW.

pan out* *v.* turn out, work, be a success; see SUCCEED 1.

pant *v.* wheeze, throb, palpitate; see BREATHE, GASP.

panties *n.pl.* pants, underpants, briefs; see UNDERWEAR.

pantomime *n.* sign, sign language, dumb show, mimicry, play without words, acting without speech, charade, mime.

pantry *n.* storeroom, larder, cupboard; see CLOSET, ROOM 2.

pants *n.pl.* **1.** [Trousers] breeches, slacks, jeans, overalls, cords, shorts, corduroys, pantaloons, bell bottoms, riding breeches, chaps, short pants, knee pants, knickers, bloomers, rompers, sun suit; see also CLOTHES. **2.** [Underclothing, especially women's] shorts, briefs, panties; see CLOTHES, UNDERWEAR.

papa* *n.* dad*, daddy*, male parent; see FATHER 1, PARENT.

paper *n.* **1.** [A piece of legal or official writing] document, official document, legal paper; see RECORD 1. *Papers include the following:* abstract, affidavit, bill, certificate, citation, contract, credentials, data, deed, diploma, indictment, grant, orders, passport, visa, plea, records, safe-conduct, subpoena, summons, testimony, voucher, warrant, will. **2.** [A newspaper] journal, daily, daily journal; see NEWSPAPER. **3.** [A piece of writing] essay, article, theme; see WRITING 2. **4.** [A manufactured product] *Paper includes the following—writing material:* typing paper, typewriter paper, stationery, bond paper, letterhead, personal stationery, ruled paper, second sheet, onion skin, carbon paper, note pad, note card, filing card; *printing paper:* coated stock, poster, linen finish, vellum, parchment, India; 50-pound, 60-pound, etc.; newsprint; *miscellaneous:* art, rice, Chinese or Japanese rice, crêpe, butcher's, wrapping, tissue, brown, tar, roofing, tracing, graph, filter, toilet, wax, photographic; wallpaper, cellophane, paper towel, cleansing tissue. —**on paper** **1.** recorded, signed, official; see WRITTEN 2. **2.** in theory, assumed to be feasible, not yet in practice; see THEORETICAL.

paper *v.* hang, paste up, plaster; see COVER 1.

paperback *n.* softcover, pocket book, reprint; see BOOK.

papers *n.pl.* **1.** [Evidence of identity or authorization] naturalization papers, identification card, ID; see IDENTIFICATION 2, PASSPORT. **2.** [Documentary materials] writings, documents, effects; see RECORD 1.

paper work *n.* office work, desk work, keeping one's desk clear, keeping records, filing, preparing reports, taking dictation, typing, keeping books.

papery *a.* flimsy, insubstantial, slight; see POOR 2.

pappy* *n.* papa*, daddy*, pa*; see FATHER 1, PARENT.

par *n.* standard, level, norm; see MODEL 2.

parable *n.* fable, moral story, tale; see STORY.

parachute *n.* chute, seat pack parachute, lap pack parachute, harness and pack, umbrella*, bailer*, silk*.

parachute *v.* fall, bail out, hit the silk*; see DIVE.

parade *n.* **1.** [A procession] spectacle, ceremony, demonstration, review, line of floats, line of march, pageant, ritual. **2.** [An ostentatious show] show, ostentation, ceremony; see DISPLAY.

parade *v.* demonstrate, display, exhibit; see MARCH.

paradise *n.* **1.** [Heaven] Kingdom Come, Celestial Home, the other world; see HEAVEN. **2.** [The home of Adam and Eve] Garden of Eden, Eden, the Garden.

paradox *n.* mystery, enigma, ambiguity; see PUZZLE 2.

paragon *n.* ideal, perfection, best; see MODEL 1.

paragraph *n.* passage, section, division of thought, topic, statement, verse, article, item, notice.

parallel *a.* **1.** [Equidistant at all points] side by side, never meeting, running parallel, coordinate, coextending, lateral, laterally, in the same direction, extending equally. **2.** [Similar in kind, position, or the like] identical, equal, conforming; see ALIKE.

parallel *n.* resemblance, likeness, correspondence; see SIMILARITY.

parallel *v.* match, correspond, correlate; see EQUAL.

paralysis *n.* insensibility, loss of motion, loss of sensation; see ILLNESS 2.
paralytic *a.* inactive, paralyzed, crippled; see DISABLED, SICK.
paralytic *n.* paralysis victim, cripple, paralyzed person; see PATIENT.
paralyze *v.* strike with paralysis, make inert, render nerveless; see DEADEN.
paralyzed *a.* insensible, nerveless, benumbed, stupefied, inert, inactive, unmoving, helpless, torpid; see also DISABLED.
paranoid *a.* affected by paranoia, unreasonably distrustful, overly suspicious, having a persecution complex.
paraphernalia *n.* gear, material, apparatus; see EQUIPMENT.
parasite *n.* **1.** [A plant or animal living on another] bacteria, parasitoid, saprophyte, epiphyte. **2.** [A hanger-on] dependent, slave, sponger*; see SLAVE.
parcel *n.* bundle, packet, carton; see PACKAGE.
parch *v.* dessicate, dehydrate, brown; see DRY 1.
parched *a.* burned, withered, dried; see DRY 1.
parchment *n.* vellum, goatskin, sheepskin; see PAPER 4.
pardon *n.* **1.** [The reduction or removal of punishment] absolution, grace, remission, amnesty, exoneration, discharge; see also MERCY.—*Ant.* PUNISHMENT, condemnation, conviction. **2.** [Forgiveness] excuse, forbearance, conciliation; see FORGIVENESS, KINDNESS 1.
pardon *v.* **1.** [To reduce punishment] exonerate, clear, absolve, reprieve, acquit, set free, liberate, discharge, rescue, justify, suspend charges, put on probation, grant amnesty to; see also FREE, RELEASE.—*Ant.* PUNISH, chastise, sentence. **2.** [To forgive] condone, overlook, exculpate; see EXCUSE, FORGIVE.
pardoned *a.* forgiven, freed, excused, released, granted amnesty, given a pardon, reprieved, granted a reprieve, acquitted, let off, sprung*, back in circulation; see also DISCHARGED, FREE 1.—*Ant.* ACCUSED, convicted, condemned.
pare *v.* scalp, strip, flay; see CUT 1, SHAVE, SKIN.
parent *n.* immediate forebear, procreator, progenitor, sire; see also FATHER 1, MOTHER 1.
parental *a.* paternal, maternal, familial; see GENETIC.
parentheses *n.pl.* brackets, enclosure, punctuation marks; see PUNCTUATION.
parish *n.* archdiocese, congregation, diocese; see AREA, CHURCH 3.
park *n.* **1.** [A place designated for outdoor recreation] square, plaza, lawn, green, village green, promenade, boulevard, tract, recreational area, pleasure ground, national park, national monument, enclosure, woodland, meadow. **2.** [A place designed for outdoor storage] parking lot, parking space, lot; see GARAGE, PARKING LOT.
park *v.* mass, collect, order, place in order, station, place in rows, leave, store, impound, deposit; see also LINE UP.
parked *a.* stationed, standing, left, put, lined up, in rows, by the curb, in the parking lot, stored, halted, unmoving.
parking lot *n.* lot, parking, space, parking space, parking garage, parking area, parking facility, parking slot, off-street parking.
Parliament *n.* national legislative body of Great Britain, House of Commons, House of Lords; see GOVERNMENT 1, LEGISLATURE.
parliamentary *a.* congressional, administrative, lawmaking; see GOVERNMENTAL, LEGISLATIVE.
parochial *a.* provincial, insular, sectional; see LOCAL 1, REGIONAL.
parody *n.* travesty, burlesque, mimicry; see JOKE.
parody *v.* mimic, copy, caricature; see IMITATE 1, JOKE.
parole *v.* discharge, pardon, liberate; see FREE, RELEASE.
parrot *n.* **1.** [A bird] parakeet, lovebird, cockatoo; see BIRD. **2.** [One who copies others] plagiarist, mimic, mimicker, ape, impersonator, imposter, mocker, copycat*; see also IMITATOR.
parson* *n.* clergyman, cleric, preacher; see MINISTER 1.
part *n.* **1.** [A portion] piece, fragment, fraction, section, sector, member, segment, division, allotment, apportionment, ingredient, element, slab, subdivision, partition, particle, installment, component, constituent, bit, slice, scrap, chip, chunk, lump, sliver, splinter, shaving, molecule, atom, electron, proton, neutron; see also SHARE.—*Ant.* WHOLE, total, aggregate. **2.** [A part of speech] modifier, preposition, conjunction; see NOUN, VERB. **3.** [A machine part] molding, casting, fitting, lever, shaft, cam, spring, band, belt, chain, pulley, clutch, spare part, replacement; see also BOLT, GEAR, MACHINE, WHEEL 1. **4.** [A character in a drama] hero, heroine, character; see ROLE. **—for the most part** mainly, mostly, to the greatest extent; see MOST. **—in part** to a certain extent, somewhat, slightly; see PARTLY. **—on one's part** privately, as far as one is concerned, coming from one; see PERSONALLY 2. **—play a part** share, join, take part; see PARTICIPATE 1.
part *v.* **1.** [To put apart] separate, break, sever; see DIVIDE. **2.** [To depart] withdraw, take leave, part company; see LEAVE 1.
partake *v.* participate, divide, take; see SHARE 2.

parted *a.* divided, severed, sundered; see SEPARATED.

part from *v.* separate, part, break up with; see LEAVE 1.

partial *a.* **1.** [Not complete] unperformed, incomplete, half done; see UNFINISHED 1. **2.** [Showing favoritism] unfair, influenced, biased; see PREJUDICED.

partiality *n.* fondness, inclination, preference; see AFFECTION.

partially *a.* partly, somewhat, in part; see PARTLY.

participant *n.* cooperator, partner, sharer; see ASSOCIATE.

participate *v.* **1.** [To take part in] share, partake, aid, cooperate, join in, come in, associate with, be a party to, have a hand in, concur, take an interest in, take part in, enter into, have to do with, get into the act*, go into, chip in*; see also JOIN 2.—*Ant.* RETIRE, withdraw, refuse. **2.** [To engage in a contest] play, strive, engage; see COMPETE.

participation *n.* partnership, joining in, sharing, support, aid, assistance, help, encouragement, seconding, standing by, taking part; see also PARTNERSHIP.

particle *n.* jot, scrap, atom, molecule, fragment, piece, shred; see also BIT 1.

particular *a.* **1.** [Specific] distinct, singular, appropriate; see SPECIAL. **2.** [Accurate] precise, minute, exact; see ACCURATE 2. —**in particular** expressly, particularly, individually; see ESPECIALLY 1.

particular *n.* fact, specification, item; see DETAIL.

particularly *a.* unusually, expressly, individually; see ESPECIALLY 1.

parting *n.* leavetaking, goodbye, farewell; see DEPARTURE.

partisan *n.* adherent, supporter, disciple; see FOLLOWER.

partition *n.* **1.** [Division] apportionment, separation, severance; see DISTRIBUTION. **2.** [That which divides or separates] bar, obstruction, hindrance; see BARRIER, WALL 1.

partly *a.* in part, partially, to a degree, measurably, somewhat, noticeably, notably, in some part, incompletely, insufficiently, inadequately, up to a certain point, so far as possible, not entirely, as much as could be expected, to some extent, within limits, slightly, to a slight degree, in some ways, in certain particulars, only in details, in a general way, not strictly speaking, in bits and pieces, by fits and starts, carelessly, short of the end, at best, at worst, at most, at least, at the outside.—*Ant.* COMPLETELY, wholly, entirely.

partner *n.* co-worker, ally, comrade; see ASSOCIATE.

partnership *n.* alliance, union, cooperation, company, combination, corporation, connection, brotherhood, society, lodge, club, fellowship, fraternity, confederation, band, body, crew, clique, gang, ring, faction, party, community, conjunction, joining, companionship, friendship, help; see also ALLIANCE 1, UNION 1.

part of *pron.* portion, section, division; see SOME.

part of speech *n.* grammatical construction, word, lexeme; see ADJECTIVE, GRAMMAR, PRONOUN, VERB, WORD 1.

partway *a.* started, toward the middle, somewhat; see BEGUN, SOME.

part with *v.* let go of, suffer loss, give up; see LOSE 2.

party *n.* **1.** [A social affair] at-home, tea, luncheon, dinner party, dinner, cocktail hour, surprise party, house party, social, reception, banquet, feast, affair, gathering, function, fete, ball, recreation, amusement, entertainment, festive occasion, carouse, diversion, performance, high tea, binge*, spree*, blowout*, bash*. **2.** [A group of people] multitude, mob, company; see CROWD, GATHERING. **3.** [A political organization] organized group, body, electorate, combine, combination, bloc, ring, junta, partisans, cabal; see also FACTION. **4.** [A specified but unnamed individual] party of the first part, someone, individual; see PERSON 1, SOMEBODY.

pass *n.* **1.** [An opening through mountains] gorge, ravine, crossing, track, way, path, passageway; see also GAP 3. **2.** [A document assuring permission to pass] ticket, permit, passport, visa, order, admission, furlough, permission, right, license. **3.** [In sports, the passing of the ball from one player to another] toss, throw, fling; see PITCH 2. **4.** [*An advance] approach, sexual overture, proposition; see SUGGESTION 1.

pass *v.* **1.** [To move past] go by, run by, run past, flit by, come by, shoot ahead of, catch, come to the front, go beyond, roll on, fly past, reach, roll by, cross, flow past, glide by, go in opposite directions; see also MOVE 1. **2.** [To elapse] transpire, slip away, slip by, pass away, pass by, fly, fly by, linger, glide by, run out, drag, crawl. **3.** [To complete a course successfully] satisfy the requirements, be graduated, pass with honors; see SUCCEED 1. **4.** [To hand to others] transfer, relinquish, hand over; see GIVE 1. **5.** [To enact] legislate, establish, vote in; see ENACT. **6.** [To become enacted] carry, become law, become valid, be ratified, be established, be ordained, be sanctioned. **7.** [To exceed] excel, transcend, go beyond; see EXCEED. **8.** [To spend time] fill, occupy oneself, while away; see SPEND. **9.** [To proceed] progress, get ahead, move on, go on; see also ADVANCE 1. **10.** [To emit] give off, send forth, exude; see EMIT. —**bring to pass**

bring about, initiate, start; see CAUSE. — **come to pass** occur, develop, come about; see HAPPEN 2.

passable *a.* open, fair, penetrable, navigable, accessible, traveled, easy, broad, graded; see also AVAILABLE.

passage *n.* **1.** [A journey] voyage, crossing, trek; see JOURNEY. **2.** [A passageway] way, exit, entrance; see ENTRANCE 2. **3.** [A reading] section, portion, paragraph; see QUOTATION 1.

pass away *v.* depart, expire, pass on; see DIE.

pass by *v.* **1.** [To go past] travel, move past, depart from; see LEAVE 1, PASS 1. **2.** [To neglect] pass over, not choose, omit; see ABANDON 1, NEGLECT 1.

passé *a.* old-fashioned, out-of-date, outmoded; see OLD-FASHIONED.

passenger *n.* commuter, tourist, wanderer; see RIDER 1.

passerby *n.* witness, traveler, bystander; see OBSERVER.

passing *a.* **1.** [In the act of going past] departing, crossing, going by, gliding by, flashing by, speeding by, going in opposite directions, passing in the night; see also MOVING 1. **2.** [Of brief duration] fleeting, transitory, transient; see TEMPORARY.

passion *n.* lust, craving, sexual excitement; see DESIRE 2, EMOTION.

passionate *a.* **1.** [Excitable] vehement, hot-headed, tempestuous; see sense 2. **2.** [Ardent] intense, impassioned, loving, fervent, moving, inspiring, dramatic, melodramatic, romantic, poignant, swelling, enthusiastic, tragic, stimulating, wistful, stirring, thrilling, warm, burning, glowing, vehement, deep, affecting, eloquent, spirited, fiery, expressive, forceful, heated, hot. **3.** [Intense] strong, vehement, violent; see INTENSE.

passive *a.* **1.** [Being acted upon] receptive, stirred, influenced; see AFFECTED 1. **2.** [Not active] inactive, inert, lifeless; see IDLE.

pass off *v.* **1.** [To pretend] pass for, make a pretense of, palm off*; see PRETEND 1. **2.** [To emit] give off, send forth, eject; see EMIT.

pass on *v.* **1.** [To decide] determine, conclude, make a judgment; see DECIDE, JUDGE. **2.** [To die] expire, depart, succumb; see DIE.

pass out *v.* **1.** [To faint] swoon, lose consciousness, black out*; see FAINT. **2.** [To distribute] hand out, circulate, deal out; see DISTRIBUTE, GIVE 1.

pass over *v.* **1.** [To traverse] travel through, go over, go across; see CROSS 1. **2.** [To ignore] dismiss, overlook, neglect; see DISREGARD.

passport *n.* pass, license, permit, safe-conduct, visa, travel permit, authorization, warrant, credentials; see also IDENTIFICATION 2.

pass the buck* *v.* transfer responsibility, assign, refer; see AVOID, DELEGATE 1.

pass up *v.* dismiss, send away, reject; see DENY, REFUSE.

password *n.* countersign, signal, phrase, secret word, watchword, identification, open sesame.

past *a.* **1.** [Having occurred previously] former, preceding, gone by, foregoing, elapsed, anterior, antecedent, prior. **2.** [No longer serving] ex-, retired, earlier; see PRECEDING.

past *n.* **1.** [Past time] antiquity, long ago, the past, past times, old times, years ago, good old days, ancient times, former times, days gone by, auld lang-syne, days of old, yesterday.—*Ant.* FUTURE, the present, tomorrow. **2.** [Past events] knowledge, happenings, events; see HISTORY.

past *prep.* through, farther than, behind; see BEYOND.

paste *n.* cement, glue, mucilage; see CEMENT.

paste *v.* glue, fix, affix, repair, patch; see also STICK 1.

pastime *n.* recreation, amusement, sport; see ENTERTAINMENT, HOBBY.

pastor *n.* priest, rector, clergyman; see MINISTER 1.

pastry *n.* baked goods, dainty, delicacy, bread, goodies*, fixings*, trimmings*; see also BREAD. *Pastries include the following:* French, Danish; tart, pie, turnover, oatcake, shortbread, pudding, eclair, cake, sweet roll.

pasture *n.* grazing land, pasturage, hayfield; see FIELD 1, MEADOW.

pasty *a.* wan, pallid, sickly, ashen, anemic; see also PALE 1, DULL 2.

pat *v.* **1.** [To strike lightly] tap, beat, punch; see HIT 1. **2.** [To strike lightly and affectionately] stroke, pet, rub; see TOUCH 2.

patch *n.* piece, mend, bit, scrap, spot, application.

patch *v.* darn, mend, cover; see REPAIR.

patch up *v.* appease, adjust, compensate; see SETTLE 7.

patchwork *n.* jumble, hodgepodge, muddle; see CONFUSION, DISORDER.

patent *n.* patent right, protection, concession, control, limitation, license, copyright, privilege; see also RIGHT 1.

patent *v.* license, secure, control, limit, monopolize, safeguard, exclude, copyright.

patented *a.* copyrighted, patent applied for, trademarked, under patent, under copyright, patent pending; see also RESTRICTED.

paternal *a.* patrimonial, fatherly, protective, benevolent.

paternity *n.* progenitorship, paternal parentage, fathership; see FATHER 1.

path *n.* trail, way, track, shortcut, footpath, crosscut, footway, roadway, cinder track, byway, path; see also ROUTE 1.

pathetic *a.* touching, affecting, moving; see PITIFUL.

patience *n.* **1.** [Willingness to endure] forbearance, fortitude, composure, submission, endurance, nonresistance, self-control, passiveness, bearing, serenity, humility, yielding, poise, sufferance, long-suffering, moderation, leniency; see also RESIGNATION 1.—*Ant.* NERVOUSNESS, fretfulness, restlessness. **2.** [Ability to continue] submission, perseverance, persistence; see ENDURANCE.

patient *a.* **1.** [Enduring without complaint] submissive, meek, forbearing, mild-tempered, composed, tranquil, serene, long-suffering, unruffled, imperturbable, passive, cold-blooded, easy-going, tolerant, gentle, unresentful; see also RESIGNED.—*Ant.* IRRITABLE, violent, resentful. **2.** [Quietly persistent in an activity] steady, dependable, calm, reliable, stable, composed, unwavering, quiet, serene, unimpassioned, enduring; see also RELIABLE.—*Ant.* RESTLESS, irrepressible, feverish.

patient *n.* case, inmate, victim, sufferer, sick individual, medical case, surgical case, patient, outpatient, bed patient, emergency ward patient, convalescent, hospital case, hospitalized person, subject.

patiently *a.* **1.** [Suffering without complaint] enduringly, bravely, impassively, resignedly, numbly, forbearingly, tolerantly, submissively, meekly; see also CALMLY. **2.** [Continuing without impatience] steadily, firmly, unabatingly; see REGULARLY.

patio *n.* porch, courtyard, square; see YARD 1.

patriarch *n.* master, head of family, ancestor; see CHIEF.

patriot *n.* lover of his country, good citizen, statesman, nationalist, volunteer, loyalist, jingoist, chauvinist.

patriotic *a.* devoted, zealous, public-spirited, consecrated, dedicated, jingoistic, chauvinistic.

patriotism *n.* love of country, public spirit, good citizenship, nationality, nationalism; see also LOYALTY.

patrol *n.* guard, watch, protection; see ARMY 2.

patrol *v.* watch, walk, inspect; see GUARD.

patrolman *n.* police, police officer, constable; see POLICEMAN.

patron *n.* philanthropist, benefactor, helper, protector, encourager, champion, backer, advocate, defender, guide, leader, friend, ally, sympathizer, well-wisher, partisan, buyer, angel*, sugar daddy*, booster.—*Ant.* ENEMY, obstructionist, adversary.

patronage *n.* **1.** [Trade] commerce, trading, shopping; see BUSINESS 1. **2.** [Condescension] deference, patronization, toleration; see PRIDE 2.

patronize *v.* **1.** [To trade with] frequent, buy from, shop with; see BUY, SELL. **2.** [To assume a condescending attitude] talk down to, be overbearing, stoop, be gracious to, favor, pat on the back, play the snob, snub, lord it over; see also CONDESCEND.

patronizing *a.* condescending, gracious, stooping; see EGOTISTIC, POLITE.

pattern *n.* original, guide, copy; see MODEL 2.

pauper *n.* dependent, indigent, destitute person; see BEGGAR.

pause *v.* delay, halt, rest, catch one's breath, cease, hold back, reflect, deliberate, suspend, think twice, discontinue, interrupt; see also HESITATE.

pause *n.* lull, rest, stop, halt, truce, stay, respite, standstill, stand, deadlock, stillness, intermission, suspension, discontinuance, breathing space, hitch, hesitancy, interlude, hiatus, interim, lapse, cessation, stopover, interval, rest period, gap, stoppage.

pave *v.* lay concrete, asphalt, gravel; see COVER 1.

paved *a.* hard-surfaced, flagged, cobblestone, asphalt, concrete, brick, bricked, surfaced with wood blocks; see also COVERED 1.

pavement *n.* hard surface, paving, paving stone, paving tile, flagging, pave. *Road surfaces include the following:* concrete, asphalt, blacktop, stone, brick, tile, macadam, gravel, cobblestone, wood blocks, flagstone.

paving *n.* hard surface, concrete, paved highway; see PAVEMENT.

paw *n.* forefoot, talon, hand; see CLAW.

paw *v.* **1.** [To strike wildly] clutch, grasp, smite; see HIT 1. **2.** [To scrape with the front foot] scratch, rake, claw; see DIG 1.

pawn *v.* deposit, pledge, hock; see SELL.

pawned *a.* deposited, pledged, hocked; see SOLD OUT.

pay *n.* **1.** [Monetary return] profit, proceeds, interest, return, recompense, indemnity, reparation, rake-off*, reward, consideration, defrayment.—*Ant.* EXPENSE, disbursement, outlay. **2.** [Wages] compensation, salary, payment, hire, remuneration, commission, redress, fee, stipend, earnings, settlement, consideration, reimbursement, satisfaction, reward, time, time and a half, double time, overtime.

pay *v.* **1.** [To give payment] pay up, compensate, recompense, make payment, reward, remunerate, charge, discharge, pay a bill, foot the bill*, refund, settle, get even with, reckon with, put down, make restitution, make reparation, hand over, repay, liquidate, handle, take care of, give, confer, bequeath, defray, meet, disburse, clear, adjust, satisfy, reimburse, kick in*, plunk down*, put up*, pay as you go, fork out*, fork over*, ante up, even the score*, chip in*.—*Ant.* DECEIVE, swindle, victimize. **2.** [To produce a profit] return, pay off, pay out, show profit, yield profit, yield excess, show gain, pay dividends.—*Ant.* FAIL, lose, become bankrupt. **3.** [To retaliate] repay, punish, requite; see REVENGE.

pay back *v.* discharge a responsibility, even up, compound for; see RETURN 2.

pay down on *v.* make a payment on, pay in on, put money down on; see PAY 1.

pay for *v.* atone for, make amends for, do penance for, compensate for, make up for, make satisfaction for, expiate, make reparation for, give satisfaction for, pay the penalty for, make compensation for.

payment *n.* **1.** [The act of paying] recompense, reimbursement, restitution, subsidy, return, redress, refund, remittance, reparation, disbursement, money down, amends, cash, salary, wage, sum, payoff, repayment, defrayment, retaliation; see also PAY 1. **2.** [An installment] portion, part, amount; see DEBT.

payoff *n.* settlement, conclusion, reward; see PAY 1, PAYMENT 1.

pay off *v.* discharge, let go, drop from the payroll; see DISMISS.

payroll *n.* employees, workers, pay list; see FACULTY 2, STAFF 2.

peace *n.* **1.** [The state of being without war] armistice, pacification, conciliation, order, concord, amity, union, unity, reconciliation, brotherhood, love, unanimity; see also AGREEMENT 1, FRIENDSHIP.—*Ant.* WAR, warfare, battle. **2.** [State of being without disturbance] calm, repose, quiet, tranquillity, harmony, lull, hush, congeniality, equanimity, silence, stillness; see also REST 1.—*Ant.* FIGHT, noisiness, quarrel. **3.** [Mental or emotional calm] calmness, repose, harmony, concord, contentment, sympathy; see also COMPOSURE, RESERVE 2, TRANQUILLITY.—*Ant.* DISTRESS, disturbance, agitation. **—at peace** peaceful, quiet, tranquil; see CALM 1, 2. **—hold** (or **keep**) **one's peace** be silent, keep quiet, not speak; see SHUT UP 1. **—make peace** end hostilities, settle, reconcile; see QUIET 1.

peaceable *a.* conciliatory, pacific, peaceful; see FRIENDLY.

peaceful *a.* **1.** [At peace] quiet, tranquil, serene; see CALM 1, 2. **2.** [Inclined to peace] well-disposed, sociable, amiable; see FRIENDLY.

peacefully *a.* **1.** [Calmly] tranquilly, quietly, composedly; see CALMLY. **2.** [Without making trouble] harmoniously, placatingly, inoffensively, temperately, civilly; see also MODESTLY.

peak *n.* **1.** [A mountain] summit, top, crown; see MOUNTAIN 1. **2.** [The maximum] zenith, highest point, greatest quantity; see HEIGHT, TIP 1, TOP 1.

peaked *a.* pointed, topped, triangle-topped; see SHARP 1.

pearl *n.* nacre, margarite, cultured pearl; see JEWEL.

peasant *n.* small farmer, farm laborer, farm worker; see FARMER, LABORER, WORKMAN.

pebble *n.* pebblestone, gravel, cobblestone; see ROCK 1, STONE.

peck *n.* **1.** [A slight, sharp blow] pinch, tap, rap; see BLOW. **2.** [One fourth of a bushel] eight quarts, quarter-bushel, large amount; see MEASURE 1, QUANTITY.

peck *v.* nip, pick, tap; see BITE 1, PINCH.

peculiar *a.* **1.** [Unusual] wonderful, singular, outlandish; see STRANGE, UNUSUAL 2. **2.** [Characteristic of only one] strange, uncommon, eccentric; see CHARACTERISTIC, UNIQUE.

peculiarity *n.* distinctiveness, unusualness, singularity; see CHARACTERISTIC.

pedal *n.* treadle, foot lever, accelerator; see LEVER.

pedal *v.* treadle, operate, work; see DRIVE 2.

peddle *v.* hawk, vend, trade; see SELL.

peddler *n.* hawker, vender, seller; see BUSINESSMAN.

pedestal *n.* stand, foundation, footstall, plinth; see also COLUMN 1, SUPPORT 2.

pedestrian *n.* foot-traveler, walker, hiker; see WALKING *a.*

peek *n.* sight, glimpse, glance; see LOOK 3.

peek *v.* glance, peep, glimpse; see SEE 1.

peel *n.* husk, bark, shell; see SKIN.

peel *v.* pare, strip, tear off, pull off, flay, uncover; see also SKIN.

peeling *n.* paring, strip, sliver; see SKIN.

peep *n.* **1.** [A peek] glimpse, glance, sight; see LOOK 3. **2.** [A peeping sound] cheep, chirp, hoot; see CRY 2.

peep *v.* **1.** [To look cautiously] peek, glimpse, glance; see SEE 1. **2.** [To make a peeping sound] cheep, chirp, squeak; see CRY 2.

peer *n.* match, rival, companion; see EQUAL.

peer *v.* gaze, inspect, scrutinize; see SEE 1.

peer group *n.* equals, social group, one's peers; see ASSOCIATE, EQUAL.

peeve* *v.* irritate, annoy, anger; see BOTHER 2.

peeved *a.* sullen, irritated, upset; see ANGRY.

peevish *a.* cross, fretful, fretting; see ANGRY.

peg *n.* pin, tack, fastener; see NAIL. **—take down a peg** humiliate, criticize, diminish; see HUMBLE.

pellet *n.* pill, bead, grain; see STONE.

pell-mell *a.* impetuously, hurriedly, indiscreetly; see FOOLISHLY.

pelt *n.* fell, hair, wool; see HIDE.

pen *n.* **1.** [An enclosed place] coop, cage, corral, sty, close, concentration camp, prison, penitentiary; see also ENCLOSURE 1. **2.** [A writing instrument] *Pens include the following:* fountain, desk, drawing, ruling, artist's, reed, quill, steel, ballpoint, felt-tip.

pen *v.* **1.** [To enclose] close in, confine, coop up*; see ENCLOSE. **2.** [To write] compose, indite, commit to writing; see WRITE 1, 2.

penalize *v.* scold, chasten, castigate; see PUNISH.

penalty *n.* fine, mortification, discipline; see PUNISHMENT.

penance *n.* mortification, purgation, repentance, retribution, compensation, self-imposed atonement, fasting, suffering, sackcloth and ashes, hair shirt, reparation; see also PUNISHMENT.

pencil *n. Types of pencils include the following:* lead, mechanical, colored, drawing, indelible, charcoal, grease, eyebrow, cosmetic, drafting; chalk, crayon, stylus.

pendant *n.* earring, locket, lavaliere; see DECORATION 2, JEWELRY.

pending *a.* continuing, indeterminate, awaiting; see OMINOUS.

pendulum *n.* swing, pendant, suspended body; see DEVICE, MACHINE.

penetrable *a.* permeable, receptive, open, passable, accessible; see also POROUS.

penetrate *v.* bore, perforate, enter, insert, go through, make an entrance, stick into, jab, thrust, stab, force, make a hole, run into, run through, punch, puncture, drive into, stick, drill, eat through, spear, impale, wound, gore, sting, sink into, knife, go through, pass through.—*Ant.* LEAVE, withdraw, turn aside.

penetrating *a.* **1.** [Entering] piercing, going through, puncturing; see SHARP 1. **2.** [Mentally keen] astute, shrewd, sharp; see INTELLIGENT.

penetration *n.* **1.** [Act of entering] insertion, invasion, perforation; see ENTRANCE 1. **2.** [Mental acuteness] discernment, perception, keen-sightedness; see INTELLIGENCE 1.

peninsula *n.* point, promontory, cape; see LAND 1.

penitentiary *n.* reformatory, penal institution, pen*; see JAIL, PRISON.

penniless *a.* poverty-stricken, lacking means, indigent; see POOR 1.

penny *n.* cent, copper, red cent*; see MONEY 1.

penny ante *a.* trifling, insignificant, petty; see TRIVIAL, UNIMPORTANT.

pension *n.* annuity, premium, payment, grant, social security, gift, reward; see also ALLOWANCE.

pent-up *a.* held in check, repressed, restrained; see RESTRAINED, RESTRICTED.

people *n.pl.* **1.** [Humankind] humanity, mankind, the human race; see MAN 1. **2.** [A body of persons having racial or social ties] nationality, tribe, community; see RACE 2. **3.** [The middle and lower classes of society] mass, folk, proletariat, rabble, masses, the multitude, the majority, democracy, crowd, common people, common herd, rank and file, the underprivileged, the public, the man in the street, bourgeoisie, riffraff, the herd*, the horde, the many, the great unwashed*, hoi polloi, John Q. Public, Jane Q. Public. **4.** [Family] close relatives, kin, siblings; see FAMILY. **5.** [Society in general] they, anybody, the public; see EVERYBODY.

peopled *a.* lived in, dwelt in, sustaining human life; see INHABITED.

pep* *n.* energy, vigor, liveliness; see ACTION 1.

per *prep.* to each, for each, contained in each, according to, through, by, by means of.

perceive *v.* **1.** [See] observe, note, notice; see LOOK 2, SEE 1. **2.** [Understand] comprehend, sense, grasp; see UNDERSTAND 1.

perceived *a.* seen, felt, touched; see UNDERSTOOD 1.

percent *a.* by the hundred, reckoned on the basis of a hundred, percentaged, in a hundred, percentile.

percentage *n.* percent, rate, rate per cent, portion, section, allotment, duty, discount, commission, winnings, cut*, rake-off*, payoff, slice*; see also DIVISION 2.

perceptible *a.* perceivable, discernible, cognizable; see OBVIOUS 1.

perception *n.* **1.** [The act of perceiving] realizing, understanding, apprehending; see ATTENTION, JUDGMENT 2. **2.** [The result of perceiving] insight, knowledge, observation; see ATTITUDE, OPINION 1, VIEWPOINT.

perceptive *a.* alert, incisive, keen; see CONSCIOUS, OBSERVANT.

perch *n.* seat, pole, landing place, resting place.

perch *v.* roost, settle down, land; see REST 1, SIT.

perfect *a.* **1.** [Having all necessary qualities] complete, sound, entire; see ABSOLUTE 1, WHOLE 1, 2. **2.** [Without defect] excelling, faultless, flawless, impeccable, immaculate, unblemished, foolproof, untainted, unspotted, absolute, classical, stainless, spotless, crowning, culminating, supreme, ideal, sublime, beyond all praise, beyond compare; see also EXCELLENT, PURE 2, WHOLE 2.—*Ant.* RUINED, damaged, faulty. **3.** [Exact] precise, sharp, distinct; see ACCURATE 2.

perfect *v.* fulfill, realize, develop; see ACHIEVE, COMPLETE.

perfected *a.* completed, developed, mature, conclusive, full, elaborate, thorough; see also FINISHED 1, FULFILLED.

perfection *n.* completion, fulfillment, finishing, consummation, supremacy, ideal, ending, realization; see also ACHIEVEMENT.—*Ant.* RUIN, destruction, neglect.

perfectly *a.* excellently, fitly, correctly, flawlessly, faultlessly, supremely, ideally.—*Ant.* BADLY, poorly, incorrectly.

perforate *v.* drill, slit, stab; see PENETRATE.

perforation *n.* break, aperture, slit; see HOLE 1.

perform *v.* **1.** [To accomplish an action] do, make, achieve, rehearse, accomplish, fulfill, execute, transact, carry out, carry through, discharge, effect, enforce, administer, complete, consummate, operate, finish, realize, go about, go through with, put through, work out, devote oneself to, come through, be engrossed in, be engaged in, see to it, bring about, engage in, concern oneself with, have effect, fall to, do justice to, do one's part, make a move, follow through, apply oneself to, deal with, do something, look to, take measures, act on, lose oneself in, make it one's business, dispose of, bring to pass, do what is expected of one, put into effect, occupy oneself with, take action, address oneself to, put in action, lift a finger*, keep one's hand in*, pull off*. **2.** [To present a performance] give, present, enact, play, offer, impersonate, show, exhibit, display, act out, dramatize, execute, put on the stage, produce, act the part of, put on an act, act one's part.

performance *n.* appearance, rehearsal, exhibition, offering, representation, spectacle, review, revue, opera, play, concert, exhibit, display, show; see also DRAMA.

perfume *n.* scent, fragrance, aroma, odor, sweetness, bouquet, incense; see also SMELL 1. *Perfumes include the following:* attar of roses, sandalwood, bay, rosemary, frankincense, myrrh, eau de Cologne, musk, spice, sachet, lavender, rose geranium.

perhaps *a.* conceivably, possibly, reasonably; see MAYBE.

perilous *a.* precarious, unsafe, uncertain; see DANGEROUS.

perimeter *n.* margin, outline, border; see BOUNDARY, EDGE 1.

period *n.* **1.** [A measure of time] epoch, time, era; see AGE 3. **2.** [An end] limit, conclusion, close; see END 2. **3.** [A mark of punctuation] point, full stop, full pause, dot, ending-pitch; see also PUNCTUATION.

periodic *a.* rhythmic, regular, recurrent; see REGULAR 3.

periodical *n.* review, number, publication; see MAGAZINE, NEWSPAPER.

periodically *a.* rhythmically, systematically, annually; see REGULARLY.

peripheral *a.* external, outer, surface; see OUTSIDE.

periphery *n.* covering, perimeter, border; see OUTSIDE 1.

perish *v.* pass away, be lost, depart; see DIE.

perjure *v.* prevaricate, swear falsely, lie on the stand; see LIE 1.

perjury *n.* false statement, violation of an oath, willful falsehood; see LIE.

perk up *v.* **1.** [Be refreshed] revive, recuperate, liven up; see RECOVER 3. **2.** [Cheer or refresh] invigorate, shake, enliven; see RENEW 1, REVIVE 1.

permanence *n.* continuity, dependability, durability; see STABILITY 1.

permanent *a.* durable, enduring, abiding, uninterrupted, stable, continuing, lasting, firm, hard, tough, strong, hardy, robust, sound, sturdy, steadfast, imperishble, surviving, living, long-lived, long-standing, invariable, persisting, tenacious, persevering, unyielding, persisting, resistant, impenetrable, recurring, wearing, constant, changeless, persistent, perennial.

permanently *a.* for all time, enduringly, lastingly; see FOREVER.

permeate *v.* pervade, saturate, fill; see FILTER 1.

permissible *a.* allowable, sanctioned, to be permitted; see PERMITTED.

permission *n.* leave, liberty, consent, assent, acceptance, letting, approbation, agreement, license, permit, allowance, authority, tolerance, toleration, authorization, approval, acknowledgment, admission, verification, recognition, concurrence, promise, avowal, support, corroboration, guarantee, guaranty, visa, encouragement, ratification, grace, authority, sanction, confirmation, endorsement, affirmation, assurance, empowering, legalization, grant, indulgence, trust, concession, adjustment, settlement, accord, nod*, OK, rubber stamp*, the go-ahead*, high sign, green light*.—*Ant.* DENIAL, injunction, interdiction.

permissive *a.* authorizing, allowing, agreeable; see PERMITTED.

permit *n.* license, grant, consent; see PERMISSION.

permit *v.* sanction, tolerate, let; see ALLOW.

permitted *a.* granted, allowed, licensed, authorized, legalized, tolerated, empowered, sanctioned, conceded, consented, favored, suffered, chartered, accorded, let, indulged, privileged; see also APPROVED.—*Ant.* REFUSED, denied, prohibited.

perpendicular *a.* vertical, plumb, straight; see STRAIGHT 1.

perpetrate *v.* commit, act, do; see PERFORM 1.

perpetual *a.* **1.** [Never stopping] continual, unceasing, constant; see ENDLESS. **2.** [Continually repeating] repetitious, repeating, recurrent; see CONSTANT.

perpetually *a.* enduringly, unceasingly, permanently; see FOREVER.

perplex *v.* puzzle, confound, bewilder; see CONFUSE.

perplexed *a.* troubled, uncertain, bewildered; see DOUBTFUL.

perplexing *a.* bewildering, confusing, mystifying; see DIFFICULT 2.

per se *a.* as such, intrinsically, alone, singularly, fundamentally, in essence, in itself, by itself, virtually; see also ESSENTIALLY.

persecute *v.* afflict, harass, victimize; see ABUSE.

persecution *n.* torture, torment, teasing, provoking; see also ABUSE.

perseverance *n.* grit, resolution, pluck; see DETERMINATION.

persevere *v.* persist, remain, pursue; see ENDURE 1.

persist *v.* persevere, pursue, strive; see CONTINUE 1, ENDURE 1.

persistence *n.* constancy, resolution, stamina; see ENDURANCE.

persistent *a.* tenacious, steadfast, determined; see RESOLUTE.

person *n.* **1.** [An individual] human being, child, somebody, self, oneself, I, me, soul, spirit, character, individuality, personage, personality, identity; see also MAN 2, WOMAN 1. **2.** [An individual enjoying distinction] distinguished person, personality, success; see CHARACTER 4. **3.** [Bodily form] physique, frame, form; see BODY 1. —**in person** personally, in the flesh, present; see NEAR 1.

personable *a.* agreeable, pleasant, attractive; see CHARMING.

personage *n.* human being, someone, individual; see MAN 2, PERSON 1.

personal *a.* **1.** [Private] secluded, secret, retired; see PRIVATE. **2.** [Individual] claimed, peculiar, particular; see INDIVIDUAL, SPECIAL. **3.** [Pertaining to one's person] fleshly, corporeal, corporal; see BODILY.

personality *n.* **1.** [The total of one's nature] self, oneself, being; see CHARACTER 2. **2.** [Individual characteristics] disposition, nature, temper; see CHARACTER 1. **3.** [A notable person] celebrity, star, cynosure; see CHARACTER 4.

personally *a.* **1.** [Viewed in a personal manner] narrowly, selfishly, with concern for self; see SELFISHLY. **2.** [From the point of view of the speaker] for me, myself, for myself, for my part, as I see it, according to my opinion; see also INDIVIDUALLY.—*Ant.* CERTAINLY, objectively, scientifically.

personify *v.* **1.** [To impersonate] represent, live as, act out; see IMPERSONATE. **2.** [To represent] copy, symbolize, exemplify; see REPRESENT 3.

personnel *n.* workers, employees, group; see STAFF 2.

perspective *n.* aspect, attitude, outlook; see VIEWPOINT.

perspiration *n.* water, exudation, beads of moisture; see SWEAT.

perspire *v.* secrete, exude, lather; see SWEAT.

persuade *v.* convince, move, induce, assure, cajole, incline, talk someone into something, win over, bring around, lead to believe, lead to do something, gain the confidence of, prevail upon, overcome another's resistance, wear down, bring a person to his senses, win an argument, make one's point, gain the confidence of, make someone see the light; see also INFLUENCE.—*Ant.* NEGLECT, dissuade, dampen.

persuaded *a.* convinced, won over, moved to, led, influenced, motivated, lured, impelled, wheedled, having succumbed to pressure, brought to see the light.

persuasion *n.* **1.** [The act of persuading] inducing, influencing, enticing; see INFLUENCE. **2.** [A belief] creed, tenet, religion; see FAITH.

persuasive *a.* convincing, alluring, luring, seductive, influential, winning, enticing, impelling, moving, actuating, efficient, effective, effectual, compelling, touching, forceful, potent, powerful, swaying, pointed, strong, energetic, forcible, plausible, inveigling; see also CONVINCING.

pertain *v.* relate to, belong to, refer to; see CONCERN 1.

pertaining to *a.* belonging to, appropriate to, connected with, having to do with.

pertinence *n.* consistency, congruity, relevance; see IMPORTANCE.

pertinent *a.* appropriate, suitable, related; see RELEVANT.

perturb *v.* pester, worry, irritate; see BOTHER 2.

perturbed *a.* uneasy, anxious, restless; see TROUBLED.

pervade *v.* suffuse, permeate, spread through; see PENETRATE.

perverse *a.* wayward, delinquent, capricious; see BAD 1.

perversion *n.* **1.** [A distortion] involution, regression, abuse; see CONTORTION. **2.** [Sexual deviation] corruption, debasement, depravity, wickedness, depredation, degeneration, degradation, impairment, bestiality, self-defilement, vice; see also LEWDNESS.

pervert *v.* ruin, vitiate, divert; see CORRUPT.

pervert *n.* sex maniac, sex criminal, transvestite, rapist, autoeroticist, lecher, nymphomaniac, satyr.

perverted *a.* distorted, deviating, corrupt; see BAD 1.

pessimism *n.* unhappiness, gloom, low spirits; see DEPRESSION 2, GRIEF, SADNESS.

pessimistic *a.* **1.** [Discouraging] worrisome, troublesome, troubling; see DISMAL. **2.** [Inclined to a discouraging view] hopeless, gloomy, cynical; see SAD 1.

pest *n.* **1.** [Anything destructive] virus, germ, insect pest, bug, harmful bird, bird of prey, destructive animal. *Common pests include the following:* house fly, mosquito, flea, louse, mite, gnat, bedbug, tick, aphid, Japanese beetle, corn borer, boll weevil, squash bug, peach moth, gypsy moth, cutworm, pear slug, mouse, rat, gopher, prairie dog, woodchuck, groundhog, rabbit, mole, weasel, coyote, hawk. **2.** [A nuisance] bore, tease, annoyance; see TROUBLE 1.

pester *v.* annoy, harass, provoke; see BOTHER 2.

pestilence *n.* epidemic, endemic, sickness; see ILLNESS 1.

pet *n.* **1.** [A term of endearment] lover, dear, love; see DARLING. **2.** [Favorite] darling, idol, adored one; see FAVORITE. **3.** [A creature kept as an object of affection] *Common pets include the following:* pony, dog, cat, horse, goldfish, rabbit, hamster, guinea pig, lamb, mouse, white rat, canary, parrot.

pet *v.* **1.** [To caress] fondle, cuddle, kiss; see TOUCH 1. **2.** [*To make love] embrace, hug, neck*; see CARESS, KISS, LOVE 2.

petal *n.* floral leaf, flower part, leaf; see FLOWER.

petition *n.* prayer, request, supplication; see APPEAL 1.

petrified *a.* stone, hardened, mineralized; see FIRM 2.

petrify *v.* mineralize, clarify, solidify; see HARDEN.

petroleum *n.* crude oil, fuel, coal oil; see OIL.

petty *a.* small, insignificant, frivolous; see TRIVIAL, UNIMPORTANT.

phantom *n.* apparition, specter, shade; see GHOST.

phase *n.* condition, stage, appearance, point, aspect; see also STATE 2.

phase out *v.* slowly get rid of, gradually dispose of, weed out*; see ELIMINATE.

phenomenal *a.* extraordinary, unique, remarkable; see UNUSUAL 1.

phenomenon *n.* aspect, appearance, happening; see EVENT.

philanthropic *a.* kindhearted, benevolent, humanitarian; see HUMANE, KIND.

philosopher *n.* logician, wise man, sage, savant, Sophist, Solon. *Major philosophers include the following:* Epicurus, Plato, Aristotle, Marcus Aurelius, St. Augustine, St. Thomas Aquinas, Thomas Hobbes, John Locke, Immanuel Kant, John Stuart Mill, Friedrich Schiller, Jean Jacques Rousseau, Arthur Schopenhauer, G.W.F. Hegel, Soren Kierkegaard, Friedrich Nietzsche, William James, Karl Marx, Ernst Cassirer, Jean-Paul Sartre.

philosophical *a.* **1.** [Given to thought] reflective, cogitative, rational; see THOUGHTFUL 1. **2.** [Embodying deep thought] erudite, thoughtful, deep; see LEARNED 1, PROFOUND.

philosophize *v.* ponder, weigh, deliberate; see THINK 1.

philosophy *n.* **1.** [The study of knowledge] theory, reasoned doctrine, explanation of phenomena, logical concept, systematic view, theory of knowledge, early science, natural philosophy; see also KNOWLEDGE 1. *Fields of philosophy include the following:* aesthetics, logic, ethics, metaphysics, epistemology, psychology, axiology, ontology, teleology. *Philosophic attitudes include the following:* idealism, realism, existentialism, nihilism, mechanism, naturalism, determinism, natural realism, intuitionism, utilitarianism, nominalism, conceptualism, pragmatism, Kantianism, Hegelianism, logical empiricism, absolutism, transcendentalism, logical positivism. **2.** [A fundamental principle] truth, axiom, conception; see BASIS, LAW 4, THEORY 1. **3.** [A personal attitude or belief] outlook, view, position; see BELIEF, OPINION 1, VIEWPOINT.

phlegm *n.* spittle, discharge, spit; see SALIVA.

phobia *n.* fear, neurosis, aversion; see HATRED, RESENTMENT.

phone *n.* pay phone, home phone, wall phone, desk phone, car phone, cellular phone, fax; see also TELEPHONE.

phonograph *n.* stereo, gramophone, juke box; see RECORD PLAYER.

phony* *a.* counterfeit, imitation, artificial; see FALSE 3.

photograph *n.* photo, print, portrait, image, likeness, snapshot, microcopy, microfilm, radiograph, X-ray, photomontage, photomural, shot, pic*, close-up, candid; see also PICTURE 2, 3.

photograph *v.* take a picture, get a likeness, film, snapshot, copy, reproduce, illustrate, make an exposure, make a picture, catch a likeness, get a film, record, make a moving picture of, microfilm, snap, shoot, get a close-up.

photographer *n.* picture-taker, cameraman, cinematographer; see ARTIST.

photographic *a.* **1.** [Of photography] camera, video, film, cinematographic. **2.** [Precise] accurate, detailed, exact; see GRAPHIC 1.

photography *n.* picture-taking, portrait photography, view photography, aerial photography, tactical photography, candid camera photography, microphotography, photomicrography, videotaping.

phrase *n.* group of words, expression, slogan, catchword, maxim, wordgroup. *Grammatical phrases include the following:* prepositional, gerund, gerundive, participial, infinitive, noun, adjective, adjectival, adverbial, conjunctive, absolute, attributive.

phraseology *n.* style, manner, idiom; see DICTION.

physical *a.* **1.** [Concerning matter] material, corporeal, visible, tangible, environmental, palpable, substantial, natural, sensible, concrete, materialistic; see also REAL 2. **2.** [Concerning the body] corporal, corporeal, fleshly; see BODILY. **3.** [Concerning physics] mechanical, motive, electrical, sonic, vibratory, vibrational, thermal, radioactive, atomic, relating to matter, dynamic.

physical *n.* medical checkup, health examination, exam, checkup.

physically *a.* corporally, really, actually; see BODILY.

physician *n.* practitioner, doctor of medicine, surgeon; see DOCTOR.
physicist *n.* biophysicist, geophysicist, nuclear physicist; see SCIENTIST.
physics *n.* natural philosophy, science of the material world, science of matter and motion; see SCIENCE 1. *Divisions of physics include the following:* heat, light, electricity, electronics, sound, mechanics, dynamics, kinetics, atomic structure, radiant energy, spectroscopy, supersonics, hydraulics, pneumatics, aerodynamics, engineering.
physiology *n.* anatomy, study of organic functions, biology; see SCIENCE 1.
physique *n.* build, structure, frame; see BODY 1.
pianist *n.* performer, piano player, virtuoso; see MUSICIAN.
piano *n.* grand, baby grand, upright, cabinet, pianoforte, concert grand, spinet, clavichord, harpsichord, keyboard, electric piano, player piano; see also MUSICAL INSTRUMENT.
picayune *a.* trivial, petty, small; see TRIVIAL, UNIMPORTANT.
pick *n.* **1.** [An implement for picking] pickax, mattock, ice pick; see TOOL 1. **2.** [A blow with a pointed instrument] peck, nip, dent; see BLOW. **3.** [A selection] choice, election, preference; see CHOICE.
pick *v.* **1.** [To choose] select, pick out, separate; see CHOOSE. **2.** [To gather] pluck, pull, choose; see ACCUMULATE. **3.** [To use a pointed instrument] dent, indent, strike; see HIT 1.
pick a fight *v.* provoke, start, foment; see FIGHT.
pick apart *v.* dissect, break up, pick to pieces; see BREAK 2, CUT 1.
picked *a.* elite, special, exclusive; see EXCELLENT.
picket *n.* **1.** [A stake] stake, pole, pillar; see POST 1. **2.** [A watchman] patrolman, guard, security person, scout, lookout, sentry.
picket *v.* **1.** [To strike] walk out, blockade, boycott; see STRIKE 2. **2.** [To enclose] imprison, fence, corral; see ENCLOSE.
picking *n.* gathering, selecting, separating; see CHOICE, PREFERENCE.
pickings *n.pl.* profits, earnings, proceeds; see BOOTY.
pickle *n.* **1.** [A relish] *Varieties of pickles include the following:* cucumber, beet, green tomato, dill, bread-and-butter, sweet, gherkin, kosher, mustard, garlic, sour, pickled peppers, pickled beans, pickled apricots, pickled cherries, pickled peaches, pickled pears, piccalilli, chutney, spiced currants, spiced gooseberries, beet relish, chili sauce, catsup. **2.** [*A troublesome situation] disorder, dilemma, evil plight; see DIFFICULTY 2.
pick off *v.* snipe, get, shoot; see KILL 1.
pick out *v.* select, make a choice of, notice; see CHOOSE.
pickpocket *n.* petty criminal, thief, purse snatcher; see CRIMINAL, ROBBER.
pick up *v.* **1.** [To acquire incidentally] happen upon, find, secure; see GET 1. **2.** [To take up in the hand or arms] lift, elevate, hold up; see RAISE 1. **3.** [To receive] get, take, acquire; see RECEIVE 1. **4.** [To increase] improve, do better, grow; see INCREASE. **5.** [To improve physically] get better, get well, recover health; see RECOVER 3. **6.** [*To call for] stop for, bring along, go to get, accompany, get, invite; see also INVITE.
picnic *n.* barbecue, cookout, fish fry; see MEAL 2.
pictorial *a.* **1.** [Having the quality of a picture] graphic, scenic, striking; see GRAPHIC 1. **2.** [Making use of pictures] decorated, embellished, illustrated.
picture *n.* **1.** [A scene before the eye or the imagination] spectacle, panorama, pageant; see VIEW. **2.** [A human likeness] portrait, representation, photo, photograph, snapshot, cartoon, image, effigy, statue, statuette, figure, icon, figurine, close-up. **3.** [A pictorial representation] illustration, engraving, etching, woodcut, cut, outline, cartoon, draft, hologram, fax, graph, halftone, still, ad*, crayon sketch, pastel, watercolor, poster, oil, chart, map, plot, mosaic, blueprint, advertisement, facsimile, animation, tracing, photograph, lithograph, print; see also DESIGN, DRAWING, PAINTING 1. *Types of pictures, as works of art, include the following:* landscape, seascape, genre painting, cityscape, historical work, religious work, battle scene, triumphal entry, detail, icon, illumination, miniature, portrait, illustration, self-portrait, nude, fresco, mural, collage, pin-up, figure, still life, center spread, animal picture, hunting print, fashion plate, photomural, poster, photomontage. **4.** [A motion picture] cinema, film, show; see MOVIE. **5.** [A description] depiction, delineation, portrayal; see DESCRIPTION. **6.** [Adequate comprehension; *usually with "the"*] the idea, understanding, survey; see KNOWLEDGE 1.
picture *v.* **1.** [To depict] sketch, delineate, portray; see DRAW 2. **2.** [To imagine] envision, think of, conceive; see IMAGINE.
picturesque *a.* pictorial, scenic, graphic, striking, arresting.
pie *n.* *Varieties of pies include the following—meat pies:* fish, chicken, chicken pot, lamb, pork, beef, steak-and-kidney, cottage; *dessert pies:* apple, banana, banana cream, chiffon, apricot, peach, pear, raisin, custard, coconut cream, rice custard, pecan, rhubarb, caramel, caramel nut, chocolate, lemon, cranberry and raisin, orange, mince, prune, cherry, gooseberry, huckleberry, blueberry, strawberry, strawberry cream; see also DES-

SERT. —**as easy as pie*** not difficult, simple, uncomplicated; see EASY 2.

piece *n.* **1.** [Part] portion, share, section; see PART 1. **2.** [Work of art] study, composition, creation; see ART. **3.** [Musical, literary, or theatrical composition] suite, orchestration, production, opus, aria, song, study, arrangement, treatise, exposition, sketch, play, novel, thesis, dissertation, discourse, discussion, treatment, essay, article, paper, memoir, homily, poem, theme, monograph, commentary, review, paragraph, criticism, play, drama, melodrama, pageant, monologue, opera, overture, prelude, étude, ballet. —**go to pieces** **1.** come apart, break up, fail; see BREAK DOWN 2. **2.** quit, collapse, lose control; see CRY 1, WORRY 2. —**speak one's piece** air one's opinions, talk, reveal; see TELL 1.

piece together *v.* combine, make, create; see ASSEMBLE 2.

pier *n.* wharf, landing, quay; see DOCK.

pierce *v.* break into, stab, intrude; see PENETRATE.

piercing *a.* **1.** [Shrill] deafening, earsplitting, sharp; see LOUD 1, SHRILL. **2.** [Penetrating] entering, boring, puncturing; see SHARP 1.

piety *n.* reverence, duty, zeal; see DEVOTION.

pig *n.* piglet, swine, shoat; see ANIMAL, HOG 1.

pigeon *n.* dove, homing pigeon, turtledove; see BIRD.

piggish *a.* selfish, dirty, ravenous; see GREEDY.

pigheaded *a.* recalcitrant, insistent, stubborn; see STUBBORN.

pigment *n.* paint, oil paint, dye; see COLOR.

pigskin* *n.* football, the ball, the sphere; see FOOTBALL 2.

pigtail *n.* plait, hairdo, braid; see HAIR 1.

piker* *n.* tightwad*, skinflint, cheapskate*; see MISER.

pile *n.* **1.** [A heap] collection, mass, quantity; see COLLECTION. **2.** [*Money] affluence, riches, dough*; see WEALTH.

pile *v.* heap, stack, gather; see ACCUMULATE, STORE.

pilgrim *n.* wayfarer, wanderer, sojourner; see TRAVELER.

pilgrimage *n.* travel, wayfaring, trip; see JOURNEY.

pill *n.* **1.** [A tablet] capsule, gelcap, caplet; see MEDICINE 2. **2.** [*A contraceptive tablet; *usually with "the"*] birth control pill, oral contraceptive, prophylactic; see DRUG.

pillage *v.* plunder, loot, rob; see DESTROY, STEAL.

pillar *n.* **1.** [A column] pedestal, mast, shaft; see COLUMN 1, POST 1. **2.** [A support] mainstay, reinforcement, buttress; see SUPPORT 2.

pillow *n.* feather pillow, down pillow, foam rubber cushion, pad, padding, rest, cushion, support, headrest.

pillowcase *n.* pillow slip, pillow casing, pillow cover; see COVER 1.

pilot *n.* **1.** [Flier] airman, fighter pilot, commercial pilot, bomber pilot, automatic pilot, mechanical pilot, aeronaut, aerial navigator, navigator, aerialist. **2.** [Guide] scout, leader, director; see GUIDE.

pilot *v.* guide, conduct, manage; see LEAD 1.

pimp *n.* procurer, whoremonger, pander; see CRIMINAL.

pimple *n.* pustule, swelling, acne, whitehead, blackhead, inflammation, bump, lump, boil, carbuncle, blister, zit*; see also BLEMISH.

pin *n.* **1.** [A device to fasten goods by piercing or clasping] clip, catch, needle, bodkin, quill, clasp, nail; see also FASTENER. *Pins include the following:* common, safety, straight, hat, knitting, hair, clothes, bobby, cotter, push. **2.** [A piece of jewelry] tiepin, stickpin, brooch, badge, stud, sorority pin, fraternity pin, school pin; see also JEWELRY.

pin *v.* close, clasp, bind; see FASTEN.

pinch *n.* squeeze, compression, nip, nipping, grasp, grasping, pressure, cramp, contraction, confinement, limitation, hurt, torment. —**in a pinch** if necessary, in an emergency, under stress; see UNFORTUNATELY.

pinch *v.* **1.** [To squeeze] nip, grasp, compress, press, cramp, grab, contract, confine, limit, torment; see also HURT 1. **2.** [*To steal] take, rob, pilfer; see STEAL. **3.** [*To arrest] apprehend, detain, hold; see ARREST.

pinchers *n.pl.* pliers, pair of pincers, wrench; see TOOL 1.

pinch-hit *v.* replace, act for, succeed; see SUBSTITUTE.

pine *n.* *Pines include the following:* white, jack, bristlecone, nut, loblolly, piñon. sugar, longleaf, lodgepole, Scotch; see also TREE, WOOD 2.

pink *a.* rosy, reddish, pinkish, flushed, ruddy.

pink *n.* rose, red, roseate, blush-rose, salmon, shocking pink, blushing pink; see also COLOR.

pinnacle *n.* zenith, crest, summit; see CLIMAX.

pioneer *a.* pioneering, initial, untried; see BRAVE, EARLY 1, EXPERIMENTAL.

pioneer *n.* **1.** [One who prepares the way] pathfinder, scout, explorer; see GUIDE. **2.** [One in the vanguard of civilization] early settler, colonist, pilgrim, immigrant, colonizer, homesteader, squatter.

pioneer *v.* discover, explore, found; see COLONIZE, ESTABLISH 2, SETTLE 1.

pious *a.* divine, holy, devout; see RELIGIOUS 2.

pipe *n.* **1.** [A tube] pipeline, drain pipe, sewer, conduit, culvert, waterpipe, aqueduct, trough, passage, duct, canal, vessel. **2.** [A device for smoking] *Varieties of smok-*

ing pipes include the following: meerschaum, corncob, Missouri meerschaum, bulldog pipe, briar pipe, clay pipe, hookah, opium pipe, water pipe, churchwarden, calabash, calumet, hash pipe*. **3.** [A musical instrument] wind instrument, flute, piccolo; see MUSICAL INSTRUMENT.

pipe down* *v.* become quiet, hush, speak lower; see STOP 2.

piracy *n.* pillage, holdup, robbery; see CRIME, THEFT.

pirate *n.* thief, freebooter, plunderer, pillager, marauder, privateer, soldier of fortune, buccaneer, sea rover; see also CRIMINAL, ROBBER.

piss* *v.* pass water, go to the bathroom, pee*; see URINATE.

pistol *n.* revolver, automatic, six-shooter, rod*, cannon*, six-gun*, Saturday night special*, iron*, forty-five*, thirty-eight*; see also GUN, WEAPON.

pit *n.* abyss, cavity, depression; see HOLE 1.

pitch *n.* **1.** [Slope] slant, incline, angle; see GRADE 1, INCLINATION 2. **2.** [A throw] toss, fling, hurl, heave, cast, pitched ball, ball, strike, delivery, offering. **3.** [Musical frequency] frequency of vibration, rate of vibration, tone; see SOUND 2. **4.** [A viscous liquid] resin, gum resin, rosin; see GUM, TAR.

pitch *v.* **1.** [To throw] hurl, fling, toss; see THROW 1. **2.** [To fall forward] plunge, flop, vault; see DIVE, FALL 1. **3.** [To slope abruptly] rise, fall, tilt; see BEND, LEAN 1.

pitcher *n.* **1.** [A utensil for pouring liquid] cream pitcher, milk pitcher, water pitcher, jug, vessel, amphora; see also CONTAINER. **2.** [In baseball, one who pitches to the batter] right-hand pitcher, right-hander, left-hand pitcher, left-hander, southpaw*, lefty*, righty*, reliever*, fireballer*, hurler*, ace*.

pitchfork *n.* fork, hayfork, three-tined fork; see TOOL 1.

pitch in *v.* volunteer, work, aid; see HELP.

pitch into* *v.* assault, blame, scold; see ATTACK, FIGHT.

pitfall *n.* snare, pit, blind; see TRAP 1.

pitiful *a.* miserable, mournful, sorrowful, woeful, distressed, distressing, cheerless, comfortless, deplorable, joyless, dismal, touching, pathetic, affecting, stirring, arousing, lamentable, poignant, heart-breaking, human, dramatic, impressive, tearful, gratifying, heart-rending, depressing, afflicted, suffering, moving, vile; see also SAD 1.—*Ant.* HAPPY, cheerful, joyful.

pitiless *a.* unfeeling, heartless, cold; see INDIFFERENT.

pitter-patter *n.* thump, patter, tap; see NOISE 1.

pity *n.* sympathy, compassion, charity, softheartedness, tenderness, goodness, understanding, forbearance, mercy, kindness, warmheartedness, kindliness, brotherly love, unselfishness, benevolence, favor, condolence, commiseration, clemency, humanity.—*Ant.* HATRED, severity, ferocity. —**have** (or **take**) **pity on** show pity to, spare, pardon; see FORGIVE, PITY 2.

pity *v.* **1.** [To feel pity] feel for, sympathize with, commiserate, be sorry for, bleed for, be sympathetic to, show sympathy, express sympathy for, grieve with, weep for; see also COMFORT, SYMPATHIZE. **2.** [To be merciful to] spare, take pity on, show pity to, show forgiveness to, be merciful to, give quarter, put out of one's misery, pardon, reprieve, grant amnesty to; see also FORGIVE.—*Ant.* DESTROY, condemn, accuse.

pivot *v.* whirl, swivel, rotate; see TURN 1.

place *n.* **1.** [Position] station, point, spot; see POSITION 1. **2.** [Space] room, compass, stead, void, distance, area, seat, volume, berth, reservation, accommodation; see also EXTENT. **3.** [Locality] spot, locus, site, community, district, suburb, country, section, habitat, home, residence, abode, house, quarters; see also AREA, NEIGHBORHOOD, REGION 1. **4.** [Rank] status, position, station; see RANK 3. —**go places*** attain success, achieve, advance; see SUCCEED 1. —**in place** fitting, timely, appropriate; see FIT 1. —**in place of** as a substitute for, instead of, taking the place of; see INSTEAD. —**out of place** inappropriate, unsuitable, not fitting; see IMPROPER. —**put someone in his place** humiliate, reprimand, shame; see HUMBLE. —**take place** occur, come into being, be; see HAPPEN 2. —**take the place of** replace, act in one's stead, serve as proxy for; see SUBSTITUTE.

place *v.* **1.** [To put in a place] locate, assign, deposit; see PUT 1. **2.** [To put in order] fix, arrange, group; see ORDER 3.

placed *a.* established, settled, fixed, located, rated, deposited, lodged, quartered, planted, set, arranged, stowed, stored, installed, situated, implanted, set up, ordered.

placement *n.* situation, position, arrangement; see ORGANIZATION 1.

plagiarism *n.* literary theft, forgery, fraud; see THEFT.

plague *n.* epidemic, pestilence, disease; see ILLNESS 2.

plague *v.* disturb, trouble, irk; see BOTHER 2.

plain *a.* **1.** [Obvious] open, manifest, clear; see OBVIOUS 1, 2, UNDERSTANDABLE. **2.** [Simple] unadorned, unostentatious, unpretentious; see MODEST 2. **3.** [Ordinary] everyday, average, commonplace; see COMMON 1. **4.** [Homely] plain-featured, coarse-featured, unattractive; see UGLY 1. **5.** [In blunt language] outspoken, candid, impolite; see RUDE 2.

plain *n.* prairie, steppe, pampas, expanse, open country, lowland, flat, level land, mesa, savanna, moorland, moor, heath, tundra, veldt, downs, the High Plains; see also FIELD 1, MEADOW.

plainly *a.* evidently, visibly; see CLEARLY 1, 2.

plan *n.* 1. [A preliminary sketch] draft, diagram, map, chart, time line, design, outline, representation, form, drawing, view, projection, rough, rough draft, road map. 2. [A proposed sequence of action] plans, scheme, project, flow chart, scope, outline, idea, handling, manipulating, projection, undertaking, method, design, tactics, procedure, treatment, intention, policy, course of action, plot, conspiracy, expedient, strategy, stratagem, arrangement, way of doing things, angle*, the picture; see also PROGRAM 2, PURPOSE 1. 3. [Arrangement] layout, method, disposition; see ORDER 3.

plan *v.* 1. [To plot an action in advance] prepare, scheme, devise, invent, outline, project, contrive, shape, design, map, plot a course, form a plan, think out, concoct, engineer, figure on, intrigue, conspire, frame, steer one's course, establish guidelines, set parameters, work up, work out, line up, plan an attack, come through, calculate on, make arrangements, take measures, bargain for, cook up*, put on ice*. 2. [To arrange in a preliminary way] outline, draft, sketch, lay out, map out, preprint, organize, prepare a sketch, chart, map, draw, trace, design, illustrate, depict, delineate, represent, shape, chalk out, rough in, block out, block in. 3. [To have in mind] propose, think, contemplate; see INTEND 1.

plane *n.* 1. [A plane surface] level, extension, horizontal, flat, sphere, face, stratum. 2. [A tool for smoothing wood] electric planer, jointer, foreplane; see TOOL 1. *Types include the following:* jack, smoothing, jointing, block, circular, rabbet, grooving, routing, scraper, dado, trying, bullnose, toothing, chamfer. 3. [An airplane] aircraft, airliner, aeroplane, airship, heavier-than-air craft, shuttle, jet, jet plane. *Kinds of planes include the following:* propeller, jet, rocket, scout, observation, reconnaissance, transport, pursuit, commercial, passenger; biplane, triplane, monoplane, racer, glider, bomber, seaplane, hydroplane, fighter, fighter-bomber, dive bomber, interceptor, turbojet, stratojet, helicopter, gunship, gyroplane, amphibian, sailplane.

plane *v.* finish, smooth, level; see FLATTEN.

planet *n.* celestial body, heavenly body, luminous body, wandering star, planetoid, asteroid, star. *The known planets are as follows:* Mercury, Venus, Earth, Mars, Jupiter, Saturn, Uranus, Neptune, Pluto, the asteroids.

plank *n.* board, planking, sheet; see LUMBER.

planned *a.* projected, budgeted, in the budget, provided for, on the drawing board, programmed, in the making, under consideration, on the docket, prospective, cut out, cut and dried, under advisement, prepared.

planning *n.* preparation, devising, outlining; see PLAN 2.

plans *n.pl.* outline, expectations, planned procedure; see PLAN 1, 2, PROGRAM 2, SKETCH.

plant *n.* shrub, weed, bush, slip, shoot, cutting, sprout, seedling, plantlet, bulb, flower.

plant *v.* put in the ground, sow, farm, set out, pot, start, transplant, seed, stock, colonize, settle, establish, locate.

plantation *n.* acreage, estate, ranch; see FARM.

planted *a.* cultivated, sown, seeded, stocked, implanted, strewn, drilled.

planting *n.* sowing, seeding, drilling; see FARMING.

plaster *n.* mortar, binding, plaster of Paris; see CEMENT.

plaster *v.* coat, bind, cement; see COVER 1.

plastic *a.* substitute, synthetic, cellulose; see SYNTHETIC.

plastic *n.* synthetic, artificial product, substitute, plastic material, processed material, polymerized substance, thermoplastic, cellophane, melamine, vinyl, nylon, PVC.

plate *n.* 1. [A flat surface] lamina, slice, stratum; see PLANE 1. 2. [A full-page illustration] photography, lithograph, etching; see ILLUSTRATION, PICTURE 3. 3. [A flattish dish] dinner plate, soup plate, salad plate, casserole, dessert plate, platter, trencher, china, serving dish; see also DISH 1. 4. [Food served on a plate] helping, serving, course; see MEAL 2. 5. [In baseball, the base immediately before the catcher] home base, home plate, home; see BASE 4.

plate *v.* laminate, stratify, layer, scale, flake, overlay, gild, nickel, bronze, chrome, silver, enamel, encrust, cover.

plateau *n.* tableland, mesa, elevation; see HILL, PLAIN.

platform *n.* 1. [A stage] dais, pulpit, speaker's platform, rostrum, stand, floor, staging, terrace. 2. [A program] principles, policies, the party planks*; see PROGRAM 2.

platoon *n.* detachment, military unit, company; see ARMY 2.

platter *n.* tray, serving platter, meat platter; see DISH 1, PLATE 3.

plausible *a.* probable, credible, supposable; see LIKELY 1.

play *n.* 1. [Amusement] enjoyment, diversion, pleasure; see ENTERTAINMENT. 2. [Recreation] relaxation, game, sport; see ENTERTAINMENT. 3. [Fun] frolic, happiness, sportiveness; see FUN. 4. [A drama] performance, musical, show; see DRAMA. 5. [Sport] exhibition, match, competition; see SPORT 1, 3. 6. [Action] activity, movement, working; see ACTION 1. **—make a play for*** make advances to, court, woo; see TRY 1.

play *v.* **1.** [To amuse oneself] entertain oneself, revel, make merry, carouse, play games, rejoice, have a good time, idle away, horse around*.—*Ant.* MOURN, grieve, sulk. **2.** [To frolic] frisk, sport, cavort, joke, dance, play games, make jokes, be a practical joker, show off, jump about, skip, gambol, caper.—*Ant.* DRAG, mope, droop. **3.** [To produce music] perform, execute, work, cause to sound, finger, pedal, bow, plunk, tinkle, pipe, toot, mouth, pump, fiddle, sound, strike, saw, scrape, twang, pound, thump, tickle. **4.** [To engage in sport] participate, engage, practice; see COMPETE. **5.** [To pretend] imagine, suppose, think; see PRETEND 1.

play down *v.* belittle, hold back, minimize; see RESTRAIN.

player *n.* **1.** [One who takes part in a game] member, athlete, sportsman, sportswoman, amateur, professional, gymnast, acrobat, swimmer, diver, trackman, champ*, pro*, semipro*, jock*; see also CONTESTANT. **2.** [An actor] performer, entertainer, thespian; see ACTOR, ACTRESS.

playful *a.* joking, whimsical, comical; see FUNNY 1.

playground *n.* playing field, park, school ground, municipal playground, yard, school yard, diamond, gridiron.

playing *a.* sportive, sporting, gamboling; see ACTIVE.

playmate *n.* comrade, neighbor, companion; see FRIEND.

plaything *n.* gadget, amusement, trinket; see DOLL, GAME 1, TOY 1.

playwright *n.* scripter, scenarist, tragedian; see AUTHOR, WRITER.

plea *n.* **1.** [An appeal] overture, request, supplication; see APPEAL 1. **2.** [A form of legal defense] pleading, argument, case; see DEFENSE 2.

plead *v.* **1.** [To beg] implore, beseech, solicit; see ASK, BEG. **2.** [To enter a plea] present, allege, cite; see DECLARE.

plead guilty *v.* confess, repent, concede; see ADMIT 2.

pleading *a.* imploring, supplicating, desirous.

pleasant *a.* **1.** [Affable] agreeable, attractive, obliging, charming, mild, amusing, kindly, mild-mannered, gracious, genial, amiable, polite, urbane, cheerful, sympathetic, civil, cordial, engaging, social, bland, diplomatic, civilized, good-humored, good-natured, soft, fun, delightful, jovial, jolly.—*Ant.* SULLEN, unsympathetic, unkind. **2.** [Giving pleasure; *said of occasions, experiences, and the like*] gratifying, pleasurable, agreeable, cheering, amusing, welcome, refreshing, satisfying, all right, satisfactory, adequate, acceptable, comfortable, diverting, fascinating, adorable, enjoyable, delightful, sociable, lively, exciting, glad, festive, cheerful, entertaining, relaxing, joyous, joyful, merry, happy, pleasing, favorable, bright, sunny, brisk, catchy, sparkling, enlivening, colorful, light, humorous, laughable, comforting.—*Ant.* SAD, unhappy, disagreeable.

pleasantly *a.* pleasingly, charmingly, welcomely; see AGREEABLY.

please *interj.* if you please, if it please you, may it please you, by your leave.

please *v.* **1.** [To give pleasure] gratify, satisfy, make up to; see ENTERTAIN. **2.** [To desire] wish, demand, command; see WANT 1. **—if you please** if you will, if I may, by your leave; see PLEASE.

pleased *a.* gratified, satisfied, charmed; see HAPPY.

pleasing *a.* charming, agreeable, delightful; see PLEASANT 1.

pleasure *n.* **1.** [Enjoyment] bliss, delight, ease; see HAPPINESS. **2.** [Will] want, preference, wish; see DESIRE 1.

pleat *n.* pleating, tuck, crease; see FOLD.

pleat *v.* ruffle, crease, gather; see FOLD.

pledge *n.* guarantee, token, agreement; see PROMISE 1.

pledge *v.* swear, vow, vouch; see PROMISE 1.

plentiful *a.* **1.** [Bountiful] prolific, fruitful, profuse, lavish, liberal, unsparing, inexhaustible, replete, generous, abundant, extravagant, improvident, excessive, copious, superabundant, over-liberal, superfluous, overflowing, flowing.—*Ant.* STINGY, niggardly, skimpy. **2.** [Existing in plenty] sufficient, abundant, copious, ample, overflowing, large, chock-full, teeming, unlimited, well-provided, flowing, full, flush, lush with, pouring, fruitful, swarming, swimming, abounding.—*Ant.* POOR, scant, scanty.

plenty *n.* abundance, fruitfulness, fullness, lavishness, deluge, torrent, sufficient, bounty, profusion, adequacy, flood, avalanche, good store, limit, capacity, adequate stock, enough and to spare, everything, all kinds of, all one wants, all one can eat and drink, more than one knows what to do with, too much of a good thing, a good bit, all one needs, all one can use, a great deal, a lot*, lots*, oodles*.

pliable *a.* limber, supple, plastic; see FLEXIBLE.

pliant *a.* limber, supple, plastic; see FLEXIBLE.

pliers *n.pl.* pinchers, wrench, pincers, tongs, forceps, tweezers.

plod *v.* trudge, hike, plug; see WALK 1.

plop *v.* thump, thud, bump; see SOUND.

plot *n.* **1.** [An intrigue] conspiracy, scheme, artifice; see TRICK 1. **2.** [The action of a story] plan, scheme, outline, design, development, progress, unfolding, movement, climax, events, incidents, enactment, suspense, structure, build-up, scenario. **3.**

[A piece of ground] parcel, land, division; see AREA, LOT 1.

plot *v.* **1.** [To devise an intrigue] frame, contrive, scheme; see PLAN 1. **2.** [To plan] sketch, outline, draft; see PLAN 2.

plow *n. Plows include the following:* moldboard, gang, steam, tractor, double, straddle, sulky, wheel, shovel, hand; lister, hoe plow or horse-hoe, garden plow or wheel hoe, (corn) cultivator; see also TOOL 1.

plow *v.* **1.** [To use a plow] break, furrow, cultivate, turn, plow up, turn over, till, list, ridge, break ground, do the plowing; see also FARM. **2.** [To act like a plow] smash into, rush through, shove apart; see DIG 1, PUSH 1.

plug *n.* **1.** [An implement to stop an opening] cork, stopper, stopple, filling, stoppage, spigot, wedge. **2.** [An electrical fitting] attachment plug, fitting, connection, wall plug, floor plug, plug fuse. **3.** [A large pipe with a discharge valve] water plug, fire hydrant, fire plug; see PIPE 1.

plug *v.* stop, fill, obstruct, secure, ram, make tight, drive in; see also STOP 2.

plug in *v.* connect, make a connection, bring in electricity; see JOIN 1, 3.

plum *n. Plums and plumlike fruits include the following:* freestone, Damson, Satsuma, Green Gage, Reine Claude, Sugar plum, French prune, Stanley prune; see also FRUIT.

plumber *n.* tradesman, metal worker, handy man; see WORKMAN.

plumbing *n.* pipes, water pipes, sewage pipes, heating pipes, bathroom fixtures, sanitary provisions; see also PIPE 1.

plummet *v.* plunge, fall, nosedive; see DIVE, FALL 1.

plump *a.* obese, stout, fleshy; see FAT.

plunder *v.* burn, steal, lay waste; see RAID, RAVAGE.

plunge *v.* fall, throw oneself, rush; see DIVE, JUMP 1.

plural *a.* few, a number of, abundant; see MANY h.

plurality *n.* majority, advantage in votes cast, favorable returns; see LEAD 1, MAJORITY 1.

plus *a. & prep.* added to, additional, additionally, increased by, with the addition of, surplus, positive; see also EXTRA.—*Ant.* LESS, minus, subtracted from.

plush* *a.* elegant, luxurious, sumptuous; see RICH 2.

P.M. *abbrev.* after noon, afternoon, evening, before midnight, shank of the evening, sunset.

pneumonia *n.* pneumonitis, lobar pneumonia, croupous pneumonia; see ILLNESS 2.

poach *v.* filch, pilfer, smuggle; see STEAL.

pock *n.* flaw, hole, mark; see BLEMISH, SCAR.

pocket *a.* small, tiny, miniature; see LITTLE 1, MINUTE 1.

pocket *n.* **1.** [A cavity] hollow, opening, air pocket; see HOLE 1. **2.** [A pouch sewed into a garment] pouch, poke, sac, pod. *Kinds of pockets include the following:* patch, slash, inset, watch, coin, invisible, pants, jacket, coat, vest, inner, outer, inside. **3.** [Small area] isolated group, enclave, survival; see AREA. **—in someone's pocket*** controlled, under control, regulated; see MANAGED.

pocket *v.* conceal, hide, enclose; see STEAL.

pocketbook *n.* wallet, pouch, coin purse; see BAG, PURSE.

pod *n.* seed vessel, bean pod, pea pod; see SEED.

poem *n.* poetry, lyric, sonnet, ballad, quatrain, blank verse, free verse, song, composition, creation; see also WRITING 2.

poet *n.* writer, poemwriter, bard, versifier, minstrel, troubadour, verse maker, maker of verses, lyrist, author of the lyric, dramatic poet, dramatist, lyric poet, writer of lyrics, lyricist, poetaster; see also ARTIST, WRITER. *Major poets include the following—British:* Geoffrey Chaucer, Edmund Spenser, William Shakespeare, John Donne, John Milton, John Dryden, Alexander Pope, Samuel Johnson, Robert Burns, William Blake, William Wordsworth, Samuel Taylor Coleridge, Lord Byron, John Keats, Percy Bysshe Shelly, Alfred Lord Tennyson, Robert Browning, Gerard Manley Hopkins, William Butler Yeats, T.S. Eliot, Dylan Thomas, Philip Larkin; *American:* Edgar Allan Poe, Walt Whitman, Emily Dickinson, Edwin Arlington Robinson, Robert Frost, Carl Sandburg, Ezra Pound, Wallace Stevens, E.E. Cummings, Robert Lowell, Marianne Moore; *Classical Greek:* Homer, Pindar, Aeschylus, Sophocles, Euripides; *Latin:* Virgil, Lucretius, Ovid, Horace, Catullus, Juvenal; *European:* Dante Alighieri, Petrarch, Ludovico Ariosto, François Villon, Jean de La Fontaine, Charles Baudelaire, Stéphane Mallarmé, Paul Verlaine, Arthur Rimbaud, Victor Hugo, Pedro Calderón, Federico Garcia Lorca, Pablo Neruda, Luis Vaz de Camões, Wolfgang von Goethe, Friedrich Schiller, Heinrich Heine, Rainer Maria Rilke, Bertolt Brecht, Alexander Pushkin, Boris Pasternak, Vladimir Mayakovski.

poetic *a.* poetical, lyric, lyrical, metrical, tuneful, elegiac, romantic, dramatic, iambic, dactylic, spondaic, trochaic, anapestic, imaginative.

poetry *n.* poem, song, versification, metrical composition, rime, rhyme, poesy, stanza, rhythmical composition, poetical writings. *Forms of verse include the following:* sonnet, Shakespearean sonnet, Italian sonnet, Miltonic sonnet, Wordsworthian sonnet, Chaucerian stanza, Spenserian stanza, heroic couplet, Alexandrine, iambic pentameter, rhyme royal, ottava rima, couplet, distich, ode, epode, triolet, rondeau, rondel, rondelet, tanka, haiku, ballade, sestine, villanelle, limerick, blank verse, free verse, stop-short, strophic verse, stanzaic verse, assonance, accentual verse, alliterative verse.

pogrom *n.* slaughter, mass murder, massacre, genocide; see also MURDER.

point *n.* **1.** [A position having no extent] location, spot, locality; see POSITION 1. **2.** [A sharp, tapered end] end, pointed end, needle point, pin point, barb, prick, spur, spike, snag, spine, claw, tooth, calk, sticker; see also TIP 1. **3.** [Anything having a point] sword, dagger, stiletto; see KNIFE, NEEDLE. **4.** [Purpose] aim, object, intent; see PURPOSE 1. **5.** [Meaning] force, drift, import; see MEANING. **6.** [A detail] case, feature, point at issue; see CIRCUMSTANCE 1, DETAIL. **—at** or **on the point of** on the verge of, close to, almost; see NEAR 1. **—beside the point** immaterial, not pertinent, not germane; see IRRELEVANT. **—make a point of** stress, emphasize, make an issue of; see DECLARE. **—to the point** pertinent, apt, exact; see RELEVANT.

point *v.* **1.** [To indicate] show, name, denote; see NAME 2. **2.** [To direct] guide, steer, influence; see LEAD 1.

pointed *a.* **1.** [Sharp] fine, keen, spiked; see SHARP 1. **2.** [Biting or insinuating] caustic, tart, trenchant; see SARCASTIC.

pointer *n.* **1.** [A pointing instrument] hand, rod, indicator, dial, gauge, director, index, mark, signal-needle, register. **2.** [A variety of dog] hunting dog, gun dog, game dog; see DOG. **3.** [*A hint] clue, tip, warning; see HINT.

pointing *a.* showing, signifying, denoting; see SHOWN 1.

pointless *a.* **1.** [Dull] uninteresting, prosaic, not pertinent; see IRRELEVANT, TRIVIAL, UNNECESSARY. **2.** [Blunt] worn, obtuse, rounded; see DULL 1. **3.** [Ineffective] useless, powerless, impotent; see INCOMPETENT, WEAK 1, 2.

point of view *n.* outlook, position, approach; see ATTITUDE.

point out *v.* indicate, show, denote; see NAME 2.

poise *n.* balance, gravity, equilibrium; see COMPOSURE, DIGNITY.

poison *n.* virus, bane, toxin, infection, germ, bacteria, oil, vapor, gas. *Poisons include the following:* rattlesnake, copperhead, black-widow-spider, tarantula venom; smallpox, yellow-fever, common-cold, flu virus; poison oak, poison ivy, carbon monoxide gas, cooking gas, arsenic, lead, strychnine, oxalic, sulfuric, hydrochloric, nitric, carbolic, prussic, hydrocyanic acid; cantharides, caustic soda, lye, belladonna, aconite, lead arsenate, blue vitriol or copper sulfate, nicotine.

poison *v.* infect, injure, kill, murder, destroy, corrupt, pervert, undermine, defile, harm, taint, make ill, cause violent illness.—*Ant.* HELP, benefit, purify.

poisoned *a.* **1.** [Suffering from poisoning] infected, indisposed, diseased; see SICK. **2.** [Dying of poison] fatally poisoned, beyond recovery, succumbing; see DYING 1. **3.** [Polluted with poison] contaminated, tainted, defiled, corrupted, venomous, virulent, impure, malignant, noxious, deadly, toxic; see also POISONOUS.—*Ant.* PURE, fresh, untainted.

poisonous *a.* bad, noxious, hurtful, dangerous, malignant, infective, venomous, virulent, vicious, corrupt, morbid, fatal, pestilential, toxic, deadly, destructive; see also HARMFUL.—*Ant.* HEALTHY, wholesome, nourishing.

poke *n.* jab, thrust, punch; see BLOW.

poke *v.* jab, punch, crowd; see PUSH 1.

polar *a.* glacial, frozen, frigid; see COLD 1.

pole *n.* shaft, flagpole, flagstaff; see POST 1.

police *n.* arm of the law, law enforcement body, FBI, police officers, policemen, police force, detective force, military police, Royal Canadian Mounted Police, New York's Finest*.

police *v.* watch, control, patrol; see GUARD.

policeman *n.* patrolman, officer, magistrate, process server, constable, cop*, copper*, flatfoot*, fuzz*, the Man*, speed cop*, bobby*, pig*. *Police officers include the following:* beat patrolman, mounted police, motorcycle police, traffic police, squad-car police, municipal police, state police, highway patrol, detective, federal agent, federal investigator, fed*, narc*, FBI agent, prefect, inspector, member of the homicide squad, member of the vice squad.

police state *n.* dictatorship, autocracy, authoritarian government; see TYRANNY.

policy *n.* course, procedure, method, system, strategy, tactics, administration, management, theory, doctrine, behavior, scheme, design, arrangement, organization, plan, order.

polish *n.* shine, burnish, glaze; see FINISH 2.

polish *v.* burnish, furbish, finish; see SHINE 3.

polished *a.* **1.** [Bright] glossy, shining, gleaming; see BRIGHT 1. **2.** [Refined] polite, well-bred, cultured; see REFINED 2.

polite *a.* obliging, thoughtful, mannerly, attentive, pleasant, gentle, mild, nice, concerned, considerate, solicitous, bland, condescending, honey-tongued, amiable, gracious, cordial, considerate, good-natured, sympathetic, interested, smooth, diplomatic, kindly, kind, kindly disposed, affable, agreeable, civil, complacent, respectful, amenable, gallant, genteel, gentlemanly, mannered, sociable, ingratiating, neighborly, friendly, respectful.—*Ant.* EGOTISTIC, insolent, pompous.

politely *a.* thoughtfully, considerately, attentively, solicitously, cordially, graciously, amiably, kindheartedly, compassionately, gently, urbanely, affably, agreeably, civilly, gallantly, complacently, sociably, elegantly, gracefully, charmingly, ingratiatingly, winningly, tactfully, in good humor, with good grace; see also RESPECTFULLY.

politeness *n.* refinement, culture, civility; see COURTESY 1.

political *a.* legislative, executive, administrative; see GOVERNMENTAL.

politician *n.* officeholder, office seeker, party man, partisan, legislator, congressman, member of parliament, politico.

politics *n.* practical government, functional government, systematic government, domestic affairs, internal affairs, foreign affairs, matters of state, campaigning, getting votes, seeking nomination, electioneering, being up for election, running for office.

poll *n.* **1.** [A census] vote, consensus, ballot; see CENSUS. **2.** [A voting place; *usually plural*] ballot box, voting machines, polling place, polling area.

poll *v.* question, register, enroll; see EXAMINE, LIST 1.

pollute *v.* deprave, soil, stain; see DIRTY, POISON.

polluted *a.* corrupted, defiled, poisoned; see DIRTY 1.

pollution *n.* corruption, defilement, adulteration, blight, soiling, fouling, foulness, taint, tainting, polluting, decomposition, desecration, profanation, abuse, deterioration, rottenness, impairment, misuse, infection, besmearing, besmirching, smirching. *Some common pollutants of the air and water include the following:* sewage, soapsuds, garbage, factory waste, detergent, carbon monoxide, automobile or bus or truck exhaust, pesticides, factory smoke.

poltergeist *n.* spirit, spook, supernatural visitant; see GHOST.

polygamy *n.* polyandry, plural marriage, bigamy; see MARRIAGE.

pomp *n.* magnificence, affectation, splendor; see MAGNIFICENCE.

pompous *a.* arrogant, haughty, proud; see EGOTISTIC.

pond *n.* fishpond, millpond, lily pond; see LAKE, POOL 1.

ponder *v.* meditate, deliberate, consider; see THINK 1.

ponderous *a.* dull, weighty, lifeless; see HEAVY.

pony *n.* Shetland pony, bronco, mustang; see HORSE.

poodle *n.* French poodle, French barbet, fancy dog; see DOG.

pool *n.* **1.** [Small body of liquid, usually water] puddle, mud puddle, pond, fishpond, millpond; see also LAKE. **2.** [Supply] funds, provisions, amount available; see EQUIPMENT. **3.** [Game] snooker, 8-ball, billiards; see GAME 1.

pool *v.* combine, merge, blend; see JOIN 1.

poor *a.* **1.** [Lacking worldly goods] indigent, penniless, moneyless, impecunious, destitute, needy, poverty-stricken, underprivileged, fortuneless, starved, pinched, reduced, beggared, emptyhanded, meager, scanty, insolvent, ill-provided, ill-furnished, in want, suffering privation, in need, poor as a church mouse, broke, hard up, down and out.—*Ant.* WEALTHY, well-to-do, affluent. **2.** [Lacking excellence] pitiful, paltry, contemptible, miserable, pitiable, dwarfed, insignificant, diminutive, ordinary, common, mediocre, trashy, shoddy, worthless, sorry, base, mean, coarse, vulgar, inferior, imperfect, smaller, lesser, below par, subnormal, under average; second-rate, third-rate, fourth-rate, etc.; reduced, defective, deficient, lower, subordinate, minor, secondary, humble, second-hand, pedestrian, beggarly, tawdry, petty, unimportant, bad, cheap, flimsy, threadbare, badly made, less than good, unwholesome, lacking in quality, dowdy, second-class, shabby, gaudy, mass-produced, squalid, trivial, sleazy, trifling, unsuccessful, second-best, tasteless, insipid, rustic, crude, odd, rock-bottom, garish, flashy, showy, loud, unsightly, affected, ramshackle, tumble-down, glaring, artificial, newfangled, out-of-date, crummy*, junky*, two-bit*, raunchy*, corny*, cheesy*; see also INADEQUATE, UNSATISFACTORY. **3.** [Lacking strength] puny, feeble, infirm; see WEAK 1. **4.** [Lacking vigor or health] indisposed, impaired, imperfect; see SICK. **5.** [Lacking fertility] infertile, unproductive, barren; see STERILE 1, 2, WORTHLESS.

poor *n.* needy, forgotten man, the unemployed, underdogs, the underprivileged, beggars, the impoverished masses, second-class citizen, have-nots; see also PEOPLE 3.

poorly *a.* defectively, crudely, unsuccessfully; see BADLY 1, INADEQUATELY.

pop *n.* **1.** [A slight explosive sound] report, burst, shot; see NOISE 1. **2.** [A carbonated drink] soda pop, ginger pop, soda water, beverage, soft drink; see also DRINK 2.

pop *v.* dart, leap, protrude; see JUMP 1.

Pope *n.* head of the Roman Catholic Church, bishop of Rome, the Holy Father; see PRIEST.

poppy *n.* bloom, blossom, herb; see DRUG, FLOWER.

populace *n.* masses, commonality, multitude; see MAN 1, PEOPLE 3.

popular *a.* **1.** [Generally liked] favorite, well-liked, approved, pleasing, suitable, well-received, sought, fashionable, stylish, beloved, likable, lovable, attractive, praised, promoted, recommended, in the public eye, celebrated, noted, admired, famous, run after*.—*Ant.* UNKNOWN, in disrepute, out of favor. **2.** [Cheap] low-priced, popular-priced, marked down; see CHEAP 1, ECONOMICAL 2. **3.** [Commonly accepted] general, familiar, demanded, in demand, prevalent, prevailing, current, in use, widespread, ordinary, adopted, embraced, having caught on, in the majority; see also FASHIONABLE, MODERN 1. **4.** [Pertaining to the common people] proletarian, accessible, neighborly; see DEMOCRATIC, REPUBLICAN.

popularity *n.* approval, general esteem, widespread acceptance, following, prevalence, universality, demand, fashionableness, the rage*.

popularly *a.* commonly, usually, ordinarily; see REGULARLY.

populated *a.* crowded, teeming, populous, peopled, urban, inhabited; see also INHABITED.

population *n.* inhabitants, dwellers, citizenry, natives, group, residents, culture, community, state, populace; see also SOCIETY 2.

porch *n.* entrance, doorstep, stoop; see ENTRANCE 2.

pore *n.* opening, foramen, orifice, vesicle; see also HOLE 1.

pork *n.* ham, bacon, chops; see MEAT.

pornographic *a.* immoral, dirty, obscene; see LEWD 2.

pornography *n.* vulgarity, obscenity, smut; see LEWDNESS.

porous *a.* pervious, permeable, acceptable; see OPEN 1.

port *n.* haven, anchorage, gate; see DOCK.

portable *a.* transportable, transferable, manageable; see MOVABLE.

portal *n.* gateway, opening, ingress; see DOOR, ENTRANCE 2, GATE.

portfolio *n.* **1.** [A flat container] briefcase, attaché case, folder; see BAG, CONTAINER. **2.** [Assets, especially stocks and bonds] holdings, selection, documents; see WEALTH.

portion *n.* section, piece, part; see DIVISION 2, SHARE.

portrait *n.* likeness, portraiture, representation; see PAINTING 1, PICTURE 4.

portray *v.* depict, characterize, reproduce; see DESCRIBE, REPRESENT 2.

portrayal *n.* depiction, replica, likeness; see DESCRIPTION, IMITATION 2.

pose *n.* artificial position, affectation, attitudinizing; see FAKE, PRETENSE 1.

pose *v.* **1.** [To pretend] profess, feign, make believe; see ACT 1, PRETEND 1. **2.** [To assume a pose for a picture] model, adopt a position, posture; see SIT.

posh* *a.* elegant, stylish, opulent; see RICH 2, FASHIONABLE.

position *n.* **1.** [A physical position] location, locality, spot, seat, ground, environment, post, whereabouts, bearings, station, point, place, stand, space, surroundings, situation, site, geography, region, tract, district, scene, setting; see also AREA, PLACE 3. **2.** [An intellectual position] view, belief, attitude; see JUDGMENT 3, OPINION 1. **3.** [An occupational position] office, employment, occupation; see JOB 1, PROFESSION 1. **4.** [A social position] station, state, status; see RANK 3. **5.** [Posture] pose, carriage, bearing; see POSTURE 1.

positive *a.* **1.** [Definite] decisive, actual, concrete; see DEFINITE 1, REAL 2. **2.** [Emphatic] peremptory, assertive, obstinate; see EMPHATIC, RESOLUTE. **3.** [Certain] sure, convinced, confident; see CERTAIN 1.

positively *a.* **1.** [In a positive manner] assertively, uncompromisingly, dogmatically, arbitrarily, stubbornly, obstinately, emphatically, dictatorially, imperatively, decidedly, absolutely, insistently, authoritatively, assuredly, confidently, unhesitatingly, with conviction. **2.** [Without doubt] undoubtedly, unmistakably, undeniably; see SURELY.

posse *n.* lynch mob, armed band, police force; see POLICE.

possess *v.* hold, occupy, control; see MAINTAIN 3, OWN 1.

possessed *a.* **1.** [Insane] mad, crazed, violent; see INSANE. **2.** [Owned] kept, enjoyed, in one's possession; see HELD, OWNED.

possession *n.* **1.** [Ownership] proprietary rights, hold, mastery; see OWNERSHIP. **2.** [Property] personal property, real estate, something possessed; see PROPERTY 1, 2.

possessions *n.pl.* belongings, goods, effects; see ESTATE, PROPERTY 1.

possessor *n.* holder, proprietor, occupant; see OWNER.

possibility *n.* **1.** [The condition of being possible] plausibility, feasibility, workableness; see CHANCE 2. **2.** [A possible happening] hazard, chance, occasion, circumstance, hope, occurrence, hap, happening, outside chance, incident, instance; see also EVENT, OPPORTUNITY 1.

possible *a.* **1.** [Within the realm of possibility] conceivable, imaginable, thinkable; see LIKELY 1. **2.** [Acceptable] expedient, desirable, welcome; see PLEASANT 2. **3.** [Contingent upon the future] indeterminate, fortuitous, adventitious; see LIKELY 1, UNCERTAIN.

possibly *a.* perhaps, by chance, potentially; see LIKELY 1, MAYBE, PROBABLY.

post *n.* **1.** [An upright in the ground] prop, support, pillar, pedestal, stake, stud, upright, doorpost; see also COLUMN 1, MAST. **2.** [The mails] postal service, post office, PO; see MAIL.

postcard *n.* postal card, note, letter card; see LETTER 2.

poster *n.* placard, bill, sign, banner, sheet, billboard, handbill, broadside; see also ADVERTISEMENT.

posterior *a.* **1.** [Subsequent] coming after, succeeding, next; see FOLLOWING. **2.** [Behind] in back of, last, after; see BACK.

posterity *n.* descendants, breed, children; see FAMILY, OFFSPRING.

postman *n.* mailman, letter carrier, postal employee; see WORKMAN.

post office *n.* mail office, postal service, PO; see MAIL.

postpone *v.* defer, put off, hold over; see DELAY, SUSPEND 2.

postponed *a.* deferred, delayed, put off, set for a later time, to be done later, withheld, shelved, tabled, adjourned, suspended; see also LATE 1.

postponement *n.* respite, suspension, adjournment; see DELAY, PAUSE.

posture *n.* **1.** [Stance] pose, carriage, demeanor, aspect, presence, condition. **2.** [Attitude] way of thinking, feeling, sentiment; see ATTITUDE.

postwar *a.* peacetime, post-bellum, after the war, peaceful.

pot *n.* **1.** [Container] vessel, kettle, pan, jug, jar, mug, tankard, cup, can, crock, canister, receptacle, bucket, urn, pitcher, bowl, cauldron, melting pot; see also CONTAINER. **2.** [*Marijuana] *cannabis sativa* (Latin), grass*, weed*; see DRUG. **—go to pot** deteriorate, go to ruin, fall apart; see SPOIL.

potato *n.* tuber, white potato, sweet potato, yam, spud*, tater*.

potency *n.* **1.** [Strength] power, energy, vigor; see MANHOOD 2, STRENGTH. **2.** [Authority] influence, control, dominion; see COMMAND, POWER 2.

potent *a.* **1.** [Strong] vigorous, robust, sturdy; see STRONG 1, 2. **2.** [Powerful] mighty, great, influential; see POWERFUL 1.

potential *a.* implied, inherent, dormant; see LIKELY 1.

potentially *a.* conceivably, imaginably, possibly; see LIKELY 1, MAYBE, PROBABLY.

potion *n.* dose, draft, liquor; see DRINK 1, LIQUID, MEDICINE 2.

pottery *n.* ceramics, porcelain, crockery, earthenware, clay ware; see also UTENSILS.

pouch *n.* sack, receptacle, poke; see BAG, CONTAINER.

poultry *n.* domesticated birds, pullets, barnyard fowls; see FOWL.

pounce *v.* bound, surge, dart; see DIVE, JUMP 1.

pound *n.* **1.** [Measure of weight] sixteen ounces, Troy pound, avoirdupois pound, commercial pound, pint; see also MEASURE 1, WEIGHT 1. **2.** [Kennel] coop, doghouse, cage; see PEN 1.

pound *v.* strike, crush, pulverize; see BEAT 1, HIT 1.

pour *v.* **1.** [To flow] discharge, emit, issue; see DRAIN 3, FLOW. **2.** [To allow to flow] replenish with, spill, splash; see EMPTY 2. **3.** [To rain heavily] stream, flood, drench; see RAIN.

pouring *a.* streaming, gushing, spouting, rushing, raining, flooding, showering, discharging, emitting, issuing, escaping, emanating, welling out, spurting, spilling, shedding, draining, running down, running out; see also FLOWING.

pout *v.* make a long face, protrude the lips, sulk; see FROWN.

poverty *n.* **1.** [Want of earthly goods] destitution, pennilessness, indigence, pauperism, want, need, insufficiency, starvation, famine, privation, insolvency, broken fortune, straits, scantiness, deficiency, meagerness, aridity, sparingness, stint, depletion, reduction, emptiness, vacancy, deficit, debt, wolf at the door*, pinch*, bite*, tough going*; see also LACK 1.—*Ant.* WEALTH, prosperity, comfort. **2.** [Want of any desirable thing] shortage, inadequacy, scarcity; see LACK 1.

poverty-stricken *a.* penniless, broke, bankrupt; see POOR 1, WANTING 1.

powder *n.* particles, film, powderiness, explosive powder, medicinal powder, cosmetic powder; see also COSMETIC, EXPLOSIVE, MEDICINE 2.

powdery *a.* sandy, gravelly, dusty; see GRITTY.

power *n.* **1.** [Strength] vigor, energy, stamina; see STRENGTH. **2.** [Controlling sway] authority, command, jurisdiction, dominion, ascendency, superiority, domination, dominance, mastery, control, sway, sovereignty, prerogative, prestige, omnipotence, supreme authority, the last word, rule, law, first-strike capability, warrant, supremacy, legal sanction, government, say-so*; see also INFLUENCE, LEADERSHIP. **3.** [Ability; *often plural*] skill, endowment, capability; see ABILITY. **4.** [Force] compulsion, coercion, duress; see PRESSURE 2, RESTRAINT 2. **5.** [Energy] horsepower, potential, dynamism; see ENERGY 2. **—in power** ruling, authoritative, commanding; see POWERFUL 1.

powerful *a.* **1.** [Wielding power] mighty, all-powerful, almighty, superhuman, omnipotent, overpowering, great, invincible, dominant, influential, authoritative, overruling, potent, forceful, forcible, compelling, ruling, prevailing, preeminent, commanding, supreme, highest, important, authoritarian, ruthless, having the upper hand, in control.—*Ant.* WEAK, incompetent, impotent. **2.** [Strong] robust, stalwart, sturdy; see STRONG 1, 2. **3.** [Effective] efficacious, effectual, convincing; see PERSUASIVE.

powerfully *a.* forcibly, forcefully, effectively, severely, intensely, with authority; see also VIGOROUSLY.

powerless *a.* impotent, feeble, infirm; see WEAK 1, 2.

(the) powers that be *n.* management, higher authorities, higher-ups*; see ADMINISTRATION 2.

practical *a.* matter-of-fact, pragmatical, unimaginative, practicable, feasible, workable, functional, useful, sound, unromantic, sound-thinking, down-to-earth, realistic, sensible, sane, reasonable, rational, to one's advantage, operative, utilitarian, possible, usable, serviceable, efficient, effective, working, in action, in operation, with both feet on the ground.—*Ant.* UNREAL, imaginative, unserviceable.

practically *a.* **1.** [In a practical manner] unimaginatively, pragmatically, efficiently, functionally, sensibly, rationally, reasonably, realistically, with regard to use, from a workable standpoint; see also EFFECTIVELY. **2.** [Virtually] for ordinary purposes, nearly, just about; see ALMOST.

practice *n.* **1.** [A customary action] usage, use, wont; see CUSTOM. **2.** [A method] mode, manner, fashion; see METHOD, SYSTEM. **3.** [Educational repetition] exercise, drill, repetition, iteration, rehearsal, recitation, recounting, relating, tuneup*, prepping*. **4.** [A practitioner's custom] work, patients, clients; see BUSINESS 4.

practice *v.* **1.** [To seek improvement through repetition] drill, train, exercise, study, rehearse, repeat, recite, iterate, put in practice, make it one's business, work at, accustom oneself, act up to, polish up*, sharpen up*, build up. **2.** [To employ one's professional skill] function, work at, employ oneself in; see WORK 2.

practiced *a.* trained, expert, exercised; see ABLE.

pragmatic *a.* realistic, utilitarian, logical; see PRACTICAL.

prairie *n.* steppe, savanna, grassland; see FIELD 1, MEADOW, PLAIN.

praise *n.* **1.** [The act of praising] applause, approval, appreciation; see ADMIRATION. **2.** [An expression of praise] laudation, eulogy, regard, applause, recommendation, handclapping, hurrahs, bravos, ovation, cheers, cries, whistling, tribute, compliment, acclaim, flattery, blessing, benediction, boost, rave.—*Ant.* BLAME, censure, condemnation.

praise *v.* **1.** [To commend] recommend, applaud, cheer, acclaim, endorse, sanction, admire, eulogize, adulate, elevate, smile on, cajole, give an ovation to, clap, pay tribute to, do credit to, have a good word for, make much of, extend credit, advocate, compliment, appreciate, admire, celebrate, honor, congratulate, flatter, rave over, boost, give a big hand, raise the roof*; see also APPROVE. **2.** [To speak or sing in worship] glorify, adore, reverence; see WORSHIP.

praised *a.* admired, aided, helped, flattered, worshiped, glorified, exalted, blessed, celebrated, paid tribute to, magnified.

prance *v.* cavort, frisk, gambol; see DANCE.

prank *n.* game, escapade, caper; see JOKE.

pranks *n.pl.* antics, capers, frolics; see TRICK 1.

pray *v.* **1.** [To ask or beg] importune, petition, plead; see ASK, BEG. **2.** [To call upon God] hold communion with God, supplicate, implore, petition, entreat, commend someone to God.

prayer *n.* **1.** [An earnest request] entreaty, request, petition; see APPEAL 1. **2.** [An address to the deity] invocation, act of devotion, supplication, devotions, benediction, litany. *Prayers include the following:* Lord's Prayer, Pater Noster, Ave Maria, grace, kaddish, matins, vespers, Angelus, general confession, Miserere, collects, hours, stations of the cross, evensong.

prayer book *n.* liturgy, mass book, missal, missalette, hymnal, holy text, guide; see also BIBLE.

preach *v.* exhort, discourse, moralize, teach, lecture, talk, harangue, inform, address.

preacher *n.* missionary, parson, evangelist; see MINISTER 1.

preamble *n.* prelude, preface, introductory part; see INTRODUCTION 4.

precarious *a.* doubtful, uncertain, dubious; see DANGEROUS.

precaution *n.* anticipation, forethought, regard; see CARE 1.

precede *v.* go before, come first, be ahead of, move ahead of, take precedence over, preface, introduce, usher in, ring in, herald, forerun, head, lead, go ahead, scout, light the way, go in advance, come before, come to the front, forge ahead, head up.—*Ant.* SUCCEED, come after, come last.

precedence *n.* preference, precession, the lead; see ADVANTAGE.

precedent *n.* authoritative example, exemplar, pattern; see EXAMPLE 1, MODEL 1.

preceding *a.* antecedent, precedent, previous, other, prior, aforesaid, ahead of, earlier, former, forerunning, past, foregoing, above-mentioned, above-named, above-cited, aforementioned, before-mentioned, above, before, prefatory, front, forward, anterior, preliminary, preparatory, introductory, aforeknown, already indicated, previously mentioned.

precious *a.* **1.** [Valuable] high-priced, costly, dear; see EXPENSIVE, VALUABLE. **2.** [Beloved] cherished, inestimable, prized; see BELOVED, FAVORITE. **3.** [Refined and delicate] overrefined, overnice, fragile; see DAINTY.

precipice *n.* crag, cliff, bluff; see HILL, MOUNTAIN.

precipitate *v.* accelerate, press, hurry; see HASTEN 2, SPEED.

precipitation *n.* **1.** [Carelessness] rashness, presumption, impetuosity; see CARELESSNESS, RUDENESS. **2.** [Condensation] hail, rain, snow; see STORM.
precise *a.* **1.** [Exact] decisive, well-defined, strict; see ACCURATE 2, DEFINITE 1, 2. **2.** [Fussily or prudishly careful] rigid, inflexible, uncompromising; see CAREFUL, SEVERE 1.
precisely *a.* correctly, exactly, definitely; see ACCURATE 2.
precision *n.* exactness, correctness, sureness; see ACCURACY.
preconception *n.* prejudice, bias, assumption; see INCLINATION 1.
predatory *a.* voracious, carnivorous, bloodthirsty; see GREEDY, HUNGRY.
predecessor *n.* antecedent, forerunner, ancestor; see PARENT.
predicament *n.* strait, quandary, plight, puzzle, perplexity, dilemma, scrape, corner, hole, impasse, tight situation, state, condition, position, lot, circumstance, mess, muddle, deadlock, pinch, crisis, bind*, fix*, pickle*, hot water*, jam*; see also DIFFICULTY 1, 2.
predicate *n.* verbal phrase, part of speech, word; see VERB.
predicate *v.* assert, declare, state; see MEAN 1.
predict *v.* prophesy, prognosticate, divine; see FORETELL.
predictable *a.* anticipated, foreseen, prepared for; see EXPECTED, LIKELY 1.
prediction *n.* prophecy, foresight, prognostication; see GUESS.
predominance *n.* reign, supremacy, control; see COMMAND, POWER 2.
predominant *a.* **1.** [Supreme in power] mighty, almighty, supreme; see POWERFUL 1. **2.** [Of first importance] transcendent, surpassing, superlative; see PRINCIPAL.
predominate *v.* dominate, prevail, rule; see GOVERN, MANAGE 1.
prefab* *n.* prefabricated building, temporary structure, standardized housing; see BUILDING.
prefabricate *v.* fabricate, preform, set up, coordinate, pre-assemble; see also ASSEMBLE 2.
preface *n.* prelude, prolegomenon, preliminary; see EXPLANATION, INTRODUCTION 4.
preface *v.* introduce, commence, precede; see BEGIN 1.
prefer *v.* single out, fix upon, fancy; see FAVOR.
preferable *a.* more eligible, more desirable, good; see EXCELLENT.
preferably *a.* by preference, by choice, by selection, in preference, first, sooner, before, optionally, at pleasure, willingly, at will; see also RATHER 2.
preference *n.* favorite, election, option, decision, selection, pick; see also CHOICE.
preferred *a.* chosen, selected, fancied, adopted, picked out, taken, elected, liked, favored, set apart, handpicked, singled out, endorsed, settled upon, sanctioned, decided upon.—*Ant.* NEGLECTED, unpreferred, overlooked.
prefix *n.* **1.** [An addition] affix, adjunct, introductory word part, prefixion. **2.** [A designation] title, cognomen, designation; see NAME 1.
pregnancy *n.* reproduction, fertilization, gestation; see BIRTH.
pregnant *a.* gestating, gravid, fruitful, with child, big with child, hopeful, anticipating, in a family way*, expecting*.
prehistoric *a.* preceding history, very early, unknown; see OLD 3.
prejudge *v.* presuppose, forejudge, presume; see DECIDE.
prejudice *n.* partiality, unfairness, spleen, bias, detriment, enmity, prejudgment, dislike, disgust, aversion, antipathy, race prejudice, apartheid, misjudgment, pique, coolness, animosity, contemptuousness, bad opinion, displeasure, repugnance, revulsion, preconception, foregone conclusion, quirk, warp, twist.—*Ant.* ADMIRATION, appreciation, good opinion.
prejudiced *a.* preconceived, prepossessed, biased, directed against, influenced, inclined, leaning, conditioned, presupposing, predisposed, dogmatic, opinionated, partisan, extreme, hidebound, narrow, intolerant, canting, racist, sexist, chauvinistic, blind, partial, narrow-minded, parochial, provincial, one-sided, not seeing an inch beyond one's nose, squint-eyed, intolerant of, disliking, having a predilection, closed against, judging on slight knowledge, smug.—*Ant.* GENEROUS, open-minded, receptive.
preliminary *a.* preparatory, preceding, prefatory; see INTRODUCTORY.
prelude *n.* preface, preliminary preparation, prelusion; see INTRODUCTION 3.
premarital *a.* before the vows, before marriage, during courtship; see BEFORE.
premature *a.* unanticipated, precipitate, rash; see EARLY 2, UNTIMELY.
prematurely *a.* too early, rash, precipitately; see EARLY 2, UNTIMELY.
premiere *n.* first night, beginning, opening; see PERFORMANCE.
premise *n.* proposition, evidence, assumption; see BASIS, PROOF 1.
premises *n.pl.* **1.** [Evidence] testimony, reason, support; see BASIS, PROOF 1. **2.** [Real estate] bounds, limits, land; see PROPERTY 2.
premium *a.* prime, superior, select; see EXCELLENT.
premium *n.* remuneration, bonus, installment; see PRIZE.
premonition *n.* omen, portent, forewarning; see SIGN 1, WARNING.

preoccupation *n.* absorption, daydreaming, amusement; see FANTASY, THOUGHT 1.

preoccupied *a.* removed, absorbed, distracted; see RAPT.

preparation *n.* **1.** [The act of preparing] preparing, fitting, making ready, manufacture, readying, putting in order, establishment, compounding, adapting, rehearsal, incubation, gestation, building, construction, formation, maturing, anticipation, development, evolution, furnishing, buildup*. **2.** [The state of being prepared] preparedness, readiness, fitness, adaptation, suitability, capacity, qualification, background, ripeness, mellowness, maturity, training, education, equipment. **3.** [Something that is prepared] arrangement, product, compound; see MIXTURE 1.

prepare *v.* **1.** [To make oneself ready] get ready, foresee, arrange, make preparations, make arrangements, fit, adapt, qualify, put in order, adjust, set one's house in order, prime, fix, settle, fabricate, appoint, furnish, elaborate, perfect, develop, prepare the ground, lay the foundations, block out, smooth the way, man, arm, cut out, warm up, lay the groundwork, contrive, devise, make provision, put in readiness, build up, provide for, provide against, make snug, be prepared, be ready; see also ANTICIPATE, PLAN 1. **2.** [To make other persons or things ready] outfit, equip, fit out; see PROVIDE 1. **3.** [To cook and serve] concoct, dress, brew; see COOK, SERVE.

prepared *a.* **1.** [Fitted] adapted, qualified, adjusted; see ABLE, FIT 1. **2.** [Subjected to a special process or treatment] frozen, precooked, processed; see PRESERVED 2. **3.** [Ready] available, on hand, in order; see READY 2.

preposition *n.* part of speech, function word, form word; see GRAMMAR, WORD 1.

prepossessing *a.* handsome, captivating, attractive; see CHARMING, PLEASANT 1.

prerequisite *n.* essential, necessity, need; see REQUIREMENT 2.

prerogative *n.* privilege, advantage, exemption; see RIGHT 1.

prescribe *v.* guide, order, give directions; see ORDER 1.

prescription *n.* direction, medical recipe, formula; see MEDICINE 2.

presence *n.* **1.** [The fact of being present] occupancy, occupation, residence, inhabitance, habitancy; see also ATTENDANCE 1. **2.** [The vicinity of a person] propinquity, nearness, closeness; see NEIGHBORHOOD. **3.** [One's appearance and behavior] carriage, port, demeanor; see APPEARANCE 1, BEHAVIOR.

presence of mind *n.* sensibility, alertness, acumen; see ATTENTION.

present *a.* **1.** [Near in time] existing, being, in process, in duration, begun, started, commenced, going on, under consideration, at this time, contemporary, immediate, instant, prompt, at this moment, at present, today, nowadays, these days, already, even now, but now, just now, for the time being, for the occasion; see also NOW 1.—*Ant.* PAST, over, completed. **2.** [Near in space] in view, at hand, within reach; see NEAR 1.

present *n.* **1.** [The present time] instant, this time, present moment; see TODAY. **2.** [A gift] grant, donation, offering; see GIFT 1.

present *v.* **1.** [To introduce] make known, acquaint with, give an introduction; see INTRODUCE 3. **2.** [To submit] donate, proffer, put forth; see OFFER 1. **3.** [To give] grant, bestow, confer; see GIVE 1. **4.** [To give a play, etc.] put on, do, offer; see ACT 3, PERFORM 2.

presentable *a.* attractive, prepared, satisfactory; see FIT 1.

presentation *n.* **1.** [The act of presenting] bestowal, donation, delivering; see GIVING. **2.** [Something presented] present, offering, remembrance; see GIFT 1.

presented *a.* bestowed, granted, conferred; see GIVEN.

presently *a.* directly, without delay, shortly; see IMMEDIATELY, SOON.

preservation *n.* security, safety, protection, conservation, maintenance, saving, keeping, storage, curing, tanning, freezing, sugaring, pickling, evaporation, canning, refrigeration.

preserve *v.* **1.** [To guard] protect, shield, save; see DEFEND 2. **2.** [To maintain] keep up, care for, conserve; see MAINTAIN 3. **3.** [To keep] can, conserve, process, save, put up, put down, store, cure, bottle, do up, season, salt, pickle, put in brine, put in vinegar, pot, tin, dry, smoke, corn, dry-cure, smoke-cure, freeze, quick freeze, keep up, cold-pack, refrigerate, dehydrate, seal up, kipper, marinate, evaporate, embalm, mummify, mothball, fill.—*Ant.* WASTE, allow to spoil, let spoil.

preserved *a.* **1.** [Saved] rescued, guarded, secured; see SAVED 1. **2.** [Prepared for preservation] canned, corned, dried, freeze-dried, dehydrated, evaporated, smoked, seasoned, pickled, salted, brined, put up, conserved, cured, marinated, tinned, potted, bottled, embalmed, mummified.

preserves *n.pl.* spread, sweet, jell*; see JAM 1, JELLY.

preside *v.* direct, lead, control; see ADVISE, MANAGE 1.

presidency *n.* office of the president, chairmanship, position; see ADMINISTRATION 2.

president *n.* presiding officer, chief director, prez*; see EXECUTIVE.

presidential *a.* official, regulatory, of the chief executive; see MANAGING.

press *n.* **1.** [The pressure of circumstances] rush, confusion, strain; see HASTE. **2.** [Publishing as a social institution] the Fourth Estate, publishers, publicists, newsmen, newspapermen, journalists, journalistic writers, editors, correspondents, political writers, columnists, periodicals, papers, newspapers.

press *v.* **1.** [To subject to pressure] thrust, crowd, bear upon, bear down on, squeeze, hold down, pin down, force down, crush, drive, weight, urge; see also PUSH 1.—*Ant.* RAISE, release, relieve. **2.** [To smooth, usually by heat and pressure] finish, mangle, roll; see IRON, SMOOTH.

press conference *n.* interview, public report, briefing; see ANNOUNCEMENT, HEARING 1.

pressing *a.* importunate, constraining, distressing; see IMPORTANT 1, URGENT 1.

pressure *n.* **1.** [Physical pressure] force, burden, mass, load, encumbrance, stress, thrust, tension, squeeze; see also WEIGHT 1.—*Ant.* RELEASE, relief, deliverance. **2.** [Some form of social pressure] compulsion, constraint, urgency, persuasion, stress, affliction, coercion, trouble, hardship, humiliation, misfortune, necessity, repression, confinement, unnaturalness, obligation, discipline.—*Ant.* AID, assistance, encouragement.

pressure *v.* press, compel, constrain; see URGE 2, 3.

prestige *n.* renown, effect, influence; see FAME.

presumably *a.* in all probability, credibly, likely; see PROBABLY.

presume *v.* consider, suppose, take for granted; see ASSUME.

presumption *n.* **1.** [An assumption] conjecture, guess, hypothesis; see ASSUMPTION 1. **2.** [Impudence] arrogance, audacity, effrontery; see RUDENESS.

pretend *v.* **1.** [To feign] affect, simulate, claim falsely, imitate, counterfeit, sham, make as if, make as though, mislead, beguile, delude, pass off for, cheat, dupe, hoodwink, be deceitful, bluff, falsify, be hypocritical, fake, put on*, let on*, go through the motions, keep up appearances; see also DECEIVE. **2.** [To make believe] mimic, fill a role, take a part, represent, portray, put on a front, play, make believe, act the part of, put on an act*, act a part, put on airs*, playact.

pretended *a.* feigned, counterfeit, assumed, affected, shammed, bluffing, simulated, lying, falsified, put on, concealed, covered, masked, cheating; see also FALSE 3.

pretense *n.* **1.** [The act of pretending] affectation, misrepresentation, falsification, act, deceit, fabrication, trickery, double-dealing, misstatement, falsifying, simulation, excuse, insincerity, profession, ostentation, assumption, dissimulation, evasion, equivocation, prevarication, egotism, brazenness, arrogance, dandyism, foppery, servility, complacency, smugness, prudishness, coyness, formality, stiffness, blind, smoke screen; see also DISHONESTY, IMITATION.—*Ant.* HONESTY, candor, sincerity. **2.** [Something pretended] falsehood, lie, falseness, affectation, mask, cloak, show, excuse, subterfuge, pretext, fraud, appearance, seeming, semblance, wile, ruse, sham, airs, claim, mannerism; see also DECEPTION, IMITATION 2.

prettily *a.* pleasingly, gently, quietly; see POLITELY.

pretty *a.* **1.** [Attractive] comely, lovely, good-looking; see BEAUTIFUL. **2.** [Pleasant] delightful, cheerful, pleasing; see PLEASANT 2. **3.** [*Considerable] ample, sizable, notable; see LARGE 1, MUCH 1, 2. **4.** [Somewhat] rather, tolerably, a little; see MODERATELY.

prevalence *n.* dissemination, occurrence, currency; see REGULARITY.

prevalent *a.* widespread, accepted, frequently met; see COMMON 1.

prevent *v.* preclude, obviate, forestall, anticipate, block, arrest, stop, thwart, repress, interrupt, halt, impede, check, avert, frustrate, balk, foil, retard, obstruct, counter, countercheck, counteract, inhibit, restrict, block off, limit, hold back, hold off, stop from, deter, intercept, override, circumvent, bar, ward off, keep from happening, nip in the bud, put a stop to, stave off, keep off, turn aside; see also HINDER, RESTRAIN.—*Ant.* HELP, aid, encourage.

prevented *a.* obviated, stopped, interfered with; see INTERRUPTED.

prevention *n.* anticipation, forestalling, arresting, obviating, bar, debarring, halt, impeding, retardation, repression, restraint, restriction, inhibition, interception, overriding, circumvention, hindering, counteraction, obstruction, opposition, warding off, staving off, keeping off, stopping, thwarting, blocking; see also REFUSAL.—*Ant.* AID, encouragement, help.

preventive *a.* deterrent, precautionary, tending to prevent, averting, defensive.

previous *a.* antecedent, prior, former; see PRECEDING.

previously *a.* long ago, earlier, beforehand; see BEFORE.

prey *n.* spoil, pillage, loot; see VICTIM.

prey on *v.* **1.** [To destroy] seize, raid, pillage; see DESTROY. **2.** [To eat] feed on, devour, consume; see EAT 1.

price *n.* expenditure, outlay, expense, cost, value, worth, figure, dues, tariff, valuation, quotation, fare, hire, wages, return, disbursement, rate, appraisal, reckoning, equivalent, payment, demand, barter, consideration, amount, marked price, asking price, estimate, output, ransom, reward, pay, prize, return, par value, money's worth, price ceiling, ceiling; see also VALUE 1. **—at any price** whatever the cost, expense no object, anyhow; see REGARDLESS 2.

price *v.* fix the price of, appraise, assess; see RATE, VALUE 2.

priced *a.* valued, estimated, worth; see COSTING.

priceless *a.* invaluable, inestimable, without price; see VALUABLE.

prick *n.* tap, stab, stick; see CUT.

prick *v.* pierce, puncture, stick; see CUT, HURT 1.

prickly *a.* thorny, pointed, spiny; see SHARP 1.

pride *n.* **1.** [The quality of being vain] conceit, vainglory, egoism, egotism, self-esteem, self-love, self-exaltation, self-glorification, self-admiration, pretension.—*Ant.* HUMILITY, self-effacement, unpretentiousness. **2.** [Conduct growing from pride or conceit] haughtiness, vanity, disdain, condescension, patronizing, patronage, superiority; see also sense 1. **3.** [Sense of personal satisfaction] self-respect, self-satisfaction, self-sufficiency; see HAPPINESS. **4.** [A source of satisfaction] enjoyment, repletion, sufficiency; see SATISFACTION 2.

pride oneself on *v.* take pride in, flatter oneself that, be proud of; see BOAST.

priest *n.* *Names for priests in various sects include the following:* father confessor, spiritual father, priest-vicar, high priest, minor canon, pontiff, vicar, care of souls, clergyman, rector, preacher, presbyter, elder, rabbi, lama, monk, friar; see also MINISTER 1.

priesthood *n.* clergy, Holy Orders, monasticism; see MINISTRY 2.

priestly *a.* ecclesiastic, episcopal, ministerial; see CLERICAL 2.

prim *a.* stiff, formal, precise, demure, decorous, nice, orderly, tidy, cleanly, trim, spruce, pat; see also POLITE.

primarily *a.* mainly, fundamentally, in the first place; see PRINCIPALLY.

primary *a.* **1.** [Earliest] primitive, initial, first; see ORIGINAL 1. **2.** [Fundamental] elemental, basic, central; see FUNDAMENTAL. **3.** [Principal] chief, prime, main; see PRINCIPAL.

primate *n.* gorilla, chimpanzee, orangutan, gibbon, great ape; see also MAN 1, MONKEY.

prime *a.* **1.** [Principal] main, first, chief; see PRINCIPAL. **2.** [Excellent] top, choice, superior; see EXCELLENT.

primitive *a.* **1.** [Simple] rudimentary, elementary, first; see FUNDAMENTAL. **2.** [Ancient] primeval, archaic, primordial; see OLD 3. **3.** [Uncivilized] crude, rough, simple, rude, atavistic, uncivilized, savage, uncultured, natural, barbaric, barbarous, barbarian, fierce, untamed, uncouth, ignorant, undomesticated, wild, animal, brutish, raw, untaught, green, unlearned, untutored, underdeveloped.

primp* *v.* make one's toilet, paint and powder, get dressed up; see DRESS, PREPARE 1.

prince *n.* sovereign, ruler, monarch, potentate; see also ROYALTY.

princely *a.* **1.** [Royal] sovereign, regal, august; see ROYAL. **2.** [Suited to a prince] lavish, sumptuous, luxurious; see EXPENSIVE, HANDSOME, RICH 1, 2.

princess *n.* sovereign, monarch, infanta; see ROYALTY.

principal *a.* leading, chief, first, head, prime, main, foremost, cardinal, essential, capital, important, preeminent, highest, supreme, prominent, dominant, predominant, controlling, superior, prevailing, paramount, greatest, incomparable, unapproachable, peerless, matchless, unequaled, unrivaled, maximum, crowning, unparalleled, sovereign, second to none.—*Ant.* UNIMPORTANT, secondary, accessory.

principal *n.* chief, head, governing officer, master; see also EXECUTIVE.

principally *a.* chiefly, mainly, essentially, substantially, materially, eminently, preeminently, superlatively, supremely, vitally, especially, particularly, peculiarly, notably, importantly, fundamentally, dominantly, predominantly, basically, largely, first and foremost, in large measure, first of all, to a great degree, prevalently, generally, universally, mostly, above all, in the first place, for the most part, for the greatest part, before anything else, in the main.—*Ant.* SLIGHTLY, somewhat, tolerably.

principle *n.* **1.** [A fundamental law] underlying truth, basic doctrine, postulate; see LAW 4. **2.** [A belief or set of beliefs; *often plural*] system, opinion, teaching; see BELIEF, FAITH 2, POLICY.

print *n.* **1.** [Printed matter] impression, reprint, issue; see COPY. **2.** [A printed picture] engraving, lithograph, photograph; see PICTURE 3, SKETCH. **—in print** printed, available, obtainable; see PUBLISHED. **—out of print** O.P., unavailable, remaindered; see SOLD OUT.

print *v.* **1.** [To make an impression] impress, imprint, indent; see MARK 1. **2.** [To reproduce by printing] run off, print up, issue, reissue, reprint, bring out, go to press, set type, compose, start the presses; see also PUBLISH 1.—*Ant.* TALK, write, inscribe. **3.** [To simulate printing] letter, do lettering, hand-letter; see WRITE 2.

printed *a.* impressed, imprinted, engraved, stamped, lithographed, multilithed, xeroxed, printed by photo-offset, silkscreened; see also REPRODUCED.

printer *n.* typesetter, compositor, linotype operator; see WORKMAN.

printing *n.* **1.** [A process of reproduction] typography, composition, typesetting, presswork. **2.** [Printed matter] line, page, sheet; see PAGE. **3.** [Publication] issuing, issuance, distribution; see PUBLICATION 1.

prior *a.* antecedent, above-mentioned, foregoing; see PRECEDING.

priority *n.* superiority, preference, precedence; see ADVANTAGE.

prison *n.* penitentiary, reformatory, prison house, guardhouse, stockade; see also JAIL.

prisoner *n.* captive, convict, culprit, jailbird, detainee, escapee, hostage, con*; see also DEFENDANT.

prisoner of war *n.* captive person, captured person, interned person, person in captivity, POW; see also PRISONER.

privacy *n.* seclusion, solitude, retreat, isolation, separateness, aloofness, separation, concealment; see also SECRECY.

private *a.* special, separate, retired, secluded, withdrawn, removed, not open, behind the scenes, off the record, privy, clandestine, single; see also INDIVIDUAL, OWN.—*Ant.* PUBLIC, open, exposed. —**in private** privately, personally, not publicly; see SECRETLY.

private *n.* enlisted man, infantryman; private first class, second class, etc.; see also SAILOR, SOLDIER.

privately *a.* confidentially, clandestinely, alone; see PERSONALLY 1, SECRETLY.

private parts *n.pl.* genital organs, organs of reproduction, privates; see GENITALS.

privilege *n.* **1.** [A customary concession] due, perquisite, prerogative; see RIGHT 1. **2.** [An opportunity] chance, fortunate happening, event; see OPPORTUNITY 1.

privileged *a.* free, vested, furnished; see EXEMPT.

prize *n.* reward, advantage, privilege, possession, honor, inducement, premium, bounty, bonus, spoil, booty, plunder, pillage, loot, award, accolade, recompense, requital, acquisitions, laurel, decoration, medal, trophy, palm, crown, citation, scholarship, fellowship, feather in one's cap, title, championship, first place, pay-off*, cake*, plum.

prize *v.* regard highly, value, esteem; see VALUE 2.

probability *n.* likelihood, possibility, chance; see CHANCE, POSSIBILITY 2.

probable *a.* seeming, presumable, feasible; see LIKELY 1.

probably *a.* presumably, seemingly, apparently, believably, reasonably, imaginably, feasibly, practicably, expediently, plausibly, most likely, everything being equal, as like as not, as the case may be, one can assume, like enough, no doubt, to all appearance, in all probability.—*Ant.* UNLIKELY, doubtfully, questionably.

problem *n.* **1.** [A difficulty] dilemma, quandary, obstacle; see DIFFICULTY 1, 2. **2.** [A question to be solved] query, intricacy, enigma; see PUZZLE 2.

procedure *n.* fashion, style, mode; see METHOD, SYSTEM.

proceed *v.* move, progress, continue; see ADVANCE 1.

proceeding *n.* [*Often plural*] process, transaction, deed, experiment, performance, measure, step, course, undertaking, venture, adventure, occurrence, incident, circumstance, happening, movement, operation, procedure, exercise, maneuver; see also ACTION 1.

proceeds *n.pl.* gain, profit, yield; see RETURN 3.

process *n.* means, rule, manner; see METHOD. —**in (the) process of** while, when, in the course of; see DURING.

process *v.* treat, make ready, concoct; see PREPARE 1.

processed *a.* treated, handled, fixed; see PRESERVED 2.

prod *v.* provoke, crowd, shove; see PUSH 1.

prodigy *n.* marvel, portent, miracle, monster, enormity, spectacle, freak, curiosity; see also WONDER 2. —**(child) prodigy** genius, gifted child, boy or girl wonder; see ARTIST, MUSICIAN, SCIENTIST, WRITER.

produce *n.* product, harvest, result, crop, return, effect, consequence, amount, profit, outcome, outgrowth, aftermath, gain, realization; see also BUTTER, CHEESE, CREAM 1, FOOD, FRUIT, GRAIN 1, MILK, VEGETABLE.

produce *v.* **1.** [To bear] yield, bring forth, give birth to, propagate, bring out, come through, blossom, flower, deliver, generate, engender, breed, contribute, give, afford, furnish, return, render, show fruit, fetch, bring in, present, offer, provide, contribute, sell for, bear fruit, accrue, allow, admit, proliferate, be delivered of, bring to birth, reproduce, foal, lamb, drop, calve, fawn, whelp, kitten, litter, hatch, usher into the world, spawn. **2.** [To create by mental effort] originate, author, procreate, bring forth, conceive, engender, write, design, fabricate, imagine, turn out, churn out, devise; see also COMPOSE 2, CREATE, INVENT 1. **3.** [To cause] effect, occasion, bring about; see BEGIN 1. **4.** [To show] exhibit, present, unfold; see DISPLAY. **5.** [To make] assemble, build, construct; see MANUFACTURE. **6.** [To present a performance] present, play, prepare for public presentation; see ACT 3, PERFORM 2.

produced *a.* **1.** [Created] originated, composed, made; see FORMED. **2.** [Presented] performed, acted, put on; see SHOWN 1. **3.** [Caused] occasioned, propagated, begot, bred, engendered, generated, hatched, induced.

product *n.* **1.** [A result] output, outcome, outgrowth; see RESULT. **2.** [Goods produced; *often plural*] stock, goods, merchandise; see GOODS 1.

production *n.* **1.** [The act of producing] origination, creation, authoring, reproduction, yielding, giving, bearing, rendering, giving forth, increasing, return, procreation, generation, engendering, blooming, blossoming; see also MAKING. **2.** [The amount produced] crop, result, stock; see QUANTITY.

productive *a.* rich, fruitful, prolific; see FERTILE.

productivity *n.* richness, potency, fecundity; see FERTILITY.

profanity *n.* abuse, cursing, swearing; see CURSE 1.

profession *n.* **1.** [A skilled or learned occupation] calling, business, avocation, vocation, employment, occupation, engagement, office, situation, position, lifework, chosen work, role, service, pursuit, undertaking, concern, post, berth, craft, sphere, field, walk of life; see also CHURCH 3, EDUCATION 3, JUDICIARY, MEDICINE 3, TRADE 2, WRITING 3. **2.** [A declaration] pretense, avowal, vow; see DECLARATION, OATH 1.

professional *a.* **1.** [Skillful] expert, learned, adept; see ABLE. **2.** [Well-qualified] acknowledged, known, licensed; see ABLE.

professional *n.* expert, trained personnel, specially trained person; see SPECIALIST.

professor *n.* educator, faculty member, sage; see TEACHER. *Teachers popularly called professors include the following:* full professor, associate professor, assistant professor, instructor, lecturer, graduate assistant, teaching assistant, tutor, school principal, fellow, teaching fellow, master docent.

proficiency *n.* learning, skill, knowledge; see ABILITY.

proficient *a.* skilled, expert, skillful; see ABLE.

profile *n.* silhouette, shape, figure; see FORM 1, OUTLINE 3.

profit *n.* **1.** [Advantage] avail, good, value; see ADVANTAGE. **2.** [Excess of receipts over expenditures] gain, returns, proceeds, receipts, take*, gate, acquisition, rake-off*, accumulation, saving, interest, remuneration, earnings.—*Ant.* LOSS, debits, costs.

profit *v.* **1.** [To be of benefit] benefit, assist, avail; see HELP. **2.** [To derive gain] benefit, capitalize on, cash in on, realize, clear, gain, reap profits, make a profit, recover, thrive, prosper, harvest, make money.—*Ant.* LOSE, lose out on, miss out on.

profitable *a.* lucrative, useful, sustaining, aiding, remunerative, beneficial, gainful, advantageous, paying, successful, favorable, assisting, productive, serviceable, valuable, instrumental, practical, pragmatic, effective, to advantage, effectual, sufficient, paying its way, bringing in returns, making money, paying well, paying out, in the black; see also HELPFUL 1.—*Ant.* UNPROFITABLE, UNSUCCESSFUL, unproductive.

profitably *a.* lucratively, remuneratively, gainfully, usefully, advantageously, successfully, favorably, for money, productively, practically, effectively, effectually, sufficiently, sustainingly.

profiteer *n.* exploiter, chiseler, cheater; see CHEAT.

profound *a.* **1.** [Physically deep] fathomless, bottomless, subterranean; see DEEP 1. **2.** [Intellectually deep] heavy, erudite, scholarly, mysterious, sage, serious, sagacious, penetrating, discerning, knowing, wise, knowledgeable, intellectual, enlightened, thorough, informed; see also LEARNED 1, SOLEMN.—*Ant.* SUPERFICIAL, shallow, flighty. **3.** [Emotionally deep] heartfelt, deep-felt, great; see INTENSE.

profoundly *a.* deeply, extremely, thoroughly; see VERY.

program *n.* **1.** [A list of subjects] schedule, memoranda, printed program; see LIST. **2.** [A sequence of events] happenings, schedule, agenda, order of business, calendar, plans, business, affairs, details, arrangements, catalogue, curriculum, order of the day, series of events, appointments, things to do, chores, preparations, meetings, getting and spending, all the thousand and one things; see also PLAN 2. **3.** [An entertainment] performance, show, presentation; see PERFORMANCE.

program *v.* **1.** [To schedule] slate, book, bill; see sense 2. **2.** [To work out a sequence to be performed] feed in, activate a computer, compute, reckon, figure, calculate, estimate, enter, compile, feed, edit, process, extend, delete, add.

programmed *a.* scheduled, slated, lined up; see PLANNED.

progress *n.* **1.** [Movement forward] progression, advance, headway, impetus, forward course, development, velocity, pace, momentum, motion, rate, step, stride, current, flow, tour, circuit, transit, journey, voyage, march, expedition, locomotion, passage, course, procession, process, march of events, course of life, movement of the stars, motion through space.—*Ant.* STOP, stay, stand. **2.** [Improvement] advancement, development, growth; see IMPROVEMENT 1. —**in progress** advancing, going on, continuing; see MOVING 1.

progress *v.* proceed, move onward, move on; see ADVANCE 1.

progressive *a.* **1.** [In mounting sequence] advancing, mounting, rising; see MOVING 1. **2.** [Receptive to new ideas] tolerant, lenient, open-minded; see LIBERAL.

prohibit *v.* interdict, put under the ban, obstruct; see FORBID, PREVENT.

prohibited *a.* forbidden, restricted, not approved; see ILLEGAL, REFUSED.

project *n.* outline, design, scheme; see PLAN 2.

project *v.* **1.** [To thrust out] protrude, hang over, extend, jut, bulge, stick out, hang out, jut out, be prominent, be conspicuous.—*Ant.* WITHDRAW, regress, revert. **2.** [To throw] pitch, heave, propel; see THROW 1.

projection *n.* **1.** [Bulge] prominence, jut, protuberance, step, ridge, rim; see also BULGE. **2.** [Forecast] prognostication, prediction, guess; see GUESS.

prolong *v.* continue, hold, draw out; see INCREASE.

prolonged *a.* extended, lengthened, continued; see DULL 4.

prominence *n.* **1.** [A projection] jut, protrusion, bump; see BULGE, PROJECTION 1. **2.** [Notability] renown, influence, distinction; see FAME.

prominent *a.* **1.** [Physically prominent] protuberant, extended, jutting, conspicuous, protruding, projecting, noticeable, rugged, rough, obtrusive, standing out, sticking out, hilly, raised, relieved, rounded.—*Ant.* HOLLOW, depressed, sunken. **2.** [Socially prominent] notable, preeminent, leading; see FAMOUS. **3.** [Conspicuous] remarkable, striking, noticeable; see CONSPICUOUS.

promiscuity *n.* lechery, looseness, sexual immorality; see LEWDNESS.

promiscuous *a.* indiscriminate, sexually immoral, loose; see LEWD 2.

promise *n.* **1.** [A pledge] assurance, agreement, pact, oath, engagement, covenant, consent, warrant, affirmation, swearing, plight, word, troth, vow, profession, guarantee, insurance, obligation, commitment, betrothal, espousal, plighted faith, marriage contract, giving one's word, gentleman's agreement, word of honor. **2.** [Hope] outlook, good omen, good appearance; see ENCOURAGEMENT.

promise *v.* **1.** [To give one's word] engage, declare, agree, vow, swear, consent, affirm, profess, undertake, pledge, covenant, contract, bargain, espouse, betroth, assure, guarantee, warrant, give assurance, give warranty, insure, cross one's heart, plight one's troth, bind oneself, commit oneself, obligate oneself, make oneself answerable, give security, underwrite, subscribe, lead someone to expect, answer for, pledge one's honor.—*Ant.* DECEIVE, deny, break faith. **2.** [To appear promising] ensure, insure, assure; see ENCOURAGE.

promised *a.* pledged, sworn, vowed, agreed, covenanted, as agreed upon, undertaken, professed, consented, affirmed, insured, warranted, vouched for, underwritten, subscribed, stipulated, assured, ensured; see also GUARANTEED.

promising *a.* likely, assuring, encouraging; see HOPEFUL 2.

promote *v.* **1.** [To further] forward, urge, encourage, profit, patronize, help, aid, assist, develop, support, boom, back, uphold, champion, advertise, advocate, cultivate, improve, push, bolster, develop, speed, foster, nourish, nurture, subsidize, befriend, benefit, subscribe to, favor, expand, improve, better, cooperate, get behind, boost.—*Ant.* DISCOURAGE, weaken, enfeeble. **2.** [To advance in rank] raise, advance, elevate, graduate, move up, exalt, aggrandize, magnify, prefer, favor, increase, better, dignify.—*Ant.* HUMBLE, demote, reduce.

promotion *n.* **1.** [Advancement in rank] preferment, elevation, raise, improvement, advance, lift, betterment, ennobling, favoring.—*Ant.* REMOVAL, demotion, lowering. **2.** [Improvement] advancement, progression, development; see IMPROVEMENT 1, INCREASE.

prompt *a.* early, timely, precise; see PUNCTUAL.

prompt *v.* **1.** [To instigate] arouse, provoke, inspire; see INCITE, URGE 2. **2.** [To suggest] bring up, indicate, imply; see PROPOSE 1.

promptly *a.* on time, punctually, hastily; see IMMEDIATELY, QUICKLY.

prone *a.* inclined, predisposed, disposed; see LIKELY 4.

prong *n.* spine, spur, spike; see FASTENER.

pronoun *n.* *Pronouns include the following:* personal, possessive, demonstrative, relative, definite, indefinite, interrogative, intensive, reflexive, reciprocal.

pronounce *v.* **1.** [To speak formally] proclaim, say, assert; see DECLARE. **2.** [To articulate] enunciate, phonate, vocalize; see UTTER.

pronounced *a.* notable, noticeable, clear; see DEFINITE 2, OBVIOUS 1, 2, UNUSUAL 1.

pronouncement *n.* report, declaration, statement; see ANNOUNCEMENT.

pronunciation *n.* articulation, utterance, voicing; see DICTION.

proof *n.* **1.** [Evidence] demonstration, verification, case, reasons, exhibits, credentials, data, warrant, confirmation, substantiation, attestation, corroboration, affidavit, facts, witness, testimony, deposition, trace, record, criterion. **2.** [Process of proving] test, attempt, assay; see TRIAL 2.

prop *n.* aid, assistance, strengthener; see POST 1.

propaganda *n.* promotion, publicity, advertisement, plug*, evangelism, proselytism, ballyhoo, handout.

propel *v.* impel forward, move, press onward; see DRIVE 2.

propellant *n.* charge, gunpowder, combustible; see EXPLOSIVE, FUEL.

propeller *n. Propellers include the following:* screw, Archimedean, fishtail, variable-pitch, feathering, marine, airplane, two-bladed, three-bladed, four-bladed, weedless, pusher, pulling.

propensity *n.* talent, capacity, competence; see ABILITY.

proper *a.* **1.** [Suitable] just, decent, fitting; see FIT 1. **2.** [Conventional] customary, usual, decorous; see CONVENTIONAL 1, 3. **3.** [Prudish] prim, precise, strait-laced; see PRUDISH.

properly *a.* correctly, fitly, suitably; see WELL 3.

property *n.* **1.** [Possessions] belongings, lands, assets, holdings, inheritance, capital, equity, investments, goods and chattels, earthly possessions, real property, personal property, taxable property, resources, private property, public property, wealth; see also BUSINESS 4, ESTATE, FARM, HOME 1. **2.** [A piece of land] section, quarter section, estate, tract, part, farm, park, ranch, homestead, yard, grounds, frontage, acres, acreage, premises, campus, grant, landed property, field, claim, holding, plot; see also LOT 1.

prophecy *n.* prediction, prognostication, augury; see IDEA 1.

prophesy *v.* predict, prognosticate, divine; see FORETELL.

prophet *n.* seer, oracle, soothsayer, prophetess, seeress, clairvoyant, wizard, augur, sibyl, sorcerer, predictor, forecaster, prognosticator, diviner, medium, witch, palmist, fortuneteller, weather forecaster, meteorologist, magus, astrologer, horoscopist.

prophetic *a.* predictive, occult, clairvoyant, oracular, sibylline.

propitious *a.* **1.** [Favorable] auspicious, encouraging, promising; see HOPEFUL 2. **2.** [Kindly] benignant, helpful, generous; see KIND.

proponent *n.* defender, advocate, champion; see PROTECTOR.

proportion *n.* relationship, dimension, share; see BALANCE 2, PART 1.

proportional *a.* proportionate, equivalent, comparable; see EQUAL.

proposal *n.* **1.** [Offer] overture, recommendation, proposition; see SUGGESTION 1. **2.** [Plan] scheme, program, prospectus; see PLAN 2.

propose *v.* **1.** [To make a suggestion] suggest, offer, put forward, move, set forth, come up with, state, proffer, advance, propound, introduce, put to, contend, assert, tender, recommend, advise, counsel, lay before, submit, affirm, volunteer, press, urge upon, hold out, make a motion, lay on the line.—*Ant.* OPPOSE, dissent, protest. **2.** [To mean] purpose, intend, aim; see MEAN 1. **3.** [To propose marriage] offer marriage, ask in marriage, make a proposal, ask for the hand of, pop the question*.

proposed *a.* projected, prospective, advised, scheduled, expected, arranged, advanced, suggested, moved, put forward, submitted, recommended, urged, volunteered, pressed, intended, determined, anticipated, designed, schemed, purposed, considered, referred to, contingent; see also PLANNED.

proposition *n.* proposal, scheme, project; see PLAN 1.

proposition *v.* ask, accost, approach; see ASK.

proprietor *n.* heritor, master, proprietary; see OWNER, POSSESSOR.

propriety *n.* aptness, suitability, advisability, accordance, agreeableness, compatibility, correspondence, consonance, appropriateness, congruity, modesty, good breeding, dignity, concord, harmony, expedience, convenience, pleasantness, welcomeness; see also FITNESS.—*Ant.* INCONSISTENCY, incongruity, inappropriateness.

prose *n.* fiction, nonfiction, composition; see LITERATURE 1, 2, STORY, WRITING 2.

prosecute *v.* contest, indict, involve in litigation; see SUE.

prosecution *n.* state, government, prosecuting attorney, state's attorney; see also LAWYER.

prospect *n.* **1.** [A view] sight, landscape, vista; see VIEW. **2.** [A probable future] expectancy, promise, hope; see OUTLOOK 2. **3.** [A possible candidate] possibility, likely person, interested party; see CANDIDATE.

prospective *a.* considered, hoped for, promised; see PLANNED, PROPOSED.

prosper *v.* become rich, become wealthy, be enriched, thrive, turn out well, fare well, do well, be fortunate, have good fortune, flourish, get on, rise in the world, fatten, increase, bear fruit, bloom, blossom, flower, make money, make a fortune, benefit, advance, gain, make good*, do well by oneself*, make one's mark, roll in the lap of luxury*, come along*, do wonders*; see also SUCCEED 1.

prosperity *n.* accomplishment, victory, successfulness; see SUCCESS 2.

prosperous *a.* flourishing, well-off, well-to-do; see RICH 1.

prostitute *n.* harlot, strumpet, lewd woman, whore, bawd, streetwalker, loose woman, fallen woman, courtesan, abandoned woman, concubine, vice girl, hustler, call girl, tramp, slut, tart*, hooker*; see also CRIMINAL.

prostitution *n.* hustling, harlotry, hooking*; see LEWDNESS.

protagonist *n.* leading character, lead, combatant; see HERO 1, IDOL.

protect *v.* shield, guard, preserve; see DEFEND 1, 2.

protected *a.* shielded, safeguarded, cared for, watched over, preserved, defended, guarded, secured, kept safe, sheltered, harbored, screened, fostered, cherished, curtained, shaded, disguised, camouflaged; see also COVERED 1, SAFE 1.—*Ant.* WEAK, insecure, unsheltered.

protection *n.* **1.** [A covering] shield, screen, camouflage; see SHELTER. **2.** [A surety] certainty, safeguard, safekeeping, assurance, invulnerability, reassurance, security, stability, strength; see also GUARANTY.—*Ant.* WEAKNESS, insecurity, frailty.

protector *n.* champion, defender, patron, sponsor, safeguard, benefactor, supporter, advocate, guardian angel, guard, shield, savior, standby, promoter, mediator, counsel, second, backer, upholder, sympathizer, big brother*, big sister*, angel*, cover*, front*; see also GUARDIAN.

protest *n.* mass meeting, rally, demonstration, peace demonstration, draft demonstration, peace rally, race riot, clamor, tumult, turmoil, campus revolt, moratorium, sit-in, love-in*.

protest *v.* demur, disagree, object; see OPPOSE 1.

protestant *a.* non-Catholic, new; Adventist, Baptist, Congregationalist, etc.; see also PROTESTANT.

Protestant *n. Protestant sects include the following:* Evangelist, Adventist, Baptist, Congregational, Episcopal, Lutheran, Methodist, Presbyterian.

protester *n.* demonstrator, dissident, rebel; see RADICAL.

protrude *v.* come through, stick out, jut out; see PROJECT 1.

proud *a.* **1.** [Having a creditable self-respect] self-respecting, self-sufficient, self-satisfied, ambitious, spirited, vigorous, high-spirted, honorable, great-hearted, fiery, dignified, stately, lordly, lofty-minded, high-minded, impressive, imposing, fine, splendid, looking one in the eye, on one's high horse, high and mighty, holding up one's head.—*Ant.* HUMBLE, unpretentious, unassuming. **2.** [Egotistic] egotistical, vain, vainglorious; see EGOTISTIC. —**do oneself proud*** achieve, prosper, advance; see SUCCEED 1.

proudly *a.* boastfully, haughtily, insolently; see ARROGANTLY.

prove *v.* justify, substantiate, authenticate, corroborate, testify, explain, attest, show, warrant, uphold, determine, settle, fix, certify, back, sustain, validate, bear out, affirm, confirm, make evident, convince, evidence, be evidence of, witness, declare, testify, have a case, manifest, demonstrate, document, establish, settle once and for all.

proved *a.* confirmed, established, demonstrated; see ESTABLISH 3.

proverb *n.* maxim, adage, aphorism, precept, saw, saying, motto, dictum, text, witticism, repartee, axiom, truism, byword, epigram, moral, folk wisdom, platitude.

proverbial *a.* current, general, unquestioned; see COMMON 1, DULL 4.

provide *v.* **1.** [To supply] furnish, equip, grant, replenish, provide with, accommodate, care for, indulge with, favor with, contribute, give, outfit, stock, store, minister, administer, render, procure, afford, present, bestow, cater, rig up, fit out, fit up, provision, ration, implement.—*Ant.* REFUSE, take away, deny. **2.** [To yield] render, afford, give; see PRODUCE 1.

provided *conj.* on the assumption that, in the event, in the case that; see IF, SUPPOSING.

provided that *conj.* on condition, in the event, with that understood; see IF, SUPPOSING.

provide for or **against** *v.* prepare for, arrange, plan ahead; see PREPARE 1.

providence *n.* divine government, divine superintendence, Deity; see GOD.

providing *conj.* provided, in the event that, on the assumption that; see IF, SUPPOSING.

providing *n.* provision, supplying, furnishing, equipping, replenishing, replenishment, contributing, outfitting, stocking, filling, procurement, affording, presenting, preparing, preparation, arrangement, planning, putting by, laying in, putting in readiness, granting, bestowing, giving, offering, tendering, accumulating, storing, saving.

province *n.* area, region, dependency; see TERRITORY 2.

provincial *a.* rude, unpolished, countrified; see RURAL.

provision *n.* **1.** [Arrangement] preparation, outline, procurement; see PLAN 2. **2.** [Supplies; *usually plural*] stock, store, emergency; see EQUIPMENT. **3.** [A proviso] stipulation, prerequisite, terms; see REQUIREMENT 1.

provisional *a.* transient, passing, ephemeral; see TEMPORARY.

provisionally *a.* conditionally, on certain conditions, for the time being; see TEMPORARILY.

provocation *n.* incitement, stimulus, inducement; see INCENTIVE.

provocative *a.* alluring, arousing, intriguing; see INTERESTING.

provoke *v.* **1.** [To vex] irritate, put out, aggravate; see BOTHER 2. **2.** [To incite] stir, rouse, arouse; see INCITE. **3.** [To cause] make, produce, bring about; see BEGIN 1.

provoked *a.* exasperated, incensed, enraged; see ANGRY.

prowl *v.* slink, lurk, rove; see SNEAK.

proxy *n.* substitute, broker, representative; see AGENT, DELEGATE.

prude *n.* prig, puritan, old maid, prudish person, priss*, sourpuss*, stick-in-the-mud*, spoilsport, wet blanket*, goody-goody*.

prudence *n.* caution, circumspection, judgment, providence, considerateness, judiciousness, deliberation, wisdom, foresight, forethought, care, carefulness, frugality, watchfulness, precaution, heedfulness, heed, economy, husbandry, concern, conservatism, conservation, discrimination, cunning, vigilance, coolness, calculation, presence of mind.—*Ant.* CARELESSNESS, imprudence, rashness.

prudent *a.* **1.** [Cautious and careful] cautious, circumspect, wary; see CAREFUL, DISCREET. **2.** [Sensible and wise] discerning, sound, reasonable; see CAREFUL.

prudish *a.* narrow-minded, illiberal, bigoted, prissy, priggish, over-refined, fastidious, stuffy, conventional, offish, stiff, smug, strait-laced, demure, narrow, puritancial, affected, artificial, scrupulous, overexact, pedantic, pretentious, strict, rigid, rigorous, simpering, finical, finicking, finicky, squeamish, like a maiden aunt, like an old maid; see also PRIM.—*Ant.* SOCIABLE, broad-minded, genial.

pry *v.* **1.** [To move, with a lever] push, lift, raise, pull, move, tilt, hoist, heave, uplift, upraise, elevate, turn out, jimmy*; see also FORCE, OPEN 2. **2.** [To endeavor to discover; *often used with "into"*] search, ferret out, seek, ransack, reconnoiter, peep, peer, peek, snoop, gaze, look closely, spy, stare, gape, nose, be curious, inquire; see also MEDDLE 1.

pseudo *a.* imitation, quasi, sham; see FALSE 3.

psyche *n.* subconscious, mind, ego; see CHARACTER 2.

psychiatrist *n.* analyst, therapist, shrink; see DOCTOR.

psychiatry *n.* psychopathology, psychotherapy, psychoanalysis; see MEDICINE 1, SCIENCE 1.

psychic *a.* **1.** [Mental] analytic, intellectual, psychological; see MENTAL 2. **2.** [Spiritual] telepathic, mystic, immaterial; see SUPERNATURAL.

psycho *a.* mad, crazy, psychopathic; see INSANE.

psychological *a.* directly experimental, subjective, experimental; see MENTAL 2.

psychologist *n.* psychiatrist, analyst, clinician; see DOCTOR, SCIENTIST.

psychology *n.* science of mind, study of personality, medicine, therapy; see also SCIENCE 1, SOCIAL SCIENCE. *Divisions and varieties of psychology include the following:* rational, existential, functional, structural, self, dynamic, motor, physiological, abnormal, differential, Gestalt, Freudian, Adlerian, Jungian, genetic, applied, popular, analytical, comparative, child, animal, mass, individual, social, behaviorism, parapsychology.

psychopath *n.* lunatic, antisocial personality, sociopath; see MADMAN.

psychotic *a.* insane, mad, psychopathic; see INSANE 1.

puberty *n.* boyhood, pubescence, adolescence; see YOUTH 1.

public *a.* **1.** [Available to the public] free to all, without charge, open, unrestricted, not private, known; see also FREE 4. **2.** [Owned by the public] governmental, government, civil, civic, common, communal, publicly owned, municipal, metropolitan, state, federal, county, city, township.—*Ant.* PRIVATE, personal, restricted.

public *n.* men, society, the community; see PEOPLE 3. **—in public** candidly, plainly, aboveboard; see OPENLY 1.

publication *n.* **1.** [The act of making public] writing, printing, broadcasting, announcement, notification, promulgation, issuing, statement, acquaintance, advisement, advertisement, communication, revelation, disclosure, discovery, making current, making available. **2.** [Something published] news, tidings, information; see BOOK, MAGAZINE, NEWSPAPER.

publicity *n.* **1.** [Public distribution] notoriety, currency, publicness; see DISTRIBUTION. **2.** [Free advertising] public relations copy, press release, report; see PROPAGANDA. **3.** [Activity intended to advertise] promotion, publicizing, advertising; see ADVERTISEMENT.

publicize *v.* announce, broadcast, promulgate; see ADVERTISE.

publicly *a.* candidly, plainly, aboveboard; see OPENLY 1.

public opinion *n.* public pressure, power of the press, popular pressure; see INFLUENCE, OPINION 1.

public relations *n.* promotion, public image, favorable climate of opinion; see ADVERTISEMENT, PROPAGANDA.

public-spirited *a.* altruistic, humanitarian, openhanded; see GENEROUS 1.

public utility *n.* public services, natural monopoly, light and power; see UTILITIES.

publish *v.* **1.** [To print and distribute] reprint, issue, reissue, distribute, bring out, write, do publishing, become a publisher, get out, put to press, put forth, be in the newspaper business, be in the book business, own a publishing house, send forth, give out; see also PRINT 2. **2.** [To make known] announce, promulgate, proclaim; see ADVERTISE.

published *a.* written, printed, made public, circulated, proclaimed, promulgated, propagated, pronounced, ventilated, divulged, made current, made known, broadcast, circulated, spread abroad, disseminated, got out, appeared, released, coming forth, seeing the light, presented, offered, voiced, noised abroad, given publicity, brought before the public; see also ADVERTISED, ISSUED.—*Ant.* UNKNOWN, unpublished, unwritten.

publisher *n.* publicist, businessman, administrator; see EDITOR.

pudding *n.* mousse, custard, tapioca; see DESSERT.

puddle *n.* plash, mud puddle, rut; see POOL 1.

pudgy *a.* chubby, chunky, stout; see FAT.

puff *n.* whiff, sudden gust, quick blast; see WIND.

puff *v.* distend, enlarge, swell; see FILL 1, 2.

puffy *a.* **1.** [Windy] airy, gusty, breezy; see WINDY. **2.** [Swollen] distended, expanded, blown; see FULL 1.

puke* *v.* throw up, retch, upchuck*; see VOMIT.

pull *n.* **1.** [The act of pulling] tow, drag, haul, jerk, twitch, wrench, extraction, drawing, rending, tearing, uprooting, weeding, row, paddle. **2.** [Exerted force] work, strain, tug; see STRENGTH. **3.** [*Influence] inclination, inducement, weight; see INFLUENCE.

pull *v.* **1.** [To exert force] tug, pull at, draw in; see WORK 1. **2.** [To move by pulling] draw, ease, drag, lift, stretch, move, jerk, haul, tear, rend, gather; see also DRAW 1. **3.** [To incline] slope, tend, move toward; see LEAN 1.

pull apart *v.* separate, split, force apart; see DIVIDE.

pull away *v.* depart, pull off, go; see LEAVE 1.

pull down *v.* raze, wreck, remove; see DESTROY.

pulley *n.* sheave, block, lift, lifter, crowbar, crow, pry; see also TOOL 1.

pull into *v.* come in, land, make a landing; see ARRIVE.

Pullman *n.* railroad sleeping car, chair car, sleeper, first-class accommodation, wagon-lit.

pull off *v.* **1.** [To remove] detach, separate, yank off; see REMOVE 1. **2.** [*To achieve] accomplish, manage, succeed; see ACHIEVE.

pull oneself together *v.* recover, revive, get on one's feet; see IMPROVE 2.

pull out *v.* go, depart, stop participating; see LEAVE 1, STOP 2.

pull over *v.* drive to the side, pull up, park; see STOP 1.

pull through* *v.* get better, get over something, triumph; see SURVIVE 1.

pull up *v.* **1.** [To remove] dislodge, elevate, dig out; see REMOVE 1. **2.** [To stop] arrive, come to a stop, get there; see STOP 1.

pulp *n.* pap, mash, sponge, paste, dough, batter, curd, jam, poultice.

pulpit *n.* **1.** [The ministry] priesthood, clergy, ecclesiastics; see MINISTRY 2. **2.** [A platform in a church] desk, rostrum, stage; see PLATFORM 1.

pulpy *a.* smooth, thick, fleshy; see SOFT 1.

pulse *n.* pulsation, vibration, throb; see BEAT 1.

pump *n.* air pump, vacuum pump, jet pump; see MACHINE, TOOL 1.

pump *v.* elevate, draw out, tap; see DRAW 1.

pun *n.* witticism, quip, play on words; see JOKE.

punch *n.* thrust, knock, stroke; see BLOW.

punch *v.* **1.** [To hit] strike, knock, thrust against; see HIT. **2.** [To perforate] pierce, puncture, bore; see PENETRATE.

punched *a.* perforated, dented, pierced, punctured, needled, stamped, imprinted, bored, wounded, bitten, tapped, impaled, spiked, gored, speared, stabbed, stuck.

punctual *a.* prompt, precise, particular, on time, on schedule, exact, timely, seasonable, regular, cyclic, dependable, recurrent, constant, steady, scrupulous, punctilious, meticulous, on the nose.—*Ant.* CARELESS, unreliable, desultory.

punctuation *n.* *Marks of punctuation include the following:* period, colon, semicolon, comma, interrogation, exclamation, parentheses, dash, brackets, apostrophe, hyphen, quotation marks, brace, ellipsis.

puncture *n.* punctured tire, flat tire, flat; see HOLE, TROUBLE 1.

puncture *v.* prick, perforate, pierce; see PENETRATE.

punish *v.* correct, discipline, chasten, chastise, sentence, train, reprove, lecture, penalize, fine, incarcerate, expel, execute, exile, behead, hang, electrocute, dismiss, debar, whip, spank, paddle, trounce, switch, cuff, inflict penalty, come down on*, attend to, crack down on*, make it hot for*, pitch into*, give a dressing-down*, lower the boom on*, ground*, throw the book at*, blacklist*, blackball*; see also BEAT 1, IMPRISON, KILL 1, SCOLD.

punished *a.* corrected, disciplined, chastened, penalized, sentenced, trained, reproved, chastised, castigated, lectured, scolded, imprisoned, incarcerated, expelled, exiled, dismissed, disbarred, defrocked, whipped, switched, cuffed, cracked down on, pitched into, grounded, given one's just deserts; see also BEATEN 1, CONFINED 3, EXECUTED 2.—*Ant.* RELEASED, cleared, exonerated.

punishment *n.* correction, discipline, reproof, penalty, infliction, suffering, deprivation, unhappiness, trial, penance, retribution, mortification, disciplinary action, fine, reparation, forfeiture, forfeit, confiscation, rap on the knuckles*.—*Ant.* FREEDOM, exoneration, release.

puny *a.* feeble, inferior, diminutive; see WEAK 1.

pup *n.* puppy, whelp, young dog; see ANIMAL, DOG.

pupil *n.* schoolboy, schoolgirl, learner; see STUDENT.

puppet *n.* manikin, figurine, moppet; see DOLL.

puppy *n.* pup, whelp, young dog; see ANIMAL, DOG.

purchase *n.* **1.** [The act of buying] procurement, getting, obtaining, shopping, installment buying, bargaining, marketing, investing; see also BUYING. **2.** [Something bought] buy, order, goods, shipment, acquisition, invoice, packages, delivery, articles, property, possession, gain, booty, acquirement, investment; see also BARGAIN, GOODS.

purchase *v.* obtain, acquire, buy up; see BUY.

purchaser *n.* shopper, obtainer, procurer; see BUYER.

pure *a.* **1.** [Not mixed] unmixed, unadulterated, unalloyed, unmingled, simple, clear, genuine, undiluted, classic, real, true, fair, bright, unclouded, transparent, lucid, straight, neat; see also CLEAR 2, GENUINE 1, SIMPLE 1.—*Ant.* MIXED, mingled, blended. **2.** [Clean] immaculate, spotless, stainless, unspotted, germ-free, unstained, unadulterated, unblemished, untarnished, unsoiled, disinfected, sterilized, uncontaminated, sanitary, unpolluted, purified, refined.—*Ant.* DIRTY, sullied, contaminated. **3.** [Chaste] virgin, continent, celibate; see CHASTE. **4.** [Absolute] sheer, utter, complete; see ABSOLUTE 1.

purely *a.* entirely, totally, essentially; see COMPLETELY.

purification *n.* purifying, cleansing, purgation; see CLEANING.—*Ant.* POLLUTION, defilement, contamination.

purify *v.* cleanse, clear, refine, wash, disinfect, fumigate, deodorize, clarify, sublimate, purge, filter; see also CLEAN.

purity *n.* **1.** [The state of being pure] pureness, cleanness, cleanliness, immaculateness, stainlessness, whiteness, clearness. **2.** [Innocence] artlessness, guilelessness, blamelessness; see INNOCENCE 2. **3.** [Chastity] abstemiousness, continence, self-command; see CHASTITY, VIRTUE 1.

purple *a.* purpled, reddish blue, bluish red; see COLOR. *Tints and shades of purple include the following:* lilac, violet, mauve, heliotrope, magenta, plum, lavender, pomegranate, royal purple, wine.

purpose *n.* **1.** [Aim] intention, end, goal, mission, objective, object, idea, design, hope, resolve, meaning, view, scope, desire, dream, expectation, ambition, intent, destination, direction, scheme, prospective, proposal, target, aspiration; see also PLAN 2. **2.** [Resolution] tenacity, constancy, persistence; see CONFIDENCE, DETERMINATION, FAITH 1. —**on purpose** purposefully, intentionally, designedly; see DELIBERATELY. —**to the purpose** to the point, pertinent, apt; see RELEVANT.

purpose *v.* aim, plan, propose; see INTEND 1.

purposeful *a.* obstinate, stubborn, persistent; see RESOLUTE.

purr *v.* hum, drone, sigh; see SOUND.

purse *n.* pouch, pocketbook, receptacle, moneybag, wallet, pocket, coin purse, billfold, money belt, sack, vanity case.

pursue *v.* **1.** [To chase] seek, hound, track down, dog, shadow, search for, search out, stalk, run after, go after, hunt down, trail, tag with, follow close upon, move behind, scout out, nose around, poke around, keep on foot, follow up. **2.** [To seek] strive for, aspire to, attempt; see TRY 1. **3.** [To continue] persevere, proceed, carry on; see CONTINUE 1.

pursuit *n.* chase, race, pursuance; see HUNT.

pus *n.* infection, discharge, mucus; see MATTER 1.

push *n.* shove, force, bearing, propulsion, drive, exertion, weight, straining, shoving, thrusting, forcing, driving, inducement, mass, potential, reserve, impact, blow; see also PRESSURE.

push *v.* **1.** [To press against] thrust, shove, butt, crowd, gore, ram, crush against, jostle, push out of one's way, lie on, shoulder, elbow, struggle, strain, exert, set one's shoulder to, rest one's weight on, put forth one's strength; see also FORCE. **2.** [To move by pushing] impel, accelerate, drive onward, launch, start, set in motion, push forward, shift, start rolling, budge, stir, shove along; see also DRIVE 2. **3.** [To promote] advance, expedite, urge; see PROMOTE 1. **4.** [*To sell illegally] sell under the counter, bootleg, black-market, moonshine; see also SELL.

push off *v.* depart, start, take off; see LEAVE 1.

push on *v.* keep going, go, make progress; see CONTINUE 1, 2.

pushover *n.* sucker, easy pickings, fool; see VICTIM.

pussyfoot* *v.* evade, avoid, dodge, sidestep, hedge; see also AVOID, EVADE.

put *v.* **1.** [To place] set, locate, deposit, plant, lodge, store, situate, fix, put in a place, lay, pin down, seat, settle. **2.** [To establish] install, quarter, fix; see ESTABLISH 2. **3.** [To deposit] invest in, insert, embed; see PLANT.

put across or **over*** *v.* succeed, fulfill, complete; see ACHIEVE.

put aside *v.* deposit, save, put out of the way; see STORE.

put away *v.* deposit, save, put out of the way; see STORE.

put back *v.* bring back, make restitution for, put in its place; see REPLACE 1, RETURN 2.

put down *v.* silence, repress, crush; see DEFEAT 2, 3.

put-down *n.* suppression, indignity, cut*; see INSULT.
put in *v.* sail for, move toward, land; see APPROACH 2.
put off *v.* postpone, defer, retard; see DELAY.
put on *v.* **1.** [To pretend] feign, sham, make believe; see PRETEND 1. **2.** [*To deceive] trick, confuse, confound; see DECEIVE.
put-on *a.* feigned, simulated, calculated; see PRETENDED.
put-on* *n.* deception, device, job*; see TRICK 1.
put on airs *v.* brag, show off, make pretensions; see BOAST.
put one's cards on the table *v.* say, display, show; see REVEAL, TELL 1.
put over* *v.* manage, do, get done; see ACHIEVE.
putrid *a.* corrupt, putrified, decayed; see ROTTEN 1.
put someone in his place *v.* reprimand, censure, correct; see SCOLD.
putter *v.* dawdle, fritter, poke; see LOITER.
put through *v.* do, manage, finish; see ACHIEVE.
put to sleep* *v.* knock out, subject to euthanasia, murder; see KILL 1.
put up *v.* **1.** [To preserve] can, smoke, pickle; see PRESERVE 2. **2.** [To build] erect, fabricate, construct; see BUILD. **3.** [To bet] speculate, wager, put one's money on; see GAMBLE. **4.** [To entertain] house, provide bed and board, make welcome; see ENTERTAIN 2.
put up with *v.* undergo, tolerate, stand; see ENDURE 2.
puzzle *n.* **1.** [The state of being puzzled] uncertainty, hardship, vexation; see CONFUSION. **2.** [A problem] tangle, bafflement, question, frustration, intricacy, maze, issue, enigma, proposition, mystification, bewilderment, query, mystery, dilemma, muddle, secret, riddle, ambiguity, difficulty, perplexity, confusion, entanglement, stickler, paradox.—*Ant.* ANSWER, solution, development. **3.** [A problem to be worked for amusement] *Varieties include the following:* riddle, cryptogram, logogram, crossword puzzle, jigsaw puzzle, anagram, acrostic, rebus, Chinese puzzle, puzzle-ring.
puzzle *v.* **1.** [To perplex] obscure, bewilder, complicate; see CONFUSE. **2.** [To wonder] marvel, be surprised, be astonished; see WONDER 1.
puzzled *a.* perplexed, bewildered, mystified; see DOUBTFUL.
puzzle out *v.* figure out, work out, decipher; see SOLVE.
puzzle over *v.* think about, consider, debate; see THINK.
puzzling *a.* **1.** [Obscure] uncertain, ambiguous, mystifying; see OBSCURE 1. **2.** [Difficult] perplexing, abstruse, hard; see DIFFICULT 2.
pyramid *n.* tomb, shrine, remains; see MONUMENT 1.

Q

quack *a.* unprincipled, pretentious, dissembling; see DISHONEST.
quack *n.* rogue, charlatan, humbug; see CHEAT, IMPOSTOR.
quadrangle *n.* geometrical four-sided figure, parallelogram, rhombus; see RECTANGLE.
quadrangular *a.* rectangular, quadrilateral, plane; see ANGULAR, SQUARE.
quadruped *n.* four-legged animal, domestic beast, mammal; see ANIMAL.
quadruple *a.* fourfold, four-way, four times as great, consisting of four parts, quadruplex, four-cycle, quadruplicate.
quaff *v.* gulp, swallow, guzzle; see DRINK 1, SWALLOW.
quaint *a.* fanciful, cute, pleasing, captivating, curious, ancient, antique, whimsical, affected, enchanting, baroque, Victorian, French Provincial, Early American, Colonial; see also CHARMING.—*Ant.* MODERN, up-to-date, fashionable.
quake *n.* temblor, tremor, shock; see EARTHQUAKE.
quake *v.* tremble, shrink, cower; see SHAKE 1.
qualification *n.* need, requisite, essential; see REQUIREMENT 1.
qualifications *n.pl.* endowments, acquirements, attainments; see EXPERIENCE.
qualified *a.* **1.** [Limited] conditional, modified, confined; see RESTRICTED. **2.** [Competent] adequate, equipped, fitted; see ABLE.
qualify *v.* **1.** [To limit] reduce, restrain, temper; see ALTER 1. **2.** [To fulfill requirements] fit, suit, pass, be capacitated for, have the requisites, meet the demands, be endowed by nature for, measure up, meet the specifications.—*Ant.* FAIL, become unfit, be unsuited.
quality *n.* **1.** [A characteristic] attribute, trait, endowment; see CHARACTERISTIC. **2.** [Essential character] nature, essence, genius; see CHARACTER 2. **3.** [Grade] class, kind,

state, condition, merit, worth, excellence, stage, step, variety, standing, rank, group, place, position, repute.

qualm *n.* indecision, scruple, suspicion; see DOUBT, UNCERTAINTY 2.

quantity *n.* amount, number, bulk, mass, measure, extent, abundance, volume, capacity, lot, deal, pile, multitude, portion, carload, sum, profusion, mountain, load, barrel, shipment, consignment, bushel, supply, ton, ocean, flood, sea, flock, the amount of, score, swarm, quite a few, army, host, pack, crowd, bunch*, heap*, mess*, gob*, batch, all kinds of*, all sorts of*; see also SIZE 2.

quarantined *a.* shut up, under quarantine, hospitalized, restrained, separated; see also ISOLATED.

quarrel *n.* **1.** [An angry dispute] wrangle, squabble, dissension; see DISAGREEMENT 1, DISPUTE. **2.** [Objection] complaint, disapproval, disagreement; see OBJECTION.

quarrel *v.* wrangle, dispute, contend, fight, squabble, row, clash, altercate, dissent, bicker, struggle, strive, contest, object, complain, disagree, argue, charge, allegate, feud, strike, engage in blows, mix it up with*, step on one's toes, get tough with*, lock horns, have words with, have a brush with*, have it out*, fall out with*, break with*; see also OPPOSE 1.—*Ant.* AGREE, accord, harmonize.

quarrelsome *a.* factious, irritable, combative, pugnacious, turbulent, unruly, passionate, violent, contentious, disputatious, fiery, cross, irascible, snappish, waspish, peevish, petulant, churlish, cantankerous, thin-skinned, touchy, huffy, pettish, peppery, impassioned, hotheaded, excitable, hasty, tempestuous, with a chip on one's shoulder*.—*Ant.* AGREEABLE, CALM, peaceful.

quart *n.* two pints, thirty-two ounces, one-fourth gallon; see MEASURE 1.

quarter *n.* **1.** [One of four equal parts] fourth, one-fourth part, portion, farthing, division, three months, semester, school term, quarter of an hour, quarter section; see also PART 1. **2.** [One quarter of a dollar; *United States*] twenty-five cents, one-fourth of a dollar, coin, two bits*; see also MONEY 1. **3.** [A section of a community] neighborhood, district, section; see AREA. **—at close quarters** at close range, cramped, restricted; see NEAR 1.

quarter *v.* **1.** [To divide into quarters] cleave, dismember, cut up; see CUT 1, DIVIDE. **2.** [To provide living quarters] lodge, shelter, house; see SHELTER.

quarterback *n.* QB, signal caller, field general*; see FOOTBALL PLAYER.

quarterly *a.* by quarters, once every three months, periodically; see REGULARLY.

quarters *n.pl.* house, apartment, room, barracks, tent, lodge, cabins, cottage, car trailer.

quartet *n.* four persons, four voices, four musicians, string quartet, principals, four-voice parts.

quartz *n.* *Types of quartz include the following:* amethyst, chalcedony, rock crystal, rose quartz, smoky quartz, bloodstone, agate, onyx, sardonyx, carnelian, chrysoprase, prase, flint, jasper; see also ROCK 1.

quasi *a.* supposedly, to a certain extent, apparently; see ALMOST.

queasy *a.* squeamish, sick, uneasy; see UNCOMFORTABLE 1.

queen *n.* ruler, female ruler, female sovereign, woman monarch, queen mother, regent, wife of a king, consort, queen consort, queen dowager, queen regent, fairy queen, May Queen, matriarch.

queen-size* *a.* medium-large, outsize, not king-size; see BROAD 1, LARGE 1.

queer *a.* **1.** [Odd] odd, peculiar, uncommon; see UNUSUAL 2. **2.** [*Suspicious] strange, questionable, curious; see SUSPICIOUS 2.

quench *v.* **1.** [To satisfy] slake, glut, gorge; see DRINK 1. **2.** [To smother] stifle, dampen, douse; see MOISTEN.

quest *n.* journey, search, crusade; see EXAMINATION 1.

question *n.* **1.** [A query] inquiry, interrogatory, interrogation, inquisition, feeler, catechism, inquest, rhetorical question, burning question, crucial question, leading question, academic question.—*Ant.* ANSWER, solution, reply. **2.** [A puzzle] enigma, mystery, problem; see PUZZLE 2. **3.** [A subject] proposal, topic, discussion; see SUBJECT. **—beside the question** not germane, beside the point, unnecessary; see IRRELEVANT. **—beyond question** beyond dispute, without any doubt, sure; see CERTAIN 2. **—in question** being considered, under discussion, controversial; see CONSIDERED. **—out of the question** not to be considered, by no means, no; see IMPOSSIBLE.

question *v.* **1.** [To ask] inquire, interrogate, query, quest, seek, search, sound out, petition, solicit, ask about, catechize, show curiosity, pry into, ask a leading question, challenge, raise a question, make inquiry, quiz, cross-examine, probe, investigate, put to the question, bring into question; see also ASK. **2.** [To doubt] distrust, suspect, dispute; see DOUBT.

questionable *a.* **1.** [Justifying doubt] doubtful, undefined, equivocal, disputable, obscure, occult, indecisive, controversial, vague, unsettled, open to doubt, indeterminate, debatable, unconfirmed, problematical, cryptic, apocryphal, hypothetical, mysterious, enigmatic, ambiguous, indefinite, contingent, provisional, paradoxical, under advisement, under examination, open to question, up for discussion, in question, to be voted on, to be decided, hard to believe, incredible; see also UNCERTAIN.—*Ant.* DEFINITE, undoubted, credible. **2.** [Having a poor appearance or reputation] dubious, disreputable, notorious, opprobrious, obnoxious, of ill repute, unsatisfactory, of little account, thought ill of, under a cloud, ill-favored, unpopular, unpleasing, ugly, unattractive, offensive, disagreeable, evil-looking, illegitimate, discreditable, unhonored, unliked, unloved; see also SUSPICIOUS 2.—*Ant.* HONORED, esteemed, liked.

questionnaire *n.* set of questions, inquiry, survey; see CENSUS.

quick *a.* **1.** [Rapid] swift, expeditious, fleet; see FAST 1. **2.** [Almost immediate] posthaste, prompt, instantaneous; see IMMEDIATE. **3.** [Hasty] impetuous, mercurial, quick-tempered; see RASH. **4.** [Alert] ready, sharp, vigorous; see ACTIVE.

quicken *v.* **1.** [To hasten] speed, hurry, make haste; see HASTEN 2. **2.** [To cause to hasten] expedite, urge, promote; see HASTEN 2.

quickly *a.* speedily, swiftly, fleetly, flying, wingedly, with dispatch, scurrying, hurrying, rushing, shooting, bolting, darting, flashing, dashing, suddenly, in haste, in a hurry, just now, this minute, in a moment, in an instant, right away, at a greater rate, without delay, against the clock, racing, galloping, loping, sweeping, light-footedly, briskly, at once, like a bat out of hell*, on the double*, in a flash*, in a jiffy*, to beat the band*, at full blast*, hellbent for leather*, hand over fist*, like mad*, by leaps and bounds, like a house afire*.—*Ant.* SLOWLY, sluggishly, creepingly.

quick-tempered *a.* temperamental, quarrelsome, sensitive; see IRRITABLE.

quiet *a.* calm, peaceful, hushed, muffled, noiseless, still, stilled, mute, muted, soundless, dumb, quieted, speechless, unspeaking, quiescent, taciturn, reserved, reticent, not excited, not anxious, not disturbed, silent, unexpressed, closemouthed, close, tight-lipped, uncommunicative, secretive.

quiet *n.* **1.** [Rest] calm, tranquillity, relaxation; see PEACE 2. **2.** [Silence] hush, stillness, speechlessness; see SILENCE 1.

quiet *v.* **1.** [To make calm] calm, cool, relax, compose, tranquilize, satisfy, please, pacify, mollify, console, subdue, reconcile, gratify, calm down, soften, moderate, smooth, ameliorate, lull, appease, restrain, sober, slacken, soothe.—*Ant.* EXCITE, increase, agitate. **2.** [To make silent] still, deaden, silence, lower the sound level, muffle, mute, stop, check, restrain, suppress, break in, confute, eliminate, repress, refute, confound, answer, quell, to stop the mouth*, put the lid on*, button up*, choke off*, put the stopper on*.—*Ant.* SOUND, ring, cause to sound.

quiet down *v.* grow silent, be hushed, hush, be subdued, be suppressed, become speechless, fall quiet, break off, be answered.

quietly *a.* **1.** [Calmly] peacefully, unconcernedly, confidently; see CALMLY. **2.** [Almost silently] noiselessly, speechlessly, as quietly as possible; see SILENTLY. **3.** [Without attracting attention] humbly, unostentatiously, simply; see MODESTLY.

quilt *n.* bed covering, coverlet, comforter, feather bed, puff, down puff, batt, bed quilt, patchwork quilt, pieced quilt, bedspread, pad; see also COVER 1.

quip *n.* jest, repartee, banter; see LANGUAGE 1.

quirk *n.* vagary, whim, caprice, fancy, whimsy, conceit, humor, turn, twist, knack, peculiarity, idiosyncrasy, quibble, equivocation, subterfuge, bee in one's bonnet*; see also CHARACTERISTIC, IRREGULARITY.

quit *v.* **1.** [Abandon] surrender, renounce, relinquish; see ABANDON 1. **2.** [To cease] discontinue, cease, halt, pause, stop, end, desist; see also STOP 2. **3.** [To leave] go away from, depart, vacate; see LEAVE 1. **4.** [To resign] leave, resign, stop work, walk out, quit, change jobs, cease work, give notice; see also RESIGN 2.

quite *a.* **1.** [Completely] entirely, wholly, totally; see COMPLETELY. **2.** [Really] truly, positively, actually; see REALLY 1. **3.** [To a considerable degree] pretty, more or less, considerably; see VERY.

quitter *n.* shirker, dropout, deserter, goldbrick*, piker*, slacker*.

quiver *n.* shudder, shiver, tremble; see VIBRATION.

quiver *v.* vibrate, shudder, shiver; see WAVE 3.

quiz *n.* test, questioning, query; see EXAMINATION 2.

quiz *v.* question, test, cross-examine; see EXAMINE.

quorum *n.* enough to transact business, majority of the membership, legal minimum; see MEMBER.

quota *n.* portion, part, division; see SHARE.

quotation *n.* **1.** [Quoted matter] excerpt, passage, citation, cite*, citing, extract, recitation, repetition, sentence, quote, plagiarism. **2.** [A quoted price] market price, current price, published price; see PRICE.

quote *v.* **1.** [To repeat verbatim] recite, excerpt, extract; see SAY. **2.** [To state a price] name a price, request, demand; see PRICE, VALUE 2.

quoted *a.* **1.** [Repeated from another] recited, excerpted, extracted, cited, instanced, copied. **2.** [Offered or mentioned at a stated price] asked, stated, announced, published, named, marked, given, priced, ticketed, tagged.

R

rabbi *n.* Jewish teacher, teacher, Hebrew theologian; see PRIEST.

rabbit *n.* hare, pika, bunny, Easter bunny; see also ANIMAL, RODENT. *Kinds of rabbits include the following:* jack rabbit, cottontail, snowshoe rabbit, Chinchilla hare, tapeti.

rabble *n.* mob, masses, riffraff; see CROWD, PEOPLE 3.

rabid *a.* **1.** [Fanatical] obsessed, zealous, keen; see RADICAL 2. **2.** [Insane] mad, raging, deranged; see INSANE. **3.** [Affected with rabies] attacked by a mad dog, hydrophobic, foaming at the mouth; see SICK.

rabies *n.* canine madness, hydrophobia, lyssa; see ILLNESS 2.

race *n.* **1.** [A major division of mankind] species, culture, variety, type, kind, strain, breed, family, cultural group, color; see also MAN 1. **2.** [Roughly, people united by blood or custom] nationality, caste, variety, type, the people, mankind, tribe, group, ethnic stock, human race, class, kind, nation, folk, gene pool, pedigree, lineage, community, inhabitants, population, populace, public, clan, breeding population; see also HEREDITY, SOCIETY 2. **3.** [A contest, usually in speed] competition, run, sprint, clash, meet, event, engagement, competitive trail of speed, competitive action, pursuit, rush, steeplechase, handicap, chase, match, derby, regatta, sweepstakes, marathon, heat, time trial; see also SPORT 3.

race *v.* **1.** [To move at great speed] speed, hurry, run, pursue, chase, tear, bustle, spurt, post, press on, run swiftly, hasten, trip, fly, hustle, dash, rush, sprint, swoop, scuttle, dart, scamper, haste, plunge ahead, whiz, bolt, scramble, whisk, shoot, run like mad, burn up the road*, gun the motor*, skedaddle*. **2.** [To compete] run a race, compete in a race, contend in running, follow a course, engage in a contest of speed, try to beat in a contest of speed, contend, enter a competition.

race prejudice *n.* racism, race hatred, bigotry; see PREJUDICE.

race riot *n.* civil disturbance, color riot, demonstration; see FIGHT, PROTEST.

racial *a.* lineal, hereditary, ancestral, genetic, ethnic, genealogical, ethnological, patriarchal, paternal, parental.

racism *n.* racial prejudice, racial bias, bigotry, racial discrimination, apartheid, segregation; see also PREJUDICE.

racist *a.* supremacist, favoring racism, bigoted; see CONSERVATIVE, PREJUDICED.

racist *n.* supremacist, believer in racism, supporter of the color line; see BIGOT, CONSERVATIVE.

rack *n.* holder, receptacle, framework, stand, shelf, ledge, perch, frame, bracket, whatnot, arbor, box, counter, trestle, hat rack, clothes rack, bottle rack, gun rack, feed rack; see also FRAME 1.

racket *n.* **1.** [Disturbing noise] uproar, clatter, din; see DISTURBANCE 2, NOISE 2. **2.** [Confusion accompanied by noise] squabble, scuffle, fracas, clash, row, wrangle, agitation, babel, pandemonium, turbulence, clamor, outcry, hullabaloo, tumult, hubbub, commotion, blare, turmoil, stir, noisy fuss, uproar, clatter, charivari, babble, roar, shouting, rumpus, riot, squall, brawl, fight, pitched battle, free-for-all, to-do*, fuss*. **3.** [A means of extortion] illegitimate business, confidence game, con game*; see CORRUPTION 2, CRIME, THEFT.

racketeer *n.* gang leader, trickster, dealer in illicit goods; see CRIMINAL.

racy *a.* **1.** [Full of zest] spicy, sharp, spirited; see EXCITING. **2.** [Not quite respectable] indecent, erotic, indelicate; see LEWD 2, SENSUAL 2.

radar *n.* radio detecting and ranging, radar principle, Missile Site Radar; see ELECTRONICS.

radial *a.* branched, outspread, radiated; see SPIRAL, SPREADING.

radiance *n.* brightness, brilliance, effulgence; see LIGHT 1.

radiant *a.* shining, luminous, radiating; see BRIGHT 1.

radiate *v.* **1.** [To send forth from a center] shed, diffuse, spread, disperse, shoot in all directions, irradiate, emit in straight lines, transmit, disseminate, broadcast, dispel, strew, sprinkle, circulate, send out in rays from a point, throw out. **2.** [To shed light or heat] beam, light up, illumine, heat, warm, circulate, expand, widen, brighten, illuminate, irradiate, glitter, glisten, glow, glare, gleam, glimmer, flare, blaze, flicker, sparkle, flash, shimmer, reflect.

radiation *n.* **1.** [Dissemination] propagation, dissipation, polarization, scattering, spread, diffraction, transmission, broadcast, emission, diffusion, dispersion, circulation, divergence, dispersal; see also DISTRIBUTION, EXTENT. **2.** [Fallout] nuclear particles, radioactivity, radiant energy; see ENERGY 2.

radical *a.* **1.** [Fundamental] original, primitive, native; see FUNDAMENTAL, ORGANIC. **2.** [Advocating violent change] extreme, thorough, complete, insurgent, revolutionary, iconoclastic, advanced, forward, progressive, abolitionist, militant, extremist, recalcitrant, mutinous, seditious, riotous, lawless, racist, insubordinate, anarchistic, unruly, nihilistic, communistic, liberal, leftist, immoderate, freethinking, ultra*, red*; see also REBELLIOUS.—*Ant.* CONSERVATIVE, reformist, gradualist. **3.** [Believing in violent political and social change] leftist, communistic, heretical; see REVOLUTIONARY 1.

radical *n.* insurgent, objector, revolutionist, revolutionary, insurrectionist, leftist, Bolshevik, anarchist, socialist, communist, pacifist, nihilist, traitor, mutineer, firebrand, renegade, extremeist, crusader, individualist, fascist, Nazi, misfit, iconoclast, eccentric, freethinker, rightist, hippie, fanatic, demonstrator, peace marcher, rioter, fifth columnist, nonconformist, left-winger, right-winger, pinko*, red*.

radically *a.* **1.** [Completely] wholly, thoroughly, entirely; see COMPLETELY. **2.** [Originally] basically, primitively, firstly, see ESSENTIALLY, FORMERLY.

radio *n.* **1.** [The study and practice of wireless communication] radio transmission, radio reception, signaling; see BROADCASTING, COMMUNICATION. **2.** [A receiving device] wireless, ship's radio, radio set, home radio, transistor radio, transistor, portable radio, pocket radio, auto radio, walkie-talkie, squawk box*; see also ELECTRONICS.

radioactive *a.* active, energetic, dangerous, hot*; see also POISONOUS.

radioactivity *n.* radiant energy, radioactive particles, Roentgen rays; see ENERGY 2.

radius *n.* space, sweep, range; see BOUNDARY, EXPANSE.

raffle *n.* sweepstakes, pool, lottery; see GAMBLING.

raft *n.* flatboat, barge, float, catamaran, life raft, swimming raft, rubber raft; see also BOAT.

rag *n.* remnant, wiper, dishrag, discarded material, hand rag, tatter, shred; see also GOODS 1. —**chew the rag*** chat, converse, have a talk; see TALK 1.

rage *n.* **1.** [A fit of anger] frenzy, tantrum, uproar, hysterics, explosion, storm, outburst, spasm, convulsion, eruption, furor, excitement, extreme agitation, madness, vehemence, fury, rampage, huff, wrath, raving, violent anger, ire, resentment, bitterness, gall, irritation, animosity, exasperation, passion, indignation, apoplexy, heat, temper, blowup*, fireworks*, hemorrhage*. **2.** [The object of enthusiasm and imitation] style, mode, fashion, vogue, craze, mania, the last word, the latest; see also FAD.

rage *v.* **1.** [To give vent to anger] rant, fume, rave, foam, splutter, yell, scream, roar, rail at, boil over, shake, quiver, seethe, shout, scold, go into a tantrum, have a fit, run amok, run riot, fly apart, flare up, carry on, show violent anger, bluster, storm, be furious, fret, lose one's temper, work oneself into a sweat*, go berserk, go into a tailspin, go up in the air*, blow one's top*, gnash one's teeth, raise Cain*, raise the devil, take on*, throw a fit*, fly off the handle*, explode, vent one's spleen, snap at, blow up*, blow a fuse*, go off at a tangent, cut loose*, have a hemorrhage*, make a fuss over*, kick up a row*, have a nervous breakdown, let off steam*, get oneself into a lather*, lose one's head*.—*Ant.* CRY, be calm, pout. **2.** [To be out of control] explode, flare, roar; see BURN, RUN 1.

ragged *a.* tattered, in shreds, patched, badly worn, rough, worn out, broken, worn to rags, frayed, frazzled, threadbare, shoddy, out at the seams, shredded, battered, the worse for wear, worn to a thread, down at the heel, moth-eaten, full of holes, torn, badly dressed; see also SHABBY, WORN 2.—*Ant.* WHOLE, new, unworn.

raging *a.* furious, irate, enraged; see ANGRY.

rags *n.pl.* old clothes, patched clothing, tatters, torn garments, scraps, castoff clothes, shreds, patches, remnants; see also CLOTHES.

raid *n.* **1.** [A predatory attack] invasion, assault, forced entrance; see ATTACK. **2.** [An armed investigation] seizure, surprise entrance, police raid, roundup, bust*; see also ARREST, CAPTURE.

raid *v.* assail, storm, plunder; see ATTACK.

raider *n.* bandit, thief, plunderer; see CRIMINAL, PIRATE, ROBBER.

rail *n.* **1.** [A polelike structure] post, railing, barrier, picket, rail fence, siding, banister, paling, rest, hand rail, guard rail, brass rail; see also BAR 1, FENCE. **2.** [A track; *often plural*] railway, monorail, railroad track; see RAILROAD.

railroad *n.* track, line, railway, trains, rails, elevated, underground, subway, commuter line, sidetrack, siding, passing track, loading track, feeder line, main line, double track, single track, trunk line, transcontinental railroad; see also TRAIN.

railway *n.* track, line, route; see RAILROAD.

rain *n.* **1.** [Water falling in drops] drizzle, mist, sprinkle, sprinkling, damp day, spring rain, rainfall, shower, precipitation, wet weather. **2.** [A rainstorm] thunderstorm, tempest, cloudburst; see STORM.

rain *v.* pour, drizzle, drop, fall, shower, sprinkle, mist, mizzle, spit, lay the dust, patter, rain cats and dogs*, come down in bucketfuls; see also STORM.

raincoat *n.* oilskin, canvas coat, mackintosh; see COAT 1, CLOTHES.

rainy *a.* moist, coastal, drizzly; see STORMY, WET 2.

raise *n.* raising, salary increment, advance; see PROMOTION 1.

raise *v.* **1.** [To lift] uplift, upraise, upheave, pull up, lift up, hold up, stand up, heave, set upright, put on its end, shove, boost, rear, mount, pry.—*Ant.* LOWER, bring down, take down. **2.** [To nurture] bring up, rear, nurse, suckle, nourish, wean, breed, cultivate, train, foster; see also PROVIDE 1, SUPPORT 3. **3.** [To collect or make available] gather, borrow, have ready; see ACCUMULATE, APPROPRIATE 2. **4.** [To erect] construct, establish, put up; see BUILD. **5.** [To ask] bring up, suggest, put; see ASK, PROPOSE 1. **6.** [To advance in rank] exalt, dignify, honor; see PROMOTE 2.

raised *a.* **1.** [Elevated] lifted, hoisted, built high, heightened, set high, in relief, erected, constructed, set up; see also BUILT.—*Ant.* REDUCED, lowered, taken down. **2.** [Nurtured] reared, brought up, trained, prepared, educated, fostered, bred, nourished, nursed. **3.** [Produced] harvested, cultivated, mass-produced; see MADE.

raise hell* *v.* carry on*, celebrate, carouse; see DRINK 2.

raise money *v.* make money by, collect, procure; see EARN 2.

rake *n.* **1.** [A debauched person] lecher, libertine, profligate; see DRUNKARD, RASCAL. **2.** [A pronged implement] *Rakes include the following:* clam, lawn, garden, moss, hay, stubble, weeding, oyster, horse, revolving; leaf sweeper; see also TOOL 1.

rake *v.* **1.** [To use a rake] clear up, collect, scratch, gather, scrape, clean up, weed, clear, grade, level. **2.** [To sweep with gunfire] strafe, machine-gun, blister; see SHOOT 1.

rally *n.* celebration, mass meeting, session; see GATHERING.

rally *v.* unite against, renew, redouble; see RETURN 1, REVENGE.

ram *n.* **1.** [An object used to deliver a thrust] plunger, pump, beam, prow, hammerhead, weight, pole, shaft, lever, spike, battering-ram, pile driver, tamping iron, punch, sledge hammer, rammer, tamper, monkey, bat, maul, hydraulic ram, spar, piston, drop weight, bow; see also BAR 1, HAMMER. **2.** [A male sheep] buck, bucksheep, bighorn; see ANIMAL.

ram *v.* **1.** [To strike head-on] bump, collide, hook; see BUTT, HIT 1. **2.** [To pack forcibly] cram, jam, stuff; see PACK 2.

ramble *v.* **1.** [To saunter] stroll, promenade, roam; see WALK 1. **2.** [To speak or write aimlessly] drift, stray, diverge, meander, gossip, talk nonsense, chatter, babble, digress, maunder, get off the subject, go on and on, expatiate, protract, enlarge, be diffuse, dwell on, amplify, go astray, drivel, rant and rave, talk off the top of one's head, go off on a tangent, beat around the bush.

rambling *a.* **1.** [Strolling] hiking, roaming, roving; see WALKING, WANDERING 1. **2.** [Incoherent] discursive, disconnected, confused; see INCOHERENT. **3.** [Covering considerable territory without much plan] spread out, strewn, straggling, trailing, random, here and there, at length, widely thrown, unplanned, sprawling, gangling; see also SCATTERED.—*Ant.* PLANNED, closely formed, compact.

ramp *n.* incline, slope, grade; see HILL, INCLINATION 2.

rampant *a.* raging, uncontrolled, growing without check, violent, vehement, impetuous, rank, turbulent, wild, luxuriant, tumultuous, profuse, plentiful, unruly, wanton, rife, prevalent, dominant, predominant, excessive, impulsive, impassioned, intolerant, unrestrained, extravagant, overabundant, sweeping the country, like wildfire*.—*Ant.* MODEST, mild, meek.

ranch *n.* plantation, grange, farmstead, ranchland, ranch house, ranch building, Western cattle farm, cattle spread; see also FARM, PROPERTY 2.

rancher *n.* ranch owner, ranchman, stockman, breeder, cattle farmer, cowherder, shepherd, drover, stock breeder, horse trainer, herdsman, herder, ranchero, broncobuster*, granger, cattleman, cowboy, cowpoke*, ranch hand, cattle baron; see also FARMER.

rancid *a.* tainted, stale, bad; see ROTTEN 1.

random *a.* haphazard, chance, purposeless, thoughtless, careless, blind, casual, fickle, eccentric, unpredictable, accidental; see also AIMLESS, IRREGULAR 1. —**at random** haphazardly, by chance, aimlessly; see ACCIDENTALLY.

range *n.* **1.** [Distance] reach, span, horizontal projection; see EXPANSE. **2.** [Extent] length, area, expanse; see EXTENT. **3.** [A series of mountains] highlands, alps, sierras; see MOUNTAIN 1. **4.** [Land open to grazing] pasture, grazing land, field; see COUNTRY 1. **5.** [A kitchen stove] gas range, electric range, portable range; see APPLIANCE, STOVE.

range *v.* **1.** [To vary] differ, fluctuate, diverge from; see VARY. **2.** [To traverse wide areas] encompass, reach, pass over, cover, stray, stroll, wander, ramble, explore, scour, search, traverse, roam, rove; see also CROSS 1, TRAVEL. **3.** [To place in order] line up, classify, arrange; see ORDER 3.

rank *a.* **1.** [Having luxurious growth] wild, dense, lush; see GREEN 2, THICK 1. **2.** [Having a foul odor] smelly, fetid, putrid, stinking, rancid, disagreeable, smelling, offensive, sour, foul, noxious, stale, tainted, gamy, musty, strong, rotten, moldy, turned, high, ill-smelling, nauseating, obnoxious, disgusting, reeking, malodorous, nasty, strong-smelling.—*Ant.* SWEET, fragrant, fresh.

rank *n.* **1.** [A row] column, file, string; see LINE 1. **2.** [Degree] seniority, standing, station; see DEGREE 2. **3.** [Social eminence] station, position, distinction, note, nobility, caste, privilege, standing, reputation, quality, situation, esteem, condition, state, place in society, status, circumstance, footing, grade, blood, family, pedigree, ancestry, stock, parentage, birth. **—pull (one's) rank on*** take advantage of, exploit, abuse subordinates; see GOVERN, HUMILIATE.

rank *v.* **1.** [To arrange in a row or rows] put in line, line up, place in formation; see ORDER 3. **2.** [To evaluate comparatively] place, put, regard, judge, assign, give precedence to, fix, establish, settle, estimate, value, valuate, include, list, rate; see also CLASSIFY. **3.** [To possess relative evaluation] be worth, stand, be at the head, have a place, go ahead of, come first, forerun, antecede, have supremacy over, have the advantage of, precede, outrank, take the lead, take precedence over, belong, count among, be classed, stand in relationship.

ranked *a.* ordered, piled, neatly stacked; see ORGANIZED.

ransack *v.* **1.** [To search thoroughly] rummage, explore, turn upside down, look all over for, look high and low for, leave no stone unturned, scour, seek everywhere, sound, spy, peer, look around, pry, scan, probe, look into, investigate, scrutinize; see also SEARCH. **2.** [To loot] pillage, plunder, ravish, rape, strip, rifle, forage, maraud, make off with, take away, seize, appropriate, spoil, poach, gut, rustle, lift*, thieve, ravage, pilfer, bag*, rob, steal, filch, pinch*.

ransom *n.* redemption money, compensation, expiation; see BRIBE.

ransom *v.* release, rescue, deliver; see FREE.

rant *v.* rave, fume, rail; see RAGE 1, YELL.

rap *n.* knock, thump, slap; see BLOW. **—beat the rap*** avoid punishment, evade, be acquitted; see ESCAPE. **—bum rap*** unfair sentence, blame, frame*; see PUNISHMENT. **—take the rap*** be punished, suffer, take the blame; see PAY FOR.

rap *v.* **1.** [To tap sharply] knock, strike, whack; see BEAT 1, HIT 1. **2.** [*To talk, often compulsively] chatter, jabber, discuss; see BABBLE, TALK 1.

rape *n.* seduction, violation, deflowering, criminal attack, assault, abduction, statutory offense, defilement, abuse, molestation, maltreatment, forcible violation of a woman; see also CRIME.

rape *v.* violate, seize, compromise, force a woman, molest, ravish, attack, assault, defile, wrong, debauch, ruin, corrupt, seduce, maltreat, abuse.

rapid *a.* speedy, accelerated, hurried; see FAST 1.

rapidly *a.* fast, swiftly, posthaste; see IMMEDIATELY, QUICKLY.

rapist *n.* raper, ravager, ravisher; see RASCAL.

rapt *a.* transported, entranced, enchanted; see HAPPY.

rapture *n.* pleasure, cheer, satisfaction; see HAPPINESS.

rare *a.* **1.** [Uncommon] exceptional, singular, extraordinary; see UNUSUAL 1, 2. **2.** [Scarce] sparse, few, scanty, meager, limited, short, expensive, precious, out of circulation, off the market, in great demand, occasional, uncommon, isolated, scattered, infrequent, deficient, almost unobtainable, few and far between; see also UNIQUE.—*Ant.* CHEAP, profuse, tawdy. **3.** [Choice] select, matchless, superlative; see EXCELLENT. **4.** [Lightly cooked] not cooked, not done, seared, braised, not overdone, nearly raw, underdone, red, moderately done, not thoroughly cooked; see also RAW 1.

rarely *a.* unusually, occasionally, once in a great while; see SELDOM.

rascal *n.* scoundrel, rogue, rake, knave, villain, robber, fraud, scamp, hypocrite, sneak, shyster*, cad, trickster, charlatan, swindler, grafter, cheat, black sheep, ruffian, tough, rowdy, bully, scalawag, mountebank, liar, blackguard, wretch, quack, fellow, tramp, beggar, bum*, idler, wastrel, prodigal, hooligan*, ne'er-do-well, reprobate, misdoer, felon, sinner, delinquent, recreant, malefactor, profligate, loafer, renegade, imposter, opportunist, vagrant, pretender, gambler, mischief-maker, sharper, faker, skunk*, bastard*, fink*, rat*, rotten egg*, con man*, con artist*, flimflammer*, dirty dog*, good-for-nothing, worm, two-timer*, stool pigeon*, case*, double-dealer*, phony*, four-flusher*, slicker*; see also CRIMINAL.—*Ant.* HERO, GENTLEMAN, philanthropist.

rash *a.* impetuous, impulsive, foolish, hotheaded, thoughtless, reckless, headstrong, bold, careless, determined, audacious, heedless, madcap, unthinking, headlong, incautious, wild, precipitant, overhasty, unwary, injudicious, venturous, foolhardy, imprudent, venturesome, adventurous, daring, jumping to conclusions, insuppressible, breakneck, irrational, fiery, furious, frenzied, passionate, immature, hurried, aimless, excited, feverish, tenacious, frantic, indiscreet, quixotic, ill-advised, unconsidered, without thinking, imprudent, unadvised, irresponsible, brash, precipitous, premature, sudden, harebrained, harum-scarum, devil-may-care*, daredevil; see also RUDE 1.—*Ant.* CALM, cool, levelheaded.

rashly *a.* brashly, impulsively, unwisely, abruptly, foolishly, impetuously, incautiously, carelessly, precipitately, imprudently, recklessly, boldly, indiscreetly, inadvisedly, ill-advisedly, thoughtlessly, unthinkingly, furiously, hurriedly, heedlessly, boldly, unpreparedly, excitedly, overhastily, wildly, frantically, irrepressibly, without due consideration, without thinking, without forethought, in a hasty manner, passionately, fiercely, feverishly, headily; see also RUDELY.

rashness *n.* frenzy, recklessness, foolhardiness; see CARELESSNESS.

rasping *a.* hoarse, grating, grinding; see HARSH.

rat *n.* **1.** [A rodent] mouse, muskrat, vermin; see PEST 1, RODENT. **2.** [*A deserter] informer, turncoat, fink*; see DESERTER, TRAITOR.

rate *n.* **1.** [Ratio] proportion, degree, standard, scale, fixed amount, quota, relation, relationship, comparison, relative, weight, percentage, numerical progression; see also MEASURE 1, 2. **2.** [Price] valuation, allowance, estimate; see PRICE. **3.** [Speed] velocity, pace, time; see SPEED.

rate *v.* **1.** [To rank] judge, estimate, evaluate, grade, relate to a standard, fix, tag, calculate, assess, class, determine, appraise, guess at; see also MEASURE 1, PRICE, RANK 2. **2.** [*To be well-thought-of] be a favorite, triumph, succeed; see SUCCEED 1.

rated *a.* ranked, classified, graded, classed, put, thought of, given a rating, weighted, measured; see also PLACED.

rather *a.* **1.** [To some degree] fairly, somewhat, a little; see MODERATELY, REASONABLY 2. **2.** [By preference] first, by choice, in preference, sooner, more readily, willingly, much sooner, just as soon, as a matter of choice; see also PREFERABLY.

rather *interj.* I should say, certainly, of course, by all means, most assuredly, no doubt about it, and how!*, you're telling me*.

ratification *n.* acceptance, confirmation, sanction; see PERMISSION.

ratify *v.* sanction, establish, substantiate; see APPROVE, ENDORSE 2.

rating *n.* grade, commission, number; see CLASS 1, DEGREE 2, RANK 2.

ratio *n.* proportion, quota, quotient; see DEGREE 1, RATE 1.

ration *n.* allotment, portion, quota; see DIVISION 2, SHARE.

ration *v.* proportion, allot, apportion; see DISTRIBUTE.

rational *a.* **1.** [Acting in accordance with reason] stable, calm, cool, deliberate, discerning, discriminating, level-headed, collected, logical, thoughtful, knowing, sensible, of sound judgment, having good sense, impartial, exercising reason, intelligent, wise, reasoning, prudent, circumspect, intellectual, reflective, philosophic, objective, far-sighted, enlightened, well-advised, judicious, analytical, deductive, synthetic, conscious, balanced, sober, systematic; see also REASONABLE 1.—*Ant.* RASH, reckless, wild. **2.** [Of a nature that appeals to reason] intelligent, sensible, wise; see REASONABLE 1. **3.** [Sane] normal, lucid, responsible; see SANE 1.

rationalize *v.* explain away, vindicate, reconcile; see EXPLAIN.

rationally *a.* sensibly, normally, intelligently; see REASONABLY 1.

rattle *n.* clatter, noise, racket; see NOISE 1.

rattle *v.* **1.** [To make a rattling sound] drum, clack, knock; see SOUND. **2.** [To talk with little meaning] chatter, gush, prattle; see BABBLE. **3.** [To disconcert] bother, put out, unnerve; see CONFUSE, DISTURB, EMBARRASS.

raucous *a.* hoarse, loud, gruff; see HARSH.

raunchy* *a.* indelicate, sexy*, suggestive; see LEWD 2.

ravage *v.* pillage, overrun, devastate, destroy, crush, desolate, despoil, overspread, wreck, waste, disrupt, disorganize, demolish, annihilate, overthrow, overwhelm, break up, pull down, smash, shatter, scatter, batter down, exterminate, extinguish, trample down, dismantle, stamp out, lay waste, lay in ruins, sweep away, raze, ruin, plunder, strip, impair, sack, consume, spoil, harry, ransack, maraud, prey, crush, rape, rob, raid, pirate, seize, capture, gut, loot; see also DAMAGE.—*Ant.* BUILD, improve, rehabilitate.

rave *v.* **1.** [To babble] gabble, jabber, rattle on; see BABBLE. **2.** [To rage] storm, splutter, rail; see RAGE 1.

ravel *v.* untwist, come apart, wind out, untangle, disentangle, unsnarl, unbraid, untwine, unweave, unravel, make plain; see also FREE, LOOSEN 2.

ravenous *a.* voracious, omnivorous, starved; see HUNGRY.

ravine *n.* gully, gorge, canyon, gulch, arroyo, valley, gap, chasm, abyss, break, crevice, crevasse, coulee.

raving *a.* violent, shouting, fuming; see INSANE.

raw *a.* **1.** [Uncooked] fresh, rare, hard, unprepared, undercooked, fibrous, coarse-grained, unpasteurized, unbaked, unfried; see also RARE 4.—*Ant.* BAKED, cooked, fried. **2.** [Unfinished] natural, untreated, crude, rough, newly cut, unprocessed, unrefined, untanned, coarse, newly mined, uncut, virgin; see also UNFINISHED 2.—*Ant.* REFINED, manufactured, processed. **3.** [Untrained] immature, new, fresh; see INEXPERIENCED. **4.** [Cold] biting, windy, bleak; see COLD 1. **5.** [Without skin] peeled, skinned, dressed, galled, scraped, blistered, cut, wounded, pared, uncovered, chafed, bruised.—*Ant.* COVERED, coated, healed. **6.** [*Nasty] low, dirty, unscrupulous; see MEAN 3, VULGAR. —**in the raw** nude, bare, unclothed; see NAKED 1.

ray *n.* beam, flash, light, stream, gleam, blaze, sunbeam, wave, moonbeam, radiation, flicker, spark, emanation, radiance, streak, shaft, pencil, patch, blink, glimmer, glitter, glint, sparkle.

razor *n.* shaving instrument, cutting edge, blade; see KNIFE. *Razors include the following:* double-edged, single-edged, straight-back, safety, hollow-ground, electric; electric shaver.

reach *n.* compass, range, scope, grasp, stretch, extension, orbit, horizon, gamut; see also ABILITY.

reach *v.* **1.** [To extend to] touch, span, encompass, pass along, continue to, roll on, stretch, go as far as, attain, equal, approach, lead, stand, terminate, end, overtake, join, come up to, sweep; see also SPREAD 2. **2.** [To extend a part of the body to] lunge, strain, move, reach out, feel for, come at, make contact with, shake hands, throw out a limb, make for, put out, touch, strike, seize, grasp; see also STRETCH 1. **3.** [To arrive] get to, come to, enter; see ARRIVE.

reaching *a.* **1.** [Extending to a point] going up to, ending at, stretching, encompassing, taking in, spanning, spreading to, embracing, joining, sweeping on to. **2.** [Arriving] coming to, landing, touching down; see LANDING 1. **3.** [Extending a part of the body] stretching, straining, lunging; see EXTENDING.

react *v.* **1.** [To act in response] reciprocate, respond, act; see ANSWER 1. **2.** [To feel in response] be affected, be impressed, be involved; see FEEL 2.

reaction *n.* reply, rejoinder, reception, receptivity, response, return, feeling, opinion, reflection, backlash, attitude, retort, reciprocation, repercussion, reflex; see also ANSWER 1, OPINION 1. *Reactions to stimuli include the following:* contraction, expansion, jerk, knee jerk, cognition, shock, relapse, exhaustion, stupor, anger, disgust, revulsion, fear, illness, joy, laughter, wonder.

reactionary *a.* rigid, retrogressive, regressive; see CONSERVATIVE.

reactionary *n.* die-hard, reactionist, conservative; see RADICAL.

read *a.* examined, gone over, scanned; see UNDERSTOOD 1.

read *v.* **1.** [To understand by reading] comprehend, go through, peruse, scan, glance over, go over, gather, see, know, skim, perceive, apprehend, grasp, learn, flip through the pages, dip into, scratch the surface, bury oneself in; see also UNDERSTAND 1. **2.** [To interpret] view, render, translate, decipher, make out, unravel, express, explain, expound, construe, paraphrase, restate, put; see also INTERPRET.

readable *a.* **1.** [Capable of being read] clear, legible, coherent, distinct, intelligible, lucid, comprehensible, plain, unmistakable, decipherable, regular, orderly, fluent, tidy, flowing, precise, graphic, understandable, unequivocal, explicit, straightforward, simple. **2.** [Likely to be read with pleasure] interesting, absorbing, fascinating, pleasurable, engrossing, satisfying, amusing, entertaining, enjoyable, rewarding, gratifying, pleasing, worth reading, pleasant, inviting, engaging, eloquent, well-written, smooth, exciting, attractive, clever, brilliant, ingenious, relaxing, stimulating, appealing.—*Ant.* DULL, dreary, depressing.

read between the lines *v.* surmise, conclude, suspect; see GUESS.

reader *n.* **1.** [One who reads habitually] editor, literary critic, proofreader; see WRITER. **2.** [A book intended for the study of reading] primer, graded text, selected readings; see BOOK.

readily *a.* quickly, promptly, immediately; see EAGERLY, EASILY, WILLINGLY.

readiness *n.* aptness, predisposition, eagerness; see WILLINGNESS, ZEAL.

reading *n.* **1.** [Interpretation] version, treatment, commentary; see INTERPRETATION, TRANSLATION. **2.** [A selection from written matter] excerpt, passage, section; see QUOTATION. **3.** [A version] account, paraphrase, rendering; see INTERPRETATION.

read up on *v.* prepare, investigate, research; see STUDY.

ready *a.* **1.** [Prompt] quick, spontaneous, alert, wide-awake, swift, fleet, fast, sharp, immediate, instant, animated; see also ACTIVE, OBSERVANT, PUNCTUAL.—*Ant.* SLOW, dull, lazy. **2.** [Prepared] fit, apt, skillful, ripe, handy, in readiness, waiting, on call, in line for, in position, on the brink of, equipped to do the job, open to, fixed for, on the mark, equal to, expectant, available, at hand, anticipating, in order, all systems go*, all squared away*, in a go condition*.—*Ant.* UNPREPARED, unready, unavailable. **3.** [Enthusiastic] eager, willing, ardent; see ZEALOUS. —**make ready** order, prepare for something, equip; see PREPARE 1.

ready-made *a.* instant, prefabricated, built; see PRESERVED 2.

real *a.* **1.** [Genuine] true, authentic, original; see GENUINE 1. **2.** [Having physical existence] actual, solid, firm, substantive, material, live, substantial, existent, tangible, existing, present, palpable, factual, sound, concrete, corporal, corporeal, bodily, incarnate, embodied, physical, sensible, stable, in existence, perceptible, evident, undeniable, irrefutable, practical, true, true to life.—*Ant.* UNREAL, unsubstantial, hypothetical. **3.** [*Very much] exceedingly, exceptionally, uncommonly; see VERY. —**for real*** actually, in fact, certainly; see REALLY 1.

real estate *n.* land, property, realty; see BUILDING, ESTATE, FARM, HOME 1.

realism *n.* authenticity, naturalness, actuality; see REALITY.
realist *n.* pragmatist, naturalist, scientist; see PHILOSOPHER.
realistic *a.* authentic, original, representative; see GENUINE 1.
reality *n.* authenticity, factual basis, truth, actuality, realness, substantiality, existence, substance, materiality, being, presence, actual existence, sensibility, corporeality, solidity, perceptibility, true being, absoluteness, tangibility, palpability.
realization *n.* understanding, comprehension, consciousness; see AWARENESS.
realize *v.* **1.** [To bring to fulfillment] perfect, make good, actualize; see COMPLETE. **2.** [To understand] recognize, apprehend, discern; see UNDERSTAND 1. **3.** [To receive] acquire, make a profit from, obtain; see EARN 2, PROFIT 2, RECEIVE 1.
realized *a.* **1.** [Fulfilled] completed, accomplished, done; see FINISHED 1. **2.** [Earned] gained, gotten, acquired, received, accrued, made, reaped, harvested, gathered, inherited, profited, taken, cleared, obtained, gleaned, netted.
really *a.* **1.** [In fact] actually, indeed, genuinely, certainly, surely, absolutely, positively, veritably, in reality, authentically, upon my honor, legitimately, precisely, literally, indubitably, unmistakably, in effect, undoubtedly, categorically, in point of fact, I assure you, be assured, believe me, as a matter of fact, of course, honestly, truly, admittedly, nothing else but, beyond any doubt, in actuality, unquestionably, as sure as you're alive*, no buts about it*, without the shadow of a doubt. **2.** [To a remarkable degree] surprisingly, remarkably, extraordinarily; see VERY.
really *interj.* indeed!, honestly!, for a fact!, yes?, is that so!, are you sure?, no fooling!, cross your heart and hope to die?, on your honor?, you don't say!*, ain't it the truth!*, you said it!*, do tell!*, no kidding!*.
realm *n.* domain, area, sphere; see DEPARTMENT, EXPANSE, REGION 1.
reappear *v.* come again, reenter, crop up again; see APPEAR 1, REPEAT 2.
rear *n.* hind part, back seat, rear end, tail, tail end, posterior, rump, butt*; see also BACK 1.
rear *v.* lift, elevate, bring up; see RAISE 1, SUPPORT 1.
rearrange *v.* do over, reconstruct, shift; see ORDER 3, PREPARE 1.
reason *n.* **1.** [The power of reasoning] intelligence, mind, sanity; see JUDGMENT 1. **2.** [A process of reasoning] logic, dialectics, speculation, generalization, rationalism, argumentation, inference, induction, deduction, analysis, rationalization. **3.** [A basis for rational action] end, object, rationale, intention, motive, ulterior motive, basis, wherefore, aim, intent, cause, design, ground, impetus, idea, motivation, root, incentive, goal, purpose, the why and wherefore; see also PURPOSE 1. **4.** [The mind] brain, mentality, intellect; see MIND 1. **—by reason of** because of, for, by way of; see BECAUSE. **—in** or **within reason** in accord with what is reasonable, rationally, understandably; see REASONABLY 1. **—stand to reason** be feasible, seem all right, appeal; see CONVINCE. **—with reason** understandably, soundly, plausibly; see REASONABLY 1.
reason *v.* **1.** [To think logically] reflect, deliberate, contemplate; see THINK 1. **2.** [To seek a reasonable explanation] suppose, gather, conclude; see ASSUME. **3.** [To discuss persuasively] argue, contend, debate; see DISCUSS.
reasonable *a.* **1.** [Rational] sane, levelheaded, intelligent, clear-cut, tolerant, endowed with reason, conscious, cerebral, thoughtful, reflective, capable of reason, reasoning, cognitive, perceiving, consistent, broad-minded, liberal, generous, sensible, unprejudiced, unbiased, flexible, agreeable; see also RATIONAL 1.—*Ant.* PREJUDICED, intolerant, biased. **2.** [Characterized by justice] fair, right, just; see HONEST 1. **3.** [Likely to appeal to the reason] feasible, sound, plausible; see UNDERSTANDABLE. **4.** [Moderate in price] inexpensive, reduced, fair; see CHEAP 1.
reasonably *a.* **1.** [In a reasonable manner] rationally, sanely, logically, understandably, plausibly, sensibly, soundly, persuasively, fairly, justly, honestly, wisely, judiciously, plainly, intelligently, soberly, agreeably, in reason, within reason, within the limits of reason, as far as possible, as far as could be expected, as much as good sense dictates, within reasonable limitations, with due restraint. **2.** [To a moderate degree] mildly, prudently, fairly, moderately, inexpensively, temperately, evenly, calmly, gently, leniently, sparingly, frugally, indulgently, tolerantly, within bounds.
reasoning *n.* thinking, rationalizing, drawing conclusions; see THOUGHT 1.
reassure *v.* convince, console, give confidence; see COMFORT 1, ENCOURAGE, GUARANTEE.
rebel *n.* insurrectionist, revolutionist, revolutionary, agitator, insurgent, traitor, seditionist, mutineer, subverter, anarchist, overthrower, nihilist, guerrilla, member of the uprising, rioter, demagogue, revolter, separatist, malcontent, schismatic, deserter, dissenter, apostate, turncoat, counterrevoluntionary, renegade, secessionist, underground worker; see also RADICAL.
rebel *v.* rise up, resist, revolt, turn against, defy, resist lawful authority, fight in the streets, strike, boycott, break with, overturn,

mutiny, riot, take up arms against, start a confrontation, secede, renounce, combat, oppose, be insubordinate, be treasonable, upset, overthrow, dethrone, disobey, raise hell*, run amok*.—*Ant.* OBEY, be contented, submit.

rebellion *n.* insurrection, revolt, defiance; see DISOBEDIENCE, REVOLUTION 2.

rebellious *a.* revolutionary, insurgent, counterrevolutionary, warring, stubborn, contemptuous, insolent, scornful, intractable, unyielding, recalcitrant, insurrectionary, attacking, rioting, mutinous, dissident, factious, seditious, disobedient, treasonable, refractory, defiant, resistant, riotous, insubordinate, sabotaging, disloyal, disaffected, alienated, ungovernable, restless, threatening, anarchistic, iconoclastic, individualistic, radical, independent-minded, quarrelsome.—*Ant.* CALM, DOCILE, peaceful.

rebirth *n.* resurrection, rejuvenation, rehabilitation; see REVIVAL 1.

rebound *v.* reflect, ricochet, spring back; see BOUNCE.

rebuild *v.* touch up, patch, build up; see REPAIR.

rebuke *n.* condemnation, reproof, reprimand; see INSULT.

rebuke *v.* reprove, reprimand, censure; see OPPOSE 1.

recall *v.* **1.** [To call to mind] recollect, think of, revive; see REMEMBER 1. **2.** [To remove from office] discharge, disqualify, suspend; see DISMISS. **3.** [To summon again] call back, reconvene, reassemble; see SUMMON.

recalled *a.* **1.** [Remembered] recollected, brought to mind, summoned up; see REMEMBERED. **2.** [Relieved of responsibility] stripped of office, dismissed, cast out, displaced, fired, replaced, ousted, suspended, laid off, cashiered, pensioned, let out, let go, removed, retired, kicked upstairs*, canned*, busted*, washed out*; see also DISCHARGED.

recapture *v.* regain, reobtain, reacquire; see RECOVER 1.

recede *v.* **1.** [To go backward] fall back, shrink from, withdraw; see RETREAT. **2.** [To sink] ebb, drift away, lower, turn down, abate, decline, go away, drop, fall off, lessen; see also DECREASE 1, FALL 2.—*Ant.* RISE, flow, increase.

receipt *n.* **1.** [The act of receiving] receiving, acquisition, accession, acceptance, taking, arrival, getting, admitting, reception; see also ADMISSION 1.—*Ant.* DELIVERY, shipment, giving. **2.** [An acknowledgement of receipt] letter, voucher, release, cancellation, slip, signed notice, stub, discharge, declaration, paid bill; see also CERTIFICATE.

receive *v.* **1.** [To take into one's charge] accept, be given, admit, get, gain, inherit, acquire, gather up, collect, obtain, reap, procure, derive, appropriate, seize, take possession, redeem, pocket, pick up, hold, come by, earn, take in, assume, draw, win, secure, come into, come in for, catch, get from; see also GET 1.—*Ant.* DISCARD, abandon, refuse. **2.** [To endure] undergo, experience, suffer; see ENDURE 2. **3.** [To support] bear, sustain, prop; see SUPPORT 1. **4.** [To make welcome] accommodate, initiate, induct, install, make welcome, shake hands with, admit, permit, welcome home, accept, entertain, invite in, show in, usher in, let through, make comfortable, bring as a guest into, introduce, give a party, give access to, allow entrance to, roll out the red carpet for*, give the red-carpet treatment to*, get out the welcome mat for*; see also GREET.—*Ant.* VISIT, be a guest, call.

received *a.* taken, gotten, acquired, obtained, honored, brought in, signed for, admitted, collected, gathered; see also ACCEPTED, ACKNOWLEDGED.—*Ant.* GIVEN, disbursed, delivered.

receiver *n.* **1.** [One who receives] customer, recipient, beneficiary; see HEIR. **2.** [A device for receiving] telephone, television, radio, satellite dish, radio telescope, walkie-talkie, headphone, car phone, beeper, pager, mission control, control center, listening device, transceiver.

recent *a.* **1.** [Lately brought into being] fresh, novel, newly born; see MODERN 1, UNUSUAL 1, 2. **2.** [Associated with modern times] contemporary, up-to-date, streamlined; see MODERN 1, 3.

recently *a.* lately, in recent times, just now, just a while ago, not long ago, a short while ago, of late, newly, freshly, new, the other day, within the recent past.—*Ant.* ONCE, long ago, formerly.

receptacle *n.* box, wastebasket, holder; see CONTAINER.

reception *n.* **1.** [The act of receiving] acquisition, acceptance, accession; see RECEIPT 2. **2.** [The manner of receiving] meeting, encounter, introduction, gathering, welcome, salutation, induction, admission, disposition; see also GREETING. **3.** [A social function] tea, party, dinner; see GATHERING.

receptive *a.* alert, sensitive, perceptive; see OBSERVANT, SYMPATHETIC.

recess *n.* **1.** [An intermission] respite, rest, pause, interlude, break, cessation, stop, suspension, interval, coffee break, intervening period, halt. **2.** [An indentation] break, dent, corner; see HOLE 1. **3.** [A recessed space] cell, cubicle, nook; see ROOM 2.

recession *n.* unemployment, inflation, decline; see DEPRESSION 3.

recipe *n.* formula, compound, receipt, instructions, prescription, cookery, formula, directions, method.

recipient *n.* receiver, beneficiary, legatee; see HEIR.

recital *n.* presentation, concert, musical; see PERFORMANCE.

recitation *n.* **1.** [The act of reciting] delivery, speaking, playing, narrating, reading, recounting, declaiming, discoursing, soliloquizing, discussion, holding forth, performance, recital, rehearsal, monologue, discourse. **2.** [A compositon used for recitation] address, talk, sermon; see SPEECH 3, WRITING 2.

recite *v.* **1.** [To repeat formally] declaim, address, read, render, discourse, hold forth, enact, dramatize, deliver from memory, interpret, soliloquize. **2.** [To report on a lesson] answer, give a report, explain; see DISCUSS, REPORT 1. **3.** [To relate in detail] enumerate, enlarge, report, account for, give an account for, impart, chant, convey, quote, communicate, utter, describe, relate, state, tell, mention, narrate, recount, retell, picture, delineate, portray; see also EXPLAIN, TELL 1.

reckless *a.* thoughtless, foolish, wild; see RASH.

recklessly *a.* dangerously, heedlessly, with abandon; see BRAVELY, CARELESSLY.

reckon *v.* consider, evaluate, judge; see ESTIMATE.

reclaim *v.* **1.** [To bring into usable condition] restore, regenerate, redeem; see RECOVER 1. **2.** [To reform] resolve, mend, improve; see REFORM 3.

reclamation *n.* redemption, repair, repossession; see RECOVERY 3.

recognition *n.* **1.** [The act of recognizing] recalling, remembering, identifying, perceiving, verifying, apprehending, acknowledging, noticing, recollection, memory, identification, recall, reidentification, recognizance, remembrance, cognizance. **2.** [Tangible evidence of recognition] greeting, acknowledgment, identification, perception, admission, verification, comprehension, appreciation, renown, esteem, notice, attention, acceptance, regard, honor.

recognize *v.* **1.** [To know again] be familiar, make out, distinguish, verify, recollect, sight, diagnose, place, espy, descry, recall, remember, see, perceive, admit, knowledge of, notice; see also KNOW 1. **2.** [To acknowledge] admit, appreciate, realize; see ALLOW. **3.** [To acknowledge the legality of a government] exchange diplomatic representatives, have diplomatic relations with, sanction, approve, extend formal recognition to; see also ACKNOWLEDGE 2.

recognized *a.* sighted, caught, perceived, realized, acknowledged, known, appreciated, admitted, recalled, remembered.

recoil *v.* turn away, shrink from, draw back; see RETREAT.

recollect *v.* recall, bring to mind, look back on; see REMEMBER 1.

recollection *n.* remembrance, reminiscence, consciousness; see MEMORY 1.

recommend *v.* **1.** [To lend support or approval] agree to, sanction, hold up, commend, extol, compliment, applaud, advocate, celebrate, praise, speak highly of, acclaim, eulogize, confirm, laud, second, favor, back, stand by, magnify, glorify, exalt, think highly of, think well of, be satisfied with, esteem, value, prize, uphold, justify, endorse, go on record for, be all for, front for, go to bat for*.—*Ant.* DENOUNCE, censure, renounce. **2.** [To make a suggestion or prescription] prescribe, suggest, counsel; see ADVISE, URGE 2.

recommendation *n.* **1.** [The act of recommending] guidance, counsel, direction; see ADVICE, SUGGESTION 1. **2.** [A document that vouches for character or ability] certificate, testimonial, reference, letter of introduction, character reference, letter of recommendation, letter in support; see also LETTER 2.

recommended *a.* urged, endorsed, suggested; see APPROVED.

reconcile *v.* **1.** [To adjust] adapt, arrange, regulate; see ADJUST 1, 2. **2.** [To bring into harmony] conciliate, assuage, pacify, propitiate, mitigate, make up, mediate, arbitrate, intercede, bring together, accustom oneself to, harmonize, accord, dictate peace, accomodate, appease, reunite, make peace between, bring to terms, bring into one's camp, win over, bury the hatchet, patch up, kiss and make up; see also SETTLE 7.—*Ant.* BOTHER, irritate, alienate.

reconciled *a.* settled, regulated, arranged; see DETERMINED 1.

reconciliation *n.* conciliation, settlement, payment; see ADJUSTMENT, AGREEMENT 1.

reconsider *v.* reevaluate, think over, rearrange, consider again, recheck, reexamine, correct, amend, revise, retrace, rework, replan, review, withdraw for consideration, reweigh, amend one's judgment; see also CONSIDER.

reconstruct *v.* rebuild, remodel, construct again, make over, revamp, recondition, reconstitute, reestablish, restore, reproduce, refashion, reorganize, replace, overhaul, renovate, modernize, rework, construct from the original, copy, remake; see also BUILD, REPAIR.

reconstruction *n.* reorganization, rehabilitation, restoration; see REPAIR.

record *n.* **1.** [Documentary evidence] manuscript, inscription, transcription, account, history, legend, story, writing, written material, document. *Types of records include the following:* register, catalog, list, inventory, memo, memorandum, registry, schedule, chronicle, docket, scroll, archive, note, contract, statement, will, testament, petition, calendar, log, letter, memoir, reminiscence, dictation, confession, deposition, inscription, official record, sworn document, evidence, license, bulletin, gazette, newspaper, magazine, annual report, journal, Congressional Record, transactions, debates, bill, annals, presidential order, state paper, white paper, blue book, budget, report, entry, book, publication, autograph, signature, vital statistics, deed, paper, diary, stenographic notes, ledger, daybook, almanac, proceedings, minutes, description, affidavit, certificate, transcript, dossier, roll, tape, disk, microfilm, microfiche. **2.** [One's past] career, experience, work; see LIFE 2. **3.** [A device for the reproduction of sound] recording, disk, phonograph record, transcription, compact disc, CD, laser disc, canned music*, cut, take, platter*. **—go on record** assert, attest, state; see DECLARE. **—off the record** confidential, unofficial, secret; see PRIVATE. **—on the record** recorded, stated, official; see PUBLIC 1.

record *v.* **1.** [To write down] register, write in, jot down, set down, take down, put on record, transcribe, list, note, file, mark, inscribe, log, catalog, tabulate, put in writing, put in black and white, chronicle, keep accounts, keep an account of, make a written account of, matriculate, enroll, journalize, put on paper, preserve, make an entry in, chalk up, write up, enter, report, book, post, copy, document, insert, enumerate; see also WRITE 1. **2.** [To indicate] point out, explain, show; see NAME 2. **3.** [To record electronically] tape, cut, photograph, make a record of, make a tape, tape-record, film, videotape, cut a record.

recorded *a.* listed, filed, on file, in black and white, in writing, inscribed, put down, registered, documented, entered, written, published, noted down, described, reported, cataloged, mentioned, certified, kept, chronicled, booked.

recorder *n.* dictaphone, recording instrument, stereophonic recorder; see TAPE RECORDER.

recording *n.* documentation, recounting, reporting; see RECORD 1.

record player *n.* phonograph, stereo, rack system, phono system, hi-fi, sound system, juke box, gramophone; see also TAPE RECORDER. *Record player parts include the following:* changer, turntable, tone arm, amplifier, preamplifier, preamp, speakers, stylus, cartridge, woofer, tweeter, spindle, needle.

records *n.pl.* documents, chronicles, archives, public papers, registers, annals, memborabilia, memoranda, lists, return, diaries, accounts.

recover *v.* **1.** [To obtain again] redeem, salvage, retrieve, rescue, reclaim, recoup, find again, recapture, repossess, bring back, win back, reacquire, obtain, regain, rediscover, resume, catch up; see also GET 1.—*Ant.* LOSE, let slip, fall behind. **2.** [To improve one's condition] gain, increase, collect; see IMPROVE 2, PROFIT 2.—*Ant.* FAIL, go bankrupt, give up. **3.** [To regain health] rally, come around, come to, come out of it, get out of danger, improve, convalesce, heal, get the better of, overcome, start anew, be restored, mend, revive, be oneself again, perk up, gain strength, recuperate, get well, get over, get better, get through, return to form, make a comeback*, get back in shape*, snap out of*, pull through*, sober up.—*Ant.* DIE, fail, become worse.

recovered *a.* renewed, found, replaced, reborn, rediscovered, reawakened, retrieved, redeemed, reclaimed, regained, revived, returned, resumed; see also DISCOVERED.—*Ant.* LOST, missed, dropped.

recovery *n.* **1.** [The act of returning to normal] reestablishment, resumption, restoration, reinstatement, return, rehabilitation, reconstruction, reformation, recreation, replacement, readjustment, improving, getting back to normal; see also SENSE 2, IMPROVEMENT 1. **2.** [The process of regaining health] convalescence, recuperation, revival, rebirth, renaissance, resurgence, resurrection, regeneration, cure, improvement, reawakening, renewal, resuscitation, rejuvenation, rehabilitation, return of health, physical improvement, healing, betterment. **3.** [The act of regaining possession] repossession, retrieval, reclamation, redemption, indemnification, reparation, compensation, recapture, recouping, return, restoration, remuneration, reimbursement, retaking, recall.

recreation *n.* amusement, relaxation, diversion, play, fun, entertainment, enjoyment, festivity, hobby, holiday, vacation, pastime, pleasure, game, avocation, refreshment; see also SPORT 1.

recruit *n.* new man, novice, beginner, selectee, draftee, trainee, volunteer, enlisted man, serviceman, soldier, sailor, marine, rookie*; see also SOLDIER.

recruit *v.* **1.** [To raise troops] draft, call up, select, supply, muster, deliver, sign up, induct, take in, find manpower, call to arms, bring into service; see also ENLIST 1. **2.** [To gather needed resources] restore, store up, replenish; see GET 1.

rectangle *n.* geometrical figure, square, box, oblong, four-sided figure, right-angled parallelogram; see also FORM 1.

rectangular *a.* square, four-sided, right-angled; see ANGULAR.

rectitude *n.* integrity, trustworthiness, responsibility; see HONESTY.

recuperate *v.* heal, pull through, get back on one's feet; see RECOVER 3.

recur *v.* return, reappear, crop up again; see HAPPEN 2, REPEAT 1.
recurrent *a.* reoccurring, repetitive, habitual; see REPEATED 1.
recycle *v.* start over, start again, restart; see BEGIN 1, RESUME.
red *n. Tints and shades of red include the following:* scarlet, carmine, vermilion, crimson, cerise, cherry red, ruby, garnet, maroon, brick red, claret, rust, red gold, magenta, pink, fuchsia, coral red, blood red, russet, terra cotta, Chinese red, Congo red, Turkey red, aniline red, chrome red, rose, rose blush, old rose; see also COLOR. **—in the red*** in debt, losing money, going broke*; see RUINED 3. **—see red*** become angry, lose one's temper, get mad; see RAGE 1.
red-blooded *a.* robust, vigorous, hearty; see HEALTHY.
redden *v.* color, tint, dye; see COLOR.
reddish *a.* flushed, somewhat red, rose; see RED, *n.*
redecorate *v.* refurbish, refresh, renew, paint, repaint, repaper, restore, recondition, remodel, renovate, revamp, reaarrange, touch up, patch up, plaster, refurnish, wallpaper, clean up, carpet, do over, fix up*; see also DECORATE.
redeem *v.* **1.** [To recover through a payment] buy back, repay, purchase; see GET 1. **2.** [To save] liberate, set free, deliver; see RESCUE 1.
redeemer *n.* rescuer, deliverer, liberator; see PROTECTOR.
redeem oneself *v.* atone, give satisfaction, make amends; see PAY FOR.
redemption *n.* regeneration, salvation, rebirth; see RESCUE 1.
redheaded *a.* auburn-haired, red-haired, sandy-haired, titian-haired, strawberry-blonde, carrot-topped, brick-topped.
red-hot *a.* **1.** [Burning] heated, sizzling, scorching; see BURNING, HOT 1. **2.** [Raging] excessive, rabid, very; see EXTREME. **3.** [Newest] latest, recent, hippest*; see MODERN 1.
redo *v.* start over, redesign, rethink, go back to the drawing board, revamp, do over again; see also REPEAT.
redone *a.* done over, refinished, fixed up; see IMPROVED.
redress *n.* compensation, satisfaction, payment; see PAY 2, PRIZE.
red tape *n.* **1.** [Delay] wait, roadblock, impediment; see DELAY. **2.** [Bureaucracy] officialism, inflexible routine, officialdom; see GOVERNMENT 1, 2.
reduce *v.* **1.** [To make less] lessen, diminish, cut down; see DECREASE 2. **2.** [To defeat] conquer, overcome, subdue; see DEFEAT 2, 3. **3.** [To humble] degrade, demote, abase; see HUMBLE, HUMILIATE.
reduced *a.* **1.** [Made smaller] lessened, decreased, diminished, shortened, abridged, abbreviated, condensed, miniaturized, transistorized, compressed, economized, cut down, shrunk, subtracted, contracted, melted, boiled down.—*Ant.* SPREAD, enlarged, stretched. **2.** [Made lower] lowered, abated, sunk, deflated, leveled, cheapened, marked down, discounted, weakened, debilitated, humbled, demoted, degraded.—*Ant.* RAISED, heightened, elevated.
reduction *n.* **1.** [The process of making smaller] conversion, contraction, abatement, reducing, refinement, diminution, lowering, lessening, shortening, condensation, decrease, loss, compression, depression, subtraction, discount, shrinkage, constriction, modification, curtailment, abbreviation, miniaturization, abridgment, modulation, mitigation, remission, decline.—*Ant.* INCREASE, increasing, enlargement. **2.** [An amount that constitutes reduction] decrease, rebate, cut; see DISCOUNT.
redundant *a.* wordy, bombastic, verbose; see DULL 3, 4.
reeducate *v.* reinstruct, readjust, rehabilitate; see TEACH.
reef *n.* ridge, shoal, sand bar; see ROCK 2.
reek *n.* stench, stink, smell; see SMELL 2.
reek *v.* smell of, give off an odor, emit a stench; see SMELL 1.
reel *n.* spool, bobbin, spindle; see ROLL 2.
reexamine *v.* go back over, review, check thoroughly; see EXAMINE.
refer *v.* **1.** [To concern] regard, relate, have relation, have to do with, apply, be about, answer to, involve, connect, be a matter of, have a bearing on, correspond with, bear upon, comprise, include, belong, pertain, have reference, take in, cover, point, hold, encompass, incorporate, touch, deal with; see also CONCERN 1. **2.** [To mention] allude to, bring up, direct a remark, make reference, ascribe, direct attention, attribute, cite, quote, hint at, point to, notice, indicate, speak about, suggest, touch on, give as an example, associate, exemplify, instance, excerpt, extract; see also MENTION. **3.** [To direct] send to, put in touch with, relegate, commit, submit to, assign, give a recommendation to, introduce; see also LEAD 1.
referee *n.* arbitrator, conciliator, judge; see UMPIRE.
reference *n.* **1.** [An allusion] mention, relation, implication; see HINT. **2.** [A book of reference] original text, source, informant; see BOOK, DICTIONARY. **3.** [A person vouching for another] associate, employer, patron; see FRIEND.
referred to *a.* **1.** [Mentioned] brought up, alluded to, spoken about; see MENTIONED, SUGGESTED. **2.** [Directed] recommended, sent on, introduced to; see PROPOSED.

refine *v.* 1. [To purify] rarefy, strain, filter; see CLEAN, PURIFY. 2. [To improve] make clear, better, clarify; see EXPLAIN.

refined *a.* 1. [Purified] cleaned, cleansed, aerated, strained, washed, clean, rarefied, boiled down, distilled, clarified, tried, drained; see also PURE.—*Ant.* RAW, crude, unrefined. 2. [Genteel] cultivated, civilized, polished, elegant, well-bred, gracious, enlightened, gentlemanly, ladylike, restrained, gentle, mannerly, high-minded, subtle, courteous; see also POLITE.

refinement *n.* 1. [The act of refining] cleansing, clearing, purification; see CLEANING. 2. [Culture] civilization, cultivation, sophistication, breeding, enlightenment, wide knowledge, lore, subtlety, science, scholarship, learning; see also CULTURE 1. 3. [Genteel feelings and behavior] elegance, politeness, polish, good manners, suavity, courtesy, grace, gentleness, tact, cultivation, graciousness, civility, affability, taste, discrimination, fineness, delicacy, dignity, urbanity; see also CULTURE 2.

refinished *a.* redone, remodeled, fixed up; see CHANGED 2, REPAIRED.

reflect *v.* 1. [To contemplate] speculate, concentrate, weigh; see CONSIDER, THINK 1. 2. [To throw back] echo, reecho, repeat, match, take after, return, resonate, reverberate, copy, resound, reproduce, reply, be resonant, emulate, imitate, follow, catch, rebound. 3. [To throw back an image] mirror, shine, reproduce, show up on, flash, cast back, return, give forth.

reflection *n.* 1. [Thought] consideration, absorption, imagination, observation, thinking, contemplation, rumination, speculation, musing, deliberation, study, pondering, meditation, concentration, cogitation; see also THOUGHT 1. 2. [An image] impression, rays, light, shine, glitter, appearance, idea, reflected image, likeness, shadow, duplicate, picture, echo, representation, reproduction; see also COPY, IMAGE 2.

reflector *n.* shiny metal, glass, reverberator; see MIRROR.

reflex *a.* mechanical, unthinking, habitual; see AUTOMATIC, SPONTANEOUS.

reform *n.* reformation, betterment, new law; see IMPROVEMENT 2.

reform *v.* 1. [To change into a new form] reorganize, remodel, revise, repair, reconstruct, rearrange, transform, ameliorate, redeem, rectify, better, rehabilitate, improve, correct, cure, remedy, convert, mend, amend, restore, rebuild, reclaim, revolutionize, regenerate, refashion, renovate, renew, rework, reconstitute, make over, remake; see also CORRECT, REPAIR.—*Ant.* CORRUPT, degrade, botch. 2. [To correct evils] amend, clean out, give a new basis, abolish, repeal, uplift, ameliorate, rectify, regenerate, give new life to, remedy, stamp out, make better, standardize, bring up to code; see also IMPROVE 1. 3. [To change one's conduct for the better] resolve, mend, regenerate, uplift, make amends, make a new start, make resolutions, turn over a new leaf, go straight*, swear off; see also sense 2.

reformation *n.* repeal, remaking, reestablishment; see RECOVERY 1.

Reformation *n.* Renaissance, Lutheranism, Protestantism, Puritanism, Calvinism, Anglicanism, Unitarianism, Counter Reformation, Protestant Movement; see also REVOLUTION 2.

reformatory *n.* house of correction, penal institution, reform school; see JAIL, SCHOOL 1.

reformed *a.* 1. [Changed] altered, transformed, shifted, reconstituted, reorganized, shuffled, reestablished, revolutionized, rectified, amended, reset, reworked, renewed, regenerated; see also CHANGED 2, IMPROVED.—*Ant.* CORRUPT, degenerated, vicious. 2. [Changed for the better in behavior] converted, improved, redeemed, gone straight*, turned over a new leaf; see also POLITE, RIGHTEOUS 1.

refrain *n.* undersong, theme, strain; see MUSIC 1, SONG.

refrain *v.* cease, avoid, forbear; see ABSTAIN.

refresh *v.* invigorate, animate, exhilarate; see RENEW 1.

refreshing *a.* invigorating, rousing, exhilarating; see STIMULATING.

refreshment *n.* tidbit, ice cream, cakes; see DRINK 1, FOOD.

refrigerate *v.* chill, make cold, freeze; see COOL.

refrigeration *n.* cooling, chilling, freezing; see PRESERVATION.

refrigerator *n.* icebox, automatic cooler, cold-storage box, refrigerator car, electric refrigerator, cooling apparatus, refrigeration equipment, deep freezer.

refuge *n.* 1. [A place of protection] shelter, asylum, sanctuary, covert, home, retreat, anchorage, nunnery, convent, monastery, poorhouse, safe place, hiding place, game preserve, safe, safe house, harbor, haven, fortress, stronghold. 2. [A means of resort] alternative, resource, last resort; see ESCAPE.

refugee *n.* exile, expatriate, fugitive, emigrant, renegade, foreigner, castaway, derelict, foundling, homeless person, leper, pariah, outlaw, prodigal, displaced person, alien, outcast.

refund *n.* return, reimbursement, repayment, remuneration, compensation, allowance, payment for expenses, rebate, discount, settlement, discharge, acquittance, retribution, satisfaction, consolation, money back; see also PAYMENT 1.

refund *v.* pay back, reimburse, remit, repay, relinquish, make good, balance, recoup, adjust, reward, restore, redeem, make repayment to, compensate, recompense, make amends, redress, remunerate, give back, settle, honor a claim, kick back*, make good*, make up for; see also PAY 1.

refunded *a.* acquitted, reimbursed, discharged; see PAID, RETURNED.

refusal *n.* repudiation, renunciation, rebuff, snub, rejection, nonacceptance, denial, disavowal, noncompliance, opposition, forbidding, veto, interdiction, proscription, ban, writ, exclusion, negation, repulse, withholding, disclaimer, nonconsent, unwillingness, regrets, declination, repulsion, reversal, dissent, prohibition, disfavor, disapproval, curb, restraint.

refuse *n.* leavings, remains, residue; see TRASH 1.

refuse *v.* dissent, desist, repel, rebuff, scorn, pass up, reject, disallow, have no plans to, not anticipate, demur, protest, withdraw, hold back, withhold, shun, turn thumbs down on, evade, dodge, ignore, spurn, regret, turn down, turn from, beg to be excused, send regrets, not budge, cut out of the budget, not budget, not care to, refuse to receive, dispense with, not be at home to, say no, make excuses, disapprove, set aside, turn away, beg off, brush off*, not buy, hold off, turn one's back on, turn a deaf ear to; see also DENY.—*Ant.* ALLOW, admit, consent.

refused *a.* declined, rejected, rebuffed, vetoed, repudiated, forbidden, denied, disowned, disavowed, forsaken, blocked, repelled, closed to, dismissed, turned down, not budgeted, not in the budget.—*Ant.* PERMITTED, allowed, consented to.

refute *v.* disprove, answer, prove false; see DENY.

regain *v.* recapture, retrieve, reacquire; see RECOVER 1.

regard *n.* **1.** [A look] gaze, glance, once-over*; see LOOK 3. **2.** [A favorable opinion] esteem, respect, honor, favor, liking, interest, fondness, attachment, deference, opinion, sympathy, estimation, appreciation, reverence, consideration, love, affection, value, devotion; see also ADMIRATION.

regard *v.* **1.** [To look at] observe, notice, mark; see SEE 1. **2.** [To have an attitude] surmise, look upon, view; see CONSIDER, THINK 1. **3.** [To hold in esteem] respect, esteem, value; see ADMIRE.

regarding *a. & prep.* concerning, with reference to, in relation to, as regards; see also ABOUT 2.

regardless *a.* **1.** [Heedless] negligent, careless, unobservant, unheeding, inattentive, reckless, inconsiderate, inadvertent, blind, unfeeling, deaf, coarse, crude, neglectful, mindless, insensitive, lax, indifferent, listless, uninterested, unconcerned.—*Ant.* OBSERVANT, alert, watchful, vigilant. **2.** [In spite of; *usually used with "of"*] despite, aside from, distinct from, without regard to, without considering, notwithstanding, at any cost, leaving aside; see also ALTHOUGH, BUT 1.

regards *n.pl.* best wishes, compliments, greetings, salutations, remembrances, respects, love, deference, commendation, love and kisses*; see also GREETING.

regenerate *v.* raise from the dead, recreate, exhilarate; see PRODUCE 2, REVIVE 1.

regeneration *n.* rebuilding, rehabilitation, renovation; see REPAIR.

regime *n.* administration, management, political system; see GOVERNMENT 2.

regiment *n.* corps, soldiers, military organization; see ARMY 2.

regimentation *n.* massing, collectivization, organization, planned economy, standardization, methodization, regulation, uniformity, arrangement, mechanization, institutionalization, classification, division, lining up, adjustment, harmonization, grouping, ordering; see also RESTRAINT 2.

region *n.* **1.** [An indefinite area] country, district, territory, section, sector, province, zone, realm, vicinity, quarter, locale, locality, environs, precinct, county, neighborhood, terrain, domain, range. **2.** [A limited area] precinct, ward, block; see AREA. **3.** [Scope] sphere, province, realm; see FIELD 3.

regional *a.* provincial, territorial, local, environmental, positional, geographical, parochial, sectional, topical, locational, insular, topographic.

register *n.* **1.** [A list] file, registry, roll; see LIST, RECORD 1. **2.** [A heating regulator] grate, hot-air opening, radiator; see APPLIANCE.

register *v.* **1.** [To record] check in, enroll, file; see LIST 1, RECORD 1. **2.** [To indicate] point to, designate, record; see NAME 2. **3.** [To show] express, disclose, manifest; see DISPLAY. **4.** [To enlist or enroll] go through registration, check into, make an entry, sign up for, check in, sign in, join.

registration *n.* **1.** [The act of registering] enrolling, signing up, certification, matriculation, recording, listing, filing, cataloging, booking, noting down, stamping, authorizing, notarization; see also ENROLLMENT 1. **2.** [Those who have registered] enrollment, turnout, registrants, voters, hotel guests, students, student body, delegation.

regress *v.* backslide, relapse, revert; see RETREAT, SINK 1.

regressive *a.* conservative, reverse, reactionary; see BACKWARD 1.

regret *n.* **1.** [Remorse] concern, compunction, worry, repentance, self-reproach, self-condemnation, self-disgust, misgiving, regretfulness, nostalgia, self-accusation, contrition, qualm, scruple, penitence, bitterness, disappointment, dissatisfaction, uneasiness, conscience, discomfort, annoyance, spiritual disturbance; see also CARE 2.—*Ant.* COMFORT, satisfaction, ease. **2.** [Grief] sorrow, pain, anxiety; see GRIEF.

regret *v.* **1.** [To be sorry for] mourn, bewail, lament, cry over, rue, grieve, repent, have compunctions about, look back upon, feel conscience-stricken, moan, have a bad conscience, have qualms about, weep over, be disturbed over, feel uneasy about, laugh out of the other side of one's mouth*, kick oneself*, bite one's tongue*, cry over spilled milk*.—*Ant.* CELEBRATE, be satisfied with, be happy. **2.** [To disapprove of] deplore, be opposed to, deprecate; see DENOUNCE, DISLIKE.

regular *a.* **1.** [In accordance with custom] customary, usual, routine; see CONVENTIONAL 1, 3. **2.** [In accordance with law] normal, legitimate, lawful; see LEGAL. **3.** [In accordance with an observable pattern] orderly, methodical, routine, symmetrical, precise, exact, systematic, arranged, organized, patterned, constant, congruous, consonant, consistent, invariable, formal, regulated, rational, steady, rhythmic, periodic, measured, classified, in order, unconfused, harmonious, systematic, normal, natural, cyclic, successive, momentary, alternating, probable, recurrent, general, usual, expected, serial, automatic, mechanical, alternate, hourly, daily, monthly, weekly, annual, seasonal, yearly, pulsating, diurnal, quotidian, menstrual, anticipated, hoped for, counted on, generally occurring, in the natural course of events, punctual, steady, uniform.—*Ant.* IRREGULAR, sporadic, erratic.

regularity *n.* evenness, steadiness, uniformity, routine, constancy, consistency, invariability, rhythm, recurrence, system, congruity, homogeneity, punctuality, periodicity, swing, rotation, conformity, proportion, symmetry, balance, cadence, harmony.

regularly *a.* customarily, habitually, punctually, systematically, unchangingly, right along, as a rule, usually, commonly, as a matter of course, tirelessly, conventionally, ordinarily, repeatedly, frequently, faithfully, religiously, mechanically, automatically, without once missing, normally, periodically, evenly, methodically, exactly, monotonously, rhythmically, steadily, unbrokenly, typically, continually, like clockwork, cyclically, day in and day out, constantly, always, ceaselessly, time and time again, invariably, redundantly, hourly, incessantly, daily, perpetually, over and over again, weekly, monthly, annually, exactly.—*Ant.* IRREGULARLY, unevenly, brokenly.

regulate *v.* **1.** [To control] rule, legislate, direct; see GOVERN, MANAGE 1. **2.** [To adjust] arrange, methodize, dispose, classify, systematize, put in order, fix, settle, adapt, standardize, coordinate, allocate, readjust, reconcile, rectify, correct, improve, temper, set; see also ADJUST 1.

regulated *a.* fixed, adjusted, arranged, directed, controlled, supervised, methodized, systematized, settled, adapted, coordinated, reconciled, improved, standardized, tempered, ruled; see also CLASSIFIED, MANAGED 2, ORGANIZED.—*Ant.* CONFUSED, disarranged, upset.

regulation *n.* **1.** [The act of regulating] handling, direction, control; see MANAGEMENT 1. **2.** [A rule] law, statute, ordinance; see COMMAND, LAW 3.

regulator *n.* adjuster, thermostat, valve; see MACHINE.

rehabilitate *v.* restore, change, reestablish; see RENEW 1.

rehabilitation *n.* rebuilding, reestablishment, remaking; see IMPROVEMENT 1, REPAIR.

rehearsal *n.* recitation, recital, trial performance, practice performance, experiment, test flight, reading, dress rehearsal, call; see also PERFORMANCE, PRACTICE 3.

rehearse *v.* **1.** [To tell] describe, recount, relate; see TELL 1. **2.** [To repeat] tell again, retell, do over, recapitulate, reenact; see also REPEAT 3. **3.** [To practice for a performance] drill, test, experiment, hold rehearsals, speak from a script, run through, hold a reading, learn one's part; see also PRACTICE 1.

reign *v.* hold power, sit on the throne, wear the crown; see GOVERN, MANAGE 1.

reimburse *v.* repay, compensate, make reparations; see PAY 1, REFUND.

reimbursement *n.* compensation, restitution, recompense; see PAYMENT 1.

rein *n.* bridle strap, line, control; see ROPE. —**give (free) rein to** authorize, permit, condone; see ALLOW. —**keep a rein on** control, check, have authority over; see MANAGE 1.

reincarnation *n.* incarnation, reanimation, rebirth; see BIRTH, RETURN 2.

reinforce *v.* buttress, pillar, add to; see STRENGTHEN.

reinforced *a.* supported, assisted, strengthened, augmented, buttressed, fortified, pillowed, banded, backed, built-up, stiffened, thickened, cushioned, lined; see also STRONG 2.

reinforcement *n.* **1.** [Support] coating, concrete block, pillar; see SUPPORT 2. **2.** [Military aid; *usually plural*] fresh troops, additional materiel, new ordnance; see HELP 1.

reject *v.* 1. [To refuse] repudiate, decline, renounce; see DENY, REFUSE. 2. [To discard] cast out, throw out, expel; see DISCARD.

rejected *a.* returned, given back, denied; see REFUSED.

rejection *n.* repudiation, denial, dismissal; see REFUSAL.

rejoice *v.* exult, enjoy, revel; see CELEBRATE 2.

rejuvenate *v.* reinvigorate, exhilarate, refresh; see STRENGTHEN.

rejuvenation *n.* reinvigoration, stimulation, revivification; see REVIVAL 1.

relapse *n.* reversion, recidivism, return; see LOSS 3.

relapse *v.* lapse, retrogress, fall, backslide, revert, regress, suffer a relapse, deteriorate, degenerate, fall from grace, fall off, weaken, sink back, fall into again, slip back, slide back, be overcome, give in to again.

relate *v.* 1. [Tell] recount, recite, retell; see DESCRIBE, REPORT 1. 2. [Connect] bring into relation, associate, correlate; see COMPARE 1.

related *a.* 1. [Told] narrated, described, recounted; see TOLD. 2. [Connected] associated, in touch with, linked, tied up, knit together, allied, affiliated, complementary, analogous, correspondent, akin, alike, like, parallel, correlated, intertwined, interrelated, similar, mutual, dependent, interdependent, interwoven, of that ilk, in the same category, reciprocal, interchangeable. 3. [Akin] kindred, of the same family, germane, fraternal, cognate, consanguine, of one blood; see also sense 2.

relate to *v.* be associated to, be connected with, affect; see CONCERN 1, REFER 1.

relation *n.* 1. [Relationship] connection, association, similarity; see RELATIONSHIP. 2. [A relative] family connection, sibling, kinsman; see RELATIVE. —**in relation to** concerning, with reference to, about; see REGARDING.

relationship *n.* relation, connection, tie, association, affinity, likeness, link, kinship, bond, dependence, relativity, proportion, rapport, analogy, homogeneity, interrelation, correlation, nearness, alliance, relevance, accord, hookup*, contact; see also SIMILARITY.—*Ant.* DIFFERENCE, dissimilarity, oppositeness.

relative *a.* 1. [Pertinent] dependent, contingent, applicable; see RELATED 2, RELEVANT. 2. [In regard to] with respect to, concerning, relating to; see ABOUT 2.

relative *n.* kin, family connection, relation, member of the family, blood relation, next of kin, sibling, kinsman. *Relatives include the following:* mother, father, parent, grandmother, grandfather, great-grandmother, great-grandfather, ancestor, aunt, uncle, great-aunt, great-uncle, cousin, first cousin, second cousin, third cousin, fourth cousin, distant cousin, wife, husband, spouse, daughter, son, nephew, niece, brother, sister, kinsman, kinswoman, mother-in-law, father-in-law, brother-in-law, sister-in-law, aunt by marriage, cousin by marriage, in-law*.

relatively *a.* comparatively, approximately, nearly; see ALMOST.

relax *v.* repose, recline, settle back, make oneself at home, breathe easy, take one's time, take a break, sit around, stop work, lie down, unbend, be at ease, take a breather*; see also REST 1.

relaxation *n.* repose, reclining, loosening; see REST 1.

relaxed *a.* untroubled, carefree, at ease; see COMFORTABLE 1.

relay *v.* communicate, transfer, send forth, transmit, hand over, hand down, turn over, deliver, pass on; see also CARRY 1, SEND 1.

release *n.* 1. [Freedom] liberation, discharge, freeing; see FREEDOM 2. 2. [That which has been released; *usually, printed matter*] news story, publicity, news flash; see PROPAGANDA, STORY.

release *v.* liberate, let go, acquit; see FREE.

released *a.* 1. [Freed] discharged, dismissed, liberated; see FREE 1, 2. 2. [Announced] broadcast, stated, made public; see PUBLISHED.

relent *v.* soften, comply, relax; see YIELD 1.

relentless *a.* unmerciful, vindictive, hard; see RUTHLESS.

relevance *n.* connection, significance, pertinence; see IMPORTANCE.

relevant *a.* suitable, appropriate, fit, proper, pertinent to, becoming, pertaining to, apt, applicable, important, fitting, congruous, cognate, related, conforming, concerning, suitable, conforming, compatible, accordant, referring, harmonious, correspondent, consonant, congruent, consistent, correlated, associated, allied, relative, connected, to the point, bearing on the question, having direct bearing, having to do with, related to, on the nose.—*Ant.* IRRELEVANT, WRONG, not pertinent.

reliability *n.* dependability, trustworthiness, constancy, loyalty, faithfulness, sincerity, devotion, honesty, authenticity, steadfastness, fidelity, safety, security.

reliable *a.* firm, unimpeachable, sterling, strong, positive, stable, dependable, sure, solid, staunch, decisive, unequivocal, steadfast, definite, conscientious, constant, steady, trustworthy, faithful, loyal, good, true, sure, devoted, tried, trusty, honest, honorable, candid, true-hearted, responsible, high-principled, sincere, altruistic, determined, reputable, careful, proved, respectable, righteous, decent, incorrupt, truthful, upright, regular, all right, kosher*, OK, on the up and up*, true-blue, safe, honest, sound, stable, solid, steady, guaranteed, sure, certain, substantial, secure, unquestionable, conclusive, irrefutable, incontestable, dependable, good, firm, strong, unfailing, infallible, authentic, competent, assured, workable, foolproof, sure-fire.—*Ant.* DANGEROUS, insecure, undependable.

reliably *a.* assuredly, presumably, certainly; see PROBABLY, SURELY.

reliance *n.* confidence, trust, hope; see FAITH 1.

relic *n.* **1.** [Something left from an earlier time] vestige, trace, survival, heirloom, antique, keepsake, memento, curio, curiosity, token, souvenir, testimonial, evidence, monument, trophy, remains, artifact, remembrance, bric-a-brac. **2.** [A ruin] remnant, residue, remains, broken stone; see also DESTRUCTION 2, RUIN 2.

relief *n.* **1.** [The act of bringing succor] alleviation, softening, comforting; see COMFORT. **2.** [Aid] assistance, support, maintenance; see HELP 1. **3.** [A relieved state of mind] satisfaction, relaxation, ease, comfort, release, happiness, contentment, cheer, restfulness, a load off one's mind; see also COMFORT. **4.** [The person or thing that brings relief] diversion, relaxation, consolation, solace, reinforcement, supplies, food, shelter, clothing, release, respite, remedy, nursing, medicine, medical care, redress, reparations, indemnities, variety, change, cure; see also HELP 1. **5.** [The raised portions of a sculptural decoration or map] projection, contour, configuration; see DECORATION 2.

relieve *v.* **1.** [To replace] discharge, throw out, force to resign; see DISMISS. **2.** [To lessen; *said especially of pain*] assuage, alleviate, soothe, comfort, allay, divert, free, ease, lighten, soften, diminish, mitigate, console, cure, aid, assist; see also DECREASE 2, HELP.

relieved *a.* **1.** [Eased in mind] comforted, solaced, consoled, reassured, satisfied, soothed, relaxed, put at ease, restored, reconciled, appeased, placated, alleviated, mollified, disarmed, pacified, adjusted, propitiated, breathing easy*; see also COMFORTABLE 1.—*Ant.* SAD, worried, distraught. **2.** [Deprived of something, or freed from it] replaced, dismissed, separated from, disengaged, released, made free of, rescued, delivered, supplanted, superseded, succeeded, substituted, interchanged, exchanged. **3.** [Lessened; *said especially of pain*] mitigated, palliated, softened, assuaged, eased, abated, diminished, salved, soothed, lightened, alleviated, drugged, anesthetized.

religion *n.* **1.** [All that centers about man's belief in or relationship to a superior being or beings] belief, devotion, piety, spirituality, persuasion, godliness, sense of righteousness, morality, theology, faithfulness, devoutness, creed, myth, superstition, doctrine, cult, denomination, mythology, communion, religious conscience, fidelity, conscientiousness, religious bent, ethical standard; see also FAITH 2. **2.** [Organized worship or service of a deity] veneration, adoration, consecration, sanctification, prayer, rites, ceremonials, holy sacrifice, incantation, holiday, observance, orthodoxy, reformism; see also CEREMONY 2. *Religions include the following:* Christianity, (Zen) Buddhism, Hinduism, Islam, Judaism, Zoroastrianism, Shintoism, Taoism, deism, theism, polytheism, dualism; see also CHURCH 3. **—get religion** become converted, believe, change; see REFORM 2, 3.

religious *a.* **1.** [Pertaining to religion] ethical, spiritual, moral, ecclesiastical, clerical, theological, canonical, divine, supernatural, holy, sacred, churchly, theistic, deistic, priestly, pontifical, ministerial.—*Ant.* WORLDLY, secular, earthly. **2.** [Devout] pious, puritanical, sanctimonious, pietistic, godly, god-fearing, orthodox, reverend, reverential, believing, faithful, Christian, fanatic, evangelistic, revivalistic, churchgoing; see also HOLY 1. **3.** [Scrupulous] methodical, minute, thorough; see CAREFUL.

relish *n.* **1.** [A condiment] seasoning, herb, savor. *Relishes include the following:* catsup or ketchup, piccalilli, cucumber relish, pickle relish, mincemeat, pickled pears, pickled peaches, chutney, chili sauce, hot sauce, cranberry sauce. **2.** [Obvious delight] gusto, joy, great satisfaction; see ZEAL.

relish *v.* enjoy, fancy, be fond of; see LIKE 1, 2.

reluctance *n.* disinclination, qualm, hesitation; see DOUBT.

reluctant *a.* disinclined, loath, unwilling, averse, opposed, tardy, backward, adverse, laggard, remiss, slack, squeamish, demurring, grudging, involuntary, uncertain, hanging back, hesitant, hesitating, diffident, with bad grace, indisposed, disheartened, discouraged, queasy.—*Ant.* WILLING, eager, disposed.

rely on or **upon** *v.* hope, have faith in, count on; see TRUST 1.

remade *a.* rebuilt, redone, made over; see IMPROVED.

remain *v.* **1.** [To stay] inhabit, stop, stay in; see SETTLE 5. **2.** [To endure] keep on, go on, prevail; see CONTINUE 1, ENDURE 1. **3.** [To be left] remain standing, outlive, outlast; see SURVIVE 1.

remainder *n.* remaining portion, leftover, residue, remains, relic, remnant, dregs, surplus, leavings, balance, residuum, excess, overplus, scrap, fragment, small piece, carryover, rest, residual portion, whatever is left, salvage.

remains *n.pl.* corpse, cadaver, relics; see BODY 2.
remake *v.* change, revise, alter; see CORRECT.
remark *n.* statement, saying, utterance, annotation, note, mention, reflection, illustration, point, conclusion, consideration, talk, observation, expression, comment, assertion, witticism.
remark *v.* speak, mention, observe; see SAY, TALK 1.
remarkable *a.* exceptional, extraordinary, uncommon; see UNUSUAL 1.
remarkably *a.* exceptionally, singularly, notably; see ESPECIALLY, VERY.
remedy *n.* **1.** [A medicine] antidote, pill, drug; see MEDICINE 2, TREATMENT 2. **2.** [Effective help] relief, cure, redress, support, improvement, solution, plan, panacea, cure-all, assistance, counteraction; see also RELIEF 4.
remedy *v.* cure, help, aid; see HEAL.
remember *v.* **1.** [To recall] recollect, recognize, summon up, relive, dig into the past, refresh one's memory, be reminded of, think of, revive, bring to mind, call to mind, think over, think back, look back, brood over, conjure up, call up, carry one's thoughts back, look back upon, have memories of, commemorate, memorialize, reminisce, carry in one's thoughts, keep a memory alive, enshrine in the memory.—*Ant.* LOSE, forget, neglect. **2.** [To bear in mind] keep in mind, memorize, know by heart, learn, master, get, be impressed on one's mind, fix in the mind, retain, treasure, hold dear, dwell upon, brood over, keep forever.—*Ant.* NEGLECT, ignore, disregard.
remembered *a.* thought of, recalled, recollected, rewarded, summoned up, brought to mind, memorialized, haunting one's thoughts, commemorated, dug up.—*Ant.* LOST, forgotten, overlooked.
remembrance *n.* **1.** [Memory] recall, recollection, recognition; see MEMORY 1. **2.** [A gift] reward, token, keepsake; see GIFT 1.
remind *v.* **1.** [To bring into the memory] bring back, make one think of, intimate; see HINT. **2.** [To call the attention of another] caution, point out, refresh the memory, remind one of, mention to, call attention to, bring up, prompt, prod, stress, emphasize, note, stir up, put a bug in one's ear, give a cue; see also WARN.
reminded *a.* warned, cautioned, prompted, put in mind of, made aware, advised, forewarned, notified, awakened, prodded.
reminder *n.* warning, notice, admonition, note, memorandum, memo, hint, suggestion, memento, token, keepsake, trinket, remembrance, souvenir.
remit *v.* make payment, forward, dispatch; see PAY 1.
remittance *n.* transmittal, money sent, enclosure; see PAYMENT 1.
remnant *n.* residue, leavings, dregs; see EXCESS 1, REMAINDER.
remnants *n.pl.* scraps, odds and ends, leftovers, particles, surplus, endpieces, remains, leavings; see also EXCESS 1, REMAINDER.
remodel *v.* renovate, refurnish, refurbish, readjust, reconstruct, readapt, rearrange, redecorate, refashion, improve, reshape, recast, rebuild, repair, modernize, repaint; see also REPAIR.
remodeled *a.* refurnished, redecorated, rebuilt; see CHANGED 2.
remorse *n.* compunction, contrition, self-reproach; see GRIEF, REGRET 1. **—without remorse** cruel, pitiless, relentless; see RUTHLESS.
remorseful *a.* contrite, penitent, repentant; see SORRY 1.
remorseless *a.* unyielding, unforgiving, vindictive; see SEVERE 1, 2.
remote *a.* **1.** [Distant] far-off, faraway, out-of-the-way, removed, beyond, secluded, inaccessible, isolated, unknown, alien, foreign, undiscovered, off the beaten track, over the hills and far away, godforsaken; see also DISTANT.—*Ant.* NEAR, close, accessible. **2.** [Ancient] forgotten, past, aged; see OLD 3. **3.** [Separated] unrelated, irrelevant, unconnected; see SEPARATED.
removal *n.* dismissal, discharge, expulsion, exile, deportation, banishment, elimination, extraction, dislodgement, evacuation, ejection, transference, eradication, extermination, replacement, translocation, the gate*, the bounce*.—*Ant.* ENTRANCE, induction, introduction.
remove *v.* **1.** [To move physically] take away from, cart away, clear away, carry away, take away, tear away, brush away, transfer, transport, dislodge, uproot, excavate, displace, unload, discharge, lift up, doff, raise, evacuate, shift, switch, lift, push, draw away, draw in, withdraw, separate, extract, cut out, dig out, tear out, pull out, take out, smoke out, rip out, take down, tear off, draw off, take off, carry off, cart off, clear off, strike off, cut off, rub off, scrape off, take in. **2.** [To eliminate] get rid of, do away with, exclude; see ELIMINATE. **3.** [To dismiss] discharge, displace, discard; see DISMISS.
removed *a.* **1.** [Taken out] extracted, eliminated, withdrawn, evacuated, dislodged, ejected, pulled out, amputated, excised, expunged, extirpated.—*Ant.* LEFT, ignored, established. **2.** [Distant] faraway, out-of-the-way, far-off; see DISTANT. **3.** [Dismissed] banished, relieved of office, retired; see DISCHARGED, RECALLED 2.
rend *v.* rip, sever, sunder; see BREAK 1.
render *v.* **1.** [To give] present, hand over, distribute; see GIVE 1. **2.** [To perform, espe-

cially a service] do, act, execute; see PERFORM 1. **3.** [To interpret; *said especially of music*] play, perform, depict; see INTERPRET.

rendition *n.* interpretation, version, reading; see TRANSLATION.

renew *v.* **1.** [To refresh] revive, reawaken, regenerate, reestablish, rehabilitate, reinvigorate, replace, revive, rebuild, reconstitute, remake, refinish, refurbish, redo, repeat, invigorate, exhilarate, restore, resuscitate, recondition, overhaul, replenish, go over, cool, brace, freshen, stimulate, recreate, remodel, revamp, redesign, modernize, rejuvenate, give new life to, recover, renovate, reintegrate, make a new beginning, bring up to date, do over, make like new; see also REVIVE 1. **2.** [To repeat] resume, reiterate, recommence; see REPEAT 1. **3.** [To replace] resume, supplant, take over; see SUBSTITUTE.

renewal *n.* resurrection, new start, renovation; see REVIVAL 1.

renewed *a.* revived, readapted, refitted; see REPAIRED.

renounce *v.* disown, disavow, give up; see DENY, DISCARD.

renovate *v.* make over, remake, rehabilitate; see RENEW 1.

renovated *a.* renewed, remodeled, redone; see CLEAN 1, REPAIRED.

renovation *n.* reform, revision, change; see IMPROVEMENT 1.

rent *v.* **1.** [To sell the use of property] lease, lend, let, make available, allow the use of, take in roomers, sublet, put on loan. **2.** [To obtain use by payment] hire, pay rent for, charter, contract, sign a contract for, engage, borrow, pay for services; see also PAY 1.

rented *a.* leased, lent, hired, contracted, engaged, let, chartered, taken, on lease, out of the market.

reopen *v.* revive, reestablish, begin again; see OPEN 2, RENEW 1.

reorganization *n.* reestablishment, reconstitution, reorientation; see CHANGE 2, IMPROVEMENT 1.

reorganize *v.* rebuild, renovate, regenerate; see RECONSTRUCT.

repaid *a.* paid back, reimbursed, refunded; see PAID.

repair *n.* reconstruction, substitution, reformation, rehabilitation, new part, patch, restoration, restored portion, replacement; see also IMPROVEMENT 1, 2.—*Ant.* BREAK, tear, fracture.

repair *v.* fix, adjust, improve, correct, settle, put into shape, reform, patch, rejuvenate, refurbish, retread, touch up, put in order, revive, refresh, renew, mend, darn, sew, revamp, rectify, right, ameliorate, renovate, reshape, rebuild, work over*, fix up.—*Ant.* WRECK, damage, smash.

repaired *a.* fixed, adjusted, rearranged, adapted, settled, remodeled, rectified, mended, corrected, righted, restored, renewed, remedied, improved, renovated, retouched, in working order, patched up, put together, put back into shape, sewn, reset, stitched up.—*Ant.* DAMAGED, worn, torn.

reparation *n.* indemnity, retribution, amends; see PAYMENT 1.

repay *v.* **1.** [To pay back] reimburse, recompense, refund, return, indemnify, give back, make amends, requite, compensate, square oneself*, settle up; see also PAY 1. **2.** [To retaliate] get even with, square accounts, reciprocate; see REVENGE.

repayment *n.* compensation, indemnity, restitution; see PAYMENT 1.

repeal *n.* annulment, cancellation, abolition; see WITHDRAWAL.

repeal *v.* annul, abolish, abrogate; see CANCEL.

repeat *v.* **1.** [To do again] redo, remake, do over, recur, rehash, reciprocate, return, rework, reform, refashion, recast, reduplicate, renew, reconstruct, reerect, revert, hold over, go over again and again. **2.** [To happen again] reoccur, recur, revolve, reappear, occur again, come again, return; see also HAPPEN 2. **3.** [To say again] reiterate, restate, reissue, republish, reutter, echo, recite, reecho, rehearse, retell, go over, play back, recapitulate, drum into, rehash, come again; see also SAY.

repeated *a.* **1.** [Done again] redone, remade, copied, imitated, reworked, refashioned, recast, done over, reciprocated, returned, reverted, reduplicated. **2.** [Said again] reiterated, restated, reannounced, reuttered, recited, reproduced, seconded, paraphrased, reworded, retold.

repeatedly *a.* again and again, many times, time and again; see FREQUENTLY, REGULARLY.

repel *v.* **1.** [To throw back] rebuff, resist, stand up against, oppose, check, repulse, put to flight, keep at bay, knock down, drive away, drive back, beat back, hold back, force back, push back, beat off, ward off, chase off, stave off, fight off.—*Ant.* FALL, fail, retreat. **2.** [To cause aversion] nauseate, offend, revolt; see DISGUST. **3.** [To reject] disown, dismiss, cast aside; see REFUSE.

repent *v.* be sorry, have qualms, be penitent; see APOLOGIZE, REGRET 1.

repentance *n.* sorrow, remorse, self-reproach; see REGRET 1.

repentant *a.* penitent, regretful, contrite; see SORRY 1.

repercussion *n.* consequence, result, effect; see RESULT.

repetition *n.* recurrence, reoccurrence, reappearance, reproduction, copy, rote, duplication, renewal, recapitulation, reiteration, return; see also WORDINESS.

repetitious *a.* boring, wordy, repeating; see DULL 4.

replace *v.* **1.** [To supply an equivalent] repay, compensate, mend; see RECONSTRUCT, RENEW 1, REPAIR. **2.** [To take the place of] take over, supplant, displace; see SUBSTITUTE. **3.** [To put back in the same place] restore, reinstate, put back; see RETURN 2.

replaced *a.* **1.** [Returned to the same place] restored, reinstated, reintegrated, recovered, recouped, reacquired, regained, repossessed, resumed, rewon, retrieved. **2.** [Having another in one's place; *said of persons*] dismissed, cashiered, dislodged; see RECALLED 2. **3.** [Having another in its place; *said of things*] renewed, interchanged, replenished; see CHANGED 1.

replica *n.* copy, likeness, model; see DUPLICATE, IMITATION 2.

reply *n.* response, return, retort; see ANSWER 1.

reply *v.* retort, rejoin, return; see ANSWER 1.

report *n.* **1.** [A transmitted account] tale, narrative, description; see NEWS 1, 2, STORY. **2.** [An official summary] proclamation, outline, release; see RECORD 1, SUMMARY. **3.** [A loud, explosive sound] detonation, bang, blast; see NOISE 1.

report *v.* **1.** [To deliver information] describe, recount, narrate, provide the details of, give an account of, set forth, inform, advise, communicate, retail, wire, cable, telephone, radio, broadcast, notify, relate, state; see also TELL 1. **2.** [To make a summary statement] summarize, publish, proclaim; see sense 1. **3.** [To present oneself] be at hand, reach, come; see ARRIVE. **4.** [To record] take minutes, inscribe, note down; see RECORD 1.

reported *a.* stated, recited, recounted, narrated, described, set forth, announced, broadcast, rumored, noted, expressed, proclaimed, made known, according to rumor, revealed, communicated, disclosed, imparted, divulged, recorded, in the air, all over town.—*Ant.* UNKNOWN, verified, certain.

reporter *n.* newspaperman, news writer, columnist, journalist, newsman, correspondent, interviewer, cub reporter, star reporter, newsgatherer; see also WRITER.

represent *v.* **1.** [To act as a delegate] be an agent for, serve, hold office, be deputy for, be attorney for, steward, act as broker, sell for, buy for, do business for, be spokesman for, be ambassador for, exercise power of attorney for. **2.** [To present as a true interpretation] render, depict, portray; see ENACT. **3.** [To serve as an equivalent] copy, imitate, reproduce, symbolize, exemplify, typify, signify, substitute, stand for, impersonate, personify.

representation *n.* description, narration, delineation; see COPY.

representative *n.* **1.** [An emissary] deputy, salesman, messenger; see AGENT, DELEGATE. **2.** [One who is elected to the lower legislative body] congressman, assemblyman, councilman, member of parliament, deputy, legislator, senator, councilor; see also DIPLOMAT.

represented *a.* **1.** [Depicted] portrayed, interpreted, pictured; see MADE. **2.** [Presented] rendered, exhibited, enacted; see SHOWN 1.

repress *v.* control, curb, check; see HINDER, RESTRAIN.

reprimand *v.* reproach, denounce, criticize; see SCOLD.

reproach *n.* discredit, censure, rebuke; see BLAME.

reproach *v.* condemn, censure, scold; see BLAME.

reproduce *v.* **1.** [To make an exact copy] photograph, print, mimeograph; see COPY. **2.** [To make a second time] repeat, duplicate, recreate, recount, revive, reenact, redo, reawaken, relive, remake, reflect, follow, mirror, echo, reecho, represent. **3.** [To multiply] procreate, engender, breed, generate, propagate, fecundate, hatch, father, beget, impregnate, progenerate, sire, repopulate, multiply, give birth.

reproduced *a.* copied, printed, traced, duplicated, transcribed, dittoed, recorded, multiplied, repeated, made identical, typed, set up, set in type, in facsimile, faxed, transferred, photographed, blueprinted, photostated, mimeographed, engraved, photoengraved; see also MANUFACTURED.

reproduction *n.* **1.** [A copy] imitation, print, offprint; see COPY. **2.** [A photographic reproduction] photostat, photoengraving, rotogravure, telephoto, wirephoto, X-ray, candid photo, closeup, pic, pix, blowup, facsimile, fax.

reproductive *a.* generative, creative, conceptive; see GENETIC.

reptile *n.* serpent, amphibian, one of the reptilia; see SNAKE.

republic *n.* democracy, democratic state, constitutional government, commonwealth, self-government, representative government; see also GOVERNMENT 2.

republican *a.* democratic, constitutional, popular; see CONSERVATIVE, DEMOCRATIC.

Republican *n.* registered Republican, GOP, Old Guard, Young Republican, Old Line Republican; see also CONSERVATIVE.

repudiate *v.* retract, repeal, revoke; see ABANDON 1.

repulse *v.* **1.** [To throw back] set back, overthrow, resist; see REPEL 1. **2.** [To rebuff] spurn, repel, snub; see REFUSE.

repulsion *n.* **1.** [Rejection] rebuff, denial, snub; see REFUSAL. **2.** [Aversion] hate, disgust, resentment; see HATRED.

repulsive *a.* **1.** [Capable of repelling] offensive, resistant, unyielding, stubborn, opposing, retaliating, insurgent, counteracting, attacking, counterattacking, defensive, combative, aggressive, pugnacious; see also STUBBORN.—*Ant.* YIELDING, surrendering, capitulating. **2.** [Disgusting] odious, forbidding, horrid; see OFFENSIVE 2.

reputable *a.* **1.** [Enjoying a good reputation] distinguished, celebrated, honored; see IMPORTANT 2. **2.** [Honorable] trustworthy, honest, worthy; see BRAVE, NOBLE 1, 2.

reputation *n.* **1.** [Supposed character] reliability, trustworthiness, respectability, dependability, credit, esteem, estimation; see also CHARACTER 2. **2.** [Good name] standing, prestige, regard, favor, account, respect, privilege, acceptability, social approval; see also HONOR 1. **3.** [Fame] prominence, eminence, notoriety; see FAME.

request *n.* call, inquiry, petition, question, invitation, offer, solicitation, supplication, prayer, requisition, recourse, suit, entreaty, demand; see also APPEAL 1. —**by request** asked for, sought for, wanted; see REQUESTED.

request *v.* **1.** [To ask] demand, inquire, call for; see ASK. **2.** [To solicit] beseech, entreat, sue; see BEG.

requested *a.* asked, demanded, popular, wished, desired, sought, hunted, needed, solicited, petitioned, appealed, requisitioned, in demand; see also WANTED.

require *v.* **1.** [To need] want, feel the necessity for, have need for; see NEED. **2.** [To demand] exact, insist upon, expect; see ASK.

required *a.* requisite, imperative, essential; see NECESSARY.

requirement *n.* **1.** [A prerequisite] preliminary condition, essential, imperative, element, requisite, provision, terms, necessity, stipulation, fundamental, first principle, precondition, reservation, specification, proviso, fulfillment, qualification, vital part, *sine qua non* (Latin); see also BASIS. **2.** [A need] necessity, necessary, lack, want, demand, claim, obsession, preoccupation, prepossession, engrossment, stress, extremity, exigency, pinch, obligation, pressing concern, urgency, compulsion, exaction.

rescue *n.* **1.** [The act of rescuing] deliverance, saving, release, extrication, liberation, ransom, redemption, freeing, salvation, reclamation, reclaiming, emancipation, disentaglement, recovering, heroism. **2.** [An instance of rescue] action, deed, feat, performance, exploit, accomplishment, heroics; see also ACHIEVEMENT.

rescue *v.* **1.** [To save] preserve, recover, redeem, recapture, salvage, retain, hold over, keep back, safeguard, ransom, protect, retrieve, withdraw, take to safety; see also SAVE 1.—*Ant.* LOSE, slip from one's hands, relinquish. **2.** [To free] deliver, liberate, release; see FREE.

research *n.* investigation, analysis, experimentation; see EXAMINATION 1, STUDY.

research *v.* read up on, do research, look up; see EXAMINE, STUDY.

resemblance *n.* likeness, correspondence, coincidence; see SIMILARITY.

resemble *v.* be like, look like, seem like, sound like, follow, take after, parallel, match, coincide, relate, mirror, approximate, give indication of, remind one of, bring to mind, catch a likeness, have all the signs of, be the very image of, be similar to, come close to, appear like, bear a resemblance to, come near, pass for, have all the earmarks of, echo, compare with, be comparable to, smack of*, be the spit and image of*, be a dead-ringer for*; see also AGREE.—*Ant.* DIFFER, contradict, oppose.

resent *v.* frown at, be vexed, be insulted; see DISLIKE.

resentment *n.* exasperation, annoyance, irritation; see ANGER.

reservation *n.* **1.** [The act of reserving] restriction, limitation, withholding; see RESTRAINT 2. **2.** [An instrument for reserving] card, pass, license; see TICKET 1. **3.** [The space reserved] seat, car, room, bus, train, box, stall, place, parking spot, table, berth, compartment.

reserve *n.* **1.** [A portion kept against emergencies] savings, insurance, resources, reserved funds, store, provisions, assets, supply, hoard, backlog, nest egg, something in the sock, something for a rainy day; see also SECURITY 2. **2.** [Calmness] backwardness, restraint, reticence, modesty, unresponsiveness, uncommunicativeness, caution, inhibition, coyness, demureness, aloofness. —**in reserve** withheld, kept back, saved; see RESERVED 2.

reserve *v.* **1.** [To save] store up, set aside, put away; see MAINTAIN 3, SAVE 3. **2.** [To retain] keep, possess, have; see HOLD 1, OWN 1.

reserved *a.* **1.** [Held on reservation] preempted, claimed, booked; see SAVED 2. **2.** [Held in reserve] saved, withheld, kept aside, preserved, conserved, stored away, funded, put in a safe, on ice*.—*Ant.* USED, spent, exhausted. **3.** [Restrained] shy, modest, backward, reticent, secretive, quiet, composed, retiring, private, controlling oneself, mild, gentle, peaceful, soft-spoken, sedate, collected, serene, placid.—*Ant.* LOUD, ostentatious, boisterous.

reserves *n.pl.* reinforcements, enlisted reserves, volunteers; see ARMY 2.

reservoir *n.* storage place, tank, reserve, store, pool, cistern, water supply.

reside *v.* dwell, stay, lodge; see OCCUPY 2.

residence *n.* house, habitation, living quarters; see APARTMENT, HOME 1.

resident *n.* house-dweller, citizen, suburbanite, tenant, inhabitant, native, denizen, occupant, inmate, householder, dweller.

residual *a.* left over, remaining, surplus, continuing, extra, enduring, lingering.

residue *n.* residual, remainder, leavings, scraps, scourings, parings, raspings, shavings, debris, sewage, dregs, silt, slag, soot, scum; see also TRASH 1.

resign *v.* **1.** [To relinquish] surrender, capitulate, give up; see ABANDON 1, YIELD 1. **2.** [To leave one's employment] quit, separate oneself from, retire, step down, drop out, stand down, sign off, end one's services, leave, hand in one's resignation, cease work, give notice, walk out of the job, walk off the job.

resignation *n.* **1.** [Mental preparation for something unwelcome] submission, humility, passivity, patience, deference, docility, submissiveness, abandonment, renunciation, acquiescence, endurance, compliance.—*Ant.* RESISTANCE, unsubmissiveness, unwillingness. **2.** [The act of resigning] retirement, departure, leaving, quitting, giving up, abdication, surrender, withdrawal, relinquishment, vacating, tendering one's resignation, giving up office, termination of one's connection.

resigned *a.* quiet, peaceable, docile, tractable, submissive, yielding, relinquishing, gentle, obedient, manageable, willing, agreeable, ready, amenable, pliant, compliant, easily managed, genial, cordial, satisfied, well-disposed, patient, unresisting, tolerant, calm, reconciled, adjusted, adapted, accommodated, tame, nonresisting, passsive, philosophical, renouncing, unassertive, subservient, deferential.—*Ant.* REBELLIOUS, recalcitrant, resistant.

resilience *n.* elasticity, snap, recoil; see FLEXIBILITY.

resilient *a.* rebounding, elastic, springy; see FLEXIBLE.

resin *n.* pine tar, pitch, gum; see GUM.

resist *v.* hold, remain, maintain, endure, bear, continue, persist, obtain, occur, repeat, stay, retain, be strong, be fixed, be immune, brook, suffer, abide, tolerate, perserve, last, oppose change, bear up against, stand up to, put up a struggle, hold off, repel, remain firm, die hard.—*Ant.* STOP, desist, cease.

resistance *n.* **1.** [A defense] stand, holding, withstanding, warding off, rebuff, obstruction, defiance, striking back, coping, check, halting, protecting, protection, safeguard, shield, screen, cover, watch, support, fight, impeding, blocking, opposition; see also DEFENSE 1.—*Ant.* WITHDRAWAL, withdrawing, retirement. **2.** [The power of remaining impervious to an influence] unsusceptibility, immunity, immovability, hardness, imperviousness, endurance, fixedness, fastness, stability, stableness, permanence. **3.** [The power of holding back another substance] friction, attrition, resistance; see RESERVE 1. **4.** [An opposition] underground movement; anti-Fascist, anti-Communist, anti-American, etc.; movement, boycott, strike, walkout, slowdown, front, stand, guerrilla movement; see also REVOLUTION 2.

resister *n.* adversary, antagonist, opponent; see OPPOSITION 2.

resolute *a.* steadfast, firm, determined; see DETERMINED 1.

resolutely *a.* with all one's heart, bravely, with a will; see FIRMLY 1, 2.

resolution *n.* **1.** [Fixedness of mind] fortitude, perseverance, resolve; see DETERMINATION. **2.** [A formal statement of opinion] verdict, formal expression, decision, recommendation, analysis, elucidation, interpretation, exposition, presentation, declaration, recitation, assertion, judgment.

resolve *v.* determine, settle on, conclude, fix, purpose, propose, choose, fix upon, make up one's mind, take a firm stand, take one's stand, take a decisive step, make a point of, pass upon, decree, elect, remain firm, take the bull by the horns; see also DECIDE.

resort *n.* **1.** [A relief in the face of difficulty] expedient, shift, makeshift, stopgap, substitute, surrogate, resource, device, refuge, recourse, hope, relief, possibility, opportunity. **2.** [A place for rest or amusement] *Resorts include the following:* seaside, mountain, rest, camping, skiing, sports, winter, lake, summer, gambling, amusement park, nightclub, spa, health spa, restaurant, dance hall, club; see also HOTEL, MOTEL. —**as a last resort** in desperation, lastly, in the end; see FINALLY 1, 2.

resort to *v.* turn to, refer to, apply, go to, use, try, employ, utilize, have recourse to, benefit by, put to use, make use of, take up.

resource *n.* reserve, supply, support, source, stock, store, means, expedient, stratagem, relief, resort, recourse, artifice, device, refuge.

resourceful *a.* original, ingenious, capable; see ACTIVE, INTELLIGENT.

resources *n.pl.* means, money, stocks, bonds, products, revenue, riches, assets, belongings, effects, capital, collateral, credit, land, holdings, real estate, investments, income, savings; see also PROPERTY 1, RESERVE 1, WEALTH.

respect *n.* esteem, honor, regard; see ADMIRATION. —**pay one's respects** wait upon, show regard, be polite; see VISIT.

respect *v.* **1.** [To esteem] regard, value, look up to; see ADMIRE. **2.** [To treat with consideration] appreciate, heed, notice, consider, note, recognize, defer to, do honor to, be kind to, show courtesy to, spare, take into account, attend, regard, uphold; see also APPRECIATE 1.—*Ant.* RIDICULE, mock, scorn.

respectability *n.* integrity, decency, propriety; see HONESTY, VIRTUE 1.

respectable *a.* presentable, upright, fair, moderate, mediocre, tolerable, passable, ordinary, virtuous, modest, honorable, worthy, estimable, decorous, seemly, admirable, correct, reputable, proper; see also DECENT 2, HONEST 1.

respected *a.* regarded, appreciated, valued; see HONORED.

respectful *a.* deferential, considerate, appreciate, courteous, admiring, reverent, attending, upholding, regarding, valuing, venerating, recognizing, deferring to, showing respect for; see also POLITE.—*Ant.* RUDE, impudent, contemptuous.

respectfully *a.* deferentially, reverentially, decorously, ceremoniously, attentively, courteously, considerately, with all respect, with due respect, with the highest respect, in deference to; see also POLITELY.—*Ant.* RUDELY, disrespectfully, impudently.

respecting *a.* regarding, concerning, in relation to; see ABOUT 2.

respiration *n.* inhalation, exhalation, expiration; see BREATH.

respite *n.* reprieve, postponement, pause; see DELAY.

respond *v.* reply, retort, acknowledge; see ANSWER 1.

response *n.* statement, reply, acknowledgment; see ANSWER 1.

responsibility *n.* 1. [State of being reliable] trustworthiness, reliability, trustiness, dependability, loyalty, faithfulness, capableness, capacity, efficiency, competency, uprightness, firmness, steadfastness, stability, ability; see also HONESTY. 2. [State of being accountable] answerability, accountability, liability, subjection, engagement, pledge, contract, constraint, restraint; see also DUTY 1.—*Ant.* FREEDOM, exemption, immunity. 3. [Anything for which one is accountable] obligation, trust, contract; see DUTY 1.

responsible *a.* 1. [Charged with responsibility] accountable, answerable, liable, subject, bound, under obligation, constrained, tied, fettered, bonded, censurable, chargeable, obligated, obliged, compelled, contracted, hampered, held, pledged, sworn to, bound to, beholden to, under contract, engaged; see also BOUND 2.—*Ant.* FREE, unconstrained, unbound. 2. [Capable of assuming responsibility] trustworthy, trusty, reliable, capable, efficient, loyal, faithful, dutiful, dependable, tried, self-reliant, able, competent, qualified, effective, upright, firm, steadfast, steady, stable; see also ABLE.—*Ant.* IRRESPONSIBLE, capricious, unstable.

rest *n.* 1. [Repose] quiet, quietness, quietude, ease, tranquillity, slumber, calm, calmness, peace, peacefulness, pacification, relaxation, rest, recreation, coffee break, rest period, siesta, doze, nap, somnolence, dreaminess, comfort, breathing spell, lounging period, loafing period, vacation, lull, leisure, respite, composure; see also sense 2. 2. [State of inactivity] intermission, cessation, stillness, stop, stay, stand, standstill, lull, discontinuance, interval, hush, silence, dead calm, stagnation, fixity, immobility, inactivity, motionlessness, pause, full stop, deadlock, recess, noon hour; see also sense 1, PEACE 2.—*Ant.* ACTIVITY, continuance, endurance. 3. [Anything upon which an object rests] support, prop, pillar; see FOUNDATION 2. 4. [*The remainder] residue, surplus, remnant; see REMAINDER. 5. [Death] release, demise, mortality; see DEATH. —**at rest** in a state of rest, immobile, inactive; see RESTING 1. —**lay to rest** inter, assign to the grave, entomb; see BURY 1.

rest *v.* 1. [To take one's rest] sleep, slumber, doze, repose, compose oneself for sleep, lie down, lounge, let down, ease off, recuperate, rest up, take a rest, take a break, break the monotony, lean, recline, couch, pillow, relax, unbend, settle down, dream, drowse, take one's ease, be comfortable, stretch out, nap, nod, snooze*. 2. [To depend upon] be supported, be seated on, based on; see DEPEND ON 2.

restaurant *n.* café, eatery, cafeteria, diner, hamburger stand. *Types of restaurants include the following;* café, hotel, dining room, inn, coffee shop, coffee house, chophouse, tearoom, luncheonette, lunch-wagon, seafood grotto, creamery, diner, fast-food place, pizzeria, lunch bar, soda fountain, milk bar, hot-dog stand, snack bar, automat, rotisserie, cabaret, nightclub, cafeteria, grill, oyster house, barbecue, spaghetti house, canteen, food court.

rested *a.* restored, refreshed, relaxed, strengthened, renewed, unwearied, unfatigued, untired, awake, revived, recovered, brought back, reanimated, revitalized, reintegrated, unworn.—*Ant.* TIRED, wearied, fatigued.

restful *a.* untroubling, untroubled, tranquil, tranquilizing, calm, peaceful, quiet, reposeful, serene, comfortable, easy, placid, mild, still, soothing, relaxing, refreshing, restoring, revitalizing, reviving, renewing.—*Ant.* LOUD, irritating, agitating.

resting *a.* 1. [Taking rest] relaxing, unwinding, reposing, composing oneself, reclining, lying down, sleeping, stretched out, at ease, quiet, dormant, comfortable, lounging, loafing, taking a breather, enjoying a lull, sleeping, dozing, drowsing, napping, taking a siesta, recessing, taking a vacation, having a holiday. **2.** [Situated] located, settled on, seated; see OCCUPYING 1, PLACED.

restitution *n.* compensation, return, restoration; see PAYMENT 1, REPARATION.

restless *a.* fidgety, skittish, feverish, sleepless, jumpy, nervous, unquiet, disturbed, uneasy, anxious, up in arms, discontented, vexed, excited, agitated, angry, disaffected, estranged, alienated, resentful, recalcitrant, fractious, insubordinate, flurried, roving, transient, wandering, discontented, unsettled, roaming, nomadic, moving, straying, ranging, footloose, itinerant, gallivanting, meandering, traipsing, restive, peeved, annoyed, impatient, flustered, twitching, trembling, tremulous, rattled*, jittery*; see also ACTIVE, EXCITED, REBELLIOUS.—*Ant.* QUIET, sedate, calm.

restlessness *n.* uneasiness, discomfort, excitability; see EXCITEMENT, NERVOUSNESS.

restoration *n.* **1.** [The act of restoring] revival, return, renewal; see RECOVERY 1. **2.** [The act of reconstructing] rehabilitation, reconstruction, reparation; see REPAIR.

restore *v.* **1.** [To give back] make restitution, replace, put back; see RETURN 2. **2.** [To recreate] reestablish, revive, recover; see RENEW 1. **3.** [To rebuild in a form supposed to be original] rebuild, alter, rehabilitate; see RECONSTRUCT, REPAIR. **4.** [To bring back to health] refresh, cure, make healthy; see HEAL.

restrain *v.* check, control, curb, bridle, rein in, hem in, keep in, handle, regulate, keep in line, guide, direct, keep down, repress, harness, muzzle, hold in leash, govern, inhibit, hold, bind, deter, hold back, hamper, constrain, restrict, stay, gag, limit, impound, bottle up, tie down, pin down, pull back, contain, sit on, come down on.

restrained *a.* under control, in check, on leash; see HELD.

restraint *n.* **1.** [Control over oneself] control, self-control, reserve, reticence, constraint, withholding, caution, coolness, forbearance, silence, secretiveness, stress, repression, self-government, self-restraint, stiffness, abstinence, self-denial, unnaturalness, self-repression, constrained manner, abstention, self-discipline, self-censorship; see also ATTENTION.—*Ant.* LAZINESS, slackness, laxity. **2.** [An influence that checks or hinders] repression, deprivation, limitation, hindrance, reduction, abridgment, decrease, prohibition, confinement, check, barrier, obstacle, obstruction, restriction, bar, curb, blockade, order, command, instruction, coercion, impediment, compulsion, duress, force, violence, deterrence, determent, discipline, assignment, definition, moderation, tempering, qualifying.—*Ant.* FREEDOM, liberty, license.

restrict *v.* delimit, limit, circumscribe, assign, contract, shorten, narrow, decrease, enclose, keep in, keep within bounds, define, encircle, surround, shut in, tether, chain, diminish, reduce, moderate, modify, temper, qualify, come down on, pin down.—*Ant.* INCREASE, extend, expand.

restricted *a.* limited, confined, restrained, circumscribed, curbed, bound, prescribed, checked, bounded, inhibited, hampered, marked, defined, delimited, encircled, surrounded, shut in, hitched, tethered, chained, fastened, secured, bridled, held back, held down, reined in, controlled, governed, deterred, impeded, stayed, stopped, suppressed, repressed, prevented, fettered, deprived, blocked, barred, obstructed, dammed, clogged, manacled, frustrated, embarrassed, baffled, foiled, shrunken, narrowed, shortened, decreased, diminished, reduced, moderated, tempered, modified, qualified, out of bounds; see also BOUND 1, 2.

restriction *n.* custody, limitation, contraction; see RESTRAINT 2.

result *n.* consequence, issue, event, execution, effect, outcome, end, finish, termination, consummation, completion, aftereffect, aftermath, upshot, sequel, sequence, fruit, fruition, eventuality, proceeds, emanation, outgrowth, outcropping, returns, backwash, backlash, repercussion, settlement, determination, decision, arrangement, payoff*; see also END 2, 4.—*Ant.* ORIGIN, source, root.

result *v.* issue, grow from, spring from, rise from, proceed from, emanate from, germinate from, flow from, accrue from, arise from, derive from, come from, originate in, become of, spring, emerge, rise, ensue, emanate, effect, produce, fruit, follow, happen, occur, come about, come forth, come out, pan out, work out, appear, end, finish, terminate, conclude.

resume *v.* take up again, reassume, begin again, recommence, reoccupy, go on with, renew, recapitulate, return, keep on, carry on, keep up; see also CONTINUE 2.—*Ant.* STOP, cease, discontinue.

résumé *n.* summary, synopsis, abstract, précis, work history, biography; see also SUMMARY.

resurrection *n.* return to life, transformation, rebirth; see RENEWAL.

retain *v.* **1.** [To hold] cling to, grasp, clutch; see HOLD 1. **2.** [To reserve services] employ, maintain, engage; see HIRE. **3.** [To remember] recall, recollect, recognize; see REMEMBER 1.

retained *a.* **1.** [Kept] had, held, possessed, owned, enjoyed, secured, preserved, saved, maintained, restrained, confined, curbed, detained, contained, received, admitted, included, withheld, put away, treasured, sustained, celebrated, remembered, commemorated; see also KEPT 2.—*Ant.* LOST, wasted, refused. **2.** [Employed] hired, engaged, contracted; see EMPLOYED.

retaliate *v.* fight back, return, repay; see REVENGE.

retaliation *n.* vengeance, reprisal, punishment; see REVENGE 1.

retard *v.* postpone, delay, impede; see HINDER.

retarded *a.* **1.** [*Said of persons*] backward, underachieving, stupid; see DULL 3. **2.** [*Said of activities*] delayed, slowed down, held back; see SLOW 1, 2, 3.

retire *v.* **1.** [To draw away] withdraw, part, retreat; see LEAVE 1. **2.** [To go to bed] lie down, turn in, rest; see SLEEP. **3.** [To cease active life] resign, give up work, sever one's connections, leave active service, relinquish, make vacant, lay down, hand over, lead a quiet life, sequester oneself, reach retirement age.

retired *a.* resigned, relinquished, laid down, handed over, withdrawn, retreated, removed, reached retirement age, leading a quiet life, secluding oneself, separating oneself, aloof.—*Ant.* ACTIVE, working, busy.

retirement *n.* **1.** [The act of retiring] removal, vacating, separation; see RESIGNATION 2. **2.** [The state of being retired] seclusion, aloofness, apartness, separateness, privacy, concealment, solitude, solitariness, isolation, remoteness, loneliness, quiet, retreat, tranquillity, refuge, serenity, inactivity; see also SILENCE 1.—*Ant.* EXPOSURE, activity, association.

retort *n.* counter, repartee, response; see ANSWER 1.

retort *v.* reply, respond, snap back; see ANSWER 1.

retract *v.* withdraw, draw away, take in; see REMOVE 1.

retraction *n.* denial, revocation, disowning; see CANCELLATION, DENIAL.

retreat *n.* **1.** [The act of retreating] retirement, removal, evacuation, departure, escape, withdrawal, drawing back, reversal, retrogression, backing out, flight, recession, retraction, going, running away, eluding, evasion, avoidance, recoil.—*Ant.* ADVANCE, progress, progression. **2.** [A place to which one retreats] seclusion, solitude, privacy, shelter, refuge, asylum, safe place, defense, sanctuary, security, cover, ark, harbor, port, haven, place of concealment, hiding place, hideaway*, resort, haunt, habitat, hermitage, cell, convent, cloister.—*Ant.* FRONT, exposed position, van.

retreat *v.* recede, retrograde, back out, retract, go, depart, recoil, shrink, quail, run, draw back, reel, start back, reverse, seclude oneself, keep aloof, hide, separate from, regress, resign, relinquish, lay down, hand over, withdraw, backtrack, leave, back off*, back down, chicken out*.—*Ant.* STAY, remain, continue.

retribution *n.* vengeance, reprisal, retaliation; see REVENGE 1.

retrieve *v.* regain, bring back, reclaim; see RECOVER 1.

return *a.* coming back, repeat, repeating, repetitive, recurring, reappearing, sent back, answering, replying, retorting, rotating, turning, rebounding, recurrent; see also REPEATED 1.

return *n.* **1.** [The act of coming again] homecoming, arrival, reappearance; see sense 2. **2.** [The act of being returned] restoration, restitution, rejoinder, recompense, acknowledgment, answer, reaction, reversion, repetition, reverberation, reappearance, reentrance, rotating, reoccurrence, rebound, recoil, reconsideration. **3.** [Proceeds] profit, income, results, gain, avail, revenue, advantage, yield, accrual, accruement, interest.—*Ant.* FAILURE, loss, disadvantage. —**in return** in exchange, as payment, as an equivalent, for a reward.

return *v.* **1.** [To go back] come again, come back, recur, reappear, reoccur, repeat, revert, reconsider, reenter, reexamine, reinspect, bounce back up, retrace one's steps, turn, rotate, revolve, renew, revive, recover, regain, rebound, circle back, double back, move back, turn back, reverberate, recoil, retrace, revist, retire, retreat.—*Ant.* MOVE, advance, go forward. **2.** [To put or send something back] bring back, toss back, roll back, hand back, give back, restore, replace, render, reseat, reestablish, reinstate, react, recompense, refund, repay, make restitution.—*Ant.* HOLD, keep, hold back. **3.** [To answer] reply, respond, retort; see ANSWER 1. **4.** [To repay] reimburse, recompense, refund; see REPAY 1. **5.** [To yield a profit] pay off, show profit, pay dividends; see PAY 2. **6.** [To reflect] echo, sound, mirror; see REFLECT 2, 3.

returned *a.* restored, given back, gone back, sent back, brought back, turned back, come back, reappeared, recurred, reoccurred, repeated, reverted, reentered, rotated, revolved, rebounded, reverberated, refunded, acknowledged, answered, repaid, yielded; see also REFUSED.—*Ant.* KEPT, held, retained.

reunion *n.* reuniting, meeting again, rejoining, reconciliation, reconcilement, homecoming, restoration, harmonizing, bringing together, healing the breach, get-together*.

reunite *v.* meet again, reassemble, reconvene, join, rejoin, become reconciled, have a reconciliation, be restored to one another, remarry, heal the breach, get together, patch it up, make up.—*Ant.* SEPARATE, go separate ways, be disrupted.

reveal *v.* disclose, betray a confidence, divulge, make known, confess, impart, publish, lay bare, betray, avow, admit, bring to light, acknowledge, give utterance to, bring out, let out, give out, make public, unfold, communicate, announce, declare, inform, notify, utter, make plain, break the news, broadcast, concede, come out with, explain, bring into the open, affirm, report, let the cat out of the bag, blab*, talk, rat*, stool*, make a clean breast of, put one's cards on the table, bring to light, show one's colors, get something out of one's system, give the lowdown*, let on*, squeal*, blow the whistle*; see also TELL 1.

revelation *n.* **1.** [A disclosure] divulgence, announcement, betrayal; see RECORD 1. **2.** [Revealed divine truth] divine word, God's word, apocalypse; see DOCTRINE, FAITH 2.

revenge *n.* **1.** [The act of returning an injury] vengeance, requital, reprisal, measure for measure, repayment, counterplay, sortie, retaliation, retribution, avenging, counterinsurgency, getting even; see also ATTACK, FIGHT 1.—*Ant.* PARDON, forgiveness, excusing. **2.** [The desire to obtain revenge] vindictiveness, rancor, malevolence; see HATRED.

revenge *v.* retaliate, vindicate, requite, take revenge, breathe vengeance, have accounts to settle, have one's revenge, pay back, make reprisal, get even with, punish for, repay, return like for like, retort, match, reciprocate, square accounts, settle up, take an eye for an eye, turn the tables on, get back at*, fight back, hit back at, be out for blood, give an exchange, give and take, give someone his deserts, even up the score, get*, fix*, get square with, return the compliment.—*Ant.* FORGIVE, condone, pardon.

revenue *n.* **1.** [Income] return, earnings, result, yield, wealth, receipts, proceeds, resources, funds, stocks, credits, dividends, interest, salary, profits, means, fruits, rents; see also INCOME, PAY 1, 2.—*Ant.* EXPENSES, outgo, obligations. **2.** [Governmental income] wealth, revenue, taxation; see INCOME, TAX 1. *Types of revenue include the following:* direct tax, indirect tax, bonds, loans, customs, duties, tariff, tax surcharge, excise, property tax, income tax, inheritance and death tax, land tax, poll tax, gasoline tax, school tax, franchise, license, grants, rates, bridge and road tolls, harbor dues, special taxation, patent stamps, stamp duties, registration duties, internal revenue, tax on spirits, tobacco tax, revenue on fermented liquors, lease of land, sale of land, subsidy.

revere *v.* venerate, regard with deep respect, respect; see ADMIRE.

reverence *n.* respect, admiration, love, regard, approval, approbation, esteem, deference, awe, fear, veneration, honor, devotion, adoration; see also PRAISE 2.—*Ant.* HATRED, contempt, disdain.

reverent *a.* venerating, esteeming, honoring; see RESPECTFUL.

reversal *n.* renunciation, repudiation, repeal; see CANCELLATION, REFUSAL, WITHDRAWAL.

reverse *n.* **1.** [The opposite] converse, other side, contrary; see OPPOSITE. **2.** [A defeat] vanquishment, catastrophe, setback; see DEFEAT.

reverse *v.* **1.** [To turn] go back, shift, invert; see TURN 2. **2.** [To alter] turn around, modify, convert; see CHANGE 2. **3.** [To annul] nullify, invalidate, repeal; see CANCEL. **4.** [To exchange] transpose, rearrange, shift; see EXCHANGE 1.

reversed *a.* turned around, turned back, backward, end for end, inverted, contrariwise, out of order, regressive, retrogressive, undone, unmade.—*Ant.* ORDERED, established, in proper order.

revert *v.* go back, reverse, recur to; see RETURN 1.

review *n.* **1.** [A reexamination] reconsideration, second thought, revision, retrospection, second view, reflection, study, survey, retrospect. **2.** [A critical study] survey, critique, criticism; see EXAMINATION 1. **3.** [A summary] synopsis, abstract, outline; see SUMMARY. **4.** [A formal inspection] parade, inspection, dress parade, drill, march, procession, cavalcade, column, file, military display, march-past; see also DISPLAY.

review *v.* **1.** [To correct] criticize, revise, reedit; see CORRECT. **2.** [To inspect] analyze, reexamine, check thoroughly; see EXAMINE.

revise *v.* reconsider, rewrite, correct; see EDIT.

revised *a.* corrected, edited, amended, overhauled, improved, altered, changed, rectified, polished, redone, rewritten, reorganized, restyled, emended.

revision *n.* reexamination, edition, editing; see CORRECTION.

revival *n.* **1.** [The act of reviving] renewal, renascence, renaissance, refreshment, arousal, awakening, rebirth, reversion, resurrection, enkindling, restoration, invigoration, vivification, resuscitation, reawakening, improvement, freshening, recovery, cheering, consolation. **2.** [An evangelical service] evangelistic meeting, prayer meeting, camp meeting; see CEREMONY.

revive *v.* **1.** [To give new life] enliven, enkindle, refresh, renew, vivify, animate, reanimate, resuscitate, recondition, rejuvenate, bring to, bring around, wake up, resurrect, make whole, exhilarate, energize, invigorate, breathe new life into, reproduce, regenerate, restore, touch up, repair.—*Ant.* DECREASE, wither, lessen. **2.** [To take on new life] come around, come to, freshen, improve, recover, flourish, awake, reawake, rouse, arouse, strengthen, overcome, come to life, grow well, be cured.—*Ant.* DIE, faint, weaken.

revoke *v.* recall, retract, disclaim; see CANCEL.

revolt *n.* uprising, mutiny, sedition; see REVOLUTION 2.

revolt *v.* **1.** [To rebel] mutiny, rise up, resist; see REBEL. **2.** [To repel] sicken, offend, nauseate; see DISGUST.

revolting *a.* awful, loathsome, repulsive; see OFFENSIVE 2, SHAMEFUL 1, 2.

revolution *n.* **1.** [A complete motion about an axis] rotation, spin, turn, revolving, circuit, round, whirl, gyration, circumvolution, cycle, roll, reel, twirl, swirl, pirouette. **2.** [An armed uprising] revolt, rebellion, mutiny, insurrection, riot, anarchy, outbreak, coup, coup d'état, destruction, overturn, upset, overthrow, reversal, rising, crime, violence, bloodshed, turbulence, insubordination, disturbance, reformation, plot, underground activity, guerrilla activity, public unrest, upheaval, tumult, disorder, foment, turmoil, uproar, uprising, row, strife, strike, putsch, subversion, breakup, secession.—*Ant.* LAW, order, control.

revolutionary *a.* **1.** [Concerned with a revolution] rebellious, revolting, mutinous, insurrectionary, destructive, anarchistic, subverting, insurgent, overturning, upsetting, destroying, breaking up, convulsive, subversive, seceding, riotous, agitating, disturbing, working underground, treasonable.—*Ant.* PATRIOTIC, loyal, constructive. **2.** [New and unusual] novel, advanced, radical; see UNUSUAL 2.

revolutionary *n.* revolutionist, traitor, insurrectionist; see REBEL.

revolutionize *v.* recast, remodel, refashion; see REFORM 1.

revolve *v.* spin, rotate, twirl; see TURN 1.

revolver *n.* automatic, gun, rod*; see PISTOL.

reward *n.* **1.** [Payment] compensation, remuneration, recompense; see PAY 1, 2. **2.** [A prize] premium, bonus, award; see PRIZE.

reward *v.* compensate, repay, remunerate; see PAY 1.

rewrite *v.* edit, fill out, cut; see EDIT.

rhyme *n.* verse, rhyming verse, vowel-chime; see POETRY.

rhythm *n.* swing, accent, rise and fall; see BEAT 2.

rhythmic *a.* patterned, measured, balanced; see MUSICAL 1, REGULAR 3.

rib *n.* **1.** [One part of the bony frame of the thorax] true rib, false rib, floating rib; see BONE. **2.** [A rod] girder, bar, strip; see ROD 1, SUPPORT 2. **3.** [A ridge] fin, nervure, vaulting; see sense 2.

ribbon *n.* strip, trimming, decoration; see BAND 1.

rich *a.* **1.** [Possessed of wealth] wealthy, moneyed, affluent, well-to-do, well provided for, worth a million, well-off, well-fixed, in clover, swimming in gravy*, in the money*.—*Ant.* POOR, poverty-sticken, destitute. **2.** [Sumptuous] luxurious, magnificent, resplendent, lavish, embellished, ornate, costly, expensive, splendid, superb, elegant, gorgeous, valuable, precious, extravagant, grand; see also BEAUTIFUL.—*Ant.* CHEAP, plain, simple. **3.** [Fertile] exuberant, lush, copious, plentiful, generous, fruitful, profuse, luxuriant, teeming, abundant, prolific, productive, fruit-bearing, propagating, yielding, breeding, superabounding, prodigal; see also FERTILE.—*Ant.* STERILE, unfruitful, barren. **4.** [Having great food value] nourishing, luscious, sweet, fatty, oily, nutritious, sustaining, strengthening, satisfying; see also HEALTHFUL.—*Ant.* INADEQUATE, not nourishing, deficient.

riches *n.pl.* fortune, possessions, money; see WEALTH.

richness *n.* copiousness, bounty, abundance; see PLENTY.

rickety *a.* infirm, shaky, fragile; see WEAK 2.

ricochet *v.* reflect, rebound, glance off; see BOUNCE.

rid *a.* relieved, quit, delivered; see FREE 2. —**be rid of** be freed from, be relieved of, have done with; see ESCAPE. —**get rid of** get free from, slough off, shed; see FREE.

rid *v.* clear, relieve, disencumber; see FREE.

riddle *n.* problem, question, knotty question, doubt, quandary, entanglement, dilemma, embarrassment, perplexity, enigma, confusion, complication, complexity, intricacy, strait, labyrinth, predicament, plight, distraction, bewilderment; see also PUZZLE 2.—*Ant.* SIMPLICITY, clarity, disentanglement.

ride *n.* drive, trip, transportation; see JOURNEY.

ride *v.* **1.** [To be transported] be carried, travel in or on a vehicle, tour, journey, motor, drive, go for an airing; go by automobile, bicycle, etc. **2.** [To control a beast of burden by riding] manage, guide, handle; see DRIVE 1. **3.** [To tease harshly] ridicule, bait, harass; see BOTHER 2.

rider *n.* **1.** [One who rides] driver, fare, passenger, motorist, horseman, hitchhiker. **2.** [An additional clause or provision, usually not connected with the main body of the work] amendment, appendix, supplement; see ADDITION 1.

ridge *n.* **1.** [A long, straight, raised portion] raised strip, rib, seam; see RIM. **2.** [A long, narrow elevation of land] mountain ridge, range, elevation; see HILL.

ridicule *n.* scorn, contempt, mockery, disdain, derision, jeer, leer, disparagement, sneer, rally, flout, fleer, twit, taunt, burlesque, caricature, satire, parody, travesty, irony, sarcasm, persiflage, farce, buffoonery, horseplay, foolery, razz*, rib*, roast*, raspberry*, horse laugh.—*Ant.* PRAISE, commendation, approval.

ridicule *v.* scoff at, sneer at, laugh at, rail at, mock, taunt, banter, mimic, jeer, twit, disparage, flout, deride, scorn, make sport of, make fun of, rally, burlesque, caricature, satirize, parody, cartoon, travesty, run down, make fun of, put down*, razz*, rib*, pull someone's leg*, roast*, pan*.—*Ant.* ENCOURAGE, approve, applaud.

ridiculous *a.* ludicrous, absurd, preposterous; see FUNNY 1, UNUSUAL 2.

rife *a.* **1.** [Widespread] prevalent, extensive, common; see WIDESPREAD. **2.** [Abundant] plentiful, abounding, profuse; see PLENTIFUL 1.

riffraff *n.* mob, masses, rabble; see PEOPLE 3.

rifle *n.* repeating rifle, carbine, automatic rifle; see GUN, MACHINE GUN.

rig *n.* tackle, apparatus, gear; see EQUIPMENT.

right *a.* **1.** [Correct] true, precise, accurate, exact, sure, certain, determined, proven, factual, correct; see also ACCURATE 2, VALID 1. **2.** [Just] lawful, legitimate, honest; see FAIR 1. **3.** [Suitable] apt, proper, appropriate; see FIT 1. **4.** [Sane] reasonable, rational, sound; see SANE. **5.** [Justly] fairly, evenly, equitably, honestly, decently, sincerely, legitimately, lawfully, conscientiously, squarely, impartially, objectively, reliably, dispassionately, without bias, without prejudice; see also JUSTLY 1. **6.** [Straight] directly, undeviatingly, immediately; see DIRECT 1. **7.** [Opposite to left] dextral, dexter, right-handed, clockwise, on the right.—*Ant.* LEFT, sinistral, counterclockwise.

right *n.* **1.** [A privilege] prerogative, immunity, exemption, license, benefit, advantage, favor, franchise, preference, priority; see also FREEDOM 2. **2.** [Justice] equity, freedom, liberty, independence, emancipation, enfranchisement, self-determination, natural expectation; see also FAIRNESS. **3.** [The part opposite the left] right hand, right side, strong side, active side. —**by rights** properly, justly, suitably; see RIGHTLY. —**in one's own right** individually, acting as one's own agent, by one's own authority; see INDEPENDENTLY. —**in the right** correct, true, accurate; see VALID 1.

right *v.* **1.** [To make upright] set up, make straight, balance; see STRAIGHTEN, TURN 2. **2.** [To repair an injustice] adjust, correct, repair, restore, vindicate, do justice, recompense, reward, remedy, rectify, mend, amend, set right; see also REPAIR.—*Ant.* WRONG, hurt, harm.

right away *a.* at once, directly, without delay; see IMMEDIATELY, NOW.

righteous *a.* **1.** [Virtuous] just, upright, good, honorable, honest, worthy, exemplary, noble, right-minded, goodhearted, dutiful, trustworthy, equitable, scrupulous, conscientious, ethical, fair, impartial, fair-minded, commendable, praiseworthy, guiltless, blameless, sinless, peerless, sterling, matchless, deserving, laudable, creditable, charitable, philanthropic, having a clear conscience; see also RELIABLE.—*Ant.* CORRUPT, sinful, profligate. **2.** [Religiously inclined] devout, pious, saintly, godly, godlike, angelic, devoted, reverent, reverential, faithful, fervent, strict, rigid, devotional, zealous, spiritual; see also HOLY 1, RELIGIOUS 2.—*Ant.* BAD, impious, irreligious. **3.** [Conscious of one's own virtue] self-righteous, hypocritical, self-esteeming; see EGOTISTIC.

righteousness *n.* **1.** [Justice] uprightness, nobility, fairness; see HONOR 1. **2.** [Devotion to a sinless life] piety, saintliness, godliness; see DEVOTION.

rightful *a.* proper, just, honest; see FAIR 1, LEGAL, PERMITTED.

rightfully *a.* lawfully, justly, fairly, properly, truly, equitably, honestly, impartially, fittingly, legitimately, in all conscience, in equity, by right, in reason, objectively, fair and square*, on the level*, by rights; see also LEGALLY.

rightly *a.* justly, properly, correctly; see WELL 2.

rigid *a.* **1.** [Stiff] unyielding, inflexible, solid; see FIRM 1. **2.** [Strict] exact, rigorous, firm; see SEVERE 1, 2. **3.** [Fixed] set, unmoving, solid; see DEFINITE 1, DETERMINED.

rigorous *a.* harsh, austere, uncompromising; see SEVERE 1.

rim *n.* edge, border, verge, brim, lip, brink, top, margin, line, outline, band, ring, strip, brow, curb, ledge, skirt, fringe, hem, limit, confine, end, terminus.—*Ant.* CENTER, middle, interior.

rind *n.* peel, hull, shell, surface, coating, crust, bark, cortex, integument; see also SKIN.—*Ant.* INSIDE, center, interior.

ring *n.* **1.** [A circle] circlet, girdle, brim; see CIRCLE 1, RIM. **2.** [A circlet of metal] hoop, band, circle; see JEWELRY. *Rings include the following:* finger, wedding, engagement, guard, signet, organization, umbrella, ankle, nose, key, harness, napkin; bracelet, earring, ear drop. **3.** [A close association, often corrupt] cabal, combine, party, bloc, faction, group, gang, monopoly, cartel, corner, pool, trust, syndicate, gang*, string; see also ORGANIZATION 2. **4.** [Pugilism] prize fighting, boxing, professional fighting; see SPORT 3. **5.** [A ringing sound] clank, clangor, jangle; see NOISE 1. —**give someone a ring***

call, call up, phone; see TELEPHONE. —**run rings around*** excel, overtake, beat; see PASS 1.

ring *v.* **1.** [To encircle] circle, rim, surround, encompass, girdle, enclose, move around, loop, gird, belt, confine, hem in. **2.** [To cause to sound] clap, clang, bang, beat, toll, strike, pull, punch, buzz, play, resound, reverberate, peal, chime, tinkle, jingle, jangle, vibrate, clang, sound the brass*; see also SOUND. **3.** [To call by ringing] give a ring, buzz for, ring up; see SUMMON.

rinse *v.* clean, flush, dip in water; see SOAK 1, WASH 2.

riot *n.* confusion, uproar, tumult; see DISORDER, DISTURBANCE 2, PROTEST. —**run riot** revolt, riot, fight; see REBEL.

riot *v.* revolt, stir up trouble, fight in the streets; see REBEL.

rip *n.* rent, cleavage, split; see TEAR.

rip *v.* rend, split, cleave, rive, tear, shred; see also CUT 1.

ripe *a.* **1.** [Ready to be harvested] fully grown, fully developed, ruddy, red, yellow, plump, filled out, matured, ready.—*Ant.* GREEN, undeveloped, half-grown. **2.** [Improved by time and experience] mellow, wise, perfected; see MATURE. **3.** [Ready] prepared, seasoned, consummate, perfected, finished, usable, fit, conditioned, prime, available, on the mark, complete; see also READY 2.—*Ant.* UNFIT, unready, unprepared.

ripen *v.* develop, evolve, advance; see GROW 2.

rise *n.* **1.** [The act of rising] ascent, mount, lift; see CLIMB. **2.** [An increase] augmentation, growth, enlargement, multiplication, heightening, intensifying, stacking up, piling up, distention, addition, accession, inflation, acceleration, doubling, advance; see also INCREASE.—*Ant.* REDUCTION, decrease, lessening. **3.** [Source] beginning, commencement, start; see ORIGIN 2. —**get a rise out of*** get a response from by teasing, provoke, annoy; see BOTHER 2. —**give rise to** initiate, begin, start; see CAUSE.

rise *v.* **1.** [To move upward] ascend, mount, climb, scale, surmount, soar, tower, rocket, surge, sweep upward, lift, bob up, move up, push up, reach up, come up, go up, surge, sprout, grow, rear, uprise, blast off, curl upward; see also FLY 1.—*Ant.* FALL, drop, come down. **2.** [To get out of bed] get up, rise up, wake; see ARISE 1. **3.** [To increase] grow, swell, intensify, mount, enlarge, spread, expand, extend, augment, heighten, enchance, distend, inflate, pile up, stack up, multiply, accelerate, speed up, add to, wax, advance, raise, double; see also INCREASE.—*Ant.* DECREASE, lessen, contract. **4.** [To begin] spring, emanate, issue; see BEGIN 2. **5.** [To improve one's station] prosper, flourish, thrive; see IMPROVE 1. **6.** [To stand] be erected, be built, be placed, be located, be put up, go up, be founded, have foundation, be situated; see also STAND 1. **7.** [To swell; *said usually of dough or batter*] inflate, billow, bulge; see SWELL.

rising *a.* climbing, ascending, going aloft, moving up, surging up, spiraling up, slanting up, inclining up, mounting, accelerating, on the rise, in ascension, upcoming, upswinging; see also GROWING.

risk *n.* **1.** [Danger] hazard, peril, jeopardy; see DANGER. **2.** [The basis of a chance] contingency, opportunity, prospect; see CHANCE 1, UNCERTAINTY 3. —**run a risk** take a chance, gamble, venture; see RISK, *v.*

risk *v.* gamble, hazard, venture, run the risk, do at one's own peril, hang by a thread, play with fire, go out of one's depth, go beyond one's depth, bell the cat, make an investment, take the liberty, lay oneself open to, pour money into, go through fire and water, leave to luck, leap before one looks, fish in troubled waters, skate on thin ice, defy danger, live in a glass house.

risky *a.* perilous, precarious, hazardous; see DANGEROUS, UNSAFE.

risqué *a.* indelicate, spicy, suggestive; see LEWD 2.

rite *n.* observance, service, ritual; see CEREMONY 2, CUSTOM.

ritual *n.* observance, rite, act; see CEREMONY 2, CUSTOM.

ritzy* *a.* elegant, luxurious, stylish; see RICH 2.

rival *a.* competing, striving, combatant, combatting, emulating, vying, opposing, disputing, contesting, contending, conflicting, battling, equal.—*Ant.* HELPFUL, aiding, assisting.

rival *n.* emulator, competitor, antagonist; see OPPONENT 1.

rival *v.* approach, match, compare with; see EQUAL.

rivalry *n.* competition, emulation, striving, contest, vying, struggle, battle, contention, opposition, dispute; see also FIGHT 1.—*Ant.* COOPERATION, combination, conspiracy.

river *n.* stream, flow, course, current, tributary, rivulet, river system, creek, brook, watercourse. *Famous rivers include the following:* Seine, Rhone, Loire, Thames, Severn, Avon, Clyde, Danube, Rhine, Elbe, Don, Volga, Vistula, Nile, Euphrates, Tigris, Ganges, Indus, Irrawaddy, Yellow, Yangtze, Congo, Zambesi, St. Lawrence, Saskatchewan, Mississippi, Missouri, Ohio, Platte, Delaware, Columbia, Gila, Colorado, Snake, Hudson, Rio Grande, Amazon, Orinoco, La Plata.

road *n.* **1.** [A strip prepared for travel] path, way, highway, roadway, street, avenue, thoroughfare, boulevard, highroad, drive, terrace, parkway, byway, lane, alley, alleyway, crossroad, viaduct, subway, paving, slab, turnpike, trail, post road, secondary road, market road, national highway, state highway, county road, military road, Roman road, freeway, the main drag*. **2.** [A course] scheme, way, plans; see PLAN 2. —**on the road** on tour, traveling, on the way; see EN ROUTE. —**one for the road*** cocktail, nightcap, toast; see DRINK 2.

roam *v.* ramble, range, stroll, rove, walk, traverse, stray, straggle, meander, prowl, tramp, saunter, knock around*, bat around*, scour, straggle, gallivant, struggle along, traipse*, hike; see also TRAVEL.

roar *n.* bellow, shout, boom, thunder, howl, bay, bawl, yell, bluster, uproar, din, clash, detonation, explosion, barrage, reverberation, rumble; see also CRY 1, 2, NOISE 1.—*Ant.* SILENCE, whisper, sigh.

roar *v.* bellow, shout, boom, thunder, howl, bay, bawl, yell, rumble, drum, detonate, explode, reverberate, resound, reecho; see also CRY 2, SOUND.

roast *v.* toast, broil, barbecue; see COOK.

rob *v.* thieve, take, burglarize, strip, plunder, deprive of, withhold from, defraud, cheat, swindle, pilfer, break into, hold up, stick up*, purloin, filch, lift*, abscond with, embezzle, pillage, sack, loot, snitch*, pinch*, swipe*, cop*; see also STEAL.

robber *n.* thief, burglar, cheat, plunderer, pillager, bandit, pirate, raider, thug, desperado, forger, hold-up man, second-story man*, privateer, buccaneer, swindler, highwayman, bank robber, pilferer, shoplifter, cattle-thief, housebreaker, pickpocket, freebooter, marauder, brigand, pickpurse, sharper, safecracker, fence, rustler*, crook*, con man*, clip artist*, chiseler*, paper hanger*, stick-up man*; see also CRIMINAL, RASCAL.

robbery *n.* burglary, larceny, thievery; see CRIME.

robe *n.* gown, dress, garment, costume, mantle, draperies, covering, cape, dressing gown, bathrobe, negligee, tea gown, kimono, house gown; see also CLOTHES.

robot *n.* **1.** [A mechanical man] automaton, android, Frankenstein, mechanical monster, humanoid, thinking machine. **2.** [A person who resembles a machine] slave, menial, scullion; see LABORER.

robust *a.* hale, hearty, sound; see HEALTHY.

rock *n.* **1.** [A solidified form of earth] stone, mineral mass, dike, mineral body, earth crust; see also METAL, MINERAL. *Rocks include the following:* igneous, sedimentary, stratified, metamorphic; concretion, gypsum, alabaster, limestone, freestone, sandstone, conglomerate, marble, dolomite, chalk, soapstone, slate, shale, granite, lava, pumice, basalt, quartz, obsidian, rhyolite, ironstone, gneiss, tufa, schist. **2.** [A piece of rock] stone, boulder, cobblestone, pebble, fieldstone, cliff, crag, promontory, scrap, escarpment, reef, chip, flake, sliver, building stone, paving block, slab. **3.** [Anything firm or solid] defense, support, Rock of Gibraltar; see FOUNDATION. **4.** [Lively dance music] rock-and-roll, popular dance, rhythm and blues; see DANCE 1, MUSIC 1. —**on the rocks*** **1.** bankrupt, poverty-stricken, impoverished; see POOR 1, RUINED 3. **2.** over ice cubes, undiluted, straight; see STRONG 4.

rock *v.* sway, vibrate, reel, totter, swing, move, push and pull, agitate, roll, shake, shove, jolt, jiggle, quake, convulse, tremble, undulate, oscillate, quiver, quaver, wobble; see also WAVE 3.

rock-bottom *a.* lowest, hopeless, way down; see POOR 2, WORST. —**hit rock bottom** drop, not succeed, plunge; see FAIL 1, FALL 1.

rocket *n.* projectile, missile, retrorocket, flying missile. *Kinds of rockets include the following:* air-to-air, air-to-surface, surface-to-surface, surface-to-air, V-2, solid-fuel, liquid-fuel; guided missile, ballistic missile, cruise missile, Polaris missile, intercontinental ballistic missile (ICBM), submarine-launched ballistic missile (SLBM), smart bomb*.

rocking chair *n.* easy chair, arm chair, rocker; see CHAIR 1, FURNITURE.

rocky *a.* stony, flinty, hard, inflexible, solid, petrified, ragged, jagged, rugged; see also STONE.—*Ant.* SOFT, flexible, sandy.

rod *n.* **1.** [A rodlike body] staff, bar, pole, wand, stave, baton, spike, pin, cylinder, bacillus, cylindrical object, rodlet, scepter, twig, switch, whip, stock, stalk, trunk; see also STICK. **2.** [A fishing rod] pole, rod and reel, tackle; see EQUIPMENT.

rodent *n.* *Common varieties of rodents include the following:* rat, mouse, squirrel, chipmunk, beaver, porcupine, rabbit, muskrat, prairie dog, gopher, marmot, groundhog, woodchuck, ground squirrel, chinchilla, mole, hare, guinea pig.

rodeo *n.* riding unbroken horses, rounding up cattle, roundup, features of a roundup. *Rodeo events include the following:* bronco-busting, bulldogging, calf-roping, cutting out steers, Brahma bull riding.

rogue *n.* outlaw, problem, miscreant; see CRIMINAL.

role *n.* function, task, part, character, title role, impersonation, leading man, leading woman, hero, heroine, ingénue, performance, presentation, acting, characterization, execution.

roll *n.* **1.** [The act of rolling] turn, turning over, revolution, rotation, wheeling, trundling, whirl, gyration. **2.** [A relatively flat object rolled upon itself] scroll, volute, spiral, coil, whorl, convolution, fold, shell, cone, cornucopia. **3.** [A long, heavy sound] thunder, roar, drumbeat; see NOISE 1. **4.** [Bread baked in a small, shaped piece] *Types of rolls include the following:* Parker House, potato, butter, finger, cinnamon, sweet, crescent, French, cloverleaf, poppy-seed, dinner; hot cross bun; see also BREAD, PASTRY. **5.** [A list] register, table, schedule; see CATALOG, INDEX 2, LIST, RECORD 1.

roll *v.* **1.** [To move by rotation, or in rotating numbers] rotate, come around, swing around, wheel, come in turn, circle, alternate, follow, succeed, be in sequence, follow in due course; see also MOVE 1, TURN 1. **2.** [To revolve] turn, pivot, spin; see sense 1. **3.** [To make into a roll] bend, curve, arch; see TWIST. **4.** [To smooth with a roller] press, level, flatten, spread, pulverize, grind.—*Ant.* CUT, roughen, toss up. **5.** [To flow] run, wave, surge; see FLOW. **6.** [To produce a relatively deep, continuous sound] reverberate, resound, echo; see ROAR, SOUND. **7.** [To function] work, go, start production; see OPERATE 2.

rolled *a.* **1.** [Made into a roll] twisted, folded, curved, bent, bowed, coiled, spiraled, arched, voluted, convoluted.—*Ant.* SPREAD, unrolled, opened out. **2.** [Flattened] pressed, leveled, evened; see FLAT 1, SMOOTH 1.

roll in *v.* **1.** [To arrive] enter, land, disembark; see ARRIVE. **2.** [To accumulate] mass, collect, assemble; see ACCUMULATE.

Roman *a.* Latin, classic, classical, late classic, Augustan, ancient, Italic.

romance *n.* **1.** [A courtship] enchantment, passion, fascination; see LOVE 1. **2.** [A tale of love and adventure] historical romance, novel, fiction; see STORY.

romantic *a.* **1.** [Referring to love and adventure] adventurous, novel, daring, charming, enchanting, lyric, poetic, fanciful, chivalrous, courtly, knightly. **2.** [Referring to languages descending from Latin; *often capital*] romanic, romance, Mediterranean, French, Italian, Spanish; see also LANGUAGE 1.

romp *v.* gambol, celebrate, frolic; see PLAY 1, 2.

roof *n.* cover, shelter, tent, house, habitation, home.

room *n.* **1.** [Space] vastness, reach, sweep; see EXTENT. **2.** [An enclosure] chamber, apartment, cabin, cubicle, cubiculum, niche, vault. *Rooms include the following:* living room, dining room, sitting room, drawing room, bedroom, music room, playroom, bathroom, guest room, family room, waiting room, boardroom, conference room, foyer, vestibule, study, library, den, kitchen, hall, master bedroom, parlor, wardrobe, closet, pantry, basement, cellar, attic, garret, anteroom, dormitory, alcove, ward, office, breakfast nook, nursery, studio, schoolroom, loft. **3.** [The possibility of admission] opening, place, resignation; see VACANCY 2. **4.** [A rented sleeping room] quarters, lodgings, digs*; see APARTMENT.

roomer *n.* lodger, occupant, dweller; see TENANT.

roommate *n.* roomie*, flatmate, bunkmate; see FRIEND.

root *n.* **1.** [An underground portion of a plant] *Types of roots include the following:* conical, napiform, fusiform, fibrous, moniliform, nodulose, tuberous, adventitious, prop, aerial, tap. **2.** [The cause or basis] source, reason, motive; see ORIGIN 2, 3. —**take root** begin growing, start, commence; see GROW 1.

rooted *a.* grounded, based, fixed; see FIRM 1.

rope *n.* cord, cordage, braiding, string, thread, strand, tape, cord, lace, cable, hawser, lariat, lasso, line, towline. —**at the end of one's rope** desperate, despairing, in despair; see EXTREME, HOPELESS. —**give someone enough rope*** permit, give freedom, concede; see ALLOW. —**know the ropes*** be experienced, comprehend, understand; see KNOW 1. —**on the ropes*** near collapse, close to ruin, in danger; see ENDANGERED.

rose *a.* rose-colored, rosy, flushed; see PINK, RED.

rose *n. Classes of roses include the following:* wild, tea, climbing tea, hybrid tea, hybrid perpetual, sweet briar, shrub, multiflora, floribunda, musk, cabbage, cinnamon, eglantine, rambler; see also FLOWER.

roster *n.* names, subscribers, program; see CATALOG, LIST, INDEX 2.

rosy *a.* **1.** [Rose-colored] colored, deep pink, pale cardinal; see PINK, RED. **2.** [Promising] optimistic, favorable, cheerful; see HOPEFUL 1, 2.

rot *n.* **1.** [The process of rotting] decomposition, corruption, disintegration; see DECAY. **2.** [*Nonsense] trash, silliness, foolishness; see NONSENSE 1.

rot *v.* decay, disintegrate, decompose; see SPOIL.

rotate *v.* twist, wheel, revolve; see MOVE 1, TURN 1.

rotation *n.* turn, circumrotation, circle; see REVOLUTION.

rotten *a.* **1.** [Having rotted] bad, rotting, putrefying, decaying, putrefied, spoiled, decomposed, decayed, offensive, disgusting, rancid, fecal, rank, foul, corrupt, polluted, infected, loathsome, overripe, bad-smelling, putrid, crumbled, disintegrated, stale, noisome, smelling, fetid, noxious.—*Ant.* FRESH, unspoiled, good. **2.** [Not sound] unsound, defective, impaired; see WEAK 2. **3.** [Corrupt] contaminated, polluted, filthy, tainted, defiled, impure, sullied, unclean, soiled, debauched, blemished, morbid, infected, dirtied, depraved, tarnished; see also DIRTY.—*Ant.* PURE, clean, healthy.

rough *a.* **1.** [Not smooth] unequal, broken, coarse, choppy, ruffled, uneven, ridged, rugged, irregular; not sanded, not finished, unfinished, not completed, needing the finishing touches, bumpy, rocky, stony, jagged, grinding, knobby, sharpening, cutting, sharp, crinkled, crumpled, rumpled, scraggly, straggly, hairy, shaggy, hirsute, bushy, tufted, bearded, woolly, nappy, unshaven, unshorn, gnarled, knotty, bristly.—*Ant.* LEVEL, flat, even. **2.** [Not gentle] harsh, strict, stern; see SEVERE 2. **3.** [Crude] boorish, uncivil, uncultivated; see RUDE 1. **4.** [Not quiet] buffeting, stormy, tumultuous; see TURBULENT. **5.** [Unfinished] incomplete, imperfect, uncompleted; see UNFINISHED. **6.** [Approximate] inexact, unprecise, uncertain; see APPROXIMATE.

rough draft *n.* outline, blueprint, first draft; see PLAN 1.

roughly *a.* **1.** [Approximately] about, in round numbers, by guess; see APPROXIMATELY. **2.** [In a brutal manner] coarsely, cruelly, inhumanly; see BRUTALLY.

roughness *n.* **1.** [The quality of being rough on the surface] unevenness, coarseness, brokenness, bumpiness, irregularity, raggedness, jaggedness, wrinkledness, shagginess, bushiness, beardedness, hairiness, woolliness; break, crack, ragged edge, scratch, nick.—*Ant.* REGULARITY, smoothness, evenness. **2.** [The quality of being rough in conduct] harshness, severity, hardness; see RUDENESS.

round *a.* **1.** [Shaped like a globe or disk] spherical, globular, orbicular, globe-shaped, ball-shaped, domical, circular, cylindrical, ringed, annular, oval, disk-shaped. **2.** [Curved] arched, rounded, bowed, looped, recurved, incurved, coiled, curled. **3.** [Approximate] rough, in tens, in hundreds; see APPROXIMATE.

round *n.* **1.** [A round object] ring, orb, globe; see CIRCLE 1, RIM. **2.** [A period of action] bout, course, whirl, cycle, circuit, routine, performance; see also SEQUENCE 1, SERIES. **3.** [A unit of ammunition] cartridge, charge, load; see AMMUNITION, BULLET, SHOT 1.

round *v.* **1.** [To turn] whirl, wheel, spin; see TURN 1. **2.** [To make round] curve, convolute, bow, arch, bend, loop, whorl, shape, form, recurve, coil, fill out, curl, mold.—*Ant.* STRAIGHTEN, flatten, level.

round *prep.* about, near, in the neighborhood of, close to; see also ALMOST, APPROXIMATELY, AROUND.

roundness *n.* fullness, completeness, circularity, oneness, inclusiveness, wholeness.

round off *v.* approximate; round off by tens, hundreds, etc.; accept a rough figure for; see also ESTIMATE.

round out *v.* expand, fill out, enlarge; see GROW 1.

rouse *v.* **1.** [To waken] arouse, raise, awake; see AWAKEN, WAKE 1. **2.** [To stimulate] stimulate, urge, provoke; see ANIMATE, EXCITE.

route *n.* **1.** [A course being followed] way, course, path, track, beat, tack, divergence, detour, digression, meandering, rambling, wandering, circuit, round, rounds, range; see also ROAD 1. **2.** [A projected course] map, plans, plot; see PLAN 2, PROGRAM 2.

routine *a.* usual, customary, methodical; see CONVENTIONAL 1, HABITUAL.

routine *n.* round, cycle, habit; see METHOD, SYSTEM.

rove *v.* walk, meander, wander; see ROAM.

row *n.* series, order, file; see LINE 1. **—in a row** in succession, successively, in a line; see CONSECUTIVE.

rowdy *a.* rebellious, rude, mischievous; see LAWLESS 2, UNRULY.

royal *a.* **1.** [Pertaining to a king or his family] high, elevated, highborn, monarchic, reigning, regnant, regal, ruling, dominant, absolute, imperial, sovereign, supreme; see also sense 2, NOBLE 3. **2.** [Having qualities befitting royalty] great, grand, stately, lofty, illustrious, renowned, eminent, superior, worthy, honorable, dignified, chivalrous, courteous, kingly, great-hearted, large-hearted, princely, princelike, majestic, magnificent, splendid, courtly, impressive, commanding, aristocratic, lordly, august, imposing, superb, glorious, resplendent, gorgeous, sublime; see also sense 1, NOBLE 1, 2, WORTHY.

royalty *n.* kingship, sovereignty, nobility, authority, eminence, distinction, blood, birth, high descent, rank, greatness, power, supremacy, primacy, the crown, suzerainty.

rub *n.* **1.** [A rubbing action] brushing, stroke, smoothing, scraping, scouring, grinding, rasping, friction, attrition; see also TOUCH 2. **2.** [A difficulty] impediment, hindrance, dilemma; see DIFFICULTY 1, 2, PREDICAMENT.

rub *v.* **1.** [To subject to friction] scrape, smooth, abrade, scour, grate, grind, wear away, graze, rasp, knead, fret, massage, polish, shine, burnish, scrub, erase, rub out, rub down, file, chafe, clean. **2.** [To apply by rubbing; *usually with "on"*] brush, cover, finish; see PAINT 2.

rubber *a.* elastic, rubbery, soft, stretchable, stretching, rebounding, flexible, ductile, lively, buoyant, resilient.

rubbish *n.* litter, debris, waste; see TRASH 1.

rub out *v.* **1.** [To cancel] eradicate, erase, delete; see CANCEL, ELIMINATE. **2.** [*To kill] destroy, murder, shoot; see KILL 1.

rude *a.* **1.** [Boorish] rustic, ungainly, awkward, crude, coarse, gross, rough, harsh, blunt, rugged, common, barbarous, lumpish, ungraceful, hulking, loutish, antic, rowdy, disorderly, brutish, boorish, clownish, stupid, ill-proportioned, unpolished, uncultured, unrefined, untrained, indecorous, unknowing, untaught, uncouth, slovenly, ill-bred, inelegant, ignorant, inexpert, illiterate, clumsy, awkward, gawky, slouching, graceless, ungraceful, lumbering, green, unacquainted, unenlightened, uneducated, vulgar, indecent, ribald, homely, outlandish, disgraceful, inappropriate.—*Ant.* CULTURED, urbane, suave. **2.** [Not polite] churlish, sullen, surly, sharp, harsh, gruff, snarling, ungracious, unkind, ungentle, obstreperous, overbearing, sour, disdainful, unmannerly, ill-mannered, improper, shabby, ill-chosen, discourteous, ungentlemanly, fresh*, abusive, forward, loud, loudmouthed, bold, brazen, audacious, brash, arrogant, supercilious, blustering, impudent, crass, raw, saucy, crusty, pert, unabashed, sharp-tongued, loose, mocking, barefaced, insolent, impertinent, offensive, naughty, impolite, hostile, insulting, disrespectful, scornful, flippant, presumptuous, sarcastic, defiant, outrageous, swaggering, disparaging, contemptuous, rebellious, disdainful, unfeeling, insensitive, scoffing, disagreeable, domineering, overbearing, high-handed, hypercritical, self-assertive, brutal, severe, hard, cocky, bullying, cheeky, nervy, assuming, dictatorial, magisterial, misbehaved, officious, meddling, intrusive, meddlesome, bitter, uncivilized, slandering, ill-tempered, bad-tempered, sassy*, snotty*, snooty*, uppity*.—*Ant.* POLITE, courteous, mannerly. **3.** [Harsh] rough, violent, stormy; see TURBULENT. **4.** [Approximate] guessed, surmised, imprecise; see APPROXIMATE. **5.** [Coarse] rough, unrefined, unpolished; see CRUDE. **6.** [Primitive] ignorant, uncivilized, barbarous; see PRIMITIVE 3.

rudely *a.* crudely, impudently, coarsely, impolitely, indecently, barbarously, roughly, harshly, bluntly, indecorously, insolently, contemptuously, brutally, dictatorially, churlishly, sullenly, gruffly, discourteously, impishly, loudly, brazenly, blusteringly, crassly, unabashedly, ribaldly, spunkily*, mockingly, snootily*.—*Ant.* KINDLY, politely, suavely.

rudeness *n.* discourtesy, bad manners, vulgarity, incivility, impoliteness, impudence, disrespect, misbehavior, barbarity, ungentlemanliness, unmannerliness, ill-breeding, crudity, brutality, barbarism, tactlessness, boorishness, unbecoming conduct, conduct not becoming a gentleman, lack of courtesy, crudeness, grossness, coarseness, bluntness, effrontery, impertinence, insolence, audacity, boldness, shamelessness, presumption, officiousness, intrusiveness, brazenness, sauciness, defiance, contempt, back talk, ill temper, irritability, disdain, bitterness, sharpness, unkindness, ungraciousness, harshness, gall*, sass*, lip*, nerve*, brass*, cheek*.

ruffle *v.* **1.** [To disarrange] rumple, tousle, ripple; see CONFUSE, TANGLE. **2.** [To anger] irritate, fret, anger; see BOTHER 1, 2.

rug *n.* carpet, carpeting, floor covering, linoleum, straw mat, floor mat, woven mat, drugget.

rugged *a.* **1.** [Rough; *said especially of terrain*] hilly, broken, mountainous; see ROUGH 1. **2.** [Strong; *said especially of persons*] hale, sturdy, hardy; see HEALTHY, STRONG 1.

ruin *n.* **1.** [The act of destruction] extinction, demolition, overthrow; see DESTRUCTION 1, WRECK 1. **2.** [A building fallen into decay; *often plural*] remains, traces, residue, foundations, vestiges, remnants, relics, wreck, walls, detritus, rubble; see also DESTRUCTION 2. **3.** [The state of destruction] dilapidation, waste, wreck; see DESTRUCTION 2.

ruin *v.* **1.** [To destroy] injure, overthrow, demolish; see DESTROY, RAVAGE. **2.** [To cause to become bankrupt] impoverish, bankrupt, beggar; see WRECK.

ruined *a.* **1.** [Destroyed] demolished, overthrown, torn down, extinct, abolished, exterminated, annihilated, subverted, wrecked, desolated, ravaged, smashed, crushed, crashed, extinguished, extirpated, dissolved, totaled*; see also DESTROYED.—*Ant.* PROTECTED, saved, preserved. **2.** [Spoiled] pillaged, harried, robbed, plundered, injured, hurt, impaired, defaced, harmed, marred, past hope, mutilated, broken, gone to the dogs*, on the rocks*, done for*.—*Ant.* REPAIRED, restored, mended. **3.** [Bankrupt] pauperized, poverty-stricken, beggared, reduced, left in penury, penniless, fleeced, brought to want, gone under*, sold up*, through the mill*.—*Ant.* RICH, prosperous, well-off.

ruins *n.pl.* remains, debris, wreckage; see DESTRUCTION 2, WRECK 2.

rule *n.* **1.** [Government] control, dominion, jurisdiction; see GOVERNMENT 1. **2.** [A regulation] edict, command, commandment; see LAW 3. **3.** [The custom] habit, course, practice; see CUSTOM. **—as a rule** ordinarily, generally, usually; see REGULARLY.

rule *v.* **1.** [To govern] conduct, control, dictate; see GOVERN. **2.** [To regulate] order, decree, direct; see MANAGE 1.

ruled *a.* administered, controlled, managed; see GOVERNED.

rule out *v.* eliminate, not consider, recant; see ABOLISH, CANCEL.

ruler *n.* **1.** [One who governs] governor, commander, chief, manager, adjudicator, monarch, regent, director; see also DICTATOR, KING 1, LEADER 2 for types of rulers. 2. [A straightedge] *Types of rulers include the following:* foot rule, yardstick, carpenter's rule, slide rule, parallel rule, stationer's rule, T-square, try square, steel square, compositor's rule, compositor's ruler.

ruling *n.* order, decision, precept; see LAW 3.

rumble *n.* reverberation, resounding, roll; see NOISE 1.

rumble *v.* resound, growl, thunder; see SOUND.

rumor *n.* report, news, tidings, intelligence, dispatch, hearsay, gossip, scandal, tattle, notoriety, noise, cry, popular report, fame, repute, grapevine, buzz*, breeze*, hoax, fabrication, suggestion, supposition, story, tale, invention, fiction, falsehood; see also LIE.

rumored *a.* reported, told, said, reputed, spread abroad, gossiped, given out, noised about, broadcast, as they say, all over town, current, circulating, in circulation, rife, prevailing, prevalent, persisting, general, going around, making the rounds.

rump *n.* posterior, buttocks, sacrum, hind end, tail end, posterior, butt end, bottom, croup, crupper, rear, backside, seat, breech, hunkers, fundament, butt*, ass*, buns*, duff*, bum*, tush*, keister*, can*.

rumple *v.* crumple, crush, fold; see WRINKLE.

run *n.* 1. [The act of running] sprint, pace, bound, flow, amble, gallop, canter, lope, spring, trot, dart, rush, dash, flight, escape, break, charge, swoop, race, scamper, tear, whisk, flow, fall, drop. 2. [A series] continuity, succession, sequence; see SERIES. 3. [In baseball, a score] record, tally, point; see SCORE 1. 4. [The average] par, norm, run of the mill; see AVERAGE. 5. [A course] way, route, field; see TRACK 1. —**in the long run** in the final outcome, finally, eventually; see ULTIMATELY. —**on the run** 1. busy, in a hurry, running; see HURRYING. 2. retreating, defeated, routed; see BEATEN 1.

run *v.* 1. [To move, usually rapidly] flow in, flow over, chase along, fall, pour, tumble, drop, leap, spin, whirl, whiz, sail. 2. [To go swiftly by physical effort] rush, hurry, spring, bound, scurry, skitter, scramble, scoot, travel, run off, run away, dash ahead, dash on, put on a burst of speed, go on the double*, light out*, have a free play, make tracks*, dart, dart ahead, gallop, canter, lope, spring, trot, single-foot, amble, pace, flee, speed, spurt, swoop, bolt, race, shoot, tear, whisk, scamper, scuttle. 3. [To function] move, work, go; see OPERATE 2. 4. [To cause to function] control, drive, govern; see MANAGE 1. 5. [To extend] encompass, cover, spread; see REACH 1, SURROUND 1. 6. [To continue] last, persevere, go on; see CONTINUE 1. 7. [To complete] oppose, contest, contend with; see COMPETE, RACE 2.

run after *v.* follow, chase, hunt; see PURSUE 1.

run amok *v.* go crazy, lose one's head, kill in a frenzy; see KILL, RAGE 1.

runaway *a.* out of control, delinquent, wild; see DISORDERLY 1.

runaway *n.* juvenile offender, lawbreaker, truant; see DELINQUENT.

run away *v.* 1. [To empty] flow, wash, pour out; see DRAIN 3. 2. [Escape] flee, depart, steal away; see ESCAPE, LEAVE 1.

rundown *n.* report, outline, review; see SUMMARY.

run down *v.* 1. [To chase] hunt, seize, apprehend; see PURSUE 1. 2. [To ridicule] make fun of, belittle, depreciate; see RIDICULE.

run-down *a.* 1. [Exhausted] weak, debilitated, weary; see WEAK 1, 2, TIRED. 2. [Dilapidated] broken-down, shabby, beat-up*; see OLD 2, CRUMBLY.

run dry *v.* dry up, stop running, cease to flow; see DRY 2.

(a) run for one's money *n.* one's money's worth, adequate payment, enough; see PAY 1.

run into *v.* 1. [To collide with] bump into, crash, have a collision; see HIT 1. 2. [To encounter] come across, see, contact; see MEET 6. 3. [To blend with] mingle, combine with, osmose; see ENTER, JOIN 1.

runner *n.* racer, entrant, contestant, sprinter, dash man, distance runner, middle distance runner, 220-man, cross-country runner, jogger, trackman, hurdler, messenger, courier, express, dispatch bearer, cinder artist*; see also ATHLETE.

running *a.* 1. [In the act of running] pacing, racing, speeding, galloping, cantering, trotting, scampering, fleeing, bounding, whisking, sprinting, flowing, tumbling, falling, pouring. 2. [In the process of running] producing, operating, working, functioning, proceeding, moving, revolving, guiding, conducting, administering, going, in operation, in action, executing, promoting, achieving, transacting, determining, bringing about. 3. [Extending] spreading, reaching, encompassing; see EXTENDING.

runoff *n.* spring runoff, drainage, surplus water; see FLOW, RIVER, WATER 1.

run off *v.* 1. [To pour out] empty, exude, draw off; see DRAIN 3. 2. [To abandon] depart, flee, go; see LEAVE 1. 3. [To produce] turn out, make, publish; see MANUFACTURE, PRINT 2.

run-of-the-mill *a.* popular, mediocre, ordinary; see COMMON 1.

run out *v.* 1. [To squander] lose, dissipate, exhaust; see WASTE 2. 2. [To stop] expire, finish, end; see STOP 2. 3. [To become exhausted] weaken, wear out, waste away; see TIRE 1. 4. [To go away] go, depart, run away; see ABANDON 2, ESCAPE, LEAVE 1. **5.** [To pour out] flow, empty, leak; see DRAIN 3. **6.** [To pass] elapse, slip by, glide; see PASS 2. **7.** [To remove physically] dislodge, throw out, put out; see EJECT.

run over *v.* trample on, drive over, run down; see HIT, KILL.

runt *n.* undersized animal or person, dwarf, midget, pygmy.

run through *v.* **1.** [To examine] check, inspect, look at; see EXAMINE. **2.** [To spend] waste, squander, lose; see SPEND.

rupture *n.* hole, separation, crack; see BREAK 1, TEAR.

rupture *v.* crack, tear, burst; see BREAK.

rural *a.* rustic, farm, agricultural, ranch, pastoral, bucolic, backwoods, country, agrarian, agronomic, suburban.—*Ant.* URBAN, industrial, commercial.

rush *n.* haste, dash, charge; see HURRY.

rush *v.* hasten, speed, hurry up; see HURRY.

rushed *a.* hurried, pressed, pressured; see DRIVEN.

rushing *a.* being quick, bestirring oneself, losing no time; see HURRYING.

Russia *n.* Union of Soviet Socialist Republics, USSR, Great Russia, Little Russia, White Russia, Muscovy, Russia in Europe, Siberia, the Soviets, Reds*, Russian Bear*; see also ASIA, EUROPE.

Russian *a.* Slavic, Slav, Muscovite, Siberian.

rust *n.* decomposition, corruption, corrosion, oxidation, decay, rot, dilapidation, breakup, wear.

rust *v.* oxidize, become rusty, degenerate, decay, rot, corrode.

rustic *a.* agricultural, pastoral, agrarian; see RURAL.

rusty *a.* **1.** [Decayed] unused, neglected, worn; see OLD 2, WEAK 2. **2.** [Unpracticed] out of practice, soft, ill-qualified; see WEAK 5.

rut *n.* **1.** [A deeply cut track] hollow, trench, furrow; see GROOVE. **2.** [Habitual behavior] custom, habit, course, routine, practice, performance, round, circuit, circle, usage, procedure.—*Ant.* CHANGE, veer, mutation.

ruthless *a.* cruel, fierce, savage, brutal, merciless, inhuman, hard, cold, fiendish, unmerciful, pitiless, grim, unpitying, tigerish, ferocious, stony-hearted, cold-blooded, remorseless, vindictive, vengeful, revengeful, rancorous, implacable, unforgiving, malevolent, surly, hard-hearted, hard, cold, unsympathetic, unforbearing, vicious, sadistic, tyrannical, relentless, barbarous, inhuman, atrocious, flagrant, terrible, abominable, outrageous, oppressive, bloodthirsty, venomous, galling.—*Ant.* KIND, helpful, civilized.

S

Sabbath *n.* day of rest, Saturday, Sunday; see WEEKEND.

sabotage *n.* demolition, overthrow, treason; see DESTRUCTION 1, REVOLUTION 2.

sabotage *v.* subvert, siege, undermine; see ATTACK 1, DESTROY.

sac *n.* welt, pouch, blister; see SORE.

sack *n.* sac, pouch, pocket; see BAG, CONTAINER. —**hit the sack*** go to bed, go to sleep, retire; see SLEEP.

sack *v.* bag, package, pocket; see PACK 1.

sacrament *n.* holy observance, ceremonial, liturgy, act of divine worship, mystery, the mysteries. *In the Roman Catholic and Eastern Orthodox churches, the seven sacraments are as follows:* baptism, confirmation or the laying on of hands, penance, Communion or the Eucharist, extreme unction or Anointing of the Sick, holy orders, matrimony.

sacramental *a.* sacred, pure, solemn; see HOLY 1, RELIGIOUS 1.

sacred *a.* **1.** [Holy] pure, pious, saintly; see HOLY 1. **2.** [Dedicated] consecrated, ordained, sanctioned; see DIVINE.

sacrifice *n.* **1.** [An offering to a deity] offering, tribute, atonement; see CEREMONY. **2.** [A loss] discount, deduction, reduction; see LOSS 1.

sacrifice *v.* **1.** [To offer to a deity] consecrate, dedicate, give up; see BLESS. **2.** [To give up as a means to an end] forfeit, forgo, relinquish, yield, suffer the loss of, renounce, spare, give up, let go, resign oneself to, sacrifice oneself, surrender, part with, go astray from. **3.** [To sell at a loss] cut, reduce, sell out; see DECREASE 2, LOSE 2.

sad *a.* **1.** [Afflicted with sorrow] unhappy, sorry, sorrowful, downcast, dismal, gloomy, glum, pensive, heavy-hearted, dispirited, dejected, depressed, desolate, troubled, melancholy, morose, grieved, pessimistic, crushed, brokenhearted, heartbroken, heartsick, despondent, careworn, rueful, anguished, disheartened, lamenting, mourning, grieving, weeping, bitter, woebegone, doleful, spiritless, joyless, heavy, crestfallen, discouraged, moody, low-spirited, despairing, hopeless, worried, downhearted, cast down, in heavy spirits, morbid, oppressed, blighted, grief-stricken, foreboding, apprehensive, horrified, anxious, wretched, miserable, mournful, disconsolate, forlorn, jaundiced, out of sorts, distressed, afflicted, bereaved, repining, harassed, dreary, down in the dumps, in bad humor, out of humor, cut up*, in the depths*, blue, stricken with grief, making a long face, in tears, feeling like hell*, down in the mouth*.—*Ant.* HAPPY, joyous, cheerful. **2.** [Suggestive of sorrow] pitiable, unhappy, dejecting, saddening, disheartening, discouraging, joyless, dreary, dark, dismal, gloomy, moving, touching, mournful, disquieting, disturbing, somber, doleful, oppressive, funereal, lugubrious, pathetic, tragic, pitiful, piteous, woeful, rueful, sorry, unfortunate, hapless, heart-rending, dire, distressing, depressing, grievous.

sadden *v.* oppress, dishearten, discourage, cast down, deject, depress, break one's heart.

saddle *n.* seat, riding seat, leather*; see CHAIR 1.

sadistic *a.* cruel, brutal, vicious; see CRUEL.

sadly *a.* unhappily, morosely, dejectedly, wistfully, sorrowfully, gloomily, joylessly, dismally, cheerlessly, in sorrow.

sadness *n.* sorrow, dejection, melancholy, depression, grief, despondency, oppression, downs, gloom, blues*.

safe *a.* **1.** [Not in danger] out of danger, secure, in safety, in security, free from harm, free from danger, unharmed, safe and sound, protected, guarded, housed, screened from danger, unmolested, unthreatened, entrenched, impregnable, invulnerable, under the protection of, saved, safeguarded, secured, defended, supported, sustained, maintained, upheld, preserved, vindicated, shielded, nourished, sheltered, fostered, cared for, cherished, watched, impervious to, patrolled, looked after, supervised, tended, attended, kept in order, surveyed, regulated, with one's head above water, undercover, out of harm's way, on the safe side, on ice*, at anchor, in harbor, snug as a bug in a rug, under lock and key.—*Ant.* DANGEROUS, unsafe, risky. **2.** [Not dangerous] innocent, innocuous, innoxious; see HARMLESS. **3.** [Reliable] trustworthy, dependable, competent; see RELIABLE.

safe *n.* strongbox, coffer, chest, repository, vault, case, safe-deposit box.

safekeeping *n.* supervision, care, guardianship; see CUSTODY, PROTECTION 2.

safely *a.* securely, with impunity, without harm, without risk, without danger, harmlessly, carefully, cautiously, reliably.

safety *n.* **1.** [Freedom from danger] security, protection, impregnability, surety, sanctuary, refuge, shelter, invulnerability. **2.** [A lock] lock mechanism, safetycatch, safety lock; see FASTENER, LOCK 1.

sag *n.* depression, dip, slump*; see HOLE 1.

sag *v.* stoop, hang down, become warped; see BEND, LEAN 1.

said *a.* pronounced, aforesaid, forenamed; see PRECEDING, SPOKEN.

sail *n.* **1.** [Means of sailing a vessel] sheets, canvas, cloth; see GOODS. *Sails include the following:* mainsail, foresail, topsail, jib, spanker, flying jib, trysail, balloon sail, spinnaker, balloon jib. **2.** [A journey by sailing vessel] voyage, cruise, trip; see JOURNEY. —**set sail** go, depart, set out; see LEAVE 1, SAIL 1.

sail *v.* **1.** [To travel by sailing] cruise, voyage, go alongside, bear down on, bear for, direct one's course for, set sail, put to sea, sail away from, navigate, travel, make headway, lie in, make for, heave to, fetch up, bring to, bear off, close with, run in, put in. **2.** [To fly] float, soar, ride the storm, skim, glide.

sailor *n.* seaman, mariner, seafarer, pirate, navigator, pilot, boatman, yachtsman, able-bodied seaman, Jack Tar, tar*, sea dog, limey*, salt*, bluejacket. *Kinds and ranks of sailors include the following—crew:* deck hand, stoker, cabin boy, yeoman, purser; ship's carpenter, cooper, tailor; steward, navigator, signalman, gunner, afterguard; *officers:* captain or commander or skipper, navigating officer, deck officer; first, second, third, boatswain's mate; boatswain or bo's'n*.

saint *n.* a true Christian, child of God, son of God, paragon, salt of the earth, godly person, martyr, man of God, unworldly person, altruist, the pure in heart, a believer.

saintly *a.* angelic, pious, divine; see HOLY.

sake *n.* **1.** [End] objective, consequence, final cause; see RESULT. **2.** [Purpose] score, motive, principle; see PURPOSE 1. **3.** [Welfare] benefit, interest, well-being; see ADVANTAGE, WELFARE 1.

salad *n.* salad greens, slaw, mixture, combination. *Common salads include the following:* green, tossed, vegetable, tomato, potato, macaroni, fruit, bean, combination, chef's, tuna, shrimp, lobster, crab, chicken, ham, Waldorf, Caesar, pineapple, banana, molded, frozen; cole slaw.

salary *n.* wages, recompense, payroll; see PAY 2.

sale *n.* **1.** [The act of selling] commerce, business, traffic, exchange, barter, commercial enterprise, marketing, vending, trade. **2.** [An individual instance of selling] deal, transaction, negotiation, turnover, trade, purchase, auction, disposal; see also BUYING, SELLING. **3.** [An organized effort to promote unusual selling] bargain sale, clearance, stock reduction, fire sale, unloading, dumping, remnant sale, going out of business sale, bankruptcy sale. —**for** or **on** or **up for sale** put on the market, to be sold, marketable, available, offered for purchase, not withheld. —**on sale** reduced, at a bargain, cut; see CHEAP 1.

sales *n.pl.* sales receipts, annual sales, business; see INCOME.

salesman *n.* **1.** [A sales clerk] salesperson, seller, counterman; see CLERK. **2.** [A commercial traveler] out-of-town representative, agent, canvasser, solicitor, seller, businessman, itinerant, field worker, traveler, traveling man, traveling salesman, sales representative, sales manager.

salesperson *n.* salesman, saleswoman, saleslady; see CLERK.

saliva *n.* water, spittle, salivation, excretion, phlegm, enzyme, spit.

saloon *n.* bar, night club, cocktail lounge, pub, beer parlor, poor man's club, joint, hangout, place; see also RESTAURANT.

salt *a.* alkaline, saline, briny; see SALTY.

salt *n.* **1.** [A common seasoning and preservative] sodium chloride, common salt, table salt, savor, condiment, flavoring, spice, seasoning. *Common types of flavoring salts include the following:* garlic, sea, celery, onion, barbecue, salad, seasoning, hickory smoked; poultry seasoning, monosodium glutamate, MSG, salt substitute. **2.** [Anything that provides savor] relish, pungency, smartness; see HUMOR 1, WIT. —**not worth one's salt** good-for-nothing, bad, worthless; see POOR 2. —**with a grain** or **pinch of salt** doubtingly, skeptically, lightly; see SUSPICIOUSLY.

salt *v.* season, make tasty, make piquant; see FLAVOR.

salty *a.* briny, brackish, pungent, alkaline, well-seasoned, flavored, well-flavored, highly flavored, sour, acrid.

salute *v.* snap to attention, dip the colors, touch one's cap, do honor to, recognize; see also PRAISE 1.

salvage *v.* retrieve, recover, regain; see SAVE 1.

salvation *n.* **1.** [The act of preservation] deliverance, liberation, emancipation; see RESCUE. **2.** [A means of preservation] buckler, safeguard, assurance; see PROTECTION 2.

salve *n.* ointment, unguent, lubricant, balm, medicine, emollient, unction, remedy, help, cure, cream.

same *a.* **1.** [Like another in state] equivalent, identical, corresponding; see ALIKE, EQUAL. **2.** [Like another in action] similarly, in the same manner, likewise; see ALIKE.

same *pron.* the very same, identical object, substitute, equivalent, similar product, synthetic product.

sameness *n.* uniformity, unity, resemblance, analogy, similarity, alikeness, identity, standardization, equality, unison, no difference.

sample *n.* specimen, unit, individual; see EXAMPLE.

sample *v.* taste, test, inspect; see EXAMINE, EXPERIMENT.

sanction *n.* consent, acquiescence, assent; see PERMISSION.

sanction *v.* confirm, authorize, countenance; see APPROVE, ENDORSE 2.

sanctity *n.* sanctification, sacredness, piety; see VIRTUE 1.

sanctuary *n.* **1.** [A sacred place] shrine, church, temple; see CHURCH 1. **2.** [A place to which one may retire] asylum, resort, haven; see SHELTER.

sand *n.* **1.** [Rock particles] sandy soil, sandy loam, silt, dust, grit, powder, gravel, rock powder, rock flour, debris, dirt; see also EARTH 2. **2.** [The beach] strand, seaside, seashore; see SHORE.

sandal *n.* slipper, thong, loafer; see SHOE.

sandwich *n.* lunch, light lunch, quick lunch. *Sandwiches include the following:* hamburger, burger*, cheeseburger, wiener, hot dog*, Denver, Western, club, tuna fish, ham, chicken, roast beef, ham and egg, cheese, deviled meat, steak, submarine, bacon and cheese, toasted cheese, tomato, egg salad, lettuce, open face, peanut butter and jelly, jelly.

sandy *a.* **1.** [Containing sand; *said especially of soil*] light, loose, permeable, porous, easy to work, easily worked, granular, powdery, gritty. **2.** [Suggestive of sand; *said especially of the hair*] fair-haired, fair, blond, light, light-haired, reddish, carrot-red, sandy-red, sun-bleached, flaxen, faded.

sane *a.* **1.** [Sound in mind] rational, normal, lucid, right-minded, sober, sound-minded, sound, in one's right mind, with a healthy mind, mentally sound, balanced, healthy-minded, reasonable, in possession of one's faculties.—*Ant.* INSANE, irrational, delirious. **2.** [Sensible] reasonable, open to reason, wise; see SENSIBLE.

sanitary *a.* hygienic, wholesome, sterile; see HEALTHFUL.

sanity *n.* sound mind, rationality, healthy mind, saneness, a clear mind, clearmindedness, wholesome outlook, common sense, intelligence, reason, reasonableness, prudence, good judgment, acumen, understanding, comprehension.

sap *n.* **1.** [The life fluid of a plant] fluid, secretion, essence; see LIQUID. **2.** [*A dupe] dolt, gull, simpleton; see FOOL.

sapling *n.* scion, seedling, slip, sprig, young tree; see also TREE.

sappy *a.* **1.** [Juicy] lush, succulent, watery; see JUICY. **2.** [*Idiotic] foolish, silly, illogical; see STUPID.

sarcasm *n.* satire, irony, banter, derision, contempt, scoffing, flouting, ridicule, burlesque, disparagement, criticism, cynicism, invective, censure, lampooning, aspersion, sneering, mockery.—*Ant.* FLATTERY, fawning, cajolery.

sarcastic *a.* scornful, mocking, ironical, satirical, taunting, severe, derisive, bitter, saucy, hostile, sneering, snickering, quizzical, arrogant, disrespectful, offensive, carping, cynical, disillusioned, snarling, unbelieving, corrosive, acid, cutting, scorching, captious, sharp, pert, brusque, caustic, biting, harsh, austere, grim.

sardonic *a.* sarcastic, cynical, scornful; see SARCASTIC.

Satan *n.* Mephistopheles, Lucifer, Beelzebub; see DEVIL.

satanic *a.* malicious, vicious, devilish; see SINISTER.

satellite *n.* **1.** [A small planet that revolves around a larger one] moon, planetoid, minor planet, secondary planet, inferior planet, asteroid. **2.** [A man-made object put into orbit around a celestial body] space satellite, robot satellite, unmanned satellite, body satellite, orbital rocket, artificial moon, spacecraft, moonlet, man-made moon, sputnik, satellite station.

satire *n.* mockery, ridicule, caricature; see IRONY.

satisfaction *n.* **1.** [The act of satisfying] gratification, fulfillment, achievement; see ACHIEVEMENT. **2.** [The state or feeling of being satisfied] comfort, pleasure, well-being, content, contentment, gladness, delight, bliss, joy, happiness, relief, complacency, peace of mind, ease, heart's ease, serenity, contentedness, cheerfulness. **3.** [Something that contributes to satisfaction] reward, prosperity, good fortune; see BLESSING 2. **4.** [Reparation] reimbursement, repayment, compensation.

satisfactorily *a.* **1.** [In a satisfactory manner] convincingly, suitably, competently; see ADEQUATELY. **2.** [Productive of satisfactory results] amply, abundantly, thoroughly; see AGREEABLY.

satisfactory *a.* adequate, satisfying, pleasing; see ENOUGH.

satisfied *a.* content, happy, contented, filled, supplied, fulfilled, paid, compensated, appeased, convinced, gratified, sated, at ease, with enough of, without care, satiated.

satisfy *v.* **1.** [To make content] comfort, cheer, elate, befriend, please, rejoice, delight, exhilarate, amuse, entertain, flatter, make merry, make cheerful, gladden, content, gratify, indulge, humor, conciliate, propitiate, capture, enthrall, enliven, animate, captivate, fascinate, fill, be of advantage, gorge. **2.** [To pay] repay, clear up, disburse; see PAY 1, SETTLE 7. **3.** [To fulfill] do, fill, serve the purpose, be enough, observe, perform, comply with, conform to, meet requirements, keep a promise, accomplish, complete, be adequate, be sufficient, provide, furnish, qualify, answer, serve, equip, meet, avail, suffice, fill the want, come up to, content one, appease one, fill the bill*, pass muster*, get by, go in a pinch*.—*Ant.* NEGLECT, leave open, fail to do.

satisfying *a.* pleasing, comforting, gratifying; see ENOUGH, PLEASANT 2.

saturate *v.* overfill, drench, steep; see IMMERSE, SOAK 1.

saturated *a.* drenched, full, soggy; see SOAKED, WET 1.

saturation *n.* fullness, soaking, overload; see EXCESS 1.

sauce *n.* appetizer, gravy, seasoning; see FLAVORING, FOOD.

saucepan *n.* stewpan, vessel, utensil; see PAN.

saucer *n.* small bowl, sauce dish, cereal dish; see DISH.

sausage *n.* link sausage, salami, liverwurst; see MEAT.

savage *a.* **1.** [Primitive] crude, simple, original; see CRUDE. **2.** [Cruel] barbarous, inhuman, brutal; see CRUEL. **3.** [Wild] untamed, uncivilized, uncultured; see UNCONTROLLED.

savage *n.* bully, ruffian, animal; see BEAST 2.

savagely *a.* cruelly, viciously, indecently; see BRUTALLY.

save *v.* **1.** [To remove from danger] deliver, extricate, rescue, free, set free, liberate, release, emancipate, ransom, redeem, come to the rescue of, defend.—*Ant.* LEAVE, desert, condemn. **2.** [To assure an afterlife] rescue from sin, reclaim, regenerate; see sense 1. **3.** [To hoard] collect, store, invest, have on deposit, amass, accumulate, gather, treasure up, store up, pile up, hide away, cache, stow away, sock away.—*Ant.* WASTE, spend, invest. **4.** [To preserve] conserve, keep, put up; see PRESERVE 2.

saved *a.* **1.** [Kept from danger] rescued, released, delivered, protected, defended, guarded, safeguarded, preserved, reclaimed, regenerated, cured, healed, conserved, maintained, safe, secure, freed, free from harm, free from danger, unthreatened.—*Ant.* RUINED, lost, destroyed. **2.** [Not spent] kept, unspent, unused, untouched, accumulated, deposited, on deposit, retained, laid away, hoarded, invested, amassed, stored, spared.—*Ant.* WASTED, squandered, spent.

savings *n.pl.* means, property, resources, funds, reserve, investment, provision, provisions, accumulation, store, riches, harvest, hoard, savings account, cache, nest egg, money in the bank, provision for a rainy day.

savior *n.* **1.** [One who saves another] deliverer, rescuer, preserver; see PROTECTOR. **2.** [Christ; *usually capital*] Redeemer, Messiah, Friend and Helper; see CHRIST.

savor *v.* enjoy, relish, appreciate; see LIKE 1.

saw *n.* power, circular, concave, mill, ice, crosscut, band, rip, hand, pruning, whip, buck, keyhole, back, butcher's, hack, jig; see also TOOL 1.

say *v.* tell, speak, relate, state, announce, declare, state positively, open one's mouth, have one's say, break silence, put forth, let out, assert, maintain, express oneself, answer, respond, suppose, assume. —**to say the least** at a minimum, at the very least, to put it mildly, minimally.

saying *a.* mentioning, making clear, revealing; see TALKING.

saying *n.* aphorism, adage, maxim, byword, motto, proverb, precept, dictum.

scab *n.* **1.** [A crust over a wound] eschar, slough, crust. **2.** [One who replaces a union worker on strike] strikebreaker, traitor, apostate, deserter.

scaffold *n.* framework, stage, structure; see BUILDING, PLATFORM 1.

scald *v.* char, blanch, parboil; see BURN.

scale *n.* **1.** [A series for measurement] rule, computation, system; see MEASURE 2. **2.** [A flake or film] thin coating, covering, incrustation; see FLAKE, LAYER. **3.** [A device for weighing; *often plural*] steelyard, analytical balance, balance, scale beam. *Varieties of scales include the following:* beam, automatic indicating, counter, cylinder, drum, barrel, platform, spring, computing, digital, household, miner's, assayer's, truck, jeweler's. **4.** [Musical tones] range, major scale, minor scale, harmonic scale, melodic scale; see also MUSIC. —**on a large scale** extensively, grandly, expansively; see GENEROUSLY. —**on a small scale** economically, in a small limited way, with restrictions; see INADEQUATE, UNIMPORTANT.

scale *v.* **1.** [To climb] ascend, surmount, mount; see CLIMB. **2.** [To peel] exfoliate, strip off, flake; see PEEL, SKIN. **3.** [To measure] compare, balance, compute; see COMPARE 1.

scalpel *n.* dissecting instrument, surgical tool, blade; see KNIFE.

scamper *v.* hasten, speed, haste; see HURRY 1, RUN 2.

scan *v.* browse, thumb over, consider; see LOOK 2.

scandal *n.* shame, disgrace, infamy, discredit, slander, disrepute, detraction, defamation, opprobrium, reproach, aspersion, backbiting, gossip, eavesdropping, rumor, hearsay.—*Ant.* PRAISE, adulation, flattery.

scandalize *v.* detract, defame, backbite; see SLANDER.

scandalous *a.* infamous, disreputable, ignominious; see SHAMEFUL 2.

scanty *a.* scarce, few, pinched, meager, little, small, bare, ragged, insufficient, inadequate, slender, narrow, thin, scrimp, scrimpy, tiny, wee, sparse, diminutive, short, stingy.—*Ant.* MUCH, large, many.

scar *n.* cicatrix, cicatrice, cat-face, mark, blemish, discoloration, disfigurement, defect, flaw, hurt, wound, injury.

scar *v.* cut, pinch, slash; see HURT 1.

scarce *a.* limited, infrequent, not plentiful; see RARE 2, UNCOMMON. —**make oneself scarce*** go, depart, run off; see LEAVE 1.

scarcely *a.* barely, only just, scantily; see HARDLY.

scarcity *n.* deficiency, inadequacy, insufficiency; see LACK 2, POVERTY 1.

scare *n.* fright, terror, alarm; see FEAR.

scare *v.* panic, terrify, alarm; see FRIGHTEN.

scared *a.* startled, frightened, fearful; see AFRAID.

scare off or **away** *v.* drive off, drive out, drive away, get rid of, dispose of; see also FRIGHTEN.

scarf *n.* throw, sash, muffler, shawl, comforter, ascot, stole, wrapper; see also CLOTHES.

scarlet *a.* cardinal, royal red, vermilion; see RED.

scat *v.* be off, begone, out of the way, get out of my way, get out from under my feet, out with you, be off with you, get out of my sight, scoot*, get out, beat it*, get going.

scatter *v.* **1.** [To become separated] run apart, run away, go one's own way, diverge, disperse, disband, migrate, spread widely, go in different directions, blow off, go in many directions, be strewn to the four winds.—*Ant.* ASSEMBLE, convene, congregate. **2.** [To cause to separate] dispel, dissipate, diffuse, strew, divide, disband, shed, distribute, disseminate, separate, disunite, sunder, scatter to the wind, sever, set asunder.—*Ant.* UNITE, join, mix. **3.** [To waste] expend, dissipate, fritter away; see SPEND, WASTE 2.

scatterbrained *a.* silly, giddy, irrational; see ILLOGICAL, STUPID.

scattered *a.* spread, strewed, rambling, sowed, sown, sprinkled, spread abroad, separated, disseminated, dispersed, strung out, distributed, widespread, diffuse, all over the place, separate, shaken out.—*Ant.* GATHERED, condensed, concentrated.

scene *n.* spectacle, exhibition, display; see VIEW.

scenery *n.* landscape, prospect, spectacle; see VIEW.

scenic *a.* beautiful, spectacular, dramatic; see BEAUTIFUL.

scent *n.* odor, fragrance, redolence; see PERFUME, SMELL 1, 2.

schedule *n.* **1.** [List] catalogue, inventory, registry; see LIST, RECORD 1. **2.** [Program] agenda, order of business, calendar; see PLAN 2, PROGRAM 2. —**on** or **up to schedule** on time, not lagging behind, being pushed along; see ACCEPTED, EARLY 2 ENOUGH.

schedule *v.* record, register, catalogue; see LIST 1.

scheduled *a.* listed, announced, arranged; see PLANNED, PROPOSED.

scheme *n.* project, course of action, purpose; see PLAN 2, SYSTEM.

scheme *v.* intrigue, contrive, devise; see PLAN 1.

scholar *n.* schoolboy, schoolgirl, learner; see STUDENT.

scholarly *a.* erudite, cultured, studious; see EDUCATED, LEARNED 1.

scholarship *n.* scientific approach, learning, intellectualism; see KNOWLEDGE 1.

scholastic *a.* academic, literary, lettered; see LEARNED 1.

school *n.* **1.** [An institution of learning] *Varieties of schools include the following:* nursery school, elementary school, high school, secondary school, parochial school, preparatory school, private school, prep school, public school, boarding school, military school, seminary, normal school, conservatory, trade school, technical school, graduate school, professional school, divinity school, art school, law school, college of arts and science, junior high school, middle school, senior high school, community college, junior college, the grades; see also COLLEGE, UNIVERSITY. **2.** [Persons or products associated by common intellectual or artistic theories] party, following, circle; see FOLLOWING. **3.** [A building housing a school] schoolhouse, establishment, institution; see BUILDING. **—go to school** attend school, attend college, matriculate; see LEARN, REGISTER.

school-age *a.* youthful, old enough to go to school, of school age; see CHILDISH, YOUNG 1.

schoolbook *n.* primer, textbook, assigned reading; see BOOK.

schooling *n.* teaching, nurture, discipline; see EDUCATION 1.

schoolmate *n.* roommate, comrade, classmate; see FRIEND.

schoolteacher *n.* educator, lecturer, instructor; see TEACHER.

school year *n.* nine months, from September to June, period school is in session; see YEAR.

science *n.* **1.** [An organized body of knowledge] classified information, department of learning, branch of knowledge, system of knowledge, body of fact; see also CHEMISTRY, MATHEMATICS, MEDICINE 3, SOCIAL SCIENCE, ZOOLOGY for commonly recognized sciences. **2.** [A highly developed skill] craftsmanship, art, deftness; see ABILITY.

scientific *a.* **1.** [Objectively accurate] precise, exact, clear; see ACCURATE 2, OBJECTIVE 1. **2.** [Concerning science] experimental, deductive, methodically sound; see LOGICAL.

scientist *n.* expert, specialist, investigator, laboratory technician, natural philosopher, student of natural history, student of natural phenomena, explorer, research worker, research assistant, learned man, serious student, PhD, scientific thinker. *Scientists include the following:* anatomist, astronomer, botanist, biologist, chemist, biochemist, geologist, geographer, mathematician, physicist, psychiatrist, psychologist, astrophysicist, ecologist, biophysicist, bacteriologist, marine botanist, oceanographer, pharmacist, chemical engineer, sanitary engineer, agronomist, entomologist, ornithologist, endocrinologist, radiologist, graphologist, geophysicist, neurologist, neurophysicist, paleontologist, mineralogist, metallurgist, anthropologist, ethnologist, archaeologist, sociologist, linguist; see also DOCTOR.

scissors *n.pl.* shears, pair of scissors, blades, hair scissors, paper scissors, garden shears, cutting instrument.

scoff *v.* mock, deride, jeer; see RIDICULE.

scold *v.* admonish, chide, chew out*, bawl out*, get after, lay down the law, jump on, jump all over, rebuke, censure, reprove, upbraid, reprimand, taunt, cavil, criticize, denounce, disparage, recriminate, rate, revile, rail, abuse, villify, find fault with, nag, lecture, have on the carpet, rake over the coals*, give one a talking to, chasten, preach, tell off*, keep after, light into*, put down; see also PUNISH.—*Ant.* PRAISE, commend, extoll.

scoop *v.* ladle, shovel, bail; see DIP 2.

scoot *v.* dart, speed, rush; see HASTEN 2, HURRY 1.

scope *n.* reach, range, field; see EXTENT.

scorch *v.* roast, parch, shrivel; see BURN.

scorching *a.* fiery, searing, sweltering; see BURNING, HOT 1.

score *n.* **1.** [A tally] stock, reckoning, record, average, rate, account, count, number, summation, aggregate, sum, addition, summary, amount, final tally, final account; see also NUMBER, WHOLE. **2.** [Written music] transcription, arrangement, orchestration; see MUSIC 1, COMPOSITION. **—know the score*** grasp, be aware of, comprehend; see KNOW 1, UNDERSTAND 1.

score *v.* **1.** [To make a single score] make a goal, a point, rack up*, chalk up, total, calculate, reckon, tally, enumerate, count, add. **2.** [To compose a musical accompaniment] orchestrate, arrange, adapt; see COMPOSE 2. **3.** [*To purchase legally or illegally] get, procure, secure; see BUY. **4.** [*To copulate] have sexual intercourse, sleep with, fornicate; see COPULATE.

scorn *v.* hold in contempt, despise, disdain; see HATE.

scornful *a.* contemptuous, disdainful, haughty; see EGOTISTIC.

scoundrel *n.* rogue, scamp, villain; see RASCAL.
scour *v.* scrub, cleanse, rub; see CLEAN, WASH 1, 2.
scout *n.* **1.** [One who gathers information] explorer, pioneer, outpost, runner, advance guard, precursor, patrol, reconnoiterer. **2.** [A Boy Scout or Girl Scout] *Degrees of scouts include the following:* Cub, Tenderfoot, Second Class, First Class, Star, Life, Eagle, Queen's (British), bronze palm, gold palm, silver palm; Brownie, Junior, Cadette, Senior.
scowl *v.* glower, disapprove, grimace; see FROWN.
scramble *v.* **1.** [To mix] combine, blend, interfuse; see MIX 1. **2.** [To climb hastily] clamber, push, struggle; see CLIMB.
scrap *n.* **1.** [Junk metal] waste material, chips, cuttings; see TRASH 1. **2.** [A bit] fragment, particle, portion; see BIT 1, PIECE 1. **3.** [*A fight] quarrel, brawl, squabble; see FIGHT 1.
scrap *v.* **1.** [To discard] reject, forsake, dismiss; see ABANDON 1, DISCARD. **2.** [*To fight] wrangle, battle, squabble; see FIGHT, QUARREL.
scrapbook *n.* portfolio, memorabilia, notebook; see ALBUM, COLLECTION.
scrape *v.* abrade, scour, rasp; see RUB 1.
scraper *n.* grater, rasp, abrasive; see TOOL 1.
scratch *n.* hurt, cut, mark; see INJURY, SCAR. **—from scratch** from the beginning, without preparation, solely; see ALONE, ORIGINAL 1.
scratch *v.* scrape, scarify, prick; see DAMAGE, HURT 1.
scratching *a.* grating, abrasive, rasping; see ROUGH 1.
scratch the surface *v.* touch on, mention, skim; see BEGIN 1, 2.
scrawl *v.* scribble, scratch, doodle; see WRITE 2.
scrawled *a.* scribbled, scratched, inscribed; see WRITTEN 2.
scrawny *a.* lanky, gaunt, lean; see THIN 2.
scream *n.* screech, outcry, shriek; see CRY 1, YELL.
scream *v.* shriek, screech, squeal; see CRY 2, YELL.
screaming *a.* shrieking, screeching, squealing; see YELLING.
screen *n.* **1.** [A concealment] cloak, cover, covering, curtain, shield, envelope, veil, mask, shade. **2.** [A protection] shelter, guard, security; see COVER 1, PROTECTION 2.
screen *v.* **1.** [To hide] veil, conceal, mask; see HIDE 1. **2.** [To choose] select, eliminate, sift; see CHOOSE.
screw *n.* spiral, worm, bolt, pin; see also FASTENER. *Screws include the following:* jack, lead, double, drive, lag, right-handed, left-handed, metric, regulating, set, winged, thumb, spiral, triple, wood, machine.
screw* *v.* **1.** [To copulate] sleep with, fornicate with, seduce; see COPULATE. **2.** [To trick or defeat] cheat, swindle, beat; see DEFEAT, HURT 2, TRICK.
screw up* *v.* bungle, foul up*, mishandle; see BOTCH.
screw-up* *n.* mistake, confusion, mess; see ERROR, CONFUSION.
screwy* *a.* odd, crazy, inappropriate; see INSANE, WRONG 2.
scribble *n.* scrawl, scrabble, scratch; see HANDWRITING.
scribble *v.* scrawl, scratch, scrabble; see WRITE 2.
scrimp *v.* limit, pinch, skimp; see ECONOMIZE.
script *n.* **1.** [Handwriting] writing, characters, chirography; see HANDWRITING. **2.** [Playbook] lines, text, dialogue, book, scenario.
scripture *n.* **1.** [Truth] reality, verity, final word; see TRUTH. **2.** [The Bible; *capital*] the Word, Holy Writ, the Book; see BIBLE.
scrub *a.* second-rate, unimportant, mediocre; see POOR 2.
scrub *v.* rub, cleanse, scour; see CLEAN, WASH 1, 2.
scrubbed *a.* cleaned, polished, immaculate; see CLEAN 1.
scruple *n.* compunction, qualm, uneasiness; see DOUBT.
scruples *n.pl.* overconscientiousness, point of honor, scrupulousness; see ATTENTION, CARE 1.
scrupulous *a.* exact, punctilious, strict; see CAREFUL.
scrutinize *v.* view, study, stare; see EXAMINE, WATCH.
scrutiny *n.* analysis, investigation, inspection; see EXAMINATION 1.
scuffle *n.* struggle, shuffle, strife; see FIGHT 1.
sculptor *n.* artist, modeler, carver, stone carver, wood carver, worker in bronze, worker in metal. *Major sculptors include the following:* Phidias, Ghiberti, Donatello, Luca della Robbia, Michelangelo, Giovanni da Bologna, Benvenuto Cellini, Gian Lorenzo Bernini, Auguste Rodin, Constantin Brancusi, Henry Moore, Jacques Lipchitz.
sculpture *n.* carving, modeling, carving in stone, modeling in clay, kinetic sculpture, op art, casting in bronze, woodcutting, stone carving, plastic art; see also ART, STATUE.
scum *n.* froth, film, impurities; see RESIDUE, TRASH 1.
sea *n.* *Important seas include the following:* Bering, Caribbean, Baltic, North, Irish, Mediterranean, Adriatic, Ionian, Aegean, Black, Caspian, Azov, Red, White, Tasman, Okhotsk, Japan, Yellow, South China, Arabian, East China, Java, Celebes, Coral; see also OCEAN. **—at sea** confused, puzzled,

upset; see BEWILDERED, UNCERTAIN. **—put (out) to sea** embark, go, start out; see LEAVE 1, SAIL 1.

sea bottom *n.* ocean floor, deep-sea floor, bottom of the sea, offshore lands, ocean bottom, ocean depths, continental shelf, undersea topography, marine farm, tidewater; see also OCEAN. *Terms for undersea topography include the following:* bank, sands, seamount, ridge, guyot, hill, tablemount, escarpment, plateau, reef, basin, canal, province, shoal, sill, channel, deep, depth, plain, trench, trough, fracture zone, rift.

seacoast *n.* seashore, seaboard, seaside; see SHORE.

sea food *n.* halibut, mollusk, marine life; see FISH, SHELLFISH.

seal *n.* **1.** [Approval] authorization, permit, allowance; see PERMISSION. **2.** [Fastener] adhesive tape, sticker, tie; see FASTENER, TAPE.

sealed *a.* secured, fixed, held together; see FIRM 1, TIGHT 2.

seal off *v.* quarantine, close, segregate; see FORBID, RESTRICT.

seam *n.* joint, line of joining, union, stitching, line of stitching, closure, suture.

seamstress *n.* sewer, needleworker, designer; see TAILOR.

sear *v.* scorch, brown, toast; see COOK.

search *n.* exploration, quest, research; see HUNTING. **—in search of** looking for, seeking, on the lookout for; see SEARCHING.

search *v.* explore, examine, rummage, look up and down, track down, look for, go through, poke into, scrutinize, ransack; see also HUNT 1. **—search me** I don't know, who knows?, how should I know?; see UNCERTAINTY 1.

searching *a.* hunting, looking for, seeking for, pursuing, in search of, ready for, in the market for, in need of, needing, wanting, on the lookout for, looking out for.

searchlight *n.* arc light, beam, ray; see LIGHT 3.

seashell *n.* conch, clam, oyster; see SHELL 1.

seashore *n.* seaboard, seaside, seacoast; see SHORE.

seasick *a.* nauseated, miserable, uneasy; see SICK.

seaside *n.* seaboard, seashore, seacost; see SHORE.

season *n.* period, term, certain months of the year; see FALL 3, SPRING 2, SUMMER, WINTER.

seasonal *a.* once a season, periodically, biennial; see ANNUAL, YEARLY.

seasoned *a.* **1.** [Spicy] tangy, sharp, aromatic; see SPICY. **2.** [Experienced] established, settled, mature; see ABLE, EXPERIENCED.

seasoning *n.* sauce, relish, spice, pungency; see also FLAVORING.

seat *n.* **1.** [A structure on which one may sit] bench, chair, stool; see FURNITURE. **2.** [Space in which one may sit] situation, chair, accommodation; see PLACE 2. **3.** [The part of the body with which one sits] buttocks, rear, breech; see RUMP. **—have** or **take a seat** be seated, sit down, occupy a place; see SIT.

seated *a.* situated, located, settled, installed, established, rooted, set, fitted in place, placed, arranged, accommodated with seats.

seating *n.* places, reservations, chairs, seats, room, accommodation, arrangement, seating space.

seaward *a.* offshore, out to sea, over the sea; see MARITIME.

seaweed *n.* kelp, tangle, sea tangle, sea meadow, algae, marine meadow; see also PLANT. *Seaweed includes the following:* sea moss, Irish moss, Sargasso weed, rockweed, sea lettuce, kelp, giant kelp, gulfweed, sea cabbage.

seaworthy *a.* fit for sea, navigable, secure; see SAFE 1.

secede *v.* withdraw, retract, leave; see RETREAT.

secession *n.* departure, seceding, retraction; see WITHDRAWAL.

seclude *v.* screen out, conceal, cover; see HIDE 1.

secluded *a.* screened, removed, sequestered; see WITHDRAWN.

seclusion *n.* solitude, aloofness, privacy; see RETIREMENT 2.

second *a.* secondary, subordinate, inferior, next, next in order, following, next to the first, next in rank, another, other. **—play second fiddle (to)** defer to, be inferior to, be less successful than; see FAIL 1.

second *n.* flash, trice, flash of an eyelid; see MOMENT 1.

secondary *a.* **1.** [Derived] dependent, subsequent, subsidiary; see SUBORDINATE. **2.** [Minor] inconsiderable, petty, small; see TRIVIAL, UNIMPORTANT.

secondhand *a.* used, not new, reclaimed, renewed, reused, old, worn, borrowed, derived, not original.

secondly *a.* in the second place, furthermore, also, besides, next, on the other hand, in the next place, for the next step, next in order, further, to continue; see also INCLUDING.

second-rate *a.* mediocre, inferior, common; see POOR 2.

secrecy *n.* concealment, confidence, hiding, seclusion, privacy, retirement, solitude, mystery, dark, darkness, isolation, reticence, stealth.

secret *a.* **1.** [Not generally known] mysterious, ambiguous, hidden, unknown, arcane, cryptic, esoteric, occult, mystic, mystical, classified, dark, veiled, enigmatic, strange, deep, buried in mystery, obscure, clouded, shrouded, unenlightened, unintelligible, cabalistic.—*Ant.* KNOWN, revealed, exposed. **2.** [Hidden] latent, secluded, concealed; see HIDDEN. **3.** [Operating secretly] clandestine, underhand, underhanded, stealthy, sly, surreptitious, close, furtive, disguised, undercover, backdoor, confidential, backstairs, incognito, camouflaged, enigmatic, under false pretense, unrevealed, undisclosed, dissembled, dissimulated, under wraps; see also SECRETIVE.—*Ant.* OPEN, aboveboard, overt.

secret *n.* mystery, deep mystery, something veiled, something hidden, confidence, private matter, code, telegram, personal matter, privileged information, top secret, enigma, puzzle, something forbidden, classified information, confidential information, inside information, an unknown, magic number, the unknown. —**in secret** slyly, surreptitiously, quietly; see SECRET 3.

secretary *n.* **1.** [A secondary executive officer] director, manager, superintendent; see EXECUTIVE. **2.** [An assistant] clerk, typist, stenographer, copyist, amanuensis, recorder, confidential clerk, correspondent.

secrete *v.* **1.** [To hide] conceal, cover, seclude; see DISGUISE, HIDE 1. **2.** [To perspire] discharge, swelter, emit; see SWEAT.

secretion *n.* discharge, issue, movement; see EXCRETION, FLOW.

secretive *a.* reticent, taciturn, undercover, with bated breath, in private, in the dark, in chambers, by a side door, under the breath, in the background, between outselves, in privacy, in a corner, under the cloak of, reserved.

secretly *a.* privately, covertly, obscurely, darkly, surreptitiously, furtively, stealthily, underhandedly, slyly, behind one's back, intimately, personally, confidentially, between you and me, in strict confidence, in secret, behind the scenes, on the sly, behind closed doors, quietly, hush-hush*.—*Ant.* OPENLY, obviously, publicly.

sect *n.* denomination, following, order; see CHURCH 3, FACTION.

section *n.* **1.** [A portion] subdivision, slice, segment; see PART 1, SHARE. **2.** [An area] district, sector, locality; see REGION 1.

sectional *a.* local, narrow, separate; see REGIONAL.

sector *n.* section, district, quarter; see AREA, DIVISION 2.

secure *a.* **1.** [Firm] fastened, adjusted, bound; see FIRM 1, TIGHT 1. **2.** [Safe] guarded, unharmed, defended; see SAFE 1. **3.** [Self-confident] assured, stable, determined; see CONFIDENT.

secure *v.* **1.** [To fasten] settle, adjust, bind; see FASTEN, TIGHTEN 1. **2.** [To obtain] achieve, acquire, grasp; see GET 1.

security *n.* **1.** [Safety] protection, shelter, safety, refuge, retreat, defense, safeguard, preservation, sanctuary, ward, guard, immunity, freedom from harm, freedom from danger, redemption, salvation.—*Ant.* DANGER, risk, hazard. **2.** [A guarantee] earnest, forfeit, token, pawn, pledge, surety, bond, collateral, assurance, bail, certainty, promise, warranty, pact, compact, contract, covenant, agreement, sponsor, bondsman, hostage; see also PROTECTION 2.—*Ant.* DOUBT, broken faith, unreliability.

sedative *n.* tranquilizer, medication, narcotic; see DRUG, MEDICINE 2.

sediment *n.* silt, dregs, grounds; see RESIDUE.

seduce *v.* decoy, allure, inveigle, entice, abduct, attract, tempt, bait, bribe, lure, induce, stimulate, defile, deprave, lead astray, violate, prostitute, rape, deflower.—*Ant.* PRESERVE, protect, guide.

see *v.* **1.** [To perceive with the eye] observe, look at, behold, examine, inspect, regard, view, look out on, gaze, stare, eye, lay eyes on, mark, perceive, pay attention to, heed, mind, detect, take notice, discern, scrutinize, scan, spy, survey, contemplate, remark, clap eyes on*, make out, cast the eyes on, direct the eyes, catch sight of, cast the eyes over, get a load of*. **2.** [To understand] perceive, comprehend, discern; see RECOGNIZE 1, UNDERSTAND 1. **3.** [To witness] look on, be present, pay attention, notice, observe, regard, heed; see also WITNESS. **4.** [To accompany] escort, attend, bear company; see ACCOMPANY. **5.** [To have an appointment (with)] speak to, have a conference with, get advice from; see CONSULT, DISCUSS.

see about *v.* attend to, look after, provide for; see PERFORM 1.

seed *n.* grain, bulbs, cuttings, ears, tubers, roots; seed corn, seed potatoes, etc. *Seeds and fruits commonly called seeds include the following:* grain, kernel, berry, ear, corn, nut. —**go** or **run to seed** decline, worsen, run out; see WASTE 3.

seed *v.* scatter, sow, broadcast; see PLANT.

seeding *n.* sowing, implanting, spreading; see FARMING.

see fit to *v.* decide to, be willing to, determine to; see WANT, WISH.

seeing *a.* observing, looking, regarding, viewing, noticing, surveying, looking at, observant, wide awake, alert, awake, perceiving, inspecting, witnessing.

seek *v.* search for, dig for, fish for, look around for, look up, hunt up, sniff out, dig out, hunt out, root out, smell around, go after, run after, see after, prowl after, go in pursuit of, go in search of.

seem *v.* appear to be, have the appearance, give the impression, impress one, appear to one, look, look like, resemble, make a show of, show, have the features of, lead one to suppose something to be, have all the evidence of being, be suggestive of, give the effect of, sound like, make out to be, give the idea, have all the earmarks of, make a noise like.

seen *a.* observed, evident, viewed; see OBVIOUS 1.

seep *v.* leak, flow gently, trickle; see DRAIN 1, FLOW.

seepage *n.* drainage, infiltration, leakage; see FLOW.

seethe *v.* simmer, stew, burn; see BOIL, COOK.

see through *v.* **1.** [To complete] finish up, bring to a successful conclusion, wind up; see COMPLETE, END 1. **2.** [To understand] comprehend, penetrate, detect; see UNDERSTAND 1.

see to *v.* do, attend to, look after; see UNDERSTAND 1.

segment *n.* section, portion, fragment; see DIVISION 2, PART 1.

segregate *v.* isolate, sever, split up; see DIVIDE, SEPARATE 2.

segregated *a.* divided along racial lines, isolated, ghettoized; see RACIAL, SEPARATED.

segregation *n.* dissociation, disconnection, separation; see DIVISION 1.

seize *v.* **1.** [To grasp] take, take hold of, lay hold of, hands on, catch up, catch hold of, hang onto, catch, grip, clinch, clench, clasp, embrace, grab, clutch, grapple, snag, pluck, appropriate, snatch, swoop up, enfold, enclose, pinch, squeeze, hold fast, possess oneself of, envelope.—*Ant.* LEAVE, pass by, let alone. **2.** [To take by force] capture, rape, occupy, win, take captive, pounce, conquer, take by storm, subdue, overwhelm, overrun, overpower, ambush, snatch, incorporate, exact, retake, carry off, apprehend, arrest, secure, commandeer, force, gain, take, recapture, appropriate, take possession of, take over, pounce on, usurp, overcome, impound, intercept, steal, abduct, snap up*, nab*, trap, throttle, lay hold of, lift, hook, collar*, fasten upon, wrench, claw, snare, bag, catch up, wring, get one's hands on, kidnap, rustle*, hold up, swipe*, scramble for, help oneself to, jump a claim*. **3.** [To comprehend] perceive, see, know; see UNDERSTAND 1.

seized *a.* confiscated, annexed, clutched; see BEATEN 1, CAPTURED.

seizure *n.* **1.** [Capture] seizing, taking, apprehending; see CAPTURE. **2.** [A spasm] spell, convulsion, breakdown; see FIT 1, ILLNESS 1.

seldom *a.* rarely, unusually, in a few cases, a few times, at times, seldom seen, usually, sporadically, irregularly, whimsically, sometimes, from time to time, on a few occasions, on rare occasions, infrequently, not often, not very often, occasionally, uncommonly, scarcely, hardly, hardly ever, scarcely ever, when the spirit moves, on and off, once in a while, once in a blue moon, once in a lifetime, every now and then, not in a month of Sundays.—*Ant.* FREQUENTLY, often, frequent.

select *v.* decide, pick, elect; see CHOOSE.

selected *a.* picked, chosen, elected; see NAMED 2.

selection *n.* **1.** [The act of selecting] choice, election, determination, choosing, preference, appropriation, adoption, reservation, separation. **2.** [Anything selected] pick, collection, excerpt; see CHOICE.

selective *a.* discriminating, judicious, particular; see CAREFUL.

self *a.* of one's self, by one's self, by one's own effort; see ALONE, INDIVIDUAL.

self *n.* oneself, one's being, inner nature; see CHARACTER 2.

self-assurance *n.* security, self-reliance, morale; see CONFIDENCE.

self-assured *a.* self-confident, assured, certain; see CONFIDENT.

self-centered *a.* self-indulgent, egotistical, self-conscious; see EGOTISTIC, SELFISH.

self-confidence *n.* assurance, courage, self-reliance; see CONFIDENCE.

self-confident *a.* fearless, secure, self-assured; see CONFIDENT.

self-conscious *a.* unsure, uncertain, shy; see DOUBTFUL, HUMBLE 1.

self-contained *a.* self-sustaining, complete, independent; see FREE 1, WHOLE 1.

self-control *n.* poise, self-restraint, reserve, self-government, reticence, discretion, balance, stability, sobriety, dignity, repression, constraint, self-regulation.—*Ant.* NERVOUSNESS, timidity, talkativeness.

self-defense *n.* self-protection, the manly art of self-defense, putting up a fight; see FIGHT 1, PROTECTION 2.

self-esteem *n.* vanity, haughtiness, egotism; see PRIDE 1.

self-evident *a.* plain, visible, apparent; see OBVIOUS 2.

self-explanatory *a.* plain, clear, distinct; see OBVIOUS 2.

self-imposed *a.* accepted, self-determined, willingly adopted; see DELIBERATE, VOLUNTARILY.

selfish *a.* self-seeking, self-centered, self-indulgent, indulging oneself, wrapped up in oneself, narrow, narrow-minded, prejudiced, egotistical, egotistic, looking out for number one*; see also GREEDY.

selfishly *a.* egotistically, stingily, greedily, in one's own interest, meanly, ungenerously, to gain private ends, from selfish motives.

selfishness *n.* self-regard, self-indulgence, self-worship; see GREED.

self-made *a.* competent, self-reliant, audacious; see ABLE, CONFIDENT.

self-reliant *a.* determined, resolute, independent; see ABLE, CONFIDENT.

self-respect *n.* morale, worth, pride; see CONFIDENCE, DIGNITY.

self-restraint *n.* patience, endurance, control; see RESTRAINT 1.

self-sacrifice *n.* altruism, kindheartedness, benevolence; see GENEROSITY, KINDNESS 1, 2.

self-satisfaction *n.* complacency, smugness, conceit; see EGOTISM.

self-satisfied *a.* smug, vain, conceited; see EGOTISTIC.

self-sufficient *a.* competent, self-confident, efficient; see CONFIDENT.

sell *v.* market, vend, auction, dispose of, put up for sale, put on the market, barter, exchange, transfer, liquidate, trade, bargain, peddle, retail, merchandise, sell over the counter, contract, wholesale, retail, dump, clear out, have a sale, give title to, put in escrow.—*Ant.* BUY, obtain, get.

seller *n.* dealer, tradesman, salesman, door-to-door salesman, retailer, agent, vender, merchant, auctioneer, shopkeeper, peddler, trader, marketer, storekeeper; see also BUSINESSMAN.

selling *n.* sale, auction, bartering, trading, vending, auctioning, transfer, transferring, commercial transaction, transacting, disposal, merchandising.—*Ant.* BUYING, acquiring, purchasing.

sellout* *n.* betrayal, deception, deal; see TRICK 1.

sell out* *v.* trick, turn in, betray, double-cross*; see also DECEIVE.

sell short *v.* undervalue, disparage, minimize; see UNDERESTIMATE.

semester *n.* six-month period, eighteen weeks, four and one-half months; see TERM 2.

semifinal *n.* next to the last match, elimination test, elimination round; see ROUND 2.

seminary *n.* secondary school, institute, theological school; see SCHOOL 1.

senate *n.* legislative body, assembly, council; see LEGISLATURE.

Senate *n.* legislative body, upper branch of Congress, the Upper House; see LEGISLATURE.

senator *n.* statesman, politician, member of the senate; see REPRESENTATIVE 2.

send *v.* **1.** [To dispatch] transmit, forward, convey, advance, express, ship, mail, send forth, send out, send in, delegate, expedite, hasten, accelerate, post, address, rush, rush off, hurry off, get under way, give papers, provide with credentials, send out for, address to, commission, consign, drop, convey, transfer, pack off, give, bestow, grant, confer, entrust, assign, impart, give out. **2.** [To broadcast, usually electronically] transmit, relay, wire, cable, broadcast, televise, conduct, communicate.

send around *v.* circulate, send to everyone, make available; see DISTRIBUTE.

send (away) for *v.* order, request, write away for; see ASK, GET 1.

send back *v.* reject, mail back, decide against; see RETURN 2.

send in *v.* submit, mail, deliver; see OFFER 1.

send word *v.* get in touch, communicate, report; see TELEPHONE.

senile *a.* aged, infirm, feeble; see OLD 1, SICK.

senility *n.* old age, dotage, feebleness, anility, infirmity, decline, senile dementia, Alzheimer's disease, senescence, second childhood; see also AGE 2, WEAKNESS 1.

senior *a.* elder, older, higher in rank; see SUPERIOR.

seniority *n.* preferred standing, ranking, station; see ADVANTAGE.

sensation *n.* **1.** [The sense of feeling] sensibility, consciousness, perception; see EMOTION, THOUGHT 1. **2.** [A feeling] response, sentiment, passion; see FEELING 1.

sensational *a.* **1.** [Fascinating] exciting, marvelous, incredible; see IMPRESSIVE, INTERESTING. **2.** [Melodramatic] exaggerated, excessive, emotional; see EXCITING.

sense *n.* **1.** [One of the powers of physical perception] kinesthesia, function, sensation; see HEARING 3, SIGHT 1, TASTE 1, TOUCH 1. **2.** [Mental ability] intellect, understanding, reason, mind, spirit, soul, brains, judgment, wit, imagination, common sense, cleverness, reasoning, intellectual ability, mental capacity, savvy*, knowledge; see also THOUGHT 1.—*Ant.* DULLNESS, idiocy, feeble wit. **3.** [Reasonable and agreeable conduct] reasonableness, fairmindedness, discretion; see FAIRNESS. **4.** [Tact and understanding] insight, discernment, social sense; see FEELING 4, JUDGMENT 1. —**in a sense** in a way, to a degree, somewhat; see SOME, SOMEHOW. —**make sense** seem reasonable, look all right, add up; see APPEAR 1, SEEM.

senseless *a.* ridiculous, silly, foolish; see ILLOGICAL, STUPID.

senses *n.pl.* consciousness, mental faculties, feeling; see AWARENESS, LIFE 1, 2.

sensible *a.* **1.** [Showing good sense] reasonable, prudent, perceptive, acute, shrewd, sharp, careful, aware, wise, cautious, capable, having a head on one's shoulders*, endowed with reason, sane, discerning, thoughtful; see also RATIONAL 1, SANE 1. **2.** [Perceptive] aware, informed, attentive; see CONSCIOUS.

sensitive *a.* **1.** [Tender] delicate, sore, painful; see SORE 1. **2.** [Touchy] high-strung, tense, nervous; see IRRITABLE, UNSTABLE 2.

sensitivity *n.* **1.** [Susceptibility] allergy, irritability, ticklishness; see FEELING 4. **2.** [Emotional response or condition] delicacy, sensibility, sensitiveness, nervousness, acute awareness, consciousness, acuteness, subtlety, feeling, sympathetic response, sympathy.

sensory *a.* **1.** [Neurological] sensible, relating to the senses, conscious; see SENSUAL 1. **2.** [Conveyed by the senses] audible, perceptible, discernible; see OBVIOUS 1, 2, TANGIBLE.

sensual *a.* **1.** [Sensory] tactile, sensuous, stimulating, sharpened, pleasing, dazzling, feeling, being, heightened, enhanced, appealing, delightful, luxurious, emotional, fine, arousing, stirring, moving; see also EXCITING. **2.** [Carnal] voluptuous, pleasure-loving, fleshly, lewd, unspiritual, self-loving, self-indulgent, epicurean, intemperate, gluttonous, rakish, debauched, orgiastic, sensuous, piggish, hoggish, bestial.

sensuality *n.* sensationalism, appetite, ardor; see DESIRE 2, EMOTION, LOVE 1.

sensuous *a.* passionate, physical, exciting; see SENSUAL 2.

sent *a.* commissioned, appointed, ordained, delegated, dispatched, directed, issued, transmitted, discharged, gone, on the road, in transit, uttered, sent forth, driven, impelled, forced to go, consigned, ordered, committed.—*Ant.* KEPT, restrained, held back.

sentence *n.* **1.** [A pronounced judgment] edict, decree, order; see JUDGMENT 3, PUNISHMENT, VERDICT. **2.** [An expressed thought] *Types of sentences include the following:* simple, complex, compound, compound-complex, kernel, transformed, declarative, interrogative, imperative, exclamatory; statement, question, command, exclamation.

sentence *v.* pronounce judgment, judge, send to prison; see CONDEMN, CONVICT, IMPRISON, PUNISH.

sent for *a.* applied for, written for, requested; see ORDERED 1.

sentiment *n.* sensibility, predilection, tender feeling; see EMOTION, FEELING 4, THOUGHT 2.

sentimental *a.* emotional, romantic, silly, dreamy, idealistic, visionary, artificial, unrealistic, susceptible, overemotional, affected, mawkish, simpering, insincere, overacted, schoolgirlish, sappy*, soupy*, gushy.

sentimentality *n.* sentimentalism, sentiment, melodramatics, bathos, mawkishness, melodrama, triteness, mush*, gush; see also EMOTION.

sentry *n.* sentinel, lookout, protector; see WATCHMAN.

separate *v.* **1.** [To keep apart] isolate, insulate, single out, sequester, seclude, rope off, segregate, intervene, stand between, draw apart, split up, break up. **2.** [To part company] take leave, go away, depart; see LEAVE 1.

separated *a.* divided, parted, apart, disconnected, partitioned, distinct, disunited, disjointed, sundered, disembodied, cut in two, cut apart, set apart, distant, disassociated, removed, distributed, scattered, put asunder, divorced, divergent, marked, severed, far between, in halves.—*Ant.* UNITED, together, whole.

separately *a.* singly, definitely, distinctly; see CLEARLY 1, 2, INDIVIDUALLY.

separation *n.* **1.** [The act of dividing] disconnection, severance, division, cut, detachment. **2.** [The act of parting] coming apart, drawing apart, parting company, breaking up.

September *n.* fall or autumn or summer month, Indian summer, back-to-school season; see FALL 3.

sequel *n.* consequence, continuation, progression; see SEQUENCE 1, SERIES.

sequence *n.* **1.** [Succession] order, continuity, continuousness, continuance, successiveness, progression, graduation, consecutiveness, flow, consecution, unbrokenness, subsequence, course. **2.** [Arrangement] placement, distribution, classification; see ORDER 3. **3.** [A series] chain, string, array; see SERIES.

serenade *n.* melody, compliment, nocturne; see MUSIC 1, SONG.

serene *a.* calm, clear, unruffled, translucent, undisturbed, undimmed, tranquil, composed, cool, coolheaded, sedate, levelheaded, content, satisfied, patient, reconciled, easygoing, placid, limpid, comfortable, cheerful.—*Ant.* CONFUSED, disturbed, ruffled.

serenity *n.* quietness, calmness, tranquility; see PEACE 2, 3.

sergeant *n.* noncommissioned officer, top kick*, sarge*. *Types include the following:* master sergeant, staff sergeant, technical sergeant, first sergeant, top sergeant, platoon sergeant, drill sergeant, sergeant major, sergeant-at-arms, police sergeant; see also OFFICER 3, SOLDIER.

serial *n.* installment, serial picture, continued story; see MOVIE.

series *n.* rank, file, line, row, set, train, range, list, string, chain, order, sequence, succession, group, procession, continuity, column, progression, category, classification, scale, array, gradation.

serious *a.* **1.** [Involving danger] grave, severe, pressing; see DANGEROUS, IMPORTANT 1. **2.** [Thoughtful] earnest, sober, reflective; see SOLEMN.

seriously *a.* **1.** [In a manner fraught with danger] dangerously, precariously, perilously, in a risky way, threateningly, menacingly, grievously, severely, harmfully.—*Ant.* SAFELY, harmlessly, in no danger. **2.** [In a manner that recognizes importance] gravely, soberly, earnestly, solemnly, thoughtfully, sternly, sedately, with great earnestness, all joking aside; see also SINCERELY.—*Ant.* LIGHTLY, thoughtlessly, airily.

seriousness *n.* **1.** [The quality of being dangerous] gravity, weight, enormity; see IMPORTANCE. **2.** [The characteristic of being sober] earnestness, sobriety, solemnity, gravity, calmness, thoughtfulness, coolness, sedateness, sobermindedness; see also SINCERITY.—*Ant.* FUN, gaiety, jollity.

sermon *n.* lesson, doctrine, lecture; see SPEECH 3.

serpent *n.* reptile, viper, ophidian; see SNAKE.

servant *n.* attendant, retainer, helper, hireling, dependent, menial, domestic, drudge, slave; see also ASSISTANT. *Servants include the following:* butler, housekeeper, chef, cook, second maid, kitchenmaid, maid of all work, general maid, laundress, chambermaid, parlormaid, lady's maid, seamstress, nursemaid, nurse, valet, doorman, footman, squire, chauffeur, groom, gardener, yardman, kennelman.

serve *v.* **1.** [To fulfill an obligation] hear duty's call, obey the call of one's country, subserve, discharge one's duty, assume one's responsibilities. **2.** [To work for] be employed by, labor for, be in the employ of; see WORK 2. **3.** [To help] give aid, assist, be of assistance; see HELP. **4.** [To serve at table] wait on, attend, provide guests with food, help.

served *a.* dressed, prepared, offered, apportioned, dealt, furnished, supplied, provided, dished up.

serve notice *v.* inform, report, give word; see TELL 1.

serve someone right *v.* deserve it, having it coming, get one's just deserts; see DESERVE.

serve time *v.* stand committed, serve a jail sentence, be incarcerated, be in jail, pay one's debt to society, go to jail, do time*, be in stir*, be in the joint*, be sent up*.

service *n.* **1.** [Aid] cooperation, assistance, aid; see HELP 1. **2.** [Tableware] set, silver, setting; see DISH 1, POTTERY. **3.** [A religious service] rite, worship, sermon; see CEREMONY 2. **4.** [Military service] the armed forces, duty, active service, stint. **—at someone's service** zealous, anxious to help, obedient; see HELPFUL 1, READY 1, WILLING. **—of service** useful, handy, usable; see HELPFUL 1.

service *v.* maintain, sustain, keep up; see REPAIR.

serviceable *a.* practical, advantageous, beneficial; see HELPFUL 1, USABLE.

serving *n.* plateful, course, portion; see MEAL 2.

session *n.* assembly, concourse, sitting; see GATHERING.

set *a.* **1.** [Firm] stable, solid, settled; see FIRM 2. **2.** [Determined] concluded, steadfast, decided; see DETERMINED 1.

set *n.* **1.** [Inclination] attitude, position, bearing; see INCLINATION 1. **2.** [A social group] clique, coterie, circle; see FACTION, ORGANIZATION 2. **3.** [A collection of (like) items] kit, assemblage, assortment; see COLLECTION.

set *v.* **1.** [To place] insert, settle, put, plant, store, situate, lay, deposit, arrange. **2.** [To establish] anchor, fix, introduce; see ESTABLISH 2, INSTALL. **3.** [To become firm] jell, solidify, congeal; see HARDEN, STIFFEN, THICKEN.

set about *v.* start, begin, start doing; see BEGIN 1.

set apart *v.* isolate, segregate, make separate; see DISTINGUISH 1, SEPARATE 1.

set aside *v.* **1.** [To save] put away, reserve, lay up; see MAINTAIN 3, SAVE 2. **2.** [To discard] abrogate, repeal, reject; see CANCEL, DISCARD.

setback *n.* hindrance, check, reversal; see DELAY, DIFFICULTY 1.

set off *v.* **1.** [To show by contrast] set in relief, enhance, intensify, enhance, intensify, make distinct. **2.** [To explode] touch off, set the spark to, detonate; see EXPLODE.

set out *v.* initiate, start, commence; see BEGIN 1.

set sail *v.* begin a voyage, shove off, weigh anchor; see LEAVE 1, SAIL 1.

set straight *v.* revise, inform properly, give the correct facts to; see CORRECT, IMPROVE 2.

setting *n.* environment, surroundings, mounting, backdrop, frame, framework, background, context, perspective, horizon, shadow, shade, distance.—*Ant.* FRONT, foreground, focus.

settle *v.* **1.** [To decide] reach a decision, form judgment on, come to a conclusion about; see DECIDE. **2.** [To prove] establish, verify, make certain; see PROVE. **3.** [To finish] end, make an end of, complete; see ACHIEVE. **4.** [To sink] descend, decline, fall; see SINK 1. **5.** [To establish residence] locate, lodge, become a citizen, reside, fix one's residence, abide, set up housekeeping, make one's home, establish a home, keep house; see also DWELL. **6.** [To take up sedentary life; *often used with "down"*] follow regular habits, live an orderly life, become conventional, follow convention, buy a house, marry, marry and settle down, raise a family, get in a rut, hang up one's hat*. **7.** [To satisfy a claim] pay, compensate, make an adjustment, reach a compromise, make payment, arrange a settlement, get squared away, pay damages, pay out, settle out of court, settle up, work out, settle the score, even the score, dispose of, account with.

settled *a.* decided, resolved, ended; see DETERMINED 1.

settlement *n.* **1.** [An agreement] covenant, arrangement, compact; see AGREEMENT 1, CONTRACT. **2.** [A payment] compensation, remuneration, reimbursement; see ADJUSTMENT, PAY 1. **3.** [A colony] principality, plantation, establishment; see COLONY.

settler *n.* planter, immigrant, homesteader; see PIONEER 2.

setup *n.* structure, composition, plan; see ORDER 3, ORGANIZATION 2.

set up *v.* **1.** [To make arrangements] prearrange, inaugurate, work on; see ARRANGE 2. **2.** [To finance] patronize, promote, support; see PAY 1.

sever *v.* part, split, cleave; see CUT 1, DIVIDE.

several *a.* **1.** [Few] some, any, a few, quite a few, not many, sundry, two or three, a small number of, scarce, sparse, hardly any, scarcely any, half a dozen, only a few, scant, scanty, rare, infrequent, in a minority, a handful, more or less, not too many.—*Ant.* many, large numbers of, none. **2.** [Various] plural, a number of, numerous; see MANY, VARIOUS.

several *n.* various ones, a small number, quite a few; see FEW.

severe *a.* **1.** [Stern] exacting, uncompromising, unbending, inflexible, unchanging, unalterable, harsh, cruel, oppressive, close, grinding, obdurate, resolute, austere, rigid, grim, earnest, stiff, forbidding, resolved, relentless, determined, unfeeling, with an iron will, strict, inconsiderate, firm, unsparing, immovable, unyielding. **2.** [Difficult or rigorous] overbearing, tyrannical, sharp, exacting, drastic, domineering, rigid, oppressive, despotic, unmerciful, bullying, uncompromising, relentless, unrelenting, hard, rigorous, austere, grinding, grim, implacable, cruel, pitiless, critical, unjust, barbarous, crusty, gruff, stubborn, autocratic, hidebound; see also DIFFICULT 1.—*Ant.* EASY, easygoing, indulgent.

severely *a.* critically, harshly, rigorously; see FIRMLY 2, SERIOUSLY 1.

severity *n.* hardness, hardheartedness, strictness; see CRUELTY.

sew *v.* stitch, seam, fasten, work with needle and thread, tailor, tack, embroider, bind, piece, baste.

sewage *n.* excrement, offal, waste matter; see RESIDUE.

sewer *n.* drain, drainpipe, drainage tube, conduit, gutter, disposal system, sewage system, septic tank, dry well, leach field, leach bed, leach ditches, sewage disposal, sanitary provisions, sanitary facility, sanitary facilities.

sewing *n.* stitching, seaming, tailoring, embroidering, darning, mending, piecing, patching, dressmaking.

sex *n.* **1.** [Ideas associated with sexual relationships] sex attraction, sex appeal, magnetism, sensuality, affinity, love, courtship, marriage, generation, reproduction. **2.** [A group, either male or female] men, women, males, females, the feminine world, the masculine world. **3.** [Gender] sexuality, masculinity, femininity, womanliness, manhood, manliness. **4.** [Sexual intercourse] making love, the sexual act, going to bed with someone; see COPULATION, FORNICATION.

sexual *a.* **1.** [Reproductive] generative, reproductive, procreative; see ORIGINAL 1. **2.** [Intimate] carnal, wanton, passionate; see SENSUAL 2.

sexuality *n.* lust, sensuality, passion; see DESIRE 2.

shabby *a.* ragged, threadbare, faded, ill-dressed, dilapidated, decayed, deteriorated, poor, pitiful, worn, meager, miserable, wretched, poverty-stricken, scrubby, seedy, gone to seed, down at the heel.—*Ant.* NEAT, new, well-kept.

shack *n.* hut, shed, hovel, cabin, shanty, shotgun shack.

shade *n.* **1.** [Lack of light] blackness, shadow, dimness; see DARKNESS 1. **2.** [A degree of color] brilliance, saturation, hue; see COLOR, TINT. **3.** [A slight difference] variation, trace, hint; see SUGGESTION 1. **4.** [An obstruction to light] covering, blind, screen; see CURTAIN.

shade *v.* **1.** [To intercept direct rays] screen, cover, shadow; see SHELTER. **2.** [To make darker] darken, blacken, obscure, cloud, shadow, make dim, tone down, black out, make dusky, deepen the shade, overshadow, make gloomy, screen, shut out the light, keep out the light. **3.** [To become darker] grow dark, grow black, become dark, grow dim, blacken, turn to twilight, deepen into night, become gloomy, be overcast, grow dusky, cloud up, cloud over, overcloud, grow shadowy.

shadow *n.* umbra, obscuration, adumbration; see DARKNESS 1.

shadow *v.* **1.** [To shade] dim, veil, screen; see SHADE 1, 2, SHELTER. **2.** [To follow secretly] trail, watch, keep in sight; see PURSUE 1.

shady *a.* **1.** [Shaded] dusky, shadowy, adumbral, in the shade, shaded, sheltered, out of the sun, dim, cloudy, under a cloud, cool, indistinct, vague; see also DARK 1. **2.** [*Questionable] suspicious, disreputable, dubious, fishy*, underhanded.

shaft *n.* **1.** [Rod] stem, bar, pole; see ROD 1. **2.** [Light ray] wave, streak, beam of light; see RAY.

shake *n.* tremor, shiver, pulsation; see MOVEMENT 1, 2.

shake *v.* **1.** [To vibrate] tremble, quiver, quake, shiver, shudder, palpitate, wave, waver, fluctuate, reel, flap, flutter, totter, thrill, wobble, stagger, waggle. **2.** [To cause to vibrate] agitate, rock, sway, swing, joggle, jolt, bounce, jar, move, set in motion, convulse.

shaken *a.* unnerved, upset, overcome; see EXCITED.

shaky *a.* **1.** [Not firm] quivery, trembling, jellylike, unsettled, not set, yielding, unsteady, tottering, unsound, insecure, unstable, infirm, jittery, nervous.—*Ant.* FIRM, settled, rigid. **2.** [Not reliable] uncertain, not dependable, questionable; see UNRELIABLE, UNSTABLE 2.

shall *v.* intend, want to, must; see WILL 3.

shallow *a.* **1.** [Lacking physical depth] slight, inconsiderable, superficial, with the bottom in plain sight, with no depth, with little depth, not deep.—*Ant.* DEEP, bottomless, unfathomable. **2.** [Lacking intellectual depth] simple, silly, trifling, frivolous, superficial, petty, foolish, idle, unintelligent, piddling, wishy-washy*; see also STUPID.

sham *a.* not genuine, counterfeit, misleading; see FALSE 3.

sham *n.* pretense, deception, counterfeit; see FAKE.

shame *n.* **1.** [A disgrace] embarrassment, stigma, blot; see DISGRACE. **2.** [A sense of wrongdoing] bad conscience, mortification, confusion, humiliation, compunction, regret, chagrin, discomposure, irritation, remorse, embarrassment, abashment, self-reproach, self-disgust; see also GUILT. **3.** [A condition of disgrace] humiliation, dishonor, degradation; see DISGRACE, SCANDAL.

shame *v.* humiliate, mortify, dishonor; see DISGRACE, HUMBLE.

shameful *a.* **1.** [Offensive] immodest, corrupt, immoral, intemperate, debauched, drunken, villainous, knavish, degraded, reprobate, diabolical, indecent, indelicate, lewd, vulgar, impure, unclean, fleshly, carnal, sinful, wicked. **2.** [Disgraceful] dishonorable, scandalous, flagrant, obscene, ribald, infamous, outrageous, gross, infernal, disgusting, too bad, unworthy, evil, foul, hellish, disreputable, despicable; see also WRONG.—*Ant.* WORTHY, admirable, creditable.

shameless *a.* brazen, bold, forward; see RUDE 2, LEWD 2.

shape *n.* **1.** [Form] contour, aspect, configuration; see FORM 1, LOOKS. **2.** [An actual form] pattern, stamp, frame; see MOLD 1. **3.** [Condition] fitness, physical state, health; see STATE 2. **—out of shape** distorted, misshapen, battered; see BENT, BROKEN 1, FLAT 1, RUINED 1, 2, TWISTED 1. **—take shape** take on form, mature, fill out; see DEVELOP 1, IMPROVE 2.

shape *v.* **1.** [To give shape] mold, cast, fashion; see FORM 1. **2.** [*To take shape] become, develop, take form; see FORM 4, GROW 2.

shaped *a.* made, fashioned, created; see FORMED.

shapeless *a.* **1.** [Formless] indistinct, indefinite, invisible, vague, without form, without shape, lacking form, unformed, unmade, not formed, with no definite outline; see also UNCERTAIN. **2.** [Deformed] misshapen, irregular, unshapely, unsymmetrical, mutilated, disfigured, malformed, ill-formed, abnormal; see also DEFORMED.—*Ant.* REGULAR, symmetrical, shapely.

shapely *a.* symmetrical, comely, proportioned; see TRIM 2.

shape up* *v.* **1.** [To obey] mind, conform, observe the rules; see BEHAVE, IMPROVE 2, OBEY. **2.** [To develop] enlarge, expand, advance; see DEVELOP 1.

share *n.* division, apportionment, part, portion, helping, serving, piece, ration, slice, allotment, parcel, dose, fraction, fragment, allowance, dividend, percentage, commission, cut*, whack*, rake-off*.

share *v.* **1.** [To divide] allot, distribute, apportion, part, deal, dispense, assign, administer.—*Ant.* UNITE, combine, withhold. **2.** [To partake] participate, share in, experience, take part in, receive, have a portion of, have a share in, go in with, take a part of, take a share of.—*Ant.* AVOID, have no share in, take no part in. **3.** [To give] yield, bestow, accord; see GIVE 1.

sharp *a.* **1.** [Having a keen edge] acute, edged, razor-edged, sharpened, ground fine, honed, razor-sharp, sharp-edged, fine, cutting, knifelike, knife-edged.—*Ant.* DULL, unsharpened, blunt. **2.** [Having a keen point] pointed, sharp-pointed, spiked, spiky, peaked, salient, needle-pointed, keen, fine, spiny, thorny, prickly, barbed, needlelike, stinging, sharp as a needle, pronged, tapered, tapering, horned. **3.** [Having a keen mind] clever, astute, bright; see INTELLIGENT. **4.** [Distinct] audible, visible, explicit; see CLEAR 2, DEFINITE 2, OBVIOUS 1. **5.** [Intense] cutting, biting, piercing; see INTENSE. **6.** [*Stylish] dressy, chic, in style; see FASHIONABLE.

sharpen *v.* **1.** [To make keen] grind, file, hone, put an edge on, grind to a fine edge, make sharp, make acute, whet, give an edge to, put a point on, give a fine point to.—*Ant.* FLATTEN, thicken, turn. **2.** [To make more exact] focus, bring into focus, intensify, make clear, make clearer, clarify, outline distinctly, make more distinct.—*Ant.* CONFUSE, cloud, obscure.

sharply *a.* piercingly, pointedly, distinctly; see CLEARLY 1, 2.

shatter *v.* shiver, split, burst; see BREAK 2.

shattered *a.* splintered, crushed, destroyed; see BROKEN 1.
shave *v.* shear, graze, barber, cut, use a razor, clip closely, strip, strip the hair from, tonsure, make bare, peel, skin, remove.
she *pron.* this one, this girl, this woman, that girl, that woman, a female animal; see also WOMAN 1.
shears *n.pl.* cutters, clippers, snips; see SCISSORS.
shed *n.* shelter, outbuilding, hut, lean-to, woodshed.
shed *v.* drop, let fall, give forth, shower down, cast, molt, slough, discard, exude, emit, scatter, sprinkle.
sheep *n.* lamb, ewe, ram; see ANIMAL, GOAT.
sheer *a.* **1.** [Abrupt] perpendicular, very steep, precipitous; see STEEP. **2.** [Thin] transparent, delicate, fine; see THIN 1.
sheet *n.* **1.** [A bed cover] covering, bed sheet, bedding; see CLOTH, COVER 1. **2.** [A thin, flat object] lamina, leaf, foil, veneer, layer, stratum, coat, film, ply, covering, expanse.
shelf *n.* **1.** [A ledge] rock, reef, shoal; see LEDGE. **2.** [A cupboard rack] counter, cupboard, mantelpiece, rack, bookshelf.
shell *n.* **1.** [A shell-like cover or structure] husk, crust, nut, pod, case, scale, shard, integument, eggshell, carapace, plastron. **2.** [An explosive projectile] bullet, explosive, torpedo; see WEAPON. **3.** [A crustaceous covering] *Varieties include the following:* tortoise, crustacean, bivalve, mollusk, clam, mussel, conch, snail; see also SEASHELL.
shell *v.* shuck, strip, peel off; see SKIN.
shellfish *n.* crustacean, mollusk, crustaceous animal, invertebrate, marine animal, arthropod, gastropod, bivalve. *Creatures often called shellfish include the following:* crab, lobster, clam, shrimp, prawn, crawfish, crayfish, mussel, whelk, cockle, abalone, snail.
shelter *n.* refuge, harbor, haven, sanctuary, asylum, retreat, shield, screen, defense, security, safety, guardian, protector, house, roof, tent, shack, shed, hut, shade, shadow.
shelter *v.* screen, cover, hide, conceal, guard, take in, ward, harbor, defend, protect, shield, watch over, take care of, secure, preserve, safeguard, surround, enclose, lodge, house.—*Ant.* EXPOSE, turn out, evict.
sheltered *a.* **1.** [Shaded] screened, protected, shady, veiled, covered, protective, curtained. **2.** [Protected] guarded, ensured, shielded; see SAFE, WATCHED.
sheriff *n.* county officer, county administrator, peace officer; see POLICEMAN.
shield *n.* bumper, protection, guard; see COVER 1.
shift *n.* **1.** [A change] transfer, transformation, substitution, displacement, fault, alteration, variation; see also CHANGE 1. **2.** [A working period] turn, spell, working time; see TIME 1.
shift *v.* **1.** [To change position] move, turn, stir; see CHANGE 2. **2.** [To cause to shift] displace, remove, substitute; see EXCHANGE 1. **3.** [To put in gear] change gears, downshift, put in drive; see DRIVE 2.
shin *n.* tibia, leg, limb; see BONE, LEG.
shindig* *n.* banquet, dance, dinner; see PARTY 1.
shine *v.* **1.** [To give forth light] radiate, beam, scintillate, glitter, sparkle, twinkle, glimmer, glare, glow, flash, blaze, shimmer, illuminate, blink, shoot out beams, irradiate, dazzle, bedazzle, flash, flicker. **2.** [To reflect light] glisten, gleam, glow, look good, grow bright, give back, give light, deflect, mirror; see also REFLECT 3. **3.** [To cause to shine, usually by polishing] scour, brush, polish, put a gloss on, put a finish on, finish, burnish, wax, buff, polish up, make brilliant, make glitter; see also CLEAN, PAINT 2.
shining *a.* radiant, gleaming, luminous; see BRIGHT 1.
shiny *a.* polished, sparkling, glistening; see BRIGHT 1.
ship *n.* *Types of ships include the following:* steamer, steamship, liner, freighter, landing barge, trawler, floating cannery, factory ship, ferry, clipper, square-rigged vessel, sailing ship, transport, tanker, pilot boat, junk, galleon, sampan, battleship, cruiser, destroyer, aircraft carrier, whaling vessel, bark, schooner, windjammer, yacht, dragger, cutter, sloop, tug; see also BOAT.
ship *v.* send, consign, ship out; see SEND 1.
shipment *n.* cargo, carload, purchase; see FREIGHT.
shipped *a.* transported, exported, delivered; see SENT.
shirk *v.* elude, cheat, malinger; see AVOID, EVADE.
shirt *n.* *Shirts include the following:* dress, undershirt, sport, work, cowboy, Western, long-sleeved, short-sleeved, cotton, silk, flannel, T-shirt, tank top, blouse, jersey, pullover, turtleneck; see also CLOTHES.
shiver *v.* be cold, vibrate, quiver; see SHAKE 1, WAVE 3.
shock *n.* **1.** [The effect of physical impact] crash, clash, wreck; see COLLISION. **2.** [The effect of a mental blow] excitement, hysteria, emotional upset; see CONFUSION. **3.** [The after-effect of physical harm] concussion, stupor, collapse; see ILLNESS 1, INJURY.
shock *v.* **1.** [To disturb one's self-control] startle, agitate, astound; see DISTURB. **2.** [To disturb one's sense of propriety] insult, outrage, horrify, revolt, offend, appall, abash, astound, anger, floor, shake up, disquiet, dismay. **3.** [To jar] rock, agitate, jolt; see SHAKE 2.
shocked *a.* startled, aghast, upset, astounded, offended, appalled, dismayed; see also TROUBLED.

shocking *a.* repulsive, hateful, revolting; see OFFENSIVE 2.

shoe *n.* footwear, boot, slipper, moccasin. *Footwear includes the following:* Oxford, high top, wingtip, brogue, hush puppy, sandal, pump, flat, clog, galosh, tennis shoe, cleat, jogging shoe, running shoe, ski boot, track shoe, sneaker, loafer, heels, tennies*, wedgie. **—in another's shoes** in the place of another, in other circumstances, reversal of roles; see SYMPATHETIC, UNDERSTOOD 1.

shoo *interj.* get away, begone, leave; see GET OUT.

shoot *v.* **1.** [To discharge] fire, shoot off, expel, pull the trigger, set off, torpedo, explode, ignite, blast, sharpshoot, open fire, rake, pump full of lead. **2.** [To move rapidly] dart, spurt, rush; see HURRY 1. **3.** [To kill by shooting] dispatch, murder, execute; see KILL 1.

shoot at *v.* **1.** [To fire a weapon at] shoot, fire at, take a shot at; see ATTACK 1. **2.** [*To strive for] aim, endeavor, strive; see TRY 1.

shoot the bull* *v.* chat idly, carry on a lengthy conversation, converse; see GOSSIP.

shop *n.* store, department store, retail store, thrift shop, drug store, discount house, novelty shop. **—set up shop** go into business, start, open a business; see BEGIN 1, 2. **—shut up shop** close up, go out of business, cease functioning; see CLOSE 4, STOP 2. **—talk shop** talk business, exchange views, discuss one's specialty; see GOSSIP, TALK 1.

shop *v.* shop for, look for, try to buy; see BUY.

shopkeeper *n.* manager, merchant, storekeeper; see BUSINESSMAN.

shopper *n.* bargain hunter, professional shopper, purchaser; see BUYER.

shopping *n.* purchasing, hunting, looking; see BUYING.

shopping center *n.* shops, mall, shopping mall; see BUSINESS 4, PARKING LOT.

shore *n.* beach, strand, seaside, sand, coast, seacoast, seashore, brink, bank, border, seaboard, margin, lakeside, lakeshore, riverbank, riverside.

short *a.* **1.** [Not long in space] low, skimpy, slight, not tall, not long, undersized, little, abbreviated, dwarfish, stubby, stunted, stocky, diminutive, tiny, small, dwarf, dwarfed, close to the ground, dumpy, chunky, compact, squat, thickset, pint-size, stumpy, sawed-off*, runty. **2.** [Not long in time] brief, curtailed, cut short, fleeting, not protracted, concise, unprolonged, unsustained, condensed, terse, succinct, pithy, summary, pointed, precise, bare, abridged, summarized, epigrammatic, compressed, short-term, short-lived. **3.** [Inadequate] deficient, insufficient, meager; see INADEQUATE. **—be** or **run short (of)** lack, want, run out of; see NEED. **—fall short** not reach, be inadequate, fall down; see FAIL 1, MISS 3. **—for short** as a nickname, familiarly, commonly; see NAMED 1, SO-CALLED. **—in short** that is, in summary, to make a long story short; see BRIEFLY, FINALLY 1.

shortage *n.* short fall, scant supply, curtailment; see LACK 1.

shortcoming *n.* fault, deficiency, lapse; see WEAKNESS 1.

short cut *n.* bypass, alternative, timesaver; see MEANS 1, WHY.

shorten *v.* curtail, abridge, abbreviate; see DECREASE 2.

shorter *a.* smaller, lower, not so long, briefer, more limited, more concise, more abrupt, lessened, diminished, reduced, curtailed.—*Ant.* HIGHER, longer, taller.

short-lived *a.* brief, momentary, temporary; see SHORT 2.

shortly *a.* presently, quickly, right away; see SOON.

shortness *n.* brevity, briefness, conciseness; see LENGTH 1.

shorts *n.pl.* underpants, briefs, underwear; see CLOTHES, UNDERWEAR.

shortsighted *a.* unthinking, foolish, unwary; see RASH, STUPID.

shot *n.* **1.** [A flying missile] bullet, ball, pellet, lead, projectile, buckshot, grapeshot. **2.** [An opportunity to shoot] occasion, chance, turn; see OPPORTUNITY 1. **3.** [One who shoots] gunner, rifleman, marksman; see HUNTER. **—call the shots** direct, command, supervise; see CONTROL. **—have** or **take a shot at*** endeavor, attempt, do one's best at; see TRY 1. **—like a shot** rapidly, speedily, like a bat out of hell*; see FAST 1, QUICKLY. **—shot in the arm** help, boost, assistance; see ENCOURAGEMENT.

shoulder *n.* upper arm, shoulder cut, shoulder joint; see ARM 1, 2, JOINT 1. **—cry on someone's shoulder** weep, object, shed tears; see CRY 1, COMPLAIN. **—turn** or **give a cold shoulder to** ignore, neglect, pass over; see INSULT.

shout *n.* roar, bellow, scream; see CRY 1, YELL.

shout *v.* screech, roar, scream; see YELL.

shouting *n.* cries, yelling, jeering; see CRY 1.

shove *v.* jostle, push out of one's way, shoulder; see PUSH 1.

shovel *n.* *Shovels include the following:* coal, snow, fire, miner's, irrigating, split, twisted, pronged, scoop, round-pointed; see also TOOL 1.

shovel *v.* take up, pick up, take up with a shovel, clean out, throw, move, pass, shift; see also DIG 1, LOAD 1.

show *n.* **1.** [An exhibition] presentation, exhibit, showing, exposition, expo*, display, occurrence, sight, appearance, program, flower show, boat show, home show, dog show, carnival, representation, burlesque, production, concert, act, pageant, spectacle, light show, entertainment; see also COMEDY,

DRAMA, MOVIE. **2.** [Pretense] sham, make believe, semblance; see PRETENSE 1, 2. —**for show** for sake of appearances, ostensibly, ostentatiously; see APPARENTLY. —**get** or **put the show on the road*** start, open, get started; see BEGIN 1. —**steal the show** triumph, get the best of it, win out; see DEFEAT, WIN 1.

show *v.* **1.** [To display] exhibit, manifest, present; see DISPLAY. **2.** [To explain] reveal, tell, explicate; see EXPLAIN. **3.** [To demonstrate] attest, determine, confirm; see PROVE. **4.** [To convince] teach, prove to, persuade; see CONVINCE. **5.** [To indicate] register, note, point; see RECORD 1.

showdown *n.* crisis, turning point, culmination; see CLIMAX.

shower *n.* **1.** [Water falling in drops] drizzle, mist, rainfall; see RAIN 1. **2.** [Act of cleansing the body] bathing, washing, sponging; see BATH 1.

shown *a.* **1.** [Put on display] displayed, demonstrated, advertised, exposed, set out, presented, delineated, exhibited, laid out, put up for sale, put up, put on the block.—*Ant.* WITHDRAWN, concealed, held back. **2.** [Proved] demonstrated, determined, made clear; see OBVIOUS 2.

showoff *n.* boaster, exhibitionist, egotist; see BRAGGART.

show off *v.* brag, swagger, make a spectacle of oneself; see BOAST.

showpiece *n.* masterpiece, prize, work of art; see MASTERPIECE.

show up *v.* **1.** [To arrive] appear, come, turn up; see ARRIVE. **2.** [To expose] discredit, defeat, belittle; see EXPOSE 1.

show window *n.* display window, store window, picture window; see DISPLAY.

showy *a.* flashy, glaring, gaudy; see ORNATE.

shred *n.* fragment, piece, tatter; see BIT 1.

shred *v.* slice, strip, cut into small pieces; see TEAR.

shrewd *a.* astute, ingenious, sharp; see INTELLIGENT.

shrewdly *a.* knowingly, cleverly, trickily, sagaciously, astutely, skillfully, ably, slyly, foxily, smartly, deceptively, cunningly, intelligently, judiciously, neatly, coolly, handily, facilely, adroitly, deftly, with skill, in a crafty manner, in a cunning manner, with consummate skill, knowing one's way around; see also CAREFULLY 1, DELIBERATELY.

shriek *n.* scream, screech, howl; see CRY 1, 3, YELL 1.

shriek *v.* scream, screech, squawk; see CRY 1, 2, YELL.

shrill *a.* high-pitched, piercing, penetrating, sharp, screeching, thin, deafening, earsplitting, blatant, noisy, clanging, harsh, blaring, raucous, metallic, discordant, cacophonous, acute; see also LOUD 1.—*Ant.* SOFT, low, faint.

shrine *n.* sacred place, hallowed place, altar; see CHURCH 1.

shrink *v.* withdraw, recoil, flinch; see CONTRACT 1.

shrinkage *n.* lessening, reduction, depreciation; see LOSS 1, 3.

shrivel *v.* parch, dry up, shrink; see CONTRACT 1, DRY 1.

shrub *n.* bush, fern, hedge; see PLANT.

shrubbery *n.* shrubs, bushes, hedge; see BRUSH 3.

shrug off *v.* forget, ignore, disapprove; see DOUBT, GESTURE.

shrunken *a.* withdrawn, withered, contracted; see DRY 1, WRINKLED.

shudder *n.* tremor, shuddering, shaking, trembling.

shudder *v.* quiver, quake, shiver; see SHAKE 1, WAVE 1.

shun *v.* dodge, evade, keep away from; see AVOID.

shut *a.* stopped, locked, fastened; see TIGHT 2.

shut *v.* close up, lock, seal; see CLOSE 4.

shut down *v.* close down, shut up, abandon; see STOP 1.

shut off *v.* turn off, discontinue, put a stop to; see CLOSE 4, STOP 1.

shut out *v.* keep out, evict, fence out; see REFUSE.

shutter *n.* blind, cover, shade; see CURTAIN, SCREEN 1.

shut up *v.* **1.** [To cease speaking] be quiet, stop talking, quiet, hush, quit chattering, silence, dry up*. **2.** [To close] padlock, close up, stop; see CLOSE 4.

shy *a.* retiring, bashful, girlish, modest, diffident, submissive, timid, passive, reticent, fearful, tentative, subservient, docile, compliant, humble, coy, restrained, timorous, demure.

shyness *n.* bashfulness, reserve, timidity, modesty, timidness, coyness, demureness, sheepishness, diffidence, apprehension, backwardness, nervousness, insecurity, reticence; see also RESTRAINT 1.

sick *a.* ill, ailing, unwell, disordered, diseased, feeble, frail, weak, impaired, suffering, feverish, imperfect, sickly, declining, unhealthy, rabid, indisposed, distempered, infected, invalid, delicate, infirm, rickety, peaked, broken down, physically run down, confined, laid up, under medication, bedridden, in poor health, at death's door, hospitalized, quarantined, incurable, out of kilter*, feeling poorly, sick as a dog*, in a bad way, not so hot*, under the weather*.—*Ant.* HEALTHY, hearty, well.

sicken *v.* **1.** [To contract a disease] become ill, take sick, fall ill, become diseased, fall victim to a disease, be stricken, run a temperature, run a fever, be taken with, come down with, catch a disease, acquire, waste away, suffer a relapse, break out with, catch one's death, pick up a bug*. **2.** [To offend] repel, nauseate, revolt; see DISGUST.

sickening *a.* **1.** [Contaminated] sickly, tainted, diseased; see SICK. **2.** [Disgusting] revolting, nauseous, putrid; see OFFENSIVE 2.

sickly *a.* ailing, weakly, feeble; see SICK.

sickness *n.* ill health, ailment, infirmity; see ILLNESS 1.

sick of *a.* tired of, disgusted, fed up; see DISGUSTED.

side *a.* to the side, indirect, roundabout; see OBLIQUE.

side *n.* **1.** [One of two opponents] party, contestant, combatant; see FACTION. **2.** [A face] facet, front, front side, rear, surface, outer surface, inner surface, top, bottom, elevation, view; see also PLANE 1. **—on the side** in addition to, as a bonus, additionally; see EXTRA. **—side by side** adjacent, nearby, faithfully; see LOYALLY, NEAR 1. **—take sides** join, fight for, declare oneself; see HELP, SUPPORT 2.

side effect *n.* influence, symptom, reaction; see ILLNESS 1, RESULT.

sideline *n.* avocation, interest, trade; see HOBBY.

side-step *v.* evade, elude, shun; see AVOID.

sidewalk *n.* footway, footpath, foot pavement; see PATH.

sideways *a.* indirectly, sloping, sidelong; see OBLIQUE.

side with *v.* join, aid, incline to; see FAVOR, HELP, SUPPORT 2.

siege *n.* offense, onslaught, assault; see ATTACK.

sieve *n.* strainer, sifter, colander, screen, bolt, bolting cloth, mesh, hair sieve, drum sieve, flat sieve, quarter-inch sieve, half-inch sieve, gravel sieve, flour sieve.

sift *v.* **1.** [To evaluate] investigate, scrutinize, probe; see EXAMINE. **2.** [To put through a sieve] bolt, screen, winnow, grade, sort, colander, size, strain; see also CLEAN, FILTER 2, PURIFY.

sigh *n.* deep breath, sigh of relief, expression of sorrow; see CRY 1.

sigh *v.* groan, moan, lament; see CRY 1, GASP.

sight *n.* **1.** [The power of seeing] perception, eyesight, eyes for, range of vision, apprehension, keen sight; see also VISION 1. **2.** [Something worth seeing; *often plural*] show, view, spectacle, display, scene, point of interest, local scene. **3.** [*An unsightly person] eyesore, hag, ogre; see SLOB. **—a sight for sore eyes*** beauty, welcome sight, delight; see BLESSING 2, FRIEND, VIEW. **—at first sight** hastily, without much consideration, provisionally; see QUICKLY. **—by sight** somewhat acquainted, not intimately, superficially; see UNFAMILIAR 1. **—catch sight of** glimpse, notice, see momentarily; see SEE 1. **—lose sight of** miss, fail to follow, slip up on; see FORGET, NEGLECT 1. **—on sight** at once, without hesitation, precipitately; see IMMEDIATELY, QUICKLY. **—out of sight (of)** disappeared, vanished, indiscernible; see GONE 1, INVISIBLE.

sightseeing *n.* vacationing, excursion, tour; see TRAVEL.

sightseer *n.* observer, tourist, voyager; see TRAVELER.

sign *n.* **1.** [A signal] indication, clue, omen, divination, premonition, handwriting on the wall, foreshadowing, manifestation, foreboding, foreknowledge, token, harbinger, herald, hint, symptom, assurance, prediction, portent, prophecy, mark, badge, symbol, caution, warning, beacon, flag, hand signal, wave of the arm, flash, whistle, warning bell, signal bell, signal light, high sign*. **2.** [An emblem] insignia, badge, crest; see EMBLEM. **3.** [A symbol] type, visible sign, token; see sense 1.

sign *v.* **1.** [Authorize] endorse, confirm, acknowledge; see APPROVE. **2.** [Indicate] express, signify, signal; see MEAN 1. **3.** [Hire] engage, contract, employ; see HIRE.

signal *n.* beacon, flag, omen; see SIGN 1.

signal *v.* give a sign to, flag, wave, gesture, motion, nod, beckon, warn, indicate.

signature *n.* sign, stamp, mark, name, written name, subscription, autograph, impression, indication, designation, trademark, one's John Hancock*.

signed *a.* endorsed, marked, autographed, written, undersigned, countersigned, sealed, witnessed, subscripted, registered, enlisted, signed on the dotted line.

signer *n.* cosigner, underwriter, endorser; see WITNESS.

significance *n.* weight, consequence, point; see IMPORTANCE.

significant *a.* meaningful, notable, vital; see IMPORTANT 1.

signify *v.* imply, import, purport; see MEAN 1.

silence *n.* **1.** [Absence of sound] quietness, stillness, hush, utter stillness, absolute quiet, calm, noiselessness, quiet, deep stillness, soundlessness, loss of signal, radio silence, security silence, security blackout, censorship, hush of early dawn.—*Ant.* NOISE, din, uproar. **2.** [Absence of speech] muteness, secrecy, reserve, reticence, inarticulateness, golden silence, respectful silence, sullen silence.

silence *v.* hush, quell, still; see QUIET 2.

silenced *a.* quieted, calmed, stilled, restrained, repressed, held down, held back, restricted, subdued, inhibited, coerced, suppressed, under duress, under compulsion; see also INTERRUPTED.

silent *a.* **1.** [Without noise] still, hushed, soundless; see CALM 2, QUIET. **2.** [Without speech] reserved, mute, speechless; see DUMB 1.

silently *a.* without noise, without a sound, as still as a mouse, like a shadow, in utter stillness, noiselessly, calmly, quietly, soundlessly, mutely, dumbly, in deathlike silence, like one struck dumb, speechlessly, wordlessly, as silently as falling snow.

silhouette *n.* contour, shape, profile; see FORM 1, OUTLINE 3.

sill *n.* threshold, beam, bottom of the frame; see LEDGE.

silly *a.* senseless, ridiculous, nonsensical, absurd, brainless, simpleminded, unreasonable, foolish, irrational, inconsistent, stupid, illogical, ludicrous, preposterous; see also CHILDISH.

silver *a.* silvery, pale, white, lustrous, bright, silvery white, silverlike, shimmering, resplendent, white as silver.

silverware *n.* silver, service, cutlery, flatware, hollow ware, silver plate. *Common pieces of silverware include the following:* knife, dinner knife, butter knife, fork, salad fork, cold meat fork, tablespoon, soup spoon, dessert spoon, grapefruit spoon, ice-cream spoon, iced-tea spoon, coffee spoon, teaspoon, soup ladle, gravy ladle, sugar spoon, salt spoon, spatula.

silvery *a.* shiny, glittering, brilliant; see BRIGHT 1.

similar *a.* much the same, comparable, related; see ALIKE.

similarity *n.* correspondence, likeness, resemblance, parallelism, semblance, agreement, affinity, kinship, analogy, closeness, approximation, conformity, concordance, concurrence, coincidence, congruity, parity, harmony, comparability, identity, community, relation, correlation, relationship, proportion, comparison, simile, interrelation, association, connection, similar form, like quality, point of likeness, similar appearance.—*Ant.* DIFFERENCE, variance, dissimilarity.

similarly *a.* likewise, thus, furthermore, in a like manner, correspondingly, by the same token, in addition, then, as well, too; see also SO.

simmer *v.* seethe, stew, warm; see BOIL, COOK.

simmer down *v.* cool off, be reasonable, become calm; see CALM DOWN.

simmering *a.* broiling, heated, boiling; see HOT 1.

simple *a.* **1.** [Not complicated] single, unmixed, unblended, mere, unadulterated, not complex, simplistic, not confusing, pure. **2.** [Plain] unadorned, unaffected, homely; see MODEST 2. **3.** [Easy] not difficult, mild, done with ease; see EASY 2.

simple-minded *a.* unintelligent, childish, moronic; see DULL 3, NAIVE, STUPID.

simpleton *n.* clod, idiot, bungler; see FOOL.

simplicity *n.* **1.** [The quality of being plain] plainness, stark reality, lack of ornament, lack of sophistication, bareness, homeliness, severity. **2.** [Artlessness] naiveté, plainness, primitiveness; see INNOCENCE 2.

simplified *a.* made easy, made plain, uncomplicated, clear, interpreted, broken down, cleared up, reduced; see also OBVIOUS 2.

simplify *v.* clear up, clarify, interpret; see EXPLAIN.

simplistic *a.* simplest, naive, oversimplified; see CHILDISH, SIMPLE 1.

simply *a.* **1.** [With simplicity] clearly, plainly, intelligibly, directly, candidly, sincerely, modestly, easily, quietly, naturally, honestly, frankly, unaffectedly, artlessly, ingenuously, without self-consciousness, commonly, ordinarily, matter-of-factly, unpretentiously, openly, guilelessly. **2.** [Merely] utterly, just, solely; see ONLY 2.

simulate *v.* imitate, feign, lie; see PRETEND 1.

simultaneous *a.* coincident, at the same time, concurrent, in concert, in the same breath, in chorus, at the same instant; see also EQUALLY.

simultaneously *a.* at the same time, as one, concurrently; see TOGETHER 2.

sin *n.* error, wrongdoing, trespass, wickedness, evil-doing, iniquity, immorality, crime, ungodliness, unrighteousness, veniality, disobedience to the divine will, transgression of the divine law, violation of God's law; see also CRIME. *Sins recognized as deadly include the following:* pride, covetousness, lust, anger, gluttony, envy, sloth.

sin *v.* err, do wrong, commit a crime, offend, break the moral law, break one of the Commandments, trespass, transgress, misbehave, go astray, fall, lapse, fall from grace, sow one's wild oats, wander from the straight and narrow*, backslide, live in sin*, sleep around*.

since *a., prep., & conj.* **1.** [Because] for, as, inasmuch as, considering, in consideration of, after all, seeing that, in view of, for the reason that, by reason of, on account of, in view of; see also BECAUSE. **2.** [Between the present and a previous time] ago, from the time of, subsequent to, after, following, more recently than, until now.

sincere *a.* truthful, faithful, trustworthy; see HONEST 1, RELIABLE.

sincerely *a.* truthfully, truly, really, genuinely, earnestly, aboveboard, seriously, naturally, candidly, frankly, profoundly, deeply, to the bottom of one's heart.

sincerity *n.* openness, frankness, truthfulness; see HONESTY, RELIABILITY.

sinful *a.* wicked, erring, immoral; see BAD 1, WRONG 1.

sinfully *a.* wickedly, immorally, unjustly; see WRONGLY.

sing *v.* chant, carol, warble, vocalize, trill, croon, twitter, chirp, raise a song, lift up the voice in song, burst into song.

singe *v.* brand, sear, scorch; see BURN.

singer *n.* vocalist, songster, chorister, soloist, minstrel, chanter; see also MUSICIAN.

singing *n.* warbling, crooning, chanting; see MUSIC 1.

single *a.* **1.** [Unique] sole, original, exceptional, singular, only, without equal, unequaled, peerless, unrivaled; see also RARE 2, UNIQUE, UNUSUAL 1.—*Ant.* MANY, numerous, widespread. **2.** [Individual] particular, separate, indivisible; see INDIVIDUAL, PRIVATE. **3.** [Unmarried] unwed, celibate, eligible, virginal, living alone, companionless, unattached, free, footloose, on the loose*, in the market*.—*Ant.* MARRIED, UNITED, wed.

single-handed *a.* without assistance, courageously, self-reliantly; see ALONE, BRAVELY.

single-minded *a.* stubborn, self-reliant, bigoted; see SELFISH.

singly *a.* alone, by itself, by oneself, separately, only, solely, one by one, privately, individually, once.

singular *a.* sole, one only, single; see UNIQUE.

sinister *a.* evil, bad, corrupt, perverse, dishonest, foreboding, disastrous, malignant, hurtful, harmful, injurious, dire, poisonous, adverse, unlucky, unfortunate, unfavorable; see also BAD 1.

sink *n.* sewer, basin, cesspool, washbasin, tub, pan, bowl.

sink *v.* **1.** [To go downward] descend, decline, fall, subside, drop, droop, slump, go under, immerse, go to the bottom, be submerged, settle, go to Davy Jones's locker, touch bottom, go down with the ship.—*Ant.* RISE, float, come up. **2.** [To cause to sink] submerge, scuttle, depress, immerse, engulf, overwhelm, swamp, lower, bring down, force down, cast down, let down; see also IMMERSE. **3.** [To weaken] decline, fail, fade; see WEAKEN 1. **4.** [To decrease] lessen, diminish, wane; see DECREASE 1.

sink in* *v.* impress, take hold, make an impression; see INFLUENCE.

sinner *n.* wrongdoer, delinquent, lawbreaker; see CRIMINAL.

sip *v.* taste, drink in, extract; see DRINK 1.

siren *n.* horn, whistle, signal; see ALARM.

sissy* *a.* weak, afraid, chicken*; see COWARDLY.

sister *n.* blood relative, member of the family, stepsister, half sister, big sister, kid sister*, sis*; see also RELATIVE.

sit *v.* be seated, seat oneself, take a seat, sit down, sit up, squat, perch, take a load off one's feet*, have a place, have a chair, sit in, take a chair, take a seat, take a place.—*Ant.* RISE, stand up, get up.

site *n.* locality, section, situation; see PLACE 3, POSITION 1.

sit-in *n.* demonstration, march, display; see PROTEST, STRIKE 1.

sit on or **upon** *v.* sit in on, take part in, be a part of; see COOPERATE, JOIN 2.

sit out *v.* ignore, abstain from, hold back; see NEGLECT 1, 2.

sitter *n.* baby sitter, attendant, companion; see SERVANT.

situated *a.* established, fixed, located; see PLACED.

situation *n.* **1.** [Circumstance] condition, state, state of one's affairs; see CIRCUMSTANCES 1, 2. **2.** [A physical position] location, site, spot; see PLACE 3, POSITION 1.

sit well with *v.* please, be acceptable to, gratify; see SATISFY 1.

size *n.* **1.** [Measurement] extent, area, dimension; see MEASUREMENT 2. **2.** [Magnitude] bulk, largeness, greatness, extent, vastness, scope, immensity, enormity, stature, hugeness, breadth, substance, volume, mass, extension, intensity, capacity, proportion; see also EXTENT, QUANTITY.

size up* *v.* judge, survey, scrutinize; see EXAMINE.

sizzle *n.* hiss, hissing, sputtering; see NOISE 1.

sizzle *v.* brown, grill, broil; see COOK, FRY.

skate *v.* slide, glide, skim, slip, skid, go quickly, race, ice skate, roller skate.

skeleton *n.* **1.** [Bony structure] skeletal frame, bone, support; see BONE. **2.** [Framework] draft, design, sketch; see FRAME 1.

skeptic *n.* doubter, unbeliever, freethinker; see CYNIC.

skeptical *a.* cynical, dubious, unbelieving; see DOUBTFUL, SUSPICIOUS 1.

sketch *n.* portrayal, picture, draft, design, outline, drawing, representation, painting, skeleton, figure, illustration, copy, likeness; see also PICTURE 2, PLAN 1.

sketch *v.* paint, describe, depict; see DRAW 2.

sketchily *a.* hastily, patchily, incompletely; see INADEQUATELY.

sketchy *a.* coarse, crude, preliminary; see UNFINISHED 1.

skid *v.* slip, glide, move; see SLIDE.

skill *n.* dexterity, facility, craft; see ABILITY.

skilled *a.* skillful, a hand at, proficient; see ABLE, EXPERIENCED.

skillful *a.* skilled, practiced, accomplished; see ABLE, EXPERIENCED.

skim *v.* **1.** [To pass lightly and swiftly] soar, float, sail, dart; see also FLY 1. **2.** [To remove the top; especially, to remove cream] brush, scoop, separate; see DIP 2, REMOVE 1. **3.** [To read swiftly] look through, brush over, scan; see EXAMINE, READ 1.

skimp *v.* scamp, slight, scrimp; see SACRIFICE 2, SAVE 3.

skimpy *a.* short, scanty, insufficient; see INADEQUATE.

skin *n.* epidermis, derma, cuticle, bark, peel, husk, rind, hide, coat, covering, surface, parchment. —**be no skin off one's back** or **nose*** not hurt one, do no harm, not affect one; see SURVIVE 1. —**by the skin of one's teeth** barely, scarcely, narrowly; see HARDLY. —**get under one's skin*** irritate, disturb, upset; see ENRAGE. —**save one's skin*** get away, evade, leave just in time; see ESCAPE, SURVIVE 1.
skin *v.* peel, pare, flay, scalp, shed, strip, strip off, pull off, remove the surface from, skin alive, husk, shuck, lay bare, bare.
skin-deep *a.* shallow, desultory, ignorant; see SUPERFICIAL, TRIVIAL.
skin diver *n.* scuba diver, submarine diver, deepsea diver, pearl diver, aquanaut, frogman; see also DIVER.
skinflint *n.* scrimp, tightwad, hoarder; see MISER.
skinny *a.* lean, gaunt, slender; see THIN 2.
skip *v.* hop, spring, leap; see JUMP 1.
skirmish *n.* engagement, encounter, conflict; see BATTLE, FIGHT 1.
skirt *n.* kilt, petticoat, miniskirt; see CLOTHES, DRESS 2.
skull *n.* scalp, cranium, brain case; see HEAD 1.
sky *n.* firmament, atmosphere, the blue yonder; see AIR 1, HEAVEN. —**out of a clear (blue) sky** without warning, suddenly, abruptly; see QUICKLY, SOON.
skyscraper *n.* tall building, high-rise building, high-rise; see BUILDING.
slab *n.* slice, chunk, lump; see PART 1.
slack *a.* relaxed, lax, limp; see LOOSE 1.
slack down or **off** or **up** *v.* decline, lessen, become slower; see DECREASE 1, SLOW 1.
slam *v.* **1.** [To throw with a slam] thump, fling, hurl; see THROW 1. **2.** [To shut with a slam] bang, crash, push; see CLOSE 2, 4.
slander *n.* defamation, calumny, scandal; see LIE.
slander *v.* defame, libel, defile, detract, depreciate, disparage, revile, dishonor, blaspheme, curse, attack, sully, tarnish, vilify, blot, cast a slur on, scandalize, belittle, backbite, malign, speak evil of, give a bad name, sling mud*.—*Ant.* PRAISE, applaud, eulogize.
slang *n.* cant, argot, colloquialism, pidgin English, vulgarism, lingo, bad grammar, jargon, shoptalk, vulgarity; see also JARGON 1, 2.
slant *v.* veer, lie obliquely, incline; see BEND, LEAN 1, TILT.
slanting *a.* inclining, sloping, tilting; see BENT.
slap *v.* strike, pat, spank; see HIT 1.
slapdash *a.* hasty, sluggish, impetuous; see CARELESS.
slap down *v.* rebuke, reprimand, worst; see DEFEAT 2, QUIET 2.
slap-happy *a.* out of one's head, badly beaten, dizzy; see BEATEN 1, SILLY.
slapstick *a.* absurd, droll, comical; see FUNNY 1.
slash *v.* slit, gash, sever; see CUT 1.
slaughter *n.* butchery, killing, massacre; see MURDER.
slaughter *v.* slay, murder, massacre; see BUTCHER 1, KILL.
Slav *n.* *Slavs include the following:* Russian, Bulgarian, Pole, Slovene, Slovak, Ukrainian, Bohemian, Moravian, Czech, Serb, Croat, Sorb, Deniker.
slave *n.* bondsman, bondservant, chattel, serf, toiler, menial, drudge, laborer, captive, bondsmaid, bondwoman, victim of tyranny, one of a subject people.
slavery *n.* **1.** [Bondage] subjugation, restraint, involuntary servitude; see CAPTIVITY. **2.** [Drudgery] toil, menial labor, grind; see WORK 2.
Slavic *a.* Slav, Slavophile, Slavonic, Old Slavonic, Church Slavonic. *Words referring to Slavic peoples include the following:* Cyrillic, Glagolitic, Russian, Polish, Bulgarian, Czech, Ukrainian, Bohemian, Serbian, Croatian or Croat, Bosnian, Montenegrin, Yugoslavian.
slay *v.* murder, slaughter, assassinate; see KILL 1.
sleazy *a.* shoddy, flimsy, slight; see THIN 1, WEAK 2.
sled *n.* hand sled, bobsled, sleigh, coasting sled, child's sled, toboggan, belly-bumper, pig-sticker.
sleek *a.* silken, silky, satin; see SMOOTH 1.
sleep *n.* slumber, doze, nap, rest, sound sleep, deep sleep, siesta, catnap, dream, hibernation, the sandman, snooze*, shut-eye*.
sleep *v.* slumber, doze, drowse, rest, nap, snooze, hibernate, dream, snore, nod, yawn, relax, go to bed, fall asleep, take forty winks*, catnap, turn in, hit the hay*, saw logs*, sack out*.
sleeping *a.* dormant, inert, inactive; see ASLEEP.
sleep on it* *v.* think about it, consider, ponder; see THINK 1.
sleep (something) off *v.* get over it, improve, sober up; see RECOVER 3.
sleepy *a.* dozy, somnolent, sluggish; see TIRED.
slender *a.* slim, slight, spare; see THIN 1, 2.
slice *n.* thin piece, chop, chunk; see PART 1.
slick *a.* sleek, slippery, glossy; see OILY 2, SMOOTH 1.
slide *v.* glide, skate, skim, slip, coast, skid, move along, move over, move past, pass along. —**let slide** ignore, pass over, allow to decline; see NEGLECT 1, 2.
slight *a.* **1.** [Trifling] insignificant, petty, piddling; see TRIVIAL, UNIMPORTANT. **2.** [Inconsiderable] small, sparse, scanty; see

INADEQUATE. **3.** [Delicate] frail, slender, flimsy; see DAINTY.

slightly *a.* a little, to some extent, hardly at all, scarcely any, not noticeably, unimportantly, inconsiderably, insignificantly, lightly, somewhat.

slim *a.* slender, narrow, lank; see THIN 2.

slime *n.* fungus, mire, ooze; see MUD.

slimy *a.* oozy, miry, mucky; see MUDDY 1, 2.

sling *v.* hurl, send, shoot; see THROW 1.

slink *v.* prowl, cower, lurk; see SNEAK.

slip *n.* **1.** [Error] lapse, misdeed, indiscretion; see ERROR. **2.** [Misstep] slide, skid, stumble; see FALL 1. **3.** [Undergarment] underclothing, panti-slip, bra-slip; see CLOTHES, UNDERWEAR. **—give someone the slip** get away, slip away, escape from; see LEAVE 1.

slipper *n.* house shoe, sandal, pump; see SHOE.

slippery *a.* glassy, smooth, glazed, polished, oily, waxy, soapy, greasy, slimy, icy, sleek, glistening, wet, unsafe, insecure, uncertain, tricky, shifty, slithery, slippery as an eel*.

slip-up *n.* oversight, mishap, omission; see ERROR.

slip up (on) *v.* overlook, miss, bungle; see FAIL 1.

slit *n.* split, cleavage, crevice; see HOLE 1, TEAR.

slit *v.* tear, slice, split; see CUT 1.

sliver *n.* splinter, thorn, fragment; see BIT 1, FLAKE.

slob* *n.* pig, hog, slattern, tramp, bum, yokel, ragamuffin.

slobber *v.* drip, salivate, dribble; see DROOL.

slogan *n.* catchword, rallying cry, trademark; see MOTTO, PROVERB.

slop *v.* slosh, wallow, splash, drip, spill, run over; see also DROP 1, EMPTY 1.

slope *n.* rising ground, incline, grade; see HILL.

sloppy *a.* clumsy, amateurish, mediocre; see AWKWARD, CARELESS.

slot *n.* aperture, opening, cut; see HOLE 1.

slow *a.* **1.** [Slow in motion] sluggish, laggard, deliberate, gradual, loitering, leaden, creeping, inactive, slow moving, crawling, slow-paced, leisurely, as slow as molasses in January*.—*Ant.* FAST, swift, rapid. **2.** [Slow in starting] dilatory, procrastinating, delaying, postponing, idle, indolent, tardy, lazy, apathetic, phlegmatic, inactive, sluggish, heavy, quiet, drowsy, inert, sleepy, lethargic, stagnant, negligent, listless, dormant, potential, latent; see also LATE 1.—*Ant.* IMMEDIATE, alert, instant. **3.** [Slow in producing an effect] belated, behindhand, backward, overdue, delayed, long-delayed, behindtime, retarded, detained, hindered.—*Ant.* BUSY, diligent, industrious. **4.** [Dull or stupid] stolid, tame, uninteresting; see DULL 3.

slow *v.* **1.** [To become slower] slacken, slow up, slow down, lag, loiter, relax, procrastinate, stall, let up, wind down, ease up. **2.** [To cause to become slower] delay, postpone, moderate, reduce, retard, detain, decrease, diminish, hinder, hold back, keep waiting, brake, curtail, check, curb, cut down, rein in, cut back.

slowly *a.* moderately, gradually, nonchalantly, gently, leisurely, at one's leisure, taking one's own sweet time*.

slowness *n.* sluggishness, apathy, lethargy; see INDIFFERENCE.

sluggish *a.* inactive, torpid, indolent; see LAZY 1, SLOW 1, 2.

sluggishness *n.* apathy, drowsiness, lethargy; see FATIGUE, LAZINESS.

slum *a.* ghetto, poverty-stricken, crowded; see POOR 1.

slum *n.* cheap housing, poor district, tenement neighborhood, rat-nest*, the wrong side of the tracks*.

slump *n.* depreciation, slip, descent; see DROP 2.

slump *v.* decline, depreciate, decay; see SINK 1.

slush *n.* melting snow, mire, refuse; see MUD.

slut *n.* wench, whore, hooker*; see PROSTITUTE.

sly *a.* wily, tricky, foxy, shifty, crafty, shrewd, designing, deceitful, scheming, deceiving, intriguing, cunning, unscrupulous, deceptive, conniving, calculating, plotting, dishonest, treacherous, underhanded, sneaking, double-dealing, faithless, traitorous, sharp, smart, ingenious, cagey*, dishonorable, crooked, mean, dirty, double-crossing*, slick*, smooth*, slippery, shady*.

slyly *a.* secretly, cunningly, furtively; see CLEVERLY.

smack down* *v.* rebuke, take aback, humiliate; see DEFEAT 2, 3, HUMILIATE.

small *a.* **1.** [Little in size] tiny, diminutive, miniature; see LITTLE 1. **2.** [Little in quantity] scanty, short, meager; see INADEQUATE. **3.** [Unimportant] trivial, insignificant, unessential; see SHALLOW 2, UNIMPORTANT.

smaller *a.* tinier, lesser, petite; see LESS, SHORTER.

smallness *n.* littleness, narrowness, diminutive size, shortness, brevity, slightness, scantiness, tininess.

small talk *n.* chitchat, light conversation, banter, table talk, babble.

smart *a.* **1.** [Intelligent] clever, bright, quick; see INTELLIGENT. **2.** [Impudent] bold, brazen, forward; see RUDE 2.

smart *v.* sting, be painful, burn; see HURT 1.

smart aleck* *n.* showoff, boaster, life of the party; see BRAGGART.

smash *n.* crash, breakup, breaking; see BLOW.

smash *v.* crack, shatter, crush, burst, shiver, fracture, break, demolish, destroy, batter, crash, wreck, break up, overturn, overthrow, lay in ruins, raze, topple, tumble.

smashed *a.* wrecked, crushed, mashed; see BROKEN 1.

smear *v.* **1.** [To spread] cover, coat, apply; see PAINT 2, SPREAD 3. **2.** [To slander] defame, vilify, libel; see INSULT, SLANDER.

smell *n.* **1.** [A pleasant smell] fragrance, odor, scent, perfume, essence, aroma, bouquet. **2.** [An unpleasant smell] malodor, stench, stink, mustiness, foulness, uncleanness, fume. **3.** [The sense of smell] smelling, detection, olfaction; see AWARENESS.

smell *v.* **1.** [To give off odor] perfume, scent, exhale, emanate, stink, stench. **2.** [To use the sense of smell] scent, sniff, inhale, snuff, nose out, get a whiff of; see also BREATHE.

smelly *a.* stinking, foul, fetid; see RANK 2.

smile *n.* grin, smirk, tender look, friendly expression, delighted look, joyous look; see also LAUGH.

smile *v.* beam, be gracious, look happy, look delighted, look pleased, break into a smile, look amused, smirk, grin; see also LAUGH.

smiling *a.* bright, with a smile, sunny, beaming; see also HAPPY.

smirk *n.* leer, grin, smile; see SNEER.

smith *n.* metalworker, forger, metallurgist; see CRAFTSMAN, WORKMAN.

smog *n.* high fog, smoke haze, haze, mist, air pollution; see also SMOKE.

smoke *n.* vapor, fume, gas, soot, reek, haze, smudge, smog.

smoke *v.* **1.** [To give off smoke] burn, fume, smudge, smoke up, smolder, reek. **2.** [To use smoke, especially from tobacco] puff, inhale, smoke a pipe, smoke cigarettes, use cigars.

smoked *a.* cured, dried, kippered; see PRESERVED 2.

smoke out *v.* uncover, reveal, find; see DISCOVER.

smoky *a.* smoking, smoldering, reeking; see BURNING.

smolder *v.* fume, consume, steam; see BURN, SMOKE 1.

smooth *a.* **1.** [Without bumps] flat, plane, flush, horizontal, unwrinkled, level, monotonous, unrelieved, unruffled, mirrorlike, quiet, still, tanquil, glossy, glassy, lustrous, smooth as glass.—*Ant.* ROUGH, steep, broken. **2.** [Without jerks] uniform, regular, even, invariable, steady, stable, fluid, flowing, rhythmic, constant, continuous. **3.** [Without hair] shaven, beardless, whiskerless, clean-shaven, smooth-faced, smooth-chinned; see also BALD.—*Ant.* HAIRY, bearded, unshaven.

smooth *v.* even, level, flatten, grade, iron, polish, varnish, gloss, clear the way, smooth the path.

smoothly *a.* flatly, sleekly, placidly; see EASILY, EVENLY 1.

smooth over *v.* conceal, cover up, hush up; see HIDE 1.

smorgasbord *n.* buffet, self-service meal, salad course; see FOOD, LUNCH, MEAL 2.

smother *v.* stifle, suffocate, suppress; see CHOKE, EXTINGUISH.

smothered *a.* **1.** [Extinguished] drenched, consumed, drowned, put out, not burning, quenched, snuffed. **2.** [Strangled] choked, asphyxiated, breathless; see DEAD 1.

smudge *n.* smirch, spot, soiled spot; see BLEMISH.

smug *a.* self-satisfied, complacent, conceited, pleased with oneself, snobbish, egotistical, self-righteous, stuck up*, stuck on oneself*.

snack *n.* luncheon, slight meal, hasty repast; see LUNCH, MEAL 2.

snack bar *n.* cafeteria, lunchroom, cafe; see RESTAURANT.

snag *n.* obstacle, hindrance, knot; see BARRIER, DIFFICULTY 1.

snake *n.* reptile, serpent, vermin. *Common snakes include the following:* viper, water moccasin, copperhead, black snake, rattlesnake, python, cobra, bull snake, coral snake, blue racer, garter snake, gopher snake, king snake, milk snake, water snake, boa or boa constrictor, adder, puff adder, anaconda, fer-de-lance.

snap *n.* clasp, fastening, catch; see FASTENER.

snap *v.* catch, clasp, lock; see CLOSE 4, FASTEN.

snap at *v.* vent one's anger at, jump down one's throat, take it out on; see GET ANGRY.

snap out of it *v.* pull through, get over, revive; see RECOVER 3.

snapshot *n.* snap*, candid camera shot, action shot; see PHOTOGRAPH, PICTURE 2, 3.

snare *n.* trap, lure, decoy; see TRICK 1.

snarl *n.* **1.** [Confusion] tangle, entanglement, complication; see CONFUSION. **2.** [A snarling sound] grumble, gnarl, angry words; see GROWL.

snarl *v.* growl, gnarl, grumble, mutter, threaten, bark, yelp, snap, gnash the teeth, bully, quarrel.

snatch *v.* jerk, grasp, steal; see SEIZE 1, 2.

sneak *v.* skulk, slink, creep, slip away, move secretly, hide, prowl, lurk; see also EVADE.

sneaky *a.* tricky, deceitful, unreliable; see DISHONEST.

sneer *v.* mock, scoff, jeer, taunt, slight, scorn, decry, belittle, detract, lampoon, ridicule, deride, caricature, laugh at, look down, insult, disdain, satirize, condemn, give the raspberry*, give the Bronx cheer*.

sneeze *n.* wheezing, cough, sniffle; see COLD 2, FIT 1.

snicker *v.* giggle, titter, chuckle; see LAUGH.

sniff *v.* detect, scent, inhale; see SMELL 2.

snip *v.* clip, slice, nip; see CUT 1.
snob *n.* showoff, pretender, upstart; see BRAGGART.
snobbish *a.* ostentatious, pretentious, overbearing; see EGOTISTIC.
snooty* *a.* conceited, nasty, egotistical; see EGOTISTIC.
snore *v.* snort, wheeze, sleep; see BREATHE.
snotty* *a.* impudent, like a spoiled brat, nasty; see RUDE 2.
snout *n.* muzzle, proboscis, nozzle; see NOSE 1.
snow *n.* **1.** [A snowstorm] blizzard, snowfall, snow flurry; see STORM. **2.** [Frozen vapor] snow crystal, snowflake, slush, sleet, snowdrift, snowbank, powder snow, snow pack, snowfall, fall of snow.
snow *v.* storm, blizzard, squall, howl, blow, cover, pelt, shower, sleet.
snub *v.* ignore, disregard, disdain; see NEGLECT 1.
snug *a.* **1.** [Cozy] homelike, secure, sheltered; see COMFORTABLE 1, WARM 1. **2.** [Close in fit] trim, well-built, close; see TIGHT 3.
so *a.* **1.** [To a degree] very, this much, so large, vaguely, indefinitely, extremely, infinitely, remarkably, unusually, so much, extremely, in great measure, in some measure; see also SUCH. **2.** [Thus] and so on, and so forth, in such manner, in this way, even so, in this degree, to this extent; see also THUS. **3.** [Accordingly] then, therefore, consequently; see ACCORDINGLY.
soak *v.* **1.** [To drench] wet, immerse, dip, immerge, water, percolate, permeate, drown, saturate, pour into, pour on, wash over, flood; see also MOISTEN. **2.** [To remain in liquid] steep, soften, be saturated, be pervaded, sink into, waterlog. **3.** [To absorb] dry, sop, mop; see ABSORB.
soaked *a.* sodden, saturated, wet, wet through, drenched, soggy, dripping, seeping, immersed, steeped, dipped, flooded, drowned, sunk into, waterlogged.
soap *n.* solvent, softener, cleanser, soapsuds. *Varieties and forms of soap include the following:* bar, liquid, glycerine, saddle, powdered, green, perfumed, bath, laundry, soap flakes; see also CLEANSER.
sob *n.* weeping, bewailing, convulsive sighs; see CRY 3.
sob *v.* lament, sigh convulsively, weep; see CRY 1.
sober *a.* solemn, serious, sedate, clear-headed, not drunk, calm, grave, temperate, abstemious, abstinent, abstaining, steady; see also MODERATE 4.
soberly *a.* moderately, temperately, abstemiously, solemnly, gravely, sedately, in a subdued manner, quietly, regularly, steadily, calmly, coolly, seriously, somberly, staidly, earnestly, dispassionately, fairly, justly.
so-called *a.* commonly named, nominal, professed, doubtfully called, allegedly, thus termed, wrongly named, popularly supposed, erroneously accepted as, usually supposed.
sociable *a.* affable, genial, companionable; see FRIENDLY.
social *a.* genial, amusing, entertaining, companionable, pleasurable, civil, polite, polished, informative, mannerly, pleasure-seeking, hospitable, pleasant.
socialist *n.* Marxist, communist, radical; see RADICAL.
socialistic *a.* Marxist, communistic, social-democrat, non-capitalistic; see also DEMOCRATIC, RADICAL.
socially *a.* politely, civilly, courteously, hospitably, companionably, entertainingly, amusingly, cordially, genially, sociably.
social science *n.* study of man and social phenomena, the humanities, science, study of society, social studies; see also ECONOMICS, GEOGRAPHY, HISTORY, POLITICS, PSYCHOLOGY, SCIENCE 1, SOCIOLOGY.
social security *n.* social insurance, old age insurance, disability insurance, unemployment insurance, the dole, social security payments, retirement.
social service *n.* welfare work, aid for the needy, charity, philanthropy.
society *n.* **1.** [Friendly association] friendship, social intercourse, fellowship; see ORGANIZATION 2. **2.** [Organized humanity] the public, civilization, culture, nation, community, human groupings, the people, the world at large, social life.
sociology *n.* study of society, cultural anthropology, social psychology, analysis of human institutions; see also SOCIAL SCIENCE.
sock *n.* stocking, hose, silk stocking; see HOSIERY.
socket *n.* holder, opening, cavity; see JOINT 1.
soda *n.* soda water, carbonated water, mineral water; see DRINK 2.
sofa *n.* couch, divan, love seat; see FURNITURE.
so far *a.* thus far, up to now, to here; see HERE, NOW 1.
soft *a.* **1.** [Soft to the touch] smooth, satiny, velvety, silky, delicate, fine, thin, flimsy, limp, fluffy, feathery, downy, woolly, doughy, spongy, mushy.—*Ant.* HARSH, rough, flinty. **2.** [Soft to the eye] dull, dim, quiet, shaded, pale, light, pastel, faint, blond, misty, hazy, dusky, delicate, pallid, ashen, tinted; see also SHADY.—*Ant.* BRIGHT, glaring, brilliant. **3.** [Soft to the ear] low, melodious, faraway; see FAINT 3. —**be soft on** treat lightly, not condemn, fail to attack; see FAVOR, NEGLECT 1.
soften *v.* dissolve, lessen, diminish, disintegrate, become tender, become mellow, thaw, melt, moderate, bend, give, yield,

relax, relent, mellow, modify, mollify, appease, mash, knead, temper, tone down, qualify, tenderize, weaken.—*Ant.* STRENGTHEN, increase, tone up.

softhearted *a.* tender, kindhearted, humane; see KIND.

softness *n.* mellowness, impressibility, plasticity; see FLEXIBILITY.

soggy *a.* mushy, spongy, saturated; see SOAKED, WET 1.

soil *n.* dirt, loam, clay; see EARTH 2.

soil *v.* stain, sully, spoil; see DIRTY.

soiled *a.* stained, tainted, ruined; see DIRTY 1.

sold *a.* **1.** [Sold out] disposed of, gone, taken; see SOLD OUT. **2.** [*Convinced] pleased with, impressed, taken with; see SATISFIED.

soldier *n.* warrior, fighter, private, enlisted man, draftee, volunteer, conscript, commando, mercenary, cadet, ranks, selectee, commissioned officer, noncommissioned officer, recruit, veteran, militant, marine, infantryman, guerrilla, guardsman, scout, sharpshooter, artilleryman, gunner, engineer, airman, bomber pilot, fighter pilot, paratrooper, machine-gunner, G.I. Joe*, grunt*.

sold out *a.* out of, all sold, out of stock, not in stock, gone, depleted.

sole *a.* only one, no more than one, remaining; see INDIVIDUAL, SINGLE 1.

solely *a.* singly, undividedly, singularly; see INDIVIDUALLY, ONLY 1.

solemn *a.* grave, serious, sober, earnest, intense, deliberate, heavy, austere, somber, dignified, staid, sedate, moody, pensive, brooding, grim, stern, thoughtful, reflective.

solemnly *a.* sedately, gravely, impressively; see SERIOUSLY 2.

solid *a.* **1.** [Firm in position] stable, fixed, rooted; see FIRM 1. **2.** [Firm or close in texture] compact, hard, substantial; see FIRM 2, THICK 1. **3.** [Reliable] dependable, trustworthy, steadfast; see RELIABLE. **4.** [Continuous] uninterrupted, continued, unbroken; see CONSECUTIVE, REGULAR 3.

solid *n.* cube, cone, pyramid, cylinder, block, prism, sphere.

solidification *n.* hardening, freezing, calcification, ossification, stiffening, setting, crystallization, fossilization, compression, coagulation, concentration.

solidify *v.* set, fix, crystallize; see COMPRESS, HARDEN, THICKEN.

solitary *a.* sole, only, alone, single, secluded, companionless, lonely, separate, individual, isolated, singular.—*Ant.* ACCOMPANIED, thick, attended.

solitude *n.* isolation, seclusion, retirement; see SILENCE 1.

soluble *a.* dissolvable, solvent, emulsifiable, dispersible, water-soluble, fat-soluble.

solution *n.* **1.** [Explanation] interpretation, resolution, clarification; see ANSWER. **2.** [Fluid] suspension, solvent, juice; see LIQUID.

solve *v.* figure out, work out, reason out, think out, find out, puzzle out, decipher, unravel, interpret, explain, resolve, answer, decode, get to the bottom of, get right, hit upon a solution, work, do, settle, clear up, untangle, elucidate, fathom, unlock, determine, hit the nail on the head, put two and two together, have it.

somber *a.* melancholy, dreary, gloomy; see DISMAL.

some *a.* few, a few, a little, a bit, part of, more than a few, more than a little, any.

some *pron.* any, a few, a number, an amount, a part, a portion, more or less.

somebody *pron.* someone, some person, a person, one, anybody, he, a certain person, this person, so-and-so, whoever.

someday *a.* sometime, one time, one time or another, at a future time, anytime, one day, one of these days, after a while, subsequently, finally, eventually.

somehow *a.* in some way, in one way or another, by some means, somehow or other, by hook or by crook, anyhow, after a fashion, with any means at one's disposal.

someone *pron.* some person, one, individual; see SOMEBODY.

something *pron.* event, object, portion, anything, being; see also THING 1, 8.

sometime *a.* one day, in a time to come, in the future; see SOMEDAY.

sometimes *a.* at times, at intervals, now and then; see SELDOM.

somewhat *a.* a little, to a degree, to some extent; see MODERATELY, SLIGHTLY.

somewhere *a.* in some place, here and there, around, in one place or another, someplace, about, around somewhere, kicking around*, any old place*.

son *n.* male child, offspring, descendant, foster son, dependent, scion, heir, boy, junior, chip off the old block, his father's son.

song *n.* melody, lyric, strain, verse, poem, musical expression; see also MUSIC 1. —**(big) song and dance*** drivel, boasting, pretense; see NONSENSE 1, 2. —**for a song** cheaply, at a bargain, for almost nothing; see CHEAP 1.

sonic boom *n.* report, crash, blast; see EXPLOSION, SOUND 2.

soon *a.* before long, in a short time, presently, in due time, shortly, forthwith, quickly, in a minute, in a second, in short order; see also SOMEDAY.

sooner or later *a.* eventually, inevitably, certainly; see SOMEDAY, SURELY.

soot *n.* carbon, smoke, grit; see RESIDUE.

soothe *v.* quiet, tranquilize, alleviate, calm, relax, mollify, help, pacify, lighten, unburden, console, cheer; see also COMFORT 1, EASE 1, 2, RELIEVE.

sophisticated *a.* refined, adult, well-bred; see CULTURED, MATURE.

sophistication *n.* elegance, refinement, finesse; see COMPOSURE.

soppy *a.* soaked, drippy, damp; see WET 1, 2.

sorcerer *n.* witch, wizard, alchemist; see MAGICIAN.

sorcery *n.* enchantment, divination, alchemy; see MAGIC 1, WITCHCRAFT.

sore *a.* **1.** [Tender] painful, hurtful, raw, aching, sensitive, irritated, irritable, distressing, bruised, angry, inflamed, burned, unpleasant, ulcerated, abscessed, uncomfortable. **2.** [*Angry] irked, resentful, irritated; see ANGRY.

sore *n.* cut, bruise, wound, boil, lesion, ulcer, hurt, abscess, gash, stab, soreness, discomfort, injury; see also PAIN 2.

sorely *a.* extremely, painfully, badly; see SO 1, VERY.

sorrow *n.* sadness, anguish, pain; see GRIEF.

sorrow *v.* bemoan, bewail, regret; see MOURN.

sorrowful *a.* grieved, afflicted, in sorrow, in mourning, depressed, dejected; see also SAD 1.

sorrowfully *a.* regretfully, weeping, in sadness; see SADLY.

sorry *a.* **1.** [Penitent] contrite, repentant, conscience-stricken, touched, softened, remorseful, regretful, sorrowful, apologetic. **2.** [Inadequate in quantity or quality] poor, paltry, trifling, cheap, mean, shabby, stunted, beggarly, scrubby, small, trivial, unimportant, insignificant, worthless, dismal, pitiful, despicable; see also INADEQUATE.—*Ant.* **ENOUGH,** plentiful, adequate.

sort *n.* species, description, class; see KIND 2, VARIETY 2. **—out of sorts** irritated, upset, in a bad mood; see ANGRY, TROUBLED.

sort *v.* file, assort, class; see CLASSIFY, DISTRIBUTE, ORDER 3.

sort of* *a.* somewhat, to a degree, kind of*; see MODERATELY, SLIGHTLY.

so-so *a.* ordinary, mediocre, average; see COMMON 1, DULL 4, FAIR 2.

sought *a.* wanted, needed, desired; see HUNTED.

soul *n.* **1.** [Essential nature] spiritual being, heart, substance, individuality, disposition, cause, personality, force, essence, genius, principle, ego, psyche, life. **2.** [The more lofty human qualities] courage, love, affection, honor, duty, idealism, philosophy, culture, heroism, art, poetry, reverence, sense of beauty. **3.** [A person] human being, man, being; see PERSON 1.

sound *a.* **1.** [Healthy] hale, hearty, well; see HEALTHY. **2.** [Firm] solid, stable, safe; see RELIABLE. **3.** [Sensible] reasonable, rational, prudent; see SENSIBLE. **4.** [Free from defect] flawless, unimpaired, undecayed; see WHOLE 2.

sound *n.* **1.** [Something audible] vibration, din, racket; see NOISE 1. **2.** [The quality of something audible] tonality, resonance, note, timbre, tone, pitch, intonation, accent, character, quality, softness, lightness, mournfulness, loudness, reverberation, ringing, vibration, modulation, discord, consonance, harmony. **3.** [Water between an island and the mainland] strait, bay, canal; see CHANNEL.

sound *v.* vibrate, echo, resound, reverberate, shout, sing, whisper, murmur, clatter, clank, rattle, blow, blare, bark, ring out, explode, thunder, buzz, rumble, hum, jabber, jangle, whine, crash, bang, boom, reflect, burst, chatter, creak, clang, roar, babble, clap, patter, prattle, clink, toot, cackle, clack, thud, slam, smash, thump, snort, shriek, moan, quaver, trumpet, croak, caw, quack, squawk.

sounding *a.* ringing, thudding, bumping, roaring, calling, thundering, booming, crashing, clattering, clinking, clanging, tinkling, whispering, pinging, rattling, rumbling, ticking, crying, clicking, echoing, pattering, clucking, chirping, peeping, growling, grunting, bellowing, murmuring, whirring, splattering, screeching, screaming, squealing.

sound out *v.* probe, feel out, feel, put out a feeler, send up a trial balloon, see how the land lies, get the lay of the land, see which way the wind blows; see also EXAMINE, EXPERIMENT.

soundproof *a.* soundproofed, silent, soundless; see QUIET.

soup *n.* *Soups include the following:* beef, broth, bouillon, consommé, split pea, noodle, vegetable, potato, French onion, chicken, tomato, celery, minestrone, borscht, clam chowder, Scotch broth, bouillabaisse; see also BROTH, FOOD, STEW.

soupçon *n.* dash, drop, hint; see DASH 3.

sour *a.* acid, tart, vinegary, fermented, rancid, musty, turned, acrid, salty, bitter, caustic, cutting, stinging, acrid, harsh, irritating, unsavory, tangy, briny, brackish, sharp, keen, biting, pungent, curdled, unripe.

sour *v.* turn, ferment, spoil, make sour, curdle.

source *n.* beginning, cause, root; see ORIGIN 2, 3.

south *a.* **1.** [Situated to the south] southern, southward, on the south side of, in the south, toward the equator, southernmost, toward the South Pole, southerly, tropical, equatorial, in the torrid zone. **2.** [Moving south] southward, to the south, southbound, headed south, southerly, in a southerly direction, toward the equator. **3.** [Coming from the south] headed north, northbound, out of the south, from the south, toward the North Pole; see also NORTH 2.

south *n.* southland, southern section, southern region, tropics, tropical region, equatorial region, southern hemisphere.

South *n.* the Sunny South, South Atlantic States, the Confederacy, the Old South, Pre-Civil War South, antebellum South, Southern United States, the New South, the Deep South, Sunbelt, way down south, Dixie, southland; see also UNITED STATES.

southeast *a. Points of the compass between south and east include the following:* east by south, east-southeast, southeast by east, southeast, southeast by south, south by east, south-southeast; see also DIRECTION.

southern *a.* in the south, of the south, from the south, toward the south, southerly; see also SOUTH 1.

southwest *a. Points of the compass between south and west include the following:* south by west, south-southwest, southwest by south, southwest, southwest by west, west-southwest, west by south; see also DIRECTION.

souvenir *n.* memento, keepsake, relic; see MEMORIAL.

Soviet Union *n.* USSR, CCCP, Union of Soviet Socialist Republics, the Soviets, New Russia, Soviet Russia; see also EUROPE, RUSSIA.

sow *v.* seed, scatter, plant, broadcast, drill in, drill seed, use a drill seeder, use a broadcast seeder, strew, put in small grain, do the seeding.

sowed *a.* scattered, cast, broadcast, spread, distributed, dispersed, strewn, planted.

spa *n.* baths, spring, curative bath; see RESORT 2.

space *n.* **1.** [The infinite regions] outer space, infinite distance, infinity, interstellar space, interplanetary space, the universe, cosmos, solar system, galaxy, the beyond; see also EXPANSE.—*Ant.* BOUNDARY, measure, definite area. **2.** [Room] expanse, scope, range; see EXTENT. **3.** [A place] area, location, reservation; see PLACE 2.

space-age *a.* twentieth-century, contemporary, recent; see MODERN 1.

spacecraft *n.* flying saucer, capsule, orbiter, space shuttle, unidentified flying object, UFO, spaceship, rocket, space station, space platform, weather satellite, spy satellite; see also SATELLITE 2.

spaced *a.* divided, distributed, dispersed; see SEPARATED.

spacious *a.* capacious, roomy, vast; see BIG 1.

spade *n.* implement, garden tool, digging tool; see TOOL 1.

Spanish *a.* Spanish-speaking, Iberian, Romance, Hispanic, Catalan, Castilian, Galician, Andalusian, Basque, South American, Spanish-American, Mexican, Latin American.

spank *v.* whip, chastise, thrash; see BEAT 1, PUNISH.

spare *a.* superfluous, auxiliary, additional; see EXTRA.

spare *v.* pardon, forgive, be merciful; see PITY, SAVE 1.

spark *n.* glitter, glow, sparkle; see FIRE 1.

sparkle *v.* glitter, glisten, twinkle; see SHINE 1.

sparse *a.* scattered, scanty, meager; see INADEQUATE, RARE 1.

spasm *n.* convulsion, seizure, contraction; see FIT 1.

spatter *v.* splash, spot, wet, sprinkle, soil, scatter, stain, dash, dot, speck, speckle, shower, dribble, spray.

speak *v.* **1.** [To utter] vocalize, pronounce, express; see UTTER. **2.** [To communicate] converse, articulate, chat; see TALK 1. **3.** [To deliver a speech] lecture, declaim, deliver; see ADDRESS 2. **—so to speak** that is to say, in a manner of speaking, as the saying goes*; see ACCORDINGLY. **—to speak of** somewhat, a little, not much; see SOME.

speaker *n.* speechmaker, orator, lecturer, public speaker, preacher, spokesman, spellbinder, talker.

speak for itself *v.* account for, be self-explanatory, vindicate; see EXPLAIN.

speaking *a.* oral, verbal, vocal; see TALKING.

speak out *v.* insist, assert, make oneself heard; see DECLARE.

speak well of *v.* commend, recommend, support; see PRAISE 1.

spear *n.* lance, javelin, bayonet; see WEAPON.

special *a.* specific, particular, appropriate, peculiar, proper, individual, unique, restricted, exclusive, defined, limited, reserved, specialized, determinate, distinct, select, choice, definite, marked, designated, earmarked; see also UNUSUAL 1, 2.

special* *n.* sale item, feature, prepared dish; see MEAL 2, SALE 1, 2.

specialist *n.* expert, devotee, master, ace, virtuoso, veteran, scholar, professional, authority, connoisseur, technician.—*Ant.* AMATEUR, beginner, novice.

specialize *v.* work in exclusively, go in for, limit oneself to; see PRACTICE 2.

specialized *a.* specific, for a particular purpose, functional; see SPECIAL.

specialty *n.* practice, work, special interest; see HOBBY, JOB 1.

species *n.pl.* class, variety, sort; see DIVISION 2, KIND 2.

specific *a.* particular, distinct, precise; see DEFINITE 1, 2, SPECIAL.

specifically *a.* particularly, individually, characteristically; see ESPECIALLY.

specification *n.* designation, stipulation, blueprint; see PLAN 1, 2, REQUIREMENT 1.

specified *a.* particularized, detailed, precise; see NECESSARY.

specify *v.* name, designate, stipulate; see CHOOSE.

specimen *n.* individual, part, unit; see EXAMPLE.

speck *n.* spot, iota, mite; see BIT 1.

speckled *a.* specked, dotted, motley; see SPOTTED 1.

spectacle *n.* scene, representation, exhibition; see DISPLAY, VIEW. —**make a spectacle of oneself** show off, act ridiculously, play the fool; see MISBEHAVE.

spectacular *a.* striking, magnificent, dramatic; see IMPRESSIVE.

spectator *n.* beholder, viewer, onlooker; see OBSERVER.

speculate *v.* contemplate, meditate, consider; see THINK 1.

speech *n.* **1.** [Language] tongue, mother tongue, native tongue; see LANGUAGE 1. **2.** [The power of audible expression] talk, utterance, articulation, diction, pronunciation, expression, locution, discourse, vocalization, oral expression, parlance, enunciation, communication, prattle, conversation, chatter. **3.** [An address] lecture, discourse, oration, pep talk*, harangue, sermon, dissertation, homily, exhortation, eulogy, recitation, talk, rhetoric, tirade, bombast, diatribe, commentary, appeal, invocation; see also COMMUNICATION.

speechless *a.* silent, inarticulate, mum; see DUMB 1, MUTE.

speed *n.* swiftness, briskness, activity, eagerness, haste, hurry, acceleration, dispatch, velocity, readiness, agility, liveliness, quickness, momentum, rate, pace, alacrity, promptness, expedition, rapidity, rush, urgency, headway, fleetness, breeze*, good clip, lively clip, steam*.

speed *v.* ride hard, go like the wind, gear up, roll, bowl, give it the gun*, go fast, cover ground, gun the motor*, give her the gas*, go all out, break the sound barrier; see also RACE 1.

speed up *v.* **1.** [To accelerate] go faster, increase speed, move into a higher speed; see RACE 1. **2.** [To cause to accelerate] promote, further, get things going; see URGE 3.

speedy *a.* quick, nimble, expeditious; see FAST 1.

spell *n.* **1.** [A charm] trance, talisman, amulet; see CHARM 1. **2.** [A period of time] term, interval, season; see TIME 1. —**cast a spell on** or **over** enchant, bewitch, beguile; see CHARM. —**under a spell** enchanted, bewitched, unable to resist; see CHARMED.

spell out *v.* make clear, go into detail, simplify; see EXPLAIN.

spend *v.* consume, deplete, waste, dispense, contribute, donate, give, liquidate, exhaust, squander, disburse, allocate, misspend, pay, discharge, lay out, pay up, settle, use up, throw away, foot the bill*, fork out*, ante up*, open the purse, shell out*, blow*.—*Ant.* SAVE, keep, conserve.

spent *a.* used, consumed, disbursed; see FINISHED 1.

sphere *n.* ball, globule, orb; see CIRCLE 1.

spice *n.* seasoning, pepper, cinnamon, nutmeg, ginger, cloves, salt, paprika, oregano, anise, coriander, allspice, savor, relish; see also FLAVORING.

spicy *a.* pungent, piquant, keen, fresh, aromatic, fragrant, seasoned, tangy, savory, flavorful, tasty; see also SALTY, SOUR.

spider *n. Common spiders include the following:* black widow, trapdoor, wolf, jumping, hunting, crab, burrowing, tarantula.

spigot *n.* plug, valve, tap; see FAUCET.

spill *v.* lose, scatter, drop, spill over, run out; see also EMPTY 2.

spilled *a.* poured out, lost, run out; see EMPTY.

spin *n.* circuit, rotation, gyration; see REVOLUTION 1, TURN 1.

spin *v.* revolve, twirl, rotate; see TURN 1.

spine *n.* **1.** [A spikelike protrusion] thorn, prick, spike, barb, quill, ray, thistle, needle; see also POINT 2. **2.** [A column of vertebrae] spinal column, ridge, backbone, vertebrae; see also BONE.

spineless *a.* timid, fearful, frightened; see COWARDLY, WEAK 3.

spinster *n.* unmarried woman, virgin, single woman, old maid, bachelor girl*; see also WOMAN 1.

spiny *a.* pointed, barbed, spiked; see SHARP 1.

spiral *a.* winding, circling, coiled, whorled, radial, curled, rolled, scrolled, helical, screw-shaped, wound.

spirit *n.* **1.** [Life] breath, vitality, animation; see LIFE 1. **2.** [Soul] psyche, essence, substance; see SOUL 2. **3.** [A supernatural being] vision, apparition, specter; see GHOST, GOD. **4.** [Courage] boldness, ardor, enthusiasm; see COURAGE. **5.** [Feeling; *often plural*] humor, frame of mind, temper; see FEELING 4, MOOD 1.

spirited *a.* lively, vivacious, animated; see ACTIVE.

spiritless *a.* dull, apathetic, unconcerned; see INDIFFERENT.

spiritual *a.* refined, pure, holy; see RELIGIOUS 1.

spit *v.* splutter, eject, drivel, slobber, drool.

spite *n.* malice, resentment, hatred; see HATE.

splash *n.* plash, plop, dash, spatter, sprinkle, spray, slosh, slop.

splash *v.* splatter, dabble, get wet; see MOISTEN.

splendid *a.* premium, great, fine; see BEAUTIFUL, EXCELLENT, GLORIOUS.

splendor *n.* luster, brilliance, brightness; see GLORY 2.
splice *v.* knit, graft, mesh; see JOIN 1, WEAVE 1.
splint *n.* prop, rib, reinforcement; see BRACE, SUPPORT 2.
splinter *n.* sliver, flake, chip; see BIT 1.
split *n.* **1.** [A dividing] separating, breaking up, severing; see DIVISION 1. **2.** [An opening] crack, fissure, rent; see HOLE 1.
split *v.* burst, rend, cleave; see BREAK 1, CUT 1, DIVIDE.
split up *v.* part, break up, isolate; see DIVIDE, DIVORCE.
spoil *v.* **1.** [To decay] rot, blight, fade, wither, molder, crumble, mold, mildew, corrode, decompose, putrefy, degenerate, weaken, become tainted. **2.** [To ruin] destroy, defile, plunder; see DESTROY.
spoiled *a.* damaged, marred, injured; see RUINED 2, WASTED.
spoiling *a.* rotting, breaking up, wasting away; see DECAYING.
spoils *n.pl.* plunder, pillage, prize; see BOOTY.
spoke *n.* rung, handle, crosspiece; see ROD 1.
spoken *a.* uttered, expressed, told, announced, mentioned, communicated, oral, voiced, unwritten.
spokesman *n.* deputy, mediator, substitute; see AGENT, SPEAKER.
sponsor *n.* advocate, patron, supporter, champion; see also PATRON.
spontaneous *a.* involuntary, instinctive, casual, unintentional, impulsive, automatic, unforced, natural, unavoidable, unwilling, unconscious, uncontrollable.—*Ant.* DELIBERATE, willful, intended.
spontaneously *a.* instinctively, impulsively, automatically; see UNCONSCIOUSLY.
spoof *n.* trickery, put on*, satire; see DECEPTION.
spoof *v.* fool, play a trick on, kid*; see TRICK.
spooky *a.* weird, eerie, ominous; see MYSTERIOUS 2, UNCANNY.
spoon *n.* teaspoon, tablespoon, ladle; see SILVERWARE.
sport *n.* **1.** [Entertainment] diversion, recreation, play, amusement, merrymaking, festivity, revelry, pastime, pleasure, enjoyment; see also ENTERTAINMENT, FUN, GAME 1. **2.** [A joke] pleasantry, mockery, jest, mirth, joke, joking, antics, tomfoolery, nonsense, laughter, practical joke. **3.** [Athletic or competitive amusement] *Sports include the following:* (deer, rabbit, duck, etc.) hunting, shooting, (the) Olympics, horse racing, automobile racing, runnning, fishing, basketball, golf, tennis, squash, handball, volleyball, soccer, gymnastics, (professional, pro*, collegiate, high-school, etc.) football, baseball, track and field sports, cricket, lacrosse, hockey, skating, skiing, fencing, jumping, boxing, wrestling.
sporting *a.* considerate, sportsmanlike, gentlemanly; see GENEROUS, REASONABLE 1.
sportsman *n.* huntsman, big game hunter, woodsman; see FISHERMAN, HUNTER.
sportsmanship *n.* **1.** [Skill] facility, dexterity, cunning; see ABILITY. **2.** [Honor] justice, integrity, truthfulness; see HONESTY.
spot *n.* **1.** [A dot] speck, flaw, pimple; see BIT 1, BLEMISH. **2.** [A place] point, locality, scene; see PLACE 3. **—hit the high spots*** **1.** hurry, travel rapidly, make good time; see SPEED. **2.** treat hastily, go over lightly, touch up; see NEGLECT 1, 2. **—hit the spot*** please, delight, be just right; see SATISFY 1. **—in a bad spot*** in danger, threatened, on the spot*; see DANGEROUS.
spot *v.* blemish, blotch, spatter; see DIRTY.
spotless *a.* stainless, immaculate, without spot or blemish; see CLEAN, PURE 2.
spotted *a.* **1.** [Dotted] marked, dappled, mottled, dotted, speckled, motley, blotchy. **2.** [Blemished] soiled, smudged, smeared; see DIRTY 1.
spouse *n.* marriage, partner, groom, bride; see also HUSBAND, MATE 3, WIFE.
sprain *n.* twist, overstrain, strain; see INJURY.
sprained *a.* wrenched, strained, pulled out of place; see HURT, TWISTED 1.
sprawl *v.* slouch, relax, lounge; see LIE 3.
spray *n.* splash, steam, fine mist; see FOG.
spray *v.* scatter, diffuse, sprinkle; see SPATTER.
spread *a.* expanded, dispersed, extended, opened, unfurled, sown, scattered, diffused, strewn, spread thin; see also DISTRIBUTED.—*Ant.* RESTRICTED, narrowed, restrained.
spread *n.* **1.** [Extent] scope, range, expanse; see EXTENT, MEASURE 1. **2.** [A spread cloth] blanket, coverlet, counterpane; see COVER 1. **3.** [A spread food] preserve, conserve, jelly; see BUTTER, CHEESE. **4.** [*A meal] feast, banquet, informal repast; see DINNER, LUNCH, MEAL 2.
spread *v.* **1.** [To distribute] cast, diffuse, disseminate; see RADIATE 1, SCATTER 2, SOW. **2.** [To extend] open, unfurl, roll out, unroll, unfold, reach, circulate, lengthen, widen, expand, untwist, unwind, uncoil, enlarge, increase, develop, branch off, expand; see also FLOW, REACH 1.—*Ant.* CLOSE, shorten, shrink. **3.** [To apply over a surface] cover, coat, smear, daub, plate, gloss, enamel, paint, spray, plaster, pave, wax, varnish. **4.** [To separate] part, sever, disperse; see DIVIDE, SEPARATE 1.
spreading *a.* extending, extensive, spread out, growing, widening.
spree *n.* revel, frolic, binge*; see CELEBRATION.
sprightly *a.* lively, quick, alert; see AGILE.
spring *n.* **1.** [A fountain] flowing well, artesian well, sweet water; see ORIGIN 2. **2.** [The season between winter and summer]

springtime, seedtime, flowering, budding, vernal, equinox, blackberry winter*; see also SEASON.

sprinkle *v.* dampen, bedew, spray; see MOISTEN.

sprout *v.* germinate, take root, shoot up, bud, burgeon; see also GROW 1.

spry *a.* nimble, fleet, vigorous; see AGILE.

spunk* *n.* spirit, courage, nerve; see COURAGE.

spurn *v.* despise, disdain, look down on; see EVADE.

spurt *n.* squirt, jet, stream; see WATER 2.

spurt *v.* spout, jet, burst; see FLOW.

sputter *v.* stumble, stutter, falter; see STAMMER.

spy *n.* secret agent, foreign agent, scout, detective, undercover man, CIA operative, observer, watcher.

spy *v.* scout, observe, watch, examine, bug*, tap, scrutinize, take note, search, discover, look for, hunt, peer, pry, spy upon, set a watch on, hound, trail, tail*, follow; see also MEDDLE 1, 2.

squabble *n.* spat, quarrel, feud; see DISPUTE.

squabble *v.* argue, disagree, fight; see QUARREL.

squad *n.* company, small company, crew; see TEAM 1.

squalid *a.* dirty, poor, foul; see DIRTY 1.

squall *n.* blast, gust, gale; see STORM.

squalor *n.* ugliness, disorder, uncleanness; see FILTH.

squander *v.* spend, spend lavishly, throw away; see WASTE 2.

square *a.* **1.** [Having right angles] right-angled, four-sided, equal-sided, squared, equilateral, rectangular, rectilinear. **2.** [*Old-fashioned] dated, stuffy, out-of-date; see CONSERVATIVE, OLD-FASHIONED.

square *n.* **1.** [A rectangle] equal-sided rectangle, plane figure, rectilinear plane; see RECTANGLE. **2.** [A park] city center, civic center, plaza, recreational area; see also PARK 1.

squat *v.* stoop, hunch, cower; see SIT.

squawk *v.* cackle, crow, yap; see CRY 2.

squeak *n.* peep, squeal, shrill sound; see CRY 2, NOISE 1.

squeak *v.* creak, peep, squeal; see CRY 2, SOUND.

squeak through* *v.* manage, survive, pass; see ENDURE 2, SUCCEED 1.

squeal *v.* shout, yell, screech; see CRY 1, 2.

squeamish *a.* finicky, fussy, delicate, hard to please, fastidious, particular, exacting, prim, prudish, queasy.

squeeze *n.* influence, restraint, force; see PRESSURE 1, 2. **—put the squeeze on** compel, urge, use force with; see FORCE, INFLUENCE.

squeeze *v.* clasp, pinch, clutch; see HUG, PRESS 1.

squeeze through *v.* survive, accomplish, get by; see ENDURE 1, SUCCEED 1.

squint *v.* screw up the eyes, peek, peep; see LOOK 2.

squirm *v.* wriggle, twist, fidget; see WIGGLE.

squirt *v.* spurt, spit, eject; see EMIT.

stab *n.* thrust, wound, puncture; see CUT. **—make a stab at** endeavor, try to, do one's best to; see TRY 1.

stab *v.* pierce, wound, stick, cut, hurt, run through, thrust, prick, drive, puncture, hit, bayonet, knife; see also KILL 1.

stability *n.* **1.** [Firmness of position] steadiness, durability, solidity, endurance, immobility, suspense, establishment, balance, permanence. **2.** [Steadfastness of character] stableness, aplomb, security, endurance, maturity, resoluteness, determination, perserverance, adherence, backbone, assurance, resistance; see also CONFIDENCE.

stab in the back *v.* deceive, undercut, turn traitor; see TRICK.

stable *a.* **1.** [Fixed] steady, stationary, solid; see FIRM 1. **2.** [Steadfast] calm, firm, constant.

stable *n.* barn, coop, corral; see PEN 1.

stack *n.* pile, heap, mound; see BUNCH.

stack *v.* heap, pile up, accumulate; see LOAD 1.

stack up *v.* become, work out to, resolve into; see RESULT.

stadium *n.* gymnasium, strand, amphitheater; see ARENA.

staff *n.* **1.** [A stick] wand, pole, stave; see STICK. **2.** [A corps of employees] personnel, assistants, men, women, force, help, workers, crew, organization, agents, operatives, deputies, servants.

stage *n.* **1.** [The theater] theater, limelight, spotlight; see DRAMA. **2.** [A platform] frame, scaffold, staging; see PLATFORM 1. **3.** [A level, period, or degree] grade, plane, step; see DEGREE 1. **—by easy stages** easily, gently, taking one's time; see SLOWLY.

stagger *v.* totter, waver, sway, weave, bob, careen, vacillate.

staggering *a.* monstrous, huge, tremendous; see LARGE 1, UNBELIEVABLE.

stagnant *a.* inert, dead, inactive; see IDLE.

stagnate *v.* deteriorate, rot, putrefy; see DECAY.

staid *a.* sober, grave, steady; see DIGNIFIED.

stain *n.* blot, blemish, spot, splotch, stained spot, smudge, stigma, brand, blotch, ink spot, spatter, drip, speck.

stain *v.* spot, discolor, taint; see DIRTY.

stairs *n.pl.* stairway, staircase, flight, steps, stair, escalator, ascent.

stake *n.* rod, paling, pale; see STICK. **—at stake** at issue, in danger, risked; see ENDANGERED. **—pull up stakes** depart, move, decamp; see LEAVE 1.

stale *a.* spoiled, dried, smelly; see OLD 2.

stalk *n.* stem, support, upright, spire, shaft, spike, straw, stock.
stalk *v.* approach stealthily, track, chase; see HUNT 1, PURSUE 1.
stall *v.* **1.** [To break down] not start, conk out, go dead; see BREAK DOWN 2. **2.** [To delay] postpone, hamper, hinder; see DELAY.
stamina *n.* strength, vigor, vitality; see ENDURANCE.
stammer *v.* falter, stop, stumble, hesitate, pause, stutter, repeat oneself, hem and haw; see also SPEAK 1.
stamp *n.* emblem, brand, cast; see MARK 1.
stamp *v.* impress, imprint, brand; see MARK 1.
stamped *a.* marked, branded, okayed; see APPROVED.
stampede *n.* rush, dash, flight; see RUN 1.
stampede *v.* bolt, rush, panic; see RUN 2.
stamp out *v.* eliminate, kill off, dispatch; see DESTROY.
stand *n.* notion, view, belief; see ATTITUDE, OPINION 1. **—make** or **take a stand** insist, assert, take a position; see DECLARE.
stand *v.* **1.** [To be in an upright position] be erect, be on one's feet, stand up, come to one's feet, rise, jump up. **2.** [To endure] last, hold, abide; see ENDURE 1. **3.** [To be of a certain height] be, attain, come to; see REACH 1.
stand a chance *v.* have a chance, be a possibility, have something in one's favor, have something on one's side, be preferred.
standard *a.* regular, regulation, made to a standard; see APPROVED.
standard *n.* pattern, type, example; see MODEL 2.
standardization *n.* uniformity, sameness, likeness, evenness, levelness, monotony; see also REGULARITY.
standardize *v.* regulate, institute, normalize; see ORDER 3, SYSTEMATIZE.
standardized *a.* patterned, graded, made alike; see REGULATED.
standby *n.* upholder, supporter, advocate; see PATRON , PROTECTOR.
stand by *v.* **1.** [To defend or help] befriend, second, abet; see DEFEND 2, HELP. **2.** [To wait] be prepared, be ready, be near; see WAIT 1.
stand for *v.* **1.** [To mean] represent, suggest, imply; see MEAN 1. **2.** [To allow] permit, suffer, endure; see ALLOW.
stand-in *n.* double, second, understudy; see SUBSTITUTE.
standing *n.* position, status, reputation; see RANK 3.
standoff *n.* stalemate, deadlock, dead end; see DELAY.
standoffish *a.* cool, aloof, distant; see INDIFFERENT.
stand one's ground *v.* oppose, fight against, resist; see FIGHT.
stand out *v.* be prominent, be conspicuous, emerge; see LOOM 2.
standpoint *n.* attitude, point of view, station; see OPINION 1.
standstill *n.* stop, halt, cessation; see DELAY.
stand up for *v.* back, protect, champion; see DEFEND.
stand up to *v.* resist, oppose, challenge; see FIGHT.
star *n.* **1.** [A luminous heavenly body] sun, astral body, pulsar, quasar, fixed star, variable star. *Familiar stars include the following—individual stars*: Betelgeuse, Sirius, Vega, Spica, Arcturus, Aldebaran, Antares, Atlas, Castor, Pollux, Capella, Algol, North Star or Polaris; *constellations:* Great Bear or Ursa Major, Little Bear or Ursa Minor, Great Dipper, Little Dipper, Orion, Coma Berenices or Berenice's Hair, The Gemini or Castor and Pollux, Cassiopeia, Pleiades, Hyades, Taurus, Canis Major or the Great Dog, Canis Minor or the Little Dog, Scorpion, Sagittarius, Corona Borealis or the Northern Crown, Pegasus, Leo, Hercules, Boötes, Cetus, Aquila or the Eagle, Cygnus or the Swan, Corona Australis or the Southern Crown, the Southern Cross. **2.** [A conventional figure] asterisk, six-pointed star, five-pointed star; see FORM 1. **3.** [A superior performer] headliner, leading lady, leading man, movie actor, movie actress, actor, actress, matinee idol, chief attraction.
stare *v.* gaze, gawk, look fixedly; see LOOK 2, WATCH.
stark-naked *a.* nude, without a stitch of clothing, in the altogether; see NAKED 1.
start *n.* inception, commencement, beginning; see ORIGIN 2.
start *v.* commence, rise, spring; see BEGIN 1, 2.
started *a.* evoked, initiated, instituted; see BEGUN.
start in *v.* commence, open, make a first move; see BEGIN 1, 2.
startle *v.* alarm, shock, astonish; see SURPRISE.
start up *v.* make run, crank up*, get something started; see BEGIN 1, 2.
starvation *n.* deprivation, need, want; see HUNGER.
starve *v.* famish, crave, perish; see DIE.
starving *a.* famished, weakening, dying; see HUNGRY.
state *n.* **1.** [A sovereign unit] republic, land, kingdom; see NATION 1. **2.** [A condition] circumstance, situation, welfare, phase, case, station, nature, estate, footing, status, standing, occurrence, occasion, eventuality, element, requirement, category, standing, reputation, environment, chances, outlook, position. **—in a state** disturbed, upset, badly off; see TROUBLED.

state *v.* pronounce, assert, affirm; see DECLARE.

stately *a.* **1.** [*Said of persons*] dignified, haughty, noble; see PROUD 1. **2.** [*Said of objects*] large, imposing, magnificent; see GRAND.

statement *n.* **1.** [The act of stating] allegation, declaration, assertion, profession, acknowledgment, assurance, affirmation; see also ANNOUNCEMENT. **2.** [A statement of account] bill, charge, reckoning, account, record, report, budget, audit, balance sheet, tab*, check.

statesman *n.* legislator, lawgiver, administrator, executive, minister, official, politician, diplomat, representative, elder statesman, veteran lawmaker.

station *n.* **1.** [Place] situation, site, location; see POSITION 1. **2.** [Depot] terminal, stop, stopping place; see DEPOT. **3.** [Social position] order, standing, state; see RANK 3. **4.** [An establishment to vend petroleum products] gas station, gasoline station, service station, filling station, petrol station, pumps, petroleum retailer; see also GARAGE. **5.** [A broadcasting establishment] television station, radio station, television transmission, radio transmission, microwave transmitter, television transmitter, radio transmitter, broadcasting station, studios, channel; see also COMMUNICATIONS, RADIO, TELEVISION.

station *v.* place, commission, allot; see ASSIGN.

stationary *a.* fixed, stable, permanent; see MOTIONLESS 1.

stationery *n.* writing materials, office supplies, school supplies; see PAPER 4.

statue *n.* statuette, cast, figure, bust, representation, likeness, image, sculpture, statuary, marble, bronze, ivory, icon.

statuesque *a.* stately, beautiful, grand; see GRACEFUL 2.

stature *n.* development, growth, tallness; see HEIGHT, SIZE 2.

status *n.* situation, standing, station; see RANK 3.

staunch *a.* steadfast, strong, constant; see FAITHFUL.

stay *n.* **1.** [A support] prop, hold, truss; see SUPPORT 2. **2.** [A visit] stop, sojourn, halt; see VISIT.

stay *v.* tarry, linger, sojourn; see VISIT.

stay put* *v.* remain, stand still, persist; see WAIT 1.

steadfast *a.* staunch, stable, constant; see FAITHFUL.

steadily *a.* firmly, unwaveringly, undeviatingly; see REGULARLY.

steady *a.* uniform, unvarying, patterned; see CONSTANT, REGULAR 3. **—go steady (with)*** keep company with, court, go together; see COURT, LOVE 1, 2.

steak *n.* filet mignon, sirloin, T-bone; see FOOD, MEAT.

steal *v.* take, filch, thieve, loot, rob, purloin, embezzle, defraud, keep, carry off, appropriate, take possession of, lift, remove, impress, abduct, shanghai, kidnap, run off with, hold up, strip, poach, swindle, plagiarize, misappropriate, burglarize, blackmail, fleece, plunder, pillage, ransack, burgle*, stick up*, hijack*, skyjack*, pinch*, mooch*, gyp*; see also SEIZE 2.

stealing *n.* piracy, embezzlement, shoplifting; see CRIME, THEFT.

steam *n.* vaporized water, fumes, fog; see VAPOR.

steam *v.* heat, brew, pressure cook; see COOK.

steamboat *n.* steamer, steamship, liner; see BOAT, SHIP.

steep *a.* precipitous, sudden, sharp, angular, craggy, uneven, rough, rugged, irregular, jagged, vertical, uphill, downhill, abrupt, sheer, perpendicular.

steer *v.* point, head for, direct; see DRIVE 2.

steer clear of *v.* stay away from, miss, escape; see AVOID.

stem *n.* peduncle, petiole, pedice; see STALK. **—from stem to stern** the full length, completely, entirely; see EVERYWHERE, THROUGHOUT.

stench *n.* odor, stink, foulness; see SMELL 2.

stenographer *n.* office girl, typist, shorthand stenographer; see CLERK, SECRETARY.

step *n.* **1.** [A movement of the foot] pace, stride, gait, footfall, tread, stepping. **2.** [One degree in a graded rise] rest, run, tread, round, rung, level. **3.** [The print of a foot] footprint, footmark, print, imprint, impression, footstep, trail, trace, mark; see also TRACK 2. **—in step (with)** in agreement with, coinciding with, similar to; see ALIKE, SIMILARLY. **—keep step** agree with, conform to, keep in line; see CONFORM. **—out of step** inappropriate, incorrect, inaccurate; see WRONG 2, WRONGLY. **—take steps** do something, start, intervene; see ACT 1. **—watch one's step** be careful, take precautions, look out; see WATCH OUT.

step *v.* pace, stride, advance, recede, go forward, go backward, go up, go down, ascend, descend, pass, walk, march, move, hurry, hop; see also CLIMB, RISE 1.

step by step *a.* by degrees, cautiously, tentatively; see SLOWLY.

step on it* *v.* go fast, make good time, speed up; see SPEED.

steppingstone *n.* help, agent, factor; see MEANS 1.

step up *v.* augment, improve, intensify; see INCREASE.

stereotype *n.* convention, fashion, institution; see AVERAGE, CUSTOM.

stereotype *v.* conventionalize, standardize, normalize; see REGULATE 2, SYSTEMATIZE.

stereotyped *a.* hackneyed, trite, ordinary; see CONVENTIONAL 1, 3, DULL 4.

sterile *a.* **1.** [Incapable of producing young] infertile, impotent, childless, barren.—*Ant.* FERTILE, productive, potent. **2.** [Incapable of producing vegetation] desolate, fallow, waste, desert, arid, dry, barren, unproductive, fruitless, bleak; see also EMPTY. **3.** [Scrupulously clean] antiseptic, disinfected, decontaminated, germ-free, sterilized, uninfected, sanitary, pasteurized; see also PURE 2.

sterilize *v.* antisepticize, disinfect, pasteurize; see CLEAN, PURIFY.

stern *a.* rigid, austere, strict; see SEVERE 1.

stew *n.* ragout, goulash, Hungarian goulash, seafood chowder, beef stew, Irish stew, mulligan*, casserole; see also FOOD, SOUP.

stick *n.* shoot, twig, branch, stem, stalk, rod, wand, staff, stave, walking stick, cane, matchstick, club, baton, drumstick, pole, bludgeon, bat, ruler, stock, cue, mast. **—the sticks*** rural areas, the back country, outlying districts; see COUNTRY 1.

stick *v.* **1.** [To remain fastened] adhere, cling, fasten, attach, unite, cohere, hold, stick together, hug, clasp, hold fast.—*Ant.* LOOSEN, let go, fall, come away. **2.** [To penetrate with a point] prick, impale, pierce; see PENETRATE.

stick around* *v.* stay, continue, be present; see WAIT 1.

stick by (someone) *v.* be loyal to, stand by, believe in; see SUPPORT 2.

stick it out* *v.* persist, endure, stay; see WAIT 1.

stick out *v.* jut, show, come through; see PROJECT 1.

stickup* *n.* burglary, robbery, stealing; see CRIME, THEFT.

stick up for* *v.* support, aid, fight for; see SUPPORT 2.

sticky *a.* ropy, viscous, adherent, sticking, gummy, waxy, pasty, gluey.

stiff *a.* **1.** [Not easily bent] solid, rigid, petrified, firm, tense, unyielding, inflexible, hard, hardened, starched, taut, thick, stubborn, obstinate, unbending, thickened, wooden, steely, frozen, solidified.—*Ant.* SOFT, flexible, softened. **2.** [Formal] ungainly, ungraceful, unnatural; see AWKWARD. **3.** [Severe] rigorous, exact, strict; see SEVERE 1, 2. **4.** [Potent] hard, potent, powerful; see STRONG 4.

stiffen *v.* jelly, harden, starch, petrify, brace, prop, cement, strengthen, thicken, clot, coagulate, solidify, congeal, condense, set, curdle, freeze, cake, crystallize.

stifle *v.* smother, suffocate, extinguish; see CHOKE.

still *a.* **1.** [Silent] calm, tranquil, noiseless; see QUIET. **2.** [Yet] nevertheless, furthermore, however; see BESIDES, BUT 1, YET 1.

stimulant *n.* tonic, bracer, energizer; see DRUG.

stimulate *v.* spur on, foster, incite; see URGE 2.

stimulated *a.* keyed up, speeded up, accelerated; see EXCITED.

stimulating *a.* intriguing, enlivening, arousing, high-spirited, bracing, rousing, energetic, refreshing, exhilarating, enjoyable, health-building, sharp, evocative, exciting, inspiring, provoking, animating.—*Ant.* DULL, dreary, humdrum.

sting *n.* **1.** [An injury] wound, swelling, sore; see INJURY. **2.** [Pain] prick, bite, burn; see PAIN 2.

sting *v.* prick, prickle, tingle; see HURT 1.

stingy *a.* parsimonious, niggardly, miserly, close, closefisted, greedy, covetous, tightfisted, tight*, grasping, penny-pinching, cheap, selfish, mean, cheeseparing, skimpy.—*Ant.* GENEROUS, bountiful, liberal.

stink *n.* stench, fetor, offensive odor; see SMELL 2.

stink *v.* smell bad, emit a stench, be offensive; see SMELL 1.

stir *v.* move, beat, agitate; see MIX 1.

stir up trouble* *v.* cause difficulty, foment, agitate; see BOTHER 2, DISTURB.

stitch *v.* join, make a seam, baste; see SEW.

stock *a.* trite, hackneyed, ordinary; see COMMON 1, DULL 4.

stock *n.* **1.** [Goods] merchandise, produce, accumulation; see PRODUCE. **2.** [Livestock] domestic animals, barnyard animals, farm animals; see CATTLE. **3.** [A stalk] stem, plant, trunk; see STALK. **—in stock** not sold out, stocked, not difficult to get; see AVAILABLE. **—out of stock** sold out, gone, not available; see SOLD OUT. **—take stock (of)** count up, inventory, figure; see ESTIMATE. **—take stock in** believe in, put faith in, rely on; see TRUST 1.

stocking *n.* hose, pantyhose, nylons; see HOSIERY.

stock-still *a.* frozen, stagnant, inactive; see MOTIONLESS 1.

stock (up) *v.* replenish, supply, furnish; see BUY.

stolen *a.* taken, kept, robbed, filched, purloined, appropriated, lifted*, abducted, kidnapped, snatched*, run off with, poached, copped*, plagiarized, misappropriated.

stomach *n.* paunch, belly, midsection, bowels, intestines, viscera, entrails, insides*, guts, gut*, tummy, pot*, middle, breadbasket*, corporation*.

stomachache *n.* indigestion, acute indigestion, gastric upset; see ILLNESS 1, 2.

stone *a.* rock, stony, rocky, hard, rough, craggy, petrified, marble, granite.

stone *n.* mass, crag, cobblestone, boulder, gravel, pebble, rock, sand, grain, granite, marble, flint, gem, jewel. **—cast the first stone** criticize, blame, reprimand; see ATTACK, SCOLD. **—leave no stone unturned** take great pains, be scrupulous, try hard; see PURSUE 1, WORK 1.

stoned* *a.* drugged, high*, turned on*; see DRUNK.

stony *a.* inflexible, cruel, unrelenting; see FIRM 2, ROUGH 1.

stool *n.* seat, footstool, footrest; see FURNITURE.

stoop *v.* bend forward, incline, crouch; see LEAN 1.

stop *interj.* cease, cut it out*, quit it; see STOP *v.*, 1.

stop *n.* **1.** [A pause] halt, stay, standstill; see END 2, PAUSE. **2.** [A stopping place] station, passenger station, wayside stop; see DEPOT. **—put a stop to** halt, interrupt, intervene; see STOP 1.

stop *v.* **1.** [To halt] pause, stay, stand still, lay over, stay over, break the journey, shut down, rest, discontinue, pull up, reach a standstill, hold, stop dead in one's tracks*, stop short, freeze, call it a day*, cut short; see also END 1. **2.** [To cease] terminate, finish, conclude, withdraw, leave off, let up, pull up, fetch up, wind up, relinquish, have done, desist, refrain, settle, discontinue, end, close, tie up, give up, call off, bring up, close down, break up, hold up, pull up, lapse, be at an end, cut out, die away, go out, defect, surrender, close, peter out*, call it a day*, knock off*, lay off*, throw in the towel*, melt away, drop it, run out, write off, run its course.—*Ant.* BEGIN, start, commence. **3.** [To prevent] hinder, obstruct, arrest; see PREVENT.

stopover *n.* layover, halt, pause; see DELAY.

stopped *a.* at a halt, off the air, cut short; see INTERRUPTED.

storage *n.* room, area, accommodation; see STOREHOUSE.

store *n.* shop, mart, retail establishment, sales outlet, market, department store, specialty shop, chain store, drygoods store, emporium, grocery store, business house, drug store.

store *v.* put, deposit, cache, stock, store away, stow away, lay by, lay in, lay up, lay down, put away, put aside, lock away, bank, warehouse, collect, pack away, set aside, set apart, amass, file, stash*, salt away*, put in mothballs*; see also SAVE 3.—*Ant.* SPEND, draw out, withdraw.

stored *a.* stocked, reserved, hoarded; see SAVED 2.

storehouse *n.* depository, warehouse, granary, silo, store, storage space, corncrib, barn, depot, cache, grain elevator, safe-deposit vault, armory, arsenal, repository.

storekeeper *n.* small businessman, purveyor, grocer; see MERCHANT.

storm *n.* tempest, downpour, cloudburst, disturbance, waterspout, blizzard, snowstorm, squall, hurricane, cyclone, tornado, twister*, gust, blast, gale, blow, monsoon.

storm *v.* blow violently, howl, blow a gale, roar, set in, squall, pour, drizzle, rain, rain cats and dogs*.

stormy *a.* rainy, wet, damp, cold, bitter, raging, roaring, frigid, windy, blustery, pouring, turbulent, storming, wild, boisterous, rough, squally, dark, violent, threatening, menacing.

story *n.* imaginative writing, fable, narrative, tale, myth, fairy tale, anecdote, legend, account, satire, burlesque, memoir, parable, fiction, novel, romance, allegory, epic, saga, fantasy; see also LITERATURE 1.

stout *a.* corpulent, fleshy, portly; see FAT.

stove *n.* range, heater, cooking stove, furnace; see also APPLIANCE.

straight *a.* **1.** [Not curved or twisted] rectilinear, vertical, perpendicular, plumb, upright, erect, in line, unbent, in a row, on a line, even, level.—*Ant.* BENT, curved, curving. **2.** [Direct] uninterrupted, continuous, through; see DIRECT 1.

straighten *v.* order, compose, make straight, untwist, unsnarl, unbend, uncoil, unravel, uncurl, unfold, put straight, level, arrange, arrange on a line, align.—*Ant.* BEND, twist, curl.

straighten out *v.* put in order, clarify, make less confused, clean up, arrange.

straighten up *v.* **1.** [To make neat] tidy, arrange, fix; see CLEAN, STRAIGHTEN. **2.** [To stand up] rise up, arise, be upright; see STAND 1.

straightforward *a.* sincere, candid, outspoken; see FRANK, HONEST 1.

strain *n.* **1.** [Effort] exertion, struggle, endeavor; see EFFORT. **2.** [Mental tension] anxiety, tension, pressure; see STRESS 2.

strain *v.* **1.** [To exert] strive, endeavor, labor; see TRY 1. **2.** [To filter] refine, purify, screen; see SIFT 2.

strained *a.* forced, constrained, tense; see DIFFICULT 1.

strainer *n.* mesh, filter, colander; see SIEVE.

strait-laced *a.* strict, severe, stiff; see PRUDISH.

stranded *a.* aground, beached, ashore; see ABANDONED.

strange *a.* foreign, rare, unusual, uncommon, external, outside, without, detached, apart, faraway, remote, alien, unexplored, isolated, unrelated, irrelevant; see also UNFAMILIAR 2, UNKNOWN 1, 2, 3, UNNATURAL 1.—*Ant.* familiar, present, close.

strangely *a.* oddly, queerly, unfamiliarly, unnaturally, uncommonly, exceptionally, remarkably, rarely, fantastically, amazingly, surprisingly, singularly, peculiarly, unusually.—*Ant.* REGULARLY, commonly, usually.

strangeness *n.* newness, unfamiliarity, novelty, abnormality, eccentricity, remoteness.
stranger *n.* foreigner, outsider, unknown person, uninvited person, visitor, guest, immigrant, intruder, interloper, new boy in town, new girl in town, drifter, squatter, migratory worker, perfect stranger, complete stranger, gate-crasher*.
strangle *v.* asphyxiate, suffocate, kill; see CHOKE.
strap *n.* thong, strop, leash; see BAND 1.
strategy *n.* approach, maneuvering, procedure; see TACTICS.
straw *n.* *Straws and strawlike fibers include the following:* oat, wheat, barley, rye, rice, buckwheat, bean; see also HAY. **—a straw in the wind** evidence, indication, signal; see SIGN 1. **—grasp at straws** or **a straw** try any expedient, panic, make a desperate attempt; see FEAR, TRY 1.
straw vote *n.* opinion poll, unofficial ballot, dry run*; see OPINION 1, VOTE 1, 2.
stray *v.* rove, roam, go astray; see WALK 1.
strayed *a.* wandered, vagrant, roaming; see LOST 1.
streak *n.* stripe, strip, ridge; see BAND 1.
stream *n.* current, rivulet, brook; see RIVER, WATER 2.
stream *v.* gush, run, flow; see FLOW.
street *n.* highway, way, lane, path, avenue, thoroughfare, boulevard, terrace, place, road, route, artery, parkway, court, cross street, alley, circle, dead end, passage.
streetcar *n.* tram, trolley, bus; see VEHICLE.
streetwalker *n.* whore, hustler, harlot; see PROSTITUTE.
strength *n.* vigor, brawn, energy, nerve, vitality, muscle, stoutness, health, toughness, sturdiness, hardiness, tenacity, soundness.—*Ant.* WEAKNESS, feebleness, loss of energy.
strengthen *v.* intensify, add, invigorate, fortify, reinforce, encourage, confirm, increase, multiply, empower, arm, harden, steel, brace, buttress, stimulate, sustain, nerve, animate, reanimate, restore, refresh, recover, hearten, establish, toughen, temper, rejuvenate, tone up, build up, make firm, stiffen, brace up, rally, sharpen, enliven, substantiate, uphold, back, augment, enlarge, extend, mount, rise, ascend, wax, grow, back up, beef up*.—*Ant.* WEAKEN, cripple, tear down.
strenuous *a.* vigorous, arduous, zealous; see DIFFICULT 1.
strenuously *a.* hard, laboriously, energetically; see VIGOROUSLY.
stress *n.* **1.** [Importance] significance, weight, import; see IMPORTANCE. **2.** [Pressure] strain, tension, force, burden, trial, fear, tenseness, stretch, tautness, pull, draw, extension, protraction, intensity, tightness, spring; see also PRESSURE 1.
stress *v.* accent, make emphatic, accentuate; see EMPHASIZE.
stretch *n.* compass, range, reach; see EXTENT.
stretch *v.* **1.** [To become longer] grow, expand, be extended, extend oneself, spread, unfold, increase, swell, spring up, shoot up, open.—*Ant.* CONTRACT, shrink, wane. **2.** [To cause to become longer, spread out, etc.] tighten, strain, make tense, draw, draw out, elongate, extend, develop, distend, inflate, lengthen, magnify, amplify, widen, draw tight.—*Ant.* RELAX, let go, slacken.
stretcher *n.* litter, cot, portable bed; see BED 1.
strew *v.* spread, toss, cover; see SCATTER 2.
stricken *a.* wounded, injured, harmed; see HURT.
strict *a.* stringent, stern, austere; see SEVERE 2.
strictly *a.* rigidly, rigorously, stringently; see SURELY.
stride *n.* step, pace, long step; see GAIT. **—take in one's stride** handle, do easily, deal with; see MANAGE 1.
strife *n.* quarrel, struggle, conflict; see FIGHT 1.
strike *n.* **1.** [An organized refusal] walkout, deadlock, work stoppage, quitting, sit-down strike, tie-up, slowdown, confrontation, sit-in; see also REVOLUTION 2. **2.** [A blow] hit, stroke, punch; see BLOW. **—(out) on strike** striking, protesting, on the picket line; see UNEMPLOYED.
strike *v.* **1.** [To hit] box, punch, thump; see BEAT 1, HIT 1. **2.** [To refuse to work] walk out, tie up, sit down, slow down, go out, be on strike, sit in, arbitrate, negotiate a contract, picket, boycott, stop, quit, resist, hold out for; see also OPPOSE 1, 2. **3.** [To light] kindle, ignite, scratch; see IGNITE.
strike it rich *v.* find oil, gold, etc.; become wealthy, make money; see SUCCEED 1.
strike out *v.* **1.** [To begin something new] start out, initiate, find a new approach; see BEGIN 1. **2.** [To cancel] obliterate, invalidate, expunge; see CANCEL. **3.** [In baseball, to be out on strikes] fan, whiff*, go down swinging, go down on strikes.
striking *a.* attractive, stunning, dazzling; see BEAUTIFUL, HANDSOME.
string *n.* **1.** [A sequence] chain, succession, procession; see SEQUENCE 1, SERIES. **2.** [Twine] cord, twist, strand; see ROPE. **—string along*** accede, go along, agree; see FOLLOW 2.
stringy *a.* wiry, ropy, woody, pulpy, hairy, veined, coarse, threadlike.
strip *n.* tape, slip, shred; see BAND 1, LAYER.
strip *v.* **1.** [Undress] divest, disrobe, become naked; see UNDRESS. **2.** [Remove] pull off, tear off, lift off; see PEEL.

stripe *n.* line, division, strip, contrasting color, band, border, ribbon; see also LAYER.
striped *a.* lined, marked, streaked, veined, ribbed; see also BARRED 1.
strive *v.* endeavor, aim, attempt; see TRY 1.
stroll *v.* ramble, saunter, roam; see WALK 1.
strong *a.* **1.** [Physically strong; *said especially of persons*] robust, sturdy, firm, muscular, sinewy, vigorous, stout, hardy, big, heavy, husky, lusty, active, energetic, tough, virile, mighty, athletic, able-bodied, powerful, manly, brawny, burly, wiry, strapping, made of iron*.—*Ant.* WEAK, emaciated, feeble. **2.** [Physically strong; *said especially of things*] solid, firm, staunch, well-built, secure, tough, durable, able, unyielding, steady, stable, fixed, sound, powerful, mighty, tough, rugged, substantial, reinformed.—*Ant.* UNSTABLE, insecure, tottering. **3.** [Wielding power] great, mighty, influential; see POWERFUL 1. **4.** [Potent in effect] powerful, potent, high-powered, stiff, effective, hard, high potency, stimulating, inebriating, intoxicating, spiked*. **5.** [Intense] sharp, acute, keen; see INTENSE. **6.** [Financially sound] stable, solid, safe; see RELIABLE.
strongest *a.* mightiest, stoutest, firmest, hardiest, healthiest, most vigorous, most active, most intense, most capable, most masterful, sturdiest, most courageous, strongest-willed, most efficient.—*Ant.* WEAK, feeblest, most timid.
strongly *a.* stoutly, vigorously, actively, heavily, fully, completely, sturdily, robustly, firmly, solidly, securely, immovably, steadily, heartily, forcibly, resolutely, capably, powerfully.
structure *n.* arrangement, composition, fabrication; see BUILDING.
struggle *n.* conflict, contest, strife; see FIGHT 1.
struggle *v.* strive, grapple, contend; see FIGHT.
stub *n.* stump, short end, snag, root, remainder, remnant.
stubborn *a.* unreasonable, obstinate, firm, dogged, opinionated, contradictory, contrary, determined, resolved, bullheaded, mulish, fixed, hard, willful, dogmatic, prejudiced, tenacious, unyielding, headstrong.
stubbornly *a.* persistently, resolutely, willfully, doggedly, tenaciously; see also FIRMLY 2.
stubbornness *n.* obstinacy, doggedness, inflexibility, pertinacity, tenacity, perverseness, perversity, stupidity, bullheadedness; see also DETERMINATION.
stuck *a.* **1.** [Tight] fast, fastened, cemented; see TIGHT 2. **2.** [Stranded] grounded, lost, high and dry*; see ABANDONED.
student *n.* learner, undergraduate, novice, high school student, college student, graduate student, pupil, docent, apprentice.
studious *a.* industrious, thoughtful, well-read, well-informed, scholarly, lettered, learned, bookish, earnest, diligent, attentive.
study *n.* research, investigation, examination; see EDUCATION 1.
study *v.* read, go into, refresh the memory, read up on, burn the midnight oil, bone up*, go over, cram, think, inquire, bury oneself in, plunge into.
stuff *v.* ram, pad, wad; see FILL 1, PACK 2.
stuffed *a.* crowded, packed, crammed; see FULL 1.
stuffed shirt* *n.* phony*, pompous person, incompetent; see FAKE.
stuffing *n.* **1.** [Material used to pad] packing, wadding, padding, quilting, filler, packing material. **2.** [Material used to stuff fowl, fish, etc.] dressing, forcemeat, filling; see DRESSING.
stuffy *a.* confined, stagnant, muggy; see CLOSE 5.
stumble *v.* miss one's step, trip, shamble; see FALL 1, TRIP 1.
stump *n.* butt, piece, projection; see END 4.
stumped* *a.* puzzled, baffled, bewildered; see UNCERTAIN.
stun *v.* daze with a blow, put to sleep, knock out; see DEADEN.
stunned *a.* dazed, astonished, amazed; see SHOCKED.
stunning *a.* striking, marvelous, remarkable; see BEAUTIFUL, HANDSOME.
stunt *n.* act, skit, comic sketch; see PERFORMANCE.
stupid *a.* senseless, brainless, idiotic, simple, shallow, imprudent, witless, irrational, inane, ridiculous, mindless, ludicrous, muddled, absurd, half-witted, funny, comical, silly, laughable, nonsensical, illogical, indiscreet, unintelligent, irresponsible, scatterbrained, crackbrained, addled, foolish, unwary, incautious, misguided, wild, injudicious, imbecile, addleheaded, lunatic, insane, mad, crazy, moronic, touched, freakish, comic, narrow-minded, incoherent, childish, senile, far-fetched, preposterous, unreasonable, asinine, unwise, thoughtless, careless, fatuous, light, lightheaded, flighty, madcap, giddy, cuckoo*, boneheaded*, goofy*, cracked*, dumb*, half-baked, in a daze, wacky*, harebrained, screwy*, cockeyed*, loony*, batty*, dopey*, nutty*.—*Ant.* SANE, wise, judicious.
stupidity *n.* **1.** [Dullness of mind] stupor, slowness, heaviness, obtuseness, sluggishness, feeble-mindedness, folly, weakness, silliness, nonsense, absurdity, imbecility, imprudence, lunacy, idiocy, brainlessness, shallowness, weakmindedness, impracticality, senility, giddiness, thick-headedness, asininity, slowness, lack of judgment, baloney*, bull*, hooey*.—*Ant.* INTELLI-

GENCE, wisdom, judgment. **2.** [Extreme folly] nonsense, absurdity, silliness; see CARELESSNESS, NONSENSE 2.

stupidly *a.* imprudently, stubbornly, obtusely; see FOOLISHLY.

sturdy *a.* firm, resolute, unyielding; see STRONG 1, 2.

stutter *v.* stumble, falter, sputter; see STAMMER.

style *n.* **1.** [Distinctive manner] way, form, technique; see METHOD. **2.** [Fashion] vogue, habit, custom; see FASHION 2.

stylish *a.* chic, smart, in fashion; see FASHIONABLE.

suave *a.* sophisticated, ingratiating, urbane; see CULTURED.

subconscious *a.* subliminal, innermost, inmost; see MENTAL 2.

subconscious *n.* the unconscious, psyche, mind; see SOUL 2.

subject *a.* governed, ruled, controlled, directed, obedient, submissive, servile, slavish, subservient, subjected, at one's feet, at the mercy of.

subject *n.* substance, matter, theme, material, topic, question, problem, point, case, matter for discussion, matter in hand, item on the agenda, topic under consideration, field of inquiry, head, chapter, argument, thought, discussion.

subject *v.* cause to experience something, lay open, expose, submit.

subjective *a.* nonobjective, biased, personal; see PREJUDICED.

subjectively *a.* internally, intrinsically, individually, egocentrically, mentally, nonobjectively, emotionally, introspectively, inherently; see also PERSONALLY 2.

sublime *a.* exalted, lofty, stately; see GRAND.

submarine *n.* underseas boat, submersible, sub; see SHIP.

submerge *v.* submerse, engulf, swamp; see IMMERSE, SINK 2.

submission *n.* obedience, meekness, assent; see RESIGNATION 1.

submissive *a.* passive, tractable, yielding; see DOCILE.

submit *v.* **1.** [To offer] tender, proffer, present; see OFFER 1. **2.** [To surrender] capitulate, yield, give in; see OBEY.

subordinate *a.* inferior, junior, smaller, low, insignificant, subnormal, paltry, not up to snuff*, below par, unequal to, not comparable to, lower, minor, depending on, lower in rank, subject, subservient, submissive, subsidiary; see also UNDER 2.—*Ant.* superior, higher, excellent.

subordinate *n.* assistant, helper, aide; see ASSISTANT.

subsequent *a.* succeeding, consequent, coming after; see FOLLOWING.

subsequently *a.* afterward, consequently, in the end; see FINALLY 2.

subside *v.* recede, sink, dwindle; see FALL 1.

subsidiary *a.* secondary, auxiliary, supplementary; see SUBORDINATE.

subsidize *v.* support, finance, back; see PROMOTE 1.

subsidy *n.* allowance, support, scholarship; see PAYMENT 1.

subsist *v.* stay alive, remain alive, live on; see LIVE 4.

subsistence *n.* **1.** [The supporting of life] living, sustenance, maintenance, support, keep, necessities of life. **2.** [The means of supporting life] means, circumstances, resources, property, money, riches, wealth, capital, substance, affluence, independence, gratuity, fortune, dowry, legacy, earnings, wages, salary, income, pension; see also FUNDS.—*Ant.* POVERTY, penury, pennilessness.

substance *n.* matter, material, being, object, item, person, animal, something, element; see also THING 1.

substantial *a.* **1.** [Real] material, actual, visible; see TANGIBLE. **2.** [Considerable] ample, abundant, plentiful; see LARGE 1, MUCH 2.

substantially *a.* extensively, considerably, largely; see MUCH 1, 2.

substitute *n.* deputy, double, dummy, relief, stand-in, understudy, proxy, replacement, ringer*, sub*, pinch-hitter; see also DELEGATE.

substitute *v.* act for, do the work of, replace, supplant, displace, take another's place, double for, answer for, pass for, go for, go as, fill in for, pinch-hit for, take the rap for*, go to bat for*, front for, be in someone's shoes.

substitution *n.* replacement, change, swap; see EXCHANGE 2.

subterranean *a.* subsurface, sunken, subterraneous; see UNDERGROUND.

subtle *a.* indirect, implied, insinuated; see MENTAL 2.

subtlety *n.* fine distinction, nuance, innuendo; see SUGGESTION 1.

subtract *v.* deduct, take away, withhold; see DECREASE 2.

subtraction *n.* deducting, deduction, diminution; see DISCOUNT, REDUCTION 1.

suburb *n.* outlying district, residential district, outskirts; see AREA.

suburban *a.* near a city, residential, rural; see DISTRICT, LOCAL 1, RURAL.

subversion *n.* overthrow, subversive activities, un-American activities; see DEFEAT, REVOLUTION 2.

subversive *a.* ruinous, riotous, insurgent; see REBELLIOUS.

subway *n.* underground (British), tube (British), rapid transit; see RAILROAD, TRAIN.

succeed *v.* **1.** [To attain success] achieve, accomplish, get, prosper, attain, reach, be successful, fulfill, earn, do well, secure, succeed in, score, obtain, thrive, profit, realize, acquire, flourish, be victorious, capture, reap, benefit, recover, retrieve, gain, receive; master, triumph, possess, overcome, win, win out, work out, carry out, surmount, prevail, conquer, vanquish, distance, outdistance, reduce, suppress, worst, work, outwit, outmaneuver, score a point, be accepted, be well-known, grow famous, carry off, pull off, come off, come through, make one's way, make one's fortune, satisfy one's ambition, make one's mark, hit it, hit the mark, live high, come through with flying colors, beat the game*, work well, overcome all obstacles, play one's cards well, crown, top, do oneself proud*, make it*, make good*, do all right by oneself, be on top of the heap*, go places*, click*, set the world on fire*, cut the mustard*, make a killing, put across*.—*Ant.* FAIL, give up, go amiss. **2.** [To follow in time] follow after, come after, take the place of, ensue, supervene, supplant, supersede, replace, postdate, displace, come next, become heir to, result, be subsequent to, follow in order, bring up the rear.

succeeding *a.* ensuing, following after, next in order; see FOLLOWING.

success *n.* **1.** [The fact of having succeeded to a high degree] fortune, good luck, achievement, gain, benefit, prosperity, victory, advance, attainment, progress, profit, end, completion, triumph, conclusion, accomplishment, the life of Riley*, bed of roses*, favorable outcome.—*Ant.* DEFEAT, loss, disaster. **2.** [A successful person or thing] celebrity, famous person, leader, authority, master, expert, man of fortune, somebody, star, VIP*, tops.—*Ant.* FAILURE, loser, nonentity.

successful *a.* prosperous, fortunate, lucky, victorious, triumphant, auspicious, happy, unbeaten, favorable, strong, propitious, advantageous, encouraging, contented, satisfied, thriving, flourishing, wealthy, ahead of the game*, at the top of the ladder, out in front, on the track*, over the hump*.—*Ant.* UNSUCCESSFUL, poor, failing.

successfully *a.* fortunately, triumphantly, luckily, victoriously, happily, favorably, strongly, thrivingly, flourishingly, famously, propitiously, auspiciously, prosperously, contentedly, beyond all expectation.

succession *n.* continuation, suite, set; see SEQUENCE 1, SERIES.

successive *a.* serial, succeeding, in line; see CONSECUTIVE.

successor *n.* heir, follower, replacement; see CANDIDATE.

such *a.* so, so very, of this kind, of that kind, of the sort, of the degree, so much, beforementioned.

such *pron.* this, that, such a one, such a person, such a thing. **—as such** in and of itself, by its own nature, more than in name only; see ACCORDINGLY, ESSENTIALLY.

such as *conj. & prep.* for example, for instance, to give an example; see INCLUDING, SIMILARLY, THUS.

such as it is *a.* as is, however poor it may be, for whatever it is worth; see INADEQUATE, POOR 2.

suck *v.* absorb, take up, swallow up; see SWALLOW.

sucker *n.* **1.** [A fish] lumpfish, sand sucker, brook sucker; see FISH. **2.** [*A victim] dupe, fool, cat's-paw; see VICTIM. **3.** [Candy] sweet, confectionary, lollipop; see CANDY.

suction *n.* sucking, the force of a vacuum, effect of atmospheric pressures; see ATTRACTION, POWER 2, PULL 1.

sudden *a.* precipitate, swift, impromptu; see IMMEDIATE, UNEXPECTED. **—all of a sudden** unexpectedly, suddenly, precipitously; see QUICKLY.

suddenly *a.* without any warning, abruptly, swiftly; see QUICKLY.

suds *n.* foam, bubbles, lather; see FROTH, SOAP.

sue *v.* prosecute, follow up, claim, demand, indict, litigate, contest, pray, entreat, plead, petition, appeal, accuse, file a plea, enter a plea, claim damages, go to law, file suit, prefer a claim, enter a lawsuit, take one to court, file a claim, have the law on one, haul into court.

suffer *v.* **1.** [To feel pain] undergo, experience, ache, smart, be in pain, be wounded; agonize, grieve, be racked, be convulsed, droop, flag, sicken, torture oneself, get it in the neck*, look green about the gills, complain of, be affected with, go hard with, match it, flinch at, not feel like anything, labor under.—*Ant.* RECOVER, be relieved, be restored. **2.** [To endure] bear, sustain, put up with; see ENDURE 2. **3.** [To permit] admit, let, submit; see ALLOW.

suffering *n.* distress, misery, affliction; see DIFFICULTY 1, 2, PAIN 2.

sufficient *a.* adequate, ample, satisfactory; see ENOUGH 1.

sufficiently *a.* to one's satisfaction, enough, amply; see ADEQUATELY.

suffocate *v.* stifle, smother, strangle; see CHOKE.

sugar *n. Common varieties and forms of sugar include the following:* sucrose, cane sugar, brown sugar, beet sugar, grape sugar, dextrose, fructose, fruit sugar, maltose, malt sugar, lactose, maple sugar; see also FOOD.

sugary *a.* sticky, granular, candied; see SWEET 1.

suggest *v.* **1.** [To make a suggestion] submit, advise, recommend; see PROPOSE 1. **2.** [To bring to mind] imply, infer, intimate; see HINT.

suggested *a.* submitted, advanced, proposed, propounded, advised, recommended, counseled, tendered, reminded, prompted, summoned up, called up, offered, laid before, put forward.

suggestion *n.* **1.** [A suggested detail] hint, allusion, suspicion, intimation, implication, innuendo, insinuation, opinion, proposal, advice, recommendation, injunction, charge, instruction, submission, reminder, approach, advance, bid, idea, tentative statement, presentation, proposition. **2.** [A suggested plan] scheme, idea, outline; see PLAN 2. **3.** [A very small quantity] trace, touch, taste; see BIT 1.

suicide *n.* self-murder, self-destruction, hara-kiri; see DEATH.

suit *n.* **1.** [A series] suite, set, group; see SERIES. **2.** [A case at law] lawsuit, action, litigation; see TRIAL 2. **3.** [Clothes to be worn together] costume, ensemble, outfit, livery, uniform; see also CLOTHES. *Kinds of suits include the following— women:* sport suit, tailored suit, man-tailored suit, jump suit, evening suit, bathing suit, sun suit, play suit; *men:* sport suit, business suit, full dress, tails*, monkey suit*, dinner jacket, tuxedo, tux*, bathing suit. —**bring suit** prosecute, start legal proceedings, initiate a case; see SUE.

suit *v.* **1.** [To be in accord with] befit, be agreeable, be appropriate to; see AGREE. **2.** [To please] amuse, fill, gratify; see ENTERTAIN 1, SATISFY 1. **3.** [To adapt] accommodate, revise, readjust; see ALTER 1.

suitable *a.* fitting, becoming, proper; see FIT 1.

suitably *a.* well, all to the good, pleasantly; see FIT 1.

suitcase *n.* case, grip, satchel; see BAG.

suited *a.* adapted, satisfactory, fitted; see FIT 1.

sullen *a.* unsociable, silent, morose, glum, sulky, sour, cross, ill-humored, petulant, moody, grouchy, fretful, ill-natured, peevish, gloomy, gruff, churlish; see also IRRITABLE.—*Ant.* FRIENDLY, sociable, jolly.

sullenly *a.* morosely, glumly, sourly; see ANGRILY, SILENTLY.

sum *n.* amount, value, worth; see WHOLE.

summarily *a.* promptly, readily, speedily; see IMMEDIATELY.

summarize *v.* review, compile, shorten; see DECREASE.

summary *n.* outline, digest, synopsis, recap, analysis, abstract, abbreviation, resume, précis, skeleton, brief, case, reduction, version, core, report, survey, sketch, syllabus, condensation, sum and substance, wrap-up*.

summer *n.* summertime, summer season, dog days, sunny season, harvest, haying time, vacation, picnic days; see also SEASON.

summit *n.* apex, zenith, crown; see TOP 1.

summon *v.* request, beckon, send for, invoke, bid, ask, draft, petition, signal, motion, sign, order, command, direct, enjoin, conjure up, ring, charge, recall, call in, call for, call out, call forth, call up, call away, call down, call together, volunteer.

sum up *v.* summarize, review, conclude; see TOTAL.

sun *n.* day-star, solar disk, eye of heaven, light of the day, solar energy, source of light; see also STAR 1. —**under the sun** on earth, terrestrial, mundane; see EARTHLY.

sunburned *a.* tanned, burned, sunburnt, brown, suntanned, bronzed, ruddy.—*Ant.* PALE, white skinned, pallid.

Sunday *n.* first day, day off, Lord's day; see WEEKEND.

sunken *a.* lowered, depressed, down; see UNDER 1.

sunlight *n.* daylight, sunshine, light of day; see LIGHT 1.

sunny *a.* shining, brilliant, sunshiny; see BRIGHT 1.

sunrise *n.* peep of day, daybreak, aurora; see MORNING 1.

sunset *n.* sundown, evening, end of the day, close of the day, nightfall, twilight, dusk; see also NIGHT 1.—*Ant.* MORNING, dawn, sunrise.

sunshine *n.* sunlight, the sun, sunbeams; see LIGHT 1.

superb *a.* magnificent, splendid, elegant; see EXCELLENT, GRAND.

superficial *a.* flimsy, cursory, hasty, shallow, short-sighted, ignorant, narrow-minded, prejudiced, partial, external, unenlightened.—*Ant.* LEARNED, deep, profound.

superficially *a.* lightly, on the surface, frivolously; see CARELESSLY.—*Ant.* CAREFULLY, thoroughly, thoughtfully.

superfluous *a.* unnecessary, excessive, exorbitant; see EXTREME.

superintendent *n.* supervisor, inspector, director; see EXECUTIVE.

superior *a.* higher, better, preferred, above, finer, of higher rank, a cut above*, more exalted; see also EXCELLENT.

superiority *n.* supremacy, preponderance, advantage; see PERFECTION.

supernatural *a.* superhuman, spectral, ghostly, occult, hidden, mysterious, secret, unknown, unrevealed, dark, mystic, mythical, mythological, fabulous, legendary, unintelligible, unfathomable, inscrutable, incomprehensible, undiscernible, transcendental, obscure, unknowable, impenetrable, invisible, concealed.—*Ant.* NATURAL, plain, common.

superstition *n.* false belief, fear, superstitious fear; see FEAR.

superstitious *a.* fearful, apprehensive, credulous; see AFRAID.

supervise *v.* oversee, conduct, control; see MANAGE 1.

supervised *a.* directed, administered, superintended; see MANAGED 2.

supervision *n.* guidance, surveillance, direction; see MANAGEMENT 1.

supervisor *n.* director, superintendent, administrator; see EXECUTIVE.

supper *n.* evening meal, tea, late refreshments; see DINNER.

supplement *n.* sequel, continuation, complement; see ADDITION 1.

supplement *v.* add to, reinforce, strengthen; see INCREASE.

supplementary *a.* additional, completing, supplemental; see EXTRA.

supplied *a.* provided, furnished, endowed; see GIVEN.

supply *n.* stock, amount, number; see QUANTITY.

supply *v.* furnish, fulfill, outfit; see SATISFY 3.

support *n.* **1.** [Aid] care, assistance, comfort; see HELP 1. **2.** [A reinforcement] lining, coating, rib, stilt, stay, supporter, buttress, pole, post, prop, guide, backing, stiffener, rampart, stave, stake, rod, pillar, timber; see also BRACE. **3.** [Financial aid] maintenance, livelihood, sustenance; see PAYMENT 1.

support *v.* **1.** [To hold up from beneath] prop, hold up, buoy up, keep up, shore up, bear up, bolster, buttress, brace, sustain, stay, keep from falling, shoulder carry, bear.—*Ant.* DROP, let fall, break down. **2.** [To uphold] maintain, sustain, back up, abet, aid, assist, help, bolster, comfort, carry, bear out, hold, foster, shoulder, corroborate, cheer, establish, promote, advance, champion, advocate, approve, stick by, stand by, stand behind, substantiate, verify, get back of, stick up for*, go to bat for*, confirm, further, encourage, hearten, strengthen, recommend, take care of, pull for, agree with, stand up for, keep up, stand back of, take the part of, rally round, give a lift to, boost. **3.** [To provide for] take care of, keep an eye on, care for, attend to, look after, back, bring up, sponsor, put up the money for, finance, pay for, subsidize, nurse, pay the expenses of, grubstake, stake, raise.—*Ant.* ABANDON, ignore, fail.

supported *a.* **1.** [Backed personally] financed, promoted, sustained; see BACKED 2. **2.** [Supported physically] held up, propped up, braced, bolstered, borne up, floating on, floated, buoyed up, based on, founded on, raised up, having a sufficient base, having an adequate foundation; see also FIRM 1.

supporter *n.* advocate, sponsor, helper; see PATRON.

suppose *v.* conjecture, surmise, deem; see GUESS.

supposed *a.* assumed, presumed, presupposed; see LIKELY 1.

supposedly *a.* seemingly, supposably, believably; see PROBABLY.

supposing *conj. & a.* if, in case that, in these circumstances, under these conditions, let us suppose, allowing that, presuming, assuming, taking for granted that.

suppress *v.* crush, overpower, subdue; see DEFEAT.

suppression *n.* abolition, suppressing, overthrow; see DEFEAT.

supremacy *n.* domination, mastery, supreme authority; see POWER 2.

supreme *a.* highest, greatest, paramount, chief; see also BEST.

sure *a. & interj.* certainly, of course, by all means, positively, absolutely, but definitely; see also SURELY.

sure *a.* positive, assured, convinced; see CERTAIN 1. —**for sure** certainly, for certain, without doubt; see SURELY. —**make sure** make certain, determine, establish; see GUARANTEE. —**to be sure** of course, certainly, obviously; see SURELY.

sure-fire* *a.* dependable, good, infallible; see EXCELLENT, RELIABLE.

surely *a.* doubtlessly, certainly, undoubtedly, definitely, absolutely, evidently, explicitly, without doubt, beyond doubt, beyond question, plainly, infallibly, most assuredly, decidedly, inevitably, indisputably, positively, unquestionably, without any doubt, admittedly, clearly, with assurance, beyond the shadow of a doubt, nothing else but, precisely, conclusively, distinctly, by all means, at any rate, with certainty, unerringly, unmistakably, at all events, undeniably, with confidence, as a matter of course, rain or shine*.

sure thing* *n.* no gamble, certainty, safe investment; see WINNER.

surf *n.* breakers, rollers, combers; see WAVE 1.

surface *n.* exterior, covering, superficies; see COVER 1, OUTSIDE 1.

surgeon *n.* specialist in surgery, surgical expert, internist; see DOCTOR.

surgery *n.* operative surgery, the knife*, operation; see MEDICINE 3, OPERATION 4.

surname *n.* cognomen, last name, patronymic; see NAME 1.

surpass *v.* excel, outdo, better; see EXCEED.

surplus *n.* residue, leftover, something extra; see EXCESS 1, REMAINDER.

surprise *n.* **1.** [A feeling] astonishment, wonderment, shock; see WONDER 1. **2.** [The cause of a feeling] something unexpected, blow, sudden attack, unexpected good fortune, sudden misfortune, unawaited event, unsuspected plot. —**take by surprise** startle, assault, sneak up on; see SURPRISE *v.*

surprise *v.* astonish, astound, bewilder, confound, shock, overwhelm, dumbfound, unsettle, stun, electrify, petrify, startle, stupefy, stagger, take aback, cause wonder, awe, dazzle, daze, perplex, leave aghast, flabbergast, floor*, bowl over*, jar, take one's breath away, strike dumb, beggar belief, creep up on, catch unaware.

surprised *a.* upset, taken unaware, astounded, caught napping, astonished, bewildered, taken by surprise, shocked, confounded, startled.

surprising *a.* extraordinary, remarkable, shocking; see UNEXPECTED, UNUSUAL 1, 2.

surrender *n.* capitulation, yielding, giving up, submission, giving way, unconditional surrender, abdication, resignation, delivery.

surrender *v.* **1.** [To accept defeat] capitulate, yield, give in; see QUIT 2. **2.** [To relinquish possession] give up, let go, resign; see ABANDON 1.

surround *v.* **1.** [To be on all sides] girdle, circle, environ, enclose, close in, close around, circle about, envelop, hem in, wall in. **2.** [To take a position on all sides] encompass, encircle, inundate, flow around, close in, close around, hem in, go around, beleaguer, blockade.—*Ant.* ABANDON, flee from, desert.

surrounded *a.* girdled, encompassed, encircled, hemmed in, fenced in, hedged in, circled about, enclosed, fenced about, enveloped.—*Ant.* FREE, unfenced, agape.

surrounding *a.* enclosing, encircling, encompassing; see AROUND.

surroundings *n.pl.* setting, environs, vicinity; see ENVIRONMENT.

survey *n.* study, critique, outline; see EXAMINATION 1.

survey *v.* **1.** [To look upon] look over, take a view of, view; see SEE 1. **2.** [To examine or summarize] study, scan, inspect; see EXAMINE.

survival *n.* endurance, durability, continuance; see CONTINUATION.

survive *v.* **1.** [To live on] outlive, outlast, outwear, live down, live out, weather the storm, make out, persist, persevere, last, remain, pull through, come through, keep afloat, get on; see also ENDURE 1. **2.** [To endure] suffer through, withstand, sustain; see ENDURE 2.

survivor *n.* descendant, heir, widow, widower, orphan.

suspect *a.* dubious, questionable, suspected; see SUSPICIOUS 2, UNLIKELY.

suspect *v.* **1.** [To doubt someone] distrust, disbelieve, mistrust; see DOUBT. **2.** [To suppose] presume, surmise, speculate; see ASSUME.

suspected *a.* doubtful, imagined, fancied; see SUSPICIOUS 2.

suspend *v.* **1.** [To exclude temporarily] reject, exclude, drop, remove; see also BAR 2, EJECT, REFUSE. **2.** [To cease temporarily] postpone, defer, put off, discontinue, adjourn, interrupt, delay, procrastinate, shelve, waive, retard, protract, lay on the table, file, lay aside, break up, restrain, desist, break off, halt, put a stop to, check, put an end to.—*Ant.* CONTINUE, carry on, proceed.

suspended *a.* pensile, postponed, pendulous; see HANGING.

suspense *n.* apprehension, indecisiveness, dilemma; see DOUBT.

suspicion *n.* misgiving, mistrust, surmise; see DOUBT. **—above suspicion** honorable, cleared, gentlemanly; see HONEST 1, INNOCENT 1. **—under suspicion** suspected, held for questioning, dubious; see SUSPICIOUS 2.

suspicious *a.* **1.** [Entertaining suspicion] jealous, distrustful, suspecting, doubting, questioning, doubtful, dubious, in doubt, skeptical, unbelieving, wondering.—*Ant.* TRUSTING, trustful, without any doubt of. **2.** [Arousing suspicion] not quite trustworthy, questionable, queer, suspect, irregular, unusual, peculiar, out of line, debatable, disputable.—*Ant.* REGULAR, usual, common.

suspiciously *a.* doubtingly, doubtfully, skeptically, dubiously, uncertainly, unbelievingly, questioningly, in doubt, having doubt, causing suspicion, with caution, with reservations, with a grain of salt.

sustain *v.* **1.** [To carry] bear, transport, pack; see CARRY 1, SUPPORT 1, 2. **2.** [To nourish] maintain, provide for, nurse; see PROVIDE 1, SUPPORT 2.

swallow *v.* consume, engulf, gulp, take, wash down, pour, swill, bolt, swig, choke down, swallow up, toss off; see also DRINK 1, EAT 1.

swamp *n.* bog, fen, quagmire, morass, marsh, slough, soft ground, wet ground, mire, peat bog, bottoms, river bottoms, lowland, bottomland, muskeg.

swampy *a.* boggy, wet, miry; see MUDDY 2.

swanky *a.* showy, elegant, swank*; see EXCELLENT, EXPENSIVE, ORNATE.

swap* *v.* interchange, trade, barter; see EXCHANGE.

swarm *n.* throng, crowd, multitude, horde, pack, troop, school.

swarm *v.* rush together, crowd, throng; see GATHER, RUN.

swarthy *a.* dark skinned, brown, tawny, dark hued, dark complexioned.

swat *v.* beat, knock, slap; see HIT 1.

sway *n.* swaying, swinging, swing, leaning, oscillation, vibration, undulation, wave, wavering, pulsation.

sway *v.* bend, oscillate, swagger; see WAVE 3.

swear *v.* **1.** [To curse] blaspheme, utter profanity, cuss*; see CURSE. **2.** [To take an oath] avow, affirm, testify, state, vow, attest, warrant, vouch, assert, swear by, give witness, cross one's heart.

sweat *n.* perspiration, beads of sweat, sweating, steam.

sweat *v.* perspire, secrete, swelter, wilt, exude, break out in a sweat.
sweater *n. Types of sweaters include the following:* coat, twin, evening, sport, long-sleeved, short-sleeved, barrel, sleeveless, crew neck, turtleneck; pullover, cardigan; see also CLOTHES.
sweaty *a.* perspiring, moist, wet with perspiration, glowing, bathed in sweat; see also HOT 1.
sweep *v.* brush up, clear, clear up; see CLEAN, MOP.
sweep under the rug* *v.* conceal, ignore, put out of sight; see HIDE 1, NEGLECT 1.
sweet *a.* **1.** [Sweet in taste] toothsome, sugary, luscious, candied, honeyed, saccharine, cloying, like nectar, delicious; see also RICH 4.—*Ant.* SOUR, bitter, sharp. **2.** [Sweet in disposition] agreeable, pleasing, engaging, winning, delightful, reasonable, gentle, kind, generous, unselfish, even-tempered, good-humored, considerate, thoughtful, companionable; see also FRIENDLY.—*Ant.* SELFISH, repulsive, inconsiderate. **3.** [Sweet in smell] fragrant, sweet-smelling, fresh, delicate, delicious, spicy, rich, perfumed, clean.
sweeten *v.* add sugar, make sweet, add sweetening; see FLAVOR.
sweetheart *n.* beloved, dear, loved one; see LOVER 1.
sweetly *a.* agreeably, pleasantly, comfortably, gently, gratefully, softly, smoothly, kindly, in a winning manner, charmingly.
sweets *n.pl.* bonbons, candy, confection, sweetmeats, preserves, candied fruit; see also CANDY.
swell* *a.* just what one wants, desirable, fine; see EXCELLENT.
swell *v.* dilate, expand, distend, increase, enlarge, grow, grow larger, puff up, be inflated, become larger, bulge, puff, inflate, bulge out, blister, round out, fill out.
swelling *n.* welt, wart, pimple, carbuncle, boil, pock, pustule, inflammation, growth, corn, lump, bunion, tumor, blister, abscess; see also INJURY.
swerve *v.* move, bend, turn aside; see TURN 6.
swift *a.* flying, sudden, speedy; see FAST 1.
swiftly *a.* speedily, rapidly, fast; see QUICKLY.
swim *n.* bath, dip, plunge, dive, jump, splash.
swim *v.* bathe, float, glide, slip through the water, stroke, paddle, go for a swim, take a dip, train for the swimming team, swim freestyle.
swimming *n.* diving, aquatic, bathing; see SPORT 3.
swimmingly *a.* successfully, smoothly, effectively; see EASILY, QUICKLY.
swindle *n.* imposition, deception, knavery; see TRICK 1.
swindle *v.* dupe, victimize, defraud; see DECEIVE.
swindler *n.* cheat, cheater, thief, impostor, charlatan, trickster, deceiver, falsifier, counterfeiter, card shark*, forger, fraud, con-man*, fourflusher*, sharper, gyp*; see also CRIMINAL.
swing *n.* sway, motion, fluctuation, stroke, vibration, oscillation, lilt, beat, rhythm; see also WAVE 2. —**in full swing** lively, vigorous, animated; see ACTIVE, EXCITING.
swing *v.* sway, pivot, rotate, turn, turn about, revolve, fluctuate, waver, vibrate, turn on an axis; see also WAVE 3.
swinger* *n.* sex deviant, sophisticated person, life of the party*, mistress, cohabitant.
switch *v.* turnabout, shift, rearrange; see ALTER 1, TURN 2.
swollen *a.* distended, puffed, swelled; see ENLARGED.
swoop *n.* plunge, fall, drop; see DESCENT 2, DIVE 1.
swoop *v.* slide, plummet, plunge; see DESCEND, DIVE, FALL 1.
sword *n.* saber, rapier, weapon; see KNIFE.
syllabus *n.* digest, outline, synopsis; see PLAN 1, PROGRAM 2.
symbol *n.* representative, token, figure; see SIGN 1.
symbolic *a.* representative, typical, indicative, suggestive, symptomatic, characteristic.
symbolize *v.* typify, signify, express; see MEAN 1.
symmetry *n.* proportion, arrangement, order, equality, regularity, conformity, agreement, shapeliness, evenness, balance, equilibrium, similarity.
sympathetic *a.* compassionate, loving, considerate; see THOUGHTFUL 2.
sympathetically *a.* sensitively, perceptively, responsively, harmoniously, in accord, in harmony, in concert, understandingly, appreciatively, emotionally, with feeling, warmly, heartily, cordially, kindheartedly, warmheartedly, softheartedly, humanely, in tune with.
sympathize *v.* pity, show mercy, comfort, understand, be understanding, love, be kind to, commiserate, express sympathy.
sympathy *n.* **1.** [Fellow feeling] understanding, commiseration, compassion; see PITY. **2.** [An expression of sympathy] condolence, consolation, solace, comfort, cheer, encouragement, reassurance; see also HELP 1.
symptom *n.* mark, sign, token; see CHARACTERISTIC.
synonymous *a.* same, like, similar, equivalent, identical, correspondent, corresponding, alike, interchangeable, convertible, compatible, coincident; see also EQUAL.—*Ant.* OPPOSITE, divergent, contrary.

synopsis *n.* outline, digest, brief; see SUMMARY.

syntax *n.* order of words, arrangement, grammatical rules; see GRAMMAR, LANGUAGE 2.

synthetic *a.* artificial, counterfeit, plastic; see FALSE 3.

syrup *n.* glucose, molasses, honey; see SUGAR. *Kinds of syrup include the following:* cane, corn, maple, simple, rock candy.

system *n.* orderliness, regularity, conformity, logical order, definite plan, arrangement, rule, systematic order, systematic arrangement, logical process; see also ORDER 3.

systematize *v.* plan, arrange, organize; see ORDER 3.

T

tab *n.* loop, stop, clip; see LABEL, MARKER, TAG 2.

table *n.* **1.** [A piece of furniture] desk, pulpit, stand, board, counter, slab, dresser, bureau, lectern, sideboard, washstand, sink; see also FURNITURE. *Tables include the following:* writing table, secretary, dining table, kitchen table, card table, drafting table, vanity table, drop-leaf table, operating table, altar table, end table, laboratory table, library table, refectory table. **2.** [A statement in tabulated form] synopsis, report, record; see SUMMARY. **—turn the tables** reverse, change, switch; see ALTER 1. **—under the table*** covertly, surreptitiously, not obviously; see SECRETLY.

tableau *n.* scene, picture, illustration; see VIEW.

tablecloth *n.* covering, spread, place mats; see COVER 1.

tablet *n.* **1.** [A thin piece of material bearing a legend] slab, stone, monument; see MEMORIAL. **2.** [Writing paper] folder, pad, sheets; see PAPER 4. **3.** [A pharmaceutical preparation] pill, dose, capsule; see MEDICINE 2.

taboo *a.* forbidden, out of bounds, reserved; see ILLEGAL, RESTRICTED.

taboo *n.* restriction, reservation, limitation; see RESTRAINT 2.

taboo *v.* inhibit, forbid, prevent; see HINDER, RESTRAIN.

tabulate *v.* formulate, arrange, index; see LIST 1, RECORD 1.

tack *n.* **1.** [A short, broad-headed nail] thumbtack, push pin, carpet tack, copper tack; see also NAIL, PIN 1. **2.** [An oblique course] tangent, deviation, digression; see TURN 6.

tack *v.* **1.** [To fasten lightly] pin, nail, stitch; see FASTEN. **2.** [To steer an oblique course] go in zigzags, zigzag, change course; see TURN 6.

tackle *n.* **1.** [Equipment] rigging, ropes and pulleys, apparatus; see EQUIPMENT. **2.** [A contrivance having mechanical advantage] pulleys, block-and-tackle, movable pulley; see TOOL 1. **3.** [In football, an attempt to down a ball-carrier] flying, running, shoulder, etc. tackle; sack, hit; see DEFENSE 1, JUMP. **4.** [In football, one who plays between end and guard] linesman, right tackle, left tackle; see FOOTBALL PLAYER. **5.** [In fishing, equipment] gear, sporting goods, fishing outfit; see EQUIPMENT. *Fishing tackle includes the following:* hook, line, fly, casting rod, casting reel, cut bait, live bait, minnow, grasshopper, fish eggs, worm, lure, spinner, fish net, landing net, pole, float, cork, sinker, creel, tackle box, shot, deep-sea tackle, leader, stringer, fish sack, basket.

tackle *v.* **1.** [To undertake] begin, turn to, make an attempt; see TRY 1, UNDERTAKE. **2.** [In football, to endeavor to down an opponent] seize, throw down, grab; see UPSET 1.

tact *n.* perception, discrimination, judgment, acuteness, penetration, intelligence, acumen, common sense, subtlety, discernment, prudence, aptness, good taste, refinement, delicacy, the ability to get along with others, finesse, horse sense*.—*Ant.* RUDENESS, coarseness, misconduct.

tactful *a.* diplomatic, civil, considerate; see THOUGHTFUL 2.

tactics *n.pl.* strategy, maneuvering, military art, generalship, plan of attack, plan of defense, procedure, stratagem, approach, disposition, map work, chalk work.

tactless *a.* stupid, unperceptive, inconsiderate, rude, discourteous, unsympathetic, unthoughtful, insensitive, boorish, misunderstanding, impolite, rash, hasty, awkward, clumsy, imprudent, rough, crude, unpolished, gruff, uncivil, vulgar.

tag *n.* **1.** [A remnant or scrap] rag, piece, patch; see REMNANTS. **2.** [A mark of identification] ticket, badge, card tab, trademark, stamp, stub, voucher, slip, label, check, emblem, insignia, tally, motto, sticker, inscription, laundry mark, price tag, bar code, identification number, button, pin. **3.** [A children's game] hide-and-seek, freeze tag, capture the flag; see GAME 1.

tag *v.* **1.** [To fit with a tag] designate, denote, earmark; see MARK 2. **2.** [*To follow closely] chase, dog, trail; see PURSUE 1.

tail *n.* rear end, rear appendage, extremity, hind part, butt*, coccyx; see also REAR. —**on one's tail** behind, shadowing, trailing; see FOLLOWING. —**with one's tail between one's legs** in defeat, humbly, dejectedly; see FEARFULLY.

tailor *n.* garment maker, clothier, dressmaker, seamstress, designer, fashion designer.

take *n.* **1.** [Something that is taken] part, cut, proceeds; see PROFIT 2, SHARE. **2.** [Scene filmed or televised] film, shot, motion picture; see PHOTOGRAPH. **3.** [*Something that is seized] holding, catching, haul*; see BOOTY.

take *v.* **1.** [To seize] appropriate, take hold of, catch, grip, grab, pluck, pocket, carry off; see also SEIZE 1, 2. **2.** [To collect] gather up, accept, reap; see RECEIVE 1. **3.** [To catch] capture, grab, get hold of; see CATCH 1. **4.** [To choose] select, settle on, opt for, make a selection, pick, decide on, prefer; see also CHOOSE, DECIDE. **5.** [To acquire] win, procure, gain, achieve, receive, attain, obtain, secure; see also EARN 2, GET 1. **6.** [To require] necessitate, demand, call for; see NEED. **7.** [To contract; *said of a disease*] get, come down with, be seized with; see CATCH 4. **8.** [To record] note, register, take notes; see RECORD 1. **9.** [To transport] move, drive, bear; see CARRY 1. **10.** [To captivate] charm, delight, overwhelm; see ENTERTAIN 1, FASCINATE. **11.** [To win] prevail, triumph, beat; see DEFEAT 2, 3. **12.** [To buy] pay for, select, procure; see BUY. **13.** [To rent] lease, hire, charter; see RENT 2. **14.** [To steal] misappropriate, loot, rob; see STEAL. **15.** [To undergo] tolerate, suffer, bear; see ENDURE 2, UNDERGO. **16.** [To lead] guide, steer, pilot; see LEAD 1. **17.** [To escort] conduct, attend, go with; see ACCOMPANY. **18.** [To admit] let in, welcome, give access to; see RECEIVE 4. **19.** [To adopt] utilize, assume, appropriate; see ADOPT 2. **20.** [To apply] put in practice, exert, exercise; see PRACTICE 1, USE 1. **21.** [To experience] sense, observe, be aware of; see FEEL 2. **22.** [To cheat] defraud, trick, swindle; see DECEIVE. **23.** [To grow] germinate, develop into, grow to be; see BECOME.

take a chance* *v.* venture, hazard, gamble; see RISK, TRY 1.

take advantage of *v.* dupe, fool, outwit; see DECEIVE.

take after *v.* **1.** [To resemble] look like, be like, seem like; see RESEMBLE. **2.** [To follow] follow suit, do like, emulate; see FOLLOW 2.

take a picture *v.* shoot, snap, film; see PHOTOGRAPH.

take away *v.* **1.** [To subtract] deduct, take from, minus*; see DECREASE 2. **2.** [To carry off] transport, cart off, carry away; see REMOVE 1.

take back *v.* **1.** [To regain] retrieve, get back, reclaim; see RECOVER 1. **2.** [To restrict] draw in, retire, pull in; see REMOVE 1, WITHDRAW. **3.** [To disavow] retract, recant, recall; see DENY, WITHDRAW.

take care *v.* beware, heed, mind, take heed; see also PREPARE 1, WATCH OUT.

take care of *v.* superintend, oversee, protect; see GUARD.

take down *v.* **1.** [To dismantle] disassemble, take apart, undo; see DISMANTLE. **2.** [To write down] inscribe, jot down, note down; see RECORD 1, WRITE 2.

take for *v.* **1.** [To mistake] misapprehend, misunderstand, err; see MISTAKE. **2.** [To assume] presuppose, infer, accept; see ASSUME.

take from *v.* take, grab, appropriate; see SEIZE 2.

take in *v.* **1.** [To include] embrace, comprise, incorporate; see INCLUDE 1. **2.** [To understand] comprehend, apprehend, perceive; see UNDERSTAND 1. **3.** [To cheat] swindle, lie, defraud; see DECEIVE. **4.** [To give hospitality] welcome, shelter, accept; see RECEIVE 1, 4. **5.** [To shorten] reduce, lessen, cut down; see DECREASE 2.

take in (one's) stride *v.* handle, do, manage; see ACHIEVE, PERFORM 1, SUCCEED 1.

take into account *v.* ponder, study, take into consideration; see CONSIDER, THINK 1.

take into consideration *v.* study, examine, ponder; see CONSIDER, THINK 1.

take into custody *v.* jail, apprehend, imprison; see ARREST.

take it *v.* **1.** [To assume] suppose, presume, gather; see ASSUME. **2.** [To endure] persevere, keep on, carry on; see ENDURE 2.

take it out on* *v.* get even with, get back at, settle with; see REVENGE.

taken *a.* **1.** [Captured] arrested, seized, appropriated; see CAPTURED. **2.** [Employed or rented] occupied, reserved, held; see RENTED.

take notice *v.* heed, perceive, observe; see SEE 1.

take off *v.* **1.** [To undress] strip, divest, expose; see UNDRESS. **2.** [To deduct] lessen, subtract, take away; see DECREASE 2. **3.** [To leave the earth] blast off, ascend, soar; see FLY 1, 4, RISE 1. **4.** [To leave] go away, depart, shove off*; see LEAVE 1.

take-off *n.* ascent, upward flight, fly-off, climb, rise, hop, jump, vertical takeoff; see also RISE 1.

take on *v.* **1.** [To hire] employ, engage, give work to; see HIRE. **2.** [To acquire an appearance] emerge, develop, turn; see BECOME, SEEM. **3.** [To undertake] attempt, handle, endeavor; see TRY 1, UNDERTAKE. **4.** [*To meet in fight or sport] engage, battle, contest; see ATTACK 1, COMPETE.

take one's chances *v.* hazard, jeopardize, try; see CHANCE, RISK.

take one's choice *v.* pick out, discriminate between, make a decision; see CHOOSE, DECIDE.

take out *v.* **1.** [To extract] cut out, pull out, draw out; see REMOVE 1. **2.** [To escort] lead, chaperon, attend; see ACCOMPANY.

take over *v.* **1.** [To take control] take charge, take command, assume control; see LEAD 1. **2.** [To seize control] take the reins of, take the helm of, overthrow; see SEIZE 2. **3.** [To convey] transport, bear, move; see CARRY 1, SEND 1.

take pains *v.* make an effort, care, endeavor; see TRY 1.

take part *v.* associate, cooperate, follow; see JOIN 2, PARTICIPATE 1, SHARE 2.

take place *v.* befall, come to pass, ensue; see HAPPEN 2.

take precautions *v.* foresee, mind, adjust; see PREPARE 1, WATCH OUT.

take seriously *v.* consider, calculate on, work on; see BELIEVE, TRUST 1.

take stock (of) *v.* **1.** [To inventory] enumerate, audit, take account of; see EXAMINE. **2.** [To consider] examine, study, review; see CONSIDER, THINK 1.

take the lead *v.* direct, guide, head; see LEAD 1.

take the place of *v.* replace, take over, supersede; see SUBSTITUTE.

take to *v.* enjoy, be fond of, admire; see FAVOR, LIKE 1, 2.

take up *v.* **1.** [To begin] start, initiate, commence; see BEGIN 1. **2.** [To raise] lift, elevate, hoist; see RAISE 1. **3.** [To shorten] tighten, reduce, lessen; see DECREASE 2. **4.** [To occupy] consume, engage, fill; see OCCUPY 2, USE 1. **5.** [To adopt as a cause] appropriate, become involved with, assume; see ADOPT 2.

tale *n.* **1.** [A story] anecdote, fairy tale, folk tale; see STORY. **2.** [A lie] tall tale, fiction, exaggeration; see LIE.

talent *n.* aptitude, faculty, gift; see ABILITY.

talented *a.* gifted, capable, skilled; see ABLE.

talk *n.* **1.** [Human speech] utterance, locution, parlance; see COMMUNICATION, SPEECH 2. **2.** [A conference] symposium, parley, consultation; see CONVERSATION, DISCUSSION. **3.** [An address] lecture, oration, sermon; see SPEECH 3. **4.** [Gossip] report, hearsay, chatter; see GOSSIP 1, RUMOR. **5.** [Nonsense] noise, rubbish, jive; see JARGON 1, NONSENSE 1.

talk *v.* **1.** [To converse] discuss, confer, chat, interview, speak, communicate, talk together, engage in a meaningful dialogue, have a meeting of the minds, chatter, gossip, yammer, remark, be on the phone with, be in contact with, talk over, reason with, visit with, parley, read, hold a discussion, confide in, argue, observe, notice, inform, rehearse, debate, have an exchange, exchange opinions, have a conference with, talk away, go on*, gab*, chew the fat*, compare notes with, talk a leg off of*, go over*, shoot off one's mouth*, spit out*, shoot the breeze*, pass the time of day, engage in conversation. **2.** [To lecture] speak, give a talk, deliver a speech; see ADDRESS 2. **3.** [To inform] reveal, divulge, notify; see TELL 2. **4.** [To utter] pronounce, express, speak; see UTTER.

talk about *v.* treat, take under consideration, deal with; see CONSIDER, DISCUSS.

talkative *a.* wordy, verbal, long-winded; see FLUENT.

talk back *v.* sass, retort, defy; see ANSWER 1.

talk down to *v.* stoop, snub, be overbearing; see HUMILIATE, PATRONIZE 2.

talker *n.* speaker, orator, speechmaker, mouthpiece, spokesman, lecturer, actor, performer, debater, storyteller, conversationalist, barker, announcer, preacher, lawyer, reader, after-dinner speaker, gossip, windbag*.

talking *a.* eloquent, chattering, mouthing, repeating, echoing, pronouncing, fluent, expressing, articulating, enunciating, ranting, spouting, haranguing, speaking, vocalizing, verbalizing, orating, verbose, conversing, discussing, holding forth.

talk over *v.* consider, consult, deliberate; see DISCUSS.

talk someone into *v.* win over, sway, affect; see CONVINCE, INFLUENCE, PERSUADE.

tall *a.* **1.** [Lofty] big, great, towering; see HIGH 1. **2.** [Exaggerated] far-fetched, outlandish, unbelievable; see EXAGGERATED.

tally *n.* reckoning, account, poll; see SCORE 1.

tally *v.* record, write down, register, mark down, count, total, add up, sum.

tame *a.* **1.** [Domesticated] subdued, submissive, housebroken, harmless, trained, overcome, mastered, civilized, broken in, harnessed, yoked, acclimatized, muzzled, bridled.—*Ant.* WILD, undomesticated, untamed. **2.** [Gentle] tractable, obedient, kindly; see GENTLE 3. **3.** [Uninteresting] insipid, monotonous, routine; see CONVENTIONAL 3, DULL 4, UNINTERESTING.

tamper with *v.* alter, diversify, vary; see ALTER 1, DESTROY.

tan *a.* brownish, sun-tanned, weathered; see BROWN.

tan *n.* light-brown, beige, natural; see BROWN, GOLD, YELLOW.

tang *n.* zest, flavor, savor; see TASTE 2.

tangible *a.* perceptible, palpable, material, real, substantial, sensible, touchable, verifiable, physical, corporeal, solid, visible, stable, well-grounded, incarnated, embodied, manifest, factual, objective, tactile.—*Ant.* SPIRITUAL, ethereal, intangible.

tangle *n.* snarl, snag, muddle; see CONFUSION, KNOT 2.

tangle *v.* involve, complicate, confuse, obstruct, hamper, derange, mix up, disorganize, upset, unbalance, unhinge, perplex, tie up, trap, mess up.—*Ant.* ORDER, fix, unravel.

tangled *a.* tied up, confused, knit together, disordered, chaotic, out of place, mixed up, snarled, trapped, entangled, twisted, raveled, muddled, messed up*, balled up*, screwy*, wires crossed*.

tank *n.* **1.** [A large container for liquids] tub, basin, vat; see CONTAINER. **2.** [An armored caterpillar vehicle] caterpillar, armored personnel carrier, armored car; see WEAPON.

tanned *a.* sunburned, bronzed, tan-faced; see BROWN.

tantrum *n.* rage, outburst, spell; see ANGER, FIT 2.

tap *n.* **1.** [A light blow] pat, rap, dab; see BLOW. **2.** [A spigot] faucet, petcock, drain; see FAUCET.

tap *v.* **1.** [To strike lightly] pat, touch, rap; see HIT 1. **2.** [To puncture in order to draw liquid] perforate, pierce, bore; see PENETRATE.

tape *n.* ribbon, line, rope. *Tapes include the following:* recording tape, cartridge, cassette, edging, tapeline, tape measure, steel tape, surveyor's chain, adhesive tape, gummed tape, draftsman's tape, Scotch tape, masking tape, packing tape, transparent tape, videotape, mending tape.

tape *v.* **1.** [To fasten] tie up, bind, bond; see FASTEN. **2.** [To record] register, make a recording, put on tape; see RECORD 3. **3.** [To bandage] tie, bind up, dress; see BIND 1, FASTEN.

taper *v.* narrow, lessen, thin out; see DECREASE 1, 2.

tape recorder *n.* recording equipment, stereo, stereophonic recorder, cassette recorder, cassette deck, cassette player, dictaphone, VCR, videotape machine, videocassette recorder; see also RECORD PLAYER.

taper off *v.* recede, rescind, diminish; see DECREASE 2.

tar *n.* pitch, mineral pitch, coal tar; see GUM.

tardy *a.* overdue, too late, delayed; see LATE 1, SLOW 2, 3.

target *n.* **1.** [A goal] objective, aim, purpose, end, destination, mark. **2.** [Bull's-eye] point, spot, butt, mark, dummy. **3.** [A prey] quarry, game, scapegoat; see VICTIM.

tarnish *v.* soil, smudge, smear; see DIRTY.

tart *a.* bitter, pungent, sharp; see SOUR.

task *n.* chore, responsibility, business; see DUTY 1.

taste *n.* **1.** [The sense that detects flavor] tongue, taste buds, palate, senses. **2.** [The quality detected by taste] flavor, savor, savoriness, aftertaste, tang, suggestion, zip*, wallop*, kick*, smack*, bang*, jolt*, zing*, punch*. **3.** [Judgment, especially esthetic judgment] discrimination, susceptibility, appreciation, good taste, discernment, acumen, penetration, acuteness, feeling, refinement, appreciation; see also JUDGMENT 1. **4.** [Preference] tendency, leaning, attachment; see INCLINATION 1. —**in bad taste** pretentious, rude, crass; see TASTELESS 3. —**in good taste** delicate, pleasing, refined; see ARTISTIC, DAINTY. —**to one's taste** pleasing, satisfying, appealing; see PLEASANT 2.

taste *v.* **1.** [To test by the tongue] sip, try, touch, sample, lick, suck, roll over in the mouth, partake of. **2.** [To recognize by flavor] sense, savor, distinguish; see KNOW 3. **3.** [To experience] feel, perceive, know; see UNDERGO.

tasteful *a.* **1.** [Delicious] delectable, pleasing, tasty, savory, rich; see also DELICIOUS. **2.** [Esthetically pleasing] delicate, elegant, fine; see DAINTY.

tasteless *a.* **1.** [Lacking flavor] unsavory, bland, dull, unseasoned, vapid, flat, watery, flavorless, without spice; see also DULL 4, ORDINARY 2.—*Ant.* DELICIOUS, seasoned, spicy. **2.** [Plain] homely, insipid, trite; see COMMON 1. **3.** [Lacking good taste] pretentious, ornate, showy, trivial, artificial, florid, ostentatious, clumsy, makeshift, coarse, useless, rude, uncouth, ugly, unsightly, unlovely, hideous, foolish, stupid, crass.—*Ant.* REFINED, civilized, cultivated.

tasty *a.* savory, palatable, appetizing; see DELICIOUS.

tattle *v.* blab, tell on, report; see GOSSIP.

tattler *n.* busybody, tattletale, snoop; see GOSSIP 2, TRAITOR.

tattletale *n.* informer, tattler, busybody, snitch*, fink*, squealer*, stool pigeon*, stoolie*, rat*.

taught *a.* instructed, informed, directed; see EDUCATED, LEARNED 1.

taunt *n.* insult, mockery, jibe; see RIDICULE.

tavern *n.* taproom, alehouse, roadhouse; see BAR 2.

tax *n.* **1.** [A pecuniary levy] fine, charge, rate, toll, levy, impost, duty, assessment, tariff, tribute, obligation, price, cost, contribution, expense; see also DUES. **2.** [A burden] strain, task, demand; see BURDEN 2.

tax *v.* **1.** [To cause to pay a tax] assess, exact from, demand, exact tribute, charge duty, demand toll, require a contribution, enact a tax. **2.** [To burden] encumber, weigh down, overload; see BURDEN.

taxation *n.* levying, assessment, money-gathering; see DUES, TAX 1.

taxed *a.* **1.** [Paying taxes] levied upon, demanded from, required from, assessed, imposed upon, subjected to tax. **2.** [Burdened] overtaxed, strained, harassed, fatigued; see also TIRED.

taxicab *n.* taxi, cab, sightseeing car; see AUTOMOBILE.

tea *n.* **1.** [An infusion made from tea leaves] beverage, brew, infusion, decoction; see also DRINK 2. *Tea and tealike drinks include the following:* black, green, Lapsang, Souchong, Oolong, Darjeeling, orange pekoe, pekoe, Gunpowder, Earl Grey, mixed, jasmine, blended, orange flower, sassafras, sage, mint, camomile, herb. **2.** [A light afternoon or evening meal] snack, refreshment, tea party; see LUNCH, MEAL 2.

teach *v.* instruct, tutor, coach, educate, profess, explain, expound, lecture, direct, give a briefing, edify, enlighten, guide, show, give lessons in, ground, rear, prepare, fit, interpret, bring up, instill, inculcate, indoctrinate, brainwash, develop, form, address to, initiate, inform, nurture, illustrate, imbue, implant, break in, give the facts, give an idea of, improve one's mind, open one's eyes, knock into someone's head*, bring home to*, cram*, stuff*; see also INFLUENCE, MOTIVATE.—*Ant.* LEARN, gain, acquire.

teacher *n.* schoolmaster, schoolmistress, schoolman, educator, public school teacher, high school teacher, tutor, mentor, pedagogue, master, guru, swami, mistress, kindergarten teacher, pupil teacher, teacher-in-training, substitute teacher, professor, lecturer, instructor, faculty member, graduate assistant.

teaching *n.* pedagogy, instruction, normal training; see EDUCATION 1, 3.

team *n.* **1.** [People working together, especially on the stage] partners, combo, troupe, company, duo, trio, foursome; see also ORGANIZATION 2. **2.** [An organization, especially in sport] squad, crew, club; see ORGANIZATION 2.

team up with *v.* attach oneself to, collaborate, corroborate; see ACCOMPANY, COOPERATE, HELP.

teamwork *n.* partisanship, collaboration, union; see ALLIANCE 1, COOPERATION, PARTNERSHIP.

tear *n.* teardrop, droplet, eyewash; see DROP 1.

tear *n.* rent, rip, hole, slit, laceration, split, break, gash, rupture, fissure, crack, cut, breach, damage, imperfection.—*Ant.* REPAIR, patch, renovation.

tear *v.* rend, rip, shred, cut, mangle, split, lacerate; see also CUT 1.

tears *n.pl.* sobbing, sob, crying, cry, weeping, lamenting, whimpering, grieving, mourning, waterworks*; see also GRIEF.

tease *v.* taunt, tantalize, torment; see BOTHER 2, RIDICULE.

teaspoon *n.* kitchen utensil, measuring spoon, 1/3 of a tablespoon, stirrer; see also UTENSILS.

technical *a.* specialized, special, scientific, professional, scholarly, mechanical, methodological, restricted, highly versed, technological, industrial.—*Ant.* ARTISTIC, nontechnical, simplified.

technician *n.* practitioner, professional, engineer; see CRAFTSMAN, SPECIALIST.

technique *n.* procedure, system, routine; see METHOD.

tedious *a.* slow, wearisome, tiresome; see DULL 4.

tedium *n.* boredom, tediousness, dullness; see MONOTONY.

teenage *a.* immature, youthful, adolescent; see YOUNG 1, 2.

teens *n.pl.* boyhood, girlhood, adolescence, early adolescence, late adolescence, awkward age*; see also YOUTH 1.

teeter *v.* seesaw, totter, wobble; see SHAKE 1.

teeth *n.* dentition, fangs, tusks; see TOOTH.

telegram *n.* wire, cable, cablegram, message, teletype copy, radiogram, call, report, summons, night message, night letter, day letter, news message, code message, signal, flash, buzzer*; see also COMMUNICATION.

telegraph *n.* Morse telegraph, wireless, transmitter; see COMMUNICATION, RADIO 2.

telegraph *v.* wire, send a wire, send a cable; see COMMUNICATE 2.

telepathy *n.* insight, premonition, extrasensory perception; see COMMUNICATION.

telephone *n.* phone, private phone, extension phone, radiophone, radiotelephone, car phone, cellular phone, cordless phone, phone machine, fax machine, mouthpiece, line, party line, long distance, extension, pay phone.

telephone *v.* call, call up, phone, ring, ring up, make a call to, dial, call on the phone, fax, put in a call to, phone up*, give a ring, give a buzz*.

telephoned *a.* phoned, radiophoned, called, communicated by telephone, faxed, reached by phone.

telescope *n.* field glasses, binoculars, opera glass, glass, optical instrument, reflecting telescope, refracting telescope, radio telescope; see also GLASSES.

television *n.* T.V., teevee, video, color television, home entertainment center, boob tube*, the tube*, the box*; see also STATION 5.

tell *v.* **1.** [To inform] communicate, explain, instruct, direct, order, divulge, reveal, make known, utter, speak, report, recite, cue in, reel off, spit it out, put before, name over, let in on, let into, open up, give the facts, blow upon, lay open, fill one in, let on, let slip, level with, leave word, hand it to, lay before, break it to, break the news, add up, keep one posted, let know, give out, leak out, give notice, declare, acquaint, advise, confess, impart, notify, represent, assert, mention, tell all, break down with, give away, cough up*, come across with*, shoot*, come clean*, make a clean breast of; see also DISCUSS, SAY.—*Ant.* HIDE, keep secret, be silent. **2.** [To deduce] know, understand, make out, perceive, ascertain, find out, recognize, be sure, differentiate, discriminate, determine, know for certain.

teller *n.* cashier, clerk, bank clerk; see WORKMAN.

telling *a.* crucial, conspicuous, significant; see EFFECTIVE, IMPORTANT 1.

tell off *v.* rebuke, reprimand, chide; see SCOLD.

temper *n.* **1.** [State of mind] disposition, frame of mind, humor; see MOOD 1. **2.** [An angry state of mind] furor, ire, passion; see ANGER, RAGE 1. **3.** [The quality of being easily angered] impatience, excitability, touchiness, sourness, sensitivity, fretfulness, peevishness, irritability, ill humor, petulence, irascibility, crossness, churlishness, pugnacity, sullenness, grouchiness, huffiness.—*Ant.* PATIENCE, calmness, equanimity. **4.** [The quality of induced hardness or toughness in materials] tensile strength, sturdiness, hardness; see FIRMNESS, STRENGTH. **—lose one's temper** become angry, get mad, fly off the handle; see RAGE 1.

temper *v.* **1.** [To soften or qualify] mitigate, pacify, moderate; see EASE 1, 2, SOFTEN. **2.** [To toughen or harden] steel, stiffen, cement; see STRENGTHEN.

temperament *n.* character, disposition, constitution, nature, inner nature, quality, temper, spirit, mood, attitude, type, structure, makeup, humor, mood, outlook, peculiarity, individuality, idiosyncrasy, distinctiveness, psychological habits, mentality, intellect, susceptibility, ego, inclination, tendency, turn of mind.

temperamental *a.* moody, sensitive, touchy; see IRRITABLE.

temperance *n.* moderation, abstinence, self-control; see RESTRAINT 1.

temperate *a.* **1.** [Moderate] regulated, reasonable, fair; see MODERATE 4. **2.** [Neither hot nor cold] medium, warm, balmy; see FAIR 3, MILD 2. **3.** [Not given to drink] abstemious, abstinent, restrained; see MODERATE 5.

temperature *n.* heat, warmth, cold, body heat, weather condition, climatic characteristic, thermal reading, degrees of temperature.

temple *n.* house of prayer, synagogue, pagoda; see CHURCH 1.

tempo *n.* pace, speed, meter; see SPEED.

temporal *a.* **1.** [Transitory] temporary, transient, ephemeral; see TEMPORARY. **2.** [Worldly] secular, earthly, mundane; see WORLDLY.

temporarily *a.* momentarily, briefly, tentatively, for a while, for the moment, for a time, provisionally, transitorily, for the time being, pro tempore, pro tem.—*Ant.* FOREVER, perpetually, perennially.

temporary *a.* transitory, transient, fleeting, short, brief, ephemeral, fugitive, volatile, shifting, passing, summary, momentary, stopgap, makeshift, substitute, for the time being, overnight, *ad hoc* (Latin), impermanent, irregular, changeable, unenduring, unfixed, unstable, perishable, provisional, short-lived, mortal, pro tem, on the go*, on the fly*, on the wing, here today and gone tomorrow*.—*Ant.* PERMANENT, fixed, eternal.

tempt *v.* lure, fascinate, seduce, appeal to, induce, intrigue, incite, provoke, allure, charm, captivate, entice, draw out, bait, stimulate, move, motivate, rouse, instigate, wheedle, coax, inveigle, vamp, make a play for*, make one's mouth water.

temptation *n.* lure, attraction, fascination; see APPEAL 2.

tempted *a.* desiring, inclined, enticed; see CHARMED.

tempting *a.* appetizing, attractive, fascinating; see CHARMING.

ten *a.* tenth, tenfold, decuple, denary, decimal.

tenant *n.* renter, lessee, householder, rent payer, dweller, inhabitant, occupant, resident, roomer, lodger, holder, possessor, leaseholder, tenant farmer; see also RESIDENT.—*Ant.* OWNER, proprietor, landlord.

tend *v.* **1.** [To watch over] care for, manage, direct, superintend, do, perform, accomplish, guard, administer, minister to, oversee, wait upon, attend, serve, nurse, mind; see also MANAGE 1. **2.** [To have a tendency (toward)] lead, point, direct, make for, result in, serve to, be in the habit of, favor, be predisposed to, be prejudiced in favor of, be apt to, gravitate toward, incline to, verge on.

tendency *n.* **1.** [Direction] aim, bent, trend; see DRIFT 1. **2.** [Inclination] leaning, bias, bent; see INCLINATION 1.

tender *a.* **1.** [Soft] delicate, fragile, supple; see SOFT 2. **2.** [Kind] loving, solicitous, compassionate; see KIND. **3.** [Touching] moving, pathetic, affecting; see PITIFUL. **4.** [Sensitive] touchy, ticklish, oversensitive; see RAW 5, SORE 1.

tenderhearted *a.* softhearted, tender, humane; see HUMANE, KIND, MERCIFUL.

tenderly *a.* **1.** [Softly] gently, carefully, delicately; see LIGHTLY. **2.** [Lovingly] fondly, affectionately, appreciatively; see LOVINGLY.

tenderness *n.* love, consideration, care; see FRIENDSHIP, KINDNESS 1.

tending *a.* **1.** [Inclined (toward)] apt to, likely to, working toward; see LIKELY 4. **2.** [Giving attention to] caring for, managing, directing; see MANAGING.

tennis *n.* lawn tennis, court tennis, tennis tournament; see SPORT 3.

tense *a.* **1.** [Nervous] agitated, anxious, high-strung, on edge, fluttery, jumpy, jittery; see also EXCITED.—*Ant.* CALM, unconcerned, indifferent. **2.** [Stretched tight] rigid, stiff, firm; see TIGHT 1.

tension *n.* **1.** [Stress] tautness, force, tightness; see BALANCE 2, STRESS 2. **2.** [Mental stress] pressure, strain, anxiety; see STRESS 2.

tent *n.* shelter, canvas, canopy, tarpaulin, covering; see also COVER 1. *Tentlike coverings include the following:* umbrella tent, awning, marquee, wigwam, tepee, booth, pavilion, pup tent, fly tent, fly, canoe tent, lean-to tent, circus tent, big top*.

tentative *a.* provisional, probationary, makeshift; see EXPERIMENTAL.

tentatively *a.* experimentally, conditionally, provisionally; see TEMPORARILY.

tepee *n.* Indian tent, wigwam, wickiup; see TENT.

term *n.* **1.** [A name] expression, terminology, phrase, word, locution, indication, denomination, article, appellation, designation, title, head, caption, nomenclature, moniker*; see also NAME 1. **2.** [A period of time] span, interval, course, cycle, season, duration, phase, quarter, course of time, semester, school period, session, period of confinement; see also TIME 2. **—come to terms** compromise, arrive at an agreement, arbitrate; see AGREE. **—in terms of** in reference to, about, concerning; see REGARDING.

terminal *a.* final, concluding, last; see LAST 1.

terminal *n.* **1.** [An end] limit, extremity, terminus; see END 4. **2.** [Part of a computer] keyboard, CRT, monitor, printer, screen; see also COMPUTER.

terminate *v.* complete, end, perfect; see ACHIEVE.

termination *n.* finish, close, terminus; see END 2.

terminology *n.* nomenclature, technology, specification; see JARGON 2, LANGUAGE 1.

terms *n.pl.* 1. [Conditions] details, items, points, particulars; see also CIRCUMSTANCES 2. **2.** [An agreement] understanding, treaty, conclusion; see AGREEMENT 1.

terrace *n.* patio, garden, lawn; see GARDEN, YARD 1.

terrain *n.* ground, region, territory; see AREA.

terrible *a.* **1.** [Inspiring terror] terrifying, appalling, fearful, awesome, horrifying, ghastly, awe-inspiring, petrifying, revolting, gruesome, shocking, unnerving; see also FRIGHTFUL.—*Ant.* HAPPY, joyful, pleasant. **2.** [Unwelcome] unfortunate, disastrous, inconvenient, disturbing, atrocious*, lousy*; see also OFFENSIVE 2.—*Ant.* WELCOME, good, attractive.

terribly* *a.* horribly, frightfully, drastically; see BADLY 1, VERY.

terrific *a.* shocking, immense, tremendous; see GREAT 1, LARGE 1.

terrify *v.* shock, horrify, terrorize; see FRIGHTEN.

territorial *a.* regional, sectional*, provincial; see NATIONAL 1.

territory *n.* **1.** [A specified area] region, township, empire; see AREA. **2.** [An area organized politically under the central government] commonwealth, colony, dominion; see NATION 1. **3.** [An indefinite area] section, area, boundary; see REGION 1.

terror *n.* fright, horror, panic; see FEAR.

terrorist *n.* subversive, revolutionary, incendiary; see REBEL.

terrorize *v.* coerce, intimidate, browbeat; see THREATEN.

test *n.* **1.** [A check for adequacy] inspection, analysis, countdown, probing, inquiry, inquest, elimination, proving grounds, training stable, search, dry run*; see also EXAMINATION 1, EXPERIMENT. *Tests include the following:* engineering, technical, structural, mechanical, chemical, countdown, psychological, mental, intelligence, IQ, intelligence quotient, aptitude, vocational, qualifying, comprehensive, written, true-false, multiple choice, objective, diagnostic, semester, term, association, psychiatric. **2.** [A formal examination] quiz, questionnaire, essay; see EXAMINATION 2.

test *v.* inquire, question, try out; see EXAMINE, EXPERIMENT.

tested *a.* examined, tried, proved; see ESTABLISHED 2, RELIABLE.

testify *v.* **1.** [To demonstrate] indicate, show, make evident; see PROVE. **2.** [To bear witness] affirm, give evidence, swear, swear to, attest, witness, give witness, give one's word, certify, warrant, depose, vouch, give the facts, stand up for, say a good word for. **3.** [To declare] assert, attest, claim; see DECLARE.

testimony *n.* **1.** [The act of stating] attestation, statement, assertion; see DECLARATION. **2.** [Evidence] grounds, facts, data; see PROOF. **3.** [Statement] deposition, affidavit, affirmation; see DECLARATION.

Texas *n.* Lone Star State, Jumbo State, Longhorn State; see SOUTH, UNITED STATES.

text *n.* **1.** [A textbook] required reading, manual, handbook; see BOOK. **2.** [A subject, expecially a verse from the Bible] quotation, stanza, passage; see SUBJECT. **3.** [Writing, considered for its authenticity] lines, textual evidence, document; see MANUSCRIPT, WRITING 2.

texture *n.* **1.** [Quality] character, disposition, fineness, roughness, coarseness, feeling, feel, sense, flexibility, stiffness, smoothness, taste; see also FIBER. **2.** [Structure] composition, organization, arrangement; see CONSTRUCTION 2, FORM 2.

thank *v.* be obliged, show gratitude, give thanks, acknowledge, show appreciation, be obligated to, be indebted to, bless, praise, bow down to, kiss, smile on, show courtesy, express one's obligation to; see also APPRECIATE 1.—*Ant.* NEGLECT, ignore, show indifference.

thanked *a.* blessed, applauded, appreciated; see PRAISED.

thankful *a.* obliged, grateful, gratified, contented, satisfied, indebted to, pleased, kindly disposed, appreciative, giving thanks, overwhelmed.

thankless *a.* **1.** [Not returning thanks] unappreciative, ungrateful, self-centered; see CRUEL, RUDE 2. **2.** [Not eliciting thanks] poorly paid, unappreciated, unrewarded; see USELESS 1.

thanks *n.pl.* appreciation, thankfulness, acknowledgment, recognition, gratitude, gratefulness.—*Ant.* BLAME, censure, criticism.

Thanksgiving *n.* Thanksgiving Day, last Thursday in November, turkey day*; see CELEBRATION, FEAST, HOLIDAY.

that *conj.* in that, so, so that, in order that, to the end that, for the reason that; see also BECAUSE.

that *a.* the, this, one, a certain, a well-known, a particular, such.

that *pron.* the one, this one, the one in question, that fact, that other, who; see also WHICH. **—all that*** so very, so, rather less; see NOT. **—at that*** even so, all things considered, anyway; see ANYHOW.

thaw *v.* dissolve, liquefy, flow, run, liquate, fuse, become liquid; see also DISSOLVE, MELT 1.—*Ant.* FREEZE, congeal, refrigerate.

the *a.* **1.** [The definite article] some, a few, a particular one, a special one, a specific one, a certain one, an individual one, this, that, each, every, these, those, the whole, the entire. **2.** [Special or unique; *often italics*] preeminent, outstanding, particular, unparalleled, unequaled, supreme, unsurpassed, unusual, uncommon, rare, singular, unprecedented, exceptional, one, sole, single, significant, distinguished, specific, choice, individual, peculiar, exceptional, occasional, unfamiliar, strange, spectacular, phenomenal, unheard of, unknown, unattainable, invincible, almighty, all-powerful; see also SPECIAL, UNIQUE.—*Ant.* COMMON, USUAL, ordinary.

theater *n.* **1.** [A building intended for theatrical productions] playhouse, concert hall, coliseum; see AUDITORIUM. **2.** [The legitimate stage] stage, drama, Broadway; see COMEDY, MOVIES 2.

theatrical *a.* ceremonious, meretricious, superficial; see AFFECTED 2.

theft *n.* robbery, racket, thievery, larceny, stealing, swindling, swindle, cheating, defrauding, fraud, piracy, burglary, pillage, pilfering, plunder, vandalism, holdup, pocket-picking, safecracking, extortion, embezzlement, looting, appropiation, shoplifting, fleece, mugging, stickup*; see also CRIME.

their *a.* belonging to them, belonging to others, theirs, of them.

them *pron.* those persons, those things, the others, the above, some people, he and she; see also EVERYBODY.

theme *n.* **1.** [A subject] topic, proposition, argument, thesis, text, subject matter, matter at hand, problem, question, point at issue, affair, business, point, case, thought, idea, line; see also SUBJECT. **2.** [A recurrent melody] melody, motif, strain; see SONG. **3.** [A short composition] essay, report, paper; see WRITING 2, STATEMENT 1.

then *a.* at that time, formerly, before, years ago, at that point, suddenly, all at once, soon after, before long, next, later, thereupon; see also WHEN 2, 3. **—but then** but at the same time, on the other hand, however; see BUT 1, 2. **—what then?** in that case?, and then?, as a result?; see WHAT 1.

theology *n.* dogma, creed, theism; see BELIEF, FAITH 2.

theoretical *a.* ideal, analytical, academic; see ASSUMED.

theory *n.* **1.** [Principles] method, approach, philosophy; see LAW 4. **2.** [Something to be proved] assumption, conjecture, speculation; see OPINION 1.

therapy *n.* remedy, healing, cure; see MEDICINE 3.

there *a.* in that place, not here, beyond, over there, yonder, in the distance, at a distance, over yonder, just there, where I point, in that spot, at that point; see also WHERE 2. **—not all there*** crazy, eccentric, demented; see INSANE.

thereafter *a.* from there on, from that day on, after that; see FOLLOWING, HEREAFTER.

thereby *a.* by way of, how, by which; see THROUGH 4, WHEREBY.

therefore *a. & conj.* accordingly, consequently, hence, wherefore, for, since, inasmuch as, for this reason, on account of, to that end, on the ground, in that event, in consequence, as a result.

thermometer *n.* mercury, thermostat, thermoregulator; see MEASURE 2.

these *a.* those, the indicated, the present, the aforementioned, the already stated, the referred to, hereinafter described, the previously mentioned, the well-known, the aforesaid, the above, the below; see also CERTAIN 4.

they *pron.* people, men, those people, all, others, he and she, both; see also EVERYBODY.

thick *a.* **1.** [Dense] compact, impervious, condensed, compressed, multitudinous, numerous, rank, crowded, close, solid, packed, populous, profuse, populated, swarming, heaped, abundant, impenetrable, concentrated, crammed, packed together, closely packed, like sardines in a can*, jam-packed.—*Ant.* SCATTERED, spacious, wide-open. **2.** [Deep] in depth, edgewise, third-[illegible]mensional; see DEEP 2. **3.** [Of heavy con-[illegible]ncy] compact, heavy, viscous, viscid, [illegible] syrupy, ropy, coagulated, curdled, [illegible]elatinous, glutinous, gummy, [illegible]otted; see also STRINGY.—*Ant.* [illegible]porous, filmy. **4.** [Not clear] cloudy, [illegible]d, indistinct; see DULL 2, MUDDY 1, OBSCURE 1. **5.** [Stupid] obtuse, ignorant, doltish; see DULL 3. **6.** [*Intimate] cordial, familiar, fraternal; see FRIENDLY. —**through thick and thin*** faithfully, devotedly, in good and bad times; see LOYALLY.

thicken *v.* coagulate, curdle, petrify, ossify, solidify, freeze, clot, set, congeal, jelly, grow thick; see also HARDEN, STIFFEN.

thickheaded *a.* stupid, ignorant, idiotic; see DULL 3.

thickness *n.* density, compactness, solidity, closeness, heaviness, stiffness, condensation, concentration, clot.—*Ant.* FRAILTY, thinness, slimness.

thief *n.* burglar, highwayman, holdup man; see CRIMINAL.

thieve *v.* loot, rob, filch; see STEAL.

thievery *n.* burglary, robbery, pilfering; see CRIME, THEFT.

thigh *n.* thigh bone, femur, ham; see LEG.

thin *a.* **1.** [Of little thickness] flimsy, slim, slight, diaphanous, sheer, rare, sleazy, permeable, paper-thin, wafer-sliced.—*Ant.* THICK, heavy, coarse. **2.** [Slender] slim, lean, skinny, scraggy, lank, spare, gaunt, bony, wan, rangy, skeletal, scrawny, lanky, delicate, wasted, haggard, emaciated, rawboned, shriveled, wizened, rickety, spindly, pinched, starved.—*Ant.* FAT, obese, heavy. **3.** [Sparse] scarce, insufficient, deficient; see INADEQUATE. **4.** [Having little content] sketchy, slight, insubstantial; see SHALLOW 1, 2. **5.** [Having little volume] faint, shrill, weak; see LIGHT 7.

thin *v.* thin out, weed out, dilute; see DECREASE 2, WEAKEN 2.

thing *n.* **1.** [An object] article, object, item, lifeless object, commodity, device, gadget, material object, being, entity, body, person, something, anything, everything, element, substance, piece, shape, form, figure, configuration, creature, stuff, goods, matter, thingumajig*, doohickey*, thingumabob*. **2.** [A circumstance] matter, condition, situation; see CIRCUMSTANCE 1. **3.** [An act] deed, feat, movement; see ACTION 2. **4.** [A characteristic] quality, trait, attribute; see CHARACTERISTIC. **5.** [An idea] notion, opinion, impression; see THOUGHT 2. **6.** [A pitiable person] wretch, poor person, sufferer, urchin; see also PATIENT, REFUGEE. **7.** [Belongings; *usually pl.*] possessions, clothes, personals; see PROPERTY 1. **8.** [Something so vague as to be nameless] affair, matter, concern, business, occurrence, anything, everything, something, stuff, point, information, subject, idea, question, indication, intimation, contrivance, word, name, shape, form, entity. **9.** [Something to be done] task, obligation, duty; see JOB 2. —**do one's own thing*** live according to one's own principles, do what one likes, live fully; see LIVE 1.

things *n.pl.* possessions, luggage, belongings; see BAGGAGE, PROPERTY 1.

think *v.* **1.** [To examine with the mind] cogitate, muse, ponder, consider, contemplate, deliberate, stop to consider, study, reflect, examine, think twice, estimate, evaluate, appraise, resolve, ruminate, scan, confer, consult, meditate, meditate upon, take under consideration, have on one's mind, brood over, speculate, weigh, have in mind, keep in mind, bear in mind, mull over*, turn over, sweat over*, stew, bone up*, beat one's brains, rack one's brains, use the old bean*, figure out, put on one's thinking cap*, use one's head, hammer away at, hammer out, bury oneself in.—*Ant.* NEGLECT, take for granted, accept. **2.** [To believe] be convinced, deem, hold; see BELIEVE. **3.** [To suppose] imagine, guess, presume; see ASSUME. **4.** [To form in the mind] conceive, invent, create; see IMAGINE. **5.** [To remember] recollect, recall, reminisce; see REMEMBER 1, 2.

thinking *a.* pensive, introspective, reflective; see THOUGHTFUL 1. —**put on one's thinking cap** begin thinking, study, examine; see THINK 1.

thinking *n.* reasoning, reason, contemplation; see THOUGHT 1.

think twice (about) *v.* reconsider, weigh, pause, be uncertain; see also HESITATE.

thinness *n.* slenderness, slimness, shallowness; see LIGHTNESS 2.

third *a.* part, after the second, next but one; see THREE.

thirst *n.* dryness, need for liquid, longing, craving, cobweb throat*.

thirsty *a.* dry, parched, arid, eager, hankering for, burning for, craving, longing for, partial to, hungry for, itching for, inclined to, bone dry*, crazy for*, wild for; see also HUNGRY.—*Ant.* SATISFIED, full, replete.

this *a.* the, that, the indicated, the present, here, aforementioned, already stated.

this *pron.* the one, this one, that one, the one in question, the aforementioned one, this person, the thing indicated; see also THAT.

thorn *n.* spine, briar, neetle; see POINT 2, SPINE 1.

thorough *a.* 1. [Painstaking] exact, meticulous, precise; see ACCURATE 2, CAREFUL. 2. [Complete] thoroughgoing, out-and-out, total; see ABSOLUTE 1.

thoroughly *a.* fully, wholly, in detail; see COMPLETELY.

those *a.* these, the above-mentioned, the indicated; see THE 1.

those *pron.* the others, they, them, not these; see also THAT.

though *conj.* despite, even if, if; see ALTHOUGH, BUT 1.

thought *n.* 1. [Mental activity] speculation, reflection, deliberation, meditation, rumination, perceiving, apprehending, seeing, consideration, reasoning, intuition, logical process, perception, insight, understanding, viewpoint, concept, brainwork, thinking, knowing, realizing, discerning, rationalizing, drawing conclusions, concluding, inferring, deducing, deriving, deduction, inducing, logic, judging, rationalization, judgment, argumentation, cogitation, contemplation, cognition, intellection, brainstorm. 2. [The result of mental activity] idea, plan, view, fancy, notion, impression, image, understanding, appreciation, conception, observation, belief, feeling, opinion, guess, inference, theory, hypothesis, supposition, assumption, intuition, conjecture, deduction, postulate, premise, knowledge, evaluation, assessment, appraisal, estimate, verdict, finding, decision, determination, reflection, consideration, abstraction, conviction, tenet, presumption, intellectualization, surmise, doctrine, principle, drift, calculation, caprice, reverie, sentiment, care, worry, anxiety, uneasiness, dream. 3. [Care or attention] heed, thoughtfulness, solicitude; see ATTENTION.

thoughtful *a.* 1. [Notable for thought] thinking, meditative, engrossed, absorbed, rapt in, pensive, considered, seasoned, matured, studied, philosophic, contemplative, studious, cogitative, examined, pondered, speculative, deliberative, reflective, introspective, clearheaded, levelheaded, keen, wise, well-balanced, judged, farsighted, reasoning, rational, calculating, discerning, penetrating, politic, shrewd, careful, sensible, retrospective, intellectual, brainy*, deep.—*Ant.* THOUGHTLESS, unthinking, irrational. 2. [Considerate] heedful, polite, courteous, solicitous, friendly, kind, kindly, unselfish, concerned, anxious, neighborly, regardful, social, cooperative, responsive, aware, sensitive, benign, indulgent, obliging, careful, attentive, gallant, chivalrous, charitable.—*Ant.* SELFISH, boorish, inconsiderate.

thoughtfulness *n.* understanding, helpfulness, indulgence; see KINDNESS 1.

thoughtless *a.* 1. [Destitute of thought] irrational, unreasoning, unreasonable, inane, incomprehensible, witless, undiscerning, foolish, doltish, babbling, bewildered, confused, puerile, senseless, driveling, inept, dull, heavy-handed, obtuse, feeble-minded, flighty; see also STUPID. 2. [Inconsiderate] heedless, negligent, inattentive, careless, neglectful, self-centered, egocentric, selfish, asocial, antisocial, unmindful, unheeding, deaf, blind, indifferent, unconcerned, listless, apathetic, boorish, discourteous, primitive, unrefined; see also RUDE 2.—*Ant.* CAREFUL, thoughtful, unselfish.

thoughtlessness *n.* inattention, oversight, heedlessness; see CARELESSNESS, NEGLECT 1.

thought (over or **through)** *a.* studied, thought about, revised; see CONSIDERED, INVESTIGATED.

thousand *a.* ten hundred, millenary, thousandfold; see MANY.

thrash *v.* trounce, whip, chasten; see BEAT 1, PUNISH.

thread *n.* yarn, string, strand; see FIBER.

thread *v.* attach, weave together, string together; see JOIN 1.

threat *n.* menace, fulmination, intimidation; see WARNING.

threaten *v.* intimidate, caution, admonish, hold over, scare, torment, push around, forewarn, bully, abuse, bluster, endanger, be dangerous, be gathering, be in the offing, imperil, be brewing, approach, come on, advance; see also FRIGHTEN, WARN.—*Ant.* HELP, mollify, placate.

threatened *a.* warned, endangered, imperiled, jeopardized, in bad straits, insecure, unsafe, unprotected, vulnerable, exposed, in a crucial state, in danger, besieged, surrounded, under attack, set upon, in a bad way.—*Ant.* SAFE, invulnerable, protected.

threatening *a.* alarming, dangerous, aggressive; see OMINOUS, SINISTER, UNSAFE.

three *a.* triple, treble, threefold, third, triform, triune, tertiary, thrice, triply.

threshold *n.* sill, gate, door; see ENTRANCE 1.

thrift *n.* saving, parsimony, frugality; see ECONOMY.

thrifty *a.* saving, careful, frugal; see ECONOMICAL 1.

thrill *n.* pleasant sensation, stimulation, tingle; see EXCITEMENT, FUN.

thrill *v.* animate, inspire, rouse; see EXCITE.

thrilled *a.* inspired, moved, touched; see EXCITED, HAPPY.

thrilling *a.* overwhelming, exciting, breathtaking; see STIMULATING.

thrive *v.* flourish, increase, succeed; see GROW 1.

throat *n.* neck, windpipe, larynx, trachea, esophagus, jugular region, gullet, gorge. —**cut each other's throats*** ruin each other, fight, feud; see DESTROY. —**cut one's own throat*** ruin oneself, cause one's own destruction, act contrary to one's best interests; see COMMIT SUICIDE, DAMAGE. —**ram down someone's throat*** impose, pressure, coerce; see FORCE. —**stick in one's throat*** be difficult to say, not come easily, be disturbing; see DISTURB.

throaty *a.* husky, hoarse, deep; see HOARSE.

throb *n.* beat, pulsation, palpitation; see BEAT 1.

throb *v.* beat, pulsate, palpitate; see BEAT 2.

throng *n.* multitude, mass, concourse; see CROWD, GATHERING.

throttle *v.* strangle, stifle, silence; see CHOKE.

through *a. & prep.* **1.** [Finished] completed, over, ended; see DONE 1, FINISHED 1. **2.** [From one side to the other] straight through, through and through, clear through; see IN 2, INTO, WITHIN. **3.** [During] throughout, for the period of, from beginning to end; see DURING. **4.** [By means of] by, by way of, by reason, in virtue of, in consequence of, for, by the agency of, at the hand of. **5.** [Referring to continuous passage] nonstop, unbroken, one-way; see CONSECUTIVE, CONSTANT, REGULAR 3.

through and through *a.* permeating, pervasive, enduring; see COMPLETELY, THROUGHOUT.

throughout *a. & prep.* all through, during, from beginning to end, from one end to the other, everywhere, all over, in everything, in every place, up and down, on all accounts, in all respects, inside and out, at full length, every bit, to the end, down to the ground, head and shoulders, from the word go, up to the brim*; see also COMPLETELY.

through thick and thin *a.* devotedly, loyally, constantly; see REGULARLY.

throw *v.* **1.** [To hurl] fling, butt, bunt, pitch, fire, let go, sling, toss, heave, lob, dash, launch, chuck, bowl, cast, hurl at, let fly, deliver, cast off*, lay across*.—*Ant.* CATCH, receive, grab. **2.** [To connect or disconnect] turn a switch, connect, start; see TURN OFF, TURN ON 1. **3.** [To force to the ground] pin*, nail*, flatten; see DEFEAT 3. **4.** [*To permit an opponent to win] submit, yield, surrender; see LOSE 3.

throw away *v.* reject, refuse, turn down; see DISCARD.

throw in *v.* add, expand, give; see INCREASE.

throw in the towel or **sponge*** *v.* give up, surrender, bow to; see QUIT 2.

thrown *a.* **1.** [Hurled] pitched, tossed, heaved; see SENT. **2.** [Beaten] knocked over, sent sprawling, heaved; see BEATEN 1.

throw out *v.* discharge, throw away, reject; see DISCARD.

throw together *v.* make quickly, do in a hurry, do a rush job; see BUILD, MANUFACTURE.

throw up *v.* **1.** [To vomit] regurgitate, retch, barf*; see VOMIT. **2.** [To quit] give up, cease, terminate; see STOP 2. **3.** [To construct, usually hastily] build overnight, patch up, knock together; see BUILD.

thrust *n.* **1.** [A jab] punch, stab, poke; see BLOW. **2.** [An attack] onset, onslaught, advance; see ATTACK. **3.** [A strong push] drive, impetus, momentum; see PUSH.

thrust *v.* poke, push, shove; see HIT 1.

thud *n.* thump, dull sound, plop; see NOISE 1.

thumb *n.* pollex, first digit, preaxial digit; see FINGER. —**all thumbs** fumbling, clumsy, inept; see AWKWARD. —**under one's thumb** under one's control, controlled, governed; see MANAGED.

thump *n.* thud, knock, rap; see NOISE 1.

thump *v.* pound, knock, rap, wallop, slap, strike, whack, hit; see also BEAT 1.

thunder *n.* crash, peal, outburst, explosion, boom, booming, roar, rumble, clap, crack, discharge, thunderbolt, uproar, blast; see also NOISE 1.

thunder *v.* peal, boom, rumble, resound, roll, deafen, crash, clamor, clash; see also SOUND, STORM.

thunderstorm *n.* electric storm, squall, downpour; see THUNDER, STORM.

thus *a.* in this manner, so, consequently, hence, in such a way, just like that, in kind, along these lines; see also THEREFORE.

thwart *v.* stop, impede, frustrate; see CONFUSE, PREVENT.

tick *n.* **1.** [A light beat] beat, click, ticktock; see BEAT 1, 2. **2.** [An insect] parasite, louse, mite; see INSECT, PEST 1.

ticket *n.* **1.** [A valid token] check, certificate, notice, badge, label, voucher, stub, countercheck, rain check, tag, slip, note, card, pass, receipt, record, license, permit, passage, credential, visa, passport, document. **2.** [Candidates representing a political party] party list, choice, ballot; see CANDIDATE, FACTION, PARTY 3.

tickle *v.* rub, caress, stroke; see TOUCH 1.

ticklish *a.* sensitive, unsteady, touchy; see IRRITABLE, UNSTABLE 2.

tidbit *n.* morsel, mouthful, bite; see BIT 1.

tide *n.* current, flow, flux, stream, course, sluice, undercurrent, undertow, drag, whirlpool, eddy, vortex, torrent, wave, tidal wave. *Tides of the sea include the following:* low, neap, ebb, spring, full, high, flood.

tidiness *n.* neatness, spruceness, uniformity; see CLEANLINESS.

tidy *a.* orderly, trim, spruce; see NEAT 1.

tie *n.* **1.** [A fastening] band, strap, bandage, zipper; see also FASTENER. **2.** [A necktie] cravat, neckerchief, bow, knot, scarf, neckcloth, choker. **3.** [Affection] bond, relation, kinship; see AFFECTION, LOVE 1. **4.** [An equal score, or a contest having that score] deadlock, draw, even game, dead heat, drawn battle, neck-and-neck contest, even-steven*, stalemate, nose finish*, standoff, wash*.

tie *v.* **1.** [To fasten] bind, make fast, attach; see FASTEN, JOIN 1. **2.** [To tie a knot in] knot, make a bow, make a tie, make a knot, do up, fix a tie, make a hitch; see also sense 1. **3.** [To equal] match, keep up with, parallel; see EQUAL.

tied *a.* **1.** [Firm] fixed, bound, made firm; see FIRM 1. **2.** [Even] evenly matched, running neck and neck, in a dead heat; see ALIKE, EQUAL.

tie up *v.* **1.** [To fasten] wrap, package, secure; see CLOSE 4, ENCLOSE. **2.** [To obstruct] hinder, stop, delay; see HINDER.

tight *a.* **1.** [Firm] taut, secure, fast, bound up, close, clasped, fixed, steady, stretched thin, established, compact, strong, stable, enduring, steadfast, unyielding, unbending, set, stuck hard, hidebound, invulnerable, snug, sturdy, see also FIRM 1.—*Ant.* LOOSE, tottery, shaky. **2.** [Closed] sealed, airtight, impenetrable, impermeable, impervious, watertight, hermetically sealed, padlocked, bolted, locked, fastened, shut tight, clamped, fixed, tied, snapped, swung to, tied up, nailed, spiked, slammed, obstructed, blocked, blind, shut, stopped up, plugged.—*Ant.* OPEN, penetrable, unprotected. **3.** [Closefitting] pinching, shrunken, snug, uncomfortable, cramping, skintight, short, crushing, choking, smothering, cutting.—*Ant.* LOOSE, ample, wide. **4.** [*Intoxicated] inebriated, drunken, tipsy; see DRUNK. **5.** [*Stingy] miserly, parsimonious, close; see STINGY. **6.** [Difficult to obtain; *said especially of money*] scarce, frozen, tied up; see RARE 2. **—sit tight** do nothing, refrain from action, stay put; see WAIT 1.

tighten *v.* **1.** [To make tight] compress, condense, squeeze, bind, contract, strangle, constrict, crush, cramp, pinch, grip more tightly, clench, screw down, add pressure; see also STRETCH 2.—*Ant.* LOOSEN, relax, unloose. **2.** [To become tight] contract, harden, congeal, stiffen, toughen, become more disciplined.—*Ant.* SOFTEN, melt, liquefy.

tightfisted *a.* thrifty, niggardly, frugal; see STINGY.

tile *n.* baked clay, flooring, roofing; see CLAY, FLOORING.

till *v.* cultivate, work, raise crops from; see FARM.

tilt *n.* slant, slope, slide; see INCLINATION 2.

tilt *v.* slant, tip, turn, set at an angle, lean, slope, slouch, shift, dip, sway, make oblique, deviate, turn edgewise; see also BEND.—*Ant.* STRAIGHTEN, level, bring into line.

timber *n.* **1.** [Standing trees] wood, lumber, timberland; see FOREST. **2.** [A beam] stake, pole, club; see BEAM 1, LUMBER.

time *n.* **1.** [Duration] continuance, lastingness, extent, past, present, future, infinity, space-time; see also TODAY. *Units of measuring time include the following:* second, minute, hour, day, term, millisecond, week, month, year, decade, generation, lifetime, century, millennium, eon. **2.** [A point in time] incident, event, occurrence, occasion, time and tide, instant, term, season, tide, course, sequence, point, generation. **3.** [A period of time] season, era, interval; see AGE 3. **4.** [Experience] background, living, participation; see EXPERIENCE. **5.** [Leisure] opportunity, free moment, chance; see FREEDOM 2. **6.** [Circumstances; *usually plural; used with "the"*] condition, the present, nowadays; see CIRCUMSTANCE 1, CIRCUMSTANCES 2. **7.** [A measure of speed] tempo, rate, meter; see BEAT 2.

time *v.* register, distance, clock, measure time; see also MEASURE 1. **—ahead of time** ahead of schedule, fast, earlier than expected; see EARLY 2. **—at one time** simultaneously, concurrently, at once; see TOGETHER 2. **—at the same time** simultaneously, concurrently, at once; see TOGETHER 2. **—at times** occasionally, sometimes, once in a while; see SELDOM. **—behind the times** out of date, archaic, antediluvian; see OLD-FASHIONED. **—behind time** tardy, delayed, coming later; see LATE 1. **—between times** now and then, occasionally, sometimes; see SELDOM. **—do time*** serve a prison term, go to jail, be imprisoned; see SERVE TIME. **—for the time being** for the present, for now, under consideration; see TEMPORARILY. **—from time to time** occasionally, sometimes, once in a while; see FREQUENTLY. **—in no time** instantly, rapidly, without delay; see QUICKLY, SOON. **—in time** eventually, after the proper time, inevitably; see FINALLY 2. **—lose time** go too slow, tarry, cause a delay; see DELAY. **—make time** gain time, act hastily, hasten; see HURRY 1. **—many a time** often, regularly, consistently; see FREQUENTLY. **—on time** **1.** at the appointed time, punctually, correct; see PUNCTUAL. **2.** by credit, in installments, on account; see UNPAID 1. **—out of time** out of pace, unreasonable, improper; see UNTIMELY. **—pass the time of day** exchange greetings, chat, converse; see GREET.

timely *a.* opportune, seasonable, in good time, fitting the times, suitable, appropriate, convenient, favorable, propitious, well-timed, modern, up-to-date, newsworthy.—*Ant.* UNTIMELY, ill-timed, inappropriate.

timepiece *n.* timekeeper, chronometer, sundial; see CLOCK, WATCH 1.

timid *a.* **1.** [Irresolute] indecisive, vacillating, wavering; see IRRESPONSIBLE. **2.** [Cowardly] fainthearted, spiritless, weak; see AFRAID, COWARDLY. **3.** [Reticent] shy, withdrawn, modest; see HUMBLE 1.

tinge *n.* tint, shade, hint; see TRACE 1, TINT.

tingle *v.* shiver, prickle, sting, itch, creep, grow excited, get goose pimples all over*.

tinker *v.* try to mend, play with, take apart; see REPAIR.

tint *n.* tinge, hue, shade, color value, cast, flush, dye, tinct, taint, glow, pastel color, luminous color, pale hue, tone, tincture, dash, touch, color tone, coloration, pigmentation, ground color, complexion; see also COLOR.

tinted *a.* tinged, painted, touched up; see COLORED.

tiny *a.* small, miniature, diminutive; see LITTLE 1.

tip *n.* **1.** [The point] apex, peak, top; see POINT 2. **2.** [A gratuity] reward, gift, compensation, fee, small change, money, handout; see also PAY 2. **3.** [*A bit of information] hint, clue, warning; see KNOWLEDGE 1, NEWS 1.

tip *v.* slant, incline, shift; see BEND, LEAN 1, TILT.

tiptop *a.* superior, prime, choice; see BEST, EXCELLENT.

tire *n.* casing, tire and tube, one of a set; see WHEEL 1. *Terms for types of tires include the following:* tubeless, belted, radial, snow, mud, puncture-proof, recapped, synthetic, low-pressure, natural rubber, solid rubber, pneumatic, oversize, airplane, motorcycle, bicycle, recap.

tire *v.* **1.** [To become exhausted] grow weary, break down, droop, flag, pall, faint, drop, puff, sink, yawn, collapse, give out, wilt, go stale, poop out*, burn out*.—*Ant.* REST, awake, relax. **2.** [To make a person exhausted] tax, overtax, harass, fatigue, exhaust, overwork, strain, overstrain, overburden, depress, dispirit, pain, vex, worry, distress, deject, dishearten, wear out, run a person ragged, do in*.

tired *a.* fatigued, weary, run-down, exhausted, overworked, overtaxed, wearied, worn, spent, wasted, worn-out, drooping, distressed, unmanned, drowsy, droopy, sleepy, haggard, faint, prostrated, broken-down, drained, consumed, empty, collapsing, all in*, finished, stale, fagged, dog-tired*, dead on one's feet*, pooped*, done in*, done for*, worn to a frazzle*, played out*, tuckered out*, fed up*.—*Ant.* ACTIVE, lively, energetic.

tireless *a.* unwearied, unwearying, untiring; see ACTIVE.

tiresome *a.* irksome, wearying, monotonous; see DULL 4.

tissue *n.* **1.** [A network] web, mesh, filigree; see NETWORK 2. **2.** [Thin fabric] gauze, gossamer, lace; see VEIL, WEB. **3.** [Protective layer, especially in living organisms] film, membrane, intercellular substance; see MUSCLE.

title *n.* **1.** [A designation] indication, inscription, sign; see NAME 1. **2.** [Ownership or evidence of ownship] right, claim, license; see OWNERSHIP. **3.** [Mark of rank or dignity] commission, decoration, medal, ribbon, coat of arms, crest, order, authority, privilege, degree; see also EMBLEM. *Titles include the following:* Sir, Doctor, Mr., Ms., Mrs., Miss, Reverend, Monsignor, Dame, King, Prince, Baron, Viscount, Earl, Marquis, Marquise, Duke, Grand Duke, Knight, Count, Sultan, Queen, Duchess, Lady, Princess, Countess, Monsieur, Madame, Mademoiselle, Don, Doña, Herr, Frau, Fräulein, General, Colonel, Major, Captain, Lieutenant, Admiral, Commander, Ensign, President, Vice-president, Secretary, Speaker, Governor, Mayor, Representative, Senator.

to *prep.* **1.** [In the direction of] toward, via, into, facing, through, directed toward, traveling to, along the line of. **2.** [Indicating position] over, upon, in front of; see ON 1. **3.** [Until] till, up to, stopping at; see UNTIL. **4.** [So that] in order to, intending to, that one may, for the purpose of. **5.** [Indicating degree] up to, down to, as far as, in that degree, to this extent. **6.** [Indicating result] becoming, until, back, ending with.

to and fro *a.* seesaw, zigzag, back and forth, backwards and forwards, in and out, up and down, from side to side, from pillar to post, off and on, round and round, forward and back.

toast *n.* **1.** [A sentiment or person drunk to] pledge, salute, acknowledgment; see HONOR 1. *Invitations for toasts include the following:* here's to you, good luck, lest we forget, your health, *prosit* (German), *skoal* (Scandinavian), *salud* (Spanish), *a votre sante* (French), down the hatch*, here's how, mud in your eye, here's looking at you. **2.** [Browned bread] *Varieties of toast include the following:* Melba, French, cinnamon; see also BREAD.

toast *v.* **1.** [To honor by drinking liquor] drink to, compliment, propose a toast; see DRINK 2, PRAISE 1. **2.** [To brown bread] put in a toaster, heat, crisp; see COOK.

tobacco *n.* *Forms of tobacco include the following:* nicotine, cigarette, cigar, chewing tobacco, pipe tobacco, snuff, stogie, weed*.

to blame *a.* at fault, culpable, censurable; see GUILTY.

to date *a.* so far, as yet, up to now; see NOW 1.

today *n.* this day, the present, our time, this moment; see also NOW 1.

to-do *n.* commotion, stir, fuss; see DISORDER, FIGHT 1.

toe *n.* digit, front of the foot, tip of a shoe; see FOOT 2. —**on one's toes*** alert, aware, attentive; see CAREFUL. —**step** or **tread on someone's toes** annoy, offend, disturb; see ANGER.

together *a.* **1.** [Jointly] collectively, unitedly, commonly; see sense 2. **2.** [Simultaneously] at the same time, concurrently, coincidentally, contemporaneously, at once, in connection with, at a blow, in unison, at one jump.

togs* *n.pl.* clothing, outfit, attire; see CLOTHES.

toil *n.* labor, occupation, drudgery; see WORK 2.

toil *v.* sweat, labor, slave; see WORK.

toilet *n.* water closet, lavatory, washroom, rest room, men's room, women's room, powder room, gentlemen's room, ladies' room, comfort station, bathroom, bath, little boy's room*, little girl's room*, head*, potty*, can*, pot*, john*.

token *n.* mark, favor, sample; see GIFT 1. —**by the same token** following from this, similarly, thus; see THEREFORE. —**in token of** evidence of, by way of, as a gesture; see BY 2.

told *a.* recounted, recorded, set down, reported, known, chronicled, revealed, exposed, made known, said, published, printed, announced, released, described, stated, set forth, included in the official statement, made public property, become common knowledge, related, depicted, enunciated, pronounced, given out, handed down, telegraphed, broadcast, telecast, confessed, admitted, well-known, discovered; see also SPOKEN.—*Ant.* SECRET, concealed, unknown.

tolerable *a.* endurable, sufferable, sustainable; see BEARABLE.

tolerance *n.* **1.** [Open-mindedness] concession, liberality, permission, forbearance, indulgence, mercy, compassion, license, sufferance, grace, understanding, sensitivity, charity, benevolence, humanity, endurance, altruism, patience, good will; see also KINDNESS 1. **2.** [Saturation point] threshold, tolerance level, end; see LIMIT 2.

tolerant *a.* understanding, receptive, sophisticated; see LIBERAL, PATIENT 1.

tolerate *v.* **1.** [To allow] permit, consent to, put up with; see ALLOW. **2.** [To endure] bear, undergo, abide; see ENDURE 2.

toll *n.* **1.** [Charges] duty, fee, customs, exaction, tollage; see also PRICE, TAX. **2.** [Loss] casualties, deaths, losses; see DAMAGE 2.

tomb *n.* vault, crypt, mausoleum; see GRAVE.

tombstone *n.* monument, gravestone, headstone, footstone, stone, marker, cross, funerary statue.

tomorrow *n.* the morrow, next day in the course of time, the future, *mañana* (Spanish); see also DAY 1.

ton *n.* two thousand pounds, short ton, metric ton, long ton, shipping ton, displacement ton, measurement ton, freight ton; see also WEIGHT 1, 2.

tone *n.* **1.** [A musical sound] pitch, timbre, resonance; see SOUND 2. **2.** [Quality] nature, trend, temper; see CHARACTER 1. **3.** [Manner] expression, condition, aspect; see MOOD 1. **4.** [A degree of color] hue, tint, coloration; see COLOR.

tone down *v.* subdue, moderate, temper; see SOFTEN.

tongs *n.pl.* pinchers, pliers, tweezers; see UTENSILS.

tongue *n.* **1.** [The movable muscle in the mouth] organ of taste, organ of speech, lingua; see MUSCLE, ORGAN 2. *Parts of the tongue used in speech are:* tip, apex, front, center, back. **2.** [Speech] speech, utterance, discourse; see LANGUAGE 1. —**hold one's tongue** refrain from speaking, hold back, keep silent; see RESTRAIN. —**on the tip of one's tongue** forgotten, not quite remembered, not readily recalled; see FAMILIAR, FORGOTTEN.

tongue-tied *a.* **1.** [Mute] silent, speechless, voiceless; see DUMB 1, MUTE 1. **2.** [Inarticulate] reticent, nervous, inarticulate; see RESERVED 3.

tonight *n.* this evening, this p.m., later; see NIGHT 1.

too *a.* **1.** [Also] as well, likewise, in addition, additionally, moreover, futhermore, further, besides; see also ALSO. **2.** [In excess] excessively, extremely, over and above; see BESIDES.

tool *n.* **1.** [An implement] utensil, machine, instrument, mechanism, weapon, apparatus, appliance, engine, means, contrivance, gadget; see also DEVICE 1. *Common tools include the following:* can opener, hammer, knife, jack, crank, pulley, wheel, bar, crowbar, lever, sledge, winch, chisel, plane, screw, brace, bit, file, saw, screwdriver, ax, corkscrew, hatchet, wrench, pliers, drill, sander, router, jimmy. **2.** [One who permits himself to be used] accomplice, hireling, dupe; see SERVANT.

too much *n.* excess, waste, extravagance, overabundance, superfluity, preposterousness, overcharge, ever so much, more than can be used, vastness, prodigiousness, immensity; see also EXCESS 1.—*Ant.* LACK, want, shortage.

tooth *n.* **1.** [A dental process] fang, tusk, saber-tooth, ivory, artificial tooth, false tooth, bony appendage. *Human teeth include the following:* incisor, canine, cuspid, eyetooth, biscuspid, premolar, molar, grinder, wisdom tooth. **2.** [A toothlike *or* tooth-shaped object] point, stub, projection; see ROOT 1. —**get** or **sink one's teeth**

into* become occupied with, involve oneself in, be busy at; see ACT 1.
toothache *n.* swollen gums, abscessed tooth, decayed tooth; see PAIN 2.
tooth and nail *a.* energetically, fervently, forcefully; see EAGERLY, FIERCELY.
toothbrush *n.* electric toothbrush, nylon bristle toothbrush, brush; see BRUSH 1.
top *a.* **1.** [Highest] topmost, uppermost, highest, on the upper end; see also HIGHEST. **2.** [Best] prime, head, first, among the first; see also BEST 1.
top *n.* **1.** [The uppermost portion] peak, summit, crown, head, crest, tip, apex, acme, cap, crowning point, headpiece, capital, pinnacle, zenith, spire; see also HEIGHT.—*Ant.* BOTTOM, lower end, nadir. **2.** [A cover] lid, roof, ceiling; see COVER 1. **3.** [A spinning toy] spinner, musical top, whistling top; see TOY 1. **4.** [The leader] head, captain, chief; see LEADER 2. **—blow one's top*** lose one's temper, become angry, be enraged; see RAGE 1. **—off the top of one's head*** speaking offhand, chatting casually, spontaneous; see SPONTANEOUS. **—on top** prosperous, thriving, superior; see SUCCESSFUL.
top *v.* **1.** [To remove the top] prune, lop off, trim; see CUT 1. **2.** [To exceed] better, beat, excel; see EXCEED. **3.** [To apply topping] cover, screen, coat; see PAINT 2.
top-heavy *a.* overweight, unstable, unbalanced; see SHAKY 1.
topic *n.* question, theme, material; see SUBJECT.
topless* *a.* almost nude, bare to the waist, exposed; see NAKED 1.
top-level *a.* leading, superior, supreme; see EXCELLENT, IMPORTANT 1.
top off *v.* finish, end, bring to a conclusion; see COMPLETE.
top-secret *a.* restricted, kept quiet, hush-hush*; see SECRET 1.
topsy-turvy *a.* confused, upside down, disordered; see DISORDERLY 1.
torch *n.* beacon, light, flare; see LIGHT 3.
torment *n.* agony, suffering, misery; see PAIN 1, 2, TORTURE.
torment *v.* mistreat, torture, irritate; see HURT 1.
tormentor *n.* oppressor, persecutor, antagonist; see ENEMY.
torn *a.* ripped, slit, split, severed, lacerated, mutilated, broken, rent, fractured, cracked, slashed, gashed, ruptured, snapped, sliced, burst, cleaved, wrenched, divided, pulled out, impaired, damaged, spoiled; see also RUINED 1.—*Ant.* WHOLE, repaired, adjusted.
torrent *n.* overflow, deluge, downpour; see FLOOD, FLOW, STORM.
torrid *a.* blazing, fiery, sweltering; see HOT 1.
torture *n.* pain, anguish, agony, torment, crucifixion, martyrdom, pang, ache, twinge, physical suffering, mental suffering, tribulation; see also CRUELTY.—*Ant.* COMFORT, enjoyment, delight.
torture *v.* annoy, irritate, disturb; see ABUSE, BOTHER 2.
toss *v.* **1.** [To throw easily] hurl, fling, cast; see THROW 1. **2.** [To move up and down] bob, buffet, stir, move restlessly, tumble, pitch, roll, heave, sway, flounder, rock, wobble, undulate, swing, rise and fall; see also WAVE 3.
tossup *n.* deadlock, bet, draw; see TIE 4.
tot *n.* child, infant, youngster; see BABY.
total *a.* **1.** [Whole] entire, inclusive, every; see WHOLE 1. **2.** [Complete] utter, gross, thorough; see ABSOLUTE 1.
total *n.* sum, entirety, result; see WHOLE.
total *v.* **1.** [To add] figure, calculate, count up, ring up, tag up, sum up, add up; see also ADD 1. **2.** [To amount to] consist of, come to, add up to; see AMOUNT TO, EQUAL.
totality *n.* everything, oneness, collectivity; see WHOLE.
totally *a.* entirely, wholly, exclusively; see COMPLETELY.
totem *n.* figure, symbol, crest; see EMBLEM.
to the contrary *a.* in disagreement with, in opposition to, in contradiction to; see AGAINST 1, ON THE CONTRARY.
totter *v.* shake, rock, careen, quake, tremble, stumble, lurch, stagger, falter, trip, weave, zigzag, reel, rock, roll, walk drunkenly, wobble, waver, hesitate, seesaw, teeter, dodder, crumple, sway, be loose, be weak; see also WAVE 3.
touch *n.* **1.** [The tactile sense] feeling, touching, feel, perception, tactility. **2.** [Contact] rub, stroke, pat, fondling, rubbing, petting, stroking, licking, handling, graze, scratch, brush, taste, nudge, kiss, peck, embrace, hug, cuddling, caress. **3.** [A sensation] sense, impression, pressure; see FEELING 2. **4.** [Skill] knack, technique, talent; see ABILITY, METHOD. **5.** [A trace] suggestion, scent, inkling; see BIT 1.
touch *v.* **1.** [To be in contact] stroke, graze, rub, nudge, thumb, finger, paw, pat, pet, caress, lick, taste, brush, kiss, glance, sweep, fondle, smooth, massage, sip, partake; see also FEEL 1. **2.** [To come into contact with] meet, encounter, reach; see MEET 1. **3.** [To relate to] refer to, regard, affect; see CONCERN 1.
touch-and-go *a.* **1.** [Hasty] rapid, casual, superficial; see SHALLOW 2. **2.** [Risky] ticklish, hazardous, tricky; see DANGEROUS, UNCERTAIN.
touched *a.* **1.** [Having been in slight contact] fingered, nudged, used, brushed, handled, rubbed, stroked, rearranged, kissed, grazed, licked, tasted, fondled. **2.** [Affected] moved, impressed, stirred; see AFFECTED 1.
touching *a. & prep.* **1.** [Referring to] regarding, in regard to, in reference to; see ABOUT 2. **2.** [Affecting] moving, pathetic, tender;

see PITIFUL. 3. [Adjacent] tangent, in contact, against; see NEAR 1, NEXT 2.

touch off *v.* 1. [To cause to explode] detonate, light the fuse of, set off; see EXPLODE. 2. [To cause to start] start, initiate, release; see BEGIN 1, CAUSE.

touch on *v.* treat, refer to, mention; see DISCUSS.

touch up *v.* renew, modify, rework; see REMODEL, REPAIR.

touchy *a.* 1. [Irritable] ill-humored, testy, sensitive; see IRRITABLE. 2. [Delicate] harmful, hazardous, risky; see UNSAFE.

tough *a.* 1. [Strong] robust, wiry, mighty; see STRONG 1, 2. 2. [Cohesive] solid, firm, sturdy, hard, hardened, adhesive, leathery, coherent, inseparable, molded, tight, cemented, unbreakable, in one piece, dense, closely packed.—*Ant.* WEAK, fragile, brittle. 3. [Difficult to chew] uncooked, half-cooked, sinewy, indigestible, inedible, fibrous, old, hard as nails, tough as shoeleather*.—*Ant.* SOFT, tender, overcooked. 4. [Difficult] hard, troublesome, laborious; see DIFFICULT 1, SEVERE 1. 5. [Hardy] robust, sound, capable; see HEALTHY. 6. [Rough and cruel] savage, fierce, ferocious; see CRUEL. 7. [*Unfavorable] bad, unfortunate, untimely; see UNFAVORABLE. 8. [*Excellent] fine, terrific*, first-class; see EXCELLENT. —**tough it out*** persevere, persist, endure; see ENDURE 1.

tour *n.* trip, voyage, travel; see JOURNEY.

tour *v.* voyage, vacation, take a trip; see TRAVEL.

tourist *n.* sightseer, vacationist, visitor; see TRAVELER.

tournament *n.* meet, tourney, match; see SPORT 3.

tow *v.* haul, pull, drag; see DRAW 1.

toward *a. & prep.* to, in the direction of, pointing to, via, on the way to, proceeding, moving, approaching, in relation to, close to, headed for, on the road to; see also NEAR 1.

towel *n.* wiper, drier, absorbent paper, sheet, toweling, napkin, cloth, rag. *Towels include the following:* linen, cotton, terry, guest, face, Turkish, hand, bath, beach, dish, tea, paper, napkin. —**throw in the towel*** admit defeat, give in, surrender; see QUIT 2.

tower *n.* spire, mast, steeple, bell tower, lookout tower, keep, belfry, monolith, radio tower, skyscraper, obelisk, pillar, column, minaret.

tower *v.* look over, extend above, mount; see OVERLOOK.

town *a.* civic, community, civil; see MUNICIPAL, URBAN.

town *n.* 1. [In the United States, a small collection of dwellings] township, village, hamlet, county seat, municipality, borough, hick town*. 2. [The people in a city, especially the prominent people] townspeople, inhabitants, society; see POPULATION.

toxic *a.* noxious, virulent, lethal; see DEADLY, POISONOUS.

toy *a.* childish, miniature, small; see LITTLE 1.

toy *n.* 1. [Something designed for amusement] game, plaything, pastime; see DOLL, GAME 1. *Toys include the following:* dolls, games, balls, toy weapons, blocks, jacks, tops, puzzles, models, jump ropes, scooters, wagons, kites, sporting goods, electronic devices, bicycles, tricycles, roller skates, marbles, skateboards, hobby horses. 2. [Anything trivial] trifle, bauble, gadget; see KNICKKNACK.

trace *n.* 1. [A very small quantity] indication, fragment, dash, dab, sprinkling, tinge, pinch, taste, crumb, trifle, shred, drop, speck, shade, hint, shadow, nuance, iota, particle, jot, suggestion, touch, suspicion, minimum, smell, spot; see also BIT 1. 2. [A track] evidence, trail, footprint; see TRACK 2.

trace *v.* 1. [To track] smell out, track down, run down; see TRACK 1. 2. [To draw] sketch, outline, copy; see DRAW 2.

tracing *n.* imitation, reproduction, duplicate; see COPY.

track *n.* 1. [A prepared way] path, course, road; see RAILROAD. 2. [Evidence left in passage] footprint, step, trace, vestige, impression, tire track, mark, footmark, footstep, trail, imprint, remnant, record, indication, print, sign, remains, token, symbol, clue, scent, wake, monument. —**keep track of** keep an account of, stay informed about, maintain contact with; see TRACK 1, WATCH. —**lose track of** lose sight of, lose contact with, abandon; see FORGET. —**make tracks*** run away, abandon, depart quickly; see LEAVE 1. —**off the track** deviant, variant, deviating; see MISTAKEN 1. —**the wrong side of the tracks*** ghetto, poor side of town, lower class neighborhood; see SLUM.

track *v.* 1. [To follow by evidence] hunt, pursue, smell out, add up, put together, trail, follow, trace, follow the scent, follow a clue, follow footprints, draw an inference, piece together, dog, be hot on the trail of, tail*, shadow. 2. [To dirty with tracks] leave footprints, leave mud, muddy, stain, soil, besmear, spatter, leave a trail of dirt; see also DIRTY.

track down *v.* pursue, hunt down, find; see CATCH 1, DISCOVER.

tracks *n.pl.* 1. [*An injection scar] needle marks, punctures, injection marks; see MARK 1, SCAR. 2. [Means of passage] road, way, path; see TRACK 1. 3. [Evidence of passage] trail, footprints, marks; see TRACK 2.

trade *n.* 1. [Business] commerce, sales, enterprise; see BUSINESS 1. 2. [A craft] occupation, profession, position; see JOB 1.

Common trades include the following: auto mechanic, bookkeeper, boilermaker, baker, barber, butcher, bookbinder, bricklayer, carpenter, cook, cabinetmaker, cameraman, dressmaker, electrician, embalmer, engraver, hairstylist, jeweler, locksmith, metallurgist, miner, machinist, optician, painter, plumber, printer, seamstress, shoemaker, tailor, textile worker, technician, toolmaker, truck driver, welder. **3.** [An individual business transaction] deal, barter, contract; see SALE 2.

trade *v.* **1.** [To do business] patronize, shop, purchase; see BUY, SELL. **2.** [To give one thing for another] barter, swap, give in exchange; see EXCHANGE. —**trade in** turn in, make part of a deal, get rid of; see SELL.

trademark *n.* brand, tag, commercial stamp; see LABEL.

trader *n.* salesman, dealer, merchant; see BUSINESSMAN.

tradesman *n.* storekeeper, retailer, merchant; see BUSINESSMAN.

trade union *n.* union, organized labor, guild; see LABOR 4.

tradition *n.* **1.** [The process of preserving orally] folklore, legend, fable; see STORY. **2.** [Cultural heritage] ritual, mores, law; see CULTURE 2, CUSTOM.

traditional *a.* folkloric, legendary, mythical, epical, ancestral, unwritten, balladic, told, handed down, anecdotal, proverbial, inherited, folkloristic, old, acknowledged, customary, generally accepted, habitual, widespread, usual, widely used, popular, acceptable, established, fixed, sanctioned, universal, taken for granted, rooted, classical, prescribed, doctrinal, conventional; see also COMMON 1, REGULAR 3.

traffic *n.* **1.** [The flow of transport] travel, passage, transportation, flux, movement, transfer, transit, passenger service, freight shipment, influx. **2.** [Dealings] commerce, transactions, exchange; see BUSINESS.

tragedy *n.* **1.** [Unhappy fate] lot, bad fortune, misfortune, doom, problem, error, mistake.—*Ant.* HAPPINESS, fortune, success. **2.** [A series of tragic events] adversity, affliction, hardship; see DIFFICULTY 1, 2.—*Ant.* SUCCESS, prosperity, good fortune. **3.** [An artistic creation climaxed by catastrophe] play, tragic drama, melodrama; see DRAMA, MOVIE, NOVEL.

tragic *a.* catastrophic, fatal, disastrous; see UNFORTUNATE.

trail *n.* trace, tracks, path; see WAY 2.

trail *v.* **1.** [To follow] track, trace, follow a scent; see HUNT 1, PURSUE 1. **2.** [To lag behind] fall back, loiter, tarry; see WAIT 1.

trailer *n.* house trailer, recreational vehicle, mobile home; see HOME 1.

train *n.* **1.** [A sequence] string, chain, succession; see SERIES. **2.** [A locomotive and attached cars] transport train, passenger train, freight train, local train, limited, supply train, express train, excursion train, commuters' train, troop train, boat train, mail train, bullet train, subway, rapid transit, underground, elevated, electric, diesel, choo-choo*; see also RAILROAD.

train *v.* **1.** [To drill] practice, exercise, discipline; see REACH 2. **2.** [To educate] instruct, tutor, enlighten; see TEACH. **3.** [To toughen oneself] prepare, grow strong, get into practice, reduce, make ready, fit out, equip, qualify, bring up to standard, whip into shape*, get a workout.—*Ant.* WEAKEN, break training, be unfit. **4.** [To direct the growth of] rear, lead, discipline, mold, bend, implant, guide, shape, care for, encourage, infuse, imbue, order, bring up, nurture, nurse, prune, weed; see also RAISE 1.—*Ant.* NEGLECT, ignore, disdain. **5.** [To aim] bring to bear, level, draw a bead; see AIM.

trained *a.* prepared, qualified, cultured, initiated, skilled, informed, schooled, primed, graduated, disciplined, enlightened; see also EDUCATED.—*Ant.* INEXPERIENCED, raw, untrained.

trainer *n.* teacher, tutor, instructor, coach, manager, mentor, officer, master, boss, handler, pilot.

training *n.* drill, practice, exercise, preparation, instruction, foundation, schooling, discipline, basic principles, groundwork, coaching, indoctrination, preliminaries, tune-up*, buildup*; see also EDUCATION.

trait *n.* habit, manner, peculiarity; see CHARACTERISTIC.

traitor *n.* betrayer, deserter, renegade, Judas, informer, spy, counterspy, agent, double agent, hypocrite, imposter, plotter, conspirator, turncoat, sneak, double-crosser*, fink*, rat*, stool pigeon*, two-timer*; see also REBEL.—*Ant.* SUPPORTER, follower, partisan.

tramp *n.* **1.** [Vagrant] hobo, wanderer, bum*; see BEGGAR. **2.** [A long walk, often in rough country] hike, excursion, stroll; see WALK 3. **3.** [*Prostitute] whore, harlot, slut; see PROSTITUTE.

trample *v.* stamp on, crush, tread on, grind underfoot, injure, squash, bruise, tramp over, overwhelm, defeat.

trance *n.* coma, daze, stupor; see CONFUSION.

tranquil *a.* composed, agreeable, gentle; see SERENE.

tranquilize *v.* calm, pacify, quell; see CALM DOWN, QUIET 1, SOOTHE.

tranquilizer *n.* sleeping pill, depressant, alleviative, palliative, soother, mollifier, calmative, sedative, placebo, pacifier; see also DRUG, MEDICINE 2.

tranquillity *n.* calmness, peacefulness, serenity; see PEACE 2, 3.

transact *v.* accomplish, carry on, conclude; see BUY, SELL.
transaction *n.* sale, proceeding, deal; see BUSINESS 4.
transcend *v.* rise above, transform, excel; see EXCEED.
transcontinental *a.* trans-American, trans-Siberian, trans-Canadian, trans-European, cross-country, intracontinental.
transcribe *v.* reprint, reproduce, decipher; see COPY.
transcriber *n.* copyist, copier, translator; see SECRETARY 2.
transcript *n.* record, reprint, reproduction; see COPY.
transfer *n.* **1.** [Ticket] token, fare, check; see TICKET 1. **2.** [A document providing for a change] new orders, instructions, new assignment; see COMMAND, DIRECTIONS.
transfer *v.* **1.** [To carry] transport, convey, shift; see CARRY 1. **2.** [To assign] sell, hand over, pass the buck*; see ASSIGN, GIVE 1.
transferred *a.* moved, removed, shifted, transported, relocated, transmitted, turned over, sent, relayed, shipped, mailed, faxed, transplanted, reassigned, transposed, restationed, conveyed, transmuted; see also SENT.—*Ant.* FIXED, left, stationed.
transform *v.* convert, mold, reconstruct; see ALTER 1.
transformation *n.* **1.** [A change] alteration, transmutation, conversion; see CHANGE 1. **2.** [A grammatical construction] transform, transformed construction, equivalent grammatical sequence; see ADJECTIVE, PHRASE, SENTENCE 2.
transformational grammar *n.* generative grammar, new grammar, string grammar; see GRAMMAR.
transfusion *n.* dialysis, blood exchange, bleeding; see EXCHANGE 1.
transgress *v.* overstep, rebel, infringe; see DISOBEY.
transgression *n.* misbehavior, trespass, infraction; see CRIME, SIN, VIOLATION.
transgressor *n.* offender, sinner, rebel; see CRIMINAL.
transient *a.* provisional, ephemeral, transitory; see TEMPORARY.
transistor *n.* portable radio, pocket radio, receiver; see RADIO 2.
transition *n.* shift, passage, flux, passing, development, transformation, turn, realignment; see also CHANGE 2.—*Ant.* STABILITY, constancy, durability.
translate *v.* decode, transliterate, interpret, decipher, paraphrase, render, transpose, turn, gloss, put in equivalent terms.
translated *a.* interpreted, adapted, rendered, transliterated, glossed, paraphrased, transposed, reworded, reworked, transferred, rewritten.
translation *n.* transliteration, version, adaptation, rendition, rendering, interpretation, paraphrase, rewording, gloss, reading.
transmission *n.* **1.** [The act of transporting] transference, conveyance, carrying; see DELIVERY 1, TRANSPORTATION. **2.** [The carrying of sound on radio waves] broadcast, telecast, conduction; see BROADCASTING. **3.** [A mechanism for adapting power] gears, gear box, automatic transmission; see DEVICE 1.
transmit *v.* **1.** [To send] dispatch, forward, convey; see SEND 1, 2. **2.** [To carry] pass on, transfer, communicate; see SEND 2.
transmitter *n.* conductor, antenna, wire; see COMMUNICATION, ELECTRONICS.
transparent *a.* **1.** [Allowing light to pass through] translucent, lucid, crystalline, gauzy, thin, permeable, glassy, cellophane; see also CLEAR 2.—*Ant.* DARK, black, smoky. **2.** [Obvious] easily seen, plain, clear; see OBVIOUS 1.
transplant *n.* transplanting, transplantation, graft; see OPERATION 4.
transplant *v.* reset, reorient, remove; see ALTER 1.
transport *v.* convey, move, bring; see CARRY 1.
transportation *n.* conveying, conveyance, carrying, hauling, shipping, carting, moving, transferring, truckage, freightage, airlift, transference, transit, passage.
transported *a.* conveyed, forwarded, transferred; see MOVED 1.
trap *n.* **1.** [A device to catch game or persons] net, box trap, steel trap, spring trap, snare, mousetrap, pit, blind, maneuver. **2.** [A trick] prank, practical joke, snare; see TRICK 1.
trap *v.* ensnare, seduce, fool; see AMBUSH, DECEIVE.
trapped *a.* ambushed, cornered, with one's back to the wall; see CAPTURED.
trash *n.* **1.** [Rubbish] garbage, waste, refuse, dregs, filth, litter, debris, dross, sweepings, rubble, odds and ends, stuff, rags, scraps, scrap, excess, scourings, fragments, pieces, shavings, loppings, slash, rakings, slag, parings, rinsings, shoddy, residue, offal, junk, sediment, leavings, droppings.—*Ant.* MONEY, goods, riches. **2.** [Nonsense] drivel, rubbish, senselessness; see NONSENSE 1.
travel *n.* riding, roving, wandering, rambling, sailing, touring, biking, hiking, cruising, driving, wayfaring, going abroad, seeing the world, sightseeing, voyaging, journeying, trekking, flying, globe-trotting, space travel, rocketing.
travel *v.* tour, cruise, voyage, roam, explore, jet to, rocket to, orbit, go into orbit, take a jet, go by jet, migrate, trek, vacation, motor, visit, traverse, jaunt, wander, journey, adventure, quest, trip, rove, inspect, make an expedition, cross the continent, cross the ocean, encircle the globe, make the grand

tour, sail, see the country, go camping, go abroad, take a trip, cover, go walking, go riding, go bicycling, make a train trip, drive, fly, set out, set forth, sightsee; see also WALK 1.

traveled *a.* **1.** [*Said of persons*] worldly, cosmopolitan, experienced; see CULTURED. **2.** [*Said of roads*] well-used, busy, operating, in use, frequented, widely known, sure, safe, well-trodden, accepted.—*Ant.* ABANDONED, little-used, unexplored.

traveler *n.* voyager, adventurer, tourist, explorer, nomad, wanderer, truant, peddler, roamer, rambler, wayfarer, migrant, excursionist, sightseer, straggler, vagabond, vagrant, hobo, tramp, gypsy, gadabout, itinerant, pilgrim, rover, passenger, commuter, globe-trotter.

traveling *a.* passing, en route, on board, shipped, freighted, transported, moving, carried, conveyed, consigned, wandering, touring, roving, on tour, vagrant, migrant, nomadic, wayfaring, itinerant, cruising, excursioning, commuting, driving, flying, sailing, riding, on vacation, migrating, voyaging; see also MOVING 2.

travesty *n.* burlesque, spoof, caricature; see PARODY.

tray *n.* platter, plate, tea wagon; see DISH 1.

treacherous *a.* deceptive, undependable, dangerous, risky, misleading, tricky, ensnaring, faulty, precarious, unstable, insecure, shaky, slippery, ticklish, difficult, ominous, alarming, menacing.—*Ant.* RELIABLE, dependable, steady.

treachery *n.* faithlessness, disloyalty, betrayal; see DISHONESTY, TREASON.

tread *v.* walk, step, step on; see TRAMPLE.

treason *n.* sedition, disloyalty, perfidy, treachery, seditionary act, seditious act, aid and comfort to the enemy, factious revolt; see also DISHONESTY, DECEPTION, REVOLUTION 2.

treasure *n.* richness, riches, nest egg; see WEALTH.

treasure *v.* prize, value, appreciate, guard; see also LOVE 1.

treasurer *n.* receiver, cashier, banker; see CLERK.

treasury *n.* exchequer, safe, depository; see BANK 2.

treat *n.* entertainment, surprise, amusement, feast, source of gratification, gift, drinks for the crowd*, setup, spree.

treat *v.* **1.** [To deal with a person or thing] negotiate, manage, have to do with, have business with, behave toward, handle, make terms with, act toward, react toward, use, employ, have recourse to.—*Ant.* NEGLECT, ignore, have nothing to do with. **2.** [To assist toward a cure] attend, administer, prescribe, dose, operate, nurse, dress, minister to, apply therapy, care for, doctor*; see also HEAL. **3.** [To pay for another's entertainment] entertain, indulge, satisfy, amuse, divert, play host to, escort, set up, stake to*.

treatise *n.* tract, paper, monograph.

treatment *n.* **1.** [Usage] handling, processing, dealing, approach, execution, procedure, method, manner, proceeding, way, strategy, custom, habit, employment, practice, mode, line, angle. **2.** [Assistance toward a cure] diet, operation, medical care, surgery, therapy, remedy, prescription, regimen, hospitalization, doctoring*; see also MEDICINE 2.

treaty *n.* agreement, pact, settlement, covenant, compact, convention, alliance, charter, sanction, bond, understanding, arrangement, bargain, negotiation, deal*.

tree *n. Trees include the following:* ash, elm, oak, maple, evergreen, birch, tulip, fir, cypress, juniper, larch, tamarack, pine, cedar, beech, chestnut, eucalyptus, hickory, walnut, sycamore, palm, willow, locust, sequoia, redwood, poplar, acacia, cottonwood, box elder, apple, cherry, peach, plum, pear, banyan, bamboo, mahogany, ebony, ironwood, bottletree; see also WOOD 1. —**up a tree*** cornered, in difficulty, trapped; see IN TROUBLE.

trees *n.pl.* wood, woods, windbreak; see FOREST.

trek *v.* hike, migrate, journey; see TRAVEL.

tremble *v.* quiver, shiver, vibrate; see SHAKE 1.

tremendous *a.* huge, great, colossal; see LARGE 1.

tremor *n.* trembling, shaking, shivering; see EARTHQUAKE.

trench *n.* rut, hollow, gully, depression, gutter, tube, furrow, drainage canal, creek, moat, dike, drain, channel, main, gorge, gulch, arroyo. *Military trenches include the following:* dugout, earthwork, entrenchment, fortification, breastwork, pillbox, excavation, bunker, machine-gun nest, foxhole.

trend *n.* bias, bent, leaning; see INCLINATION 1.

trendy* *a.* stylish, popular, contemporary; see FASHIONABLE.

trespass *v.* encroach, invade, infringe; see MEDDLE 1.

trespasser *n.* encroacher, invader, infringer; see INTRUDER.

trial *a.* tentative, test, preliminary; see EXPERIMENTAL.

trial *n.* **1.** [An effort to learn the truth] analysis, test, examination; see EXPERIMENT. **2.** [A case at law] suit, lawsuit, fair hearing, hearing, action, case, contest, indictment, legal proceedings, claim, cross-examination, litigation, counterclaim, arraignment, prosecution, citation, court action, judicial contest, seizure, bill of divorce, habeas corpus, court-martial, impeachment. **3.** [An ordeal] suffering, misfortune, heavy blow; see DIFFICULTY 1, 2.

triangle *n. Triangles include the following:* equilateral, isosceles, right-angled, obtuse-angled, scalene, acute-angled.

triangular *a.* three-cornered, three-sided, trigonal; see ANGULAR.

tribal *a.* tribalistic, racial, kindred; see RACIAL.

tribe *n.* primitive group, ethnic group, association; see RACE 2.

tributary *n.* stream, branch, sidestream; see RIVER.

tribute *n.* applause, recognition, eulogy; see PRAISE 2.

trick *n.* **1.** [A deceit] wile, fraud, deception, ruse, cheat, cover, feint, hoax, artifice, decoy, trap, stratagem, intrigue, fabrication, double-dealing, forgery, fake, illusion, invention, subterfuge, distortion, delusion, ambush, snare, blind, evasion, plot, equivocation, concealment, treachery, swindle, feigning, impersonation, duplicity, pretense, falsehood, falsification, perjury, disguise, conspiracy, circumvention, quibble, trickery, beguiling, chicanery, humbug, maneuver, sham, counterfeit, gyp*, touch*, phoney*, come-on*, fast one*, dodge*, plant*, clip*, sucker deal*, con game*, bluff, shakedown*, sell-out*, con*, funny business*, dirty work*, crooked deal, front*, gimmick*; see also LIE.—*Ant.* HONESTY, truth, veracity. **2.** [A prank] jest, sport, practical joke; see JOKE. **3.** [A practical method or expedient] skill, facility, know-how*; see ABILITY, METHOD.

trick *v.* dupe, outwit, fool; see DECEIVE.

trickle *v.* drip, leak, run; see FLOW.

tricky *a.* **1.** [Shrewd] clever, sharp, keen-witted; see INTELLIGENT. **2.** [Delicate or difficult] complicated, intricate, critical, touchy, involved, perplexing, knotty, thorny, complex, unstable, ticklish, catchy, likely to go wrong, hanging by a thread*; see also DIFFICULT 1, 2.—*Ant.* EASY, clearcut, simple.

tricycle *n.* trike*, wheel*, three-wheeler; see VEHICLE.

tried *a.* dependable, proved, used; see USED 1.

trifle *n.* **1.** [A small quantity] particle, piece, speck; see BIT 1. **2.** [A small degree] jot, eyelash, fraction; see BIT 2. **3.** [Something of little importance] triviality, small matter, nothing; see INSIGNIFICANCE.

trifling *a.* petty, small, insignificant; see TRIVIAL, UNIMPORTANT.

trim *a.* **1.** [Neat] orderly, tidy, spruce; see CLEAN 1, NEAT 1. **2.** [Well-proportioned] shapely, well-designed, streamlined, clean, slim, shipshape, delicate, fit, comely, well-formed, symmetrical, well-made, clean-cut, well-balanced, graceful, well-molded, harmonious, beautiful, classical, compact, smart; see also HANDSOME.—*Ant.* DISORDERED, shapeless, straggly.

trim *v.* **1.** [To cut off excess] prune, shave, lop; see CUT 1. **2.** [To adorn] ornament, embellish, deck; see DECORATE. **3.** [To prepare for sailing] ballast, rig, outfit; see SAIL 1.

trimming *n.* **1.** [Ornamentation] accessory, frill, tassel; see DECORATION 2. **2.** [The act of cutting off excess] shearing, lopping off, shaving off; see REDUCTION 1.

trinity *n.* trio, trilogy, triplet, triplicate, threesome, triad, the Godhead; Father, Son, and Holy Ghost; the Triune God, Trinity; see also GOD 1.

trinket *n.* gadget, novelty, bauble; see JEWEL, JEWELRY.

trio *n.* **1.** [A combination of three] threesome, triangle, triplet; see TRINITY. **2.** [Three musicians performing together] string trio, vocal trio, swing trio; see BAND 3.

trip *n.* **1.** [A journey] voyage, excursion, tour; see JOURNEY. **2.** [A psychedelic experience] hallucinations, LSD trip, being turned on; see DRUG.

trip *v.* **1.** [To stumble] tumble, slip, lurch, slide, founder, fall, pitch, fall over, slip upon, plunge, sprawl, topple, go head over heels.—*Ant.* ARISE, ascend, get up. **2.** [To cause to stumble] block, hinder, bind, tackle, overthrow, push, send headlong, kick, shove, mislead.—*Ant.* HELP, pick up, give a helping hand.

triple *a.* in triplicate, by three, threefold; see THREE.

trite *a.* hackneyed, prosaic, stereotyped; see COMMON 1, DULL 4.

triumph *n.* conquest, achievement, success; see VICTORY.

triumphant *a.* victorious, successful, lucky, winning, conquering, in the lead, triumphal, jubilant, dominant, laurel-crowned, champion, unbeaten, topseeded, out front, triumphing, victorial, elated, in ascendancy, with flying colors.—*Ant.* BEATEN, defeated, overwhelmed.

trivial *a.* petty, trifling, small, superficial, piddling, wee, little, insignificant, frivolous, irrelevant, unimportant, nugatory, skin-deep, meaningless, mean, diminutive, slight, of no account, scanty, meager, inappreciable, microscopic, atomic, dribbling, nonessential, flimsy, inconsiderable, vanishing, momentary, immaterial, indifferent, beside the point, minute, inessential, paltry, inferior, minor, small-minded, beggarly, useless, inconsequential, worthless, mangy, trashy, pitiful, of little moment, dinky*, small-town*, cutting no ice*, cut and dried; see also SHALLOW 2.—*Ant.* IMPORTANT, great, serious.

troops *n.pl.* soldiers, armed forces, fighting men; see ARMY 1.

trophy *n.* citation, medal, cup; see PRIZE.

tropic *a.* **1.** [Related to the tropics] tropical, equatorial, jungle; see HOT 1. **2.** [Hot] thermal, torrid, burning; see HOT 1.

tropics *n.pl.* torrid zone, equator, Equatorial Africa; South America, Amazon, the Congo, the Pacific Islands, hot countries, jungles; see also JUNGLE.

trot *v.* single-foot, jog, amble; see RUN 2.

trouble *n.* **1.** [A person or thing causing trouble] annoyance, difficult situation, bother, bind, hindrance, difficulty, task, puzzle, predicament, plight, problem, fear, worry, concern, inconvenience, nuisance, disturbance, calamity, catastrophe, crisis, delay, quarrel, dispute, bad news, affliction, intrusion, irritation, trial, pain, ordeal, discomfort, injury, adversity, hang-up*, case, bore, gossip, problem child, meddler, pest, tease, tiresome person, inconsiderate person, intruder, troublemaker, fly in the ointment, headache*, brat, holy terror*, peck of trouble*.—*Ant.* HELP, aid, comfort. **2.** [Illness] malady, ailment, affliction; see ILLNESS 1, 2. **3.** [Civil disorder] riot, turmoil, strife; see DISTURBANCE 2. **4.** [A quarrel] argument, feud, bickering; see DISPUTE, FIGHT 1. **—in trouble** unfortunate, having trouble, in difficulty; see IN TROUBLE.

trouble *v.* **1.** [To disturb] disconcert, annoy, irritate; see BOTHER 2, DISTURB. **2.** [To take care] be concerned with, make an effort, take pains; see BOTHER 1.

troubled *a.* disturbed, agitated, grieved, apprehensive, pained, anxious, perplexed, afflicted, confused, puzzled, overwrought, aggravated*, uptight, bothered, harassed, vexed, plagued, teased, annoyed, concerned, uneasy, discomposed, harried, careworn, mortified, badgered, baited, inconvenienced, put out, upset, flurried, flustered, bored, tortured, goaded, irritated, displeased, tried, roused, disconcerted, pursued, chafed, ragged, galled, rubbed the wrong way, tired, molested, crossed, thwarted, fazed, distressed, wounded, sickened, griped, restless, irked, pestered, heckled, persecuted, frightened, alarmed, terrified, scared, anguished, harrowed, tormented, provoked, stung, ruffled, fretting, perturbed, afraid, shaky, fearful, unsettled, suspicious, in turmoil, full of misgivings, shaken, dreading, bugged*, in a quandary, in a stew, on pins and needles*, all hot and bothered*, worried stiff, in a tizzy*, burned up*, miffed*, peeved*, riled*, floored*, up a tree*, hung-up*, up the creek without a paddle*.—*Ant.* CALM, at ease, settled.

troublemaker *n.* rogue, knave, recreant; see CRIMINAL.

troublesome *a.* bothersome, annoying, difficult, irritating, oppressive, repressive, distressing, upsetting, painful, dangerous, damaging.

trough *n.* dip, channel, hollow; see HOLE 2.

trousers *n.pl.* slacks, breeches, knickerbockers; see CLOTHES.

trout *n. Trout include the following:* speckled, brook, rainbow, cutthroat, lake, salmon, steelhead, blue-backed, brown; see also FISH.

trowel *n.* blade, scoop, implement; see TOOL 1.

truant *a.* missing, straying, playing hooky; see ABSENT.

truce *n.* armistice, peace agreement, lull; see PEACE 1.

truck *n.* carriage, van, lorry, car; see also VEHICLE. *Types of trucks include the following:* delivery wagon, moving van, police van, patrol wagon, laundry truck, pickup truck, freight truck, logging truck, army truck, trailer, piggyback trailer, truck trailer, truck and trailer, truck train, cement mixer, refrigerator truck, four-wheel drive truck, freighter, garbage truck, dump truck, semi*, halftrack.

trudge *v.* plod, step, tread; see WALK 1.

true *a.* **1.** [Accurate] precise, verified, proved, certain, certified, definite, checked, exact, correct; see also VALID 1. **2.** [Loyal] sure, reliable, trustworthy, faithful, dependable, sincere; see also FAITHFUL, RELIABLE. **3.** [Genuine] authentic, virtual, substantial, tangible, genuine, actual, pure; see also REAL 2, VALID 2. **—come true** become a fact, be actualized, come about; see DEVELOP 1, HAPPEN 2.

truly *a.* honestly, exactly, definitely, reliable, factually, correctly, unequivocally, sincerely, scrupulously, fairly, justly, validly, rightfully, righteously, faithfully, worthily, scientifically, without bias, without prejudice, fairly and squarely*.—*Ant.* WRONGLY, dishonestly, deceptively.

trumped up *a.* falsified, concocted, magnified; see EXAGGERATED, FALSE 2.

trumpet *n.* horn, bugle, cornet; see MUSICAL INSTRUMENT.

trump up *v.* think up, devise, concoct, falsify, present fraudulent evidence, misrepresent; see also DECEIVE, LIE 1.

trunk *n.* **1.** [A container for goods] chest, case, foot locker; see CONTAINER. **2.** [The torso] body, soma, thorax; see BACK 1, STOMACH. **3.** [The stem of a tree] column, stock, log; see STALK. **4.** [A proboscis] prow, snoot, snout; see NOSE 1.

trust *n.* **1.** [Reliance] confidence, dependence, credence; see FAITH 1. **2.** [Responsibility] guardianship, account, liability; see DUTY 1. **3.** [A large company] corporation, monopoly, institution; see BUSINESS 4. **—in trust** in another's care, held for, reserved; see SAVED 2.

trust *v.* **1.** [To believe in] swear by, place confidence in, confide in, esteem, depend upon, expect help from, presume upon, lean on, have no doubt, rest assured, be sure about, have no reservations, rely on, put faith in, look to, count on, assume that, presume that, be persuaded by, be convinced, put great stock in, set great store by, bank on*, take at one's word; see also BELIEVE.—*Ant.* DOUBT, mistrust, disbelieve. **2.** [To hope] presume, take, imagine; see ASSUME, HOPE. **3.** [To place in the protection of another] lend, put in safekeeping, entrust; see sense 1. **4.** [To give credit to] advance, lend, loan, let out, grant, confer, let, patronize, aid, give financial aid to.—*Ant.* BORROW, raise money, pawn.

trusted *a.* trustworthy, dependable, reliable, trusty, tried, proved, intimate, close, faithful, loyal, true, constant, staunch, devoted, incorruptible, safe, honorable, honored, inviolable, on the level*, regular*, right, sure-fire*.—*Ant.* DISHONEST, questionable, unreliable.

trustee *n.* guardian, custodian, controller, lawyer, stockholder, guarantor, regent, board member, appointee, administrator, member of the directorate.

trusting *a.* trustful, credulous, confiding, gullible, unsuspecting, easygoing, open, candid, indulgent, obliging, well-meaning, good-natured, tenderhearted, green, with a glass jaw*; see also NAIVE.—*Ant.* SUSPICIOUS, skeptical, critical.

trustworthiness *n.* integrity, uprightness, loyalty; see HONESTY.

trustworthy *a.* accurate, honest, true; see RELIABLE.

trusty *n.* trusted person, trustworthy convict, prison attendant, privileged prisoner; see also PRISONER.

truth *n.* **1.** [Conformity to reality] truthfulness, correctness, sincerity, verity, candor, openness, honesty, fidelity, frankness, revelation, authenticity, exactness, infallibility, precision, perfection, certainty, genuineness, accuracy, fact, the gospel truth*, straight dope*, inside track*, the nitty-gritty, the facts, the case.—*Ant.* LIE, deception, falsehood. **2.** [Integrity] trustworthiness, honor, probity; see HONESTY. —**in truth** in fact, indeed, really; see TRULY.

truthful *a.* correct, frank, just; see HONEST 1.

truthfully *a.* honestly, honorably, veraciously; see SINCERELY, TRULY.

truthfulness *n.* integrity, frankness, accuracy; see HONESTY.

try *v.* **1.** [To endeavor] attempt, undertake, exert oneself, contend, strive, make an effort, risk, have a try at, contest, wrangle, labor, work, aspire, propose, try to reach, do what one can, tackle, venture, struggle for, compete for, speculate, make every effort, put oneself out, vie for, aspire to, attack, make a bid for, beat one's brains*, bear down, shoot at*, shoot for*, drive for, chip away at*, do one's best, make a pass at, go after, go out of the way, give a workout*, do all in one's power, buckle down, lift a finger, break an arm*, lay out, do oneself justice, have a go at*, make a go of it*, go all out, leave no stone unturned, move heaven and earth, knock oneself out*, break one's neck*, bust a gut*, take a crack at*, give it whirl*. **2.** [To test] assay, investigate, put to the proof; see ANALYZE, EXAMINE. **3.** [To conduct a trial] hear a case, examine, decide; see JUDGE.

trying *a.* troublesome, bothersome, irritating; see DIFFICULT 1, 2.

try on *v.* fit, have a fitting, try on for size; see WEAR 1.

tryout *n.* test, demonstration, rehearsal; see EXAMINATION 1.

try out for *v.* go out for, audition for, compete; see REHEARSE 3.

tub *n.* keg, bucket, tank; see CONTAINER.

tube *n.* **1.** [A pipe] conduit, hose, test tube, tubing, tunnel, loom, subway; see also PIPE 1. **2.** [A metal container] package, paste tube, squeeze tube; see CONTAINER. **3.** [An electronic device] cell, electric eye, vacuum tube; see DEVICE 1, MACHINE.

tuck *n.* crease, folding, pleat; see FOLD.

tuck in *v.* insert, squeeze in, add; see INCLUDE 2.

tuft *n.* clump, cluster, group; see BUNCH.

tug *v.* pull, haul, tow; see DRAW 1.

tuition *n.* fee, cost, expenditure; see PRICE.

tumble *v.* drop, plunge, descend; see FALL 1, TRIP 1.

tumor *n.* neoplasm, tumefaction, cyst; see SWELLING.

tumult *n.* agitation, uproar, turbulence; see CONFUSION, DISTURBANCE 2, FIGHT 1.

tune *n.* melody, air, strain; see SONG. —**change one's tune*** change one's mind, alter one's actions, be transformed; see ALTER 1. —**sing a different tune*** change one's mind, alter one's actions, be transformed; see ALTER 1.

tune *v.* adjust the pitch, attune, put in tune, tune up, tighten the strings, use the tuning fork, set the tune; see also HARMONIZE.

tune in (on)* *v.* participate, become part of, enter into; see JOIN 1, 2, LISTEN.

tune up* *v.* enliven, refine, make better; see REPAIR.

tunnel *n.* hole, burrow, underground passage, subway, tube, crawl space, crawlway, shaft, mine, pit.

turbulence *n.* disorder, commotion, fracas; see CONFUSION, DISTURBANCE 2, FIGHT 1.

turbulent *a.* riotous, violent, stormy, disturbed, noisy, restless, raging, howling, buffeting, thunderous, tumultuous, excited, passionate, uncontrolled, vehement, roaring, tempestuous, rampant, rowdy, lawless, disorderly, untamed, disordered, chaotic, agitated, fierce, wild, rude, rough, blustering, angry, storming, uproarious, clamorous, mutinous, rebellious, destructive, hard, stern, bitter, fiery, rabid, boisterous, perturbed, foaming, shaking, vociferous, demonstrative.—*Ant.* PEACEFUL, tranquil, at ease.

turf *n.* earth, peat, lawn; see GRASS 1.

turkey *n.* turkey cock, turkey hen, tom, bird, fowl, Thanksgiving bird, Christmas bird, gobbler, turkey gobbler, wild turkey, domestic turkey.

turmoil *n.* agitation, turbulence, riot; see CONFUSION, DISTURBANCE 2.

turn *n.* **1.** [A revolution] rotation, cycle, circle, round, circulation, pirouette, gyre, gyration, spin, round-about-face, roll, turning, circumrotation, spiral; see also REVOLUTION 1. **2.** [A bend] curve, winding, twist, wind, hook, shift, angle, corner, fork, branch. **3.** [A turning point] climax, crisis, juncture, emergency, critical period, crossing, change, new development, shift, twist. **4.** [A shock] fright, jolt, blow; see SURPRISE 2. **5.** [An action] deed, accomplishment, service; see HELP 1. **6.** [A change in course] curve, detour, deviation, corner, ground loop, stem turn, jump turn, telemark, kick turn, inside loop, outside loop, wing spin, tight spin, tight spiral. **—at every turn** in every instance, constantly, consistently; see REGULARLY. **—by turns** taking turns, in succession, alternately; see CONSECUTIVE. **—call the turn** anticipate, predict, foretell; see EXPECT 1. **—take turns** do by turns, do in succession, share; see ALTERNATE 1. **—to a turn** correctly, properly, to the right degree; see PERFECTLY.

turn *v.* **1.** [To pivot] revolve, rotate, roll, spin, wheel, whirl, circulate, go around, swivel, round, twist, twirl, gyrate, ground, loop; see also SWING. **2.** [To reverse] go back, recoil, change, upset, retrace, face about, turn around, capsize, shift, alter, vary, convert, transform, invert, subvert, return, alternate. **3.** [To divert] deflect, veer, turn aside, turn away, sidetrack, swerve, put off, call off, turn off, deviate, dodge, twist, avoid, shift, switch, avert, zigzag, shy away, redirect, draw aside. **4.** [To become] grow into, change into, pass into; see BECOME. **5.** [To sour] curdle, acidify, become rancid; see SOUR. **6.** [To change direction] swerve, swing, bend, veer, tack, round to, incline, deviate, detour, loop, curve. **7.** [To incline] prefer, be predisposed to, favor; see LEAN 1, TEND 2. **8.** [To sprain] strain, bruise, dislocate; see HURT 1. **9.** [To nauseate] sicken, make one sick, revolt; see DISGUST. **10.** [To bend] curve, twist, fold; see BEND. **11.** [To transform] transmute, remake, transpose; see ALTER 1. **12.** [To make use of] apply, adapt, utilize; see USE 1. **13.** [To point] direct, set, train; see AIM. **14.** [To repel] repulse, push back, throw back; see REPEL 1.

turn about *v.* turn around, pivot, reverse; see TURN 1.

turn against *v.* revolt, disobey, defy; see OPPOSE 1, 2, REBEL.

turn aside *v.* avert, deflect, divert; see TURN 3.

turn back *v.* retrogress, retrograde, revert; see RETURN 1, 2.

turn down *v.* **1.** [To decrease in volume, etc.] hush, lower, curb; see DECREASE 2. **2.** [To refuse] reject, decline, rebuff; see REFUSE.

turned *a.* **1.** [Revolved] spun, rounded, circled, circulated, rotated, rolled, whirled, gyrated, set going. **2.** [Deflected] switched, twisted, dodged, avoided, shied away from, shifted, shunted, changed.

turn in *v.* **1.** [To deliver] hand over, transfer, give up; see GIVE 1. **2.** [*To go to bed] lie down, retire, hit the hay*; see REST 1.

turning *a.* twisting, shifting, whirling, rotating, revolving, bending, curving, shunting; see also GROWING, CHANGING.—*Ant.* PERMANENT, static, fixed.

turning *n.* whirling, revolving, rotating; see REVOLUTION 1.

turning point *n.* peak, juncture, culmination; see CLIMAX, CRISIS.

turn into *v.* **1.** [To change] transform, alter, transmute; see ALTER 1. **2.** [To become changed] be converted, transform, modify; see CHANGE 2.

turn loose *v.* liberate, emancipate, set free; see FREE.

turn off *v.* stop, shut off, douse, turn out, log off, halt, close, shut, extinguish, shut down, kill the light, turn off the juice, cut the motor, hit the switch.

turn on *v.* **1.** [To start the operation of] set going, switch on, set in motion, log on, put in gear; see also BEGIN 1. **2.** [To attack] strike, assail, assault; see ATTACK. **3.** [*To take drugs] smoke marijuana, get high*, take a trip*, smoke pot*, get stoned*, freak out*, blow pot*, trip out*, get wasted*. **4.** [*To arouse] titillate, stimulate, stir up; see EXCITE. **5.** [*To depend on or upon] hinge on, be dependent on, be based on; see DEPEND ON 2.

turnout *n.* **1.** [Production] output, result, volume; see PRODUCTION 1. **2.** [A gathering] assembly, attendance, group; see GATHERING.

turn out *v.* **1.** [To stop the operation of] extinguish, shut off, stop; see TURN OFF. **2.** [To dismiss] discharge, evict, send away; see DISMISS, OUST. **3.** [To produce] make, put out, build; see MANUFACTURE, PRODUCE 2. **4.** [To get out of bed] get up, rise, wake up; see ARISE 1, WAKE 2. **5.** [To finish] end, complete, perfect; see ACHIEVE.

turn over *v.* **1.** [To invert] overturn, reverse, subvert; see UPSET 1. **2.** [To transfer] hand over, give over, deliver; see ASSIGN, GIVE 1.

turn over a new leaf *v.* get better, change for the better, make New Year's resolutions; see IMPROVE 2, REFORM 3.

turn sour *v.* putrefy, rot, spoil; see SPOIL.

turn the tables *v.* reverse conditions, reverse circumstances, give one his own medicine; see ALTER 1, UPSET 1.

turn to *v.* **1.** [To rely upon] confide, appeal to, depend upon; see TRUST 1. **2.** [To start] start to work, become interested in, take up; see BEGIN 1.

turn up *v.* **1.** [To find] disclose, learn, come across; see DISCOVER, FIND. **2.** [To arrive] enter, come, roll in; see ARRIVE. **3.** [To increase the volume, etc.] amplify, augment, boost; see INCREASE, STRENGTHEN.

tusk *n.* canine tooth, fang, incisor; see TOOTH 1.

tutor *n.* instructor, tutorial assistant, private tutor; see TEACHER.

tutoring *n.* coaching, training, instruction; see EDUCATION 1.

TV *n.* video, cable, idiot box*; see TELEVISION.

tweak *v.* twitch, squeeze, jerk; see PINCH.

tweezers *n.pl.* forceps, nippers, tongs; see TOOL 1.

twelve *a.* dozen, twelvefold, twelfth; see NUMBER.

twenty *a.* twentieth, vicenary, twentyfold, vicennial.

twice *a.* double, doubly, once and again, over again, once over.

twig *n.* offshoot, limb, sprig; see BRANCH 2.

twilight *n.* dusk, nightfall, late afternoon, early evening, sunset, dawn, break of day; see also NIGHT 1.

twin *a.* identical twin, fraternal twin, look-alike, identical two, fellow, twofold, second, accompanying, joint, coupled, matched, copied, duplicating; see also SECOND, TWO.—*Ant.* SINGLE, lone, solitary.

twine *n.* braid, cord, string; see ROPE.

twinge *v.* twitch, shiver, smart; see TINGLE.

twinkle *v.* shimmer, flicker, sparkle; see SHINE 1.

twinkling *a.* sparkling, glimmering, flashing; see BRIGHT 1.

twirl *v.* spin, rotate, twist; see TURN 1.

twist *v.* wring, wrap, twine, twirl, spin, turn around, wrap around; see also TURN 1.

twisted *a.* **1.** [Crooked] contorted, wrenched, bent, knotted, braided, twined, wound, wreathed, writhing, convolute, twisting.—*Ant.* STRAIGHT, even, regular. **2.** [Confused] erroneous, perplexing, wrong-headed, awry, puzzling, unintelligible, disorganized, tangled, perverted; see also WRONG 2.—*Ant.* CLEAR, simple, logical.

twitch *v.* **1.** [To pluck] pull, tug, snatch; see PULL 2. **2.** [To jerk] shiver, shudder, have a fit, kick, work, palpitate, beat, twinge, pain.

two *a.* twin, dual, binary, both, double, forked, bifid.

two *n.* two of a kind, twins, couple; see PAIR. **—in two** halved, divided, split; see SEPARATED. **—put two and two together*** reason, sum up, reach a conclusion; see DECIDE.

two-faced *a.* deceitful, hypocritical, treacherous; see FALSE 1.

tycoon *n.* magnate, mogul, director; see BUSINESSMAN, EXECUTIVE.

type *n.* **1.** [Kind] sort, nature, character; see KIND 2, VARIETY 2. **2.** [Representive] representation, sample, example; see MODEL 1, 2. **3.** [Letter] symbol, emblem, figure, character, sign; see also LETTER 1. *Styles of types include the following:* Gothic, black letter, old style, new style, modern, roman, italic, script, sans serif, Old English, text. *Sizes of types include the following:* Excelsior or 3-point, Brilliant or 3-1/2-point, Diamond or 4-1/2-point, Pearl or 5-point, Agate or 5 1/2-point, Nonpareil or 6-point, Minion or 7-point, Brevier or 8-point, Bourgeois or 9-point, Long Primer or 10-point, Small Pica or 11-point, Pica or 12-point, English or 14-point, Columbian or 16-point, Great Primer or 18-point. *Fonts of types include the following:* standard, lightface, boldface, extra-bold, cursive, open, extended, condensed, shaded, upright, expanded, wide.

type *v.* **1.** [To use a typewriter] typewrite, copy, transcribe, teletype, input, touchtype, hunt and peck. **2.** [To classify] categorize, normalize, standardize; see CLASSIFY.

typed *a.* **1.** [Set down on a typewriter] typewritten, copied, set up, written, transcribed; see also PRINTED. **2.** [Classified] labeled, characterized, analyzed, symbolized, classed, prefigured, sampled, marked, regulated, exemplified, made out to be, patterned, standardized, stylized, cast, formalized.

typewriter *n.* typing machine, office typewriter, portable, noiseless, electric typewriter, electronic typewriter, word processor, memory typewriter, ticker, teletypewriter.

typewritten *a.* written on a typewriter, transcribed, copied; see PRINTED.

typical *a.* characteristic, habitual, usual, representative, symbolic, normal, illustrative, conventional, archetypical, ideal, expected, suggestive, standardized, standard, patterned, ordinary, average, common, everyday, regular.—*Ant.* SUPERIOR, exceptional, extraordinary.

typify *v.* exemplify, symbolize, embody; see MEAN 1.

typing *n.* typescript, typewriting, typed copy; see WRITING 1.

typist *n.* secretary, typewriter operator, teletyper, office girl, inputter, clerk, clerical worker.

tyrannical *a.* dictatorial, domineering, totalitarian; see ABSOLUTE 2.

tyranny *n.* oppression, cruelty, severity, reign of terror, despotism, absolutism.

tyrant *n.* despot, absolute ruler, czar; see DICTATOR.

U

ugliness *n.* unsightliness, homeliness, hideousness, repulsiveness, loathsomeness, unseemliness, offensiveness, deformity, bad looks, ill looks, ill-favored countenance, plainness, disfigurement, grim aspect, foulness, horridness, monstrousness, inelegance, frightfulness, fearfulness.—*Ant.* BEAUTY, fairness, attractiveness.

ugly *a.* 1. [Ill-favored] unsightly, loathsome, hideous, homely, repulsive, unseemly, uncomely, deformed, bad-looking, plain, disfigured, monstrous, foul, horrid, frightful, revolting, repellent, unlovely, appalling, haglike, misshapen, misbegotten, grisly, looking a mess*, looking like the devil*, not fit to be seen*.—*Ant.* BEAUTIFUL, handsome, graceful. 2. [Dangerous] pugnacious, quarrelsome, bellicose, rough, cantankerous, violent, vicious, evil, sinister, treacherous, wicked, formidable.—*Ant.* REASONABLE, mild, complaisant.

ulcer *n.* boil, abscess, infection; see SORE.

ultimate *a.* final, terminal, latest; see LAST 1.

ultimately *a.* eventually, at last, in the end, sooner or later, as a conclusion, to cap the climax, sequentially, after all, at long last, climactically, at the close, in conclusion, conclusively, in due time, after a while, in after days, presently, by and by; see also FINALLY.—*Ant.* EARLY, in the beginning, at present.

ultimatum *n.* demands, requirements, terms.

ultraviolet *a.* beyond violet, having wavelengths of more than 4,000 angstroms, beyond the range of sight; see INVISIBLE.

umbrella *n.* parasol, sunshade, beach umbrella; see HAT.

umpire *n.* referee, moderator, mediator; see JUDGE 1.

unabbreviated *a.* unabridged, complete, whole; see WHOLE 1.

unable *a.* incapable, powerless, weak, incompetent, unskilled, impotent, not able, inept, incapacitated, inefficacious, helpless, unfitted, inefficient, unqualified, inadequate, ineffectual, inoperative.—*Ant.* ABLE, capable, effective.

unaccompanied *a.* sole, solitary, deserted; see ALONE.

unaccustomed *a.* 1. [Unfamiliar] strange, unknown, unusual; see UNFAMILIAR 1. 2. [Unpracticed] unskilled, incompetent, untrained; see NAIVE.

unacquainted *a.* ignorant, out of touch, unknown; see UNFAMILIAR 1.

unaffected *a.* 1. [Genuine] spontaneous, candid, simple; see NATURAL 3. 2. [Uninfluenced] unmoved, unchanged, steady; see CALM 1.

un-American *a.* undemocratic, underground, subversive; see FOREIGN.

unanimous *a.* united, single, collective, combined, unified, concerted, harmonious, concordant, concurrent, public, popular, undivided, of one accord, agreed, common, communal, shared, universal, accepted, unquestioned, undisputed, uncontested, consonant, consistent, with one voice, homogeneous, accordant, assenting.—*Ant.* DIFFERENT, dissenting, irreconcilable.

unanimously *a.* with one voice, harmoniously, all together, by acclamation, universally, unitedly, singly, collectively, without a dissenting voice, by common consent, by vote, in unison, cooperatively, concurrently, popularly, commonly, undisputedly, consonantly, consistently, in agreement.

unanswered *a.* without reply, unrefuted, not responded to, unnoticed, unchallenged, unquestioned, demanding an answer, filed, ignored, unsettled, undecided, in doubt, disputed, moot, debatable, vexed, open, pending, under consideration, undetermined, tabled, up in the air.—*Ant.* DETERMINED, answered, responded to.

unapproachable *a.* withdrawn, hesitant, aloof; see DISTANT.

unarmed *a.* weaponless, defenseless, peaceable; see WEAK 5.

unasked *a.* uninvited, not asked, unwelcome; see UNPOPULAR.

unattached *a.* independent, unbound, ungoverned; see FREE 1, 2, 3.

unauthorized *a.* unofficial, unapproved, unlawful; see ILLEGAL.

unavoidable *a.* inescapable, impending, sure; see CERTAIN 2.

unaware *a.* uninformed, oblivious, ignorant, not cognizant, unmindful, unknowing, heedless, negligent, careless, insensible, forgetful, unconcerned, blind, deaf, inattentive, without notice, deaf to, caught napping, in a daze, not seeing the forest for the trees*.—*Ant.* CONSCIOUS, aware, cognizant.

unbalance *v.* **1.** [To upset] capsize, overturn, tumble; see UPSET 1. **2.** [To derange] dement, craze, obsess; see DISTURB.

unbalanced *a.* **1.** [Deranged] unsound, crazy, psychotic; see INSANE, TROUBLED. **2.** [Unsteady] wobbly, shaky, treacherous; see UNSTABLE 1.

unbearable *a.* intolerable, unacceptable, too much*; see TERRIBLE 2.

unbeaten *a.* victorious, triumphant, winning; see SUCCESSFUL.

unbecoming *a.* unsuitable, unfitted, awkward; see IMPROPER.

unbelievable *a.* beyond belief, incredible, inconceivable, staggering, unimaginable, not to be credited, dubious, doubtful, improbable, questionable, implausible, open to doubt, a bit thick*; see also UNLIKELY.—*Ant.* LIKELY, believable, probable.

unbelievably *a.* remarkably, horribly, badly; see STRANGELY.

unbend *v.* become more casual, be informal, relax; see REST 1.

unbind *v.* unfasten, disengage, untie; see FREE.

unblemished *a.* spotless, flawless, unmarked; see PERFECT 2.

unborn *a.* embryonic, incipient, expected, future, prospective, potential, latent, anticipated, awaited.

unbound *a.* loose, untied, unfastened; see FREE 1, 2, 3.—*Ant.* BOUND, stapled, tied.

unbreakable *a.* indestructible, durable, everlasting, cast-iron, lasting, unshakeable, solid, firm, unchangeable, invulnerable, incorruptible, resistant, rugged, tight, unyielding.—*Ant.* DAINTY, fragile, brittle.

unbroken *a.* **1.** [Whole] entire, intact, unimpaired; see WHOLE 2. **2.** [Continuous] uninterrupted, continuous, even; see REGULAR 3, SMOOTH 1, 2.

unburden *v.* **1.** [To unload] dump, dispose of, relinquish; see LIGHTEN, RELIEVE. **2.** [To reveal] disclose, confess, divulge; see ADMIT 2.

unbutton *v.* undo, open up, unfasten; see OPEN 2.

uncalled for *a.* unjustified, redundant, not needed; see UNNECESSARY.

uncanny *a.* weird, unnatural, supernatural, preternatural, superhuman, ghostly, inexplainable, mystifying, incredible, mysterious, magical, devilish; see also MAGIC.

uncertain *a.* undecided, undetermined, unsettled, doubtful, changeable, unpredictable, improbable, unlikely, unfixed, unsure, indeterminate, haphazard, random, chance, casual, provisional, contingent, alterable, subject to change, possible, vague, conjectural, questionable, problematic, suppositional, hypothetical, theoretical, open to question, equivocal, perplexing, debatable, dubious, indefinite, unascertained, ambiguous, unresolved, debated, conjecturable, unknown, unannounced, imprecise, in abeyance, up in the air, in doubt.

uncertainty *n.* **1.** [The mental state of being uncertain] perplexity, doubt, puzzlement, quandary, mystification, guesswork, conjecture, indecision, ambivalence, dilemma.—*Ant.* BELIEF, certainty, decision. **2.** [The state of being undetermined or unknown] questionableness, contingency, obscurity, vagueness, ambiguity, difficulty, incoherence, intricacy, involvement, darkness, inconclusiveness, indeterminateness, improbability, unlikelihood, low probability, conjecturability; see also DOUBT.—*Ant.* DETERMINATION, sureness, necessity. **3.** [That which is not determined or not known] chance, mutability, change, unpredictability, possibility, emergence, contingency, blind spot, puzzle, enigma, question, blank, vacancy, maze, theory, risk, leap in the dark.—*Ant.* TRUTH, fact, matter of record.

unchangeable *a.* fixed, unalterable, inevitable; see FIRM 1.

unchanged *a.* unaltered, the same, unmoved, constant, fixed, continuing, stable, permanent, durable, unvarying, eternal, invariable, consistent, persistent, firm, unvaried, resolute, perpetual, continuous, maintained, uninterrupted, fast.—*Ant.* CHANGED, altered, modified.

uncivilized *a.* barbarous, uncontrolled, barbarian; see PRIMITIVE 3.

unclassified *a.* not classified, disordered, out of order; see CONFUSED 2, UNKNOWN 1.

uncle *n.* father's brother, mother's brother, elder; see RELATIVE.

unclean *a.* soiled, sullied, stained, spotted, filthy, bedraggled, smeared, befouled, nasty, grimy, polluted, rank, unhealthful, defiled, muddy, stinking, fetid, rotten, vile, decayed, contaminated, tainted, rancid, putrid, putrescent, moldy, musty, mildewed, besmirched, smirched, filmed over, bleary, dusty, sooty, smudgy, scurvy, scurfy, clogged, slimy, mucky, tarnished, murky, smudged, daubed, blurred, spattered; see also DIRTY 1, IMPURE 1.—*Ant.* CLEAN, pure, white.

uncomfortable *a.* **1.** [Troubled in body or mind] distressed, ill at ease, uneasy, nervous, disturbed, pained, miserable, wretched, restless, annoyed, angry, in pain, smarting, suffering, upset, vexed, on pins and needles, weary, tired, fatigued, exhausted, strained, worn, aching, sore, galled, stiff, chafed, cramped, agonized, hurt, anguished.—*Ant.* QUIET, rested, happy. **2.** [Causing discomfort] ill-fitting, awkward, annoying, irritating, distressful, galling, wearisome, difficult, hard, thorny, troublesome, harsh, grievous, dolorous, bitter, excruciating, afflictive, distressing, torturing, painful, agonizing, disagreeable.—*Ant.* EASY, pleasant, grateful.

uncomfortably *a.* distressfully, uneasily, dolefully, agonizingly, painfully, miserably, wretchedly, restlessly, sadly, fretfully, annoyingly, disturbingly, awkwardly, irritatingly, troublesomely, harshly, grievously, bitterly, poignantly, sharply, keenly, excruciatingly, disagreeably, unhappily, dismally, in anguish.

uncommitted *a.* **1.** [Neutral] unpledged, unaffiliated, free; see NEUTRAL 1. **2.** [Reserved] evasive, reticent, shy; see WITHDRAWN.

uncommon *a.* unusual, out of the ordinary, different, extraordinary, unheard of, unique, rare, exceptional, out of the way, strange, exotic, arcane, remarkable, startling, surprising, fantastic, unaccustomed, unfamiliar, freakish, irregular, uncustomary, unconventional, unorthodox, abnormal, aberrant, peculiar, odd, bizarre, eccentric, original, nondescript, prodigious, fabulous, monstrous, curious, wonderful, unaccountable, noteworthy, queer, unparalleled, outlandish, extreme.—*Ant.* COMMON, usual, ordinary.

uncompromising *a.* strong, inflexible, determined; see FIRM 1.

unconcern *n.* apathy, aloofness, coldness; see INDIFFERENCE.

unconcerned *a.* careless, apathetic, inattentive; see NONCHALANT, INDIFFERENT.

unconditional *a.* positive, definite, absolute, unconstrained, without reserve, outright, final, certain, complete, entire, whole, unrestricted, unqualified, unlimited, actual, thorough, thoroughgoing, genuine, indubitable, assured, determinate, unequivocal, full, categorical, decisive, unmistakable, clear, unquestionable.

unconditionally *a.* absolutely, thoroughly, unreservedly; see COMPLETELY.

unconnected *a.* **1.** [Separate] divided, detached, disconnected; see SEPARATED. **2.** [Irrelevant] impertinent, unrelated, inapplicable; see IRRELEVANT.

unconscious *a.* insensible, swooning, in a state of suspended animation, torpid, lethargic, inanimate, senseless, drowsy, motionless, benumbed, stupefied, numb, inert, paralyzed, palsied, tranced, entranced, in a stupor, in a coma, in a trance, raving, out of one's head, out like a light*, knocked out.—*Ant.* CONSCIOUS, vivacious, awake.

unconscious *n.* [*Usually used with "the"*] psyche, instinct, motive force; see MEMORY 1, MIND 1.

unconsciously *a.* abstractedly, mechanically, carelessly, automatically, habitually, by rote, unintentionally, inattentively, heedlessly, without reflection, negligently, disregardfully, thoughtlessly, neglectfully, hurriedly, unthinkingly, without calculation, unguardedly.—*Ant.* DELIBERATELY, intentionally, willfully.

unconstitutional *a.* un-American, undemocratic, lawless; see ILLEGAL.

uncontrollable *a.* ungovernable, stubborn, insurgent; see UNRULY.

uncontrolled *a.* open, clear, free, unchecked, unhindered, boundless, ungoverned, unsuppressed, limitless, unbridled, unfettered, unobstructed, independent, unburdened, unbounded, unhampered, unlimited, uncurbed, unconstrained, unconfined.

unconventional *a.* novel, individual, different; see UNIQUE, UNUSUAL 2.

uncouth *a.* awkward, clumsy, crude; see RUDE 1, 2.

uncover *v.* unseal, uncork, unscrew, pry open, lift the lid, dig up, reveal, tap, lay open, unclose, fish out, fish up; see also OPEN 2.—*Ant.* CLOSE, cover, seal up.

uncovered *a.* exposed, conspicuous, unsafe; see OPEN 4.

undamaged *a.* uninjured, safe, unharmed; see WHOLE 2.

undecided *a.* undetermined, in the balance, unsettled; see DOUBTFUL, UNCERTAIN.

undefeated *a.* unbeaten, victorious, winning; see SUCCESSFUL.

undefined *a.* **1.** [Infinite] limitless, boundless, forever; see INFINITE. **2.** [Vague] dim, unclear, indistinct; see IRREGULAR 4, OBSCURE 1.

undeniable *a.* proven, sound, sure; see ACCURATE 1.

undependable *a.* careless, unsound, inconstant; see IRRESPONSIBLE, UNRELIABLE.

under *a. & prep.* **1.** [Referring to physical position] on the bottom of, below, covered by, 'neath, concealed by, held down by, supporting, pinned beneath, on the underside of, pressed down by, beneath.—*Ant.* ABOVE, over, on top of. **2.** [Subject to authority] governed by, in the power of, obedient to; see SUBORDINATE. **3.** [Included within] belonging to, subsequent to, following; see BELOW 3.

underachiever *n.* slow learner, retarded child, underprivileged person, backward child, misfit, problem child, foreigner, nonnative speaker, foreign-born pupil; see also FOOL.

underage *a.* juvenile, youthful, minor; see YOUNG 1.

under arrest *a.* arrested, caught, apprehended, taken into custody, seized, taken in, handcuffed, confined, jailed, imprisoned, detained, shut up, penned up, put in irons, sent to prison, sent to jail, busted*, pinched*, booked, collared*, nabbed*, sent up the river*.

underbrush *n.* thicket, brush, brushwood, jungle, second growth, tangle, hedge, cover, scrub, bush; see also FOREST.

underclothes *n.pl.* lingerie, undies*, underthings; see CLOTHES, UNDERWEAR.

under construction *a.* in production, in preparation, being built, going up.

undercover *a.* **1.** [Secret] hidden, surreptitious, clandestine; see SECRET 3. **2.** [Secretly] privately, surreptitiously, stealthily; see SECRETLY.

underdeveloped *a.* backward, retarded, slowed down; see WEAK 1, 2, 3, 5.

underdog *n.* loser, underling, low man on the totem pole*; see FAILURE 2, VICTIM.

underestimate *v.* miscalculate, come short of, undervalue, depreciate, underrate, disparage, slight, minimize, think too little of, hold too lightly, make light of, deprecate.

under fire *a.* in action, at the front, embattled; see FIGHTING.

underfoot *a.* **1.** [Beneath] down, at bottom, below; see UNDER 1. **2.** [In the way] annoying, tiresome, impeding; see DISTURBING.

undergo *v.* sustain, submit to, support, experience, feel, know, be subject to, bear, meet with, endure, go through, encounter, bear up under, put up with, share, withstand.—*Ant.* AVOID, ESCAPE, RESIST.

undergone *a.* sustained, submitted to, supported, experienced, felt, suffered, borne, met with, known, endured, gone through, encountered, put up with, shared, seen, withstood.

underground *a.* **1.** [Subterranean] buried, covered, earthed over, under the sod, in the recesses of the earth, hidden from the eye of day, gone to earth; see also UNDER 1. **2.** [Secret] hidden, undercover, clandestine; see SECRET 3. **3.** [Unconventional] experimental, radical, avant-garde; see UNUSUAL 2.

undergrowth *n.* underwood, tangle, scrub; see BRUSH 3.

underhanded *a.* secret, sneaky, secretive; see SLY.

underlie *v.* carry, bear, hold up; see HOLD 7.

underline *v.* **1.** [Emphasize] stress, mark, indicate; see EMPHASIZE. **2.** [To make a line under] underscore, mark, interline, bracket, check off, italicize.

undermine *v.* impair, ruin, threaten; see WEAKEN 2.

underneath *a. & prep.* beneath, below, lower than; see UNDER 1.

undernourished *a.* underfed, mistreated, afflicted with malnutrition; see HUNGRY.

underpass *n.* bridge, culvert, cave; see TUNNEL.

underprivileged *a.* indigent, destitute, educationally handicapped; see POOR 1.

undershirt *n.* shirt, T-shirt, turtleneck; see CLOTHES, UNDERWEAR.

underside *n.* underneath, base, root; see BOTTOM, FOUNDATION 2.

understand *v.* **1.** [To comprehend] apprehend, fathom, take in, grasp, figure out, seize, identify with, know, perceive, appreciate, follow, master, conceive, be aware of, sense, recognize, grow aware, explain, interpret, see through, learn, find out, see into, catch, note, be conscious of, have cognizance of, realize, discern, read, distinguish, infer, deduce, induce, make out, become alive to, have been around*, experience, have knowledge of, be instructed in, get to the bottom of, get at the root of, penetrate, possess, be informed of, come to one's senses, see the light, make out, register*, savvy*, get the gist of, catch on, get the point of, dig*, read between the lines, be with it*, get the idea. **2.** [To suppose] guess, conjecture, surmise; see ASSUME. **3.** [To accept] concede, take for granted, count on; see AGREE.

understandable *a.* comprehensible, conceivable, appreciable, expected, to be expected, natural, normal, regular, making sense, intelligible, in harmony with, readable, reasonable, logical, right, customary, recognizable, justifiable, imaginable, acceptable, apprehensible, credible.

understanding *n.* **1.** [The power to understand] sharpness, intelligence, comprehension; see JUDGMENT 1. **2.** [The act of comprehending] recognition, knowing, perception; see JUDGMENT 2, THOUGHT 1. **3.** [That which comes from understanding] conclusion, knowledge, perception; see BELIEF, OPINION 1. **4.** [Informal agreement] meeting of minds, common view, harmony; see AGREEMENT 1. **5.** [The intellect] head, brain, mentality; see MIND 1.

understood *a.* **1.** [Comprehended] penetrated, realized, appreciated, known, discovered, grasped, reasoned out, rationalized, explained, experienced, discerned, distinguished, made out, learned, fathomed, searched, explored, analyzed, mastered, conned, taken to heart.—*Ant.* UNKNOWN, overlooked, uncomprehended. **2.** [Agreed upon] concerted, ratified, assumed, stipulated, pledged, tacitly agreed upon, engaged for, settled, concluded, fixed upon, endorsed, subscribed to, accepted.

undertake *v.* endeavor, engage, set out, promise, try out, try, begin, offer, set in motion, volunteer, initiate, commit oneself to, embark upon, venture, take upon oneself, answer for, hazard, stake, move, devote oneself to, take up for, take on, set about, go in for, put one's hand to, have one's hands in, have in hand, launch into, address oneself to, enter upon, busy oneself with, tackle, pitch into*, fall into, buckle down, take on, take the plunge, fall to, have a try at, go for in a big way.

undertaken *a.* set in motion, begun, launched, embarked upon, initiated, pushed forward, ventured, started, endeavored, assumed, taken up, promised, offered, volunteered, hazarded, chanced, risked, pledged, tackled, essayed, tried, aimed at, attempted, striven for, engaged for.

undertaker *n.* mortician, funeral director, embalmer, body snatcher*.

undertaking *n.* enterprise, attempt, engagement; see ACTION 1, 2.

undertone *n.* buzz, murmur, hum; see WHISPER 1.

undertow *n.* whirlpool, undercurrent, riptide; see FLOW, TIDE.

underwater *a.* submarine, sunken, marine; see UNDER 1.

under way *a.* initiated, started, under construction; see BEGUN.

underwear *n.* undergarments, underclothing, unmentionables*, lingerie, intimate things, underlinen, underclothes; see also CLOTHES. *Types of underwear include the following—men*: shirt, shorts, briefs, drawers, red flannels, union suit, jockey shorts, T-shirt, boxer shorts, long underwear; *women*: underskirt, slip, petticoat, girdle, brassiere, garter belt, bra-slip, bra, panty slip, halfslip, corset, corselet, bodice, *cache-sexe* (French), vest, briefs, foundation garment, panty girdle, panties, pantyhose, shorts, knickers (British), falsies*; *infants*: shirt, drawers, pants, diaper, slip, rubber pants.

underweight *a.* skinny, undersized, puny; see THIN 2.

underworld *n.* **1.** [Hell] Hades, Inferno, netherworld; see HELL. **2.** [Crime] gangdom, rackets, organized crime; see CRIME.

undesirable *a.* objectionable, shunned, disliked, to be avoided, unwanted, outcast, rejected, defective, disadvantageous, inexpedient, inconvenient, troublesome, unwished for, repellent, loathed, unsought, dreaded, annoying, insufferable, unacceptable, scorned, displeasing, distasteful, loathsome, abominable, obnoxious, unpopular, bothersome, unlikable, unwelcome, unapprovable, useless, inadmissible, unsatisfactory, disagreeable, awkward, embarrassing, unfit.—*Ant.* WELCOME, proper, suitable.

undeveloped *a.* potential, incipient, unactualized; see HIDDEN.

undisputed *a.* unchallenged, unquestioned, assured; see CERTAIN 2.

undistinguished *a.* ordinary, commonplace, plain; see COMMON 1, CONVENTIONAL 3, DULL 4.

undisturbed *a.* settled, unruffled, untroubled; see CALM 1, 2.

undivided *a.* **1.** [Unified] united, full, collective; see WHOLE. **2.** [Undistracted] exclusive, complete, entire; see WHOLE 1.

undo *v.* mar, destroy, ruin, wreck, break, bring to naught, subvert, injure, overthrow, unsettle, turn topsy-turvy, upset, defeat.

undoing *n.* ruination, downfall, reversal, destruction, misfortune, calamity, overthrow, trouble, grief, catastrophe, defeat, shipwreck, smash, wrack, subversion, collapse, casualty, accident, mishap, misadventure, misstep, mischance, bad luck, adversity, reverse, blow, trial, affliction, stroke of fate, slip, blunder, fault, omission, difficulty, failure, error, miscalculation, trip, stumble, fumble, blunder, repulse, discouragement, deathblow, last straw.—*Ant.* ADVANTAGE, good omen, godsend.

undone *a.* **1.** [Unfinished] left, incomplete, unperformed; see UNFINISHED 1. **2.** [Distraught] upset, disturbed, agitated; see TROUBLED. **3.** [Ruined] betrayed, destroyed, killed; see DEAD 1, RUINED 1, 2.

undoubtedly *a.* assuredly, without doubt, of course; see UNQUESTIONABLY.

undress *v.* strip, take off one's clothes, disrobe, dismantle, divest, become naked, peel*, pile out of one's clothes*.—*Ant.* DRESS, put on one's clothes, attire oneself.

undue *a.* improper, illegal, indecorous, unfair, unseemly, unjust, underhanded, sinister, forbidden, excessive, unnecessary, extreme, extravagant, disproportionate, immoderate.—*Ant.* NECESSARY, proper, requisite.

unduly *a.* improperly, excessively, extremely; see UNNECESSARILY.

undying *a.* everlasting, perpetual, deathless; see ETERNAL.

unearned *a.* won, gratis, unmerited; see FREE 4.

unearth *v.* reveal, find, uncover; see LEARN.

unearthly *a.* frightening, ghostly, supernatural; see UNNATURAL 1.

uneasiness *n.* disquiet, restlessness, agitation; see FEAR.

uneasy *a.* unquiet, anxious, fearful, irascible, troubled, harassed, vexed, perturbed, alarmed, upset, afraid, apprehensive, nervous, frightened, shaky, perplexed, agitated, unsettled, suspicious, peevish, irritable, fretful, worried, anguished, in turmoil, disquieted, shaken, full of misgivings, fidgety, jittery, on edge, all nerves, jumpy, snappish, uncomfortable, molested, tormented, in distress.—*Ant.* QUIET, placid, soothed.

uneducated *a.* illiterate, unschooled, untaught; see IGNORANT 2.

unemotional *a.* reticent, apathetic, insensitive; see INDIFFERENT, QUIET.

unemployed *a.* out of work, in the bread lines, receiving charity, jobless, idle, inactive, loafing, unoccupied, without gainful employment, on the dole, cooling one's heels*, on the shelf.—*Ant.* BUSY, employed, at work.

unemployment *n.* work stoppage, layoff, strike conditions; see IDLENESS.

unending *a.* everlasting, infinite, neverending; see ETERNAL.

unequal *a.* **1.** [Not alike] odd, ill-matched, dissimilar; see UNLIKE. **2.** [One-sided] uneven, unbalanced, inequitable; see IRREGULAR 1.

unequaled *a.* unmatched, unrivaled, supreme; see UNIQUE.

unethical *a.* sneaky, immoral, unfair; see DISHONEST, WRONG 1.

uneven *a.* **1.** [Rough] bumpy, rugged, jagged; see ROUGH 1. **2.** [Irregular] notched, jagged, serrate; see IRREGULAR 4. **3.** [Variable] intermittent, spasmodic, fitful; see IRREGULAR 1. **4.** [Odd] remaining, leftover, additional; see ODD 4.

unevenly *a.* roughly, intermittently, irregularly, spottily, bumpily, with friction, haphazardly, jumpily, all up and down, fitfully, off an on.

unexpected *a.* unforeseen, surprising, unlooked for, sudden, startling, unpredicted, coming unaware, astonishing, staggering, stunning, electrifying, amazing, not in the cards, not on the books, unanticipated, not bargained for, left out of calculation, wonderful, unprepared for, instantaneous, eye-opening, like a bolt from the blue.—*Ant.* EXPECTED, predicted, foreseen.

unexpectedly *a.* surprisingly, instantaneously, suddenly, startlingly, without warning, like a bolt from the blue; see also QUICKLY.—*Ant.* REGULARLY, according to prediction, as anticipated.

unfair *a.* **1.** [Unjust] wrongful, wrong, low, base, injurious, unethical, bad, wicked, culpable, blamable, blameworthy, foul, illegal, inequitable, improper, unsporting, shameful, cruel, shameless, dishonorable, unreasonable, grievous, vicious, vile, undue, unlawful, petty, mean, inexcusable, unjustifiable, immoral, criminal, forbidden, irregular.—*Ant.* FAIR, proper, sporting. **2.** [Not in accord with approved trade practices] unethical, criminal, discriminatory; see sense 1.

unfairly *a.* unjustly, unreasonable, irregularly; see BRUTALLY.

unfaithful *a.* **1.** [Not faithful] false, untrue, deceitful; see UNRELIABLE. **2.** [Having broken the marriage vow] adulterous, incontinent, unchaste; see BAD 1.

unfamiliar *a.* **1.** [Unacquainted] not introduced, not associated, unknown, not on speaking terms, not versed in, not in the habit of, out of contact with.—*Ant.* FRIENDLY, intimate, acquainted. **2.** [Strange] alien, outlandish, exotic, remote, novel, original, different, unusal, extraordinary, unaccustomed, unexplored, uncommon.—*Ant.* COMMON, ordinary, usual.

unfashionable *a.* outmoded, antiquated, obsolete; see OLD-FASHIONED.

unfasten *v.* unsnap, untie, unlock; see LOOSEN 1.

unfavorable *a.* inopportune, untimely, unseasonable, adverse, calamitous, unpropitious, inexpedient, bad, ill-chosen, ill-fated, ill-suited, ill-timed, unsuitable, improper, wrong, abortive, untoward, inauspicious, unlucky, ill, unfortunate, regrettable, premature, tardy, late, unfit, inadvisable, objectionable, inconvenient, disadvantageous, damaging, destructive, unseemly, ill advised, obstructive, troublesome, embarrassing, unpromising, awkward.

unfavorably *a.* adversely, negatively, opposingly, oppositely, conflictingly, antagonistically, obstructively, malignantly, on the contrary, counteractively, contrarily, in opposition, in the negative, by turning thumbs down, by giving the red light; see also AGAINST 3.

unfilled *a.* vacant, void, drained; see EMPTY.

unfinished *a.* **1.** [Not completed] uncompleted, undone, half done, incomplete, under construction, unperformed, imperfect, unconcluded, deficient, unexecuted, unaccomplished, in preparation, in the making, not done, in the rough, sketchy, tentative, shapeless, formless, unperfected, unfulfilled, undeveloped, unassembled, defective, found wanting, cut short, immature, faulty, crude, rough.—*Ant.* DONE, completed, perfected. **2.** [Without a finish] unpainted, unvarnished, bare, raw, rough, crude, unprotected, uncovered, plain, undecorated, unadorned.

unfit *a.* **1.** [Incompetent] unqualified, feeble, unpracticed, inexperienced, weak, impotent, inept, clumsy, debilitated, incapacitated, badly qualified, incompetent, unable, unprepared, ineffective, unapt.—*Ant.* ABLE, fit, effective. **2.** [Unsuitable] improper, ill-adapted, wrong, ill-advised, unlikely, unpromising, inexpedient, inappropriate, inapplicable, useless, valueless, mistaken, incorrect, inadequate, flimsy.—*Ant.* FIT, suitable, correct.

unfold *v.* shake out, straighten, release, display, unwind, spread out, uncurl, unwrap, reel out, unbend, open, flatten, loosen, unroll.—*Ant.* FOLD, roll, lap.

unforeseen *a.* surprising, abrupt, sudden; see UNEXPECTED.

unforgettable *a.* notable, exceptional, extraordinary; see IMPRESSIVE.

unforgivable *a.* inexcusable, unpardonable, unjustifiable, indefensible, inexpiable; see also WRONG 1.

unformed *a.* not formed, formless, incomplete; see UNFINISHED 1.

unfortunate *a.* unlucky, luckless, unhappy, afflicted, troubled, stricken, unsuccessful, without success, burdened, pained, not prosperous, in adverse circumstances, broken, shattered, ill-fated, on the road to ruin, in a desperate plight, ruined, out of luck, in a bad way, jinxed*, behind the eight ball*, gone to the dogs*, down on one's luck; see also SAD 1.—*Ant.* HAPPY, lucky, prosperous.

unfortunately *a.* unluckily, unhappily, miserably, sadly, grievously, disastrously, dismally, calamitously, badly, sickeningly, discouragingly, catastrophically, horribly, if worst comes to worst.—*Ant.* HAPPILY, favorably, prosperously.

unfounded *a.* baseless, unproven, groundless; see UNTRUE.

unfriendly *a.* **1.** [Hostile] opposed, alienated, ill-disposed, against, opposite, contrary, warlike, competitive, conflicting, antagonistic, estranged, at variance, irreconcilable, not on speaking terms, turned against, with a chip on one's shoulder*.—*Ant.* FRIENDLY, intimate, approving. **2.** [Lacking friendly qualities] grouchy, bearish, surly, misanthropic, gruff, ill-disposed, envious, uncharitable, faultfinding, combative, quarrelsome, grudging, malignant, spiteful, malicious, vengeful, resentful, hateful, peevish, aloof, unsociable, suspicious, sour.—*Ant.* GENEROUS, frank, open.

ungainly *a.* clumsy, gawky, inexpert; see AWKWARD, RUDE 1.

ungodly* *a.* dreadful, atrocious, immoral; see BAD 1.

ungovernable *a.* unmanageable, wild, uncontrollable; see UNRULY.

ungrateful *a.* thankless, selfish, lacking in appreciation, grasping, demanding, forgetful, self-centered, unmindful, heedless, careless, insensible, dissatisfied, grumbling, unnatural, faultfinding, oblivious.—*Ant.* THANKFUL, grateful, obliged.

unguarded *a.* thoughtless, frank, careless; see CARELESS.

unhandy *a.* awkward, ill-arranged, unwieldy, ill-contrived, clumsy; see also TROUBLESOME.

unhappily *a.* regrettably, lamentably, unluckily; see UNFORTUNATELY.

unhappiness *n.* sorrow, woe, sadness; see DEPRESSION 2, GRIEF.

unhappy *a.* **1.** [Sad] miserable, sorrowful, wretched; see TROUBLED. **2.** [Unfortunate] afflicted, troubled, in a desperate plight; see UNFORTUNATE.

unharmed *a.* unhurt, uninjured, intact; see SAFE 1, WHOLE 2.

unhealthy *a.* sickly, sick, in a decline, in ill health, infirm, delicate, feeble, shaky, undernourished, rickety, spindling, ailing, weak, in a run-down condition.—*Ant.* HEALTHY, robust, hale.

unheard *a.* noiseless, soundless, hushed; see QUIET.

unheard-of *a.* unprecedented, unique, new; see UNKNOWN 1.

unhinge *v.* **1.** [To detach] dislodge, disjoint, disunite; see REMOVE 1. **2.** [To upset] unbalance, disorder, derange; see UPSET 1.

unhoped-for *a.* incredible, unforeseen, unexpected; see UNIMAGINABLE.

unhurried *a.* leisurely, deliberate, nonchalant; see SLOW 1.

unhurt *a.* uninjured, all right, whole; see SAFE 1.

unidentified *a.* nameless, unnamed, not known; see UNKNOWN 1, 2.

unified *a.* made one, united, joined, combined, concerted, synthesized, amalgamated, conjoined, incorporated, blended, identified, coalesced, federated, centralized, intertwined, consolidated, associated, cemented, coupled, allied, wedded, married, confederated.—*Ant.* SEPARATED, distinct, disjoined.

uniform *a.* **1.** [Even] symmetrical, smooth, straight; see REGULAR 3. **2.** [Alike] equal, well-matched, similar; see ALIKE.

uniform *n.* costume, suit, dress; see CLOTHES.

uniformity *n.* **1.** [Regularity] steadiness, sameness, evenness; see REGULARITY. **2.** [Harmony] unity, accord, concord; see AGREEMENT 1.

unify *v.* consolidate, ally, conjoin; see UNITE.

unimaginable *a.* inconceivable, incomprehensible, incredible, unbelievable, unheard-of, indescribable, unthinkable, improbable; see also IMPOSSIBLE.

unimaginative *a.* barren, tedious, usual; see COMMON 1, DULL 4.

unimportance *n.* immateriality, triviality, worthlessness; see INSIGNIFICANCE.

unimportant *a.* trifling, inconsiderable, slight, worthless, inconsequential, insignificant, unnecessary, immaterial, indifferent, beside the point, frivolous, useless, of no account, worthless, trivial, paltry.—*Ant.* IMPORTANT, weighty, great.

unimproved *a.* ordinary, in a natural state, untutored; see NATURAL 3.

uninformed *a.* unenlightened, naive, unacquainted; see IGNORANT 1, 2.

unintentional *a.* unthinking, involuntary, erratic; see AIMLESS.

unintentionally *a.* involuntarily, casually, inadvertently; see ACCIDENTALLY.

uninterested *a.* apathetic, impassive, detached; see INDIFFERENT.

uninteresting *a.* tedious, boring, tiresome, dreary, wearisome, prosaic, fatiguing, monotonous, dull, stale, trite, commonplace, irksome, stupid, humdrum, prosy, flat, depressing, insipid, unentertaining, dismal, banal.—*Ant.* INTERESTING, exciting, lively.

uninterrupted *a.* continuous, unending, unbroken; see CONSECUTIVE, CONSTANT.

uninvited *a.* unasked, unwanted, not invited; see UNPOPULAR.

union *n.* **1.** [The act of joining] unification, junction, meeting, uniting, joining, coupling, embracing, coming together, merging, fusion, mingling, concurrence, symbiosis, amalgamation, confluence, congregation, reconciliation, conciliation, correlation, combination, connection, linking, attachment, coalition, conjunction, consolidation, incorporation, centralization, affiliation, confederation, copulation, coition.—*Ant.* DIVORCE, separation, severance. **2.** [A closely knit group] association, federation, society; see ORGANIZATION 2. **3.** [A marriage] wedlock, conjugal ties, matrimony, cohabitation, nuptial connection, match, matrimonial affiliation. **4.** [A labor union] laborers, workingmen, employees; see LABOR 4.

Union *n.* **1.** [The United States] the States, Columbia, America; see UNITED STATES. **2.** [The North in the American Civil War] the Free States, Antislavery States, the Northern States; see NORTH.

unique *a.* single, peerless, matchless, unprecedented, unparalleled, novel, individual, sole, unexampled, lone, different, unequaled.—*Ant.* COMMON, frequent, many.

unison *n.* concert, unity, harmony; see UNITY 1.

unit *n.* **1.** [A whole] entirety, complement, total, totality, assemblage, assembly, system. **2.** [A detail] section, segment, part, fraction, piece, joint, block, square, layer, link, length, digit, member, factor.

unite *v.* join, meet, ally, combine, solidify, harden, strengthen, condense, confederate, couple, affiliate, merge, band together, blend, mix, become one, concentrate, consolidate, entwine, intertwine, grapple, amalgamate, league, band, embody, embrace, copulate, associate, assemble, gather together, conjoin, keep together, tie in, pull together, hang together, join forces, coalesce, fuse, wed, marry, mingle, stick together, stay together.—*Ant.* DIVIDE, separate, part.

united *a.* unified, leagued, combined, affiliated, federal, confederated, integrated, amalgamated, cooperative, consolidated, concerted, congruent, associated, assembled, linked, banded, in partnership; see also ORGANIZED.—*Ant.* SEPARATED, distinct, individual.

United Kingdom *n.* the British Isles, Great Britain, U.K.; see EUROPE.

United Nations *n.* UN, peace-keeping force, international society, community of nations. *Divisions and function of the United Nations include the following:* General Assembly, Security Council, Economic and Social Council, Trust and Non Self-Governing Territories Trusteeship, Trusteeship Council, International Court of Justice, Secretariat.

United States *n.* America, US, United States of America, U.S.A., Columbia, the Union, the States, US of A, the land of liberty*, the land of the free and the home of the brave, God's country*, the melting pot*, stateside*, the mainland.

unity *n.* **1.** [The quality of oneness] homogeneity, homogeneousness, sameness, indivisibility, identity, inseparability, singleness, similarity, uniqueness, integration, universality, all-togetherness, ensemble, uniformity, wholeness; see also WHOLE.—*Ant.* DIFFERENCE, diversity, divorce. **2.** [Union] federation, confederation, compact, combination, correspondence, alliance, agreement, concord, identity of purpose, unification, aggregation; see also ORGANIZATION 2. **3.** [Harmony] concord, agreement, accord; see HARMONY 1.

universal *a.* **1.** [Concerning the universe] cosmic, stellar, celestial, sidereal, astronomical, cosmogonic. **2.** [Worldwide] mundane, earthly, terrestrial, sublunary, terrene, human, wordly.—*Ant.* LOCAL, restricted, district. **3.** [General] entire, all-embracing, prevalent, customary, usual, whole, sweeping, extensive, comprehensive, total, unlimited, limitless, endless, vast, widespread, catholic, common, regular, undisputed, accepted, unrestricted.—*Ant.* SPECIAL, limited, peculiar.

universally *a.* entirely, prevailingly, comprehensively; see COMPLETELY.

universe *n.* cosmos, creation, the visible world, astral system, universal frame, all created things, everything, nature, the natural world.

university *a.* professional, advanced, graduate, college, collegiate, undergraduate, freshman, sophomore, junior, senior, learned, academic, educational.

university *n.* educational institution, institution of higher learning, multiversity, megaversity, normal school, state university; see also COLLEGE, SCHOOL 1.

unjust *a.* wrong, inequitable, wrongful; see UNFAIR.

unjustifiable *a.* unallowable, unforgivable, unjust; see WRONG 1.

unjustly *a.* brutally, cruelly, meanly; see WRONGLY.

unkind *a.* malignant, spiteful, mean, malicious, inhuman, inhumane, sadistic, cruel, hateful, malevolent, savage, barbarous; see also RUDE 1, 2.—*Ant.* KIND, benevolent, helpful.

unknown *a.* **1.** [Not known; *said of information*] uncomprehended, unapprehended, undiscovered, untold, unexplained, uninvestigated, unexplored, unheard-of, unperceived, concealed, hidden, unrevealed.—*Ant.* KNOWN, established, understood. **2.** [Not known; *said of people*] alien, unfamiliar, not introduced, unheard-of, obscure, foreign, strange, unacknowledged, ostracized, outcast, friendless, private, retired, aloof, forgotten. **3.** [Not known; *said of terrain*] unexplored, far-off, remote, far, distant, foreign, undiscovered, exotic, transoceanic, transmarine, at the far corners of the earth, faraway, outlandish, unheard-of, unfrequented, untraveled, desolate, desert, unvisited, legendary, strange.

unlawful *a.* forbidden, illicit, outlawed; see ILLEGAL.

unlawfully *a.* illegally, unjustly, unjustifiably; see WRONGLY.

unlearned *a.* unlettered, rude, boorish, uneducated, ignorant, illiterate, clownish, untutored, untaught, unread, savage, uncivilized, doltish, crass, half-taught, ill-bred, half-educated, uninitiated, unversed, uninstructed, unguided, unenlightened, dull, misguided, empty, unaccomplished, backward, superficial, pedantic, low-brow*.—*Ant.* LEARNED, educated, adept.

unless *prep.* saving, without the provision that, if not, except, except that, excepting that.

unlike *a.* dissimilar, different, incongruous, contradictory, hostile, opposed, inconsistent, heterogeneous, diverse, contrasted, conflicting, contrary, disparate, dissonant, discordant, clashing, separate, opposite, divergent, various, variant.—*Ant.* LIKE, similar, correspondent.

unlikely *a.* improbable, unheard-of, incredible, implausible, not to be thought of, unbelievable, absurd, unconvincing, not likely, scarcely possible, apparently false, contrary to expectation, inconceivable, doubtful, dubious, questionable, extraordinary, marvelous, out of the ordinary, strange.—*Ant.* LIKELY, probable, credible.

unlimited *a.* infinite, limitless, boundless, unending, extensive, universal, unrestricted, unconditional, unfathomable, inexhaustible, unconfined, immense, illimitable, measureless, incalculable, interminable, without number, unfathomed, unsounded, untold, countless, numberless, incomprehensible, immeasurable, endless.

unload *v.* disburden, discharge, dump, slough, lighten, cast, unpack, relieve, remove cargo, disgorge, empty, deplane, unburden, break bulk.—*Ant.* FILL, load, pack.

unlock *v.* unbar, unfasten, open the lock; see OPEN 2.

unlocked *a.* free, unbarred, unlatched; see OPEN 1, 2.

unloved *a.* disliked, detested, despised; see HATED.

unlucky *a.* **1.** [Unfortunate] luckless, unhappy, afflicted; see UNFORTUNATE. **2.** [Unpropitious] ill-chosen, ill-fated, untimely; see UNFAVORABLE.

unmanageable *a.* uncontrollable, irrepressible, ungovernable; see UNRULY.

unmarried *a.* celibate, unwed, single, virgin, maiden, eligible, chaste, unwedded, spouseless, footloose and fancy-free.—*Ant.* MARRIED, wed, wedded.

unmistakable *a.* conspicuous, distinct, evident; see CLEAR 2, OBVIOUS 1.

unmoved *a.* **1.** [Not moved physically] firm, stable, motionless, static, solid, durable, immovable, firm as a rock, staunch, fast, moveless, statuelike, rooted, steady, immobile, unshaken, changeless, unwavering. **2.** [Not moved emotionally] impasssive, stoic, quiet, cold, cool, calm, collected, deliberate, resolute, dispassionate, calculating, unaffected, unemotional, indifferent, judicious, unflinching, nerveless, cool as a cucumber.

unnatural *a.* **1.** [Contrary to nature] monstrous, phenomenal, malformed, unaccountable, abnormal, preposterous, marvelous, uncanny, wonderful, strange, incredible, sublime, freakish, unconforming, inhuman, outrageous, unorthodox, miraculous, contrary to known laws.—*Ant.* COMMON, ordinary, usual. **2.** [Artificial] synthetic, imitation, manufactured, ersatz, concocted, made-up, fabricated, false, pseudo, mock, spurious, phony*.—*Ant.* NATURAL, occurring, naturally.

unnecessarily *a.* needlessly, by chance, carelessly, fortuitously, casually, haphazardly, wantonly, accidentally, unessentially, redundantly, inexpediently, uselessly, exorbitantly, superfluously, undesirably, objectionably, disadvantageously, optionally, avoidably, without cause, without reason, gratuitously; see also FOOLISHLY.—*Ant.* NECESSARILY, indispensably, unavoidably.

unnecessary *a.* needless, fortuitous, casual, chance, haphazard, wanton, accidental, unessential, nonessential, beside the point, irrelevant, futile, extraneous, additional, redundant, useless, exorbitant, superfluous, worthless, undesirable, optional, avoidable, objectionable, disadvantageous, random, noncompulsory, dispensable, adventitious, without compulsion, uncalled-for, gratuitous.—*Ant.* NECESSARY, essential, required.

unnoticed *a.* unobserved, unseen, unheeded, overlooked, inconspicuous, secret, hidden, passed by, unobtrusive, disregarded, unconsidered, unattended, neglected, unmarked, unremembered, unscrutinized, unremarked, unrecognized, slurred over, uninspected, winked at, glossed over, lost sight of, ignored, shoved into the background, undistinguished, unexamined, unwatched, unlooked at.—*Ant.* SEEN, watched, noticed.

unoccupied *a.* 1. [Vacant] uninhabited, empty, deserted, unfurnished, void, voided, disfurnished, blank, untenanted.—*Ant.* FULL, inhabited, tenanted. 2. [Idle] loitering, inactive, unemployed; see IDLE.

unofficial *a.* unconstrained, personal, casual; see INFORMAL.

unopposed *a.* unchallenged, unrestricted, unhampered; see FREE 1, 2, 3.

unorganized *a.* chaotic, random, disorganized; see CONFUSED 2.

unorthodox *a.* unconventional, irregular, eccentric; see UNUSUAL 2.

unpack *v.* unload, uncrate, unwrap; see REMOVE 1.

unpaid *a.* 1. [Owed; *said of debts*] due, payable, not discharged, past due, overdue, delinquent, unsettled, unliquidated, undefrayed, outstanding.—*Ant.* PAID, discharged, defrayed. 2. [Working without salary] voluntary, unsalaried, amateur, freewill, donated, contributed.

unpleasant *a.* 1. [Not pleasing in society] disagreeable, obnoxious, boring; see RUDE 2. 2. [Not pleasing to the senses] repulsive, obnoxious, abhorrent; see OFFENSIVE 2.

unpopular *a.* disliked, despised, out of favor, abhorred, loathed, shunned, avoided, ostracized, scorned, detested, unloved, unvalued, uncared-for, obnoxious.—*Ant.* POPULAR, liked, agreeable.

unprecedented *a.* unparalleled, novel, original; see UNIQUE.

unpredictable *a.* random, inconstant, variable; see IRREGULAR 1.

unprepared *a.* unready, unwarned, unwary, unexpectant, surprised, taken aback, unguarded, unnotified, unadvised, unaware, unsuspecting, taken off guard, napping, in the dark, going off half-cocked.

unproductive *a.* unprolific, impotent, barren; see STERILE 1, 2.

unprofitable *a.* ill-requited, ill-paid, profitless, costly, expensive, unlucrative, unremunerative.—*Ant.* PROFITABLE, gainful, productive.

unpromising *a.* discouraging, unfavorable, adverse; see UNLIKELY.

unprotected *a.* defenseless, unarmed, unguarded; see UNSAFE.

unpublished *a.* unprinted, still in manuscript, manuscript; see UNKNOWN 1.

unqualified *a.* 1. [Absolute] downright, utter, outright; see CERTAIN 2. 2. [Incompetent] inexperienced, unprepared, incapable; see UNFIT.

unquestionable *a.* 1. [Certain] sure, obvious, clear; see CERTAIN 2. 2. [Faultless] unexceptionable, superior, flawless; see EXCELLENT.

unquestionably *a.* certainly, without a doubt, surely, indubitably, indisputably, definitely, reliably, absolutely, positively, incontrovertibly, indeed, assuredly, of course, undoubtedly, undeniably, past a doubt, beyond doubt, beyond a shadow of a doubt, past dispute.

unravel *v.* unwind, disengage, undo; see FREE.

unreal *a.* visionary, delusive, deceptive, illusory, imagined, hallucinatory, ideal, dreamlike, unsubstantial, nonexistent, fanciful, misleading, fictitious, theoretical, hypothetical, fabulous, notional, whimsical, fantastic; see also UNBELIEVABLE.—*Ant.* REAL, substantial, genuine.

unrealistic *a.* unworkable, not practical, nonsensical; see UNRELIABLE.

unreasonable *a.* 1. [Illogical] irrational, biased, fatuous; see ILLOGICAL. 2. [Immoderate] exorbitant, extravagant, inordinate; see EXTREME. 3. [Senseless] foolish, silly, thoughtless; see STUPID.

unreasonably *a.* illogically, irrationally, stupidly; see FOOLISHLY.

unregulated *a.* uncontrollable, unchecked, chaotic; see UNCONTROLLED.

unrelated *a.* independent, unattached, irrelevant; see SEPARATE.

unreliable *a.* undependable, unstable, wavering, deceitful, tricky, shifty, furtive, underhanded, untrue, fickle, giddy, untrustworthy, vacillating, fallible, weak, unpredictable; see also DISHONEST.

unrest *n.* 1. [Lack of mental calm] malaise, distress, discomfort, perturbation, agitation, worry, sorrow, anxiety, grief, trouble, annoyance, tension, ennui, disquiet, soul-searching, irritation, harassment, upset, vexation, chagrin, mortification, perplexity, unease, disease, moodiness, disturbance, bother, dither, tizzy*. 2. [Social or political restlessness] disquiet, agitation, turmoil, strife, disturbance, uproar, debate, contention, bickering, change, altercation, crisis, confusion, disputation, contest, controversy, quarrel, sparring, uncertainty, insurrection, suspicion, dissatisfaction.

unrestricted *a.* allowable, not forbidden, free; see OPEN 3.

unripe *a.* green, tart, immature; see RAW 1.

unroll *v.* display, uncover, present; see EXPOSE 1.

unruffled *a.* collected, smooth, serene; see CALM 1, 2.

unruly *a.* uncontrollable, willful, headstrong, forward, violent, impulsive, uncurbed, impetuous, ill-advised, rash, reckless, dashing, heedless, perverse, intractable, recalcitrant, self-assertive, refractory, rebellious, wayward, inexorable, restive, impervious, hidebound, unyielding, incorrigible, intemperate, drunken, lawless, vicious, brawling, unlicensed, rowdy, bawdy, quarrelsome, immovable, unwieldy, resolute, inflexible, forceful, dogged, mulish, fanatic, irrational, unreasonable, irrepressible, high-spirited, impudent, abandoned, profligate, stubborn, obstinate, turbulent, disorderly, self-willed, opinionated, bullheaded, ungovernable, stiff-necked, ornery*, mean, skittish, dangerous.

unsafe *a.* hazardous, perilous, risky, threatening, treacherous, fearsome, unreliable, insecure, venturesome, unstable, alarming, precarious, ticklish, giddy, dizzy, slippery, uncertain, unpromising, shaky, explosive.—*Ant.* SAFE, harmless, proof.

unsaid *a.* unspoken, not expressed, unstated; see QUIET.

unsatisfactorily *a.* poorly, crudely, inefficiently; see BADLY 1.

unsatisfactory *a.* disappointing, below expectation, displeasing, undesirable, regrettable, disconcerting, disquieting, vexing, distressing, upsetting, disturbing, offensive, unacceptable, disagreeable, unwelcome, shocking, deficient; see also POOR 2.—*Ant.* EXCELLENT, satisfactory, gratifying.

unsavory *a.* disagreeable, unpleasant, revolting; see OFFENSIVE 2.

unscientific *a.* irrational, impulsive, inconclusive; see ILLOGICAL.

unscrew *v.* screw out, unfasten, untwist; see LOOSEN 1.

unscrupulous *a.* unprincipled, bad, wicked; see DISHONEST.

unseal *v.* free, remove, crack; see OPEN 2.

unseemly *a.* **1.** [In bad taste; *said of conduct*] improper, unbecoming, inept; see RUDE 1. **2.** [In bad taste; *said of things*] vulgar, tawdry, cheap; see POOR 2.

unseen *a.* imagined, imaginary, hidden, obscure, unobserved, veiled, occult, sensed, unperceived, unnoticed, unsuspected, curtained, unobtrusive, viewless, invisible, sightless, dark, shrouded, impalpable, imperceptible, inconspicuous, undiscovered, impenetrable, dense.

unselfish *a.* disinterested, selfless, charitable; see KIND.

unselfishly *a.* openhandedly, bountifully, lavishly; see FREELY 1, 2, GENEROUSLY 1, 2.

unselfishness *n.* charity, kindness, liberality; see GENEROSITY.

unsettle *v.* disrupt, displace, disarrange; see BOTHER 2, DISTURB.

unsettled *a.* **1.** [Undetermined] undecided, unfixed, unresolved; see UNCERTAIN. **2.** [Unstable] confused, agitated, troubled, changing, explosive, shifting, precarious, ticklish, unpredictable, uneasy, unbalanced, perilous, complex, complicated, fluid, kinetic, active, busy, critical.—*Ant.* SIMPLE, stable, solid.

unshaken *a.* unmoved, unaffected, undaunted; see FIRM 1.

unsheltered *a.* unprotected, exposed, uncovered; see UNPREPARED, UNSAFE.

unsightly *a.* hideous, deformed, homely; see REPULSIVE 1, UGLY 1.

unskilled *a.* untrained, uneducated, amateur; see IGNORANT 2.

unsophisticated *a.* ingenuous, innocent, simple; see INEXPERIENCED, NAIVE.

unsound *a.* **1.** [False] ill-founded, erroneous, incongruous; see ILLOGICAL. **2.** [Insecure] unreliable, unbacked, weak; see UNSTABLE 2.

unspeakable *a.* horrid, unutterable, abominable, horrible, fearful, inexpressible, unimaginable, dreadful, dire, shocking, appalling, frightful, frightening, alarming, beastly, inhuman, calamitous.

unspeakably *a.* greatly, unbelievably, terribly; see MUCH 1, 2.

unspecified *a.* general, undefined, indefinite; see VAGUE 2.

unspoiled *a.* unblemished, spotless, faultless; see PERFECT 2, PURE 2.

unspoken *a.* tacit, implicit, inferred; see UNDERSTOOD 1.

unstable *a.* **1.** [Having a high center of gravity] unsteady, wavering, unbalanced, giddy, wobbly, wiggly, weaving, shifty, precarious, top-heavy, teetering, shifting, uncertain, rattletrap, beetling, jutting, lightly balanced.—*Ant.* FIRM, steady, solid. **2.** [Easily disturbed] variable, changeable, giddy, capricious, fluctuating, shifty, volatile, rootless, dizzy, unpredictable, uncertain, sensitive, oversensitive, thin-skinned, timid, delicate.

unsteady *a.* **1.** [Wobbly] wiggly, wavering, shaky, treacherous, unbalanced, top-heavy, leaning, ramshackle, giddy, weaving, heaving, precarious, teetering, uncertain; see also IRREGULAR 1. **2.** [Inconstant] changeable, fluctuating, vacillating, variable, uncertain, unfixed, capricious, volatile, unreliable, tricky, shifty, shaky, jerky, fluttering.

unstuck *a.* unfastened, unglued, rattling; see LOOSE 1.

unsubstantiated *a.* unconfirmed, unattested, unsupported; see FALSE 2.

unsuccessful *a.* defeated, disappointed, frustrated, aborted, disastrous, unprosperous, unfortunate, unlucky, futile, failing, fruitless, worthless, sterile, bootless, unavailing, ineffectual, ineffective, immature, useless, foiled, shipwrecked, overwhelmed, overpowered, broken, ruined, destroyed, thwarted, crossed, disconcerted, dashed, circumvented, premature, inoperative, of no effect, balked, left holding the sack*, skunked*, stymied, jinxed*, out of luck, stuck*.—*Ant.* SUCCESSFUL, fortunate, lucky.

unsuitable *a.* inadequate, improper, malapropos, disagreeable, discordant, incongruous, inharmonious, incompatible, clashing, out of place, jarring, dissonant, discrepant, irrelevant, uncalled-for, dissident, inappropriate, ill-suited, unseemly, conflicting, opposite, contrary, unbecoming, unfitting, unfit, disparate, disturbing, mismatched, disproportionate, divergent, mismated, inapplicable, unassimilable, inconsistent, intrusive, amiss, interfering, disagreeing, inept, unbefitting, inadmissible, absurd, senseless, unseasonable, unfortunate, ill-timed, unsympathetic, not in keeping, out of joint, at odds, at variance, repugnant, out of kilter*, cockeyed*.—*Ant.* FIT, suitable, proper.

unsure *a.* unreliable, hesitant, doubtful; see UNCERTAIN.

unsurpassed *a.* unexcelled, unequaled, matchless; see UNIQUE.

unsuspecting *a.* **1.** [Gullible] undoubting, confiding, credulous; see TRUSTING. **2.** [Naive] innocent, inexperienced, simple; see NAIVE.

unsympathetic *a.* unmoved, apathetic, cold; see INDIFFERENT.

untangle *v.* clear up, put in order, disentangle; see ORDER 3.

unthinkable *a.* inconceivable, unimaginable, improbable; see UNLIKELY.

unthinking *a.* heedless, rude, inconsiderate; see CARELESS.

untidy *a.* slovenly, unkempt, disorderly; see DIRTY 1.

untie *v.* unlace, unknot, loosen, unfasten; see also LOOSEN 1.

untied *a.* unfastened, slack, unbound; see FREE 2, 3, LOOSE 1.

until *prep.* till, to, between the present and, in anticipation of, prior to, during the time preceding, down to, continuously, before the coming of, in expectation of, as far as; see also UNTO.

untimely *a.* unseasonable, awkward, ill-timed, inauspicious, badly timed, too early, abortive, too late, unpromising, ill-chosen, improper, unseemly, inappropriate, wrong, unfit, disagreeable, mistimed, intrusive, badly calculated, inopportune, out-of-date, malapropos, premature, unlucky, unfavorable, unfortunate, inexpedient, anachronistic.—*Ant.* EARLY, timely, seasonable.

untiring *a.* inexhaustible, powerful, persevering; see STRONG 1.

unto *prep.* to, toward, till, until, contiguous to, against, up to, next to, beside, in the direction of, to the degree of, to the extreme of.

untold *a.* uncounted, countless, unnumbered, many, innumerable, beyond measure, inexpressible, incalculable, undreamed of, staggering, unimaginable, multitudinous, manifold, multiple.

untouchable *a.* taboo, forbidden, denied; see ILLEGAL.

untouched *a.* **1.** [Not harmed] intact, whole, secure, unbroken, in good order, unharmed, in good condition, in a good state of preservation, safe and sound, out of danger, shipshape. **2.** [Not contaminated] virgin, clear, pure; see CLEAN 1.

untrained *a.* green, new, novice; see INEXPERIENCED.

untried *a.* untested, uninitiated, new; see INEXPERIENCED.

untroubled *a.* composed, serene, placid; see CALM 1, 2.

untrue *a.* false, misleading, specious, lying, hollow, deceptive, delusive, untrustworthy, deceitful, sham, spurious, incorrect, prevaricating, wrong.

untruth *n.* falsehood, misrepresentation, evasion; see LIE.

untruthful *a.* insincere, crooked, deceitful; see DISHONEST.

unused *a.* **1.** [Not used] fresh, available, usable; see NEW 1. **2.** [Surplus] additional, remaining, superfluous; see EXTRA.

unusual *a.* **1.** [Remarkable] rare, extraordinary, strange, outstanding, great, uncommon, special, distinguished, prominent, important, noteworthy, awe-inspiring, awesome, unique, fine, unheard-of, unexpected, seldom met with, surprising, superior, astonishing, amazing, prodigious, incredible, inconceivable, atypical, conspicuous, exceptional, eminent, significant, memorable, renowned, refreshing, singular, fabulous, unprecedented, unparalleled, unexampled, unaccountable, stupendous, unaccustomed, wonderful, notable, superior, marvelous, striking, overpowering, electrifying, dazing, fantastic, startling, astounding, indescribable, appalling, stupefying, ineffable, out of sight*.—*Ant.* COMMON, familiar, customary. **2.** [Different] unique, extreme, uncommon, particular, exaggerated, distinctive, choice, little-known, out of the ordinary, marked, forward, unconventional, radical, exceptional, peculiar, strange, foreign, unnatural, puzzling, perplexing, confounding, disturbing, novel, advanced, startling, shocking, staggering, uncustomary, breaking with tradition, infrequent, mysterious, mystifying, surprising, extraordinary, unparalleled, deep, profound, aberrant, singular, unorthodox, unconformable, not to be expected, eccentric, unbalanced, unprecedented, inconsistent, individual, original, refreshing, newfangled, new, modern, recent, late, fresh, curious, unfamiliar, irregular, odd, unaccountable, alien, queer, quaint, freakish, bizarre, far-fetched, neurotic, exotic, outlandish, old-fashioned, out-of-the-way, abnormal, irrational, monstrous, anomalous, fearful.—*Ant.* COMMON, ordinary, normal.

unusually *a.* **1.** [Not usually] oddly, curiously, peculiarly; see ESPECIALLY 1. **2.** [To a marked degree] extraordinarily, remarkably, surprisingly; see VERY.

unveil *v.* uncover, reveal, make known; see EXPOSE 1.

unwanted *a.* undesired, rejected, outcast; see HATED, UNPOPULAR.

unwarranted *a.* unjust, wrong, groundless; see UNFAIR 1.

unwelcome *a.* uninvited, unwished for, repellent; see UNPOPULAR.

unwholesome *a.* unhealthful, toxic, dangerous; see POISONOUS.

unwieldy *a.* awkward, clumsy, cumbersome; see HEAVY 1.

unwilling *a.* backward, resistant, reluctant, recalcitrant, unenthusiastic, doubtful, wayward, unready, indisposed, disinclined, averse, opposed, against, contrary, indifferent, indocile, intractable, demurring, shrinking, flinching, hesitating, shy, slack, evasive, loath, shy of, malcontent, slow, remiss, grudging, uncooperative, contrary, against the grain.—*Ant.* READY, willing, eager.

unwillingly *a.* grudgingly, resentfully, involuntarily; see ANGRILY.

unwind *v.* **1.** [To undo] separate, loose, undo; see UNWRAP. **2.** [To uncoil] untwist, unravel, untwine; see FREE, LOOSEN 2. **3.** [To relax] recline, get rid of one's tensions, calm down; see RELAX.

unwise *a.* ill-considered, ill-advised, rash; see STUPID.

unwitting *a.* chance, inadvertent, accidental; see AIMLESS.

unwittingly *a.* ignorantly, in ignorance, without awareness; see UNCONSCIOUSLY.

unworthy *a.* undeserving, reprehensible, contemptible; see OFFENSIVE 2.

unwrap *v.* untie, undo, unpack, take out of wrappings, unroll, disclose, free, uncover, strip, lay bare, divest, dismantle, peel, husk, shuck, flay, expose, lay open, unclothe, denude.—*Ant.* COVER, wrap, pack.

unzip *v.* unfasten, undo, free; see OPEN 3.

up *a. & prep.* **1.** [Situated above] at the top of, at the crest of, at the summit of, at the apex of, nearer the top of, nearer the head of, nearer the source of.—*Ant.* DOWN, nearer the bottom of, farther from the head of. **2.** [Moving from the earth] upward, uphill, skyward, heavenward, away from the center of gravity, perpendicularly, into the air, higher, away from the earth. **3.** [Expired] lapsed, elapsed, run out, terminated, invalid, ended, come to a term, outdated, exhausted, finished, done. **4.** [Happening] under consideration, being scrutinized, moot, live, current, pertinent, timely, relevant, pressing, urgent. **5.** [Next] after, in order, prospective; see FOLLOWING.

up* *v.* elevate, raise up, boost; see INCREASE.

up and around *a.* improved, improving, getting better; see WELL 1.

up-and-coming *a.* industrious, prospering, alert; see ACTIVE.

upbringing *n.* rearing, bringing up, instruction; see CHILDHOOD, TRAINING.

upcoming *a.* expected, future, imminent; see FORTHCOMING.

update *v.* modernize, bring up to date, refresh; see RENEW 1.

up for grabs* *a.* available, open to applications, not allocated; see FREE 4.

upheaval *n.* outburst, explosion, eruption; see OUTBREAK 1.

upheld *a.* supported, maintained, advanced; see BACKED 2.

uphill *a.* up, toward the summit, toward the crest, skyward, ascending, climbing.—*Ant.* DOWN, downhill, descending.

uphold *v.* **1.** [To hold up] brace, buttress, prop; see SUPPORT 1. **2.** [To maintain] confirm, sustain, back up; see SUPPORT 2.

up in arms *a.* agitated, indignant, riotous; see EXCITED, REBELLIOUS.

up in the air *a.* undecided, confused, indecisive; see UNCERTAIN.

upkeep *n.* **1.** [Maintenance] conservation, subsistence, repair; see CARE 1. **2.** [Cost of maintenance] expenses, outlay, expenditure; see PRICE.

upon *a. & prep.* **1.** [On] on top of, in, attached to, visible on, against, affixed to, above, next to, located at, superimposed on. **2.** [At the time of] consequent to, beginning with, at the occurrence of; see SIMULTANEOUS.

upper *a.* top, topmost, uppermost, above, higher, more elevated, loftier, overhead.—*Ant.* UNDER, lower, bottom.

upper-class *a.* well-born, cultivated, genteel; see NOBLE 3.

upper hand *n.* sway, dominion, superiority; see ADVANTAGE.

upright *a.* **1.** [Vertical] erect, perpendicular, on end; see STRAIGHT 1. **2.** [Honorable] straightforward, honest, fair; see HONEST 1.

uprising *n.* rebellion, riot, upheaval; see REVOLUTION 2.

uproar *n.* babble, confusion, turmoil, ado, hassle, commotion, clamor, disturbance, tumult, din, racket, clatter, hubbub, fracas, clangor, jangle, bustle, bickering, discord, row.

uproot *v.* tear up by the roots, pull up, weed out; see REMOVE 1.

ups and downs *n.pl.* troubles, complications, uncertainties; see DIFFICULTY 1, 2.

upset *a.* disconcerted, amazed, shocked; see CONFUSED 2.

upset *n.* overthrow, destruction, subversion; see DEFEAT.

upset *v.* **1.** [To turn over] overturn, upturn, subvert, turn bottom-side up, turn inside out, upend, reverse, keel over, overset, topple, tip over, turn topsy-turvy, overbalance, invert, capsize, tilt, pitch over, overthrow.—*Ant.* STAND, erect, elevate. **2.** [To disturb] agitate, fluster, perturb; see BOTHER 2. **3.** [To beat] conquer, outplay, overpower; see DEFEAT 2, 3.

upside-down *a.* topsy-turvy, tangled, bottomside up, inverted, rearend foremost, backward, the wrong way, wrongside uppermost, cart-before-the-horse, head over heels.—*Ant.* STEADY, upright, right side up.

upstairs *a.* in the upper story, above, up the steps; see UPPER.

upstairs *n.* the upper story, the penthouse, the rooms above the ground floor; see FLOOR 2.

upstanding *a.* honorable, upright, straightforward; see HONEST 1.

upswing *n.* growth, boom, acceleration; see INCREASE.

uptight* *a.* **1.** [Troubled] worried, concerned, apprehensive; see TROUBLED. **2.** [Cautious] conventional, old-fashioned, strict; see CONSERVATIVE.

up to *prep.* **1.** [Until] before, preceding, previous to; see UNTIL. **2.** [*Doing] occupied with, engaged in, carrying out, dealing with. **3.** [*Dependent upon] assigned to, expected of, delegated to, enjoined upon.

up-to-date *a.* in vogue, in fashion, fashionable, conventional, stylish, modern, modernistic, streamlined, popular, faddish, brand-new, current, up-to-the-minute, according to the prevailing taste, modish, the latest, all the rage, trendy*, in*, with-it*.

up to one's ears (or **neck**) **in** or **with** *a.* occupied with, busy with, absorbed in; see BUSY 1.

upturned *a.* tilted, tipped, upside-down, inclined, sloped, slanted, oblique, expectant, upward-looking, turned up, extended.

upward *a.* up, higher, skyward, in the air, uphill, away from the earth, up the slope, on an incline, up north.

urban *a.* **1.** [Concerning city government] city, municipal, civil; see PUBLIC 2. **2.** [Concerning city living] big-city, civic, municipal, metropolitan, within the city limits, inner-city, central-city, downtown, zoned, planned, business-district, civil, nonrural, ghetto, shopping, residential, apartment-dwelling.

urban renewal *n.* rebuilding the inner city, modernization, bringing up to date; see IMPROVEMENT 2.

urge *v.* **1.** [To present favorably] favor, further, support; see APPROVE. **2.** [To induce] charge, beg, plead, adjure, influence, beseech, implore, ask, command, entreat, desire, request, press, inveigle, talk into, incite, move, allure, tempt, attract, influence, prompt, instigate, exhort, advise, solicit, inspire, stimulate, conjure, coax, wheedle, maneuver, draw, put up to*, prevail upon.—*Ant.* RESTRAIN, deter, discourage. **3.** [To drive] compel, drive, propel, impel, force, coerce, constrain, press, push, make, oblige, goad, prod, spur.—*Ant.* DENY, block, withhold.

urged *a.* **1.** [Supported] favored, furthered, proposed; see BACKED 2. **2.** [Pressed] begged, charged, implored, asked, commanded, entreated, desired, requested, inveigled, talked into, incited, moved, motivated, allured, lured, tempted, seduced, attracted, influenced, prompted, instigated, exhorted, advised, solicited, inspired, whipped up, stimulated, coaxed, wheedled, maneuvered, put up to*, prevailed upon, compelled, obliged, propelled, driven, induced, impelled, coerced, forced, constrained.

urgency *n.* import, need, seriousness; see IMPORTANCE, NECESSITY 3.

urgent *a.* **1.** [Of immediate importance] pressing, critical, necessary, compelling, imperative, important, indispensable, momentous, wanted, required, called for, demanded, salient, chief, paramount, essential, primary, vital, principal, absorbing, all-absorbing, not to be delayed, crucial, instant, leading, capital, overruling, foremost, exigent, crying. **2.** [Insistent] compelling, persuasive, imperious, solemn, grave, weighty, impressive, earnest, importunate, clamorous, hasty, breathless, precipitate, frantic, impetuous, imperative, convincing, beseeching, seductive, commanding, imploring, eager, zealous, anxious, moving, excited, impulsive, vigorous, enthusiastic, overpowering, masterful.

urgently *a.* **1.** [Critically] pressingly, instantly, imperatively, necessarily, indispensably, momently*, requisitely, essentially, primarily, crucially, capitally. **2.** [Insistently] compellingly, persuasively, solemnly, gravely, weightily, impressively, earnestly, importunately, clamorously, hastily, breathlessly, precipitately, frantically, impetuously, convincingly, beseechingly, seductively, commandingly, imploringly, eagerly, anxiously, zealously, movingly, emotionally, excitedly, impulsively, vigorously, irresistibly, enthusiastically, overpoweringly, masterfully, compulsively.

urging *n.* begging, persuading, pleading; see REQUEST.

urinate *v.* go to the restroom, go to the bathroom, go to the lavatory, have to go*, excrete, use the urinal, use the bedpan, make water, tinkle*, wizz*, peepee*, take a leak*.

usable *a.* available, at hand, useful, employable, unused, good, serviceable, applicable, ready, subservient, helpful, valuable, beneficial, profitable, advantageous, fit, desirable, efficacious, instrumental, fitting, conformable, suitable, proper, practical, convenient.—*Ant.* USELESS, worthless, no good.

usage *n.* **1.** [Custom] practice, rule, habit; see USE 1. **2.** [Accepted language] good usage, grammatical usage, approved diction; see GRAMMAR.

use *n.* **1.** [The act of using] practice, employment, application, usage, appliance, effecting, manner, adoption, utilization, manipulation, bringing to bear, management, handling, performance, conduct, recourse, resort, exercise, treatment, method, technique, control, resolution, realization, association.—*Ant.* NEGLECT, disuse, dismissal. **2.** [The state of being useful] utility, usefulness, usability, employment, application, value, advantage, excellence, helpfulness, convenience, suitability, expedience, aid, serviceability, merit, profit, practicability, practicality, fitness, subservience, effectiveness, applicability.

use *v.* **1.** [To make use of] avail oneself of, employ, put to use, exercise, exert, put forth, utilize, apply, bring to bear, practice, play on, do with, draw on, adopt, take advantage of, make do, accept, work, put in practice, relate, make with, put to work, make shift with.—*Ant.* DISCARD, reject, refuse. **2.** [To make a practice of; *now used principally in the past tense*] be accustomed to, practice, adapt, conform, habituate, regulate, suit, familiarize, attune. **3.** [To behave toward] deal with, handle, bear oneself toward; see MANAGE 1.

used *a.* **1.** [Employed] put to use, utilized, applied, adopted, adapted, accepted, put in service, practiced, turned to account.—*Ant.* DISCARDED, rejected, unused. **2.** [Accustomed] practiced, customary, suited; see HABITUAL. **3.** [Secondhand] castoff, depreciated, repossessed; see OLD 2.

useful *a.* valuable, beneficial, serviceable; see HELPFUL 1.

usefulness *n.* application, value, advantage, excellence, convenience, suitability, usability, range, versatility, helpfulness, utility, serviceability, merit, profitableness, practicality, practicability, fitness, propriety, adaptability; see also USE 2.

useless *a.* **1.** [Unserviceable] worthless, unusable, ineffectual, expendable, incompetent, of no use, ineffective, inoperate, dysfunctional, counterproductive, inefficient, unprofitable, no damn good*.—*Ant.* EFFICIENT, usable, operative. **2.** [Futile] vain, pointless, fruitless; see HOPELESS.

use up *v.* consume, exhaust, squander; see SPEND, WASTE 1, 2.

using *a.* employing, utilizing, applying, adopting, taking advantage of, accepting, working, practicing, manipulating, controlling, putting in service, trying out, testing, proving, wearing out.

usual *a.* **1.** [Ordinary] general, frequent, normal; see COMMON 1. **2.** [Habitual] prevailing, accustomed, customary; see CONVENTIONAL 1.

usually *a.* ordinarily, customarily, habitually; see REGULARLY.

utensils *n.pl.* [Implements; *especially for the kitchen*] equipment, tools, appliances, conveniences, wares; see also TOOL 1. *Kitchen utensils include the following:* sieve, egg beater, knife, fork, spoon, measuring cup, grater, spatula, skewer, pancake turner, can opener, egg slicer, meat grinder, butcher knife, peeler, paring knife, pastry cutter, squeezer, knife sharpener, coffee grinder, blender, food processor, mixer, vegetable brush, pan scourer, frying pan, saucepan, cake pan, pie pan, roaster, bottle brush, dishpan, draining pan, sink strainer, dishmop, mixing bowl, pan lid, rolling pin, pastry board, coffee pot, bread pan, cookie sheet.

utilities *n.pl.* services, public utilities, conveniences, current necessities of modern life, household slaves. *Utilities include the following:* heat, light, power, gas, water, telephone, electricity, cable, garbage disposal, sewage disposal.

utility *n.* **1.** [Usefulness] service, advantage, convenience; see USE 2. **2.** [Utility company] gas company, electricity company, water company; see BUSINESS 4.

utilize *v.* employ, appropriate, turn to account; see USE 1.

utmost *a.* ultimate, chief, entire, whole, full, unreserved, complete, unstinted, total, absolute, unlimited, unsparing, thorough, exhaustive, highest, maximum, most, top, undiminished, undivided, thoroughgoing, unmitigated, sheer, unqualified, unconditional, all-out.

utter *a.* complete, total, thorough; see ABSOLUTE 1.

utter *v.* pronounce, talk, express, articulate, voice, whisper, mutter, shout, exclaim, enunciate, air, speak, tell, disclose, declare, say, assert, affirm, ejaculate, vocalize, proclaim, give tongue to, recite, blurt out, let fall, announce, come out with.

utterance *n.* declaration, saying, assertion, announcement, pronouncement, ejaculation, vociferation, talk, speech, statement, query, expression, sentence, proclamation, recitation, spiel, rant, jargon, response, reply, oration.

uttered *a.* asserted, expressed, announced; see ORAL.

utterly *a.* wholly, thoroughly, entirely; see COMPLETELY.

V

vacancy *n.* **1.** [A vacated position] opening, vacated post, post without an incumbent, unfilled position, unheld office, job. **2.** [A vacated residence] empty apartment, tenantless house, uninhabited house, vacant house, unoccupied house, deserted house, house for rent, house for sale.

vacant *a.* **1.** [Without contents] devoid, void, unfilled; see EMPTY. **2.** [Without an occupant] unoccupied, untenanted, tenantless, uninhabited, idle, free, deserted, abandoned, without a resident, not lived in.—*Ant.* INHABITED, occupied, tenanted.

vacate *v.* go away, relinquish, depart; see LEAVE 1.

vacation *n.* respite, rest, recreation time, intermission, recess, holiday, leave of absence, sabbatical, time off*.

vaccinate *v.* inoculate, immunize, prevent, treat, mitigate, protect, inject, shoot.

vaccinated *a.* immunized, inoculated, given injections; see PROTECTED.

vaccination *n.* **1.** [The act of administering vaccine] injection, inoculation, shots; see TREATMENT 2. **2.** [A result of vaccination] protection, immunization, inoculation; see IMMUNITY 2.

vacuum *n.* space, void, hollowness, emptiness.

vacuum cleaner *n.* vacuum sweeper, carpet sweeper, vacuum; see APPLIANCE.

vagrant *a.* **1.** [Having no home] roaming, itinerant, nomadic; see TRAVELING. **2.** [Having no occupation] begging, mendicant, profligate, idling, prodigal, loafing, beachcombing, panhandling*, bumming*, mooching*. **3.** [Having no fixed course] wayward, capricious, erratic; see AIMLESS.

vagrant *n.* beggar, idler, loafer; see TRAVELER.

vague *a.* **1.** [Not clearly expressed] indefinite, unintelligible, superficial; see OBSCURE 1. **2.** [Not clearly understood] uncertain, undetermined, unsure, doubtful, dubious, questionable, misunderstood, enigmatic, puzzling, nebulous, inexplicable, unsettled, bewildering, perplexing, problematic.—*Ant.* CERTAIN, sure, positive. **3.** [Not clearly visible] dim, nebulous, dark; see HAZY.

vaguely *a.* uncertainly, unclearly, hazily, foggily, confusedly, mistily, shiftily, unreliably, dubiously, eccentrically, unsurely, illegally, evasively, unpredictably, indefinitely, obscurely, without clear outlines, incapable of being determined.

vagueness *n.* ambiguity, obscurity, difficulty; see CONFUSION, UNCERTAINTY 1, 2.

vain *a.* **1.** [Possessing unwarranted self-esteem] proud, arrogant, haughty; see EGOTISTIC. **2.** [Useless] worthless, hopeless, profitless; see FUTILE, USELESS 1.

valentine *n.* sentimental letter, St. Valentine's Day greeting, love verse; see LETTER 2.

valiant *a.* courageous, unafraid, dauntless; see BRAVE.

valiantly *a.* courageously, boldly, fearlessly; see BRAVELY.

valid *a.* **1.** [Capable of proof] sound, cogent, logical, conclusive, solid, well-grounded, well-founded, tested, accurate, convincing, telling, correct, determinative, compelling, persuasive, potent, stringent, strong, ultimate, unanswerable, irrefutable.—*Ant.* WRONG, erring, misleading. **2.** [Genuine] true, original, factual, real, actual, pure, uncorrupted, authentic, confirmed, authoritative, trustworthy, credible, attested, efficient, legitimate, adequate, substantial, proven, unadulterated.—*Ant.* FALSE, fictitious, counterfeit.

validate *v.* confirm, sanction, legalize; see APPROVE.

validity *n.* soundness, value, advantage; see USEFULNESS.

valley *n.* vale, glen, canyon, depression, trough, notch, channel, lowland, river valley, stream valley, hollow, plain, dell, valley floor, coulee, dale, river bottom; see also GAP, RAVINE.—*Ant.* MOUNTAIN, ridge, hilltop.

valor *n.* bravery, heroism, boldness; see COURAGE.

valuable *a.* salable, marketable, in demand, high-priced, commanding a good price, costly, expensive, dear, priceless, precious, of value, in great demand, hardly obtainable, scarce, without price, good as good*.—*Ant.* CHEAP, unsalable, unmarketable.

value *n.* **1.** [Monetary value] price, expense, cost, profit, value in exhange, equivalent, rate, amount, market price, charge, face value, assessment, appraisal. **2.** [The quality of being desirable] use, benefit, advantage; see sense 3. **3.** [Quality] worth, merit, significance, consequence, goodness, condition, state, excellence, distinction, desirability, grade, finish, perfection, eminence, superiority, advantage, power, regard, importance, mark, caliber, repute. **4.** [Precise signification] significance, force, sense; see MEANING.

value *v.* **1.** [To believe to be valuable] esteem, prize, appreciate; see ADMIRE. **2.** [To set a price upon] estimate, reckon, assess, appraise, fix the price of, place a value on, assay, rate, figure, compute, evaluate, judge, repute, consider, enumerate, account, charge, levy, ascertain, price.

valued *a.* evaluated, appraised, charged; see MARKED 2.

valve *n.* flap, lid, plug; see PIPE 1. *Valves include the following:* automatic, alarm, check, cutoff, side, overhead, dry-pipe, gate, lift, piston, rocking, safety, slide, throttle, sleeve, intake, exhaust, butterfly.

vandal *n.* despoiler, rapist, thief; see PIRATE.

vandalism *n.* piracy, demolition, wreckage; see DESTRUCTION 1.

vanish *v.* fade out, go away, dissolve; see DISAPPEAR.

vanishing *a.* disappearing, going, fading; see HAZY.

vanity *n.* ostentation, display, conceit, show, self-love, narcissism, self-glorification, self-applause, pretension, vainglory, conceitedness, affection, complacency, smugness.

vanquish *v.* conquer, overcome, subdue; see DEFEAT 2, 3.

vapid *a.* flat, boring, uninteresting; see DULL 3, 4.

vapor *n.* mist, steam, condensation, smog, exhalation, breath, fog, gas, haze, smoke.

vaporize *v.* diffuse, vanish, dissipate; see EVAPORATE.

variable *a.* inconstant, shifting, unsteady; see IRREGULAR 1, 4.

variance *n.* change, fluctuation, deviation; see VARIATION 2.

variation *n.* **1.** [Change] modification, alteration, mutation; see CHANGE 1. **2.** [Disparity] inequality, difference, dissimilarity, distinction, disproportion, exception, contrast, irregularity, aberration, abnormality, disparity.—*Ant.* SIMILARITY, conformity, likeness.

varied *a.* discrete, different, diverse; see MIXED 1, VARIOUS.

variety *n.* **1.** [Quality or state of being diverse] diversity, change, diversification, difference, variance, medley, mixture, miscellany, disparateness, divergency, variation, incongruity, fluctuation, shift, change, modification, departure, many-sidedness. **2.** [Sort] kind, class, division, species, genus, race, tribe, family, assortment, type, stripe, nature, ilk, character, description, rank, grade, category, classification, quality.—*Ant.* EQUALITY, equalness, similarity.

various *a.* different, disparate, dissimilar, diverse, diversified, variegated, varicolored, many-sided, several, manifold, numerous, unlike, many, sundry, variable, changeable, inconstant, uncertain, of any kind, all manner of, of every description, distinct; see also MULTIPLE 1.—*Ant.* ALIKE, undiversified, identical.

variously *a.* varyingly, inconsistently, unpredictably; see DIFFERENTLY.

varnish *v.* finish, paint, shellac, lacquer, wax, size, enamel, japan, surface, coat, luster, polish, gloss, adorn, refinish, glaze, gloss over.—*Ant.* EXPOSE, remove the finish, strip.

vary *v.* dissent, diverge, differ, deviate, digress, swerve, depart, fluctuate, alternate, diverge from, be distinguished from, range, be inconstant, mutate, be uncertain.—*Ant.* REMAIN, be steady, hold.

varying *a.* diverse, differing, diverging; see CHANGING.

vase *n.* vessel, urn, jar, pottery, porcelain, receptacle, flower holder, ornament.

vast *a.* **1.** [Large] huge, enormous, immense; see LARGE 1. **2.** [Extensive] broad, far-flung, wide, spacious, expansive, spread-out, ample, far-reaching, widespread, comprehensive, detailed, all-inclusive, astronomical, prolonged, stretched out, expanded.—*Ant.* NARROW, limited, confined.

vastness *n.* hugeness, extent, enormity; see EXPANSE, SIZE 2.

vat *n.* vessel, tub, barrel; see CONTAINER.

vault *n.* **1.** [A place for the dead] tomb, crypt, grave; see MONUMENT 1. **2.** [A place for preserving valuables] safe-deposit box, time vault, burglar-proof safe; see SAFE.

veal *n.* calf, beef, baby beef; see MEAT. *Cuts of veal include the following:* chops, leg, loin, rack, neck, breast, chuck. *Veal dishes include the following:* breaded veal cutlet, veal stew, calf's liver, Wiener schnitzel, veal Parmigiano, veal scallopini.

veer *v.* swerve, bend, divert; see TURN 1, 2, 3.

vegetable *a.* plantlike, herblike, floral, blooming, blossoming, growing, flourishing.

vegetable *n.* plant, herbaceous plant, herb, edible root. *Common vegetables include the following:* cabbage, potato, turnip, bean, carrot, pea, celery, lettuce, parsnip, spinach, squash, tomato, pumpkin, asparagus, onion, corn, lentil, leek, chicory, kale, garlic, radish, cucumber, artichoke, eggplant, beet, scallion, pepper, okra, kohlrabi, parsley, chard, rhubarb, cauliflower, Brussels sprouts, broccoli, endive, Chinese cabbage, watercress, rutabaga.

vegetate *v.* **1.** [To germinate] sprout, bud, blossom; see BLOOM, GROW 1. **2.** [To stagnate] hibernate, stagnate, languish; see WEAKEN 1.

vegetation *n.* plants, plant growth, trees, shrubs, saplings, flowers, wildflowers, grasses, herbage, herbs, pasturage, weeds, vegetables, crops.

vehicle *n.* *Vehicles include the following:* carriage, buggy, wagon, sleigh, cart, motor car, jeep, rover, automobile, truck, van, motorcycle, taxicab, railroad car, cab, hack, taxi.

veil *n.* **1.** [A thin fabric] scarf, kerchief, mask; see WEB. **2.** [A curtain] screen, cover, shade; see CURTAIN.

vein *n.* **1.** [A fissure] cleft, aperture, opening, channel, cavity, crack, cranny, rift, chink, break, breach, slit, crevice, flaw, rupture. **2.** [A persistent quality] strain, humor, mood, temper, tang, spice, dash; see also CHARACTERISTIC, TEMPERAMENT. **3.** [A blood duct leading to the heart] *Important veins include the following:* jugular, pulmonary, subclavian, portal, iliac, hepatic, renal.

velocity *n.* quickness, rapidity, impetus; see SPEED.

velvet *a.* silken, shining, plushy; see SOFT 2.

velvet *n.* cotton velvet, rayon, corduroy; see GOODS.

veneer *n.* surface, exterior, covering; see COVER 1.

venerable *a.* revered, old, aged, ancient, hoary, reverenced, honored, honorable, noble, august, grand, esteemed, respected, dignified, imposing, grave, serious, sage, wise, philosophical, experienced.—*Ant.* INEXPERIENCED, callow, raw.

venerate *v.* revere, reverence, adore; see LOVE 1, WORSHIP.

veneration *n.* respect, adoration, awe; see REVERENCE, WORSHIP 1.

vengeance *n.* retribution, return, retaliation; see REVENGE 1.

vengeful *a.* spiteful, revengeful, rancorous; see CRUEL.

venom *n.* poison, virus, toxin, bane, microbe, contagion, infection.

vent *n.* ventilator, vent hole, venting hole, ventiduct, liquid-vent, vent faucet, molding, touchhole, drain, smoke hole, flue, aperture.

vent *v.* let out, drive out, discharge; see FREE.

ventilate *v.* freshen, let in fresh air, circulate fresh air, vent, air cool, air out, free, oxygenate; see also AIR.

ventilated *a.* aired out, having adequate ventilation, not closed up; see AIRED 1, COOL 1, OPEN 1.

ventilation *n.* airing, purifying, oxygenating, freshening, opening windows, changing air, circulating air, air conditioning.

venture *n.* adventure, risk, hazard, peril, stake, chance, speculation, dare, experiment, trial, attempt, test, gamble, undertaking, enterprise, investment, leap in the dark, plunge*, flyer*, crack*, fling*.

venture *v.* attempt, experiment, try out; see TRY 1.

ventured *a.* risked, chanced, dared; see DONE 1.

verb *n.* *Verbs include the following:* finite, active, neuter, passive, transitive, intransitive, modal, auxiliary, linking, reciprocal, copulative, reflexive, strong, weak, regular, irregular.

verbal *a.* told, unwritten, lingual; see ORAL, SPOKEN.

verbal *n.* *Verbals in English include the following:* infinitive, gerund, participle, gerundive, verbal noun, present participle, verbal adjective, past participle, verbal phrase, absolute construction.

verbally *a.* orally, by word of mouth, person-to-person; see SPOKEN.

verbatim *a.* exactly, *literatim*, to the letter; see LITERALLY.

verdict *n.* judgment, finding, decision, answer, opinion, sentence, determination, decree, conclusion, deduction, adjudication, arbitrament.

verge *n.* edge, brink, terminus; see BOUNDARY.

verge *v.* end, edge, touch; see APPROACH 2.

verification *n.* verifying, attestation, affirmation; see CONFIRMATION 1.

verify *v.* establish, substantiate, authenticate, prove, check, test, validate, settle, corroborate, confirm.

veritable *a.* authentic, true, real; see GENUINE 1.

vermin *n.* flea, louse, mite; see INSECT.

versatile *a.* many-sided, adaptable, dexterous, varied, ready, clever, handy, talented, gifted, adroit, resourceful, ingenious, accomplished; see also ABLE.

versatility *a.* flexibility, utility, adjustability; see ADAPTABILITY.

verse *n.* **1.** [Composition in poetic form] poetry, metrical composition, versification, stanza, rhyme, lyric, sonnet, ode, heroic verse, dramatic poetry, blank verse, free verse. **2.** [A unit of verse] line, verse, stanza, stave, strophe, antistrophe, hemistich, distich, quatrain.

version *n.* **1.** [One of various accounts] report, account, tale; see STORY. **2.** [A translation] paraphrase, redaction, transcription; see TRANSLATION.

vertebrae *n.* spine, spinal column, backbone, chine. *Parts of the vertebra include the following:* atlas, axis, cervical, thoracic, lumbar, caudal, disk, spinous process, neural arch, anterior and posterior zygapophysis, transverse process.

vertical *a.* perpendicular, upright, on end; see STRAIGHT 1.

very *a.* extremely, exceedingly, greatly, acutely, indispensably, just so, surprisingly, astonishingly, incredibly, wonderfully, particularly, certainly, positively, emphatically, really, truly, pretty, decidedly, pressingly, notably, uncommonly, extraordinarily, prodigiously, hightly, substantially, dearly, amply, vastly, extensively, noticeably, conspicuously, largely, considerably, hugely, excessively, imperatively, markedly, enormously, sizably, materially, immensely, tremendously, superlatively, remarkably, unusually, immoderately, quite, indeed, somewhat, rather, simply, intensely, urgently, exceptionally, severely, seriously, in a great measure, to a great degree, beyond compare, on a large scale, ever so, beyond measure, by far, in the extreme, in a marked degree, to a great extent, without restraint, more or less, in part, infinitely, very much, real*, right, pretty, awfully*, good and*, powerful*, powerfully*, hell of a*, precious*, so*, to a fault, a bit of, no end*.

vessel *n.* **1.** [A container] pitcher, urn, kettle; see CONTAINER. **2.** [A ship] boat, craft, bark; see SHIP. **3.** [A duct; *especially for blood*] blood vessel, artery, capillary; see VEIN 2.

vest *n.* waistcoat, jacket, garment; see CLOTHES.

vestige *n.* trace, remains, scrap; see REMAINDER.

veteran *n.* **1.** [An experienced person] master, one long in service, old hand, one of the old guard, old bird*, old dog*, old timer*.—*Ant.* AMATEUR, new man, youngster. **2.** [An experienced soldier] ex-soldier, seasoned campaigner, ex-service man, re-enlisted man, old soldier, war horse*, ex-G.I.*, vet.

veterinarian *n.* animal specialist, vet, animal doctor; see DOCTOR.

veto *n.* prohibition, declination, negative; see DENIAL, REFUSAL.

veto *v.* interdict, prohibit, decline; see DENY, REFUSE.

vetoed *a.* declined, rejected, disapproved; see NO, REFUSED.

via *prep.* by way of, by the route passing through, on the way to, through the medium of; see also BY 2, THROUGH 4.

vibrant *a.* energetic, vigorous, lively; see ACTIVE.

vibrate *v.* **1.** [To quiver] fluctuate, flutter, waver; see WAVE 3. **2.** [To sound] echo, resound, reverberate; see SOUND.

vibration *n.* quake, wavering, vacillation, fluctuation, oscillation, quiver, shake; see also WAVE 3.

vice *n.* corruption, iniquity, wickedness; see EVIL 1.

vice versa *a.* conversely, in reverse, the other way round, turn about, about face, in opposite manner, far from it, on the contrary, in reverse.

vicinity *n.* proximity, nearness, neighborhood; see ENVIRONMENT, REGION 1.

vicious *a.* bad, debased, base, impious, profligate, demoralized, faulty, vile, foul, impure, lewd, indecent, licentious, libidinous; see also BAD 1.—*Ant.* PURE, noble, virtuous.

vicious circle *n.* chain of events, cause and effect, interreliant problems; see DIFFICULTY 1, 2.

viciously *a.* cruelly, spitefully, harmfully; see BRUTALLY, WRONGLY.

victim *n.* prey, sacrifice, immolation, sufferer, wretch, quarry, game, hunted, offering, scapegoat, martyr.

victimize *v.* cheat, swindle, dupe, trick, fool; see also DECEIVE.

victor *n.* conqueror, champion, prize winner; see WINNER.

victorious *a.* winning, triumphant, mastering; see SUCCESSFUL.

victory *n.* conquest, mastery, subjugation, overcoming, overthrow, master stroke, lucky stroke, winning, gaining, defeating, subduing, destruction, killing, knockout, pushover.

vie *v.* contend, strive, rival; see COMPETE.

view *n.* glimpse, look, panorama, aspect, show, appearance, prospect, distance, opening, stretch, outlook, way, extended view, long view, avenue, contour, outline, scene, spectacle. **—in view** visible, in sight, not out of sight, perceptible, perceivable; see also OBVIOUS 1. **—on view** displayed, on display, exposed; see SHOWN 1. **—with a view to** in order to, so that, anticipating; see TO 4.

view *v.* observe, survey, inspect; see SEE 1.

viewer *n.* spectator, watcher, onlooker; see OBSERVER.

viewpoint *n.* point of view, perspective, standpoint, angle, slant, position, stand, aspect, light, respect, attitude, ground, point of observation, outlook.

vigor *n.* **1.** [Activity] exercise, action, energy; see VITALITY. **2.** [Health] well-being, endurance, vitality; see HEALTH.

vigorous *a.* **1.** [Done with vigor] energetic, lively, brisk; see ACTIVE. **2.** [Forceful] powerful, strong, potent; see EFFECTIVE.

vigorously *a.* energetically, alertly, eagerly, quickly, nimbly, agilely, strenuously, resolutely, firmly, forcibly, forcefully, urgently, unfalteringly, purposefully, actively, boldly, adventurously, zealously, lustily, robustly, stoutly, hardily, wholeheartedly, earnestly, warmly, fervidly, passionately, sincerely, devoutly, appreciatively, with heart and soul, healthily, fearlessly, mightily, decidedly, by brute force, like blazes*; see also POWERFULLY.—*Ant.* CALMLY, aimlessly, slowly.

vile *a.* sordid, corrupt, debased; see SHAMEFUL 1, 2.

village *n.* hamlet, crossroads town, small town; see TOWN 1.

villain *n.* scoundrel, knave, brute; see CRIMINAL.

vindicate *v.* **1.** [To clear] acquit, free, absolve; see EXCUSE. **2.** [To justify] prove, bear out, warrant; see PROVE.

vindication *n.* defense, acquittal, clearance; see PROOF 1.

vindictive *a.* revengeful, resentful, spiteful; see CRUEL.

vine *n.* creeper, climbing plant, creeping plant, trailing plant, stem climber, leaf climber, tendril climber; see also PLANT. *Vines include the following:* grapevine, honeysuckle, trumpet vine, English ivy, Virginia creeper, poison ivy, blackberry, raspberry, briar, rambler, teaberry, dewberry, morning-glory, hopvine, bougainvillea, jasmine, pea vine, watermelon, cantaloupe, cucumber, wild cucumber, passion flower.

violate *v.* **1.** [To transgress] outrage, disrupt, infringe, break, tamper with; see also MEDDLE 1. **2.** [To rape] dishonor, profane, defile, ravish.

violation *n.* infringement, negligence, misbehavior, nonobservance, violating, shattering, transgressing, forcible trespass, trespassing, contravention, breach, breaking, rupture, flouting; see also CRIME.

violence *n.* **1.** [Violent disturbance] rampage, tumult, disorder, clash, onslaught, struggle; see also CONFUSION, DISTURBANCE 2, UPROAR. **2.** [Violent conduct] fury, force, vehemence, frenzy, savagery; see also INTENSITY.

violent *a.* strong, powerful, forceful, forcible, rough, mighty, great, potent, coercive, furious, mad, savage, fierce, passionate, splitting, vehement, frenzied, demoniac, frantic, fuming, enraged, disturbed, agitated, impassioned, impetuous, urgent, maddened, aroused, inflamed, distraught, infatuated, hysterical, great, vehement, extreme, unusual, destructible, murderous, homicidal, rampageous.—*Ant.* CALM, GENTLE, QUIET.

violently *a.* destructively, forcibly, forcefully, combatively, powerfully, strongly, coercively, flagrantly, outrageously, overwhelmingly, compellingly, disturbingly, turbulently, stormily, ruinously, stubbornly, with violence, in a violent manner, abruptly, noisily, with a vengeance, like fury, rebelliously, riotously, furiously, angrily, vehemently, frantically, fiercely, hysterically, hilariously, passionately, urgently, madly, frenziedly, ardently, enthusiastically, impulsively.—*Ant.* MILDLY, gently, undisturbedly.

violet *a.* lavender, mauve, purplish; see PURPLE.

violin *n.* fiddle, viola, Stradivarius; see MUSICAL INSTRUMENT.

VIP* *n.* very important person, notable, important figure; see LEADER 2.

virgin *a.* **1.** [Chaste] pure, modest, virginal; see CHASTE. **2.** [Original or natural] undisturbed, new, untamed; see NATURAL 3, ORIGINAL 1, 3.

Virgin *n.* Madonna, Blessed Virgin Mary, Queen of Saints, Our Lady, Mother of God, Mary, the Queen of Heaven, Queen of Angels, Star of the Sea, The Virgin Mother, Immaculate Conception, Immaculate Mary; see also SAINT.

virginity *n.* maidenhood, girlhood, celibacy; see VIRTUE 1.

virile *a.* masculine, potent, manlike; see MALE, MANLY.

virility *n.* potency, masculinity, manliness; see MANHOOD 2.

virtually *a.* for all practical purposes, practically, implicitly; see ESSENTIALLY.

virtue *n.* **1.** [Moral excellence] ideal, ethic, morality, goodness, righteousness, uprightness, ethical conduct, good thing, respectability, rectitude, honor, honesty, candor, merit, fineness, character, excellence, value, chastity, quality, worth, kindness, innocence, generosity, trustworthiness, faithfulness, consideration, justice, prudence, temperance, fortitude, faith, hope, charity, love.—*Ant.* EVIL, immorality, depravity. **2.** [An individual excellence] quality, characteristic, attribute, temper, way, trait, feature, accomplishment, achievement, property, distinction, capacity, power.—*Ant.* LACK, inability, incapacity. **3.** [Probity in sexual conduct] virginity, purity, decency; see CHASTITY. —**by virtue of** on the grounds of, because of, looking toward; see BECAUSE.

virtuous *a.* good, upright, moral; see HONEST 1, WORTHY.

virus *n.* **1.** [An infection] sickness, communicability, illness; see ILLNESS 2. **2.** [An organism] microorganism, bacillus, bacteriophage; see GERM.

vise *n.* clamp, holder, universal vise; see FASTENER.

visibility *n.* perceptibility, discernibility, distinctness; see CLARITY.

visible *a.* apparent, evident, noticeable; see OBVIOUS 1.

vision *n.* **1.** [The faculty of sight] sight, perception, perceiving, range of view, optics, eyesight. **2.** [Understanding] foresight, discernment, breadth of view, insight, penetration, intuition, divination, astuteness, keenness, foreknowledge, prescience, farsightedness. **3.** [Something seen through powers of the mind] imagination, poetic insight, fancy, fantasy, image, concept, conception, ideality, idea; see also THOUGHT 1, 2. **4.** [Something seen because of an abnormality] revelation, trance, ecstasy, phantom, apparition, ghost, wraith, specter, apocalypse, nightmare, spirit, warlock; see also ILLUSION.

visionary *a.* **1.** [Impractical] ideal, romantic, utopian; see IMPRACTICAL. **2.** [Imaginary] chimerical, delusory, dreamy; see IMAGINARY.

visit *n.* social call, call, appointment, interview, formal call, talk, evening, stay, weekend, holiday, visitation.

visit *v.* stay with, stop by, call on, call upon, come around, be the guest of, make a visit, sojourn awhile, revisit, make one's compliments to, look in on, visit with, call for, stop off, stop in, stop over, have an appointment with, pay a visit to, tour, take in, drop in on, hit, look around*, look up, go over to, look in, drop over, pop in, have a date.

visitor *n.* caller, visitant, official inspector; see GUEST.

visual *a.* seen, optic, of the vision; see OBVIOUS 1.

visualize *v.* see in the mind's eye, picture mentally, conceive; see IMAGINE.

vital *a.* **1.** [Necessary] essential, indispensable, requisite; see NECESSARY. **2.** [Alive] live, animate, animated; see ALIVE. **3.** [Vigorous] lively, energetic, lusty; see ACTIVE.

vitality *n.* life, liveliness, animation, vim, vigor, intensity, continuity, endurance, energy, spirit, ardor, audacity, spunk, fervor, verve, venturesomeness.

vitals *n.pl.* organs, intestines, entrails; see INSIDES.

vitamin *n. Types of vitamins include the following:* vitamin A, vitamin B complex, vitamin C, vitamin D, vitamin E, vitamin K, riboflavin, flavin, nicotinic acid, ascorbic acid, thiamin, thiamine, niacin, pantothenic acid, nicotinamide, pyridoxine, tocopherol; see also MEDICINE 2.

vivid *a.* **1.** [Brilliant] shining, rich, glowing; see BRIGHT 1. **2.** [Distinct] strong, vigorous, lucid; see CLEAR 2, DEFINITE 2.

vividly *a.* glowingly, strikingly, flamingly; see BRIGHTLY.

vocabulary *n.* wordbook, dictionary, lexicon, thesaurus, stock of words, glossary, scientific vocabulary, literary vocabulary; see also DICTION.

vocal *a.* **1.** [Verbal] expressed, uttered, voiced; see ORAL, SPOKEN. **2.** [Produced by the voice; *said especially of music*] sung, scored for voice, vocalized; see MUSICAL 1.

vocalist *n.* chorister, songstress, caroler; see MUSICIAN, SINGER.

vocation *n.* calling, mission, pursuit; see PROFESSION 1.

voice *n.* **1.** [A vocal sound] speech, sound, call, cry, utterance, tongue, whistle, moan, groan, song, yell, hail, howl, yowl, bark, whine, whimper, mutter, murmur, shout, bleat, bray, neigh, whinny, roar, trumpet, cluck, honk, meow, hiss, quack; see also NOISE 1.—*Ant.* SILENCE, dumbness, deaf-mutism. **2.** [Approval or opinion] decision, conclusion, assent, negation, approval, recommendation, wish, view; see also CHOICE, OPINION 1. —**with one voice** all together, by unanimous vote, without dissent; see UNANIMOUSLY.

voice *v.* assert, cry, sound; see TALK 1, TELL 1.

voiced *a.* vocal, sonant, sounded; see ORAL, SPOKEN.

void *a.* barren, sterile, fruitless, meaningless, useless, invalid, vain, voided, unconfirmed, unratified, null and void, worthless, unsanctioned, set aside, avoided, forceless, voted out, ineffectual, ineffective, voidable.—*Ant.* VALID, in force, used.

volatile *a.* **1.** [Having the qualities of a gas] gaseous, airy, buoyant; see LIGHT 5. **2.** [Having a sprightly temperament] lively, vivacious, playful; see ACTIVE.

volley *n.* round, discharge, barrage; see FIRE 2.

voltage *n.* electric potential, potential difference, charge; see ENERGY 2.

voluble *a.* talkative, glib, loquacious; see FLUENT.

volume *n.* **1.** [Quantity] bulk, mass, amount; see EXTENT, SIZE 2. **2.** [Contents] cubical, size, dimensions; see CAPACITY. **3.** [A book] printed document, tome, pamphlet; see BOOK. **4.** [Degree of sound] loudness, amplification, strength; see SOUND 2.

voluntarily *a.* by preference, willingly, deliberately, optionally, spontaneously, freely, intentionally, by choice, of one's own choice, on one's own, in one's own sweet way, heart in hand, of one's own free will, on one's own hook, to one's heart's content, at one's discretion, on one's own initiative, with all one's heart.

voluntary *a.* willing, freely, spontaneous; see OPTIONAL.

volunteer *n.* enlistee, enlisted man, taker; see CANDIDATE, RECRUIT.

volunteer *v.* come forward, enlist, sign up, submit oneself, take the initiative, offer oneself, do on one's own accord, do of one's own free will, take the initiative, take upon oneself, speak up, stand up and be counted, go in*, chip in*, do on one's own hook*, take the bull by the horns, stand on one's own feet, take the bit between one's teeth, paddle one's own canoe, take the plunge; see also JOIN 2.

volunteered *a.* offered, proffered, signed-up; see JOINED.

volunteers *n.* all comers, everybody, anyone; see RECRUIT.

vomit *v.* throw up, eject, bring up, spit up, dry heave, be seasick, hurl forth, retch, ruminate, regurgitate, give forth, discharge, belch forth, spew up, puke*, barf*, toss one's cookies*.

voracious *a.* insatiable, gross, ravening; see GREEDY.

vote *n.* **1.** [A ballot] tally, ticket, slip of paper, ball, yes or no, rising vote, Australian ballot, secret ballot. **2.** [A decision] referendum, choice, majority; see ELECTION. **3.** [The right to vote] suffrage, the franchise, manhood suffrage, universal suffrage, woman suffrage; see also RIGHT.

vote *v.* ballot, cast a vote, cast a ballot, give a vote, enact, establish, determine, bring about, effect, grant, confer, declare, suggest, propose; see also DECIDE.

voted *a.* decided, willed, chosen; see NAMED 2.

vote down *v.* decide against, refuse, blackball; see DENY.

vote for *v.* give one's vote to, cast a ballot for, second; see SUPPORT 2.

vote in *v.* elect, put in, put in office; see CHOOSE.

vote out *v.* reject, remove from office, vote down; see DEFEAT, DISMISS.

voter *n.* elector, balloter, registered voter, member of a constituency, member of the electorate, vote caster, native, naturalized citizen, taxpayer, voter by proxy, one of the folks back home*, ballot-box stuffer*; see also CITIZEN.

vouch *v.* assert, attest, affirm; see ENDORSE 2.

vow *n.* pledge, solemn assertion, asseveration; see PROMISE 1.

vowel *n.* vocoid, open-voiced sound, vowel sound, glide, diphthong, digraph; see also LETTER 1. *Linguistic terms referring to vowel sounds include the following:* high, mid, low, front, back, rounded, unrounded, tense, slack, stressed, unstressed, nasal, nasalized, clipped, diphthongized. *In English spelling, symbols used to represent vowels include the following:* a, e, i, o, u and sometimes y.

voyage *n.* tour, trip, excursion; see JOURNEY.

vulgar *a.* sordid, ignoble, mean, base, obscene, indecent, gross, filthy, villainous, dishonorable, unworthy, fractious, inferior, disgusting, base-minded, mean-spirited, malicious, ill-tempered, sneaking, deceitful, slippery, loathsome, odious, foul-mouthed, brutish, debased, contemptible, abhorrent, profane, nasty.—*Ant.* NOBLE, high-minded, lofty.

vulgarity *n.* impudence, discourtesy, crudity; see RUDENESS.

vulnerable *a.* woundable, exposed, assailable; see UNSAFE, WEAK 2, 5.

W

wad *n.* **1.** [A little heap] bundle, pile, gathering; see BUNCH. **2.** [*A considerable amount of money] fortune, purse, bankroll; see WEALTH.

wad *v.* stuff, pad, cushion; see PACK 2.

wade *v.* walk in the surf, paddle, get one's feet wet; see SWIM.

wafer *n.* biscuit, cracker, slice; see BREAD.

wag *v.* waggle, swing, sway; see WAVE 3.

wage *v.* conduct, make, carry on; see DO 1.

wager *n.* risk, hazard, challenge; see BET.

wages *n.pl.* salary, earnings, payment; see PAY 2.

wagon *n.* pushcart, buggy, truck, coach, carriage, caravan, car, covered wagon, prairie schooner, Conestoga wagon, cab.

wail *v.* moan, weep, lament; see MOURN.

waist *n.* waistline, middle, midriff; see STOMACH.

wait *n.* halt, interim, time wasted; see DELAY, PAUSE.

wait *v.* **1.** [To await] expect, anticipate, tarry, pause, wait for, look for, watch for, abide, dally, remain, idle, bide one's time, mark time, stay up for, lie in wait for, ambush, lie low*, hole up*, hang around*, stick around, cool one's heels*.—*Ant.* LEAVE, hurry, act. **2.** [To serve food at a table] serve, deliver, tend, act as waiter, act as waitress, arrange, set, ready, place on the table, help, portion, bus the dishes.

waiter *n.* headwaiter, steward, attendant, footman, boy, servant, innkeeper, host, lackey, counterman, soda jerk.

wait for *v.* await, expect, stay up for; see WAIT 1.

waiting *a.* standing, languishing, in line, next in turn, expecting, hoping for, marking time, in wait, cooling one's heels*.—*Ant.* MOVING, hurrying, acting.

waiting room *n.* restroom, salon, lounge, terminal, reception room, hall, antechamber, foyer, preparation room, depot, station.

wait on *v.* accommodate, serve, attend; see WAIT 2.

waitress *n.* female attendant, servant, maidservant, hostess, counter girl, restaurant employee, car hop.

wait up (for) *v.* wait for, expect, stay awake; see WAIT 1, WORRY 2.

waive *v.* forgo, neglect, reject; see ABANDON 1.

wake *v.* **1.** [To waken another] call, rouse, bring to life, arouse, awaken, wake up, prod, shake, nudge, break into one's slumber. **2.** [To become awake] get up, awake, be roused, get out of bed, open one's eyes, rise, arise, stir, stretch oneself.

wake up *interj.* rise and shine, arise, get up, awake, get going*, get cracking.

walk *n.* **1.** [Manner of walking] gait, tread, stride; see STEP 1. **2.** [Course over which one walks] pavement, sidewalk, pathway, footpath, track, trail, sheepwalk, boardwalk, pier, promenade, avenue, street, road, alley, dock, platform, gangway; see also STREET. **3.** [A short walking expedition] stroll, ramble, turn, hike, promenade, airing, saunter, tramp, trek, march, circuit, jaunt, tour.

walk *v.* **1.** [To move on foot] step, pace, march, tread, amble, stroll, hike, saunter, wander, ramble, go out for an airing, take a walk, promenade, trudge, tramp, trek, tour, take a turn, roam, rove, meander, traipse about, patrol, file off, knock about*, knock around*, hoof it*, toddle along, shuffle, wend one's way, cruise. **2.** [To cause to move on foot] lead, drive, exercise, train, order a march, escort, accompany, take for a walk.

walk (all) over* *v.* subdue, trample on, beat up; see ABUSE.

walk away *v.* vanish, depart, split*; see ABANDON 1, 2, LEAVE 1.

walkie-talkie *n.* portable transmitter and receiver, field radio, battery-operated two-way communication; see RADIO 2.

walking *a.* strolling, rambling, trudging, hiking, touring, ambling, sauntering, tramping, marching, promenading, passing, roaming, wandering, wayfaring, trekking*.

walk off *v.* depart, go one's own way, stalk off; see LEAVE 1.

walk off or **out on** *v.* desert, leave, walk off from; see ABANDON 2.

walk off with *v.* take, pilfer, pick up; see STEAL.

walkout *n.* protest, boycott, demonstration; see STRIKE 1.

wall *n.* **1.** [A physical barrier] dam, embankment, dike, ditch, bank, levee, stockade, fence, parapet, retainer, rampart, bulwark, palisade, fort, cliff, barricade, floodgate, sluice. **2.** [An obstacle; *figurative*] barrier, obstruction, bar, cordon, entanglement, hurdle, resistance, defense, snag, hindrance, impediment, difficulty, limitation, restriction, retardation, knot, hitch, drawback, stumbling block, check, stop, curb, red tape, fly in the ointment, bottleneck, red herring, detour.

wallet *n.* billfold, purse, moneybag; see BAG, FOLDER.

wallop *v.* thump, thrash, strike; see HIT 1.

wallow *v.* grovel, welter, flounder, lie in, roll about in, bathe in, toss, immerse, be immersed in, besmirch oneself.

wall up *v.* close up, surround, wall in; see ENCLOSE.

wander *v.* **1.** [To stroll] hike, ramble, saunter; see WALK 1. **2.** [To speak or think incoherently] stray, shift, digress; see RAMBLE 2.

wanderer *n.* adventurer, voyager, gypsy; see TRAVELER.

wandering *a.* **1.** [Wandering in space] roving, roaming, nomadic, meandering, restless, traveling, drifting, straying, going off, strolling, ranging, prowling, ambulatory, straggling, on the road, peripatetic, itinerant, roundabout, circuitous.—*Ant.* IDLE, home-loving, sedentary. **2.** [Wandering in thought] incongruous, digressive, disconnected; see INCOHERENT.

wane *v.* decline, subside, fade away; see DECREASE 1, FADE 1.

want *n.* **1.** [Need] privation, dearth, shortage; see LACK 2. **2.** [Desire] wish, craving, demand; see DESIRE 1.

want *v.* **1.** [To desire] require, aspire, fancy, hanker after, have an urge for, incline toward, covet, crave, long for, lust for, have a fondness for, have a passion for, have ambition, thirst after, hunger after, be greedy for, ache*, have a yen for*, have an itch for. **2.** [To lack] be deficient in, be deprived of, require; see NEED.

wanted *a.* needed, necessary, desired, in need of, sought after, in demand, requested, asked for.—*Ant.* SATISFIED, fulfilled, filled.

wanting *a.* **1.** [Deficient] destitute, poor, in default of, deprived of, bereft of, devoid of, empty of, bankrupt in, cut off, lacking, short, inadequate, defective, remiss, incomplete, missing, substandard, insufficient, absent, needed, unfulfilled, on the short end. **2.** [Desiring] desirous of, covetous, longing for; see ENVIOUS, GREEDY.

want in or **out*** *v.* desire, be anxious, be impatient; see ARRIVE, LEAVE 1.

wanton *a.* **1.** [Unrestrained] extravagant, capricious, reckless, unreserved, unfettered, free, wayward, fluctuating, changeable, whimsical, fitful, variable, fanciful, inconstant, fickle, frivolous, volatile. **2.** [Lewd] wayward, lustful, licentious; see LEWD 2.

war *n.* fighting, hostilities, combat. *Types of wars include the following:* air, guerrilla, shooting, ground, sea, jungle, desert, mountain, amphibious, three-dimensional, trench, naval, aerial, land, push-button, hot, cold, total, limited, civil, revolutionary, religious, preventive, world, offensive, defensive, biological, bacteriological, germ, chemical, atomic, nuclear, psychological, war to end all wars, war of nerves, war of attrition, campaign, crusade, *Blitzkrieg* (German).

war *v.* fight, battle, go to war, wage war on, make war against, engage in combat, take the field against, contend, contest, meet in conflict, march against, attack, bombard, shell, kill, shoot, murder.

ward *n.* **1.** [A territorial division] district, division, territory; see REGION 1. **2.** [A juvenile charge] orphan, foster child, adopted child; see CHILD. **3.** [Hospital room] convalescent chamber, infirmary, emergency ward; see HOSPITAL.

warden *n.* official, officer, overseer, superintendent, guardian, tutor, keeper, head keeper, jailer, bodyguard, guard, governor, prison head.

wardrobe *n.* **1.** [A closet] chest, bureau, dresser; see CLOSET. **2.** [Clothing] apparel, garments, attire; see CLOTHES.

warehouse *n.* wholesale establishment, storehouse, stockroom, storage place, distributing center, repository, depot, shed, stockpile, depository, bin, elevator, storage loft, barn.

wares *n.pl.* goods, lines, stock, products, commodities, manufactured articles, merchandise, range, stuff.

warfare *n.* military operations, hostilities, combat; see WAR.

warlike *a.* belligerent, hostile, offensive; see AGGRESSIVE.

warm *a.* **1.** [Moderately heated] heated, sunny, melting, hot, mild, tepid, lukewarm, summery, temperate, clement, glowing, perspiring, sweaty, sweating, flushed, warmish, snug as a bug in a rug*.—*Ant.* COOL, chilly, chilling. **2.** [Sympathetic] gracious, cordial, compassionate; see FRIENDLY.

warm *v.* heat up, warm up, put on the fire; see COOK, HEAT 2.

warmth *n.* **1.** [Fervor] fever, passion, feeling; see EMOTION. **2.** [Affection] friendliness, kindness, sympathy; see FRIENDSHIP. **3.** [Heat] light, glow, warmness; see HEAT 1, TEMPERATURE.

warn *v.* forewarn, give notice, put on guard, give fair warning, signal, advise, prepare, alert, inform, remind, enjoin, hint, prepare for the worst, offer a word of caution, admonish, counsel, exhort, dissuade, reprove, threaten, forbid, predict, remonstrate, deprecate, prescribe, urge, recommend, prompt, suggest, advocate, cry wolf, tip off*, give the high sign, put a bug in one's ear*.

warned *a.* informed, admonished, made aware, cautioned, advised, given warning, prepared for the worst, told, forewarned, tipped off*, put on the lookout.

warning *n.* caution, admonition, notice, advice, forewarning, alert, intimation, premonition, notification, sign, omen, alarm, indication, token, hint, lesson, information, example, distress signal, prediction, signal, injunction, exhortation, high sign, word to the wise, tip-off, SOS*, handwriting on the wall.

warp *v.* curve, twist, pervert; see BEND.

warrant *n.* authorization, certificate, credential, official document, license, summons, subpoena, security, pass, testimonial, passport, credentials, permit, permission, verification, authentication.

warrant *v.* **1.** [To guarantee] assure, insure, vouch for; see GUARANTEE. **2.** [To justify] bear out, call for, give grounds for; see EXPLAIN.

warranty *n.* guaranty, guarantee, pledge; see GUARANTY.

warrior *n.* battler, fighter, hero; see SOLDIER.

warship *n.* fighting ship, armored vessel, gunboat, man-of-war, frigate, ship-of-the-line; see also BOAT, SHIP. *Warships include the following:* battleship, cruiser, destroyer, destroyer escort, submarine, guided-missile frigate, guided-missile destroyer, missile cruiser, attack submarine, dreadnought, capital ship, landing ship, submarine chaser, aircraft carrier, escort carrier, torpedo boat, PT-boat, raider, flagship.

wart *n.* protuberance, spots, mole, projection, blemish, growth, bulge, lesion, tumor.

wary *a.* circumspect, cautious, alert; see CAREFUL, SLY.

wash *n.* **1.** [Laundry] wet wash, washing, linen, family wash, soiled clothing, clean clothes, washed clothing, rough-dry wash, flat pieces, finished laundry. **2.** [The movement of water] swishing, lapping, roll, swirl, rush, surging, eddy, wave, undulation, surge, heave, flow, murmur, gush, spurt. **3.** [A stream bed that is usually dry] arroyo, gulch, canyon; see GAP 3. **4.** [A prepared liquid] rinse, swab, coating; see LIQUID.

wash *v.* **1.** [To bathe] clean, cleanse, shine, immerse, douse, soak, take a bath, take a shower, soap, rub the dirt off, scour, scrub, rinse, wipe, sponge, dip, fresh up*, wash up, clean up, brush up. **2.** [To launder] clean, starch, scrub, put in a washing machine, boil, soap, send to the laundry, scour, rinse out, soak, drench.—*Ant.* DIRTY, stain, spoil. **3.** [To brush with a liquid] swab, whitewash, color; see PAINT 2. **4.** [*To be convincing] be plausible, stand up, endure examination; see ENDURE 1, SUCCEED 1.

washable *a.* tubfast, fast, unfading, launderable, permanent-press, colorfast, preshrunk.

washed *a.* **1.** [Laundered] cleaned, scrubbed, bleached, boiled, put through the wash, soaped.—*Ant.* DIRTY, soiled, foul. **2.** [Watered] bathed, dipped, drenched, sponged, doused, soaked, cleansed, submerged, showered.—*Ant.* DRY, scorching, desert.

washed up* *a.* finished, defeated, done for*; see RUINED 1, 2.

washer *n.* dishwasher, washing machine, laundry machine; see APPLIANCE, MACHINE.

washing *n.* laundry, soiled clothes, dirty clothes; see WASH 1.

Washington *n.* the nation's capital, the national government, the Capitol; see ADMINISTRATION 2, CITY, UNITED STATES.

washout* *n.* disaster, disappointment, mess; see FAILURE 1, 2.

waste *a.* futile, discarded, worthless, valueless, useless, empty, barren, dreary, uninhabited, desolate, profitless, superfluous, unnecessary, functionless, purposeless, pointless, unserviceable.

waste *n.* 1. [The state of being wasted] disuse, misuse, dissipation, consumption, uselessness, devastation, ruin, decay, loss, exhaustion, extravagance, squandering, wear and tear, wrack and ruin; see also WEAR.—*Ant.* USE, PROFIT, VALUE. 2. [Refuse] rubbish, garbage, scrap; see TRASH 1. 3. [Unused land] desert, wilds, wilderness, wasteland, fen, tundra, marsh, marshland, bog, moor, quagmire, dustbowl, badlands, swamp, wash.

waste *v.* 1. [To use without result] dissipate, spend, consume, lose, be of no avail, come to nothing, go to waste, misuse, throw away, use up, misapply, misemploy, labor in vain, cast pearls before swine.—*Ant.* PROFIT, use well, get results. 2. [To squander] burn up, lavish, scatter, splurge, spend, be prodigal, indulge, abuse, empty, drain, fatigue, spill, impoverish, misspend, exhaust, fritter away, ruin, be spendthrift, divert, go through, gamble away, throw money away*, run through, hang the expense*, blow*, burn the candle at both ends.—*Ant.* SAVE, be thrifty, manage wisely. 3. [To be consumed gradually] decay, thin out, become thin, wither, dwindle, lose weight, be diseased, run dry, wilt, droop, decrease, disappear, drain, empty, wear.—*Ant.* GROW, develop, enrich.

wasted *a.* squandered, spent, destroyed, lost, consumed, eaten up, thrown away, shriveled, gaunt, emaciated, decayed, depleted, scattered, drained, gone for nothing, missapplied, useless, to no avail, down the drain, unappreciated, of no use, worthless.

wasteful *a.* extravagant, profligate, dissipated, prodigal, liberal, immoderate, overgenerous, cavalier, incontinent, thriftless, lavish, squandering, profuse, unthrifty, improvident, careless, reckless, wild, destructive, with money to burn*, easy come easy go, out of bounds.

wastefully *a.* extravagantly, carelessly, improvidently, wildly, immoderately, thriftlessly, recklessly, prodigally, destructively, foolishly, lavishly, inconsiderately, openhandedly, imprudently, ruthlessly, profusely, overgenerously, with no thought for tomorrow, without a second thought, without restraint, without good sense, without consideration.

waste time *v.* malinger, dawdle, drift; see LOAF.

watch *n.* 1. [A portable timepiece] wristwatch, pocket watch, stopwatch, digital watch, analog watch, sportsman's watch, fashion watch, ladies' watch, men's watch, children's watch, chronometer; see also CLOCK. 2. [Strict attention] lookout, observation, observance, awareness, attention, vigilance, guard, heed, watchfulness.—*Ant.* NEGLECT, sleepiness, apathy. 3. [A period of duty or vigilance] patrol, guard duty, nightwatch; see GUARD. 4. [Persons or a person standing guard] guard, sentry, sentinel; see GUARDIAN 1.

watch *v.* 1. [To be attentive] observe, see, scrutinize, follow, attend, mark, regard, listen, wait, attend, take notice, contemplate, mind, view, pay attention, concentrate, look closely. 2. [To guard] keep an eye on, patrol, police; see GUARD.

watched *a.* guarded, spied on, followed, held under suspicion, scrutinized, observed, marked, kept under surveillance, noticed, noted, bugged*.

watchful *a.* on guard, vigilant, prepared; see CAREFUL.

watchfulness *n.* vigilance, alertness, caution; see ATTENTION.

watching *a.* vigilant, wary, alert; see CAREFUL.

watchman *n.* day watchman, watcher, sentinel, scout, spy, ranger, observer, spotter, signalman, flagman, shore patrol, night watchman, curator, guard, guardian, patrolman, detective, policeman, sentry, keeper, caretaker, lookout.

watch out *v.* take care, heed, be cautious, proceed carefully, mind, go on tiptoe, take precautions, be on one's guard, make sure of, be doubly sure, keep an eye peeled, handle with kid gloves*.

watch over *v.* protect, look after, attend to; see GUARD.

water *n.* 1. [Water as a liquid] rain, rainwater, liquid, drinking water, city water, mineral water, salt water, spa water, distilled water, limewater, H_2O. 2. [Water as a body] spring, lake, ocean, sea, gulf, bay, sound, strait, marsh, loch, puddle, pond, basin, pool, river, lagoon, reservoir, brook, stream, creek, waterfall, bayou.

water *v.* sprinkle, spray, irrigate; see MOISTEN.

water down *v.* dilute, restrict, make weaker; see WEAKEN 2.

watered *a.* 1. [Given water] sprinkled, showered, hosed, sprayed, washed, sluiced, bathed, drenched, wetted, irrigated, flooded, baptized, doused, soused, sodden, slaked, quenched; see also WET 1. 2. [Diluted] thinned, weakened, adulterated, lessened, contaminated, mixed, debased, impure, corrupt, blended, weakened, spread out, inflated, cheapened.

water power *n.* hydraulics, waterworks, water pressure, electricity, electric power; see also ENERGY 2.

waterproof *a.* impermeable, tight, airtight, vacuum-packed, oiled, rubber-coated, watertight, insulated, impervious, hermetically sealed.

watery *a.* moist, damp, humid, soggy, sodden, wet, thin, colorless, washed, waterlike.—*Ant.* DRY, parched, baked.

wave *n.* **1.** [A wall of water] comber, swell, roller, heave, tidal wave, billow, tide, surge, crest, bore, breaker, whitecap, curl*. **2.** [A movement suggestive of a wave] surge, gush, swell, uprising, onslaught, influx, tide, flow, stream, come and go, swarm, drift, rush, crush, fluctuation. **3.** [Undulating movement] rocking, bending, winding; see sense 2.

wave *v.* **1.** [To flutter] stream, pulse, flow, shake, fly, dance, flap, swish, swing, tremble, whirl.—*Ant.* FALL, droop, hang listless. **2.** [To give an alternating movement] motion, beckon, call, raise the arm, signal, greet, return a greeting, hail. **3.** [To move back and forth] falter, waver, oscillate, vacillate, fluctuate, pulsate, vibrate, wag, waggle, sway, lurch, bend, swing, dangle, seesaw, wobble, reel, quaver, quiver, swing from side to side, palpitate, move to and fro; see also ROCK.

waver *v.* fluctuate, vacillate, hesitate, dilly-dally, seesaw, deliberate, reel, teeter, totter, hem and haw, pause, stagger.

wavy *a.* **1.** [Sinuous] bumpy, crinkly, curved; see ROUGH 1, TWISTED 1. **2.** [Unsteady] wavering, fluctuating, vibrating; see UNSTABLE 1.

wax *n. Waxes include the following:* paraffin, resin, spermaceti, beeswax, honeycomb, sealing wax, earwax, cerumen, carnauba wax, automobile wax, floor wax, furniture polish.

waxy *a.* slick, glistening, polished, slippery, smooth, glazed, sticky, tacky, glassy; see also SMOOTH 1.

way *n.* **1.** [Road] trail, walk, byway; see HIGHWAY. **2.** [Course] alternative, direction, progression, trend, tendency, distance, space, extent, bearing, orbit, approach, passage, gateway, entrance, access, door, gate, channel. **3.** [Means] method, mode, means, plan, technique, design, system, procedure, process, measure, contrivance, stroke, step, move, action, idea, outline, plot, policy, instrument. **4.** [Manner] form, fashion, gait, tone, guise, habit, custom, usage, behavior, style. —**by the way** casually, by the by, as a matter of fact; see INCIDENTALLY. —**by way of** routed through, detoured through, utilizing; see THROUGH 4. —**get out of the** or **one's way** go, remove oneself, retire; see LEAVE 1, REMOVE 1. —**make one's way** progress, succeed, do well; see SUCCEED 1. —**make way** draw back, give way, withdraw; see LEAVE 1. —**on the way out** declining, no longer fashionable, going out; see OLD-FASHIONED, UNPOPULAR. —**out of the way** disposed of, terminated, taken out; see GONE 1. —**parting of the ways** breakup, agreement to separate, difference of opinion; see FIGHT 1, SEPARATION 1. —**under way** going, prospering, making headway; see MOVING 1.

way out *n.* means of escape, salvation, loophole; see ESCAPE.

way-out* *a.* very different, revolutionary, strange; see EXTREME.

ways and means *n.pl.* methods, approaches, devices; see MEANS 1.

wayward *a.* unruly, disobedient, perverse, headstrong, capricious, delinquent, refractory, willful, unruly, unmanageable, insubordinate, incorrigible, recalcitrant, self-indulgent, changeable, stubborn.—*Ant.* OBEDIENT, stable, resolute.

we *pron.* you and I, he and I, she and I, they and I, us.

weak *a.* **1.** [Lacking physical strength; *said of persons*] delicate, puny, flabby, flaccid, effeminate, frail, sickly, debilitated, senile; see also SICK.—*Ant.* STRONG, healthy, robust. **2.** [Lacking physical strength; *said of things*] flimsy, makeshift, brittle, unsubstantial, jerry-built, rickety, tumbledown, sleazy, shaky, unsteady, ramshackle, rotten, wobbly, tottery.—*Ant.* STRONG, shatterproof, sturdy. **3.** [Lacking mental firmness or character] weak-minded, nerveless, faint-hearted, irresolute, nervous, spineless, unstrung, palsied, wishy-washy, hesitant, vacillating, frightened.—*Ant.* BRAVE, courageous, adventurous. **4.** [Lacking in volume] thin, low, soft, indistinct, feeble, faint, dim, muffled, whispered, bated, inaudible, light, stifled, dull, pale.—*Ant.* LOUD, strong, forceful. **5.** [Lacking in military power] small, paltry, ineffectual, ineffective, inadequate, impotent, ill-equipped, insufficiently armed, limited, unorganized, undisciplined, untrained, vulnerable, exposed, assailable, unprepared. **6.** [Lacking in capacity or experience] unsure, untrained, young; see UNSTABLE 2.

weaken *v.* **1.** [To become weaker] lessen, lose, decrease, relapse, soften, relax, droop, fail, crumble, halt, wane, abate, limp, languish, fade, decline, totter, tremble, flag, faint, wilt, lose spirit, become disheartened, fail in courage, slow down, break up, crack up*, wash out*.—*Ant.* STRENGTHEN, revive, straighten. **2.** [To make weaker] reduce, minimize, enervate, debilitate, exhaust, cripple, unman, emasculate, castrate, devitalize, undermine, impair, sap, enfeeble, unnerve, incapacitate, impoverish, thin, dilute, take the wind out of, wash up*; see also DECREASE 2.—*Ant.* REVIVE, quicken, animate.

weakling *n.* puny person, feeble creature, dotard, coward, crybaby, milksop, jellyfish*, softy*, sissy*, pushover*, namby-pamby.

weakness *n.* **1.** [The state of being weak] feebleness, senility, delicacy, invalidity, frailty, faintness, prostration, decrepitude, debility, impotence, enervation, dizziness, infirmity.—*Ant.* STRENGTH, good health, vitality. **2.** [An instance or manner of being weak] fault, failing, deficiency, defect, disturbance, lapse, vice, sore point, gap, flaw, instability, sin, indecision, inconstancy, vulnerability.—*Ant.* VIRTUE, good, strength. **3.** [Inclination] liking, tendency, bent; see HUNGER, INCLINATION 1.

wealth *n.* capital, capital stock, economic resources, stock, stocks and bonds, securities, vested interests, land, property, labor power, commodities, cash, money in the bank, money, natural resources, assets, means, riches, substance, affluence, belongings, property, fortune, hoard, treasure, resources, revenue, cache, cash, competence, luxury, opulence, prosperity, abundance, money to burn*.—*Ant.* POVERTY, pauperism, unemployment.

wealthy *a.* opulent, moneyed, affluent; see RICH 1.

weapon *n.* armament, protection, weaponry, deadly weapon, military hardware, sophisticated hardware, lethal weapon, defense. *Weapons include the following:* club, spear, arrow, knife, catapult, bullet, dart, missile, ABM (antiballistic missile), MRV (multiple re-entry vehicle), MIRV (multiple independently-targetable re-entry vehicle), CAM (cybernetic anthropomorphic machine), CBW (chemical and biological warfare), bomb, stick, ax, firearm, cannon, gun, musket, rifle, blackjack, whip, sword, pistol, revolver, bayonet, machine gun, warhead, airplane, tank, destroyer.

wear *n.* depreciation, damage, loss, erosion, wear and tear, loss by friction, diminution, waste, corrosion, impairment, wearing away, disappearance, result of friction.—*Ant.* GROWTH, accretion, building up.

wear *v.* **1.** [To use as clothing or personal ornament] bear, carry, effect, put on, don, be clothed, slip on, have on, dress in, attire, cover, wrap, harness, get into*; see also DRESS 2.—*Ant.* UNDRESS, take off, disrobe. **2.** [To consume by wearing] use up, use, consume, wear thin, wear out, waste, diminish, cut down, scrape off, exhaust, fatigue, weather down, impair. **3.** [To be consumed by wearing] fade, go to seed, decay, crumble, dwindle, shrink, decline, deteriorate, decrease, waste, become threadbare.

wear and tear *n.* depletion, wearing, effect of use; see DAMAGE 1, 2, DESTRUCTION 2.

wear down *v.* wear out, get thinner, get worn out; see DECREASE 1, WASTE 3.

weariness *n.* tiredness, exhaustion, dullness; see FATIGUE.

wear off *v.* go away, get better, decline; see STOP 2.

wear out *v.* become worn, be worthless, get thinner; see WASTE 1, 3.

weary *a.* exhausted, fatigued, overworked; see TIRED.

weary *v.* **1.** [To make weary] annoy, vex, distress, irk, strain, overwork, exhaust, fatigue, tire, harass, bore, disgust, dishearten, dispirit, wear out, cause ennui, leave one cold, depress, glut, overstuff, burden, sicken, nauseate. **2.** [To become weary] pain, flag, be worn out, sink, droop, lose interest, fall off, tire, grow tired, drowse, doze, sicken.—*Ant.* ENJOY, excite, be amused.

weather *n.* climate, atmospheric conditions, air conditions, drought, clear weather, sunny weather, foul weather, tempest, calm, windiness, the elements, cloudiness, heat, cold, warmth, chilliness.

weather *v.* **1.** [To expose to the weather] dry, bleach, discolor, blanch, whiten, pulverize, tan, burn, expose, harden, petrify. **2.** [To pass through adversity successfully] overcome, stand up against, bear the brunt of; see ENDURE 1, SUCCEED 1.

weather-beaten *a.* decayed, battered, weathered; see OLD 2, 3, WORN 2.

weatherman *n.* weather reporter, weather prophet, weather forecaster, meteorologist, climatologist, weather bureau, weather station, newsman.

weather report *n.* weather picture, weathercast, meteorological forecast; see FORECAST.

weave *n.* pattern, design, texture; see WEB.

weave *v.* **1.** [To construct by interlacing] knit, sew, interlace, spin, twine, intertwine, crisscross, interlink, wreathe, mesh, net, knot, twill, fold, interfold, ply, reticulate, loop, splice, braid, plait, twist. **2.** [To move in and out] sidle through, make one's way, twist and turn, snake, zigzag, beat one's way, insinuate oneself through, wedge through.

web *n.* cobweb, lacework, netting, plait, mesh, mat, matting, wicker, weft, warp, woof, network, interconnection, reticulation, intermixture, entanglement, tracery, filigree, interweaving, trellis.

wed *v.* espouse, join in wedlock, take in marriage; see MARRY 1, 2.

wedded *a.* married, espoused, in holy matrimony; see MARRIED.

wedding *n.* wedlock, nuptials, matrimony; see MARRIAGE.

wedge *n.* spearhead, prong, drive; see MACHINE, TOOL 1.

weed *n.* **1.** [Wild plant] noxious weed, unwanted plant, prolific plant; see PLANT. *Common weeds include the following:* ragweed, nettle, wild morning-glory, pigweed, buckthorn, dandelion, lamb's quarters, buttonweed, dog fennel, plantain, quack grass, jimson weed, ironweed, wild sunflower, wild hemp, horsemint, foxtail, milkweed, wild barley, wild buckwheat, mullein, cheat grass, Russian thistle, tumbleweed, burdock, wild carrot, wild parsley, tarweed, vervain, wild mustard. **2.** [*Cigarette or cigar] coffin nail*, fag*, joint*; see TOBACCO. **3.** [*Marijuana] pot*, Mary Jane*, grass*; see MARIJUANA.

week *n.* wk., seven days, six days, forty-hour week, working week, work week.

week after week *a.* continually, right along, regularly; see REGULARLY.

weekday *n.* working day, Monday through Friday, not a Sunday or Saturday; see DAY 1.

weekend *n.* end of the week, Saturday to Monday, short vacation, English weekend.

weekly *a.* once every seven days, once a week, occurring every week.

weep *v.* wail, moan, lament; see CRY 1.

weigh *v.* **1.** [To take the weight of] measure, scale, put on the scales, hold the scales, put in the balance, counterbalance, heft*; see also MEASURE 1. **2.** [To have weight] be heavy, carry weight, be important, tell, count, show, register, press, pull, be a load, burden, tip the beams*. **3.** [To consider] ponder, contemplate, balance; see CONSIDER.

weigh down *v.* pull down, burden, oppress; see DEPRESS 2.

weight *n.* **1.** [Heaviness] pressure, load, gross weight, net weight, dead weight, molecular weight, gravity, burden, mass, density, ponderability, tonnage, ballast, substance, G-factor*; see also MEASUREMENT 2, PRESSURE 1.—*Ant.* LIGHTNESS, buoyancy, airiness. **2.** [An object used for its weight] counterbalance, counterweight, counterpoise, ballast, paperweight, stone, rock, lead weight, sinker, anchor, plumb, sandbag. *Common weights include the following:* ounce, pound, ton, long ton, kilogram, centigram, gram, gram molecule, milligram, metric ton, metric carat, carat (grain), assay ton. **3.** [Importance] influence, authority, sway; see IMPORTANCE.

weird *a.* uncanny, ominous, eerie; see MYSTERIOUS 2.

welcome *interj.* greetings, come right in, make yourself at home, how do you do?, glad to see you, won't you come in?.

welcome *a.* gladly received, gladly admitted, desired, appreciated, honored, esteemed, cherished, desirable, agreeable, pleasant, grateful, good, pleasing, joy-bringing, delightful.—*Ant.* UNDESIRABLE, disagreeable, unpleasant.

welcome *n.* greetings, salute, salutation, a hero's welcome, handshake, warm reception, free entrance, entree, hospitality, friendliness, the glad hand*.—*Ant.* rebuke, snub, cool reception. **—wear out one's welcome** bore others, stay too long, make others weary with one; see WEARY 1.

welcome *v.* embrace, hug, take in; see GREET.

welcomed *a.* received, accepted, initiated; see WELCOME.

weld *v.* fuse, unite, seam; see JOIN 1.

welfare *n.* **1.** [Personal condition] health, happiness, well-being, prosperity, good, good fortune, progress, state of being. **2.** [Social service] poverty program, social insurance, health service; see INSURANCE.

well *a.* **1.** [In good health] fine, sound, fit, trim, healthy, robust, strong, hearty, high-spirited, vigorous, hardy, hale, blooming, fresh, flourishing, rosy-cheeked, whole, in fine fettle, hunky-dory*, great*, fit as a fiddle, chipper*.—*Ant.* SICK, ill, infirm. **2.** [Satisfactorily] up to the mark, suitably, adequately, commendably, excellently, thoroughly, admirably, splendidly, favorably, rightly, properly, expertly, strongly, irreproachably, capably, soundly, competently, ably.—*Ant.* BADLY, poorly, unsatisfactorily. **3.** [Sufficiently] abundantly, adequately, completely, fully, quite, entirely, considerably, wholly, plentifully, luxuriantly, extremely.—*Ant.* HARDLY, insufficiently, barely. **—as well** in addition, additionally, along with; see ALSO. **—as well as** similarly, alike, as much as; see EQUALLY.

well *n.* **1.** [A source of water] spring, fountain, font, spout, geyser, wellspring, mouth, artesian well, reservoir. **2.** [A shaft sunk into the earth] pit, hole, depression, chasm, abyss, oil well, gas well, water well. **3.** [Any source] beginning, derivation, fountainhead; see ORIGIN 3.

well-balanced *a.* steady, sensible, well-adjusted; see RELIABLE.

well-behaved *a.* mannerly, courteous, civil; see POLITE.

well-being *n.* prosperity, happiness, fortune; see HEALTH, WELFARE 1.

well-fixed* *a.* well-to-do, wealthy, in comfortable circumstances; see RICH 1.

well-informed *a.* informed, advised, well-read; see EDUCATED, LEARNED 1.

well-known *a.* famous, reputable, recognized, renowned, familiar, widely known, noted, acclaimed, popular, public, celebrated, in the public eye.—*Ant.* UNKNOWN, obscure, undiscovered.

well-off *a.* prosperous, well-to-do, wealthy; see RICH 1.

well-rounded *a.* well-informed, built-up, having a good background; see BALANCED.

well-to-do *a.* wealthy, well-off, prosperous; see RICH 1.

welt *n.* wound, bruise, weal; see INJURY.

west *a.* facing west, westerly, westwards; see WESTERN 1.

West *n.* **1.** [Western Hemisphere] New World, the Americas, North and South America; see AMERICA 1, 2. **2.** [European and American Culture] Occident, Western civilization, Christian society; see EUROPE, UNITED STATES. **3.** [Western United States;

especially the cowboy and mining culture] the range, the prairies, Rocky Mountain country, Far West, Northwest, Southwest, where men are men*, wild-and-woolly country*, the wide open spaces*, Cow Country*, buffalo range*.

western *a.* **1.** [In or toward the west] westwards, westerly, occidental, in the west, on the west side, where the sun sets, facing west, from the east, westernly, westernmost, westbound.—*Ant.* EASTERN, easterly, oriental. **2.** [Having characteristics of the western part of the United States; *sometimes capital*] cowboy, middle-western, southwestern, far-western, in the sagebrush country, on the Western plains, in the wide open spaces, in the wild west, in the Rockies, in God's country, in the wild-and-woolly West*, out where the men are men*.

westward *a.* to the west, in a westerly direction, westbound; see WESTERN 1.

wet *a.* **1.** [Covered or soaked with liquid] moist, damp, soaking, soaked, drenched, soggy, muggy, dewy, watery, dank, slimy, dripping, saturated, sodden.—*Ant.* DRY, dried, clean. **2.** [Rainy] drizzly, slushy, snowy, slippery, muddy, humid, foggy, damp, clammy, showery, drizzling, cloudy, misty.—*Ant.* CLEAR, sunny, cloudless.

wet *v.* sprinkle, dampen, splash; see MOISTEN.

whack *n.* stroke, thump, wham; see BLOW. **—out of whack*** out of order, not working, spoiled; see RUINED 1, 2.

wham *n.* hit, knock, whack; see BLOW.

wharf *n.* boat landing, quay, pier; see DOCK.

what *pron.* **1.** [An indication of a question] which?, what sort?, what kind?, what thing?, what means?. **2.** [Something indefinite] that which, whatever, something, anything, everything, whichever, anything at all. **—and what not** etcetera, and other things too numerous to mention, some more; see ANYTHING, EVERYTHING.

what about *conj. & prep.* but what, remember, and then; see BUT 1, 2, 3.

whatever *pron.* anything, everything, no matter what, whatsoever.

what for *conj.* but why, to what end, for what purpose; see WHY.

what have you* *n.* other things, almost anything else, the rest; see ANYTHING, EVERYTHING.

what if *conj.* but suppose, imagine, supposing; see BUT 1, 2, 3, IF.

what it takes* *n.* capacity, competence, aptitude; see ABILITY.

what's what* *n.* the facts in the case, the truth, the lowdown*; see ANSWER 1, 2.

wheat *n.* staff of life, breadstuff, wheat flour; see GRAIN 1.

wheel *n.* **1.** [A thin circular body that turns on an axis] disk, ratchet, ring, hoop, roller, caster, drum, ferris wheel, wheel trolley, flywheel, cogwheel, steering wheel, sprocket, wheel, chain wheel, water wheel. **2.** [*An important person] personage, VIP, big shot*; see CELEBRITY, EXECUTIVE. **—at the wheel** driving, in control, running things; see RUNNING 1, 2.

wheel and deal* *v.* play fast and loose, take chances, cut corners; see OPERATE 2, 3.

wheels* *n.pl.* car, vehicle, buggy*; see AUTOMOBILE.

wheeze *v.* breathe heavily, puff, pant; see GASP.

when *a. & conj.* **1.** [At what time?] how soon?, how long ago?, in what period?, just when?, at which instant?. **2.** [Whenever] if, at any time, at the moment that, just as soon as, in the event that, on the condition that; see also IF. **3.** [During] at the same time that, immediately upon, just as, just after, at, while, meanwhile; see also DURING.

whenever *conj.* at any time, at any moment, on any occasion, at the first opportunity, if, when, should.

where *a. & conj.* **1.** [A question as to position] in what place?, at which place?, at what moment?, whither?, in what direction?, toward what?. **2.** [An indication of position] wherever, anywhere, in whatever place, at which point, in which, to which, to what end.

whereabouts *n.pl.* location, spot, site; see PLACE 3.

whereas *conj.* since, inasmuch as, insomuch as, forasmuch as, considering that, when in fact, while, while on the contrary.

whereby *a.* by which, through which, in accordance with which, with the help of which, how.

wherefore *a.* why?, for what?, for which reason?, therefore, so, accordingly, thereupon.

whereupon *a.* at which point, thereupon, at the conclusion of which, whereon, upon which, consequently.

wherever *a. & conj.* where, in whatever place, anywhere, in any place that, wheresoever, regardless of where, in any direction.

whether *conj.* if, either, even if, if it follows that.

whether or not *a. & conj.* **1.** [Surely] in any case, certainly, positively; see SURELY. **2.** [If] whether, yes or no, whichever; see IF.

which *conj.* what, whichever, that, whatever, and that, and which.

which *pron.* what, that, one, who.

whichever *a. & conj.* whatever, which, whichsoever, no matter which, whoever.

whiff *n.* scent, puff, fume; see SMELL 1, 2.

whiff *v.* inhale, sniff, scent; see SMELL 2.

while *conj.* **1.** [As long as] during, at the same time that, during the time that, whilst, throughout the time that, in the time that.

2. [Although] whereas, though, even though; see ALTHOUGH.

whim *n.* notion, vagary, caprice; see INCLINATION 1.

whimper *v.* fuss, weep, object; see COMPLAIN, WHINE.

whimsical *a.* playful, capricious, comical; see FUNNY 1.

whine *v.* sing, hum, whistle, whimper, drone, cry, moan, murmur, grumble, complain, gripe*, beef*.

whip *n.* switch, strap, rod, cane, lash, scourge, knotted cord, knout, cat-o-nine-tails, thong, blacksnake, dog whip, ox whip, bullwhip, horsewhip, buggy whip, riding whip, quirt.

whip *v.* thrash, strike, scourge; see BEAT 2, PUNISH.

whipping *n.* beating, thrashing, strapping; see PUNISHMENT.

whir *v.* whiz, swish, vibrate; see HUM.

whirl *n.* **1.** [Rapid rotating motion] swirl, turn, flurry, spin, gyration, reel, surge, whir; see also REVOLUTION 1. **2.** [Confusion] hurry, flutter, fluster, ferment, agitation, tempest, storm, rush, tumult, turbulence, commotion, hurly-burly, bustle.

whirl *v.* turn around, rotate, spin; see TURN 1.

whiskers *n.pl.* beard, mustache, sideburns, goatee, hair, face hair, bristles, muff, chin armor, weeds.

whiskey *n.* bourbon whiskey, rye whiskey, corn whiskey, Scotch whiskey, Irish whiskey, Canadian whiskey, hard liquor, spirits, aqua vitae, firewater*, hooch*, home-brew, moonshine*, mountain dew*; see also DRINK 2.

whisper *n.* **1.** [A low, sibilant sound] rustle, noise, murmur, hum, buzz, drone, undertone, hissing. **2.** [A guarded utterance] disclosure, divulgence, rumor; see SECRET.

whisper *v.* speak softly, speak in a whisper, speak under one's breath, speak in an undertone, tell, talk low, speak confidentially, mutter, murmur, speak into someone's ear.—*Ant.* YELL, speak aloud, shout.

whispering *a.* rustling, sighing, buzzing, humming, murmuring, droning, hissing.

whistle *n.* **1.** [A shrill sound] cry, shriek, howl, blast, piping, siren call, fire alarm, birdcall, signal, toot, blare; see also NOISE 1. **2.** [An instrument that produces a shrill sound] fife, pipes, siren; see ALARM.

whistle *v.* **1.** [To produce a shrill blast] fife, pipe, flute, trill, hiss, whiz, wheeze, shriek, howl, blare, toot, tootle; see also SOUND. **2.** [To call with a whistle] signal, summon, warn; see SUMMON.

white *a.* **1.** [The color of fresh snow] ivory, silvery, snow-white, snowy, frosted, milky, milky-white, chalky, pearly, blanched, ashen, pale, wan, albescent.—*Ant.* DARK, black, dirty. **2.** [Colorless] clear, transparent, clean, blank, spotless, pure, unalloyed, neutral, achromatic, achromic. **3.** [Concerning the white race] fair-skinned, light-complexioned, Caucasian; see EUROPEAN, WESTERN 2. **4.** [Pale] ashen, wan, pallid; see PALE 1.

whiten *v.* **1.** [To become white] grow hoary, blanch, turn white, turn gray, grow pale, be covered with snow, be silvered, change color, fade. **2.** [To make white] bleach, blanch, silver, paint white, whitewash, apply powder, chalk.—*Ant.* DIRTY, smudge, blacken.

whitewash *v.* **1.** [To cover with a lime wash] whiten, apply a white coating, wash; see PAINT 2. **2.** [To give the appearance of innocence] gloss over, cover up, prove innocent; see EXCUSE.

whittle *v.* pare, carve, shape, fashion, shave, model, chip off, lessen, diminish, shave, decrease, pare down.

who *pron.* what, that, which, he, she, they, I, you, whoever, whichever.

whoever *pron.* he who, the one who, whatever person, whatever man, no matter who.

whole *a.* **1.** [Entire] all, every, inclusive, full, undivided, integral, complete, total, aggregate, indivisible, organismic, inseparable, indissoluble, gross, undiminished, utter.—*Ant.* UNFINISHED, partial, incomplete. **2.** [Not broken or damaged] thorough, mature, developed, unimpaired, unmarred, full, unbroken, undamaged, entire, in one piece, sound, solid, untouched, without a scratch, intact, uninjured, undecayed, completed, preserved, perfect, complete, safe, in A-1 condition, shipshape, in good order, together, unified, exhaustive, conclusive, unqualified, fulfilled, accomplished, consummate.—*Ant.* BROKEN, mutilated, defective. **3.** [Not ill or injured] hale, hearty, sound; see HEALTHY, WELL 1.

whole *n.* unity, totality, everything, oneness, entity, entirety, collectivity, sum, assemblage, aggregate, aggregation, body, lump, gross, entire stock, length and breadth, generality, mass, amount, bulk, quantity, universality, combination, complex, assembly, gross amount.—*Ant.* PART, portion, fraction.

wholehearted *a.* sincere, earnest, candid; see HEARTY.

wholesale *a.* **1.** [Dealing in large lots] large-scale, in the mass, quantitative, in bulk, bulk, to the retailer, by the carload, loose, in quantity, in job lots; see also COMMERCIAL. **2.** [Indiscriminate] sweeping, widespread, comprehensive; see WHOLE 1.

wholesome *a.* nutritive, nourishing, beneficial; see HEALTHFUL.

wholly *a.* totally, entirely, fully; see COMPLETELY.

whom *pron.* that, her, him; see WHO, WHAT 2.
whoops *interj.* oh-oh*, sorry; oh, no; see NO.
whore *n.* call girl, harlot, streetwalker; see PROSTITUTE.
whose *pron.* to whom, belonging to what person, of the aforementioned one, from these.
why *a. & conj.* for what reason?, how so?, how?, how is it that?, on whose account?, what is the cause that?, to what end?, for what purpose?, on what foundation?, how do you explain that?, how come?*.
whys and wherefores *n.pl.* reasons, explanations, causes; see REASON 3.
wicked *a.* sinful, immoral, corrupt, evil, base, foul, gross, dissolute, wayward, irreligious, blasphemous, profane, evil-minded, vile, bad, naughty, degenerate, depraved, incorrigible, unruly, heartless, shameless, degraded, debauched, hard, toughened, disreputable, infamous, indecent, mean, remorseless, scandalous, atrocious, contemptible, nasty, vicious, fiendish, hellish, villainous, rascally, devilish, malevolent, plotting, conspiratorial, flagrant, criminal, heinous, murderous, tricky, sinister, ignoble, monstrous, rotten*, low-down*, good-for-nothing, dirty, felonious, dangerous, cutthroat, ratty*, slippery, crooked.—*Ant.* HONEST, just, kind.
wickedness *n.* evil, depravity, immorality; see EVIL 1.
wide *a.* **1.** [Broad] extended, spacious, deep; see BROAD 1. **2.** [Loose] broad, roomy, full; see LOOSE 1. **3.** [Extensive] large-scale, all-inclusive, universal; see GENERAL 1.
wide-awake *a.* alert, watchful, vigilant; see CAREFUL.
widely *a.* extensively, generally, publicly, nationally, internationally, universally, in many places, broadly, comprehensively.
widen *v.* **1.** [To make wider] add to, broaden, stretch, extend, increase, enlarge, distend, spread out, give more space, augment. **2.** [To become wider] unfold, grow, open, stretch, grow larger, increase, swell, multiply.
widespread *a.* extensive, general, sweeping, broad, comprehensive, far-reaching, widely accepted, boundless, popular, public, unrestricted, unlimited, on a large scale, overall.—*Ant.* OBSCURE, secret, limited.
widow *n.* widow woman, dowager, divorcée, husbandless wife, dead man's wife; see also WIFE.
widower *n.* surviving husband, grass widower, widowman*; see HUSBAND.
width *n.* breadth, wideness, girth, diameter, distance across, amplitude, cross dimension, cross measurement, expanse.—*Ant.* LENGTH, height, altitude.
wield *v.* handle, manipulate, exercise; see HOLD 1.
wiener *n.* frankfurter, sausage, hot dog*; see MEAT.
wife *n.* married woman, spouse, lady, dame, madam, matron, helpmate, consort, mate, housewife, better half*, the missis*, the little woman*, wifey*, the old lady*.—*Ant.* WIDOW, spinster, old maid.
wig *n.* artificial hair, fall, hairpiece; see HAIR 1.
wiggle *v.* wag, waggle, wriggle, squirm, shimmy, shake, flounce, dance sensually.
wild *a.* **1.** [Not controlled] unrestrained, unmanageable, boisterous; see UNRULY. **2.** [Uncivilized] barbarous, savage, undomesticated; see PRIMITIVE. **3.** [Not cultivated] luxuriant, lush, exuberant, dense, excessive, desolate, waste, desert, weedy, untrimmed, impenetrable, uninhabited, native, natural, untouched, virgin, overgrown, uncultivated, untilled, uncared for, neglected, overrun, free, rampant. **4.** [Inaccurate] erratic, off, unsound; see WRONG 2. **5.** [Stormy] disturbed, raging, storming; see TURBULENT. **6.** [Excited] hot, eager, avid; see EXCITED. **7.** [Dissolute] loose, licentious, profligate; see LEWD 2. **8.** [Imprudent] reckless, foolish, incautious; see CARELESS.
wilderness *n.* primitive area, wastelands, back country, the woods, the North woods, primeval forest, uninhabited region; see also DESERT, FOREST.
wildly *a.* hastily, rashly, fiercely, violently, ferociously, uncontrollably, carelessly, quixotically, savagely, unwittingly, recklessly, confusedly, pell-mell.—*Ant.* CAREFULLY, prudently, judiciously.
will *n.* **1.** [Desire] inclination, wish, disposition, pleasure, yearning, craving, longing, hankering. **2.** [Conscious power] resolution, volition, intention, preference, will power, mind, determination, self-determination, decisiveness, moral strength, discretion, conviction, willfulness.—*Ant.* DOUBT, vacillation, indecision. **3.** [Testament for the disposition of property] bequest, disposition, instructions, last wishes, bestowal, dispensation, last will and testament. **—at will** whenever one wishes, at any time, at any moment; see ANY TIME.
will *v.* **1.** [To exert one's will] decree, order, command, demand, authorize, request, make oneself felt, decide upon, insist, direct, enjoin. **2.** [To wish] want, incline to, prefer; see WISH. **3.** [An indication of futurity] shall, would, should, expect to, anticipate, look forward to, hope to, await, foresee, propose.
willful *a.* intentional, premeditated, contemplated; see DELIBERATE.
willing *a.* energetic, prompt, reliable, active, obedient, enthusiastic, zealous, responsible, agreeable, prepared, voluntary, ready, compliant, amenable, tractable, feeling, like, in

accord with.—*Ant.* OPPOSED, averse, unwilling.

willingly *a.* gladly, readily, obediently, agreeably, voluntarily, with relish, at one's pleasure, on one's own account, of one's own accord, with open arms, with good cheer, freely, with pleasure, cheerfully, with all one's heart, at the drop of a hat*, like a shot*.

willingness *n.* zeal, enthusiasm, readiness, earnestness, eagerness, alacrity, cordiality, hospitality, courteousness, compliance, good will, geniality.

wilt *v.* droop, wither, weaken, shrivel, flag, dry up, fade, become flaccid, lose freshness, faint.—*Ant.* GROW, STAND, stiffen.

win* *n.* triumph, conquest, victory; see SUCCESS 1.

win *v.* **1.** [To gain a victory] be victorious, prevail, get the best of, come out first, conquer, overcome, overwhelm, triumph; see also SUCCEED 1. **2.** [To obtain] get, acquire, gain; see GET 1. **3.** [To reach] attain, accomplish, effect; see APPROACH 2, 3.

wind *n.* draft, air current, breeze, gust, gale, blast, flurry, whisk, whiff, puff, whirlwind, flutter, wafting, zephyr, trade wind, sirocco, northeaster, southwester, tempest, blow, cyclone, typhoon, twister, hurricane, sandstorm, prevailing westerlies, stiff breeze, Chinook. **—get** or **have wind of*** hear about, have news of, trace; see HEAR 1. **—take the wind out of one's sails** best, get the better of, overcome; see DEFEAT 2, 3.

wind *v.* **1.** [To wrap about] coil, reel in, entwine, wreathe, shroud, fold, cover, bind, tape, bandage. **2.** [To twist] convolute, screw, wind up; see BEND. **3.** [To meander] zigzag, weave, snake, twist, loop, turn, twine, ramble, swerve, deviate.

winding *a.* turning, gyrating, gyring, spiraling, twisting, snaky, serpentine, convoluted.—*Ant.* STRAIGHT, direct, vertical.

window *n.* skylight, porthole, bay window, bow window, picture window, casement, dormer, stained-glass, show window, rose window, transom, peephole.

windowpane *n.* pane, square of glass, glass; see WINDOW.

windpipe *n.* airpipe, bronchus, trachea; see THROAT.

windshield *n.* windscreen, protection against the wind, wraparound; see SCREEN 1.

wind up *v.* conclude, be through with, come to the end of; see END 1.

windy *a.* breezy, blustery, raw, stormy, wind-swept, airy, gusty, blowing, fresh, drafty, wind-shaken, tempestuous, boisterous.—*Ant.* CALM, quiet, still.

wine *n. Wines include the following:* fine, sparkling, still, fortified, dry, sweet, heavy, light, white, rosé, red, green, blackberry, cherry, currant, gooseberry, dandelion; sacramental, dessert, dinner, medicinal, aperitif, cooking; California, New York State, French, Italian, sherry, Tokay, port, muscatel, Burgundy, Bordeaux, Champagne, Haut Sauterne, Rhine wine, Riesling, Traminer, Chablis, Chardonnay, white Chianti, red Chianti, Pinot, Concord, Catawba, Sauvignon blanc; see also DRINK 2.

wing *n.* **1.** [An organ or instrument of flight] appendage, aileron, airfoil; see FEATHER. **2.** [An architectural unit or extension] annex, addition, projection, hall, section, division, part. **3.** [An organized group of aircraft] flying unit, formation, air squadron; see UNIT. **—take under one's wing** favor, help, guarantee; see ADOPT 2.

wink *v.* squint, blink, flirt, make eyes at, bat the eyes.

winner *n.* victor, conqueror, prize winner, champion, winning competitor, hero, successful contestant, leading entrant, Olympic champion, title-holder, champ*, front runner.

winning *a.* **1.** [Engaging] attractive, appealing, agreeable; see CHARMING. **2.** [Victorious] champion, conquering, leading; see SUCCESSFUL.

winter *n.* cold season, frosty weather, wintertime, Christmastime, Jack Frost.

wintry *a.* chilly, frosty, icy, snowy, frigid, cold, bleak, raw, biting, cutting.—*Ant.* WARM, summery, balmy.

wipe *v.* rub, clean, dry, dust, mop, clear, wash, swab, soak up, obliterate.

wipe out *v.* slay, annihilate, eradicate; see DESTROY, KILL 1, REMOVE 1.

wire *n.* **1.** [A metal strand] line, electric wire, cable, aerial, circuit, wiring, live wire, coil, conductor, filament, musical string, wire tape, wire cord. **2.** [A metal net] barbed wire, wire fence, wire cage; see FENCE. **3.** [A telegraphic message] cablegram, message, cable; see TELEGRAM. **—down to the wire** to the very end, at the last, eventually; see FINALLY 2. **—get (in) under the wire** just make it, succeed, squeak through*; see ARRIVE.

wire *v.* **1.** [To install wire] set up a circuit, install electricity, lay wires, connect electric cables, prepare for electrical service, pipe*; see also ELECTRIFY. **2.** [To send a message by wire] flash, telegraph, notify; see TELL 1.

wiring *n.* wirework, electric line, cable work, cables, electrical installations, facilities for electric power, circuit system, electrical wire distribution, tubing, circuit pattern, circuiting, threading, process, route, line, path, pattern, trail.

wiry *a.* agile, sinewy, tough; see STRONG 1.

wisdom *n.* prudence, astuteness, sense, reason, clear thinking, good judgment, brains, sagacity, understanding, sanity, shrewdness, experience, practical knowledge, carefulness, vigilance, tact, balance, poise, stability, caution, solidity, hardheadedness, common sense, horse sense*, savvy*.—*Ant.* STUPIDITY, irrationality, rashness.

wise *a.* **1.** [Judicious] clever, sagacious, witty; see THOUGHTFUL 1. **2.** [Shrewd] calculating, cunning, crafty; see SLY. **3.** [Prudent] tactful, sensible, wary; see CAREFUL. **4.** [Erudite] taught, scholarly, smart; see EDUCATED, LEARNED 1. **5.** [Informed] wise to*, acquainted with, aware of; see FAMILIAR WITH.

wisely *a.* tactfully, prudently, circumspectly, sagaciously, shrewdly, judiciously, discreetly, carefully, admirably, discerningly, sagely, knowingly, reasonably, sensibly, intelligently.—*Ant.* FOOLISHLY, stupidly, unthinkingly.

wise up* *v.* become informed, get acquainted with, learn one's way around; see LEARN.

wish *n.* longing, yearning, hankering, desire, thirst, disposition, request, hope, intention, preference, choice, want, prayer, invocation, liking, pleasure, injunction, command, order.

wish *v.* **1.** [To desire] covet, crave, envy; see WANT 1. **2.** [To express a desire] hope, request, entreat, prefer, want, pray for, invoke, command, order, solicit, beg, look forward to, require; see also NEED.

wishful *a.* desirous, longing, eager; see ZEALOUS.

wishy-washy *a.* cowardly, mediocre, feeble; see WEAK 3.

wit *n.* wittiness, smartness, whimsicality, pleasantry, drollery, banter, burlesque, satire, jocularity, witticism, sally, whimsy, repartee, joke, aphorism, jest, quip, epigram, pun, wisecrack*, gag. **—at one's wits' end** downhearted, desperate, helpless; see TROUBLED. **—have** or **keep one's wits about one** be ready, take precautions, be on one's guard; see WATCH OUT. **—live by one's wits** use sharp practices, live dangerously, take advantage of all opportunities; see TRICK.

witch *n.* sorcerer, warlock, magician, enchantress, charmer, hag, crone.

witchcraft *n.* sorcery, magic, black magic, necromancy, witchery, divination, devil worship, enchantment, spell, bewitchment, voodooism, shamanism, demonology.

with *prep.* by, in association, in the midst of, among, amidst, along with, in company with, arm in arm, hand in glove, in conjunction with, among other things, beside, alongside of, including.

withdraw *v.* **1.** [To retire] depart, draw back, take leave; see RETREAT. **2.** [To remove from use or circulation] revoke, rescind, abolish, repeal, annul, abrogate, veto, suppress, repress, retire, stamp out, declare illegal, ban, bar, nullify, repudiate, reverse, retract, throw overboard, invalidate, quash, dissolve.

withdrawal *n.* removal, retreat, retraction, resignation, alienation, abandonment, recession, revulsion, abdication, relinquishment, departure.—*Ant.* PROGRESS, advance, appearance.

withdrawn *a.* retired, secluded, isolated, removed, departed, cloistered, recluse, drawn back, gone into retirement, taken out, absent, retreated.—*Ant.* ACTIVE, involved, progressing.

wither *v.* shrivel, shrink, droop, wilt, decay, die, grow brown, dry up, dry out, fade, lose freshness, deteriorate, fall away.—*Ant.* REVIVE, reawaken, bloom.

withered *a.* shriveled, wilted, decayed, deteriorated, shrunken, dead, browned, faded, parched, dried up, drooping, wrinkled.—*Ant.* FRESH, blooming, alive.

withheld *a.* concealed, held back, hidden, checked, restrained, delayed, denied, kept on leash, on ice*.—*Ant.* FREE, opened, made visible.

withhold *v.* hold back, reserve, keep; see DENY.

within *a. & prep.* inside, indoors, in, not further than, not beyond, not over, in reach of, in a period of, not outside; see also INSIDE 2.

with-it* *a.* up to date, informed, contemporary; see MODERN 1.

without *a. & prep.* **1.** [Outside] out, outdoors, outwardly, externally, on the outside, standing outside, left out. **2.** [Lacking] not with, not having, in the absence of, free from, deprived of.

withstand *v.* face, confront, oppose, resist, endure, stand up to, hold out.

witness *n.* observer, onlooker, eyewitness, bystander, spectator, testifier, beholder, signatory.

witness *v.* see, observe, be a witness, be on the scene, behold, be present, testify, vouch for, stand for, look on, say under oath, depose, be on hand.

witnessed *a.* sworn to, vouched for, alleged, borne out, validated, valid, established, verified, authenticated, substantiated, supported, upheld, endorsed, brought forward.

witty *a.* quick-witted, clever, bright; see INTELLIGENT.

wizard *n.* magician, soothsayer, witch, witch doctor, sorcerer, fortuneteller, astrologer, medicine man, conjurer, shaman, enchanter, hypnotist, diviner, seer, clairvoyant, palmist, augurer, medium.

wobble *v.* shake, quaver, flounder, vacillate, tremble, quiver, move unsteadily, dodder, teeter, totter, be unsteady, waver, quake, stagger, shuffle, waggle.

wobbly *a.* wavering, unbalanced, precarious; see UNSTABLE 1.

wolf *n.* wild dog, coyote, timber wolf; see DOG.

woman *n.* **1.** [An adult female] lady, dame, matron, gentlewoman, maid, spinster, debutante, nymph, virgin, girl, old woman, chick*, doll*, babe*, broad*. **2.** [A wife or mistress] love, lover, wife; see WIFE. **3.** [Womankind] femininity, fair sex, womanhood, the world of women, the female of the species*.

womanhood *n.* adulthood, maturity, majority, womanliness, sexual prime, nubility, marriageable age, maidenhood, matronhood, spinsterhood.

womanly *a.* effeminate, ladylike, feminine, female, gentle, modest, compassionate, wifely, sisterly, motherly, protective, womanish, fair.—*Ant.* MANLY, virile, masculine.

womb *n.* uterus, female cavity, belly; see STOMACH.

won *a.* gained, achieved, conquered, taken, got, triumphed, overwhelmed.—*Ant.* BEATEN, lost, failed.

wonder *n.* **1.** [Amazement] surprise, awe, stupefaction, admiration, wonderment, astonishment, puzzlement, wondering, stupor, bewilderment, perplexity, fascination, consternation, perturbation, confusion, shock, start, jar, jolt, incredulity. **2.** [A marvel] miracle, curiosity, oddity, rarity, freak, phenomenon, sensation, prodigy, act of God, portent, wonderwork, spectacle, perversion, monstrous birth, prodigious event, something unnatural, the unbelievable.

wonder *v.* **1.** [To marvel] be surprised, be startled, be fascinated, be amazed, be dumbfounded, be confounded, be dazed, be awestruck, be astonished, be agape, be dazzled, stand aghast, be struck by, be unable to take one's eyes off, admire, gape, be taken aback, stare, be flabbergasted. **2.** [To question] be curious, query, hold in doubt; see ASK.

wonderful *a.* fine, enjoyable, pleasing; see PLEASANT 2.

wonderfully *a.* beautifully, admirably, excellently; see WELL 2.

wood *a.* wooden, made of wood, hard; see WOODEN.

wood *n.* **1.** [A forest; *often plural*] grove, woodland, timber; see FOREST. **2.** [The portion of trees within the bark] log, timber, lumber, sapwood, heartwood. *Varieties of wood include the following:* oak, chestnut, mahogany, sugar maple, red maple, cherry, cedar, walnut, hickory, butternut, hemlock, spruce, hornbeam, ebony, linden, beech, birch, poplar, tamarack, white pine, yellow pine, gumwood, elm, cypress, redwood, fir, Douglas fir, ash, red oak, live oak, white oak, willow, cottonwood, bamboo.

wooded *a.* timbered, forested, tree-covered, wild, tree-laden, treed, reforested, woody, jungly, having cover, timber-bearing, lumbering, uncut, not lumbered, not cut over, with standing timber, primeval, below the timberline, jungle-covered.

wooden *a.* wood, frame, frame-built, long-built, boarded, clapboarded, plank, built of slabs, pine, oak, elm, ash, mahogany.

woodwork *n.* molding, fittings, paneling, stairway, wood finishing, doors, window frames, sashes, jambs, wood trim.

wool *n.* fleece, lamb's wool, Angora wool, Shetland wool, glass wool, mineral wool, tweed, flannel, gabardine, worsted, woolen, suiting, serge, broadcloth, frieze, mohair, felt, blanketing, carpeting; see also GOODS 1.

word *n.* **1.** [A unit of expression] term, name, expression, designation, concept, vocable, utterance, sound, a voicing, form of speech, speech, locution, free morpheme, lexeme. *Classes of words include the following:* common noun, proper noun, personal pronoun, possessive pronoun, demonstrative pronoun, relative pronoun, interrogative pronoun, indefinite pronoun, definite article, indefinite article, transitive verb, intransitive verb, descriptive adjective, quantitative adjective, participial adjective, adverb, coordinating conjunction, subordinate conjunction, preposition, modifier, subject, predicate, root, primitive word, parent word, source word, synonym, antonym, etymon, cognative word, analogous word, derivative, slang, colloquialism, jargon, slang word, dialect word, provincialism, translation, native word, foreign word, idiom, connotative word, denotative word. **2.** [Promise] pledge, commitment, word of honor; see PROMISE 1. **3.** [Tidings] report, message, information; see NEWS 1. **—a good word** favorable comment, recommendation, support; see PRAISE 2. **—by word of mouth** orally, verbally, spoken; see ORAL. **—have words with** argue with, differ with, bicker; see ARGUE, FIGHT. **—in so many words** succinctly, cursorily, economically; see BRIEFLY. **—take at one's word** trust in, have confidence in, put one's trust in; see BELIEVE. **—the word** information, the facts, the lowdown*; see KNOWLEDGE 1.

word-for-word *a.* exactly, accurately, verbatim; see LITERALLY.

wordiness *n.* redundance, redundancy, diffuseness, circumlocution, repetition, verbiage, verbosity, bombast, tautology, indirectness, vicious circle, flow of words, rhetoric, copiousness, tediousness.—*Ant.* SILENCE, conciseness, succinctness.

wordy *a.* tedious, bombastic, long-winded; see DULL 4.

work *n.* **1.** [Something to be done] commitment, task, obligation; see JOB 2. **2.** [The doing of work] performance, endeavor, employment, production, occupation, practice, activity, manufacture, industry, operation, transaction, toil, labor, exertion, drudgery, functioning, stress, struggle, slavery, trial, push, attempt, effort, pains, elbow grease*, muscle*. **3.** [The result of labor; *often plural*] feat, accomplishment, output; see ACHIEVEMENT. **4.** [Occupation] profession, craft, business; see JOB 1. **—at work** working, on the job, engaged; see BUSY 1. **—in the works*** prepared for, budgeted, approved; see READY 2. **—make short** or **quick work of** finish off, deal with, dispose of; see DO 1. **—out of work** not hired, dismissed, looking for a job; see UNEMPLOYED.

work *v.* **1.** [To labor] toil, slave, sweat, do a day's work, do the chores, exert oneself, apply oneself, do one's best, overexert, overwork, overstrain, get to work, work overtime, work day and night, work one's way up, tax one's energies, pull, plod, tug, chore, struggle, strive, carry on, do the job, punch a time clock*, put in time, pour it on*, work one's fingers to the bone*, buckle down, bear down, work like a horse*, work like a dog, work like a slave, keep at it, stay with it, put one's shoulder to the wheel, burn the candle at both ends, burn the midnight oil. **2.** [To be employed] earn a living, have a job, hold a post, occupy a position, report for work, be off the welfare rolls, be among the employed, be on the job. **3.** [To function] go, run, serve; see OPERATE 2. **4.** [To handle successfully] control, accomplish, manage; see ACHIEVE, OPERATE 3. **5.** [To fashion] give form to, sculpture, mold; see FORM 1.

workable *a.* useful, practicable, functional; see WORKING 1.

work at *v.* attempt, endeavor, do one's best; see TRY 1.

worker *n.* laborer, toiler, mechanic; see WORKMAN.

work in *v.* introduce, find a place for, squeeze in; see INCLUDE 1.

working *a.* **1.** [Functioning] toiling, laboring, moving, in process, in good condition, in force, in gear, in collar, in exercise, going, twitching, effective, practical, on the job, never idle, on the fire. **2.** [Employed] with a job, engaged, on the staff; see BUSY 1.

workman *n.* operator, mechanic, machinist, craftsman, artist, artisan, technician, journeyman, master worker, handworker, skilled workman, white-collar worker, field workman. *Skilled workers include the following:* carpenter, cabinetmaker, upholsterer, paperhanger, plasterer, bricklayer, plumber, electrician, metalworker, locksmith, boilermaker, pipefitter, coppersmith, printer, pressman, linotype operator, glassworker, concrete worker, tiler, automobile mechanic, punch press operator, addressograph operator, multigraph operator, cost accountant, secretary, computer programmer, clerk, file clerk, stenographer, bookkeeper, salesman, packager, assembler, darkroom operator, photographer, proofreader, conductor, brakeman, locomotive engineer, fireman, barber, custodian, truck driver, bus driver, carpet installer, carpet cleaner, gardener, tree surgeon, seamstress, tailor, baker, butcher, farm worker, cowboy, dairyman, waiter, waitress, laundry worker, welder, drill operator, hydraulic press operator, diesinker, mason, lathe operator, gear-cutting machine operator, threading machine operator, telegrapher, teletype operator, operator, radio repairer, pattern builder, textile worker, tool designer, postal clerk, policeman, painter, galvanizer, draftsman, furrier, jewelry repairman, appliance repairman, TV repairman, cameraman, meat cutter, packer, medical technician, nurse's aide, dental hygienist.

workmanship *n.* craftsmanship, skill, quality of work, performance, handicraft, working ability, handiwork, achievement, manufacture, execution.

work on or **upon** *v.* try to encourage, use one's influence with, talk to; see INFLUENCE.

workout *n.* exercise, conditioning, gymnastics; see DISCIPLINE 2.

work out *v.* **1.** [To solve] come to terms, compromise, reach an agreement; see AGREE. **2.** [To satisfy a requirement] finish, do what is necessary, get something done; see ACHIEVE.

work over *v.* **1.** [To repair] fix up, go over, redo; see REPAIR, REPEAT 1. **2.** [*To beat or punish] thrash, beat up*, abuse; see BEAT 1, PUNISH.

works *n.pl.* **1.** [Working parts] cogs, belts, cams, wheels, gears, pistons, springs, coils, chains, rods, pulleys, wires; see also INSIDES. **2.** [*Punishment] beating, thrashing, wallop; see ABUSE, ATTACK 1. **3.** [*Everything] totality, entirety, the whole; see ALL, EVERYTHING.

world *n.* **1.** [The earth] globe, wide world, planet; see EARTH 1. **2.** [The universe] cosmos, nature, creation; see UNIVERSE. **3.** [A specific group] realm, division, system; see CLASS 1. **4.** [All one's surroundings] environment, atmosphere, childhood, adolescence, adulthood, experience, life, inner life, memory, idealization. **—bring into the world** give birth to, bear, have a baby; see PRODUCE 1. **—in the world** anywhere at all, wheresoever, in the universe; see ANYWHERE, WHEREVER. **—on top of the world** feeling fine, exuberant, successful; see HAPPY. **—out of this world** extraordinary, strange, remarkable; see UNUSUAL 1, 2.

worldly *a.* mundane, earthly, ungodly, practical, matter-of-fact, secular, strategic, grubbing, money-making, unprincipled, power-loving, self-centered, opportunistic, sophisticated, cosmopolitan, terrestrial, profane, human, natural, temporal.

worldwide *a.* global, universal, extensive; see GENERAL 1.

worm *n.* caterpillar, grub, larva, maggot, leech, parasite, helminth. *Common worms include the following:* angleworm, earthworm, threadworm, tapeworm, silkworm, flatworm, gordian worm, ribbon worm, marine worm, hookworm, pinworm, planarian, tubifex worm, horsehair worm, blindworm, slowworm, roundworm, annelid worm, cutworm, army worm, wireworm.

worm *v.* inch, creep, slink; see CRAWL, SNEAK.

worm out of *v.* evade, get out of, slip out of; see AVOID, ESCAPE.

worn *a.* **1.** [Used as clothing] carried, put on, donned, displayed, exhibited, used, sported*. **2.** [Showing signs of wear] frayed, threadbare, old, secondhand, ragged, shabby, impaired, used, consumed, deteriorated, torn, patched, the worse for wear.—*Ant.* FRESH, new, whole.

worn-out *a.* used up, gone, destroyed; see RUINED 1, 2, USELESS 1.

worried *a.* troubled, bothered, perturbed, vexed, distressed, miserable, annoyed, concerned, upset, suffering, torn, in conflict, pained, burdened, ill at ease, racking one's brains, uptight*, all hot and bothered*, anxious, hung up*.

worry *n.* **1.** [The state of anxiety] concern, anxiety, misery; see DISTRESS. **2.** [A cause of worry] problem, upset, disturbance; see FEAR, TROUBLE 1.

worry *v.* **1.** [To cause worry] annoy, trouble, bother; see DISTURB. **2.** [To indulge in worry] fret, chafe, grieve, take to heart, break one's heart, despair, stew, be anxious, worry oneself, have qualms, wince, agonize, writhe, suffer, turn gray with worry, become sick with worry, sweat out*; see also BOTHER 1.

worse *a.* more evil, not so good, deteriorated; see POOR 2.

worship *n.* **1.** [Adoration] prayer, devotion, homage, adulation, benediction, invocation, supplication, beatification, veneration, offering, burnt offering, reverence, honor, religious ritual. **2.** [A religious service] Mass, services, devotions; see CHURCH 2.

worship *v.* sanctify, pray to, invoke, venerate, glorify, praise, exalt, offer one's prayers to, pay homage to, recite the rosary, give thanks, offer thanks to, sing praises to, reverence, celebrate, adore, revere, laud, extol, magnify, chant, sing, bow down, canonize; see also PRAY 2.

worshiper *n.* churchgoer, communicant, pilgrim, supplicant, devotee, devotionalist, adorer, pietist, pious person, devout person, celebrant, saint, priest, priestess.—*Ant.* SKEPTIC, atheist, agnostic.

worst *a.* most terrible, most harmful, most lethal, poorest, lowest, least, most ghastly, most horrible, most pitiful, least meaningful, meanest, least understanding, least effective.

worst *n.* calamity, catastrophe, ruin; see DESTRUCTION 2. **—at worst** under the worst possible circumstances, unluckily, grievously; see BADLY 1, UNFORTUNATELY. **—(in) the worst way** unluckily, disastrously, horribly; see UNFORTUNATELY.

worth *a.* deserving, meriting, equal in value to, priced at, exchangeable for, valued at, worth in the open market, pegged at, cashable for, good for, appraised at, having a face value of, reasonably estimated at, bid at, held at. **—for all one is worth** greatly, mightily, hard; see POWERFULLY.

worth *n.* goodness, value, quality, character, importance, significance, meaning, estimation, benefit, excellence, merit; see also VALUE 1, 3.

worthless *a.* profitless, counterproductive, barren, unprofitable, unproductive, unimportant, insignificant, counterfeit, bogus, cheap, sterile, waste, wasted, no good, trashy, inconsequential, petty, piddling, paltry, trivial, trifling, unessential, beneath notice, empty, good-for-nothing, no-account*, not worth a damn*, not worth the trouble*, not worth speaking of*, not able to say much for*.

worthlessness *n.* uselessness, impracticality, inefficiency; see WASTE 1.

worthwhile *a.* good, serviceable, useful, important, profitable, valuable, remunerative, estimable, worthy, helpful, beneficial, meritorious, excellent, rewarding, praiseworthy.

worthy *a.* good, true, honest, honorable, reliable, trustworthy, dependable, noble, charitable, dutiful, philanthropic, virtuous, moral, pure, upright, righteous, decent, incorruptible, meritorious, creditable, deserving, right-minded, worthy of, model, exemplary, sterling, sinless, stainless, blameless.—*Ant.* WORTHLESS, bad, evil.

would-be *a.* anticipated, assuming, supposed; see HOPEFUL 1.

wound *a.* twisted, coiled, wrapped; see WOVEN.

wound *n.* bruise, hurt, scar; see INJURY.

wound *v.* **1.** [To hurt the body] gash, scrape, injure; see HURT 1. **2.** [To hurt the feelings] trouble, upset, pain; see BOTHER 2, DISTURB.

wounded *a.* injured, hurt, disabled, stabbed, cut, shot, scratched, bitten, gashed, hit, beaten, attacked, winged, nicked.

woven *a.* spun, interlinked, netted, netlike, dovetailed, wreathed, sewn, intertwined, united, interlaced, interwoven, worked into.

wow* *v.* triumph, overcome, be a success; see DEFEAT 2, 3.

wrap *v.* roll up, swathe, muffle, bind, fold about, encircle, coil, enclose, swaddle, bandage, envelop, enwrap, protect, encase, sheathe, cover up, shelter, clothe, cover with paper, enclose in a box.—*Ant.* UNWRAP, unsheathe, open up.

wrapped *a.* covered, sheathed, swaddled, swathed, enclosed, papered, protected, enveloped, encased, shrouded, concealed, hidden, clothed, done up.—*Ant.* OPEN, unwrapped, uncovered.

wrapped up in *a.* in love with, devoted to, affectionate; see LOVING.

wrapper *n.* envelope, folder, book cover; see COVER 1.

wrap up* *v.* finish off, bring to an end, polish off*; see COMPLETE.

wrath *n.* fury, vengeance, madness; see ANGER.

wreck *n.* **1.** [Anything wrecked] junk, ruins, skeleton, hulk, stubble, collapse, bones, scattered parts, rattletrap, relic, litter, pieces, shreds, waste, wreckage, debris. **2.** [A person in poor physical condition] incurable, invalid, consumptive, nervous case, overworked person, cripple, mess*, goner*, washout*, shadow, skin-and-bones*, walking nightmare*.

wreck *v.* spoil, ruin, destroy, disfigure, mangle, smash, tear down, break, split, efface, batter, torpedo, tear to pieces, put out of order, impair, injure, bash in, mess up, play hell with*, put out of commission.—*Ant.* REPAIR, restore, rebuild.

wreckage *n.* remains, ruins, hulk, remnants; see also WRECK 1.

wrecked *a.* demolished, destroyed, broken up, knocked to pieces, ruined, smashed to bits, shipwrecked, stranded, beached, grounded, scuttled, capsized, put out of order, blown to bits, junked, dismantled, shattered, on the rocks*, gone to pot, shot to hell*.

wrench *n.* **1.** [A violent twist] jerk, strain, sprain, tug, pull, dislodgement, extrication, dislocation. **2.** [A spanner] *Wrenches include the following:* monkey, single-head, double-head, pipe, Stillson, crescent, spark-plug, hubcap, flat, S-socket, bearing, connecting-rod; see also TOOL 1.

wrench *v.* twist, strain, distort; see BEND.

wrestle *v.* grapple, struggle with, contend with, perform in a wrestling bout, wrassle*, tangle*, tussle; see also FIGHT.

wrestling *n.* contention, grappling, bout; see FIGHT 1.

wretched *a.* **1.** [Afflicted] distressed, woeful, sorrowful; see SAD 1. **2.** [Poor in quality] weak, faulty, cheap; see POOR 2.

wring *v.* squeeze out, compress, press; see TWIST.

wrinkle *n.* crease, furrow, crinkle, ridge, fold, corrugation, line, crow's foot, pucker, pleat.

wrinkle *v.* rumple, crease, furrow, screw up, pucker, twist, crumple, compress, crinkle.—*Ant.* STRAIGHTEN, smooth out, iron.

wrinkled *a.* creased, rumpled, furrowed, puckered, warped, twisted, crumpled, crinkled, dried up, withered, unironed, unpressed, shrivelled.—*Ant.* SMOOTH, ironed, pressed.

write *v.* **1.** [To compose in words] set forth, record, formulate, draft, turn out, give a report, note down, transcribe, pen, put in writing, comment upon, go into, typewrite, communicate, rewrite, produce fiction, do imaginative writings, correspond, scribble. **2.** [To set down in writing] inscribe, sign, scrawl, address, print, letter, autograph, reproduce, dash off, put in black and white. —**write off** charge off, take a loss on, recognize as a bad debt; see LOSE 2. —**write up** expand, work up, deal at length with; see WRITE 1, 2.

writer *n.* author, journalist, reporter, newspaperman, magazine writer, contributor, poet, novelist, essayist, biographer, dramatist, playwright, literary critic, foreign correspondent, feature writer, sports writer, fashion writer, shorthand writer, stenographer, anecdotist, amanuensis, ghostwriter, songwriter, copyist, scribe, editor, contributing editor, war correspondent, special writer, freelance writer, representative, member of the Fourth Estate, scribbler, pen pusher*, hack, newshound*. *Major writers include the following— British:* Henry Fielding, Sir Walter Scott, Charlotte Brontë, George Eliot, Jane Austen, Charles Dickens, Thomas Hardy, D.H. Lawrence, James Joyce, Joseph Conrad, Samuel Beckett, George Orwell, Virginia Woolf; *American:* James Fenimore Cooper, Edgar Allan Poe, Ralph Waldo Emerson, Henry David Thoreau, Nathaniel Hawthorne, Herman Melville, Samuel Langhorne Clemens (Mark Twain), Henry James, Stephen Crane, Theodore Dreiser, William Faulkner, John Steinbeck, Ernest Hemingway, F. Scott Fitzgerald, Norman Mailer, Saul Bellow, Edith Wharton, Flannery O'Connor; *French:* (François-Marie Arouet de) Voltaire, Jean Jacques Rousseau, Victor Hugo, Honoré de Balzac, Gustave Flaubert, Alexandre Dumas, Jules Verne, Albert Camus, André Malraux; *Italian:* Niccolo Machiavelli, Giovanni Boccaccio, Alessandro Manzoni, Ignazio Silone; *German:* Thomas Mann, Franz Kafka, Günter Grass; *Russian:* Fyodor Dostoevsky, Leo Tolstoy, Ivan Turgenev, Anton Chekhov, Boris Pasternak; *Spanish:* Miguel de Cervantes, Jorge Luis Borges; *Yiddish:* I.B. Singer.

write-up* *n.* report, account, publicity; see WRITING 2.

writhe *v.* contort, move painfully, squirm, distort, suffer, twist and turn, undergo agony, turn with pain, throw a fit*.—*Ant.* REST, be at ease, move easily.

writing *n.* 1. [The practice of writing] transcribing, inscribing, reporting, corresponding, letter-writing, copying, typewriting, penmanship, lettering, printing, graphology, signing, autographing, stenography. 2. [Anything written] literature, written matter, document, composition, article, poem, prose, paper, theme, editorial, discourse, essay, thesis, dissertation, book, manuscript, novel, play, literary production, scenario, drama, piece, work, signature, letter, pamphlet, tract, treatise, disquisition, comment, commentary, review, recitation, certificate, record, bill, bit*, item, piece. 3. [The occupation of a writer] journalism, reporting, literature, authorship, freelance writing, professional writing, auctorial pursuits, the pen, the Fourth Estate, creative writing; novel-writing, verse-writing, feature-writing, etc.; newspaper work, the writers' craft, pencil-pushing, hack writing, writing for the slicks*, ghostwriting.

written *a.* 1. [Composed] set forth, authored, penned, drawn up, reported, signed, turned out, fictionalized, arranged, rearranged, adapted, ghostwritten, recorded, dictated. 2. [Inscribed] copied, scriptural, transcribed, printed, lettered, autographed, signed, put in writing, in black and white, under one's hand.

wrong *a.* 1. [Immoral] evil, sinful, wicked, naughty, salacious, base, indecent, risqué, blasphemous, ungodly, amoral, dissolute, dissipated, wanton, profane, sacrilegious, depraved, corrupt, profligate, shady*, low-down*, smutty.—*Ant.* GOOD, righteous, virtuous. 2. [Inaccurate] inexact, erroneous, mistaken, in error, incorrect, fallacious, untrue, erring, astray, amiss, ungrounded, spurious, unsubstantial, unsound, erratic, deceiving oneself, in the wrong, under an error, beside the mark, laboring under a false impression, out of line, at fault, to no purpose, not right, awry, faulty, mishandled, miscalculated, misfigured, misconstructed, misconstrued, mismade, altered, not precise, perverse, wide of the mark, not according to the facts, badly estimated, a mile off*, all off, crazy*. 3. [Inappropriate] unfitted, disproportionate, ill-fitting; see IMPROPER.

wrong *n.* vice, sin, misdemeanor, crime, immorality, indecency, transgression, unfairness, imposition, oppression, foul play, prejudice, bias, favor, unlawful practice, villainy, delinquency, error, miscarriage, mistake, blunder, offense, wrongdoing, violation, tort, hurt, persecution, malevolence, cruelty, libel, abuse, harm, damage, spite, slander, false report, slight, misusage, outrage, inhumanity, overpresumption, insult, discourtesy, raw deal*, bum steer*, dirt.—*Ant.* KINDNESS, good deed, consideration.

wrong *v.* hurt, oppress, defame; see ABUSE.

wrongdoer *n.* lawbreaker, rogue, fugitive; see CRIMINAL.

wrongly *a.* unfairly, prejudicially, wrongfully, partially, badly, unjustifiably, illegally, disgracefully, sinfully, unreasonably, unlawfully, criminally, inexcusably, unsuitably, improperly, awkwardly, incongruously, incorrectly, unbecomingly, indecorously, out of the question, imprudently, rashly, unnaturally, illogically; see also INADEQUATELY.—*Ant.* APPROPRIATELY, tastefully, prudently.

wrung *a.* twisted, squeezed out, pressed; see TWISTED 1.

x *n.* unknown quantity, unknown, y; see QUANTITY.

Xmas *n.* the Nativity, Christmas holiday, Yule; see HOLIDAY.

X-rays *n.pl.* Roentgen rays, radioactivity, radium emanation, actinic rays, actinism, encephalogram, CAT scan, ultraviolet rays, refractometry, radiant energy, cathode rays; see also ENERGY 2, RAY.

xylophone *n.* carillon, vibraphone, vibes*, glockenspiel, marimba; see also MUSICAL INSTRUMENT.

Y

yacht *n.* pleasure boat, sloop, racing boat; see BOAT, SHIP.

yammer *v.* nag, whine, whimper; see COMPLAIN.

yank *n.* twitch, jerk, wrench; see JERK 1.

yank* *v.* haul, tug, drag, jiggle, jerk*, flip, wrench, twitch; see also DRAW 1, PULL 2.

Yank* *n.* American, soldier, Yankee, doughboy*, GI Joe*.

Yankee *a.* **1.** [Having New England qualities] homespun, individualistic, conservative; see MODERATE 3, 4, 5, PRACTICAL. **2.** [Concerning the United States] North American, Western, Americanized; see AMERICAN.

Yankee *n.* **1.** [A New Englander] Northerner, Easterner, early settler, Abolitionist, Unionist. **2.** [A person from the United States] American, American citizen, North American, westerner, Occidental, Yank*.

yap* *v.* jabber, rant, chatter; see BABBLE, TALK 1.

yard *n.* **1.** [An enclosure, usually about a building] court, courtyard, barnyard, back yard, corral, fold, patch, patio, terrace, play area, lawn, grass, garden, clearing, quadrangle, lot; see also PLAYGROUND. **2.** [An enclosure for work] brickyard, coalyard, junkyard, navy yard, dockyard, railroad yard, stockyard, lumberyard. **3.** [Tracks for making up trains; *often plural*] railroad yard, switchyard, railway yard, marshalling yard, terminal. **4.** [A unit of measurement] three feet, pace, step, arm-span, thirty-six inches; see also MEASURE 1.

yardstick *n.* **1.** [A rule three feet long] thirty-six-inch ruler, measuring stick, molding rule, yard, yard measure; see also RULER 2. **2.** [A unit for comparison] criterion, basis for judgment, standard; see MEASURE 2.

yarn *n.* **1.** [Spun fiber] spun wool, twist, flaxen thread, cotton fiber, rug yarn, crochet thread, knitting yarn, alpaca yarn; see also FIBER. **2.** [A tale] anecdote, sea story, adventure story, fictional account; see also STORY. **3.** [A lie] fabrication, tall story, alibi, fish story*, cock-and-bull story*; see also LIE.

yawn *v.* **1.** [To open wide] gape, split open, spread out; see DIVIDE, GROW 1. **2.** [To give evidence of drowsiness] gape, be sleepy, make a yawning sound, show weariness; see also SLEEP, TIRE 1.

yea *interj.* okay, aye, well; see YES.

year *n.* twelve months, annual cycle, continuum of days; see AGE 3, TIME 1, 2. *Kinds of years include the following:* civil, legal, calendar, lunar, solar, astronomical, natural, sidereal, tropical, equinoctial, leap, school, fiscal.

year after year *a.* year by year, annually; year in, year out; see also YEARLY.

yearbook *n.* annual, almanac, yearly report; see CATALOG, RECORD 1.

yearling *n.* suckling, nursling, weanling; see ANIMAL, BABY.

yearly *a.* annually, once a year, every winter, every spring, every summer, every autumn, year by year; see also REGULARLY.

yearn *v.* want, crave, long for, fret, chafe, grieve, mourn, droop, pine, languish, be eager for, be desirous of, be ardent, be fervent, be passionate, wish for, thirst for, hunger for, aspire to, set one's heart upon, hanker for, have a yen for*; see also TRY 1.—*Ant.* AVOID, be content, be indifferent.

yearning *n.* want, longing, craving; see DESIRE 1, WISH.

years *n.pl.* agedness, oldness, senescense; see AGE 2.

yell *n.* **1.** [A shout] bellow, cry, yelp, roar, whoop, howl, screech, shriek, squeal, holler*, hoot, yawp*, hubbub, hullabaloo, hue and cry, protest; see also NOISE 1. 2. **2.** [Organized cheering] hip-hip-hurrah, rooting, cheer; see ENCOURAGEMENT.

yell *v.* bellow, cry out, scream, shout, yelp, yap, bawl, roar, halloo, vociferate, whoop, howl, screech, shriek, shrill, squeal, squall, yammer, hoot, cheer, call, yip, give encouragement, call down, raise one's voice, holler, whoop it up; see also SOUND.

yelling *a.* boisterous, clamorous, noisy, bawling, uproarious, turbulent, drunken, aroused, riotous, cantankerous, blatant, vociferous; see also HARSH, LOUD 2.—*Ant.* QUIET, subdued, silent.

yelling *n.* cry, scream, shout, outcry, vociferation, screeching, bawling, yowling, bellowing, howling, yelping; see also NOISE 1, 2, YELL.

yellow *n. Tints and shades of yellow include the following:* cream color, ivory color, old ivory, ivory-yellow, tan, lemon color, orange-yellow, saffron, jasmine, tawny, sand, gold, sallow, buff, brilliant yellow, chrome yellow, Dutch pink-yellow, Dutch yellow, golden yellow, Imperial yellow, platinum yellow, yellow carmine, yellow madder, yellow ocher; see also COLOR, GOLD.

yellow *a.* **1.** [Having a yellowish color] yellowish, golden, jaundiced-looking. **2.** [*Cowardly] tricky, deceitful, low, cringing, sneaking, white-livered, craven, treacherous; see also COWARDLY, VULGAR. **3.** [Sensational; *said especially of some newspapers*] tabloid, unethical, unprincipled; see EXCITING, OFFENSIVE 2.

yelp *v.* howl, screech, hoot; see CRY 2, SOUND.

yen* *n.* longing, craving, hunger; see DESIRE 1.

yes *interj.* surely, of course, certainly, good, fine, aye, true, granted, very well, all right, OK*, okay*, oke*, okey-dokey*, Roger, we copy, over to you, most assuredly, by all means, agreed, oh yes!, amen, naturally, without fail, just so, good enough, even so, in the affirmative, you bet*.

yesterday *a.* recently, previously, earlier; see BEFORE.

yesterday *n.* the other day, the day before, recently, last day, not long ago; see also PAST 1.

yet *a.* **1.** [Nevertheless] notwithstanding, however, in spite of, despite, still, but, though, although, at any rate, on the other hand. **2.** [Thus far] until now, till, hitherto, prior to, still; see also UNTIL. **3.** [In addition] besides, additionally, further; see BESIDES.

yield *v.* **1.** [To surrender] give up, capitulate, succumb, resign, abdicate, relinquish, quit, cede, bow, lay down arms, cease from, let go, submit, give oneself over, relent, admit defeat, suffer defeat, forgo, humble oneself, waive, throw in the towel*, call quits*, back down*, holler uncle*, eat crow*; see also ABANDON 1.—*Ant.* RESIST, withstand, repulse. **2.** [To produce] bear, bring forth, blossom; see BLOOM, PRODUCE 1, 2. **3.** [To grant] accede, concur, acquiesce; see ADMIT 2, AGREE.

yielding *a.* **1.** [Producing] green, fruitful, productive; see FERTILE, RICH 3. **2.** [Flexible] pliant, plastic, malleable; see FLEXIBLE. **3.** [Docile] submissive, pliable, tractable; see HUMBLE 1, OBEDIENT 1.

yogi *n.* mystic, fakir, anchorite, ascetic, practitioner of yoga, guru, devotee.

yokel *n.* rustic, bumpkin, hayseed; see BOOR.

yolk *n.* yellow, egg-yellow, egg yolk; see CENTER 1, EGG.

yonder *a.* farther, away, faraway; see DISTANT, REMOTE 1.

you *pron.* yourself, you yourself, thee, thou, all of you, you too, you alone, you all*.

young *a.* **1.** [In the early portion of life] puerile, boyish, girlish, adolescent, juvenile, budding, in one's teen's, childlike, youthful, pubescent, boylike, girllike, new-fledged, blooming, burgeoning, childish, half-grown, growing, blossoming, at the breast, babe in arms, knee high to a grasshopper.—*Ant.* OLD, aged, senile. **2.** [Inexperienced] callow, green, immature, tender, raw, untutored, unlearned, junior, subordinate, inferior, unfledged, ignorant, undisciplined, tenderfoot, not dry behind the ears; see also INEXPERIENCED, NAIVE.—*Ant.* EXPERIENCED, veteran, expert. **3.** [New] fresh, modern, recent, newborn; see also FASHIONABLE.

youngster *n.* child, boy, girl, pupil; see also YOUTH 3.

you're welcome *interj.* my pleasure, forget it, think nothing of it, don't mention it, it's nothing.

youth *n.* **1.** [The state or quality of being young] boyhood, adolescence, girlhood, childhood, early manhood, early adulthood, puberty, tender age, minority, youthfulness, teen age, virginity, bloom, teens, age of ignorance, age of indiscretion, awkward age, salad days.—*Ant.* MATURITY, old age, senility. **2.** [Young people] the younger generation, the rising generation, the next generation, children, the young, college youth, working youth. **3.** [A young person] boy, junior, teenager, lad, youngster, stripling, minor, young man, miss, girl, maiden, fledgling, juvenile, urchin, adolescent, student, kid*, teen, pre-teen, gosling, pup, calf; see also CHILD.

youthful *a.* **1.** [Possessing youth] young, childlike, adolescent; see ACTIVE, YOUNG 1, 2. **2.** [Suited to youth] keen, enthusiastic, zestful, vigorous, active, buoyant, lighthearted, prankish, fresh, lithe, full-blooded, full of life, full of animal spirits, limber, athletic, lightfooted, bubbling over, full of the devil; see also MODERN 1.—*Ant.* SLOW, cautious, serious.

yowl *n.* howl, yelp, wail; see CRY 1, YELL 1.

yule *n.* Christmas, Xmas, Nativity, Christmas season, Christmastide.

Z

zeal *n.* **1.** [Enthusiasm] ardor, eagerness, fervor, enthusiasm. **2.** [Industry] earnestness, hustle, hustling, bustle, bustling, intensity, industry, willingness, inclination, application, determination, promptitude, dispatch, diligence, perseverance, intentness, readiness, aptitude, enterprise, initiative, push*, what it takes*, stick-to-itiveness*; see also ATTENTION, CARE 1, COOPERATION.—*Ant.* IDLENESS, slackness, indolence.

zealot *n.* partisan, fan, bigot, fanatic, lobbyist, devotee, dogmatist, opinionist, missionary, fighter, cultist, follower, disciple, propagandist, bitter-ender*, crank*, addict, bug*, faddist, fiend.

zealous *a.* fervent, earnest, intense, fanatic, industrious, diligent, intent, dogmatic, devoted, ardent; see also ENTHUSIASTIC.

zealously *a.* with zeal, assiduously, fiercely; see INDUSTRIOUSLY, VIGOROUSLY.

zero *n.* **1.** [A cipher] naught, nothing, nadir, love, below freezing, the lowest point, goose egg*, nix*. **2.** [Nothing] nullity, oblivion, void; see BLANK 1.

zest *n.* **1.** [Relish] gusto, enjoyment, pleasure; see HAPPINESS. **2.** [Savor] taste, tang, piquancy, spice, bite, nip, pungency, punch, snap, ginger, kick, guts, body; see also FLAVOR.

zigzag *a.* oblique, inclined, sloping, awry, crooked, sinuous, twisted, askew, transverse, diagonal, curved, bent, crinkled, serrated, jagged, straggling, meandering, devious, erratic, rambling, oscillating, fluctuating, waggling, undulatory, vibratory, indirect, spiral, tortuous; see also ANGULAR, IRREGULAR 4.—*Ant.* STRAIGHT, parallel, undeviating.

zip* *n.* energy, vigor, vim; see STRENGTH.

zip* *v.* run, dash, rush; see RUN 2.

zodiac *n.* celestial meridian, signs of the zodiac, sky signs, groups of stars, constellations; see also PLANET, STAR 1. *The twelve signs of the zodiac are as follows:* Aquarius or Water Bearer, Pisces or Fish, Aries or Ram, Taurus or Bull, Gemini or Twins, Cancer or Crab, Leo or Lion, Virgo or Virgin, Libra or Scales, Scorpio or Scorpion, Sagittarius or Archer, Capricorn or Goat.

zone *n.* **1.** [A band] circuit, meridian, latitude; see BAND 1, STRIPE. **2.** [An area] region, district, territory; see PLACE 3, POSITION 1. *Specific zones include the following:* Torrid, Frigid, Temperate, Variable, Canal, traffic, parking, danger, building, quiet, school; Tropic of Cancer, Tropic of Capricorn, Arctic Circle, Antarctic Circle.

zoo *n.* menagerie, terrarium, aquarium, aviary, vivarium, zoological garden.

zoological *a.* animal, mammalian, marsupial, zoologic, mammalogical, ornithological, herpetological, ichthyological, ascidiological, echinological, conchological, entomological, arachnological, crustaceological, zoophytological, spongiological, protozoological, helminthological; see also ALIVE, BIOLOGICAL.

zoology *n.* life science, biological science, natural history; see LIFE 1, SCIENCE.

zoom *v.* speed, rush, hum; see CLIMB, HURRY 1, RISE 1.

SYNONYMIES

The following paragraphs, listing and discriminating groups of closely related terms, are arranged alphabetically under those words which may generally be considered the most basic or comprehensive for each group. Although synonyms have similar, sometimes virtually identical, meanings in isolation, they are not always interchangeable with one another in every context. The subtle differences that distinguish such synonyms are briefly stated here, and typical examples of usage are given where they may be helpful. Note that although a term may have multiple meanings, only the relevant meaning is discussed within a given synonymy.

able implies power or ability to do something [*able* to make payments] but sometimes suggests special power or skill [an *able* speaker]; **capable** usually implies that only ordinary requirements are met [a *capable* machinist]; **competent** and **qualified** both imply that the necessary qualifications for something are met, but qualified emphasizes that certain specified requirements are complied with [a *competent* critic of modern art; a *qualified* voter]

abridgment describes a work that is shortened from a larger work, but that keeps the main contents more or less unchanged; an **abstract** is a short statement of the main contents as of a court record or a technical writing; a **summary** usually restates the main points of the matter that has gone before; a **synopsis** is a condensed, orderly treatment, as of the plot of a novel; a **digest** is a concise, systematic treatment, generally broader in scope than a synopsis

absurd means so inconsistent with what is judged as reasonable or true as to be laughable [an *absurd* hypothesis]; **ludicrous** is applied to what is so incongruous or exaggerated as to be laughable [a *ludicrous* facial expression]; **preposterous** is used to describe anything extremely absurd or ludicrous; **foolish** describes that which shows lack of good judgment or of common sense [I don't take *foolish* chances]; **ridiculous** applies to whatever causes amusement or contempt because of its extreme foolishness

adjacent things may or may not be in actual contact with each other, but they are not separated by things of the same kind [*adjacent* angles; *adjacent* buildings]; that which is **adjoining** something else touches it at some point or along some line [*adjoining* rooms]; things are **contiguous** when they touch along the whole or most of one side [*contiguous* lots]; **tangent** implies contact at a single point on a curved line or surface [a line *tangent* to a circle]

agile and **nimble** both imply quickness and lightness of movement, but **agile** stresses general skill and ease in the use of the limbs, while **nimble** suggests quick sureness in carrying out a particular act [*nimble* fingers at the keyboard]; **quick** implies speed or promptness with no indication of the degree of skill; **spry** suggests nimbleness, esp. as displayed by a vigorous, elderly person; **sprightly** suggests liveliness, gaiety, etc.

agree is the general term used to express a fitting or going together without conflict; **conform** emphasizes agreement in form or basic character [specifications must *conform* to the building code]; **accord** emphasizes fitness for each other of the things being considered together [his story does not *accord* with the facts]; **harmonize** implies a combining of different things in an orderly or pleasing arrangement [*harmonizing* colors]; **correspond** is applied to that which matches, complements, or is comparable to something else [their Foreign Office *corresponds* to our State Department]: **coincide** stresses that the things being considered are identical [their interests *coincide*]

amiable and **affable** both suggest friendliness and an easygoing temperament that makes one likeable, **affable** also implying a readiness to talk and be sociable; a **good-natured** person is one who tends to like others as well as to be liked by them, and is sometimes easily imposed on; **obliging** implies a ready, often cheerful, desire to be helpful [the *obliging* clerk answered my questions]; **genial** suggests cheerful sociability [our *genial* host]; **cordial** suggests sincerity and warmth [a *cordial* welcome]

appreciate implies enough understanding and judgment to see the value or to enjoy [he *appreciates* good music]; to **value** is to rate highly because of worth [I *value* your friendship]; to **prize** is to think highly of or take great satisfaction in [he *prizes* his art collection]; to **treasure** is to regard as precious and implies special care and protection; to **esteem** is to hold in high regard or respect [an *esteemed* statesman]; to **cherish** is to prize or treasure, but connotes greater affection for the thing cherished [he *cherished* his family]

argument refers to a discussion in which there is disagreement and suggests the use of reasoning and the bringing forth of facts to support or disprove a point; **dispute** basically refers to a disagreement involving debate in which there is strong feeling or anger [an international boundary *dispute*]; **controversy** suggests a disagreement that lasts a long time and has to do with a matter of some importance [the continuing *controversy* over some of Freud's theories]

avenge and **revenge** both refer to the inflicting of punishment for a wrong done, but **avenge** suggests that the motive is a wish to see justice done, whereas **revenge** implies that one wishes to get even, usually for an injury against oneself, and suggests bitter feelings of hatred and resentment

banish means to force to leave a country (not necessarily one's own) as a punishment; **exile** implies being forced to leave one's own country, either because the government has ordered it or events have made it necessary; **expatriate** suggests more strongly exile by one's own choice and often implies the getting of citizenship in another country; to **deport** is to send (an alien) out of the country, either because he entered unlawfully or because he is considered undesirable

base implies a putting of one's own interests ahead of all else, as because of greed or cowardice [*base* motives]; **mean** suggests a pettiness of character or conduct [his *mean* attempts to slander her]; **ignoble** suggests a lack of high moral qualities [to work for an *ignoble* end]; **abject** implies lowness of character and a lack of self-respect [an *abject* coward]; **sordid** suggests a depressing drabness of something mean or base [the *sordid* details of their scam]; **vile** is a somewhat archaic term suggesting disgusting foulness or wickedness [**vile** conduct, a **vile** wretch]; **low** suggests coarseness and corruption, esp. in reference to taking unfair advantage [so *low* as to rob the poor]

beautiful is applied to that which gives the most pleasure and suggests that the thing that delights one comes close to one's ideal; **lovely** refers to that which delights by causing one to feel affection or warm admiration; **handsome** is used of that which attracts by its pleasing proportions, elegance, etc. and in certain contexts suggests a masculine quality; **pretty** implies daintiness or gracefulness and often suggests a feminine quality; **comely** applies to persons only and suggests a wholesome attractiveness rather than great beauty; **fair** suggests beauty, esp. of complexion or features, that is fresh, bright, or perfect; **good-looking** generally equals either **handsome** or **pretty**; **beauteous**, a poetic synonym for **beautiful**, is now often used in a joking or belittling way

belief is the general term for the acceptance of something as true, even without being completely certain; **faith** implies complete acceptance, even without proof and, esp., of something not supported by reason; **trust** implies assurance, often based on intuition, that someone or something is reliable; **confidence** also suggests such assurance, esp. when based on reason or proof

belligerent implies a taking part in war or fighting or in warlike actions [*belligerent* nations]; **bellicose** implies a warlike nature, suggesting a readiness to fight [a *bellicose* mood]; **pugnacious** and **quarrelsome** both suggest eagerness to start a fight, but **quarrelsome** more often suggests willingness to fight for no good reason; **contentious** suggests a readiness to keep on arguing or quarreling in an annoying way

bodily refers to the human body as apart from the mind or spirit [*bodily* organs]; **physical** is often used like **bodily**, but may suggest less directly the organs or parts, etc. of the body [*physical* labor]; **corporeal** refers to the matter that makes up the body and is opposed to *spiritual* [his *corporeal* remains]; **corporal** refers to the effect of something upon the body [*corporal* punishment]; **somatic** is the word used, as in a scientific description, to refer to the body as distinct from the mind [the *somatic* differences between individuals]

bright implies in a general way the giving forth or reflecting of light, or a being filled with light [a *bright* day, star, shield, etc.]; **radiant** emphasizes the sending out of rays of light; **shining** implies a steady, continuous brightness [the *shining* sun]; **brilliant** implies strong or flashing brightness [*brilliant* sunlight, diamonds, etc.]; **luminous** is used of objects that are full of light or give off phosphorescent light; **lustrous** is used of objects whose surfaces gleam by reflected light and suggests glossiness [*lustrous* silk]

bulk, mass, and **volume** all refer to a quantity of matter or number of units making up a whole; **bulk** implies a body of great size, weight, or numbers [the lumbering *bulk* of an elephant; the *bulk* of humanity]; **mass** suggests a group or number of parts forming a single, unified body [an egg-shaped *mass*; the *mass* of workers]; **volume** implies a moving or flowing mass, often one that keeps changing [*volumes* of smoke; the *volume* of production]

calm, basically applied to the weather, suggests a lack of movement or excitement [a *calm* sea; a *calm* reply]; **tranquil** implies a deeper or more permanent peace and quiet than calm [a *tranquil* old age]; **serene** suggests a dignified tranquillity, as of a person who is at peace with himself; **placid** implies total calmness, often to the point of being dull and uninteresting [leading a *placid* existence]; **peaceful** suggests freedom from disorder or from a show of strong feeling [a *peaceful* gathering]

caricature refers to an imitation or drawing of a person, as in a cartoon, that exaggerates outstanding features in a comical way; **burlesque** implies the handling of a serious subject in a light and flippant way or of a trivial subject in a way that pretends to be serious; a **parody** imitates the style of a writer or some writing very closely, but makes fun of it by using an absurd subject or a nonsensical approach; a **travesty**, on the other hand, deals with the same subject as the original but in a ridiculous style or laughable language; **satire** refers to a literary composition or play, etc. in which follies, vices, stupidities, and abuses in life are held up to ridicule and contempt

cause refers to something that produces an effect or result [carelessness is often a *cause* of accidents]; **reason** implies thinking that is engaged in to explain some act or idea [she had a *reason* for laughing]; a **motive** is a thought, emotion, or desire that leads to action [the *motive* for the crime]; an **antecedent** is an event or thing that comes before, and is responsible for, a later event or thing [war always has its *antecedents*]; an **occasion** is a situation or event that allows a cause to have an effect [the court case was an *occasion* for stating a new legal principle]

cheat implies the use of dishonesty in dealing with someone, in order to get some advantage or gain; **defraud** stresses the use of deliberate deception in taking away a person's rights, property, etc. in a way that is against the law; **swindle** stresses the winning of a person's trust in order to cheat or defraud him of money, etc.; **trick** implies the use of a clever scheme or device to mislead someone, but does not necessarily suggest dishonesty; **dupe** suggests the tricking of someone who is foolish and too willing to trust others; **hoax** implies the use of a complicated scheme to dupe others, often simply in fun

childlike and **childish** are both applied to persons of any age in referring to qualities considered typical of a child, **childlike** suggesting the favorable qualities such as innocence, honesty, curiosity, zest, etc., and **childish** the unfavorable ones such as immaturity, foolishness, lack of self-control, self-centeredness, etc.

clever implies a quickness of mind or wit, as in solving a problem, in conversation, etc. [a *clever* idea; a *clever* reply]; **cunning** implies cleverness of a sly, tricky, or crafty kind [a *cunning* thief]; **ingenious** suggests cleverness in thinking up or inventing something [an *ingenious* explanation; an *ingenious* designer]; **shrewd** suggests cleverness or sharpness in dealing with practical matters [a *shrewd* analysis: a *shrewd* bargainer]

comfort suggests any attempt to make someone less sorrowful or unhappy as by trying to cheer him up or inspire him with hope: **console** suggests the offering of help or relief to someone who has lost someone or something or has been disappointed [to *console* someone whose best friend has died]: **solace** suggests any thing or any action that makes a person less sad. depressed. bored. lonely. etc. [he *solaced* himself by playing the guitar]: **relief** suggests the easing. often just for a time. of misery or discomfort so that one can bear it more easily [to *relieve* the poor on welfare]: **soothe** implies trying to calm or lessen pain or distress [to *soothe* a child with a lullaby]

compare implies a noting of likenesses and differences and an examining of features side by side to see how they are alike or different [to *compare* Shaw with Chekov]: **contrast** implies a comparing for the express purpose of showing differences [to *contrast* city life with living in the country]

concise stresses briefness in speaking or writing so that no more words are used than are needed to express something clearly [a *concise* statement]: **terse** suggests extremely clipped and abrupt expression. as when one must be brief and to the point [the captain's *terse* command]: **laconic** implies a very brief. sometimes vague statement. as by someone who habitually says very little [the cowboy's *laconic* reply]: **succinct** indicates very brief. clear. and compact expression in which only what is essential is dealt with [a *succinct* record of the proceedings]: **pithy** suggests that what is stated in highly compressed form is important and full of meaning [a *pithy* proverb]

consent implies giving in to something proposed or requested when one has the power to do so or not [to *consent* to serve as chairman]: to **assent** is to express one's acceptance or approval of something [she *assented* with a nod]: **agree** implies accord reached by settling differences of opinion or overcoming resistance [to *agree* on a fair price for the property]: **concur** implies agreement arrived at formally on a specific matter. often with regard to a line of action [all the doctors *concurred* in the decision to operate]: to **accede** is to yield one's assent to a proposal [he *acceded* to the union's request for arbitration]: **acquiesce** implies a giving in quietly when one may have some doubts

continual applies to that which happens again and again or goes on without stopping over a long period of time [*continual* arguments]: **continuous** applies to that which goes on without a break in either space or time [a *continuous* area of land]: **constant** stresses being steady or regular in happening or happening again and again [the *constant* beat of the heart]: **incessant** implies activity that goes on or seems to go on without being stopped or interrupted [*incessant* chatter]: **perpetual** applies to that which lasts or remains for an indefinitely long period of time [a *perpetual* nuisance]: **eternal** stresses an endless or timeless quality [the *eternal* truths]

copy is the broadest of the terms here referring to anything that is made to be like the original or patterned after it [a carbon *copy*: a *copy* of a designer's dress]: **reproduction** implies a close imitation of the original. often. however. with differences. as of material. size. or quality [a *reproduction* of a painting]: a **facsimile** is an exact reproduction. sometimes one differing in scale [a photostated *facsimile* of a document]: a **duplicate** is a double. or counterpart. of something. serving all the purposes of the original [all the books of a single printing are *duplicates*]: a **replica** is an exact reproduction of a work of art

criticize. in this comparison. is the general term for finding fault with or disapproving of a person or thing: **reprehend** suggests severe disapproval. usually of faults. errors. etc rather than of people: **blame** stresses the fixing of responsibility for an error. fault. etc. [don't *blame* your laziness on the heat]: **censure** implies the expression of severe criticism or disapproval. as by a person in authority: **condemn** suggests the passing of harsh. final judgment on a person or thing considered guilty or to blame: **denounce** implies a speaking out publicly against persons or actions thought to be immoral. corrupt. evil. etc.

danger is the general word for any kind of exposure to injury. loss. etc [the *danger* of falling on icy walks]: **peril** suggests great danger that is near at hand [flood waters put the town in *peril*]: **jeopardy** emphasizes exposure to extreme danger [reckless driving puts one's life in *jeopardy*]: **hazard** implies danger of which one may be aware but over which one has little control [the *hazards* of combat duty]: **risk** implies willingness to take a dangerous chance [she rescued the documents at the *risk* of her life]

deceive implies a deliberate telling of lies or acting dishonestly, usually with the expectation of personal gain [*deceived* into buying fraudulent stocks]: to **mislead** is to cause to follow the wrong course or do the wrong thing, although not always on purpose [*misled* by the sign into going to the wrong floor]: **beguile** implies the use of charm, tempting promises, etc. in deceiving or misleading [*beguiled* by promises of great wealth]: to **delude** is to fool someone so completely that he accepts as true or real something that is false: **betray** implies a breaking of faith while seeming to be loyal, true, or friendly

delusion implies belief in something that is contrary to fact or reality, resulting from trickery, a misunderstanding, or a mental disorder [to have *delusions* of grandeur]: **illusion** suggests or gives an appearance of something real as by copying it or making something that looks like it [movies give us the *illusion* of seeing and hearing real people]: **hallucination** gives one the impression of experiencing as though it were real something that is not actually there, as when one is drugged or has a mental disorder

dexterous implies an ability to do things with skill and precision [a *dexterous* weaver]: **adroit** adds to this the idea of cleverness, now esp. in dealing with people, ideas, etc. [*they* admired her *adroit* handling of an awkward situation]: **deft** suggests a nimbleness and sureness of touch [a seamstress *deft* with the needle]: **handy** suggests skill, usually without training, at a large variety of tasks [he is very *handy* around the house]

discern implies a making out of something or recognizing it clearly with the eyes or in the mind [to *discern* someone's motives]: **perceive** implies a recognizing by means of any of the senses, and often, in addition, implies keen understanding or insight [to *perceive* differences in pitch: to *perceive* a change in attitude]: **distinguish** implies a perceiving clearly by sight, hearing, etc. [he *distinguished* the voices of men and women down the hall]: **observe** and **notice** both connote paying attention to some degree, and usually suggest use of the sense of sight [to *observe* an eclipse: to *notice* a sign]

disparage means to cast doubt on the worth or reputation of someone or something, often in subtle ways, as by praising with little enthusiasm or making an unfair comparison [to *disparage* a modern dramatist by comparing him with Shakespeare]: to **depreciate** is to suggest that something has less value than it is generally supposed to have: to **belittle** is to indicate, often spitefully or scornfully, one's low opinion of something's or someone's worth [always *belittling* his fellow scientists' achievements]: to **minimize** is to make seem as small as possible [a biased biographer who *minimized* her subject's faults]

distinguish implies a recognizing or setting apart from others by means of special features or characteristic qualities [to *distinguish* the Asian elephant from the African elephant]: **discriminate** suggests a distinguishing of minute or subtle differences between similar things [to *discriminate* between synonyms]: **differentiate** suggests noticing or pointing out specific differences between things by comparing them in detail [his duties as a son as *differentiated* from those as a brother]

dwarf refers to an individual that is much smaller than the usual kind and sometimes implies that the parts are deformed or not in normal proportion: **midget** refers to a very small human being who has normal form and proportions: **Pygmy**, in strict use, refers to a member of any of several small-sized African or Asian peoples, but it is sometimes used (written **pygmy**) as a synonym for **dwarf** or **midget**

ecstasy implies very strong feeling, now usually intense delight, that overpowers one's senses and lifts one into a kind of trance: **bliss** implies a state of happiness and contentment so great as to suggest the joys of heaven: **rapture** now generally suggests the intense feeling one has when something causing great joy or pleasure captures all of one's attention: **transport** implies a being carried away by any powerful feeling

eject implies generally a throwing or casting out from within [to *eject* saliva from the mouth]: **expel** suggests a driving out, as by force, specif., a forcing out of a country, organization, etc., often in disgrace [*expelled* from school]: **evict** refers to a forcing out by the use of legal means [to *evict* a tenant]: **oust** implies the getting rid of something that is not wanted, as by the use of force or the action of the law [to *oust* corrupt officials]

enormous implies a going far beyond what is normal in size, amount, or degree [an *enormous* room; *enormous* expenses]; **immense** implies size beyond the usual measurements but suggests that great size is normal for the thing described [redwoods are *immense* trees]; **huge** usually suggests a great mass or bulk [a *huge* building; *huge* profits]; **gigantic**, **colossal**, and **mammoth** originally implied a likeness to a *giant*, the *Colossus* of Rhodes, and an extinct elephant (the *mammoth*), and therefore these words emphasize the idea of great size, force, importance, etc., now often in an exaggerated way; **tremendous** literally suggests that which causes awe or amazement because of its great size

epicure refers to a person whose taste in food and drink is highly refined and who takes great pleasure in eating and drinking good things; a **gourmet** is one who is very fond of fine things to eat and drink, has expert knowledge about their selection and preparation, and takes pride in his ability to appreciate subtle differences in flavor and quality; **gourmand**, occasionally used to mean the same thing as **gourmet**, is more often applied to a person who has such a hearty appetite for good food that he tends to overeat

essential is applied to that which is the basic essence or fundamental nature of a thing and therefore must be present for the thing to exist, function, etc. [food is *essential* to life]; an **indispensable** person or thing cannot be done without if the specified purpose is to be achieved [he had become *indispensable* to his boss]; **requisite** is applied to that which is required by the circumstances or for the purpose and often suggests a requirement that is demanded or insisted upon [the *requisite* skills for the job]; **necessary** implies an urgent or pressing need but not always for something that is indispensable

excessive applies to that which goes beyond what is needed, right, or usual [*excessive* demands]; **exorbitant** is applied esp. to charges, prices, etc. that are unreasonably or unfairly high [*exorbitant* profits]; **extravagant** and **immoderate** both imply excessiveness resulting from a lack of control or careful judgment [*extravagant* praise; *immoderate* smoking]; **inordinate** implies a going beyond the orderly limits of convention or good taste [his *inordinate* pride]

explain implies a making clear of something that is not known or understood [to *explain* how a machine operates]; **expound** implies an orderly and thorough explanation, often one made by a person having expert knowledge [to *expound* a theory]; **explicate** implies a scholarly analysis or explanation that is developed in detail [the *explication* of a Biblical passage]; **elucidate** implies a shedding light upon by clear and specific explanation, illustration, etc. [to *elucidate* the country's foreign policy]; to **interpret** is to bring out meanings not immediately clear, as by translation, personal insight, or special knowledge [how do you *interpret* his silence?]; **construe** suggests a particular interpretation of something that can be understood in several ways [his statement is not to be lightly *construed*]

extract implies a drawing out of something, as if by pulling [to *extract* testimony from an unwilling witness]; **educe** suggests a bringing out or evolving of something that is undeveloped [to *educe* a theory from the known facts]; **elicit** suggests difficulty or skill in drawing forth something [his jokes *elicited* no smiles]; **evoke** implies a calling forth, as of a mental image, by stimulating the mind or emotions [the odor *evoked* a memory of childhood]

fantastic implies a completely free use of the imagination, and suggests that which is unreal or dreamlike in a striking way [*fantastic* stage sets]; **bizarre** suggests that which is extremely strange or unusual because of startling contrasts or extreme incongruities [a *bizarre* chain of events]; **grotesque** suggests something that appears comic or frightening because it is a distortion of the real or natural [pain twisted his face into a *grotesque* mask]

fatal implies that death or disaster has occurred or will surely occur [a *fatal* disease; a *fatal* mistake]; **deadly** is applied to a thing that can and probably will cause death [a *deadly* poison]; **mortal** is applied to that which has just caused or will soon cause death [a *mortal* wound]; **lethal** is applied to that which is intended or designed to cause death [a *lethal* weapon]

flagrant applies to anything that is so clearly bad or wrong that it deserves to be criticized or condemned [a *flagrant* violation of the law]; **glaring** is used of something bad that stands out even more clearly so that it is noticed immediately [a *glaring* error in arithmetic]: **gross** implies badness or wrongness which is so extreme or disgusting that it cannot be excused or forgiven [*gross* neglect of a child]

flash implies a sudden, brief, brilliant light: **gleam** suggests a steady, narrow ray of light shining through darkness; **sparkle** implies a number of brief, bright flashes from many points of light; **glitter** implies the reflection of such bright flashes, as from metal or a jewel; **glisten** suggests the reflection of a bright light, as from a wet surface; **shimmer** refers to a soft, wavering reflection of light, as from the surface of gently moving water

frank applies to a person, remark, etc. that is free or blunt in expressing the truth or an opinion and is not held back by the usual restraints [a *frank* criticism]: **candid** implies a basic honesty that makes it impossible for one to deceive or be sly, sometimes to the point where the listener could be embarrassed [a *candid* opinion]: **open** implies a lack of secrecy and often suggests a genuine and innocent quality [her *open* admiration for him]: **outspoken** suggests a lack of restraint in offering opinions, esp. when it might be better to keep quiet

funny is the simple, general term for anything that appeals to one's sense of humor or causes laughter: **laughable** is a usually scornful term for that which is fit to be laughed at [what a *laughable* excuse!]: something that is **amusing** brings laughter or smiles by its pleasant, entertaining quality; that which is **droll** amuses one because it is quaint or strange or because of its twisted humor; **comic** is applied to that which is like a comedy in amusing one in a thoughtful way; **comical** is used of that which brings on uncontrolled laughter; **farcical** suggests a comical quality that is based on nonsense, broad humor, etc.

gaudy applies to that which is brightly colored and highly decorated but which is regarded as being in bad taste [*gaudy* furniture]: **tawdry** is used of something cheap and poorly made that is also gaudy [*tawdry* jewelry]: **garish** implies a glaring brightness of color and too much decoration [*garish* wallpaper]: **flashy** and **showy** imply a brightness or display that attracts attention, but **flashy** implies that it is offensive to those with more conservative tastes [a *flashy* sport coat], while **showy** does not always imply this [*showy* blossoms]

ghastly suggests the horror caused by the sight or suggestion of death [a *ghastly* smile on the dead man's face]: **grim** implies extremely disagreeable or even terrifying aspects [the *grim* life of the very poor]: **grisly** suggests an appearance or nature that causes one to be horrified [the *grisly* sights of the concentration camp]: **gruesome** suggests the fear and disgust caused by something horrible and evil [the *gruesome* details of a murder]: **macabre** implies a being concerned or fascinated with the gruesome aspects of death [a *macabre* tale]

greedy implies a desire to get or have more of something than is one's share or than one needs; **avaricious** stresses greed for money or riches and often suggests a being miserly; **grasping** suggests a strong eagerness for gain that shows itself in a seizing of every opportunity to get what one wants; **acquisitive** stresses the drive to keep gathering more and more wealth or possessions; **covetous** implies a strong desire for something that belongs to another person

group is the basic, general word expressing the simple idea of an assembly of persons, animals, or things without any added meaning; **herd** is applied to a group of cattle, sheep, or similar large animals feeding, living, or moving together; **flock**, to goats, sheep, or birds; **drove**, to cattle, hogs, or sheep; **pack**, to hounds or wolves; **pride**, to lions; **swarm**, to insects; **school**, to fish, porpoises, whales, etc.; **bevy**, to quail; **covey**, to partridges or quail; **flight**, to birds flying together. In extended use, **flock** connotes guidance and care, **herd**, **drove**, and **pack** are used as terms of contempt for people, **swarm** suggests a large mass or throng moving together, and **bevy** and **covey** are often used of girls or women

happy generally suggests a feeling of great pleasure, contentment, etc. [a *happy* marriage]: **glad** more strongly implies a feeling of joy [your letter made her so *glad!*], but both **glad** and **happy** are commonly used in merely polite phrases expressing pleasure [I'm *glad*, or *happy*, to have met you]: **cheerful** implies a steady display of bright spirits, optimism, etc. [she is always *cheerful* in the morning]: **joyful** and **joyous** both imply very high spirits and rejoicing, the former generally because of a particular event [the good news made them *joyful*], and the latter usually because of a continuing situation [they were a *joyous* family]

hate implies a feeling of great dislike or a strong

wish to avoid, and, with persons as the object, suggests a wish to harm them; **detest** implies extreme dislike; **despise** suggests a looking down with great contempt upon the person or thing one hates; **loathe** implies intense dislike together with extreme disgust; **abhor** implies great dislike or disgust joined with feelings of moral disapproval

hesitate implies a temporary stopping because of feeling uncertain, unwilling, or confused [he *hesitated* before entering]; **vacillate** implies a shifting back and forth in a decision, opinion, etc. [she *vacillates* in her affection]; **waver** is often applied to a holding back or hesitating after a decision has been made [she never *wavered* in her determination]; **falter** suggests a pausing or slowing down, as in fear or indecision [they never *faltered* in the counterattack]

high and **tall** both refer to something which extends farther upward than is normal for its kind, and **high** also refers to something in a place far above a given level [a *high* mountain; *high* clouds], but **tall** is usually applied to people, animals, and other growing things [a *tall* woman; a *tall* tree]; **lofty** and **towering** suggest great, imposing, or very noticeable height [*lofty* peaks; a *towering* castle]

ignorant implies a lack of knowledge, either in general [an *ignorant* man] or on some particular matter [*ignorant* of the reason for their quarrel]; **illiterate** implies an inability to read or write; **unlettered** is sometimes used as a milder substitute for **illiterate**, but often implies unfamiliarity with fine literature [although a graduate engineer, he is relatively *unlettered*]; **uneducated** and **untutored** imply a lack of formal schooling [she had a brilliant, though *uneducated*, mind]

impertinent is used of speech or behavior that shows a lack of respect by not following the usual rules of politeness and good manners; **impudent** suggests bold, open, deliberate rudeness or impertinence; **insolent** implies extreme disrespect shown in speech or behavior that is deliberately insulting or filled with contempt; **saucy** suggests a light, flippant manner and improper informality in dealing with someone to whom respect should be shown

include implies a containing as part of a whole; **comprise**, in careful use, means to consist of and takes as its object the various parts that make up the whole [his library *comprises* 2,000 volumes and *includes* many first editions]; **comprehend** suggests that the object is contained within the total scope or range of the subject, sometimes by being implied [the word "beauty" *comprehends* various qualities]; **embrace** emphasizes the variety of objects comprehended [he had *embraced* a number of hobbies]; **involve** implies that an object is included because of its connection with the subject as a cause or result [acceptance of high office *involves* responsibilities]

infer suggests the arriving at a decision or opinion by reasoning from known facts or evidence [from your smile, I *infer* that you are pleased]; **deduce** stresses the use of logical and systematic reasoning in inferring something [the existence of the planet Neptune was *deduced* before its actual discovery]; **conclude** strictly implies an inference that is the final, logical result in a process of reasoning [I must, therefore, *conclude* that you are right]; **judge** stresses the careful checking and weighing of statements, arguments, etc. in reaching a conclusion [your proposal was *judged* the better of the two]; **gather** is an informal substitute for **infer** and **conclude** [I *gather* that you don't care]

instance refers to a person, thing, or event that is given as proof or support of something [the gift is an *instance* of his generosity]; **case** is implied to a happening or situation of a specified kind [a *case* of mistaken identity]; **example** is applied to something that is mentioned as typical of the members of its group [his novel is an *example* of science fiction]; **illustration** is used of an instance or example that helps to explain or make something clear [this sentence is an *illustration* of the use of a word]

intrude implies the forcing of oneself or something upon another without being asked or wanted or without having the right to do so [to *intrude* upon another's privacy]; **obtrude** suggests even more strongly that the intrusion causes an unwanted distraction or great unpleasantness [side issues keep *obtruding*]

irritate is the most general of the words here and may suggest mild impatience, continued annoyance, or a flare-up of anger [their smugness *irritates* her]; **provoke** suggests the causing of strong feelings of annoyance, resentment, or anger, often with a wish to get even [*provoked* by the insult]; **nettle** implies irritation caused as by petty, nagging remarks or actions that hurt one's pride [subtle taunts that *nettled* him]: **exasperate** implies great irritation caused by something that makes one lose one's patience or self-control [*exasperated* by the clerk's many careless mistakes]

join is the general term meaning a bringing or coming together of two or more things and may suggest direct contact, becoming a member of a group, etc.: **combine** implies a mingling together of things or a complete merging of distinct elements [to *combine* milk and water]: **unite** implies a joining or combining of things to form a single whole [the *United* States]: **connect** implies attachment by some fastening or relationship [roads *connected* by a bridge; the duties *connected* with a job]: **link** stresses firmness of a connection [*linked* together in a common cause]: **consolidate** implies a merger of distinct and separate units into a single whole for making something compact, strong, efficient, etc. [to *consolidate* one's debts]

laugh is the general word for the sounds made in expressing happiness, amusement, ridicule, etc.: **chuckle** implies the soft laughter in low tones that expresses mild amusement or inner satisfaction; **giggle** and **titter**, both often associated with children or girls, refer to a half-suppressed laugh consisting of a series of rapid, high-pitched sounds, suggesting embarrassment, silliness, etc.: **snicker** is used of a sly, half-suppressed laugh, as at another's embarrassment, confusion, etc.: **guffaw** refers to loud, hearty, coarse laughter

liberal implies tolerance of others' views as well as open-mindedness to ideas that challenge tradition, established institutions, etc: **progressive** is the opposite of *reactionary* or *conservative* and is applied to persons who favor progress and reform in politics, education, etc. and are inclined to take direct action; **radical** is applied to those who favor fundamental or extreme change, specifically of the social structure; **left** is applied to those who are liberal or radical in their political views

liquid refers to a substance that flows readily and takes on the form of its container but stays the same in volume [water that is neither ice nor steam is a *liquid*]: **fluid** applies to any substance that flows [all liquids, gases, and viscous substances are *fluids*]

loiter implies either staying around a place without having anything to do there or moving along in a slow, rambling way [to *loiter* on street corners]: **dawdle** implies wasting time over trifles or taking more time to do something than is necessary [to *dawdle* over dinner]: **dally** suggests spending time in silly or pointless activity; **idle** suggests laziness or avoidance of work [to *idle* away the hours]

love implies intense fondness or deep devotion and may apply to various relationships or objects [sexual *love*, brotherly *love*, *love* of one's work, etc.]: **affection** suggests warm, tender feelings, usually not as powerful or as deep as those implied by **love** [she remembered her high-school coach with *affection*]: **attachment** implies connection by ties of affection, loyalty, devotion, etc. and may be felt for non-living things as well as for people [an *attachment* for an old hat]: **infatuation** implies a passion or affection that is foolish or shows poor judgment, often one that lasts only a short time [*infatuation* with a rock star]

lure suggests a strong force, as desire, greed, curiosity, etc., that attracts someone, often to something harmful or evil [*lured* on by false hopes]: **entice** implies a clever or skillful luring [the witch *enticed* Hansel and Gretel into her house]: **decoy** implies the use of false appearances in luring into a trap [artificial birds are used to *decoy* wild ducks]: **beguile** suggests the use of subtle tricks in leading someone on [*beguiled* by her sweet words]: **tempt** suggests a powerful attraction that tends to overcome doubts or judgment [*tempted* by a chance for profit to invest his savings]

malice implies a deep hatred or dislike causing one to get pleasure from hurting others or seeing them suffer; **ill will** implies unfriendly feelings that lead one to wish harm, unhappiness, etc. to others; **malevolence**, a formal term for **ill will**, may also suggest that the unfriendly feelings are stronger and more evil; **spite** suggests a mean desire to get back at others by hurting or annoying them, esp. in nasty, petty ways; **rancor** implies bitter, long-lasting ill will; **malignity** suggests great malevolence that shows itself in acts of cruelty without pity

material is applied to anything that is formed of matter or substance [chairs are *material* objects]: **physical** applies either to material things known through the senses or to forces that can be measured scientifically [the *physical* world: the *physical* properties of sound]: **corporeal** applies only to material objects that have bodily form and can be touched [a house is *corporeal* property]

meaning is the general word for what is intended to be expressed or understood by something [the *meaning* of a sentence]: **sense** refers especially to any of the various meanings of a word or phrase [this word has several slang *senses*]: **import** refers to all of what is being implied by something said or done, including any subtle or hidden meanings [the full *import* of his remark came to me later]: **purport** refers to the general meaning, or main point, of something [what was the *purport* of her letter?]: **signification** is applied especially to the meaning that a certain sign, symbol, character, etc. commonly suggests to people [the *signification* of the ace of spades in fortunetelling]

memory refers to the ability or power of keeping in or bringing to mind past thoughts, images, ideas, etc. [to have a good *memory*]: **remembrance** applies to the act or process of having such events or things come to mind again [the *remembrance* of things in the past]: **recollection** implies a careful effort to remember the details of some event [his *recollection* of the campaign is not too clear]: **reminiscence** implies the thoughtful or nostalgic recollection of long-past events, usually pleasant ones, or the telling of these [he entertained us with *reminiscences* of his childhood]

mirth implies gaiety, gladness, or great amusement, esp. as expressed by laughter: **glee** implies a great, open display of joy, or it may suggest delight over another's suffering or unhappiness: **jollity** and **merriment** imply very great mirth or joy like that displayed at an especially lively and merry party or celebration: **hilarity** implies noisy and lively merriment and sometimes suggests an excessively loud display of high spirits

mix implies a combining of things so that the resulting substance is the same throughout, whether or not the separate elements can be distinguished [to *mix* paints]: **mingle** usually implies that the separate elements can be distinguished [*mingled* feelings of joy and sorrow]: **blend** implies a mixing of different varieties to produce a desired quality [a *blended* tea, whiskey, etc.] or the mingling of different elements to form a pleasing whole [a novel *blending* fact and fiction]

mood refers to a temporary state of mind and emphasizes a specified feeling [she's in a happy *mood*]: **humor** emphasizes an uncertain or changing quality in the mood [in the *humor* for fighting]: **temper** applies to a mood marked by a single, strong emotion, especially that of anger [my, he's in a nasty *temper*]

moral implies living according to accepted standards of goodness or rightness in conduct or character, sometimes especially in sexual conduct [a highly *moral* person]: **ethical** implies following a carefully planned ideal code of moral principles, often the code of a particular profession [an *ethical* lawyer]: **virtuous** implies a morally excellent character concerned about justice, integrity, and, often, chastity: **righteous** implies taking a moral stand based on good or just reasons [*righteous* anger]

murmur implies a steady flow of words or sounds in a low, indistinct voice and may suggest either a contented or discontented feeling [to *murmur* a prayer]: **mutter** usually suggests angry or complaining words or sounds of this kind [to *mutter* curses]: to **mumble** is to utter words or sounds in low tones and with the mouth almost closed so that they are very hard to hear or understand [*mumbling* to herself as she rummaged in the drawer]

naive implies a being simple and innocent in a trusting way, but sometimes suggests an almost foolish lack of worldly wisdom [his *naive* belief that all advertising is honest]: **ingenuous** suggests a childlike frankness or straightforwardness [her *ingenuous* delight in any kind of flattery]: **artless** implies the appealing open and natural quality of one who is indifferent to the effect he has on others [a simple, *artless* style of folk singing]: **unsophisticated** implies a lack of poise, worldliness, subtlety, etc. resulting from a limited experience of life [an *unsophisticated* freshman]

need is the simple, direct word and **necessity** the more formal term referring to a lack of something that is wanted or must be had, or to the thing that is required [they are in *need* of food: food is a *necessity* for all living things]: **exigency** refers to a necessity brought about by some emergency or by specific events [the *exigencies* created by the flood]: **requisite** applies to something that cannot be done without in order to carry out some activity [a sense of rhythm is a *requisite* in a dancer]

new is applied to that which has never existed before or which has only just come into being, possession, use, etc. [a *new* coat, plan, etc.]; **fresh** is used of something so new that it still has its original appearance, quality, strength, etc. [*fresh* eggs, a *fresh* start]; **novel** implies a newness that is very strange or unusual [a *novel* idea, combination, etc.]; **modern** and **modernistic** refer to that which is associated with the present time rather than an earlier period and imply up-to-dateness, with **modernistic** sometimes being used to suggest contempt as well [*modern* dance, a *modernistic* painting]; **original** is used of that which not only is new but is also the first of its kind [an *original* plan, melody, etc.]

obscure applies to that which is unclear to the senses or to the mind either because it is concealed, veiled, or imprecisely stated or because of dullness or lack of insight in the perceiver [his motives remain *obscure*]; **vague** applies to that which is so lacking in precision or exactness that it is indistinct or unclear [a *vague* notion]; **enigmatic** and **cryptic** are used of that which baffles or bewilders, the latter word implying a deliberate intention to puzzle [his *enigmatic* behavior, a *cryptic* warning]; **ambiguous** applies to that which puzzles because it can be understood in more than one way ["The Lead Horse" is an *ambiguous* title]; **equivocal** is used of something ambiguous that is used to mislead or confuse [an *equivocal* answer to a rude question]

offend implies a causing displeasure or resentment in another, either on purpose or without meaning to, by hurting his feelings or by behaving in a way he considers improper [she will be *offended* if she is not invited]; **affront** implies an open and deliberate showing of disrespect or contempt [his uncalled-for criticism of their school *affronted* the graduates]; **insult** implies an affront so insolent or rude that it causes deep humiliation and resentment [to *insult* someone by calling him a liar]

ominous is used of something that seems to threaten but does not necessarily suggest that a disaster will result [his request was met by an *ominous* silence]; **portentous** is applied literally to a sign or warning, esp. of evil, but is now more often used of that which causes awe or amazement because of its wonderful or extraordinary character [the first landing on the moon was a *portentous* event]; **fateful** may imply control by or as if by fate, but is now usually applied to that which is of very important or crucial significance [a *fateful* truce conference]; **foreboding** implies a feeling that something evil or harmful will happen [a *foreboding* anxiety]

opinion is used of a conclusion or judgment which seems true or probable to one's own mind even though it may still be argued [it's my *opinion* that he'll agree]; **belief** refers to the acceptance by the mind of an idea, esp. a doctrine or dogma that others accept [religious *beliefs*]; a **view** is an opinion affected by the personal way one looks at things [she gave us her *views* on life]; a **conviction** is a strong belief about whose truth one has no doubts [I have a *conviction* of his innocence]; **sentiment** refers to an opinion that is the result of careful thought but that is influenced by emotion; **persuasion** refers to a strong belief that cannot be shaken because one wishes to believe in its truth

oppose implies attacking something that threatens or interferes with one; **resist** implies defending against something that is already actively opposed to one [one *opposes* a legislative action under consideration, one *resists* a law already passed by refusing to obey it]; **withstand** usually implies resistance that keeps the attack from being successful [can they *withstand* the heavy bombing?]

oral refers to that which is spoken, rather than written, to communicate something [an *oral* promise, request, etc.]; **verbal**, though often used in the same way as **oral**, in careful discrimination refers to the use of words, either written or oral, rather than pictures, symbols, etc., to communicate an idea or feeling [a *verbal* image, portrait, etc.]

origin is applied to that from which a person or thing has its very beginning [the word "rodeo" has its *origin* in Spanish]; **source** is applied to the point or place from which something arises, comes, or develops [the sun is our *source* of energy]; **beginning** is the general term for a starting point or place [the *beginning* of a friendship]; **inception** is specifically applied to the beginning of an undertaking, organization, etc. [Smith headed the business from its *inception*]; **root** suggests an origin so deep and basic as to be the very first cause from which something stems [an error in arithmetic was the *root* of all our trouble]

pacify implies a making quiet and peaceful that which has become noisy or disorderly [to *pacify* a crying child]: **appease** suggests a pacifying by giving in to demands [to *appease* one's hunger]: **mollify** suggests a soothing of wounded feelings or calming of anger [his compliments failed to *mollify* her]: **placate** implies the changing of an unfriendly or angry attitude to a friendly or favorable one [to *placate* an offended colleague]: **propitiate** implies a calming or preventing of hostile feeling by winning the good will of a higher power [to *propitiate* a deity]: **conciliate** implies the use of arbitration, concession, persuasion, etc. in an attempt to win someone over

part is the general word for any of the components of a whole [a *part* of one's life]: **portion** often suggests a part given or assigned as a share [his *portion* of the inheritance]: a **piece** is either a part separated from the whole [a *piece* of pie] or a single unit from a collection of related things [only one *piece* missing from her set of china]: a **division** is a part formed by cutting, partitioning, classifying, etc. [the fine-arts *division* of a library]: **section** means much the same as **division** but usually suggests a smaller part [a *section* of a bookcase]: **segment** implies a part separated along natural lines of division [a *segment* of a tangerine]: a **fraction** is strictly a part contained by the whole a certain number of times without remainder, but generally it suggests a small, unimportant part [he received only a *fraction* of the benefits he was entitled to]: a **fragment** is a relatively small part separated as by breaking [a *fragment* of rock]

pay is the simple, direct word meaning to give money, etc. due for services provided, goods received, etc.: **compensate** implies a return, whether of money or something else, thought of as equal to the service given, the effort made, or the loss suffered [he could never be *compensated* for the loss of his son]: **remunerate** emphasizes the idea of payment for a service provided, but it often also implies a reward [a bumper crop *remunerated* the farmer for his labors]: to **reimburse** is to pay back what has been spent [the sales rep was *reimbursed* for her traveling expenses]

perseverance implies a continuing to do something in spite of difficulties, obstacles, etc.: **persistence** may imply either steadfast perseverance that is usually admired or stubborn continuance that is usually annoying: **tenacity** and **pertinacity** both imply firmness in holding to some purpose, action, or belief, but **tenacity** suggests that such firmness is admirable, while **pertinacity** suggests a being obstinate in a way that annoys

petty is applied to that which is small, minor, unimportant, etc. compared with others of its kind, and it is often used to imply small-mindedness [*petty* cash, a *petty* grudge]: **trivial** applies to that which, because it is both petty and ordinary, has no special value [a *trivial* remark]: **trifling** applies to something so small and unimportant that it can be ignored [a *trifling* matter]: **paltry** is applied to something so small or worthless that it deserves contempt [a *paltry* wage]: **picayune** is used of a person or thing thought of as small, mean, or insignificant [a *picayune* objection]

pity implies sorrow felt for another's suffering or misfortune and sometimes suggests slight contempt as well, because the person's troubles are considered to be the result of his own weakness or inferiority [she felt *pity* for a person so ignorant]: **compassion** implies pity along with an urge to help or spare [she was moved by *compassion* and did not demand payment of the debt]: **sympathy** implies a feeling of such closeness to another that one is able to understand and even share emotionally his sorrow, etc. [he always turned to his wife for *sympathy*]

pleasant and **pleasing** are both applied to the effect of giving satisfaction or delight, but **pleasant** stresses the effect produced [a *pleasant* smile] and **pleasing**, the ability to produce such an effect [his *pleasing* ways]: **agreeable** is used of that which suits one's personal likes, mood, etc [*agreeable* music]: **enjoyable** implies the ability to give enjoyment or pleasure [an *enjoyable* picnic]: **gratifying** implies the ability to give pleasure by satisfying someone's wishes, hopes, etc. [a *gratifying* experience]

plentiful implies a large or full supply [a *plentiful* supply of books]: **abundant** implies a very plentiful or very large supply [a forest *abundant* in wild game]: **copious**, now used chiefly to refer to quantity produced, used, etc., implies a rich or continuing abundance [a *copious* harvest, a *copious* discharge, etc.]; **profuse** implies a giving or pouring forth abundantly or very generously, often beyond what is needed or wanted [*profuse* in his thanks]; **ample** applies to that which is large enough to meet all demands [his savings are *ample* to see him through this crisis]

pliable and **pliant** both suggest something that can be easily bent, as a thin wooden stick, and in a more general way, a nature that gives in or adapts easily; **plastic** is used of substances, such as plaster or clay, that can be molded into various shapes which they keep after they become hard, and is also used of persons who can be easily influenced or persuaded; **ductile** suggests that which can be drawn or stretched out [copper is a *ductile* metal]; **malleable** suggests that which can be hammered, beaten, or pressed into various forms [copper is *malleable* as well as ductile]

ponder implies a weighing mentally and suggests careful consideration of a matter from all sides [to *ponder* over a problem]; **meditate** suggests quiet, deep study or thought [he *meditated* on the state of the world] or careful thinking about some plan [to *meditate* revenge]; **muse** implies a dreamlike series of thoughts [to *muse* over the past]; **ruminate** suggests turning a matter over and over in the mind [the loser *ruminated* on the cause of his defeat]

position is used of any kind of work done for salary or wages, but often only of work done by a white-collar or professional worker; **situation** now usually refers to a position that needs to be filled or to one that is desired [*situation* wanted as salesman]; **office** refers to a position that gives one authority or power, esp. in government, a corporation, etc.; a **post** is a position or office that carries important responsibilities, esp. one to which a person is appointed; **job** is now the common, basic term which can be used in place of any of the preceding terms.

possible is used of anything that may exist, occur, be done, etc., depending on circumstances [a *possible* solution to a problem]; **practicable** applies to that which can easily be brought about under the existing conditions or by the means available [a *practicable* plan]; **feasible** is used of anything that is likely to be carried through to a successful conclusion and, thus, may seem worth doing [a *feasible* enterprise]

praise is the simple, basic word that refers to the expressing of approval, respect, or admiration [to *praise* a student's work]; **laud** implies great, sometimes excessive praise [the critics *lauded* the actor to the skies]; **extol** implies high, often formal praise that is meant to make the one who receives it feel proud and happy [the scientist was *extolled* for his work]; **eulogize** suggests formal praise in a speech or writing, esp. of someone who has recently died

presume implies a taking something for granted or accepting it as true, usually on the basis of probable evidence in its favor and the absence of proof against it [the man is *presumed* to be of sound mind]; **presuppose** suggests a taking something for granted without good reason [this writer *presupposes* too large a vocabulary in children]; **assume** implies the taking of something for granted as a basis for argument or action [let us *assume* her motives were good]; **postulate** implies the assuming of something as an underlying factor, often something that cannot be proved [his argument *postulates* the natural goodness of man]

previous generally implies a coming before in time or order [a *previous* meeting]; **prior** adds to this the idea of greater importance or claim as a result of being first [a *prior* obligation]; **preceding**, esp. when used with the definite article, implies a coming just before [the *preceding* night]; **antecedent** adds to the meaning of **previous** the idea of directly causing what follows [events *antecedent* to the war]; **foregoing** applies specif. to something previously said or written [the *foregoing* examples]; **former** always implies a comparison between the first and the last (called *latter*) of two persons or things just mentioned

prone, in strict use, implies a position in which one lies on one's belly [he fell *prone* upon the ground and drank from the brook]; **supine** implies a position in which one lies on one's back, and may suggest a listless feeling or passive attitude [lying *supine* on the grass and gazing lazily at the clouds]; **prostrate** implies the position of one thrown or lying flat in a prone or supine position or the state of one completely beaten, helpless, exhausted, etc. [lying *prostrate* on the ground after the grueling march]; **recumbent** suggests a lying down or back in any position one might assume for rest or sleep [she was *recumbent* upon the couch]

punish implies making a wrongdoer suffer for his wrongdoing by paying a penalty, usually with no idea of reforming or correcting him [to *punish* a murderer by hanging]: **discipline** suggests punishment that is intended to control the wrongdoer or to establish in him habits of self-control [to *discipline* a naughty child]: **correct** suggests punishment of a wrongdoer for the purpose of overcoming his faults [to *correct* unruly pupils]: **chastise** implies punishment, usually physical punishment, along with an attempt to correct the wrongdoer

push implies the use of force or pressure by a person or thing in contact with someone or something to be moved ahead, aside, etc. [to *push* a baby carriage]: **shove** implies a pushing of something so as to force it to slide along a surface, or it suggests rough handling in pushing [*shove* the box into the corner]: to **thrust** is to push with sudden force, sometimes so as to put one thing into another [he *thrust* his hand into the water]: **propel** implies a driving forward of something by a force that makes it move [the wind *propelled* the sailboat]

puzzle implies that a problem, situation, etc. is so involved or complicated that it is very hard or difficult to understand or solve: **perplex**, in addition, implies uncertainty or even worry as to what to think, say, or do: **confuse** implies a becoming mixed up mentally to a greater or lesser degree: **confound** implies a becoming so confused that one is completely frustrated or greatly astonished: **bewilder** implies such complete confusion in one's mind that one can no longer think clearly

quarrel implies a sharp disagreement full of angry words and feelings and often suggests that those arguing become unfriendly: **wrangle** suggests a noisy, fairly lengthy dispute in which each person stubbornly refuses to change his mind: **altercation** suggests a heated argument which may or may not come to blows: **squabble** implies undignified, childish arguing over a small matter: **spat** is the colloquial word for a petty quarrel and suggests a brief, angry outburst that has little lasting effect

range refers to the full extent over which something is recognizable, effective, etc. [the *range* of his knowledge]: **reach** refers to the furthest limit of effectiveness, influence, etc. [beyond the *reach* of my understanding]: **scope** is used of the area covered by a particular activity, written work, etc. having set limits [does it fall within the *scope* of the text?]: **compass** suggests completeness within limits thought of as the outer edge of a circle [to do all within the *compass* of one's power]: **gamut**, in this connection, refers to the full range of shades, tones, etc. within the limits of something [the full *gamut* of emotions]

rational implies the ability to reason in an orderly, carefully controlled way so as to reach conclusions logically without being swayed by emotion [Holmes's *rational* explanation of the mysterious events]: **reasonable** suggests the calm, careful use of the mind in making decisions, choices, etc. that are fair and practical [the teacher was *reasonable* in the amount of homework she required]: **sensible** implies the use of common sense based on sound judgment and practical experience [a *sensible* man who bought no more than he needed]

rebellion implies organized, armed, open resistance to the authority or government in power, and when applied to a historical event, suggests that it failed [Shay's *Rebellion*]: **revolution** applies to a rebellion that succeeds in overthrowing an old government and establishing a new one [the American *Revolution*] or to any movement that brings about a drastic change in society [the Industrial *Revolution*]: **insurrection** suggests an outbreak that is smaller in scope and less well organized than a rebellion [the Philippine *Insurrection*]: **revolt** stresses a casting off of allegiance or a refusal to submit to established authority [a *revolt* of students against the dress code]: **mutiny** applies to a forcible revolt of soldiers or, especially, sailors against their officers [*mutiny* on the Bounty]: **uprising** is a simple, direct term for any outbreak against a government and applies specifically to a small, limited action or to the beginning of a general rebellion [local *uprisings* against the Stamp Act]

recover implies a finding or getting back something that one has lost in any manner [to *recover* stolen property, one's self-control, etc.]: **regain** emphasizes a struggle to win back something that has been taken from one [to *regain* a hill from the enemy]: **retrieve** suggests that something is beyond easy reach and requires some effort to get it back [he was determined to *retrieve* his honor]

regard usually implies a judging of someone or something according to its worth or value [the book is highly *regarded* by critics]; **respect** implies a judging to have great worth or high value, as shown by courtesy or honor [a jurist *respected* by lawyers]; **esteem**, in addition, suggests that the person or object is highly prized or desired [a friend *esteemed* for his loyalty]; **admire** suggests a feeling of enthusiastic delight in appreciating something or someone that is superior [one must *admire* such courage]

relevant implies a close, logical relationship with, and importance to, the matter being considered [*relevant* testimony]; **germane** implies such close natural connection as to be highly suitable or fitting [your memories are not really *germane* to this discussion]; **pertinent** implies an immediate and direct bearing on the matter at hand [a *pertinent* suggestion]; **apposite** applies to that which is both relevant and happily suitable or fitting [referring to an *apposite* passage in Shakespeare]; **apropos** is used of that which is right for the purpose as well as relevant [an *apropos* remark]

reliable is used of a person or thing that can be counted upon to do what is expected or required [his *reliable* assistant]; **dependable** refers to a person or thing that can be depended on, as in an emergency, and often suggests personal loyalty, levelheadedness, or steadiness [she is a *dependable* friend]; **trustworthy** applies to a person, or sometimes a thing, whose truthfulness, honesty, carefulness, etc. one has complete confidence in [a *trustworthy* source of information]; **trusty** applies to a person or thing that has in the past always been trustworthy or dependable [his *trusty* horse]

reluctant implies an unwillingness to do something, as because of dislike, uncertainty, etc. [she was *reluctant* to marry]; **disinclined** suggests a lack of desire for something, as because it fails to suit one's taste [I feel *disinclined* to argue]; **hesitant** implies a holding back from action, as because of caution, uncertainty, etc. [don't be *hesitant* about asking]; **loath** suggests a strong feeling of unwillingness [they were *loath* to testify against him]; **averse** suggests a deep-seated, long-lasting unwillingness [she is *averse* to borrowing money]

remark applies to a brief, more or less casual statement of opinion, etc., as in calling attention to something [a *remark* about clothes]; an **observation** is an expression of opinion on something to which one has given special attention and thought [the warden's *observations* on prison reform]; a **comment** is a remark or observation made in explaining, criticizing, or interpreting something [*comments* on a novel]

remember implies a putting oneself in mind of something, often suggesting that the thing stays so vividly alive in the memory that one becomes conscious of it without effort [he'll *remember* this day]; **recall** and **recollect** both imply some effort to bring something back to mind, **recall**, in addition, often suggesting that one tells others what is brought back [let me *recall* what was said; to *recollect* the days of one's childhood]

replace implies a taking the place of someone or something that is now lost, gone, destroyed, worn out, etc. [to *replace* a defective pump]; **displace** suggests the forcing or driving out of a person or thing by another that replaces it [he had been *displaced* in her affections by another man]; **supersede** implies a replacing with something superior, more up-to-date, etc. [the steamship *superseded* the sailing ship]; **supplant** suggests a displacing that involves force, trickery, or an introduction of new methods [the prince had been *supplanted* by an imposter]

restrain suggests the use of strong force or authority either in preventing, or in putting down or controlling, some action [try to *restrain* your enthusiasm]; **curb**, **check**, and **bridle** get their meanings from the various uses of a horse's harness, **curb** implying a sudden, sharp action to bring something under control [to *curb* one's tongue], **check** implying a slowing up of action or progress [to *check* inflationary trends], and **bridle** suggesting a holding in of emotion, feelings, etc. [to *bridle* one's envy]; **inhibit**, as used in psychology, implies a holding down or keeping back of some thought or emotion [her natural warmth and affection had become *inhibited*]

ridicule implies a making fun of a person or thing by way of showing disapproval [he *ridiculed* her new hat]; **deride** suggests contempt for or a strong dislike of what is being made fun of [to *deride* another's beliefs]; *mock* suggests a ridiculing by the unkind imitation of another's mannerisms or habits [it is cruel to *mock* his lisp]; **taunt** implies insulting ridicule, esp. as shown by jeering at another and harping on something that makes him feel ashamed [they *taunted* him about his failure]

rise and **arise** both imply a coming into being, action, notice, etc., but **rise** carries an added suggestion of upward movement [empires *rise* and fall] and **arise** is often used to show a cause-and-effect relationship [accidents *arise* from carelessness]

roam implies a traveling about over a large area without a fixed goal and carries suggestions of freedom, pleasure, etc. [to *roam* about the country]; **ramble** implies an idle moving or walking about, esp. in a carefree or aimless way [we *rambled* through the woods]; **rove** suggests a wandering over a wide area, but usually implies a special purpose or activity [a *roving* reporter; *roving* bands of looters]; **range** stresses the wide area covered and sometimes suggests a search for something [hunters *ranging* the western plains]; **meander** is used of streams, paths, etc., and, less often, of people and animals, that follow a winding, seemingly aimless course

rural is the general word referring to life on the farm or in the country as distinguished from life in the city [*rural* schools]; **rustic** emphasizes the contrast between the supposed crudeness and lack of sophistication of country people and the polish and refinement of city people [*rustic* humor]; **pastoral** suggests an ideally simple sort of life as lived in the country, originally by shepherds; **bucolic**, in contrast, suggests a down-to-earth, rustic simplicity or crudeness [her *bucolic* suitor]

sarcastic implies a deliberate attempt to hurt by ridicule, mocking, sneers, etc. [a *sarcastic* reminder that work begins at 9:00 AM]; **ironic** is used of a form of sarcasm in which the meaning of what is said is directly opposite to the usual sense ["My, you're early," was his *ironic* taunt to the latecomer]; **sardonic** implies sneering or mocking bitterness in a person, or, more often, in what he says or how he looks [a *sardonic* smile]; **caustic** implies a cutting, biting, or stinging wit or sarcasm [a *caustic* tongue]

satisfy implies the fact of meeting wishes, needs, expectations, etc. fully; **content** implies a filling of needs to the degree that one is not disturbed by a desire for something more [it takes great wealth to *satisfy* him, but she is *contented* with their modest but steady income]

scream is the general word for a loud, high, piercing cry, made as in fear, pain, or anger; **shriek** suggests a sharper, more sudden or anguished cry than **scream** and is also used of loud, high-pitched, uncontrolled laughter; **screech** suggests a shrill or harsh cry that is painful or unpleasant to hear

sentimental suggests emotion of a kind that is felt in a longing or tender mood [*sentimental* music] or emotion that is exaggerated, artificial, foolish, etc. [a trashy, *sentimental* novel]; **romantic** suggests emotion stirred up by that which appeals to the imagination as it is influenced by stories of love and adventure [a *romantic* girl waiting for her knight in shining armor]; that is **mawkish** which is sentimental in a disgustingly weak, insincere, or exaggerated way [the *mawkish* lyrics of a popular love song]; that is **maudlin** which is tearfully or weakly sentimental in a foolish way [to become *maudlin* when drunk]

sharp and **keen**, both apply to that which is cutting, biting, penetrating, or piercing, as because of having a very thin edge, but **sharp** may imply a harsh, disagreeable cutting quality [a *sharp* pain, tongue, etc.] and **keen**, a pleasantly biting or stimulating quality [*keen* wit, delight, etc.]; **acute** is used literally to describe an angle or end formed by lines or edges that meet in a sharp point, but may be used to suggest a very clear awareness of small differences [*acute* hearing, an *acute* intelligence] or the quality of being sharply painful to the feelings [*acute* distress]

shrewd implies a keen mind, sharp insight, and often a crafty approach in practical matters [a *shrewd* comment, businessman, etc.]; **sagacious** implies a keen insight and farsighted judgment [a *sagacious* advisor]; **perspicacious** suggests the keen mental vision or judgment that helps one clearly to see and understand what is vague, hidden, etc. [a *perspicacious* judge of character]; **astute** implies shrewdness combined with wisdom [an *astute* politician]

silly implies ridiculous or unthinking behavior that seems to show a lack of common sense, good judgment, or seriousness [it was *silly* of you to dress so lightly]; **stupid** implies slowness in thinking or a lack of normal intelligence [he is *stupid* to believe that]; **fatuous** suggests stupidity or dullness joined with smug, mistaken satisfaction with the way things are [a *fatuous* smile]; **asinine** implies the extreme stupidity traditionally thought of as characteristic of the ass, or donkey [an *asinine* argument]

small and **little** are often used interchangeably, but **small** is preferred in referring to something of slightly less than the usual size, amount, value, importance, etc. [a *small* man, tax, matter, etc.] and **little** is more often used when no comparison is being stressed [he has his *little* faults], in expressing tenderness [his *little* sister], and in suggesting unimportance, pettiness, etc. [of *little* interest]; **diminutive** implies extreme, sometimes delicate, smallness or littleness [a *diminutive* teacup]; **minute** and the more informal **tiny** suggest that which is extremely diminutive, often to the degree that it can be noticed only by looking very closely [a *minute*, or *tiny*, difference; a *minute* flaw in the weave]; **miniature** applies to a copy, model, etc. on a very small scale [*miniature* paintings]; **petite** refers specifically to a girl or woman who is small and trim in figure

sorrow refers to the deep, long-lasting mental pain caused by loss, disappointment, etc. [his secret, life-long *sorrow*]; **grief** suggests briefer, more intense mental pain resulting from a particular misfortune, disaster, etc. [her *grief* over the loss of her child]; **woe** suggests grief or misery so intense that it cannot be relieved [the war-torn nation's *woe*]

speech is the general word for a piece on some subject spoken before an audience, with or without preparation; **address** implies a formal, carefully prepared speech and usually suggests that the speaker or the speech is important [an *address* to a legislature]; **oration** suggests an eloquent or sometimes merely pompous and showy speech, esp. one delivered on some special occasion [a Fourth of July *oration*]; a **lecture** is a carefully prepared speech intended to inform or instruct the audience [a *lecture* to a college class]; **talk** suggests informality and is applied either to an unprepared speech or to an address or lecture in which the speaker purposely uses a simple, conversational approach

steep suggests a slope so sharp that it makes going up or down difficult [a *steep* hill]; **abrupt** implies a very sharp incline in a surface that breaks off suddenly from the level [an *abrupt* bank at the river's edge]; **precipitous** suggests the sudden, almost vertical drop of a precipice [*precipitous* canyon walls]; **sheer** indicates an incline that is straight up and down, or almost so, with a surface that is smooth and unbroken [cliffs falling *sheer* to the sea]

strong is the most general of these terms, implying power that can be used actively as well as power that resists destruction [a *strong* body, fortress, etc.]; **stout** implies ability to stand strain, pressure, wear, etc. without breaking down or giving way [a *stout* rope, heart, etc.]; **sturdy** suggests the strength of that which is solidly developed or built and thus difficult to shake, weaken, etc. [*sturdy* oaks, faith, etc.]; **tough** suggests the strength of that which is firm and resistant in quality [*tough* leather, opposition, etc.]; **stalwart** emphasizes firmness, loyalty, or reliability [a *stalwart* supporter]

stupid implies such lack of intelligence or inability to understand, learn, etc. as might be shown by one in a mental daze [a *stupid* answer]; **dull** implies a mental slowness that may be in one's makeup or may result from overfatigue, illness, etc. [the fever left him *dull* and listless]; **dense** suggests lack of sensitivity or an irritating failure to understand quickly or to react intelligently [too *dense* to take a hint]; **slow** suggests that the quickness to learn, but not necessarily the ability to learn, is below average [a pupil *slow* in his studies]

summit refers to the topmost point of a hill or similar high place or to the highest reachable level, as of achievement or rank; **peak** refers to the highest of a number of high points, as in a mountain range or in some changing action or condition [at the *peak* of his powers as a writer]; **climax** applies to the highest point in interest, force, excitement, etc. in a scale of rising values; **acme** refers to the highest possible point of perfection in the development or progress of something; **apex** suggests the highest point of a geometric figure or of a career, process, etc.; **pinnacle**, in its figurative uses, can be substituted for **summit** or **peak**, but sometimes suggests a dizzy or unsteady height [the *pinnacle* of success]; **zenith** refers to the highest point in the heavens and thus suggests fame or success reached by a spectacular rise

surprise, in this connection, implies a causing wonder because unexpected, unusual, etc. [I'm *surprised* at your concern]; **astonish** implies a surprising with something that seems unbelievable [to *astonish* with magic tricks];

amaze suggests an astonishing that causes confusion [*amazed* at the sudden turn of events]; **astound** suggests shocking astonishment that leaves one unable to act or think [I was *astounded* when he offered me a bribe]

talent implies a natural ability to do a certain thing and suggests that the ability has been or can be developed through training, practice, etc. [a *talent* for drawing]; **gift** suggests a special ability that is thought of as having been given, as by nature, rather than gotten through effort [a *gift* for making friends]; **aptitude** implies a special ability which makes it likely that one can do a certain kind of work easily and well [no *aptitude* for a desk job]; **faculty** implies a special ability or skill that is either natural or acquired [she has developed the *faculty* of getting along with others]; **knack** implies an ability, gained through practice or experience, to do something easily and cleverly [the *knack* of writing limericks]; **genius** may imply any great natural ability [he has a *genius* for always saying the right thing], but more often suggests an extraordinary natural power to do creative, original work in the arts or sciences [the *genius* of Leonardo da Vinci]

theory, as compared here, implies a general principle for which there is much evidence explaining how something works or comes to be [the *theory* of evolution]; **hypothesis** implies an explanation which, although there is little evidence for it, is assumed to be true, esp. as a basis for further experimenting [the nebular *hypothesis*]; **law** implies an exact principle that has been worked out by observing how certain events in nature occur over and over again under the same conditions [the *law* of the conservation of energy]

throw is the general word meaning to cause to move through the air by a rapid movement of the arm, etc.; **cast,** the preferred word in special uses [to *cast* a fishing line], has in general use a more archaic or formal quality [they *cast* stones at him]; to **toss** is to throw lightly or carelessly and, usually, with an upward or sideways motion [to *toss* a coin]; **hurl** and **fling** both imply a throwing with force or violence, but **hurl** suggests that the object thrown moves swiftly for some distance [to *hurl* a spear], while **fling** suggests that the object is thrust sharply so that it strikes a surface with considerable force [she *flung* the plate to the floor]; **pitch** implies a throwing with a definite aim or in a definite direction [to *pitch* a baseball]

transform implies a change either in outer form or inner nature, in use, etc. [the opportunity to study *transformed* her life]; **transmute** suggests a change in basic nature that seems almost like a miracle [*transmuted* from a shy youth into a man about town]; **convert** implies a change in details so as to be suitable for a new use [to *convert* an attic into an apartment]; **metamorphose** suggests a surprising change produced as if by magic [a tadpole is *metamorphosed* into a frog]; **transfigure** implies a change in outward appearance which seems to make splendid or glorious [plain features *transfigured* with tenderness]

trite is applied to an expression or idea which has been used so often that it has lost its original freshness and force (e.g., "like a bolt from the blue"); **hackneyed** refers to expressions which through constant use have become just about meaningless (e.g., "last but not least"); **stereotyped** applies to those fixed expressions which seem almost sure to be used in certain situations (e.g., "I point with pride" in a political speech); **commonplace** is used of any obvious remark or idea that is familiar to just about everybody and is used merely as a matter of course and without any real thought (e.g.: "it isn't the heat, it's the humidity")

turn, the most general word here, implies motion around, or partly around, a center or axis [a wheel *turns*]; **rotate** implies movement of a body around its own center or axis [the earth *rotates* on its axis]; **revolve** is sometimes substituted for **rotate,** but in exact use it suggests movement, usually circular or elliptical, around a center outside itself [the earth *revolves* around the sun]; **gyrate** implies movement in a spiral course, as by a tornado; **spin** and **whirl** suggest very fast and continuous rotation or revolution [a top *spins*; the leaves *whirled* about the yard]

universal is used of that which applies to every case or individual, without exception, in the class, category, etc. concerned [a *universal* practice among primitive peoples]; **general** refers to that which applies to all or nearly all of the members of a group or class [a *general* favorite among college students]: **generic** is used of that which applies to every member of a class or, specif. in biology, of a genus [a *generic* name]

use implies the putting of a thing into action or service for a given purpose, esp. its intended purpose, or, in the case of a person treated as a thing, for one's own selfish purposes [to *use* a pencil, a suggestion, etc.; he *used* his brother to advance himself]: **employ**, a more formal term, implies the putting to useful work of something not in use at that moment [to *employ* a vacant lot as a playground] and with reference to persons, suggests a providing of work and pay [he *employs* five mechanics]: **utilize** implies the putting of something to a practical or profitable use [to *utilize* byproducts]

vagrant refers to a person without a fixed home who wanders about from place to place, supporting himself by begging, etc., and in legal usage refers to any person, as a prostitute or disorderly person, whose way of living may cause him to be arrested: **vagabond**, orig. implying laziness, roguishness, etc., now often suggests no more than a carefree, roaming existence: **bum**, **tramp**, and **hobo** are informal substitutes for **vagrant** and **vagabond**, in some senses, but **bum** specifically brings to mind a homeless drunkard who never works, **tramp**, a vagrant who lives by begging or by doing odd jobs, and **hobo**, a migratory laborer who follows seasonal work

view is the general word for that which can be seen [the *view* is cut off by the next building]: **prospect** suggests a view from a position that allows one to look out over a wide area and to a great distance [a grand *prospect* of snowy mountains and deep valleys]: **scene** suggests an attractive or dramatic view of objects, persons, etc. placed or arranged as they might be in a painting or a play [a peaceful country *scene*]: **vista** suggests a distant view seen through a long, narrow passage [at the end of the valley lay a *vista* of rolling hills and winding rivers]

wage (or **wages**) applies to money paid an employee at regular periods of time, as at hourly or piecework rates, esp. for skilled or manual labor: **salary** applies to fixed amounts usually paid monthly or twice a month, esp. to clerical or professional workers: **stipend** is a somewhat overly formal substitute for **salary**, or it is applied to a fixed payment, as an amount of money granted to a student: **fee** applies to the payment requested or given for professional services, as of a doctor, lawyer, etc.: **pay** is the general term that may be substituted for any of these words

weak, the most general of these words, implies having very little, or less than normal, physical, mental, or moral strength [a *weak* muscle, mind, character, etc.]: **feeble** is used of that which is so weak or ineffective as to be pitiable [a *feeble* old dog, a *feeble* joke]: **frail** refers to that which is extremely delicate or weak, or easily broken or shattered [a *frail* body, *frail* support]: **infirm** suggests a loss of strength or soundness, as through illness or old age [his *infirm*, old grandfather]: **decrepit** implies a being broken down or worn out, as by old age or long use [a *decrepit* old horse, a *decrepit* sofa]

wise implies the ability to judge and deal with persons, situations, etc. rightly, based on a broad range of knowledge, experience, and understanding [a *wise* parent]: **sage** suggests the great wisdom of age, experience, and philosophical thought [*sage* advice]: **judicious** implies the ability to make wise decisions based on sound judgment [a *judicious* approach to a problem]: **prudent** suggests the wisdom of one who is able to recognize the most suitable or careful course of action in practical matters [a *prudent* policy]

wit refers to the ability to see contradictions, weaknesses, etc. in people and things and to make quick, sharp, often sarcastic remarks about them that delight or entertain: **humor** is applied to the ability to see and express that which is comical, or ridiculous, but suggests a kindly or sympathetic quality in the use of this ability to amuse others: **irony** refers to the humor that is implied in the difference between what is actually said and the meaning that is intended, or in the difference between appearance and reality in life

worth and **value** both refer to the amount of money or goods a thing can be exchanged for [the *worth* or *value* of the jewels]: when the terms are distinguished, **worth** refers to the basic excellence of a thing as judged by its moral or cultural qualities and the like, while **value** refers to excellence as measured by how useful, important, profitable, etc. a thing is [the true *worth* of Shakespeare's plays cannot be measured by their *value* to the commercial theater]

zealot implies great, often too great, devotion to a cause and intense activity in its support [*zealots* of reform]: **fanatic** suggests the unreasonable attitude of one who goes to any length to preserve or carry out his beliefs [a *fanatic* on a suicidal mission]: an **enthusiast** is one who shows a strong, eager, lively interest in an activity, cause, etc. [a sports *enthusiast*]

NOTES

NOTES